THE OFFICIAL HISTORY
OF THE
AUSTRALIAN ARMY MEDICAL SERVICES
IN THE WAR OF 1914-1918
VOLUME II
THE WESTERN FRONT

1. MAJOR-GENERAL SIR NEVILLE R. HOWSE, DIRECTOR OF MEDICAL SERVICES, AUSTRALIAN IMPERIAL FORCE, 1915-19

Aust. War Memorial Collection No. A1189.

Frontispiece.

THE
AUSTRALIAN ARMY MEDICAL SERVICES
IN THE
WAR OF 1914-1918

VOLUME II

BY
COLONEL A. G. BUTLER, D.S.O., V.D.,
B.A., M.B., Ch.B. (Camb.)

With 212 illustrations, maps, and graphs

The Naval & Military Press Ltd

AUSTRALIAN WAR MEMORIAL, CANBERRA
1940

Published by

The Naval & Military Press Ltd
Unit 5 Riverside, Brambleside
Bellbrook Industrial Estate
Uckfield, East Sussex
TN22 1QQ England

Tel: +44 (0)1825 749494

www.naval-military-press.com
www.nmarchive.com

In reprinting in facsimile from the original, any imperfections are inevitably reproduced and the quality may fall short of modern type and cartographic standards.

PREFACE

WHEN the first volume of this history was published, the whole history was envisaged as a two-volume work. Before the second volume was completed, however, it became evident that if the medical experiences of the A.I.F. in the War of 1914-1918 were to be of full benefit to the nation the difficult and costly problems of repair and pensioning must be part of this history; and the clinical issues involved in the post-war problems of "attribution" and treatment called for much study and space. The writer found himself unable to confine the results of this study within the covers of a single volume. He was accordingly permitted to transfer those chapters, together with others on certain technical aspects of surgery, gas warfare, influenza, and venereal disease, and on the Dental, Nursing and Massage Services, and the R.A.N. and R.F.C.—already partly complete —to a final volume. The present volume deals solely with the experiences of the 1st A.I.F. at the main theatre of war and some of its implications.

Apart from the narrative chapters, a particular study has here been made of the problems of siting and working the machinery of evacuation, from front line to general hospital and back; of prevention of disease and promotion of health— the statistics (which, however, are mostly deferred till the next volume) being based on a classification not hitherto adopted, it is believed, in military medical history; and of the influence of the determination by its medical director to keep the 1st A.I.F. an "*A.1.*" force. The comparison made in *Appendix No. 9* of the evolution and methods of the medical services of the chief nations engaged in the war may also prove useful. To members of the A.A.M.S. who contemplate active service *Appendices 3* and *4* are commended as a goldmine of exact information regarding medical duties in the field as these were laid down for the B.E.F. and interpreted in the Australian Corps at the zenith of its efficiency.

In the authorised scheme of this work it was assumed that the detailed technique of the *regional surgery* of war wounds belonged to text book and manual rather than to history. This argument does not, however, apply to the evolution, during the war, of the *general surgery* of war wounds, and treatment of wounded men. Similarly, on the "medical" side, the therapeutic and diagnostic problems of disease in the war did not differ essentially from those of peace and are not studied here. But the machinery for their *prevention* did, and this has been made the subject of particular examination in three special chapters.

The passages in small type are mainly concerned with exposition or discussion of military or technical matters; this method is intended to provide more detailed information than would otherwise have been possible, and to make the perusal of these passages in some degree optional to the reader. Each of the technical chapters is introduced by a synopsis of the matters dealt with.

By far the most important source of the information on which this volume is based has been the records supplied by the Australian War Memorial—war diaries, personal records, official files from the overseas registries and so forth. Often, unfortunately, it has been impossible to show by actual quotation the value of admirable memoranda by members of the Service. The files of the *Medical Journal of Australia* and the *R.A.M.C. Journal* also have been of service. Of the various medical histories of the war, official and other, most use has been made of the *British Official Medical History*, from which, by special permission, a number of diagrams have been reproduced. That comprehensive study of the medical problems of the war, the vast American history, stands alone in having an international outlook, as do the German volumes in their system and completeness. An official French medical history has not been published.

For assistance by information and advice the writer is deeply indebted to so many friends and other helpers that mention of them all would be impossible and acknowledgment to a few invidious. For other assistance his personal thanks are due, first, to Mr. A. J. Withers, who throughout the production of this and the first volumes, has been retained by the Gov-

PREFACE vii

ernment as his assistant; to him chiefly fell the task of providing the general and replacing the unhappily destroyed clinical statistics, and in the next volume his name will be linked with the author's in connection with the chapter on statistics. Mr. J. Balfour, of the Official Historian's staff, has devoted nearly a year of labour and care to ensure that, so far as possible, the volume should be free from error. That Miss M. Ordish, who has translated my MS into typescript, has earned an expression of my gratitude, my friends will readily admit.

As the reader will doubtless observe, the final revision of this volume was complete before the present war began.

A. G. B.

CANBERRA,
10th January, 1940.

CONTENTS

INTRODUCTION: THE A.I.F. ON THE WESTERN FRONT:
THE WAR OF ATTRITION 1

SECTION I

I. THE NEW INTERMEDIATE BASE 7
II. THE NEW SEAT OF WAR 21
III. TRENCH-WARFARE: THE BATTLE OF FROMELLES . . 35
IV. THE SOMME: POZIÈRES AND MOUQUET FARM . . 49
V. THE SOMME WINTER 74
VI. THE GERMAN RETIREMENT, 1917 104
VII. BULLECOURT 129
VIII. THE FLANDERS OFFENSIVE: THE BATTLE OF MESSINES . 158
IX. THE FLANDERS OFFENSIVE (continued): THIRD BATTLE OF YPRES 183
X. THE END OF ATTRITION WARFARE 232

SECTION II

INTRODUCTION: EVOLUTION IN THE MEDICAL SERVICE DURING ATTRITION WARFARE 260
XI. EVACUATION WITHIN THE ARMY ZONE—MOVEMENT . 267
XII. THE GENERAL SURGERY OF WOUNDS IN THE GREAT WAR 297
XIII. EVACUATION: THE CASUALTY CLEARING STATION . . 354
XIV. EVACUATION: EXPEDITIONARY BASE, THE GENERAL HOSPITALS 388
XV. EVACUATION: LAST STAGE, DISTRIBUTION . . . 423
XVI. THE HUMAN GRINDSTONE: REPAIRS AND REPLACEMENTS 444
XVII. PREVENTIVE MEDICINE IN THE WAR— (I) THE FACTORS INVOLVED 482
XVIII. PREVENTIVE MEDICINE IN THE WAR— (II) THE PROMOTION OF HEALTH 513

CONTENTS

XIX. PREVENTIVE MEDICINE IN THE WAR—(III) THE PREVENTION OF DISEASE 533

SECTION III

INTRODUCTION: THE WAR OF MOVEMENT: THE OFFENSIVES OF 1918 603
XX. THE GERMAN THRUST FOR VICTORY 606
XXI. THE ALLIED COUNTER-OFFENSIVE: AUSTRALIAN CORPS PREPARES 647
XXII. THE BATTLE OF AMIENS 679
XXIII. "OPEN WARFARE" AND HARGICOURT—THE PROBLEM OF FIGHTING STRENGTH 703
XXIV. THE HINDENBURG LINE—A STUDY IN CO-OPERATION . 735
XXV. THE END OF THE WAR AND THE BEGINNING OF THE PEACE 767
XXVI. AN ESTIMATE OF THE MEDICAL DIRECTION OF THE A.I.F. 802

APPENDICES 859
1 Statistics of casualties in the Great War . . 860
2 Documents relating to Australian Army Medical Services overseas 866
3 Orders and instructions illustrating the technique of medical administration in the field . . 874
4 Standing Orders for A.A.M.C., Australian Corps 889
5 Extracts from correspondence concerning the fitness of recruits sent oversea 900
6 Physical standard of A.A.M.C. personnel . . 904
7 Employment of "B" Class men 906
8 Medical establishments, A.I.F. 911
9 Some national systems for dealing with casualties 913
10 Some constant factors which determine the arrangements required for the transportation of battle-casualties 926
11 Various types of huts and tents in common use. 931
12 Sanitation on the Western Front . . . 935
13 Front-line application of the Thomas splint . 942
14 Wound shock and haemorrhage: Resuscitation in the field 946

INDEX 961

LIST OF ILLUSTRATIONS

Surgeon-General Sir Neville Howse	*Frontispiece*
Headquarters of A.I.F. Depots in the United Kingdom	18
A parade at the A.A.M.C. Training Depot, Parkhouse	18
No. 1 Australian Auxiliary Hospital, Harefield	19
Ward 31 at Harefield	19
An Australian medical unit marching through Marseilles ..	32
Air-photograph of the opposing trench systems at "The Lozenge," near Armentières	33
The famous "Chalk Pit" near Pozières	64
"Sausage Valley," Pozières	65
Stretcher-bearers passing through the exposed area south of Mouquet Farm	68
Dressing wounded in Bécourt Château	68
Colonel G. W. Barber	69
Colonel A. H. Sturdee	69
Colonel A. Sutton	69
Colonel A. T. White	69
Colonel C. H. W. Hardy	69
British ambulance bearers carrying a stretcher through the Somme mud	76
Stretcher-bearing in the Somme Winter	76
Men with trench feet being carried from A.D.S. to motor ambulance	77
Sick parade at an R.A.P. on the Somme front	77
Trolley with wounded being pushed by bearers along light railway	112
Main dressing station at Contalmaison	112
Scene of a typical fight during the "Alberich" retreat	113
Open country north-west of Doignies	113
The exposed carry at Second Bullecourt	150
Collecting and relay post in the sunken road at Noreuil	150
The "forward" advanced dressing station in front of Vaulx-Vraucourt	151
The advanced dressing station at "Kandahar Farm" during the Battle of Messines	172

ILLUSTRATIONS

The A.D.S. on the Menin Road	173
The A.D.S. for walking wounded, Menin Road	173
Wounded temporarily held up at The Culvert on the Menin Road	200
The advanced dressing station on the Menin Road	201
Zonnebeke church, October 1917	232
The plank roads and dump at Birr Cross-road	233
Wounded at a relay post near Zonnebeke railway station	240
"Ideal House"	241
Stretcher-bearers worn out on the Zonnebeke railway enbankment	241
The shoulder-high carry	288
A motor ambulance of the Australian Voluntary Hospital	288
A British motor transport park	289
Panoramic diagram showing the successive stages of evacuation and return to duty in the Army area	292
Plan of the 1st Division's rest station at Wippenhoek	293
A demonstration of three stages in the application of the Thomas splint	348
Preparing a patient for operation at No. 1 A.C.C.S.	349
A ward in No. 2 A.C.C.S.	349
An operation at No. 1 A.C.C.S.	364
No. 3 A.C.C.S. at Gézaincourt	365
"Nissen bow" hospital huts	412
Part of the tent lines of No. 3 A.G.H.	412
A tent ward at No. 3 A.G.H.	413
A hut ward at No. 1 A.G.H.	413
Model showing the embarkation of wounded on hospital ferry at Boulogne	428
The central kitchen of No. 3 A.G.H.	428
Bishop's Knoll hospital	429
The electro-therapeutic ward at No. 1 A.A.H.	429
No. 7 Camp, Codford	452
No. 2 Camp, Codford	452
A "temporary dressing station" of the 17th Field Ambulance during training	453
Medical examination at No. 4 Command Depot	453
A hutted camp at Dickebusch	524
A company cook-house	524
Supplying fresh vegetables for the 5th Division	525
Australian soldiers in winter kit	528
Hot food containers	528

ILLUSTRATIONS

An officer inspecting feet during the Third Battle of Ypres	529
Water-carts at the water point, Montauban	529
Foden disinfectors	580
Bath house of the 5th Australian Division	581
Fly-proof latrine seat	581
A standard ablution bench	581
The Somme valley near Corbie	628
The southernmost huts of the old "Edgehill" C.C.S. after "Michael"	629
General Birdwood visiting a rest station	629
The advanced dressing station on the Franvillers-Bonnay road	660
The congestion of wounded at the loading post near 4th Brigade headquarters during the Battle of Hamel	661
Operating room in the model dressing station, Franvillers road	661
Gassed men at an R.A.P.	661
Bearers of a field ambulance waiting for the second stage of the Infantry's advance, 8th August, 1918	692
Bearers of the 7th Field Ambulance after the fighting on 10th-11th August, 1918	693
German prisoners carrying Australian wounded during the Battle of Bray	708
Wounded being brought to the R.A.P. by German prisoners during fighting at Bray	709
Loading wounded at the A.D.S., Bray	732
The M.D.S. at Buire, beyond Péronne, September, 1918	732
Engineers repairing the plank road to Bellicourt	733
Stretcher-bearers near Martinpuich	772
An Australian and an American stretcher-bearer during the Battle of Hamel	773
A relay post during the Battle of the Hindenburg Line	773
The dismantling of No. 3 A.G.H.	808
The last draft of Australian sisters leaving France for demobilisation	808
A.I.F. Administrative Headquarters, London	809
Horseferry-road, London	809
Key to conventional signs used in maps	959

LIST OF MAPS

1	The I Anzac Corps area, July-September, 1916	68
2	Medical arrangements on the Somme battlefield, November, 1916	88
3	The I Anzac Corps front, February, 1917	93
4	The Battle of Messines—medical arrangements of II Anzac Corps	164
5	The Battle of the Menin Road—scheme of clearance ..	206
6	The Battle of Polygon Wood—scheme of clearance	216
7	The Battle of Broodseinde—scheme of clearance	224
8	Stages of evacuation from front line to railhead	273
9	Australian Auxiliary Hospitals and Command Depots ..	452
10	Medical arrangements of 1st Australian at Strazeele, April, 1918	645
11	Medical arrangements, Battle of Hamel	668
12	Moves of forward medical positions, 29th September-2nd October, 1918	760
13	The Fourth Army's advance, August-November, 1918 ..	769

LIST OF DIAGRAMS

Scheme of Medical Administration, Western Front	24
The organisation of medical services from a corps front to a sea base	28
Insulated shed for drying clothes	95
A method of applying heat by hot air	343
The technique of the blanket	344
Small Thomas splint for arm	348
Hypodermic morphia outfit for field work	349
Working scheme of a casualty clearing station	371
The cock-up splint	373
Portable hot-air cradle for use in resuscitation ward	376
Plan of No. 1 A.C.C.S.	381
Scheme of method of running an ambulance train	392
Plan of No. 3 A.G.H.	400
Disposal of sick and wounded on the Lines of Communication in France	419
Evacuation and return to duty in the A.I.F. on the Western Front	440
Distribution and disposal of Australian sick and wounded arriving in the United Kingdom	481
Methods of protection against shell and bomb splinters adopted by field ambulances	521
The Australian boot	525
Beds arranged in "Adrian" hut to avoid mucous interchange ..	557
Plan of Australian Corps baths	576
The small pit incinerator	587
Russian type of improvised delouser	588
The two-gallon petrol tin	592
The "flying fox" transporter	636
The underground dressing station on the Franvillers-Bonnay road	660

xvi   DIAGRAMS AND GRAPHS

Two methods of "leapfrogging" 686
The main dressing station at Buire 729
Battle of Hindenburg Line, showing situation on Australian Corps
  front, 29th and 30th September, 1918 743
Dressing station at Ste. Emilie 755
French method of disposition in depth of the medical stations behind
  the fighting forces 784
Scheme of French evacuation 917
Scheme of American evacuation in a divisional area .. 920
German scheme of evacuation in a divisional area 923
The distance time-factor in evacuation .. 928
The "brigading" of marquees 934
A front-line application of the Thomas splint 943
Glass milk-bottle adapted for the purpose of saline infusion 951

LIST OF GRAPHS

1 Wounded admitted to No. 2 A.C.C.S., January-September, 1918   372
2 Admissions to No. 2 A.C.C.S., July 1916 to June, 1918 .. 385
3 Australians under treatment in British Hospitals in the United
     Kingdom and in Australian Auxiliary Hospitals 436
4 Sickness in the A.I.F. Depots in U.K., October 1916 to December, 1918 454
5 Source of men flowing into Command Depots and destination
     of those flowing out, July 1917 to December 1918 .. 469
6 Numbers of the A.I.F. sent from Western Front to hospital
     and subsequently returned to duty 480
7 Total casualties in the A.I.F. on Western Front 492
8 Percentage of total evacuations of A.I.F. on the Western
     Front 493
9 Comparison of A.I.F. sick rates in Gallipoli and on the Western Front 494
10 Course of a mumps epidemic in II Anzac 556
11 Mortality among troops in A.I.F. Depots in the United Kingdom 562
12 Sick and wounded of the German armies in the field .. 863

INTRODUCTION

THE A.I.F. ON THE WESTERN FRONT

THIS volume of the history of the Australian Army Medical Services in the Great War is chiefly concerned with the operations on the Western Front. So far as land armaments played their part in attaining victory, this front is generally acknowledged to have been the decisive, as it certainly was the major, theatre of war. It is of course axiomatic that the part of the sea forces, and, in less measure, the efforts in the air, were in certain respects essential to the attainment of supremacy[1]; and that political, economic, and moral factors, such as the British blockade, the German strategic bombing, the campaigns of propaganda and other operations on the home front had an important place in the final result; and furthermore that the strategic moves of 1915, in particular the Russian offensives and Gallipoli Campaign, were in their sphere and their moment powerful to influence the decision. But it nevertheless remains true as a general thesis that the war was won and lost on the battlefields of France and Belgium. From the military side then the work of the Medical Services in this sphere of action has a special significance.

The historian of Medical Service therefore enters on this part of his task with a deepened sense of responsibility. And this is immensely augmented by a very remarkable and momentous development in the attitude of military students of war towards the work of the Medical Service. This relates especially to the fighting on the Western Front and is very clearly stated in the text-book on strategy written by Sir Frederick Maurice.[2]

[1] It is to Winston Churchill that we owe the epigram that Jellicoe was the only man on either side who could have lost the war in an afternoon.

[2] *British Strategy*, by Maj.-Gen. Sir F. Maurice, Professor of Military Studies in the University of London. Director of Military Operations, Imperial General Staff, 1915-18. With Introduction by Field-Marshal Sir G. Milne, Chief of the Imperial General Staff. (Constable & Co. Ltd., London, 1929.) The quotation is from pp. 1-8.

"It is said commonly that the principles of war are immutable. While this is a claim which requires some consideration, it is indisputable that the methods of applying these principles vary constantly.[3] ... War in its highest development is, in fact, as we have good reason to know, a tremendous social cataclysm, affecting every part of the national life. It is primarily because war is a social rather than a purely military development that its nature is progressively changing. ... What are the factors which made the Great War so entirely different from any other war? There have been in the past many wars which were of longer duration. There have been none in which the opposing armies were permanently in contact. There have been none in which the numbers engaged have been so huge. ... The feature that was without precedent was that from the first day to the last the guns never ceased firing. This was the consequence of the establishment of a continuous barrier of trenches, which limited manoeuvre and kept the opposing armies permanently in contact.

"To what was the continuous barrier of trenches due? Primarily to the vast numbers engaged on either side. For the first time in history entire nations were in arms. But the appearance of this phenomenon in the years between 1914 and 1918 was not caused by any drastic change in the machinery for making armies. ... This remarkable change, which, as I have endeavoured to show, altered the form and nature of war far more drastically than did any development of weapons or of military methods, was the consequence of other changes that had no direct connection with war.

"The prime cause of the expansion in the size of armies, which took place at the beginning of the twentieth century, was the expansion which had taken place in the means of transportation ... the application of the internal combustion engine to road transport. ... The motor lorry could carry from three to four times as much as the horse-drawn vehicle occupying a similar space on the road, and could travel six times as fast. ... Transportation had ceased to be a limiting factor in the size of armies.

"There remained one difficulty to be overcome before vast armies could be maintained for any length of time in the field. In all wars before the Great War disease had proved to be at least as great a cause of loss as the enemy's bullets and shells, in most of them a greater one. ... But while scientists of one kind were giving their minds to the solution of the problems of transportation, those of another kind were solving the problems of sanitation and of the prevention of disease, with the result that in the Great War armies of unprecedented size were kept healthy, though the men in the ranks were living under conditions such as human beings had never before been called upon to endure for a like period. ... It was no longer necessary to calculate how many men could be fed and kept healthy at any given time and place; the question became how many men capable of bearing arms were available. ..."

---

[3] In Lord Rosebery's *Napoleon: The Last Phase* (p. 191), Napoleon is reported to have once said, at St. Helena, "War is a strange art. I have fought sixty battles, and I assure you that I have learned nothing from all of them that I did not know in the first." This epigram of the great master of the art of war supports the contention that the fundamental principles of warfare are immutable and reflect the operation of natural laws. But *tempora mutantur et nos mutamur in illis*: science has revolutionised the arts of peace and it is impossible but that it should have a like influence on the art, though not on the essential principles, of war.

INTRODUCTION

Study of the conditions under which the formations of the A.I.F. were maintained in the field leads to the conclusion that, in maintaining the strength of the force in the field, a factor of almost equal importance to the prevention of disease was the improvement of methods of treatment—in particular of wounds —and the system of return to duty that was associated with it. This is borne out by a study of the medical statistical records of the German Army.

However brought about, this new status of the Medical Service in the machinery of war has come to stay. The part of the Medical Services in the war was to maintain the national army at the highest point of strength and fitness. In this it co-operated with other services of maintenance and with each of the three great branches of the army.[4] In its task it met with problems of the most diverse kind, the nature of which it is the special purpose of this work to demonstrate and develop. The more strictly professional and scientific aspect of these problems is dealt with in the third (and final) volume. We are here concerned rather with the effect that laboratory and clinical researches had upon the *organisation* and *procedure* of the Army Medical Service of Great Britain and, as part and parcel with this, of Australia and the other self-governing dominions.

The three Sections into which for greater clarity the volume is divided relate chiefly to the fighting on the Western Front. *Section I* deals with warfare of the type which during 1915, 1916, and 1917 developed as a direct result of the special conditions described by Sir Frederick Maurice. In *Section II*, for reasons that are there fully set out, a general review is made of the new methods of the fully developed Medical Service, as seen at the end of that phase of the war. *Section III* deals with the work of this remodelled service in the operations of the final phase of the war, in which the static warfare of the previous years was replaced by immense drives by each side, with the final victorious push-through by the Allies and the end of active military operations.

Section I—The war of attrition
While, therefore, the previous volume, dealing with the Gallipoli, Palestine, and New Guinea campaigns, was concerned with more

---
[4] *See Vol. I, Appendix No. 2, p. 813.* The function of humane alleviation is not here in question.

or less traditional methods of making war by strategic manœuvres (with all the medical complications that these involved) *Section I* of the present volume describes the experiences of the A.A.M.C. in a campaign greatly different from any that had ever before been waged. The combined result of improved means of mechanical transport and of preventive medicine in conjunction with a highly developed system of entrenchment and protection by machine-guns and barbed-wire, had been to make an entrenched force inviolate save to highly organised attack and immense expenditure of high explosive or "gas" shell. The so-called "race for the sea," which followed the Battles of the Marne and Aisne in 1914, had been a supreme effort by the Command on both sides to maintain opportunity for open manœuvre. It failed and the result was the permanent engagement of the opposing forces, which became closely locked in two lines extending continuously 50 to 1,000 yards apart, from the sea to Switzerland. Thereafter the numbers engaged in each side and their concentration were on a scale never before known or even imagined.

Out of these unique conditions there arose a method of warfare also without precedent; and this in respect not only of its actual methods but of its human involvements. There developed on this, the decisive front, a condition of stalemate from which the normal methods of strategy and tactics were insufficient to extricate the leaders of either side; and which resulted (whether rightly or wrongly, necessarily or unnecessarily, it is not the part of a medical historian to conjecture) in an experience which the human race can hardly contemplate with any pride or satisfaction as a phase in its *iter ad astra* or an element in its cultural evolution; and which the most ardent advocate of war as a factor in the elevation of humankind must find difficult to exploit for argument in support of his thesis. For it involved, in actual practice, this truly shocking result that, to destroy the continuity of the trench line and compel strategically decisive success, it was first necessary to accomplish a sufficient measure of human attrition by prolonged mechanical slaughter—continued deliberately until the opposing fronts reached a stage of tenuity at which the side emerging more intact and efficient in material and morale might effect, by some surprise or original combination, a breach in the ramparts sufficient to be exploited with decisive effect.

Such, speaking broadly, was the nature of the fighting with which the chapters in this first section of the present volume are concerned. The first two chapters relate to the transfer of the Australian infantry to the Western Front, and the changes in organisation and method involved therein for the Medical Service, and furnish also a brief survey of the military conditions in the British Expeditionary Force in France in 1916. The succeeding chapters are occupied wholly with a narrative of those aspects and events of the fighting on this front in which the Australian force directly participated until the end of 1917. The course of the fighting is followed chronologically from the preliminary sorties and feints leading up to the Battle of the Somme until the Third Battle of Ypres. The Battle of Cambrai, big in its import and omen if slight in its direct effects, completes the old and points the new phase of the war. *Section I* concludes with the reorganisation of the Australian force in France and concentration of its formations from two Anzac Corps into the single Australian Corps which was to play an important, even commanding, part in those decisive operations of 1918 that had been made possible by the attrition of 1916-17.

CHAPTER I

THE NEW INTERMEDIATE BASE

THE year of our Lord 1916 found the nations that composed the greater part of the western world spending themselves, with an *abandon* possible only to those engaged in the fulfilment of some great purpose, in that process of human "attrition" to which the science and art of war had been driven by the entrenched line, the machine-gun, and the internal combustion engine. This year was to be made memorable for humanity by the two most destructive and terrible of those "weird battles of the west" that marked the progress of this "war to end war." And it was now to see, as an incident of some local if of no great cosmic import, the arrival in Europe of the Australian Imperial Force and the absorption into the inferno of the Western Front of the manhood of the island continent of the Pacific, as part of the great war-machine into which the British nation was in process of being organised.[1]

It is not easy, even from the vantage ground provided by some twenty years of retrospect and a huge war literature, to accomplish a mental picture of the vast system of ordered movement and activities organised for destruction into which the Australian force, and within its lesser gambit the Australian Army Medical Services, were now being fitted as a factor in what is perhaps the most interesting experiment of modern times in national organisation—the British Commonwealth of Nations.

The year 1915 had been on the whole a bad one for the Allied powers. It had seen the final battles of the Masurian

---

[1] The magnitude of the British military effort to this date is illustrated by the following figures. By the end of March, 1916, 2,660,806 troops had enlisted for the Regular Army and the Territorial Force: the British strength in France was 1,146,357. During the same period 385,631 sick and wounded had reached England from France, and 98,626 from the Mediterranean Expeditionary Force, 12,297 of the latter being Australians.

7

Lakes, the elimination for the time being of the gallant Russian ally as an active factor in the war, the failure of the impulsive Italian offensive against Austria, and—following the Allied failure to force the Dardanelles—the withdrawal of their defensive front in the East to the very brink of the Suez Canal, the main British line of communication with India, Australia, and New Zealand. On the Western Front the year had been marked by the introduction of poison gas and—for a time—unrestricted submarine campaigning as instruments of war; and by fierce, but wholly ineffective local Allied offensives in France, at Neuve Chapelle and Loos, and in Champagne. On December 19th—the day of the evacuation of Anzac and Suvla—Sir Douglas Haig had replaced Sir John French as Commander-in-Chief of the British Expeditionary Force in France.

The general military situation

At the end of 1915 the German higher command had decided that the time and events were ripe for a supreme bid for victory on the Western Front. The French nation was selected for the blow, the impact of which came in February, 1916, at Verdun—"the northern gateway into France." At the time when the Australian force became active on the Western Front this battle had been in progress for over three months and had cost the French 190,000 casualties. In the opinion of the French nation and its military staff the time had come—was, in fact, overdue—for an effort on the part of the British on a corresponding scale, to relieve by a counter-offensive an onslaught that was fast becoming a death grapple. To this the British Government and Imperial General Staff had agreed. The moment also had just arrived when such an effort was possible. British munition factories were now in full swing. The "New Army" of Great Britain—a body of young volunteers of a spirit that can hardly have been surpassed in the long history of the world's conflicts—had completed its organisation and training. The stage was being set for Britain's supreme effort in the Great War.[2]

The requirements of the coming offensive made it necessary that the Australian troops to take part should reach France in time to receive preliminary training in the methods of warfare peculiar to the Western Front. Accordingly the first troops of the four

The A.I.F. arrives

---

[2] *See Vol. I, p. 512.*

infantry divisions into which the main part of the Australian force in Egypt had just been reorganised began to arrive at Marseilles on March 20th, the Australian cavalry (the Light Horse) being left in the Near East where it served for the remainder of the war.[3] A necessary concomitant of the absorp-

tion of the A.I.F. in the British Expeditionary Force in France was a reorganisation of the Intermediate Base of the force and readjustment of its special lines of communication, particularly in the matter of providing for the disposal of its casualties. Of these military adjustments, which deeply concerned the medical service, a brief account must now be given.

The medical arrangements for the British force in France were throughout the war based on the principle, laid down at the beginning of the war by the French Government, that the British casualties should be evacuated at once to England. This principle, which would appear a natural and mutually

General arrangements for Australian casualties

---
[3] Except the corps mounted regiments, which accompanied the infantry to France.

advantageous one, imposed a considerable strain in practice; and the enemy's policy of ruthless submarine warfare afterwards accentuated this almost to breaking point. The general scheme of evacuation to England hinged on a system of rapid clearance by hospital ships carrying patients from groups of general hospitals at the British expeditionary bases in France to the ports of Southampton and Dover. With the decision early in March, 1916, that the Australian infantry should be sent to France, the problem of the disposal of A.I.F. casualties became a matter of urgent concern to the War Office. The

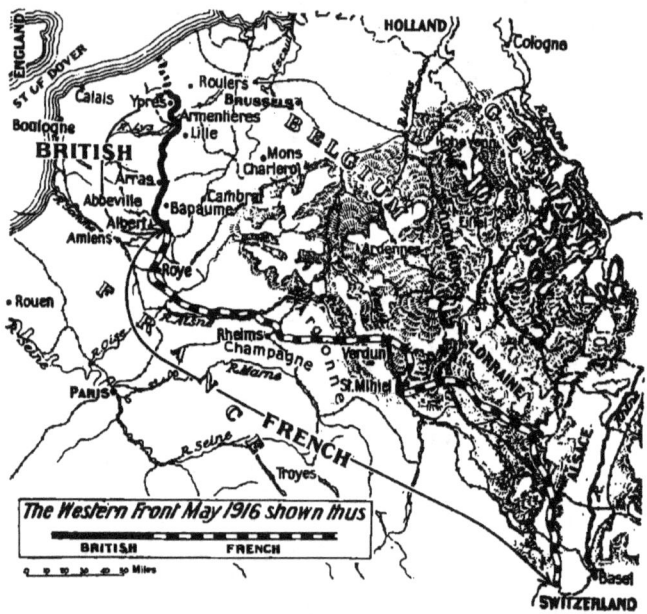

policy put forward by the Defence Department early in 1915, and reiterated during that year, was that as many casualties as possible should be returned for treatment to Australia; and this, together with the view of the Commonwealth Government regarding the risk of transfer from the Egyptian summer to an English winter,[4] was accepted by the Director-General, Army Medical Services (Sir Alfred Keogh)[5] as having sufficient weight to warrant departure from the normal British procedure. Arrangements were therefore, at first, made to base Australian evacuation from France not on England but on Egypt, via Marseilles. On 7th March, 1916, the Director-General of the Medical Services, B. E. F. (Sir Arthur Sloggett) was advised to this effect[6] and tentative arrangements were made to meet the requirements of this policy. On March 31st a War Office conference (attended by Surgeon-General Williams, D.D.M.S., Australians in England[7]) decided that "officers and men likely to be fit for duty in a month should be retained in France," those "likely to be fit for duty within three months should be sent to England," others "not likely to be fit for duty within three months should be despatched to Egypt for onward conveyance to Australia."

On April 4th the G.O.C., A.I.F. Lieut.-General Birdwood with I Anzac Corps Headquarters arrived in France, and on April 1st No. 2 Australian General Hospital[8] opened at Marseilles a tented hospital to receive the sick from the now rapidly following transports. With this unit arrived also Lieut.-Colonel T. E. V. Hurley, A.A.M.C. representing Surgeon-General Howe, the D.M.S., A.I.F., with instructions "to furnish the British authorities with all possible information concerning the A.I.F. medical units and organisation." Proceeding to northern France this officer discussed with the Australian Headquarters staff, and later with Sir Arthur Sloggett, the arrangements to be made for the Australian sick and wounded. Already the "Commandant A.I.F. troops in United Kingdom" (Brigadier-General Sir Newton Moore) had realised that the provision made to meet the wishes of Australia must involve the War

---

[4] This view was urged on the War Office by the High Commissioner, Sir George Reid. In January, 1916, Sir George was replaced by Mr. Andrew Fisher, who resigned the Prime Ministership of Australia.

[5] On 3 October, 1914, Sir Alfred Keogh (D.G., A.M.S., 1904-10), was recalled to the position to replace Sir Arthur Sloggett who had been appointed to the position of Director-General of the Medical Services in the British Expeditionary Force.

[6] In coming to this decision "War Office authorities were guided by the expressed wish of the Minister for Defence of many months ago that Australian sick and wounded be not sent to England." The scheme it may be noted was identical with that in operation for the Indian Expeditionary Force.

[7] *See Vol. I, p. 510.*

[8] The establishment of Nos. 1 and 2 Australian General Hospitals had been raised to 750 beds before leaving Egypt, with a 25 per cent. increase in nurses.

Office in considerable difficulties.[9] Lieut.-General Birdwood also, on his arrival in France, became impressed by the military defects of the scheme proposed. The Australian Government had cabled its desire that before final arrangements were made, General Howse should be consulted and that he should "personally arrange regarding hospital accommodation"; but the proposals were to be submitted to Australia before final adoption.

Before General Howse's arrival in England, however, the Australian High Commissioner (Mr. Fisher) at a second War Office conference[10] on April 21st, definitely proposed that Australian evacuation should be based on England, and reinforcement camps established there; and pledged himself to accept any risk involved, provided only that hutted accommodation be provided for the troops. The War Office, through the Adjutant-General, stated that Great Britain "had accommodation" in existence and would make the same provision for Australian troops as they made for their own. This would also apply to hospital accommodation. The latter (the conference was informed) increased automatically with the number of troops in France. The conference agreed:—

A crucial conference—New arrangements

"That there should be three categories of sick and wounded as they recover: 'A,' those fit for general service; 'B,' those likely to be fit within six months; 'C,' those unlikely to be fit in six months. No man should be sent back to Australia or New Zealand who was likely to be fit in six months. Those who were medically certified as likely to be unfit for over six months should be sent back to Australia and New Zealand." [11]

On April 26th the Director of Medical Services, A.I.F., Surgeon-General Howse, arrived at Marseilles, was rejoined by his staff officer, Colonel Hurley, and proceeded direct to England. On April 28th he attended a third conference at the War Office, at which the decision was finally made

D.M.S., A.I.F. arrives. Medical policy finalised

---

[9] For appreciation of this fact the War Office had relied on the vision of those responsible for advising the Australian Government. It is nowhere expressed in the official correspondence.

[10] The War Office was represented by the Adjutant-General, the Director-General, Army Medical Services, the Deputy Quartermaster-General, and the Directors of Organisation and of Movements; Australia by the High Commissioner, the Commandant A.I.F. troops in U.K., and the Deputy-Director of Medical Services; New Zealand by the High Commissioner and Commandant New Zealand troops in U.K. Lieut.-General Birdwood was present as General Officer Commanding the Australian Imperial Force.

[11] Army Council Instruction No. 1023 of 19 May, 1916, prescribed 6 months as the basis for categorisation of sick and wounded of the British Expeditionary Force.

"that Australian sick and wounded in France would be dealt with under exactly similar arrangements to those in existence for Imperial troops."[12]

The War Office further agreed that, though it was impossible to send all Australian sick and wounded to Australian hospitals, nevertheless any of them "arriving at a base at which Australian hospitals are located shall, whenever possible, be sent to the Australian hospital located there"[13] and that in England, as soon as fit, they should be transferred from the British hospitals to Australian "auxiliaries." All venereal cases would be treated in France. The Australian Government was advised of this policy, and arrangements were made by General Howse to bring over the Australian hospitals still in Egypt.

Consideration is given in later chapters (*Section II*) to the provision made to meet the new situation, and the very important medical problems that soon arose in connection with the maintenance at strength of the Australian force, and disposal of its casualties, are also studied there in some detail. It is, however, desirable to indicate here the immediate course of events in England consequential on the arrival of the Australian force in the western sphere of operations.

The decision arrived at in the conferences referred to above—confirmed by the Commonwealth Government—involved the formation in England of an Australian "Intermediate Base." The organisation of this was discussed with the War Office by Lieut.-General Birdwood, as "G.O.C., A.I.F.,"[14] during his visit to England. The essential components of such a base were, first, an administrative headquarters for dealing with matters concerning the maintenance of the force such as pay, personal records, movements of personnel, and so forth; and second, an organisation for the reception and training of recruits

An A.I.F. Intermediate Base

---

[12] The system of military hospitals and convalescent (command) depots in Great Britain is described in *Vol. I, pp. 492-6.*

[13] On April 4 the Director-General of Medical Services in Australia, Surgeon-General Fetherston, had written to Howse that "our own Australian hospitals should be placed in good positions in France and should treat large numbers of men there." The D.M.S., A.I.F. agreed that the right policy was "to place as many as possible of our hospitals in France where they would get primary rather than second and third hand cases."

[14] The matter of administrative command of the A.I.F. and its internal organisation and economy, medical and other, are dealt with elsewhere. See in particular index to *Vol. I* and *Chapter xxvi* of this work. The matter is fully dealt with in *Vol. III* of the *Australian Official History of the War.*

arriving from Australia as reinforcements, and for the treatment and disposal of Australian casualties.

It was decided that the "Australian Intermediate Base Depot," (A.I.B.D.), in Egypt,[15] should be brought to England and should form an "Australian Administrative Headquarters," in London. Salisbury Plain was proposed by the War Office as the site of the training camps for Australian reinforcements and for new "Command Depots" for recovered casualties. Under instructions from General Birdwood, General Howse, with Sir Newton Moore made a survey of the area and selected sites for the training battalions as well as for the last of the five infantry divisions of the A.I.F., the 3rd, which was due to arrive in June from Australia in order to complete its training in England.

The "Australian Intermediate Base Depot" arrived from Egypt on May 22nd—having left an Egyptian section behind—and was established at Horseferry-road as "A.I.F. Headquarters in England." In view of the desire of the War Office that there should be "one person responsible in England," its commanding officer, Brigadier-General V. C. M. Sellheim, took over the dual control hitherto exercised over Australian military affairs in England by the High Commissioner and Sir Newton Moore. The various sections of the Australian Intermediate Base Depot —finance, medical, ordnance, police, postal, records, and veterinary—were developed to meet the now vastly increased requirements and became the "Administrative Headquarters, A.I.F." The functions of this headquarters were set out by the A.I.F. chief-of-staff, Brigadier-General White, as follows:

> To fulfil all War Office requirements in the administration of the Australian Imperial Force.
>
> To ... act as a representative in England of the Australian Defence Department.
>
> To form a Home record office for the A.I.F.
>
> To provide all the administrative power and machinery necessary to enable the exercise of the power granted to the G.O.C., A. & N.Z. Army Corps, by the Australian Government.

Medical Section. The existing medical organisation at Horse-

---

[15] See *Vol. I, pp. 54-6, 488.*

ferry-road, built up during 1915,[16] became merged into the medical section of Administrative Headquarters, and Surgeon-General Howse, as Director of Medical Services, A.I.F., took over medical control in England from Surgeon-General Williams. That officer was given the option of remaining in England as D.D.M.S. on Howse's staff, but he elected to go before a medical board, by which he was marked "permanently unfit for general service." He embarked for Australia on June 1st, and in the Birthday Honour List issued on the 3rd he was created a Knight Commander of the Order of St. Michael and St. George. He died in May, 1919.

D.M.S., A.I.F. The responsibilities of the D.M.S., A.I.F., were defined by the A.I.F. chief-of-staff to comprise—

Maintenance of strength of A.A.M.C., A.I.F. (including the Light Horse in Egypt).

Fitness of general reinforcements before absorption into drafts for the front, and employment of "B" class men.

Supervision of Australian sick and wounded in Great Britain, disposal of fit discharged from British hospitals, including boarding, convalescents and returned to duty, and invaliding.

Medical care of A.I.F. troops in United Kingdom in particular, "including V.D."

Administration of Australian Dental, Nursing and Pharmaceutical Services.

General supervision of the activities of the Australian Red Cross Society.

Surgeon-General Howse's position as "D.M.S., A.I.F.," was confirmed by the Commonwealth Government on 27th January 1916.[17] His control over medical affairs in Egypt was maintained through an A.D.M.S. By the War Office the question of his administrative designation—whether as "Director" or "Deputy-Director"—was tacitly dropped, and his status as chief administrative medical officer for the whole Australian force overseas was accepted "without prejudice" to any difficulties that might arise in giving effect to it. Howse established official relations with the Director-General, A.M.S., General Keogh, though not on any very intimate or exact basis. At the desire of the latter, at the end of May, 1916, he left on a visit to the

---

[16] *See Vol. I, p. 503.* [17] With effect from 22 November, 1915.

Italian, French, and British fronts, and on return furnished him with a summary of his impressions. While in France he reported to A.I.F. Headquarters in the field (to which while there he was attached as *"liaison* officer") and visited the Director-General of Medical Services at British General Headquarters—then General Sloggett. With the approval of the War Office, and the concurrence—indefinitely extended—of the British Command in France,[18] he inspected a number of the Australian medical units and advised the G.O.C., A.I.F., in regard to certain matters of medical organisation wherein a departure had been made in the Australian service from British establishment or procedure.

Pari passu with the administrative reconstruction noted above new machinery was created for dealing with reinforcements and recovered men. Based on the British system of "commands" an Australian organisation was built up which derived in part from the A. & N.Z. training depots in Egypt, in part from the Australian "convalescent depots" already established in England.

Training and convalescent depots

1. Reinforcements: The Training Brigades. This part of the system derived from Egypt.

In the reorganisation after Gallipoli arrangements for dealing with reinforcements had received exact attention at the hands of General Birdwood's Chief of General Staff, Brigadier-General C. B. B. White. In particular the "training battalions" which held and trained the reinforcements arriving from Australia for their corresponding brigades at the front were to be "training brigades," each such brigade representing a division in the field. Thus when the force came to the Western Front there were at hand a system and a skeleton staff, which required only a headquarters' staff and instructors together with suitable camps and training areas to become at once a "going concern."

This matter was an urgent one. A large surplus of troops had remained over when the two new divisions (4th and 5th) were complete, and though a batch of reinforcements went to the Base Depots in France, more would soon be coming (now round the Cape) direct from Australia, whence also the 3rd Australian Division would arrive in June.

---

[18] The arrangement with Canada is very clearly stated in *The War Story of the Canadian Army Medical Corps, 1914-1915* by Col. J. G. Adami, *pp. 81-2*, and in the *Official History of the Canadian Forces in the Great War 1914-19, The Medical Services*, by Sir Andrew Macphail. See also *The New Zealand Medical Services in the Great War, 1914-18* by Lieut.-Col. A. D. Carbery, *pp. 366-7*.

The Camps on Salisbury Plain. As a result of the inspection by Surgeon-General Howse and Sir Newton Moore of the accommodation on and around Salisbury Plain in the British Southern Command, made available by the War Office for Australian use, camp sites partly in huts, partly in tents, were selected for some 60,000 to 70,000 troops: for the 3rd Division at Lark Hill, for the training brigades here and at Rollestone, Parkhouse and Perham Downs. The whole centre was subdivided into three training groups as hereunder, each to be under a "group commander"[19]:—

Military Commands in the United Kingdom. (London and Aldershot are separate commands. The H.Q. of both the Eastern Command and the London District are in London.)

HEADQUARTERS at Bhurtpore Barracks, Tidworth.

TRAINING GROUP "A" at Perham Downs and Parkhouse. (Distance from Tidworth, 3 miles.) Accommodation for approximately 12,000 troops.

TRAINING GROUP "B" at Rollestone. (Distance from Tidworth, 12 miles.) Accommodation, 22,000.

TRAINING GROUP "C" at Lark Hill. (Distance from Tidworth, 10 miles.) Accommodation, 30,000.

These were placed under the command of Brigadier-General Spencer Browne. As in Egypt, the first instructional staff was supplied by the War Office.

---

[19] This decision was the result of a conference early in June between the War Office and representatives of the A.I.F.—the latter the "Commandant A.I.F. troops in England" (Brigadier-General Sellheim) and Sir Newton Moore.

Training of A.A.M.C. On May 11th instructions were issued by General Howse that

all A.M.C. men in England are to be trained in Field Ambulance work and carry out a course of training in stretcher drill.

A special "medical company" was formed at Weymouth under Captain M. B. Johnson

for training as a separate unit in special drill, first aid, and all subjects peculiar to the medical branch of the army.

In June an A.A.M.C. training depot—No. 2 Camp—was formed at Parkhouse with 656 details—"collected from reinforcements and the flotsam and jetsam of the A.A.M.C., who had drifted in from various hospitals, the Overseas Base and Convalescent Depots in Egypt"—who on June 14th "marched in" under Lieut.-Colonel J. S. Purdy. Among these was the nucleus of a Sanitary Section formed by Lieut.-Colonel Purdy in Egypt.

2. *Convalescents: the "Command Depots."* The other side of the Base Depot system—the "convalescent depots"—was founded on the scheme already existing in Great Britain.

Here, as we have seen,[20] there had been built up during 1915, under Sir Newton Moore and Surgeon-General Williams, a system of convalescence, medical and military, along the lines of the British Command (convalescent) Depots (which themselves had replaced the "military convalescent hospitals"). The very efficient British organisation was adapted to meet the new needs of the A.I.F. After the evacuation of Gallipoli the pressure on the Australian depots in England had greatly relaxed; save for invalids awaiting return to Australia they had been almost emptied.[21]

The old "intermediate depot" at Bostal Heath (Abbey Wood) was now vacated and a new "A.I.F. Command Depot"—"No. 1"—was formed at Perham Downs, to receive convalescents "likely to be fit for return to duty in *less than three months.*" The original Australian Base Depot at Weymouth with Major D. M. McWhae as S.M.O. after serving for a time as a "general base depot" became "No. 2 Command Depot"; it took

---

[20] *In Chapter xxiii of Vol. I.*
[21] The distribution of Australian troops in the United Kingdom at the end of May, 1916, was as follows:—

Australian Base Depot, Weymouth	2,624 including 1,273 fit	
Intermediate Depot, Abbey Wood	839 ,,	185 ,,
Hospitals and furlough	1,368	—
TOTAL	4,831 ,,	1,458 ,,

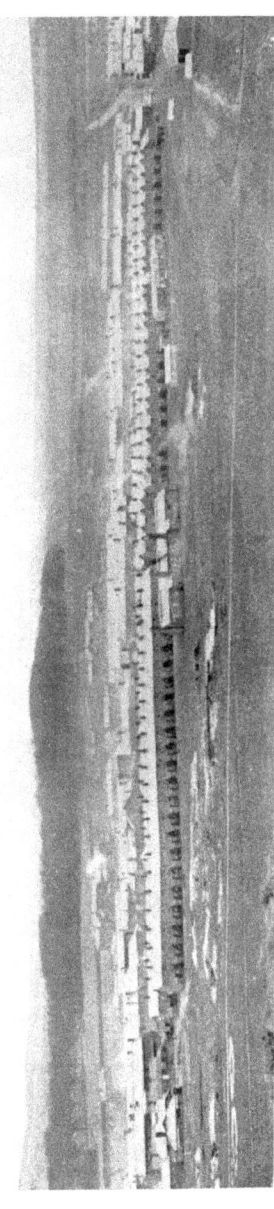

2. HEADQUARTERS OF A.I.F. DEPOTS IN THE UNITED KINGDOM
Bhurtpore Barracks at Tidworth, Salisbury Plain.

Aust. War Memorial Official Photo. No. D477.

3. A PARADE AT THE A.A.M.C. TRAINING DEPOT, PARKHOUSE

Lent by Major A. C. Fraser, A.A.M.C.
Aust. War Memorial Collection No. A1871.

To face p. 18.

4. No. 1 AUSTRALIAN AUXILIARY HOSPITAL, HAREFIELD
Australians skating on the pond.

Lent by Miss J. Jennings, Aust. Massage Service.
Aust. War Memorial Collection No. A11165.

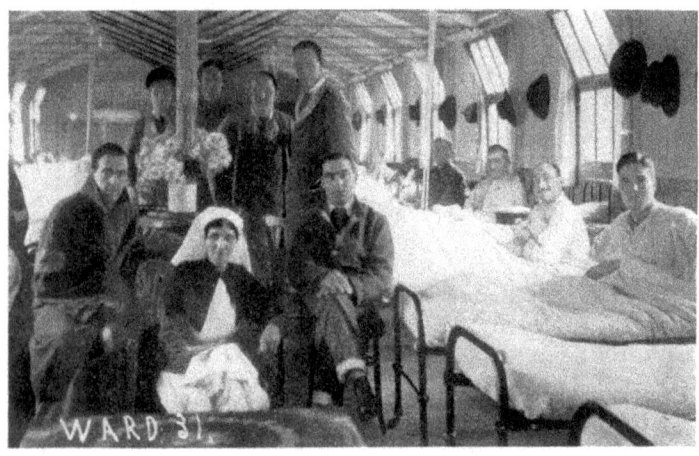

5. WARD 31 AT HAREFIELD

Lent by Sister A. C. Stone, A.A.N.S.
Aust. War Memorial Collection No. H16435. *To face p. 19.*

chiefly the more serious cases transferred from British hospitals and the Australian Auxiliaries. In particular it received (for treatment and retraining) men "unlikely to be fit for duty within *three* months," and (for "B" class duties, or for return to Australia as invalids) those "unlikely to be fit within *six* months."[22]

"*A.I.F. Depots in U.K.*" In June the reinforcement and convalescent depots were combined as the "A.I.F. Depots in U.K." under the command of Brigadier-General Sir Newton Moore, with headquarters at the Bhurtpore Barracks, Tidworth.[23] Colonel R. J. Millard was appointed to his staff on General Howse's nomination as "A.D.M.S., A.I.F. Depots in U.K." Responsibility for "higher" control on the medical side was shared vaguely by the D.D.M.S., Southern Command[24] and the D.M.S., A.I.F., the first named being responsible for medical arrangements, the latter for personnel. A "Senior Medical Officer" (S.M.O.) was appointed to each Command Depot; in June twelve medical officers and seven dental units were detailed by the D.M.S. for depot service. Each training battalion had, as part of its official establishment, an "attached" corporal and 4 other ranks, A.A.M.C., "for medical and sanitary duties." Small "brigade camp hospitals" were soon established at Perham Downs and at No. 2 Camp, Parkhouse, but in general the hospital requirements of the depots were served by British units. A medical staff for the A.I.F. Depots was slowly built up; but partly because the immense casualties, and consequent flow of convalescents, were not foreseen, partly (and chiefly) through the serious shortage of A.I.F. medical officers at this time, it was some time before the staff approached adequacy. And within a few weeks venereal disease and mumps were creating problems which occupied the attention of the medical staff to the detriment of more important matters.

---

[22] For the significance of the term "command" in the present reference *see Vol. I, p. 504*. Strictly speaking, the reinforcement depots on Salisbury Plain also were "Command" Depots, but the term came to signify only the Convalescent Depots.

[23] This was contrary to the original proposal of Surgeon-General Howse and Sir Newton Moore. The former did not, until 1917, exercise the degree of control of the machinery for return to duty after convalescence that would have been expected in view of his great interest in this matter.

[24] This was Surgeon-General W. G. Birrell, A.M.S., whom we have already met as D.M.S., M.E.F.

The Training Depots Fill Up. By the end of June (a record states) the training battalions were a "hive of activity." By the third week 12,765 reinforcements had marched in from Egypt, at the end of the month a further 11,000 troops arrived—9,256 direct from Australia. The 3rd Division came in during the month and the depots contained, beside this formation, 17,123 fully effective troops. The Command Depots held 2,592.[25]

Hospital treatment
The system that had been built up in England for the treatment of Australian sick and wounded arriving from overseas was retained, without any immediate modification. By this arrangement all Australian patients on arrival in England were dispersed in the British hospital system[26] where they remained till convalescent, being then transferred to the Australian Auxiliary Hospital at Harefield, or else sent direct to a convalescent depot.[27]

The "A.I.F." A national "unit"
The transfer of A.I.F. Headquarters and overseas base to England completed the unification of the A.I.F. and opened up a new phase of Australian co-operation in the Imperial war effort. The scheme for the internal control of the A.I.F., devised on a basis of experience acquired during the first year of the war, was now given form in administrative departments, whose activities covered every aspect of the "interior economy," working, and maintenance of an expeditionary force—except one: all its munitions and most of its supplies and military equipment were now obtained from British sources and paid for on a capitation basis.[28] Its component parts in England and Egypt and at the respective fronts were united under one supreme administrative "command." Like most new machinery the system at first worked stiffly.

---

[25] The surplus of recruits available in Australia at this time was such that the offer was made in May of a sixth Australian division, the special purpose of which was to permit the formation of an Australian "army." The offer included a new Australian hospital of 1,040 beds. With a prescience begotten of experience, the War Office suggested that the problem of maintaining existing divisions at strength must be the first consideration and might involve very heavy demands. Upon its advice the proposal was dropped.

[26] For a description of this the reader is referred to *Vol. I, p. 493n* of this history, and to the *British Official Medical History of the War, General, Vol. I.*

[27] For further developments, *see Chapter xv.*

[28] For details of this arrangement, which was completed in 1916, *see Chapter xxvi.* See also *Vol. I, p. 57.*

CHAPTER II

THE NEW SEAT OF WAR

THE "nursery sector" of the British front in France, to which the Australian Divisions, organised (together with the New Zealand Division) as the I and II Anzac Corps, were now sent for training, lay close in front of the River Lys near the old Flemish towns of Hazebrouck and Armentières, a few miles from the Belgian border. This sector was part of that of the British Second Army, commanded by General Sir Herbert Plumer. During the months of April, May, and June the four Australian Divisions, with their medical units together with Corps and Divisional Headquarters, arrived at Marseilles and moved, in a picturesque and colourful journey of three days, to the new front, where they took over a sector of the line south of Armentières. The combatant troops were set to learn the art of war in France; the services of maintenance took over the system of supply, replacement, and medical aid which had been built up by generations of British troops since November 1914, when the front had crystallized on the line of the Lys.

To understand the structure and fully to appreciate the international and military significance of the British Expeditionary Force in France would call for a particular study of the fighting of September and October 1914, and of the events that followed this. For such a study the reader must be referred elsewhere,[1] but it will assist to a better understanding of the situation as it appeared to the Australian force and its medical service in the months of April and May, 1916, if a brief résumé be made of the more significant developments.

The B.E.F.

---

[1] For example, to the admirable account of this given in the *British Official Medical History of the War, General, Vol. II; The Great War and the R.A.M.C.* by Lieut.-Col. F. S. Brereton; and *The War Story of the Canadian Army Medical Corps, 1914-1915*, by Col. J. G. Adami.

At the end of September, 1914, the three British army corps which had helped the five armies of France to check the German push through
Military developments in France: 1914-15
Belgium and make possible the ultimate victory of the Allies, were withdrawn from the Aisne to the Flanders front. In the middle of November, following the bitter and confused fighting of the First Battle of Ypres, Field-Marshal French took over a defined sector of the newly-entrenched line in Flanders. New formations arrived—the Indian Army Corps, and the IV and V British Corps—organised from the Regular Army reserves. With his force thus increasing, on December 25th Sir John French authorised the formation of the First and Second British Armies. The Canadian Division arrived in February, and the "First 100,000" of the British "New Armies" in May, 1915. A Third Army was formed in July, 1915, and a Fourth in March, 1916. The British Front in France and Belgium was organised on normal military lines in army areas, lines of communication, and expeditionary bases. General Headquarters of Sir John French with that of the D.G.M.S. were placed at St. Omer, but in 1916 both G.H.Q. and the medical headquarters that formed part of it were removed to Montreuil. The Headquarters of the Inspector-General of Communications and of his Director of Medical Services were placed at Abbeville.

The British Front, June, 1916

The growth of the British Expeditionary Force in France, and *pari passu* the development of the services of maintenance, were marked by stirring incident and rapid moves related to the German threat to Paris and later by the "race for the open flank" on the North Sea and the German retirement to a defensive position—chosen with a skill which the A.I.F. was afterwards to appreciate by bitter experience. This permitted the placing of British bases so far north as Calais and Boulogne—a circumstance the importance of which is amply illustrated in the medical history of the British effort in France. Through this system of Bases there passed, from England to the front, the prodigious stream of effectives, munitions and supplies, and back across the Channel the not less remarkable flow of casualties.[2]

The first eighteen months of the war had seen an amazing increase in the medical service with the B.E.F. not only in size
British Medical Service in France
to cope with the ever augmenting numbers, but (and even more remarkably) in complexity. When the Australians arrived in France, the

---
[2] *See sketch maps at pp. 30, 397.*

medical service there had entered upon a cardinal phase in its development. Its part in maintaining the strength and efficiency of the force in the field—now, probably, the supreme concern of the Commander-in-Chief—had been impressed on the military command by huge losses from wounds and sickness. At the same time its place as the proper medium for voluntary efforts of humane alleviation and treatment (evoked with intensity of feeling by the dreadful experiences of the troops in the fighting of 1914 and by the hardships of two winters) had been accepted by the recognised voluntary aid societies. That this position had not been achieved without "dust and heat" and some tragic events is made clear from outspoken comment by lay writers and not less definitely, if with greater restraint and understanding, in official writings.

Its Organisation. At the period under review the Service had become established on lines which changed comparatively little during the war. The general scheme of administration will be clear from the subjoined diagram. The machinery for prevention of disease was in great measure self-contained and distinct from that concerned in the movement and treatment of casualties, as were also the executive units for these two purposes. From early in 1915 a sanitary section formed part of the medical organisation of each division in the line, while "mobile laboratories," both bacteriological and hygienic, were attached to each Army.

Between the administrative departments and the executive units, and having immediate relations with each, was a system of "specialists" and "consultants." These, with various advisory commissions and councils, at the seat of war and at the War Office, formed a consultative and advisory body that played a very important part in directing the development of medical policy.

In addition to the above, certain departments of medical work had by this time become so important as to call for a separate administrative as well as executive staff. In particular must be mentioned the duties associated with the problem of medical *railway transport,* the prodigious growth of which led in March, 1915, to the appointment of a special officer and staff under the Inspector-General of Communications. *Gas warfare* had in-

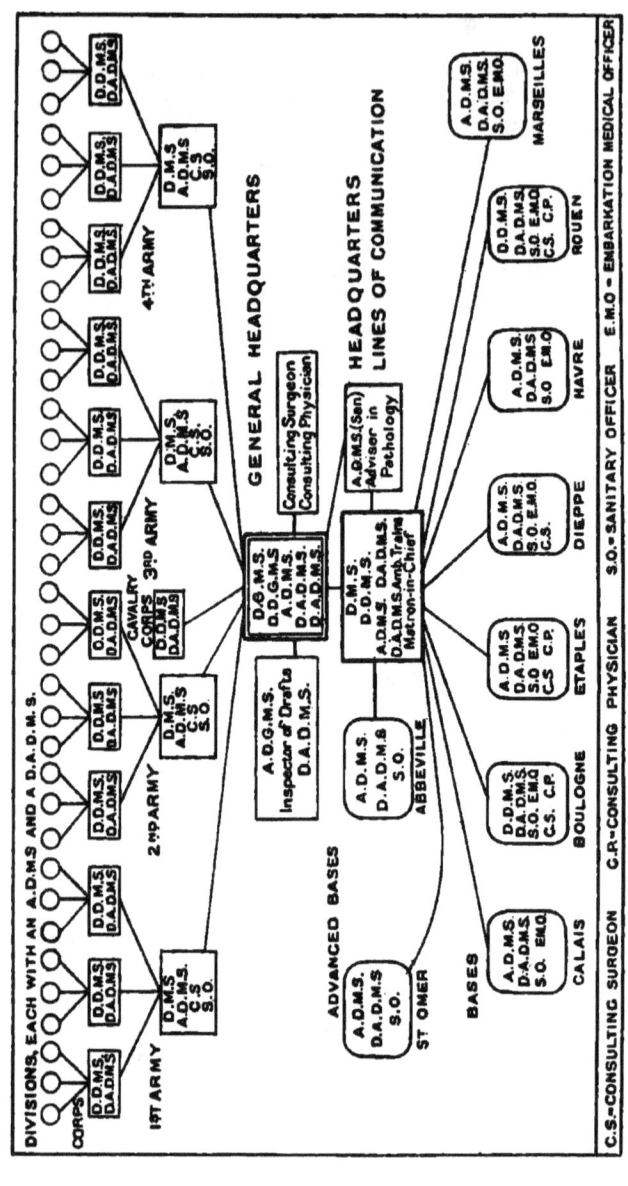

SCHEME OF MEDICAL ADMINISTRATION, WESTERN FRONT, 1918

The scheme here shown is for a force of four armies of three corps each, with sea bases and advanced bases.

*From the British Official Medical History;
by courtesy of the Historian.*

volved the medical service in onerous and difficult problems and duties, and for a time in heavy non-medical responsibilities. This matter is dealt with in a special chapter,[3] but occasional reference must be made to it in the account of the military operations.

Its Methods: Cardinal Phase. In respect of control and executive the medical service of the B.E.F. had achieved a stable and efficient system, fully adapted to meet the special requirements of warfare in France; but in respect of its methods, including in greater or less degree most of its prime functions, it was still in a state of flux. The chief feature of this was a revolt against those principles and methods which, derived from the experience of previous wars, had proved wholly inapplicable to the conditions on the Western Front. There had arisen, indeed, a compelling sense of the need for research and experiment in quest of a scientific basis for more effective action. In particular the huge mortality from *wound shock* and *wound infection* had brought a resolute campaign for improvement which embraced every aspect of the problem. This campaign was developing along two broad lines corresponding with the two prime elements in "evacuation"—transport and treatment. The treatment of wounds in war is of necessity closely related to the process of the removal of the wounded from the battle area. The growth of the military medical service has been largely moulded by the need for fulfilling at the same time these two fundamental purposes; and, in the change of medical methods in the Great War also, these two functions moved hand in hand. The story of their parallel development will be found one of surpassing interest. Here it must suffice to say that by the beginning of 1916 the dominant purpose of the medical service at the front was on the one hand to shorten the time and improve the conditions prior to effective surgical treatment and after-treatment and, on the other, in conjunction with experimental and clinical research in the field, at the base, and in the research institutions in Britain, to ascertain the exact nature of the morbid processes concerned and to find means to offset their effects.

Transport: Motor Ambulance Convoys. The equipping of

---
[3] *In Vol. III.*

the British field ambulances with motor-transport had been vetoed before the war by military members of the Army Council:[4] that of the B.E.F. was at first all horse-drawn. The evacuation of the wounded from the British force in the retreat from Mons would seem to compare unfavourably even with that[5] of the Landing on Gallipoli. Motor-transport was (officially) attached to field ambulances in November 1914;[6] and when the Australians arrived in France each of these units had an establishment of three horse-drawn ambulance waggons and seven motor ambulance cars, including two light Ford cars. To clear from the "stations" established by the field ambulances to those of the casualty clearing stations and thence to ambulance train (L. of C.), in September 1914 "motor ambulance convoys" had been formed. Of these there were now some twenty—each consisting of some fifty cars—working on the British front as well as twenty-five ambulance trains, the number of both having a definite ratio to that of the troops in France.

Treatment: Casualty Clearing Stations. Treatment of wounds and clinical research were now centring in the casualty clearing stations; since the middle of 1915, save in rushes, most of the urgent surgery had been carried out there.[7] The rôle of the field ambulance was becoming more and more that of subserving, by appropriate treatment and rapid transport, the work of the C.C.S.; as that of the great general hospitals at the Base was to carry it on. When therefore in May, 1916, the Australian Casualty Clearing Stations arrived in France they found themselves sited within a few miles of the front line and called on to undertake immediate surgery of all kinds, and to keep pace with improvements that were soon to transform the medical system at the front and very greatly to improve the outlook, immediate and remote, of the wounded man.[8]

Prevention of Wastage. To prevent the evacuation of slight cases from "army" areas (or, in technical terms, to "reduce

---

[4] *British Official Medical History, General, Vol. I, p. 12.*
[5] Described in this work, *Vol. I, Chapter viii*, and in *The Great War and the R.A.M.C., loc. cit. See also Chapter xi* of this volume.
[6] The history of medical motor-transport in the British Army is discussed in the chapter of this volume dealing with transport (*Chapter xi, pp. 285-91*).
[7] In November of 1914 provision was made for a female nursing staff in the casualty clearing stations. In January of 1915 approval was given for their undertaking systematic operative work, heretofore done entirely in the field ambulances, and suitable equipment was provided. *See also Chapters xii and xiii.*
[8] See, however, in this connection, *Chapter xxv.*

'army' wastage") ambulance "rest stations" had been formed. "convalescent depots" were also formed at the Base, at Boulogne, Rouen, Le Havre, Etaples, and other centres.

A great system of baths and divisional laundries was induced by the vast wastage caused during 1915 through various minor infections and physical traumata—pediculosis, scabies, "I.C.T." (Inflammation of Connective Tissue), sore feet, trench foot, and so forth—the whole system being conducted by the medical service. Further, the fundamental medical duty of preventing infection was at a peculiarly interesting stage in its development. Not only were scientific diagnosis and research in full swing, with their advanced-guard in the mobile laboratories at the front, but there was also beginning the process of devolution whereby much of the executive work was being passed to the department of the Quartermaster-General.

Even more important as regards the development of the medical service than any specific advance in methods was the birth within it of an ardent spirit of scientific adventure, which in its call for high endeavour to the members of the medical profession—and, by repercussion, to all members of the corps—was hardly less compelling than the emotional appeal for service in relief of suffering. In solid results it was perhaps as helpful as the highest acts of heroism in the field and devotion to duty in the hospital wards. Efficient and flexible as the British army medical system had proved, it was in the highest degree advantageous that the moral sentiment sustaining its personnel should be fed by the adventurous spirit of youth and warmed by the steady glow of scientific and professional enthusiasm.

A new outlook

Such in outline was the situation when the Australian force took its place among the performers already moving towards their appointed stations in preparation for the stupendous opening scene of the Somme Battle.

When on April 7th the 2nd Australian Division entered the quiet line south of Armentières, the 5th and 7th Field Ambulances took over the duty of clearance, with the 6th in reserve at Erquinghem baths. On May 5th the first enemy raid was sustained, and on June 6th the first counter-raid was made by a party from the 26th and 28th Battalions. By the

Australian formations arrive in France

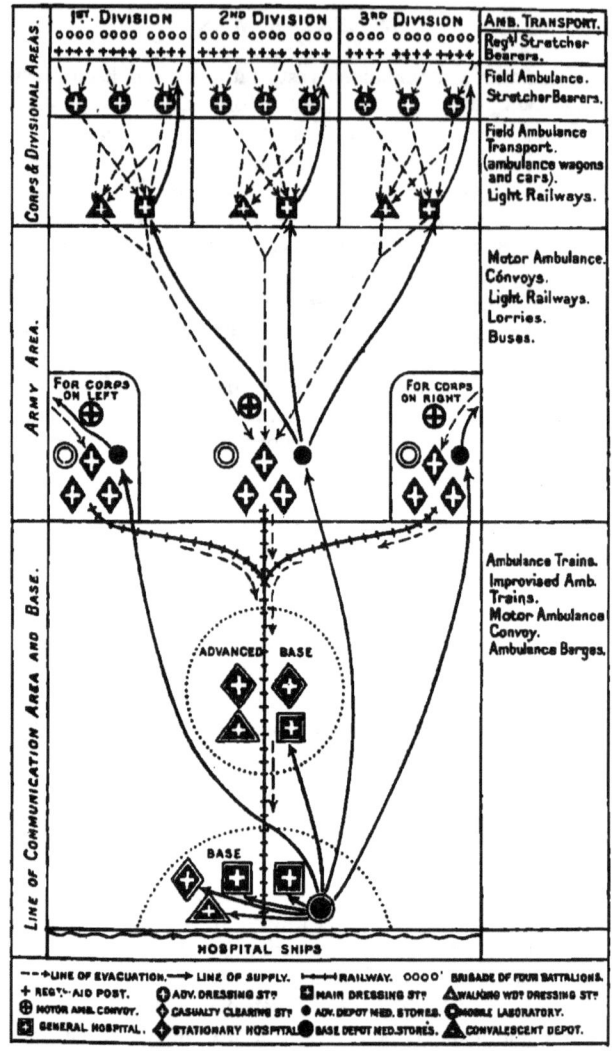

THE ORGANISATION OF MEDICAL SERVICES FROM A CORPS FRONT
OF THREE DIVISIONS IN AN ARMY TO A SEA BASE

NOTE.—The signs for Motor Ambulance Convoy, Advanced Depot of Medical Stores, Base Depot of Medical Stores, Walking Wounded Dressing Station, Mobile Laboratory, and Convalescent Depot differ from those used in the present volume.

*From the British Official Medical History:
by courtesy of the Historian.*

middle of April the whole of I Anzac Corps had arrived in France; II Anzac followed during June. The order of battle of the Australian medical units and the dates of their arrival are shown in the subjoined table.

I. ANZAC CORPS

G.O.C.: Lieut.-General Sir W. R. Birdwood.
D.D.M.S.: Colonel C. C. Manifold, I.M.S.

1st Australian Division		*2nd Australian Division*	
G.O.C.: Maj.-Gen. H. B. Walker		G.O.C.: Maj.-Gen. J. G. Legge	
A.D.M.S.: Col. A. H. Sturdee		A.D.M.S.: Col. A. Sutton	
	Arrived France		Arrived France
1st Fld. Amb.	30/3/16	5th Fld. Amb.	25/3/16
2nd Fld. Amb.	31/3/16	6th Fld. Amb.	26/3/16
3rd Fld. Amb.	3/4/16	7th Fld. Amb.	20/3/16
No. 2 San. Sectn.	3/4/16	No. 1 San. Sectn.	23/3/16

II. ANZAC CORPS

G.O.C.: Lieut.-General Sir A. J. Godley.
D.D.M.S.: Colonel E. Reuter Roth, A.A.M.C.

4th Australian Division		*5th Australian Division*	
G.O.C.: Maj.-Gen. Sir H. V. Cox		G.O.C.: Maj.-Gen. J. W. M'Cay	
A.D.M.S.: Col. G. W. Barber		A.D.M.S.: Col. C. H. W. Hardy	
	Arrived France		Arrived France
4th Fld. Amb.	9/6/16	8th Fld. Amb.	23/6/16
12th Fld. Amb.	11/6/16	14th Fld. Amb.	27/6/16
13th Fld. Amb.	13/6/16	15th Fld. Amb.	28/6/16
No. 4 San. Sectn.	8/6/16	No. 5 San. Sectn.	9/6/16

L. OF C. UNITS

No. 1 C.C.S.	23/3/16	No. 1 Gen. Hospital	5/4/16
No. 2 C.C.S.	27/4/16	No. 2 Gen. Hospital	1/4/16

In accordance with the new Australian organisation, a Dental Section accompanied each field ambulance.

The New Zealand Division (A.D.M.S. Colonel C. Mackie Begg) arrived with I Anzac in April, but on the advent of II Anzac its place was taken by the 4th Australian Division, and the New Zealand Division together with the 5th Australian then formed the II Anzac Corps. The 3rd Division, it will be recalled, was at this time arriving in England from Australia.

Army, and Lines of Communication Units. On April 12th No. 1 Australian General Hospital, arriving at Rouen, was established in the great hospital centre outside the town, and it received its first patients on April 30th. On June 2nd No. 2 left Marseilles to reopen at Wimereux near Boulogne. The two Australian stationary hospitals also were offered to the Director-General, B.E.F., but were declined by him since "no suitable sites were available." No. 1 Australian Casualty Clearing Station arrived with I Anzac Corps and opened at Estaires, serving the Divisions of I Anzac. The 2nd was located at Trois Arbres, north-west of Armentières, near Steenwerck. From this time till the end of the war the experience of all these units was no longer as heretofore involved with that of the Australian Divisions. As Army or Line of Communication units they found themselves sited in close relation to highly stabilised channels of movement—the "lines of communication" between the railheads and the Base—their activities being controlled by static administrations of "Army" and "I.G.C." The Divisions, on the other hand, being essentially mobile formations, were transferred from one Army to another. From the outset General

The Lines of Communication and Bases in the Northern Sector of the British Front.

Haig insisted that the Australian Divisions, like all the rest, should be available for independent service.[9] Since the present chapters deal with the work of the field formations the experience of the Line of Communication units is narrated in special chapters. By reason of the particular nature of their work, the same course is adopted with the sanitary sections, though these formed part of the Divisions.

The assimilation of the Australian units was accomplished smoothly and rapidly. They contained a solid nucleus of men who had been trained in the hardest and most individualistic school of arms on any front. All the medical administrative officers were by now experienced in war, as were also the commanding officers and the senior N.C.O's of the field medical units. Routes of evacuation were taken over from British formations, at first on a single divisional front, but in July, when II Anzac had arrived, from two and, later, from three Divisions in the line. Regular divisional reliefs were organised, and by the end of May the Australian troops were an integral part of the British Army front, which (with a short gap in Belgium held by the Belgian Army or, for political reasons, by French troops) then extended from Dixmude on the North Sea to the Somme.

The New Conditions. The Australian soldiers, especially those who had known Gallipoli, were at first highly pleased with their new surroundings and conditions. The forests and fertile fields of Flanders were green and fresh in the early spring, the stately and well ordered towns and quaint villages held solid comfort as well as piquant novelty. The field ration, though it differed little from that of Gallipoli, was greatly improved by local purchase by the Supply Department. Relief from the line was regular, and leave to England or Paris was available. The medical service found itself in a new world where medical comforts, official and Red Cross, were almost unlimited, and the equipment "additional to mobilisation table" was governed only by transport facilities.

The Australian force which took its place on the Allied side of the great No-Man's Land, which stretched unbroken for

---

[9] On his part, however, General Haig promised that this should be exceptional. For details the reader is referred to *The Official History of Australia in the War 1914-1918, Vol. III.*

400 miles, with a man to each three yards, was composed of troops of the finest physique, in perfect health, and attuned to a very high pitch of *élan*. At no time in its history was the force in a higher state of physical and moral fitness for deeds of high emprise. The sustenance of its morale was a responsibility of those who directed these endeavours; and in the maintenance of its health and strength the medical service was closely concerned, and certain matters germane thereto require reference here.

Health of troops

Exclusion of Exotic Diseases. Great concern had been felt by British General Headquarters at the transfer of Australian troops from the East. Events in Gallipoli had conferred on any force that served there a sinister reputation for infection, and more than a suspicion of sanitary slackness. All armies in the Great War were louse-infested; and to such forces typhus, the historic foe of field armies, was a real menace. The measures taken to prevent the entry of this and other diseases are described elsewhere;[10] here it will suffice to say that only two cases of smallpox, and five of relapsing fever escaped the sieve established by No. 2 Australian General Hospital at Marseilles, where several cases of typhus among British troops were intercepted.

Sanitary Conference. Early in May two important conferences were held between specialists—engineers, medical, and "Q"—of Second Army and representatives from the Australian formations. At the first conference, the arrangements for water (to be dealt with in *Chapter XIX*) were discussed. The second, on May 5th, concerned sanitation in general and measures for disease prevention. At the latter the Australian Deputy Assistant Directors of Medical Services, and officers commanding the Australian and New Zealand Sanitary Sections conferred with the Second Army "Sanitary" authorities represented by Captain Bullock, R.A.M.C. commanding No. 14 "Mobile Bacteriological Laboratory,"[11] chiefly concerning dysentery, including the details of sanitary routine, food and cooking, and the training of cooks; and as well discussed methods for the

---

[10] In *Chapter xix.*
[11] The enthusiasm and ability, and not less the cordiality, of the officers who commanded these mobile laboratories deeply impressed the Australians.

6. AN AUSTRALIAN MEDICAL UNIT MARCHING THROUGH MARSEILLES

Lent by Chaplain the Rev. C. W. Tomkins.
Aust. War Memorial Collection No. A1061.

To face p. 32.

7. THE OPPOSING LINES ON THE WESTERN FRONT IN 1916

Air-photograph of the opposing trench systems at "The Lozenge," near Armentières, showing the British trenches below and the German above. The width of No-Man's Land varies from 350 yards on the left to 200 on the right. On the right a bend in the British line has been remedied by making a "chord" trench. The photograph was taken after a raid, and the actual track of the Australian party across No-Man's Land can be seen on the right.

British Air Force Photograph.
Aust. War Memorial Collection No. G1534bc.

technical and administrative control of contacts and "carriers" (described in *Chapter XIX*). The establishing of personal relations was of great and lasting importance to both parties to the conference; it was characteristic of the new spirit in the medical service.

The peaceful invasion—for it was nothing less—of France by Britain during 1914-18 brought inevitably problems of social co-operation which were of quite first-rate importance, not only for the winning of the war by the Allies, but as a guide in a far greater problem, namely, the possibility of a peaceful international democracy as the basis of human society. Among the multifarious elements of this—economic, temperamental, intellectual, sexual, and the like—was one in which the medical service took the leading part, namely, the professional relations with the civil communities of France and Belgium. The matter is given some attention in *Chapter XXV*, but we may note here that the medical officers of the A.I.F. found a *modus vivendi* evolving along three distinct lines:—

Problems of alliance: the civil population

(1) Rescue of civilians involved in military action. Here the "dictates of humanity" left no room for uncertainty. (2) Sickness in the civil population in billeting areas and occupied towns. This problem was not so clear-cut, and will call for a note. (3) The involvement of the troops in risk from civil foci of infection, either from persons (as in cases of diphtheria, scarlet fever, tuberculosis, cerebro-spinal fever, and, in particular, V.D.) or from places, such as billeting areas or trench zones where the water supplies were contaminated with typhoid or dysentery.

The reorganisation—then but recently carried out in Egypt —of the Australian field ambulances as two-section units could not be maintained; it was considered by the British authorities that it involved the risk of confusion on interchange with British units, and in the supply of rations, stores, and equipment. Permission to retain it was therefore refused by the War Office.[12]

Two-Section Field Ambulance

---

[12] It is only fair to Surgeon-Generals Howse and Williams to note that their innovation forestalled changes embodied in the post-war units. *See Vol. I (pp. 41, 482).*

With each Division there came to France reinforcements of 10 per cent. of the divisional infantry and a smaller proportion for other services, together with a small administrative staff from the Australian depots in Egypt. Four Australian Base Depots, one for each of the 1st, 2nd, 4th, and 5th Divisions, were established as part of the great British Infantry Base Depot at Etaples. Into them passed, as required, reinforcements and recovered men from the training battalions and Command Depots in England, together with convalescents from the Base Hospitals in France; and from them were drawn the drafts for the front. These drafts were "demanded" by units in the field sending in a "field return" (Army Form B.213) to the Australian Section of the "3rd Echelon" of G.H.Q.—the Adjutant-General's Branch, situated at Rouen.

Reinforcements

The first experience of the Australian force in the evacuation of wounded from a major operation in France—the Battle of Fromelles—was typical of the kind of warfare in vogue at this period. Intended as a comparatively unimportant feint, it became for the Australian force a most serious and tragic affair. Its medical events indeed were of sufficient significance to call for a special chapter.

CHAPTER III

TRENCH-WARFARE : THE BATTLE OF FROMELLES

THE battle line in France which for three years determined in great measure the nature and course of the fighting was for the most part that selected by the German General Staff after its failure to effect a breakthrough in October, 1914. It was a defensive position and sited to control an extensive field of observation and artillery fire. Its chief features should be known to any student of the war in France. They have been well set out as follows :—[1]

The trench line in France

"The German General Staff . . selected as the buttress of its new line a series of eminences that lay more or less continuously from the sea to Switzerland. Examples of high ground thus selected are Passchendaele Ridge, Messines Ridge, Aubers Ridge, Vimy Ridge, and there were many others. Their tactical importance was amply evidenced by the sanguinary struggles which eventually centred round most of them. . . . Defences were invariably flung out some thousands of yards in front of the dominating ridges [so that] the typical German position consisted of a considerable width of low-lying ground, trenched, wired, and studded with strong points, behind which rose in tiers ridge after ridge of higher ground, culminating finally in a feature that conferred command over all the adjacent terrain for miles."

In the Flanders area this command derived not so much from the height of the ridges as from the uniform flatness of the rest of the country. In the sector south-west of Armentières, with which this chapter is concerned, the British line was in front of the River Lys, and routes of access and egress were therefore determined by existing bridges. The land was rescued from swamp only by a vast reticulation of ditches. The place of trenches, which when dug in the lowlands became water-

---

[1] *See The Story of the Fifth Australian Division, pp. 88-89, by Captain A. D. Ellis.*

logged, was taken by sandbagged parapets and duckboard tracks. Roads, except the cobbled ones, were soon cut up.

The system of breastworks around the eastern edge of Armentières and thence to the south-west—about nine miles in all—was held on a two-divisional front, first by I Anzac, and later, in mid-July, by II Anzac which disposed the newly-arrived 5th Australian Division on the right, and the veteran New Zealand Division on the left. The conditions of fighting in this area permitted the close approximation of medical posi-

The Second Army Area, May 1916.

tions to the firing line. Peasants worked in the fields and children attended school within a few miles of the front line with only occasional mishaps. But in its place and time the fighting here was fierce enough.

Scheme of Clearance. Field ambulance dressing stations[2] were formed in front of the Lys in schools or breweries, mostly little damaged though only a few miles behind the line. Evacuation to these and clearance from the regimental aid-posts were straightforward though at times eventful. Regimental bearers, commonly attached to companies, carried wounded from the front lines through narrow saps to the aid-posts in sandbagged cupolas or cellars outside the field of machine-gun fire. Thence clearance to the horse- or motor-ambulance post was chiefly by wheeled stretcher. Roads were seldom severely shelled except during raids. The general scheme of dressing and rest stations, and of clearance to casualty clearing stations will be made clear by the maps and sketches.

Trench-warfare. In this trench-warfare casualties from the sniping, machine-gunning, and occasional artillery "hates" averaged not more than ninety to a hundred per week for the Corps. A sharp rise from time to time shows the shelling of a relief or of a billet; through their excellent system of ground observation the Germans could inflict such losses almost at will.[3] The total Australian battle casualties in May and June were, 499 killed or died of wounds and 1,579 wounded.

Raids. In May the serenity of this warfare was broken, never, for the A.I.F., to return till the end of the war. On May 5th the force sustained the first German "raid."

The "raid" was simply a trench-line battle on a small scale, and all the great battles of 1916-17 were in tactical method not unlike large-scale raids. Raids were undertaken for various purposes, but chiefly to take prisoners for identification of their units, to inflict casualties and to promote the morale and the "offensive spirit" of the attacking side and lessen those of the enemy. At times they served a tactical or even strategic purpose. But unless it was specially desired to improve the sector of line or to eliminate a strong-post, the enemy trench entered was not retained. In 1918 the Australian troops raided for fun. Combatant preparations for these miniature battles were often very detailed and at this time included elaborate artillery action of the kind known as the "box barrage." Casualties sustained or inflicted varied from five or six up to a hundred or more.

---

[2] On March 27 the 7th Field Ambulance opened a large dressing station at Morbecque. On April 5 it moved to Fort Rompu, taking over an M.D.S. with A.D.S's at Bois Grenier, Fleurbaix and Port à Clous.

[3] Thus on April 20 the 9th Battalion sustained 74 casualties in a company billet. In this first sharp test of morale the regimental medical officer and bearers kept their heads and were commended. The Regimental Medical Officer, Capt. A. McKillop, and five bearers were wounded; one bearer was killed.

One or more squads of regimental bearers usually accompanied the raiders. General medical arrangements dovetailed in with the normal scheme of evacuation and do not call for special description, and space precludes a detailed account of

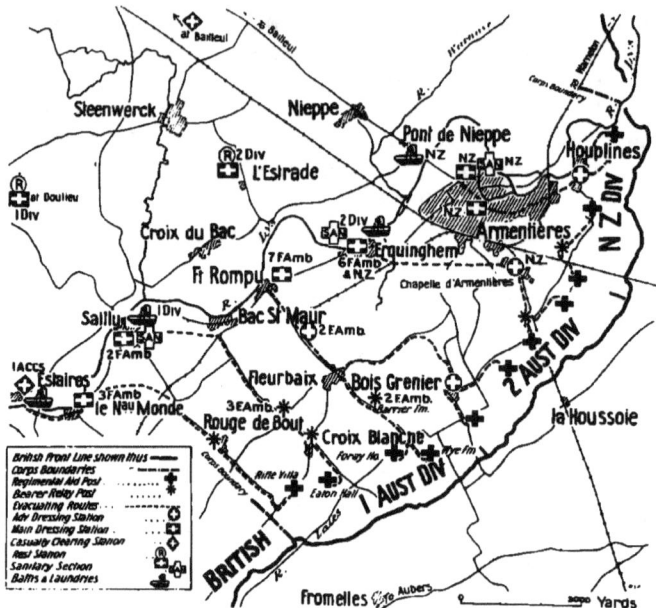

The "Nursery" Front during the Tenure of I Anzac, June 1916, showing Medical Arrangements.

any one raid. Casualties were chiefly due to the shelling, mainly to the preliminary bombardment, which was often very severe. That preceding the German raid at Bois Grenier on July 3rd is described by the regimental medical officer[4] as

the fiercest I ever saw during the war, though I experienced some that continued for hours, even for days on end. When it ceased parapet and parados had been replaced by a line of gaping holes. And yet a few dazed men not only survived but fought with the raiders.

---

[4] Capt. R. C. Winn, R.M.O. of the 14th Bn.

This feature of intense shelling became familiar, and was an important element both in battlecraft and in medical work.[5] At the beginning of June, in fulfilment of a pledge to the French High Command raiding became an element in the British operations in relief of Verdun. In all thirteen were undertaken at this time by units of the I Anzac Corps. To the A.I.F. and its medical service they were of great value both as training for attack and in welding the various units and services into an efficient weapon of war.

TABLE I.—Casualties of A.I.F. on Western Front to 30th June, 1916.

Battle Casualties		Non-Battle Casualties	
Killed in action	418	Died of Disease ..	51
Died of wounds	178	Accidentally killed	24
Died of Gas Poisoning	2	Sick	5,437
Wounded in action	1,725	Accidentally injured	40
Gassed ..	9	Self inflicted injuries	23
Shell Shock	50		
Prisoners of war	24		

It was unhappily far otherwise with the operation of the same kind but on far greater scale, carried out by Australian and English troops at the end of this series.

Battle of Fromelles
The Battle of the Somme had then opened some three weeks before, on July 1st. On the 3rd the I Anzac Corps (Lieut.-General Sir William Birdwood) had been replaced by II Anzac (Lieut.-General Sir Alexander Godley) and, after moving to Bailleul,[6] entrained on July 11th for the south to join the "Reserve" Army. On the 19th—the day on which the transferred units began to move up to the Somme battle line—the 5th Division, which had been left in Flanders, was called on—only three weeks after arrival from

---

[5] The purpose and events of these raids in May-July, 1916 are described in detail in *Vol. III* of the *Official History of Australia in the War of 1914-18*. This form of warfare was one of which the Australian troops became the acknowledged masters (*Ibid., Vol. VI*).

[6] While there the I Anzac Corps staff, instructed by Second Army, reconnoitred medical positions for a British attack on Messines, preparations for which were in progress.

Egypt—to undertake an action that involved some fifty per cent. of casualties to its infantry engaged.

The Battle of Fromelles has been called "an important raid" (British Official), an "attack on a sector of the line" (German Official), and an "attack at Fromelles" (Official Chronology). The Australian Official Historian properly names it a Battle. The plan was the outcome of an ambitious scheme of the British XI Corps to assist the Somme offensive by repeating a previous unsuccessful attack threatening the important Aubers Ridge that dominated the western approach to Lille. Forestalled by the Battle of Albert the local general staff was loth to give up its scheme, which then became a "feint" to divert attention from the Somme. The objective finally proposed was a small German salient facing the First and Second Armies, known as the "Sugar-loaf," formed through a slight rise which had been developed as a machine-gun fortress. This strong point together with some 2,000 yards of the German reserve line, presumed to run parallel with the front, were to be captured and held. On July 15th General Haig gave a tentative and general approval; thereafter the project moved confusedly to its *dénouement*.

The military plan

The Sugar-loaf was faced on the north by the right of the newly arrived 5th Australian Division and on the west by the left of the 61st, a Territorial division, also newly sent to France, and forming the left of the First Army just as the 5th Division formed the right of the Second. For the attack, the 5th Division was to concentrate all its three brigades on the front of its right brigade, the 15th, and the 61st Division similarly concentrated itself upon its own left. The XI Corps would direct the attack. After several delays the well advertised operation was fixed for 5.45 p.m. on July 19th.

Across No-Man's Land ran a muddy stream, the Laies, usually three to four feet deep. The attack was made late in the afternoon, and darkness fell soon after, about 8.30 p.m.

The artillery preparation had left the German machine-gun posts on the Sugar-loaf for the most part intact. As a consequence the 61st Division and 15th Brigade failed in their assault on this strong-post. The centre and left brigades (14th and 8th) of the 5th Division crossed No-Man's Land, seized two lines of German trench, and moved on 300 yards to what was noted in their maps as the third trench—their objective, some 600 yards from the front line. This however proved to be no more than a ditch filled with water. The night was spent in desperate attempts to consolidate the positions occupied; but the morning found each Brigade partly surrounded by the enemy and compelled to fight its way back to, and across No-Man's Land, with appalling loss.

Course of the Battle

Casualties occurred chiefly in No-Man's Land, but also in the approach trenches—which were heavily shelled during the assembly—and large numbers of men were killed or wounded in the confused fighting which took place in and beyond the German lines.

Responsibility for the medical arrangements in rear of the 5th Division lay with the D.M.S. of Second Army, who detailed No. 2 Australian C.C.S. for "sitting cases"; stretcher cases were to go to a British unit at Bailleul.[7] Fifty motor ambulances of No. 14 Motor Ambulance Convoy were allotted to the D.D.M.S. II Anzac Corps for evacuation to C.C.S., and twenty-one were lent to the 5th Division, whose motor-transport had not yet arrived. A special rest station was formed at Port à Clous Farm for slight casualties.

Medical arrangements

The 5th Division's sector of the front of attack had previously been held by the 15th Brigade with two battalions in

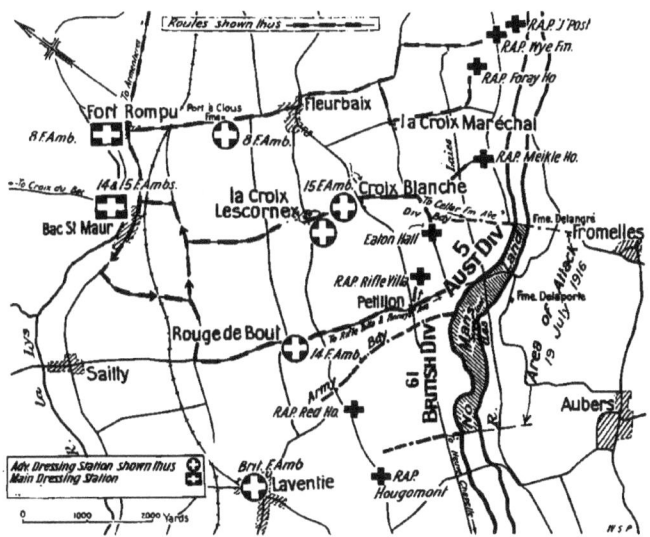

Scheme of Clearance from Fromelles Sector, July 1916.

line. Regimental aid-posts had been at "Pinney's Avenue" (58th Bn.) and at Cellar Farm Avenue (57th). These normally cleared through advanced dressing stations at Rouge de Bout

---

[7] The use of No. 1 Aust. C.C.S., situated at Estaires, only five miles from the front line, for this duty was precluded by the arrangements for road traffic.

and Croix Blanche to the main dressing station at Fort Rompu, staffed by the 8th Field Ambulance. For the battle the latter station was retained to serve the left sector, and a new main dressing station was opened in a factory at Bac St. Maur to serve the right. The latter was elaborately equipped with wards to be staffed by two units (14th and 15th Field Ambulances) which would work independently. Ample supplies of stretchers, splints, dressings, blankets and medical comforts were provided.

Like the plans of the battle itself the arrangements made by the A.D.M.S. (Colonel C. H. W. Hardy) for clearing his front were unusual. No single field ambulance was charged with the sole duty of controlling clearance from the front; instead, different sectors of it were allotted for each unit and "definite routes were arranged and set apart." The two existing regimental aid-posts at "Pinney's Avenue" and "Cellar Farm" were retained, together with those in use by the reserve battalions at "Rifle Villa" and "Eaton Hall." All were well stocked with extra dressings and comforts, issued officially or procured through individual initiative.[8] *"Liaison"* between the ambulance "bearer" officers and the regimental medical officers appears to have been defective. Most of the latter had however reconnoitred the front line, as also had those of the reserve battalions. Though new to the conditions on the Western Front some medical officers and a considerable proportion of their N.C.O's had been trained and tried out at Gallipoli, and there was among them a general apprehension of very heavy casualties—an apprehension which does not appear to have been felt by the British commander concerned—Lieut.-General Haking.[9]

The chief medical features of Fromelles were, *first*, a military failure with exceptionally heavy casualties, sustained in a brief time, and on a very small front; **General course of events** *second*, the fact that the distance of the advanced and main dressing stations from the front line was much less than usual. These features, and the

---

[8] Thus one R.M.O. (Capt. K. H. Grieve of the 56th Bn.) records that "strong scissors," were bought with regimental funds and issued to each bearer, and were found of great service.

[9] "The Battalion officers all realised it would be a very bloody business. The Gallipoli ones said it would be much worse than the German Officers' Trench." (Major E. F. Lind, 15th Fld. Amb.) *See also Vol. I, p. 293* "Steele's. August 7."

comparative absence of intense shelling in the back areas, determined the nature of the medical problem and in great measure also the results achieved. While they promoted a rapid evacuation by wheeled transport from the dressing stations they also made inevitable a period of congestion in the zone of hand-carry. The medical interest of the battle centres therefore in the collecting of casualties from the field of battle and their clearance in the zone served by the regimental and ambulance bearers.

Partly through the excess of casualties on the Australian right, but chiefly through the existence there of more direct routes of clearance and special means of escape from the sphere of fighting,[10] the streams of wounded passed chiefly along the right hand routes of clearance.[11] The first casualties, from the German shelling, reached the field ambulances in the M.D.S. at Bac St. Maur at 12.30 p.m. on the 19th. Early reports received by the A.D.M.S. from the advanced dressing station were very favourable; but at about midnight the 14th Brigade reported

numbers of casualties exceeds the capacity of the medical staff and stretcher bearers. Our old line very full of wounded. . . . Very Urgent.

Action was taken in response to this call by both the Army Corps and the 5th Division staffs. Assistance was obtained from the New Zealand Division on the left, whose A.D.M.S. (Colonel Begg) sent substantial help in officers and bearers to the 14th Field Ambulance at Rouge de Bout, and from the 8th Field Ambulance at Fort Rompu. The 184th Brigade of the 61st Division lent a hand. At 4.35 a.m. a message was received by the A.D.M.S. from the II Anzac Corps Commander (General Godley) congratulating "all ranks on your splendid work"; at 4.45 a.m. the D.A.D.M.S. II Anzac reported that "all was going most satisfactorily, and that there were then no further bearers or medical officers wanted."

This complaisance, born of the muddle that dogged this dreadful affair, was rudely shaken when, at 7.12 a.m., an urgent wire

---

[10] As at Lone Pine, "saps" were dug into No-Man's Land during the night of the battle. These were a factor in the rescue of the wounded, though not a great one.

[11] As in all military treatises, the terms "right" and "left" are of course used with reference to the front, and not to the rearward direction of the stream of casualties.

was received at Divisional Headquarters from the 15th Brigade that "there is still a large number of men wounded during the action awaiting to be dealt with." The experienced Officer Commanding the 14th Field Ambulance, Lieut.-Colonel A. H. Tebbutt, had on his own initiative made a personal reconnaissance of the front line and now reported that whereas the wounded who had reached the dressing stations were being evacuated satisfactorily, the front line and the battlefield itself, through shortage of regimental bearers and their exhaustion, had certainly not been "cleared." This was confirmed by reports from the 15th Brigade, and it soon became evident that a serious medical tragedy was impending on the military one. From that hour onwards it was recognised that the collecting of wounded from the zone of fighting to the regimental aid-posts and thence to the advanced dressing stations was a problem demanding the utmost efforts of the whole medical service and combatant troops alike. We may now pick up the actual course of "medical" events in this tragic affair.

No-Man's Land on this front varied in depth from 400 yards at the Sugar-loaf to some 100 in front of the 8th Brigade. From zero hour at 5.45 p.m. onwards men were being wounded and now lay scattered thickly over the whole of the area covered in the attack, in particular around the "sallyports" and on the right, in the sphere of the 15th Brigade's advance across No-Man's Land. The problem of collecting and clearance of battle casualties is essentially a matter of numbers; and with the figures now available we can envisage more clearly than could the actors at Fromelles the nature of their problem.

Collecting the wounded

As at Lone Pine these officers remained for the most part in their aid-posts, sending their bearers forward in charge of the N.C.O's.[12] Collecting of wounded in and beyond No-Man's Land was at first undertaken entirely by the regimental bearers. Retiring troops

R.M.O's

---

[12] The R.M.O. 60th Battalion (Capt. F. W. D. Collier) records his own experience—"I was at first ordered to go over with the last wave but that was changed and I was to stay back and clear up till the new position was captured, and then go over. But I had orders that my sixteen regimental bearers were to go over with the last wave, and collect wounded at once. I think now that this was a great mistake but it was my first battle. Nine out of my sixteen bearers were knocked out soon after they jumped over and I never saw any more of them after that night."

assisted those who could walk, and with this help and that of the regimental bearers of reserve battalions, and later of infantry fatigue parties, and of ambulance bearers, large numbers of wounded reached the front line and thence the aid-posts, or were "dumped" in the nearest trench or dugout.

The aid-posts at Pinney's Avenue and Cellar Farm Avenue were behind the support trenches and some 300 yards from the front line. The R.A.P's at Rifle Villa **At the regimental aid-posts** and Eaton Hall became waggon loading posts. In Pinney's five and at Cellar Farm three medical officers worked together. At 10 p.m. a "forward post" was established in Pinney's, close to the front line; another was organised in Mine Avenue beyond Cellar Farm by the R.M.O. 31st Battalion (Captain E.

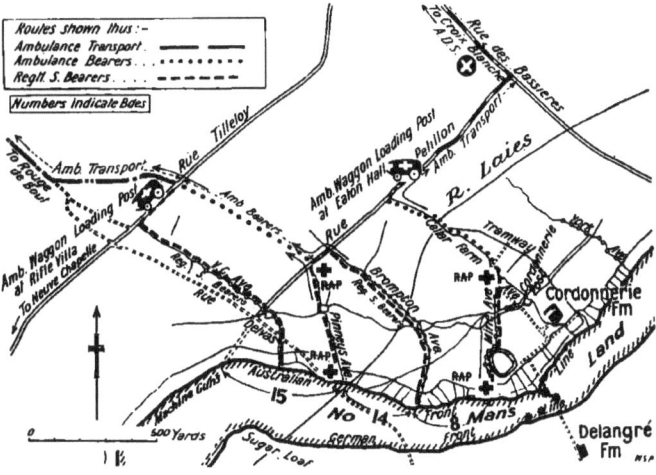

Collection and Clearance at Battle of Fromelles, 19-20 July 1916.

Russell), but on this officer's being wounded the post was abandoned. Finally at 9 a.m. on the 20th when the last troops of the 14th Brigade withdrew across No-Man's Land, not only all the regimental aid-posts but the whole of the front line and approach trenches were thickly thronged with wounded. Thereafter, no further collecting from the scene of the fighting could be done by normal means.[13]

The work in the aid-posts was very heavy.

"We worked all that afternoon (19th) that night and all next day without ceasing [writes Captain Collier]. We could not show a light and when we came to a wounded man we would ask him where he was hit and feel for his wound with hands covered with dried blood and mud. There was no time and no water to wash hands, and of course the wounded had their first dressing at the regimental aid-post."

Through the night the burthen of appeal by regimental medical officers and brigade staff was for additional help in the clearance from aid to ambulance post. When in the early hours of the 20th the nature of the catastrophe became known, helpers, medical and other, were freely available. Aid-posts, trenches, and dugouts were searched and by 10 a.m. the front line was "practically" clear.

Field ambulances

The work at the advanced dressing stations was largely in supplement—it would seem even in duplication—of that of the regimental aid-posts. Of five advanced dressing stations that were formed, all save those at Croix Blanche and Rouge de Bout faded out at an early hour and their personnel moved forward to the more advanced posts. Eaton Hall and Rifle Villa became the most important field ambulance positions in front of the main dressing stations, since here mechanical transport was

Advanced dressing stations

---

[13] Early on the 20th there occurred an episode of great interest. A man of the 29th Bn. searching for a wounded officer in No-Man's Land was challenged by a Bavarian officer, who insisted that the action must be regularised if it was to be permitted. A combatant officer of the 29th (Major A. W. Murdoch) then made a rough Red Cross flag and, passing over No-Man's Land, asked if a mutual cessation of hostilities could be arranged. The Bavarian officer telephoned for instructions, and in the meantime the men of both sides took advantage of the curious situation. The firing ceased and the wounded were brought in on our side while the Germans repaired their parapets. Major Murdoch returned safely, but as his action was not confirmed by the Australian Divisional Commander (who considered himself bound by standing instructions from the Higher Command), the informal truce ceased. During the whole of the next week, however, parties or individuals went out by night and brought in men marked down during the day. The last was carried to Captain H. Rayson's aid-post nine days after wounding. He had crawled to a shell-hole and though he could not reach the water had kept himself alive by continuously soaking and sucking a strip of his tunic.

available. It is noted however that the work at the "advanced dressing stations" was "very heavy." Clearance thence to the main dressing station was smooth and without incident. The front lines were not fully relieved till the 21st.

At both of the main dressing stations treatment and evacuation to casualty clearing station were carried out with a smoothness and celerity probably not exceeded in the history of the Australian Medical Service in this war. The rate of clearance indeed reached as high as two cases per minute. Ample provision had been made and it was effectively exploited; the dressing of wounds—in particular splinting—brought high commendation from the Second Army authorities.[14] At Bac St. Maur and Fort Rompu recordings of woundings by sites were kept as well as of the number of walking, sitting, and lying-down cases.

Main dressing stations

The casualties sustained in the operation are shown in the following table. They are a measure at once of the extraordinary medical problem and of the cost to the A.I.F. of this "feint"—really a subsidiary attack, wholly futile and unnecessary, made by inexperienced troops against unduly distant positions with insufficient preparation, particularly by the artillery, which itself was insufficient for the enterprise. They represent a casualty list of 50 per cent. of the troops engaged. Normally in the A.I.F. the proportion of wounded and died of wounds to killed in action was approximately as four to one. In the 15th Brigade at Fromelles it was less than one and a half to one. This increased proportion is due to men being shot to death as they lay wounded in No-Man's Land, or dying there through lack of assistance. The small number of medical casualties, one officer and four other ranks wounded, is due to the comparatively slight shelling of the ambulance bearer routes in rear. Regimental bearers working in the front area lost very heavily, more so, possibly, than in any other engagement of the A.I.F.

---

[14] This operation is, indeed, selected by the British Official Historian as illustrating a smooth and successful evacuation. *British Official Medical History, General, Vol. III, pp. 7-10.*

TABLE II.—Casualties sustained by the 5th Division at Fromelles between noon on 19th July and 8 p.m. of 21st July:—

	Killed in action	Died of wounds	Prisoners of war	Wounded in action	Total
8th Inf. Bde	477	51	166	1,086	1,780
14th „	438	58	283	948	1,727
15th „	726	98	5	904	1,733
Other units	60	9	16	208	293
Totals	1,701	216	470	3,146	5,533[15]

Wounded passed through main dressing stations:—

	Walking	Sitting	Lying down	Total
8th Fld. Amb	17	211	358	586
14th „	453	324	637	1,414
15th „	347	373	557	1,277
Totals	817	908	1,552	3,277

Percentage of wounds according to site:
Upper limb	31·79 per cent
Lower limb	31·00
Head and neck	16·67
Thorax	7·93
Abdomen	4·27
Back	2·22
"Shell Shock"	6·12
Total	100·00

On this sector and on the whole Second Army front the tumult and shouting died down as quickly as it arose. The 5th Division, badly shaken, went back from the XI Corps to II Anzac and remained in this sector till the autumn.

Shortly after Fromelles Colonel R. E. Roth[16] was replaced as D.D.M.S., II Anzac Corps, by Colonel C. Mackie Begg, N.Z.M.C.[17]

---

[15] The 61st British Division during the same period lost 1,547 of whom approximately 934 were admitted to field ambulances and the remainder were killed or died of wounds, or were taken prisoner.
[16] This officer was invalided to Australia. He died in 1924.
[17] Comparisons and contrast of great medical interest may be made between the Battle of Fromelles and certain operations of the Gallipoli and Palestine Campaigns. Thus the Landing at Anzac, and the Amman raid illustrate clearance in a retreat, and the attack on Krithia, the collection and clearance of casualties reaching fifty per cent. in a few hours. In the *Australian Official History* Fromelles is compared with the raid at Lone Pine, and the medical problems were also very similar. *See Vol. I, pp. 138-45, 153-7; 293-5, 691-5.*

CHAPTER IV

THE SOMME: POZIÈRES AND MOUQUET FARM

"IN our trenches after seven o'clock on that morning our men waited under a heavy fire for the signal to attack. Just before half-past seven, the mines at half a dozen points went up with a roar that shook the earth and brought down the parapets in our lines. Before the blackness of their burst had thinned or fallen the hand of Time rested on the half-hour mark, and along all that old front line of the English there came a whistling and a crying. The men of the first wave climbed up the parapets, in tumult, darkness, and the presence of death, and having done with all pleasant things, advanced across the No Man's Land to begin the Battle of the Somme."[1]

It is becoming clear to the most casual observer of world events that the Great War has had an important influence on the fate of this present era of culture. The question therefore, which was the decisive battle of the war is a proper and an important one. It may be answered Socratically—what is meant by a "Battle"? and what by "decisive"? That the Marne was both decisive and a battle needs no debating; but with the war of entrenched lines a new concept must be formed of both. Thus in the British official names of battles the "Operations on the Somme" in the latter half of 1916 comprise twelve "battles" and three "attacks."[2] As for decisiveness, after the first battle of Ypres it began to be suspected that two distinct processes might be necessary before a decision could be reached; the attainment of a commanding position leading, as at Blenheim or Sedan, to a military checkmate might not be possible until, by a process of "wearing down" or attrition, physical and moral

---

[1] John Masefield, *The Old Front Line*, p. 128; London, William Heinemann, 1917.

[2] The Battle of Albert, July 1-13. Attack on Gommecourt Salient July 1. Battle of Bazentin Ridge 14-17. Attack at Fromelles 19. Attacks on High Wood 20-25. Battle of Delville Wood July 15-Sept. 3, of Pozières Ridge July 23-Sept. 3, of Guillemont 3-6, Ginchy 9, Flers-Courcelette 15-22, Morval 25-28, Thiepval Ridge 26-28, Le Transloy Ridges Oct. 1-18, Ancre Heights Oct. 1-Nov. 11, Ancre Nov. 13-18. The course of the most important of these is shown in sketch on *p. 51*.

dominance had been achieved. And, as it turned out, of these two phases the latter was incomparably the more important as a means to the decision of the Great War; and on both counts this first combined Anglo-French offensive in the Somme area has strong claims to being the most decisive operation. At its end the balance of moral and physical dominance, though small, was definitely on the side of the Allies, and it sufficed in the long run to win the war. Through all the vicissitudes of 1917 and even in the great German offensive of 1918 it was never really lost.[3] Of strategical manœuvres the most effective during this period was probably the German "Alberich" withdrawal to the Hindenburg Line in March 1917.

On the medical side also the first Somme campaign has no less claim to consideration. In its course can be seen the initiation of a movement in the treatment of wounds that was to exercise a decisive influence on the whole scheme of medical work in the army zone; here also the psychical traumata so characteristic of this war were first scientifically observed and effectively dealt with.

The selection, as a point of attack of sufficient strategic importance, of that part of the German bastion that included the watershed between the Somme and the Scarpe was intended chiefly to permit of French participation in a decisive "break-through."[4] The region through which run the Somme and the Ancre consists of rolling chalk downs, and a striking feature opposite the British front was the strong buttress of Thiepval on the extreme left. This natural fortress had been greatly strengthened, and it determined the course both of the main operations and incidentally of the Australian part in them.

The terrain

Throughout most of July and August the weather was hot and dry, and the operations presented three phases. The offensive was opened

---

[3] This is generally accepted by British writers. Thus Lord Esher writes (*The Tragedy of Lord Kitchener, p. 207*) "One month later, (i.e. after the death of General Galliéni) Sir Douglas Haig's guns began that battle on the Somme, which, taken together with what Jellicoe had achieved off Jutland, settled the inevitable issue of the War." Yet both Verdun and the German check before Amiens in 1918 have been held by others to be the decisive factor.

[4] Major-General Rt. Hon. J. E. B. Seely, who commanded the Canadian Cavalry Brigade expected that the cavalry would be called on to operate behind the German front within a week of the first attack.

on July 1st with a bombardment of a severity hitherto unknown.[5] The first attacks were made on a wide front, and, except on the British left the advance penetrated to a depth which promised well. The "Battle of Albert" was followed up by further smashing blows. Later attacks failed to sustain the progress. The casualties were enormous—the toll on the New Armies, the flower of British manhood, reached proportions that caused to the Cabinet grave concern and to many of the British people a feeling akin to consternation—the first realisation of the nature and involvements of the new phase of the war.

Military operations

The failure was due in large measure to the salient created by the fortress of Thiepval, which held up the capture of the neighbouring and commanding Pozières ridge. On the south also Guillemont held out, and must be captured to align the British advance with that of the French. A combined advance was planned for July 23rd, and the I Anzac Corps was brought in for the attack on Pozières village. The result was inconclusive. The village was captured, but elsewhere the attacks failed—a result not unexpected. Already on July 23rd an order by General Haig initiated the second phase of the British operations—a deliberate recourse to the "wearing-down" battle. To this the I Anzac Corps was wholly committed. During the next six weeks only local offensives were undertaken; and the whole force of the German artillery was concentrated on smashing these. This second period, which ended with a loosely combined and unsuccessful offensive on September 3rd-5th, coincided with the tour of I Anzac in the battle.

The Battle of the Somme, 1916: Stages of the Advance.

The third phase was begun on September 15th when the British secret weapon, the tank, was used by General Haig in an endeavour to compel the strategic success which otherwise seemed beyond attainment. The whole Allied front pressed forward. The Thiepval salient (which had caused the A.I.F. casualties heavier, in proportion to the numbers engaged, than those sustained in any other battle) was "mopped up" in the general advance. This ended on November 18th in the attainment of im-

---

[5] "No thunder was ever so terrible as that tumult. It broke the drums of the ears when it came singly, but when it rose up along the front and gave tongue together in full cry it humbled the soul. With the roaring, crashing, and shrieking came a racket of hammers from the machine guns till men were dizzy and sick from the noise, which thrust between skull and brain, and beat out thought." (John Masefield *loc. cit. p. 127.*)

portant if not of commanding positions. In these triumphs however the I Anzac Corps did not participate, since on September 5th it was withdrawn from the Somme.

The attempt, begun on July 23rd, to reduce Thiepval had, as we have seen, included as its most important feature, an attack on Pozières village carried out by the new Reserve Army (I Anzac and II British Corps)[a] into which the I Anzac Corps had been re-

The Australian fighting ceived. The first Australian objective set was the "village" of Pozières, lying something short of the crest. Through this ran the road from Albert to Bapaume; to the left lay Thiepval and the strongly fortified "Mouquet Farm;" on the right were the ruins of captured Contalmaison and the long shallow depression known as "Sausage Valley." After two days of bombardment the 1st Division with the 48th Division on the left advanced with a fine determination, to complete success. On the 25th the attack was pushed through the strong German entrenchments that occupied the powdered remains of the village, and the Australians joined hands with the 48th, successfully sustaining repeated counter-attacks. By this time the German artillery concentration was intense; but on August 4th, after an initial repulse on July 29th, the 2nd Division with the 12th British Division captured the crest of the ridge—the highest point in the whole Allied objective. A wide vista opened to and beyond Bapaume—for eight months the Mecca of Australian hopes.

The 4th Division held the captured crest through several days of the most intense bombardment and counter-attack, and then, with Suffolk troops on the left, thrust strongly towards Mouquet Farm threatening the rear of the Thiepval salient. Thereafter, however, in a second tour of the line, each Division was thrown, by a somewhat unintelligent interpretation on the part of Reserve Army of General Haig's intention, in a series of unsuccessful frontal attacks on a diminishing front against the underground trench fortress known as "Mouquet Farm."

The Australian effort may thus be summarised as follows:—

First Stage.—Capture of Pozières Heights.
1. First attack on Pozières. 1st Division, 23rd-27th July.
2. Capture of Pozières Heights, 2nd Division, 28th July-6th August.
3. Holding the crest: thrust towards Thiepval. 4th Division, 6th-12th August.

Second Stage.—Attacks on Mouquet Farm.
4. 1st Division, 14th-20th August.
5. 2nd Division, 21st-24th August.
6. 2nd and 4th Divisions, 26th August—3rd September.
7. 1st Canadian Division and 13th Brigade, 4th Australian Division, 3rd-5th September.

In these operations the Australian force in France lost in

---

[a] This was formed on 23 May, 1916, with General Sir Hubert Gough in command. On 30 October, 1916, it became the Fifth Army. The sectors occupied by the Reserve Army and the Fourth Army (General Rawlinson) are shown in the sketch map on *p. 54.*

battle casualties some 33 per cent. of its strength. The fighting thus curtly summarised contained an experience of endeavouring and enduring of which, for want of adequate analogy, it is not possible to convey to non-participants any adequate picture. It was largely concerned in frontal attacks on trenches and strongpoints defended by machine-guns. The actual fighting was hand-to-hand homeric contests, for the most part—with the weapon of universal application in trench fighting, the hand grenade—interspersed with periods of occupation of captured trenches under a concentrated bombardment with high explosive shell, chiefly howitzer, of every calibre. The German bombardment fell in these battles almost entirely on the front and reserve trench lines. On the first it was poured with the deliberate intention of destruction, or in preparation for a counter-attack: on the second usually in the form of a "barrage," to prohibit communication between the front line trenches and the rear. Necessarily it was in this area that the regimental and forward ambulance posts were largely situated, and in the clearance of wounded, as in the maintenance of supplies, the transit of the barrage zone was a constant and very dreadful feature of the problem. Clearance of casualties in the trench line hinged on this hostile barrage. Fortunately, owing chiefly to Allied supremacy in the air, the depth of habitual shelling was far less than in some later battles, and when the barrage was once passed, evacuation was unimpeded, so that wheeled transport was available often within a mile or so of the front lines.

The actions were for the most part fought on a divisional front of from 500 to 1,000 yards with, usually, two brigades in the attack employing from three to six battalions.

On its arrival on the Somme the I Anzac Corps was wedged in between the III Corps (Fourth Army) on the right, and the II Corps (Reserve Army) on the left and established its Headquarters at Contay. It was allocated an area the boundaries of which were precisely defined, a long narrow strip extending to the rear for nine miles. Within this area the Corps was more or less self-contained, especially in its administrative services, having its own routes and stations for supply and evacuation. The Australian line of evacuation may thus be visualised as a single strand, more and more closely involved with others, in a cord

Medical arrangements

which linked the British battle line with the hospital centres at the expeditionary base. From the regimental aid-posts the Australian thread of evacuation ran singly to the "main dressing station" where, in the motor ambulance convoy, it merged with the general stream of British casualties.

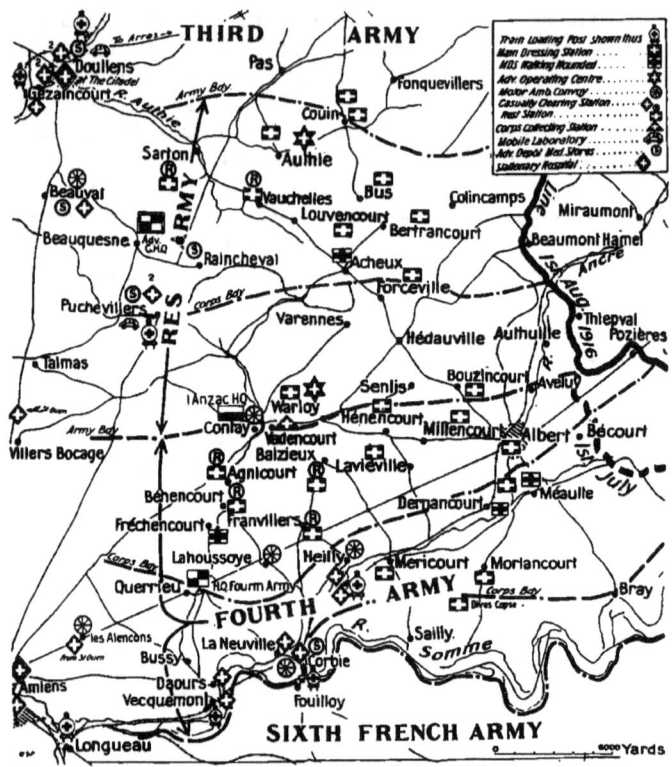

The Somme Battlefront, July 1916, showing Main Medical Stations as on July 1. This sketch map is compiled from the British Official Medical History (General, Vol. III, p. 31). It illustrates (i) the "forward" positions of M.D.S. first adopted; (ii) the "Divisional" as against the "Corps" M.D.S. The A.D.S's are not shown.

The British scheme of evacuation was based chiefly on Rouen, to which casualties were conveyed mostly by train, ambulance or improvised, but also by barges down the Somme and by *char-à-bancs*. Casualty clearing stations were allocated in pairs to each Corps and, by instruction of the D.G.M.S., B.E.F., General Sloggett, were sited well beyond the range of artillery. As the line moved forward their distance from the front became extreme. By General Sloggett's orders "advanced operating centres" were formed in each Army—that for the Reserve Army being at Warloy in the Australian Corps area. Nos. 3 and 44 British Casualty Clearing Stations at Puchevillers were allotted to the I Anzac Corps as was No. 6 Motor Ambulance Convoy.[7]

General scheme of evacuation

The Australian Deputy and Assistant Directors had little more than a week in which to prepare, but they found in existence an already highly organised and stable system of clearance and evacuation. Something of a crisis had however been reached through the strain imposed on the services of maintenance by the immense concentration of troops on this front, and through the fact that each advance had lengthened the routes of supply and evacuation by adding a further stretch of battle-torn country. The Australian Directors moreover found that all the best sites for medical stations within the Corps area (which had been newly created from the territory of its neighbours) were already occupied.[8] Much debate ensued between Army and the respective Corps headquarters—and more effectively between the formations directly concerned—and a concordat of "give and take" in sites and routes was reached.[9] The most formidable problem lay in the clearance of the forward area. The direct route—the Albert-Bapaume road which led through Pozières— was too exposed, being visible from the Thiepval salient and intensely shelled, as was the valley north of it. Albert itself, allotted as the site for an advanced dressing station, was often

Medical arrangements—I Anzac Corps

---

[7] For the Somme Battle there were provided over twenty casualty clearing stations, twenty-three ambulance trains, nine motor ambulance convoys, and three mobile laboratories—two bacteriological and one hygienic. The employment of the motor omnibus for evacuation became general.

[8] Picardy was poor country compared to Flanders, the villages feudal in structure, with wattle and daub cottages adjoining the historic *châteaux* used as headquarters.

[9] Under ordinary circumstances the handing and taking over between formations and units was automatic and carried out on prescribed lines. The conditions in this battle were exceptional.

shelled. The most protected outlet was on the right, down the Sausage Valley, but this lay largely in the area of III Corps. Some heart-to-heart talk, however, brought an invitation to the A.D.M.S. 1st Division (Colonel A. H. Sturdee) to arrange his clearance down the valley and to share with a field ambulance of the 19th Division a safe and commodious though battered *château* in Bécourt Wood near the valley's southern exit. The medical units concerned established cordial and co-operative relations.

Colonel Sturdee, issued his "medical arrangements" on July 20th. They provided for regimental aid-posts at the positions shown in the sketch map. These would be cleared by ambulance bearers who, if necessary, would assist the regimental bearers in the collection and clearance of the front line.[10] Three field ambulance collecting posts were formed, the most important at Casualty Corner (at the head of Sausage Valley, near "Bailiff Wood") close to a loading post at "Gordon Dump." At the latter horsed-waggons and wheeled stretchers were available for transport to the advanced dressing station and a loading party of twenty-four men was stationed. A trolley line would take "walkers" to a "walking wounded post" outside Albert, to be cleared thence by motor lorries of supply or by omnibus. Clearance of the advanced dressing station was arranged chiefly by motor ambulance waggons for which a park was formed in a factory in Albert known as the "North Chimney," the preliminary selection for the advanced dressing station. A "collecting post" for slightly wounded and stragglers was formed by the Assistant Provost Marshal on the Albert-Bapaume road (Bapaume Post). These stations and all forward posts were put under the officer commanding 3rd Field Ambulance (Lieut.-Colonel H. N. Butler) who had also at his disposal the bearers of the 1st and 2nd Field Ambulances and as many of their ambulance waggons as could be spared, supplemented through the D.D.M.S. with some from the other Divisions.

The supply of dressings, equipment and "medical comforts" was ample. As a main dressing station the auxiliary to a British

Collection and clearance, 1st Division

---

[10] Only sixteen bearers were at this time allotted to regimental medical officers.

Field Ambulance in Warloy[11] was taken over and placed under the direction of the officer commanding 1st Field Ambulance (Lieut.-Colonel C. Gordon Shaw). Arrangements were made whereby for a time "abdominal, head, and serious cases" were to be sent to the British Field Ambulance which ran the "Main Hospital" at Warloy. A station for slight wounds and walking wounded was opened near by at Vadencourt by the 2nd Field Ambulance (Lieut.-Colonel W. W. Hearne).

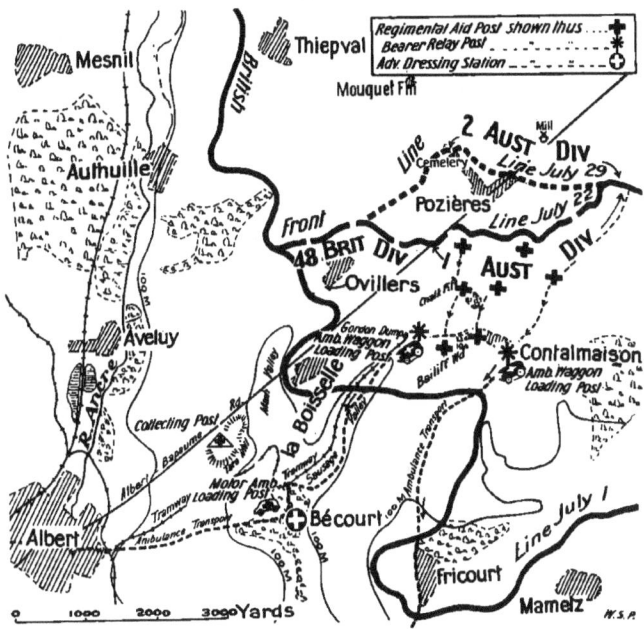

Scheme of Clearance, 1st Aust. Division, July 22-29.

The problems of clearance and of treatment within the battle-torn area controlled by the officer in command at the advanced dressing station were quite distinct in kind from those which concerned the reception of the same casualties in the treat-

Problems of evacuation

---

[11] This village was in the I Anzac Corps area. The "give and take" arrangement permitted the retention by British units of the other positions occupied.

ment centres far in the rear—the main dressing, lightly wounded, and casualty clearing stations. The junction of the two zones of responsibility lay approximately in the "bottle neck" at Albert.

When the attack on the village was launched at 12.30 a.m. on July 23rd, the regimental aid-posts were soon found to be too far from the advanced line, and forward posts were formed. That of the R.M.O. 2nd Battalion (Captain R. L. Henderson), for example, was made in a double (German) dugout 50 yards from the front line, his previous post being 800 yards in the rear. From an early hour the regimental bearers suffered heavily and ambulance bearers worked with them to clear to the aid-posts. Even with the bearers increased to some 300 in all by the help from other Divisions the clearance of stretcher cases from the aid-posts required the assistance of infantry fatigues who paid toll in heavy casualties, as did all bearers, runners, fatigues, signallers and others whose business it was to traverse the barrage zone. As the line advanced, bearer relays and reliefs were organised. In the early operations, however, many of these carried till exhaustion made them useless. By July 26th the shell-fire on Sausage Valley and the Chalk Pit road diminished, and ambulance bearers were able to level the surface for wheeled stretchers as far forward as Bailiff Wood.

Capture of Pozières village

The scene at the 2nd Battalion aid-post is thus described:—[12]

"Our dugout seems right in the barrage line, for shells are falling thick and fast all round this place. Stretcher-bearers have not returned in numbers sufficient to clear. In the aid-post the scene was terrible. Outside it is worse where we have to dress wounds out in the open roadside or in trenches. Many were hit, unable to move, others buried alive.

"It is marvellous how the wounded stand the agony of their wounds, many shot to pieces but never a murmur, others when forced to cry out apologise for it. One old chap who was dying kept saying "stop the bleeding boys and I'll get back to the Mrs. and Kids," alas, am afraid his wife and children will never see him again in this world. . . . Eventually with the help of volunteers all were carried back or walked. It is awful to see crippled men staggering back with the help of a shovel, stick, or anything, just crawling along until at last they either reach help or fall exhausted on the road, some to be picked up later, others to be buried where they fall."

---

[12] In the diary of No. 8353 Lance-Corporal Roger Morgan, 1st Fld. Amb., who was attached to the 2nd Battalion.

Clearance from the waggon loading post was, after the first few days, impeded only by the prodigious accumulation of guns and stream of traffic in this the main avenue of access and egress from the battle zone.[13]

The Australian casualties in the capture of Pozières Village (19th-26th July) totalled 5,892 as follows:

Killed in action	1,260	Wounded in action (including Shell Shock "W")	4,411
Died of wounds ..	162		
Died of Gas Poisoning	2	Gassed	37
Prisoners of war	20		

Pozières village having been taken, the 1st Division was on July 25th relieved by the 2nd[14] which had the duty of capturing the summit of the ridge beyond, crowned by the old German second line (the well-known trenches O.G.1 and O.G.2). On the 29th in response to pressure by the Reserve Army a premature and ill-prepared attack was made. It was repulsed with heavy loss, to be followed by twelve days of shelling which in its sustained intensity, the Australian Official Historian records, was unequalled in the history of the Australian force. By this time however routes, medical posts, and reliefs had been organised, and bearers were becoming skilled in avoiding the worst features of the barrage. On the other hand the advance of the line made the carry to aid-posts longer, over ground even more shell-

Pozières Heights

---

[13] The work of the medical personnel of the artillery brigades lay in this area. The following note is from a record by the R.M.O., 2nd Field Artillery Brigade (Capt. H. R. J. Harris, A.A.M.C.).

"I had an aid-post in Sausage Valley but quickly realised that, to be of much use to the wounded I would have to move among the batteries. Accordingly I did so and was also able to daily superintend the evacuation of infantry wounded down Sausage Valley.

"It was here I first saw badly gassed cases with cyanosis, dyspnoea, frothing at the mouth etc., the result of chlorine. We (the R.M.O's) had been handed supplies of atropine sulphate and of ammonia, but as the best course was to get the men gassed evacuated as soon as possible, these supplies were hardly ever used. In any case I early realised how comparatively useless both these drugs were in the treatment of badly gassed cases . . .

"At Pozières there were many cases of genuine 'shell shock.' In evacuating cases of 'shell shock,' I do not consider it mattered much if the case was one of stark fear or genuine 'shell shock'—the former had to be evacuated to the ambulance because of the disastrous moral effect of a badly frightened man on his comrades."

[14] The collecting zone was placed under the officer commanding the 5th Field Ambulance (Lieut.-Col. J. H. Phipps) who had the bearer divisions of the 6th and 7th Field Ambulances together with part of their motor-transport.

riven than the old; nor could there yet be made any advance of the waggon loading posts.[15]

The attack on August 4th-5th, whereby the Pozières heights were taken, was well prepared, and a measure of surprise was achieved. With the 12th British Division on the left, an advance of a mile was made on a front of some 3,000 yards, and the new line was held in spite of repeated counter-attacks, and the use of liquid fire.

The collecting of the wounded was helped by the official addition of eight regimental bearers to the usual sixteen. Regimental aid-posts also were advanced. But the terror of the barrage remained, and the great length of the bearer carry made clearance a terrible problem still.

The nature of the service required of the R.M.O's at this time is very well illustrated by the following note by Brigadier-General R. L. Leane—then commanding the 48th Battalion—anent the work of his R.M.O., Major H. H. Woollard.[16]

"It was at Pozières that he [Major Woollard] really proved his great worth. . . . On the night of 5th August . . . the enemy shelling was the worst I experienced during the war, being all directed on Pozières over a narrow front of some 500 yards. Walking along Tramway Trench just forward of the town of Pozières, I came upon Woollard surrounded by wounded men, the trench being torn with heavy shell fire. I questioned him as to his reason for being in the position I found him in view of the fact that the aid-post was at the chalkpits. He told me that many of the men needed immediate attention and that the carry was too far to enable medical aid to be given to badly wounded men in time. I can see him now as he looked up at me and said, 'I'm frightened as hell, Colonel.' I patted him on the back. . . ."

The difficulty of obtaining water, food, and dressings for the

---

[15] From the medical standpoint the tragic reverse of the 7th Brigade on the 29th was relieved by an event that influenced the fate of the gravely wounded in the terrible fighting that was to come. From the shell-holes over the stretch of No-Man's Land, under cover of a morning mist, Australian regimental and ambulance bearers collected wounded near our trenches. German bearers collected the Australian casualties in front of their own. In this way many were rescued, but continuance of the informal truce was not permitted. Large numbers remained out, of whom a few were got back later. The rest, as at Russell's Top and Fromelles, died where they lay, of wounds and thirst. But from this time onwards, though frowned on by authority, the bearers of both sides often co-operated.

[16] The late Professor Woollard's work in the A.A.M.C. was of outstanding merit. *See pp. 455, 457-60, 463, 774.*

front was extreme.[17] The casualties in the 2nd Division's offensive (27th July-6th August) were as shown below:—

Killed in action	1,605	Wounded in action (including Shell Shock "W")	4,663
Died of wounds	246		
Died of gas poisoning	5	Gassed	47
Prisoners of war	69		
		Total casualties	6,635

On August 6th the 2nd Division was relieved by the 4th. The 12th Field Ambulance took over the advanced dressing station. From the first moment the 4th Division was called on to sustain counter-attacks whose character was determined—as were the German casualties in these operations—by the order of General von Below that—

Holding the Heights

"at any price Hill 60 (Pozières Heights) must be recovered ... troops who first reach the plateau must hold on until reinforced whatever their losses."

—and by an unexampled bombardment. These efforts were repelled and on the 10th, 13th and 14th the Australian force struck home again, now in pursuance of a new tactical scheme. An advance to the left over a front of some 600 yards took the line to within 200 yards of Mouquet Farm.

The series of operations, of which this was the first, initiated a distinct and a more sombre and—because of its futility—more terrible phase of the Australian fighting on the Somme. They consisted of an attempt to drive a wedge on an ever narrowing front into the flank of the German salient caused by the fortress at Thiepval, whose front had defied the whole force of the British offensives, and already had taken in toll almost half of the British New Armies. The direction and course of the attacks are made clear in the sketch map and the exposed and desolate nature of the terrain in the official photographs. The tactical purpose was wholly unattainable, and the other aim —of wearing down the enemy—could be achieved only at the cost of a much greater wearing down of the attacking side.

---

[17] In these operations for the first time the two-gallon petrol tin became an official issue and the recognised method of supply of water for the trenches, being adapted to chlorination. Its use first was suggested by Australian officers on the basis of Gallipoli experience. *See Chapter six and Vol. I, p. 300.*

The clearance of the front in these operations opens also a new phase. Even before the advance on the 10th the A.D.M.S. 4th Division (Colonel G. W. Barber) had found himself faced with bearer carries so lengthy and formidable as to make the

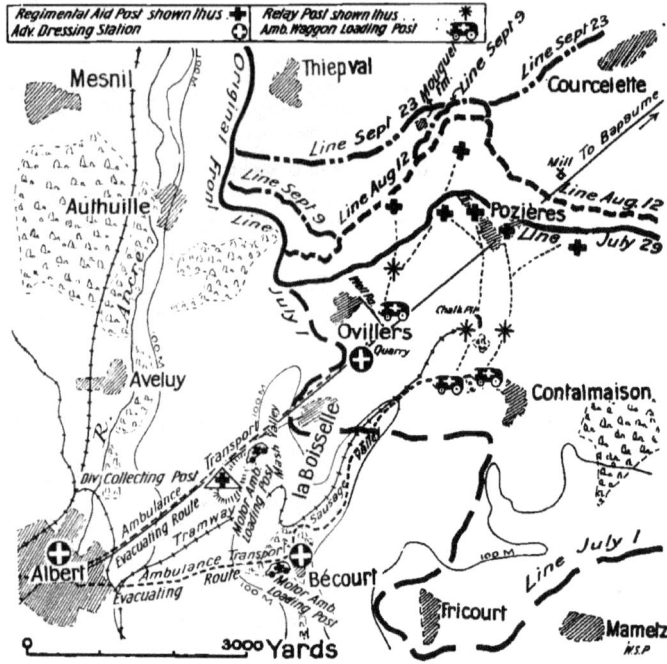

Scheme of Clearance, end of August.

clearance of the line a matter of the utmost danger and difficulty. At his instance the regimental aid-posts were pushed forward to the cemetery, west of Pozières village:[18] advanced posts, and

---

[18] *The History of the 24th Battalion* says (*pp. 94-6*): "The village of Pozières was no longer in existence, churned up earth, heaps of powdered masonry and blasted tree stumps alone marked the site. The only structure which had withstood the bombardment was Cement House also known as Gibraltar, a former German dugout with a concrete observation post surmounting it.

"The vicinity of Gibraltar was a terrible death trap. It lay right on the route of all movement to and from the lines and as shells crashed in salvos around the structure men fell right and left. Every track over the remains of the village changed shape a dozen times a day under the deluge of shells that fell there."

loading posts followed, as shelling permitted. "Casualty Corner" and the "Chalk Pits" became "forward advanced dressing stations" (*sic*). The number of regimental bearers was greatly increased (in the 14th Battalion, for example, to no less than 40 in addition to 16 partly trained men).

Owing to the extension of the routes through the area of heavy shelling, clearance by the 4th Division was as difficult as at any time during the operations. The aid-post of the R.M.O. 14th Battalion (Captain R. C. Winn)

"was a deep German dugout. Two regimental medical officers worked in a sap near the entrance. This was moreover choked with wounded many of whom would be wounded afresh or killed out-right while being attended to. The earth for miles behind the line was like a ploughed field and changed like the waters of a rain-swept lake. The dugout rocked with concussions. Many wounded were brought in who were out days before being rescued. Some of their wounds were crawling with maggots but looked surprisingly clean. I was led to judge with sympathy those evacuated with shell shock and formed the opinion that loss of sleep was one of the main contributing factors."

The R.M.O. of the 47th Battalion (Captain J. T. Jones) notes that nearly all the casualties were due to high explosive shell. Wounded from the front line were generally brought in within three hours, a distance of 300 to 500 yards.

"Most had been dressed by the bearers and improvised splints applied. Most had been so well attended to that they could be sent straight to the advanced dressing station. Casualties near the regimental aid-post were conveyed there and dressed by the medical officer, there was no shortage of dressings or splints—which were often those improvised by the bearers. At the regimental aid-post right angle splints were used for the arm and Long Liston's for the thigh. Morphia was used when the patient was suffering much. It was realised here how simple are the supplies required at the R.A.P—an abundance of shell dressings, a pair of scissors, a bottle of morphia solution and syringe, and a supply of water are all that are absolutely essential."[19]

In this last stage of the Australian fighting all three Divisions were thrown again in quick succession in a series of costly frontal attacks on Mouquet Farm. In the last effort a brigade of the 4th Division attacked, being supported and eventually relieved by the 1st Canadian Division. The "Farm" was still uncaptured when the I Anzac Corps left the Somme, and it took

---

[19] Observations made by these officers on the production of "shell shock" at this time are referred to in *Vol. III*.

toll of the Canadians to the extent of some 5,000 before it was mopped up in the general British advance of September 26th.

With the Australian advance to the left new lines of clearance and evacuation became possible. At first alternatively, and later as the main route of clearance, the Albert-Bapaume road came into use, and the "Right" and "Left" sectors of clearance, always intended, now became a *fait accompli*. On August 26th a "forward advanced dressing station" was formed at "The Quarry" on the Bapaume road. At this time the reliefs and offensives were becoming progressively shorter since battalions were in numbers mere skeletons. For the last operation school buildings in Albert were taken over as an advanced dressing station, replacing Bécourt Château. Early in September Albert school became the main dressing station.

Clearance, Aug. 16 to Sept. 5

At the end of August the weather changed: dust was replaced by mud, from which many of the wounded had to be dug out. Under these conditions collection of the wounded under a white flag[20] became habitual. In front of the 13th Battalion bearers of both sides divided No-Man's Land between them, each side handing over the other's wounded. In these dreadful conditions, indeed, with the troops on each side living in full view of each other, an almost friendly spirit arose between them although both kept a sharp look-out for its abuse. Often one side informed the other of the position of wounded men in No-Man's Land and so made their rescue possible.

On this human note of mutual respect in men who in this grim process of wearing down had tried the temper of each other's metal and had found it good, we may fittingly close this brief and formal account of medical work on the fighting front in this, the most terrible trial by battle to which the Australian force was exposed in the Great War.

Treatment— The A.D.S.

During the period of this fighting the work at the advanced dressing station and its forward posts, and clearance therefrom, had gone on smoothly and without special event, though at very high pressure. At this time the system of treatment of the wounded

---

[20] A handkerchief or scrap of white cloth, constantly—and quite illegally though innocently—used by Australian stretcher-bearers in the absence of Red Cross flags, and largely respected by the Germans.

8. THE FAMOUS "CHALK PIT" NEAR POZIÈRES

The trees on the Bapaume road near Pozières can be faintly seen on the horizon to the left. This was the safest near rendezvous for bearers, but a large dump here was blown up on August 11th-12th.

Aust. War Memorial Official Photo. No. EZ112.

To face p. 64.

9. "SAUSAGE VALLEY," POZIÈRES

Showing the traffic down the valley from "Gordon Dump" (at its head) towards Bécourt (outside the left of the picture). The German bombardment of Pozières can be seen on the horizon on the right.

From a painting by F. R. Crozier in the Australian War Memorial.
Aust. War Memorial Official Photo. No. D515.

To face p. 65.

was at a critical stage in its evolution and the defects incidental to change and of growth are evident. The very terms used had a varying connotation. "Forward stations" and "advanced posts" were formed as the front advanced, for the most part as relay and holding stations for bearers. The work done at Bécourt Château has been described thus by Captain P. A. C. Davenport:—

"During the 2nd Division's stay in the line the 5th Field Ambulance did all the A.D.S. work, the 6th and 7th acting as collecting and forwarding stations in the rear behind Albert. The two furthest A.D.S's treated casualties as quickly as possible, doing only first-aid, and they were then sent . . . to us at Bécourt Château, about a mile. Here we were the main A.D.S. All wounds were most thoroughly treated, cleaned and rendered as antiseptic as possible. Fractures were put up in splints, etc., and were sent on by motor ambulance through the forwarding stations to the casualty clearing station. We generally had about eight medical officers. On July 29th we dressed 800 casualties in twelve hours. The private chapel of the Château was used as the dressing room, and six officers slept in the family vault. . . . During our ten days we treated just under 4,000 casualties."

There is clear evidence that the work done here tended to overlap with that at the main station. But the wounded were exceedingly well cared for, and were dealt with expeditiously. The provision for nourishment and rapid clearance were indeed not surpassed in any action of the A.I.F. in the war,[21] a result due in great part to the admirable organisation of the transport, at first under Divisional and later under Corps administration.

Casualties comprised stretcher and sitting cases sent to Warloy; and minor injuries and cases of exhaustion and "shock" sent to the Rest Station at Vadencourt.

Evacuation: Transport

To carry the former, the pooled motor ambulance cars parked at "the North Chimney" Albert were, by an ingenious control scheme, despatched as required to Bécourt. For the lightly wounded *char-à-bancs* were supplied from "Army." From 8 p.m. on July 28th the divisional supply lorries were utilised under an arrangement that cen-

---

[21] In these operations the Australian Red Cross Society set a precedent which received the flattery of imitation by the British. By a nice admixture of bluff, cajolery and pressure, its officer obtained permission to work as far forward as Albert, and took an active part in the provision of comforts, additional to the admirable efforts of the divisional supply departments, specialising in beef tea, sweet biscuits and cocoa.

tralised their disposal in the Quartermaster-General's Department at Corps Headquarters.[22]

By these various means the distance between the front line and the main dressing station was bridged and the heavy casualties very successfully cleared. This result was made possible only by the employment of special methods of organisation,

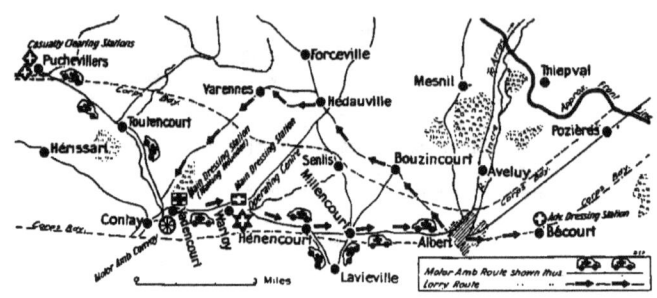

Routes of Clearance from A.D.S. to C.C.S. during Pozières Fighting.

and required considerable administrative adjustments. These it is necessary to describe in some detail since the medical service was intimately involved.

The change was presaged by a memorandum from General Sloggett, the D.G.M.S., B.E.F., to the D's.M.S. Armies dated July 25th in which he pointed out that, when **Corps control of administrative services** Corps were operating on narrow fronts, the work of the main dressing stations should be concentrated at some suitable central place in the Corps area, and that the commanding officer of one of the ambulances should remain in charge, and not be changed while his Division remained in the area. An "administrative memorandum" issued on August 2nd by I Anzac Corps

---

[22] The scheme handed down in *Field Service Regulations* that the wounded should be taken up by "returning empty waggons of supply" was in France impracticable by reason of the fact that the routes of supply very seldom coincided with those of evacuation. By the new arrangement on the entry of a division to the line at Pozières a precise scheme came automatically into operation whereby the divisional supply column arranged a regular service of lorries for the evacuation of walking wounded. Advantage was taken of the fact that normally supply lorries remained empty for twelve hours, to provide that from 8 p.m. to midnight ten—and from midnight to 8 a.m. four—lorries reported to the collecting post, where an officer of supply was stationed. In the daytime twenty-four were made available. For later developments—as the "Corps Motor Relay Post"—*see pp. 657-8*.

after setting out the exact boundaries of the Corps area, defined a "forward area" (for the troops engaged), a "central area" (for the assembly of those next to be engaged), and a "resting area" (for those who had been through the mill). The memorandum continued as follows:—

"While only one Division is in the front line, and reliefs of infantry are necessarily frequent, the Corps Commander has decided that the relief of administrative divisional units need not be simultaneous, as this would entail congestion of traffic and unnecessary movement."

The movements of infantry divisions were to be carried out to a programme issued by Corps Headquarters.[23] It was noted that:—

"in order to deal with the evacuation of wounded from the front it is necessary to modify to a certain extent the divisional organisation of medical units."

An appendix laid down in detail a list of duties of the Assistant-Directors in the "forward and collecting areas"; in the "reserve area" (which largely corresponded to the administrative "control area") for evacuation; and in the back or resting area. The A.D.M.S. of the Division in the line was to be responsible for all clearance. The ambulance in charge of this would, on relief, move out with its Division to the rest area. In the "reserve" or "central" area, in charge of the main dressing and rest stations, were concentrated all tent divisions of field ambulances, except those in the "forward" and "rest" areas. These units were responsible also for such duties as control of baths and laundries, care of Corps and Divisional attached troops,[24] supply of personnel for the casualty clearing station, and so forth. The administration of this area was vested in the A.D.M.S. of the Division in transit, to whom returns were rendered. All the bearer divisions except those engaged in the front line and those of the resting units were held here as a reserve. In effect they were, as in pre-war days, a separate "bearer company" but located with the tent-divisions.

---

[23] The approximate time occupied by a Division in its cycle of movements was a week in the line, a week in moving to and resting in the back area, and another in return via the "staging camp" (in the well known "Brickfields") behind Albert. The facilities for rest in the reserve area, it may be noted, were very good.

[24] Owing chiefly to the successive development of heavy artillery and supply services, "Corps Troops" numbered at this time some thousands. They greatly increased later.

Map No. 1

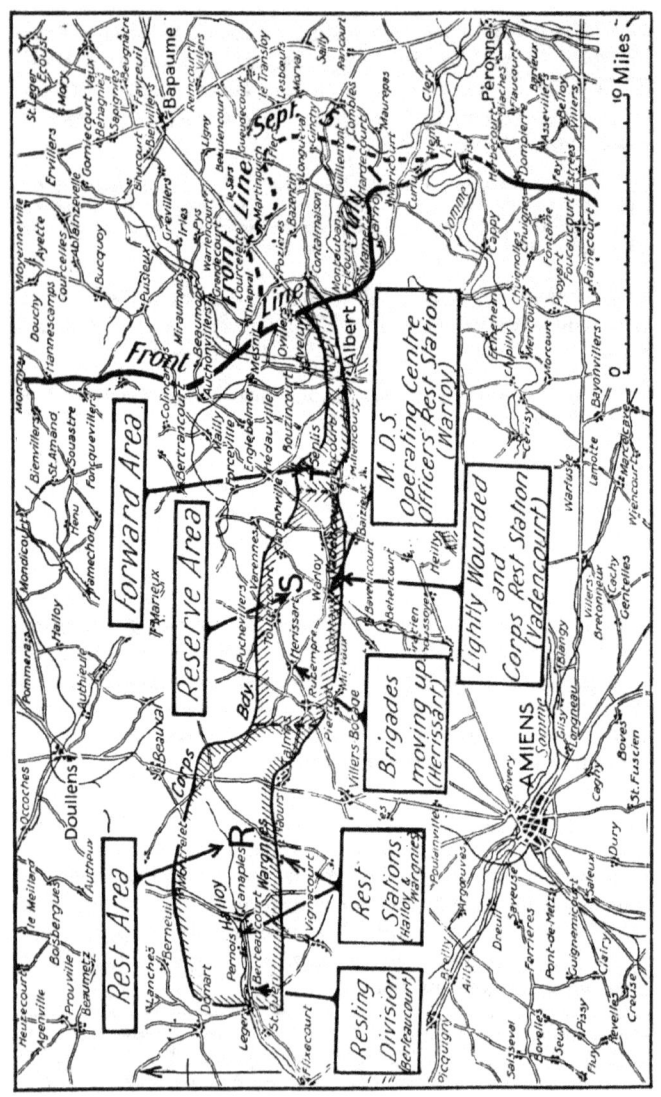

The I Anzac Corps area, July–September, 1916

10. STRETCHER-BEARERS PASSING THROUGH THE EXPOSED AREA
SOUTH OF MOUQUET FARM

The carriage of stretchers "shoulder high" had not yet been adopted. Collection under the "white flag," though not official, was constantly employed.

*Aust. War Memorial Official Photo. No. E4946.
Taken 28th August, 1916.*

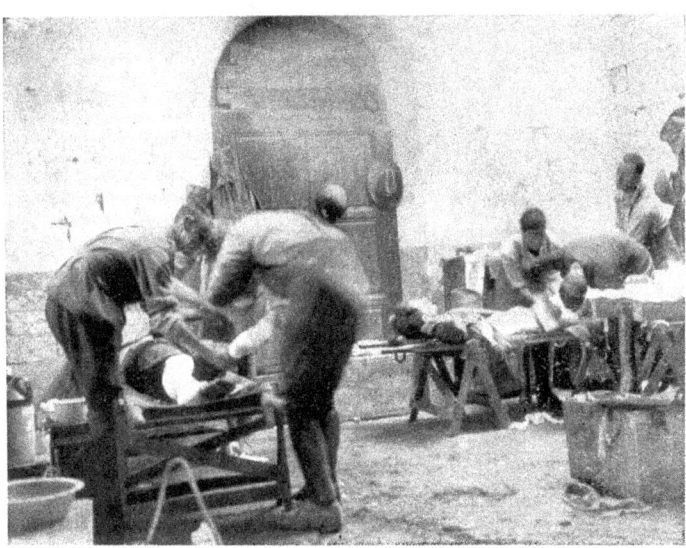

11. DRESSING WOUNDED IN BÉCOURT CHÂTEAU

Aust. War Memorial Official Photo. No. EZ66.   *To face p. 68.*

12. THE D.D.M.S., AUSTRALIAN CORPS, 1918, AND THE A.D's.M.S. OF THE AUSTRALIAN INFANTRY DIVISIONS WHEN THEY ARRIVED ON THE WESTERN FRONT

Centre: Colonel G. W. Barber, D.D.M.S., Australian Corps, 1918, and original A.D.M.S., 4th Division; *top left*: Colonel A. H. Sturdee, 1st Division; *top right*: Colonel A. Sutton, 2nd Division; *bottom left*: Colonel A. T. White, 3rd Division; *bottom right*: Colonel C. H. W. Hardy, 5th Division.

All changes and reliefs were initiated by the Deputy Director from Corps Headquarters; but the selection of units and the issue of executive orders remained with the Divisions. Thus at a stroke the Corps, instead of the Division, became the unit[25] for the organisation of evacuation. In the medical service the change was not made without some friction; like the Divisions themselves, the Assistant Directors of Medical Services were very jealous of encroachment on their importance and status. Happily the Deputy Director in the I Anzac Corps, Colonel Manifold, had a wide experience in such matters, and was moreover possessed of great tact, and, if somewhat impulsive in personal initiative, was deeply concerned to promote the smooth working of the Service which he had been called upon to direct. By a system of conferences he ensured that his own views, and those of each Assistant Director should not conflict in matters of real moment. Ultimately the waxing and waning of Corps control followed automatically on the military situation.

The treatment centres During this time the field ambulances had been engaged in the task of developing a series of secondary treatment centres.

Main Dressing Station. Under its experienced commanding officer (Lieut.-Colonel C. G. Shaw) the 1st Field Ambulance built up in Warloy a tented hospital capable of dealing expeditiously with very large numbers of wounded. The site conveniently adjoined the Corps Motor Repair Workshop, and the Motor Ambulance Convoy Park. The work at times was very strenuous—four operating tables going at one time. In this unit the splinting of fractures was made a specialty.

On August 2nd the 13th Field Ambulance (Lieut.-Colonel J. B. St. V. Welch) opened a second tented station. A small ward was fitted up in the chapel of the *château* at Warloy under Major Piero Fiaschi for the treatment of shocked and urgent

---

[25] It was stated indeed by Maj.-Gen. N. Malcolm, the chief of the general staff of Reserve Army, that "the inclination to look upon the Division instead of the Corps as the proper fighting unit is a relic of our pre-war army . . . the Corps must be regarded not as three separate Divisions but as a single organisation." Developments in later phases of the war, however, made it clear that such a pronouncement was misleading. General Haig never relaxed his decision that the Division was the true Army unit, and used them accordingly. A memorandum by the Chief of General Staff, I Anzac Corps, (Brig.-Gen. C. B. B. White,) laid down specifically that "while it is intended to maintain the Corps as a fighting unit this will be done with a minimum of interference in the powers and responsibilities of divisional commanders . . . . Corps control will be limited to the most efficient and economic distribution of our fighting power."

cases which were held for some days. A note by the officer commanding 12th Field Ambulance (Lieut.-Colonel T. G. Ross) states that

"almost invariably the condition of the wounded was good as the transport was rapid between the trenches and this place, and all the cases had been recently dressed further up. The Field Ambulance was somewhat of the nature of a casualty clearing station, and had an abdominal injury hospital attached. The condition of the wounded pointed to the advisability of having the casualty clearing station well forward so that thorough dressing under anaesthetics could be done early. Cases rarely arrived which could not by thorough dressing have the sepsis fairly well controlled."

Perhaps the most striking feature of wound treatment during these operations was a lack of co-ordination in the functions of treatment and of movement. There is discernible no clear-cut purpose and aiming point. The casualty clearing station was not yet the Mecca to the attainment of which in good condition by the wounded the efforts of all engaged in transport or in treatment would be wholly centred. Yet the records of both stations are in agreement regarding the general good condition of the wounded on arrival. Gassed cases were treated in the general wards.[26] Anti-tetanic serum was given at the advanced station.

That the lack of special incident in the work of the main dressing stations had the same significance as absence of noise in efficient machinery, is shown by unimpeachable evidence in the high commendation of the Advisory Consulting Surgeon B.E.F. (Sir Anthony Bowlby) from whom the stations received the compliment of frequent visits.[27]

Walking wounded were efficiently dealt with in the station at Vadencourt.

The special station at Warloy for abdominal, head, and other urgent cases was staffed by special surgical "teams" from field ambulances with a female nursing staff from the casualty clearing station. It was commonly known as the "main hospital," and occupied a small but well built civil hospital of 75 beds together with accommodation for 375 in tents, huts,

Advanced operating centre, Warloy

---

[26] Gas shells were used first on the Somme. Cloud gas was not employed.
[27] Disproportionate space is given in this chapter to the work of collecting and clearance for two reasons: first, that the experience of this battle was cardinal in the development of the regimental medical service; second—and of general application—that the clinical work of the medical units with which the main stations were chiefly concerned is fully dealt with elsewhere (*Chapters xi and xii*).

and other buildings. Personnel from Australian units were from time to time attached.[28] On August 1st a detachment from a casualty clearing station was placed in charge.[29] From Warloy stretcher and sitting cases went by No. 6 M.A.C. to the casualty clearing stations at Puchevillers. Walking wounded from Vadencourt, if not returned to duty, went by lorry to casualty clearing station or direct to railhead. The distance traversed by the convoy was less than ten miles; and though transport arrangements were good there is ample evidence that on arrival at the clearing stations the condition of the wounded had very often gravely deteriorated.[30] The staff of the C.C.S's was supplemented by officers and other ranks from the field ambulance personnel, detailed for the duty and attached for brief periods.[31] One of these[32] relates that on his arrival (on July 23rd)

Motor Ambulance Convoy

Casualty clearing stations

---

[28] An Australian Officer, Maj. J. W. B. Bean, acted as anaesthetist during the Pozières battle.

[29] The formation of these centres is of great historic interest in relation to the evolution both of wound surgery and of the scheme of evacuation and treatment in general. They were organised for these operations under instructions from General Headquarters, B.E.F. The ambulance personnel did not move with its unit but remained attached for administration. It has been stated (by Col. Langford Lloyd, R.A.M.C.) that an abdominal wound was successfully operated upon within one and a half hours of the opening of the Somme Battle on July 1.

[30] *German experience.* In a report of these operations General Sixt von Armin commanding the Fourth German Army Corps, which faced I Anzac, makes some interesting comments on the medical service.

"*Reliefs.*" The medical units of the Corps "went into line with the Divisions" and were relieved with them. "The duties of the medical service during continuous fighting in trench warfare are so strenuous that the medical personnel urgently requires relief at the same time as the troops. Furthermore, the medical personnel takes greater pleasure in its difficult task and carries it out with more devotion if it is assisting the formation to which it belongs."

"*Motor Ambulances.*" "The attaching of a motor ambulance column to the Army Group proved itself very useful." Only "a small proportion" of the cars were placed at the disposal of the Field Ambulances (Hauptverbandplätze). The reserve "was principally used to transport cases to hospital trains."

"*Stretcher-bearers.*" To meet the "great demand for stretcher-bearers, which was universal" fifty reserve bearers were trained in each of the "Divisional Field Recruit Depots" (Reinforcement camps).

"*Communication between medical units.*" "In consequence of the wide distribution of the medical arrangements" it was found desirable to insist by regulation on the importance of ample telephone communications between the various medical units in the line.

[31] In these battles though "the necessity of good front-line surgery" was agreed upon "it was very evident that .... much more was required." (*British Official History, Surgery, Vol. I, p. 219*). The mortality from wounds was indeed at this time very high. The nature of the work done in these units may be judged from the following wire from the D.M.S., Fourth Army to the D.G.M.S., B.E.F. dated 12 July, 1916: "Mobile X-Ray unit absolutely essential for this Army. There is now no X-Ray apparatus working for either Fourth Army or Reserve Army." The 1st A.C.C.S. left Australia with a portable X-Ray apparatus. *See Vol. I, p. 29.*

[32] Capt. P. A. C. Davenport.

"a most terrific amount of work was going on. We had six operating tables going continuously day and night and for the first three days had very little rest."

During the second week in August No. 49 C.C.S. was established at Contay to deal with lightly wounded.

Close to the junction of the lorry switch with the main Albert Road, in the fine grounds of the Château Vadencourt, the 2nd Field Ambulance built up a station which was to serve the Australian troops under many and varied circumstances. On July 27th the 7th Field Ambulance (Lieut.-Colonel R. B. Huxtable) formed a Corps Rest Station in the field near by in order to minimise the evacuation of light casualties from the Reserve Army's zone. During the period July 22nd-16th August, excluding 1,112 cases of sickness, 7,183 casualties passed through this unit. Analysis of the returns reveals as the outstanding feature of the experience the emergence, as a major medical problem of the war (as it was to be of the peace), of the condition then known as "shell shock." The term had been in use for some time and was loosely applied to all cases of physical and mental breakdown within the battle zone without apparent wound. It had become indeed a diagnostic shibboleth and an open sesame to the Base. Its importance in these operations is shown by the following figures of cases admitted to this unit during the 1st Division's offensive, July 22nd-26th:—

Rest stations

Admissions	July 22	July 23	July 24	July 25	July 26
Shell Shock ..	11	31	72	205	57
Walking wounded	43	687	180	730	184

A report on the matter was furnished to the D.D.M.S., I Anzac Corps by Colonel W. W. Hearne on August 18th. On November 12th a general Army Order initiated special machinery for dealing with the condition on scientific lines by the formation of special diagnostic centres in the Army zone.

Health

Throughout these operations the general health of the Australian troops was good.[33] The

---

[33] *The British Official Medical History, General, Vol. III, p. 49* records that the health of the troops during the Somme battles was good, but that cases of diarrhoea and dysentery began to appear in August and went on increasing. Scabies also was prevalent.

weekly sick evacuation rate per cent. on weekly average strength was as follows:—

15 July, ·42 per cent.;   5 Aug., ·46 per cent.;   26 Aug., ·82 per cent.
22 July, ·74   „   12 Aug. ·55   „   2 Sept., 1·00   „
29 July, ·36   „   19 Aug. ·70   „   9 Sept., ·37   „

Baths and Laundries. The maintenance of personal hygiene reached an important stage in the proposal initiated by Divisions for the organising of baths and laundries on a Corps instead of a Divisional basis. General sanitation was largely concerned in the prevention of fly-breeding and control of latrines in the staging areas. Sanitary Sections were in general allotted to the three "areas" to which reference has been made rather than moving always with their Divisions.

On August 25th the 1st Division was relieved by the 1st Canadian Division and entrained for the north followed by the 2nd and 4th. On September 3rd I Anzac Corps was replaced by the Canadian Corps whose D.D.M.S., Colonel G. L. Foster, became responsible for medical arrangements in this area. The A.I.F. left the Somme profoundly disillusioned but still ignorant of the full extent of the involvements of this new type of warfare. The next five months were to bring almost complete enlightenment.

Move north

TABLE I.—Casualties sustained by the A.I.F. on the Somme between July 19th and September 5th.

	Killed in action	Died of wounds	Died of Gas	Prisoners of war	Wounded in action	Gassed in action	Total
1st Division	1,904	456	4	70	6,087	60	8,581
2nd „	1,917	418	5	152	5,759	66	8,317
4th „	1,704	320	1	167	4,995	7	7,194
Other troops	8	4	–	–	35	–	47
Total	5,533	1,198	10	389	16,876[84]	133	24,139

TABLE II.—Casualties sustained by the field ambulances and regimental stretcher-bearers during the period, July 19th to September 5th.

	Killed		Wounded		Missing		Prisoners		Total
	Amb.	Regtl.	Amb.	Regtl.	Amb.	Regtl.	Amb.	Regtl.	
1st Division	18	31	71	137	1	4	—	—	262
2nd Division	7	20	59	72	3	7	—	—	168
4th Division	13	12	47	103	—	—	16	3	194
Total	38	63	177	312	4	11	16[35]	3	624

[84] The wounded in action figure includes 405 who were evacuated as shell shock "wound."
[35] The circumstances of this loss are recorded on *p. 278n.*

CHAPTER V

THE SOMME WINTER

THE action with which in the wider sphere the present chapter is concerned relates to the final phase of the Somme offensive and its immediate aftermath, and to the preparations for a British offensive in the spring of 1917. The experience of the A.I.F. during this period falls naturally in three periods namely, six weeks of rest in the Ypres Salient, followed by return to the Somme for a brief immersion in the dregs of the great battle, and then by three months spent in the occupation of trenches there in front of Flers and Gueudecourt.

The three Divisions of I Anzac Corps reached the Second Army in Flanders between August 30th and September 14th, replacing the Canadian Corps in the line between Menin Road and Groote Vierstraat in front of Ypres.[1] Corps Headquarters were located at Abeele.

I. Rest in the Salient

The Ypres Salient had not hitherto been peaceful, but the Somme and Verdun had now drained the front of active Divisions[2] and during the tour of I Anzac in the north, the warfare there, apart from an occasional raid, was uneventful. The trenches were sparsely held on a three Divisional front, each Division having two brigades in the line; casualties were insignificant.

In the belief that they were to winter here the Australian troops set to work to make themselves safe and comfortable. As elsewhere, the Canadians had left their mark on the roads

---

[1] The 5th Division at this time was still in II Anzac and held a sector in front of Fleurbaix.
[2] In July the Battle of Verdun was relaxed. On August 29 General von Falkenhayn was replaced as Chief of Staff by Marshal von Hindenburg, with General Ludendorff as "Chief-Quartermaster-General."

and railways, water-supplies, baths and laundries. No troops, however, in the British Army surpassed the Australian in the making and maintenance of trenches, and those in front of Ypres were now fortified and organised as never before.

Change in Administration. The exceptional character of the administrative system introduced during the Somme Battle is shown by the fact that on their arrival in the Ypres area the Australian Divisions automatically resumed control of administrative affairs in their own sectors. Apart from the care of "Corps troops" the medical department of the Corps became for the time little more than a record office for consolidating returns.

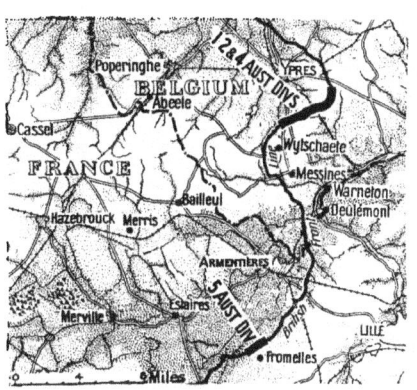

Fronts held by Australian Divisions in Second Army, Sept. 1916.

The Deputy-Director supervised Divisional arrangements, suggesting rather than requiring action. In particular he concerned himself energetically in preparations for the winter, and in the improvement of the rest stations and officers' hospitals.

Medical Arrangements. As part of this reversion the A.D's.M.S. of the Divisions now made their own arrangements.[3] Each Division had its own medical stations and routes of clearance, each brigade was served by its "own" field ambulance.[4]

---

[3] On the left sector of the Corps front the 2nd Division had three "advanced dressing stations," the two forward converging on a third behind Ypres, which evacuated to a "main dressing station" at Vlamertinghe. In the centre the 1st had two, with a main station at Brandhoek. The 4th cleared via A.D.S's at Dickebusch and La Clytte to a main dressing station at Ouderdom. No. 11 Motor Ambulance Convoy was allotted to the Corps. Divisional rest stations, baths, and laundries, were taken over as going concerns from the Canadians.

[4] Though strictly divisional troops, each field ambulance was commonly attached to its corresponding brigade.

Rest stations were "Divisional," as also were baths and laundries.

Organisation and Training. The heavy casualties and severe ordeal of the Somme required, first, that the force be again brought to strength, and, second, that health be recuperated and spirits restored. For this purpose the conditions at this time in the Ypres sector were ideal. The most direct and obvious effect on the A.I.F. of the Somme Battle had been an acute crisis in the matter of reinforcements. The drain on the training battalions had been enormous, recovery and return to duty of

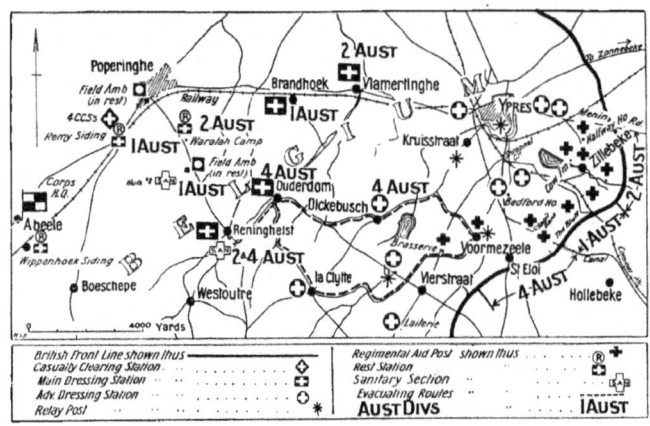

I Anzac Medical Arrangements, Ypres Area, Sept.-Oct. 1916.

casualties took time; and these, together with a drop in recruiting in Australia, brought about a serious depletion of the depots in trained effectives. The outcome of the crisis and the means adopted for maintaining intact the five Divisions are related elsewhere.[5] But it may here be said that means were found to bring

---

[5] *See pp. 448-9.* As affecting the present narrative it is proper here to note that the circumstances led to an endeavour to introduce compulsory service into Australia as had been done in Great Britain. The A.I.F. participated in the referendum on the matter, the vote being taken while in this area. The A.I.F. as a whole gave a small "Yes" majority, but the vote of the men in the field was against compulsion, as also was that of the majority in Australia. The decision threw a heavy burden on the early volunteers: and it greatly enhanced the military importance of the work of the medical service with the A.I.F. and the responsibility falling on its Medical Director.

13. SEVEN BRITISH AMBULANCE BEARERS CARRYING A STRETCHER THROUGH THE SOMME MUD ABOUT THE END OF 1916
Aust. War Memorial Collection No. J642.

14. STRETCHER-BEARING IN THE SOMME WINTER
Bearers of the 12th Field Ambulance near Longueval.
Aust. War Memorial Official Photo. No. E49. *To face p. 76.*

15. MEN WITH TRENCH FEET BEING CARRIED FROM A.D.S. TO MOTOR AMBULANCE AT BERNAFAY

Aust. War Memorial Official Photo. No. E81.

16. SICK PARADE AT AN R.A.P. ON THE SOMME FRONT

Taken at Eaucourt-l'Abbayé in February, 1917. Note the use of sandbags instead of puttees.

Aust. War Memorial Official Photo. No. E233. *To face p. 77.*

each Division almost to strength without—as for a time was contemplated—breaking up the 3rd which was still training in England. Regimental bearers were established at sixteen per battalion. Losses in medical units were fully replaced.

Recuperation. The recovery of physical resilience and moral tone was promoted by the facilities for relaxation and personal comfort to be found in this rich Flemish district. Leave, local and general, was available, rations were fully adequate, personal opportunity for the expenditure of pay was good. No Army was better organised than the Second, and no sector more adequately furnished with the means for promoting health than that now occupied by the Australian troops.

Maintenance of Health. In the prevention of disease in respect both of administrative measures (detection and isolation of infection) and of general sanitation the Sanitary Sections, which on the Somme had in some measure lost touch with their Divisions, here regained it, and once more worked in close conjunction with the Divisional deputy assistant directors. There is visible also at this time in the A.I.F. the early stage of a development of great importance, namely the assumption by the Quartermaster-General's Branch of responsibility for execution in many matters of health hitherto placed under the medical department, leaving to the latter the duty of expert advice and direction.

General Hygiene—Water. The methods adopted for maintaining pure supplies of water for the troops call for only brief reference in these narrative chapters. In the Hazebrouck area the supply had been derived chiefly from shallow wells, on the Somme from deep wells and streams. Here first the A.I.F. was introduced to a fully organised reticulation which reached even to the front line. Purity was secured by chlorination both in the water cart and in petrol tin, the degree of chlorination being controlled by the "Horrocks test case." At the water points controlled by the Sanitary Sections were stationed the water duty men of battalions as "water wardens" whose duties (exactly laid down) comprised in addition to general oversight and prevention of waste, ensurance of the efficient chlorination of all supplies.

Personal Hygiene. In this stable and well appointed area the provision for "personal hygiene," was fully adequate—in marked contrast to that possible on the Somme. The Canadian Divisional baths, accepted as models in the British Army, were taken over by the Australian formations, and were a factor of first rate importance in promoting health.[6]

Gas Defence. Ypres the first scene of a gas attack was the centre of British defensive measures against this weapon; the enemy was known to contemplate a great extension in the amount used and also a change in its nature. On arrival in France the troops had been issued with a "P.H. Helmet" and trained in methods of defence against this new weapon, and this training now became intensive. A cardinal stage had just been reached through the introduction for general use of the "British small box respirator" and the recognition of the fact that the instruction of troops and supervision of all defensive measures against gas were not properly duties of the medical service. During their stay in the Salient in addition to general training, medical officers received instruction in the measures for protecting aid-posts and so forth, and were issued with special stores; and were also fully informed of the methods of treatment then in vogue. In addition one officer from each field ambulance attended a special course at the Army Gas Centre at Cassel.

Winter Preparations. The Australian force had been duly impressed by warnings on the need to prepare for this its first winter on the Western Front, especially as regards bronchitis and colds, local skin infections and infestations, and "trench foot," but also in general, for the maintenance of health by food, warmth, and comfort. The fact that Australia is in large part a dry sub-tropical country increased the concern of the medical department of the Corps. Vigorous action was taken. The troops worked enthusiastically to improve the trenches and communications and to provide drainage. The Quartermaster-

---

[6] The provision of baths and laundries was a "Q" Branch matter but they were still controlled by medical orderlies under an officer detailed from the field ambulance. A laundry staffed by local women was attached to each and a staff of needlewomen. Each man banded in his dirty underlinen on entrance to the bath and received a clean outfit after he had bathed. These laundries undertook to supply a clean dry pair of socks daily to each man. Outer clothes were deloused and disinfected and brushed.

General's Branch and the medical department co-operated in measures that might promote the purpose in view.

The Call South. These preparations were well advanced when on October 9th instruction was received by the Second Army that the Australian Division most fitted for offensive operations should be sent at once to the Somme and that all the other Australian Divisions were to follow. In response, on October 17th the 5th Division from II Anzac, though not yet fully up to strength, entrained for the south and joined the XV Corps (Fourth Army) and on October 23rd took over a sector of the line in front of Flers. The 1st Division went next and on October 30th entered the line on the right of the 5th. The 2nd and 4th followed in that order. On October 30th the I Anzac Corps took over from the XV British—which like most of the higher British headquarters in the battle area had been continuously in the line since July 1st—and on November 2nd all four Australian Divisions in France were united in the one command under General Birdwood.

It is not easy in writing the medical history of this period to maintain the narrative on a note of detachment or even to form a balanced judgement on the events that led up to the "Somme Winter." In the first place the Aus-

II. The Battle of the Ancre tralian force was subjected to a trial which, though successfully surmounted, left its mark in a long-sustained sense of resentment and a lasting heritage of ill-health "due to or aggravated by war service." And in the second the historian, in a study of "wearing-down" warfare, finds himself compelled to record, and required to explain or excuse, a winter wastage on this front from sickness which in its totality went far to rival in numbers, if not in gravity,[7] that sustained in the summer fighting and was in excess of all previous experience of white British troops on the Western Front. Moreover this was in a great measure brought about by the existence of conditions that compel the impression that questions regarding the effect of tactical schemes on the problems of food and health, and on the well-being of the human

---

[7] For the proportion of sick and wounded returned to duty, *see diagram at p. 440.*

material available for attrition, did not at this time enter greatly into the mind of the British General Staff.

The military situation
The military events which brought about this experience in the British Expeditionary Force and in the A.I.F. must briefly be stated.

The advance on a broad front made on September 14th and October 4th had carried the British Army's front beyond the high ground facing Bapaume—it now lay near the bottom of the valley, crowning whose farther side stood that long desired objective. Short of a breakthrough, the general purpose of the offensive had been achieved. The balance of casualties and morale was reported as highly favourable.[8] General Haig held however that the conditions in "an ordinary winter" need not compel the cessation of "pressure," and he proposed to deliver on October 14th and 16th an attack by the Third, Fourth, and Fifth Armies which should reach the opposite slope of the valley.

The season, however, broke early and wet. The shell-riven country became a sodden swamp. On the 12th he decided to break off the battle, and prepare for winter and a large scale spring offensive, which it was hoped would bring victory. Two factors, however, conspired to make him change this wise decision. In the first place strong pressure was brought to bear on him from the French Command—Marshal Joffre and General Foch—who for political reasons desired more to show for the Somme. The other was the operation of the policy of "wearing-down," the supposed success of which, when the "break-through" had failed, supplied the chief justification for the appalling expenditure of life and loss of "effectives." In the hope of better weather, the offensive was resumed by the Fourth and Fifth Armies. On the left the Fifth, after repeated postponements, carried out on November 15th-18th, a very successful attack (Battle of Ancre) which, while it did little if anything to improve the tactical situation brought 7,500 prisoners at the cost of not more than the same number of British casualties. On the right (Fourth Army), however, the only result of repeated attacks was to push the front line into the morass until it stuck fast, and to postpone for a month the urgent preparations for the winter. It was to participation in this fighting on the Fourth Army front that the I Anzac Corps was consigned.

Haig's Intentions. When the I Anzac Corps arrived on the Somme those responsible for its command and administration found themselves committed to the pursuance of two imperious but mutually conflicting purposes—arrangements for the proposed advance, and preparations for the wintering of the troops, always with a view to the resumption of the offensive in the early spring, which it was hoped would bring victory to the

---

[8] The optimistic tone of this report is now known to have had much less justification than its author supposed.

Allies. For the immediate offensive an enormous concentration of troops, munitions, and artillery was in progress—that of guns being greater than in any previous phase of the Somme Battle; but General Haig proposed, when these operations should end, to form in each Army (Fourth and Fifth)—army corps each of four divisions, of which in turn two would maintain pressure in the line while the others were, one in reserve and one in rest and training.

The Terrain. The terrain of this present fighting was again the stretch of low ridges with shallow intervening valleys that reached out from the Somme plateau to separate the lower from the upper valley of the Ancre, which here runs in a semi-circle. The Fourth Army front lay along the broad well-tilled upper valley from Morval, where it joined the French, to Le Sars where it met the Fifth Army front. The 4,000 yards of the I Anzac Corps front line (now occupied by the 5th and 1st Divisions) lay before Gueudecourt and Flers, some two to three miles in advance of the crest of the ridge.

Communications. The one formed road ran along the spur on which once lay Montauban, Mametz, and Fricourt, diverging near Bécordel—on the one hand to Méaulte and villages along the lower Ancre, Dernancourt, Buire, Ribemont, Heilly, and on the other via Albert to Amiens and Vignacourt. Railhead was at Mericourt near Dernancourt.[9]

Conditions in the Forward Area. From the old British front line near Fricourt to the new front, a distance of from eight to ten miles, every yard of ground had been fought over, nearly everything standing had been razed, every inch of soil turned and re-turned by some of the heaviest bombardments of the war and by entrenchments. Continuous rains through October had converted the whole of this area into a very sea of mud. To Mametz the main two-way road was passable; but forward on the one way circuit to Montauban the wet, and the excessive use for carriage of heavy munitions, had destroyed the metal surface, causing heavy waste of vehicles and constant traffic

---

[9] *See Map No. 3 (at p. 93)* which represents the situation in February. The French railway could be used in parts only. The French gauge was less than the British but could take British rolling stock with care. Light railway lines (60 cm. gauge) were reaching out at various points in the forward area.

4

blocks, which at times extended for miles and lasted for hours. Tracks and non-metalled roads had become quagmires. Duckboards, revetments, indeed all supplies, reached the front in doles; even rations were held up. The supply dumps (refilling points) had been forced back to Albert; delivery points were at Montauban and Quarry railhead.[10]

I Anzac Corps back area, Nov. 1916.

The area over which the Corps assumed control[11] was organised and administered on lines already made familiar.[12] The D.D.M.S. at Corps Headquarters resumed administrative control, and on November 9th issued a full scheme of "medical arrangements" for evacuation and treatment. Assistant Directors of Medical Services became again in great measure merely executive officers, their initiative being chiefly confined to the clearance of the forward area. In this duty, however, they found themselves fully occupied.

The I Anzac Corps arrives

In this administrative integration each branch and every department, of the Corps and Divisions alike, was involved. The

---

[10] *See diagram in Vol. I, p. 208.*

[11] The Corps boundaries and most important features of this area are shown in the accompanying sketch map. It was divided into three areas, respectively: (1) the fighting zone (front line to Fricourt), (2) reserve and approach zone (to Ribemont), (3) rest and training zone (extending back to Montigny with facilities for billeting in villages as remote as Vignacourt). The striking feature was its length and the consequent great distance for the movement of troops, casualties, and supplies—a feature due to the immensity of the impedimenta required for this type of warfare. Staging camps were at Montauban (Pommiers Redoubt) and Ribemont.

[12] *See Chapter iv, pp. 66-9.*

situation in which the force now found itself was indeed obviously such as to make imperative the pursuance, with the utmost possible vigour, of well concerted measures designed to safeguard not merely the comfort and welfare of the troops and the care and clearance of casualties, but the very existence of the Corps as an effective fighting force.

The Corps Scheme of Works. A scheme of works—maintenance and development—was put in hand at once, being set out on November 2nd by General Birdwood's chief of staff (Brigadier-General C. B. B. White). It embraced every branch and department of the Corps and Divisions.[13] The official diary of the D.D.M.S. (Colonel C. C. Manifold) records that on November 3rd he himself "wrote into the D.A. & Q.M.G.[14] a strong letter on the vital necessity of taking measures to minimise the occurrence of trench foot, and pointed out that it was as much a military necessity as bringing up ammunition, if efficiency was not to be impaired."[15]

With the offensive continuing, however, little could be done to prepare for the winter before it should set in.

The scheme of clearance and evacuation taken over from the XV Corps ran roughly parallel to, and south of, that used during the Battle of Pozières. From the Upper Ancre the routes ran across low ridges to meet that river again near Albert, and thence along its course to Nos. 36 and 38 Casualty Clearing Stations at Heilly.

Medical Arrangements

Collection and clearance were based on advanced dressing

---

[13] The scheme was implemented by frequent conferences and consultations between headquarters staff and the executive departments. Its most important elements in respect of maintenance were an ambitious scheme of railways—British broad gauge, and Decauville—undertaken by the C.R.E. I Anzac (Brig.-Gen. A. C. de L. Joly de Lotbinière) with the co-operation of a specially appointed officer for light railway construction and working; the repair of roads; housing and feeding facilities and staging camps; and the organisation of the front lines. The scheme involved heavy calls on the infantry for fatigues to supplement the Pioneer Battalions. Any improvement in the front lines and approaches and in conditions of living and medical service were wholly dependent on the progress of this work.

[14] Brig.-Gen. R. A. Carruthers. As representing both "A" and "Q" branches of I Anzac Corps Headquarters, this officer was directly responsible for the medical department. (*See Vol. I, p. 127.*)

[15] The diary of the D.M.S., Fourth Army has the following entries at this time:— October 31 (in a summary) "Operations almost completely stopped, the troops being literally stuck in the mud." November 3. "The sick wastage of all divisions in the front line is going up rapidly. . . . It is impossible while fighting is going on to do anything to alleviate it."

stations at "Thistle Dump" and "Bernafay Wood" (left and right sectors). These were tented stations, respectively 3,000 and 6,000 yards from the regimental aid-posts in the front line area. This distance was covered in parts by horsed-transport and Decauville; but a bearer carry of two to six thousand yards of mud unbridged by duckboards remained. Bearer relay and "field collecting" posts had been formed where facilities for shelter and safety were available[16] and at the points of junction of hand carriage with wheeled transport. Bearer, store, and horsed-waggon depots had been formed in connection with advanced dressing stations. The position of all these, and the routes of collecting and clearance changed but little from those shown in the map at *page 88*.

Clearance to main dressing station, some five miles from the advanced dressing station, was, for stretcher cases, by field ambulance motor transport via Montauban and Mametz—and later by train; for walkers it was by lorry and army buses, and later by railway. Treatment and evacuation centred on a Corps Main Dressing Station and a Corps Collecting Station at Bécordel siding where the road and railway lines met. A Corps Rest Station had been formed at Buire. All these were under the immediate direction of the Deputy Director at Corps. The whole system of collection, clearance, treatment, and distribution hinged on the condition of the routes of transport. For reasons already set out these were inadequate to maintain normal communications with the fighting front. Records of this time show that the system of clearance taken over by the I Anzac Corps had reached a stage where breakdown was imminent: by ordinary military standards indeed this stage had already been passed.

The continual postponement and resumption of plans for the Fourth Army's offensive action, embarrassing alike to commanding officers and administrative departments,[17] ended on November 5th with operations

---

[16] Medical work here as elsewhere was heavily dependent on the captured German deep dugout.

[17] Thus Lord Cavan commanding the XIV Corps, at the end of October "desired to know whether it was deliberately intended to sacrifice the British right in order to help the French left. No one (he wrote) who has not visited the front can really know the state of exhaustion to which the men are reduced . . . all my officers agree that they are the worst they have seen owing to the enormous distance of the carry of all munitions."
Already he had lost 3,520 men in these minor operations.

on all three corps fronts (XV, XIV and I Anzac). On the I Anzac Corps front the attacks were chiefly in the left sector. For these the 2nd Division relieved the 5th. The results in all were as unsatisfactory as were the conditions under which they were carried out. With no ultimate gain the 2nd Division sustained 549 and the 1st 243 casualties.

I Anzac in Ancre Battle

November 5th to 19th. With this military failure, active operations ceased on the Fourth Army front, except on a reduced scale designed to assist the long delayed blow by the Fifth Army. Road repair and other winter preparations, except railway construction, were almost completely held up. By the middle of the month the main road had become almost impassable; on November 17th it was closed to all motor traffic. The final offensive in this "battle" was launched on November 14th. On the left, moving off high ground, the Fifth Army, as already mentioned, advanced its line astride of the Ancre. Operations in the Fourth Army were confined to minor and unsuccessful operations by the 2nd Australian and 48th British Divisions.

Collecting and Clearance in October. While in the line (October 23rd to November 4th) the 5th Division—8th Field Ambulance (Lieut.-Colonel A. E. Shepherd)—had built up a working system of clearance. The problem of the bearer carry however was rendered almost insuperable by the mud which lay deep over the whole 6,000 yards of the carry, and in the communication trenches was in parts up to the thigh so that bearers perforce carried in the open.

"Under average conditions [says the diary of the 8th Field Ambulance] the time for a carry from the regimental aid-post to the advanced dressing station was over six hours and required thirty-six bearers in relays for each stretcher case. After their relay, bearers were exhausted. Eight hourly reliefs would not work as too much time was spent on the road; a system of forty-eight hours on duty with eighteen hours rest was adopted."

Some relief was obtained by the use of flat-bottomed sledges which slid over the mud.[18]

Medical Arrangements for November 5th. For these operations the 2nd Division (7th Brigade) relieved the 5th. The 6th Field Ambulance (Lieut.-Colonel A. H. Moseley) replaced the 8th at Thistle Dump A.D.S. and had the bearers of the 7th.

[18] The idea originated with Warrant Officer A. E. Roberts, 8th Field Ambulance. With the co-operation of Captain H. A. C. Irving, A.A.M.C., a horse-drawn sledge was designed whereby, under favourable conditions, a case might reach the advanced dressing station in less than two hours, a stretcher-bearer and driver only being required. The Army Service Corps helped also with horses. *See also Vol. I, pp. 564-5.*

The relieving units took over the divisional collecting station at "Medical Dump" near Mametz. Large dumps of stretchers, blankets, dressings, and medical comforts were made.[19] The A.D.S. for the right sector was run by the 2nd Field Ambulance on the Longueval-Bernafay road.

In this action all movement was greatly hampered by a peculiarly gluey and tenacious quality of the mud, composed of clay and chalk which had partly dried.[20]

The 7th Brigade (2nd Division) attacked at 9.10 a.m. on the 5th. Colonel Moseley that night

"found the sledge track very bad. Two horses required to each sledge. Wounded came in from 12 noon to the advanced dressing station; the horses completely knocked up. Stretcher cases had to be carried requiring six to eight bearers to each relay. A hundred men of the 21st Battalion reported to assist."

The medical arrangements were officially reported adequate but in spite of the comparatively small number of casualties, clearance of stretcher cases was not complete till the following day and from individual records it is clear that serious delay occurred at the aid-posts where in some instances the battalions (which had just moved in) had made little or no provision for the care of stretcher cases awaiting clearance, and some of these died from exposure. The weather was damp and bitterly cold.

The 1st Division—which had been a week in the line—had attempted its part in drenching rain in the small hours of the morning. Its wounded were cleared by the 2nd Field Ambulance by dusk on the following night; the officer commanding (Lieut.-Colonel W. W. Hearne)[21] himself worked in No-Man's Land, where the regimental medical officer 1st Battalion (Captain N. E. B. Kirkwood) had prepared a German dugout as his prospective aid-post.

By this time the clearance of the sick had become the major, if the less urgent, medical problem. In his report for November

---

[19] It was in the Somme Winter that the provision of blanket and stretcher "dumps" and the issue to field ambulance of equipment "additional to Mobilisation Store Table" first became a major feature of medical arrangements.

[20] It is recorded that in one instance the attempted extrication of an unwounded officer led to a fracture—dislocation of the spine. Horses when bogged were shot. "The place (says one record) is dotted with them."

[21] On November 20 this officer replaced Colonel C. H. W. Hardy as A.D.M.S. 5th Division. He was succeeded by Lieut.-Col. A. H. Marks.

3rd to 6th when one hundred wounded passed through his aid-post the R.M.O. 27th Battalion (Captain J. S. Mackay) noted that he

"was obliged to return many men who were really unfit for duty. . . . The greater number of the Battalion are at present suffering from an early stage of Oedema of the feet. There is slight swelling, redness, extreme tenderness, and burning pains. Some show marked swelling."

Already indeed the problem of "trench foot" was dominating the military and medical situation alike.

Medical Arrangements for November 14th. By now, in the fighting zone, the situation had deteriorated almost to chaos. Approach trenches were impassable. Each sledge took three horses, those of the Field Ambulance being supplemented by the Army Service Corps. To extricate and clear the four hundred casualties, slight and severe, in this action, required the utmost efforts of two bearer divisions and the help of some 400 infantry. Both Divisional and Brigade commanders took the matter in hand. "Officers and N.C.O's shouldered stretchers with their men."[22]

Clearance to Bécordel by Road. The approach road to Montauban soon became almost impassable; by the middle of November the main circuit itself was in the same condition; and on the 17th all motor traffic along it was stopped for some days to permit of repair. By this time about eighty per cent. of the divisional motor ambulance transport was in the workshops, and clearance by this route was chiefly by cars of No. 27 Motor Ambulance Convoy.[23]

By Rail. Communication was saved from a complete breakdown by the energy with which the broad gauge railway was pushed up the valley from Fricourt. From mid-November trains ran from "Quarry siding"; at the end of the month three trains

---

[22] The medical situation was brought home to the Corps Staff by the death of Brig.-Gen. D. J. Glasfurd, commanding 12th Inf. Bde. Wounded on Nov. 12 near the front line, his transport over 3,000 yards to the advanced dressing station took ten hours. He died in No. 38 Casualty Clearing Station at Heilly.
[23] This departure from the rule which forbade the use of M.A.C. cars in advance of the "main dressing station" was permitted by the D.M.S., Fourth Army Surgeon-General M. W. O'Keeffe. No officer concerned in clearance at this time would forgive neglect to record the value of this service or to appreciate the spirit in which it was rendered by the British Motor Convoy.

per day were specially allocated to the clearance of wounded and sick from the forward area. An ambulance station with adequate staff under a particularly energetic officer,[24] with adequate provision for warmth and sustainment, controlled the railway clearance of casualties and the replacement of returnable equipment from the siding at Bécordel.

Treatment and Disposal at Bécordel. Within a short time Bécordel became a very large centre for the reception, treatment, and disposal of casualties arriving by road and rail from the Corps front. The main dressing station—one field ambulance complete with three or more tent sub-divisions attached—accommodated between 400 and 500 patients and contained "three large operating tents each with three tables." Elaborate arrangements were made "in tents of all sorts for every conceivable purpose."[25]

The "Corps Collecting Station" was staffed by one field ambulance (less bearer division) and received all slight and walking cases. The problem of classification and distribution of casualties was admirably solved for both stations by a most efficient system of reception at a special railway siding. A quartermaster's store was placed here with a "dump" of blankets and a staff to collect and check all blankets and stretchers and return them to railhead at The Quarry. This post was well run by the Dental Officer, Lieutenant A. F. Sutton.

From these two stations patients obviously unlikely to recover within fourteen days went to casualty clearing station,[26] others to the Corps Rest Station at Buire. The function of this extraordinary establishment lay outside the normal scheme of field

---

[24] Lieut.-Col. J. B. St. Vincent Welch.

[25] The D.D.M.S. (Colonel Manifold) was himself "not in favour of the huge main dressing stations which had been formed under Army instruction. The whole thing (he wrote) simply meant usually that the wounded were dressed unnecessarily, with long delay in getting back to the casualty clearing station, where the whole procedure would be again undertaken." (Personal memorandum to the D.M.S., A.I.F.) It would seem indeed that the conditions of the Battle of Pozières were accentuated here through circumstance rather than individual misjudgement. However keen the desire to observe the instructions contained in the official manual, *Treatment of War Wounds*, the ambulance surgeon could not but feel—as was indeed the case—that in the existing conditions the majority of seriously wounded men were unfit for a further journey: yet to retain them often meant a deliberate surgical procedure under anaesthetic. The situation is disclosed by an official request by Corps (which could not at the time be fulfilled) for an advanced operating centre or a casualty clearing station here.

[26] Special stations, Corps and Army, were set apart for the treatment of particular conditions—nervous and gassed cases, and infectious disease—scabies, and, for the Australian units, mumps.

Map No. 2

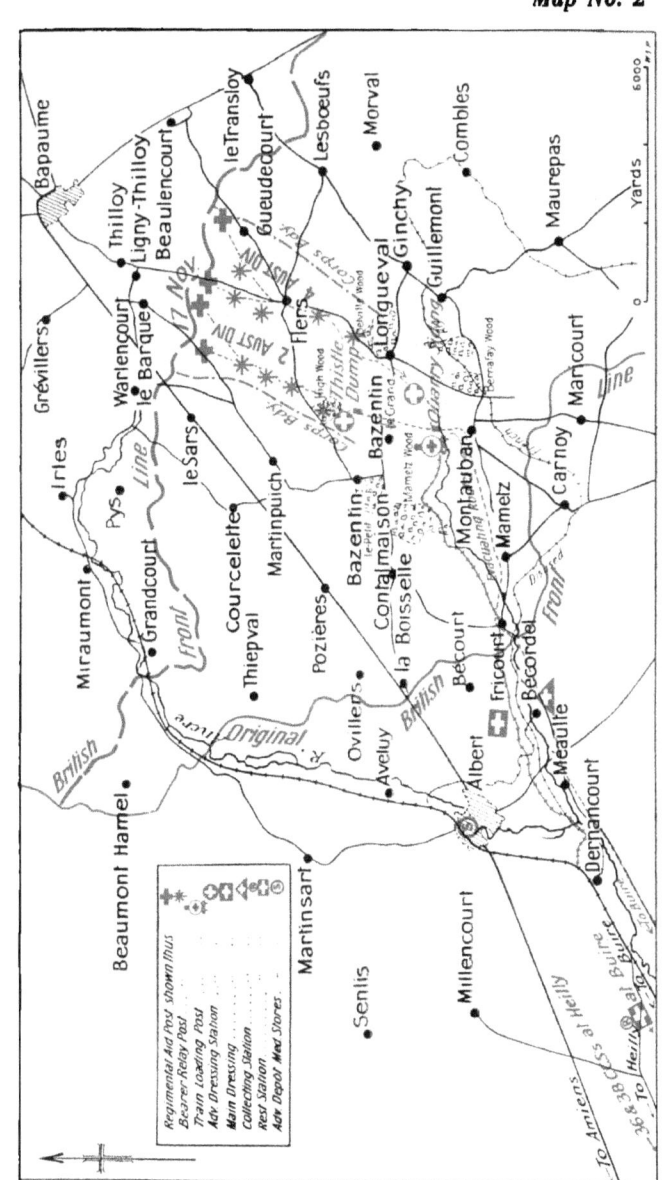

Medical arrangements on the Somme battlefield, mid-November, 1916

ambulance work, wide though this was. It was intimately related to the military problem of the control of wastage and is conveniently considered under that heading.[27]

The First Battle of the Somme, begun with what brave hopes, sustained with what unsurpassed devotion, petered out officially on November 19th. A summary of casualties and results is deferred till the close of the "Somme Winter" is dealt with. During the period under review,

End of First Somme Battle apart from the regimental personnel, strain fell on the officers and men of the "bearer divisions" and the motor ambulance transport. The conditions on the fighting front imposed on the troops the extreme limit of sordid discomfort and suffering in the process of dying for their country; and the same conditions required of those officers and other ranks of the A.A.M.C., whose duty and privilege it was to succour these men, an organising and administrative ability, and qualities of physical endurance and mental and moral fortitude to a degree never exceeded in the history of the Australian Medical Service.

No one who saw, as did the writer, the troops of the 7th Brigade moving out from the fighting line on November 7th toward Montauban could fail to realise that he looked on men who had reached the limit of their resources,

III. The Somme Winter physical and moral. The men of the 1st Division had come out of the Battle of Pozières as from the Valley of the Shadow of Death; but the troops of the 2nd Division who dragged themselves step by step through the mud from Flers seemed to reach a further degree of reaction —being almost past caring. Nor were the conditions to which they emerged such as should bring any quick recovery. The weather was bitterly cold. The "staging camps" at this time were bare huts in a sea of mud, fuel was scarce, heating stoves few, cooking difficult. In the front line to which within a few days they must return, men must sustain the fighting spirit on shell-hole water and hard rations.[28] Almost everything neces-

---

[27] See pp. 293-6.
[28] Divisional reliefs were fortnightly. Battalions were relieved after two days in the trenches. Asked by Colonel Manifold whether the divisional reliefs could not be more frequent, General Birdwood pointed out that the time spent in the process and the exertion involved made it not worth the while to make any change.

sary to ameliorate the conditions was at first lacking. Neither time nor opportunity had been given to battalions to exercise the ingenuity in improvising and compelling comfort which was an outstanding characteristic of the Australian infantry.

Discipline certainly was needed— but discipline that would reach the highest as well as the lowest, and would include command and organisation as well as executive. Consulted on November 12th by Colonel Manifold, the D.A. & Q.M.G. Fourth Army had said he looked upon "Trench Foot as wholly a matter of disciplinary measures being carried out." General Rawlinson, the Army Commander, more constructively pointed out that "sickness really resolved itself into a matter of communications." The course of events during the next two months were to prove the wisdom of General Rawlinson's advice.

Aftermath of Ancre Fighting. On November 10th the diary of the D.M.S. Fourth Army records:—

"Reported to 'A' that very large numbers of Australians are going sick. They are not suffering from any disease but are merely tired and exhausted."

But the initial stage of disease was clear to the R.M.O's. The conditions in the 24th Battalion were typical:—

"sick parades [says its historian] largely attended, everybody had a cold, some developing bronchitis. Rheumatism as common as iron rations."

For the week ending the 19th the weekly sick evacuation rate for the divisions in the line averaged 2·4 per cent. of ration strength, and the rest station expanded to 1,200. On November 22nd the 5th Division replaced the Guards in a general move to the right. Snow had been succeeded by rain and fog. During the week ending December 3rd 1,132 sick were evacuated from this formation—8·13 per cent. of ration strength.[29] The discipline of the Division was questioned—that of the Australians in general was already suspect. The Director-General (General Sloggett) from British General Headquarters and Deputy Director-General (General Macpherson) from the Lines of

---

[29] Because it interfered with a man's ability to march the disorder of function known as "trench foot" (more properly "frost-bite") was at this moment the most important element in the health situation—causing 699 out of the 1,132 evacuations in the 5th Division. It became the touchstone of health discipline.

Communications made direct enquiry. The D.D.M.S. made personal investigation and reported to the Corps Commander:—

"The large casualty list is, I believe, the result of avoidable causes, and centres mainly upon four factors. (1) An wholly inadequate supply of trench boots, and neglect to wear those issued. (2) An almost complete lack of dugouts and dry standing places to which men could resort to rub their feet and change their socks. Such dugouts . . . did not exist and none have as yet been made. (3) Neglect to remove boots and socks and to use the whale oil whilst in the firing line, and often similar neglect in the intermediate line. (4) The fourth cause is in my opinion the root of the whole matter. The Australian officer has not learned to look after his men; he lacks that knowledge which is usually only acquired by experience and careful training, and fails to exercise that immediate and close supervision over small details which bears so much upon the health of his men. It is only fair to state (he added) that this Division has occupied a deplorably bad front line with an immense carry . . . all this is being rapidly remedied. The 4th Division who occupied the left sector have had time to prepare trenches properly for the winter and the Division which preceded them belonging to this Corps had already put in an immense amount of work."

"Drastic steps," as Colonel Manifold was aware, had already been taken by the Corps Commander to deal with the matter last referred to.[30] It is certain that both these sincere and experienced British officers were unduly severe on the "junior Australian officer," as were the British medical authorities in their comments on the Division concerned and on the Australian force as a whole.[31] For the picture changes with a rapidity too marked to be the effect of these somewhat ill-timed, if salutary admonitions, and too sustained to be mere coincidence. From December 10th weekly returns of "trench foot" were required by Fourth Army. For the week ending on the 16th the XV Corps had a total of 1,585. I Anzac Corps 242. On December 23rd the totals were 721 and 141 respectively, while the Guards

[30] The chief measure had taken the form of a circular to all officers suggesting that the high Australian sick rate was due to lack of care and concern for their men by junior combatant officers.

[31] Personal testimony by Brig.-Gen. E. Tivey, who kept close touch with his Battalions, and the A.D.M.S. Col. W. W. Hearne, who himself carried hot food containers from the cooks' lines in Bernafay Wood to Needle Trench to test out the problem, and the diaries of the R.M.O's seem to prove that in the 5th Division debacle, the factor of discipline played a minor part. The conditions were deplorable. The formation it is true had not fully recovered from Fromelles: its units were much below strength, its commanding officer had lost his grip on his juniors. But the trenches taken over had become degraded beyond any casual redemption. Gen. Tivey has placed on record that then, as always, "it was a matter of honour with the Australian units to get their rations to the front line." The R.M.O., 32nd Battalion (Capt. E. W. B. Woods), records "every spare minute occupied rubbing feet with whale oil. All the men have thigh-high waders." On relief, in his "very large sick parade" he found that "practically every man had partial loss of voice and a heavy cough, very often so severe as to induce vomiting after a spasm."

Division alone (which had taken over a shocking sector from the French) evacuated 345, over double that for the whole I Anzac Corps.

Molière incurred the wrath of the orthodox medical profession of his day and delighted the Philistine laity with the epigram "medicine is the art of amusing the patient while nature effects a cure." In this enlightened age of "preventive medicine" it is the profession itself that is at pains to extol the *vis medicatrix naturae,* and to commend the virtue of self-help in the matter of preserving both personal and the public health. In its reaction to the inexorable law of the Great War—"root, hog, or die"—medicine, like other scientific techniques sloughed all unessentials and found its proper place in the scheme of things. In the conditions of the "Somme Winter" the part of the medical service in maintaining the health of the army in the field lay, as it happened, chiefly in giving admonition and expert advice; its special concern and preoccupation were the prevention of "army" wastage by treating minor non-battle casualties in the rest stations. The clinical analysis of the sick records is in accord with what "commonsense" would expect. The chief morbid states were those due to the direct influence of environment. Battle casualties and gassing became negligible; major epidemic infections (as it chanced) were also comparatively inconspicuous. In place of the acute psychic breakdown of Pozières we find those types of disorder and dysfunctions that are brought about by continued subjection to adverse physical and physiological agencies—cold, wet, malnutrition, exhausting toil, dirt—in general, "hardship." A note of the most important will be given later.

Prevention of Wastage, Winter 1916-17

In its essence the maintenance of health as distinct from the prevention of disease is largely a matter of wresting from the environment conditions favourable to physiological living. And, in a proper order of precedence in the prevention of wastage, the prosecution of the Corps scheme of works must be placed first. It does not however fall within the province of medical history to enter upon the technical and military problems involved in

The Corps Scheme of Works—Effort to " Return to Normality "

Map No. 3

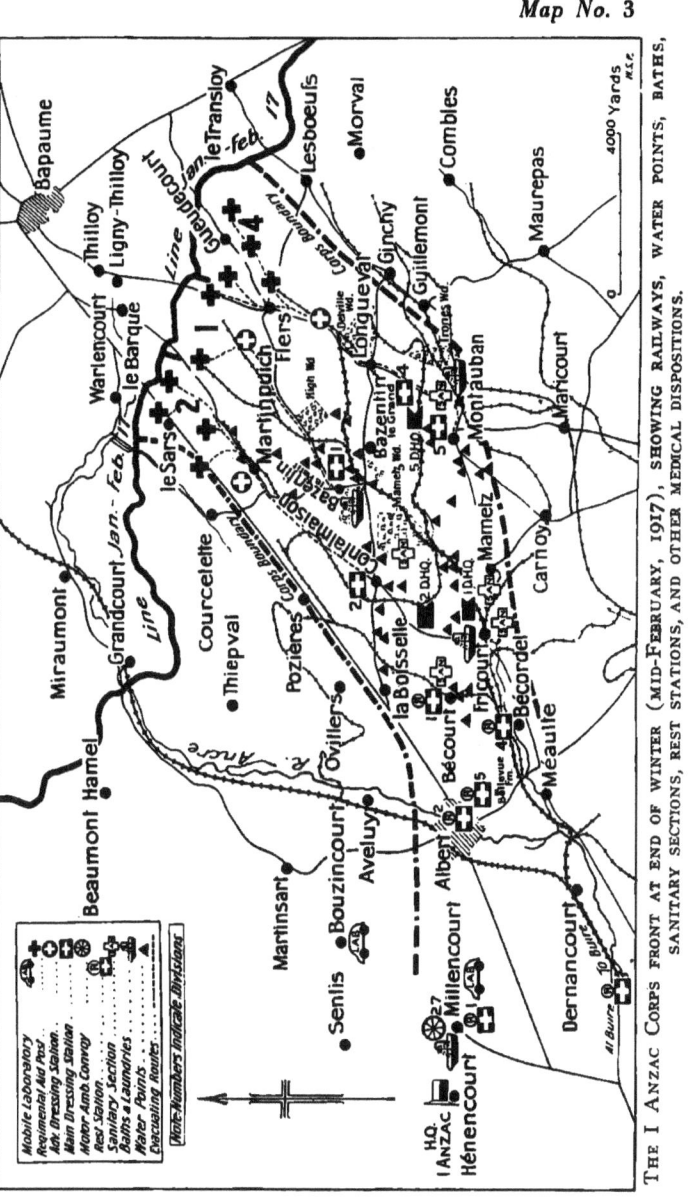

THE I ANZAC CORPS FRONT AT END OF WINTER (MID-FEBRUARY, 1917), SHOWING RAILWAYS, WATER POINTS, BATHS, SANITARY SECTIONS, REST STATIONS, AND OTHER MEDICAL DISPOSITIONS.

the process of creating a working system for reaching, feeding, housing and warming, resting, clothing, cleaning, and drying the vast numbers of men who must in this war be maintained in a few hundred yards of waterlogged trench, or within striking distance of it. The nature of the problem will have become evident. Railways, broad and light gauge, were pushed forward, roads repaired, wire-covered duckboard tracks laid down, trenches drained, the staging camps improved, reliefs organised. By the end of January the new railway lines were in full work;[32] communication with the front was complete, the trenches dry and comfortable.

Special Military Measures. Physical Amelioration. With these major works were associated those divisional activities and unit self-help which were perhaps the most important individual factors in maintaining health. The problem of providing hot food in the trenches was solved by the provision of special thermos-containers to bring it at night from the cooks' lines; braziers, burning charcoal, and solidified alcohol, ameliorated the conditions of life. In the approach area, drying rooms and stores—for the exchange of socks and trench boots and for the care of feet—were divisional responsibilities. Stoves warmed the staging huts. The organising of baths and laundries became a large and important function of the "Q" Branch of I Anzac Corps Headquarters—the establishment formed at Cagny in September by the Corps was greatly enlarged and admirably worked under a very efficient staff. Its output of disinfected and mended clothes was enormous.[33] Closely related to these and even more important as a factor in health was the provision for disinfestation (delousing). For this duty sanitary sections were largely responsible, but they worked in close conjunction with the "Q" branch of divisions. A special portable disinfesting chamber on lorry designed by the A.Q.M.G. (Lieut.-Colonel M. G. Taylor) brought delousing facilities within easy reach of the front line.

Psychical Stimulation. The gradual re-establishment of normal conditions of trench life and reliefs brought the means for exploiting "yet more excellent" ways. In the rest and

---

[32] *See also sketch map on p. 112.*
[33] A special sub-department of the "Q" Branch was formed in Sept., 1916, under Lieut. H. H. R. Macknight who retained the position until the end of the war.

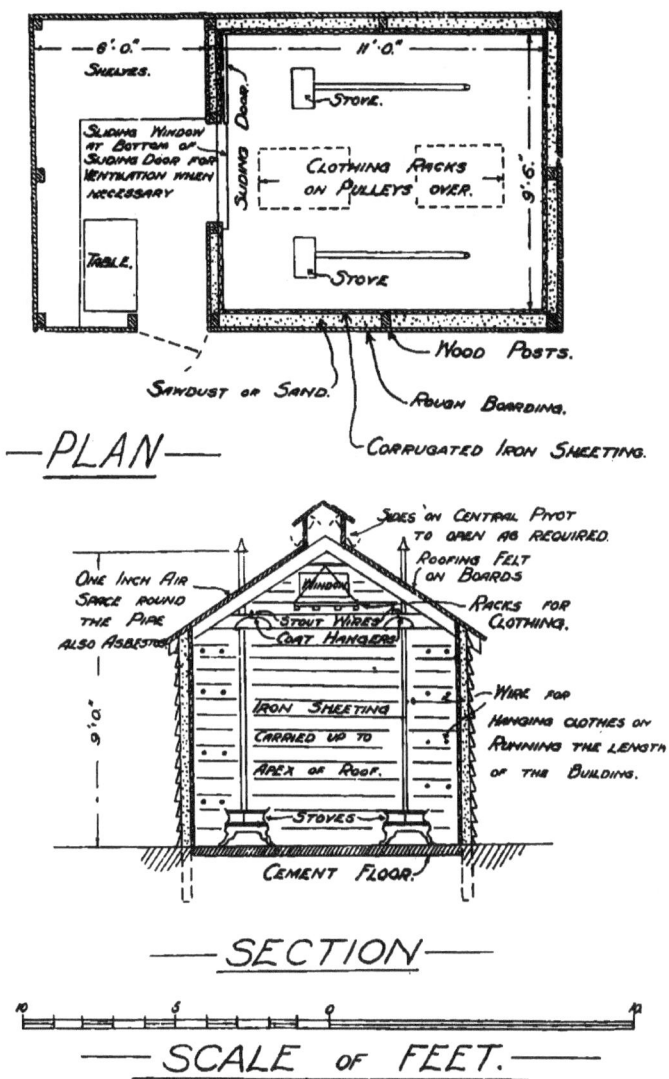

INSULATED SHED FOR DRYING CLOTHES
Designed by Lieut.-Colonel A. D. Sharpe, R.A.M.C.T.

training area north of Amiens social recreation was fostered.
Leave, local and general, was freely given. These and like
measures had results which illustrated again—as always throughout this war—the amazing resilience of man. The sense of
humour revived. By the end of December there emerged a
spirit of emulation in this contest with the elements and pursuit
of health; the source of which and its impulse were closely
similar to those which brought the troops through Pozières, as
also were its results. More powerful than almost anything
else in its effect on the health and spirits of the Australian
troops was the clear, bright, hard cold frost that arrived in
January with the most severe winter in France for a quarter
of a century. With frost and sunshine trench foot disappeared
as by magic—to reappear with any rain or snow, and in the
thaw.

Rôle of the Medical Service. In this struggle for health the
medical service was the *deus ex machina*. If at this time and in
these conditions its work was definitely ancillary to that of other
departments, its activities were yet of high and in some respects
of commanding importance. Its special activities in the detection
of epidemic disease, the elucidation of the scientific problems
relating thereto, and the designing of measures of prevention,
are dealt with elsewhere.[34] It need only be noted here that, in
this wider health field, the British force was at this time on the
eve of two important developments. "Trench fever" can be
seen—a small cloud on the horizon—in the increase of "P.U.O."
And in the Interallied Sanitary Conference of this year the
problem of food and rations was a subject of
grave debate. It should also be noted that this
was the time at which there was reached a
cardinal phase in the work of the Australian
sanitary sections, and their rôle in the army system. That development is examined elsewhere,[35] and it suffices here to record
that during the Somme Winter the sections were stationed in
areas: No. 2 at Vignacourt for the reserve area, No. 1 at Ribemont for the rest area, No. 5 at Montauban for left and right
divisional forward areas, and No. 4 for the intermediate zone.

The Sanitary Sections

---

[34] *Chapters xvii, xviii, and xix, and Vol. III.*
[35] *In Chapter xix (pp. 594-600).*

It is necessary, however, at this point to refer to certain matters of direct medical concern in the control of wastage, and also to give a brief summary of the most important morbid states which were influenced by the action that has been described.

The conditions on the Somme made inevitable an immense extension of the system of rest stations, in the endeavour to escape the effects of the high sick rate. With Corps control tented stations grew up rivalling a town in extent and population. In these the facilities for comfort and treatment were perforce meagre; these immense stations were at best a drab and dispiriting solution to the problem of minor maladies and debility. Without a time limit for the retention of cases, with no purpose other than to prevent wastage, and with few provisions for recreation, discipline was defective. The I Anzac Corps rest station at Buire was quite unsuited for winter conditions, undrained, bare, and with inadequate facilities for comfort. Over 1,200 men at one time were here treated in small marquees without floorboards. The Deputy-Director, Colonel Manifold, was indefatigable in his efforts to mitigate the conditions, and in this he was greatly helped by the Australian Red Cross Society. At the end of November the D.M.S., A.I.F., Surgeon-General Howse, inspected these medical units, his visit having special connection with his own increasing responsibility in relation to the maintenance of strength of the A.I.F. At his instance a new site was found at Bellevue Farm, where, under an enthusiastic officer (Lieut.-Colonel A. H. Moseley, 6th Field Ambulance) a not inadequate system of rest and relief was achieved. But the "Corps rest station" died with the Somme campaign, reverting afterwards to Divisional control. It had proved at least a convenient means for the camouflage (as "I.C.T."[36] or "sore feet") of much trench foot.

The weekly sick rates per cent. of strength together with the

---

[36] Inflammation of connective tissue. Battalions sometimes copied their superiors in this. The effect of the practice is exposed in the following passage from *Backs to the Wall* (p. 47), by Captain G. D. Mitchell. "The battalion hospital . . . , an ordinary hut, was filled with trench feet cases whose feet were swollen to two or three times normal size. . . . Two orderlies laboured manfully but could not catch up with the arrears of filth and neglect. . . . A battalion was in disgrace in having a large number of men evacuated sick, so these unfortunates were kept in this makeshift hospital . . . instead of being sent to England. How the devil the 'heads' expected to man the Somme without a big sick list beats me, but I suppose the pain of those poor blighters made their honour white."

actual numbers evacuated from casualty clearing stations to the base i.e. "Army Wastage" were as follows:—[37]

Week ended	1st Division			2nd Division			4th Division			5th Division		
	Sick	Per cent.	Wounded	Sick	Per cent.	Wounded	Sick	Per cent.	Wounded	Sick	Per cent.	Wounded
5/11/16	395	2·17	98	126	·73	13	28	·20	14	560	3·55	230
12/11/16	632	2·48	298	766	3·96	641	239	1·99	8	250	2·20	39
19/11/16	326	2·46	92	441	2·46	675	183	·69	64	189	1·27	24
26/11/16	284	2·44	24	617	3·18	159	372	1·40	98	431	2·15	62
3/12/16	642	4·85	16	304	1·61	36	413	1·59	84	1,132	8·13	150
10/12/16	406	1·78	26	452	2·48	13	231	1·64	46	468	3·56	83
17/12/16	371	1·76	56	293	1·72	10	284	1·88	5	475	3·62	89
24/12/16	298	1·40	33	274	1·42	2	132	·87	8	195	1·48	41
31/12/16	419	1·65	93	456	2·85	30	223	1·49	18	312	1·95	11
7/1/17	342	1·53	67	368	2·04	36	217	1·40	9	252	1·57	14
14/1/17	263	1·45	39	338	1·86	40	277	1·38	19	221	1·11	6
21/1/17	217	1·21	2	373	2·23	13	164	·82	31	264	1·47	12
28/1/17	322	1·51	7	348	1·65	8	233	1·17	68	396	1·86	73
4/2/17	412	2·00	32	327	1·63	9	275	1·37	72	340	1·70	81
11/2/17	173	·89	45	192	1·04	51	176	·78	379	269	1·21	89
18/2/17	160	·82	48	136	·73	26	98	·44	23	125	·58	15

[37] Attention may be drawn to the fine results achieved by the 4th Division whose figures (for evacuation) were invariably below "Army" average. Both the Assistant-Director of the formation (Colonel G. W. Barber) and his Deputy achieved high distinction in the Australian Army Medical Service.

The figures for sickness given in this table are taken from the "weekly returns of sickness" issued by the D.M.S., Fourth Army. There being no means of verification, some obvious inaccuracies in the percentages cannot be corrected.

The subject of disease prevention is dealt with in special chapters of this volume,[38] and statistically in the final volume. A list of the morbid states most prevalent and important at this time, however, will help to link up this objective narrative with those subjective studies.

"Disease"

Due to Physical Factors. By far the most important single cause of wastage was *Trench Foot*;[39] and the measures taken to minimise its incidence were a prominent element in the problems of administration and command during this period. It came indeed to constitute an index to the morale of a battalion and therein of the efficiency of its command. It was at this time that the so-called French method of treatment and prevention came into vogue. *Traumatic abrasions* (chiefly sore feet) merged with trench foot as a convenient euphemism; *Rheumatism; Bronchial catarrh; Gastritis; Diarrhoea; Haemorrhoids; Physical and Psychic Exhaustion.*

Local and Non-specific Infections. Septic Traumatic Abrasion ("S.T.A.") and *Inflammation of Connective Tissue* ("I.C.T.")—congeners of trench foot and traumatic abrasion; *Bronchitis; Coryza; "Influenza"*—forerunners of Upper Respiratory Tract Infection ("U.R.T.I.") and *"pulmonary fibrosis"*; *Colitis* and *Enteritis.*

Skin Infestations. Scabies—among the most important diseases in the armies on the Western Front; *Pediculosis*—not yet incriminated as the cause of trench fever and, in the absence of typhus, a "minor horror" only.

General Infections. Venereal Disease; Dysentery—outbreaks in Fourth and Fifth Armies in January, Lieut.-Colonel C. J. Martin, A.A.M.C. begins his historic work on the disease, at Rouen; *P.U.O.—* now to be recognised as chiefly "trench fever"; *Pneumonia*—not extraordinarily prevalent; *Mumps*—accompanied the 3rd Australian Division to France in December and became epidemic in the II Anzac Corps.

Chronic and Pre-existing Disorders. "*Debility*"; *Varicose veins; Varicocele; Hernia; Asthma;* and so forth were very prevalent—for obvious reasons.

"Trench Foot"

The pathology of this peculiarly interesting form of physical injury will be examined in *Volume III,* but it is convenient here, at the scene of its apotheosis, to give a note on its aetiology and prophylaxis.

The characteristic clinical syndrome of swelling (oedema), pain, and functional disablement in the part affected, most commonly the feet, which might pass on to actual gangrene, was clinically indistinguishable from "frost-bite," and, like this condition, was the result of circulatory stasis and a local neuritis. For reasons that need not be discussed here the combination of cold and "wet" was a much more potent exciting

---
[38] *Chapters xvii, xviii and xix.*
[39] The following figures show the number of cases of "trench foot" admitted to medical units from the A.I.F. during the period October, 1916-May, 1917: 1st Division, 1,020; 2nd Division, 1,190; 3rd Division 46; 4th Division, 490; 5th Division, 1,673. The figures are from British Official "returns."

cause than was cold *per se*, and the chief objective in the campaign of prophylaxis was to keep the troops dry.

Only less potent as causal factors were conditions in the environment which tended to bring about stagnation in the capillary circulation—lack of muscular movement, as through standing or sitting in the semi-frozen slush of the trenches, pressure from knee breeches and tight puttees, and lowered vitality through malnutrition and excessive toils.

A third factor put forward at this time by French observers, which formed the basis for the so called "French" method of treatment, attributed the condition to a fungoid infection of the sodden epidermis, and the subsequent invasion of the devitalised dermis by the mycelium. The condition was, in fact, looked on as a "disease," and was treated as such. Though these observations were not confirmed, septic infection, even tetanus, were not infrequent complications. Anti-tetanic Serum ("A.T.S.") was official.

Prophylaxis. The means and methods, individual and collective, employed to combat these several factors can be summed up as—drainage and duckboards, facilities for foot-care in the line, forward-placed drying rooms and wash-houses, gum boots, dubbing, and spare socks; movement and massage, whale oil, sandbags instead of puttees, hot food containers, and solidified alcohol in "Tommy cookers"; the systematic use of soap and warm water, and of "French powder" (borated talc and camphor); morale.

The value or otherwise of "whale oil" was hotly debated. The troops for the most part greatly disliked it. But in a battalion (the 1st) whose record of trench foot was so good that a special report was desired by Corps Headquarters on the methods adopted, the regimental medical officer (Captain N. E. B. Kirkwood) attributed his success to its use, in conjunction with the general measures outlined above. "It did good" (he reported) "in the following ways: (1) It ensured the removal of boots and socks at frequent intervals. (2) It ensured a careful supervision of the men's feet by officers and N.C.O's as 'whale-oiling' was a parade. (3) The friction and rubbing, alone, helped the circulation. (4) The coating of animal oil reduced the loss of heat from the feet and so encouraged a good blood supply. (5) The oil helped to prevent the skin from becoming sodden. (6) It very considerably lessened the discomfort of wet socks and boots. . . . As far as possible 'islands' were formed—i.e. dry spots where men could dry their feet and change their socks." "Whale oil" in fact was only the pivot of a campaign. The real secret is revealed in the statement: "The C.O. and all officers entered enthusiastically into the spirit of the game."

The prophylaxis of "trench foot" can in fact be summed up in two words, morale and organisation.

The end of December saw a marked change in the disease picture of this extraordinary episode in the history of the force; from then onwards the health experience became normal, and no examination of it in detail is therefore required in the narrative chapters.

For the I Anzac Corps (at least) it may be said that in the matter of health the war on the Western Front had two periods, respectively before and after the Somme Winter of 1916-17. Even more than those of Gallipoli, this experience clothed with life the dry bones of the *Field Service Regulations* which made the promotion of health "the duty of every officer and man." The term hygiene took a wider significance. Wastage from disease was not, as largely heretofore, the act of God and default of the medical service, but was known to be as much a matter of cause and effect as were the results of a raid. No longer was sanitary discipline merely the affair of the regimental medical officer, and sanitation that of his "sanitary detachment." Ability to keep down his sick rate became an element in the selection of an officer for appointment to, or retention of, battalion command.

The training and reorganisation prescribed by Haig were adequately fulfilled in the I Anzac Corps. As usual the medical service had little time for such diversions. But in the medical

January and February

stations by February work was running smoothly. On January 24th an extension of the Corps front put a third Division in the line with advanced dressing station at Bazentin-le-Petit, clearing to Bécordel. By the 31st all four Divisions were in the line, the 2nd that day replacing on the left the 15th (Scottish) Division, the 5th Field Ambulance taking over an A.D.S. at Martinpuich. The four Divisions now occupied a front of 6,000 yards from Le Sars to Gueudecourt.

By this time routes of clearance and medical stations had greatly improved. Light railways brought casualties almost from the front line—

"many will still remember the wild rides on the return trips down the inclines, and the language when the trucks jumped the rails and pitched all and sundry in the snow."[40]

Large medical dugouts had been made at Needle Dump (right brigade headquarters) and Bernafay. Advanced dressing stations became main dressing stations, that at Bécordel was taken over by the 4th Division as a rest station. Evacuation was

---

[40] From a narrative by L/Cpl. O. R. Burton, 1st Field Amb.

now by broad-gauge train from Bernafay and Bazentin, direct to the 45th and 1/1st Midland Casualty Clearing Stations at Edgehill.

With approaching spring spirits rose, and the mind of the staff turned inevitably to thoughts of battle. To have travelled so far hopefully did not content; Bapaume beckoned. But on February 24th the German Army began the initial stage of a strategic movement which was to bring to naught any tactical gains in position achieved by the fighting of 1916, and was largely to determine the course of the fighting throughout the rest of the war.

An exact comparison of the Allied and German losses at the Somme is not possible owing to the different systems on which the casualty lists were compiled. In the *British Official History*[41] it is noted, "We may fairly assume that the real total (German casualties during the Somme operations) is something under 600,000, just as the Allied total is something just over it."[42]

Cost of the Somme

The total figures in battle casualties for the Australian Divisions engaged on the Somme are as follows:—

TABLE I.—A.I.F. casualties on the Somme and at Fromelles, 1st July to November 30th.

	Killed in action	Died of wounds	Died of Gas	Wounded in action	Gassed	Prisoners of war	Total
1st Div.	2,205	618	4	7,027	75	80	10,009
2nd „	2,807	640	5	7,949	79	193	11,673
4th „	1,950	481	5	5,778	20	179	8,413
5th „ ..	2,171	459	1	4,955	22	499	8,107
Corps troops	53	11	—	123	19	—	206
Totals	9,186	2,209	15	25,832	215	951	38,408

[41] See *The British Official History, Military Operations, France and Belgium, 1916*, Vol. I, p. 497. The matter is dealt with exhaustively in the *Australian Official History*, Vol. III, pp. 942-6 and Vol. IV, p. 943.

[42] The *British Official Medical History, General*, Vol. III, p. 50, states that "between the 1st July and 30th November, 1916, 316,073 wounded were admitted to the field ambulances of the Fourth, Fifth (Reserve), and Third Armies." On a ratio of approximately 1 killed to 3·3 wounded (*British Official Medical History, Statistics*, p. 149, also Table below) this would give a total battle casualty list of some 412,000. Over the whole British front during this period battle casualties numbered 498,054. The *British Official History* states that the battle was, after the first fortnight, "a ding-dong struggle of attrition, with no tactical objective"; and the claim of the Allies to victory is based on the moral superiority gained, which is candidly acknowledged by authoritative German military writers. See *British Official History, Military Operations, France and Belgium*, Vol. I, pp. 494-5.

The total wastage in battle and non-battle casualties in the British Expeditionary Force and the A.I.F. in France in 1916 is shown in the following table.

TABLE II.—Total Numbers and Classification of Casualties during 1916 (B.E.F. and A.I.F. compared).[43]

	Numbers		Percentages of Respective Total Cas.	
	B.E.F. (including A.I.F.)	A.I.F.	B.E.F.	A.I.F.
(a) Killed	107,411	9,948	8·29	11·31
(b) Died of wounds	36,879	2,593	2·85	2·95
(c) Missing and prisoners	43,675	992	3·37	1·13
(d) Wounded less (b)	463,697	28,734	35·79	32·68
A. Total battle casualties	651,662	42,267	50·30	48·07
(e) Died of disease or injury	5,841	299	0·45	0·34
(f) Sick or injured less (e)	638,080	45,358	49·25	51·59
B. Total non-battle casualties	643,921	45,657	49·70	51·93
Total A and B	1,295,583	87,924	100·00	100·00

Numbers alone do not fully disclose the cost of this year to the British nation or to Australia. It has been well stated by one who saw clearly and could share his vision with others.[44]

"Never before in our history had such an army been gathered, and never again would such an army be seen. . . . True, we launched greater armies, and won greater victories in the two years that followed; but—the very flower of a race can bloom but once in a generation. The flower of our generation bloomed and perished during the four months of the First Battle of the Somme. We shall not look upon their like again."

---

[43] In this table the "B.E.F." figures are taken from the *Brit. Off. Med. History—Casualties and Medical Statistics, p. 149.* They differ from those in the *Statistics of the Military Effort of the British Empire, pp. 256-260*, but not to an extent which would greatly alter the percentages shown.

[44] "Ian Hay" (Major J. H. Beith), in *The Willing Horse, pp. 154-5.*

CHAPTER VI

THE GERMAN RETIREMENT, 1917

The remaining part of this Section relates to the two great campaigns in which Great Britain carried the main burden of war on the Western Front through the year 1917. The subject of the present chapter is the work of the medical service with the I Anzac Corps in the British spring offensive—that is, during the Battle of Arras and in the attacks on the Hindenburg Line.

The failure of the Allies at Gallipoli was felt this year in the locking up of half a million effectives facing Turkey and Bulgaria, in Palestine and Macedonia,[1] and in the isolation of Russia. This power though even now building her Phoenix pyre of revolution, still had cannon-fodder in plenty and generals, not unable, to lead them though, unfortunately, to a martyrdom that was neither inspired nor inspiring. The armies of Roumania and Serbia like that of Belgium had survived defeat (in some part at least) and were still a force behind the Russian and the Balkan fronts respectively. The fact that in this way some hundred German divisions were still held, though precariously, in the East, made possible a renewal in 1917 of the Allied offensive in the West. Italy, also, though she would not move until she felt safe in doing so, itched to prove by right of conquest her claim to possess Trieste; and hoped incidentally to aid the general Allied cause.

The general situation 1917

From the fighting on this front in 1916 the Allies claimed a

---

[1] General Ludendorff (*My War Memories 1914-1918, p. 209*) contends that the Allied operations in the Middle East were solely for aggrandizement and hampered them in their conduct of the war. His estimate of the Gallipoli Campaign on the other hand is wholly opposed to that of the extreme "Western" school of strategy whose protagonists, it seems clear, failed to observe that the year 1915 could not be decisive but must be devoted by each side to the achievement of strategic advantage in preparation for the decisive struggle by attrition on the Western Front. *See Vol. I, pp. 342-4.*

total credit balance in respect of man-power and of morale. France had survived Verdun, Britain and France had pushed back their enemy on the Somme. The German leaders, losing hope of victory on land, were led to attempt a complete sea blockade of Great Britain by submarines, to take effect from February 1st, rapid and complete success being guaranteed by Admiral von Tirpitz. Meanwhile her field armies would push with vigour on the East while maintaining in the West a strictly defensive battle, to further which an important strategic move was designed and special tactical methods devised.[2]

The Western Front in 1917

Britain and France were indeed still in a position to strike a blow of immense strength: only now was Britain reaching zenith in her ability to supply "effectives" and munitions. Such a blow, it had been proposed,[3] should be delivered in the spring of 1917 by all the Allied powers, and it was expected to have decisive results.

Thus 1917 was confidently designed by both sides to be the year of victory—to be achieved by the Entente powers on land, by the Central powers on the sea. Each belligerent held a second string to his bow, the Allies in the success of the British naval blockade of Germany, Germany in the release, by the expected collapse of Russia, of her Eastern force for a Western offensive in 1918.

The conference of the Allied military leaders at Chantilly had proposed a vigorous resumption of the Somme offensive in the spring and new offensives by Russia and Italy in May. The first would continue the process of "wearing down" the enemy's line of resistance by means of repeated assaults covered by bombardment of unprecedented ferocity, with a view to a strategic breakthrough when opportunity should arise. General Haig obtained agreement also to his suggestion that afterwards an offensive might be undertaken to drive the Germans from the vital position of their right flank in Flanders. The preparations for the

Military plans for 1917

---

[2] Essentially, defence by means of counter-attack: the troops disposed in depth, the front line thinly manned, and sheltered from the terrific bombardments (which were the Allied reply to barbed-wire and machine-guns) in deep dugouts or concrete strongholds. The nature of the tactical methods employed for offence and defence were of great importance in the work of the regimental stretcher-bearers.

[3] At a conference, in which Britain, France, Italy, and Russia were represented, held in November at Chantilly.

concerted spring advance by the British and French on the fronts from Arras to the Oise were immediately begun.

In December, 1916, however, these plans sustained a dramatic amendment. Both the British and French nations—especially the latter, worn by its long sustainment of the chief burden—were eager for methods that should involve "no more Sommes." Unhappily for the Allied cause there appeared at the height of this reaction a will-o-the-wisp of quite exceptional brightness and allure in the form of a supposed shortcut to victory. On the strength of a striking success in the counter-offensives at Verdun, achieved by adopting an unlimited objective and without initial "wearing down," the commander of the French Second Army, General Nivelle, had inspired French politicians with the belief that like methods applied on a grand scale might achieve the desired "knock-out blow." On December 13th he superseded General Joffre in command on the Western Front, and in February, through the action of Mr Lloyd George (who had replaced Mr Asquith as head of the British Coalition Government) he was given what was in effect the supreme command of both British and French forces in France and a free hand to carry through a battle plan that was to end the war. For a combined French and British advance on the Somme, to be made in steps, each covered by sustained bombardments, there was substituted a French whirlwind push, to attain victory by the new methods in the Champagne. To this a British offensive on the Ancre and Scarpe would give support.

The French attack was timed for April 1st, the British for the end of March. The French—and to less extent the British—armies were reorganised on more strongly "offensive" lines: a new drill and training were put in hand. Six new British divisions were sent to France, and the British front was extended 20 miles southwards to a point opposite the town of Roye. The formation of a sixth Australian Division was again mooted—this time by the Army Council—and authorised, and on February 15th the nucleus of its 16th Infantry Brigade and the "16th Australian Field Ambulance" were formed from the contents of the Command Depots.[4]

The new plan for the British spring offensive involved an

---

[4] See pp. 475-6.

assault by the First, Third, and Fifth Armies. The First and
Third Armies would attack the northern side of
the German bastion, from the key point, Vimy
Ridge, southwards to the apex of the German
salient created by the Allied advance on the Somme. The Fifth
Army would attack the southern side of this salient from
the old battlefield on the Ancre, its right flank hinging on the
Fourth Army's left
at Le Transloy.
During January
and February ex-
tensive local raids
were undertaken to
"maintain pressure"
and as a prelude to
the general offen-
sive. In these the
I Anzac Corps took
its part. From
where it stood the
Corps would also
be responsible for
the right wing of
the great attack,
being transferred
for that purpose to the Fifth Army, which then comprised the
II, V, XIII and I Anzac Corps.

The British Offensive

Whatever hope of success may have lain in these ambitious
plans was gravely prejudiced by a clever move made by the
German High Command to abandon the unfavourable positions into which its troops had
been forced on the Somme, and also—by resort
to a shorter and more secure front—to release formations and
save man-power, and thus promote an offensive defence. During the winter the Germans had created, behind the Somme front
and farther north, one of the most remarkable defensive lines
that warfare has seen. Its southern element, the "Hindenburg"
or "Siegfried" Line, stretched with accessory switches across the
chord of the great Vimy-Soissons salient. In the waterlogged
country of Flanders a complete line of shell-proof ferro-concrete

The Hindenburg Line

blockhouses (nicknamed by the British infantry "pill-boxes") was built along the whole front.[5]

Against this fortress system or its northern continuation—wide trenches, broad belts of barbed wire, machine-gun strongposts, and deep dugouts—the Australian Imperial Force was to be thrown several times during the remainder of the war. In its first great fight in 1917 it thrust deeply into them; in its last battle in the war it broke through one of the strongest sectors. The present chapter relates to the first of these impacts, preceded, as it was, by the retirement of the First German Army to its new front followed closely by the British Fifth Army.

Though the existence of this new German line far in rear of the old was known to the British General Staff in January it was not taken seriously into account. Early in February however the intention of the enemy to abandon his present front was suspected; on February 23-24 a retirement of the Fifth Army front was disclosed by patrols. The involvements of the move soon became clear[6]; pursuit across the morass of the Ancre battlefield must be slow, and, with nothing to strike at, the British full dress offensive could not now include a main stroke by the Fifth Army. The French offensive had been postponed until April 17th. The date for the British was now fixed for the 7th, with the bastion of Vimy Ridge in front of Arras as the chief objective; the assault would be made by the First Army (Horne) and Third (Allenby). The ultimate rôle of the Fifth Army would depend on the rate of its advance following up the enemy; its immediate task was that of vigorous pursuit, its advanced troops harassing the enemy while the main force dragged itself clear, through and across the mud field. In this task for the next four weeks it was very strenuously occupied.

The German plan of retirement—the code name for which was appropriately "Alberich"[7]—was designed to cover five weeks, mainly for
"**Alberich**" preparation and destruction, the actual withdrawal of the infantry occurring in the last few days. The first day of preparation was February 9; but the pressure of British winter activity forced the Germans to a previously unintended preliminary withdrawal to the first, and later to the second reserve lines (R.I and R.II). These were respectively in front of and behind Grévillers, a distance of about three miles. The general retirement over the whole salient was arranged for March 16th. In this second phase the whole force would retire along prepared routes to the Hindenburg Line. As it turned out the line was not ready, and the

---

[5] "Hindenburg Line" was the Allies' name for the whole system. The Germans called the main line, from the neighbourhood of Soissons to that of Arras, the "Siegfried Line." To bar any attempt to advance from Arras they built northwards, from between Quéant and Bullecourt, a switch known to the British as the Drocourt-Quéant switch and to the Germans as the "Wotan Line."

[6] The comment of the I Anzac Corps Chief of Staff (General C. B. B. White) was, "I am afraid it is a very clever thing the Germans have done." *Australian Official History, Vol. IV, p. 69.*

[7] The malignant dwarf in Wagner's opera *Die Rheingold.*

villages in front of it were therefore still to be held as outposts until it was quite complete. A third phase was thus added to the actual withdrawal.

Fifth Army's pursuit

The most important feature of the pursuit was the fact that, till roads should be repaired and railways pushed forward, the advanced British force had now to leave farther and farther behind it the artillery, the railheads, supply depots, workshops, reserve and rest areas, billets, medical bases—all the vast paraphernalia of static trench warfare. The enemy on the other hand was moving into an area prepared to give him the greatest assistance and his pursuer the greatest hindrance. The British advance had to conform closely to the German plan of retirement. Save for the fact that the raids in February induced the German army group commander to order the forestallment of the time-table, already mentioned, the retiring formations were not seriously incommoded by British or French action.[8] The first stage of the pursuit was carried out by the Divisions in the British line, the boundary between I Anzac Corps and its northern neighbour being, at first, the Albert-Bapaume road. The progress of the main force was in a great measure determined by the condition of this highway.

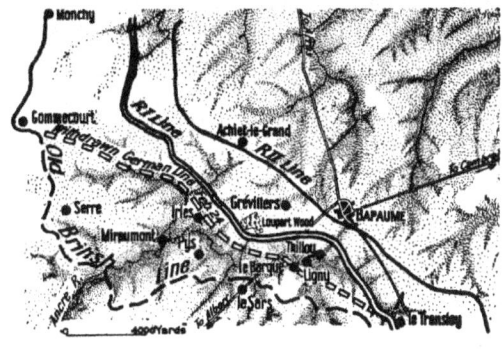

First Phase: Feb. 25-Mar. 17, I Anzac Corps

On February 23rd the 4th Division had sustained 37 casualties in an attack on "Stormy Trench." These were evacuated along the well established routes. On the 24th this formation was taken out of the line[9] and the Anzac front was held by the 1st, 2nd, and 5th Divisions, in that order from the right. Medical arrangements were adjusted between the assistant-directors concerned. On the same date the British pursuit began. The battalions in line moved forward as a whole, feeling their way across the old battlefield by their own scouting and raiding parties, with constant outpost bicker-

---

[8] The analogy between this retirement of the German force and the Evacuation of Gallipoli is interesting both in the methods employed and in the ease and safety with which it was accomplished. The German losses entailed by this apparently formidable operation were comparatively insignificant. *See Vol. I, Chapter xx.*

[9] For rest, and training in the new infantry tactics and drill, and to reorganise for offensive. Of medical personnel, only the Bn. stretcher-bearers were concerned in this special training; their disposal with the companies became general, and their distinction from the other combatant troops was made less marked.

ings and occasional serious engagements. The course of the fighting, and the problems of the medical service were largely determined by the fact that the right flank of the I Anzac Corps (5th Division) and the whole Fourth Army were held stationary by the enemy, the German retirement (and British advance) swinging on Le Transloy. The first two weeks of February were frosty and clear; thereafter rain or snow often fell, the spring thaw began, and fogs sometimes lay heavy, day and night.

On February 24th the 1st Division occupied with little opposition "The Maze," "Chord line," and "Gird" trenches—the scene of the bitter struggles of November. On February 27th, by active fighting involving over a hundred casualties, the Germans were forced by the 1st Division from the villages of Le Barque, Thilloy and Ligny-Thilloy. By the 28th the corps had advanced within a mile and a half of Bapaume. On March 2nd the first German reserve line at Loupart Wood was uncovered by the capture by the 2nd Division of "Malt Trench." On the 10th this Division occupied Grévillers, the enemy having evacuated his first reserve line and, on the whole Fifth Army front, retired to his second reserve line running through and around Bapaume. A projected advance by the whole of the Fifth Army was forestalled by his general retirement to the Hindenburg Line on March 16th and 17th.

"A.A.M.C. Order No. 51" of the Deputy Director for February 4th had directed that:—

the four main dressing stations of the divisions now in the line are the four advanced positions occupied by their field ambulances in the forward area.

The position of these, when the advance began, and of the other collecting, clearing, and evacuating stations, and the routes of clearance, are shown in map at *page 93*. The

Medical situation February 24th
vast "Corps Rest Station" at Bellevue Farm had been replaced by Divisional rest stations.[10] The Corps Mumps Station, however, at Bécourt Château, and the Corps Scabies Station at Buire, retained their titles as "Corps" establishments and they also were on a considerable scale. Throughout the advance of the I Anzac Corps at the Hindenburg Line the field ambulances mostly worked with their sections in tandem, each unit clearing through its own advanced posts and stations to its own main dressing station by its own routes.

The collecting and clearing of the casualties sustained in the small initial clashes with rearguards was a routine matter, but

---

[10] 1st Division had a rest station at Millencourt, 2nd and 4th at Bécordel, and 5th at Bellevue Farm.

with the sharp fights that resulted when the battalion lines advanced across the Ancre valley it became a most difficult problem. At the end of February the great frost broke; and with the mud the work of the bearers came closely to resemble that described of November and December of 1916.[11] Furthermore the repair of roads and extension of the narrow and broad-gauge railways could not keep pace with the advance of the battalion fronts. As these drove deeper and deeper into the morass of the old German trench area, not only the road- and rail-heads available for the mechanical transport of casualties but the regimental aid-posts also fell far behind, so that "bearer carries" lengthened inordinately. The first result of this initial extension of the lines of clearance was that regimental bearers could not collect to the aid-posts and ambulance bearers were obliged to clear the field in front of these.[12]

Medical operations—First Phase

The direction of the flow of casualties, and hence the position of new relay and treatment stations, was determined by the swing forward of the left front of I Anzac across the line of the Bapaume road, while the right remained relatively immobile. In front of Flers the conditions were such as to prevent any rapid opening up of new lines of communication. All routes of advance by road and rail converged on the main road from Albert to Bapaume, creating a bottle-neck through which must flow the whole impedimenta of the army.

For a time the urgent and relentless drive to advance paralysed all efforts at improvement in the medical situation. Where and when available the light railways[13] were an immense

---

[11] The resemblance is made the closer through the coincidence of the most potent causal factor—the forcing through of enormous weights of heavy artillery and shells required for the type of warfare then in vogue.

[12] The clearance of casualties in the central sector (1st Division) was considered by the bearers of the 3rd Field Ambulance (Bazentin-le-Petit) to have been one of their worst experiences in the war. "My worst time" (says one) "was early in 1917 in front of Warlencourt where we often had calls well beyond the aid-posts. There were no duckboard tracks and with six bearers to a squad, one to each handle and two in between, it often took three hours from one relay-post to another. With a heavy man in the stretcher the bearers often bogged; one, I recall, bogged almost to the waist, could not be released till night, owing to sniping. The physical strain was shocking; the mental anguish of the patient hardly greater than that of the bearers." (Private O. R. Dunstan, 3rd Fld. Amb. who served as O. R. Kollosche.)

[13] The British light railways gauge 60 cm. was some two inches narrower than the German and the rolling stock much less substantial—far too light indeed for the service required of it at this time.

relief to the bearers; for the patients, however, even for lightly wounded and sick, this form of transport was at this time distressing. The small open trucks were hand-pushed, the track bumpy, and the service very irregular, being largely monopolised for ammunition.[14]

Broad-Gauge Railways and I Anzac Corps Light Railways, Jan. 1917.

It was not till the general advance that motor ambulance waggons were of service much beyond the original lines.

On March 2nd there was made the formal and carefully prepared assault by the 7th Brigade (2nd Division) north of the Bapaume road against "Malt Trench"—a strongly defended outlier of the enemy's first reserve (Loupart Wood) line. The casualties in this tough little fight were relatively high, totalling 238; the wounds were caused chiefly by bullets at close range, and were therefore very severe, with a large proportion of killed. For this action the regimental medical officers (26th, 27th and 28th Battalions) formed aid-posts close behind the battalion fronts. In the 26th Battalion

At Malt Trench

"the regimental aid-post" (says the R.M.O., Capt. F. L. Bignell) "was formed in a sunken road 200 yards behind the front line and consisted of a shelter eight feet square formed of broken timber. A reserve

---

[14] In his diary of March 1 the D.D.M.S. records: "Found Colonel Sutton (A.D.M.S. 2nd Division) waiting to see me about evacuation from Martinpuich. The trucks on the Decauville are a great strain on the men, trucks often not available and no timing of trains. The C.O. Corps Light Railways (Colonel A. C. Fewtrell) said trucks were very scarce and timing difficult, as ammunition went up at all sorts of times."

17. TROLLEY WITH WOUNDED BEING PUSHED BY BEARERS ALONG LIGHT RAILWAY NEAR EAUCOURT-L'ABBAYÉ, 27TH FEBRUARY, 1917, WHEN THE GERMANS BEGAN TO FALL BACK

Aust. War Memorial Official Photo. No. E250.

18. MAIN DRESSING STATION AT CONTALMAISON CHÂTEAU, SOMME BATTLEFIELD, MARCH, 1917

Aust. War Memorial Official Photo. No. E1833.   *To face p. 112.*

19. SCENE OF A TYPICAL FIGHT DURING THE "ALBERICH" RETREAT
Cross-roads south-west of Beaumetz, site of a German counter-attack. The rifles taken from prisoners can be seen above the "pozzies" in the sunken road-bank.
Aust. War Memorial Official Photo. No. E529.

20. OPEN COUNTRY NORTH-WEST OF DOIGNIES (TAKEN BY THE 5TH DIVISION ON 2ND APRIL, 1917)
Aust. War Memorial Official Photo. No. E1367. *To face p.* 113.

R.A.P. was in 'Little Wood' about 500 yards in rear of this. During the day 117 cases passed through; the stretcher-bearers carried the cases to the first relay station at the side of the Bapaume road, 1,000 yards."

The casualties were cleared by the 5th Field Ambulance, by bearer relay and ambulance waggon, stretcher cases being sent to the advanced dressing station, still at Contalmaison. Walking wounded went by light railway to Bazentin.

Following this operation vigorous efforts were made to improve the medical situation. Fortunately the battle casualties were few, averaging, after March 2nd, only 42 daily for the whole corps; a minor recurrence of trench foot occurred in the 1st Division, but in general the "sick" evacuation was small. As a result of combined Corps and Divisional action (by the D.D.M.S. and A.D's.M.S.) the medical stations were moved up, and the claim that battle casualties should have consideration in the struggle for transport was accepted by General Staff of I Anzac.

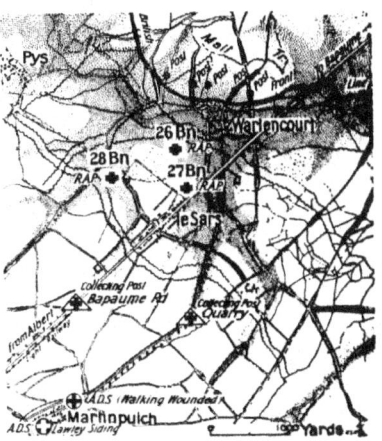

Medical Arrangements, 7th Brigade, in Malt Trench Attack, 2 March 1917.

Early in March the C.R.E. I Anzac began to extend the broad-gauge line[15] of the corps from Contalmaison to Pozières, with Bapaume (still in German hands) as the next objective.

By the second week in March G.H.Q. became convinced that the Fifth Army could not reach the Hindenburg Line in time

---

[15] The II Corps also at this time used this railway, and the competition for medical sites at railhead and for use of rolling stock was acute. Ultimately the I Anzac Corps scheme was thrown out and the civilian French railway along the valley of the Ancre was used to provide the rail connections for the new area.

to participate effectively in the British offensive on April 9th. Steps were therefore immediately taken to reduce its strength, which was greater than was justified by its present rôle of merely following the enemy. Most of its heavy artillery was transferred to the First Army; it was decided that on March 16th the II Corps should be withdrawn for a rest, and the XIII Corps also was transferred on March 18th to the First Army, leaving the Fifth Army Commander with only the V British and I Anzac Corps. Even of these a portion could be relieved as the line shortened; on March 7th the 1st Australian Division went into reserve for rest and training, the pursuit being carried on for I Anzac by the 5th and 2nd Divisions alone.

At this stage the D.D.M.S. directed[16] that

"The A.D.M.S. 2nd Australian Division will establish an advanced dressing station in the neighbourhood of Le Sars or at whatever place is best suited, and will also establish a dressing station at Pozières on a site suitable for the reception and evacuation of wounded by road and by railway."

Nissen huts and equipment were brought up to Pozières and a "main" dressing station was formed there by the A.D.M.S. 2nd Division and was opened on March 17th by the 5th Field Ambulance. On March 12th the A.D.M.S. 5th Division formed a new "advanced" dressing station near the old front line, at Factory Corner.

The second phase—the main advance to the Hindenburg Line—began when early on March 17th it was discovered that the Germans were withdrawing from their position at Bapaume.

Second Phase: Advance to the Hindenburg Line This indeed was the main withdrawal and occurred on the date long since planned, extending along a very wide front, from Arras in the north almost to Soissons, and affecting not only the Fifth but the Fourth British and Sixth French Armies. At this stage the main bodies of both sides went temporarily out of the picture, that of the Germans withdrawing behind the Hindenburg Line, that of the British taking up a strong defensive position immediately beyond Bapaume and the old Somme battlefield. Meanwhile the Allies' advanced guards followed the German rearguards across a wide, new No-Man's Land of

---

[16] In D.D.M.S. "Medical Instruction No. 1" of March 4th. By desire of General White (Chief of the General Staff I Anzac Corps), from March 4 onwards, Colonel Manifold conveyed his wishes to the Assistant-Directors by "Instructions," not as heretofore by "Orders." The decisions of the Assistant-Directors were conveyed to units as "Orders." When the I Anzac Corps entered the Somme Battle in 1916, the Deputy Director obtained from Surgeon-General W. G. Macpherson, the D.D.G.M.S. at G.H.Q., suggestions regarding the issue of instructions. (*See Appendix No. 3 of this volume and Appendix No. 4 of Vol. 1.*)

from seven to twenty miles, until about March 26th they brought up against strong resistance from a line of villages within artillery range of the Hindenburg Line, some of which could not be taken until, by April 2nd, the artillery of the main force came up.[17]

The Advanced Guards
The advanced guards of I Anzac, which moved out from either side of Bapaume on March 18th, consisted of two strong brigade-columns of the 5th and 2nd Divisions complete with field artillery, light horse, supply units, and medical detachments. The 15th Brigade (General Elliott) composed the right, the 6th (General Gellibrand) the left. These columns advanced, with a vigour and *élan* that gained the commendation of the army commander, on a front of seven miles, the inter-column boundary line being slightly to the left of the Bapaume-Cambrai road.

In spite of the German retreat preventing the Fifth Army from playing its intended part in the coming British offensive, General Gough informed his Corps Commanders that he wished to attack the Hindenburg Line and get behind the flank of the Germans facing the Third Army. The ultimate results of this decision were momentous for the Australian force, and its immediate effect was felt in every service of maintenance—in none more than in those concerned with the evacuation and treatment of casualties.

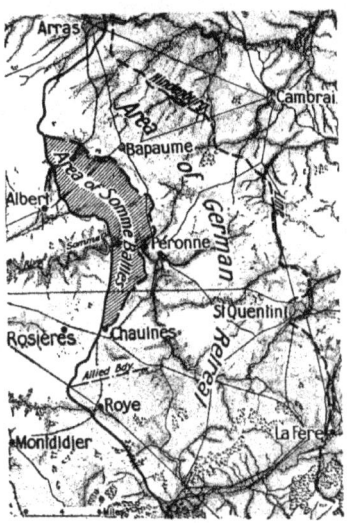

The German Retirement to the Hindenburg Line in the Spring of 1917.

This phase of the war stands out clean and exhilarating in the annals of the A.I.F. in France. The troops were freed, for the moment, from the dark shadow of "attrition." To the uplift in morale and in physical well being, that came with the

---

[17] As a tactical precaution in his retreat the enemy systematically—in some instances wantonly—blew up roads, bridges, houses, and destroyed also wells and trees along the high roads. The rubble from the houses was a godsend to the road repairers.
The emotional outbursts in the Allied press were largely propaganda. If half the indignation that is wasted on "atrocities" were directed against the supreme atrocity, scientific warfare, humanity and civilization might begin to see some daylight.

spring and with the prospect of a rest and reinforcements, the German retreat gave an impetus that sent men's spirits soaring as they had not done since the beginning of the Somme offensive, when the A.I.F. along with the British New Armies had thrilled to the hopes and the high emprise which preceded that first great effort—and passed with it.

The medical interest attaching to this brief and picturesque interval, in which the casualties of I Anzac were practically confined to the two brigade-columns,[18] derives mainly from the fact that during it the medical units concerned built up a system of treatment and transport which served the corps well in the hard fighting that followed. The withdrawal of the Germans from Bapaume had brought immediate improvement in one respect; on the 18th the light railway was extended to Warlencourt and casualties went by it to the main dressing station at Bazentin. Petrol tractors now came into use on it, and reduced the time of passage from its railhead to main dressing station by three to four hours.

Clearance— Communications

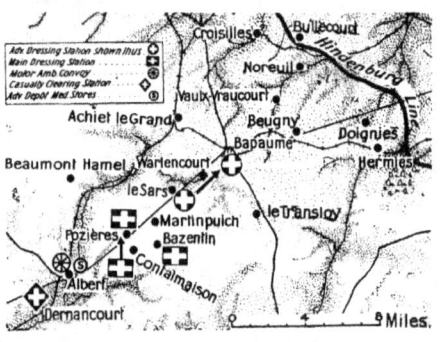

Movement of Field Ambulances, March 18.

But with the advance from Bapaume the depth of the corps area, already extended, was further increased by as much as ten miles. The administrative departments now had on their hands three sets of troops: first the advanced columns and men engaged forward in railway construction and road repair; second the main defensive line of the corps, near Bapaume; and third the divisions passed back to reserve near Fricourt, Bazentin, and Albert on or behind the old battle area, and to rest and

Move up of medical treatment stations

---

[18] *See Table on p. 128.*

training still farther back round Warloy, Millencourt, and the Ancre villages. From the front to rear the total distance was, in a direct line, some twenty miles.

When the advanced guards moved off on March 18th "advanced dressing stations" had been formed in Bapaume by each of the field ambulances responsible for clearance from the columns and from the main defensive line in front of Bapaume. The 15th Field Ambulance opened in the town on the 18th with accommodation for sixty stretcher cases and forty-five A.M.C. personnel. The diary of the 6th Field Ambulance records of March 20th—

" 'A' Section moved up to Bapaume and commenced to take in wounded. Horsed-waggons working in front two miles past Beugnâtre bringing wounded into A.D.S. Walkers sent to head of Decauville at the Butte, where Captain Fraser opened a depot with tents, stoves, etc. The Albert-Bapaume road blocked till noon, and during the night trains delayed through derailment."

But till the end of March these "advanced" stations were separated from their "main" stations by the slough of the old battlefield, bridged only by the old Roman road between Albert and Bapaume, along which must pass almost the whole traffic of the army. The main stations themselves were connected with the casualty clearing stations by roads which had in many parts broken down with the spring thaw. The journey to the C.C.S's at Edgehill "took longer than on the Somme in 1916." During the next four weeks the history of the medical service of the Corps, like that of its fighting formations, is largely one of struggle to secure access to traffic routes; a struggle for the most part not against the elements and effects of enemy action but against the imperious drive to force the heavy artillery and ammunition through in time for the great British offensive.

But with the advance of the broad and narrow gauge railways and the opening of the Albert-Bapaume road[19] that followed the advance of the forward troops on March 17th, the static elements of the army—concerned with supply and ammunition railheads, engineering workshops, medical stations, rest and training areas—began to shift forwards. The movement

---

[19] For some three weeks this thoroughfare served two Army Corps; both the outer flanks—the right of the I Anzac and the left of the II British Corps—were devoid of traffic routes.

may be compared not inaptly to that of an amoeba: preceded by the advanced guards as by a pseudopod the army oozed forward in pursuit of its prey. The treatment stations that had served the old front line moved up; new transport routes were formed: the "rest and training" area passed from "army" to "lines of communication," and was replaced by the old "reserve" area. The move proceeded with accelerating speed, involving the main dressing stations and, later, the casualty clearing stations, until ultimately the whole Fifth Army medical system lay in front of the old Somme battlefield. In terms of movement the crux of the medical problem at this time, like that of every service concerned in movement and maintenance, lay in the Bapaume bottle-neck.[20]

Leaving the main body of the force halted for a fortnight in the defensive line in front of Bapaume (R.III) we follow now the fortunes of the medical detachments with the advanced guards.

The medical detachment that accompanied the Right Brigade Column was taken from the 15th Field Ambulance. With some ten miles to traverse, it comprised "A" Section complete with light transport, and the bearers of "B" and "C" Sections. Between March 17th and 20th the column covered six miles and captured eight villages, with a loss of only 65 casualties (47 wounded). On the 21st Beaumetz was occupied. The Germans counter-attacked and retook it, but on the 23rd it was recaptured with casualties amounting to 85 (62 wounded). Further advance was held

Right Column—collecting and clearance

---

[20] The *pavé* in the Bapaume road was only some 20 feet wide; off this was mud. Till sanity was restored by Field-Marshal Haig's order on March 28, that repair of roads should precede their excessive use, an obstinate vicious circle obtained—the more the half-made roads were broken up by tractors and lorries, and the advance thus delayed, the more relentless was the drive to force them through at all costs.

The following from *The Story of the Fifth Australian Division, p. 193* pictures the situation south of the Bapaume road:

"The great problem was how to convey, across the trackless waste of shell-hole country that intervened, water, food, and ammunition to the forward troops. For at least three miles the whole area was a morass of mud in which waggon loads of brick and stone rubble sank completely out of sight in a few minutes . . . at first glance the work seemed hopeless. For a few critical days the success of the whole Division had depended entirely on the engineering and pioneering and transport services. . . ."

The dates of the opening up of the road and railway connection between the old and new areas and the new front (which determined the moves of the medical treatment stations) are epitomised as follows:

By March 18 the Albert-Bapaume road was rendered fit for horse and light motor transport, but it was not till the beginning of April that this artery was serviceable for heavy traffic. On March 28 the broad-gauge railway was opened to Achiet-le-Grand, and on April 3 to Bapaume.

up on the line of villages Hermies—Doignies—Lagnicourt,[21] now occupied as outposts of the Hindenburg Line.

The medical detachment reported to the headquarters of the column at Riencourt-les-Bapaume on March 18th. A relay post was established at Bancourt and bearers got in touch with the forward battalions. The tent sub-division and transport of "A" Section at once moved to Frémicourt and on the 19th opened there a "forward A.D.S." Every available man was put on to make a route round an immense mine crater in the road, which for a time blocked all motor traffic. On March 20th an additional "advanced dressing station" was formed at Beaulencourt, clearing by bearer relays via the Transloy-Bapaume road to the central A.D.S. in Bapaume. By the 21st the R.A.P's were at Beugny; all hands were put to work to make a route for motor cars on the shell-cratered road, and by March 22nd the aid-posts were being cleared by the Ford cars. On the 24th the "forward A.D.S." was pushed up from Frémicourt to Beugny, a good treatment post was improvised, and the battle casualties from the fighting at Beaumetz were easily dealt with. These were brought in from the R.A.P's by bearer relays and horsed ambulance, and went by Ford cars to Frémicourt, and thence by the Sunbeams and Daimlers to Bapaume, or through to the light railhead loading post formed by 6th Field Ambulance at Le Sars and The Butte.

Left Column — The first halt of the Left Column (6th Brigade) was made on the outskirts of Vraucourt, which was captured on March 18th. A night attack on Noreuil on the 19th failed, with 296 casualties. On March 20th the 6th Brigade was relieved by the 7th.

This column was accompanied by the bearers and light transport of the 5th Field Ambulance, who cleared chiefly by wheeled stretchers and horse waggon down the Noreuil-Bapaume road to the A.D.S., which lay first at Le Sars but after March 20th in Bapaume. In the attack on Noreuil the tent division moved up and formed a "forward A.D.S." in Vaulx, which was served by ambulance bearer relays, and cleared by motor ambulance waggon to the central A.D.S. in Bapaume.

---

[21] On the right of this column the advanced guards of the Fourth Army were furnished by the Cavalry Corps.

On March 26th, just before daylight, the two brigade columns combined to capture and, by hard fighting, to hold the strong outpost village of Lagnicourt. In this action the 7th Brigade sustained 240 casualties (162 wounded), and the 15th 156 (126 wounded). From this date the brigade columns ceased to function as independent units, and were absorbed in the "advanced line of defence."

Capture of Lagnicourt: March 26

Clearance. Each brigade cleared its own wounded, the 15th through Beugny, the 7th through Vaulx. Captain Bignell, the R.M.O. of the 26th Battalion (7th Brigade), wrote:—

"The R.A.P. was formed in an old German gun-pit about 1,000 yards from Lagnicourt. Early in the day it was roofed by wire-netting and branches; later a decent shelter was built by the Pioneers . . . 120 cases came through. The ambulance bearers were in two relays, one from the R.A.P. to Shelter Crater about half a mile from Vaulx. The second relay from Shelter Crater by wheelers to the A.D.S. near the Corps line [i.e. the main defence line] now situated behind Vaulx."

After the capture of Lagnicourt the 4th Division relieved the 2nd. From now onwards movement and action centred on the left sector fronting the junction, near Quéant, of the Wotan line (Drocourt-Quéant switch) with the main Siegfried Line—an area which, as zero day of the great British offensive drew near, became charged with tremendous if still vague possibilities. The medical duties there now fell on Colonel Barber. On March 27th the 13th Field Ambulance replaced the 6th in the advanced dressing station (railway yard, Bapaume) and took charge of evacuation from the front line. The main dressing station at Pozières (5th Field Ambulance) also was administered by the A.D.M.S., 4th Division.

Reliefs and Moves. March 26-April 2

On March 22nd the first broad-gauge train ran from Pozières railhead with casualties to the C.C.S. at Edgehill, and next day "A" Section 5th Field Ambulance was detailed for special duty, under the D.M.S., Fifth Army, with the "Fifth Army Advanced Operating Centre" which was established at the Pozières dressing station for the treatment of abdominal and urgent chest wounds, serving both Corps.[22] On

Evacuation to C.C.S. March 17-April 2

---

[22] The C.C.S. personnel forming this centre comprised three operating surgeons and twelve other ranks R.A.M.C. and four army nursing "sisters." The centre was housed in a Nissen hut and some large marquee tents. Fifteen A.A.M.C. bearers were attached. Most of the cases were severely shocked and the death rate was heavy.

March 28th the "Special Operating Centre" of the Fifth Army also opened at Pozières for the treatment of urgent wounds of other types.[23] For the time Pozières became the pivot for distribution of casualties to the casualty clearing and rest stations for both the Army Corps. Patients marked for the two "operating centres" came from the advanced dressing stations at Bapaume by a special service of motor ambulance convoy cars, thus allowing the divisional transport to be used for clearance in front of the advanced stations. On March 26th the A.D.M.S. 5th Division transferred his main dressing station (15th Field Ambulance) from Bernafay to Bapaume, leaving behind one section for the treatment of the slightly wounded and sick.

On April 2nd, when the advanced troops were ready to assault the villages of the outpost line, the main defensive line of the corps was advanced from near Bapaume to the old German third reserve line (Ytres-Beugny line), and the front of the advanced brigades became the "advanced line of resistance." Roads had been repaired and railheads advanced with great vigour. Concurrently, the medical treatment stations began to move into the new area. Battle casualties now came to Bapaume by the field ambulance transport and after treatment went to Pozières by motor ambulance convoy, returning lorries, and (after April 3rd) by light railway, for which a loading post was formed behind Bapaume. Evacuation by this route meant a ride of from three to five hours in open unprepared trucks exposed to rain and snow. On April 1st the advanced dressing station was moved up from Bapaume to Vaulx and was replaced by a main dressing station (13th Field Ambulance) with a "walking wounded station" (4th Field Ambulance) adjoining it. The main dressing stations at Bazentin and Pozières were now converted into "entraining centres" respectively for the transmission of cases to the rest stations at Bécordel, Bellevue Farm and Millencourt, and to the casualty clearing stations, which were still at Edgehill. A site for a divisional rest station was found in Avesnes-les-Bapaume.

On March 24th by order of the D.D.M.S. a forward treatment centre for gassed cases was formed behind Bapaume.

---

[23] These two centres acted in effect as an advanced casualty clearing station—conforming closely in their function if not in their structure, to that of these units as now laid down in British Army Manuals.

This grew to be a large station, accommodating 50-100 cases in marquee tents.[24]

It remains to follow the third phase of the "pursuit" to the Hindenburg Line.

Third Phase— Capture of Outpost Line, April 2-9

At the end of March the Fifth and part of the Third Armies were still held off the German front (the Hindenburg Line) by the line of outpost villages, and on April 2nd both Armies launched an attack to eliminate this buffer zone. On the I Anzac Corps front Noreuil covered the Riencourt re-entrant; on the V Corps front the villages of Ecoust and Longatte covered the Bullecourt salient. On the right the captured village of Lagnicourt had stood sentinel to a formidable row of fortified villages reaching southwards to the Fourth Army front, a distance of eight to nine miles.

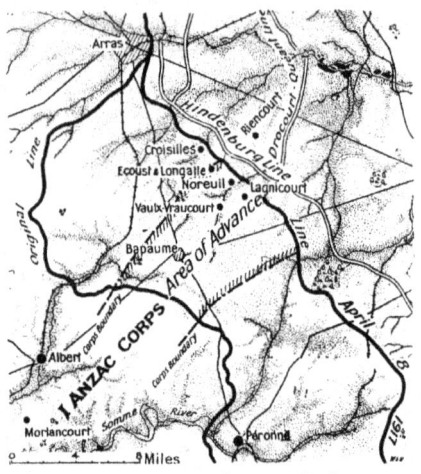

The significance of the events that now occurred differed very greatly on the two sectors of the corps front. On the left the next stage of the advance was to lead, through the capture of Noreuil, to the terrible "First" and "Second" battles of Bullecourt; on the right, it resulted in a series of highly successful battalion actions which, though hard fought and sometimes costly, suggest, in comparison with those battles, the mimic affairs of peace time

Northern Sector of German Retirement, showing Area of I Anzac Advance, Feb.- April 1917.

training. Meanwhile engineers and pioneers opened up routes, by roads and rail, for the heavy artillery and other machinery of warfare. The forward brigades ceased to be known as the advanced guards and more active control was now taken by the divisional commanders.

Right Divisional Front

To take first the operations on the right division's front—the capture of these villages was effected by a series of individual operations undertaken between April 2nd and 11th by the 5th and 1st Divisions. On April 2nd the 5th Division captured Louverval and Doignies; on the 8th and 9th the 1st Division took Boursies, Demicourt, and Hermies.

---

[24] The subject of chemical warfare will be examined in detail in *Vol. III*.

The nature of the fighting in the right sector was peculiarly congenial to the Australian aptitudes, temperament and training. In each of these miniature battles the problems of collecting to aid-post and clearing to the advanced dressing station called for skill and soldier-craft, in particular for close co-operation of regimental medical officers with the battalion and company commanders on the one hand and with the field ambulance bearer division officers on the other—as well as for individual enterprise and resource.

On April 2nd the 55th and 56th Battalions (5th Division), attacking at 5 a.m. captured Louverval and Doignies at a cost of 395 casualties (294 wounded). The regimental aid-posts were cleared by 4.30 p.m. to A.D.S. at Beugny and thence to M.D.S. at Bapaume (15th Field Ambulance)—gassed cases going to the special centre at Avesnes. From Bapaume all casualties went to Pozières for distribution, having travelled from the front, in all, about fifteen miles.

On April 6th the right sector was taken over by the 1st Division. The 2nd Field Ambulance with headquarters at Frémicourt relieved the 15th Field Ambulance at the advanced dressing station at Beugny and cleared the seven miles of front, via a motor relay and urgent treatment post at Frémicourt, to the main dressing station in Bapaume (3rd Field Ambulance). The problem of equipment and supplies was still very difficult. The only stores handed over in the forward posts were 60 stretchers and some 110 blankets.

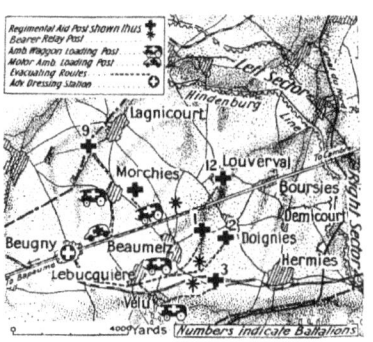

Right Sector, April 9.

The collecting and clearance of casualties in the next action —the triple attack on Boursies, Demicourt and Hermies, on April 8th-9th—illustrates the medical problems in all these small

124 THE WESTERN FRONT [22nd Mar.-9th Apr., 1917

operations.[25] The marginal sketch shows the position of the aid-posts in this attack and the routes of clearance to advanced dressing station at Beugny.

From personal diaries which record the attack on these villages a picture of the marching and fighting of this time can be constructed:

A Medical Orderly.[26] "*March 22nd* to *April 3rd* billetted at Ribemont (on the Ancre) a typical Somme village, dirty and miserable to look at. Houses for the most part of mud and straw made into a plaster and filled in between laths. *April 3rd.* Departed from Ribemont in the good old fashion, packs up. After padding the hoof ten miles reached Montauban. *April 4th.* The country through which we had to pass is the old forward area. Moved along duckboards for some miles, many missing—in such cases had to plough through the mud—snow storm during the march; find it difficult to even imagine more adverse circumstances. Near Gueudecourt (of painful memory) the duckboards finished and remainder of trip had to be got over somehow. The Germans had to retire from the area as it was untenable owing to mud—a regular sea of it. Reached Haplincourt after hours of struggling (not marching) having traversed twelve miles of country.[27]

"*April 8th.* Went into action near Doignies. Established aid-post in sunken road to right of Doignies, and not far from Hermies. Getting on for midnight, and as our battalion attacks at dawn we prepare for the stunt."

The "stunt" in question was the attack on Hermies undertaken on April 9th by the 2nd and 3rd Battalions of the 1st Brigade, whose R.M.O's took over from those of the 55th and 56th. The following abbreviated extract from the diary of a bearer officer supplies the link between the R.A.P's and the 2nd Field Ambulance A.D.S. at Beugny.

A Bearer Officer.[28] "*7/4/17.* Packed my things and set out [from Bapaume] in the cold driving snow for 2nd Field Ambulance. At Beugny

---

[25] The closest analogy to these operations in the experience of the A.I.F. is to be found in some of the fighting in the Sinai and Palestine Campaign. *See Vol. I, pp. 587-99.*

[26] Lance-Corporal R. Morgan, 2nd Battalion. This and the following quotations are somewhat abbreviated.

[27] The bearer division of the 2nd Field Ambulance (Lieut.-Col. W. E. Kay), moving up to Bapaume, had a very similar experience.

[28] Abbreviated from diary kept by Major L. May, who with a bearer section of the 3rd Field Ambulance was attached to the 2nd. The regimental medical officers of the 2nd and 3rd Battalions were Captain H. M. North and Major F. T. Beamish, and of the 55th and 56th Captain H. A. Wyllie and Captain G. S. Elliott. (Captain North had been acting as R.M.O. of the 2nd Battalion since November in place of Captain R. L. Henderson, who had been invalided. On this day Henderson returned and North went to the 3rd Battalion, replacing Major Beamish who was evacuated sick.)

was the A.D.S. and after a short rest here we went on to Lebucquière (Ambulance Bearers' Headquarters). It is a little empty village, the houses all destroyed and broken, so that it was hard to find a decent room. Willcocks and I went along to Vélu and saw the 4th Bn. and Mackay their M.O., and then went across to Major Beamish (3rd) who was in railway cutting with his battalion; they live in small dugouts scooped out of the embankments. This was the real thing at last—all the rails torn up and removed, sentries up on watch, and we had to peer up over the edge carefully, though there was no shooting at all. Had a fossick round and left a squad of men there in a dugout away from the cutting in a wood. And then back to Lebucquière about 2.30.

"*8/4/17.* Wakened about 3.30 by bombardment. . . . I went along to Mackay and went out with him to select his R.A.P. for Hermies and its taking. . . . My men repaired the road with broken bricks. . . . Capt. Mackay and North came along and after tea I took 18 bearers with me and disposed them in relays with good cover in sunken roads. 2nd Battalion did not move up till 9 p.m. Walked 8 kilos. to do the rounds and it was dark when I returned, to find Capt. Lee of 1st Field Ambulance there with 25 more bearers. He took charge and I went round the R.A.P's again. Then at 1.30 a.m. went up to find the 2nd Battalion M.O. Found them in a sunken road near where I had left my bearers. . . . Had a burst of machine-gun fire but got home safely after 4 a.m. About 6.30 a.m. a terrible barrage started in the north which we found to be the beginning of the Great Offensive. [Battle of Arras.]

"*9/4/17.* To-day the 1st Brigade attacked Hermies and took it. I had no sleep nor laid down at all. This morning went round and saw that the relays and R.A.P's were running well and spent the rest of the day seeing the wounded and loading them. Three died here. Our fellows fed the wounded Fritzes and gave them cigarettes. The other prisoners were made to carry stretchers and load waggons, while the bearers robbed them of buttons, badges, etc. . . . Cases poured in all day and now at 7 p.m. all is cleared. We had horsed ambulances at Vélu to carry and unload here for tea, etc. . and three cars from here to Beugny."

The affair is characterised by the Official Historian as "a completely successful action."[29] The brunt of the fighting fell on the 2nd Battalion attacking from the north through Doignies and this unit sustained 181 casualties, the 3rd 72. The proportion of killed to wounded was 1 in 3. 2nd Battalion wounded were cleared from their aid-post by bearers of the 2nd Field Ambulance[30] through waggon loading post just south of Doignies.

---

[29] *Australian Official History, Vol. IV, p. 247.* The account continues (*p. 251*): "It is significant that, of important operations, the attack upon Hermies was the first, within the experience of Australian infantry, to develop from start to finish almost precisely in accordance with plan."
[30] Under Capt. G. C. Willcocks.

In this action casualties were cleared to advanced dressing station at Beugny (2nd Field Ambulance) to which four officers and 102 bearers were attached from the other two units; 500 casualties passed through the A.D.S. in forty-eight hours. After receiving A.T.S., food and urgent treatment cases went by Sunbeam cars to Bapaume (3rd Field Ambulance) which was "just able to cope with the work."

On April 9th on the initiative of the Deputy-Director, the A.D.M.S. 1st Division (Colonel R. B. Huxtable) moved the main dressing station (3rd Field Ambulance) to Beugny and the A.D.S. to Lebucquière. Both stations were shelled but without much harm, and they were soon able to offset the inordinate length of the evacuation route. The M.D.S. was indeed commended by the D.D.M.S. to the Corps Commander for his inspection as a model of comfort and order. "There is no doubt" he observed (Official Diary April 22nd)

"that for a main dressing station much more tentage is required than the regulation three operating tents. The A.D.M.S. 11th British Division was very agreeably surprised when he saw the number of tents we had put up, and they were not one too many. Reception tent, two dressing tents, evacuation tent, buffet, walking wounded reception and dressing tents, tents for gassed cases treatment, store tent, blanket and stretcher tent; and in this bitterly cold weather we have to keep a dump of 1,000 blankets as one could not depend [for their return] on C.C.S., who had only recently moved up without much transport."

The special features of collecting and clearance in the right division's sector were, first, the long bearer carries over rolling downs country or along the valleys that sloped up from the Siegfried Line. Each relay of bearers carried from 1,500 up to 2,000 yards; but by adopting the "shoulder high" method such "carries" were easily negotiated by squads of four.[31] A second feature was the use of horsed, and even light motor, ambulance waggons (Fords) far up in the forward area, at times even to the aid-posts. This was possible for example, at an early stage on the right of Lebucquière, and at Hermies and Doignies after the roads were clear. Heavy motor ambulance waggons also pushed forward far along the Bapaume-Cambrai road in advance of Beugny, and often came under shell-fire. In this sector the

---

[31] See Chapter xi and *Australian Official History, Vol. XII, Plate 293*. During this period carriage shoulder high became universal throughout the I Anzac Corps.

"advanced line of defence" extended to nearly eight miles, astride of the Bapaume-Cambrai road. By April 11th this front was consolidated some 1,000 yards from the Hindenburg Line.

In the left (4th) Division's sector, the Hindenburg Line was, throughout, much closer and the fighting more cramped. On April 2nd Noreuil was captured by the 50th and 51st Battalions with 570 casualties (413 wounded), and on the same date the V Corps on the left took Ecoust and Longatte. These captures uncovered the proposed Fifth Army objective—the Bullecourt salient and the sharp re-entrant angle between Bullecourt and the Quéant bastion, which guarded the junction of the "Wotan Line." By April 4th, both corps had "dug in" some 1,000 yards from the broad triple belt of barbed-wire, and faced at striking distance the great Siegfried Line. Zero day for the Battle of Arras had been fixed for April 9th.

Left Divisional Front

In the attack on Noreuil (launched just before dawn) casualties were cleared from the aid-posts to a waggon loading post in the long valley of the little Hirondelle stream leading down past Noreuil and thence to advanced dressing station (4th Field Ambulance) now in a distillery behind Vaulx-Vraucourt and so by the ambulance cars eight miles to Bapaume. On April 5th, on account of shelling, the advanced station was moved back some half mile from Vaulx to the open fields; and on the 6th for the same reason[32] the main station was moved about two miles forward from Bapaume to "a very good site" selected by the A.D.M.S. (Colonel Barber) at cross roads near Beugnâtre. Here, two miles from Vaulx, a fine tented station was laid out to accommodate 100-150 stretcher cases, with a walking wounded station adjoining. These were served respectively by the motor ambulance convoy, and by buses and returning supply lorries.

Medical arrangements, 4th Division, April 2

For an assault on such a position as the Hindenburg Line at Bullecourt a minimum of ten days' bombardment would be required. Enormous efforts were made to bring up guns and ammunition in time. The railway had reached Achiet-le-Grand on March 28th, and some bombardment began on April 4th. By

Siegfried Line to be attacked

---

[32] On April 6 twenty-nine heavy shells fell into this station of which nineteen were "duds." Some of the latter had buried themselves beneath marquee tents. Only one man was wounded.

6

April 6th light and medium artillery was massed in the Noreuil valley,[33] and heavier guns and howitzers behind Vaulx, and all "worked overtime." But on April 9th, when the Battle of Arras opened, the wire was still uncut.

A.I.F. Battle Casualties on the Somme, during the German retirement, 25th February-9th April, 1917.

1917	Killed in action	Died of Wounds	Died of Gas	Wounded	Gassed	Prisoners of War	Total Casualties
25 Feb.-17 Mar.	407	256	1	1,577	18	52	2,311
18 Mar.-26 Mar.	238	62	—	824	300	55	1,479
27 Mar.-2 Apr.	341	68	1	883	68	85	1,446
3 Apr.-9 Apr.	290	108	1	548	35	19	1,001
Totals	1,276	494	3	3,832	421	211	6,237

---

[33] This valley sloped *from* the German lines not, as did most, toward them. On this feature the medical route of clearance for the Bullecourt battles was based. The guns were placed for the most part about 600 yards in front of the waggon loading post—described in the next chapter. The relation of medical positions to those of artillery (and of supply) was a matter of constant concern. The artillery behind Noreuil were field guns and 4·5-inch howitzers; behind Vaulx were the naval guns and the heavy howitzers. The upper end of the valley was subjected to one of the heaviest bombardments with "irritant" shell gas (phosgene and "di-phosgene") experienced by the A.I.F.

CHAPTER VII

BULLECOURT

THESE operations began on April 9th with the battles of Vimy (First Army) and Scarpe (Third Army) and ended officially on May 15th. They present two distinct phases, in each of which the A.I.F. was involved.

The operations in front of Arras

Heralded by the heaviest bombardment yet laid down by British artillery,[1] the "Battle of Arras"[2] was launched at 4 a.m. in snow and darkness, a typical "dual-purpose" Haig offensive. In these initial battles, success was achieved beyond expectation. The German defences were broken through on wide fronts, positions of great tactical—indeed of ultimate strategic—importance were gained; the Sixth German Army was badly mauled and suffered heavy loss. The confidence of the German Staff was undoubtedly shaken, in particular as to the efficiency of their new method of waging "the defensive battle"—a strategy to which the German force on the west was now fully committed.

The initial impetus, however, was not sustained. The Cavalry "broke through" but was ineffective. A second effort (Second Battle of the Scarpe) fell far short of the success of the first. The Germans counter-attacked with effect and by April 28th both First and Third Armies were held up. The part played by the Fifth Army in this phase of the operations was the raid on the Siegfried Line, known officially as the "attack on Bullecourt, April 11th," and in Australian history as "First Bullecourt."

Field-Marshal Haig, it is known, would have been well pleased to break off the offensive and proceed with his Flanders offensive; but a transfer of effort to the north was prevented by the swift and complete failure of Nivelle's offensive—an event which changed the course of the war, and brought an immediate crisis on the Western Front. The Arras offensive was accordingly resumed on May 3rd to support

---

[1] The British had a gun to every nine yards of front.

[2] The operations commonly referred to as the Battle of Arras are known officially as "The Arras Offensive," and include the following "battles" and attacks:—Battle of Vimy Ridge April 9-14; First Battle of Scarpe, April 9-14; Second Battle of Scarpe, April 23-24; Battle of Arleux, April 28-29; Third Battle of Scarpe, May 3-4. Flanking operations:—First attack on Bullecourt, April 11; German attack on Lagnicourt, April 15; Battle of Bullecourt, May 3-17; Actions on Hindenburg Line, May 20-June 16.

a renewed French offensive on May 4th, a battle being launched by the First, Third, and Fifth Armies on a very wide front but mainly with tired troops. In this anticlimax only minor successes were achieved. The contribution of the Fifth Army to this second phase was the "Battle of Bullecourt," in which the Australian force played the most prominent part. It became known to them as "Second Bullecourt."

The Fifth Army's objective was substantially the same in both Bullecourt battles. From the point of view of the services concerned in maintaining supplies and clearing casualties, the most important feature was the narrowness of the Riencourt re-entrant. Penetration at this point—unless the Bullecourt salient were promptly effaced—would (as in the event it did) create a situation entirely analogous to that which faced the Light Brigade at Balaclava. A further feature of great importance was the railway embankment along which the Australian line partly lay—a substantial earth wall which faced the re-entrant and provided the real jumping-off line for attacks upon it. Along the German front ran a broad barbed-wire belt. The re-entrant was bisected by the "Central Road", running from the Australian position into the German. Behind the embankment a low ridge sloped up toward Noreuil, from which

Medical features of terrain

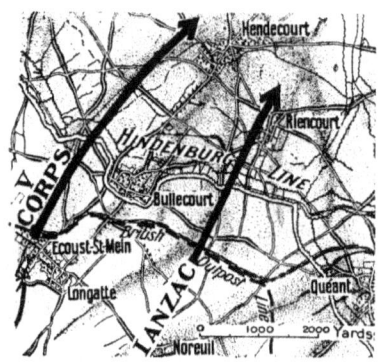

The Fifth Army Objectives, Bullecourt.

point communications mostly veered into the long valley leading down and back to Vaulx. "Sunken" roads ran from Noreuil to Bullecourt and to Longatte. Between the first and the railway was an open stretch, some 2,000 yards across at its widest; from the second a like stretch led to the valley below Noreuil.

These features set the stage for two of the finest exploits in the history of the A.I.F. and two of the most difficult tasks ever faced by its Medical Service.

The obvious importance of a thrust at the junction of the Drocourt-Quéant (Wotan) line led the Fifth Army commander to attempt a
tactical coup. In its concept, its course, and it must
"**First** be added, its results, First Bullecourt is painfully
Bullecourt" reminiscent of Fromelles. On April 7th General
Gough informed Field-Marshal Haig that the Fifth
Army was not ready to assault. The Corps Commanders were warned
however that the Divisions in line (4th Australian and 62nd British)
must be ready to advance at short notice on two-brigade fronts; the
Divisional Staffs, including the A.D.M.S. 4th Division, made arrangements. The 4th and 12th Brigades dug in on the right and left of
the Central Road slightly in advance of the railway. On April 9th the
British farther north attacked Arras. Unduly optimistic reports from
General Allenby unhappily coincided with a suggestion by the officer
in command of the tanks[3] that these might take the place of the absent
artillery, and led to orders for an attack before dawn on the 10th.
The British 62nd Division would flatten out the Bullecourt salient, the
4th Australian would drive a lane through the Siegfried Line at the
apex of the re-entrant and open a way for a cavalry dash to cut off the
German force which should be retiring before the main British thrust
at Arras to the Wotan line.

During the period covered by the events narrated the move up of medical stations continued—and, as will be seen, somewhat overshot itself.

In Fifth Army. The driving force behind these forward moves of the medical units was the D.M.S., Fifth Army,
Surgeon-General G. B. M. Skinner. This
"**First** officer held views on the disposition and use
Bullecourt" of medical units that had this much in com-
Medical arrange-
ments (April mon with those of the Army Commander,
2-10) that he envisaged large and most desirable
ends, but with inadequate consideration of
the method of achieving them, or of possible untoward results.
As D.D.M.S. III Corps on the Somme, he was among the first
to adopt the "forward" policy and he resolutely—even obstinately—adhered to his purpose.[4] His determination to bring skilled surgical treatment and nursing at the earliest possible moment within reach of the wounded man was, it must be said,

---

[3] Seventeen in all. The British Commanders had been at no great pains to work out the tactical use of this new arm. French, Haig, Allenby, and Gough were officers of cavalry—the arm of the military chieftain. *The History of the Royal Army Service Corps* as told by Sir J. W. Fortescue is illuminating of much British military history even in the War of 1914-1918.

[4] *See British Official Medical History of the War, General, Vol. III, pp. 155-6,* and this volume, *Chapter xx (pp. 609, 621n).*

entirely in accord with developments in medical organisation and surgical technique that were greatly to advantage the wounded and to assist the nation in the problem of manpower.[5] On April 8th he moved No. 3 Australian Casualty Clearing Station from Edgehill to railhead at Grévillers, and shortly afterwards placed two more C.C.S's at Grévillers and two at Achiet-le-Grand to serve the II Corps. The two operating centres[6] at Pozières closed down, and this station became an entraining centre for walking wounded and sick, who were evacuated by ambulance waggons and lorry along the Albert road, and by "Decauville" light railway.

In Corps and Divisions. The 27th Motor Ambulance Convoy carried back from Beugnâtre. On April 6th Colonel Manifold urged on the A.D.M.S., 4th Australian Division, Colonel Barber, that his "main" should replace his "advanced" station, and that the latter should move beyond Vaulx. Barber strongly demurred and got his way, but he agreed to maintain a "dump" of tents in Vaulx for the rapid transformation of the A.D.S. in the event of the troops making a swift advance.

It was not until April 7th that Colonel Barber was informed of the intention to attack the Hindenburg Line.[7] On the information then received he made arrangements for a break-through and advance on a two-brigade front, and allotted Field Ambulances (13th and 12th) to the two brigades (4th and 12th). For the left (12th) Brigade he formed a new forward advanced station in front of Vaulx; both stations were to be cleared by motor ambulance waggons and bearers stationed behind Vaulx. A horsed-waggon loading post was formed in the open fields some 1,500 yards behind the Noreuil-Longatte road, visible to the enemy from a great part of his area. Regimental aid-posts were, in the 4th Brigade, stationed at the railway embankment, and, in the 12th, in the Noreuil-Longatte "sunken" road. As usual, the regimental stretcher-bearers were to go forward with the companies. Colonel Barber's "orders" issued on April 7th included the following:—

---

[5] In particular, the organisation of "surgical teams" and discovery of improved methods of treating shock and wounds. *See Index*—"Wounds, treatment."

[6] *See pp. 120-1.*

[7] On April 5 the D.D.M.S., Col. Manifold himself, "was informed that nothing of great importance was likely to take place."

"In the event of an advance R.M.O's will instruct bearers with companies to form an advanced R.A.P., and when necessary will move R.A.P. to that point. R.A.P's normally will be in the vicinity of Battalion Headquarters.

"Regimental bearers will not be allowed in rear of the R.A.P's. Ambulance bearers will not be allowed in front.

"R.M.O's will inform the A.D.M.S. [of] the location of their R.A.P's through Brigade Headquarters. All gassed cases must be carried on stretchers."

The events of this fight are part and parcel with its medical history, and call for some description :—

April 10th. The night of April 9th-10th was wild and bitterly cold, with a fierce wind and occasional sleet and snow. The Battalions of the 4th and 12th Brigades reached the tapes on time and undetected by the enemy. But the tanks failed to get up and at daylight the troops marched back to Noreuil. On this day, in the main battle away to the north-west, Allenby's Cavalry advance was checked. Patrols found the German front opposite Fifth Army also held in strength, but General Gough adhered to his plan, and the assault by the 4th Division on the Siegfried Line began on April 11th at 5.45 a.m.

"**First Bullecourt**"

The tanks again proved unequal to the demands made upon them[8] and were of no great assistance. The British frontal attack on Bullecourt was first countermanded and later, when partly undertaken, was cut up. The infantry of the 4th and 12th Brigades passed through or over the barbed-wire belt unaided, losing heavily. By noon the remnants of the 48th Battalion, the last to retire, were making their way back across the German wire from one of the worst disasters, but most notable feats-of-arms, in the history of the Australian force.[9] The course of events is summed up in the *Australian Official History*[10] as follows :—

The Battle

"Thrown between two pylons of the enemy's line, despite failure of the tanks which were to cut the wire and replace the barrage, the 4th Australian Division had achieved what most soldiers then in France would previously have believed impossible—broken, without artillery barrage, the Hindenburg Line. But when after this, misled by reports of mythical success, the artillery had continued to withhold its support, the German machine-gunners had with impunity closed a gate behind the Australian infantry, and forced it to withstand attack until its supplies ran out, when most of the unwounded survivors made the brave effort to run the gauntlet and escape. The six and a half battalions

---
[8] These were the old Mark I tank, slow, vulnerable, difficult to manoeuvre, and ill-ventilated. Of their crews—103 officers and men—52 were killed, wounded or missing. Cavalry was moved up behind the railway embankment but was promptly forced back by shell-fire.

[9] The account of this battle in the *Australian Official History of the War (Vol. IV)* is commended to the reader as one of the most inspiring writings in Australian literature, and as presenting a sane and balanced judgment on the event.

[10] *Vol. IV, pp. 341-3.*

and accompanying units of the 4th Division engaged lost over 3,000 officers and men, of whom 28 officers and 1,142 men were captured, much the largest number of Australians taken by the enemy in a single battle. As few men who were wounded beyond the first wire escaped, the number of prisoners includes a great part of the wounded."

The Cost. The proportionate loss in killed, wounded, missing and prisoners of war was the heaviest ever sustained by any Australian formation in a single action. In the 4th Brigade casualties averaged four-fifths of each battalion engaged—2,339 out of 3,000; in the 12th they were 950 out of less than 2,000. For the medical service the events of this battle were as tragic as those of Fromelles. Of the large number of wounded, 1,090 reached the advanced dressing stations. The collecting of these to the aid-posts and the fate of the remainder call for more than casual note.

Collecting Wounded from the Lines. As at Fromelles the problem presented itself in two phases, respectively before and after daylight.[11] In both Brigades, especially in the 4th, the casualties before the attack and during the advance over the wire were heavy. Many of these were brought into the aid-posts by the regimental bearers, and, for a time, wounded men came back even from the fighting zone, mostly arriving unassisted. In the fighting in the trenches which followed, the seriously wounded moved aside as best they might; many were placed in dugouts by the bearers or by comrades, or were carried to the old German front line, which they greatly cumbered. In the 4th Brigade wounded were tended with admirable devotion by two captured German medical orderlies, who at a later stage continued their humane endeavours after their own rescue by the German counter-attack. On this sector, when full daylight came and supplies and reinforcements were cut off, the alternatives presented to the "walking" wounded as to the uninjured were—either to be captured or to face the re-crossing of the old No-Man's Land (including the wire belt) under continuous aimed rifle and machine-gun fire. The majority attempted to escape, and on the less exposed 12th Brigade front many reached the lines; but a very large number, especially in the 4th Brigade,

---

[11] Before daylight the German machine-guns were not able to prevent runners, carriers, and walking wounded from making their way back. But "about 6 o'clock, with sunrise, the whole battlefield came suddenly into view." Thereafter movement between opposing lines was only at the utmost risk.

were killed on the wire[12] or were wounded and lay about until captured or, as the Australian Official Historian properly states, "were put to death by a merciful enemy."

When the action was over it was seen that, in spite of our artillery and machine-gun fire, German medical orderlies were attending the wounded in the shell-holes in No-Man's Land and on the wire. The firing was therefore stopped, and, after display of a white flag, for some two hours our regimental bearers and fifty infantry were permitted to assist in collecting wounded. Most of those who were picked by the Germans off the wire were carried by them to their own trenches, but in some instances they placed badly wounded men on its outer edge to be picked up by our bearers. By 6 p.m. snow was falling; the Germans shouted "finish hospital," and both sides withdrew. During this night, however, many further rescues were made and for several nights afterwards survivors crawled or were helped back to the railway embankment.

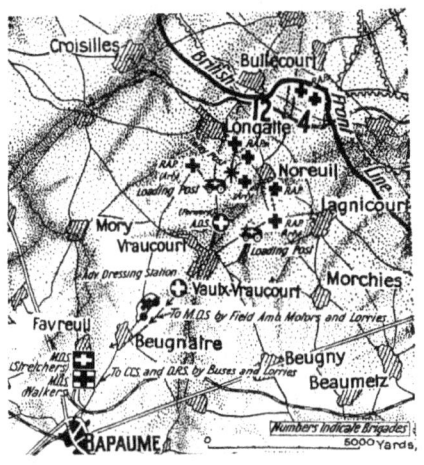

First Bullecourt—Medical Situation during the Attack, April 11. (The two forward R.A.P's in each sector were those of the battalions engaged.)

Clearing the Wounded. The routes from the two groups of aid-posts converged to independent bearer relay and waggon posts in the Noreuil Valley. "The Sunken Road," where lay the 12th Brigade's R.A.P's, was to become one of the landmarks in the history of the Australian Medical Service. On both sectors the route from the railway ran over the open fields, in

---

[12] Seen before the battle this wire showed up a broad red patch "like a poppy field."

full view from the German lines. On this "carry" and in the course of the two battles (April 11th-May 17th) 234 A.A.M.C. men were killed or wounded. But during this first battle the experience was one rather of endurance than of danger.

The task of the regimental and ambulance bearers respectively differed greatly on the two Brigade fronts. In the 12th Brigade the battalion bearers faced an immense carry but the ambulance bearers one of a few hundred yards only. Consequently—though against the orders of the A.D.M.S.—the task was shared between the two classes of bearers.

"The wounded," writes Captain J. T. Jones, R.M.O. of the 47th, "began to reach the R.A.P's (Sunken Road) shortly after the attack opened, and they came in a continuous stream all day, and, considering the numbers, were passed through quickly. Some delay was caused later in the day by the disappearance of the ambulance bearers. So, to supplement the number carrying, men were detailed from the 47th and 51st Battalions."

In the 4th Brigade the situation was reversed but the results *mutatis mutandis* were similar. An unpublished history of the 4th Field Ambulance says:—

"*April 10th.* [At M.D.S. Beugnâtre] 'A' and 'C' Sections with two ambulance waggons set out at 7.30 p.m. for temporary duty with the 12th and 13th Field Ambulances. As the C.O. came out to wish his men 'Good Luck,' a feeling came over one that something was doing. *11th.* All departments were kept busy. [At the M.D.S.] almost a record number of patients were put through [in the time], and the doctors with their assistants never stopped. [At the front] the stretcher-bearers had one continuous stream of wounded and barely had time to eat. Every possible man helped to carry the wounded in. For the first time the method of carrying on the shoulders was adopted by all, and from that date it was never dropped. The weather kept fine till the afternoon and then the snow came and it was frightfully difficult for the bearers to pick their tracks. The men were drenched and cold, but as nothing compared to the wounded who lay out in the snow. It was a sight to see the smaller men stick to their job, backwards and forwards. Finally, with strength almost gone, a party of infantry relieved them in what was the most solid day's carrying in France."

The work of clearance was made unduly heavy and some "congestion" was caused by the method adopted by the A.D.M.S. Colonel Barber has indeed himself ensured that this be put on record:—

"On this occasion I placed an Ambulance Commander in charge of the right and left sectors, one behind each Brigade, as the operations proposed an advance. This led to complications in connection with the supply of reinforcement bearers from the reserve ambulance; and, as the prospective advance did not take place, it would have been better if one C.O. only had been in charge of the whole evacuation from the front line."[13]

Advanced Dressing Stations. Clearance from the horsed- and motor-waggon loading posts, to advanced dressing stations "proceeded satisfactorily." The "forward advanced station" in the left sector (12th Field Ambulance) was used as a relay and motor loading post. In the advanced dressing station behind Vaulx (12th Field Ambulance) the work was "extremely heavy." At the main dressing station (4th and 13th Field Ambulances) 446 stretcher cases and 671 walking wounded passed through in 24 hours after the attack. Stretcher cases went to Grévillers, walking wounded and "sitters" to Pozières for distribution.

Reliefs. On April 14th the 4th Division was relieved by the 2nd and after two weeks' rest was transferred to II Anzac Corps (Second Army) for the first blow in the great British offensive now being prepared in Flanders. In handing over medical control in the sector, Colonel Barber (as his diary records) "urged on Colonel Sutton" that pressure from above should not induce him to move his stations forward; he referred to "the risk of shelling, even of capture," and the fact that even now motor ambulance waggons could not pass through Vaulx.[14]

On April 13th the 1st Division advanced to within 1,000 yards of the Hindenburg Line, holding now a front of nearly eight miles. The tenuity gave the enemy a much desired chance to
German counter retaliate and on the 15th he raided in force. Though
raid: Lagnicourt repulsed with heavy loss the attack was highly dramatic and eventful. Lagnicourt was captured and held for four hours. The raiding parties (two Divisions) destroyed some field-guns, and came within 500 yards of 5th Brigade Head- quarters—incidentally within 600 yards of the advanced dressing station. The regimental medical officer of the 12th Battalion narrowly escaped capture. The loss to the attackers was 2,313; to the defenders, 705 in the 1st Division and 305 in the 2nd.

---

[13] *Memorandum to the D.M.S., A.I.F., 1919.*

[14] On April 24, with the approval of Major-General Holmes commanding the division, Colonel Barber issued "Standing Orders for the A.A.M.C. of this (4th) Division based on his experience on the Somme." At a later time these formed the basis for the Standing Orders for the Australian Corps.

Collecting and Clearance. The regimental bearers had a very heavy time. From the 2nd Division wounded were evacuated through the forward A.D.S. and there was no congestion at any point. From the 1st Division wounded went through Morchies to the main dressing station at Beugny. Casualties from the Australian counter-attack arrived at the main station in less than four hours after wounding, but of the men who had been wounded in the first enemy assault many lay for twelve hours before rescue. The wounds were chiefly by bullet and were found "very severe," partly—and this is of some moment—because all the wounded—and therefore all serious cases—were brought in. Stretcher cases went to the casualty clearing stations at Grévillers, others to Bapaume and thence via entraining centre to Pozières and so to C.C.S. at Edgehill and Aveluy, about twenty miles in all; the last stage was "still a long and dreadful journey, sometimes taking five hours."

Two days later the great French offensive was launched and, as already mentioned, completely failed. Its influence on the course of events calls for examination at this stage.

The events of this month, indeed, were of cardinal importance. On April 6th America declared war on Germany, an offset to the menacing situation created by the success of Germany's submarine blockade and by her progressive elimination of the whole eastern front as a major military problem.[15]

Course of the World War

But the failure of the French offensive led to results perhaps even more serious than these. There followed a depression and loss of morale in the French Army that threatened disaster to the Allied cause. Field-Marshal Haig, at a meeting on April 24th with General Nivelle, agreed to postpone his Flanders offensive and continue the Arras operations. A result of this decision was the Third Battle of the Scarpe, with Second Bullecourt as its "flanking operation."[16]

---

[15] On March 12 the Russian Proletariat revolted against the ruling class, and the promised co-operation was delayed. From this time, indeed, the history of Russia, and her anguish, belongs to herself not to the Great War.

[16] It is clear that at this time agreement was general that "wearing down" must for the present be the major element in the Allied strategy. Even Gough accepts this (*The Fifth Army p. 130*). At a meeting of the British and French staffs (the Australian Official Historian states) "all agreed that grandiose enterprises aimed at breaking through were now out of the question. The enemy must be worn down by well prepared local offensives." Throughout this critical time the character of Field-Marshal Haig stands out in strong relief: he was more than willing to act alone, but ready at all times to co-operate and if need be to efface himself. "As true of war in its modern scientific methods as of the battles of past centuries, character remains the supreme essential, alike in the rank and file, in the subaltern, in the leader of armies." (*Sir Douglas Haig's Command, 1915-1918, Vol. I, p. 414*, by G. A. B. Dewar and J. H. Boraston.)

From as early as April 15th the Fifth Army Commander pressed for permission to intervene *fortiore* in the *diminuendo* of the British offensive. The front of attack for May 3rd was arranged to include that of the Fifth Army.

Preparations in Fifth Army

Artillery in Noreuil Valley. The history of the three weeks that intervened between the First and Second Bullecourt belongs to the artillery. Emplaced almost wheel to wheel in "death valley"—the upper Noreuil Valley—the light and medium artillery brigades of I Anzac sustained at this time casualties only exceeded in the Third Battle of Ypres. Special arrangements were made for clearance from this area. The medical officer to the 4th Field Artillery Brigade (Captain B. H. Mack) was killed on April 10th.[17] The heavy artillery beyond Vaulx, also was subject to severe shelling. Between the two, part of the Noreuil Valley was less heavily shelled, and it was through this gap that the stream of casualties from the Riencourt re-entrant passed.

Improvement of Corps Area. During April the Fifth Army completed its move up. Roads were metalled; on April 30th the light railway reached Vaulx. On April 13th Colonel Manifold moved to advanced Corps Headquarters at Grévillers and concerned himself actively in the problem of maintenance in the new area. These were difficult enough. Beside the Divisions the I Anzac Corps contained at this time some hundred odd units[18] comprising personnel to the number of many thousand. For the medical arrangements for these troops the D.D.M.S. was directly responsible.

The Corps area was an enormous one. The old reserve area on the Ancre was retained for rest and training, a new one was created in front of the old battlefield—a wide belt of useless waste now however bridged by roads and light railways. The housing of troops in the forward area was however a tremendous problem. In muddy trenches, far from billets, baths, and

---

[17] Some details of medical service with the artillery will be found on *pp. 279-80*. *See also Vol. I, p. 207n.*

[18] These were of the most varied kind. They included the 15th Mobile Hygiene Laboratory, 13th Mobile Bacteriological Laboratory, a Special Medical Operating Centre, 2nd Section Water Column, Tunnelling Companies, Pigeon lofts, Wireless Sections, Corps Schools, Reinforcement Camps, Veterinary Detachments, and so forth, not to mention the Heavy Artillery and Corps Supply Columns, a number of Engineer and Labour units and other technical services.

laundries[19] the men lived in great discomfort. The weather was cold—often bitterly cold—and wet. April 24th was the first spring day—beautifully mild and sunny. These conditions were not without effect on health and morale. The rest—promised for training and needed after the winter's trials—was held to be long overdue and though the military situation did not permit of this—indeed, a great battle loomed instead—vigorous efforts were made within the Corps to improve matters. The Divisions not in the line went to rest and training behind Albert. Leave was free, sports, concerts and so forth were organised.[20]

The part of the medical service in these amenities was physical rather than "moral." But no "lesson of the war" is more clear than this—that these two were made one and may not by man be put asunder. Nor is there question that the work of the medical service at this time was of very material concern in maintaining man-power in the field, and in promoting the "offensive" spirit. It is not necessary to enter into details regarding these various activities.[21] Some reference must however be made to the problem of "sanitation" during this period.

The swift transition from static to moving warfare affected no element in the medical system of the I Anzac Corps more than the Divisional Sanitary Sections. In particular it brought out the involvements of the new policy which had bound these units to areas

Sanitary Sections

---

[19] All the French inhabitants had been removed behind the German lines and all the villages destroyed. Baths and laundries at this time had been taken over by Fifth Army—to the great disadvantage of the Australian formations.

[20] In the 5th Division medical schemes of training included (*inter alia*) lectures and instructions on gas, enemy mines and booby traps, on first-aid in gas poisoning, on feet, on conduct as prisoners of war, camp sanitation, care of tilled land, trees, and crops, discipline and *esprit de corps*. Unit, service, and divisional sports were in full swing at the beginning of May, when the Second Battle of Bullecourt began.

[21] We find the Deputy-Director, Colonel Manifold, concerned, as were his A.D's.M.S., in promoting baths, laundries, and the supply of clean underclothing (with the D.A. and Q.M.G.); in delousing arrangements (to combat a great recrudescence of this pest); in conferring with the D.M.S., A.I.F., General Howse (who at this time was much at the front) and with the Dental Staff Officer in France (Major L. B. Day), in the matter of dental service for the troops in the field; in the subject of rations, in which he advocated discrimination in favour of front line troops (discussed in March in the Interallied Sanitary Conference). He tried (without avail) to obtain permission for Australian troops to retain one blanket during summer. In particular, he made the improving of rest stations his special concern, and made great use of the Australian Red Cross Society in promoting this purpose. Inspecting the stations at Bellevue Farm, Bécordel, and Buire in April General Howse "expressed himself highly pleased." Early in May a site was selected in Bapaume for an "Advanced Rest Station."

rather than to formations. When the advance began the four Australian sections were put under Corps control. On March 11th the Deputy-Director conferred with their commanding officers, and a policy was approved which permitted very direct contact with the Australian formations. But Colonel Manifold kept himself closely in touch with their work, and "supported them against any attempt by combatant officers to dispute their authority or by Army to interfere with their independence."

The new area had been heavily fouled by the retiring enemy, and water purification was a serious problem. On April 14th each Division was required to provide the officer commanding its Sanitary Section with a Ford car for his greater mobility, but requests for reversion to Divisional control were refused by Army. The rapid moves, however, showed up to advantage the active rôle favoured for these units in the Australian force as against the passive one imposed by the British sanitary authorities. In the forward zone indeed, the "area" idea was perforce in abeyance, and the Section allotted to that region (2nd Sanitary Section) employed with conspicuous success the methods of co-operative supervision, and education in self-help, which were becoming the keynote of the sanitary system and sanitary discipline of the A.I.F.[22]

Casualty Clearing Stations. From the second week in April the C.C.S. groups at Grévillers and Achiet-le-Grand received all battle casualties, only sick being sent through Pozières to the rest stations.

Fifth Army advances medical units

The M.D.S. In the quiescent period between the Bullecourt battles the Fifth Army staff found time to intervene in a very unusual way in the medical arrangements of the I Anzac Corps. Accepting the advice of his A.D's.M.S., Colonel Manifold had ceased to press for the advancing of the main station. The Fifth Army's chief-of-staff, however (at the instance of the army commander), pressed insistently for the move and the Deputy-

---

[22] Though his headquarters were in Albert the officer-in-charge of this unit (Capt. M. J. Holmes) was in Bapaume on the day after its capture, and he was also an early visitor to Lagnicourt—where he and his sergeant, caught in No-Man's Land, achieved the compliment of being sniped at by "Pip-squeaks" (the German 37-mm quick-firing gun).

Director of I Anzac was overborne. After a further effort to retain his walking wounded collecting station at Beugnâtre, Colonel Sutton obeyed a direct order received through the General Staff.[23] The 5th Field Ambulance moved up the station for walking wounded, the 6th that for stretchers. An enormous tented station grew up behind Vaulx in preparation for the now imminent battle.[24] On April 25th the 1st Division, holding the southern sector of the Corps, was relieved by the 11th British and went to reserve. On the same day definite orders were issued by General Gough for the attack on May 3rd.

For this offensive the First, Third, and Fifth British Armies were to attack on a front of sixteen miles—a British "record." *Fifth Army.*
The intentions and objective of the Fifth Army in
Third Battle this battle, as finally whittled down by the corps
of Scarpe commanders, were substantially the same as for those
for the attack of April 11th. The 62nd British Division was to efface the Bullecourt salient, while the 2nd Australian would break through the re-entrant and push out some 3,000 yards beyond. This would be followed by a cavalry drive.

If no more difficult task was ever set the Australian force, no more careful or exact steps were ever taken to ensure suc-
I Anzac cess. Nor, it must be added were the qualities
of the Australian soldier of all ranks and in every service ever seen to better advantage. On the experience of the first battle, and working to a ground plan of the battlefield, every problem of the battle was worked out, and not least exactly those of supply, maintenance and the clearance of casual-

---

[23] In view of *dénouements* the circumstances of this move have a general interest. They are recorded in Col. Manifold's diary:—"*April 15:* In reference to a request from 2nd Australian Division that they should not move their dressing station forward I told General White (the I Anzac chief-of-staff) that the movement had been ordered by the D.M.S. and on the wishes of the army commander, who had now for the second time drawn attention to the M.D.S. not being far enough forward. (On his advice) I sent a memo to the D.M.S. forwarding memorandum from the A.D.M.S., 4th Division giving the objections of his "G" Staff, (to the move).
"*April 27:* Enquiry from the Fifth Army General Staff asking why we had not moved up the M.D.S.; that to dress cases at the A.D.S. and re-dress again at the M.D.S. was very bad for the wounded. I pointed out that the so-called A.D.S. was only used as a waggon post . . . however as the matter had reached this stage I advised our chief-of-staff that any objection to moving forward should be over-ruled. Orders were issued to move it at once to Vaulx."

...[24] On April 28 at the instance of General Birdwood the D.D.M.S. urged Colonel Sutton to lay-off somewhat in his preparations. With "all preparations made for a very severe offensive," Colonel Sutton was placed between the devil and the deep sea. He agreed as to the risk and "would see what could be done."

ties. Saps were dug, or designed, and the potentialities of the railway embankment and of all sunken roads exploited.

The evacuation scheme of the D.M.S. Fifth Army was based on the two groups of clearing stations at Grévillers and Achiet-le-Grand.[25] Visiting No. 3 A.C.C.S. on May 2nd the D.M.S., A.I.F. (General Howse) found "all preparations made for a very severe offensive."

Medical arrangements

Anzac Corps. Like those of the Infantry, medical preparations for this battle were complete and exact. By this time indeed the medical service with the A.I.F. was fully equipped both in direction and executive for any military task.

The order of battle provided for only one Division (two brigades) in the active line, and the course of evacuation from aid-posts to main dressing station was therefore directed by the A.D.M.S. of the 2nd Division (Colonel Sutton). As the battle progressed however, Division after Division was drawn in to replace the fighting formation, and the medical situation came to resemble that seen in combined operations.[26] In view of expected heavy casualties the Deputy-Director made available bearers and transport from other Divisions and from the Corps. For the walking wounded he arranged transport by light railway from a siding behind Vaulx to the detraining post at Bapaume, which was well equipped for the event. No. 27 M.A.C. attached to the Corps had great difficulty in finding a site forward, and parked precariously behind the M.D.S. Buses for walking wounded were supplied by Army.

Collecting and Clearance. Regimental work was based on three groups of aid-posts behind the railway embankment or in sunken roads. Elephant iron cupolas provided shelter from weather and some psychic easement. The rear side of the embankment was safe in most parts even from enfilade fire for a space of at least a few yards.

---

[25] The Director-General of Medical Services, B.E.F. in his diary for April 4 refers to a request from the Fifth Army Commander urging that "Army" should control the moves of these units. Reply was made that the general scheme of evacuation must be considered as well as the advantage of the particular Army to which the units should be allotted. There were at the time, he noted, in the Fifth Army six stations in excess of the proper allotment by divisions.

[26] Though composed of units from several divisions, the main dressing station was not termed a "Corps Main Dressing Station."

Field Ambulances. Colonel Sutton disposed his field units in echelon, with the 7th Field Ambulance (Lieut.-Colonel J. J. Black) in charge of clearance from aid-posts to M.D.S. The routes of clearance, transport circuits and posts were not

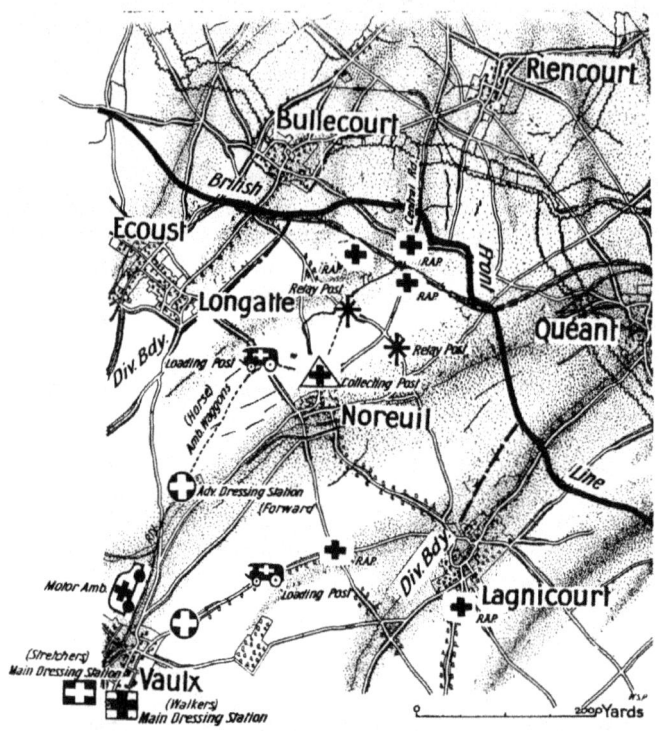

Second Bullecourt—Medical Arrangements for Action of May 3.

changed materially from the first battle. Special officers were put in charge of the bearer and transport circuits, and reserves of bearers were posted at the main and advanced stations and collecting posts.

The main dressing station, both walking section (5th Field

Ambulance) and stretcher section (6th Field Ambulance), was staffed and equipped for heavy casualties.

The battle as a whole was an anticlimax, and its results accorded. "In the whole sixteen miles of battle-front, except for one minor gain south of the River Scarpe, the only troops who on the morning of May 4th still held any substantial part of the ground won were the 1st and 6th Canadian Brigades at Fresnoy on the extreme left of the offensive, and the 6th Australian Brigade on the extreme right." During the next two weeks the active fighting on the British front in France centred in this "flanking operation" which developed from the "attack" into the "battle" of Bullecourt.

Progress of main Battle

The events of the battle of Bullecourt have a dramatic quality not often seen in the operations of this phase of the war. In the first place a great battle was fought in a space that brought its events almost within the view of a single observer. The battle itself was a prolonged homeric hand to hand struggle, continued for a fortnight; the cost in Australian casualties almost equalled those from all the previous spring fighting. These features were due in part to the nature of the battlefield; but much more to the quality of the men who opposed each other in a contest in which each side fought berserk.[27]

Battle of Bullecourt

The battle began at 3.45 a.m. and presents three phases: (1) *May 3-4*. The Australian 5th Brigade and British 62nd Division were quickly thrown back. But the 6th Brigade broke through and held on, and at night, in spite of very heavy losses, retained some 400 yards of both German lines. By 9 p.m. the 2nd Pioneer Battalion had run a trench "fringed with their dead bodies" 1,150 yards along the Central Road, one of the most notable feats of sapping in Australian history. Through this artery, circulation was maintained within the forward area. Battalions of the 1st Division were drawn in, and in 48 hours the position was extended and consolidated. (2) *May 5-9*. On May 5th, Australian parties bombed towards Bullecourt, and on the 7th the Gordon Highlanders and Devons made a frontal attack there and gained a footing. On the 9th-10th the 5th Australian Division took over the Anzac front. (3) *May 11-15*. The whole Bullecourt salient was captured and held.

In all there were seven major and perhaps a dozen minor counter-attacks. The last, made on the 15th, was a full-dress affair ordered by von Below himself, the new commander of the Sixth German Army. On May 20th a British division took over the Anzac front and the territory gained was incorporated in the British line.

On May 9th Haig's orders moved most of the heavy artillery from this front, including three Australian field artillery brigades—the first move in preparation for the Flanders offensive.

---

[27] "The opposing troops were massive big men and fight like fury, very few of them were taken prisoners. Speaking to one he told me (in French) they 'were the élite regiment of the Prussian Guards,' the Kaiser's Cockchafers as I understood from him." (Diary of Lance-Corporal Morgan, A.A.M.C. attached 2nd Battalion.) The troops were in fact some of the finest regiments in the German Army.

With the Battle of Bullecourt ended to all intents the great Arras offensive. Its last stages went far to wipe out in man-power, if not perhaps in morale, the credit balance achieved in the first assault. Had it been possible to break it off and shift the powerful reserves to the Flanders front for an early offensive, it is hard to say what might not have been achieved, what attrition avoided.

The Battle of Bullecourt, Haig has said, was "among the great achievements of the war." It remains to see how the Australian medical service sustained its part in this achievement.

In point of numbers the medical problem in this battle presents itself as follows:—

TABLE I.—Wounded and Gassed Evacuated (including D. of W.)

	1st Div.	2nd Div.	4th Div.	5th Div.	Total
May 3-4	315	2,431	31	42	2,819
May 5-9	1,717	324	23	91	2,155
May 10-17	83	56	25	1,118	1,282
Totals	2,115	2,811	79	1,251	6,256

The medical problem . To pass so large a number of casualties along a single route of clearance, so that in no transport circuit or at no treatment centre should there be any check to the steady flow of the stream, would in any circumstances be a serious problem. Here the task was made peculiarly difficult by the course of the battle and the nature of the battlefield. During the first day the wounded were made with a rapidity and in a concentration not exceeded in Australian fighting, and in the narrow battle zone their removal was urgent. At the aid-posts conditions were such that any concentration would be at terrible risk; even a brief stay there would have been little (if at all) less dangerous than to remain in the fighting line. At the other end of the zone the facilities of an elaborate and well organised scheme of transport circuits and posts ensured that, from the time the casualty reached the waggon loading post, clearance would be rapid. Within the re-entrant no vehicular circuit could be formed. The gap—a matter of nearly two miles from the fighting line—must be bridged by two bearer circuits, regimental and ambulance, linked at the aid-posts. The manner in which this problem was faced by those responsible gives a distinctive character to the medical events of this battle.

The collecting of casualties from the fighting zone in a great battle is part and parcel with the battle itself. The regimental bearers were combatants and lived and moved for the most part with the companies, and in all heavy fighting their work was shared by the troops themselves.[28] In the first days of this battle the severity of the fighting gave little scope for systematic collecting—

Regimental collecting of casualties

"Men could not be spared for stretcher-bearing—the wounded made their own way to the rear 'unless absolutely mangled.' The firing line became crowded with men with ghastly wounds."[29]

That these were collected—and with expedition—to the regimental aid-posts is shown by the fact that, by clearing across 1,000 yards of country more severely shelled than the front line itself, the regimental bearers imposed on the ambulance bearers within a very brief time one of the heaviest tasks in their experience.[30]

From May 4th onwards some aid-posts were moved up to the fighting zone (as at Lone Pine) where they should be cleared by ambulance squads, and, as the situation in rear permitted, the bearer squads worked up to these.

The conditions at the 2nd Battalion aid-post (Major M. V. Southey)[31] is described in the diary of his lance-corporal (R. Morgan):—

"The aid-post was a small place built overnight (May 3rd) by the Pioneers—one sandbag overhead, not enough to stop the smallest shell made, and we had for the most part to tend wounded in the roadway.

---

[28] For a discussion of this problem of collecting see *Chapter xi, and Vol. I (Index—under Stretcher-bearers; and Regimental Medical Service)*. The story belongs to General as much as to Medical history. This is accepted by the Australian Official Historian, and the matter receives appropriate attention in volumes of the *Official History*. The reader is particularly referred to the chapters which deal with this battle—*Volume IV, Chapters xii-xiii*—from which much of the detail of front-line experience given here is taken. ("Regimental" signifies "battalion.")

[29] From *Australian Official History Vol. IV, p. 484.*

[30] In the *Australian Official History loc. cit.* an account is given of an episode of rescue which (as the Historian rightly remarks), was worthy the award of the Victoria Cross. The reason for the fact that no such award was ever made in the Australian force for deeds of rescue will be discussed in *Vol. III*. It may be said here that such acts of impulsive courage or daring with remote possibility of results of tangible value was alien to the type of bravery most proper in the stretcher-bearer. In the case in question more lives were lost than were saved by rescue, which might well have been left till nightfall. But the value of the tradition thus maintained and of the morale thus encouraged went far beyond that price.

[31] Major Southey had replaced Captain R. L. Henderson, who was mortally wounded on May 3 as the battalion moved in, and died on July 31.

fortunately sunken, with a little shelter from the banks. At times the shelling was so fierce that we were all forced to lie alongside the bank. Casualties passed through our hands in one endless procession; mangled bodies and shattered limbs, but one cannot be but callous and indifferent as practical assistance is needed here, not sympathy. To be sympathetic one would soon become useless. Working practically for 48 hours without rest and very little food, blood to the elbows as there is not enough water to drink much less to wash."

At the regimental aid-posts along the railway the conditions in the first week of this battle became proverbial in ambulance history. The zone of comparative safety was very narrow, and outside it casualties were only less frequent than in the fighting line itself.[32] A rigid selection of men for clearance had to be made so as not to include hopeless cases.

With the advance to Bullecourt and its capture the routes of collecting and aid-posts moved round to the left. After May 8th the regimental problem ceased to be a serious one.

Ambulance circuits

In the ambulance circuits Colonel Black disposed his personnel as follows:—

Headquarters at M.D.S. Officer-in-Command, Transport Officer, One Tent Sub-division in reserve.

A.D.S. Right. Tent Sub-division. *Left.* Tent personnel.

Advanced Collecting Posts. Officer-in-Charge forward clearance—Tent Division personnel.

Waggon Loading Post. Transport Officer. Tent Sub-division in reserve. Two Bearer squads.

First R.A.P. Group. Sixteen squads (four battalions).
Second R.A.P. Group. Ten squads (two battalions).
Third R.A.P. Group. Twelve squads (two battalions).

It is clear that officers and other ranks alike saw well the gravity of the problem they would have to face, and provided for it so far as this could be done by the assembling and distribution of ample supplies and the careful disposal of personnel and transport. The aid-posts were reconnoitred, and the bearer squads found the battalions beforehand. The sunken roads afforded adequate sites for collecting and reserve bearer posts. Behind these, clearance should not cause anxiety. There remained one problem stark and simple—to clear the aid-posts

---

[32] Thus on the 5th, two ambulance squads were almost wiped out at an R.A.P. by a high explosive shell.

by man-carry across 1,200 yards of open hillside in full view and rifle range and with no alternative routes. The left group might be cleared down the sap but (as one bearer put it) "it would have taken a fortnight to do it." The ambulance bearers found that if they would keep pace with the regimental bearers they must carry by day and night across the open, "shoulder high." Faced with an extraordinarily difficult and dangerous task, they took stock of the situation as it developed and, meeting the problems in their own way and with their own standards of duty and fortitude, played their part in such a manner that, after the first rush, at no time was there at the R.A.P's any hold-up of stretcher cases marked by R.M.O's for removal by the bearer squads. Casualties began to arrive at the R.A.P's within half-an-hour of the opening bombardment, and thereafter the stream rapidly increased in volume.

"Evacuation" (the O.C., 7th Field Ambulance, Colonel Black, reported) "was carried out without any hitch. . . . The morale of the stretcher-bearers was remarkable. Their casualties were very heavy but there was no hesitation. Heavy shelling tends to immobilise bearers but this was not seen."

By the afternoon heavy casualties among the bearers and the large number of wounded made evident the serious nature of the problem in this circuit. The Assistant-Director, Colonel Sutton, called up the reserves allotted by the Corps and by evening all the bearers of the 2nd and 3rd Field Ambulances were also in the line. Some local relief was arranged, the bearers resting in the two sunken roads. The experience of one[33] is typical of their work in this battle.

Experience of a Bearer Squad of 5th Field Ambulance, attached 17th and 18th Battalions. "Evening of the 2nd we dumped our packs at Headquarters (M.D.S.) at Vaulx. Orders came out to wear brassards. We marched through Vaulx, reached the A.D.S. and joined the 17th and 18th Battalions and on through Noreuil, ghostly in the moonlight. We carried stretchers loaded with blankets, splints, and dressings. Arrived at our front line (a sunken road) where we formed an R.A.P. There was no protection, the R.A.P. a galvanised shanty against the bank. Just before dawn our guns opened, the shells bursting a few hundred yards in front of us. As it eased, cases came in and soon the road was packed with stretchers and walking wounded. The M.O. put on a rough dressing and we carried the cases back one and a half miles to the sunken road. Fritz shelled our track from one end to the other, on our second trip one of my squad was hit in the thigh,

[33] Lance-Cpl. E. C. Munro.

we carried him out and got another man. On our next trip another of our squad got a small piece of H.E. in his leg but carried on till we reached the dressing station. We went on throughout the day. At dusk a H.E. shell wounded two of the rear squad and hit our patient. We hurried on and returned but found that another shell had killed one of those previously wounded, and wounded the patient and another bearer. We fixed them up as best we could and carried them back. At night we were relieved."

The two bearer routes from right and left brigades, and also the walking wounded, converged on the "forward collecting and relay post"—some fifty yards or so of sunken road lined with sheet iron shelters and "pozzies." Here the wounded were dressed and got a drink, and reserve bearers rested; and from this station the officer-in-charge of the bearer circuit directed operations. Officers with bearers from other units came under him. While in circuit, bearer squads and their N.C.O's worked from the aid-posts, and after delivering their patient they returned to the aid-posts with supplies. A mental picture of what was done at the collecting post may be formed from the diary of a tent-division private:—[34]

The Collecting and Relay Post: "Sunken Road"

"The dressing room was a place made in the bank of the road with room for one or two stretchers. It was still the 27th Battalion R.A.P. Half-an-hour after the bombardment the wounded came pouring in. There are always a majority of walkers, though, when a stunt is on, many walk who should be stretcher cases. There is nothing else quite like the sight of a stream of wounded passing back. A man with a broken arm supports on the other side a man with a big flesh wound in the leg, another with wounded feet hobbles along with the aid of a pick handle. Many did not wait to have their wounds dressed at the R.A.P., they were so anxious to get away. I was kept busy for hours fixing up such cases. Many came through with no dressings at all or a very hasty one. We fixed up as many of these as we could, but the best we could do often was to send them on. At one time, when the rush was worst, the stretchers were lined up three abreast for almost a hundred yards along the road, but by means of constant work the squads managed to get the road cleared, and by 1 p.m. the worst of the rush was over. Shells came close enough to shake the place. I was going hard all the day of the stunt and the following night; though the worst of the rush was soon over, cases kept coming through in a constant stream. About midnight of the 5th the whole of the 5th Field Ambulance bearers were relieved and we trudged back to the M.D.S. beyond Vaulx."

From this relay a safe and easy carry to the Noreuil-Longatte sunken road linked up with the waggons.

---

[34] Pte. K. S. Cunningham, 5th Field Ambulance.

21. THE EXPOSED CARRY AT SECOND BULLECOURT
Shell bursting over bearers on their way back to Noreuil Valley,
4th May, 1917.
Aust. War Memorial Official Photo. No. E443.

22. SECTION OF THE COLLECTING POST IN THE SUNKEN ROAD, NOREUIL,
ON 7TH MAY, 1917, DURING THE SECOND BATTLE OF BULLECOURT
Aust. War Memorial Official Photo. No. E514. *To face p. 150.*

23. The "forward" advanced dressing station in front of Vaulx-Vraucourt, near the head of Noreuil Valley

Aust. War Memorial Official Photo. No. E591.

In this battle the horsed-waggons played an unusually important part. The circuit was controlled and carried through with great coolness, judgement and courage, relieving the bearers of a heavy additional carry. Its work is recorded by the Commanding Officer (Lieut.-Colonel J. J. Black) as follows:—

Horsed-waggon circuit

Horsed-waggons. "The transport officer (Captain J. H. B. Brown), moved from M.D.S. at 3 a.m. with ten ambulance waggons and three G.S. waggons, each fitted to carry five stretchers. He posted a waggon some 200 yards short of the Noreuil-Longatte road, in about half-an-hour the rush of stretcher cases commenced and the waggons moved right up to the road. From that time till about 4 p.m. the waggons loading at this point were able to take away stretcher cases as fast as they arrived though they were fully extended to do so. The waggons carried to A.D.S. and returned. The post was shelled at times severely but only one horse was wounded. At 4 p.m. the rush subsided somewhat. The G.S. waggons were withdrawn to A.D.S. and the post moved back as the risk of keeping it forward was not now justified. At 8 p.m. on the 4th, a complete relief of horses and waggons was made. In all, horsed-transport was used from nine field ambulances of all four Divisions—a total of 5 sergeants, 50 drivers, 94 horses, 12 waggons, and 14 G.S. waggons."

After the first day no difficulty was experienced in this circuit in keeping pace with the bearers.

The nebulous function of the advanced dressing station is seen by frequent reference to it as "the A.D.S. so-called"—a matter of some interest from the point of view of medical field technique. In effect this A.D.S. became a motor ambulance loading post and bearer reserve, with provision for holding, in emergency, a few cases. The circuit behind it extended only a mile and a half, with little danger and no delay.

Advanced dressing station

The course of events in this combined station is described by the respective Commanding Officers (Lieut.-Colonels J. H. Phipps and A. H. Moseley) as follows:—

Main dressing station

Walking Wounded. 5th Field Ambulance: "At 6 a.m. a rush of wounded set in and 600 were cleared by noon the same day and 1,534 till midnight. During the 3rd-8th 868 sick and 3,508 wounded were cleared. Six motor-lorries and four motor-buses cleared from M.D.S. to C.C.S. Grévillers. At Decauville-tramway entraining-point at Vaulx, two Red Cross trucks were available as well as others; trains ran at regular times to detraining point outside Bapaume where tent cover for

100 patients and medical comforts were maintained by 3rd Field Ambulance."

Stretcher Cases. 6th Field Ambulance: "Stretcher cases began to arrive at 7 a.m. and came steadily all night of 3rd-4th. All patients were housed and none kept waiting for cars to C.C.S. 720 passed through by 7 p.m."

Visiting this station at 7 a.m. on May 3rd the D.D.M.S. (Colonel Manifold) found the arrangements

"excellent. The 5th Field Ambulance had two tent sub-divisions with one large and three small hospital marquees (new pattern) in a continuous stretch, opening one into another, also one marquee for Q.M. stores, one for buffet.... I ordered the large store tent to be pitched for men who were waiting and that two sets of A. & D. books should be going at different ends. I ordered up a tent division from the 3rd Field Ambulance to work in another tent.

"The 6th Field Ambulance had ... for stretcher cases two hospital marquees (large) and one (small) for dressing tent, and large marquee for waiting cases.... I ordered up a fourth tent sub-division to assist the other three. The 7th Field Ambulance Headquarters were here with all bearer divisions forward and one tent sub-division in the event of an advance."

Motor Ambulance Convoy

As in every Australian battle on the Western Front, the British motor ambulance convoy played its part without default.

General Howse, who watched the evacuation on the 3rd at the advanced waggon post, "expressed great satisfaction, and said it went like clockwork."

The flow of wounded from the front line eased a little on May 4th but on the 5th the rush recommenced. Some squads had worked unrelieved for 48 hours.[35] The chief trouble was due to the length of the bearer carry. Relays were formed, but any halt on the route involved great risk. On the 5th the officer in charge, Colonel Black, reported that a complete relief was urgent. This was provided by the Deputy-Director who called on the 4th Division units. A British field ambulance of the 11th Division lent a hand and readjustments were made at the aid-posts.[36] By the 6th regular

May 4-8

---

[35] Colonel Manifold records a report to him of a bearer who had traversed forty-two miles without respite. Many squads, without relief, made fifteen double trips or more.

[36] The disposition of the bearers in the line on the 5th was as follows. *First R.A.P. Group*, 14 squads. *Second*, 9. *Third*, 6. *First relay*, 4. *Collecting post*, 6, with 2 in reserve and 2 at the waggon post. From 15 to 18 squads were held in reserve at the Noreuil-Longatte sunken road.

twenty-four hour reliefs were arranged, and later the bearers served 24 hours on and 48 hours off.

In the attack on Bullecourt on May 7th many Gordon Highlanders, Royal Welch, and Devonshire troops passed through the Anzac stations. Satisfaction in this assistance was mutual and cordial.[87]

Relief
The A.D.M.S. 2nd Division (Colonel Sutton) continued to direct evacuation until May 9th when orders were issued for relief of the 2nd by the 5th Division. Colonel Hearne took charge on the 10th. By this time the scheme of clearance from the front was well organised and the medical problem caused no undue concern. The casualties from the counter-attack on the 15th were cleared by routes formed on the left flank.

The A.A.M.C. casualties during the period are shown hereunder. The question whether, from the military point of view, heavy casualties are justified in such rescue work is of interest. At this time, and again when much heavier losses occurred at the end of the year, General Howse called for report and comment—the reinforcement rate for the medical service did not allow for such wastage. From the point of view of commanders in the field the saving of stretcher cases was chiefly a matter of morale—from the point of view of man-power it was expensive.

TABLE II.—Battle casualties in A.A.M.C. April 11-May 17.

	K.I.A.	D. of W.	Wounded	Total
1st Div.	8	6	58	72
2nd	14	3	59	76
4th	5	1	26	32
5th	4	7	43	54
Totals	31	17	186	234

In addition the ambulance diaries record that many bearers with minor wounds were treated in their own units.

---

[87] Maj.-Gen. T. H. Shoubridge, Commanding 7th Division, in conveying to Headquarters, 2nd Aust. Div., his own appreciation, forwarded also a letter from the Brigadier of the 22nd Inf. Bde. (Brig.-Gen. J. Steele): "Will you be so good as to convey to the 2nd Aust. Division my great appreciation of, and thanks for, the work done by their Medical Staff and Field Ambulances in assisting in the evacuation of wounded of this Brigade during the recent attack on Bullecourt. The whole of this Brigade are most grateful for their assistance."

Shelling of M.D.S. During the relief of the 5th Division the M.D.S. was involved in heavy shelling with casualties among personnel, patients, and transport, and serious dislocation of work. The 6th Field Ambulance moved back to Beugnâtre, and the walking wounded station to a point three-quarters of a mile in rear of the position shelled. Here, however, it was again shelled, and on May 8th was relieved by the 8th Field Ambulance.[38]

The proportion of stretcher cases to walking wounded in this battle was exceptionally high. As a feat in evacuation these operations were indeed among the most spectacular and successful of any undertaken by the Australian service.

Most of the Australian wounded were received at Grévillers; between May 3rd and May 9th No. 3 A.C.C.S. passed through a total of 2,545 casualties. The Deputy-Director

Casualty clearing station

I Anzac was informed by the D.M.S., Fifth Army that "the operating surgeons at the C.C.S. were greatly struck with the admirable condition in which the wounded reached them."

The sick rate in the spring was less by some 50 per cent. than in the winter. For reasons already discussed the improvement was not fully maintained. The detailed

Health of the troops, March-May

analysis of causes of wastage in *Chapter XVII* should be studied in relation to the conditions described.

Trench fever first received official recognition early in 1917 but appears at this time chiefly as "P.U.O." Nephritis gave some concern. Throughout the period "shell shock" was notably inconspicuous.

During these operations poison gas (phosgene) was freely used by the enemy, entirely as shell gas. On May 16th Colonel

Poison gas

Manifold records 50 cases under treatment, "the first time this Corps has ever suffered from more than a stray gas shell case."

---

[38] This attack on the medical units, as also shelling and machine-gun fire on the ambulance bearers throughout the operation, was probably in some measure deliberate. Stretcher parties were certainly shelled. There was, however, little resentment on the spot. Mingling as they did with other parties, the bearers formed a mixed target. The M.D.S. was intentionally pushed back by the enemy—as is clear from the repetition of the shelling. The explanation current at the time (recorded by Pte. O. R. Dunstan, 3rd Field Ambulance) was that the British had shelled a German Ambulance train—this being brought about by the fact that a British aeroplane had been fired at by infantrymen who were travelling in the train—he reported to the British artillery, who on his direction shelled the train.

The peculiar delayed effects of phosgene caused some curious problems in treatment and prognosis. These are dealt with elsewhere.[39] It may be noted here however that recognition of the need for a special diagnostic centre, and the field diagnosis "N.Y.D. gas," were the result of experiences in the gas centres of the field units during this time.

The Australian formations had occupied continuously some part of the front since their arrival in France and had been in some of the fiercest fighting of the war. A prolonged rest had been promised and now was pressed for by General Birdwood. The moment was opportune, and, at the end of May the 1st, 2nd and 5th Divisions went into billets for training and recuperation in the pleasant country behind Albert.

Relief of Australian Divisions

From time to time, in relation both to major spheres of action and to those of minor or only local concern, some special part of the machinery for maintaining man-power, some group of persons engaged serving the Army in medicine, stands out as notably promoting the purpose in view. Certain features of Australian experience at this time invite comment in this respect.

Comment and elucidation

The period of the British spring offensive marks a definite stage of advance in the treatment of the wounded soldier, the result of experimental and clinical research in wound surgery and wound treatment, implemented by improved methods at the front in the employment of field medical units.

1. Improved methods

The Casualty Clearing Stations. We find more surgical teams and improved surgical methods; with a correspondingly greater proportion of operations, and improved results therefrom. The study of these matters—which rank with the great things of the war—belongs elsewhere.[40]

Field Technique. The influence of this technical progress can be discerned at the periphery—in the field medical units. Thus, during April, Colonel S. Maynard-Smith, the Consulting Surgeon, Fifth Army, demonstrated the Thomas knee-splint in the first-aid treatment of fractured femurs. Methods of *réchauffement*, of first-aid technique, and of sustainment were more exactly taught and practised. To offset the dreadful transport journeys of March and April the exhaust pipes of motor ambulance waggons were used to warm the interior of the vehicles.

---

[39] In *Vol. III*.

[40] *Chapters xii and xiii.* It may be noted here that during the Arras offensive (April 9 to May 31) over 90,000 wounded passed through the clearing stations of First, Third and Fifth Armies, of whom some 20 per cent. were operated upon. There was a large fall in the incidence of gas-gangrene, sepsis, and secondary haemorrhage. (Sir A. Bowlby, in *The British Official Medical History, Surgery, Vol. I, p. 221.*)

The Field Hospital. In the moves of wounded men during the advance in March and April the conditions of transport were often such as to compel the "advanced" stations to fill the part commonly assigned to the "main" stations. A result of this experience was to push forward the field hospital, whether as an "A.D.S." or an "M.D.S."

A more elusive and curious interest and significance attaches to the move, at the instance of "Army," of the main field hospital to Vaulx. The real interest of the failure by the D.M.S., Fifth Army, while striving to ensure that surgical treatment should be *cito et jucunde,* to observe the precept, *tuto,* does not lie in any question as to the propriety of his interference or as to the justification of running the risk, but in the fact that *it served no real purpose.* The following entries in the diary of the D.D.M.S., I Anzac Corps point the moral of much narrative in previous chapters and suggest an interest in those to come. "*May 13th,* D.M.S. asked that we might utilise the A.D.S. at Vaulx for wounded and pass them right through from there. This was impossible owing to shell-fire . . . but I agreed to use a station still further forward, namely, the Collecting Post (*sic*) at C.20 (in front of Vaulx), and to send the wounded direct back to C.C.S. and not utilise A.D.S. or M.D.S. at all. This virtually turned the C.C.S. into M.D.S., and was a step towards the C.C.S. discharging its proper functions. With the C.C.S. within five miles of the firing line there was no necessity to have an M.D.S. or any other post intervening. *May 20th.* Rode out with A.D.M.S., 5th Division to see M.D.S. and arrange for the opening of what could be called the M.D.S. at C.20, where two cupolas had been completed."

The medical service gained regard and status in the army by efficiency and devotion in two spheres of duty—related and even overlapping, but quite distinct in their purpose. These **2. Rescue work** were, its duty in the service of humanity, and its duty in the service of war. The events of the Battles of Bullecourt are a milestone in the history of the Medical Service with the A.I.F., through the fact that, on this small stage, its work of rescue caught for a moment the limelight commonly reserved for major performers. The commendations of the work of the stretcher-bearers, regimental and ambulance, were spontaneous and remarkable. Bullecourt gained for the ambulance bearers two important things: notably increased respect from their military comrades, and a greater measure of personal self-regard. These were to stand them well in the more terrible and prolonged testing of Third Ypres.[41]

TABLE III.—Battle-casualties in the A.I.F. during the Bullecourt fighting: presented by periods.

	Killed in Action	Died of Wounds	Wounded (inc. Gas)	Prisoners of War	Total
11 Apr. ..	825	32	1,059	1,275	3,191
12 Apr.-2 May	470	258	1,366	412	2,506
3 May-4 May	990	76	2,754	38	3,858
5 May-9 May	469	180	2,003	12	2,664
10 May-17 May	259	139	1,156	9	1,563
Totals	3,013	685	8,338	1,746	13,782

[41] These commendations were not only official—as from the Army Commander, and his D.M.S., and the Corps Divisional Commanders—but from Staff Officers, artillery observers, and so forth.

TABLE IV.—The same showing relative percentages and ratios.

	Killed	Wounded and gassed (incl. d. of wounds)	Prisoners of War	Ratio of killed to wounded
11 Apr.	25·86	34·19	39·95	1 : 1·36
12 Apr.-2 May	18·76	64·80	16·44	1 : 3·45
3-4 May	25·66	73·35	0·99	1 : 2·86
5-9 May	17·61	81·94	0·45	1 : 4·65
10-17 May	16·57	82·86	0·57	1 : 5·00

NOTE.—The figures given in these two tables are based on the records kept by the Australian Section of 3rd Echelon, B.E.F., finalised to include all "missing." The terrible character of the proportions of killed to wounded and died of wounds reflects accurately the nature of the fighting. In the battles of April 11 and May 3-4 men who "died of wounds" died for the most part without rescue. See in this connection *p. 787.*

CHAPTER VIII

THE FLANDERS OFFENSIVE: THE BATTLE OF MESSINES

IN this important battle, the first blow in the third (and last) of the Allied offensives of attrition, the A.I.F. was represented by two Divisions—the 3rd,[1] which with the 25th British and the New Zealand Divisions had for some time formed the II Anzac Corps; and the 4th, which had been brought to strength and joined the Corps for this battle.

In this terrible campaign Great Britain took up the part sustained in the first phase of the war by France and Russia. During six months she maintained, without

The Flanders Offensive,[2] June 7th-Nov. 10th respite and almost unaided, an unceasing "pressure" on the Western Front. The full involvements of the task unfolded themselves only during the campaign, in which battle after battle was launched under conditions for the most part shockingly adverse to the attacking side.

Military plan and methods Haig's intentions in this campaign are thus summed by the Australian Official Historian:—[3]

"He envisaged a return to the principles of the Somme offensive, a combination of 'wearing-down' and 'breaking-through' tactics, but with improved methods for the former and a more definite strategic aim for the latter. When the other generals at the conference [at Paris on May 4th] agreed that 'it is now a question of wearing down and exhaust-

---

[1] *See Vol. I, p. 515.* This formation, raised and partly trained in Australia, arrived in England in June and July 1916 and during the succeeding months was organised and trained under Major-General J. Monash on Salisbury Plain. It arrived in France in November 1916 and was put in the II Anzac Corps. Its A.D.M.S. Colonel A. T. White had commanded No. 2 Australian Stationary Hospital at the Dardanelles; the D.A.D.M.S. (Major J. H. Anderson) had served from the outbreak of war in field units. Of the officers commanding the Field Ambulances—9th, 10th and 11th—two had seen service in the South African War.

[2] Beginning with the Battle of Messines, June 7-14, these operations comprised officially nine battles, with two subsidiary actions. The Australian force was engaged in seven of these.

[3] In *Vol. IV, p. 553.*

ing the enemy's resistance,' it was surely his insistence which caused them to add: 'and, if and when this is achieved, to exploit it to the fullest extent possible.'"

Strategic objective. A thrust at Bruges through Roulers from the apex of the Ypres Salient would threaten the German communications in the north and would moreover threaten the submarine base at Zeebrugge, then a matter of immense importance, and would fulfil the first requirement of Haig's strategy. His second object—attrition by killing, maiming, capture, and the creation of fear and "moral" depression—would be effected chiefly by exploiting the Allied superiority in artillery. As the campaign progressed an increasing prominence was thrust upon the medical service as a factor for success in the process of wearing down.

Tactical objective. The German line before Ypres lay on a semicircle of ridges nowhere very high but of great tactical importance in that low country. This range had been the scene of hard-fought battles in the first year of the war. To the south, where it ran into the British line, it buttressed a German salient in front of Wytschaete and Messines. To eliminate this salient and its buttress as prelude to a general advance in front of Ypres, the battle of Messines was fought on June 7th-14th by the British Second Army.[4] The objective in this battle was the German reserve line along the chord of the salient beyond the Messines heights.

In its thoroughness and attention to detail the Second British Army reflected the character of its Commander, Sir Herbert Plumer. Since the First Battle of Ypres its staff had studied the methods of attrition warfare, and these were exploited to the utmost in the Battle of Messines.[5] The reflection of these methods in the work of the Second Army Medical Service as seen in this battle gives the *motif* for this chapter.

Battle of Messines: General preparations

Preparations for the battle had been in hand since 1915, and since early in 1917 had been pressed with immense energy, and with no thought save to ensure complete success. Nineteen immense mines had been prepared[6] and the artillery offensive

[4] The importance attached by Field-Marshal Haig to the human element (as it may be termed) of his strategy *i.e.*, the destruction of the German man-power and morale, in contrast with the physical—the capture of positions and high ground—is shown by his great anxiety lest the enemy should abandon the ridge to him without a fight by a premature retirement, a course actually proposed to the German Army Group Commander (Crown Prince Rupprecht of Bavaria) by his Chief of Staff.

[5] This battle has been held by Sir John Monash to be the type and exemplar of the "set piece" battle of which he himself became the most notable exponent.

[6] 25,000 feet of gallery were driven in these immense operations and over a million pounds of explosive was used. No. 1 Australian Tunnelling Company played an important part in this work (see *Australian Official History, Vol. IV, Appendix No. 1*). Australian medical officers were attached to these units as R.M.O's but took no part in the special rescue work associated with mine warfare, which was of a highly specialised and technical kind. It may however be noted that the most important

7

worked out with unexampled accuracy. An elaborate system of roads and railways, broad and narrow gauge, served every part of the proposed battle-front. On his side the enemy had been hardly less assiduous. His defences included a series of concrete blockhouses covering each line of entrenchments.

Plans for the attack had been worked out by every branch and in each formation with a like exactitude and attention to detail, but perhaps in none so fully as in the 3rd Division. The **Second Army Battle Plan** first objective ("Black Line") lay just beyond the zone of the minefields. A second wave would pass through or "leap-frog"[7] the first and move against the second (main) objective—the Green Line—broadly, the Oosttaverne line at the bottom of the eastern slope of Messines Heights.

The battle was fought by the X and IX British, and II Anzac Corps, in that order from the north. The II Anzac Corps objective was 1,000 yards of the Oosttaverne line, and the **Order of battle** Corps started with its right just north of Ploegsteert Wood. The first and main advance would be made by three divisions, 25th British on left, New Zealand in centre, 3rd Australian on right. The 4th Australian Division would leap-frog the 25th British and New Zealand Divisions and together with the left of the 3rd would capture the II Anzac section of the Oosttaverne line.[8]

In this battle there will be seen in an incomplete stage the technical and administrative evolution in the medical service which, with its reflection in field methods, was **Medical arrangements. General** to reach its zenith at the beginning of 1918. In the very elaborate medical arrangements for "Messines" every possible factor in the problem of collecting, clearing, treating and evacuating casualties, was foreseen and exactly provided for. As it turned out, "events" were in so close accord with "arrangements" that, as an exposition of military medical technique, an account of the medical features of the battle might be based on either. This, however, is far from saying that the methods adopted are suited to general

---

problem was that of dealing with poisoning by carbon monoxide against which the gas-mask was powerless. In the *British Official History* (*Diseases in the War, Vol. II*) a very full study of the problems connected with mine warfare sums up the essential factor to success as exact organisation, and the training of the special staff (and of all personnel engaged) in the use of the oxygen apparatus—which, it is emphasised, must be fool-proof and kept under constant inspection. The Schafer method of artificial respiration was found most satisfactory.

[7] This was becoming a usual method of advance and was adopted for medical units. See sketch map at *p. 685*, and diagram at *p. 686*.

[8] The other British Corps each contained four Divisions; their tactical schemes were generally similar.

application, or were even in the best interests of the wounded at the time.

Second Army. Treatment and transport
In a report by the D.M.S. (Surgeon-General R. Porter) to G.H.Q. the principles adopted by his staff were summed up as follows:—

"The scheme . . . for the evacuation of casualties from the area of operations followed a principle previously laid down—that the A.D's. M.S. of Divisions were responsible for the evacuation of wounded from the fighting line to the Corps main dressing stations and the Corps collecting posts. The D.D's.M.S. of the Corps were responsible for the evacuation from these to the casualty clearing stations. From this point the evacuation to the base was carried out under the direction of the D.M.S."

Army evacuation to the Base was directed chiefly to Boulogne, but trains ran also to Calais and Rouen. The three Army Corps cleared to casualty clearing stations at Proven (two), Remy Siding (three), Bailleul (five, including No. 1 A.C.C.S.) and Steenwerck (one—No. 2 A.C.C.S.). Each station "expanded" to accommodate 1,000 patients, and two days before the battle each was reinforced by the Director-General with surgical teams. A motor ambulance convoy was allotted to each Corps, and, with thirty lorries for walking wounded, was put under the Corps Deputy-Director. Co-operation of Army with Corps, and of these with Divisions, was promoted by a system of regular "consultations," a method brought to perfection in this Army.

A "Memorandum on the treatment of wounds in regimental aid-posts and field ambulances" was sent to all medical officers concerned. Under appropriate headings this gave exact instructions on the immediate treatment of wounds and of the wounded, in accordance with the principles then in vogue. These instructions are epitomised hereunder.[9]

1. Dressing of Wounds. Picric acid instead of Iodine (to prevent blistering). Eusol as "a standard lotion." Gauze cut in squares in "flamed" tea-tins.

2. Minor Cases. Those that will not require dressing at casualty clearing station should have their Card envelope marked "C" with time and date.

3. Operations. These to be mainly restricted to arrest of haemorrhage and removal of shattered limbs.

---

[9] A detailed account of these technical matters will be found in *Chapters xi and xii*.

4. *Haemorrhage.* Tourniquets to be removed at M.D.S. or an orderly to accompany the case. Haemorrhage to be arrested by (a) Ligature; (b) failing this by pressure forceps; (c) by cone shaped gauze packing to the depth of the wound. Anaesthetics to be given only exceptionally; fluids to be given freely, morphia sparingly.

5. *Amputations.* Only for completely shattered limbs; surface to be smeared with B.I.P. To be retained for twenty-four hours before sending to C.C.S.

6. *Fractures.* Thomas splints should be applied as the initial treatment for all fractures of the femur. . . . if possible in the regimental aid-post. To be applied over the boot and extension applied to the end of the splint.

7. *Abdominal Wounds.* To be sent to C.C.S. with least possible delay. "Large doses of morphia (more than ¼ gr) increase operation mortality." Patients (it was stated) "travel more comfortably in semi-prone position than on the back."

8. *Wounds of Thorax.* Except during gas attacks severe cases should be retained at the M.D.S. and kept absolutely at rest till shock etc., have subsided. If they are bleeding or air is entering freely, to be closed by suture and plugged.

9. *Shock.* "Plenty of blankets" to be applied—under and over. If profoundly shocked, to be retained and resuscitated before moving. Hypertonic saline (Sodium, Potassium, and Calcium Chloride) Camphor hypodermically.

10. *Gassed Cases.* Absolute rest is essential. Outer clothing to be removed to prevent further inhalation of gas. If badly gassed, venesection (10 to 18 ozs). Restlessness (if conscious) to be dealt with by ¼ gr. of morphia. Emetic of salt and water (early). If collapsed—warmth; and continuous oxygen if cyanosed and pallid collapse.

11. *Morphia.* Time and amount to be noted on Field Medical Card.

It was laid down that all ranks should wear brassards. To meet the unusual conditions of the battle the Deputy-Director, II Anzac (Colonel C. Mackie Begg), employed somewhat novel methods. In particular the field ambulances, normally divisional units, were (in effect) pooled; they were resolved into their component sections, and these used to serve a very elaborate scheme, the success of which would depend on close and continued co-operation of all concerned—who embraced every branch of the Army.

In II Anzac Corps

A memorandum ("Medical arrangements, II Anzac Offensive Operations") issued early in May sets out the general plan of evacuation as follows:—

"In the proposed scheme the principle of working with one Corps

Main Dressing Station has had to be modified by the fact that the area is divided by Hill 63 into two equal parts. In order to fall in with the general scheme of traffic control[10], it is necessary to establish two corps main dressing stations. One of these will deal with cases from the north, the other from the south of Hill 63. The line of communication from the north area will be to casualty clearing stations in Bailleul, from the South to Trois Arbres."

"Medical arrangements" were based on a very exact separation of stretcher cases from the "walking wounded" and sick.[11] Beginning at the regimental aid-posts this segregation was carried through combined corps main dressing stations and collecting posts to the casualty clearing stations of which one was set apart for the "slightly wounded."[12] Corps rest stations for sick, and for very slight wounds and "shell shock,"[13] and also a corps gas station, were formed from existing divisional stations.

Divisional responsibility was defined as follows:—

"Responsibility for the conveyance of wounded to the R.A.P's rests with battalions and brigades. The arrangements necessary to reinforce the small regimental establishments should be made before the action. . . . From advanced dressing stations cases are conveyed by divisional transport to the corps main dressing stations where divisional responsibility ceases.

"*Walking cases.* Special provision must be made for these. They must on no account be allowed to enter the A.D.S. Divisional collecting posts should be formed as convenient, not near an A.D.S. Walking cases will be fed, dressed if necessary, and sent by returning empty transport, 60 cm. railway, and lorries. The routes for walking cases to be well marked."

All records were to be kept at the "Corps Main Dressing Station" where also the anti-tetanic serum would be given.

The main dressing stations of II Anzac were placed at

---

[10] This vital matter of road control devolved on the Quartermaster-General's Branch and the department of the Provost-Marshal.

[11] Readers of *Vol. I* will recall the peculiar importance attached to such "classification" in the scheme of evacuation from Gallipoli.

[12] The subsequent report on the Second Army's medical arrangements says that this one "did not prove satisfactory and was therefore done away with."

[13] A practical and common sense classification of these cases distinguished two types:—

(1) Those with obvious shell shock—to be evacuated to C.C.S. with diagnosis of "N.Y.D." Shell shock.

(2) Doubtful cases, including exhaustion, nervousness and malingering—to be sent to rest station diagnosed as exhaustion.

Westhof Farm (left sub-sector) for the New Zealand and 25th British Divisions, and Pont d'Achelles (right sub-sector) for the 3rd Division. The 4th Division, advancing later in front of the centre and left would naturally be served mainly by the left station.[14] On May 25th the officer commanding the 9th Field Ambulance, Lieut.-Colonel F. A. Maguire, (3rd Division) was seconded to the Corps to organise (and command for the operations) a Corps combined "dressing station" and "collecting post," which was to replace a Divisional station already established about 8,000 yards behind the front line near the main Bailleul-Armentières road. No. 2 A.C.C.S., to which its cases were cleared, was something less than a mile away. Personnel was provided by allocating one tent sub-division from each of the six Australian field ambulances with a New Zealand bearer sub-division and a fatigue party of 60 infantry.

C.M.D.S.
Pont d'Achelles

Colonel Begg laid down as "the primary principle for successful evacuation" that of "saving transport," by forward regimental aid-posts "to save regimental stretcher-bearers," and by planning routes for medical stations "so far as possible at right angles backward from the line of advance—to save ambulance transport." The use of "Corps main dressing stations," he stated, was "to save motor ambulance convoy cars." It lay with the Assistant Directors to interpret these principles into "arrangements." The 3rd Australian Division was peculiarly fitted to deal with the problem of this type of battle. The personality of its Commander, Major-General Monash, dominated every department. With a genius for organising he combined a no less remarkable flair for lucid exposition and for co-ordinating the work of his staff officers. He saw his command as a machine whose several parts interlocked, and none was held to be undeserving of his direct attention. The A.D.M.S. (Colonel

The Divisions

---

[14] In this narrative, however, we confine attention to arrangements and events in the southern sub-sector (3rd Division) with a brief excursion to the advanced zone occupied by the 4th. The C.M.D.S. at Westhof Farm through which passed almost all the wounded from the 4th Australian Division was commanded by a New Zealand officer (Lieut.-Colonel E. J. O'Neill). In this sub-sector until June 9 the clearance of wounded was controlled by the A.D.M.S., New Zealand Division (Colonel D. J. McGavin). Events here are very fully described in *The New Zealand Medical Services in the Great War, 1914-18*, the author of which, Colonel A. D. Carbery, was at the time D.A.D.M.S. in the Division.

Map No. 4

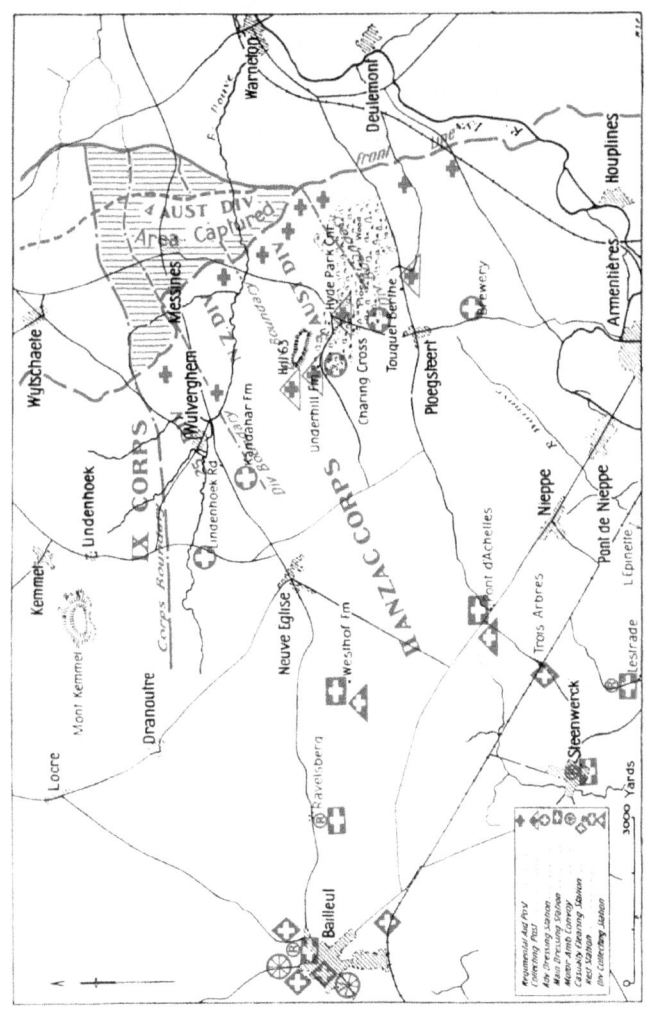

THE BATTLE OF MESSINES—MEDICAL ARRANGEMENTS OF II ANZAC CORPS

A. T. White) was not only permitted but required to attend staff conferences in any matter that concerned his department. The formation was fortunate also in the fact that its medical units had been trained by the D.A.D.M.S. (Major J. H. Anderson) on lines laid down to secure uniformity, and (as he said),

"they had not had time to develop individuality. This made possible the interchange of sections."

Regimental. Colonel White's "scheme for *Magnum Opus*" was issued on May 21st. Eighty "other ranks" were allotted to assist the regimental bearers. Regimental medical officers had been required to certify the efficiency of their personnel and to keep a file of instructions which they passed to their successor. Four regimental aid-posts were built for the battle, not to be occupied till zero day.[15] These were fully stocked, in particular each with two Thomas splints.[16]

The names of the advanced posts on this front bring an echo of "unhappy far off things and battles long ago." The central advanced dressing station was at "Charing Cross," the divisional collecting posts at "Hyde Park Corner" and Touquet Berthe. These were south of Ploegsteert Wood and all adjoined the 60 cm. railway and well-made roads. The dressing station had ample accommodation for personnel and was fully equipped for dressing cases under good conditions. Tent sub-divisions were allotted to these advanced stations from all three ambulances.

An unusual plan was adopted for controlling and co-ordinating the work of the several treatment centres and transport circuits. The commanding officers of the 10th and 11th Field Ambulances (Lieut.-Colonels J. S. Purdy and M. H. Downey) were relieved of other duties and put in charge of the bearer and transport circuits respectively, working directly under the A.D.M.S.

Advanced treatment centres

Transport circuits

---

[15] With the help of the engineers these were strongly built to provide dressing room, sleeping room for two officers (for whom the scheme provided) and a resting room for the ambulance bearer squads to be attached.

[16] It is believed that this was the first occasion in the war that exact provision was made for the use of this splint in the aid-posts. After demonstration of the splint in first aid by Major Meurice Sinclair, R.A.M.C., the D.A.D.M.S. tried them in the front line with dummies. These experiments proving successful, he obtained supplies by visiting as many advanced depots as possible and getting a few from each. Two were sent to each R.A.P. at the last minute. Dressing stations held supplies and each car had one to replace those sent down with the case; the rule of exchange was the same as for blankets.

Bearer Circuit. In this were comprised all duties relating to hand carry from R.A.P. "up to but not including the A.D.S." The bearer divisions were pooled and exactly organised to work in shifts from the R.A.P's. Reliefs and reserves were held at Charing Cross. Routes were surveyed and marked for night and day.[17]

Transport Circuit—"A.D.S. to C.M.D.S." The ambulance waggons and allotted transport were pooled and controlled by a special executive officer (the Dental Officer 11th Field Ambulance) from a central park near Pont d'Achelles, where also the officer-in-charge had his office. Two transport circuits for casualties by road and rail respectively were arranged in addition to transport by "returning empties." That by road ran direct to Pont d'Achelles. The train service centred on the "Connaught Siding" conveniently placed for walking wounded. So early as May 1st the officer-in-charge reported that

"all officers are making themselves acquainted with the positions and routes in the advanced area, and ambulance cars are being sent over and are familiarising themselves with the (ambulance) routes."

Supplies. An exact scheme was arranged to provide the forward units with food, comforts, and dressings through returning transports. Water was sent in two gallon petrol tins in special carts.

Co-ordination. "The officers in command (in these special spheres and in the advanced stations) were directly under the A.D.M.S., and he was the medium of communication, except in trivial matters that could be settled direct."[18] The whole scheme was made automatic through bearer squads and transport drivers, whereby all medical stations from R.A.P. to C.M.D.S., were linked up in both directions. Thus the D.A.D.M.S. at Divisional Headquarters had a dual control on the course of events.

---

[17] These were exactly prescribed by the A.D.M.S. in his orders (which occupied six pages of foolscap): Thus from "Anscroft Avenue" R.A.P., the following routes were prescribed:
Stretcher cases. Seaforth tramline—Corps tramline (or wheeled stretcher carriage)—Charing Cross A.D.S. Alternative Routes (1) Wheeled stretchers along Cook's Way—Messines Road—Hyde Park Corner—Charing Cross A.D.S. (2). (If not used for incoming troops) Hand carriage Anscroft Avenue—Charing Cross A.D.S.
Walking cases. Cook's Way—Messines Road—Hyde Park Corner Divisional Collecting Post. Alternative Routes—Anscroft Avenue—Hyde Park Corner D.C. Post.
[18] Report by Major J. H. Anderson, D.A.D.M.S. 3rd Division.

The Move Up. Medical stations were manned only a few days before zero. Fifty per cent. of the men were in position at midnight of June 5th-6th, the remainder by 11 p.m. on the 6th.

The Battle occupied officially eight days, June 7th to 14th and, with minor vicissitudes, went "according to plan." Over the whole front long before sunset on the 7th the main objective had

Battle of Messines

been occupied. In one terrific onslaught the German salient from Hooge to the Lys was bitten off; 7,000 prisoners were taken. Hard fighting followed on the 8th, but the capture was confirmed and on the 14th the German force fell back on the Lys. A table at *page 180* shows the total British losses and the comparative incidence of casualties in the British and Anzac Corps. The weather throughout was hot, with thunderstorms on the 7th and 12th.

Zero hour was 3.10 a.m.—the first streak of dawn. From 7 p.m. of the 6th until

II Anzac Corps

2 a.m. of the 7th the II Anzac lines of approach were drenched with shell-gas so that the battalions of the 3rd Division reached their take off lines barely on time.[10] At 3.10 a.m. the mines were set off and a creeping barrage loosed, behind which the first line advanced. Even to the attacking side "the earth seemed to vomit fire and was shaken as by an earthquake. The air screamed shells and above all was the roar of the guns. . . . It would be impossible to describe the inferno, or to conjecture the condition of the enemy lines under this hail of shot and shell."[20]

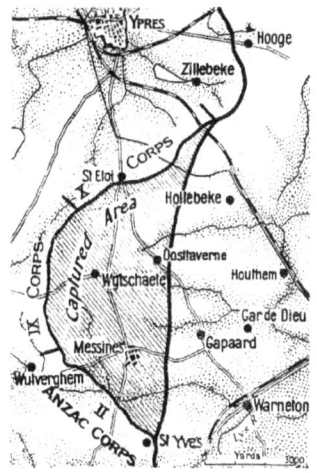

Area Captured in Battle of Messines.

By 8 a.m. on the Anzac front all the first objective (Green Line) had been captured. It was fully consolidated, and occupied in force. At 3.15 p.m. the 4th Australian Division "leap-frogged" the 25th British and the New Zealand and, with the left flank of the 3rd, moved on to take by hard hand-to-hand fighting the final objective of the II Anzac Corps, and (as it turned out) part of that of the IX Corps whose troops were too late on that flank. At nightfall the two Australian Divisions

---

[10] The gas was partly lethal ("Green Cross" and Phosgene), partly lachrymatory. All troops wore the small box respirator which had been issued early in 1917. This conferred adequate protection against the gasses then employed but made any heavy or prolonged exertion most distressing and any but the simplest actions almost impossible especially at night. An account of this episode illustrating the effect of gas as a weapon will be found in *Vol. III.*

[20] Captain R. C. Grieve, V.C., 37th Battalion, A.I.F.

held exactly half the whole battle line of Messines, and had sustained thirty per cent. of the total British casualties in wounded. Gaps were filled in the night. The 8th brought minor assaults, counter-attacks and more heavy casualties. From June 9th onwards both Divisions were employed in desultory fighting and consolidation. The battle ended with voluntary withdrawals of the Germans on June 10th and 12th to positions beyond the British objective.

Like the assault evacuation went "according to plan" on the whole front—the medical machine worked smoothly throughout.

Evacuation : Second Army

"The total number of wounded" (the D.M.S., Second Army—Surgeon-General R. Porter—reported to G.H.Q.) "was considerably less than was anticipated." The course of this stream of casualties must now rapidly be surveyed, from its source, in the stretcher cases collected by the regimental bearers of the 3rd and 4th Divisions and in the other wounded who fell out of the fighting and made their own way or were helped back, to its confluence with the general stream that moved to the Base.

We have to do first with the casualties from the gas barrage; and thereafter with two streams, "stretchers" and "walkers,"

3rd Australian Division : Collecting and Clearance

each including a proportion of "sitters" which, diverging at the regimental aid-posts, moved by their own routes and posts to converge and meet at Pont d'Achelles. In equal accord with the high-lights of the medical scheme the account of events might follow these or might focus in turn on the two zones. In so complex a web some confusion of time and place was unavoidable; and, since clearance is primarily movement, the natural course of narrative moves with the streams.

In terms of time (days) and of mass (casualties) the medical problem presents itself as follows :—

TABLE I.

	June 6	June 7	June 8	June 9-11	June 12-15	Total Wounded
3rd Div.	74	1,444	826	717	83	3,144
4th „	15	1,052	252	561	164	2,044
Gassed ..	16	214	65	128	10	433
Shell Shock	3	14	10	20	11	58
Total	108	2,724	1,153	1,426	268	5,679

The barrage of shell-gas, especially in Ploegsteert Wood,

disorganised the troops in their move up to the jumping-off tapes and interfered very greatly with medical work. Between 11 p.m. on the 6th and zero hour of the 7th (when the gas shelling ceased) the bearers carried under conditions that are described as "hellish and well-nigh unbearable." At "Charing Cross" for a time there was great confusion—

June 6th: The gas barrage

"All through the night of 6th-7th June the personnel had to work in gas masks. A large number of slightly gassed and walking cases rushed for shelter at the A.D.S., and made the work very difficult."

For a time this station was unable to cope with the casualties and the stream was diverted to "Underhill Farm" (New Zealand). In two hours "all was running smoothly and the decks cleared" for the wounded from the aid-posts who began to arrive at 4.30 a.m.[21]

Regimental, June 9th-15th. The collecting of wounded by regimental bearers, and the work of the R.M.O's, is for the most part unrecorded in the official documents. Their work must be judged chiefly on results, as seen in the task set by them to the ambulance squads, and reports by the treatment centres.

3rd Division. From the first advance casualties were collected to aid-posts with exceptional promptness, but, in spite of the rate at which they came through, the ambulance bearers easily coped with them. When the "Green Line" was captured "advanced aid-posts" were formed beyond the trench tramways, and here the squads were hard put to it to keep pace. There is particular as well as indirect proof that the regimental work was very well done. The C.C.S. reported that no casualties had been left out for long—which was perhaps partly due to the fact

---

[21] Official records (Australian Section 3rd Echelon, G.H.Q., B.E.F.) show that on June 6 and 7 the 3rd Division sustained 227 casualties from gassing, (but no deaths from "gas poisoning") distributed as follows:—9th Infantry Brigade 95; 10th, 31; 11th, 44; and Pioneers, Machine Gun Companies, Trench Mortar Batteries, Artillery and Engineer units 57. On the 8th 65 were gassed in this division and 52 on the 9th. In the 4th Division 3 are recorded as gassed on the 7th and 5 during the remainder of the operation. The Official Historian records "at least 500 men, most of them gassed, had been put out of action," and adds that "some estimates put the number as high as 1,000." The O.C. 11th Field Ambulance records 25 of his personnel "gassed" between 4th and 11th. The reason for this large discrepancy (which has far-reaching bearings both in the war and its aftermath) is discussed in *Vol. III.* (*See also pp. 693-4, 699* of the present volume.)

that the bearer squads helped to search the battlefield. At the A.D.S. many dressings could be franked through. The Thomas splint was used at all the R.A.P's and at least once was applied in a front line trench.

The regimental aid-posts behind the old front line were cleared with a celerity certainly not exceeded in any of the Australian battles. At 10.45 a.m. on the 7th the officer-in-charge of bearers reported:—

Stretcher cases: R.A.P. to A.D.S.

"Clearance from the R.A.P's to the A.D.S. proceeding well—quicker than can be cleared from the A.D.S.; train lines working well—all R.A.P's cleared a few minutes ago. Fifty gas cases at Touquet Berthe C.P. await clearance."

Arrangements were good, conditions favourable. Every aid-post was near a trench tramway, by which route "by far the greater number of casualties were cleared." The elaborate scheme of reliefs and routes was adhered to:—

"In clearing from the R.A.P. to A.D.S. each bearer captain kept to his own line. A squad of bearers was always at each aid-post and as these came down the same number at once set out. The men who brought down the case had a rest for food and went up again in their turn. When their tour of duty was over they went off to sleep. On the way back to the R.A.P. food was taken up to the ambulance squads there and medical stores to the R.M.O's. The trucks that took up food and water and munitions brought down the wounded."[22]

The advance on the right brought trials and some casualties, but broadly speaking in the 3rd Division the squads easily kept pace with the regimental bearers in front and with the ambulance waggons behind them.

Between the circuit of the field ambulance bearers and that of the ambulance waggons lay the advanced posts of treatment. By far the most casualties cleared by motor-transport passed through the Charing Cross A.D.S. It was in a direct line from the front to the main dressing station and though it was all among the guns it escaped—with warnings. Here all dressings were examined, splints adjusted, urgent haemorrhage dealt with,

The A.D.S. Charing Cross

---

[22] The statement is that of the D.A.D.M.S., Major J. H. Anderson.

and morphia given if necessary.[23] The arrangements for sustenance were fully adequate. The medical scheme made these advanced stations in a great measure autonomous—they were cleared and supplied automatically through the motor-transport circuit.

From 2 a.m. on June 2nd to midnight on the 11th 3,003 cases passed through the station, including 1,156 for the twenty-four hours beginning at 2 a.m. on the 7th.

Of this service and of the work of the A.D.S. the officer-in-charge, Lieut.-Colonel Downey, reported to Colonel A. T. White (the A.D.M.S.) that "it ran smoothly and without a hitch: motor-drivers and orderlies did splendid work." Colonel Downey's station at the Cawnpore lines was both motor ambulance park and medical supply depot, the former in charge of a special officer,[24] the latter of the Quartermaster 11th Field Ambulance (Captain J. F. S. Murray). Connaught siding on the 60 cm. railway near by had an ambulance officer in charge of clearance by this route. Little (it would seem) was required of the directing officer, the system of demand and supply being self-sufficient. Major Anderson's report says:—

3rd Division: Transport circuit

"The motor ambulance waggons were sent up from the transport park as required, the cars were pooled and ran in circuits, one always at the A.D.S. Departure of those in circuit from the controlling point depended on the arrival at the M.D.S. Every driver reported there the number of cases in sight at the A.D.S. and also at the park. Thus the transport officer knew if he could cut down or should add to the number in circuit.

"Supplies were sent in the same way. Blankets and stretchers were replaced at the M.D.S. The M.A.C. cars from C.C.S. unloaded at one side of the pile and the field ambulance cars from the A.D.S. uploaded at the other. Roads and arrangements allowed a straight run—everything came in from one side and went out at the other. The Q.M. of the forward area sent up his food, water and medical stores in this way. The A.D.S. could thus be supplied within an hour of demand."

During the operations over 2,100 walking wounded reached

---

[23] The part played in the medical scheme by this station was perhaps, of those we have seen, most like that filled on the Somme by Bécourt Château during the Pozières fighting, but with more concern for movement and less for treatment.

[24] The Dental Officer 11th Field Ambulance (Capt. H. C. D. Taunton) was detailed for this duty. In major battles dental officers filled at times such positions with distinction. *See for example p. 88 and Vol. I p. 307.*

Pont d'Achelles through the divisional collecting posts by the light railways with some help by returning empty waggons of supply, and some special vehicles.²⁵ From the R.A.P's the walking wounded, directed by bearers, made their way to the divisional collecting posts chiefly by trench trolley. The separation of the two streams (as required by the D.D.M.S.) was fairly well maintained. The posts for walking cases were, however,

The Walking Wounded 3rd Division

"placed near the A.D.S. as the Corps Collecting Post and Main Dressing Station were also together. This allowed ready reinforcement of personnel from one to the other and transfer." After zero "nearly all stretcher cases came to A.D.S. and walking cases to D.C.P's."

As always, the walkers took the safest route, and went by Hyde Park Corner. At the collecting posts dressings were adjusted and there were "hot drinks and something to eat." From here they went on foot to the light railway and so by train to the Connaught siding, 1,200 yards from the "Corps Collecting Post" at Pont d'Achelles.

By these two routes during the first four days of the battle some 3,000 wounded were cleared from the 3rd Division and transferred to Army Corps control.

The special and in some ways unusual conditions under which the 4th Division advanced—in front of the line gained by the New Zealand and 25th Divisions, which still maintained their positions behind it—gave a very different aspect to its medical experience, and were the cause of difficulties for which its own authorities were in no way responsible. (1) The Division took off from a new formed line some 1,500 yards in front of the old. (2) The advance went another 1,500 yards deep on a wide stretch of country. (3) Though the Division was to clear by its own bearers these were put under the A.D.M.S. New Zealand Division. Colonel Barber himself issued no special orders. (4) Regimental aid-posts and collecting of casualties were wholly under combatant control.

4th Australian Division

---

²⁵ It is recorded that the transport of casualties to the C.M.D.S. during this battle was "by walking, hand-carriage, wheeled-stretcher, horsed-ambulance, motor-ambulance, trench tram-line, 60 cm. railway line, broad-gauge line, returning empty transport (horsed and motor)."

24. THE ADVANCED DRESSING STATION AT "KANDAHAR FARM" DURING THE BATTLE OF MESSINES, 7TH JUNE 1917
The photograph was taken during the afternoon.

Aust. War Memorial Official Photo. No. E482.

To face p. 172.

25. THE A.D.S. ON THE MENIN ROAD, 20TH SEPTEMBER, 1917

The Walking Wounded A.D.S. was across the road. At this spot on the road Lieutenant-Colonels J. J. Nicholas and S. G. Gibbs were killed.

A drawing by Pte. A. S. H. Picking (5th F. Amb.) in "Abroad With the Fifth."

26. THE A.D.S. FOR WALKING WOUNDED, MENIN ROAD, 20TH SEPTEMBER, 1917

Aust. War Memorial Official Photo. No. E1909. *To face p. 173.*

When contact with ambulance bearers was indirect and *liaison* maintained through headquarters, the clearing of aid-posts was always imperfect; the maladjustments of this Division are not less instructive than the ultra-perfect arrangements in the 3rd.

June 7th. The R.M.O's formed new aid-posts well in advance of the "Black Line" (the objective of the first phase) but the old posts were retained for the New Zealand Division entrenched there. Between these two groups lay a wide stretch of battle-torn and well barraged country, and this tract became for a time a medical No-Man's Land. A more important cause of miscarriage was the novel front line feature, the German concrete "pill-box" whose tempting security led to disaster through the fact that their sites were known to the enemy and were always shelled.

The points of view respectively of the regimental medical officers and of the medical units are seen in the following reports:—

R.M.O. 47th Battalion (Captain J. T. Jones):—"June 7th. The M.O. moved forward with the C.O. and reached the right edge of Messines just after the attack was launched. Fighting was going on fiercely, and the party was met by a salvo of whizz-bangs. Search was made for a suitable R.A.P. Battalion Headquarters took a concrete pill-box. At one end was a wicker structure, banked up, which opened into a sap. . . . This was used as R.A.P. and the A.D.M.S. notified. . . The A.D.S. was built of concrete close to the front line and not used till the attack started. . . . Nearly all the wounded from the first attack and many of the earlier cases from the second were carried there by the regimental stretcher-bearers. . . .[26] The New Zealand Division had charge of evacuation . . . but no bearers arrived during the first night and wounded were carried back to the A.D.S. by regimental bearers or by passing fatigue parties. Casualties came through in a constant stream all night. . . . Next morning bearers of the 4th Division came forward in sufficient numbers to keep the R.A.P's clear. (Other R.A.P's—45th, 48th and 51st—were in front.) . . . In the afternoon the R.A.P. was hit, four ambulance bearers killed and others wounded with many casualties in the forward area. [The Officer] in charge of evacuation [declined] to send more bearers until another R.A.P. was formed in a safer locality. This action was strongly to be condemned, as the position of the R.A.P. is a matter over which the C.O. Battalion concerned has control, and the duty of the ambulance is to clear it."

In the night of the 8th-9th regimental bearers again carried

---

[26] The station thus described was in point of fact "Spring Street," one of the original regimental aid-posts; the A.D.S., Kandahar Farm, was 3,000 yards in rear.

through the New Zealand lines to the old R.A.P's. On the 9th the bearer squads cleared again under their sectional officers:—

> *A Bearer Captain* (Captain R. C. Winn, 4th Field Ambulance): "I was ordered by my section commander to take the bearers to pick up eleven wounded which had accumulated at Captain Parker's R.A.P. 45th Battalion. Near the Headquarters pill-box we struck a heavy barrage ... a shell splinter cut my eyebrow. ... As we reached the top of the ridge near the R.A.P. a machine-gun opened fire on us, as we came against the skyline. ... The R.A.P. was in a large shell crater with two heavy beams across as the only cover. ... Four stretchers were loaded and we set off back. About twenty yards beyond the ridge I was struck on the right foot by a large piece of shell. ... Parker took my boot off and the front part of my foot fell back on my ankle."

With the casualty here recorded began a tragic succession of deaths and woundings among the bearer captains; the response of the field ambulance officers to the challenge tacit in the bearing of the regimental medical officers toward the medical units.

On June 9th the II Anzac Corps front was readjusted to the "Green Line." Colonel Barber, 4th Division, relieved Colonel D. J. McGavin, A.D.M.S. New Zealand Division; the 4th Field Ambulance took over Kandahar Farm.[27] The bearers worked from the old R.A.P's (Boyle's Farm and Spring Street) as a base, returning to Kandahar Farm when relieved. Relays were pushed forward and waggon loading posts formed. The war diary of this unit (Lieut.-Colonel H. H. B. Follitt) records events thus:—

> "Evacuation of wounded has been materially hampered by the number of R.A.P's which have been established. There are six on this Divisional front. There has been a noticeable tendency on the part of R.M.O's each to choose his R.A.P. quite irrespective of the others, so that at present south of Messines there are three strung out in a line and regimental and ambulance bearers are working over the same ground. The R.A.P. south-east of Messines (47th Battalion) is at a strong cement dugout but well known to the enemy and a number of casualties amongst the bearers occurred in approaching it. Ultimately a longer but safer route was found, avoiding the southern spur of Messines ridge."

---

[27] In connection with these readjustments a note in the diary of the D.D.M.S. II Anzac for June 9 is instructive. In connection with the medical readjustments involved in the interchange of formations he says, "Representations were made to the 'G' and 'A' Branches of Corps asking that information of the movements of troops and changes in command" should be furnished to his office "so that it will not in future be necessary for the D.D.M.S. to obtain this information through the A.D's.M.S. of Divisions."

Throughout the operations this Division was cleared through the New Zealand main dressing station at Westhof Farm.

The Corps Stations
The scheme of the II Anzac Corps stations worked smoothly,[28] and in spite of the rapid arrival of casualties congestion occurred only at 5 p.m. on June 7th, when Westhof Farm was compelled for a time to switch to Pont d'Achelles. Over the period 7th-9th June, 8,867 wounded passed through these two stations; up to midnight on the 7th the motor ambulance convoy carried 4,403 cases, lying and sitting.[29]

In a later chapter the work of a field hospital is appraised as a constructive human effort, but here such a station is seen as a cog in the wheels of warfare, and its work

C.M.D.S. Pont d'Achelles
as a brief but important event in the swift movement of the casualty from the battlefield to the base for repair and reconditioning. In the Australian station at Pont d'Achelles we find treatment and movement admirably combined in a single process: surgery, sustenance, the making of records and rendition of returns, carried out so as least to check this movement. In human undertakings (as in the human body) structure and function are intimately correlated; so the layout of a major treatment centre was a very important factor in efficiency. In both respects this station has been extolled as a model.[30]

Layout. The station was designed to ensure that the walking wounded and stretcher cases should be kept separate, the "Main Dressing Station" and "Corps Collecting Post" (*sic*) being run by separate staffs though under one command. The following description is based on "Notes on the Work of a Corps M.D.S." by Lieut.-Colonel F. A. Maguire and Captain E. Selwyn Harrison (9th Field Ambulance) :—

---

[28] The IX British Corps (central sector) made dispositions that differed greatly from those of II Anzac. Both within the Corps (R.A.P. to M.D.S.) and without (M.D.S. to C.C.S.) the distances were much greater; and it happened that the casualties were much less. Four main dressing stations were formed which, though called "Corps" main stations, worked Divisionally with the field ambulances disposed in column. Comparison of results is not possible.

[29] Colonel Begg records that the Director-General considered the arrangements at the Corps station "very fine" and that the Senior Consulting Surgeon said that "the condition of patients from the Corps on arrival at the C.C.S. was unusually good."

[30] The station was selected by the Australian War Memorial for exact and artistic reproduction in plaster, to illustrate the evacuation of the wounded. This model is now in the War Memorial at Canberra.

"The dressing station consisted of four large Nissen huts (60 feet by 20 feet) and fourteen small Nissen huts (30 feet by 14 feet), with pack store, kitchens etc., and quarters. Huts were set aside for admitting, dressing, wards, and evacuation. Cases were received in the admitting hut and from there were passed direct to dressing room, wards, or evacuation hut, where they were picked up by the M.A.C."

Method of Clearance. Stretcher cases brought by car passed in one direction through the private road ("the boomerang") of the station and thus kept the main road clear. At the admitting hut the cars were unloaded by bearer squads and patients seen there by the special admitting officer, recorded ("Buff slip"),[31] and given A.T.S. Cases for redressing, etc., went to the dressing room; moribund patients to the special ward; others straight through from the admitting hut to the evacuating hut. From here they went by M.A.C. to C.C.S. or special "Army" Stations.

The account given in this report of the work might serve, *mutatis mutandis* for that of a casualty clearing station. The Dressing Station was organised in departments: "Admissions, Dressings, Wards, Evacuations, Special Wards, Records, Quartermaster, Pack Store, Mortuary, Accessories." As staff for this formidable enterprise Colonel Maguire had twelve medical officers, some 100 nursing orderlies, a bearer section, and combatant fatigues. Save for one short period the staff worked in twelve hour shifts.[32]

The following is an epitome of the general principles laid down beforehand:—

Records. A full record of every case is essential. From these records, returns are compiled. Special attention must be paid to accuracy in regard to regimental number, initials and spelling of names.

Clearing must be rapid to prevent blocking of divisional clearing which would react on the front line. It is estimated that the average stay of patients in C.M.D.S. will be two hours.

---

[31] The "Buff slip" (Army Form W. 3210) was filled in by the medical officer who should first attend to the sick or wounded man at the dressing station ("Advanced" or "Main") where records were kept. It identified the soldier and recorded the identity and nature of his casualty and the treatment given—*e.g.* A.T.S. Its sole purpose was to inform the recording clerk of the entry to be made in the "Admission and Discharge book" and on the "A 36." Similar entries were made at the same time on the A.F.W. 3118—Field Medical Card—which however remained attached to the soldier and accompanied him to the Base—was, in effect his "pass" along the line of evacuation. An account of the system of "Records and returns" will be given in *Vol. III*.

[32] "The system," writes Major Anderson, "dovetailed in exactly" with that of the transport circuit and "was on the principle that, since ample resources were available in men and vehicles, additional requirements could be met, not by demanding extra work from the men engaged, but by increasing the number employed." "As the rush passed (working units) were relieved in turn for food and sleep. All had been prepared at the start and got into work in rota. Clerical work, equipment, fatigues, and the quartermasters were co-ordinated with the work of the operating units and relieved or taken on with them."

Dressing. Only urgent dressing must be done. No case should go on with a tourniquet unless the patient can be operated on in a short time. All fractures should be splinted, only urgent amputations done, and only dressings which have slipped off the wounds or from which the blood is oozing.

Cases fit to travel, and marked at the A.D.S. as effectively dressed, should be given A.T.S. and hurried through and also head, chest and abdominal cases. To minimise wastage all slightly wounded men likely to be fit for duty in a few days will be dressed and sent to Corps Rest Station. All cases suffering severely from shock should receive special attention but only be held if removal would endanger their lives.

Detailed instructions were issued and special provision made for consolidating records and returns[33] from the "Buff slips." The duties of the admitting officer were described as follows:—

"To see all cases; classify in order of urgency; separate as requiring dressing, no further dressing, shock treatment moribund, and gassed; and to draft them to wards or to dressing room as required, the latter in order of urgency."

The dressing room was staffed by one tent sub-division when things were quiet, and by two during busy times.

"Each tent sub-division supplied two officers and eight trained dressers who worked in pairs." The dressing hut accommodated eight "dressing units," each "unit," complete in itself for the treatment of any case, and consisting of operating table (stretcher on trestles) with dressing table and shelves," and a steriliser to each four tables. Each "unit" was self-contained. Sections supplied their own instruments.

"During heavy work eight tables were continuously employed with two trained dressers at each. One officer was found sufficient per three tables or in very busy times one per two. The work of the officers consisted in performing urgent operations and in directing and supervising the dressers, who did the actual dressings."

Ward accommodation was provided for 300 stretcher cases, and could expand to 600. Officers' wards, moribund wards, and gas wards were equipped, the latter to treat 20 cases simultaneously with continuous oxygen by means of a special apparatus designed by the D.D.M.S.

In his report Colonel Maguire urged the importance "in running a dressing station of this size" of a special ward with beds and other equipment for treating post operative cases and for resuscitation. "Eighty per cent. of the cases set aside as moribund rallied sufficiently with rest, quiet, and shock treatment, to justify operation or evacuation."

---

[33] Such as A. & D. Books, A.F.W. 3185, A36, Nominal rolls and daily wires.

Accommodation for 700 was provided in marquees and the walking wounded were well served by the Y.M.C.A. They were cleared "according to classification" by motor-lorries which ran to a time-table—to C.C.S. or rest station.

Corps Collecting Post

These arrangements were carried out with great exactitude. By 6.45 a.m. on the 7th some 200 gassed cases were awaiting evacuation. The greatest number passing through the station at any one time was 3,000 in twenty hours from 6 a.m. of the 7th to 2 a.m. of the 8th. Colonel Maguire records,

"the cases came down from the front remarkably quickly, many abdominal wounds being in C.C.S. within two hours of wounding. In general they came from the A.D.S. very well dressed, all fractured thighs with Thomas splints and suspended." The excessive use of tourniquets was reported, and (it is stated) "remedied."

TABLE II.—Admissions to C.M.D.S's from II Anzac Corps.

1917	25th Brit. Div.	N.Z. Div.	3rd Aust. Div.	4th Aust. Div.	Corps Troops	Prisoners of war	Total
7th June	306	470	567	18	178	3	1,542
8th	1,198	1,433	1,298	534	173	381	5,017
9th	138	773	627	662	111	96	2,407
10th „	92	218	266	176	96	21	869
Total	1,734	2,894	2,758	1,390	558	501	9,835

From Pont d'Achelles the two streams, "stretchers" and "walkers," diverged again. Of the various special "Corps" stations only one received large numbers—that run at Steenwerck by the 4th Field Ambulance. It is clear that, in the rush, classification slipped somewhat; and also that, being out of the limelight, this station suffered some neglect. On June 5th the O.C. was required to expand for 600 "wounded and shell shock cases" and protested that his facilities were inadequate. On the 7th he recorded "hospital overcrowded—562 patients whose adequate treatment and feeding overtax the personnel of one and a half tent subdivisions." The provision of such a station, he considered, was an excellent plan, but called for more exact arrangements.

Distribution of casualties

"Shell Shock." The very small number of "shell shock" cases in this well-ordered battle was a matter of special com-

BATTLE OF MESSINES

ment, and is of great professional interest. It is referred to elsewhere.[34]

Casualty Clearing Stations

The total casualties passed through the various groups of clearing stations between June 7th and 9th are shown hereunder.[35]

TABLE III

	Trois Arbres.	Bailleul.	Remy Siding.	Proven.	Total.
7 June	1,015	3,587	1,404	708	6,714
8 June	1,483	3,078	2,533	1,308	8,402
9 June	416	989	958	892	3,255
	2,914	7,654	4,895	2,908	18,371

Early on the 7th all stations in Bailleul were congested, but this was soon adjusted.[36]

The Australian Stations. Most cases marked for the Base from Pont d'Achelles went to No. 2 A.C.C.S., a few minutes' run in the M.A.C. cars. The relations permitted by personal intimacy made special arrangements possible. In particular an endeavour was made to mitigate the situation created by the proximity to the M.D.S.

"We arranged," says the D.A.D.M.S., "that the cases marked in a special way be sent right through to the base without being taken down at the C.C.S. The marking really amounted to a statement that redressing would not be required for from twelve to twenty hours."

No. 2 received its first rush at 7 a.m. on the 7th when about 100 gas cases arrived. The full flow of wounded began about 11 a.m. During the 48 hours of 7th-8th June 2,830 casualties

---

[34] In *Vol. III*.

[35] The following facts and figures are taken from the *British Official Medical History, Vol. III, p.* 136. The proportion of "stretcher cases" to others was estimated at 35·8 to 64·2. The difficulty of ascertaining the allocation of "sitting" to "stretchers" or "walkers" made the figures, however, uncertain. By reason of the rapid clearance from field units only 14 per cent. of cases passing through the clearing stations came to operation as compared with 20 per cent. in the Arras offensive. The corresponding figures for the Australian units will be found in *Chapter xiii.*

[36] It was chiefly due to the large number of casualties in the II Anzac Corps, and the rapidity with which these arrived from the front. The congestion was relieved by switching evacuations to the Remy Siding group and by sending 400 stretchers to the St. Omer group. The plan whereby adjoining units worked in rotation had not been exactly developed. On June 9 the stations in Bailleul were involved in the shelling of this town and sustained considerable casualties. On July 22 Steenwerck was bombed and No. 2 A.C.C.S. was damaged—four patients were killed and fifteen wounded. Though it was less than five miles from the front, this was the only occasion on which this unit was in trouble. No. 1 was moved to a site near Oultersteene.

were admitted and 2,579 evacuated: During the month this station put through 7,441 cases of which 1,025 came to operation.

No. 1 A.C.C.S. in Bailleul worked in conjunction with Nos. 2, 11, and 53 British. Between June 6th and 9th this station admitted 2,450 patients.

Evacuation to Base. The first ambulance train left Bailleul at 7.30 a.m. on the 7th; thirty ambulance and five adapted trains were used in the first three days and carried 18,265 patients.

On June 12th, after a brief period of rest, the New Zealand Division relieved the 3rd in the trenches south of the Douve; the 4th Division also was relieved by the 25th British. Already the British artillery was taking up its positions for the bombardment preparatory to the main British offensive in front of Ypres. The artillery of the Australian divisions still in the Somme area left for the north on July 8th. Meanwhile the infantry of those Divisions, in the peaceful back areas of Picardy in perfect summer weather were enjoying the longest and best relief and rest that the force experienced in the war.

Reliefs and Movements

TABLE IV.—Total Battle casualties during the Messines Operations, 6th-15th June 1917.

(1) In the
Corps engaged.	II Anzac	IX Corps	X Corps	Total
	15,303	4,000 (Approx.)	8,000 (Approx.)	27,303

(2) In II Anzac Corps	25th Brit. Div.	N.Z. Div.	3 Aust. Div.	4 Aust. Div.	Total
	3,379	4,978	4,264	2,682	15,303

(3) In Aust. Divs.	KIA	DOW	POW	WD.	GAS	S/Shock	Total
3rd Aust. Div.	661	147	1	2,997	425	33	4,264
4th Aust. Div.	592	113	13	1,931	8	25	2,682
Totals	1,253	260	14	4,928	433	58	6,946

The Battle of Messines is a central event of a cardinal phase in the evolution of the Medical Service in the war. The success achieved in this battle and its methods have invested its conduct with a certain juggernaut quality of over-powering efficiency; and part of this reputation has adhered to the performances of the Medical Services and placed them also on a plane of their own among the medical battle-efforts of the war. That in large measure reputation reflects reality may be conceded. The German historians regard the

Messines— appreciation and criticism

BATTLE OF MESSINES

event as a major disaster to the German arms; and in the medical field the arrangements made in II Anzac for evacuation ran with unusual exactitude to plan, and greatly pleased both Army Command and General Headquarters B.E.F.[87]

But weight of authority and tradition notwithstanding, critical comment seems to be called for. Dispassionate examination of the medical events of this battle in the light of other experience compels a conviction that while on the one hand the medical work in this battle may strongly be commended as an example of what may be achieved by co-operation and organisation, yet—in so far as the scheme of the II Anzac Corps and 3rd Division reflect the intention of the D.M.S.—no battle in the war is less suitable to serve as a model for medical arrangements under less static conditions of warfare.

Critical comment focuses on two spheres of action—the treatment of casualties and method of using the field units.

Treatment. The medical problem of evacuation (we may remind ourselves) connotes concurrent movement and treatment. But in the surgery of wounds (as of disease) action inevitably must move to a definite occasion, namely, the "operation"; in which under an anaesthetic and with sufficient deliberation, the surgeon does what he may, in accord with current surgical technique, to restore a structural and functional *status quo*. All other action prepares the patient for this, or follows up the treatment. At this time developments in wound surgery pointed strongly to the casualty clearing station as the proper venue for this vital occasion in the course of evacuation. Its function was already very different from that of a mere clearing house between the field units and the base hospitals, doing only such major surgery as could not be postponed.

In the II Anzac Corps, the main dressing stations interposed an elaborate system of redressing and resuscitation within a few minutes' run of their casualty clearing stations.[88] The station for the walking wounded at Pont d'Achelles filled a necessary function; but the conviction impresses itself that, for stretcher cases, a recording and distributing centre adjoining the C.C.S., served by both M.A.C. and ambulance cars would have saved the wounded a double handling, *extempore* operation, and "an average of two hours" waiting—all-be-it in admirable circumstances.

The cause of this defect—for such, in the light of later developments, it must be held to be—can be traced to the fact that the technical progress in the treatment of wounds and of wound shock had not yet definitely fixed the place and part of the various treatment centres, so as to serve an exact technique; "dressing" was still a fetish. The Corps

[87] The Director-General B.E.F., Sir Arthur Sloggett, and Deputy Director-General, Maj.-Gen. W. G. Macpherson, were both present. The former expresses high approval; the latter as Editor-in-Chief of the *British Official Medical History* selected the orders of the D.M.S. II Anzac Corps for reproduction in full as a model, and has no criticism to offer of the medical scheme.

[88] The bearer officer whose wounding has been reported notes of his move from aid-post to operation in Bailleul that, after leaving the A.D.S., he passed through "an advanced casualty clearing station (?)" (*sic*)—*i.e.* the Corps Main Dressing Station.

M.D.S. at Pont d'Achelles was, in fact, the last bright flicker of the old régime.[39]

Field units. The interchange of field units was devised to take advantage of certain specially advantageous conditions, which need not be recapitulated. In any unforeseen event, such as advance or counter-offensive, it must have led to great confusion; as it was, in the re-assembling of units there was some confusion and intermixture of equipment. In the operation itself however the end may be held to have fully justified the means.[40]

The Thomas Splint. If, in the domain of general treatment, the medical arrangements for the wounded may be open to criticism as retrograde, in one special sphere at least a notable advance is to be recorded. In this battle the Thomas knee splint came fully to its kingdom. Contemporary records and later experience agree that for fractured femurs its advent was a landmark in the history of first aid, military and civil.[41] The results of its use in this battle were dramatic. For those who went through the first years of the war a very poignant sense of tragedy attaches to this triumph of war surgery in the thought that it was in December of 1914 that Robert Jones, in a special report to the War Office and special article in the *B.M.J.*, commended this splint for the transporting of wounded men with fractured femurs, adducing in support of his advice the fact that, put up in this splint, he himself had "often sent the patient home in a cab."

---

[39] The anomaly was indeed seen, and an attempt was made to offset its effects. The idea of "franking" cases through without redressing was, says the D.A.D.M.S., "easy to work in the division (A.D.S. to M.D.S.) but it was an Australian C.C.S. that made it possible for us to carry it further." "Two features (he naively adds) which might have led to trouble were first, the M.D.S. was under corps. This I think was a mistake. In the second place, the division should have controlled the motor-transport as far back as the C.C.S." The field ambulance served, in fact, as an annexe of the C.C.S. and relieved the pressure on its staff. But this supposed a degree of co-operation not normally obtainable.

[40] Colonel Barber held that the medical plan was over-elaborate and inelastic, and that, had the casualties been as great as expected, it would have "broken down." He strongly disapproved the system of Corps stations—"particularly if any advance is contemplated after the objective has been gained." He agreed however that "the scheme looked well on paper."

[41] The reader is commended to an article in the *Medical Journal of Australia* (*May, 1936*) by Colonel John C. Storey, A.A.M.C. and A. J. Thomas on the application of this splint to ambulance work in civil life. The article is based on the war experience of Colonel Storey, and on experiments carried out in N.S.W. by his co-writer in his capacity as Superintendent, Sydney Municipal Council Division of the St. John Ambulance Brigade.

CHAPTER IX

THE FLANDERS OFFENSIVE (CONTINUED): THIRD BATTLE OF YPRES

THE second phase of the Flanders offensive was a thrust towards Bruges; and the British Commander-in-Chief hoped that it would bring victory itself within sight. That, instead, it paved the way for the terrible battles of 1918 must be held a disaster for *all* the actors in this vast tragedy of humankind. The campaign was for both sides one of the most dreadful in the war[1]: in terms of casualties the cost to the British and German nations was 720,000 in killed and wounded. It very effectively completed the business of mutual attrition.

The British offensive was made possible, (1) by an overpowering superiority in material of war, and (2) by the Allied advantage in man-power on the Western Front —due in some part to the fact that the Eastern Front was still an active seat of war. By the German plan of defence the human element was either sheltered in steel and concrete strong-posts disposed in echelon over the whole front, or else was held behind the barrage zone. British offensive tactics were designed to oppose to this material rampart a material force, namely, overpowering artillery bombardment. By each bombardment, or series of them, the infantry would be enabled to gain certain ground. Advance would therefore be made in a series of "set-piece" battles.[2]

The "step by step" offensive

These methods of attack and defence, together with the nature of the terrain and the weather, determined the nature of the medical problem and the experience of the medical service in these operations.

---

[1] Some German historians place it in this respect above the Somme and even Verdun, but in the Australian force, as a test of morale, it did not compare with the Somme.

[2] The "Third Battle of Ypres" has been called "the greatest battle of 'material'" in history. It was the logical consummation of methods evolved for attrition at Verdun, on the Somme, and at Arras.

The tactical objectives were, first, the capture of the whole line of heights culminating at the village of Passchendaele, which dominated the Ypres Salient. The moral and material attrition achieved in the process would then (it was hoped) permit of a second stage—a "break-through" and general advance to Roulers, forcing the Germans to abandon the Belgian coast.

Plan of campaign

The British Force. For this offensive the Fourth and Fifth Armies were brought up from the Somme. The Fifth took over from Second Army most of the front for the coming conflict. General Gough was charged with the conduct of the campaign, the Fourth Army placed on the coast for use in the second stage, after the capture of the high ground which it was hoped would be achieved by the end of August. A small French army was brought in to assist the Fifth Army's left.

The campaign opened on July 31st with the fairly successful Battle of Pilckem.³ This victory was followed by a month of almost continuous rain, which held up road and rail construction and movement of artillery.⁴ Unhappily, in the intervals between battles imposed by the weather, British man-power and morale were squandered in a series of minor offensives after the manner of Mouquet Farm. In little over a month, August 5th-September 9th, British losses totalled 109,000.⁵

First phase. July 31-August

In the operations of August the Australian force was represented only by its artillery although on July 31st the 3rd Division had played a minor part in the Second Army's holding offensive near Messines.

These huge losses compelled a halt and drastic change of method. (*a*) The plan of "set-piece" battles, in fine weather, was to be strictly followed, and minor diversions eliminated; (*b*) though still kept in view, the purpose of a break-through and strategic advance was to be subordinated to that of attrition; (*c*) the Second Army was put in charge of the major sphere of action, though the Fifth remained in control of the left.

Second phase. Sept. 20-Oct. 12

The new offensive began on September 20th with the Battle of Menin

---

³ For the successive advances see *sketch map on opposite page*.
⁴ The terrain of this offensive had been reclaimed from swamp by an elaborate system of drains. In the terrific bombardments these were destroyed, and with the rains—expected in autumn—the low, flat countryside reverted to primitive morass. In the experience of Australian stretcher-bearers the mud of Flanders was less tenacious than on the Somme; but, as the fighting occurred largely in the rain, its influence on the course of the campaign was far greater—it was indeed a factor second to none in importance in the military situation. An epigram attributed to Napoleon affirms that to the four "primitive elements," earth, air, fire, and water, a fifth should be added, "mud." In the Great War, in no mere figure of speech, the qualities that inhere in *mud*, as such, made it a thing individual and elemental in its malignity.
⁵ At the end of August Field-Marshal Haig combed the ancillary services in France—cavalry, transport, railway-construction, labour corps, medical corps and clerical staffs—for "effectives" for the infantry.

Road, and was followed by the battles of Polygon Wood (September 26th), Broodseinde (October 4th), Poelcappelle[6] (October 9th), and the "first" battle of Passchendaele (October 12th). The first three were among the most successful fought by the British Army in the war. Had it been followed by fine weather the great battle of Broodseinde might well have come to rank with the "decisive battles of the world." In it Haig struck at the central point of the German defensive line in Flanders and the blow was a staggering one. But on October 5th came disaster, relentless and tragic, for from this date it rained persistently, and the whole shell-torn battlefield became a gigantic quagmire. To push forward the plank roads or duckboard tracks and light railways so as to move up the vast impedimenta of the set-piece battle surpassed human powers. In the battles of October 9th and 12th the Second Army offensives were thrown back with heavy loss, both in man-power and morale.

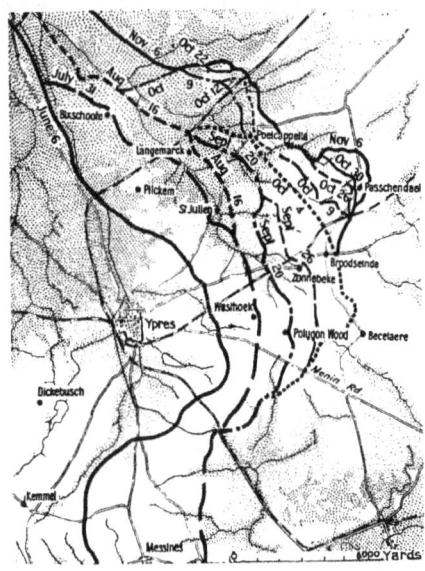

Successive Advances during Third Battle of Ypres.

Throughout this phase of the offensive the Anzac formations played the leading part.

Third phase. Oct. 14–Nov. 10
After the "first" battle of Passchendaele the idea of a push through and strategic advance in 1917 was abandoned. The Canadian Corps was brought up to take the leading rôle and the offensive was, however, continued into November in a series of battles in the mud, the purpose of which was to achieve a better tactical position. Both in

---

[6] The names and dates given here to the confused series of "battles" that made up the last stage of the Flanders offensive follows the official British nomenclature. The *Australian Official History* names the battle of October 9 "First" and that on October 12 "Second Battle of Passchendaele." Officially the "Second Battle of Passchendaele" began with the Canadian attack on October 26 and ended on November 10 after the capture of Passchendaele.

its purpose and its circumstances the fighting of this stage resembles that of the I Anzac Corps in November of 1916. The crest of the ridge was gained at enormous cost, to be held for a few months. When next year the Germans retook Messines ridge and the heights behind it, the British command voluntarily abandoned the ridges at Ypres in whose capture it had shortly before expended almost the whole British reserve of man-power.

In this last stage of the Passchendaele offensive the Australian force did little more than hold the line, but it sustained heavy casualties from shelling, especially with mustard gas, and from bombing.

The preparations for the offensive of July 31st, made by the Director-General of Medical Services, B.E.F. (General Sloggett) and by the Director of Medical Services, Fifth Army (Surgeon-General G. B. M. Skinner) illustrate the major problems of these vast attrition battles. They mirror moreover a cardinal phase in the evolution of the medical services in this war the outstanding feature of which was the fact that casualty clearing stations were now organised with a clearly defined purpose in view—namely, early surgical operation.

Third Battle of Ypres. General medical scheme

The Director-General's part
"The preparations made for the offensives, more especially those for which the D.M.S., Fifth Army was responsible, were based upon an anticipation of the complete success of the operation."[7]

On May 29th the D.G.M.S. held a conference of D's.M.S. of all Armies in which the needs of the Fifth Army were considered. These required the transfer of various medical units from other armies "in order to build up a medical strategical position in preparation for the part this Army was to play after Messines ridge had been captured by Second Army." By the end of July Surgeon-General Skinner had under his control 15 casualty clearing stations, 3 advanced depots of medical stores, 4 mobile laboratories, 2 X-ray units, 5 motor ambulance convoys, and 14 sanitary sections.

The casualty clearing stations were disposed as follows:—At Proven (Mendinghem) 3, for cases of lachrymatory gas and head injuries; at Dozinghem 3, self-inflicted injuries, infectious, and N.Y.D. Gas; Brandhoek 3 (including No. 3 A.C.C.S.), abdominal, severe chest injuries and compound fractures of thigh; Remy Siding 4 (including Nos. 2 and 3 Canadian); Haringhe (Bandaghem) 2, N.Y.D.N.

Approximately 1,300 marquees and 60 huts were provided for sick and wounded, of whom each marquee could take 10 and each hut 20. Accommodation was thus provided for 14,200, which in emergency could be increased to 20,000, at one time. Thirteen ambulance and four

---

[7] *British Official Medical History, General, Vol. III, pp. 140-144, 166.*

adapted trains were available for 12,000 cases on the first and 11,000 on the second day of the opening battle. "A special feature of the work of the medical services during these battles was the provision made for the surgical treatment of wounds in casualty clearing stations. For this purpose the number of surgical teams and other personnel sent to Fifth Army was greatly in excess of what had been possible during previous battles. . . . In the final phases the additional personnel in these units consisted of 46 surgical teams, 21 medical officers, and 195 other ranks in Second Army, and 28 surgical teams, 15 medical officers, and 140 other ranks R.A.M.C. in the Fifth Army."[8]

During the four months August to November nearly 8,000 stretchers were sent up to the Armies. The British Historian comments: "What became of the enormous number of stretchers sent up to armies was at all times a mystery to those whose duty it was to endeavour to recover them." It is suggested that an answer could readily have been supplied by those who took an active part in the medical events of these battles. Like most quantities of other war gear, they were destroyed by shells or in exploded ammunition dumps, or they were left leaning against the sides of abandoned trenches, or around the inside or outside of pill-boxes, or in the sea of mud beside the duckboard tracks, where thousands of them were soon broken and broken again until (sometimes with their human burdens) they fed the soil from which the crops of Flanders spring to-day.

The dominant purpose in the general plan of the D.M.S., Fifth Army was to *shorten the time* between wounding and surgical operation. In making his arrangements Surgeon-General Skinner built on the policy which we have seen at work on the Somme. In this he was strongly backed on the clinical side by the Advisory Consulting Surgeon, B.E.F., Sir Anthony Bowlby. As much as the Army Medical Directors themselves, though from a different outlook, this officer was responsible for initiating experiments in evacuation, transport, and treatment that made these operations notable in the medical history of the B.E.F. These experiments involved: (1) The staffing of the Casualty Clearing Stations and their venue, and (2) the method of clearing the front. The first is part of the subject of a later chapter and calls only for brief reference here. The second provides the key-note to medical administration in these operations.

The part of D.M.S., Fifth Army

The Forward Policy—(1) *The Casualty Clearing Stations*. An ambitious but, as it turned out, ill-judged attempt was made in July and August to advance the venue of the surgeon on the principle of moving Mahomet up to the mountain. For

---

[8] *Ibid. Vol. III, p. 165.*

three clearing stations brought up from the Somme (Nos. 32 and 44 British, and No. 3 Australian) a site was selected on a railway siding at Brandhoek on the main broad-gauge railway and adjoining the Ypres-Poperinghe road, only five miles from the front and on the direct road and railway routes from there through the Lines of Communication to the medical bases at Boulogne and Calais. At the end of July No. 32 British C.C.S. was made an advanced operating centre for "abdomens and chests." No. 44 British and No. 3 Australian arrived soon after it. Unfortunately, though otherwise admirably suited for the end in view, the site had the grave disadvantage that some British 15-inch guns were near by, and huge supply and ammunition dumps covered the adjoining area. All these were legitimate and obvious targets for German artillery. No. 32 British C.C.S. began work on July 31st with no less than 30 medical officers and 33 nursing sisters, with 8 tables going continuously. No. 44 British and No. 3 Australian C.C.S's opened on August 14th. But all three stations were subject to such severe shelling and bombing that their removal was ordered by the D.A. and Q.M.G., Fifth Army. No. 3 Australian and No. 44 British C.C.S. were moved back to "Nine Elms"—five miles behind Poperinghe. No. 32, but with its female nursing staff removed, remained as a C.C.S. "for walking wounded only."

The Forward Policy—(2) *Direct Evacuation.* Another experiment, initiated by General Skinner and implemented by his Deputy-Directors in order to promote the same end, attacked the problem from the side of transport. Instead of advancing the major treatment centres, an endeavour was made to facilitate the rearward movement of the wounded to them. To achieve this purpose methods tentatively exploited by Fifth Army in the Battle of Arras were carried to their logical conclusion.[9] A systematic attempt was made to short-circuit to the C.C.S. the general stream of casualties as well as "abdominals," "heads," and "thighs" by reducing to a minimum the treatment to be given in the "main" dressing station. Casualties were to be retained there only for inspection, recording, and urgent treatment. The injection of anti-tetanic serum was to be carried out at the C.C.S. Further to reduce "overhead" a "central record bureau" was created, which freed the advanced treatment centres from this time-consuming procedure. The problem of transport was met by pooling the ambulance vehicles allotted to the army corps (Motor Ambulance Convoy) and those of the divisions.

---

*See p. 156

The experiment began with arrangements for the Battle of Pilckem. These were developed during August and were taken over in September by Second Army (and by the I Anzac Corps, which formed the spearhead of that Army). The reaction of the Deputy- and Assistant-Directors of Fifth Army to the new policy, as expressed in their several schemes of evacuation, though not part of the history of the Australian service, has a direct bearing on the development of its methods and calls for brief notice.

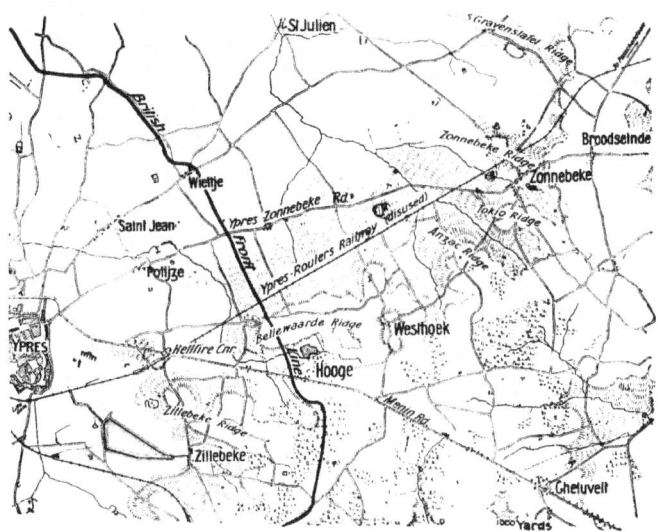

Chief Features of Terrain in "Third" Ypres

The Ypres Salient. The chief features of the terrain—main ridge and its spurs, with intervening swampy streams (beeks) and lakes—will be clear from the maps, which show also the British lines of advance. Of the communications, the most important from the medical standpoint were the historic Ypres-Menin road, and the Ypres-Zonnebeke road, which had survived three years of war and the traffic of ever vaster armies, and the Ypres-Roulers railway; although east of Ypres this then afforded little more than a landmark and boundary.

Fifth Army: Medical Arrangements July-August

For the Battle of Pilckem each of the four Corps of Fifth Army organised its own medical posts and routes. D.D's.M.S. were made responsible for the evacuation of wounded to C.C.S. from "main" and "advanced" dressing stations. The collecting of wounded from the battlefield and their removal to collecting posts and advanced dressing stations were carried out by the Assistant-Directors of the Divisions engaged. The methods adopted varied considerably.

II Corps. The arrangements for II and XIX Corps for the Battle of Pilckem, which were afterwards taken over by the Australian formations, are shown in the sketch map. The II Corps formed near Dickebusch two "main" dressing stations, one for severely and one for walking wounded. The first was manned by a full tent-division and sub-divisions from no less than seven field ambulances. Three advanced

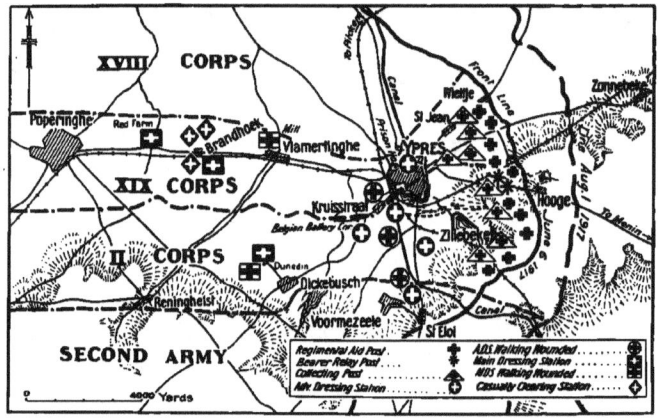

Medical Arrangements for II and XIX Corps, Battle of Pilckem Ridge.

dressing stations and four collecting posts were established. To clear from the advanced dressing station a "Corps combined motor ambulance convoy" was formed; the Ypres-Menin road served this Corps and the XIX.

XIX Corps. For the XIX Corps two main dressing stations were formed, one at Brandhoek and one at the "Red Farm" with a Corps walking wounded station at Vlamertinghe Mill; with one A.D.S. in the Prison House, Ypres, and an alternative station at Kruiss-straat. Ambulance motor-transport was not pooled but remained under orders of the A.D.M.S.

XVIII Corps. In the XVIII Corps, on the other hand, a divisional arrangement was adopted. An A.D.S. and collecting post for each division in line were cleared entirely by its own transport to a "corps main dressing station" for stretcher and walking cases, organised on a strictly divisional basis.

XIV Corps. With one corps main dressing station, advanced stations were formed for each division in the line with special transport to clear direct to C.C.S. The A.D.M.S. of the Guards Division (Colonel Fawcus), in his diary, makes an interesting comment on clearance from this battle.[10] Orders had been issued by the D.D.M.S. to the effect that "all the cases were to be dressed before being sent back direct to casualty clearing stations." The A.D.M.S. observes that "if such a procedure was to hold good on future occasions more medical officers would have to be provided and larger accommodation made at the advanced dressing stations; and this would have necessitated the advanced dressing station being established much further back." He considers that "for an advance it was best to move and keep the advanced dressing station as near the line as possible, moving it as the line advanced; in fact, to make the advanced dressing station a loading post only and to clear all cases from it as rapidly as possible to a place further back, where the necessary dressings could be carried out in comfort." This procedure (the British Historian comments) "would have been in accordance with *R.A.M.C. Training Manual* and *Field Service Regulations*; an advanced dressing station, as laid down in them, was not intended to be more than a post at the place where wounded brought back on stretchers could be loaded on to wheeled traffic."

The questions raised by these two very distinguished officers[11] have a direct and intimate bearing on the experience of the Australian service in this and in later battles.

3rd and 4th Divisions. After Messines both these Divisions were employed in II Anzac under Second Army in the hard local fighting which followed that battle; in this the Australian force sustained 870 casualties killed, 386 died of wounds, and 3,928 wounded. The medical work was at times very arduous and of no little interest but it did not present features calling for special study. At the end of August both Divisions were relieved for rest, reorganisation, and training.

**A.I.F.
July-August**

A.I.F. Artillery. The greater part of the Australian artillery was attached to Fifth Army for the opening battles of the Flanders offensive and was stationed around Zillebeke lake. For medical administration these artillery brigades came

---

[10] The reference is from the *British Official Medical History of the War, General*, Vol. II, p. 154.

[11] Col. (later Lieut.-General Sir) H. B. Fawcus, who became D.G., A.M.S. at the War Office during the years 1929-34; and Major-General Sir W. G. Macpherson, Deputy D.G.M.S., B.E.F. and Editor-in-Chief, *Official History of the War, Medical Services*.

chiefly under the British II Corps: the arrangements made for clearing their casualties are indicated later in this chapter.

The experience of these artillery brigades was not only unique in their own history but was of outstanding interest in that of the A.I.F. In this battle the British guns by reason of their vast number—one to each six yards of front—were emplaced in the open so that the incidence of casualties in the gun teams was limited mainly by the weight of metal that the enemy could throw against them. The courage and staunchness of the medical personnel attached were severely tested, and, with the gunners, they came through the ordeal in a manner that much enhanced the prestige of the Australian troops.

TABLE I.—Casualties in the Australian formations during July and August 1917.

	Killed or Died of wounds	Wounded or Gassed	Total
Artillery	298	1,077	1,375
A.A.M.C.	18	37	55
Others	937	2,815	3,752
Totals	1,253	3,929	5,182

The British Second Army which at the end of August took over the conduct of the offensive from the Fifth had from early 1916 until Messines been a military backwater; the conservative "safety first" policy of its D.M.S. (Surgeon-General Porter) was in strong contrast with the aggressive methods of Surgeon-General Skinner. But the movement in the medical service, which we have called the "forward policy" in respect of the treatment centres, was not a mere matter of individual initiative—it was the implement of a revolution in surgical technique born of new ideals and urgent needs; and under Second Army, during September and October 1917, the Australian Medical Service, *con amore*, exploited its possibilities to the utmost. Inasmuch as the line advanced, but the loading posts did not, the need for passing wounded men quickly along the transport routes became more and more urgent. The medical interest of these operations is found chiefly in the toils and trials of the bearer divisions, who with every advance must "drag at each remove a lengthening chain" of relays. The problem that faced the medical directors and ambulance commanders was—how best to offset this

Second Army: September

handicap, so as to save alive not only "abdomens," "chests" and "femurs," but any man severely wounded in or near the front line.

During June, July and August the I Anzac Corps—1st, 2nd and 5th Australian Divisions[12]—was "happy in having no history." No trials of battle could so effectively have prepared the Australian force for the part it had to play in this last terrible battle of attrition, and in the war of movement in 1918, as did these three months of rest, training and reconstruction during the summer of 1917 in Picardy. All the formations were brought to strength,[13] and the medical units were never better equipped or more exactly trained.

I Anzac Corps. 1st, 2nd, 4th, 5th Divisions

Early in August the 1st, 2nd, and 5th Divisions moved to the Hazebrouck-St. Omer area, and there under Second Army during six weeks[14] were prepared for a part in the decisive blow.[15] From the end of August the medical officers concerned reconnoitred the battle-front and prepared for the coming battle. On September 1st Colonel A. B. Soltau, Consulting Physician of Second Army, lectured to medical officers on "the treatment of mustard gas effects."[16]

Move to Flanders

---

[12] The 4th Division rejoined the Corps at the end of August.

[13] The ambulance transport service in all field ambulances was reorganised; drivers instead of being "A.A.M.C." were made "A.A.S.C." Seven motor ambulances were provided in place of seven of the horsed-waggons, three of the cars being light Fords.

The fighting of Bullecourt and Messines had effectively killed the project of forming a 6th Division; the personnel already allotted to it was absorbed as reinforcements together with large numbers from the Command Depots. *See Chapter xvi.*

[14] All medical unit diaries for September are emphatic in recording a high standard of strength, efficiency and morale. On September 2 the 1st Field Ambulance (1st Division) was at full strength with 10 officers and 231 other ranks together with 41 additional to establishment. The 5th Field Ambulance (2nd Division) near St. Omer was in billets "which gave admirable facilities for training and recreation. The morale of the men had rarely been better; a common opinion (was) prevalent of big things in the near future, and that the Australians would be given a prominent part."

[15] Like the battalions the medical units at this time, having spare time on their hands, were officially encouraged to help in the harvesting. For the 10 days, August 13-23, the 3rd Field Ambulance returned to Brigade a total of 520 hours' work done by 35 men and 10 horses using 5 G.S. waggons for "harvesting and potato digging."

[16] This gas had been used for the first time in the second week in July when Ypres and Nieuport were heavily shelled with "Yellow Cross." The British respirator in use was, however, effective and within a fortnight defensive measures and treatment had been designed. But from this time till the end of the war these shells were an important weapon and the conditions of these operations were peculiarly suited to their use. For a detailed consideration of the subject of chemical warfare, *see Vol. III.*

Even before the decision to replace Fifth Army by Second for the next advance, I Anzac Corps had been selected to take the place of the II British Corps as the spearpoint of the assault against the main ridge, about the point where it was crossed by the Menin Road. Against this high ground —Glencorse Wood, Nonne Bosschen, and the slope towards Zonnebeke beyond the Bellewaarde and Westhoek spurs—during August attack after attack had been launched by the Fifth Army at terrible cost—casualties in the II Corps alone amounted to 27,300.

Second phase— Second Army and I Anzac

The two first battles in the new phase were closely related in their tactical objective and military circumstances, and also in the nature of their medical problems. Each was a typical "set-piece" battle—their purpose, to place the British front line astride the main ridge in preparation for a general advance on Passchendaele.

The first battle, that of the Menin Road, was to be fought by the Second and Fifth British Armies (Generals Plumer and Gough) and First French Army (General F. P. Anthoine). The British order of battle was, from right: X British and I Anzac Corps (Second Army), and V and XVIII Corps (Fifth Army). The attack was on a front of ten miles; the objective was limited by a map line whose attainment would advance the British front some 1,000-1,500 yards.

Between September 12th and 15th the 1st, 2nd, and 5th Divisions moved up to the Reserve area behind Ypres. Relief of the II Corps was effected on September 16th and 18th by attaching to the I Anzac Corps the British 25th and 47th Divisions which held the line, while the four Australian brigades which were to attack moved up.

Rôle of I Anzac

The Australian force was set the chief task—an advance on a two divisional front from the Hooge and Westhoek spurs through Glencorse Wood and Nun's Wood—"Nonne Bosschen" of dreadful memory. Behind the front line the divisional areas and traffic routes were separated by a dismal swamp—the Bellewaarde "lake." The advance was planned for three successive leaps to the "Red Line" (800 yards in 44 minutes from zero, followed by a halt of one hour); to "Blue Line" (4-500 yards, two hours from zero, with a halt of two hours); to "Green Line" (2-300 yards, four and a half hours from zero).[17]

The Divisions. The 1st and 2nd Divisions, right and left, were to attack in the direction of Polygon Wood, each with two brigades in line and one in reserve, the attacking brigades mostly using all their battalions, which "leap-frogged" one another at the several stages.[18]

Administration. In the area transferred to Second Army

---

[17] The long halts on the intermediate objectives were arranged in order to allow the line of attack to be reorganised. They were an important factor in regimental medical work.

[18] For the Battle of Menin Road the light and medium batteries of I Anzac Corps were for the most part massed about the level of Bellewaarde and Hooge. The approximate positions of the artillery are indicated in the sketch map, at *p. 202.*

the replacement of Fifth Army by Second went *pari passu* with that of II Corps by I Anzac. Instead of the incoming Australians, as on the Somme, being wedged at briefest notice between two formations, in the present operations an established system of relay and treatment posts was taken over from the II and XIX Corps and modified to suit the tactical developments. Save for some general rules similar to those laid down for the Battle of Messines, the medical arrangements for the Corps were for the most part left by the D.M.S., General Porter, to the Deputy-Director, Colonel Manifold, and his Divisional staffs. In the I Anzac Corps the spheres of action and initiative proper to Corps and Divisions were by now clearly defined, and the relations between the officers concerned were cordial and co-operative. At the same time the field ambulances could be relied on to give prompt effect to orders and instructions, and their commanding officers were closely in touch with the Assistant-Directors and Deputy Assistant-Directors. In other words, direction and executive had been integrated in a very effective *unit of action*,[19] which was now to be tested as perhaps at no other time in the history of the Australian force.

Battle of Menin Road. Medical arrangements

The General Scheme. On September 5th Corps Headquarters moved to Hoograaf: on the same day Colonel Manifold conferred with the Assistant-Directors, and the essential features of the Corps scheme were arranged. All cases "fit to travel the distance" would go direct from the A.D.S. to the C.C.S group at Remy Siding, which had been allotted to the I Anzac and a British Corps. A "Corps Main Dressing Station" would be maintained only "for such cases as could not be taken further." For the duty of clearing the front line to the A.D.S. in the first battle the A.D's.M.S. 1st and 2nd Divisions (Colonels R. B. Huxtable, and A. Sutton) nominated the 3rd and 5th Field Ambulances, and during the next week the officers commanding these units (Lieut.-Colonel A. G. Butler and Major J. J. Nicholas) and the D.A.D's.M.S. (Majors W. J. Stack and H. K. Fry) reconnoitred the routes. A novel and interesting

---

[19] Evidence of this efficiency is found in the consecutive orders and instructions issued by the several formations and units; in the admirable operation and progress reports furnished to the A.D's.M.S. by commanding officers; and in the frequent conferences, formal and informal, and prompt action contingent thereon.

scheme of clearance and evacuation was devised for the pending battle which with necessary adjustments served the Corps throughout the operations.

The Situation. The front to be taken over extended some 2,000 yards from the Menin Road south of Glencorse Wood—slightly in rear of the crest of the ridge—to Westhoek spur. It was held on a two-brigade front by the 47th (British) Division and was cleared from aid-posts at "Clapham Junction" and Westhoek via "collecting" and "loading" posts on the Menin Road at "The Culvert" and "Birr Cross-Road" to an advanced and walking wounded dressing station on the Menin Road some mile in front of Ypres. The scheme was quite inadequate to the requirements of two Divisions in a great battle. Moreover certain features in the situation made necessary some departure from the normal method of working the field units. These features were:—

(1) The fact of the A.D.S. being used as the chief ambulance treatment centre and pivot of evacuation. (2) Certain peculiarities of the terrain—in particular the circumstance that the Bellewaarde swamp and the morass of Nonne Bosschen lay between the routes from the two fronts, which converged to common loading posts on the Menin Road. (3) The fact that motor-transport to the A.D.S. was wholly confined to a stretch of some 2,000 yards of the Menin Road, constantly shelled, and shared by the two Divisions for every purpose of communication with their fronts.

Wheel Traffic Routes. Another factor, of vital importance in the medical problem, as it was in the military, was that of traffic routes. From early in September, under the direction of C.R.E. I Anzac, the Divisional Engineers and the Pioneer and Labour Battalions were occupied at high pressure constructing roads and light railways, the extension of which was essential to continued advance by the troops, and not less so to any scheme for the retirement of their wounded. At this time the situation was briefly as follows:—

Roads. The sketch map on *page 202* shows the two main circuits, rear and forward, on which the use of wheeled-transport was based. The rearmost of these—completed by September 20th—was a metalled or double plank road; the forward circuit, a "one-way" single plank road, was under construction. In addition to these roads, double and single duckboard tracks reached out across the waste. Off these, even before the rains, movement on foot was difficult, and transport by wheel almost impossible.

Light Railways and Tramways. The I Anzac Corps specialised in these and (in spite of previous adverse experience on the Somme) they were expected to play an important part in evacuation. By September 20th the light line ran from Birr Cross-Road past Zillebeke and Dickebusch, to supply railhead near Remy Siding. A switch with a special siding ran to the A.D.S.

The Detailed Plan, I Anzac Corps   The scheme arranged by the Deputy- and Assistant-Directors was set forth by the former[20] as follows:—

"A.D's.M.S. of the Divisions concerned will be responsible for (1) The arrangements for the evacuation of wounded from their Divisional front to collecting posts in the vicinity of Menin Road from which the A.D.M.S. 1st Australian Division will be responsible for the evacuation by ambulance-car to A.D.S. of all stretcher cases, of both Divisions, and the A.D.M.S. 2nd Australian Division for the evacuation of all lightly wounded of both Divisions. In the event of evacuation along Menin Road by Ambulance-car being impossible, arrangements must be made for carriage by wheeled-stretchers or bearers. A.D's.M.S. will mutually arrange the necessary details.[21]

"These officers will arrange also for (2) the staffing of all Ambulance posts and their stocking with equipment, water and dressings. (3) the 'flagging' for all routes of clearance; (4) the formation of new advanced dressing stations."

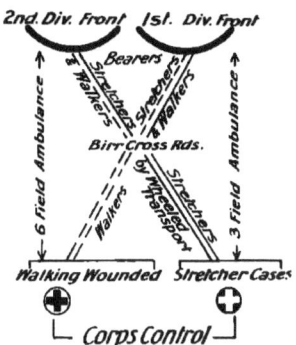

Scheme Showing Allocation of Responsibility, Battle of Menin Road.

Evacuation from the A.D.S. would "be under Corps arrangements."

Transport. The elimination of the main dressing station made necessary a complete readjustment of ambulance transport. The motor ambulance transport of the Corps (No. 20 Motor Ambulance Convoy) and of the Divisions was pooled to form a "Corps combined convoy" of 82 cars (50 M.A.C. and 8 from each Division). This was put under the Officer Commanding the M.A.C. and was parked at Dickebusch to serve the rear circuit (A.D.S. to C.C.S.). For the forward circuit loading post

---

[20] In "Medical arrangements, operations No. 5," issued on September 15. These occupied 10 pp. of foolscap. Orders of the two A.D's.M.S. were issued on September 13. A particularly interesting contrast is afforded by those for the A.I.F's last battle of the war, 29 Sept., 1918, *q.v.*, *pp. 739-42*.

[21] The diagram, above, shows that this scheme could claim at least an anatomical analogy.

to A.D.S. a small convoy, formed by pooling 3 large and 3 Ford cars from each Division in the line, was put at the disposal of the A.D.M.S. 1st Division. The horsed-waggons remained with Divisions.

Special provision was made for the use of light railways for both stretcher cases and walking wounded. For the latter a lorry "convoy" of 20 lorries (Corps) and 20 buses (Army) was to be available for the A.D.M.S. 2nd Division.

Regimental Establishments. It was accepted generally in I Anzac Corps that brigades and battalions were responsible for clearing all casualties from their fronts to the Regimental Aid-Posts, and for first aid in the field.[22] The duty of maintaining *liaison* between the R.M.O. and the ambulance bearers was accepted by the field ambulances. A paragraph in the orders of the A.D.M.S. 1st Division laid down that

Medical Arrangements: The Divisions

"the commanding officer" [of the 3rd Field Ambulance] "will ensure that contact is kept with all new R.A.P's which may be established during the advance and will clear the wounded from them and the ground over which advance has been made."

At this time, however, the dual allegiance of the R.M.O. to his regiment and to the Medical Service was often imperfectly adjusted and defects in this matter were not infrequent.

The regimental bearers—commonly 32—invariably went into battle with their companies. The R.M.O. commonly kept with him his medical orderly and "A.A.M.C. corporal."

Base and Reserves. The technical details that follow are epitomised from Divisional diaries. The arrangements were applicable only to the requirements of a battle of attrition.

The resources of the two field ambulances responsible for clearing the line were disposed in echelon to serve the purpose of relief, reinforcement, and supply to the front. (1) Both units established headquarters, depot, and transport lines behind Ypres, the 3rd Field Ambulance at "Château Hendrique," the 5th at "Belgian Battery Corner." Here bearers, when relieved, were rested and fed; and from here, as a base, the forward stations and posts were supplied and rationed by the quartermasters. In each unit many hundreds of two-gallon petrol

---

[22] At least in the 4th and 5th Divisions this was laid down precisely in Standing Orders. The officer in charge of the 5th Division's field ambulance bearers, when taking over the line for the Battle of Polygon Wood, "met the Divisional Commander, General Hobbs, who enquired as to my dispositions. I was directed by him emphatically to confine my bearers solely to relaying wounded from the R.A.P's to the rear."

tins were collected and marked with red cross to be sent with water in specially fitted carts to the front. Rations were done up in sandbags labelled for each forward post and were sent by supply waggon to the advanced dressing station or waggon loading post for further distribution by returning bearer squads. Each unit built field ovens to roast for 600-700 men and fitted up comfortable sleeping quarters. By such means the bearer divisions were sustained in their immense labours. Medical and Red Cross stores were assembled and dressings prepared and sandbagged for distribution to the forward ambulance posts and to the R.M.O's.[23]

These stations served successive units throughout the operations.

(2) *Advanced Reserve Stations.* Quarters to accommodate a full bearer division were formed by both field ambulances, by the 3rd in immense cellars beneath the "Ypres ramparts" some 20 minutes by route march from the advanced dressing station; by the 5th in the "canal dugouts."

(3) *Local Reserves* of personnel, transport, and stores were held at the advanced dressing station and in various advanced posts on the lines of clearance.

Reserves of Bearers—Divisional. The bearers of those field ambulances that were not themselves in the line, but whose Divisions *were,* remained with their units. For the battle they were "attached for duty" to the unit clearing the front and were controlled by the A.D.M.S.

Corps. The bearers of the Divisions in reserve constituted the "corps reserve," controlled by the Deputy-Director.

Lines of Clearance. Special officers were detailed by both units (1) to direct the work of the bearers; (2) to control the motor circuit; (3) to supervise treatments and evacuation at the A.D.S.

Bearer Circuit: 1st Division. The 1st Division's front lay some 3,000 yards in advance of Birr Cross-Road and was reached by the Hooge Ridge, along which ran the Menin Road —available for traffic only as far as "The Culvert." A vast mine crater marked the site of Hooge whence, beneath the road, as far as the crest of the ridge at Clapham Junction, ran the remains of the "Hooge Tunnel."[24]

The "chief difficulties" met were:—

---

[23] The importance of the work of the ambulance quartermasters achieved general recognition in these operations. It is perhaps permissible in a technical history to commend to prospective commanders of field units the "lessons" of this war on the matter.

[24] This remarkable work had been constructed by the Germans with typical thoroughness to protect their reliefs. It was some 6 ft. wide by 8 ft. high, and was protected by from 5 ft. to 6 ft. of roadway, with a buffer space of 2 ft. above steel girders. It was lined with solid baulks of timber.

(1) Lack of accommodation for R.A.P's and relay posts. (2) Direct enemy observation of the whole left brigade front. (3) The exposed carry down the Menin Road from Clapham Junction. (4) The nature of the country on each side of this road which almost cut out alternative routes. (5) Complete absence of supplies in the forward posts.

By vigorous initiative and hard work by the bearers[25] most of these had been at least partly met before zero day.

Temporary aid-posts were formed in conjunction with the X Corps at Clapham Junction in a sector of the tunnel (right); and in a much-shelled pill-box (left).[26] For relays and depots the Engineers opened up various sections of the Hooge Tunnel, in particular a fifty yards stretch at the point where the routes from right and left brigades should converge. Here side galleries were dug and accommodation was provided for personnel and stores, and a dressing room for 30-40 stretcher cases. The left front was cleared, till the line should advance, through Clapham Junction. A new track was made along the south side of the Menin roadway and an alternative route for walking wounded through the X Corps posts, "Stirling Castle" and "Woodcote House" A.D.S.—historic names in the annals of the Salient. In return, the X Corps would clear its left brigade through the Menin Road posts and the I Anzac A.D.S. Stores and equipment were brought by transport to the loading posts and man-handled to the forward posts.

2nd Division. "A preliminary estimate of 2,000 wounded was made; of this 500 were reckoned as stretcher cases. Our line ran about 800 yards in front of Westhoek Ridge. It was decided to use Bellewaarde ridge as our main forward post and dump for materials, with a rear dump at Birr Cross-Road. At Bellewaarde the one pill-box was reserved for shelter, and two 'elephants'[27] were built by ambulance bearers, one for material and one for a dressing post. The advanced depot supplied 200 Thomas splints and other equipment; dressings were prepared for 2,000 cases. Bearers were posted at the two R.A.P's on Westhoek Ridge, and directing signs were placed on the very difficult tracks leading back to Bellewaarde Post." (Report of the officer-in-charge of the bearers—Maj. C. L. Chapman.)

Two bearer carries were worked out: (1) north of Bellewaarde Lake clearing to Birr Cross-Road via "Simon's Post" relay; and (2) south of the lake by Château Wood, clearing to "The Culvert."

Waggon Posts. This stretch of road—some 500 yards— "lined with its blasted tree stumps, flanked by a continual ridge built of dead mules and horses, limbers, waggons, guns, ammunition, ambulances

---

[25] The divisional bearer reserves were used for such fatigue work as well as the personnel of the units clearing the line.

[26] Near the front line shelter for aid-posts or for relays or any other purpose (such as Battalion headquarters) was to be found only in the captured German strong-posts. But these had the grave disadvantages that they were a focus for enemy shells as well as for all and sundry wayfarers, and that the entrance faced toward the enemy. In spite of this it is hard to see how the offensive could have continued without them—they played the same part as the deep German dugouts on the Somme.

[27] That is, "elephant iron" shelters.

27. WOUNDED TEMPORARILY HELD UP AT THE CULVERT ON THE MENIN ROAD DURING THE BATTLE OF 20TH SEPTEMBER, 1917
The officer with bandaged arm is Major G. A. M. Heydon, R.M.O., 8th Battalion. A dump of stretchers is seen on the right.

Aust. War Memorial Official Photo. No. B711.

To face p.

28. THE ADVANCED DRESSING STATION ON THE MENIN ROAD DURING THE FIGHT OF 20TH SEPTEMBER, 1917

The chamber shown is a cellar under the building in *plate* 25. The clerk in the foreground is filling in field medical cards which were tied on to patients.

Aust. War Memorial Official Photo. No. E715.

To face p.

and the whole paraphernalia of war, wrecked on that highway and tossed aside,"[28] formed a bottle-neck through which in the next two months was to pass a not inconsiderable part of all the casualties sustained by the A.I.F. in France. At this time here were the loading post and focus of clearance for all the "stretchers" and "walkers" of the two Divisions, and the headquarters of the staff allotted for this work, and in addition the road- and railhead, and medical supply dump for the two Divisional fronts. This was the testing point of the "mutual co-operation" which Corps orders enjoined on commanding officers. Both field ambulances worked to provide accommodation at Birr Cross-Road and "The Culvert" and both supplied personnel for the posts there. At Birr Cross-Road, in "some deep and damp dugouts," racks were put up to hold a few stretcher cases. At "The Culvert" four elephant cupolas were built by the Engineers.

"*Stretchers.*" The "forward" ambulance convoy carried stretcher cases from here to the A.D.S.

"*Walkers.*" Duckboard tracks north and south of the Menin Road were marked with notices directing the walking wounded to the A.D.S. To short circuit that post a route was arranged from Birr Cross-Road by light railway or duckboard tracks past the Zillebeke Bund to an "ambulance post" at "Shrapnel Corner."

Advanced Dressing Station : Menin Road
The combined advanced and walking wounded dressing station taken over from II Corps was located in two ruined buildings on the Menin Road about a mile east of Ypres and had been in use for medical purposes since 1915. It was now by Colonel Manifold's orders reorganised as separate stations :—

"(a) for all stretcher cases, on the north side of Menin Road, under the A.D.M.S. 1st Australian Division (3rd Field Ambulance) ; (b) for lightly wounded, directly opposite south of the Menin Road, under the A.D.M.S. 2nd Australian Division (5th Field Ambulance).

"Every effort must be made to clear casualties as soon as possible after the treatment their condition requires. Without causing undue delay all wounded will be supplied with hot drinks and so forth."

---

[28] Quotation from *Reveille*, Sept. 1936, *p. 22*.

The site was only a few hundred yards from heavy artillery positions, and throughout the operations the stations were subject to shell-fire. They sustained a few serious disasters, and had many narrow escapes.

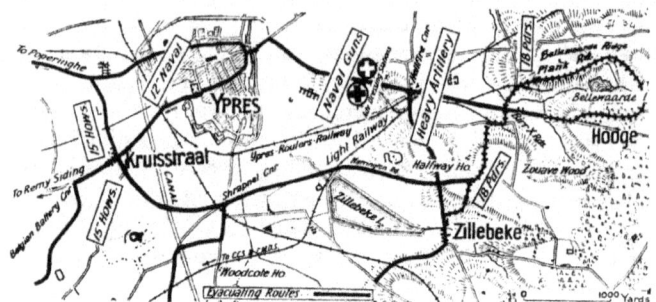

Routes of Evacuation from Birr Cross-Road, Sept. 20-26; and Artillery Positions.

A.D.S. to C.C.S.
" Corps
arrangements "

The elaborately detailed "arrangements" of the Deputy-Director for evacuation from this point to the C.C.S. can be epitomised as follows :—

"Lightly wounded" to be evacuated by narrow-gauge railway from a special siding, or by lorries or buses "which will go direct to C.C.S. by the shortest route permissible; and will NOT go to the Corps Main Dressing Station." Stretcher cases to go by light railway or motor ambulance waggons of the "Corps combined convoy." These to be classified (A) "long distance," fit for through journey to C.C.S. by the long route via Corps main dressing station; (B) "short distance" —shock, gas, haemorrhage, etc., to go direct to M.D.S.; (C) immediate operation—abdominals, etc.—to be sent direct to C.C.S. via Poperinghe road. Vacant places on "C" class cars to be filled by "A" class cases. Others to go whenever possible by light railway for which an hourly service of trains would run, consisting of eight trucks, each truck to take eight stretchers. Otherwise "A" cases would go by cars of the motor ambulance convoy.[29]

Corps Main
Dressing Station

The scheme prescribed that at the Corps main dressing station at Dickebusch

"All cars and trains will be met by an officer, who will unload all 'B' class patients—haemorrhage, shock, and so forth, and all gas cases; only cases requiring immediate treatment to be given attention; no redressing to be done unless absolutely necessary."

---

[29] The A, B, and C Circuits and Scheme of Evacuation for Sept. 20 are shown in the map at p. 273. See also *Appendix No. 9* for the French system.

A gas treatment centre was formed and accommodation found for the Corps Reserve of bearers and medical stores—for which 2,000 blankets and 1,500 stretchers were supplied by the D.G.M.S., B.E.F., through Second Army.

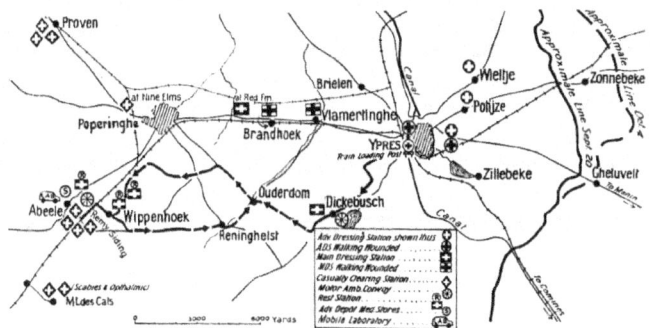

Scheme of Evacuation, " Third " Ypres, Oct. 1917. The arrows show main route of evacuation to C.C.S.; urgent cases went to Remy via Poperinghe. (Inserted here to show C.C.S's. See p. 223.)

Records. Further to promote the idea of rapid evacuation it was arranged that no records would be kept at the A.D.S. or M.D.S. "except those of deaths, and of cases treated and returned to duty." The "Corps Central Record Bureau" was moved from Dickebusch to the 5th Divisional Rest Station at Remy Siding, and arrangements were made to take the prescribed particulars of casualties at the admitting room of the C.C.S. Divisional returns would be made up and consolidated at the Central Bureau. The Officer Commanding the 6th Field Ambulance (Lieut.-Colonel A. H. Moseley)[30] was put in charge and a clerical staff drawn from each Division.

This renowned centre of surgical work and research comprised at this time four units—2nd and 3rd Canadian, and 10th and 17th British. Among the extra staff were surgical teams from No. 1 A.G.H. at Rouen. During the operations tent sub-divisions from each field ambulance in turn were "attached for duty."

The C.C.S. Group Remy Siding

---

[30] Later it was under Major D. S. Mackenzie, 3rd Field Ambulance who had special experience in this matter.

The move up—Sept. 17-19

On September 17th the 1st Field Ambulance (Lieut.-Colonel E. T. Brennan) took over the Corps main dressing station. Rest stations for each Division had already been occupied. Between September 14th and 18th the Commanding Officers of the 3rd and 5th Field Ambulances took over the forward posts clearing the brigades in line and replaced the 6th London Field Ambulance in the advanced dressing station. Through this post during the next eight weeks were to pass approximately 15,000 Australian battle casualties.

Each commanding officer had available for zero day 3 bearer divisions at full strength, totalling 12 officers and 324 other ranks. On the 17th the Divisional reserves—1st, 2nd, 6th, and 7th Field Ambulances—moved up to the Ramparts and Canal Dugouts. A tent division was posted to the A.D.S. and one tent sub-division to the walking wounded post. Till zero hour every available man was at work. Posts were sandbagged and gas-proofed and routes surveyed. Shelling on the front and on traffic routes was heavy and casualties, chiefly from the Pioneer Battalions, Engineers and Artillery, were severe.[31]

On the 19th bearer officers moved their Divisional reserve squads to the forward stations along the Menin Road and Bellewaarde Ridge. In the 1st Division bearers for the R.A.P's were posted at Clapham Junction to clear the right brigade; those for the left were stationed in the Hooge Tunnel, to move up when the battle opened.

In the 2nd Division

"by dint of great efforts" the bearers completed the work at the collecting post on Bellewaarde Ridge at 3 a.m. on the 20th. Reliefs were posted without casualty and details set out for the R.A.P's. By 5.40 a.m., when the barrage opened, "all the arrangements were complete and everybody was confident."[32]

Battle of Menin Road

The Battle of Menin Road "is easily described inasmuch as it went almost precisely in accordance with plan. The advancing barrage won the ground; the infantry merely occupied it."[33] Casualties occurred chiefly from shell-fire in the approach and on the tapes and later around the strong-points. The counter-attacks were shattered

---

[31] On the 18th a single shell from a long range gun searching for the artillery emplacements killed 5 bearers of the 1st Field Ambulance and wounded 14 others in front of the A.D.S.

[32] From a report by Major C. L. Chapman.

[33] *Australian Official History. Vol. IV, p. 761.*

by artillery before they approached the line and were quite ineffective. Casualties in the two Divisions on the 20th and 21st numbered 947 killed, and 3,283 wounded, of whom 114 died.

The staggering effect of this first blow upon the enemy was reflected in the conditions under which the wounded were evacuated. The A.D.M.S. 1st Division (Colonel Huxtable) summed up the day in his war diary as follows:—

Evacuation of Casualties

"*September 20th, 11 p.m.* The O.C. 3rd Field Ambulance called at Headquarters to report, and states everything going very satisfactorily. Cases have been cleared from the front line with amazing rapidity. Blocking of Menin Road occurred from time to time but it was due to the amount of traffic, ammunition limbers, lorries, etc., which held up the ambulance waggons. Practically no delay by enemy shelling on the road, which we all so greatly feared."

This immunity (it should be said) did not include the area over which the troops advanced, nor did it last beyond the first thirty-six hours.

In each division in this battle, as in the later ones, the R.M.O's of the five or six attacking battalions worked in groups of two or three, and for the most part followed closely after the advancing battalions, often going forward before the regimental bearers had cleared the wounded from the first objective to the old aid-posts. These rapid moves, together with some failure on both sides—regimental and ambulance— in the very difficult matter of "keeping touch," led at times to delay in locating wounded—and this to some mutual criticism.

The Divisional fronts

1st Division. From the right (2nd Brigade) 2nd Field Ambulance bearers cleared casualties via Clapham Junction, which became the first relay, to the new Hooge Tunnel post, whence they were "relayed" to "The Culvert" loading post. In the left (3rd Brigade) the R.A.P. of the 11th and 12th Battalions was "blown out" and the R.M.O. of the 12th Battalion, Major Johnston, was wounded. Runners sent from this R.A.P. to direct the ambulance bearers were wounded and the first "bearer party" failed to locate the R.M.O's. At 8 a.m., therefore, the bearer officer responsible (Captain L. May)

Map No. 5

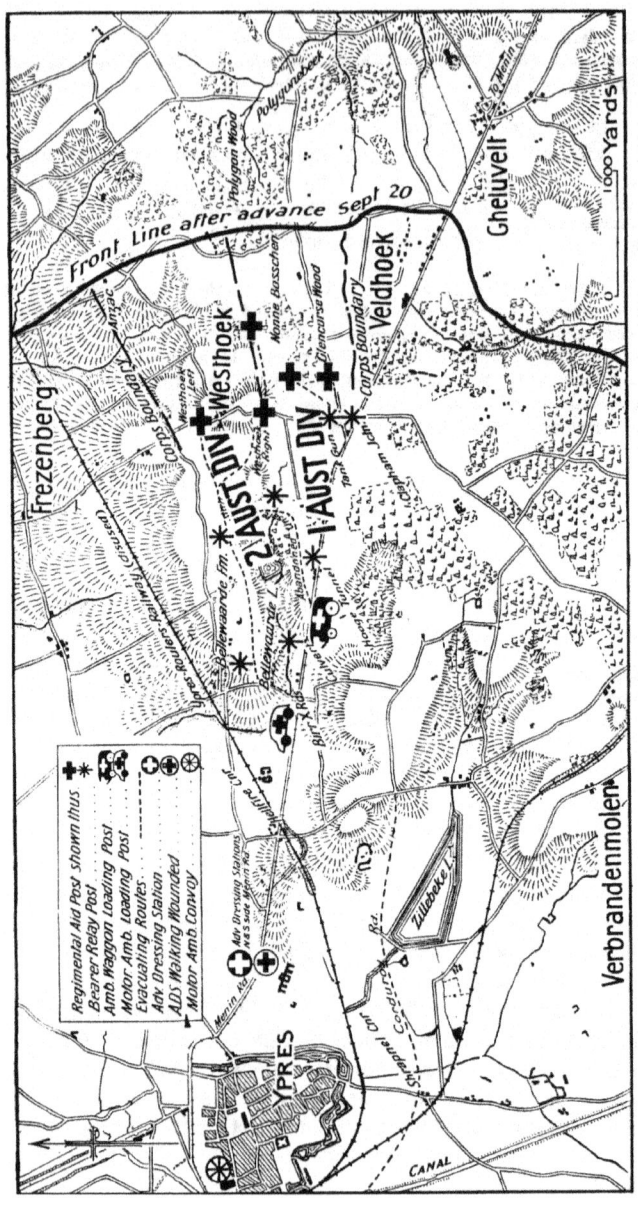

"with eight squads pushed out into Glencorse Wood to find the R.A.P. Shelling terrific but the loose soil saved casualties. Found 11th and 12th R.A.P., set my squads to work, and soon had things in order."

The R.M.O's of the 9th and 10th Battalions (Captain R. K. Rae and Major S. V. Appleyard) were found "in a fine strong post, containing four rooms, in a sunken road." During the morning the R.M.O. 8th Battalion (Major Heydon) was wounded. At 3 p.m. Major H. H. Willis, acting R.M.O. in the 7th Battalion, reported that he was

"badly in need of bearers and stretchers. Despite our distance from the line the regimental bearers are now clearing us more rapidly than the ambulance is clearing back."

By 3.30 p.m. the Corps reserve of bearers—from the 12th and 13th Field Ambulances—was *en route*, and proved quite adequate, and by nightfall the bearers were clearing the two brigades by routes which converged to "Tunnel Post," now some 1,000 yards from the front line.

Throughout the day shell-fire was severe in the captured area. Captain May (3rd Field Ambulance) records that he

"ended up with four fit squads, fifteen men wounded, five missing and five worn out. Bearers all thoroughly done up."

Collecting Post. From about 8 a.m. casualties went through rapidly, "fifteen (stretcher cases) the first hour and then (about) forty an hour." The officer-in-charge found himself compelled to carry out much surgical treatment, chiefly for haemorrhage—to adjust or replace splints—and for "redressing," this work being done for the most part in the open but, on this day, with comparative impunity.

2nd Division. The clearing of the left sector of the front was not less satisfactory.

"It was not till 8.30 a.m. that the wounded began to come through to the collecting post in large numbers; from then on there was a constant stream, but the bearers were quite able to cope with the work, and German prisoners of war were made free use of. At midday shelling was severe and the new Bellewaarde station knocked in. As the line advanced nearly a mile, and R.A.P's had moved on, the 7th bearers (Divisional Reserve) were brought up. In the meantime the 19th Battalion had lent over 100 men at a critical moment. The tram trollies were blocked by the ammunition coming forward. Reinforcement of bearers (Corps Reserve) at 5 p.m. cleared the line. In less than ten hours nearly 600 stretcher cases were cleared without any congestion."[34]

The Loading Posts—Stretchers. For the first thirty-six hours the officer-in-charge of transport had little trouble. Horsed-waggons worked as far as Bellewaarde and The Crater. A "hold up" at The Culvert about 11 a.m.—when as many as forty-five stretcher cases lined the road—was met by forming a local circuit of Ford cars, which cleared between the two loading posts, connecting at Birr Cross-Road with the circuit of heavy cars, augmented for a few hours from the Corps Convoy.[35]

Walkers. The 3rd Field Ambulance diary remarks that walkers "had no difficulty" when once past the forward relay posts. At 6 p.m. trains cleared walking wounded direct from a light-railway siding near Birr Cross-Road via M.D.S. to Remy Siding group.

Advanced Dressing Station— Stretcher cases The advanced dressing station had been established by dint of much hard work on the part of previous occupants, and the incoming unit had spared no pains to fit the station for its most unusual rôle.

The station at Menin House was formed [says Major Crowther][36] by clearing out the cellars, reinforcing the ruins with sandbags, and erecting "elephant iron" cupolas. Patients were slid from the road down an inclined plane into the "operating room" where 3-4 "teams" could work at once. Good lighting was received by day from the road and by night from the portable acetylene outfits. At one end of the dressing room was a small cellar used by medical personnel—the rest bivouacked among the ruins or in the open. An excellent "mustard gas" treatment room was formed in a cupola with special staff and full supply of pyjamas (Red Cross) and blankets. Full and exact rules were laid down for the treatment of these cases.

Stretcher cases began to arrive at 9 a.m. and the numbers reached a maximum about 11 a.m. At that time "some congestion occurred owing to the difficulty of passing wounded

---

[34] From the war diary of the 5th Field Ambulance. Estimates made by officers in forward posts were almost always excessive. The number of stretcher cases admitted to the A.D.S., Menin Road, by 4 p.m. was 205; in addition 30 cases were waiting at The Culvert and 40 at Hooge.

[35] The Officer-in-Charge of the Convoy—Major Stack, R.A.M.C.—combined enterprise and initiative with excellent discretion in his novel command. Officially motor ambulance convoy cars worked only *behind the M.D.S.;* here, motor ambulances as well as lorries from the "combined" convoy worked in *front of the A.D.S.!*

[36] Of the 14th Field Ambulance, who, a few days later took over this station.

through the station quickly enough." It was relieved by cutting out for a time the "A" circuit and the A.D.S. All wounded arriving from the front who did not require immediate care were sent direct to C.C.S. or M.D.S.

The nature of the work done at this station varied somewhat with circumstances. In this battle (says Major Crowther) "casualties were taken in rotation to the 4 tables, splints adjusted, haemorrhage treated, resuscitation done—carried again to the Motor Ambulance Convoy, and thence to the C.C.S. group."

Walking Wounded began to arrive at the A.D.S. at 7 a.m. and then "came in a steady stream." Prisoners of war for the most part went past the Bund to "Shrapnel Corner"; the officer-in-charge (Major A. L. Buchanan) observed that their wounds were often very severe.[37] At the A.D.S. a quite elaborate station had been designed for the walking wounded. The R.M.O. of the 5th Field Artillery Brigade (Captain G. B. Lowe), who was assisting, noted:—

"The ground floor of a ruined house was used as a dressing room; elephant cupolas for cases awaiting dressing and evacuation. A sand-bagged cupola outside formed a very efficient buffet, run by the Y.M.C.A. The dressing room was manned by three M.O's and a large staff of dressers, with two clerks. An officer posted outside classified the cases and passed them along for dressing or clearance."

This officer found his chief difficulty in the fact that

"every man no matter how slightly wounded, is convinced that his wound must be redressed at the A.D.S., and also that he must have a 'ticket' (A.F.W. 3118) to take him further. This conviction was not easy to alter and men pressed on automatically into the dressing room."

The first train cleared both stations at 7.20 a.m., and then for a time this service ceased. Lorries came to the rescue[38] but at 10.30 a.m. the train service was resumed, and cleared a large portion of the casualties.

In the first twenty-four hours, ending 6 a.m. on the 21st, 2,200 Australian and about 1,000 British wounded passed through the two

---

[37] Wounded prisoners of war were always cleared by the same routes and procedure as other casualties, but usually took turn after those of a like severity. A larger proportion therefore, as here, went on foot, helped by their comrades.

[38] While directing the loading of these, Lieut.-Col. Nicholas, together with the D.A.Q.M.G. I Anzac, Lieut.-Col. S. G. Gibbs, was killed by a shell outside the A.D.S. Both were splendid officers—the former had been promoted from D.A.D.M.S. 1st Division.

stations; and, in the next, 800 and 550. The proportion of "stretchers" to "walkers" was roughly 1 to 3; that of killed to died of wounds, wounded, and gassed, was 1 to 3·6.

Evacuation, and the work at the M.D.S., went "without a hitch." Approximately 58 per cent. of stretcher cases went by "A" route, 27 per cent. by "B" route and 15 per cent. by "C." At Remy Siding the casualties from the I Anzac and X Corps arrived so rapidly as to cause some embarrassment, but the difficulty was met by a system of "rosters" whereby, when full, the station receiving was at once relieved by the next for duty.

Evacuation to C.C.S.

September 22nd-23rd. On both fronts the clearing of casualties quickly became systematised. By the method of trial and error—on a balance of the prime factors concerned, namely, distance, danger, and the duckboard tracks—the bearers and their officers and N.C.O's worked out the best routes and posts. By the 23rd in the 1st Division arrangements were adequate and personnel sufficient, though the bearers "had a heavy time" and casualties were considerable.

In the 2nd Division (says the diary of the 5th Field Ambulance)

"hot tea or coffee and fancy biscuits provided by Y.M.C.A. and Red Cross, and cigarettes, were provided at the collecting and all relay posts and at the A.D.S. For the first day personnel had bread and tinned meat, and thereafter cooked meat sent up on G.S. waggons to Bellewaarde ridge."

In both Divisions a good supply of food and "medical comforts" was maintained. In the 1st Division this was "one of the most satisfactory features of the operations."[39]

After this battle the Deputy-Director enquired regarding the system of "direct evacuation." Replies were entirely favourable. The A.D.M.S., 1st Division (Colonel Huxtable) described the method as

Battle of Menin Road : Comments by officers

"most satisfactory, cases were saved from delay and redressing which must occur when the wounded pass from A.D.S. to M.D.S. and then on to the C.C.S." Of the "Corps Central Bureau" the A.D.M.S.

---

[39] Diary of the 3rd Field Ambulance.

2nd Division wrote that its continuance was "very advisable." If records had been kept at the A.D.S. "congestion or inefficient recording or both would have occurred."

Major Chapman, in charge of bearers in the 2nd Division, appreciated "the lesson of this battle" as follows:—[40]

Difficulties: (1) Absence of roads—one main road had to be used which reached only to within 3,000 yards of any part of the front. (2) Lack of organised stations. (3) The great depth of the German shell-fire and its volume. (4) Mustard-gas shelling.

Main Features: (1) Keeping touch with advancing R.A.P's. This was done by ensuring that two squads at least of bearers moved forward with each R.M.O. or group of R.M.O's. (2) Use of returning combatants to carry wounded (*vide F.S. Regs.*). (3) Failure of trams and light railways. (4) Need for bearer reserves at close call. The bearer divisions of five field ambulances were used in a period of less than eight hours.

Results. In spite of the great success achieved the battle was, from the medical point of view, not without disturbing features. The A.D.M.S., 1st Division wrote to the Deputy-Director:—

"If losses are severe during any further offensive it is likely that there will be a grave shortage of stretcher-bearers. Casualties in this division among bearers total seventy, and the bearers have had very little rest."

Reliefs. On September 23rd the 1st and 2nd Divisions were replaced by the 5th and 4th and during the next two days the medical units of these formations swung into line for the next battle.

In the slow but inexorable advances (in low gear, as it were) of these "attrition" battles—with each stage 1,000-1,500 yards at most and each "battle," with dreadful iteration, providing its temporary crescendo of slaughter (commonly 2,000-3,000 killed or wounded) in the sustained carnage of the "offensive"—the machinery for clearing our own casualties had to move with the same clock-work precision as that designed by us to create them in the enemy. From zero hour of each "battle" the engineers, pioneers, and labour corps, with "fatigues" from the infantry in reserve, worked furiously to prepare traffic routes for the next advance,

Step by step

---

[40] Epitome of report in diary of 5th Field Ambulance.

five or six days hence. Field-guns were rushed up to gun-pits already dug by night in No-Man's Land, and ammunition and all other supplies to forward dumps. With even greater—and a twofold—urge for haste, the medical service must collect the human débris and clear what of it remained sentient from beneath the very wheels of the advancing juggernaut. Then, after some forty-eight hours the new divisions began to move in; and the officer-in-charge of the field ambulance detailed to clear the wastage of the next advance took over posts and stores, the bearer officers and N.C.O's got touch with the new aid-posts, formed new relays, and equipped and prepared them to meet the deluge from the next zero day; providing, meantime, for the stream of casualties from counter-attacks and bombardments.

Though charged with poignant memories for those who trod these tracks and manned the posts, who sustained the terrible toils, the moral conflicts, and the personal tragedies of these dreadful battles, by no weaving of words—even were space available—could the mere naming and locating on maps of all the new aid-posts, relays, and carries be made to convey much of interest or instruction to those for whom they must remain names—*et praeterea nihil.* In general, the medical scheme arranged for each battle was an extension, at most a variant, of that for the preceeding one; they were built up, as the line advanced, on the general "arrangements" described in the preceeding pages. The dominant motive always was that of advancing the scope of the wheeled-transport.

No attempt therefore is made to present a detailed picture of the medical work in each of the several battles. In maps and sketch maps provided throughout this chapter, the successive advances can be followed: R.M.O's move up and form new aid-posts, the bearer captains select from those abandoned the most safe and suitable for new ambulance posts, and, if possible, move up the "collecting post" and most forward treatment centre. The most striking changes in the medical scheme were due to the "side-slipping" of the I Anzac Corps to the left, as the line bestrode the ridge, this being necessary in order to direct the Australian thrust farther north, towards the new main objectives, Broodseinde and Passchendaele.

The battle launched on September 26th continued the advance some three-quarters of a mile. The I Anzac Corps was still the apex of the attack, its right directed along the main ridge, its left against the "Tokio" ridge. The attack, which was rendered much more difficult by a German thrust against the right on the previous day, began at 5.40 a.m. on the 26th; its methods and course were almost a replica of those of September 20th. With some minor vicissitudes, and not without hard fighting, the final objective was occupied by 7.30 a.m.: it placed the front in position for an attack against the main part of the ridge at Broodseinde.

September 23-29 : Battle of Polygon Wood

The casualties on the 26th and 27th were 787 killed and 2,770 wounded, of whom 124 died.

Medical Arrangements. I Anzac General Staff orders for the battle were issued on September 21st, and the "medical instructions" of the D.D.M.S. on the same day. The A.D.M.S. 5th Division (Colonel W. W. Hearne) would

"take over the right sector of the Corps front utilising such of his field ambulances for this purpose as may be necessary." In similar terms the A.D.M.S. 4th Division (Col. G. W. Barber) was instructed to relieve the 2nd; the A.D's.M.S. of the Divisions relieved were to hold 200 bearers in readiness for emergency "as Corps Reserve."

The outgoing units went with their brigades through the great staging camps behind Ypres—scene now of nightly bombings more ferocious and effective than any others experienced by the Australian force in the war[41]—to camps around Steenvoorde, Wippenhoek, and Ouderdom.[42] In these camps the facilities for bathing, recreation, and recuperation in general, were very good.

The 3rd Field Ambulance was relieved on September 23rd by the 14th (Lieutenant-Colonel Clive W. Thompson).[48] The A.D.M.S. 5th Division, Colonel Hearne, an officer of tireless energy who took nothing on trust, after inspecting his own aid-posts in Glencorse Wood explored also the circuit road laid on planks round Bellewaarde Lake. What he saw made him gravely

Right Sector : 5th Division

---

[41] On three successive nights casualties from Corps troops and formations in the staging camps averaged over 600.

[42] During the brief rests between the battles the medical units had little respite. Field hospitals were formed and the officers and tent divisions kept fully employed in the treatment and weeding out of sick from the relieved battalions. At this time the problem of "B" class men was becoming one of great importance in the A.I.F.

[48] On September 23 Lieut.-Col. Thompson was wounded and the unit was commanded for the battle by the senior officer, Major W. E. L. H. Crowther.

apprehensive for the impending and future battles. He advised the Deputy-Director that the use of wheeled-transport in advance of the Menin Road would be precarious, and the problem of clearing the front lines a very difficult one.

"In addition to the 100 (bearers) promised for the 25th and another 100 for the 26th (zero day), we shall almost certainly require 200 infantry to act as emergency bearers."

Bearers Move In. The bearers of the 14th, who had rejoined their unit at 11 a.m. on the 22nd after 48 hours duty in the line as "corps reserve,"

"were given [says Major Crowther] the best we could in the way of food and rest," but at 6 p.m. were required to move up to the Ramparts. At 3 a.m. on the 23rd they fell in for the route march to man the posts along the 5th Division line of clearance—the loading posts (Crater Post and Hooge Tunnel) and the Tank Gun post; and thence, through Glencorse Wood—"where the gas lay so thick as to nauseate"—to the 55th and 56th Battalion R.A.P's in "pill-boxes." Here *liaison* squads were left, "who, when the line advanced, would move with the R.M.O. to his new R.A.P., and work back his wounded." By noon all bearers were posted and settling down to the normal routine of clearing occasional casualties from the two R.A.P's; until zero hour this was done via two relays and the collecting post, to The Culvert—a little over 3,500 yards.

The bearer divisions of the 8th and 15th Field Ambulances (divisional reserve) reported at the Ramparts for duty at 6 p.m. on the 25th.

On the same day the shelters at The Culvert were heavily shelled, and a new post was formed in the Brigade Headquarters at Hooge Crater. Here

"in some deep, steep, and very wet dugouts wounded were lowered or raised by a hoist, and casualties held till they could be cleared by handcarry or Ford."

Left Sector: 4th Division

For this battle the 4th Division, which took over the left sector of the Corps, moved up from a fortnight's rest in the First Army area. The medical units had been reinforced, though not to strength. On September 24th the 4th Field Ambulance (Lieut.-Colonel H. H. B. Follitt) relieved the 5th (Major A. L. Buchanan). On this front the regimental aid-posts were now on Anzac Spur and cleared via right and left relay posts on

Westhoek ridge to Bellewaarde and thence via "Simon's Post" relay to Birr Cross-Road. The war diary of the 4th Field Ambulance states:—

"All the advanced posts except Westhoek left are concrete pill-boxes—that at 'Nun's Wood' (right relay) being a group of three all fairly roomy. The carry to Birr Cross-Road is 3,000 yards but the going is good. A timber track (the forward circuit) runs from Birr Cross-Road to within 100 yards of Bellewaarde post, but is a one-way track and has no turning points. Horsed-ambulances will be used if traffic conditions permit."

Rearward of the collecting posts the posts were unchanged, except that The Culvert was cut out.

Clearance, Sept. 26
The course of medical events in this battle followed closely those of September 20th. The weather throughout was fine, but the shelling of transport routes was far more severe.

5th Division. 14th Field Ambulance. With zero at 5.50 a.m.,

"from about 5 a.m.[44] the wounded came in a steady stream to the A.D.S. no congestion, prisoners of war carried many cases and were used to unload the ambulance cars. The fact that three Divisions—4th and 5th Australian and 33rd British—were clearing along the Menin Road caused some congestion there, but approximately 2,000 casualties from the 5th were cleared without serious delay or hitch.[45] In 24 hours 599 stretchers were cleared through the A.D.S."

The Divisional and Corps bearer reserves were brought in, and in addition 190 infantry were employed—approximately 600 in all. Until the 28th only a few Fords could get through to the Hooge Crater, and the carry from R.A.P's to Birr Cross-Road was over 4,000 yards. The preceding enemy counter-attack on the flank, which involved very stubborn and difficult fighting, made the tour of duty of this Division a very heavy one.

4th Division. 4th Field Ambulance. Casualties from this Division were much less than in the 5th and were cleared without hitch; but all reserves were used, and as well prisoners of war

---

[44] Heavy casualties were sustained by the 15th Brigade during the previous day and night through an enemy attack on the X Corps, supporting the right flank.

[45] A complaint of neglect on the part of the 14th Field Ambulance made by the officer commanding the 29th Battalion was taken up with vigour by the A.D.M.S. After searching enquiry Colonel Hearne reported to the A.A. & Q.M.G. that, on the contrary, the ambulance and attached infantry bearers had cleared for the battalion, whose own "arrangements had broken down."

Map No. 6

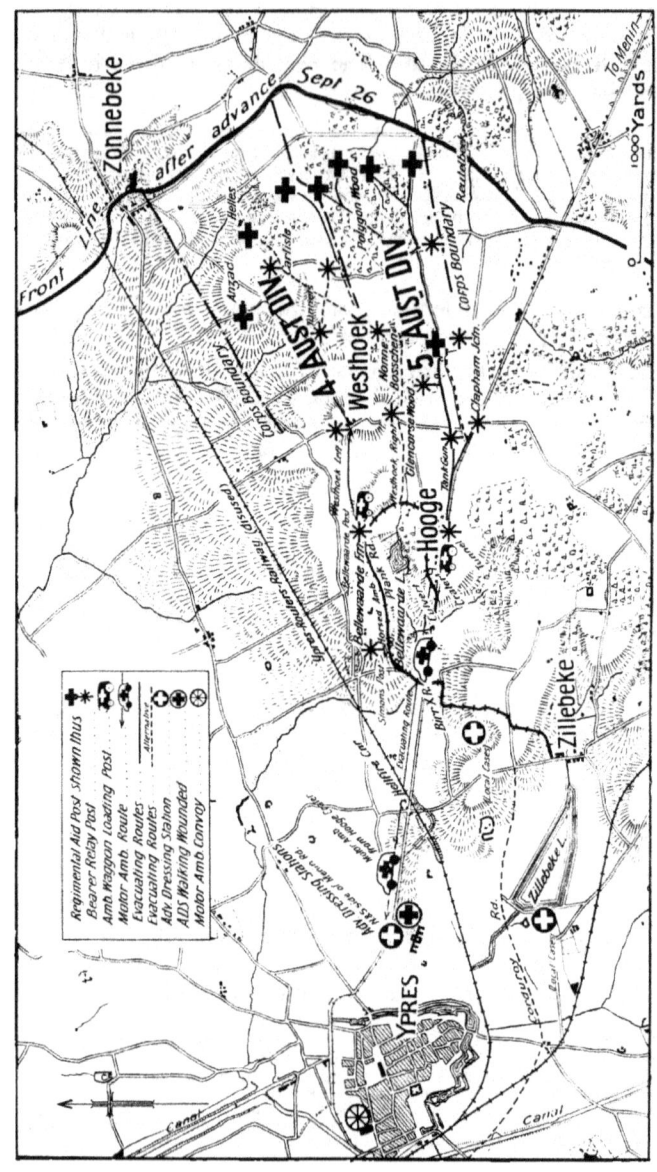

and fatigues of infantry. On September 26th alone these two divisions sustained 2,656 battle casualties, made up as follows:—

	K. in A.	D. of W.	Wounded	Gas	Total
4th Division	154	18	778	9	959
5th Division	412	30	1,250	5	1,697
Totals	566	48	2,028	14	2,656

Aid-posts were pushed forward to "right," "middle" and "left," R.A.P's at Helles, Garter Point, and Anzac clearing through relay posts at the Tunnels, Westhoek left and Bellewaarde posts in succession. Most casualties passed through a new post, "Garter Point."[46] The track that led through "Nun's Wood" was now abandoned and that on the left via Westhoek became the effective route for clearing casualties from the whole of the I Anzac front. By the 28th horse-drawn ambulance waggons worked systematically, though precariously, on the plank road from Bellewaarde to Birr Cross-Road.

Walking Wounded came through to the A.D.S. very rapidly. The war diary of the 4th Field Ambulance states:—

"by 9.45 p.m. the station was glutted with wounded, the majority 5th Division—remainder 4th and 33rd British (X Corps)." While time permitted wounded were re-dressed whenever there was any sign of haemorrhage or of derangement of dressings, "but since 5 a.m. no cases have been re-dressed at A.D.S. except those who obviously needed it. Others sent to C.C.S. after food and hot drinks."

The light railway could then take only 180—the rest went by lorry and bus.

An Accessory A.D.S. On the 27th on the instructions of the Deputy-Director, who feared for the safety of the stations on the Menin Road, the 4th Field Ambulance opened an accessory station in Ypres near the Lorry Park—"a site" (the Ambulance Commander reported) "at least as susceptible."

During the 24 hours ended 5 a.m. on the 27th 599 stretcher cases were admitted to the A.D.S. and 338 on the 28th. In the first 24 hours

[46] From this post "a message [stating that there was congestion] was received through A.D.M.S. Bearers and stretchers were at once sent up [from the A.D.S.] but no congestion whatever was found, the normal complement of squads having cleared without difficulty." This entry, from the Ambulance diary, illustrates the inefficiency of *liaison* through the official channel—Battalion, Brigade, Division, A.D.M.S., Ambulance Headquarters, to the forward ambulance posts. *See p. 283.* (The position of Garter Point is shown in map on *p. 224.*)

1,530 Australian wounded and 1,300 others (British, and prisoners of war) passed through the two stations. The proportion of killed to died of wounds, wounded or gassed was 1 to 3·7.

On October 1st, again in order to bring I Anzac opposite the crucial sector for the next attack, the Corps shifted northwards. The 14th Field Ambulance handed over to units of the 7th and 21st British Divisions (X Corps), and the old route of evacuation was not again used by the I Anzac Corps. By October 2nd, the new sector of I Anzac was held by the 1st and 2nd Australian Divisions, the 4th and 5th having been relieved. Between September 26th and that date the bearers of every Division in the Corps were used. In effect, indeed, the several bearer divisions were treated as a single unit or company.

After the Battle of Polygon Wood, at the instigation of the D.M.S., A.I.F. (Surgeon-General Howse), the Deputy-Director I Anzac Corps (Colonel Manifold) wrote to commanding officers of field ambulances:—

"Casualties amongst the A.A.M.C. are of serious gravity.[47] . . . Please see that all bearer officers fully realise that bearers should not take undue risks . . . crowding of men at the advanced posts should be avoided. . . . Have you any suggestions?"

All officers agreed that some form of cover should be found for bearers at the R.A.P's and relay posts—always badly shelled. Battalion commanders reporting collections of wounded should get in touch direct with bearer captains, giving in their message the time and exact location —often neglected.

"It is often impossible," says one reply, "to concentrate bearers where most wounded will be, because this is impossible to foresee."

But the fact was stressed that casualties to bearers were received in the course of their duty—"which they understand to be that of clearing R.A.P's and relay posts irrespective of conditions, and depending only on the requirements of the wounded. I think (wrote the O.C. 3rd Field Ambulance) the large number is due to the keen desire of the A.A.M.C. bearers . . . not to let their comrades in the infantry suffer through any lack of courage or keenness. . . . While bearers are resolutely determined not to allow wounded men to remain under fire, casualties will occur.

"My bearers are instructed to avoid unnecessary risk, but no urgent call from an R.A.P. has ever been held up."

The next battle, that of Broodseinde, must (as already has

---

[47] In this battle the 4th Division field ambulances sustained 15 casualties, the 5th, 47. Among the wounded (it may be mentioned) was Pte. W. A. Oldfield who served as a stretcher-bearer in the 15th Fld. Amb.

been suggested) be held to mark an important phase in the
war: after a most successful stroke made in
the morning of October 4th, there passed, at
4 in the afternoon all possibility that the great
British offensive in Flanders could attain
further important—not to say decisive—success. At that hour there began to fall rain
which thereafter (though no one could then prophesy this with
certainty) never allowed the ground to dry sufficiently to carry
the massive impedimenta necessary for success in this kind of
warfare.

Battle of Broodseinde, Sept. 29- Oct. 6

In the medical history, also, of this offensive a new outlook
opens up. From the afternoon of October 4th with dramatic
suddenness, a note of failure enters—deepening during the
month to one of tragedy, at times almost of despair.

Entry of II Anzac. Hitherto in this history we have been
concerned with the "medical arrangements" of a single corps,
clearing by a single route from one or two divisions: now—and
for the only time—two "Anzac" Army Corps, and two corps
schemes of clearance and evacuation, come together into the
picture.

Plans and objective. The attainment of the map-line objective[48]
set for this battle would advance the front on a width of 14,000 yards
to a depth, at its apex, of 2,500 yards, and would plant it athwart the
main ridge near Broodseinde—whence, since 1915, the Germans had
"looked out on the famous British salient as on a spread-out map."
(*Australian Official History, Vol. IV, p. 834.*)

In this advance the spearpoint of the attack was directed north-east,
towards Passchendaele, and was formed by the I and II Anzac Corps.
The order of battle from the right was IX and X Corps, I and II
Anzac (Second Army); and XVIII and XIV Corps (Fifth Army).
Mention has already been made of the relief by I Anzac Divisions
(1st and 2nd) on a front slightly more northward than that previously
held. On September 29th II Anzac Corps replaced the V British, the
3rd and New Zealand Divisions taking over the line fronting "Abraham
Heights" and the Gravenstafel Ridge (abandoned in the first gas attack
of the war, in April, 1915). The Roulers railway formed the boundary
between I and II Anzac.

Communications. The weakness, as the strength, of the "step by
step" advance lay in the shortness of the steps and their destructive

---

[48] In the "set-piece" battle the objective was a map line defined on the ground
partly by visible landmarks, partly by distance and compass bearings, partly by the
known location of enemy trenches etc. afforded by aeroplane and balloon observations.
R.M.O's were occasionally able to decide beforehand on the site for their aid-post.

violence. More and more completely, through the tearing up of the ground by bombardment, the fighting front, men and guns, were cut off from the rear, and communication had to be maintained through a few single roads and light railways, which came to have a significance akin to that of the main arterio-venous supply to a limb. In this offensive a collateral flow, often a matter of most urgent need, could but slowly be created, and almost always was inadequate to maintain an effective circulation.

Roads and Rail. After the Battle of Polygon Wood stupendous efforts were made to force forward the road and rail circuits from Birr Cross-Road to and beyond Westhoek. The Bellewaarde-Hooge plank circuit, 3,200 yards, had been completed in time for "Polygon Wood"; a new one, begun on September 20th, eventually linked this with Westhoek. In preparation for October 4th "Smith's Road" was thrust out from Westhoek toward Zonnebeke, but it exceeded the combined resources of Second Army and I Anzac Corps to plank it beyond Westhoek, and this accordingly remained a "dirt" track till the rains, when it became mud, and almost impassable.[49]

It had been found impossible also to complete the duckboard tracks across the country captured on September 26th. The II Anzac area was even worse off in this respect. Across the Zonnebeke swamp itself the II Anzac engineers laid some duckboard tracks but the roads and railways left to this Corps by the V Corps were far behind those of I Anzac.

Medical Arrangements I Anzac

The problem of clearing the front line had become now a most difficult one. The bearer divisions were much below strength;[50] at the same time their task was far harder. The slide of the Corps front to the left had sheared across its forward lines of supply and of clearance; the route via Hooge had been lost, and no new one taken over. Already the aid-posts were along Tokio Ridge. The foot tracks from the line converged to Anzac Ridge. The next advance would carry the front five miles from the loading posts on the Menin Road.

It was agreed, however, at a conference, that the notable success achieved in previous battles justified a continuance of the same methods.

The 1st Field Ambulance (Lieut.-Colonel Brennan) was to clear the 1st Division stretcher cases "to where motor-ambulance cars can

---

[49] The task of laying the duckboard tracks and roads was a terrible one. An average "duckboard" was 6 feet long by 18 inches wide and weighed, when wet, some 35-40 lb. The planks for the traffic roads (as on the Zonnebeke and Westhoek circuits) were 10 feet by 2½ to 4 inches by about a foot. The work of those concerned in this "service of maintenance" is commended by the Australian Official Historian in terms reserved by him for service of exceptional merit. Very heavy casualties were sustained in men, animals and vehicles by all the units engaged.

[50] In the 5th Division on Sept. 25 less than 200 bearers were available instead of 324. The 1st Division was even more reduced.

pick them up," and walking wounded of both divisions from Westhoek to C.C.S. The 6th (Lieut.-Colonel A. H. Moseley) was to clear the 2nd Division, and stretchers of both "from motor-loading post to A.D.S." Motor-transport was re-arranged—A.D.M.S. 2nd Division was to have 16 large cars and 16 Fords. A reserve of 16 large cars from the 4th and 5th Divisions was held at the C.M.D.S. The units clearing the line retained their horsed-waggons to clear stretchers "whenever circumstances render evacuation by motor impossible."

After each of the first two battles the A.D's.M.S. concerned had urged that as soon as possible the advanced dressing station be moved up. Hitherto, however, only a precarious service of horsed-waggons and Fords had worked in front of Birr Cross-Road; but now, in anticipation of an advance, the 1st Field Ambulance was instructed

"The forward policy— The A.D.S.

"to see to the preparation and equipping of the ambulance post at Westhoek Ridge, in view of its use as an A.D.S. should circumstances permit."

The Engineers began work here on October 1st, and by October 4th the station was ready. To offset the inordinate length of the clearing circuit the Deputy-Director arranged that a service of broad-gauge trains should evacuate wounded direct to C.C.S. from a siding in Ypres. Arrangements were complete for an "advanced operating centre" at the C.M.D.S. (2nd Field Ambulance), but the idea was not favoured by Second Army and was dropped.

The Divisions. The problem faced by the Assistant-Directors was common to every element in the Army—communications and cover. The O.C. 1st Field Ambulance reported:—

"Owing to the formation of the ground and heavy fighting there was no natural cover save in the block-houses, and all that had survived were in great demand for Brigade, Battalion and Company headquarters, signal and A.A.M.C. posts."

In particular, the siting of R.A.P's—the crux of the problem of clearing the front—was a most difficult matter.[51]

1st Division: 1st Field Ambulance. Infantry fatigues from

---

[51] In the maps the position only of those which were retained as ambulance posts is shown. In each battle they must be conceived as scattered, from soon after zero, over the captured area or just behind it, from one to three posts serving each brigade in line.

the battalion in reserve were used in making the preparations, so as to rest the ambulance bearers for the actual battle. In the four days available great efforts were made to push forward the focal point in the scheme for clearing the front.

To this end "Westhoek relay" was developed as a "forward A.D.S." Thirteen "splinter-proof cupolas" were dug in by the Engineers behind the ridge, water tanks installed, and the staff at Bellewaarde transferred thither. Large reserves of stretchers, blankets, Thomas splints, and dressings were stored along the route from the Menin Road to the R.A.P.'s; rations and medical comforts were carried up to Westhoek.

Dispositions. For this battle bearer officers were stationed at "Helles" (relays) and "Garter Point" (controlling the R.A.P.'s). The commanding officer himself was at Westhoek, the transport officer at Bellewaarde, and an officer-in-charge at the A.D.S. by the Menin Road. The bearer divisions of all three field ambulances were available.

2nd Division: 6th Field Ambulance. During its tour of the front, October 2nd-11th, the 6th Field Ambulance faced three distinct problems in succession:—

(1) On account of the side-slip to the left, new ambulance posts had to be found, and a new line of clearance formed for the battle of October 4th. (2) New routes were opened up and new relay posts formed to meet developments in the military situation. (3) To straighten out the division's line of evacuation, after the advance northwards, a new scheme was created by which casualties were cleared down the left flank along the Ypres-Zonnebeke road, instead of by the right flank.

For October 4th the following arrangements were made:—

The 6th Field Ambulance took over on October 1st. The crowded condition of the Ypres-Zonnebeke road and lack of cover on the left flank and centre decided the commanding officer (Colonel Moseley) to clear from Anzac Ridge down the right to Westhoek Ridge. The only line of strong-posts affording suitable shelter for this lay along the boundary line between the two divisions and was claimed by both. The two medical units concerned agreed to work together "by a process of mutual give and take." The three main posts—Bellewaarde loading post, Westhoek collecting post, and the "Tunnels" relay (three concrete-covered steel cupolas) were held in common. At Carlisle's Post and Ideal House, R.A.P. and relay posts were formed. The aid- and relay-posts and routes from the left and right brigade fronts met at Westhoek, whence casualties were cleared by light railway, horsed-waggons and hand carry.

Before the action 750 blankets, 300 stretchers, and many Thomas and other splints and dressings were sent up to the forward posts. Three large dumps had to be placed in the open, and these suffered much from shell-fire.

Colonel Begg's scheme reflected the methods of Second Army and Messines. It was based on a "corps main dressing station" and "walking wounded collecting station," each staffed by several field ambulances. All casualties were to be admitted there, passed through the A. and D. Books, and given A.T.S. A "Corps combined convoy" was formed to clear both A.D.S. and M.D.S.

II Anzac Corps

3rd Division.[52] The intimate *aura* of "The Salient" surrounds the names of the ambulance posts taken over by the New Zealand and 3rd Australian Divisions; the routes of clearance were those used by the Canadians in the Second Battle of Ypres in April and May, 1915. The main dressing and walking wounded collecting stations (11th Australian and 4th New Zealand Field Ambulances) were at "Red Farm" and the Vlamertinghe Mill on the Ypres-Poperinghe road. The 10th Field Ambulance took over the "gas-treatment centre" at Brandhoek and a "sick distributing centre."

In the cellars of the "Prison House" in Ypres, the 9th Field Ambulance (Lieut.-Colonel F. A. Maguire) formed headquarters and accessory A.D.S., and an advanced dressing station at Potijze (the "White Château") a mile from Ypres. The "walking wounded collecting post" at "Mill Cott" cleared by lorries and light railway to Vlamertinghe. Here the Y.M.C.A. ran a "buffet." Heavy motors loaded at Bavaria House clearing down the Zonnebeke Road; Fords and horsed-waggons worked from "Frost House."

Bearers Move In. On the night of October 3rd-4th the bearers of the 10th and 11th Field Ambulances manned the regimental and relay posts relieving those of the 9th who were then held as reserve at the Prison House.

The orders of the Deputy-Director required that R.M.O's should "notify immediately the nearest Field Ambulance post of any change in the position of the R.A.P."[53]

---

[52] A very full account of medical work during October on the II Anzac front is given in the *New Zealand Medical Service in the Great War, 1914-1918*, by Lieut.-Col. A. D. Carbery.

[53] From diary of A.D.M.S. 1st Division.

Map No. 7

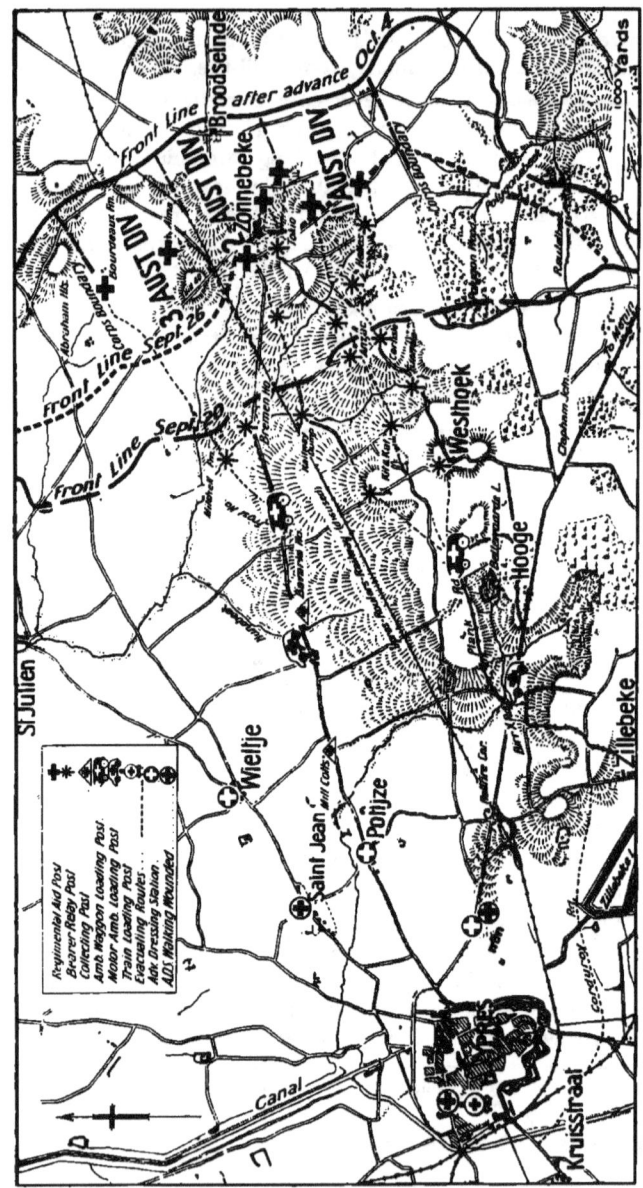

The Battle of Broodseinde—The scheme of clearance after the Advance of 4th October, 1917. Subsequent extensions of the plank road are not shown.

4th-5th Oct., 1917] THIRD BATTLE OF YPRES 225

Broodseinde (October 4th). The Battle. The actual battle of Broodseinde was fought mainly in the hours before the rain fell. The effect of the impasse due to the mud was not felt in it, and its success was even more dramatic than that of the two preceding battles. From zero hour, at 6 a.m. the advance on both Anzac fronts was almost exactly to time. The Australian attack met a German counter-attack timed for the same hour, and completely shattered it, capturing or killing both the troops and many of their headquarters. The line reached in the three divisions is shown in the map.

The casualties sustained by the Australian Divisions in the two Corps on October 4th and 5th were:—*I Anzac*: 1st Division, killed 518, wounded, 1,381. 2nd Division, killed 403, wounded 1,332. Ratio of killed to wounded and died of wounds, 1 to 3·0. *II Anzac*: 3rd Division, killed 400, wounded 1,459. Ratio of killed to wounded and died of wounds, 1 to 3·6.

Broodseinde: Clearing the Battlefield. From this great battle the wounded were collected, cleared and evacuated with a celerity which in the circumstances is remarkable. For, unlike the battle itself, which by 10 a.m. had been well won, in neither Corps did "medical arrangements" work out "according to plan." The rain caught the retiring stream of wounded intermingled on the narrow plank roads with artillery and other material of attrition moving up to prepare for an intended advance to victory five days hence. On the I Anzac front the waggon loading posts were forced back to the Menin Road, on that of II Anzac to Bavaria House.

I Anzac Corps The general course of events is described by the Deputy-Director (Colonel Manifold) :—[54]

Oct. 4th. The attack opened at 6 a.m.: at 9 a.m. walking wounded came in fairly large numbers and the service of lorries (2 every 5 minutes) had to be augmented. At 10 a.m. stretcher cases began to arrive. A broad-gauge train was despatched at 10.45 a.m. with 300 cases, 24 being stretchers. A.D.M.S. 1st Division short of bearers—12th Field Ambulance (4th Division) bearers in (Corps) reserve at M.D.S. sent up in returning ambulance waggons. By mid-day both A.D's.M.S. had asked for two bearer divisions additional to their own three. This extra demand (which used up all reliefs) was occasioned by the inability to use horsed-waggons to effect on the slippery planked road, a one-way circuit, with passing points, but made useless by artillery limbers making short (two-way) journeys. With this road out of use the bearer carry was 8,000 yards, but when it was used to Westhoek the carry was reduced by (some) 3,000 yards. Infantry put at my disposal as emergency were sent up at 6 a.m. on the 5th and German prisoners were freely used.

Before 2 p.m. (on 4th) 500 stretcher cases had passed through the A.D.S. and about 1,500 walking wounded. Of the latter some 600 went

[54] The account has here been epitomised.

by broad-gauge train from Ypres together with about 40 stretcher cases, and another 260 by light railway, of whom 200 with some stretcher cases were sent from Bellewaarde straight to C.C.S. This saved ambulance cars considerably, and it was the only occasion [in these battles] on which the light railways have been of any real service in evacuation.

1st Division. 1st Field Ambulance. The bombardment preparatory to the German counter-attack fell on this division as it lay out on its jumping-off tapes, and, though the counter-attack was immediately afterwards shattered, heavy casualties had been suffered on the tapes. These were carried by the regimental bearers to the aid-posts, and very quickly cleared by prisoners, who worked under ambulance bearers in parties of ten to twenty. During the morning most of the R.M.O's moved up and the bearer carry to Westhoek lengthened accordingly.

"Wounded began to arrive at Westhoek at 7.15 a.m. 100 prisoners of war carrying to Bellewaarde ridge from the front. Our men all working right forward" (chiefly in the captured area).[55]

Enemy shell-fire was fierce and at 4 p.m. it began to rain. From this moment the task of the bearers was one of constant and most dreadful toil. At 8 p.m. the officer in control at Helles reported:—

"Carry from right and left R.A.P's impossible until dawn. At 7 p.m. about 40 stretcher cases remain beyond the (Zonnebeke) swamp at R.A.P., all under cover."

2nd Division. 6th Field Ambulance. This front was cleared with expedition, but only by using very large numbers of bearers.

"Before the battle," Colonel Moseley reported, "the infantry bearers were replaced by the Ambulance reserves, and on the 4th the fine weather prevailing [till the afternoon] made evacuation easy and rapid." Clearing in common, though it caused some confusion in checking stores, saved much labour and ensured an ample supply—"an important matter since the stream of stretcher cases was very rapid, owing to the great use made of German prisoners."

The report continued:—

"The following figures show that the field of battle was entirely cleared within 10 hours of the beginning of the attack: stretcher cases evacuated to C.C.S. from A.D.S.—8 a.m. to 12 noon, 216; noon to 4 p.m., 316; 4 p.m. to 9 p.m., 96—Total 628."

---

[55] From the war diary of A.D.M.S. 1st Aust. Division. At 10 a.m. the A.P.M. prohibited the use of the German prisoners for stretcher-bearing after they had got as far back as Bellewaarde.

The officer-in-charge of the bearers (Major E. L. Hutchinson) reported of his "hand carry" that

On the whole everything went smoothly, though the work of the stretcher-bearers was very heavy, chiefly through the fact that for some days there were no duckboards forward.

During this night and on the following day horsed-waggons for stretcher cases and lorries for walking wounded plied precariously on the plank circuits. The advancing (by the Canadians) of the medium light railhead to Anzac Ridge on October 5th helped to relieve the situation,[56] but on the 7th stretcher cases were being hand-carried from the R.A.P's right through to Birr Cross-Road, a matter of five miles! And in the 1st Division only eleven ambulance squads were available to the A.D.M.S for reliefs, though the bearers of both units had been augmented by large infantry fatigues.

The following from a personal diary[57] describes the work at a combined relay:—

"*C.M.D.S. October 2nd.* The Gothas over again to-night—it will be quite a pleasure to be up the line.

"*Oct. 3rd. Tunnel Relay Post, Westhoek.* 3rd Field Ambulance bearers (1 officer, 2 N.C.O's, 52 privates) relieve the 1st for a spell, but we may be in for the 'stunt.' By lorries to A.D.S. then walk to Westhoek and on to 'the Tunnel'—3 connected German cupolas—leaving squads at each. Through shell-holed country to 'left R.A.P.' near Anzac, and another ¼ mile to 'Helles,' 2nd Battalion R.A.P. Left squads, and returned to the Tunnels, pretty knocked up. Bearers to-day have carried both 2nd and 1st Division casualties back to Westhoek. . . . We are just N. of our old September 20 stunt, and can see Polygon Wood.

"*Oct. 4th.* Prisoners streaming in and casualties pouring through; our 8 squads stationed here are out all the time. I am doing a few dressings and keeping hot coffee and drinks going. All in great heart. *Later.* It has been a cruel day for the bearers; the enemy pounded our supports and the guns in front of us. At Helles Major Hunt killed and the M.O's cut off by shell-fire all day. Prisoners carried here from "Ideal House" for 2 or 3 carries; then as we were congested I pushed them off (to the rear) in twos. The bearers worked without stopping—I gave them rum and hot drinks and their rations. In the afternoon it rained and the tracks were frightful—there were continual slips and falling into holes. When the rain stopped it was sloppy and sticky and the men absolutely done up, but they kept cheery and worked till 8 when I made them rest till midnight as few cases were coming down to us from the front and the 4th Division (bearers) eased us.

---

[56] Like the D.D.M.S. the 1st Field Ambulance diary states that this was "the only occasion during the offensive when the light railways were of real use to the walking wounded."

[57] Of Capt. L. May, 3rd Field Ambulance.

"*Oct. 5th.* Going again—dugout[58] crowded, almost impossible to move. The 3rd Brigade moved up on a daylight relief (of the 1st and 2nd Brigades). Battalions working in our valley digging new gun-posts and building railways. Cases poured in pretty fast for a while—wounded who had been collected and housed in pill-boxes for the night. Rain made the mud less sticky—it was cruel to see the bearers wilted up and almost dropping, with staring eyes and listless faces but ready when another case came in to get it away. 2 *p.m.* 15th Field Ambulance bearers (relief) came along. Went to Ideal Post and to Helles, and got the men down and sent them along to Westhoek. I appreciated the awful time the bearers had on their carries, as I slipped and slopped along without any weight to bother me. Met my men from Nun's Wood Post and went along the Decauville track and on to the Corduroy Road with its dead horses on the sides and overturned limbers; with guns and waggons and howitzers and mules in hundreds, and carrying parties, squeezing us off the track into the muddy shell holes. At Birr Cross-Road on familiar ground, and on to A.D.S., the road thick with lorries and ambulances, horsed and motor. At C.M.D.S. hot food, rum issue, cigarettes and an extra blanket.

"The bearers compare the carry this time as being worse than Flers, owing to the mud and the number of cases—Flers mud was deeper and worse, but they had only 4 carries a day there; and to Bullecourt, when it was fine weather but the shells were thick and the carries long."

The relief was for twenty-four hours only; on the night of October 6th these bearers were again in the line.

Waggon Posts. The advance greatly relieved the Menin Road. On October 8th Westhoek was heavily shelled and the "A.D.S." was transferred *pro tem.* to the Tunnels waggon post. This sector, however, was not again involved in heavy fighting, and, though a large flow of sick, gassed, and casual wounded passed along the Menin Road by Hooge, the major stream from the I Anzac Corps was again directed leftwards, henceforth to be evacuated down the Ypres-Zonnebeke route. To this route, between October 6th and 8th, the 6th Field Ambulance with great labour transferred its posts, routes and relays.

The attack of II Anzac advanced the front across country which the rain turned into a dreadful morass. The R.A.P's moved up some mile and a half to the vicinity of "Bordeaux" and "Alma," the two brigades clearing respectively north and south of "Hill 40" to Bremen House relay. By 10 a.m., according to the diary of the 9th Field Ambulance,

II Anzac Corps.
3rd Division

"all the bearers (of the 3rd Division) are employed in the forward area and all reserve used up."

---

[58] All protected posts were termed "dugouts."

"Fords" could no longer clear from Frost House; after the rain even horsed-waggons cleared Bavaria only by using four horses to each waggon. At 2 p.m. Major R.J. Taylor (in charge of bearers) was asking for yet more bearers:—

"The carrying is extremely heavy and very slow, as there are no made paths, and the country is a continuous chain of shell-holes and the ground very muddy."

At 4 p.m. it was "raining heavily and very cold; ground extremely heavy and sticky with mud." At 9 p.m. bearers were

"dead beat. Still 12 cases to clear from R.A.P's. Things practically at a standstill."

An infantry fatigue appeared at 10 p.m. and most bearers were relieved for the night, but next morning they had to be rushed up to deal with a "congestion" at the aid-posts. At 5 p.m. on the 5th Major Taylor reported "all clear at R.A.P's."

Clearance to A.D.S. Fords and horsed-waggons were used to convey stretcher cases to the A.D.S. at the Prison House, Ypres, from the most advanced point that could be reached by road—Frost House or Bremen—the heavy cars of the division in the line starting every five minutes were used to evacuate the A.D.S. via the Prison House to the M.D.S. "This system" (Colonel Begg observed) "was quite effective and casualties were cleared in a minimum time." Walking wounded were evacuated by light railway and lorries.

Advanced Dressing Stations. In the II Anzac Corps the "advanced" dressing stations were no more than treatment and transport relays to the "main" dressing station at Red Cottage.

Between 6 a.m. and noon of October 4th 314 stretcher cases were cleared through the Prison House and Potijze A.D.S's. It is recorded that "Practically all wounded were from high explosive—no gassed, very few bullet and shrapnel wounds."

C.M.D.S. "Red Farm." Though his orders prescribed that all casualties should be cleared through the C.M.D.S. the Deputy-Director paid homage to the new ideas by instructing that

"As few dressings will be done as is compatible with efficient surgical treatment. At A.D.S. only dressings of an urgent nature . . . all cases of fractured femur to be adjusted with Thomas splint. Tourniquets must be removed—except in most exceptional cases—and never sent to C.C.S. At M.D.S. cases will not again be dressed except for definite reason. Officers should remember that all cases are redressed at the C.C.S."

In his interpretation of this order the A.D.M.S., 3rd Div., "played for safety"; 6 officers and 140 other ranks were employed in the M.D.S. The diary of the 9th Field Ambulance says:—[59]

> In the admitting huts (3 medical officers and 10 O/r) records were taken—hot drinks and warm clothing provided, A.T.S. given and cases sorted out: "E"—Evacuation, "D" Dressing, "R" Resuscitation. In the dressing room 6 tables worked, 2 orderlies at each table, one of which was reserved for "aseptic work"; 5 medical officers were always in attendance, with one for "urgent cases not unloaded." Returns were made up in a special "recording room."

Evacuation. Battle casualties were evacuated to thé Nine Elms group—chiefly to No. 3 A.C.C.S.

This remarkable battle marks the climax of a well defined stage in the evolution of the British Medical Service, as in the course of the war itself. Until the final advance to victory it was the last which involved the problem of moving up the medical posts. It illustrates at their best the methods evolved during attrition warfare. The technique of "evacuation"—implying, as its prime purpose, the prompt removal of wounded from the battlefield—was never in the A.I.F. more effectively applied. In spite of the immense extension of the bearer circuit, the rate of flow to the C.C.S. was as rapid as in any previous or subsequent engagement in which the A.I.F. was involved. And the prime factor in this achievement was the efficient work of the bearer divisions and their prompt exploitation of success. It is convenient here, as the scene of their worst trial, to discharge a bounden duty and service by recording the fine work of *the drivers,* both horse and motor.

Battle of Broodseinde : comment

The conduct of medical affairs by the 1st and 2nd Divisions stands out in the history of the service for team work and enterprise.[60] The 3rd Division was confronted by peculiar diffi-

---

[59] The account is here epitomised.
[60] The field messages that passed between the Commanding Officer of the 1st Field Ambulance and his junior officers in charge of posts and stations were assembled as this unit's war diary. They illustrate medical co-operation in battle at its best. The 6th Field Ambulance compiled a special report for the Deputy-Director.

culties largely due to the fact that II Anzac, with shortened time for preparation, could not extend its duckboard tracks over a large part of the morass. Reports from medical and combatant officers of the division also strongly complained that there was undue allocation of trained ambulance bearers for the corps dressing station. Something approaching a breakdown in evacuation occurred,[61] for which, however, the medical service of the division seems to have been in no way responsible.

From October 5th onwards the weather was bitter and the problem of "wound shock" became a major factor in the medical situation. On the 7th, 150 "walking" cases of trench foot were cleared through the 1st Field Ambulance.

---

[61] See *Australian Official History, Vol. IV, p. 882*. In a "review" of this battle for the A.D.M.S., Colonel Maguire complained that "the three ambulances were 60 under strength to start with, and some of the men unfit for more than one carry." Even the full quota of bearers was (he urged) "far too small for a division—they are quite unable to cope with any (large) number of casualties . . . and for efficient reliefs a reserve of at least 300 infantry bearers should be available."

CHAPTER X

THE END OF ATTRITION WARFARE

WITH the next series of battles we enter upon a sombre and terrible phase of this offensive. For the Allies the sands of time ran out fast; the glass must soon be turned for the Central Powers, whose corps after corps, relieved (as was soon to be known) from the Russian front, were even then beginning to be sent west to force victory in 1918. The Battles of Poelcappelle (October 9th) and First Passchendaele (October 12th) were pushed through to their bitter failure in a desperate effort to achieve a break-through in the north before the winter.[1] As the last stroke in the warfare of attrition they and their sequels closed the penultimate phase of the war on the Western Front. Cambrai, battle of surprises, herald of the dawn and of open warfare, was ready for launching—held up (as Haig himself has revealed) only through fear that the Germans might strike at the French if the pressure of the British offensive at Ypres was relaxed for a moment.[2]

The Achilles heel of the "step by step" advance was revealed in the failure along the whole British front to push forward the road and rail circuits. The rains laid bare the weak spot; accurate shelling of all available traffic routes effectively hamstrung the attacking force.

Both Second and Fifth British Armies moved against a deep objective. In the II Anzac Corps the 3rd and N.Z. Divisions were replaced on October 6th by two British ones, the 49th and 66th. In I Anzac Corps the 1st and 2nd remained in the line and took some part in the battle. On the level ground Fifth Army made progress, but Second Army's attack

**Poelcappelle,
October 9**

---

[1] For a concise and exact statement of the conditions which induced Haig to continue the offensive, *see Sir Douglas Haig's Despatches, p. 127.*

[2] ". . . The probability of the French Army breaking up in 1917 compelled me to go on attacking. It was impossible to change sooner from the Ypres front to Cambrai without Pétain's coming to press me not to leave the Germans alone for a week on account of the awful state of the French troops. You, even, did not know the facts as Pétain told them to me in confidence." (Letter to Brigadier-General Charteris quoted in *The Fighting Forces, Vol. XIII, No. 1, April 1936, p. 33.*)

29. ZONNEBEKE CHURCH, OCTOBER, 1917

The photograph looks over the Broodseinde Ridge into the country beyond. Passchendaele lies just below the left-hand top corner, and the railway cutting through Broodseinde Ridge can be seen near the right-hand top corner. A shell is bursting on the ridge half-way between the two. The woods at the top of the picture are in the open country beyond.

British Air Force Photograph.
Aust. War Memorial Collection No. A3321.

To face p. 232.

30. THE PLANK ROADS AND DUMP AT BIRR CROSS-ROAD, OCTOBER, 1917

The road in the foreground is a one-way loading track at the dump. On the left in the distance can be seen a train on the light railway to Bellewaarde Ridge.

Aust. War Memorial Official Photo. No. E4613.

To face p. 233.

on Passchendaele was a disastrous failure; the circumstances of the assault by the 66th Division are among the most dreadful in the whole history of the war. The 2nd Australian Division attacked with one brigade which during the whole of the previous 24 hours had been employed, under dreadful conditions, on road and rail repair. Its attack, like that of the 66th, failed; farther south, from a minor feint by the 1st Division, of 85 who went out only 14 returned unwounded.

On both Anzac fronts the approach to the line lay now for the most part across a trackless waste of shell-torn soil, or in the low ground of the Ravebeek through deep swamp and slush. After the advance, until duckboard tracks could be pushed out, troops, walking wounded, and stretcher-bearers must thread their way along the mounds of loose soil or mud between shell-holes "as closely placed as the cells in a honeycomb."[3]

Medical arrangements

2nd Division. Though "medical arrangements" were unchanged, in effect each division now cleared its own casualties. The 2nd Division's scheme was based chiefly on the "emergency A.D.S." near the Ramparts, which evacuated by both broad-gauge train and M.A.C.

The front. From the report of Colonel Moseley (6th Field Ambulance) :—

On October 6th . . . plans were made to abandon the right flank and evacuate entirely down the left and to post waggons as far up the Ypres-Zonnebeke road as possible. Stores were sent by road and across country to the loading post at Frost House and on the 8th we were able to cut out the right line and clear to the Ypres-Zonnebeke road forming new relays near Zonnebeke (at the "Brick-kiln" and "Cordial factory"). By the night of October 8-9 all the new posts were manned.

From the personal diary of Colonel Sutton (A.D.M.S. 2nd Australian Division) :—

6/10/17. Very cold, heavy rain. We are again to side-step to the left. . . . Asked D.D.M.S. for 250 more bearers. *7th.* Cold and foggy—rain, rain, rain. Up at 4 a.m. (new time)[4] picked up Moseley to reconnoitre; road very bad from half mile in front of Potijze, thousands of men working at it. Daimlers can ply to Potijze and Fords to Bavaria House. *8th.* A.D.M.S. 66th British Division tried to warn me off Zonnebeke road, but I told him straight I was going on with it as it was our only means. The weather is damnable.

---

[3] The bearers of the 2/3rd East Lancs. Field Ambulance relieving the 9th Field Ambulance on the 6th were 8 hours late at the posts. Moving up for the battle on the 9th, the attacking troops of the 66th Division took 12 hours to traverse 5 miles, and barely arrived on the tapes, exhausted, by zero hour.

[4] On Oct. 7 the clocks were retarded an hour, reverting to true (or "winter") time. "Summer" time had begun on March 24.

During the battle of October 9th only horsed-waggons could work to Frost House and the bearer carry was about three miles. Some duckboard tracks had been pushed out, but regimental bearers and many of those from the ambulances had to carry across the unbridged mudfield.

"From the 8th to the 11th," Major Hutchinson records, "the work was so heavy that for a large part of the time 6 men had to carry one stretcher—8 and even 12 men were used in parts. Under these conditions the stretcher-bearers rapidly became exhausted, and absolutely so after 24 hours' work. Usually they were relieved after 24 hours, but owing to the universal shortage some 36 and even 48 hour shifts were done. About 200 bearers (ambulance and infantry) were continually at work. The infantry suffered more, if possible, than the ambulance men as their shoulders were not hardened to the stretcher handles. The only serious block, however, was at an R.A.P. in the front line on the railway near Zonnebeke where the cases were held up for 12 hours by shell-fire on the railway line [the only way out]. The continued wet and cold made it necessary to use 3, 4, and even 5 blankets per patient and we had just enough to see us through.[5] Ground sheets, sent up in large numbers on the 8-9th to cover the wounded, were of great service. Blankets, stretchers, splints, dressings were fed up to the advanced posts by returning squads from relay to relay but when the bearers were exhausted it was difficult to keep this stream constant right up to the line."

Waggons. The Ypres-Menin road was very much congested and on the Zonnebeke Road the waggons could only very slowly get up to the loading posts at Potijze and Frost House and, at times, took three hours to return.

A.D.S. These delays were reflected at the A.D.S., Ypres, where stretcher cases did not begin to arrive till 1 p.m. By 4 p.m. 115 stretchers and 350 others had passed through. Much time was saved here by having all patients examined and classified on the road; many were sent direct to C.C.S., by M.A.C. or ambulance train.

In a report by the Officer Commanding the 6th Field Ambulance, the comment is made that

"the stretcher-bearers of a Division are insufficient to cope with the casualties of a modern battle, especially in wet weather, and with a long carry."

In any retirement, however orderly and devoted the efforts of the bearers, many severely wounded men must die. In this

---

[5] The wastage of medical stores—stretchers, blankets, food and so forth—in these operations was enormous, and was a constant source of anxiety to those concerned. At this time even for the Allies the problem of *material* including food-stuffs (especially fats) was becoming serious, and the co-operation of field units in the work of salvage was strongly pressed by rewards and punishments.

action the 2nd Division had 334 "killed in action" in a battle casualty list of 961—a proportion of 1 "killed in action" to 1·9 "wounded," as compared with 1 to 4·2, the average in the A.I.F. over the war.

In the *1st Division* attempt was made by bearers under Red Cross flag to search for the wounded from this division who were left in front of the line, but those who went out were at once shot down.[6]

October 10th-15th. With this check, which on the 12th was turned to check-mate, the medical work in these battles, like the offensive itself, takes the character of anti-climax. "Medical arrangements" changed but little; the problem that confronted administrative and commanding officers alike became more and more how to maintain in the forward zone a strength of bearer squads and supply of medical stores sufficient to offset the increasing needs of wounded men and the retarded pace of the transport units and their wastage through mud, enemy action, exhaustion, and break-down. On a few occasions, indeed, the work of rescue in some part failed; that at no time did it do so completely was achieved only by the use of infantry fatigues for stretcher-bearing to an extent not approached on any other occasion in the experience of the A.I.F. or perhaps in the history of warfare.

On October 14th the enemy began a series of heavy bombardments with gas shell, chiefly "yellow cross." The casualties from gassing in the Australian Divisions from October 14th to November 10th numbered 30 per cent. of the total for that period, and the wide diffusion of "mustard" gas materially increased the difficulty of the medical problem.

First Battle of Passchendaele. October 12
The success of the Fifth Army on October 9th, and intense desire of Field-Marshal Haig and the Second Army staff to reap some fruit from the great British victories that culminated at Broodseinde, led them to repeat on the 12th the thrust toward Passchendaele. In this battle I and II Anzac Corps (Second Army) and XVIII and XIV Corps (Fifth Army) were engaged. On October 10th and 11th the 5th and 4th Divisions

---

[6] Instances of this occurred at this time on both sides commonly through suspicion of treachery, or as the result of the spreading of atrocity stories as "propaganda"—the malignant influence of which was constantly felt by the medical services during the war. There is no record of any member of the 1st Australian Division having been made a prisoner of war during this week, although some 50 were "missing" at Celtic Wood.

relieved the 1st and 2nd, and the 3rd and N.Z. Divisions relieved the 66th and 49th British. On the II Anzac front the conditions were now appalling. The 66th Division front was found by the 3rd only after perilous scouting across the mudfield.[7]

The Battle. With a much deeper objective, and under conditions even worse than on October 9th, the 3rd and New Zealand Divisions of II Anzac with the 4th Divison of I Anzac on their right set out to capture the Passchendaele ridge, advancing against a line of concrete machine-gun posts. The New Zealand Division stuck fast in the uncut wire on Bellevue Spur, losing nearly 3,000 in killed, wounded, and missing. The 3rd reached part and the 4th the whole of its first objective, but each division, finding its left flank in the air, fell back to its starting point. In these three formations during the course of ten hours, 5.35 a.m. to 3.30 p.m., some 6,000 men had been killed and wounded, or were bogged. Of the latter some were rescued by comrades and regimental bearers, many were shot by snipers, but at nightfall not a few still lay out in the almost impassable mud of the Ravebeek. The 3rd Division's casualties for October 12th and 13th were 651 killed and 1,772 wounded, of whom 40 died after rescue (the ratio of killed to wounded and died of wounds being 1 to 2·7). The 4th Division suffered much less heavily, losing 317 killed and 677 wounded of whom 32 died (ratio of killed to wounded and died of wounds 1 to 2·1).

Medical Arrangements. I Anzac (Ypres-Menin Road). The A.D.M.S. 5th Division took charge of all Australian casualties passing down the Menin Road via Westhoek, and ran the walking wounded A.D.S. The work of this division does not call for particular reference save to record one heavy loss: on October 17th, when visiting his forward posts, the A.D.M.S. Colonel Hearne, a gentle and lion-hearted man, was killed by a fragment of H. E. shell.

I and II Anzac (Ypres-Zonnebeke Road). The 12th Field Ambulance (Lieut.-Colonel C. E. Wassell) took over the Menin Road A.D.S. and the 13th Field Ambulance (Lieut.-Colonel J. B. St. Vincent Welch) that in the Ramparts and also the Railway Siding, and cleared the left (4th Division's) sector of the I Anzac front. The 3rd Division was again cleared by the 9th Field Ambulance. With the approval of the Deputy-Directors the A.D's.M.S. pooled their wheeled-transport for evacuation down the Zonnebeke Road. On each front the aid-posts, scattered at first in the pill-boxes like islands in a sea of mud, had for the most part converged to the safer spots.

---

[7] Posts were found full of dead and dying men cut off from any contact with the rear.

Ambulance bearers pushed up the forward relay and collecting posts; the Cordial Factory in Zonnebeke, the Brick-kiln, Railway Dump, St. Joseph's—later destroyed by shell-fire, with heavy casualties—are names familiar to bearers who served in these battles. The bearer carry varied from 3,000 to over 6,000 yards, with relays 500-600 yards apart. Loading posts had moved up—horsed-waggons as far as Bremen House, motors and lorries to Frost House.

4th Division. To assist the ambulance bearers, 150 infantrymen were attached and were sent to the forward posts; but even with these the whole strength of three bearer divisions could not cope with the task.[8] By reason of features of the landscape regimental bearers from the 3rd Division converged to the safe and commodious 4th Division post at the Cordial Factory, and at 6.30 p.m. Captain D. M. Steele (in charge) asked for more infantry

"to replace or probably to supplement the men I have at present. We could manage if we were only serving our own Division but the present is an enormous contract."

One hundred men were sent to the forward posts in the vain hope of clearing the aid-posts by night. The situation at these is well described by the R.M.O. 47th Battalion (Captain J. T. Jones) :—

"On October 11th went over the ground, studied maps and collected equipment. The battlefield had become much worse since October 1st; it was difficult now to move over the area unencumbered—to bring up supplies in the enormous quantities required for an offensive was a task so huge that words fail to describe it adequately. Shelter of any sort was scarce, the only post available for the M.O. was a small chamber in Battalion headquarters pill-box. The attack started at daybreak and at once a heavy barrage fell on all the forward area. Almost all the men attached to headquarters were killed or wounded—24 around the pill-box. 'Walkers' were sent back and messages sent to the A.D.S. (*sic*) at the Cordial factory Zonnebeke, for bearers. None arrived—of three runners sent, two were killed and one wounded. The battle continued fiercely the whole day—wounded were collected in shell-holes and trenches. Early in the afternoon the medical orderly and A.M.C. corporal were wounded, and the M.O. left without assistance. Soon afterwards the Division was outflanked with heavy casualties, and the

---

[8] Colonel Barber complained of the physical standard of the medical reinforcements at this time. After the Battle of Broodseinde the D.D.M.S. I Anzac arranged with the Chief of Staff (General White) that "Divisions in the line should supply all extra bearers needed, so that Divisions in reserve should not be called upon." The effect of this was to substitute infantry fatigues for the Corps bearer reserve.

O.C's 47th and 48th Battalions wounded. As darkness fell the R.M.O. 48th Battalion, Captain A. J. Collins, arrived back with some squads of ambulance bearers. The most urgent cases were sent away at once, the rest later. Next morning the ground around the R.A.P. was littered (with wounded who had died) who had to be piled in heaps to clear the trenches; and along the track from the R.A.P. to Zonnebeke a distance of over a mile, the dead lay every few yards. From the medical point of view this operation was one of the most depressing that could be imagined."

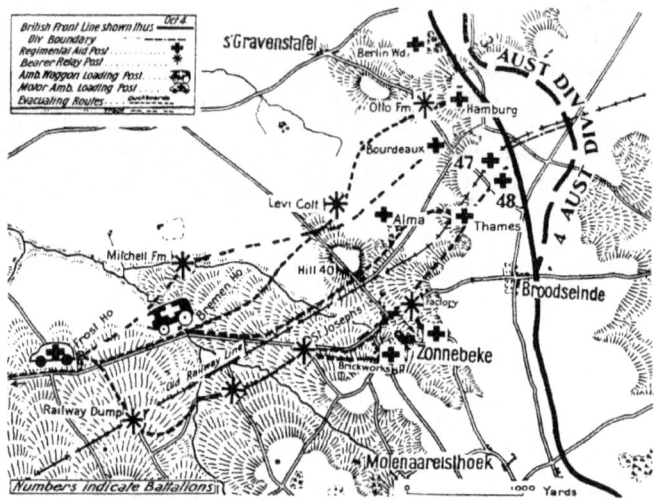

Lines of Evacuation, 3rd and 4th Aust. Divisions, 12th-14th Oct. 1917.

Waggon Posts and A.D.S. During the 24 hours ended 6 a.m. on October 13th 535 casualties were cleared from the 4th Division front. They arrived at the A.D.S.

"soaked through, covered from head to foot with thick mud, . . . having been exposed all night to heavy rain before they attacked."[9]

First Passchendaele. 3rd Division. The work of the regimental bearers in this battle is described in the *History of the 38th Battalion (page 38)* :—

October 12th. "A word for the (regimental) stretcher-bearers will not be out of place. It was quite a common occurrence for men to sink to their thighs and waists into the soft slimy mud, which drew one

---

[9] D.D.M.S. I Anzac and War Diary of 4th Field Ambulance.

10th-13th Oct., 1917] END OF ATTRITION WARFARE 239

down, down, for ever downward like some live thing. To carry a wounded man from the front line to the R.A.P. was a terrible undertaking. The distance to be covered was less than a thousand yards, but it took six men four, five, and even six hours to do the trip. . . . The heroic deeds performed at Ypres and Passchendaele have never been excelled!"

In their first 24 hours in the line (October 10th-11th) the ambulance stretcher-bearers of the 3rd Division cleared 123 stretcher cases—including 87 from the 66th Division most of whom were wounded four days before[10]—and faced their tremendous task on the 12th already very tired. The conditions of cold, wet, and mud were even worse than on the 9th; the carry by stretcher-bearers had extended to 6,000 yards—160 infantrymen were detailed to help and, in groups of twelve, each with four trained bearers, these accompanied the attacking battalions on the approach march, in the course of which heavy casualties were sustained. By 7.15 p.m. of the 12th the officer-in-charge (Major R. J. Taylor) reported:—

"All my men are done—many of the emergency infantry have run off.[11] A good few cases will have to remain out all night—it is impossible to carry now—too dark and no tracks. Must have fresh bearers, all you can get together, at 5 a.m. It will take 150 fresh men to clear the field by to-morrow evening."

Colonel Maguire at once communicated with his officers at the Prison House and Potijze:—

"Cut your staff (he ordered) so that you have no more than sufficient to carry on. Cut down work at the A.D.S. and send on every case which is not haemorrhaging, and with dressing in position . . . use (your men) 24 hours on end. . . . Cut out the canteen and sanitary squad, officers' mess, batmen, cooks' offsiders—send every available man up at 5 a.m. to-morrow."

The 85 men thus made available went forward at 5 a.m. on the 13th, but at 6 a.m. a heavy thunderstorm brought things to a climax. At 10.30 Major Taylor reported:—

"the great majority of bearers physically exhausted and unable to do

---

[10] See *Australian Official History, Vol. IV, pp. 907, 927*, a study of which is strongly commended. Wounded from the Manchester Regt. (66th Division) were rescued as long as seven days after wounding.

[11] In his comments on this battle, the Deputy-Director of II Anzac noted:—"when infantry are detailed as additional stretcher-bearers it is imperative that their N.C.O's and if possible officers should accompany them. Otherwise they soon become dispersed, and are of little use."

more than one or two carries. The country over which the bearers are working is one continuous sea of shell-holes full of soft mud."

In response to an urgent appeal from Colonel Maguire—
"the bearers in the forward area will be exhausted by evening. . . . I have no reserve"
—the A.D.M.S. obtained 200 ambulance bearers of the 66th British Division, who at 9 p.m. on the 13th relieved the 3rd Division bearers for 24 hours.

October 16th-November 10th. By October 17th a precarious equilibrium of bearers and casualties had been established. In the 4th Division the officer-in-charge Lieut.-Colonel J. B. St. Vincent Welch, reported that

"as soon as duckboarding is completed to Zonnebeke Road it will be possible, in ordinary times, to clear the whole Divisional front with the bearers of one Field Ambulance."

The casualties in this division at this time averaged 120 daily.

With the decision to abandon the attempt at a break-through in this year, the "step by step" advance was resumed. The pavement of the Ypres-Zonnebeke road was dug out and repaired and this traffic route extended to link up with Smith's Road at Zonnebeke. The motor loading post was moved up to Frezenberg.[12]

End of attempt to break through

By a costly and painful process of selection and survival, the safest and best routes and posts were found and the latter improved, so that on the fronts of both I and II Anzac (at Westhoek and Zonnebeke) casualties could be retained for a time in the forward zone and cleared at convenience. But throughout their whole tour of the line, October 11th-24th, the bearers of 3rd and 4th Divisions

"had an unspeakable time. A step from the narrow duckboard track meant that the bearer would sink to the waist in mud. . . . So arduous was the work that even fit men could not stand the strain and it was necessary to relieve them very frequently. . . . All spare men and all specialists, dispensing, nursing, even dentists went up in their turn to

---

[12] "Could the plank roads have been made more rapidly (the Australian Official Historian has stated—*p. 931, Vol. IV*) they might have solved the problem of communication even on this battlefield." In this respect the efforts of I Anzac Corps were outstanding: 18,300 yards of plank road and 10 miles of metal road were made in 27 days.

31. WOUNDED AT A RELAY POST NEAR ZONNEBEKE RAILWAY STATION DURING THE ATTACK ON PASSCHENDAELE, 12TH OCTOBER, 1917

Aust. War Memorial Official Photo. No. E4503.

To face p. 240.

32. "IDEAL HOUSE," AN OLD GERMAN PILL-BOX USED AS RELAY POST AND HEADQUARTERS, OCTOBER, 1917

The photograph shows the importance of the duckboard tracks for clearance in the forward area.

Aust. War Memorial Official Photo. No. E1213.

33. STRETCHER-BEARERS OF THE 9TH FIELD AMBULANCE WORN OUT ON THE ZONNEBEKE RAILWAY EMBANKMENT, 10TH OCTOBER, 1917

The photograph was taken in front of "Thames House" pill-box.

Aust. War Memorial Official Photo. No. E941. *To face p. 241.*

act as stretcher-bearers. . . . There was hardly a man in the forward lines who was not suffering from the effects of gas."[13]

Relief of I and II Anzac. On October 21st II Anzac Corps was relieved by the Canadian Corps, which on the 26th embarked on the struggle that ended on November 10th with the occupation of the whole of the Passchendaele height. I Anzac held a sector of the front till the close of the offensive. The 1st Division replaced the 4th and the 2nd the 5th, their medical clearance being carried out respectively down the Zonnebeke Road by broad-gauge railway from Ypres direct to the Godewaersvelde group, and down the Menin Road by M.A.C. to Remy Siding. As roads and duckboard tracks were pushed forward and building material was made available the conditions at the front were greatly improved.[14]

On November 14th II Anzac Corps came back into the line, relieving I Anzac. But as the 3rd Division was at the same time transferred to I Anzac, all the Australian divisions were withdrawn from the Ypres front. I Anzac went to the now quiet sector in front of Messines.

The close resemblance—so far as the fighting experience of the A.I.F. went—between the conditions on the Somme in the Autumn of 1916 and those of October in the Flanders offensive will have been apparent. Here however the parallel ends. The months spent at Messines were extremely quiet, and a striking feature both of the last operations at Ypres and of the trench-warfare that followed at Messines, was the comparatively light incidence of the disabilities commonly associated with an autumn campaign and a winter spent in the trenches. To this, in the A.I.F., the physical and moral fitness of the troops conduced; but still more did the fact that of the two prime factors in trench foot,

Health of the troops

---

[13] From a report quoted in the histories of the 4th (unpublished) and 9th Field Ambulances.

[14] The diary of the 2nd Field Ambulance (Nov. 11) says: "At 'Railway Dump' was a long concrete pill-box sheltering under the bank of the Ypres-Roulers railway; we had a room about 12 feet by 9, and a gallery in which cases were stored and bearers rested. Medical stores and Q.M's material and rations were distributed from here and [here] the officer-in-charge of the forward evacuation lived. . . . The main features of our stay in the line this time were the long lines of evacuation from the Front Line to A.D.S., about 6 to 7 miles over all, the long carries by the Bearers, and the shelling of the back areas."

wet and cold, the degree of cold had not reached the danger point before the Australian part in the offensive ended. On October 8th, however, 130 cases of "slight" trench foot passed through the 1st Division field ambulances—chiefly from the 2nd Division—and when the corps was relieved the sick rate was rising, reaching on occasions 1·65 per cent. per week. But in spite of the prevalence of trench fever the rate among the Australians fell steeply after relief, and (it may be noted here) remained at a very low figure throughout the winter of 1917-18.

The measures taken in the 4th Division identify the cause of the notable success achieved by this formation in keeping down the sick rate, but not less exactly illustrate the situation at this stage of the war in the British Army and, indeed, in greater or less degree, in every national force. On October 8th the A.D.M.S. issued a circular on "sick wastage."

"The principal causes of the sick wastage during the winter 1916-17 on the Somme," he noted, "were due to the following preventable diseases—Trench Feet, Septic Traumatic Abrasions of Feet, Trench Fever, Scabies and Diarrhoea. Considerable success attended the measures taken by this Division for the prevention of these disorders and it is recommended that they again be put in practice during the coming winter."

These measures he traversed seriatim, indicating in respect to the prevention of each condition the duties of company officers, R.M.O's, commanding officers, brigade and divisional headquarters staffs.

The importance of conserving man-power had indeed at the end of 1917 brought about an attitude on the part of "Higher Commands" toward disease prevention which ensured that every measure for promoting health and maintaining man-power should be an integral element in the organic life of the Army, and not merely an activity of the Medical Service.[15] It can be said indeed that, in the matter of conserving strength by preventing disease, the British Expeditionary Force was well prepared for the supreme trials of 1918.

---

[15] The evolution of the sanitary conscience (as seen, for example, in the transfer of wide spheres of action from the Medical Department to the Quartermaster-General's Branch) is followed more exactly in the special chapters which deal with disease prevention. The new attitude is illustrated by the following:—On October 10 the D.D.M.S. I Anzac complained to the Corps Commander of the high sick rate in the 5th Division (which in 1916 had achieved a bad reputation) pointing out that this was double that of the 4th. The A.D.M.S. riposted sharply, urging that greater freedom and greater responsibility be given to the divisional administration. Within three weeks the position was reversed—the rate in this Division was 1·33 per cent., that of the 4th 2·42 per cent.; the general Army rate being 1·06 per cent. Tenure of the front line was constantly associated with a rise in the sick rate.

TABLE I.—Classification of A.I.F. Casualties by Months.
July to December, 1917.

BATTLE CASUALTIES:	July	Aug.	Sept.	Oct.	Nov.	Dec.	Total
a. Killed	535	385	2,570	4,411	323	135	8,309
b. Died of wounds	198	181	666	1,233	205	85	2,568
c. Died of gas poisoning	1	3	3	28	34	1	70
d. Prisoners of war	50	10	25	91	12	18	206
e. Wounded less b. and g.	2,188	1,325	9,067	12,378	1,032	431	26,416
f. Gassed less c.	292	97	332	1,675	1,086	150	3,632
g. Shell shock "W"	20	12	255	245	26	3	561
NON-BATTLE CASUALTIES:							
h. Died of disease	8	13	5	11	9	17	63
i. Died of other causes	6	8	7	7	10	19	57
j. Self-inflicted wounds	20	6	15	23	15	15	94
k. Accidental wounds	80	38	32	36	17	33	236
l. Sick or injured less h., i., j., or k.	7,092	6,081	5,906	8,299	6,142	6,401	39,871
Totals	10,485	8,059	18,883	28,437	8,911	7,308	82,083

TABLE II.—The Various Causes of Casualty in the A.I.F. shown as a Percentage of the Total by Months.
July to December, 1917.

BATTLE CASUALTIES:	July	Aug.	Sept.	Oct.	Nov.	Dec.	Total
a. Killed	5.10	4.16	13.61	15.51	3.63	1.85	10.12
b. Died of wounds	1.89	2.25	3.53	4.34	2.30	1.16	3.13
c. Died of gas poisoning	0.01	0.04	0.02	0.10	0.38	0.01	0.09
d. Prisoners of war	0.48	0.12	0.13	0.32	0.13	0.25	0.25
e. Wounded less b. and g.	20.82	16.44	48.01	43.58	11.58	5.90	32.18
f. Gassed less c.	2.78	1.20	1.76	5.89	12.19	2.05	4.42
g. Shell shock "W"	0.19	0.15	1.35	0.86	0.29	0.04	0.68
NON-BATTLE CASUALTIES:							
h. Died of disease	0.08	0.16	0.03	0.04	0.10	0.23	0.08
i. Died of other causes	0.06	0.10	0.04	0.02	0.11	0.26	0.07
j. Self-inflicted wounds	0.19	0.07	0.08	0.08	0.17	0.21	0.11
k. Accidental wounds	0.76	0.47	0.17	0.13	0.19	0.45	0.29
l. Sick or injured less h., i., j. or k.	67.64	74.84	31.27	29.18	68.93	87.59	48.58

To permit a closer study of the actual divisional losses the figures are presented in the following tables by weeks covering the period of A.I.F. participation in the actual operations:—

TABLE III.—The weekly incidence of battle-casualties in the Australian divisions during the Ypres operations.

Week ended		K.I.A.	D.O.W.	D.G.P.	Total	Wounded	Gas	S/sh.	P.O.W.	Total	Grand Total
22nd Sept.	1st Div.	575	118		693	2,009	3	12	1	2,025	2,718
	2nd "	524	103		627	1,845	8	13	1	1,867	2,494
	3rd "	11	3		14	66	1	1		68	89
	4th "	12	4		16	77	3			81	97
	5th "	14	10		24	112	15	1		128	152
	Corps Tps.	25	14		39	97	9			106	145
29th "	1st Div.	19	41		60	56	1	4		57	117
	2nd "	38	61		99	182	18	7		204	303
	3rd "	22	12		34	135	12	28		154	188
	4th "	357	89	1	447	1,305	28	28	1	1,357	1,804
	5th "	798	121	1	920	2,373	59	171	18	2,621	3,541
	Corps Tps.	21	13	1	35	134	41	3		178	213
6th Oct.	1st Div.	659	121		780	1,752	29	56		1,837	2,617
	2nd "	500	98		598	1,608	4	50		1,662	2,260
	3rd "	479	98	1	578	1,634	41	27	1	1,703	2,281
	4th "	53	53		106	192	3	9		198	304
	5th "	50	44		94	276	34	7		317	411
	Corps Tps.	35	13		48	106	17	7		180	178
13th "	1st Div.	135	73		208	297	2	4		308	511
	2nd "	461	74		535	980	21	11		969	1,497
	3rd "	700	81	1	782	1,880	57	30	5	1,922	2,704
	4th "	421	45		466	877	17	8	84	986	1,452
	5th "	99	31		130	292	7	15		314	444
	Corps Tps.					13	4	1		18	18
20th "	1st Div.	27	26	2	55	54	81	3		138	193
	2nd "	8	33		41	49	62	1		112	153
	3rd "	113	97	4	214	387	105	3		495	709
	4th "	190	93	4	287	657	197	8	1	863	1,150
	5th "	129	47	2	178	374	215	1		590	768
	Corps Tps.	9	2		11	36	21	1		58	69

END OF ATTRITION WARFARE

27th "	1st Div.	82		114	286	24		428
	2nd "	22		41	52	38		133
	3rd "	1		37	6	14		57
	4th "	44		75	147	75		298
	5th "	97		159	321	66		551
	Corps Tps.	16		28	63	1		88
3rd Nov.	1st Div.	114		162	312	263		737
	2nd "	89		129	231	398		763
	3rd "		10	10				10
	4th "	2		17	37	17		71
	5th "	16		33	88	105	5	173
	Corps Tps.	11		22	38	107	1	167
10th "	1st Div.	88		117	257	194	2	568
	2nd "	38		73	168	257	8	499
	3rd "	2		9	2			11
	4th "	1		5	5			18
	5th "	3		15	27	66	2	110
	Corps Tps.	6		11	50	28	3	92
Total ..		7,116	1,998	9,171	21,790	2,768	116	34,342

TABLE IV.—Summary of weekly incidence of battle-casualties in the Australian divisions during the Ypres operations.

Week ended							
Sept. 22	1,161	259	3	1,418	4,206	39	27	5,688
" 29	1,255	887	1	1,595	4,185	154	213	19	6,166
Oct. 6	1,776	427	1	2,204	5,568	198	150	1	8,051
" 13	1,816	304	12	2,121	4,289	108	69	89	6,626
" 20	476	298	11	786	1,557	681	17	1	3,042
" 27	262	176	16	449	875	218	13		1,555
Nov. 3	232	125	18	873	651	890	7		1,921
" 10	188	79		230	509	545	6	3	1,293
Total	7,116	1,998	57	9,171	21,790	2,768	502	116	34,342

[columns: 25,171]

As with every agency in the Army which had to do with the maintaining of strength at the front, during the last half of 1917 the work of the rest stations, the first check to "Army" wastage, was subject to close oversight and made much more exact and purposeful,[16] in particular by limiting the number of cases admitted, and the duration of their stay.

Return to duty—
The Rest
Stations

"The difficulty of running a Rest Station," wrote the C.O. of the 3rd Field Ambulance, "is to determine a standard of fitness for discharge. To avoid overcrowding I have to evacuate many in 3 or 4 days if I am to keep men till they are really fit for fighting."

Though the need for controlling wastage from the front was never greater, it was realised that undiscriminating retention within the Army area of all men with mild complaints did not serve the end in view. At the end of September the D.M.S., A.I.F. (Surgeon-General Howse) inspected the 1st Division's rest station at Wippenhoek. The chief purpose of his visit was that of conserving man-power for the front—a problem which he had made the keynote of his administration from the outset of his career in the A.I.F.; yet he condemned the general practice of retaining in the Army rest stations cases of trench foot, of P.U.O.—usually trench fever—chronic ulcers, sore heels, and "I.C.T."[17] With a view to saving wastage during the winter, the scope of the rest station was extended by using the casualty clearing stations for this purpose. On December 6th No. 1 A.C.C.S. was made a "Corps Rest Station" for the reorganised "Australian Corps."

The casualties sustained by the A.I.F. in Flanders during the latter half of 1917, as presented in the preceding tables, illustrate the extent of Australian participation in the Third Ypres operations.[18]

Casualties
Third Battle
of Ypres

[16] On October 20 the Corps Commander, General Sir William Birdwood, when inspecting the 1st Division's Rest Station at Wippenhoek, commented on the importance of the Quartermaster's Department and of cooking; and approved a unit canteen at which light beer was supplied to the men.

[17] For the month ending October 31 in this station 1,030 cases (sick and wounded) were admitted. Of these 622 were evacuated and 392 "returned to duty," the average stay being 6 days for the former and 11 days for the latter.

[18] The average strength of the A.I.F. on the Western Front (i.e. in the B.E.F.), July-December, 1917, was as follows:—

| July | 121,259 | Sept. | 123,842 | Nov. | 112,651 |
| Aug. | 121,996 | Oct. | 116,249 | Dec. | 113,610 |

During the eight weeks that the A.I.F. were engaged in the Third Ypres fighting the A.A.M.C. sustained 697 casualties equalling 2·03 per cent. of the total A.I.F. battle losses; the weekly variation in the percentage was:—

Week ending	Sept. 22nd	Sept. 29th	Oct. 6th	Oct. 13th	Oct. 20th	Oct. 27th	Nov. 3rd	Nov. 10th
Percentage	2·2	1·9	1·4	1·0	3·8	3·4	4·0	2·5

TABLE V.—Summary of weekly incidence of battle-casualties in the A.A.M.C. during the Ypres operations.

Week ended	K.I.A.	D.O.W.	D.G.P.	Total	Wounded	Gas	S/sh.	P.O.W.	Total	Grand Total
Sept. 22	19	9	—	28	95	4	—	—	99	127
„ 29	12	18	—	30	67	11	7	—	85	115
Oct. 6	19	11	—	30	66	12	1	—	79	109
„ 13	14	7	—	21	42	4	—	—	46	67
„ 20	8	6	—	14	47	54	2	—	103	117
„ 27	12	9	1	22	25	6	—	—	31	53
Nov. 3	7	1	—	8	21	47	1	—	69	77
10	9	2	—	11	11	10	—	—	21	32
Total	100	63	1	164	374	148	11	—	533	697

Medical Officers. In the course of these battles (September 16th-November 10th) 12 medical officers of the bearer divisions and 2 R.M.O's were wounded. During the same period 10 medical officers were killed in action or mortally wounded; they comprised an A.D.M.S. (Colonel Hearne), 4 field ambulance officers, and 5 R.M.O.'s.[19]

"**Lessons**" **from Third Battle of Ypres**   Certain features of the Flanders Campaign call for a special note.

1. Technique of Evacuation: Transport v. Treatment. I Anzac Corps. By order, surgical treatment at the A.D.S. or "up the line" was reduced to absolute essentials; but with each advance this irreducible minimum expanded: more patients were held for treatment at the corps main dressing station, more ample provision was made for sustainment and resuscitation in the advanced ambulance posts. At the end of October a "ward" was constructed in the A.D.S. in Ypres "for the treatment of shock cases. Here," says the diary of the 2nd Field Ambulance on

---
[19] The commander of the 19th Battalion, Lieut.-Col. C. R. A. Pye (a medical practitioner of Windsor, N.S.W.) was killed in action on October 4.

October 31st, "a patient may rest for some hours until he is in a fit condition to stand the journey to C.C.S." But, in I Anzac the significance of the time element in evacuation and importance of rapid movement took hold of administrative and executive officers alike.[20]

In II Anzac (on the other hand) the corps main dressing station was avowedly a treatment (not a transport) link in the line of evacuation.[21]

Facts and figures available do not permit of an exact evaluation of the results achieved by the "forward movement" which involves the whole question of the results of war surgery. "To compare surgical results" of the Battle of Pilckem with those of Messines the British Official Historian examines the number of deaths among wounded treated in C.C.S's, and the hospitals on Lines of Communications between 7th-13th July, and 31st July-6th August. It showed a slight advantage in favour of Messines—4·3 per cent. against 4·6 per cent. Though complete figures are not available it is certain that the proportion of deaths among the rescued increased greatly in the last phase of the offensive. Over the whole campaign the number operated on—which varied inversely in the various casualty clearing stations with the numbers admitted—was 28 per cent. in the Remy group and 48 per cent. in No. 1 and No. 2 A.C.C.S. (Bailleul and Steenwerck). During June the percentage in the latter was 13·8.

From the point of view of the stations themselves the arrival of a full train-load of wounded at once caused great inconvenience.

The balance in favour of the methods of Messines may well be explained by the weather. But the experience (or experiment) laid bare a fallacy. Even during the operations exact research—on the battlefield, in the casualty clearing stations, and in the laboratories at home—revealed the importance of physiological factors in the treatment of wounded men as equipotent in the conservation of man-power with the time-factor in the aseptic treatment of war wounds. The result of excessive regard for the time element in dictating the sites of the casualty clearing stations, and the outcome of the observations made in the course of the battles on the matter of treatment in the field units, are among the most dramatic and interesting medical events of 1918.

2. *Humanity v. Efficiency—Stretchers and Walking Wounded.* A study of the emotional content of the medical events of Third Ypres, and statistical analysis of its facts and figures, if read together reveal "lessons" and lines of thought which lead to curious and far-reaching results. Out of the welter of strivings and sufferings of these battles and their immense toll of casualties, one amazing fact emerges which throws light not only on the local and immediate medical problems, and the reason for all this medical to-do, but on the *raison d'être* of medical service in warfare. The clue to it lies in the figures which give the

---

[20] In a memorandum to the Deputy-Director the officer directing the Corps Central Bureau (Major D. S. Mackenzie) made suggestions for still further expediting the movement of the wounded to the Base. "In busy times the walking wounded arrive without field medical cards. . . . If cards were supplied it would . . . save congestion at the C.C.S. and allow the cases to be pushed right through instead of having to take the dressing down. . . . By reports from C.C.S's it would appear that the wounded arrive dressed 'as well as ever.'" In this connection, *see also Chapter xi and Appendices Nos. 9 and 10.*

[21] In his diary of October 12 it is referred to by the D.D.M.S. II Anzac Corps as an "Advanced Clearing Station."

proportion of "killed" to "wounded," and in the latter of *stretcher cases* to *walking wounded*. On an average of the whole war, the proportion in the A.I.F. of killed to wounded and died of wounds, gassed, and shell shock was as 1 : 4·2. For the period October 1st to 31st this proportion was maintained at 1 : 3·5. Thus the number of seriously wounded men rescued from death on the battlefield, in relation to the total casualties, was so small, or varied so little with circumstances, that even under conditions so adverse as those of October the ratio was influenced only to the extent here shown.

At the same time records and statistics are eloquent of the immense resources required to achieve this rescue: transport and personnel were expended almost entirely in the collecting and clearing of stretcher cases. And yet from the standpoint of maintaining the numerical strength of the army, the walking wounded were incomparably the more important: here was spoil from the grindstone, that might be used for further attrition, whereas of stretcher cases only an insignificant number came back to the mill. But in the complex of motives, instinctive and rational, which determined the relation between man and man in the war, none was more potent than the impulse to attempt the rescue of helpless men. However inexorably he might be compelled, or rashly induced to sacrifice his men in the attainment of victory, no Army Commander could afford seriously to neglect the service of humanity even in the interests of efficiency.

3. *Cost of Rescue: the Bearer Divisions.* Summing up the experience of these operations the Deputy-Director II Anzac (Colonel Begg) gave his opinion that "when the conditions are bad and hand carriage long, at least 600 fresh stretcher-bearers are required on each Divisional front every 12 hours. Thus 9,900 are required in addition to the Field Ambulance bearers"—almost the equivalent of a division of troops. The estimate must, it is true, be discounted, as applicable only to heavy casualties under extraordinary conditions. But the fact that the opinion is given by a responsible and very able officer justifies an examination of the type of strategy which should bring about such a situation.

4. *The Price of Attrition: quis custodiet ipsos custodes?* It is not the place of the Medical Service to comment on matters of military strategy and tactics. The decision of the Commander-in-Chief to expend or risk his effectives in wastage through disease and physical disablement is subject to the same principles of military science—conservation of force and so forth—as obtains in the case of battle-casualties. But in a service of maintenance whose *raison d'être* rests on its knowledge of the physical potentialities and limitations of the human machine,[22] it may be permissible, perhaps, to ask, with the A.D.M.S. 2nd Division (in reference to the task set this division on October 9th), "when will these Generals learn that we are but men?"[23]

---

[22] On the question of responsibility for deciding on physical grounds the fitness for duty of a soldier in the field, both General Howse, the D.M.S., and General White, Chief of General Staff A.I.F., have since the war strongly affirmed, in discussion with the writer, the authority and the responsibility of the Medical Service—as against (for example) the Company or Platoon Commander.

[23] Colonel Sutton's personal diary October 9th.
An article in *The Fighting Forces* of August 1936 on "The Human Element in War" examines the problem of human limitations in relation to the new warfare. "We must," the writer properly urges, "make allowance in our estimate for failure in the human element as well as technical breakdown. In fact we will do well to remind ourselves we are but human after all."

5. Results of Attrition; the Human Material. There is nothing recorded of the Great War more worthy the attention of the human race than the proofs multiplied a million times of the triumph of the spirit of man over his physical self and his material environment. Of both sides it can be said that the heaviest bombardments left always some intrepid spirits ready to hold a strong-post against the enemy advancing behind his barrage, and to inflict heavy damage before death unfeared took their bodies. That it was much more true of the first three years of the war than of the last is a tribute to the ingenuity and energy of those whose business it was to find means for breaking the stoutest hearts and for driving all but the noblest spirits to women, wine, or a "war neurosis." We have Ludendorff's word that the German morale was severely shaken by the Flanders offensive.

"The enormous material resources of the enemy had given his attack a considerable preponderance over our defence, and this condition would become more and more apparent as our best men became casualties, our infantry approximated more nearly in character to a militia, and discipline declined."[24]

The events of 1918 were to show that this attrition had been mutual.

The Third Battle of Ypres stands a landmark in the course of the war on the Western Front—the watershed between the battles of siege and attrition, and those which achieved movement and the promise of victory. As their final effort of 1917 both sides staged a rehearsal of their own conception of the new tactics.

End of attrition: Battle of Cambrai

On December 5th the 4th Division, settling down to enjoy a long promised rest near Abbeville, had its pleasant anticipations suddenly broken by orders to entrain at a few hours' notice for Péronne. This sudden move, strikingly prescient of an even more urgent occasion, marks an event so significant and crucial in the history of the Medical Service and of the war as to demand attention though the Australian Medical Service was but slightly involved.

By the middle of November the Salient had settled down to its normal state of stagnant desolation. On the scene of these dreadful battles the fitful gleam of autumn suns lit up a waste more Stygian than any conceived by Dante or pictured by Doré. Haig's General Staff had shed its belated tear over the swamps of Passchendaele; a realisation of the true cost of the great British offensive had fallen with stunning impact on the British nation and its statesmen. Then on November 21st

---

[24] General Ludendorff, *My War Memories, Vol. II, p. 541-2.*

there came news from the front that set bells in England pealing for a famous victory. By a surprise effect of massed tanks, sudden bombardment, secrecy, a success was achieved that was dramatic, unprecedented and, for most onlookers, unexpected. The Hindenburg Line was broken at Cambrai; the advance was not for a paltry thousand yards or so, but a deep bite far beyond the enemy artillery—and this had been accomplished in a matter of some 48 hours, with a capture of guns and prisoners hitherto achieved only by weeks or months of expensive attrition.

The German Counter-attack. But the British offensive was a flash in the pan—there was no charge to explode. No provision had been made not merely for any strategic exploitation of a break-through but even for effective and co-ordinated tactical exploitation of a local success. For want of further purpose or possibilities the British force stayed where it was, in a sharp salient—to receive one of the most shocking reverses in the history of British arms, delivered by a foe not slow to seize the chance to try out, with a definite and tremendous purpose in view, his own scheme for exploiting the results of attrition. Ludendorff's counter-stroke was immediate and terrible. Starting on November 30th by a swift concentration of specially trained troops, sudden intense bombardment, and intelligent penetration of the breach to the extreme limit of available resources, the German General Staff in the course of three days' fighting not only restored a practical *status quo*, but achieved a tactical success such that circumstances only precluded its exploitation into a major disaster for the Allies.

The methods used by both sides were precisely those employed in 1918; and the medical events of both phases of the battle are not less illuminating of the future than the military.

Medical events

First Phase. In the expectation that the advance would be rapid and considerable, arrangements were made in the III Corps to bring the patients direct from the A.D.S. to the C.C.S., the M.D.S. being held in reserve. The result was a very rapid concentration of wounded in the C.C.S. group at Ytres four miles behind the old front line.

From the point of view of transit the "experiment" was most successful, the casualty clearing stations being indeed almost overwhelmed. Their experience is used by the British Historian to point a favourite moral.

"This experience of a system of direct evacuation from advanced dressing stations to casualty clearing stations is important, as it emphasizes the fact that wounded as a whole are not more advantageously dealt with in battle under such a system than they are under the normal system. The rule, however, that the comparatively small number requiring urgent operations . . . should be sent direct to the nearest casualty clearing station or advanced operating centre always held good; but there was no advantage in dealing with all the lying down wounded in the same way. The general result was that wounded were held up for long periods either at advanced dressing stations pending the return of cars, or at casualty clearing stations until the cars could be unloaded or until the congestion at the casualty clearing stations could be relieved."[25]

It must be said, however, that the surgeons, seeking to eradicate gas gangrene and sepsis from *all* war wounds, saw in successful transport not a menace but an opportunity.

Second Phase (November 30th-December 6th). The chief features of medical experience in the second phase were the heavy losses in material and personnel in the field units, the large number of "missing," and the grave risk of capture run by the casualty clearing stations.

"The disadvantage of having large immobile dumps of medical stores in advanced centres and casualty clearing stations near the front line became prominent.... In the VI Corps ... seven cars of No. 21 M.A.C. were ditched and had to be abandoned, but the drivers carried the wounded away with them. ... In the III Corps one (medical) officer was killed, three wounded, and six missing. Amongst other ranks, 1 was killed, 21 were wounded, and 163 missing...."[26]

Casualties in the other Corps were only less serious.

"The casualty clearing stations at Ytres were in imminent danger of capture. Orders were consequently issued for the nursing sisters to be sent back by ambulance cars, and the surgical teams distributed. ... The remainder of the personnel were to salve as much of the equipment as possible and retire to places of safety, leaving sufficient personnel in charge of wounded until all could be got away."

In all 29,068 wounded were evacuated from this battle. The Australian units involved (No. 2 Squadron, A.F.C., and 55th Siege Battery) lost only twelve (eight wounded). The 4th, 12th and 13th Field Ambulances of the 4th Division partly opened up for their brigades around Péronne, but were not called on to deal with any battle casualties.

Comments. For those who now, facing a future dark with rumours of warfare even more dreadful than that with which this history is concerned, seek a sign from the experiences and reactions of the human material caught in the madness of mutual "attrition" of the "Great War," or from the failures or successes of those who determined its strategy and tactics, Cambrai stands out clear against the sombre background of the years 1916 and 1917; token at least that the deliberate

---

[25] *British Official Medical History, General, Vol. III, p. 195.*
[26] *Ibid., pp. 197-8.*

END OF ATTRITION WARFARE

"attrition" of the manhood of nations may be "war" but it is not strategy —is not even "scientific."

For the Medical Service we see in Cambrai a miniature of the greater events of 1918. During three years of "stationary warfare" a vast and immensely complex system of transport and treatment had been built up which subserved and conformed to the methods of attrition warfare—and its purpose not less than its methods. For if (on the side of technique) the system of collection, evacuation, and distribution of casualties was speeded up as never before, the effect—indeed, the deliberate purpose—of this was chiefly to feed the war machine for further "attrition." From Cambrai onwards the consumption of manpower ceased to be an end in itself.

The military[27] problem of both sides was now essentially one of man-power. At the end of 1917 both the Allies and the Central Powers were set on victory, not on a settlement. The Central Powers, in spite of the failure of the U-boat blockade, were encouraged in their hopes by their successful defence in the West, the reduction of Russia, and victory at Caporetto; the Allies looked forward to the prospect of tapping the vast man-power of America. In the wearing-down competition the Allies had fared badly in respect of man-power, if not of morale.[28] An exact comparison of their casualties with those of the Germans is impossible, since the published figures for the various contending armies are based on different categories. For example the figures for the German loss are said to exclude all casualties except those evacuated from the "Army" area. Even after making large allowances, however, it seems certain that the losses of the Allies in "wearing down" the German Army were greater than the loss in the German Army itself.[29]

The Medical Service and Man-power

It was known that on the Western Front, which now, at least, was the crucial one for the Allies, they must be prepared to sustain an attack supported by some 40 fresh Divisions which the enemy could now bring from the Russian front.

The new defensive rôle to which the Allies were thus forced

---

[27] The medical involvements of the war of civil attrition, economic and morale (blockade, bombing, and propaganda), are examined in *Vol. III*.

[28] To what extent the success in this respect of the Central Powers was due to superior strategic methods; to the advantage of defence over attack; to the quality of the German race; or to a greater success in preventing disease and promoting repair, are matters of the highest moment for those whose duty it is to provide for national defence.

[29] See *Australian Official History, Vol. IV, p. 943*.

at the end of 1917 called for action in two directions:—(1) the
construction of material ramparts and accumu-
lation of defensive equipment and material,
together with the formulation of defensive tactics and training of the troops therein; (2) the building up of a sufficient reserve of man-power and its maintenance. In respect of (1) the Medical Service had to create a technique to meet its own special problems. An account of the response to the new conditions by the Director-General of Medical Services B.E.F. will be found in a later chapter.[30] In respect of (2) Haig at least was under no misapprehension of the serious nature of the problem. Conscription had failed to find drafts to make good the heavy drain of casualties.[31] In the British Army on the Western Front the number of battalions in each division was reduced from 12 to 9 and a reduction in the effective strength of battalions was tacitly accepted as inevitable. Moreover the quality of recruits had deteriorated, consisting as these now largely did of boys under 19 or the siftings of rejects.[32] It thus came about that in the effort to maintain the British front (apart from the tactical use of the troops) the Medical Service was called on to play the part of a veritable *deus ex machina*.

Allies on the Defensive

For the Australian Imperial Force, not less than for the British Army and the Allies, the end of 1917 marked a critical occasion in the war. In the A.I.F. the problem was twofold: (1) the maintenance of the striking power of the Australian formations in the field, and (2) the organisation and command of those on the Western Front.[33] In effect the two problems were closely related.

The Australian Imperial Force

1. *The Problem of Man-power and Maintenance.* The prob-

---

[30] Chapter xx (*pp.* 608-9).

[31] To save the situation on the Italian front after Caporetto, French and British reinforcements had to be sent thither, including a British force of two Army Corps—5 Divisions—under General Plumer. With the medical personnel went a number of Australian medical officers and a strong contingent of Australian nurses.

[32] In the British Army the age of enlistment was reduced to 18 years at the end of January 1917, and in the French Army at the end of 1916. In the German Army "the 1917 class"—*i.e.* 20 years of age in 1917—was called up some 18 months before its time, the 1918 class at the end of 1916—*i.e.* at 18 years of age. The 1919 class was called up for the most part between 17½ and 18 years. The 1920 class was being used early in 1918.

[33] For the situation of Australian troops in Egypt and Palestine see *Vol. I (Part II)* of this work.

lem of man-power in the Australian Force was in one respect special to it. Of all the important homogeneous self-governing States involved in the Great War Australia alone had seen fit to adhere to the principle of voluntary enlistment for military service abroad.[34] One effect of this was greatly to increase the importance of the Medical Service as a factor in the maintenance of man-power. This was foreseen at the outset of the war by Lieutenant-Colonel Howse[35] and we now find him, as D.M.S., A.I.F., closely in the confidence of its commander, and himself active in initiating lines of action, in connection with both aspects of the military problem as set out above.

Particular study of the situation in the A.I.F. in respect of man-power is made in later chapters.[36] Briefly, the losses in the Flanders offensive—42,000 of the 77,000 battle-casualties sustained by the Australians in France during 1917—left all the divisions much below strength. At the same time recruiting had fallen off and enlistments were now far below the demands. Nor was the question of strength the only pressing one. As Surgeon-General Howse had always insisted,[37] to achieve and maintain reputation as a *Corps d'élite*, to which the A.I.F. aspired, the quality of its reinforcement was as important a matter as strength; and his virtual control of the policy and methods of the Command Depots, and close oversight of the new recruits arriving, now put him in a position to enforce this view. This policy (as he was at no pains to disguise) would still further reduce the numbers available to reinforce the front line units. His estimate for the sick wastage in the A.I.F. for

---

[34] In *Canada* "after a violent political struggle the Military Service Act was signed by the Governor-General on 28 August, 1917, and was put into operation as soon as the necessary arrangements could be made." (*Official History of the Canadian Forces: Medical Services, p. 154.*) In New Zealand " 'the Military Service Act, giving power to use compulsion, where volunteers were insufficient, became law on the 1 August, 1916. . . .' " (*The Empire at War, Vol. III, p. 383.*)

The decision of the Australian people, and its influence upon the efficiency of the A.I.F. are discussed in *Vols. III, V,* and *XI* of the *Australian Official History of the War*. Its influence on the pensions problem is examined in *Vol. III* of this work.

[35] *Vol. I, p. 41.*

[36] In *Chapter xvi*, dealing with the procedure of "return to duty" and the "B class" problem; and in *Chapters xxi* and *xxiii* concerning the problem of strength in the final clash. It may be well however to record here that the terrific drain on national manhood brought about by the mass-slaughter of attrition warfare was such as to make necessary demands for reinforcement quotas far in excess of any hitherto conceived to be necessary (*see Vol. I, p. 369*). The proportion of their national manhood absorbed into the Armies of the various belligerents in the Great War and other features of the military problem of man-power germane to medical history are examined in *Vol. III* (Recruiting in Australia).

[37] *See Vol. I, p. 90.*

the winter 1917-18 was 4 per 1,000 per day (that for 1916-17 being 3·2).[38] Some drastic action was clearly necessary in the direction either of increasing the supply of effectives, or of reducing the demand in the field formations, or, more probably, of both.[39] On the political side the idea of conscription was again taken up; on the military a reduction in the number of battalions per division and the disbandment of a division to reinforce the rest were debated. The substitution of "B" for "A" class men at the base both in Britain and France, and to some extent also at the front, was taken in hand systematically.[40]

2. *Organisation and Command*. By the terms of its inception[41] the A.I.F. was predestined to ultimate autonomy as surely as the Australian people to some form of nationhood; but it would be an autonomy contained no less definitely within the British Army than the Australian Commonwealth was contained within the British Empire. In the accomplishing of this autonomy two factors were involved: first, the grouping of the Australian divisions under Australian command for military action,[42] and, second, the replacement of British regular officers in command and on the staff by Australian citizen soldiers.[43] At this time a proportion of the Corps, Divisional, and (to a

---

[38] He based his forecast "on the fact that men having once had Trench Foot would more readily go down again under adverse conditions; also the Australians being used to a warm climate would feel the second winter far worse than the first." (Diary of D.D.M.S., I Anzac, 27 October, 1917.) That the estimate proved excessive was in part due to the fact that it was made early, and appropriate action instituted.

[39] On November 4 the G.O.C., A.I.F. Depots in U.K. (Maj.-Gen. J. W. M'Cay) prepared at the request of the D.M.S., A.I.F. a statement of the situation in the depots, which was sent to A.I.F. Headquarters in France. On figures supplied by "3rd Echelon" he found that the "Army" wastage from the Australian formations amounted to 12,000 per month (in almost equal numbers of sick and wounded). Examining the situation in respect of new recruits, and of convalescents recovering in the Command Depots and at the Base in France, General M'Cay concluded that by March 1 this deficiency would amount to 21,000 and in May to 35,000 below establishment.

[40] A.I.F. Order No. 1,000 of 4 December, 1917, gave effect to a War Office letter of November 3 instructing the replacement of R.A.M.C. personnel attached to battalions for "water duties" by "B" class men. The reaction in the A.I.F. to this retrograde step and to the whole problem of the "B" class soldier, is examined later. (*See p. 716*).

[41] *See Vol. I, p. 31.*

[42] The circumstances of the accomplishment of autonomy for the purposes of interior self-government are narrated in *Vol. I, Chap. xxii*.

[43] The infantry element of the Canadian Force consisted of a single Corps of 4 Divisions with one "Depot" Division. Command and administration were almost wholly by Canadian officers. The Canadian Corps and Divisions as well as the Canadian Medical Service as a whole were directed by Canadian officers. The advantages and drawbacks associated with this are admirably discussed in the *Official History of the Canadian Forces in the Great War 1914-19 (Medical Services) by Sir Andrew Macphail*.

less extent) Brigade staffs, were British Regular officers. The Medical Service was the least concerned since only one British officer of the "Regular" Army[44] had been appointed—namely the Deputy-Director of I Anzac Corps, Colonel Manifold. A second result of the years of war—and a constructive one—lay in the fact that of those who had sustained its trials and its chances a large proportion had by now fully mastered the technique of mutual destruction—in the case of the Medical Service, of retrieving the flotsam and jetsam of attrition. And this proficiency reached from the comparatively simple craft of the private soldier to the highest and most responsible positions. Furthermore, trial by battle had brought to the front those most fully qualified for leadership or direction. Self-consciousness of ability to stand alone came to the A.I.F. coincidently with the necessity for reorganisation. Of this coincidence was born the "Australian Corps."

That the desire for autonomy was not a matter of individual feelings or ambitions but of "national" aspirations is made clear by correspondence between General Howse, the D.M.S., and General White, the A.I.F. chief of staff, which appears to have initiated the movement. In a letter dated 20th July, 1917 Surgeon-General Howse wrote: "A very strong feeling exists and is spreading among the A.I.F. that we should have an Australian Corps," and that so far as possible it should be staffed by Australian officers.

"It looks a rotten thing to even discuss the question of replacing Imperial Officers who have done so well, but we cannot overlook the fact that we are now nearly three years at war and we should have made our officers competent during that time."

He added that he was "blamed for the continuance of the system so far as the Medical Services are concerned"—not, he stated emphatically, on personal grounds—in relation to Colonel Manifold—but "as a reflection on the (Australian Medical) Corps."

As the urgency of the crisis in Allied affairs became evident this combined problem of man-power, reconstruction, and autonomy was debated with increasing directness and purpose between the A.I.F., the War Office and Imperial Government,

---

[44] Colonel Manifold was an officer of the Indian Army Medical Service.

and Australia. In this work it is necessary only to state the results.[45]

The steps taken

1. Man-power. To increase the available supply of effectives action was taken along a number of independent lines related only in their purpose.

Recruits. With a view to a radical solution of the problem of manpower the Prime Minister of Australia, Rt Hon. W. M. Hughes, initiated a second referendum, which on December 20th asked authority from the people—including the A.I.F.—for a modified and controlled form of conscription. In view of this project the question of breaking up A.I.F. Battalions or a Division was temporarily postponed. The vote of the Australian people, however, again rejected conscription, with the result that during 1918 reinforcements consisted largely of recovered men.

Return to Duty. (a) *Convalescent ("Command") Depots.* The military control of the depots in England was tightened up and medical and combatant activities were closely co-ordinated. At the same time the facilities were improved for return to duty direct from the Hospitals in France through the Australian Base Depot at Le Havre.

(b) *Army Zone Rest Stations.* The use of casualty clearing stations for this purpose greatly extended the facilities for early treatment in the field of mild complaints.

Wintering. As the result of initiative on the part of General White, the Australian Divisions in France took over for strictly defensive action a sector in front of Messines; the original intention had been for them to winter in the Salient in preparation for a spring offensive, the idea of which was soon afterwards abandoned.

Promoting Health. During the winter 1917-18 the staffs of Australian divisions entered with vigour into the drive for promoting the health and morale of the troops which marked this fourth winter of the B.E.F. in France. Important features of this campaign were Corps and Divisional Schools of Sanitation, Cookery, Ambulance and C.C.S. work; a great development of Baths and Laundries; increased facilities for the treatment and prevention of skin infections and infestations and of trench foot; dental work; physical and psychical tonics—amusements, recreation, local and general leave; and—most important perhaps of all—a close study of dietetic requirements. These measures will be considered later.

Promoting Recovery. The developments in war surgery at this time, and the effect of these on "return to duty" are an important part of the general military history of this period.

Discipline. A strong move to lessen the great amount of illegal

---

[45] The matter is dealt with at length in the *Australian Official History, Vol. V, Chapter i.*
There can be no question more interesting to Imperial and Dominion statesmen and jurists, and none the solution of which would more effectively resolve the problem of the constitution of the British Commonwealth, than that which seeks to determine the nature and genesis of the instincts and sentiments that caused the Australian Imperial Force to desire so ardently and to respond so effectively to the "unification" of the Australian formations into a single Corps, commanded and administered by Australian officers.

absence ("A.W.L.") in the A.I.F.[46] led to a prolonged triangular discussion between Australia, the British Government, and the British and A.I.F. Field Commands with important and far-reaching results. The close affinity between "crime" and the medical problems of "shell shock" and "malingering" brings this matter within the scope of the chapter in *Volume III* dealing with mental disorders in the war. Efforts to diminish the incidence of Venereal Disease are also dealt with in a special chapter in that volume.

It will thus be seen that there occurred at this time an important integration of all activities relating to the maintenance of man-power.

2. *Disbandment Temporarily Avoided.* As already mentioned, to decrease the requirements of the A.I.F. the War Office proposed that the Divisions be reduced to four and the establishment of these cut down. Happily this negative and defeatist line of action was, for the time avoided. By promise of vigorous efforts to promote recruiting it was secured that the Australian formations remained intact. At the same time the military objections of the Commander-in-Chief to the formation of a five Division Australian Corps—a departure from the now normal four divisional establishment—was adroitly escaped by the suggestion of General Birdwood that the 4th Division should act as a depot to the other four Divisions of an Australian Corps. The Corps was formed in November but took on its new name on January 1st. Similarly, with General Birdwood's sympathetic understanding and advocacy, the Australian desire for autonomy now resulted in the early replacement of the remaining British officers in the Corps by Australians.

The arrangements outlined above were arrived at in December 1917 and the spring of 1918. But before full effect could be given to them the German thunderbolt had been launched, and the Australian divisions were scattered over the British front, serving wherever pressure was greatest.

---

[46] At the beginning of March, 1918, nearly 9 Australians per 1,000 were in field imprisonment as against a maximum of 2 per 1,000 in the other Dominion Forces. The explanation of this, however, lay chiefly in the fact that the release of first offenders had to be restricted in the A.I.F. in which no death penalty was applicable. *See Australian Official History, Vol. V, Chap.* 1.

SECTION II

EVOLUTION IN THE MEDICAL SERVICE DURING
ATTRITION WARFARE[1]

INTRODUCTION

WE have said that by the winter of 1917-18 the need of the armies for maintenance of their waning man-power had forced upon the medical service the rôle of *deus ex machina*.

There are solid grounds for the statement that in the swinging fortunes of the desperate struggle in the first eight months of 1918 this "administrative" service was a material factor in the final issue. For this rôle it was now very fully equipped—it may in fact be said that in the fundamental problems of the prevention of disease, and of rescue, repair, and return to duty of casualties, only refinements of technique were made after the end of 1917.

It is suitable therefore (as it is convenient) at this stage to examine, from an objective service standpoint, the technique of both these methods of conserving man-power, as seen in the activities of the Australian Army Medical Corps. Accordingly in the chapters of this section we shall follow the course of a casualty (as seen in the experience of the A.I.F. on the Western Front) from the regimental aid-post through the various stages and levels of transport and treatment in the field, at the Expeditionary Base, and at Home, to the Command Depots and Overseas Training Brigade. In a final chapter of the section we examine the technique of disease prevention as it evolved in the Great War.

The chapters of the previous section carry the narrative in

---

[1] The process of "evacuation" as described in the chapters of this section should be interpreted in terms of facts and figures by reference to the diagram given on *p. 440* and to the statistical (nosological) analysis on *pp. 495-6, 501-4*, and in *Vol. III*.

point of time to the military *dies non* of the winter 1917-18; and in point of events to the eve of the final act in the war. The next chapter in the series will deal with the first scene of this—which ended in a German break-through. The reason for the check made in the narrative at this stage is not so much to prepare for that dramatic *dénouement* as the simple fact that, from the point of view of technical history, the narrative of the medical events of the war has outrun description of the medical machinery of the warfare. So much, indeed, has the *mise en scène* changed that, to enter with understanding into the action of this momentous year, the stage must be reset and stage directions in some measure revised.

An earlier chapter of this work[2] described the system in the British Medical Service for carrying out its duties. This (it may be recalled) had been revised during the years 1905-10 to accord with the experiences of the South African War and "Reports of the British officers attached to the Japanese and Russian Forces in the Field" in the Russo-Japanese War.[3] The effect of these two wars, in particular the first, on the British Army and on the organisation and methods of its Medical Service were very great. Defects however remained, in particular in respect to the means of transport for "stretcher cases," the machinery for "return to duty," and the military status of the Service, to which may be traced certain unfortunate not to say tragic happenings in the first year of the war, both in France and in the East. The early months of 1915, which saw the birth of a vast British Continental Army and the issue of *Part VII New Armies*[4] saw also far-reaching changes in the Medical Service, of which an outline was given in *Chapter II*.

The South African War and the Great War

As the war progressed this process of evolution moved with increasing momentum. *Pari passu* with a progressive degradation of the human material of warfare, we find a truly amazing

---

[2] *Chapter i, Vol. I.*

[3] Lieut.-Col. (later Maj.-Gen. Sir) W. G. Macpherson, A.M.S., was attached to the Japanese forces.

[4] *Id est* the "establishment" or tables on which, with the corresponding "mobilisation store tables," the New Army units created by Lord Kitchener were built. In April 1915 *War Establishments Part VII New Armies* replaced those for an Expeditionary Force published in January 1914. Revised editions of *Part VII* were issued in August 1915 and September 1916. In April 1917 *Part VIIA* was issued for France, and in October 1918 this was revised as *Series I, II and III*.

advance in the perfection of methods for keeping the apparatus of warfare in good order and repair. In respect to the human component it were indeed not outside debate to propose that the medical features of warfare on the Western Front at the end of the war differed from those of 1914 almost as widely as did the latter from the conditions at the Crimea.

Evolution of Medical Service in the war

High water mark in elaboration of methods had, in effect, been reached at the end of 1917: during this winter the observations made during three years of the travail and agony of this vast experiment in human vivisection—in methods of field work, in equipment, in research, in technique, in system, in the identification of essential problems—were focussed in a perfect machine admirably equipped not only for alleviating human suffering but for promoting the waging of war. In all the belligerent nations at this time their Frankenstein monster had for the time being taken control of all human affairs: the "world war" was being waged as if "victory" were the one aim and supreme purpose of the human race—as, indeed, during the madness of war, it must be.

From the manifold elements of this warfare itself; from services and organisations dragged, in regardless profusion, from the ordered normality of modern life; from the young manhood and womanhood of the world there had been created a new social cosmos; ephemeral, indeed, as must be all "cultures" that make of death and destruction an end in themselves and a fetish for worship;[5] but, for its time and in its place, ordered and sustained by a dynamic energy and singularity of purpose such as, could it be sublimated to the service of a true "league of nations," might yet save the world. Within this cosmos and its own sphere of action the medical service had become a complete and highly developed system of social service—its duties performed by a military department which, in the weight of its authority, the extent of its activities, and (it should be added) its efficiency for the purpose in hand, could not be exceeded

[5] The very important question whether the effect of war and in particular the "Great War" in the progress of the human race was constructive or destructive will be examined in *Vol. III.* In *Vol. XI (p. 864)* of the *Australian Official History*, Professor Sir Ernest Scott repudiates on behalf of Australian sentiment "such perverted opinions as that of Moltke that 'war is an essential element of God's scheme of the world' . . ."

and perhaps not equalled by any of the organised medical services of civil life.

The chapters of this section attempt no less a task than to pass in a rapid survey the methods of life and work in this new world. It need hardly be said that such a review can embrace only the broadest features of its vast subject. As such it may with advantage be preceeded by some general observations that will serve to identify the sundry matters of medical concern that call for attention.

As we follow the course of the casualties, sick and wounded, from the front through the various levels of evacuation to their distribution and final disposal, and examine the system whereby, **The allegiances** in the last years of the war, temporary "wastage" **of the Medical** from the front and loss of strength through present **Service** "unfitness for service" were reduced to their minimum and the morale and health of the force maintained, we find three prime purposes intermingling in the manifold activities of the medical service, each related to a specific responsibility and mandate. To the military command it owed service to promote and conserve man-power for the purpose of war. To the nation at large, it was responsible for promoting by intelligent anticipation the efforts of the civil institutions whose duty it should be to prepare for useful return to civil life the soldiers unfitted for further military service. By Humanity, as represented by the nations who had suscribed to the International Conventions of Geneva and the Hague, it was charged with minimising so far as possible the individual sufferings of the combatants of both sides.[6] These three strands of purpose, inextricably interwoven as they were, in a self-contained and consistent scheme of medical service, nevertheless furnished each an end in itself—all three entering at every stage into the medical problem, and now one, now another, providing its dominating motive.

Most writers who deal with the part of medicine in the war tacitly accept as a postulate—as it is also a matter of general **The military** belief—that the one essential feature of the work of **allegiance :** the medical service in the late war was to bring about **maintenance of** a greatly diminished incidence of disease. As will **man-power** be shown, close study of facts and figures makes clear that this attitude must be modified.

The many problems associated with civilian participation in military activities on the one hand, and with the reinstatement as civilians of the wastage from warfare on the other, will be found to open up in the chapters of this section. They do so along two lines—positive, in the vast domain of "reparative" treatment, surgical and medical; and negative, in the only less arduous and exacting work of the military boards and the military machinery for implementing the system of "categories." For Australia, on both these counts, the conditions differed from those

---

[6] It may be pointed out here and is amplified elsewhere (*Vol. III*) that if—as seems to have been accepted—in the next war every man, woman, and child will be regarded as a "combatant" the terms of this mandate must be revised.

of all other participants in the war (with the exception perhaps of India and South Africa) by reason of the distance that separated the greater part of her overseas force from its home base. Her problem—also on both counts—is summed up in the "six months' policy," which divided sharply the military from the civil involvements of the sustainment of casualty. On the military side, in the person of "convalescents," the problem was faced overseas, in the great system of "Command Depots."[7] On the civil, in the person of the "invalids," it was transferred *en bloc* to Australia for the "necessary action," whither it will be followed in *Volume III*.

<small>Civil allegiance :
Reparative
treatment ; and
the Military
Medical Boards</small>

A good case could be made in support of a thesis that if our civilisation should survive through the 20th century the philosopher of the next, contemplating the War of 1914-18, will select as its most significant result the jettisoning of the international move to "humanise" and ultimately to eradicate war by restricting its worst horrors to the specially-enlisted armed and uniformed forces of the nations at war; by seeking to eliminate its more degrading cruelties; and by ensuring humane treatment for the wounded. Of this movement only the Geneva Convention remains.[8] That this survives is probably due to the fact that the decision rested not with those whose business it was to direct the conduct of the war, but with those on whom chiefly it fell to sustain the direct impact of its sufferings and tragedies—the fighting troops and their womenfolk. The position of the Medical Service as the executive of the Geneva Convention, and its relation therein to the various civilian services of humanity and amelioration—Red Cross activities, Y.M.C.A., Comforts Funds, and so forth—are examined in *Volume III*. It is however desirable here to emphasise, and strongly, the fact—too often lost sight of or even unknown—that the continuance of the official Army Medical Service in its modern form, *i.e.* as a strictly non-combatant and essentially humanitarian service, hangs wholly on the continuance of international adherence to the terms of the Geneva Convention.

<small>The International
allegiance :
Geneva
Convention</small>

Whether in the future the Army Medical Service will be able to sustain this threefold allegiance is the greatest question that faces it to-day—perhaps, in its involvements, the greatest that faces humanity. It is not the purpose of this work to give an answer to this question, but rather to follow the course of development of medical work in the Great War so that in any future war the Medical Service shall not find itself involved in conflicting, as well as in independent, allegiances.

It remains to accommodate our vision and relate the per-

---

[7] Of 92,116 men returned to Australia up to 31 Dec. 1918 for all reasons, only 4,234 re-embarked, and of these it is probable that an inconsiderable proportion served again in the line. A small uncertain number re-enlisted in Australia.

[8] "One by one in the course of the war the Regulations [of the Hague Convention] were broken until not one was left." (*Brit. Off. Medical History, Surgery, Vol. I, p. 4.*)

spective of this introductory analysis to the specific problems that are the concern of these chapters. And here it will be profitable to make a preliminary survey of the route and to identify the main objectives.

The Medical Service: technique and equipment

Function and Structure in the Medical Service. Advances in medical and surgical technique, devised to meet novel medical problems and a new environment, bring a demand for better equipment and improved opportunities—for new establishments and organisation, for improved housing and transport, for inflated "equipment store tables," and for greater consideration in the matter of sites. These, in their turn bring further needs, opportunities and calls to action. In no sphere of medical work in the Great War were the developments greater and the changes in method more striking than in the complex of problems of the "evacuation of sick and wounded"; but in no other do the constants and immutables emerge more clear and illuminating.

(1) *Treatment Constants.* From our tarsoid ancestors we have inherited a hold on life and natural powers of recovery from physiological damage beyond that of most animals with whom we compete. But the limits of reaction against trauma, physical, mental, moral, impose a series of constants which, in conjunction with the conditions of battle and with military exigencies, determined the location and equipment of treatment centres on the evacuation route, for the various theatres of war and conditions of warfare. Speaking broadly *wound surgery is dominated by the time-factor.* Both in first aid and in the "urgent," "immediate" and "secondary" surgery of wounds, physiological and pathological time-constants determine the course of events. Haemorrhage —immediate, reactionary, secondary; wound shock; the influence of morphia; the safety limit of the tourniquet; the onset of peritonitis; the development of gangrene, of ischemic paralysis, of deformities: and, in particular, the course of the various forms of wound infection—all of these follow an inexorable time-table, which determines, often within narrow limits, the time within which the surgeon must intervene if he is to assist or direct to advantage the *vis medicatrix naturae*. At the same time, the military situation decides the extent to which such intervention may be expedient or even possible. Military medical units, from the regimental medical officer back to the base hospital, were organised and equipped for a dual purpose: first, to provide appropriate surgical treatment for each phase in the clinical and pathological course of battle wounds; and, second, to promote to the utmost the clearance of the wounded from the sphere of operations.

(2) *Transport Constants.* These depend on a wide variety of factors—in the Great War chiefly on the internal combustion engine. The adaptation of available means of transport to the requirements of treatment is the major problem of evacuation.

(3) *The Objective.* In the preceding narrative chapters dealing with the attrition phase of the war, the trend of clinical developments in war surgery—in particular, of the method of "excision" as applied to war wounds—has been indicated sufficiently to identify the casualty clearing station as the new *point d'appui* of treatment; already, with the formation of the motor ambulance convoy, it had become the fulcrum for

evacuation. In the chapters of this section, we shall follow the remarkable series of researches, clinical and experimental, that led to this clinical triumph and shall examine its influence on medical organisation and methods, on the immediate outlook for the wounded, and on the development of reparative surgery. In the chapters of *Section III* (which complete the narrative of the fighting in France) the move to extend to the field ambulance some of the refinements of surgical technique is seen as the natural outcome of new ideals and a new outlook.

The outlook of this series of chapters, dealing with the technique of the Medical Service in the war of 1914-18, is objective and impersonal—independent even of the particular experience of the A.I.F. It is, however, in no sense "textbook"; that is unnecessary, in as much as all significant war experience, except where outmoded by post-war developments, has been embodied in military establishments and manuals.[9] Nor is it intended to form a reservoir of relevant and useful facts—a proper service which, however, conditions of space forbid. The object rather is to suggest principles, indicate lines of thought, and identify those factors that are independent of scientific advances and are thus applicable to any type of warfare.

Outlook and intention

One of the purposes of this work though of necessity a secondary one, is to provide an individual record of the service in the Great War of the various medical units which served in the A.I.F. As this section is concerned to so great an extent with the line of communications and base, some space in each chapter is devoted to an account—of necessity little more than a summary—of the movements and special experiences of the Australian organisations chiefly concerned—the casualty clearing stations and general hospitals, and the medical attachments at the depots in England. In the final chapter, which deals with the prevention of disease in the B.E.F. and the general developments in military hygiene, the work of the Australian Sanitary Sections, and their special function, as accepted in the Australian Imperial Force, are critically examined.

The Australian Line of Communication Units

---

[9] For example, *R.A.M.C. Training*; *Army Manual of Hygiene and Sanitation*; *Organisation, Strategy and Tactics of the Army Medical Services in war* by T. B. Nicholls (London: Baillière, Tindall and Cox. 1937).

SYNOPSIS OF CHAPTER XI

EVACUATION WITHIN THE ARMY ZONE—MOVEMENT
The "Army" Zone.
Line of approach: function v. structure.
"Battle-casualties" and "Sick."
The Fundamental combination—Transport and Treatment.

MOVEMENT OF WOUNDED MEN
Methods of transport.
Stretchers.
Wheeled transport.
"Stretcher cases" and "Walking wounded."

IN THE REGIMENTAL AREA—THE STRETCHER-BEARER
Regimental bearers—collecting the wounded.
Regimental tactics.
The R.A.P. and the R.M.O.
Position of the Aid-post.
Medical work with the Artillery.
Personnel.
Evacuation of battery casualties.

R.A.P. TO MOTOR LOADING POST
The Stretcher case: the Bearer relays.
Organisation.
The Bearer as Soldier.
The Bearer Officer.
"*Liaison.*"
Status of the Bearer Officer.

THE WHEELED-TRANSPORT CIRCUITS
Motor-conveyance of stretcher cases—its origin.
1914.
The first battles: clearance to railhead.
At the Base.
Voluntary Aid in Transport.
The Motor Ambulance Convoys.
Motor-conveyance of Walking wounded—the motor lorry, etc.
Transport developments.

CO-ORDINATION OF MOVEMENT AND TREATMENT: "TRIAGE"

MOVEMENT, OR RETENTION, OF SICK MEN
Prevention of wastage by early treatment.
The sick parade.
The Field Ambulance "Rest station."
Diagnostic stations.
The treatment stations.

CHAPTER XI

EVACUATION WITHIN THE ARMY ZONE—MOVEMENT

THE study of medical military technique in this and the next eight chapters, relates to a very specialised type of warfare which is not likely to recur in precisely the same form in the present era of civilisation. Even on the Western Front the conditions varied greatly and "development" of technique by no means necessarily connoted "advance." Like the warfare itself, the prodigious expansion of medical units in 1916 and 1917 must, it is suggested, be looked on as abnormal and retrograde. And this comment is pertinent to the more intimate medical problems, as of surgical treatment; the virulent "mass infection" of wounds met with in the war on the Western Front was in some measure the product of "mass" warfare.

The developments in the medical service of the B.E.F. reflect, moreover, essentially conditions on the Western Front and the "western" outlook and ideas; and it is entirely legitimate for a student of warfare in general to question the value to military medicine of much of this experience—just as one may doubt the value of much "western" strategy and tactics to the science of war. Failing, however, a frank resort in future wars to promiscuous aerial bombing as the major weapon of strategy and tactics—in which event the whole fabric of warfare, and especially its medical aspect, must profoundly change—neither complete escape from entrenched warfare in some form nor any radical reconstruction of the military machine seems likely, so that the experiences of the Great War must form the groundwork for the constructive preparations for the next. Furthermore, the interplay of the constant factors that compose the medical problem—*time and distance, mass and movement, human powers, human limitations*—which are common to any type of warfare, is well seen in the war on the Western Front. The substitution, for example, of aeroplanes for motor and train transport in urgent cases simply involves calculations of speed and distance, accommodation, military conditions, medical facilities, and so forth; it would not change the basic factors in the medical problem.

In this chapter and in *Chapter XIII* (The Casualty Clearing Station) we are concerned with the handling of "casualties" within the "Army zone;" that is to within the administration of the headquarters staff of "Army" in distinction from that of the Inspector-General of Communications, who controlled the area next in rear.

The "Army" zone

The "Army" area was an administrative rather than a geographical one, and generally speaking was defined by the railheads. It included the field formations, the transport units operating in advance of railhead, and the medical units evacuating casualties to the ambulance train for the Base.

As applied to medical work at the seat of war the demarcation between Army and Lines of Communication was fundamental. When, on evacuation from the C.C.S., the casualty entered the ambulance train at railhead, he became *ipso facto* an element in "Army wastage" and entered on a series of movements wherein the time-factor was of an entirely different order from that which obtained within the Army zone itself. Conceiving (as it is convenient to do) the process of evacuating as a chain of movement circuits,[1] the time within which a "casualty" could be returned to duty lengthened at once from an order of days to one of weeks, if he was sent to the Expeditionary Base —or of months, if he was sent to the Home Base. If sent only as far as the field ambulance or C.C.S. men rejoined their units direct, or through the reinforcement camp. But from the Lines of Communication hospitals (Expeditionary Base) all casualties, even those whose condition did not involve evacuation overseas to the Home Base, normally went through a "Base Depot," and regained their units only as "reinforcements" in response to a "demand" for these, made by the unit through 3rd Echelon.

Each of the several structural elements in the medical system of evacuation and return to duty—field ambulance, motor ambulance convoy, casualty clearing station and so forth—furnishes a self-contained subject for study. But however useful and educative may be exact knowledge of the lines of development and methods of work of these several units, the

Line of approach: function v. structure

---

[1] The concept applies both to the *journeys of the transport units*, and the *movements of the casualty* in his return to duty from the various posts and stations along the line of clearance and evacuation.

experiences in the Great War proved that it is even more important to achieve a full appreciation of the fact that, in the last resort *all this was but the means to an end*: that, under whatever scheme it may be carried out, "evacuation" is essentially a series of co-ordinated episodes of transportation and treatment, whose sequence and inter-relation are in part only determined by the structure of the machinery by which they are effected.[2] Thus, while the organisation of medical units in the various national armies, and their direction and tactical employment, differed greatly, the process of "evacuation" was essentially the same in all.[3]

"*Battle-casualties*" *and* "*Sick.*" The distinction between "battle-casualty" and "sick" strikes deeply into the whole fabric of military medical activity, and not less drastically into its civil reflections and post-war social repercussions. In this chapter we are concerned only with the direct and immediate consequences.

The sustaining by a soldier of a "battle-casualty" carried the right to a "wound stripe," and commonly a trip to "Blighty"; and precise definition therefore became necessary. It was laid down by the D.G.M.S., B.E.F., in 1916, that:—

"(1) A 'Wound' means an injury caused by or arising from the enemy, and includes injuries by rifle and gunfire, by bombs, bayonet, liquid fire, etc. Shock to the nervous system caused by bursting shell, and the effects of inhalation of poison gases, although producing no visible trauma, are to be regarded as wounds. (2) Casualties due to injuries independent of any act of the enemy are to be entered as 'Sick' but may be marginally noted as 'injury accidental.' (3) When a casualty arrives from the front suffering from any trauma not marked 'wound';

---

[2] To promote the attitude suggested above, the statistical study made in this work of the activities of the medical units is exactly related to the movement of casualties. The statistical data assembled from the "admission and discharge books" of Australian medical units have been analysed nosologically, on the basis of pathogenesis, into types, classes, groups, and individual "diseases," and they show, for each of the several treatment centres except the regimental aid-post, both the dimensions and composition of the streams passing toward the Base, and of those diverted for local treatment and "return to duty." See *Chapters xvii, xviii*, and *xix*; and also *Vol. III*.

[3] Though such doubtless have been written, the author is not acquainted with any comprehensive study of the evolution of the modern Army Medical Service and its technique. For a particularly interesting outline of advances in the technique of medical work in war the reader is referred to the address of the President, (Maj.. Gen. R. M. Downes, D.G.M.S., Australian Military Forces) at the "Centenary" year meeting of the Victorian Branch, B.M.A., Dec. 1935; published in the *Medical Journal of Australia, Jan., 1936, p. 73*, and also in the *Journal of the Royal Army Medical Corps, Dec., 1936*. For a note on the evacuation systems in various armies during the war of 1914-18 *see Appendix No. 9*. The reader is referred also to the system of evacuation on Gallipoli and in the Sinai and Palestine Campaign. See *Vol. I* of this work.

such casualty will be classified as sick notwithstanding any statement made by the patient as to the trauma having been caused by the act of the enemy."

The evacuation of wounded was incomparably the most engrossing and difficult of medical problems and was intimately bound up with the treatment of "wounds" and of their physiological effects. In contrast, the collection and evacuation of the sick was little more than a matter of providing transport for sitting cases, and was commonly carried out by horsed ambulance waggon or by lorry. Yet for the medical authorities in the "Army" area the sick soldier was the chief element in the problem of direct control of army wastage; at the front medical interest in the *immediate* wastage through wounding was almost confined to the rendition of casualty returns, since the great majority of wounded were sent to the Base.

Following the convenient and practical—if arbitrary—convention which relates the medical problem of evacuation specially to *battle-casualties*,[4] the present study of evacuation will examine the rescue of the wounded, their movements toward the Base, and their treatment at various stages on the route. The medical problem of *sickness*, on the other hand, will be related particularly to the *prevention of wastage* in the field, with special reference to the problem of providing facilities for the diagnosis and discrimination of the several types of disease.

As an element in the professional technique of the Medical Service, "evacuation" presents for examination two distinct procedures: (1) the *movement* of the casualty and (2) his *treatment*. With these must go, in practice, consideration of the technical equipment required for both procedures—vehicles, stretchers, medical and "Red Cross" stores and "comforts," surgical instruments and appliances and so forth. This third consideration, however, is far too embracing to be dealt with in such a work as this, which must therefore confine itself almost entirely to the other two. Of these, movement will be discussed in this chapter and treatment will be dealt with only so far as it is necessary to touch upon it in explaining movement.

The fundamental combination—Transport and treatment

---

[4] On the Western Front, at least, battle-casualties were responsible for all, or nearly all, the crises in the process of evacuation.

MOVEMENT OF WOUNDED MEN

Movement, it may be postulated, as a practical problem, must always take first place as the prime factor in successful evacuation.[5] The development of the art and practice of war surgery and in particular its limitations, hinge on this fact.

Methods of Transport. On the Western Front transportation resolved itself broadly into *hand carry*, and carriage by *wheeled vehicle* on road or rail. The "success" claimed for evacuation after any major battle depended largely on the encroachment by the more hardy elements of wheeled transport—horsed-waggons, Fords, trench tramways, or light railway—on the man-power bearer circuit, with the wheeled stretcher-carrier as a connecting link when the road or track-way would permit the use of this somewhat uncertain piece of apparatus.[6]

Stretchers. The negotiation of the trench traverse and narrow communication trench brought a great crop of more or less useful and ingenious inventions in "trench stretchers." They were an important part of the equipment of the aid-post in strictly stationary warfare. The two-handed chair, single bearer back support, and overhead pulley are figured in the service handbooks of each side. The principle of the "flying fox" was called in for the passage of ravines and rivers.[7] The technique of the "shoulder high" carriage has been referred to. It was one of the important advances in service technique in the war.

Wheeled Transport.[8] Various forms of light wheel and axle—two wheel and mono-wheel—were used to support the loaded stretcher for clearing to waggon post and various types were on issue to R.M.O's and field ambulances. On occasion they were useful. Horsed ambulance waggons were retained by the field ambulances; although for the evacuation of battle-casualties they were largely replaced by the light two-stretcher Fords, they filled a definite place in the scheme of clearance. Tram-trolley, light railway, motor and train transport are dealt with elsewhere.

---

[5] This is brought out in the accounts given of medical work in the retreat from Mons 1914. See *e.g. Unwilling Passenger* by Lieut.-Col. Arthur Osburn. But it cannot too strongly be emphasised that *movement* and *treatment* must go hand in hand.

[6] A very complete account with illustration of the various apparatus of transport used in the war is given in the *British Official Medical History, General, Vol. IV*, *Chapter xxiii*.

[7] See p. 636.

[8] Animal transport was little used in France. For the use of *donkeys* at Gallipoli and *camels* in the Sinai desert see *Vol. I*. For the evacuation from C.C.S. to the Base, *ambulance barges* were found ideal when facilities existed. 70,059 British casualties were thus transported in France. They were extensively used by the Germans. In the First Battle of Bullecourt one of the *tanks* carried back a few wounded infantrymen and, by deliberate arrangement, returning empty tanks lent a hand at the Battle of Hamel (July, 1918). For the use of sledges in France *see p. 85*.

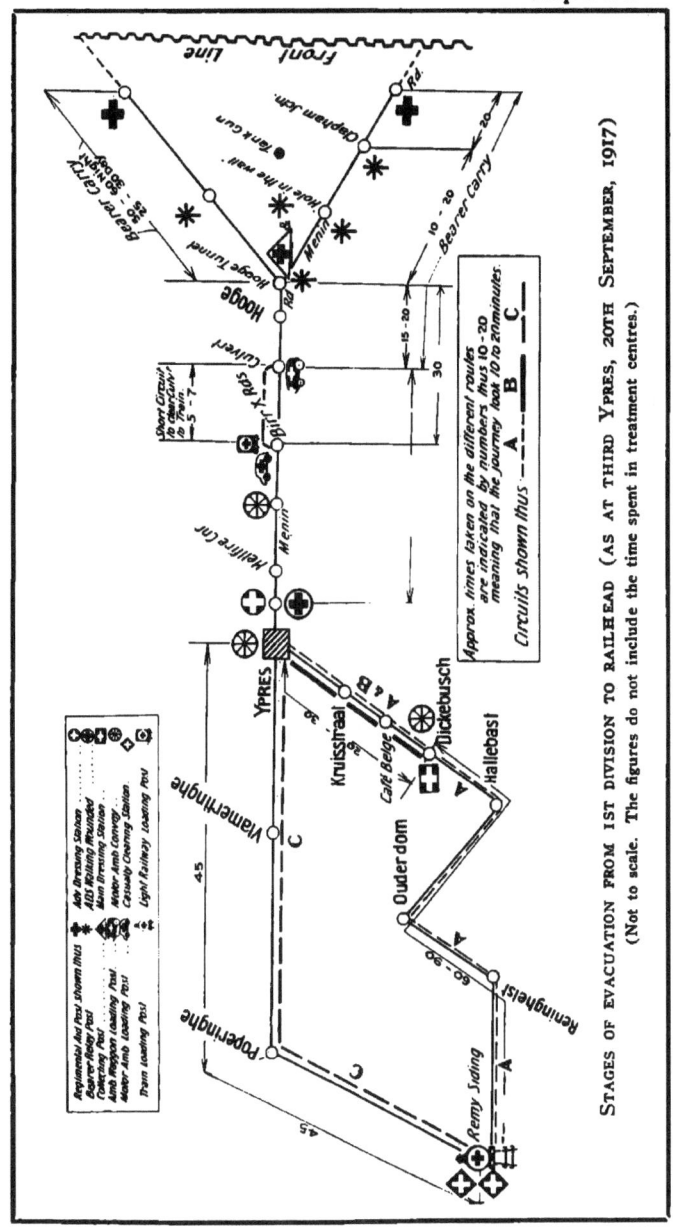

Map No. 8

Stages of evacuation from 1st division to railhead (as at Third Ypres, 20th September, 1917)
(Not to scale. The figures do not include the time spent in treatment centres.)

"Stretcher Cases" and "Walking Wounded." For the purpose both of movement and of treatment casualties were classified into "walking wounded" and "stretcher cases." The distinction is primitive, and is fundamental; it has determined the organisation of the modern Medical Service, and it profoundly influenced medical strategy and tactics. The personnel, transport, and equipment of field medical units were organised essentially to serve the needs of the helpless man—the "stretcher case." The arrangements for expediting the movement and serving the needs of the walking wounded, on the other hand, were part of the combatant machinery of warfare even more than of the medical. The "sitting cases" formed an element which varied inversely with the pressure on the transport available. The following is pertinent:—

"If there is any doubt whatever about a man being able to walk, make him a stretcher case. His chances of ultimate recovery will undoubtedly be increased thereby. Where the number of casualties, however, is in excess of the stretcher-bearers available to carry them out, this principle does not hold. Obviously the thing to do is to get them out of the Forward Area, the zone of greatest danger, as soon as possible. Every effort should be made to avoid congestion of wounded in the Forward Area, even if extra pain and discomfort are occasioned to men by making them walk a few extra miles until transport is obtainable."[10]

Exact figures of the proportion of stretcher cases, "sitters," and "walking wounded" are curiously difficult to arrive at. But it may be said that, in general, the ratio of stretcher cases to others was roughly 50-50.

In respect neither of transport nor of treatment was more important service rendered to the severely wounded man than by the regimental stretcher-bearers. The function of these men was essentially unchanged since their creation by Napoleon's great surgeon Baron Percy; it was—to be at hand in battle armed with apparatus and knowledge sufficient to enable them to render first-aid as soon as possible after wounding, and

In the regimental area—the stretcher-bearer

---

[9] From an admirable study of medical work in France written for the Australian War Memorial by Major J. H. B. Brown.

[10] It need hardly be said that under some circumstances a wounded man must walk or die. See *Vol. I p. 294* (Light Horse at the Nek) and *pp. 134-5* of the present volume.

to remove the wounded man towards safety and succour in rear of the fighting. They constituted the first line of *liaison* between "combatant" and "non-combatant." Not members of the medical service, "combatants" though non-combatant, this body of men formed the outposts of rescue, as servants at once of humanity and of hatred, of the Geneva Convention and of the Military Command. That in the war of 1914-18 this "impossible" dual allegiance was rendered—that the two masters were faithfully served—the records of rescue and of "return to duty" amply prove. But it was possible only because men were found who in this service would tread again the Via Dolorosa.[11]

Regimental Bearers— collecting the wounded
Death "killed in action" is commonly preceded by mortal struggle to survive the wounding;[12] the outcome of this was very often determined by the regimental stretcher-bearer.[13]

"When a soldier is wounded his first thought is to save himself, if possible, from further harm. . . . If he is able, he will walk, crawl, or drag himself to the nearest position of comparative safety, and there wait to be picked up by the stretcher-bearers."

"When a lad was hit he would crawl to some sheltered portion of the trench and there wait patiently. The fighting was so continuous and heavy that the wounded had to be left almost entirely to the stretcher-bearers. . . As the morning wore on our casualties were mounting up, and stretcher-bearer after stretcher-bearer was shot down."

---

[11] Though exact records are not available the casualties among these men are known to have been very heavy indeed. In any major battle all the bearers might be "laid out," by wounding and exhaustion. Thus, during the two days of the 1st Division's attack on Pozières the R.M.O. 3rd Battalion (Capt. S. C. Fitzpatrick) lost "nearly every one of his sixteen stretcher-bearers." In one action on the Somme it is recorded "the whole of the R.S.B's of one battalion, 32 in number, became casualties in one morning, and the clearing from the front line devolved upon the ambulance bearers alone." ("A.A.M.C. Work with the Infantry"—memorandum by Major James Sprent.)

[12] The term "died of wounds" has been the source of much confusion in military writings. To assist the General Staff, men who died from their wounds before evacuation to the Base are commonly included with "killed in action." From the medical point of view obviously they should be counted with the "wounded." In this volume this is done except where otherwise stated.

[13] As laid down in *Field Service Regulations* the duty of regimental stretcher-bearers was "to afford first aid to the wounded; to carry cases not able to walk to . . . cover; to assist the medical units after an action. . . ." The official record of their work—and indeed of that of the R.M.O's—is meagre. Until June, 1918—and then so far as can be ascertained only in the Australian Corps—the R.M.O. kept no official diary nor did he furnish routine reports to the A.D.M.S. Casualties among regimental stretcher-bearers, being combatants, were not recorded separately in casualty returns. The only records available of "sick parades" are those made by individual enthusiasts. From June, 1918, onwards, at the request of the Australian War Records Section, the D.D.M.S. Australian Corps arranged for a monthly report by the R.M.O. to the A.D.M.S.

"A wounded man may die of a broken heart if he is kept waiting long in the trenches; for the pain of his wound is, in most cases, nothing to compare to his agony of mind. And herein lies the peculiar privilege and reward of the stretcher-bearer. What he can do for the physical hurt is little: a bandage, an improvised splint, and perhaps a tourniquet are his only aids. But what he can do for the mind is incalculable. Even if he does not speak a word, with a pair of strong arms he can raise a man from hell to heaven in half an hour."[14]

First aid, the first duty of the stretcher-bearer, will be touched upon in the next chapter, dealing with the technique of wound treatment. With it went the equally vital duty of transportation for the half-mile or so to the "regimental aid-post."

Regimental Tactics. In the Australian forces the "moral" status in the battalion of the regimental bearers steadily rose during the war. After Pozières the use of bandsmen generally ceased and bearers were specially selected "for their physique and guts."[15] At the same time regimental tactics crystallised. In most battalions 32 men were trained.[16]

"Prior to a battle," says a record of the 27th battalion, "the bearers were attached 8 to a company—in normal times 4; one from each company would go into the line with the R.M.O. to carry the extra material and learn the location of the Aid Post. These men rejoined their companies, but the Bearer Sergeant remained at the R.A.P."

In a major battle it was seldom that the battlefield could be cleared without extra fatigue parties being allotted from the combatant troops.

The R.A.P. and the R.M.O. The following notes have the authority of experienced and successful officers.[17]

"As a rule the place for the R.M.O. is at his R.A.P. This is where he can best do his job of attending to casualties and supervising

---

[14] Quotations are from (1) Appendix 10, 5th Field Ambulance war diary, June, 1918: notes by Private G. L. Davidson, "Cost of a Casualty." (2) *The Red and White Diamond (Official History of the 24th Battalion)*, p. 156. (3) *Field Ambulance Sketches* by "A Corporal" p. 45.

[15] From a narrative by Sergt. J. R. Edwards, 27th Battalion.

[16] A much larger reserve of bearers was sometimes trained. Thus for the 4th Division offensive at Pozières the R.M.O. 14th Battalion had 14 attached to each company of whom 8 bore arms and fought in the battle. In many units every soldier was given some instruction in the use of his first field dressing and arrest of urgent haemorrhage.

[17] They are selected from a large number of admirable memoranda written by officers and other ranks of the A.A.M.C. for the purpose of the medical history, to which it is impossible to do justice by casual quotation. Those quoted here are (in order) by Major W. W. S. Johnston, R.M.O. 12th Bn.; Capt. J. C. M. Harper, R.M.O. 28th Battalion, and from a medical record whose source cannot be traced.

their evacuation.[18] His stretcher-bearers, if efficient and properly trained, can be depended on to carry out the necessary first-aid dressings and to collect the stretcher-cases. Occasionally it may be permissible for the R.M.O. to go forward and attend to specially bad cases but, in my experience, it has never been necessary to go out and search for wounded. The stretcher-bearer is too thorough and conscientious for that. There should be an N.C.O. in charge who can direct the operations of the bearers away from the direct control of the R.M.O."

"I had 32 stretcher-bearers and a Corporal (Lance-Sergeant) in charge. These went forward with their companies in a stunt. The R.M.O. (was) in his R.A.P. 6-800 yards behind the line with a couple of squads, his orderly, and an A.A.M.C. man attached. (The) R.M.O. looked at the dressings when brought in but more often did not touch them."

"Position of R.M.O. This is a matter which the R.M.O. himself will have to decide. Personally I think the R.M.O. should be at his R.A.P., but as a matter of policy he must move up to the firing line if he is to gain and retain the goodwill and confidence of the unit he is attached to. Nothing is more damning to the efficient work of an R.M.O. than to be thought a cold footer. Once he has established his reputation and gained the confidence of all, then he can hang back a bit as undoubtedly his place is not in the firing line."

To every R.M.O. there came a moment when he knew that in battle his arms were held up by his regimental bearers.

"From this—the first experience of the Bn. in the front line in France —one learned that no instruction in modern warfare however thorough, no word picture however vivid, no imagination however fertile, can furnish one with a proper conception of the actualities of a modern battle. But at the same time one learned and appreciated the value of training. . . The thing that counts most of all in connection with the medical work of a battalion during a battle is the work of the regimental stretcher-bearers. They displayed great skill in dressing the wounded and wonderful courage and powers of endurance in conveying men back. The battalion lost about half its men; casualties among the Regimental Bearers were numerous; those who were unwounded on the third day were absolutely exhausted."[19]

Every medical officer who writes of regimental work has stressed the importance of thorough training of the regimental

---

[18] This view it is believed is that of all experienced R.M.O's who served with the A.A.M.C. The antithesis is supplied by the terms of the recommendation for which Capt. N. G. Chavasse, V.C. (R.A.M.C.) was awarded a bar to the Victoria Cross. ". . . . Though severely wounded early in the action whilst carrying a wounded soldier to the dressing station, Capt. Chavasse refused to leave his post, and for two days not only continued to perform his duties, but in addition went out repeatedly under heavy fire to search for and attend to the wounded who were lying out. During these searches, although practically without food during this period, worn with fatigue and faint with his wound, he assisted to carry in a number of badly wounded men over heavy and difficult ground. . . This devoted and gallant officer subsequently died of his wounds."

[19] "Medical Report" 1916-17 by Major J. T. Jones, R.M.O. 47th Bn.—4th Division's first attack on Pozières. See pp. 61-63.

bearers and the following points are constantly made: that their powers of endurance should be conserved in battle; and that their establishment should include the proper proportion of non-commissioned officers. The great influence of stretcher-bearers on the morale of their units affords ample justification for this.

The Regimental Aid-Post. The "regimental aid-post" was the official post of succour for the battalion in a battle; it was also the consulting room and headquarters of the R.M.O. where, in times of "peace" he held his sick parade. Selection of a site was important but difficult.

"Don't expect the ideal, because you will never find it. It should be *central* and accessible from all parts of the unit's front and therefore behind the forward line. The Aid Post must be *within touch* of unit headquarters but not too close. All officers, stretcher-bearers, and as many others as possible should know its site.[20] Room to store a few stretcher cases (in particular, chests) for a short time is a great help and as well a place near the R.A.P. where a few men can secure a rest —such as slightly 'shell-shocked' or those unnerved through lack of sleep." (From notes by Major W. W. S. Johnston, R.M.O., 12th Battalion.)

Acting under advice from the Commanding Officer—who, in the last resort, was responsible—R.M.O's often selected beforehand by map reference a site for a new aid-post in enemy territory. Others in battle did not arrange previously a fixed location for their R.A.P. but worked from a shell-hole or some such convenient spot. Unless *liaison* was very effective, this often caused trouble with the bearer division.[21]

A short reference is called for here to the work of the

---

[20] "Trouble may arise from improper choice of a R.A.P. An unhappy experience was when an R.M.O., one of the bravest men I ever met, put his R.A.P. in the broken and sketchy front line at Pozières. As most of his casualties occurred behind the R.A.P., and wounded men won't go forward, the greater number were dealt with by adjoining R.M.O's or by the Field Ambulance. On 31st August, 1916 trying to reach this R.A.P. at dusk under Battalion guides in response to a message for help, 15 of my (Ambulance) men, with the guides, got through a break in the line and were taken prisoners." (Abridged from a memorandum by Major James Sprent). The R.A.P. was that of Capt. N. C. Shierlaw, R.M.O. 13th Bn.—of notable memory. This officer, more perhaps than most, identified himself with the battle outlook. He was mortally wounded in the First Battle of Bullecourt.

[21] The "greatest difficulty was experienced in connection with those medical officers who would not form an R.A.P. but dumped 2 or 3 wounded here and there all over his Battalion area. In such a case it was usually necessary for the S.B. Officer to visit that unit frequently, run the R.M.O. to earth, and get him to yield up information as to the location of wounded." (From notes by Major H. Boyd Graham.)

medical officer attached to a brigade of artillery.[22] This differed greatly from that of the R.M.O. of a battalion; and the work with field artillery was also somewhat different from that with a brigade of heavy artillery.

Medical work with the Artillery

Personnel. The medical establishment provided for an artillery brigade included, beside A.A.M.C. "attached," only a bombardier and a gunner, the latter combatants. The first and most important task of the R.M.O. therefore was to build up a scheme whereby each of his batteries was self-contained in its trained personnel, and had sufficient equipment for these to carry out first aid, and to supervise sanitation.

The following from the records of a successful R.M.O.[23] may be taken as representative.

"I was fortunate in obtaining from each battery two intelligent men who saved me more work and anxiety than they knew. They were coached for two weeks by my bombardier at Headquarters until I found that they had a good knowledge of first aid, could bandage, improvise and use splints, and apply a foment. They had learnt something about sanitation and knew the reason for the various sanitary precautions and devices; and the use of the commoner drugs. Their duties were to take charge of medical stores and comforts, attend to or report any cases of sickness and wounds, to arrange evacuations in my absence, and to keep an eye on the sanitation of their camps or billets and gun positions. There was always an orderly at the guns and one in the billets or waggon lines. In each battery also was a sanitary man and a man whose duty it was to see that the water was chlorinated and to clean out the water cart."

Evacuation of Battery Casualties. In general, successful evacuation was achieved by maintaining a close *liaison* with the field ambulance most adjacent to the several batteries which, in the case of the heavy artillery, might be scattered over several miles of front.[24] In this dispersion lay

---

[22] See in this connection pp. 59n, 139, and *Vol. I, p. 207n*. Australia supplied in France fifteen Field Artillery Brigades, one Headquarters of a Heavy Artillery Brigade, and two Siege Batteries. In 1915 a Field Artillery Brigade had an R.M.O. and 2 combatant "orderlies." In 1916 Australian brigades (3 batteries only) had, as well, 4 A.A.M.C. "attached." In France (with 4 batteries) they had 5; which number, however, was in 1918 reduced to 1.

[23] Capt. A. H. Barrett, A.A.M.C. (who took over from Major R. W. Whiston Walsh who had been R.M.O. to the 36th Australian Heavy Artillery Bde., since its formation in 1915).

[24] It will be possible for the reader to appreciate the involvements of the work of the R.M.O. to a Heavy Artillery Brigade by locating on the relevant maps the gun positions occupied by the batteries of the 36th (Australian) H. A. Bde.

1st Aust. Siege Bty. (8" hows.) Red Lodge Road behind Hill 63; billets in Bailleul and at the battery.

2nd Aust. Siege Bty. (9·2" hows.) in Ploegsteert Wood close to Hyde Park Corner.

155th Siege Bty. (6" hows.) behind the Messines ridge; billets north of Wulverghem.

353rd Siege Bty. (6" hows.) behind the Wytschaete ridge.

151st Heavy Bty. (60-pounders) Wytschaete road; waggon lines behind Neuve-Eglise.

140th Heavy Bty. (60-pounders) north of Armentières; waggon lines six miles away not far from La Clytte.

It was not possible to visit all these stations in one day.

the chief problem in connection with casualties (as well as with sick parades and sanitation) and it was met *secundum artem* by each R.M.O.
The general, situation of the batteries in relation to the various field ambulance positions—W.L.P., A.D.S., M.D.S.—was an important factor in the clearing of casualties. Though practice varied, it was not usual to form an R.A.P.; the R.M.O. went, if required, to the gun positions for which he might be equipped with a motor cycle, or (on occasion) with a motor ambulance. To quote the same officer:
"The amount of casualty work (done by the R.M.O. himself) was small because, first, the battery positions were almost always within easy carrying distance of the A.D.S. or Bearers' Relay Post; and, secondly, casualties might occur at any odd time and it was not possible to make special preparation. (I took care) to ensure that there was always at least one medical orderly in the position with stretchers and adequate supply of dressings, and to see that he, and all the battery, were informed of the location of the nearest relay post or A.D.S."
Success in this difficult job was to be achieved only by mutual co-operation between the R.M.O. and the staff at headquarters and of each battery. Personal records make it clear that in the artillery the influence of the R.M.O. in promoting "morale" and efficiency was not less assured than in the infantry.

R.A.P. to Motor Loading Post

The R.A.P. was, officially, the place of intersection of the two major bearer circuits and, as well, was the watershed between combatant and medical responsibility for the wounded; it was the focal point of the all-important *"liaison"* between the field ambulance and the regiment. Thence *walking wounded* made their way, via routes surveyed and posts formed by officers and N.C.O's of the field ambulance, to the divisional collecting post or "walking wounded A.D.S." They usually "hopped" such transport as should be available—trench tramway, light railway, or supply lorry. From the collecting post they were sent by lorry or light railway under Divisional arrangement to a "walking wounded dressing station" for recording and care. From here, under "Army Corps" arrangements but with the help of "Army" transport, they were conveyed by lorry, bus, or rail to the C.C.S. The arrangements—transport and treatment—for this clearance of walking wounded are fully described in the narrative in the chapters of this volume dealing with the actual fighting.[25]

---

[25] As will have been observed, the designation of the posts of succour for the "walking wounded" varied greatly—a cause of almost hopeless confusion in the records. Clarity of thought can be achieved only by fixing attention on the purpose in view. The following is quoted from the memorandum by Major Brown cited above. It sufficiently sums up all that need be said on this subject.
"Walking wounded and sick should be kept at the R.A.P. until a few have collected, and then sent back to the Advanced Collecting Post or Motor Loading Post, but *never* without one or two bearers as guides. These guides are frequently

The Stretcher Case: the Bearer Relays. On leaving the R.A.P. the badly wounded man entered upon a series of transport circuits which were devoid of facilities for treatment otherwise than for "re-dressing" and sustainment, but which, via relay posts, advanced collecting station, and loading posts, ended at a field ambulance "dressing station." The first mile or more—sometimes over three—of this passage was covered by relays of field ambulance bearers; the next 3-8 miles by the wheeled transport of the field ambulance or by light railway. For the severely wounded man this provided his most dreadful ordeal, for the medical service its most difficult task. Its problems are largely described in the chapters dealing with the fighting; only a few general matters call for notice here.

Organisation. It will be recalled[26] that the "bearer division" of the 3-section field ambulance replaced the independent "bearer company" of the South African War. The tactics of this new unit, worked out in militia training during the decade of 1904-14 were incomplete in two respects: (a) Inadequate account was taken of the immense increase in battle casualties that must result from machine-guns and massed artillery. (b) Inadequate attention was given to the problem of co-operation (*"liaison"*) with the R.M.O. and the regimental bearers.[27]

The increase of casualties was met by pooling the bearer divisions under Corps control and attaching combatant fatigues. This need for resort to a system closely akin to the original led not a few able officers to suggest return to this.[28] The consensus of opinion however favoured the combined unit and, notwithstanding the differing practice of most foreign armies this was probably right. The practical advantages of mutual co-operation between the transport and treatment elements (bearer and tent divisions) of the field ambulance were manifold. For the bearers, a well found and well equipped home base—so to speak—for their excursions to the front lines; for the tent division a source of essential "fatigues." For both a balanced and diversified military unit, a focus for strong and useful loyalties, service and social.

The Bearer as Soldier. But for all this the field ambulance bearers

---

required to attend to dressings which have become displaced or perhaps to render assistance to a man who has become faint or fatigued. They know the track and can lead the men back by the shortest and safest route. No sick or wounded man should be allowed to find his own way back to the A.D.S. If this is allowed, he will frequently lose his way and almost always will arrive at the A.D.S. in a more fatigued condition than he would have had he been guided over the easiest track.

"Directing sign posts should be placed at frequent intervals along the track for the benefit of stray casualties."

[26] See Vol. I p. 8.
[27] The experiences of "The Landing" may be recalled. See Vol. I p. 139.
[28] Thus Colonel A. E. Shepherd, A.D.M.S. 2nd Division in his War Diary for 13 October, 1917 writes—"A return to the old bearer companies, or the formation of a bearer battalion with infantry officers trained in First Aid, would solve these difficulties." For developments in the open warfare of 1918 see *Chapters xxiii and xxiv.*

were, in the words of one of them,[29] "very much a class apart, and had not much in common with a tent division. Their duty was to carry stretcher cases not to dress them." This technical task was the particular *métier* of a specialised body of soldiers who in its performance, through the years of war, developed in high degree individuality, ideals, and a technique of their own. Much could be said of these of great interest but space does not permit of more than cursory comment.

Two prime qualities were required, namely, physical strength and stamina, and courage. The first could be much improved by muscular adjustment, thorough training, and by technique—such as shoulder-high carriage, the use of shoulder pads, adjustment of height, and so forth.[30] The courage required of the stretcher-bearer was of a peculiar and (so to speak) unnatural quality; not the instinctive response of the courageous animal to attack, but an acquired and "conditioned" inhibition of the instinct to flight; a deliberate disciplining of the mind and will through the impulse of "self-respect"—the "self-regarding sentiment" of McDougall.[31]

The stretcher-bearers (Dunstan found) were much more scared when going back to the R.A.P. as individuals, and would duck and take cover—quite without advantage. But with a stretcher on their shoulders the intense preoccupation with their task minimised the sense of danger; as a squad they simply had to carry right on. Conversation was a great help and mutual support; the four men of the squad, with their patient, formed (so to speak) a social *unit of courage*. Field ambulance bearers did not have the personal interest in their patient which helped to sustain the regimental bearers—it was replaced by a compelling sense of professional pride and duty.

It is desirable specially to emphasise the importance of maintaining the highest standard in the non-commissioned officers of the bearer division. Colonel Barber, in his official résumé of the war, refers to "the magnificent work done by bearer sergeants (in Australian Field Ambulances) throughout the war; their duties required infinite tact, resource, and great courage."[32]

---

[29] Private O. R. Dunstan, A.A.M.C. from whose notes this and other quotations are made, observes that only once in 16 months on the Somme and in the Salient was he called on to do an important emergency dressing. First aid was commonly applied by the regimental bearer or R.M.O., and any adjustments required between the R.A.P. and the A.D.S. were done by the bearer captains or N.C.O's at the relay posts—chiefly by the former. The duty of the N.C.O's was that of directing squads, finding routes, maintaining *liaison*, maintaining supplies and so forth.

[30] Infantrymen loathed the task of bearing and could not support the toil as did the trained stretcher-bearers. "Often to the physical exertion of the journey is added the imminent fear of death. In any event, stretcher-bearing is the most exhausting task on active service. At the end of a spell a man is commonly dripping with sweat without, bone dry within, and so exhausted that he can sleep in his equipment in the adjacent mud." (*The Somme* by A. D. Gristwood, London: Jonathan Cape *p. 87.*)

[31] *Introduction to Social Psychology* 17th Edition *pp. 193-208*. In the combatant arms the supreme test of this type of courage was the holding of captured trenches through the retaliatory bombardment. In it we can glimpse "the utter difference between man's soul and body: the body so weak and frail a stuff, so easily broken, shattered, torn to rags, and trodden indistinguishably into mire: the soul so resolute, so untouched and unconquerable." (Professor Gilbert Murray *Collected Essays and Addresses*). It was this unnatural demand for continued inhibition, with its physical concomitants, lack of sleep and so forth, that gave to the medical history of this war its peculiar "psychic" quality.

[32] The reader is invited to turn here to the illustration by Lieut. Will Dyson (*p. 772*) entitled "Stretcher-Bearers near Martinpuich," and in particular to his dedication of the sketch.

EVACUATION WITHIN ARMY ZONE

The Bearer Officer. The officers of the bearer division were all registered medical practitioners. They had to organise and, through their N.C.O's, lead the bearers in the interests of the wounded. They had to direct the tactics of movement, to hold back or to push on and seize the moment; to press for help from engineers, and to use their own squads to provide shelter; to ensure sustainment and interim first aid for the casualty on the long line of relays; and, (in particular) to maintain *liaison* at the one end with the R.M.O., at the other with the field ambulance transport officer and Ambulance Headquarters.

"*Liaison.*" "It has always been evident to me that whenever there has been friction in the clearing of a battlefield from the R.A.P., half the fault only rested with the Ambulance bearers, and the R.A.P. contributed the other half."[33]

"The R.M.O. has a fixed post at his R.A.P., which only moves when the unit moves; but the one ambulance is clearing several of these. When and where are the casualties to be expected? Where can the line be staffed with a few squads only and where are extra bearers likely to be most needed?"[34]

These are some of the questions that *liaison* has to answer. Its technique and methods, as worked out in the war, should be held fast by the Medical Service as tradition—by far the most effective form of "history"—together with such hard-won and precious gifts from the dead as "excision of wounds," the Thomas splint, the stretcher-bearer's soldierly sense of self-respect, and the *esprit de corps* of the whole service. Two distinct problems presented themselves:—

(1) What should be the method of *normal liaison and co-operation in the normal clearing of trenches and battlefield?*

(2) What was the *best channel for any special demand for bearers* by R.M.O. or Battalion Commander?

With the "set-piece" battle and narrow fronts of attrition warfare, much of the teaching based on the South African War "went by the board" and the resulting confusion was slow in resolving. In the Australian force the spheres of responsibility of the R.M.O. and Field Ambulance were officially defined in 1918 as lying respectively in front of and behind the aid-post.[35]

In the Australian force divisional orders usually placed the responsibility for initiative on the field ambulance.

---

[33] Major Leonard May, 3rd Fld. Amb. and 11th Bn. (Summary to his final "official" report to A.D.M.S. 1 Dec., 1918.)

[34] Major James Sprent, *loc. cit.*

[35] In *Standing Orders for A.A.M.C.* (*see Appendix No. 4*). Ambulance bearers often complied with requests by the R.M.O. to help clear the battlefield in front of the R.A.P. but most often required that they be given in writing. In the more open warfare of 1918 overlapping was frequent.

The records of units and administrative officers lay stress on the importance of telephonic communication as a means for promoting exact co-ordination of battalion needs with field ambulance facilities for clearing wounded. The longer the war went on the more liberally, in the Australian formations, were the field medical units served by the signal service in this matter.

The following notes are by men with a wide experience of regimental and ambulance work.[36]

"As an R.M.O.," says one, "I never established *liaison* with the Field Ambulances—they did it with me. I used to decide on the map where my aid-post would be, and the Brigade sent it to the field ambulance. As a Bearer Captain I was told where the aid-posts were and used to take squads up to each Battalion served."

"*Liaison* was a dual responsibility," writes another, "on both the R.M.O. and the S.B. Captain. As R.M.O. I always sent runners back to tell the bearer captain where the aid-post was. The R.M.O. should have been a Bearer Captain himself."

"The S.B. Officer," says a third, "would detail one or two squads and a L/Cpl. to form a 'bearer post' at the R.A.P. This odd man formed a link in *liaison* and was available to receive and transmit written messages between the R.A.P. and the Relay, and moved up with the R.M.O. With R.M.O's who did not stay at their R.A.P. it was arranged that, if it moved, he (the R.M.O.) would find a guide and send a written message."

Status of the Bearer Officer. The question was often raised, especially (as in 1917) after heavy casualties among these men, whether it was necessary or advisable that they be qualified medical men. It was urged that transport work of the bearers might well be directed and command exercised by officers commissioned from the rank and file of the field ambulance. Medical officers might be stationed, as required, for treatment at strategic points on the line of relays, as at the "collecting post." Certainly, the employment of fully qualified medical men on the task of transport is difficult to justify; indeed, in a major national war, it is a gross misuse and waste of essential resources. The type of first aid required was (it was widely held) within the compass of trained N.C.O's, and the provision of an opportunity for rising to commissioned rank would be fairer to the rank and file who in the Great War—and indeed at the time of writing this volume—had no such chance. On the other hand there is undoubtedly one cogent argument in favour of the medical "bearer captain"—that it was from these officers that R.M.O's were drawn, and that experience as a bearer captain fitted a man for this important post and helped to ensure the effective *liaison* without which the best efforts of regiment and field ambulance on behalf of the wounded were nugatory. The consensus of opinion is probably summed up in the view that "for all practical purposes the bearer captain need not be a medical man, but it helps morale if he is."[37]

---

[36] The quotations are from Major M. V. Southey, 2nd Bn.; Capt. J. C. M. Harper, 28th Bn.; and Major H. Boyd Graham, an Australian serving in the R.A.M.C. For developments in 1918 see *Chapters xxiii* and *xxiv*.

[37] The personal opinion of the writer, however, based on war experience and post-war study is definitely in favour of the creation of a body of commissioned officers recruited from the ranks of the bearers themselves. Their work should, as at present, be directed by professional medical officers.

In an informal enquiry instituted by the Medical Collator after the Armistice, to ascertain the views of combatant officers on medical work, the combatant officers consulted (Brig.-Gen. J. H. Cannan and others) were definitely of the opinion that the ambulance bearers should be organised as an independent unit within each division. Such a unit, they suggested, might be organised on the lines of the pioneer battalion and its personnel be available for other duties. Bearer captains, they thought, were often poorly trained for their special work—as in map reading, the siting of posts and routes to best advantage, selection of cover, and problems of supply.

At the other end of the line of relays the bearer squads linked up with the horsed-waggons and "Fords" at the "waggon loading post." Strictly a rendezvous, the site of this post was determined by the normal range of the enemy field guns. At the "motor loading post," which in its turn was defined chiefly by the range of the enemy's medium artillery, these lightest vehicles met the rather larger cars—Sunbeams, Daimlers, Talbots, etc.—of the field ambulance; and with these again the motor ambulance convoy linked at the "main" dressing station. The tactics of wheeled-transport on these circuits and the use of trench tramways and light railways may be gathered from the narrative chapters,[88] but the history of medical motor transport calls for a brief review, since it has a permanent bearing on the evolution of military medical service.

The wheeled-transport circuits

Though motor-transport was in every civilised country the normal form of road transport, at the outbreak of the Great War, not one motor ambulance was allotted to the Medical Service of Great Britain.[39] Moreover, the method then proposed for using the general motor-transport of the army for the evacuation of wounded was of a kind that foredoomed it to failure. Together, these made inevitable one of the most tragic experiences that has befallen British wounded. The evolution of the extraordinarily successful system for ensuring the rapid evacuation of battle-casualties from the place of wounding to that of effective treatment is second to no other in its interest and instructiveness; even a bare outline such as is possible here will, it is thought, serve a useful purpose. The matter presents itself in two aspects, relating respectively to

---

[88] The value of the narrow-gauge *rail-run* transport for evacuation varied directly with the degree of co-operation between the several branches of the staff on Divisional or Corps headquarters, and inversely with the pressure of "military exigency." The following "appreciation" represents the viewpoint of a field ambulance officer; it may be contrasted with the experience in the final stage of the war as recorded (e.g.) in *Chapter xxiv*:—
"*Light Railways.* If pushed by hand, they are more or less under control and may be very useful. But if drawn by an engine, as is usually the case, they are not to be seriously relied on, for the following reasons:—(i) Patients have to be kept waiting often for hours until there are sufficient numbers for a load, or until the scheduled time of departure of the train arrives. (ii) They are never reliable. Their primary function is to convey ammunition and material to the troops, and naturally they pay more attention to this than to the evacuation of the wounded." (Major J. H. B. Brown, *loc. cit.*)

[39] The situation in the Australian Medical Service at the outbreak of war and the developments in the Eastern theatre are given fully in *Vol. I.*

the two fundamental types of battle-casualty, the *stretcher case*, and the *walking wounded*.

It is possible to identify a fundamental defect in the pre-war organisation of the Medical Service of Great Britain (and in consequence of her Dominions) in the **Motor-conveyance of stretcher cases; its origin** failure to provide for the evacuation of the stretcher case between the "Field" and "Clearing" Hospitals and thence to railhead. Under the system then existing the severely wounded man at this stage had to take his chance in the rough and tumble for securing space in supply or ammunition waggons or lorries returning empty from the front, or in "requisitioned" transport.[40] As seen in the somewhat conflicting accounts available, the first impact of real warfare on the British Medical Service brought a situation depicted as follows:—

1914. Before the Expeditionary Force embarked, a momentous conference was held at the War Office between the Quartermaster-General, the Adjutant-General, the Director of Transport, Director of Supplies, and Director of Medical Services regarding the evacuation of wounded. "It would appear" (to quote the British Official Historian) "that at this conference the immediate removal of wounded from the battlefield was not considered feasible, or advisable, and that the clearing hospitals, supplemented by personnel from the medical units on lines of communication, would have to attend to wounded in villages and houses, possibly over a large area; and that the wounded be cared for then by the R.A.M.C. personnel until such time as they were fit to be moved and transport was available. The D.M.S. had emphatically given as his opinion that, whatever theory might be held to the contrary, the removal of the wounded to railhead would necessarily occupy many days."[41]

The First Battles: Clearance to Railhead. In the first important British engagement in the war (Battle of Mons, August 22nd and 23rd) casualties for the II Corps totalled 3,784 killed, wounded and missing. "The means of clearing the wounded [to the dressing stations] were scanty"—for the II Corps they consisted of 20 horsed ambulance waggons. "For carrying wounded from the refilling points to railhead reliance had been placed in accordance with *F.S. Regs.* on the empty lorries of the supply column. . . . The position of the refilling points however was not always known to the medical units, or had been moved elsewhere before the ambulance waggons with wounded reached them. The system of evacuation by supply columns thus broke down in some

---

[40] Wounded were to be cleared to field ambulance by the horsed ambulance waggons; but from there to the "clearing" hospitals and L. of C. they were to be sent under arrangements made by the Q.M.G's branch of the staff. Transport was to be provided by the Inspector-General of Communications. "The empty waggons of supply columns and ammunition parks may be utilised" or means of transport might "be provided by hire or requisition"; or "specially organised sick and wounded convoy sections may be attached to the clearing hospitals." (*Field Service Regs., Part II, 1914.*)

[41] *British Official History of the Great War. Medical Services, General, Vol. II, p. 178.*

EVACUATION WITHIN ARMY ZONE

respects on the first occasion when it was put to a practical test."[42] The organised ambulance trains were not yet running on the railway lines but the arrangements made were sufficient for the evacuation by rail to Amiens of all sick and wounded who should arrive at the railheads.

At the Base. While the wounded at the front were thus held up and unable to reach railhead, a like situation developed at the other end of the railway. "It was no doubt anticipated" (says the *British Official History*) "that local vehicles would be requisitioned and adapted for transport of the sick and wounded [from railway terminus to the base hospital] but it was soon recognised that only motor transport would be satisfactory."[43]

Voluntary Aid in Transport. Two results accrued. The *first* was a serious break-down of evacuation.

"No amount of enthusiasm [on the part of the Army Medical Service] could relieve on the instant what presently became a critical condition of affairs. It was not indeed until many precious weeks had passed . . . that motor ambulance convoys and a free supply of motor ambulances were at last able to cope with the situation. Writing dispassionately of the transport of mobile units one can merely state the bitter facts. Intelligent anticipation on the part of a far-seeing Director-General[44] had produced a medical service capable of dealing with the casualties of an Expeditionary Force. Government parsimony and the narrow outlook of ignorant or perverse individuals had combined to limit the efficiency of its most vital article of equipment. The result was disastrous. It well-nigh wrecked the utility of an organisation otherwise efficient. The cost, small enough had it been met prior to the war, was increased tenfold, and the price was paid not in national gold, but with the lives and liberty of gallant soldiers—paid in full with bloody interest."[45]

The *second* result (which merits closer attention than it has received) was a serious discrediting of the military medical service both as the mandatory for Geneva and as a department of the Army; and its replacement for a time on sections of the lines of communication by the admirable but necessarily uncertain and promiscuous efforts of voluntary aid societies and even of private individuals. Such a situation could be in the interests neither of the wounded nor of the Army. The purpose of

---

[42] Evacuation by ambulance train was at first controlled by the French authorities. The first ambulance trains were improvised at Amiens from covered goods vans and were ready to move to railhead by the last week in August. They were however transferred to Rouen and during September moved up toward railhead where they served, in effect, as the only "clearing hospitals."

[43] Effective action at the front was impeded by the fact that the D.M.S. (Surgeon-General T. P. Woodhouse) was refused attachment to General French's headquarters. The situation was partly met by allocating thereto the D.D.M.S. of the I Army Corps—a position which itself at that time was not authorised by the Adjutant-General. In October Sir Arthur Sloggett went to France from the War Office as Director-General of Medical Services to the force which now was termed the "British Expeditionary Force." The curiously parallel situation which developed at "The Landing" in Gallipoli is described in *Vol. I, p. 162*, of the present work.

[44] Sir Alfred Keogh, Director-General during the Ministry of Lord Haldane, and subsequently throughout the greater part of the war.

[45] Quoted from *The Great War and the R.A.M.C. Vol. I Mons, The Marne, The Aisne*, by Lieut.-Col. F. S. Brereton, R.A.M.C. (London: Constable & Co., 1919, p. 49). Lieut.-Col. Brereton was in charge of the official British medical records throughout the war.

"voluntary aid" must be surely to supplement not to supplant the Army Medical Service.⁴⁶

In the second week of August, 1914, permission to improvise ambulance waggons on the chassis of local taxi-cabs was sought by the D.D.M.S., L. of C., but was refused by the Inspector-General of Communications. On the 18th however the latter agreed to ask the War Office for 60 motor ambulance cars for use at Rouen and Boulogne, and on August 25th these cars began to dribble into France.

"It was this action," the British Historian states, "which initiated the introduction of motor ambulance cars to the British Expeditionary Force in France, and brought about the subsequent formation of motor ambulance convoys as essential units of the Royal Army Medical Corps."

On September 16th (during the Battle of the Aisne) 10 motor ambulances were lent by the French; and on 20th the British Service at the front was equipped with a few cars.⁴⁷

As has been noted earlier, the first complete motor ambulance convoy was formed in September, and field ambulances were equipped with motor transport in November, 1914.⁴⁸

Thus no Army motor ambulance transport at all was available for the Retreat from Mons; nor until the end of 1914 was

---

⁴⁶ The issues in 1914-15 as between the official Medical Service and Voluntary Aid have interesting and instructive analogies with the Crimea. The following from *The Tragedy of Lord Kitchener, p. 60*, by Lord Esher records the *dénouement* as seen by the layman—who always favours Voluntary Aid and the "V.A.D."

"When these facts [the 'failure' of the medical service and refusal by the D.M.S. to permit voluntary aid in front of Rouen] were reported to Lord Kitchener, when he was told that every statement could be corroborated by Sir Alfred Keogh, at that time Commissioner of the British Red Cross . . . he was deeply angry. . . . Within a few moments of becoming acquainted with all these facts he rang his bell and summoned the acting Head of the R.A.M.C. [this was Surgeon-General W. G. Macpherson] . . . and in short, sharp sentences . . . issued verbal instructions ordering the Red Cross hospitals to be freed, and granting every request which the British Red Cross had made. Within a few hours Sir Alfred Keogh had been recalled from France, and appointed Director-General of Medical Services at the War Office, and from that moment dates the efficiency to which the Royal Army Medical Corps attained." The last sentences (it is suggested) conveys an implication that is unfair to the British Army Medical Service.

⁴⁷ Among the earlier motor ambulances sent from England to France were some representing an Australian gift.

⁴⁸ *Evacuation in a retreat*. It is desirable to add to the above that the British Official Historian, Sir W. G. Macpherson (*Vol. II, General, pp. 226 et seq.*) states that in the retreat from Mons "it is doubtful if the presence of motor ambulance cars would have made much difference owing to the impossibility for any motor transport making its way forward to the positions and rear-guards where casualties were occurring through the retreating columns of transport, or of getting back through them with wounded, had they been able to do so;" and notes further that Sir A. Lee, who was sent to France by Lord Kitchener to report on the working of the medical services, drew attention to the same difficulty in connection with the First Battle of Ypres. The sudden move at the end of August of the British bases from the Channel to the Atlantic—"a terrible blow to the medical services"—had thrown the lines of evacuation almost at right angles to the organised lines of communication of the British force.

"In these [various] circumstances (he states) preparations for methodical evacuation during the retreat were not possible, and the field ambulances seized what-

34. THE SHOULDER-HIGH CARRY
Stretcher-bearers passing through Le Sars, 1917
Aust. War Memorial Official Photo. No. E431.

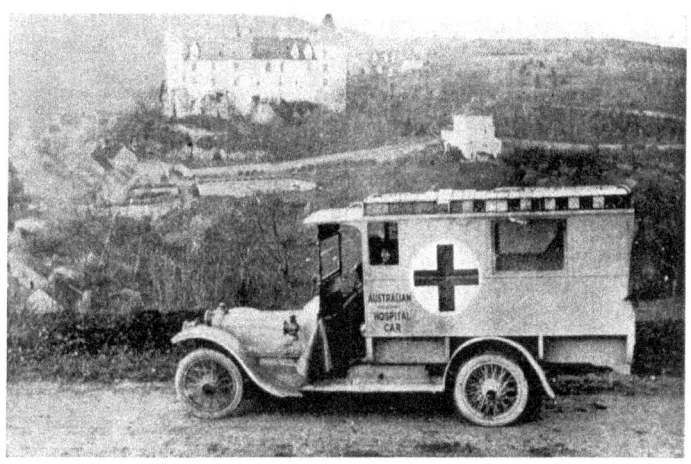

35. AN IMPROVISED MOTOR AMBULANCE OF THE AUSTRALIAN VOLUNTARY HOSPITAL AT LENS, NEAR ROUEN, IN FRANCE, OCTOBER, 1914
Lent by Lieut.-Col. L. J. Hurley, Army Ordnance Corps.
Aust. War Memorial Collection No. C1327.

36. A BRITISH MOTOR TRANSPORT PARK OUTSIDE ROUEN

Motor ambulances, cars, lorries, and, in the distance, steam-roller and tractor are shown.

British Official Photograph
Aust. War Memorial Collection No. H9498.

To face p. 289.

there sufficient to influence materially the medical situation. But a voluntary service of motor transport had for some time been in full swing.

The Motor Ambulance Convoys. The function and distribution of these, when early in 1916 the Australians arrived in France, has been introduced in the account of that event.[49] The motor ambulance convoy was a very important unit—the pivot on which turned the *movement* of casualties. The Australian Medical Service did not include one, and in France the A.I.F. was served by those of the British Army—how well served, the narrative chapters show. They were solely *transport units*; their one purpose—to fill the gap between the field ambulance and casualty clearing station by a circuit of motor ambulances wholly independent of other Army transport, and working under the aegis of the Geneva Convention. The establishment of the unit in 1918 was as follows:—

Headquarters "A" Section	20 cars
"B" and "C" Sections	30 cars
Total	50 cars

	Officers	Other ranks	Total
Medical	4	17	21
A.S.C. attached	2	103	105

ever opportunities presented themselves for transferring to empty supply lorries, other vehicles or trains, the sick and wounded whom they were able to carry with them." Very large numbers were left behind. Such a situation is, of course, expressly provided for under the Geneva Convention on occasion in "civilised warfare" it is indubitably in the interests of the seriously wounded to be left, with personnel accredited under the mandate of the Convention, to the "mercy" of the enemy. Australian records do not, moreover, negative such action. The German played the game with our wounded much as we did with his. In clearing the battlefield the enemy wounded took second place, but then was treated with equal care and consideration as our own.

The satisfactory clearance of wounded in the Fifth Army retreat of 1918 is said to be explained by "essential differences" in the circumstances of the two operations. That these were profound seems clear, and not less clear that, from the medical point of view, the most important factor was that in 1914 the disposal of wounded, and the Medical Service, were at this time looked on by the General Staff as a nuisance—hardly even a necessary one.

But all this notwithstanding, it is impossible to concur in the *reductio ab absurdum* that in a retreat speed has no place in the problem of the wheel-transport of the wounded.

The fact that the Australian Force had the good fortune never to be involved in a full dress retreat, and in very few retirements, leaves a serious gap in its medical history as a technical study. The narrative in the *British Official History* of the two great retreats of the British Army on the Western Front gives an admirably clear and (so far as can be judged) ingenuous account of these events, and may be commended. The following general works are helpful to an appreciation of the circumstances: *Unwilling Passenger* (Lieut.-Col. Arthur Osburn, R.A.M.C.), *Episodes and Reflections* (Sir Wyndham Childs), *Liaison, 1914* (Brig.-Gen. E. L. Spears), Capt. (now Professor) Marshall Allan's little book, *Letters from a Young Queenslander* (1916) describes how the "retreat from Mons" appeared to an R.M.O.

[49] *Chapter ii, p. 26.*

For working, the cars were allotted in groups of 5. The total stretcher capacity of the convoy was thus 200 cases. The convoy was self-contained as to workshop for running repairs. A forward repair shop was sometimes formed in the vicinity of the main dressing station.

The maximum number of motor ambulance convoys employed in front area work was 14 in 1915, 22 in 1916, 23 in 1917, and 25 in 1918.

Since 1914 the nature of war and its technique have been largely determined by motor road transport.

Motor conveyance of walking wounded—the motor lorry, etc.
Through the problem of "walking wounded" the medical service was intimately concerned in the evolution of a system whereby non-technical motor transport was made available for the general purposes of warfare.[50]

The provision and distribution of road transport other than the technical vehicles of artillery, engineer, flying and medical units, was the duty of the Director of Transport on the Q.M.G's branch of G.H.Q. Practically the only motor transport available in the field formations at the outbreak of the war was that allotted to the Divisional Supply Column and the Divisional Ammunition Park. The motor-transport requirements of other services were met by diverting such part of these units as could be spared. When *the front line became fixed* an immense mass of motor-transport (not, be it noted, the animal transport of "first line" and "train" consisting of pack-mules and G.S. waggons) was set free, and made potentially available to supply the needs of the engineering and medical services, both of which greatly increased their importance in the attrition warfare that followed.

Transport Developments. The developments that ensued—in effect, the attuning of war to the internal combustion engine—took two forms (a) enormous production of new transport units, (b) improved methods for making full use of these for all army purposes. The history of this development is one of extraordinary interest, but it cannot be told here. Briefly, it consisted in (1) the development of control of motor-transport by Army and Corps in place of the I.G.C. (2) The establishing of a *virtual* "pool" of motor-transport from the Divisional "parks" and "columns" from which the requirements of engineers, medical services, and so forth—even troop movements—were served. (3) The establishing at the front (in army areas) of repair workshops for the treatment

---

[50] In this evolution the Australian motor transport companies under Lieut.-Col. W. H. Tunbridge attached to the V British Corps in June 1915 were pioneers in important developments.

As to the rôle of motor-transport see *Chapter xxi*; also *Vol. I, Diagram No. 4, p. 208*. The *History of the Royal Army Service Corps* (*Vol. I* Sir John Fortescue, *Vol. II* Colonel R. H. Beadon) is only less interesting to the medical service than to that corps itself.

Knowledge of the working of the system of transport and supply in the field was very imperfect in the Australian Army Medical Service. Little or no attention was devoted to this matter in peace training. It is a "lesson" of the war that the military significance of the so-called "administrative" services should be much more generally recognised than in the past.

and return to duty of vehicles with minor engine trouble, and exact provision for the evacuation to the Base of those more seriously disabled. (4) The formation of new motor-transport companies in Army and Corps[51] for general purposes (*i.e.* apart from "supply" and ammunition) *e.g.* the extensive use of omnibuses for troop transport. (5) Administrative devices such as the "Corps relay posts" developed in 1918. (6) Not least important, the development of an *esprit de corps* and devotion to a difficult and dangerous duty in the personnel of the motor-transport companies A.S.C., not inferior to that of any other branch of the army.[52]

It was these sources that provided the transport of the walking wounded.

Readers of the first volume will recall the constant recurrence in the evacuation problems of Gallipoli of the need at almost every link in the long journey for the "classifi-

Co-ordination of movement and treatment: "triage"

cation" of casualties,[53] as a factor of first-rate importance in success. In the British scheme of evacuation in France specific arrangements for the discrimination of various types of casualty for special distribution were "conspicuous by their absence." This contrasts with the schemes evolved in the French and American Armies.[54] In these a vital element was "*triage*," a term signifying both the procedure of "classification"[55] and the special station at which it was carried out. The purpose of *triage* was, of course, discrimination between casualties with a view to exact distribution for treatment and disposal in accordance with their nature. Thus a *Triage* (station) was placed

---

[51] In Sept., 1915, a Corps transport officer ("Senior Mechanical Transport Officer," S.M.T.O.) was appointed in V Corps (Second Army) to control all transport within the Corps for purposes other than the *regular* work of the mechanical transport units, the supply columns and ammunition parks. The practice soon became general.

[52] Army companies were chiefly omnibus—for the rapid advance of reinforcements and troops and retirement of walking wounded. The formation in the Australian Corps of a Mechanical Transport Company was put in hand by Colonel Tunbridge, who early in 1916 rejoined I Anzac from V British Corps as Senior Mechanical Transport Officer, and later was made Director of Transport A.I.F. The Armistice was signed, however, before the company was formed. The writer is indebted to General Tunbridge for these notes.

[53] *See e.g. pp. 144, 290, 310.*

[54] The system in the American Army in France was in a great measure based on French procedure.

[55] In ordinary speech, the French word *triage* means choosing, sifting or sorting. As applied to medical work in the field the function of *triage* has been stated as follows: First, the grouping of casualties, by degree, for disposal. Second, classification as to type—G.S.W. nervous, gassed, fracture, sick. In addition it included, according to circumstance, minor surgical aid and readjustments, the administration of A.T.S. and morphia, and the provision of hot drinks and food. "The *triage* is not a collecting station but a means of separating and evacuating with all possible speed, through the proper channels to the assigned units." (*American Off. Med. History.*) In some form, and to suit the circumstances, the functions outlined herein were required at every stage of movement.

at the points where streams of wounded concentrated and diverged—in particular, (1) where it could make the primary differentiation into urgent ("untransportable") wounds, for immediate attention, severe wounds for rapid evacuation, slight wounds and sick, gassed and so forth; and (2) in the neighbourhood of railheads, in connection with the "Evacuation Hospital."

By the British system the field ambulance and C.C.S. took "classification" or *"triage,"* so to speak in their stride. The general principles involved and rationale of the British procedure are examined elsewhere;[56] for the present purpose it may be said that while a process of *triage* began in the front lines and R.A.P., and was continued at the collecting and loading posts, the deliberate classification of casualties for treatment was the duty of the "advanced" or the "main" dressing station, according to the nature of the medical arrangements. The final act of *triage* took place in the admission room of the C.C.S.

The following illustrates the essentially mobile outlook on this matter in the Australian force. Speaking of the work done at the advanced dressing station at Ypres Railway Station in October 1917, the C.O., of the 6th Field Ambulance, wrote:—

"Great time was saved by having all cases examined in the road and classified 'A,' 'B,' or 'C.' This allowed of a large number being sent direct to C.C.S. or to the Ambulance Train at the Ypres Railway Station. Only those requiring fresh dressings or re-splinting or those suffering from shock or threatened haemorrhage were brought in and attended to."

It has already been stated that the number of wounded retained in the "Army" zone—that is to say, returned to duty after treatment by the R.M.O., field ambulances, or C.C.S.—was comparatively small; when once a man was wounded he had to get his anti-tetanic serum at the field ambulance, and, especially in the rushes of battle, the great majority were sent through to the Base. With men who were gassed, as will be seen later, the case was entirely different, a large proportion of gas casualties returning to the front through special treatment centres without leaving the "Army" zone. And this was also the case with men in the second great category of evacuation—that of the

[56] *Pp. 764-6, 782-7 and Appendix No. 9. See also Vol. I, Chapters vii and viii.*

37. Panoramic diagram showing the successive stages of evacuation and return to duty in the Army area. The key to the conventional signs used in this plate will be found on p. 959.

*From drawings by Messrs. T. H. Robinson and F. R. Crozier.
Aust. War Memorial Official Photo. No. J6703.*

To face p. 292.

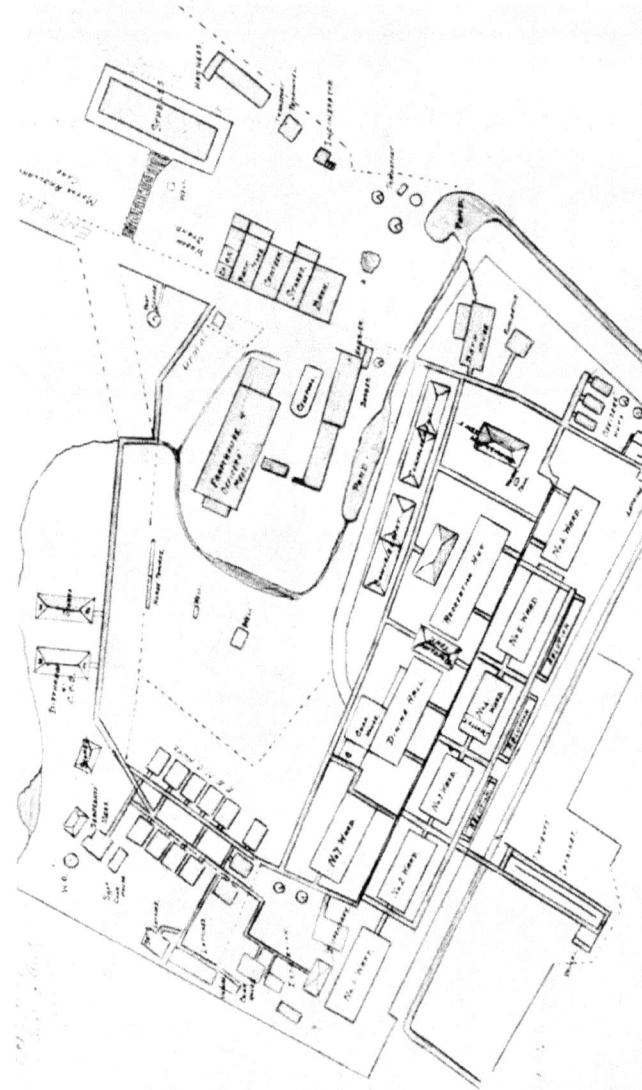

38. Plan of the 1st Division's rest station at Wippenhoek, Flanders, September, 1917

From diary of 3rd Field Ambulance.
Aust. War Memorial Official Photo. No. J6440.

To face p. 293.

sick, to which we must now turn. The technique of the prevention of disease calls for full discussion later,[57] but the processes by which the movement of a sick man, or his retention at the front, were determined, are properly described here.

MOVEMENT, OR RETENTION, OF SICK MEN

The complaint of the civilian practitioner that he is "consulted too late" had no place in the army. On the side of prevention, the "promotion of health" was "the duty of every officer and man"; on that of cure, prompt investigation of any malaise, and early treatment of trivial complaints was part of the normal routine of army life. Co-operation in this purpose by the soldier was a military obligation, and "concealment of disease" a military "crime." The necessity for this was one of the important "lessons" of the war. The correlation of prevention with treatment was perhaps most exactly achieved in the prophylaxis of venereal disease, as carried out in the Australian Imperial Force.[58]

Prevention of wastage by early treatment—the sick parade

Within the Division only two classes of officer, the R.M.O. and the Ambulance Commander (or his deputy),[59] had authority under the Medical Director, to undertake treatment and to decide on medical grounds whether a soldier was or was not physically "fit" for duty; and there were only two treatment centres, the regimental aid-post and the main dressing station, where sick men might be sorted out, and either held for treatment or "cleared" back. First, and the more important, of the two authorities concerned was the Regimental Medical Officer.

In the familiar formula, "medicine and duty," is contained—in no mere figure of speech—the worth to his regiment of the R.M.O.; who is judged by the influence that his personality and special knowledge exerts upon the efficiency and morale of his unit.

The same function in the civil community has been claimed as the social *raison d'être* for the General Practitioner of the future. (Presidential address by Sir Farquhar Buzzard; Annual Meeting B.M.A.

[57] In *Chapters xvii, xviii and xix.*
[58] This is fully described in *Vol. III.*
[59] The authority of these officers was on this matter subject only to the A.D.M.S. of the Division and could be overruled—if at all—only by the General Officer Commanding.

Oxford, 1936.) The Australian Official Historian has said that the C.O., medical officer and padre formed a trinity which set the tone of a battalion.

The Regimental Medical Officer's "sick parade" was strictly a "parade," and the finding of this officer on each case paraded to him by the orderly corporal was as binding as that of the C.O. The formula most commonly adopted ordered the soldier "medicine and duty," "light fatigue duty," "no duty," or "to hospital." To order "duty," alone, implied in most units a suspicion of fraud. Using the phrase *"Medicine and Duty"* as the title to his entertaining and useful "War Diary" (London: William Heinemann Ltd., 1928) Capt. H. Dearden, R.A.M.C., subtly sums up the ideals and aims of regimental medical work.

The following comments relevant to this matter are by men who each in his sphere speaks with authority.[60]

"Experienced Battalion Commanders have often told me they consider a good R.M.O. as a most important factor for discipline during action, for it is he who can hearten the exhausted and those suffering from trivial wounds or injuries and induce them to return to the line. It is also the good R.M.O. who can prevent so much wastage out of the line by refusing to allow men to magnify their ills and efficiently treating trivial complaints instead of evacuating such cases to the base. A properly trained R.M.O. is perhaps the most valuable Officer in the A.M.C., as prevention of disease commences at the unit and so much depends upon his initiative and resource. I invariably found that the best men from a professional point of view make the best R.M.O's."

"The R.M.O. must never evacuate in a lighthearted fashion; on the other hand every man in the unit must be able to pull his weight. . . . The same ailment may call for evacuation at one time or may be held at another. The new R.M.O. is inclined to over-estimate malingering; in my experience there was very little of it. Give a man the benefit of the doubt on his first sick parade, and if in doubt consult the Company or Platoon Commander. If the R.M.O. gives the men a fair deal they will give him one—especially in the line. Moreover they will trust him, and the knowledge that they have a medical man whom they trust behind them is a support."

"Our chief duties when out of the line were connected with the daily sick parade. This was fixed at an early hour, 7 a.m., to keep down the numbers. Men for dressings, suffering from boils, cuts, burns, sprains, blisters, chafes, and the like, were passed to the A.M.C. men who became expert dressers and only if in doubt referred the man back to the Doctor.[61] The temperature was always taken [this was, indeed, the chief diagnostic criterion—'P.U.O.' was, in effect, a 'disease.' *Ed.*] Aspirin was the chief medicine as the majority of the cases suffered from severe colds. 'No. 9' ran second, with—a good third—castor oil for diarrhoea, for which, with starvation, it stands alone."

---

[60] The quotations, slightly abbreviated, are from (1) Col. G. W. Barber, D.D.M.S. Australian Corps: (2) Major W. W. S. Johnston, RM.O. 12th Bn.; (3) Sgt. J. R. Edwards, A.A.M.C., attached to 27th Bn.

[61] It is not without significance that in the A.I.F. the Regimental Medical Officer is referred to most often as "the Doctor" or "Doc" rather than as the "Medical Officer" or "M.O." (Some relevant figures will be found on *p.* 529.)

From these fringes of disease an average of about 0·3 per cent. daily of battalion strength were sent on to the field ambulance. Those of the sick who were not sent to "hospital" were treated *secundum artem*—and as circumstances allowed.

The Field Ambulance "Rest Station." Before the Great War the time limit for retaining patients in the field ambulance was restricted to 24 or 48 hours. The "rest station" originated in a demand, made after the Battle of Neuve Chapelle[62] by the D.M.S. First Army, for "convalescent companies" to check wastage through loss of slightly wounded men. But the search for effectives soon shifted from the battle-casualties to those caused by disease, and during the "attrition" years 1916-17 these units were called on to organise within army zone a vast campaign of treatment of minor disablements—chiefly those due to *physical agencies*, such as marching, the cold and wet of trench life, or coarse food,[63] or to *infestation* by insects and moulds and to the minor microbic infections.[64] Beside these measures, in Australian units was built up a great system of early and prophylactic dental treatment. In addition steps were taken for early treatment of the great group of exhaustion, debility, and the assorted "neuroses" characteristic of this war. The extent to which these "fringes of disease" influenced the medical problem in every sphere, from that of front line wastage to that of post-war pensions, is worthy of the closest attention.[65]

Diagnostic Stations. Less extensive and important than these treatment stations were the diagnostic stations, also established within the "Army zone"; for discriminating among casualties marked at the field ambulance " N.Y.D.N.," or " N.Y.D. Gas." These are dealt with in special chapters of *Volume III.*

The Treatment Stations. The question of the employment of the supposedly mobile field ambulance for the treatment of

---

[62] Fought on 10 March 1915 by First Army.

[63] As strains and sprains, chafes, traumatic abrasion, trench foot and I.C.T., diarrhoea, "rheumatism" and fibrositis, laryngitis, minor gas effects, and so forth.

[64] Especially of the skin and respiratory tract, septic traumatic abrasions, I.C.T., acute upper respiratory tract infections, colds, coughs, sore throat, and neuralgias. Not less than 50 per cent. (as a rule) of the R.M.O's sick parade was for dis-ease without disablement and carried the award "medicine and duty."

[65] The pathogenic composition of the disease-picture at the front is described in *Chapter xix* (Prevention of Disease) and is shown more fully in *Vol. III.* See also diagram on *p. 440.*

disease on a large scale merits some attention. Though this
duty has been blessed by the British Official Historian, it was
outside their proper purpose and was not liked in the A.I.F.
The following statements made in 1917 are pertinent:—

"The A.M.C. have been continually at work since arrival in France,
and it is very often just as heavy when the Division is at rest as when
it is in the line—sometimes heavier owing to their having to carry out
work such as that at large Divisional Rest Stations and Scabies Stations,
which might reasonably be expected to be done by Stationary Hospitals. . . .

"If the personnel for a 400-bed Stationary Hospital was allotted to
Corps to take over the duties of Corps Rest Station, Scabies Station,
and Mumps Hospital, I think it would result in less sick wastage both in
the A.M.C. Units and the troops, and leave Field Ambulances mobile."

"The only way to avoid choking up the Rest Station and losing track
of cases is for the C.O. to see each day every man retained over 14
days. At the Corps Rest Station, Buire, in 1916, more than 500 of the
men on the books when we took over [from a British unit] could not
be found or accounted for. Some had been there for 6 months; many
lived in the village, came in to get their meals, and otherwise did as
they liked. At Millencourt in 1917 300 [British troops] remained permanently unaccounted for. This was largely due to the immense numbers held (at Buire over 1200) and small field ambulance staff. Large
Rest Stations cannot be run with a fair deal for each (man)—some
stay in too long, others are sent out before fit."

At the end of 1917 the D.M.S., A.I.F., Surgeon-General
Howse,[66] criticised the policy of holding at the front cases of
trench foot, trench fever, P.U.O., and so forth which he considered could not be efficiently treated in the field ambulance
rest stations. After 1917 this responsibility for treatment in
the field and "return to duty" was placed chiefly on the casualty
clearing stations.[67]

---

[60] The occasion was a visit to France in Sept., 1917, in connection with the acute problem of military strength in the field. *See p. 243.*

[67] Notes are by Col. G. W. Barber, A.D.M.S. 4th Australian Division (Correspondence with D.M.S., A.I.F. 19 April, 1917), and from War Diary 3rd Australian Field Ambulance 5 Oct., 1917.

SYNOPSIS OF CHAPTER XII

THE GENERAL SURGERY OF WOUNDS IN THE GREAT WAR

The evacuating hospitals.
Their function: the operative centre of gravity.
The objective.
The factors in wound surgery.
Return to Lister and Hunter.

THE PATHOLOGY OF WOUNDING:

1. The Wound.
   The traumatic agent.
   (A) Missiles—rifle bullets—Shrapnel and pistol bullets—H.E. Shell and "Bombs."
   (B) Types of wound—Physical features.
   (C) The diseases of wounds: sepsis.
   The infective agents of the Western Front.
2. Pathology in the wounded man:
   (A) Effects of wounding *per se*—physiological injury and reaction.
   (B) Effects of septic infection—General microbial injury and reaction—wound diseases.
   Specific morbid states—Clinical "diseases"—"Tetanus"—"Gas gangrene"—Pyogenic infection.

THE TREATMENT OF WOUNDING:—
TREATMENT OF THE WOUND ITSELF:
The search for asepsis.

FIRST STAGE: Beginnings—1914.
   The surgical debacle.
   1. Reversion to pre-aseptic methods—crude antiseptics—lavage—primitive asepsis.
   2. Initiation of Experiment and Research.
   Progress of "reaction" at the Base.
   Reaction at the front—the genesis o: asepsis.
   End of the first stage. The "Memorandum on Treatment."

SECOND STAGE: Organised experiment and observation, 1915-17
   "Surgery" moves towards the front.
   At the Base: the search for antisepsis.
   "Physiological" antisepsis: serum lavage.
   Scientific antisepsis: "Carrel-Dakin" lavage.

SYNOPSIS OF CHAPTER XII

Wright v. Carrel; nature v. art.
Front and Base—The effort for continuity.
1. Methods—The salt pack—B.I.P.
2. Means: scientific antiseptics—neutral chlorine compounds—oxidisers—synthetic dyes.
The triumph of asepsis: excision.
The last step: immediate suture of excised wounds.
End of experimental stage.

THIRD STAGE: Exploitation. March, 1917—March, 1918.

FOURTH STAGE: 1918.
THE TREATMENT OF THE WOUNDED MAN:
The problem of pain—Pain and "Shock"—Measures of relief—Morphia.
Haemorrhage
Vital depression—"Wound shock"—The nature of traumatic shock.

STAGES OF TREATMENT DURING EVACUATION:
The elements in early treatment—rest—warmth—fluid and food.
Treatment at divisional posts and stations.
By the Regimental Stretcher-bearers.
By the R.M.O.
First aid—technique—equipment.
The relay posts and collecting posts.
Dressing station and Field hospital.
Walking casualties (sick and wounded).
Stretcher cases.
Gas centre—disposal of gassed casualties.
The resuscitation centre.
"*Triage*" and the "untransportable" case.

CHAPTER XII

THE GENERAL SURGERY OF WOUNDS IN THE GREAT WAR

THE *movement* of the casualty has been followed to a place of comparative safety at railhead; the other component in evacuation now calls for notice namely, concurrent *treatment* in the several posts or stations along the route.

The position of these posts, and the facilities for treatment there, were determined in part by military exigency, in part by physiological importunity. Developments in the scheme of evacuation were efforts to co-ordinate the physical time-constants of transport with the physiological time-constants of treatment. Geographically, the main problem centred on the location of the Hospitals of Evacuation.

At the end of the static warfare of 1916-17, some 10 to 20 miles on each side of No-Man's Land, the zones of the **The evacuating hospitals** "Hospitals of the Front,"[1] Allied and German, stretched almost unbroken from the sea to Switzerland—the main line of defence in the treatment of wounds and of wounded men against wound infection and wound shock, and—what was only less important—against wastage through needless evacuation to the Base. In the warfare of the Western Front, these units may be visualised as a receiving, digesting, and discharging system for the whole of the vast outflow of sick and wounded from the front line. This stream flowed in continuously, with intermittent spates and occasional floods; less those "returned to duty," flowed out again by ambulance train, car, or barge to the expeditionary base (or the "hospitals of the interior")—a total for the B.E.F. for 1914-18 of 3,528,486 sick and 1,988,969 wounded admitted to medical units.

---

[1] British "Casualty Clearing Station" (C.C.S.); French "Hôpital d'Evacuation" (H.O.E.); American "Evacuation Hospital" (E.H.); German "Feldlazarett" (F.L.). The Feldlazarett seems to have combined in some respects the functions of our field ambulance "tent" division and casualty clearing station. *See also Appendix No. 9.*

It may be roughly estimated[2] that the battle-casualty reached this stage in his journey some 4 to 48 hours after wounding, the average being probably 8-12; and here, in the latter years of the war, he entered the atmosphere of a "hospital," laid out, organised, and equipped for *effective treatment* as well as for *movement*; beds with sheets, arranged as "wards" in huts or "brigaded" tents,[3] operating theatre, highly organised quartermaster's department, a nursing staff of fully trained women "attached" to the army as a "Nursing Service,"[4] surgical, medical, and radiological specialists. Here "first aid" and emergency treatment gave place to "resuscitation," operating under anaesthetic, and rest in a bed and skilled nursing.

On the Western Front, in respect of wounding—which we have accepted as the prime interest in the problems of evacuation —the casualty clearing station was essentially

Their function: the operative centre of gravity a centre for classifying (*"triage"*) and treatment, in particular for *operating*. From "the end of 1915" onwards, says the *British Official History*, the prime urge in the evolution of the C.C.S. from the "clearing hospital," the dominating feature of its activities, and the place of the unit in the military system, derived chiefly from the *progress made in the science and art of military surgery*, in particular in the *general surgery of wounds*. The natural line of approach, therefore, to an account of the functions, structure, and methods of work of the C.C.S., which will be given in the next chapter, is through a study of the evolution in the Great War of the *general treatment of wounds and of wounded men*. The evolution of the special surgery of regions and organs, though closely related to this, is an independent subject, and will be dealt with, so far as the scope of this work permits, in the next volume.

The clinical and experimental history of war surgery can without distortion be epitomised as a striving for *asepsis in the*

The objective *wound*, and for *counter measures to traumatic shock, in the wounded man*. A full study of these two problems would occupy—as it does in the great British, American and German medical histories of the Great War—

---

[2] For obvious reasons exact records of this are non-existent.
[3] *See plate at p. 413, and Appendix No. 11.*
[4] For status and duties of the Female Nursing Service *see Vol. III*. Female nurses were not used at the front in the French and German Armies.

many hundred pages. On the other hand a mere statement of the theory and practice of wound surgery as at the end of the war would tend to set up an artificial end-point to what must be a progressive evolution.[5] Greater advantage it is thought will accrue from an endeavour to follow (in outline) the evolution of war surgery, from the mistakes and crudities of 1914 to the triumphs of 1918. For it cannot be thought that the Great War will be the last in which the road to success will be rough and toilsome, or that the study of the lines of research found most fruitful will not be of value. To this end, first of all we epitomise briefly the chief *pathogenic and clinical factors* in the problem that faced the surgical profession at the beginning of the war, as seen in the light of our post-war knowledge.

Wound surgery, it must be repeated, presents two distinct and well-defined groups of practical problems—(a) those which relate to the wound as such, and (b) those which derive from the function and structure of the part or organ wounded.

The factors in wound surgery

The British Historian says:—

"If it had been possible at the beginning of the war, as it was at the end, to prevent or control the spread of the septic process in wounds in the early stage, then the remedial operations on nerves, tendons and other structures which were so numerous when the wounds were healed or healing, would also have been greatly reduced in numbers and would have been more successful in their result."[6]

And it does not overstate the case. On the Western Front till the end of the war, the problem of the *wound, per se,* dominated the whole domain of surgery almost as imperiously as in the days of Hippocrates, of Paré, of Hunter, of Lister. Crowned though it was by ultimate success so dramatic as to wipe out the memory of early disasters, the history of the surgery of wounds on the Western Front in the Great War[7] is

---

[5] For example, through the achievement of Ehrlich's ideal of a "therapia sterilisans magna," for the coccal group, by the agency of drugs of the sulphanilamide type.

[6] *History of the Great War. Medical Services. Surgery of the War Vol. I p. 343.* "Wound Treatment in Hospitals in the United Kingdom" by Colonel C. J. Bond, A.M.S.

[7] The history of the surgery of the War as seen from an international and scientific standpoint has not yet been written. The nearest approach seems to be the American, an immense work of over 3,000 pages. From the standpoint of British experience the *British Official History* is admirable. No "Official" French history has been published—the works mainly consulted have been *Le Service de Santé* (Mignon), *Le Service de Santé de la III Armée* (Bassères), and the *Military Medical Manuals*—English translation edited by Sir Alfred Keogh. The German

yet a painful and tragic one, by reason of the huge case mortality and morbidity associated with wounding, and of the fact that this was due chiefly to wound disease for which the medical service was nearly three years in finding and applying an effective remedy. And though the results ultimately achieved in the prevention of wound infection must be accepted as very remarkable, and certainly as calling for record for the benefit of warring posterity, and even, in some small degree, of civil practice, yet, like many other "lessons of the war" from which civilisation has been exhorted to find the basis for a new and higher plane of existence, the surgery of the war was in many respects a *réchauffé* of sordid experiences which it was thought had been swept into the scientific dustbins as relics of an unpleasant past.[8]

From the first impact, in August-September of 1914, of virulent anaerobic infections with primary or secondary streptococcal involvements, in a degree increasing with the trench bombing warfare and high explosive bombardments of 1915-16, the medical profession found itself thrown back on the beggarly rudiments of its art, and called on to face anew the elemental problems of

Return to Lister and Hunter[9]

Medical History of the war consists of (1) *Handbuch der Arztlichen Erfahrungen im Weltkriege 1914-18*, Vols. 1 to 9; edited by Prof. Dr. Otto v. Schjerning, Chief of the German Medical Services during the War. (2) *Sanitätsbericht über das Deutsche Heer (Deutsches Feld-und Besatzungsheer) im Weltkriege 1914-1918*, Vols. I and III (Official History). Vol. II was published in 1938 but was not available for this work.

[8] There are two sides in the interesting controversy that has been waged around these issues. "Perhaps nothing more forcibly demonstrates the change in conditions of surgical practice between those days" [*i.e.* "two hundred years ago" when "the craft of surgery had not been separated from the craft of barbery"] "and the present time than the fact that there is no worse training for the modern surgeon than that given by the necessarily slapdash treatment of war casualties." (Sir Alan Newton, Halford Oration, *M.J.A. 9th Jan., 1937, p. 41*). And again, "The work of a military surgeon develops quickness and resourcefulness; but in one respect military surgery is not good as an example—the personal responsibility is much greater in civil life. Younger men will have to bear that in mind when they go home and operate." (Lieut.-General Makins at the 11th Session of the Research Society of the American Red Cross in France, 22-23 Nov., 1918).

The first few editions of "Rose and Carless'" *Surgery* published after the war included a chapter on war surgery. In the editions subsequent to 1927 this was omitted as of no particular value to the civil surgeon.

On this, however, two comments should be made. First, that the enormous increase of road accident has some—though not it would seem a great—bearing on the matter. Second, and of great military importance, that (as pointed out by Sir Anthony Bowlby in the *British Official Medical History*) the surgery of war wounds demanded technical expertness of a very high order. It is indubitable that other important qualities were required as rapid decision, courage, restraint and great powers of endurance. Indeed a race of expert wound surgeons was evolved in the war, chiefly from the young men who learned their surgery on war wounds; and, in Australia at least, they have "made good" in civil life.

[9] It would hardly overstate the lapse to say, instead, "to de Mondeville and Paré."

wound healing; this experience it had to suffer before it could even begin to tackle with effect the gargantuan feast of clinical experiences, experiments, and problems in regional and reparative surgery, provided by the War Lords of Attrition in the shape of hordes of desperately wounded men, emerging not only from the major offensives of the Somme, Arras, and the Salient, but from the normal quietude of the Western Front. It was found necessary indeed (and the fact is one which gives food for thought) to begin *de novo* where Lister did, *i.e.*, with the knowledge given to humanity by Louis Pasteur that, whatever might be the cause of organic "disease" and nature of its "inborn factors," the pathogenesis of "diseases" due to "germs" was definitely, even crudely, mechanistic; to be tackled with mechanical weapons—selective chemical poisons, ablutions, drainings, excisions, as well as anti-toxins, vaccines, lymphogogues and vitamins. At the same time never in the history of scientific medicine was it more intimately understood that surgery is successful only in proportion as rational interference co-operates with the organic and instinctive processes that we identify in the *vis medicatrix naturae*.[10]

Apart from some disorder of the *"milieu intérieur"*—as by avitaminosis, diabetes, or chronic nephritis; or by some non-specific or temporary physiological disturbance, such as fatigue, or lack of food and water[11]—two factors militate against prompt

[10] The treatment of wounds is concerned with two processes, namely, *organic reaction* and *intelligent intervention*. The rational conduct and control by man of his physical health involves deliberate incursion into the domain of those primitive vital (biochemical and physical) processes, the central nervous control of which is vested in the lower cerebral centres and vegetative nervous system, whose activities in promoting healing we term the *"vis medicatrix naturae."* Of the origin of this term little seems to be known although the process was recognised by the ancients. *Hippocrates B.C. 460-357 c.* taught that "treatment is expectant though intervention may be profitable." *Ambroise Paré A.D. 1510-1590*: "I dressed the wound, God healed the patient." *John Hunter A.D. 1728-1793*: "The injury done has in all cases a tendency to produce the disposition and the means of cure." *Lister A.D. 1827-1912*: "I believe I happened to be the first to direct attention to the antiseptic agency of living structures, and there is, perhaps, no one who attaches greater importance to it than I do." *Colonel H. M. W. Gray*, Consulting Surgeon, B.E.F., *1918*: "The greatest principle of all is that of wisely assisting nature in her attempts to cure." The phrase *"vis medicatrix naturae"* appears to have been coined by the Glasgow physician William Cullen, 1710-1790.

[11] A matter of considerable importance, but one into which it is not possible to enter, concerns what has been termed the "Physiology of the Soldier." While there would seem inadequate grounds for postulating (as has been done) a peculiar physiological and psychic constitution referable to the war environment in effect universal among those who served in the front lines, it is indubitable that specific departures from normality on occasion can be discerned. In particular may be instanced the physiological degradation on Gallipoli from deficiency in accessory food factors, of water, and perhaps of carbohydrates; the "barcoo rot" of the Sinai-Palestine campaign; and on the Western Front the psychic shock of the "First Somme," and in general the great incidence of infection and of secondary

recovery from a wound *viz.*, the effect of the *physical trauma, per se*, and that of *microbial infection*. Since our forebears saw in "laudable" pus an essential element in the natural healing of wounds, the processes of healing and the local reaction against infection have been envisaged as running hand in hand. The problems of war surgery revolved round these elements in the situation.[12]

THE PATHOLOGY OF WOUNDING

Physical trauma in itself is, obviously, a cause of dis-ease, and it evokes "reactions," local and general, which do not differ fundamentally from those elicited by "pathogenic" organisms. Each has its internal components both of trauma —physical and toxic respectively—and of reaction general and local. We are concerned then with (1) the physical and psychic concomitants of wounding in general, such as pain, haemorrhage, and "traumatic shock," together with the specific physiological effects of regional and systemic traumata: and (2) with the infective concomitants—general intoxication, and local trauma from absorption of bacterial toxins or invasion by parasitic micro-organisms.

Having in mind these divisions and cross divisions of the subject, we may set it out simply for examination as follows:—

1. Pathology of the Wound. (*A*). Types of *missiles;* (*B*). Types of *wounds;* (*C*). Types of *infection.* 2. Pathology in the Wounded Man. (*A*). Effects of wounding *per se;* (*B*). Effects of "septic" infection.

The Traumatic Agent. (*A*). *Missiles.* Some 85 per cent.

1. The wound of all wounds (*i.e.*, of those admitted to field ambulance), including gassing, sustained by the A.I.F. on the Western Front were caused by

---

wound shock. One factor in the production of the latter, it is suggested, was a gycogen deficiency brought about by the frequent coincidence, while in the line, of defective nutrition, in particular of carbohydrates, with excessive physical and mental strain. The effects of haemorrhage were augmented by the concurrence of inadequate fluid intake with "sweat and fighting."

[13] It is entirely pertinent to an account of the evolution of antisepsis and asepsis in the war of 1914-18 to recall that de Mondeville in the 14th century taught aseptic principles, and that Larrey in the 18th-19th knew the value and the limitations of immediate suture and of antiseptic substances.

missiles.[13] The history of missile wounds in war as well as the mechanical factors concerned in their production has a direct bearing on the surgery of the Great War.

Rifle Bullets. The introduction at the end of the 13th century of "fire-arms" was associated (it would seem) with a much more lethal type of "wound" than heretofore. The "poisoning" of the wound attributed to the first "fire-arms," which made them for a time anathema, was doubtless the sepsis which developed in the large contaminated wounds caused by the low velocity soft leaden bullets which often themselves lodged in the wound. The velocity of the "rifle" bullet increased, but no fundamental change in small arm ballistics or wounding took place till the eighteen-eighties when the introduction of small calibre high velocity rifles burning "smokeless" powder, of which the French "Lebel" rifle was the first, throwing a hard small conical bullet with enormous velocity, opened up a new era in military surgery, as it did in warfare. Two new types of wound appear namely, the clean drilled wound with small aperture of entrance and larger of exit, and that brought about by the "explosive" effect of the high velocity bullet at close range. The ensuing debates concerned first the cause of these effects and their military significance, second their relation to the new international drive to eliminate "unnecessary suffering" in warfare, which, inspired by the success of the Geneva Convention, culminated in the agreement of The Hague. Factual contributions to this debate came from big-game shooters and from British warfare with "fanatical" warriors of the non-stop type, and concerned the comparative lethal or "stopping" effect of the small hard and the large leaden bullet and opened up the "dum dum" controversy. This carries through to the Boer War where the "humane" nature of the h.v. wound—which in that war was seldom sustained at less than half a mile—seemed soundly established. But when in 1905 Germany introduced the sharp-nosed-stream-lined-bullet, with a greatly increased muzzle velocity, the whole situation, military, medical and humane, was transformed. The experiments of Mann (America) into the ballistics of the new bullet, of Fessler (Germany) into its effect on the animal body, and of Sir Victor Horsley using wet modelling clay, pointed to an extension of the "explosive" effects on viscera, on bones, and on the aperture of exit at ranges from 200 yards up to 500. The tendency of the pointed bullet to assume an oblique position in space (the "Querschläger") and its easy deflection made for disruptive effects.

British surgeons, however, apparently continued to think—when they thought at all on these things—in terms of South African experience.

The Great War provided an unlimited supply of human rabbits and a wide range of experimental conditions. The German experimental findings were confirmed. In particular the close range of attrition warfare made common some degree of the "explosive" effect or severe disrup-

[13] For relative incidence of missile wounds, *see p. 495;* for regional incidence, *see Vol. III.* Death rates—K.I.A. and D. of W.—of various weapons of war show the comparative efficiency as *lethal* agents, but not their value in the furtherance of victory. Thus in the Great War "chemical warfare" introduced a weapon in which the mortality was insignificant in proportion to the numbers disabled. The ratio of "killed" to "wounded" recorded of ancient battles was often immensely greater than in those of modern times.

tion; ricochet increased the "Querschläger" effect. The clean drilled wound of soft tissue and cancellous bone, and stellate fracture of long bones, were often replaced by severe or gross disruption of the former and comminution of the latter.[14]

Shrapnel and Pistol Bullets. These produced a large but not "explosive" wound but were much more liable to introduce foreign substances and to lodge.

H.E. Shell and "Bombs." The severity of the average wound was also accentuated by the stupendous expenditure of high-explosive shell and grenade. The great variation in the shape and size of the fragments from these, and their comparatively low velocity, resulted in a very wide range of wound. Fragments often lodged and lacerated severely; and a distinct and important element in their action was that they almost invariably carried portions of clothing and other matter. They did not, however, as a rule cause local necrosis. The wounds inflicted were often multiple, and of a truly "shocking" nature.

(*B*). *Types of Wound.* For clinical purposes, the wounds caused by these various missiles were classified (1) by their physical and anatomical features, and, in particular by whether they involved a long bone; (2) by the region and organ chiefly involved; (3) by their local effect on the tissues.

Physical Features. The following *types of wounds* were of clinical significance apart from their regional involvements. (*i*) Through and through bullet wounds without explosive effects, or with moderate wound of exit. Such wounds were often sterile. With these may be classed minor open wounds. (*ii*) Cul-de-sac wounds, large and small, with lodgement of missile. (*iii*) "Explosive" bullet wounds, and extensive shell wounds, with wide destruction of tissues. (*iv*) Multiple wounds. (*v*) Fractures.[15] As in civil life but "more so" the involvement of a

---

[14] The true exploding bullet was not used as a man-killing missile in the Great War. The "critical" velocity to produce "explosive" effects in an ordinary bullet is placed at 2,100 feet per second (*British Official History, Surgery, Vol. I, p. 22*); or "close range . . . up to a mile" (*American Official Medical History*). The subjoined table shows the relative velocity of the British and German bullets fired from the service rifle in feet per second.

Type of Bullet	Muzzle Vel.	At 500 yds.	At 1,000 yds.
1. Mark VII. (British)	2,420	1,510	1,020
2. Spitzegeschoss (German) ..	2,980	1,780	1,090

In general the effects of missiles on the interior of the body depend on their (1) velocity, (2) weight, and (3) size and shape. The rifle and machine-gun bullets were identical. It may be recalled that the pointed bullet flies "true" in virtue of the rotation on its long axis—3·4,000 times per second—imposed by "rifling."

[15] Figures showing the proportion of these are not available from Australian records. An estimate, based on the analysis of 206,976 woundings, is made in the *British Official Medical History (Statistics, p. 284*). Applied to Australian wounded admitted to field ambulances on the Western Front, the incidence of fractures appears as follows:

Wounds with major fractures	11,278	9·10 per cent.
Wounds with minor fractures	5,788	4·67 per cent.
Other wounds	106,866	86·23 per cent.

One of the most striking features of the surgery of the Great War was the fact that the appalling surgical problem created by the wounds involving the femur, tibia and humerus, found its mechanical solution awaiting the moment in the "Thomas" type of splint.

long bone or large joint was a grave matter making necessary an elaborate and special technique, or amputation.

Apart from the wounding of vital organs and structures, and of blood vessels, nerves and muscle with resulting haemorrhage, pain and other morbific nervous stimuli, and perhaps the release of "toxic" (depressant) substances, the most important local effect of a war missile was to produce a zone of necrotic tissue sown with germs; together most often with gross foreign bodies, in particular particles of clothing and missiles. This was the central fact of war wounds around which revolved the actions and reactions of wounds, and the art and practice of wound surgery.[16]

(C). The Diseases of Wounds: Sepsis. Rupture of the skin, by wounding, opens the way to a further trauma by pathogenic micro-organisms. The woundings of the Western Front did more—they drove these deeply into the tissues and provided them with pabulum, so that on the often grave *trauma* of wounding was imposed that of "infection."[17] Further, as already said, microbic invasion itself constitutes a "cause" of disease not less extrinsic and mechanistic, if more subtle, than a "wound": eliciting in its turn an organic reaction not very dissimilar.

The Infective Agents on the Western Front. Two biologically differentiated groups were prominent. (1) Certain groups of *anaerobic sporing bacilli,*[18] chiefly of faecal habitat, strictly saprophytic but intensely toxicogenic. These did not evoke a typical "inflammatory" reaction, but, in symbiosis, produced by local action the condition known as "gas gangrene"; or by neurotropic intoxication that of "tetanus." They also (it was generally believed) promoted the action of the next group.

(2) *The Pyogenic Cocci*—in particular the haemolytic streptococci.[19] Present in all stages of wound infection and especially important as "re-infection," these groups of organisms were responsible for the microbic

---

[16] Borst (*Researches into the Morbid Anatomy of War Injuries* Leipzig 1917) describes three zones in gunshot injuries of soft parts. The first, or innermost zone is represented by the wound channel or wound cavity, which is filled with necrotic tissue, extravasated blood, foreign bodies, and shreds of torn muscles. Next comes the zone of direct traumatic destruction with cauterisation of tissue. This is of variable width, according to the physical and morphological peculiarities of individual tissues and projectiles. Bacteria find the best possible culture-medium in the necrotic or semi-necrotic tissue. In the third, or outer zone, the tissue is not necrotic, although greatly reduced in vitality. (From *History of the Medical Department* of the United States Army in the World War, *Vol. XI, Surgery, Part 1, p. 294.*)

[17] For definition of infection see footnote 58, p. 329.

[18] Apart from the Bacillus tetani and Bacillus Welchii these were for long very vaguely identified. In 1919 the Medical Research Committee found that the three types of pathogenic anaerobes most concerned in the production of gas gangrene were in order of importance *Bacillus Welchii, Vibrion septique* and *Bacillus oedematiens.* ("Report on the Anaerobic Infections of Wounds and of the Bacteriological and Serological problems arising therefrom" *Medical Research Council Special Report Series, No. 39, 1919, p. 17.* Quoted by W. J. Penfold and Jean C. Tolhurst "Formol-Toxoids in the Prophylaxis of Gas Gangrene" *M.J.A. 26 June, 1937 p. 982.*)

[19] One of the achievements of the Great War was to unmask in this group an enemy of wide-spread activities and great menace to the public health. See also under Measles, in which disease immense epidemics of streptococcal pneumonia occurred chiefly in America.

trauma which produces the "pyogenic" inflammatory and febrile reactions and most of the secondary surgical problems of war wounds.

Bacillus Coli, Bacillus Proteus and *Bacillus Pyocyaneus* and other organisms were occasionally met with, chiefly as secondary ("hospital") infections.

The local reaction against these groups or organisms is the physiological basis of wound surgery.

The effects of the wound *per se* on the wounded man were, pain, loss of blood and anoxaemia, and vital depression. On the other hand the general damage—

2. Pathology in the wounded man "disease"—brought about in the system by subsequent microbial infection, is reflected in a variety of more or less specific clinical morbid states which, here too, comprise two groups, those brought about by the anaerobes and those caused by pyogenic cocci.

(A). *Effects of Wounding per se—Physiological injury and reaction*: pain, anaemia ("haemorrhage"), vital depression ("shock" and "collapse"). It will be convenient to defer discussion of these until we deal, later in this chapter, with developments in their treatment.[20] It may be observed here, however, that these reactions interacted with each other and with *septic infections* to produce a pathological state and a corresponding clinical picture of great complexity,[21] and this fact will be found to dominate the practical problem of treating the seriously wounded man.

(B). *Effects of Septic Infection—General microbial injury and reaction—wound diseases*. The traumatic effects of the two chief groups or organisms differ fundamentally, both in their mode of action (pathogeny) and the course, results and clinical features of the "diseases" produced. Thus in tetanus we have to do with an almost purely traumatic and general effect with little obvious clinical reaction, or none; in pyogenic infection with a disease in which the reaction is the prominent component;

---

[20] *See p. 333.* A further appreciation of the actual war-time studies into the ultimate nature of the clinical syndromes is given in *Appendix No. 14.*

[21] Thus we find:—

"Shock (Path.) state of prostration following overstimulation of nerves by sudden pain as of wound." (*Concise Oxford Dict.*)

"Haemorrhage is so constantly associated with shock, and plays such an important part in its production, that the great majority of cases are examples of shock-haemorrhage rather than of pure shock." (Gray *Early treatment of War Wounds p. 82.*)

"The condition caused by acute sepsis may so closely simulate shock as to be indistinguishable from it." (*Manual of Injuries and Diseases of War, Jan. 1918, p. 18.*)

in gas gangrene with a condition pathogenically intermediate between these.

Specific Morbid States. Briefly, three clinical entities were prominent: (1) *tetanus*, (2) *gas gangrene* (both manifestations of intoxication), and (3) *pyogenic inflammation and septicaemia* (parasitic invasion). These three morbid states induced by "infection" formed a trio, each with special clinical, pathological, and immunological features; but from the point of view of surgical prophylaxis all were part of the general problem of "sepsis." Much was hoped from the biological process of artificial immunisation both for prophylaxis and treatment, and the production of passive immunity (by anti-sera) was fully tried out. Only anti-tetanic serum was of practical value in the war,[22] though an anti-gas-gangrene serum (against Bacillus Welchii and Vibrion septique) was produced and tried during 1918.[23] At the end of the war both the French and Germans were using a polyvalent serum.

Clinical "Diseases." "Tetanus." Though fully specific this disease was closely associated, both in its pathogenesis and incidence, with "infection" by the other anaerobes. It is pertinent here to note that the success achieved in civil wounds in the U.S.A. by the prophylactic use of anti-serum was fully confirmed in the Great War. An order issued in October, 1914, that every wounded man should receive a prophylactic dose of A.T.S. as soon as possible after the injury, led to a drop from 9 cases per 1,000 wounded in September to 1·4 in December—an improvement which, with fluctuations due to the circumstances of the fighting, was maintained throughout the war. The influence on this disease of the reduction of sepsis in general by improved surgical technique is stated in *The British Official History*,[24] as follows:—"It remains one of the great surgical lessons of the war that the excision of damaged and infected tissues, when it can be carried out effectively, does in practice prevent tetanus as in theory it ought to do. . . . It is obvious that this radical measure cannot be carried out in all cases," and therefore "the alternative method of administering anti-serum to the wounded cannot be dispensed with."

The importance of the reduction achieved is shown by the fact that (as stated—*loc. cit. p. 158*—by Prof. Sir F. W. Andrewes): "Had a ratio of 8 cases per 1,000 wounded and a case mortality of 78·2 per cent. been maintained during the war, there would have been 13,683 cases of tetanus [in the British force] on the Western front with 10,700 deaths, in place of 2,529 cases and 1,265 deaths." But it is necessary also to record that the incidence over the whole war was 1·7 per thousand wounded with case mortality of 50·0 per cent.; as compared with

---

[22] It is of interest that early in 1915 the D.M.S., A.I.F., Surgeon-General Williams, purchased large supplies of sera, anti-tetanic and anti-dysenteric, for the A.I.F. in anticipation of Gallipoli. In view of the urgency of the situation in France, the bulk of this was handed over to the War Office. The organisation for the British system of supply, and a note on arrangements for vaccines and sera will be found in *Vol. III*.

[23] The production of an active immunity did not in the war get very far beyond the experimental stage, but will perhaps be the method of election in future wars. Reference may be made to recent experimental work in Australia by Penfold and Tolhurst at the Baker Institute, Melbourne, into the production of active immunity against B. Welchii by formal-toxoids.

[24] *Surgery, Vol. I, p. 157.*

3·5 per thousand in the Franco-German war with case mortality of 90 per cent. Particulars of the incidence of the disease in the A.I.F. are not available owing to the destruction of clinical records.[25]

"*Gas Gangrene.*" This disease was comparatively rare before the war. In no previous campaign had it figured to any great extent, but it quickly assumed a position of tragic importance on the Western Front, especially in the first months when everything was in its favour.[26]

Its most important features and the surgical treatment of it are described in the next volume; for our present purpose it is sufficient to note that the disease appeared most commonly in grossly traumatised, contaminated, and neglected wounds, especially if closed, or in those in which the circulation had been interfered with. Haemorrhage, shock, and prolonged fatigue were potent disposing factors as also was the "dose" received, in which fragments of clothing were the most potent agent.

Infection might be well established within a few hours of the receipt of the wound. In its usual form ("group" type) it developed as a local gangrene with gas formation and intense toxaemia, spreading, through the action of chemical toxins, from the zone of traumatic necrosis in the wound—most commonly in muscle but often in haematoma or other devitalised tissue. The case mortality is stated as 22 per cent. in the B.E.F. Its incidence varied from 5 to 6 per cent. of all wounds in 1915 to a little over 1 per cent. in June, 1918.

Pyogenic Infection. (Staphylococci and Streptococci). Taken together—as to some extent they may be—as the cause of the "pyogenic" type of infection, these agents were incomparably the most important factor in the problem of war wounds. No stage in the whole surgical campaign was free from their menace. It may be that, on this side of No-Man's Land, this group was the soldiers' "Public enemy No. 1." Recent advances in the knowledge of chemotaxis seem to promise a different outlook in the next war.

THE TREATMENT OF WOUNDING

Treatment of the wound itself

We have now to follow the evolution of wound treatment in the Great War, first as applied to the wound itself. And here there may at once be noted a most striking feature: that, whereas (as we shall see later) treatment of the direct effects, physical and physiological, of the trauma moved away from the wound to the wounded man and came to centre on a vaguely defined clinical syndrome identified as "secondary wound shock," on

---

[25] The *German Official Medical History, Vol. III, pp. 77-81*, records a total of 3,600 cases in four years of whom 2,542 were on the Western Front—about 0·8 per thousand of all wounded. Among the Germans on that front 1,656 cases occurred between August and December, 1914—*i.e.* 3·8 per thousand. Serum treatment was carried out from the beginning, and from April, 1915, intensively. The injection was repeated before any operation up to three months after wounding. The figures given in that history are obviously in many cases tentative.

[26] Sir Cuthbert Wallace in the *British Official Medical History, Surgery, Vol. I, p. 134.*

the other hand till the end of the war, except in one disease, tetanus, the treatment of microbic wound disease was almost wholly confined to local action on the wound itself. The following account of "treatment of wounds" will relate almost wholly to the prevention of sepsis. In this account we have to neglect the ligature and the suture although they were the first word in the art of wound surgery. But so far as the history of the Great War is concerned they belong to the past just as the chemotactic treatment of infection belongs to the future.

The objective in this vast campaign of war surgery was asepsis. The search for this comprised four stages:—

THE SEARCH FOR ASEPSIS.

FIRST STAGE. (1914-15). *Open warfare.*
Beginnings: Unintelligent reliance on the supposed asepticity of missile wounds which were closed by suture. Effective surgery entirely done at the Base.
Reaction. (*i*) Crude chemical antisepsis—strong solutions, pastes. (*ii*) Irrigation and lavage. (*iii*) Surgical common sense, wounds cleaned, drained and left open.
Experiment—official and individual, laboratory and clinical.

SECOND STAGE. (1915-17). *Static warfare.* Experiment and experimental application; technical advances, technical training, technical organisation. The foundations laid for a continuous campaign from Front to Base.

THIRD STAGE. (1917-18). *Static warfare.* Scientific wound surgery in static warfare—antiseptic and aseptic.

FOURTH STAGE. (1918). *Open warfare.* Scientific surgery in open warfare—aseptic and antiseptic.

FIRST STAGE: "Nothing," says Sir George Turner, "impressed me more during my work in the Great War than the ignorance of the younger generation of surgeons, who had been brought up on antiseptic or aseptic surgery, of what it was necessary to do when a case went septic."[27]

1914. The medical profession entered into the war in 1914 with an interesting and very remarkable handicap. Well up in the methods of ensuring asepsis in surgical wounds, for the most part it knew little of *"septic"* wounds. In the early stages of the war the more fulminant forms of wound infection,

---

[27] From *Unorthodox Reminiscences* by Lieut.-Col. Sir George Turner. (From review *The Times Literary Supplement* 17/9/1931.)

familiar to an earlier generation as "hospital gangrene" and pyaemia, fell like the scourge of an unexpected pestilence on a race of surgeons grown complacent in the atmosphere of prophylactic asepsis, with whose toilsome and tedious evolution they were acquainted chiefly by tradition and Listerian Orations. The experience of the South African War and (with surprisingly moderate variation) of the Russo-Japanese, led to the belief that, in a large proportion of wounds, superficial or very casual chemical antisepsis with immediate suture was not only permissible but desirable. For the best part of a year, indeed, at the beginning of the Great War, the treatment of wounds in the field was vitiated by neglect of the fact that the *infection was contained within the wound itself,* so that for the most part paints of iodine or of picric alcohol were as whiting to a sepulchre, and repeated "dressings" of little more use than were the antics and the offerings of the priests of Baal.[28]

In the field ambulances during the first five or six months of the war, and later in the first "clearing hospitals," wounds were superficially disinfected and sutured. The time between first aid at the front and effective operation at the Base was commonly several days. The results were appalling. During the first six months the mortality and morbidity from "septic" infection dealt to the surgical profession in every nation concerned a staggering blow, from which it recovered only through tedious and painful apprenticeship.

The Surgical Debacle. For the situation in respect to the surgery of wounds in the first few months of the war the term "chaotic" would seem not too strong an epithet. In serious wounds, treated as they were for the most part by immediate suture, with or without some superficial antisepsis, sepsis was practically universal; "gas gangrene" was very common, tetanus

---

[28] In Jan., 1915, as A.D.M.S. 1st Australian Division Colonel (later Major-General Sir) N. R. Howse who in civil life was a surgeon of distinction, duly shocked but impressed an R.M.O. before the Landing by suggesting that, in the treatment of "abdominals" if he should spit on the wound and then move heaven and earth to get the man quickly to operation he would do more good than by fussing about with "dressing."

"A great deal of waste continues in medical units. Many of the wounded are dressed far too frequently between the firing line and the C.C.S." (Report by Lieut.-Col., later Sir H. S. Newland to D.M.S., A.I.F. Jan., 1918.)

"I generally had a look at the first field dressing myself, and usually changed them and applied picric spirit because men in my own battalion seemed more satisfied if I had seen them, and the psychological factor was worth considering" (R.M.O.).

an ever-present Sword of Damocles. The difficulties of the surgical problem were greatly enhanced by the nature of the wounds, the conditions of the fighting, and the absence of medical motor transport.

Within a matter of almost weeks an intense reaction against all this took place and followed two broad lines:—(1) a rever-
Reaction sion to pre-aseptic surgical principles and practice, and (2) the initiation of research and experiment, clinical and laboratory. From these two can be traced the avenues of thought and action along which evolved the great surgical developments of the war. Only an epitome of this illuminating episode in the history of surgery can be given here.

1. Reversion to Pre-aseptic Methods. The immediate suturing of wounds was abandoned, and three chief alternatives were adopted. Each of these contained the seed of more important later developments. Of the beginnings in this "reaction" a brief note only is required.

(*i*) *Crude Antiseptics.* Almost every known antiseptic substance was tried and much ingenuity expended in combining them—as instanced in Sir Lenthal Cheatle's solution of perchloride of mercury and carbolic. Most were futile, some grossly harmful. Of the cresol paste and salicylic and boric dusting powder—"Borsal"—devised in February, 1915, by Sir Watson Cheyne, Lister's most ardent disciple, the *British Official History*[29] notes that in cases arriving at the Base "the wound aperture was often blocked . . . or a dark evil-smelling discharge was exuding. The limbs were swollen and acute progressive infection of the tissues was present. When opened up a surface resembling . . . necrotic liver substance was exposed."[30]

(*ii*) *Lavage.* This aimed at the production, by means partly mechanical, partly chemical, of a virtual asepsis and a granulating wound, permitting sometimes the secondary suturing of the wound. "Irrigation" and the "continuous bath" had been almost a sheet anchor in the treatment of the less fulminant forms of sepsis in the "nineties"

---

[29] *Surgery, Vol. I, p. 259.*
[30] An explanation of the failure of this futile and wasteful "antiseptic" campaign may be found in failure to recognise the fact that Lister endeavoured to prevent wound "infection" rather than to cure. The "evil" brought about by the implantation in the wound of a particle of "dry septic pus," he wrote, "cannot be corrected by any antiseptic wash that is now at our disposal or that the world is ever likely to see." (Quoted by *British Official Medical History, Surgery, Vol. I, p. 258.*) As stated by Burghard, Leishman, Moynihan, and Wright ("Office international d'hygiène publique," 1915, *vol. vii, p. 946*—quoted by Carrel, *loc. cit. p.4*) "the treatment of suppurating wounds by means of antiseptics is illusory, and . . . founded upon false reasoning;" and by Sir Almroth Wright (*B.M.J. 24 Apr. 1915, p. 721*) "if it were ever to come about that an antiseptic sterilised heavily infected wounds, that would be a matter to announce in all the evening and morning papers." Carrel's quotation of these opinions was made with the purpose of vigorous refutation. It was, he implied, a matter of using antiseptics—"with brains."

and the early years of the 20th century, and proved a useful grapnel in the storms of 1914. The experimental developments of this quest, such as the historic researches of Sir Almroth Wright and of Doctors Carrel and Dakin and their co-adjutors at Compiègne, both of which began in 1914, are examined later.

(*iii*) *Primitive Asepsis.* The most important immediate practical result of the "reaction" was the return to surgical tradition and experience in the commonsense procedure of *mechanical removal of obvious foreign matter*, such as missiles, fragments of muscles, fascia, and loose bone, combined with incision and drainage. Later, when from this line of treatment there was developing the general practice of excising wounds, this earlier procedure was still for two years the recognised method of dealing with all major wounds; and, combined with improved "antiseptic" methods and thorough drainage, it continued to be applied until the end of the war in the treatment of very large and awkward wounds and—a matter of first rate importance—of fractures.

2. Initiation of Experiment and Research. Laboratory research—for a time regarded coldly by the older surgeons—was initiated in 1914 at Boulogne, and, with clinical research, centred for a time chiefly in the hospitals established there.[31]

An authentic picture of the progress of this "reaction" is presented in the following epitome of notes of a discussion, held in February, 1915, under the auspices of the Australian Voluntary Hospital, on the *treatment of wounds involving fracture of the femur arriving at the Boulogne Base Hospitals.*[32]

Progress of "reaction" at the Base

Lieut.-Colonel G. Horne,[33] introducing the discussion said: "This is all new ground, and new means must be employed. The experience of the Boer War does not entirely cover this; in particular we have a bacterial flora of greater virulence and variety. The drilled hole of a rifle bullet is seldom seen in this campaign; the commonest wound is the smash of shrapnel and shell fragments. The chief problems are those of *suppuration* and *secondary haemorrhage*, and of the indications for *suturing*." The discussion proceeded as follows:—

No. 11 General Hospital: "The question of free drainage is the first essential." *No. 13 General:* "The great difficulty has been the treatment of secondary haemorrhage—very large numbers are fatal.

---

[31] This will be dealt with in *Vol. III*.

[32] These notes, obtained from Lieut.-Col. Piero Fiaschi, through the courtesy of Lieut.-Col. George Bell, were distributed by the Acting D.M.S., A.I.F., Col. T. M. Martin, to the Australian Medical units in Egypt in May, 1915. Officers from all the Hospitals at this Base took part in the discussion and as well the Consulting Surgeon to the B.E.F. Bases Colonel (later Lieut.-General Sir G. W.) Makins and Colonel Sir Alexander MacCormick, A.A.M.C. (of Sydney, N.S.W.) Consulting Surgeon to the D.D.M.S. at the Boulogne Base. The Officer Commanding this unit was Col. (later Major-General, A.A.M.C.) W. L'Estrange Eames.

[33] Lieut.-Col. Horne was in civil life a highly esteemed and cultured gynaecological surgeon, of Melbourne.

Survival is rare after second occurrence without prompt amputation."
No. 14 General and Nos. 2 and 7 Stationary dealt at length with the
many varieties of splints in use. No. 13 Stationary: "Is it worth while
going in for these elaborate splints? If the leg is properly opened up
at the front, the patient should be sent straight home (to England) in
the splint without waste of time. How many limbs are taken off when
they get to England after lengthy treatment here? We would suggest
—open up the wound, irrigate with 1 in 20 carbolic or even 1 in 10,
insert large draining tubes, and apply a long interrupted Bryant splint."
Rawalpindi Hospital (Indian Army) suggested that men in the field
ambulance should use more free draining. *Westminster Hospital.*
Recommends drainage and irrigation, oxygen preferred to H_2O_2 "as
it gets in where the latter cannot." *Lahore Hospital* (Indian Army):
"Our practice is drainage and continuous irrigation." *Major Gordon
Watson*[84] favoured treatment of femurs in France. *Major G. A. Moore*
(Director of ambulance trains): "The ambulance trains now include a
theatre in a special bogey van, where secondary haemorrhage can be
treated." *Sir Alexander MacCormick* (Consulting Surgeon Boulogne
Base) emphasised the influence of the method of transport from the
front on the outcome of the case. He suggested that the field ambulances at the front should be supplied with the Thomas splint, "as it can
be applied immediately and would obviate a lot of subsequent movement."
Colonel G. W. Makins[85]: "A most important thing is to seek for the most
efficient means of disinfection—wounds are treated well mechanically by
means of drainage. Of anaerobic and streptococcal infection the first is
more easily dealt with and more easy to control. Gas gangrene effects
are soon over; the streptococcus is the more important as causing septicaemia, with much suffering and subsequent trouble. We look to the
bacteriologists for a prophylactic vaccine." *Sir Almroth Wright*[86] dealt
with the bacteriological aspect. "Everyone is surprised at the amount of
sepsis, not only strepto and staphylococci but B. perfringens, B. Tetani,
and other anaerobes. The whole fighting area is one of intense cultivation; this may even be called a war of faecal infection—streptococcus
and anaerobes. The missile goes through clothes soiled with faeces.
Bathing and clean clothes may help to prevent contamination, in conjunction with use of carbolic in the Field Ambulances. Drainage is only
the first and crude stage [of treatment], for lymph is the only real
purifying agent." Methods of treating infection recommended by him
were: (1) *Drainage*—promoting the exit and current flow of clear
lymph; lymph lavage; use of hypertonic salt solution which causes
secretion of lymph. (2) Prophylactic inoculation (streptococcal vaccine). (3) Antisepsis. But "no antisepsis will sterilize a wound, a
small sowing is as bad as a big, if in a good cultivation medium; antiseptics reduce the sowing only." (4) "Frequent dressing, which removes
pus and so far is useful. Irrigation is ideal."

---

[84] Col. Sir Charles Gordon-Watson, Consulting Surgeon Second Army.

[85] Colonel Makins was the author of the textbook of war surgery chiefly in use
Surgical Experiences in South Africa. In the *British Official Medical History of the
Great War* he was responsible for the following articles:—"Injuries to the Pericardium and Heart," "Wound treatment in General Hospitals in France," and
"Injuries to the Blood vessels."

[86] Consultant, B.E.F. Sometime Demonstrator of Physiology, University of
Sydney. See also *pp. 319-22.* His chapter in the *British Official Medical History,
Pathology,* on "The physiology of wounds" is of quite exceptional interest.

While this reaction was proceeding at the Base, surgical work at the front was passing from the field ambulance to the casualty clearing station and developing along lines that was to make the C.C.S. the focal centre for effective surgery. In *March, 1915,* the D.G.M.S., B.E.F. issued "Circular Memorandum No. 6" which dealt with "The principles of the treatment of wounded before evacuation from the front: based on the experiences of the last six months." The points emphasised therein were as follows:—

Reaction at the front—the genesis of asepsis

1. "All wounds should be regarded as infective or septic: sutures should consequently not be used as a rule. . . . 'Aseptic' (*sic*) surgery is out of place in septic wounds." (2) "No one antiseptic can be said to be superior to all others." [Solutions of Tincture of Iodine, carbolic, lysol, hydrogen peroxide, were recommended.] 3. "Men left lying out for a day or two are often severely collapsed," and require "saline," food, and stimulants "before dressing." 4. Strict precaution must be taken against tight bandages: "it is of the utmost importance that the first field dressing should always be removed as soon as possible." 5. Operations except those of emergency were not to be done in field ambulances, because "asepsis" could not be secured. 6. "Arrangements are now usually made to enable a certain number of patients to be retained in the C.C.S., and nurses have therefore been added to the personnel." 7. "Bad compound fractures . . . should as a rule be cleaned up at the clearing station under anaesthetic when time permits." 8. "Wounds of the skull or brain . . . can safely be sent to the base." If operation were done on these wounds at the C.C.S. "the wound itself should be excised and, if too extensive for this, its edges should be cut away."[37] 9. Chest cases should be retained in the C.C.S. for a week at least. 10. For "abdominals" as regards operations no fixed rule could be laid down "as much depends on the experience in surgery of the operator."

End of the First Stage. In July, 1915, there was issued the "Memorandum on the Treatment of Injuries in War." This important statement drawn up by the "Committee of Consultants," B.E.F., as a general guide to surgical practice, marks in effect the end—in the British Army—of our first stage.[38]

In this manual a considerable range of operative intervention was allotted to the field units—field ambulances and C.C.S. The following method was laid down for "the dressing" of large wounds "at the front."

"If it be an open wound, portions of clothing, obvious fragments of

---

[37] This was Colonel Gray's procedure.
[38] It formed the basis for surgery in the B.E.F. until its re-issue in Jan., 1918. In the period between the two issues is contained the creative period of war surgery in the B.E.F.

GENERAL SURGERY OF WOUNDS

shell, and torn or hopelessly damaged portions of tissue should be removed by forceps and scissors. If the wound be not sufficiently open to drain of itself, large drainage tubes should be inserted; and in cases where more must be done an anaesthetic should be given, and the wounds enlarged and held open by retractors so that all recesses may be washed out and drained. A good method of mechanically cleaning the track of a perforating wound consists in drawing backwards and forwards through it a piece of gauze twisted to form a rope. Very large drainage tubes (5/8-7/8 inch) should be used, with numerous large lateral openings. For large deep wounds counter-openings are necessary."

Antiseptics had been found of no avail "to inhibit bacterial growth within fouled wounds." *Drainage*, "in conjunction with the mechanical methods of cleansing, forms the essential element in the primary treatment of gunshot wounds." At the Base "the use of a blunt spoon may now be added as it removes blood clot, muscle and soft tissues well. Free removal of dead tissue is very important." The application of "powerful antiseptic media" to the wound was "undesirable"; but there was a "large consensus of opinion" favourable to the principles advocated by Sir Almroth Wright, "that the course of healing is most effectively furthered by means tending to increase the activity of vital processes concerned in its production." "*Gas gangrene and gaseous cellulitis*"—"the most important complication of wounds in this war"—was fully described but without reference to any special muscular involvements, and perhaps the more accurately for this! Treatment was to consist in "the removal of as much blood clot and devitalised tissue as possible, provision for free access to the air, and efficient drainage"—or by amputation.[30]

SECOND STAGE:
Organised
experiment and
observation,
1915-17

"In the first Aphorism of Hippocrates it is written that experience is fallacious. ... Yet we must confess that when experience leads us astray or experiment makes us stumble the cause is our faulty interpretation of facts which would be clear if we had eyes to see. ... In diagnosis and treatment experience is unavailing unless that common sense, which has been said to be the least common of all the senses, is also brought to bear upon the problem."[40]

There followed some two more years of experiences, experiments, and sufferings in this orgy of human vivisection, in which some millions of wounded men of both sides were subjected to the method of trial and error in the search for the best means of treating infected wounds of every kind and every organ, and the wounded man in every stage of his wounding. Like most evolution, that of wound surgery was

---

[30] No attempt was made in the memorandum to apportion the operative responsibilities of the Field Ambulance and C.C.S. respectively, nor to correlate treatment with movement. The use of the Thomas splint was mildly advocated, but no attempt made to ensure its general use at the front.

[40] "Medical Facts and Fallacies" by Maurice E. Shaw, *B.M.J.*, *14 March, 1936, p. 515.*

a slow and painful process in which improved methods strove against an immense inertia of structure and habit. For the Allies this phase may be held to have reached a climax with the *Interallied Surgical Conferences of March and May, 1917*, when the results of experiences and researches of the past two years were summarised and principles laid down for the technique of combined movement and treatment which the two subsequent years of the war did little to modify, though very much to implement.

Like that of all creative periods the history of these two years is full of interest—more so, perhaps, than that of the year in which the principles and methods so painfully won were successfully applied. In the present work, however, the most that can be attempted is to indicate the course of the evolution, and to present the lines of reasoning on which experimental and clinical research were based; and perhaps to suggest reasons for the success of some and failure of others.

By far the most important outward sign of the progress of surgery during this period was the gradual transfer of very much of what may be termed "essential" or "effective" surgery from the Base to the front. This was made possible, (1) by the stability of the Western Front, which permitted the building up of a system of highly organised medical units, and (2) by the development of a method of treatment—excision—whose purpose was the prevention of wound diseases or so great a mitigation as would permit the immediate or an early closure of many wounds, or, failing this, to promote the efficacy of secondary types of treatment. To achieve this end, operation must be undertaken within some 6 to 24 hours of wounding, though in exceptional cases it could be effective as late as 48 hours after the man was hit. Meanwhile, however, from 1914 onwards important developments had been taking place at the Base—designed in part to deal with declared or developing sepsis, in part to bridge the time-gap occupied by the ambulance train between the C.C.S. at the front and the General Hospital at the Base.

In the B.E.F. during the first two years of the war, and

to some extent throughout, the time-distance factor in this journey placed the British general hospitals out-
At the Base: the side the scope of prophylactic surgery, with
search for
antisepsis the result that the trend of research and clinical observation at those hospitals converged
naturally along the line of *cure*. It is to the resulting adventures
in laboratory research and clinical technique that we must now
turn—and primarily to those of Sir Almroth Wright at the
British Base, with which must be associated those of Carrel
and Dakin behind the French front at Compiègne.

Physiological Antisepsis: Serum Lavage. The vision of an
El Dorado was never followed with greater eagerness than
the pursuit in the war of the ideal means of combating sepsis.
In his "Memorandum on the treatment of infected wounds
by physiological methods" Colonel Sir Almroth Wright sets
out the principles of his method as follows:—[41]

"The ideal of physiological treatment is to give intelligent aid to
the organism in combating the bacterial infection. Saline dressings
supply a means for evoking, in the infected wound, certain requisite
physiological reactions. By their aid we can, while at the same time
inhibiting bacterial growth, drain the tissues, resolve infiltration, and
promote the separation of the sloughs—besides giving other assistance."

The therapeutic procedures involved were stated thus:—

"(1). . . . We have to promote the destruction of the microbes
which have been carried into the deeper tissues, to re-establish normal
conditions in those tissues . . . and to prevent 'the corruption of the discharges' and to inhibit microbic growth in the cavity of the wound.
During the whole period occupied by these operations we have to be
constantly on our guard to prevent active and passive movements which
would propel bacteria along the lymphatics, and carry poisonous bacterial products into the blood. (2). When the microbes in the deeper
tissues have been exterminated and the physiological conditions have
been restored and the wound rendered to naked eye inspection perfectly
clean, the time has come for dealing with the surface infection. (3). As
soon as this has been suppressed . . . all our thought ought to be
given to promoting the processes of repair, bringing together the tissues,
and covering over the denuded surfaces."

These purposes Wright sought to achieve by exploiting the
antiseptic and "tryptic" powers of the lymph and its contained

---

[41] For systematic presentation of the genesis of the methods of Wright and those of Carrel and Dakin and of the researches on which they were based the reader may be referred, for that of Wright to his article—a classic—in the *British Official Medical History, Pathology;* and for that of Carrel to the *Treatment of Infected Wounds* by Carrel and Dehelly (English translation *Military Medical Manuals*).

leucocytes, by the use of hypertonic (5 per cent.) solution of sodium chloride with or without the addition of 0·5 per cent. sodium citrate to prevent coagulation of the lymph; applied *secundum artem* to reach every part of the wound[42] with the purpose of

"drawing out from the infected tissues lymph which has spent all its antibacterial energy, and drawing into the tissues from the blood stream lymph inimical to microbic growth."[43]

This was complemented by measures—in particular the use of normal (0·85 per cent.) salt solution—for inhibiting lymph-flow, and promoting phagocytosis and (by trypsin released from the broken-down leucocytes) the removal of slough, inducing subsequent granulation.

Results. The method was perforce applied chiefly in wounds which had reached the stage of progressive infection, in many of which preliminary cleansing had been very crude. At times it seems events went "according to plan"; but on the whole the results were disappointing. In particular secondary haemorrhage was thought to be more frequent; granulations were often flabby and hydraemic, and the stage of healing slow. The method has probably no permanent place as a technique; it was based for the most part on deduction from hypotheses, themselves the result of laboratory experiment inspired by the cult of "the teat and capillary glass tube" which had imperfect contact with clinical observation. Wright's claim to a place in history rests rather on the creation of an attitude of mind, a reaction from "muddle through" methods.

Scientific Antisepsis: "Carrel-Dakin" Lavage. The method of treating contaminated and infected wounds which has been associated particularly with the names of Dr. Alexis Carrel and Professor Henry Dakin, has retained a place in the technique of civil and military surgery.

Begotten at the end of 1914 from deep resentment at the surgical disasters of the first few months, and from a robust belief in the efficacy of Listerian antisepsis if applied with due regard for scientific criteria, the experiment comprised perhaps the most complete single campaign of combined laboratory and clinical research and typical American "team work" that was occasioned by the war. The researches, laboratory and clinical, on which it was based were made in laboratories

[42] Wright employed irrigation, gauze dressings, and for deep wounds the not very effective device of gauze wicks, the wound being covered by gutta-percha tissue to keep the dressing constantly wet.
[43] *Brit. Off. Med. History. Pathology, p. 5.*

established at Compiègne under the auspices of the Rockefeller Foundation, and in the "Temporary Hospital" ("No. 21") staffed by surgeons of the French Colonial Forces and controlled by the French Medical Service under the Secretary of State for the Interior.

Important as are the details of the technique, they do not to-day call for description. But the principles on which the system was based, and on which it was built up in the very "dust and heat" of war, have a very definite historical and educational value.

The Method. The hypothesis on which the system was based is stated thus:—

"The surgical infection, at the outset, is always local. In war-wounds, it is carried by projectiles, and especially by fragments of clothing, impregnated with micro-organisms. Before crossing the boundaries of the wound, these flourish on the surface of the tissues. Therefore, during a period more or less long [placed by Carrel at broadly 12-48 hours] the infection is under control, since the microbes are, so to speak, within reach of the hand. The question then is simply, how to destroy them without harming the tissues?"

Professor Dakin's search for a substance[44] unirritating to the tissues but of sufficient bactericidal power to "kill all microbes present in a wound" led to the chloramines and thence to a neutral solution of sodium hypochlorite, prepared by special process.

Technique of Application. The method was in the first place applied to "old wounds," subsequently, in preference, to recent ones. The two essential factors in the technique were, first, the evolution of a method whereby the solution could be brought continuously in contact with *every* part of the wound, by the now well known scheme of perforated tubes and glass applicators, the intermittent flow being maintained by syphonage or gravity.[45] A second prime object in the method was to control the progress of disinfection to the point of a "virtual sterilisation" of the wound by means of daily counts[46] of the bacterial content of the wound, the purpose being to arrive at a measurable criterion of safety for *secondary suture.*

It is right to note that the conditions under which this remarkable experiment was carried out were exceptional; though the facilities were those of a base hospital, the position of Compiègne allowed casualties to arrive within time-limits that corresponded to those characteristic of a casualty clearing station.

Wright v. Carrel: Nature v. Art. Dakin himself has stated that the methods of Wright and Carrel were not fundamentally different. It is nevertheless certain that the two were at first conceived as antithetic. It is difficult for the present generation of surgeons to appreciate the

---

[44] Dakin and others *Proceedings of Royal Society 1916, Vol. 89, p. 232.* Quoted by Carrel *p. 2.*

[45] During ambulance-train transport, on the suggestion of Bowlby, irrigation was maintained by syringing.

[46] These were quantitative only.

bitterness of the quarrel between the a- and the anti-septists—which recall indeed the civil wars of Brobdingnag. British surgeons, it is clear, were "rattled" by the tragic failure of what they conceived to be Listerian principles; Carrel and Dakin helped to restore courage and sanity.[47] The method of "chemio-therapy" was adopted for reasons which are fundamental in the problem of the surgery of war wounds. "It seemed probable," Carrel states, "that the infection of war-inflicted wounds would be unsuitable for treatment by vaccines or serums. As the inoculation of the tissues by projectiles or fragments of clothing is massive, and *as the germs protected by necrosed tissues or blood-clots multiply beyond the reach of lymph-flow, it is extremely unlikely that such therapeusis could be effective.*"

The words here italicised state the essential difference between Wright's problem and that of Carrel, and also supply the key to their respective methods. Further, they presage both the success of Carrel's method and its ultimate supersession by the more direct method of excision. Indeed, the details of the preliminary surgical treatment required by Carrel make clear that—at this time, at least—only one consideration lay between irrigation with secondary suture and the immediate closure of the wound, namely the feeling expressed by Carrel in the statement that "*a surgeon has not the right to cause a single wounded man to risk useless dangers.*"[48]

Results. There is no gainsaying that, when this method could be applied as directed, it was very effective in achieving its purpose. Yet, though fully effective from September of 1915, it was not taken into general use in the British Army till the beginning of 1917 and little earlier, if at all, in the French. This neglect on the part of the French surgical profession seems to have been due in some part to the failing which so nearly killed Louis Pasteur—professional jealousy—but also, *pace* Carrel, to the progress in the French Army of *débridement* and suture. British failure to take it up must in part be set down to the physical factor which in no small measure determined the evolution of the surgery of wounds in the B.E.F.—namely the hiatus between the hospitals of the front and those of the Base.

The most general employment of this method in the B.E.F. occurred about the time of the Third Battle of Ypres. The notebooks of Australian surgeons working at Remy Siding show many cases sent to the Base under "Carrel" treatment, for which, by order of the D.G.M.S., special arrangements were made on the ambulance trains. Even then however there was strong competition by simpler methods, in particular the physiological "salt pack" and antiseptic "B.I.P." Acriflavine was on trial, and—as is strongly evident in the records of the Australian casualty clearing stations—there can be discerned a growing appreciation of the fact that the British

---

[47] Dakin (*loc. cit.*) refers to Sir Berkeley Moynihan as undertaking experiments allied to those of Carrel.

[48] *loc. cit.* The italics here are in the original.

Army was far behind the French in the courage of its conviction that the time had come for the immediate closure of wounds without the intervention of either physiological or chemical intermediaries.

These procedures, though trespassing on prophylaxis, were primarily at least intended for the treatment at the General Hospitals, and chiefly for that of declared

Front and Base— infection rather than of contamination. We
the effort for
continuity pass now to other methods and means designed to provide a short cut between the front line and the Base.

Under *methods* we have (1) the "salt packing" of Lawson and Gray and the Bismuth, Iodoform and Paraffin paste of Rutherford Morison (B.I.P.). (2) Under *means* came the "scientific" antiseptics, of which eusol, Dakin's solution, "acriflavine," and chloramine T, are types.

1. Methods. Methods of both types, "physiological" and "antiseptic," were devised in the B.E.F. with the purpose of ensuring continuity for the treatment by irrigation during the interval necessarily interposed by the ambulance train. Special arrangements were made for "Carrel" treatment. Wright's was applied by the ingenious device of the "salt pack."

The Salt Pack. In the idea of promoting serum lavage without mess and bother and of getting it going at the C.C.S. early in 1915 Lieut.-Colonel C. B. Lawson packed wounds with tablets of sodium chloride covered in gauze. The idea was taken up with enthusiasm by the Consultant Colonel Gray, and achieved a wide if transient vogue especially in the Rouen group of hospitals. Employed on the conditions laid down by Gray—(i) that the wound must be religiously cleaned up (in effect, *débrided*), (ii) that, unless specifically contra-indicated, the pack should be left *in situ* for a week or more, the offensive odour being dealt with *secundum artem*—results were obtained which justified its temporary vogue.

B.I.P. Surgeons familiar with the post-war history of this mode of treatment as developed by Winnett Orr[49] may perhaps find ground

---

[49] Vaseline alone is employed with gauze packing, especially in chronic suppurating bone conditions; rest is enforced by plaster casing. See *MJ.A.* 9 June 1934—article by A. V. Meehan.

Morison's own idea of his treatment is told thus:—

"I have discovered an antidote to true sepsis, and we are now about to leave dirty wounds undressed for a whole month. Think of what this means for compound fractures. *Programme*: Open up and clean the wound; mop it out with spirit, then fill it with paste and cover with dressing. *Paste*: Iodoform, 2 parts; bismuth sub-nitrate, 1 part; paraffin, q.s. to make a paste." (*B.M.J. 21 Jan., 1939, p. 140*—Obituary by Mr. R. J. Willan.) Mr. Willan's claim that " 'bipp'. . . is probably the only important new surgical measure introduced during the Great War which has survived and is still in use" is perhaps open to question. In passing, in the use "B.I.P." we follow the *British Official History*.

for philosophic doubt as to the antiseptic rôle assigned to it. However this may be, the records of Australian units confirm the consensus of opinion that, though this procedure devised by Rutherford Morison in the middle of 1916, in the hope that it would provide a short-cut to early suture, fell somewhat short of its ambitious aims—and, perhaps, claims —it yet proved a most effective implement for bridging the gap between the front and the Base. The technique does not call for description— roughly, after exact surgical attention the paste was rubbed in to the recesses of the wound and all excess carefully wiped away and the wound commonly closed by suture but without tension. In August, 1917, the General Hospitals were required to furnish a report on the condition of the "Bipped" cases received. The report from No. 1 A.G.H. was that it should be "confined to such cases as offer a reasonable chance of excising damaged soft parts fairly thoroughly and in the case of fractures where it could be applied to the bone surfaces" (Lieut.-Colonel Balcombe Quick). "I regard B.I.P. as very useful, providing the wound has been efficiently cleansed and dried. I regard its use as reprehensible unless the surgeon is sure that the wound is free from foreign material and haemorrhage completely stopped" (Lieut.-Colonel T. P. Dunhill). The method had great vogue in Britain and in particular was exploited at the Great Endell Street Hospital staffed by women. As with other methods, the most important "lesson," it would seem, is that there is no royal road through antisepsis to asepsis.

2. Means: Scientific Antiseptics. The genesis of the idea of these derives, in part at least, from a source that has a peculiar interest for Australians. Professor Dakin[50] extolled the researches of C. J. Martin and Miss Harriette Chick as having "done much to supply accurate information as to the laws of disinfection"—in particular that they stressed the analogy between ordinary chemical reactions and the process of disinfection.

Neutral Chlorine Compounds. "Dakin's solution" (neutral sodium hypochlorite) and "eusol" (Lorrain Smith, July, 1915) made available the powerful antiseptic properties of chlorine. By the use of polybasic acid—such as phosphoric, carbonic, or boric—the irritant alkaline reaction became amphoteric, thus making available to the surgeon "buffer solutions" of considerable antiseptic power but withal congenial to the human tissues. Both were widely employed for immediate disinfection as well as for irrigation and lavage.

Oxidisers. Hydrogen peroxide was widely used throughout the war; ozone had a vogue for a time.

The Synthetic Dyes. Flavine. ("Acri-flavine" or "trypaflavine.") Created some years before the war in Ehrlich's laboratory and used as a trypanicide, the antiseptic qualities of the drug were tried out by Carl Browning and co-workers in January, 1917. It was tested clinically at the Base and in June, 1917, more exactly in Third Army experimental C.C.S. by McNee and Drummond. Their report showed that used in

[50] "Biochemistry and War problems"—*British Medicine in the War, 1914-17, p. 13.*

strengths of 1 in 1,000 or for irrigation 1 in 5,000 while it "prevented inflammation," flavine did not sterilise rapidly any but slight wounds, and most ran the usual course—anaerobes predominating at first and later giving place to streptococci which persisted for from 2 to 3 weeks. Briefly the same conclusion was reached as with all other methods and means employed—*good results could be achieved by antiseptics provided the wound were first given effective surgical treatment.*

Logically, the subject of excision (the French *débridement*) presents itself in two distinct forms—(*a*) as a rational procedure evolved from the crude process of "mechanical cleansing of the wound," and (*b*) as a fortuitous, but not infrequent experience, by myiasis in men who had remained for some days unrescued. Of this many instances are recorded, salutary and otherwise, both in France and at Gallipoli.

The triumph of asepsis: excision

"Colonel David Cade, A.A.M.C., recalls a case at Pozières of a German who was wounded in No-Man's Land and brought in after four days to the R.A.P. with a leg smashed above the knee, and the wound such that gas gangrene would have been expected. It had however been flyblown, was full of maggots and all necrotic tissue had been consumed. There was no gas gangrene, and a clear 'line of demarcation' had formed. At the M.D.S. a 'butcher's' amputation removed the limb and next day the man was asking for a sausage; and was evacuated very well." (Note made in 1918 by the Medical Collator, A.I.F.)[51]

In remarkable and suggestive contrast with the antiseptic and physiological methods, the technique which initiated a new era in the surgery of war wounds, and far more than any other factor was the *raison d'être* of the new strategy for the casualty clearing stations, had behind it no elaborate campaign of research; rather, it was the direct result of clinical common sense applying established principles.

The practice known as excision or *débridement* of wounds was a logical extension of the crude methods of mechanical cleansing and draining of the "reaction" period, and probably suggested itself soon to many surgeons.[52] For developing this method of treatment, as also in its logical consequence—that

---

[51] This treatment was known to the Greeks. It may be suggested that the analogy to it is found in the use of B.I.P. and the salt pack rather than of excision; and that the action is chiefly mechanical and physiological—by promoting drainage—and only secondarily "antiseptic."

[52] A medical history of the war from a scientific and international standpoint is yet to be written—perhaps under the auspices of the League of Nations. The bibliography given in the *American Official Medical History* is international in character; that of the British History is somewhat parochial. Opportunity for assessing the surgical work of the Central Powers has not been available to the writer.

more searching and perilous adventure in wound surgery, the return to the immediate suture—the credit both of priority and precedence must be given to the French Service.

The idea of "*débridement*" as the essential factor in wound surgery would seem first to have been voiced by P. Riche[53] in October, 1914. M. Depage is commonly credited with its scientific development and most energetic advocacy. At the Interallied Surgical Conference in March, 1917, the French surgeons referred to the method as well established. Its combination with primary suture was rapidly developed during 1917.

In the British Service, with increasing care in the general clean up of wounds, individual surgeons both at the Base and the front were experimenting with procedure more exact than hitherto. The first published accounts of deliberate "excision" are those by Gray and Milligan.[54] The latter was an Australian, and his article, dated June, 1915, is here reproduced.

"**Excision**" in the B.E.F.

"After eight months of experience of the early treatment of projectile wounds . . . I desire to place on record a method of treatment which has given most gratifying results, and which, if practised thoroughly, will materially lessen the time a wounded man is absent from the firing line. In a modern projectile wound we have to deal with a varying amount of devitalised tissue and a varying amount of ingrained infected material, both of which are always present. The devitalised tissue varies in different wounds from a microscopical amount, through all quantities, to the gross obvious slough. The ingrained infected material is inseparably fixed to this devitalised tissue, and nothing short of the complete removal of the tissue can possibly get rid of the infected matter. Cleansing measures are placed at a great disadvantage, for only those

---
[53] *Bulletins et memoires de la Societé de Chirurgie, Paris, 14 Oct., 1914*—Quoted by *American Medical History, Vol. XI Surgery, Part I, p. 297.* The credit has also been claimed for Drs. Leriche and Gaudier of the French Army (Proceedings of the International Red Cross Conference at Paris, 1937).

The comparative slowness of the British Service in this development was doubtless largely due to the fact that the Anglo-French agreement required that so far as possible British casualties should be treated in Britain. This involved their rapid transit to the sea bases, and the Channel crossing. Development of *treatment* at the front was therefore made subservient to the prime purpose of *movement*. Moreover the structure of the British Medical Service, like that of the British Army, was primarily based on the needs of expeditions overseas. The "stationary" hospitals were intended to serve a long Line of Communications. The structure of the French, on the other hand, was based on readily accessible Hospital Centres; their front line and rear hospital systems were very closely co-ordinated.

[54] E. T. C. Milligan, late Major in the R.A.M.C., a graduate of Melbourne University who, at the outbreak of war, was engaged in special study in England and joined the R.A.M.C., author of "The Early Treatment of Projectile Wounds by Excision of the Damaged Tissues," *British Medical Journal, 26 June, 1915*. It will be recalled that the Battles of the Somme began on 1 July, 1916.

Colonel (later Sir Henry) Gray, Consulting Surgeon, B.E.F. (Rouen Base and Third Army), author of "Treatment of Gunshot Wounds by Excision and Primary Suture," *Journal of the Royal Army Medical Corps, June, 1915*; also *The Early Treatment of War Wounds* (London, Oxford University Press, 1919).

organisms which are spread loosely broadcast on the surfaces can be removed or inhibited in growth by antiseptics. The more important natural protective powers of the healthy body in which these wounds occur are also placed at a great disadvantage, for no vigorous opposition can be offered by devitalised tissue, and the healthy tissue is separated from the loosely scattered infected material on the surface of the wound by the layer of devitalised tissue bounding the wound, and this tissue also acts as a perfect culture medium.

"*The Method.* This consists in the extirpation of the devitalised tissues. An anaesthetic is given where indicated [local or general]. . . . The *wound of the skin* is boldly cut out with a sharp scalpel. It should be so completely removed that a clean healthy incised wound replaces the contused and infected wound made by the projectile. There should be nothing of the old wound remaining. The *wound of the superficial and deep fascia* should be treated in the same way. The *wound of the muscle* is dealt with in the same fashion. It presents, however, more difficulties because of the retraction of severed fibres, and because of the distance of the depths of the wound from the surface of the body. This latter difficulty can be happily overcome in many cases by making larger incisions.

"Removal of loose and fixed bits of obvious foreign and dead matter is, of course, essential. Ample exposure and drainage of the wound is necessary, and those wounds which are too extensive after the above treatment to retain a drainage tube do better than those in which a tube is necessary on account of their depth and narrowness. By this procedure the wound is put in the best possible conditions for the bactericidal actions of the tissues and the outpoured lymph. It is important to remark that it is not wise to impair the resisting and offensive powers of the artificially obtained healthy tissue surfaces by the use of strong or injurious antiseptics.

"*Results.* This method, when combined with the surgical essentials of perfect rest, cleanliness, and frequent suitable dressings has resulted in the healing of projectile wounds, without any appearance of pus in wounds of the skin and of the superficial fascia. In many wounds of muscle and bone, also, this gratifying result has been attained. In the treatment of some wounds of bone and muscle anatomical problems have prevented these principles of treatment from being thoroughly carried out, so that the results have not been as good. There have been no cases of generalised blood infection, nor of any spreading infection in the neighbourhood of the wound."

In a note, furnished for the purpose of the present history, and pointing a moral not likely to be superfluous in future wars,[55] Major Milligan wrote:—

Note by Major Milligan

"Quite early in the war, in 1914, while working at a Casualty Clear-

---
[55] Colonel Gray says: "It is curious . . . that the technique laid down for treatment of complicated types of wounds should have been so widely accepted as correct, although only after considerable delay, while that for the simpler types was neglected. . . . Several British and Colonial surgeons, however, practised the method in the early days of 1915. . . . It was not blessed by the general body of English-speaking surgeons, however, until it was discovered that our French confrères had also satisfactorily demonstrated its advantages." (*The Early Treatment of War Wounds*, H. M. W. Gray, *p. 158.*)

ing Station in Flanders, I was impressed with the idea that excision was called for. Opposition came from three quarters:—1. From the administrative officers of the R.A.M.C.; for it meant increase in staff, alteration of equipment and allotment of work, and more accommodation in order to submit the greater numbers of wounded to anaesthesia and operation. 2. From some consulting surgeons, who felt that it was unjustifiable to submit a man already badly wounded to further trauma even with a scalpel. Undoubtedly confidence in antiseptic treatment, and fear of spread of infection after operative interference, made some surgeons bitterly hostile to the procedure. 3. From junior medical officers who disliked the comparatively uninteresting work of administering the large numbers of anaesthetics required for carrying out excision of wounds.

"Opposition was so great locally that I first carried out excision of wounds under local anaesthesia, and general anaesthetics induced by myself and continued by an orderly; and this often at late hours and unknown to those in authority. At the request of a Consulting Surgeon of the Army, who opposed this treatment, my Commanding Officer ordered me to discontinue surgery; and only allowed me to return with the request that I should cease excision of wounds. . . . Sir Anthony Bowlby, the chief consultant of the B.E.F., expressed himself in agreement with my publication at the time. Sir Henry M. W. Gray, to whom War surgery owes so much, was carrying out the treatment independently at the Base in France, and soon afterwards advocated it energetically at the front. Under pressure of these opinions, and from their own convictions, many surgical specialists now took up the treatment; and the necessary administrative alterations were made by the R.A.M.C. for carrying it out.

"1. All early operative work was delegated to the Casualty Clearing Stations which were altered accordingly.

"2. Surgical Specialists and Anaesthetists were appointed to organise the surgery of Casualty Clearing Stations.

"3. Accommodation was made to enable four to six surgeons with their teams to operate at the same time so that large numbers of wounded were dealt with, teams working in shifts night and day during active fighting.

"The success of all antiseptic treatment depends on the preliminary excision of the wounds; as did also the good results of the Carrel-Dakin treatment; . . . and [it] paved the way for primary and secondary suture of wounds."[56]

Transition to new method

The technical experiments of Gray, Milligan, and doubtless hosts of others in the British Service were the reflections of action being taken along various lines, the general purpose of which was to procure *asepsis* in contaminated wounds. Of these lines of action the most important were the dissemination and co-

---

[56] A report of an address by Major Milligan, delivered in 1917, will also be found in the *M.J.A.*, 10 March, 1917, p. 201.

Some details of the technique necessary to the success of excision and of *débridement* will be given in *Vol. III*.

ordination of knowledge by extension of the system of *consultant surgeons* to the Armies in the field, and the creation of *surgical teams*. The arrangements for the Battle of the Somme included, indeed, a general move up of immediate surgery to the C.C.S. with the deliberate purpose of forestalling infection. During this great series of battles unlimited opportunity presented both for experiment and for the diffusion of knowledge.[57] From this time onward the surgical centre of gravity shifts to the front. Very gradually, in the B.E.F., "antiseptic" methods of treatment become adjuvant and secondary, being replaced, as the method of election, by "asepsis."[58]

The transition stage is illustrated by Fifth Army procedure during the German "Alberich" withdrawal to the Hindenburg Line.[59] A Circular Memorandum by Consulting Surgeon, Fifth Army (Colonel Maynard Smith, A.M.S.), 2nd April 1917, says:

"In practically all severe wounds admitted to C.C.S. it is found necessary to give anaesthetics to enable the damaged muscle, fascia, etc., bordering on the wound to be excised and foreign bodies removed, and to enable the surgeon to provide sufficient drainage. This is a preliminary to any form of treatment whether by 'Carrel,' salt pack or any drier method of dressing. It is this measure alone which diminishes the danger of severe anaerobic infection. The early and thorough adoption of this line of treatment (which is now the universal practice in casualty clearing stations) is interfered with if anaesthetics have been administered shortly before their arrival at the C.C.S." [They should be given] "only where the medical officer considers it absolutely essential and . . . when an anaesthetic has to be given for such an emergency operation, an attempt should be made to carry out the complete operation mentioned above."[60]

While effective operating was thus moving up from the Base Hospital to the C.C.S., urgent operating was moving rearwards, from the

---

[57] For the means whereby technical improvements were translated into practice see pp. 395-6.

[58] The "antiseptic" and the "aseptic" schools have fought, each for its pet abstraction, oblivious of the fact that the purpose of each is to promote, by direct action against the microbe, the efforts of nature in her fight against infection. Continental surgeons faced the verbal issue clearly if not very helpfully. Thus M. Depage (Interallied Surgical Conference) "On utilisera uniquement les pansements secs: qu'ils aient été préparés par la méthode *aseptique* (*chaleur*) ou par la méthode *antiseptique* (*action chimique*), peu importe." (*Archives de Médecine et de Pharmacie, Tome lxviii—1917, p. 49.*) Such narrow usage seems unhelpful. A wound through the protective layer of body cells must if possible be kept or made aseptic, *i.e.* free from pathogenic germs. By action promoting asepsis we seek to exclude germs from the wound; by antiseptic measures—heat, light, chemicals—we attack the germs directly.

"*Infected*" and "*contaminated*" *wounds*. These terms as applied to wounds were often used indiscriminately, but clinically the distinction was fundamental. *The time limits which distinguish contamination of the wound from infection of the tissues determined the structure of the medical scheme of evacuation.*

[59] See Chapter vi.

[60] To obviate the necessity of their use in fractured femurs the Thomas splint was advised and instructions for the first time given as to the method of its use in first aid—even "at times" at a R.A.P.

Field Ambulance to the C.C.S., as is evidenced by the following incident. On 11th April, 1917, the officer commanding No. 45 C.C.S., wrote to D.M.S., Fifth Army, that cases from the 13th Australian Field Ambulance had been anaesthetised and partly operated upon at the field ambulance and "had to be re-anaesthetised at the C.C.S." He sent a list of cases "excised and drained" and "excised and dressed" at the field ambulance. *13/4/17.* D.M.S. Fifth Army writing to D.D.M.S. I Anzac, required an explanation and referred him to the "instructions." *19/4/17.* O.C., 13th Field Ambulance (Lieut.-Colonel J. B. St. Vincent Welch) replied to the following effect: Seven officers attended to 771 cases. "We had six tables in commission all the time and thus did not hold up any which would have reached the C.C.S. earlier." The serious cases were numerous and the medical officers believed that the general washing up and placing patients in pyjamas, excising of wounds, and draining had been of assistance. "We always found that recent wounds can be excised without anaesthetic and with no pain to the patient, later they appear to become sensitive again."

The last step: immediate suture of excised wounds

In the meantime, chiefly in the French Army, individual surgeons had been experimenting—as did Larrey in the 18th-19th century—with the possibilities of immediate suturing. In the British Army in August, 1916, Rutherford Morison envisaged the immediate closure of wounds in connection with his B.I.P.[61] In the French Army *débridement* was widely exploited with the same end in view.[62]

End of experimental stage

The "new surgery" of the Great War cannot better be summed up than by quoting the conclusions unanimously arrived at in the Interallied Surgical Conference of March, 1917.[63]

"(1) It is desirable that the organization of the Medical Service should be so directed as to permit of continuity in the supervision of the treatment of the wounded men.

"(2) At the first aid stations, and especially in the trenches, surgical measures should be restricted to the minimum. They should be limited to dealing with complications which might prove immediately fatal in

---

[61] Used for this purpose B.I.P. gave poor results, but as an accessory to *débridement* it maintained a place throughout the war in the "delayed primary suture."

[62] In particular by René Lemaitre. "It is generally conceded that the first primary sutures were performed in July of 1915, by René Lemaitre. From July, 1915, to July, 1917, in 1,046 primary sutures, he had 944 complete cures, 39 partial cures, and 13 failures. . . . From July, 1917, to February, 1918, Lemaitre performed 1,618 primary sutures, with 1,555 complete cures, 44 partial cures, and 19 failures." *American Official Medical History, Vol. XI, Pt. 1, p. 296,* quoting *Medical Bulletin, Paris,* 1918, i, Supplement, March, 292.

[63] *Archives de Médicine et de Pharmacie Militaires, comptes-rendus de la Conférence Chirurgicale Interalliée pour l'étude des Plaies de guerre*—1st Session 15-16 March, 1917, pp. 103-4. A summary of the discussions at this and the next conference was published in the B.E.F. in October, 1917, as "General Principles guiding the treatment of Wounds in War."

character, and to the protection of the wounds from repeated contamination. The wound is never to be explored or washed, and should be covered by a dry dressing either sterile or antiseptic in character.

"(3) Rapid transport to one of the casualty clearing stations is essential.

"(4) It is an advantage if each of these units has one or more advanced sections nearer to the firing line, for the reception of patients seriously wounded (such as those suffering from shock, profuse haemorrhage, wounds of the chest, abdomen, etc.)

"(5) All wounds of war must be considered to be either contaminated or infected.

"(6) The object of treatment should be:—(a) To prevent development of infection if the wound is still in the stage of contamination, or to procure sterilization if infection has already developed. (b) To permit of secondary suture, when sterilization is realized.

"(7) In the primary treatment of the wound, excision of contused and lacerated tissue and the removal of fragments of clothing or foreign bodies must be considered as the rule, except in certain cases where the patient cannot be kept under supervision.

"(8) When the wound has thus been properly prepared, primary suture may give good results, especially in the case of wounds of the joints. Primary suture is not to be undertaken unless the wound is only of some hours' standing (at the most eight hours), and only when the surgeon can retain the patient under his own observation for fifteen days.

"(9) If primary suture be not undertaken, secondary suture should be performed when the clinical signs indicate that the wound is surgically sterile.

"(10) The progress towards sterilization should be systematically controlled by a series of bacteriological examinations, and a 'curve' should be constructed to allow the degree of sterility to be determined.

"(11) When patients have to be hurriedly evacuated, and definite preparation of the wound postponed, a dressing, the action of which should continue during the period of transport, may be usefully applied. Further researches on this subject are needed.

"(12) Several methods for the progressive sterilization of wounds are available, which allow of the routine practice of secondary suture."

The year 1917 offered unrivalled opportunity for the tryout of methods which experiment had shown worthy of further exploitation, and for implementing these by

THIRD STAGE: Exploitation March, 1917– March, 1918 extension of the system of casualty clearing stations and making the work in the field ambulances subservient to theirs; the effort in the ambulances was now more particularly directed to treatment of the man rather than of the wound. The huge casualties of Arras and Third Ypres[64] coincided with

---

[64] During 1917-18 1,140,398 wounded were admitted to British casualty clearing stations in France (*British Official Medical History Statistics, p. 27*).

the extreme developments of stationary warfare. This circumstance made it easier for the C.C.S., its equipment and establishment, and in particular the use of specially trained operating teams, to be developed to the utmost so as to ensure that as many as possible of the wounded who required it should receive operation under anaesthetic.[65] In particular, the possibility of the immediate or early closing of wounds was exploited to the utmost. "Experimental stations" in the various armies[66] investigated the possibilities of excision with suture—"primary" and "delayed primary";[67] and of various antiseptic and lymphagogue accessories, flavine, B.I.P., salt pack, etc., which have already been described, although experiment with them continued actively throughout this stage.

The situation at the end of this stage is shown in the report of the Surgical Specialist of No. 2 A.C.C.S. (Lieut.-Colonel Balcombe Quick) for February, 1918.

"During the month," it says, "both Lieut.-Colonel Quick and Major Barton have visited the Research Centre—No. 10 C.C.S., Remy Siding —to see the work that is being done there in connection with the early closure of wounds. The object of this research has been to find out in what class of case, with how much safety and how much success, recently inflicted wounds may be closed after thorough excision; or, when it is not judged safe to close at once, whether early secondary closure is not practicable. A very considerable degree of success has been obtained, both by primary suture and by packing for 48-72 hours with flavine gauze and suturing at the end of this period. The balance of opinion at this centre appears to show:—(1) that the excision is the essential feature of the operation, the actual antiseptic (flavine, B.I.P., ether,

---

[65] The proportion of patients operated on under anaesthetic in the casualty clearing stations varied very greatly with the conditions of the fighting. This is shown in the graph on *p. 372*, which gives the experience of No. 2 A.C.C.S. Of the figures quoted 30 per cent. received operative treatment. Sir Anthony Bowlby (*Surgery, Vol. I, p. 239*) states that "in quiet periods in a casualty clearing station, medical officers put 50 per cent. of wounded on the operating table, and, to avoid dangerous operations at the base, had to operate on 25 per cent." The figures for the Battle of Arras are placed at 24 per cent. In the Battle of Estaires (April, 1918) the proportion varied from 9 per cent. on 9 April and 14 per cent. on the 10th (2,615 cases) to 53 per cent. on the 16th (252) and 51 per cent. on the 19th (395), an average of 23.5 per cent. for some 13,000 cases over two weeks. The balance would require operation in the General Hospitals at the Base.

[66] No. 26 General Hospital at Etaples was the first of these and was set apart in June, 1916. Subsequently the First, Second and Third Armies set aside casualty clearing stations for research and experimental work in wound treatment in connection with antiseptics, excision, primary and secondary suture, and the prophylaxis and treatment of wound shock.

[67] For the technique of these procedures *see Vol. III*. Here it may be said that by "primary" suture was meant suture at the time of excision; "delayed primary" suture was that done after a delay of 24 hours or so to permit evacuation to the Base—but not involving the approximation of granulating surfaces ("secondary suture").

etc.) then applied being of secondary importance; and (2) that packing, with early secondary closure, is the safest procedure if early evacuation of the patient be necessary.

"For some time past we have been carrying out operations on the same, if rather a less ambitious plan, and the results have been satisfactory, and in no case, as far as I am aware, has harm resulted. It is perhaps a little doubtful if operations of this type, which take up a fair amount of time, can be carried out as successfully in times of stress."

FOURTH STAGE: 1918

On 21st March, 1918, Ludendorff struck. Thereafter, the war enters a new phase. The narrative of military events in that phase is found in the last section of this volume, and consideration of the fourth and final stage of wound treatment during the war is therefore deferred to a later page.[68]

THE TREATMENT OF THE WOUNDED MAN

The results of wounding *per se* to the wounded man were, as we have seen, pain, haemorrhage, and vital depression ("collapse" and "wound shock"). It is obvious that if "excision" or any other form of surgical intervention was to serve the seriously wounded man, treatment of these direct effects was of extreme importance. Its several therapeutic activities were to him as vitamins are to infection.

Though perhaps the most conspicuous weapon of warfare, the infliction of pain is not in itself the most important.[69]

The problem of pain

But its association with wounds is so general as to make alleviation an important humane duty of a medical service in modern warfare.

The immediate nervous and psychic effect of a severe wounding was a "primary shock" in which the element of pain might be inconspicuous. The local analgesia produced might permit of the removal of shattered limbs and of much manipulation without obvious pain, though possibly to the patient's detriment. And though after reaction had set in, the pain from wounds might at times be great—even to make men beg for death—with effective management it might even in the worst

---
[68] See Chapter xxv (pp. 782-7).
[69] The only weapon used in the Great War in which pain *per se* was the sole effective agent was the gas diphenyl-chlorarsene, the inhalation of which through the nasal passages even in a concentration of 1 part in 200 million of air, though devoid of any risk to life or serious after effects, produced for a short time such agony as wholly to disable.

wounds be surprisingly moderate.[70] "Management" includes the whole complex of movement and treatment—"pain" may in effect be a reactive demand for rest as well as a reflex call to action. Hilton's testament of "Rest and Pain" has full support from the war.

Pain and "Shock." One of the most striking features of very severe wounding was the progressively diminished general sensibility to pain and stimulation that was associated with "secondary" wound shock.[71]

Measures of relief. The influence of rescue on *psychic pain* has been referred to.[72] The one conspicuous and permanent measure for the relief of physical pain of wounds was to *remove its cause, i.e.* the wound itself when acting as a *noxium*. If furnished by the ideal method, as by excision and primary suture, relief might be immediate and absolute; and even far less effective measures of treatment if combined with *rest*, often wholly replaced anodynes. Foreign bodies, if not producing tension, were often left for a more convenient season without causing pain. The rôle in war of "anaesthesia," local and general is dealt with in *Vol. III.*

Morphia. As in civil medicine, opium, chiefly in the form of morphia, was the most important drug in the military pharmacopoeia. It was given at the direction of the R.M.O. or other officer, usually in ¼ to ½ grain hypodermically from a 5 per cent. solution. The technique of its "exhibition" was one of the most important aspects of front line work; many men died from its misuse, many others sustained great needless pain. The action taken to ensure the co-ordination of procedures at each stage of evacuation by the Field Medical Card included the administration of morphia and A.T.S. and was the subject of the first entry in the long train of "records and returns" which followed the wounded man from R.A.P. to "Con. Camp" and ended with the Medical Board Paper (*Army Form W. 179*).

The following from the war diary of No. 3 A.C.C.S. (Lieut.-Col. R. D. Campbell), February, 1918, brings this matter of morphia into the general scheme of evacuation:—

"It is undoubted that, in spite of moderately favourable weather, wounded cases have arrived frequently in poor condition. That this is due to delay in collection and transport I cannot agree, as for all stretcher wounded admitted in this month, an average of 6 hours

---

[70] The pain from an ordinary severe bullet wound of a limb not involving a long bone is described by Capt. Frank Kerr, an Australian who was wounded on 8 Aug., 1916, on the Somme while serving with the R.A.M.C. ". . . Dressed all wounded found in open . . . getting into communication trench, seen by snipers. . . . Hot needle sensation in right hip and concussion down bone to foot—knocked into trench on to left shoulder and temporarily paralysed left arm. Sensation as if hot fluid being poured all over limb—grab femoral artery. . . . Crawl along trench on one leg to find stretcher. . . . Car to Mametz (F. Amb.) then to Doullens (C.C.S.). Uncomfortable ride, quiet night, wound drained and dressed. *9.8.16.* Feeling of absolute bliss. Wound painful at times. *11.8.16.* Left for Rouen, very comfortable."

[71] Professor Sherrington explained this phenomenon by the interesting hypothesis that the ingoing impulses are "blocked" by an increase in the natural resistance at the synapse between the afferent nerve cells or neurones lying wholly within the central nervous system. Sherrington's view that this is a protective reaction seems difficult to accept for secondary shock on clinical grounds, which suggest rather a morbific (exhaustion) effect of the trauma producing the morbid state. (*c.f. British Official Medical History, Surgery, Vol. I, p. 89.*)

[72] See pp. 275-6.

10 minutes has elapsed between wounding and arrival at this C.C.S. In many cases, and notably in cases of urgency, only three hours might elapse between wounding and arrival, in spite of the fact that the C.C.S. is about ten miles behind the line. The factors which have been operative in producing the generally unsatisfactory condition of patients on admission are in my opinion:

"(1) The severe type of case admitted. . . .

"(2) Too frequent handling. . . .

"(3) The very limited use of Morphia. Out of 66 stretcher wounded only 10 had had morphia, and in each case only one dose. In only two was the dose of ¼ gr. exceeded. This abstention from the use of Morphia is the direct result of the present teaching in the Army, largely based on the 'acidosis' theory. While realising that some months ago Morphia was given in excess, I am not satisfied that the pendulum has not now swung too far the other way, and think that the influence of intolerable pain in the aggravation of shock should be considered."[73]

The means prescribed by teaching and tradition and implemented by equipment for the control of haemorrhage are briefly referred to later. The only significant development in this connection in the war, but one of major importance, was the scientific and very extensive use of intra-venous infusion of saline fluid and transfusion of blood for the treatment or prophylaxis of its graver effects. The matter is so intimately related to the treatment of "wound shock" that it may properly be examined in that connection.

Haemorrhage

In the course of the war the term *"wound shock"* came into general use to identify the clinical syndrome associated with the collapse of the vital powers which may follow on the sustaining of serious physical injury. The physiological and therapeutic problems presented by it were of great complexity. The reason for this may readily be discerned in the fact that the clinical syndrome thus identified derives from the very sources of organic life. The self-sustaining chemical actions and reactions and corresponding physiological processes that are the physical component of life are of immense complexity and diversity; and it might well have been foretold that their degradation, whether gradual or rapid, to the simplicity and quietude of death, would be characterised by a corresponding complexity in the resulting disorders of function not readily amenable to discrimination by clinical analysis into specific "syndromes," "disorders," or "diseases."

Vital depression

---

[73] It is perhaps permissible in this connection to refer to recent work on the prevention of wound shock by spinal anaesthesia—proposed in the war.

That such prescience were fully justified in relation to gradual decay, the never ending problems of "chronic disease" as met with in peace give ample proof. The Great War, first in the history of medical science, showed that it is scarcely less true of the rapid failure of the various vital functions brought about by physical injury, such as severe wounding. One of the most striking features of medical work in the war is to be found in the initial emergence of the pre-war concept "surgical shock" as a specific and unique syndrome, "wound shock," and its subsequent gradual resolution in a complex of pathological degradations. These, under continued adverse conditions, might move inexorably to an irreversible master-failure in a reduction of the total blood-volume to below 60 per cent. and its stagnation in the peripheral circulation indicated by a persisting fall of systolic blood-pressure to below 80 mm. of Hg.; further descent would lead to total heart failure and death. The identification of the causes that might bring about such an impasse, and the detection and exploitation of any opportunity for therapeutic intervention, constitute a remarkable episode in the history of scientific medicine. Until the last years of this present decade the subject remained much as left by the war and its immediate aftermath of war-engendered experiment. As with its *vis-à-vis*, the problem of streptococcal infection, if with less dramatic results, the past few years have seen a renewed interest and experiment; so that indeed on the scientific side the interest of war experience is chiefly historical.[74] From the orgy of clinical observation on unanaesthetised animals (battle-casualties) and corresponding series of laboratory experiments on anaesthetised animals, (cats or rabbits in England, and dogs, in America and on the Continent) the concept "traumatic shock" emerged from the war an almost crudely clinical

---

[74] The whole subject of "Shock" is much in need of comprehensive analysis and re-integration of relevant facts and current ideas regarding its essential nature and pathogenesis. The evolution of the general concept "shock" as connoting specific clinical syndromes each with a corresponding morbid anatomy and—to coin a needed term—morbid physiology is a peculiar and not particularly illuminating one. In effect, we say "Shock"—of various designations—is caused by the shock of a "shock." Lieut.-Col. Sir F. W. Mott, F.R.S., in 1917-18 investigated "the changes in the central nervous system occurring in various forms of shock"; the material employed including: "Brains of fatal cases of shell shock, with and without burial, and probable gas-poisoning. Brains of three cases of fatal wound shock. Brain of shock from extensive burns. Brains of anaphylactic shock. Brain of fatal shock from contusion of heart. Three brains of animals injected with histamine. Brain from death under anaesthetic." (*Medical Research Committee's Report No. 26, dated 14 March, 1919, pp. 44-5.*)

one, reflecting on the pathogenic side a curious congeries of causative and contributing agencies and their effects, such as psychic and physiological "pain," and their reflex effects such as acapnia; "excitement" and fear and their related glandular (hormonic) reactions; haemorrhage, with resulting anoxaemia, and acidosis; thermogenic failure; cardio-vascular failure; neurogenic failure; septic toxaemia; other intoxications as by an "H" substance. On the other hand the technique developed for the prevention and treatment of the morbid states concerned was very exact and successful. An account of war research will be found in *Appendix No. 14*. It must suffice here to define the syndrome and note the progress of ideas on the matter as reflected in official instructions.

The Nature of Traumatic Shock. From early in the war the clinical syndrome to which the term "wound shock" came to be applied was somewhat vaguely conceived as having a dual constitution as "primary" and "secondary." Precise definition and discrimination between the two did not however reach the plane even of clinical exactitude. The indiscriminate use of the word "shock" had, indeed, brought about a veritable "Babel," whereby causes and effects, morbific agents and morbid states, were confused. We may perhaps trace the genesis of the idea of a "primary" and a "secondary" type of wound shock in every-day experiences of the front. The first picture presents a robust and healthy soldier in a state of collapse—pallid, forehead bedewed with cold sweat, *facies* anxious and apprehensive, pulse imperceptible, himself presently to become unconscious—the cause of the condition being the fact that he is about to receive a hypodermic injection of T.A.B. or is being given first aid for some trifling wound. A second picture presents a similar man seen within a short time of the receipt of a serious wound. The clinical syndrome of vascular hypotension, faintness, and collapse might again be present as a temporary phenomenon; to pass off with reaction. A third experience showed the wounded man who, leaving the R.A.P. in good condition arrives at the C.C.S. pallid, cold, collapsed, requiring major acts of resuscitation before reaction may be induced. The superficial resemblance between the psycho- and neuro-genic collapse after wounding, and the clinical syndrome characteristic of "secondary" shock as commonly understood[75] (which reflects and "is proportionate to the sum of the intensities" of a congeries of morbific agencies) led to the creation of a clinical artefact, "primary" wound shock, as a distinct morbid entity; instead of a functional disorder, reflecting chiefly the psycho- and neuro-genic elements in vital collapse. At the

---

[75] It would seem that this confusion may have come as well from the other end (so to speak) by the confusing of "secondary" shock with the condition so known in the earliest days of "shock"—the 1870's—wherein death ensued many days after the injury (see *e.g.* O'Shaughnessy, *B.M.J.*, 13 April, 1935, p. 793). The official "Manual of Injuries and Diseases of War," *Jan., 1918*, is content to confound this confusion, so the clinical picture is clear, thus:—"*Wound shock.* The condition known as shock is familiar to all. A precise definition has yet to be found.

end of the war the idea of wound shock as a continuous development from morbid processes set in train at once by the wound was accepted as a proper, if a provisional, basis for treatment.

The onset and course of this terrible condition[76] has conveniently been described[77] as falling in three types or groups: (i) compensated; (ii) partially compensated; (iii) uncompensated. In the first type of case the patient's general condition is good with no symptoms of distress except for the local pain of the wound and general weakness. He may be pale, the pulse rate 90-110, systolic blood pressure above 100 mm., and the blood volume not below 80 per cent. In the second group the patient's general condition is not so good. "There is usually a history of a smart haemorrhage. He is very pale, restless, thirsty, and vomits readily. The extremities are cold and partially anaesthetic to painful stimuli. The pulse-rate is rapid, 120-140, and difficult to count; the systolic blood-pressure is, as a rule, below 90, usually 70-80 mm. Hg. The blood volume ranges between 65-75 per cent." In an uncompensated case the patient is in an extremely serious condition; as a rule restless, very thirsty but liable to vomit at once if given fluid by the mouth. The extremities are very cold to the touch, the pulse cannot be felt, the blood pressure has fallen below 60 mm. Hg. On auscultation the heart-rate will be found to be 120-160. The blood volume is below 65 per cent. of the normal.

Professor J. Fraser[78] sums up the situation in the severely shocked man as a therapeutic problem:—

"With the establishment of a low blood pressure, something in the nature of a vicious circle comes into play. . . . It will continue to a fatal issue [or] until some link in the chain is broken and the error of the blood pressure is overcome."

The following notes on the four official statements from

: . . . Pure shock, that is a state of extreme depression of the vital functions, without apparently adequate cause and possibly ending in death, has been met with. On the other hand, shock as seen in war is usually the result of one or more of the following factors. . . . Shock may be (a) primary or (b) secondary. (a) Primary shock comes on almost immediately after the receipt of the wound. The patient passes into a state of collapse. . . . At this stage the pulse rate and blood pressure may or may not show a great departure from the normal. (b) Secondary shock manifests itself later. . . . Both (a) and (b) are greatly aggravated by loss of blood, sepsis (sic), and mental perturbation." Gray (loc. cit. 1919, p. 81) finds it "necessary to distinguish between two conditions, namely, *primary shock*, or the collapse immediately supervening on the infliction of a severe wound, and *secondary shock*, which develops later as the result of such factors as exposure to cold, pain, haemorrhage, movement, anxiety, exhaustion, and all the other harmful influences associated with a long journey to the casualty clearing station."

[76] Thus Prof. John Fraser whose war work was of outstanding merit.—"Operation shock or surgical shock . . . is one of those factors which have delayed and curtailed the evolution of surgical progress. Were it possible to eliminate its appearance, the surgical horizon would correspondingly enlarge. . . . In the surgery of childhood and of accident, and in that most extreme form of accidental surgery, the surgery of war, surgical shock has ever played a formidable part." (Sixth meeting of the International Society of Surgery: *British Journal of Surgery*, 1923-4, Vol. 11, p. 410.)

[77] By Capt. N. M. Keith, R.A.M.C., "Blood volume in wound shock," *M.R.C. Reports, 1919, Series 26, p. 39.* The idea of *reaction* is preserved.

[78] *British Official Medical History, Surgery Vol. I, p. 97.*

headquarters B.E.F. on surgical procedure brings the subject to the beginning of 1918. So far as such official pronouncements may do so, these reflect the constantly changing picture of current practice at the front. There in the last phase of the war, largely through the influence of the Consulting Surgeons medical practice reacted to advances in knowledge with a facility scarcely approached in peace.

(1) In *"Circular Memorandum No. 6"* (March, 1915) the term "shock" does not appear. Reference is confined to the statement that "men who have been left lying out for a day or two are often so severely collapsed that it is advisable to use subcutaneous injections of saline solution, and to administer food and stimulants before attempting to dress the wounds."

(2) The official *Memorandum on the treatment of injuries in war* (July, 1915) devotes a single paragraph to "the condition of wounded men." "The majority of gunshot wounds," it says, "do not inflict very serious injury, and so do not cause material shock or collapse"—a statement which perhaps reflects the restrictions of rescue work at this time—but "in every convoy there are always some men in a serious state of collapse." The "causes" of this had by this time been clearly identified. Normal saline by subcutaneous or intravenous injection, or per rectum "if collapse very severe," was commended.

By this time the casualty clearing stations had become the chief operating centre, and the modern technique of war surgery was developing. " 'Moribund' patients were put into warm beds"; in special wards. 1916 and "The Somme" were, however, tragic for the wounded man. To the terrors of transport to the C.C.S. far in rear, was added the fact that the peculiarly British fetish, saline infusions, dominated the situation. The tragedies that lie behind the term "most disappointing," applied by the British Official Historian to the results, can readily be visualised against the background of our *Chapters IV-VII*. Though Professor Bayliss' historic paper on the use of colloidal infusions was published in August, 1916,[79] and in February, 1917, the Medical Research Committee issued a special memorandum on "Surgical shock and allied conditions," neither Australian records nor the British history disclose any official publication until the following, in October, 1917:—

(3) *General principles guiding the treatment of wounds in war* was based on the conclusions adopted by the Interallied Surgical Conference of May, 1917. Here we find "traumatic shock" defined as "a disturbance in functional equilibrium, characterised by reactions of the depressing class, which may even extend to death," the "essential elements" of which are discerned as "a fall in the body temperature and the arterial blood pressure." The treatment set out features "alkaline infusion" against "acidosis"; neither gum-saline infusion nor blood transfusion are mentioned.

August, 1917, saw the formation by the Medical Research Committee of its "Special Investigation Committee" for the study of "surgical

---

[79] *Proceedings of the Royal Society, B., Vol. 39, 1916.*

shock and allied conditions"; and about the same time, the initiation in the armies in France of the campaign of research in surgical treatment to which reference has already been made. Thereafter events move with increasing momentum. ·An event of major importance was the attachment from the American Expeditionary Force of men of world-wide repute in this subject.

(4) The *Manual of injuries and diseases of war* issued in January, 1918, contains ten pages devoted to "wound shock" and another two to "transfusion of blood." Part of its reference, in relation to "primary" and "secondary" shock has been quoted.[80] The treatment prescribed was designed to combat "three main conditions" (a) loss of body heat, (b) a low blood pressure, and (c) a decreased alkalinity of the blood; and was divided into that to be adopted in (a) the "forward area," and (b) the casualty clearing station.

Here, for the present, the matter may be left and the reader referred to *pages 659-64, 782-7*, and to *Appendix No. 14*.

STAGES OF TREATMENT DURING EVACUATION

It is hoped that the reader will have derived from the foregoing some useful information concerning the problems associated with the pathology of wounds and their treatment by general surgery during the Great War. But no valid concept of military surgery on the Western Front can be obtained unless full allowance is made for the two factors which most of all determined its clinical application in the field, namely, *military exigency* and *medical organisation*.

(1) *Military Exigency*. In heavy engagements the rush of casualties made movement more urgent than treatment. The surgical centre of gravity was forced back again to the base, and only the most severe and urgent types of wound were then dealt with in the zone of the field formations.[81]

(2) *Medical Organisation: Co-ordination of Procedures*. As the war progressed the treatment of wounds and of wounded men developed into an ordered and progressive campaign of surgical intervention, interposed with increasing deliberation and precision, at critical stages in the clinical situation, or in convenient eddies in the course of the stream of casualties moving from the front line in France to the hospitals in Britain. The procedure at each point, and in each type of trauma, was determined by accumulated tradition, which gradually crystallised in official instructions. More and more exactly these various stages were determined by the *needs of the case* rather than by the *structure of the medical system*.

With the proviso that the facilities for treatment conformed,

---

[80] See footnote *pp. 337-8*.
[81] See footnote 65 on *p. 332*; footnote 31 on *p. 407*; and *pp. 621-22*.

perforce, closely to the military "situation"[82] the surgical procedures proper to the various stages of evacuation of an Australian from the Western Front may roughly be defined as follows:—

The elements in early treatment

1. "First aid" was given at the hands of the regimental stretcher-bearers and at the R.A.P. where also, as well as at the ambulance relays and collecting post, pain was assuaged and some mental and physiological rest, sustainment, and warmth were often provided.

2. Surgical emergencies were met, A.T.S. administered and measures for the prevention of "secondary" wound shock and first-aid treatment of gassing carried out, sustainment (warmth, fluid, and food) provided, and if necessary rest secured, at the A.D.S. and Field Hospital (M.D.S.); or at an advanced operating or "shock" centre for special "untransportable" cases.

3. Contingent on the military situation, effective operation—such as excision and primary suture—was performed, and the treatment of secondary wound shock and of gas wounding carried out, at the advanced operating centres, the C.C.S., or the Base Hospitals.

4. Secondary surgery, and after-treatment, were carried out at the Expeditionary Base Hospitals and hospitals in England; and the former also undertook:—

(a) Primary operation, particularly in slighter cases during "rushes" of wounded; (b) the completion of delayed primary suture; continued treatment of salt pack, B.I.P. and Carrel-Dakin cases; (c) surgery of foreign bodies; (d) surgery of secondary "septic" infections—in particular by the strepto- and staphylococci; (e) surgery of special types of wounds, such as femurs, spinal and head cases, and extensive and multiple woundings unfit for the Channel crossing.

5. "Consecutive" surgery (as it may for convenience be termed) such as the consecutive treatment of fractures and the surgery of sequestra, foreign bodies, fistulae, and sinuses, the empyema stage of chests; secondary amputations; the secondary consequences of cerebral, vascular, neural and tendon injuries, were undertaken in the General Hospitals in Britain.

6. Convalescence took place in the Australian and British Auxiliaries; which also dealt with cases coming under headings 5 and 7.

7. Reparative—orthopaedic and prosthetic—surgery, and artificial replacements, were carried out chiefly in special hospitals in Britain, such as Southall and Sidcup, and in Australia.

8. For Australian soldiers interim treatment in preparation for the last-named—as massage, electrical stimulation, and remedial exercises; and also "vocational training" and "re-education" were carried out at No. 2 Command Depot, on hospital ships and hospital transports.

Leaving the major surgical problems special to the C.C.S.,

---

[82] Readers of *Vol. I* will recall instances of overlapping—as in the work done by field ambulance on the "black ships" at Gallipoli. Apparently the same conditions obtained in the first phase of the war in France. Only at the relatively static extremes, the front line and the home base, were the factors in the situation more or less stable.

Base Hospitals, and hospitals in Britain to be referred to in the succeeding chapters, we now pass to a review, necessarily cursory and incomplete, of the treatment of wounds and wounded men at the various posts and stations between the front line and the C.C.S.[83] Certain therapeutic problems, however, namely the procuring for the wounded men of rest, warmth, fluid and food—in brief the problem of vital maintenance—entered into the situation at every stage, and a word must first be said about these.

Rest. "The therapeutic value of rest has been recognised by surgeons of all periods. It constituted the fundamental principle of Hunter's practice."[84]

"The most important elements in combating the development of profound secondary shock are rest, both mental and physical, and warmth."[85]

"In every case the infected man will need to be kept at rest; and the really heavily infected will require to be kept at *absolute rest*."[86]

Of all therapeutic measures this was in the war the most difficult to achieve. Its great importance was at times lost sight of—as in the *furore* for rapid evacuation which in 1917 followed the discovery that sepsis might be prevented by early operation. From the front line to the C.C.S. the promotion of rest, local and corporal—as by careful handling, effective splinting, timely postponement of movement or of operation, and alleviation of pain—often made the difference between the success or failure of subsequent treatment. That the quest for rest only too often fails is one of the most poignant agonies of war. It could be promoted by exact training and routine, by forethought in the maintenance of equipment, such as splints and stretchers, and of transport; and by effective *liaison* between the officers responsible for movement and treatment respectively.

Warmth. Experience in France emphasised the profound therapeutic importance of a clear recognition of the fact that two distinct factors are concerned in body heat—(a) the internal production of heat, and its conservation, and (b) the artificial supply. Thus unwarmed blankets were of little use to a man whose thermogenic powers were in abeyance; so were hot drinks without conservation, as by dry clothes, effectively applied blankets, and "ground sheet." The following list of appropriate measures reflects every-day experience on the French front—

Positive (by external supply). Food and oxygen for internal com-

---

[83] Apart from the strictly surgical manuals no official handbook was provided to guide medical officers in their field work. This serious hiatus in training and instruction was met by special action in each army. A handbook *The Treatment of Wounded Men in Regimental Aid Posts and Field Ambulances*, compiled for Third Army by Col. H. M. W. Gray, A.M.S., and Capt. K. M. Walker, R.A.M.C., and printed in the field on 8 Dec., 1917, was a model of what such manuals should be. It is not proposed to enter here into details which should be available in convenient form in official handbooks.

[84] Sir Arthur Keith, *Menders of the Maimed*, *p.* 25.

[85] Colonel H. M. W. Gray, *Early Treatment of War Wounds*, *p.* 6.

[86] Sir Almroth Wright, Official Memorandum, May, 1916, *Treatment of Infected Wounds*, *p.* 19.

bustion. Administration of warmth by hot drinks and hot food, clysters and saline infusions; or of warmed air, from fuel and primus stoves and car exhaust; hot bottles and bricks, and warmed blankets.

Negative (by conservation). Blankets, dry clothes, ground sheet, shelter, such as dugouts, huts and tents.

The supply of oxygen in the form of blood is dealt with under transfusion.[87] In heat *conservation* apart from the external temperature the most serious adverse factor was wet, and mal-use of blankets. To be effective *the technique of the blanket* called for procedure as exact as the application of the Thomas splint and it should equally be a part of the routine drill of the Medical Corps. The supply of blankets to the R.A.P. lay with the bearer division and Battalion Q.M. The duty of forming dumps of these supplies lay equally with units, Division, Corps, and Army.

For every type of hurt or stage of treatment no act of sustainment was of greater importance than the "administration" of artificial warmth. Probably the most effective mode of administration of heat was by hot drinks; less so by parenteral intravenous infusions. In the Great War the oil stove was an invaluable item of equipment, and an article of this nature should be a liberal issue at every level of evacuation. With its help it was possible even in the R.A.P. to apply

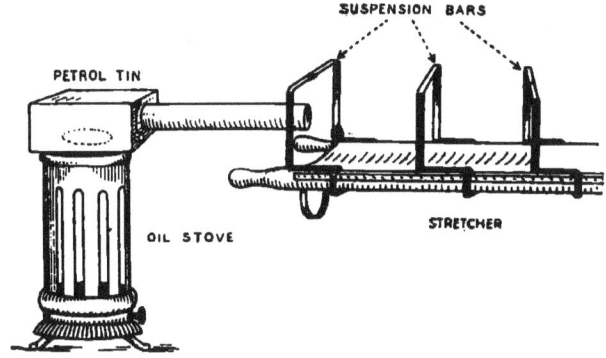

A METHOD OF APPLYING HEAT BY HOT AIR

The "Cradle" is made from Thomas Splint suspension bars. Hot air is led from an oil stove to the cradle by means of a two-gallon petrol tin, adapted as in the drawing.

From "The Early Treatment of War Wounds," by Colonel H. M. W. Gray.

artificial heat as in the manner illustrated. At the M.D.S. or shock centre, and especially at the "resuscitation hut" at the C.C.S., it could be used with even greater effect. The use of stoves to warm dugouts, huts and tents, and that of the car-exhaust to warm the motor ambulance, were measures of first-rate importance.

---

[87] *See Appendix No. 14.*

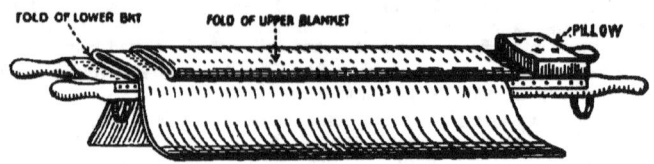

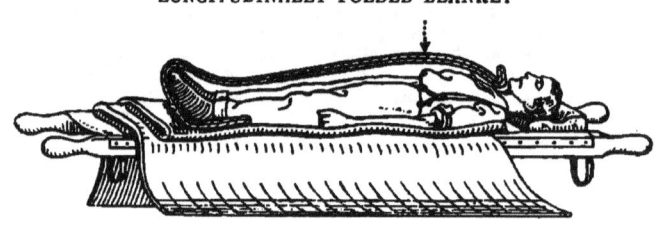

LONGITUDINALLY FOLDED BLANKET

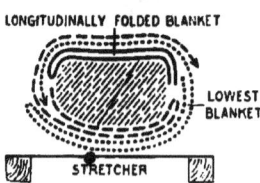

The Technique of the Blanket.

This was to meet a prime need in preventing wound shock, the maintenance of body heat. "The patient should be stripped of wet outer garments and placed on a dry stretcher on trestles with a primus stove underneath. This stretcher is prepared with two blankets folded three times lengthwise, so that there are four folds beneath the patient and one hanging down on either side to complete the hot air chamber. Thus while dressings and splints are applied the patient is being warmed. The third blanket now covers the patient, and hot water bottles are applied." (D.M.S., First Army: "Suggestions for prevention and early treatment of Wound Shock"; dated 2 Nov., 1917.)

Diagrams reproduced from "The Treatment of Wounded Men" (1917), by Colonel H. M. W. Gray, A.M.S., and Captain K. M. Walker, R.A.M.C.; and "The Early Treatment of War Wounds" (1919), by Colonel Gray.

The actual technique of the blanket and hot-air cradle will doubtless be exactly described and figured in all military medical training manuals, and only a brief note is required of the practice on the Western Front. The figures here shown illustrate the practice at the end of 1917 in the British Third Army, from which most of all the Australian Service drew its inspiration. The procedure described was to be followed from the front line to C.C.S.; warmth was to be applied in conjunction with the blanket technique. A sheet issued by the D.M.S., First Army in November, 1917, figures a stretcher on trestles with the side folds of blanket let down to form a hot-air chamber beneath the stretcher.[88] Prophylaxis was based on the premise "that two varieties of wound shock may be recognised: (a) primary, the direct result of the wound; and (b) secondary, induced by cold and the disturbance of transport"; and that "by appropriate means (a) can be reduced and (b) prevented or minimised."

Fluid and Food. Together with warmth, the chief physiological need of the wounded man—and always an urgent one—was for fluid, a need which haemorrhage and the sweat of battle greatly increased. A good "second" to these was the call for glycogen. This was reflected in the soldier's preferences: hot tea, with plenty of sugar, was better liked and was more often retained against the nausea of impending "shock," than were beef extract, cocoa or condensed milk. To neutralise the acidosis found in declared "shock," alkalis were given—as sodium bicarbonate in tea. The artificial administration of fluid and food such as glucose-saline by intravenous infusion is dealt with elsewhere. Alcohol had little place, if any, in the treatment of wounded men. For the "walkers," solid food in plenty from the "Soyers" cookers; and here also Red Cross "amenities" had a legitimate and useful place in the problem of "medical comforts."

Treatment at divisional posts and stations Next to the actual effects of his injury, the journey from the trenches to the C.C.S. was the most potent factor in the fate of the wounded man and nothing that might contribute to his safety and comfort during the journey was so trifling as not to merit consideration. The good work of an ambulance might be said to rest on attention to these details rather than on efficiency in the performance of surgical operations. What follows should be read against such a background of details, and in the light of previous chapters of action.

Treatment by the Regimental Stretcher-Bearers. This was only less vital than the rôle of the bearers in transport. The first field dressing was usually applied by the wounded man himself or by a comrade; but effective first aid—arrest of

---

[88] The method is also figured in *Report No. 2 of the Special Investigation Committee of the M.R.C., p. 86, Dec., 1917.*

serious haemorrhage, immediate splinting, if necessary improvised, and effective protection of the wound by "shell" dressing and bandage—was the duty of the stretcher-bearer.

These processes have already been described and discussed in the narrative, in which there has been also noted the fact that dressings applied by regimental stretcher-bearers often went through unchanged to the A.D.S. The statement of the R.M.O. of the 12th Battalion, Major W. W. S. Johnston, has already been quoted:—
"The R.M.O. looked at the dressings when brought in, but more often did not touch them. The bearer squads had tourniquets but no morphia, and became very expert at splints (including the Thomas splint) and dressings."

It is pertinent here again to note that these men did not belong to the Medical Service, and that their only training was that given by their R.M.O.

Treatment by the R.M.O. A Regimental Medical Officer[89] says:—

"At the R.A.P. in battle the great thing is to get the wounded away—not what you can do for them; fix them up and get them away with a hot drink and ¼ grain of morphia—see to haemorrhage, splints, morphia, hot drinks, and evacuate."

The performance of such urgent surgery as haemostasis by ligation or clip-forceps, plugging or occlusion of "sucking" chest wounds by a flap and removal of the dangling limbs[90]— the first stage in the surgical campaign; the selection of cases for transport by stretcher—the first stage of *triage*—and the keeping of records; the general oversight of first aid; the inspiring of his personnel; the maintaining of supplies and liaison

---

[89] Capt. J. C. M. Harper, R.M.O., 28th Bn.
[90] The following from A.A.M.C. records is relevant to various aspects of wound-treatment:—
"One chap, named Iredell, was brought in with his right arm shorn off at the shoulder. The upper arm had been blown clean away, and his shoulder was exposed like red beef clean cut with a cleaver. The forearm, including the elbow, was attached by a few threads of tissue. Dr. Ross said, 'Cut it off, Sergeant,' and with a scissors I snipped off the forearm. The hand, forearm, and elbow, were completely intact, the piece of shell having simply blown away the humerus, biceps and surrounding flesh. Iredell was a fine stamp of a man, and, though conscious, never batted an eyelid. The Doctor picked up artery and vein with a couple of nickelled forceps. I then bound up the lot with shell dressings and wool, and sent the poor chap on." (From *Aid Post Chronicles* (unpublished), by Sgt. J. R. Edwards, *p.* 72, 20 Sept., 1917.)
From his "B. 103" and a personal note by Mr. Iredell, Dec., 1938, we find that the wound was sustained at about 4 p.m. on Sept. 20 and the aid-post was reached about 7. He was attended to at the C.C.S., and evacuated at once. Operation 1 Oct., 1917. Now has "about 4 inches of stump," is bimanual, and is "able to 'carry on' and can do anything on the farm (except make money)!"

with the bearer division; and the making of provision for hot drinks and "comforts"—all these were functions of the R.M.O. in battle. His most useful contribution to the welfare of the wounded was probably that of inspiring his personnel and training his bearers in bandaging, splinting, immediate haemostasis, and above all in the prevention of shock by skill and care in handling, assiduity in the use and replacement of blankets and by ensuring skilful transport. In the British system, the R.A.P. formed a focus through which must pass, as through a bottleneck, all the wounded from the unit's front. It is open to question whether this system of collecting was always to the advantage of the wounded.[91]

First Aid: Technique—Haemorrhage. The most important act of treatment to the wound at the aid-post, A.D.S., or M.D.S., was to ensure that haemorrhage had been effectively controlled. As the most important factors in "wound shock" and sepsis, "haemorrhage and sepsis go hand in hand" (Gray).

In the early part of the war the amount of blood *per se* that might be lost without mortal hurt was under-estimated; natural haemostasis was under-rated[92]; and the tourniquet was much abused.

It was found by Captain Winn at Pozières that patients arrived at the R.A.P. bleeding despite the tourniquet. He found that the tourniquet, by obstructing the venous circulation, promoted bleeding, which he stopped by removing the constriction. At this time, largely through the co-ordinating activity exercised by the Consulting Surgeons, not only operating surgeons in the Field Ambulance but R.M.O's and Regimental bearers came to appreciate the danger attending the use of this implement and the narrow time-factor of safety,[93] and the crudities of Pozières and Arras do not appear in the records of 1918. The use of the tourniquet, and of voluminous "dressings" changed at each halt, gave way to plugging, local pressure by bandage, or the use of haemostatic forceps, left *in situ* by the R.M.O. and replaced by ligation at the A.D.S. or C.C.S.

The final developments will be described in the narrative of 1918.[94]

First Aid: Sepsis. By the end of 1917, though the ritual gesture

[91] It often entailed serious risk of drawing enemy fire. In the French Army professional first aid was less exactly centralised.

[92] It is recorded of Hieronymus Braunschweig (1497) that he commended as a treatment for haemorrhage to put the patient in the dark so that he could not see the bleeding, and tell him that it had stopped. Major-General R. M. Downes (in "What Medicine owes to War and War owes to Medicine," *p.* 5—published in *R.A.M.C. Journal, Dec., 1936*, and *M. J. A., Jan., 1936*) recalls the use by the ancient Egyptians of pads of "fresh flesh—no doubt to stop haemorrhage—a method we relearnt in the Great War."

[93] The incidence of gangrene in limbs on which the rubber tourniquet was retained for over 4 hours was placed as high as 80 per cent. On the other hand, "blind groping" for a bleeding vessel was generally condemned as useless, even dangerous; and a well applied tourniquet preferred.

[94] *See Chapter xxi.*

of painting the skin with iodine or picric persisted and was perhaps of some service against coccal infection, it was well understood that the function of the field personnel was to get the wounded man to the C.C.S., and that the application of "dressings" was for the purpose of protection, haemostasis, and rest. "Antiseptic" "dressings" went out of favour—the mode of application was found more important than the material. Liquid paraffin to prevent caking came into vogue in some Armies.

First Aid: "Shock." "Primary"—neuro-genic —shock was an obvious commonplace of battle and was treated by commonsense methods— rescue and rest, a smoke, hot tea, morphia. Strychnine and camphor were popular early in the war, but dropped out. But although the campaign of research brought out the importance of the work done at the R.A.P. and A.D.S. in preventing "secondary" wound shock, the possibilities of the aid-post in this respect were commonly over-estimated. Among the chief aids to advance were the Thomas splint, the technique of the blanket and primus stove, and early treatment of "chests." Most potent of all was the improved co-ordination of all elements in the service of succour, of which special note is made in chapters of the next section (1918).

First Aid: "Dressings." As foretold by Fessler in 1910, the "First Field Dressing" was wholly inadequate for the majority of wounds in this war. Stretcher-bearers accordingly carried supplies of "shell dressings." The R.M.O. indented on the field ambulance for his supply of dressings—an important responsibility of the ambulance, which sometimes sterilised and sent them up in improvised containers.[95]

First Aid: Fractures. The Femur. "My experience of the rifle splint," wrote an R.M.O. (Major M. V. Southey), "was that it was damnable and so was any other splint but the Thomas." And it cannot be too strongly stated that, excepting the treatment of wounds by excision and primary suture, no greater advance in wound treatment was made in the war than the use of the Thomas splint in the front line to prevent shock. The unedifying history of this advance has already been stressed.[96] Of the use of this splint in the

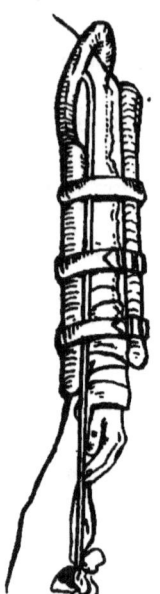

Small Thomas Splint for arm, as applied. (From "The Early Treatment of War Wounds," by Col. H. M. W. Gray.)

---

[95] Wool gauze and other dressings were for the most part supplied to the B.E.F. by the War Office in large packets unsterilised—a wasteful and dirty system. In the French Army it would seem dressings were sent out in packets of suitable size and commonly sterilised.

[96] *See Index.* Some points on the technique of the use of this splint in the war are given elsewhere. For neglect to use it in civil ambulance practice see *M.J.A., 24 Nov., 1934, p. 678.*

39-40-41. A DEMONSTRATION AT THE OLD A.D.S., YPRES, OF THREE STAGES IN THE APPLICATION OF THE THOMAS SPLINT

See also *Diagram* at p. 943.

Aust. War Memorial Official Photos. Nos. E5252-5253-5251.
Taken in June, 1919.   To face p. 348.

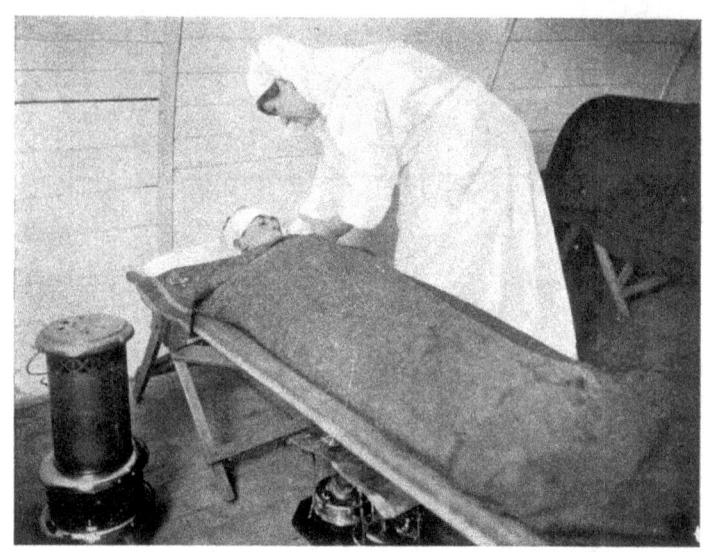

42. PREPARING A PATIENT FOR OPERATION AT NO. 1 A.C.C.S., OULTERSTEENE, IN NOVEMBER, 1917

Note the heating by primus and kerosene stove.

Aust. War Memorial Official Photo. No. E1305.

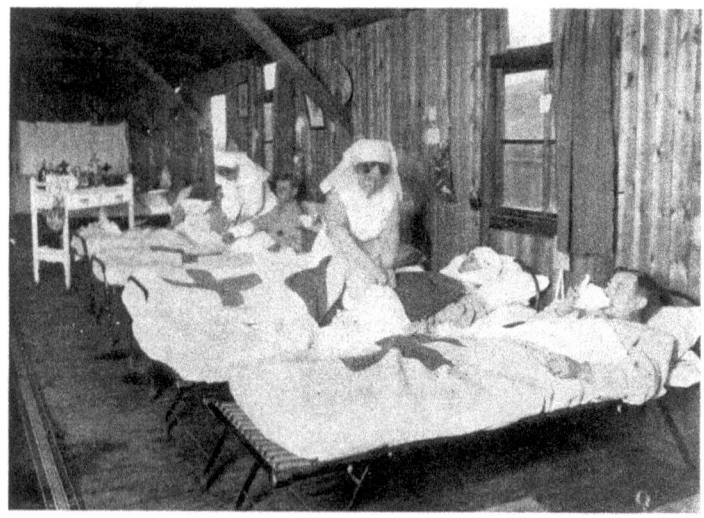

43. A WARD IN NO. 2 A.C.C.S. AT TROIS ARBRES, STEENWERCK, NOVEMBER, 1917

Aust. War Memorial Official Photo. No. E4623.   *To face p. 349.*

Palestine Campaign, the officer in charge of the Desert Mounted Corps Operating Unit[97] writes:
"In one of the Amman raids, one of our colleagues, then a combatant officer, received a gunshot fracture of the thigh. He was put in a Thomas splint by Vance and travelled all the way to Jerusalem, some of the journey on a camel cacolet, the roughest ride imaginable, yet he had an excellent result. At the same time a brave New Zealand officer died at my feet about two minutes after his arrival at Jericho simply because he had travelled with a fracture of the thigh unfixed."[98]

It is interesting to note that Sir Alexander MacCormick was one of the first, if not the first, to advocate strongly in the Great War the use of the Thomas knee splint for the transport of patients with fractures of the femur due to gunshot wounds. It is claimed that he actually bought and took across to France, early in 1915, the first Thomas knee splints used for transport purposes in this war.[99]

Humerus. An effective "first aid" splint for the humerus was found to be the patient's chest, and the most useful apparatus a roller bandage. For the forearm an internal angular splint was found to make the best of this bad job—the *bête noir* of the orthopaedist. Gooch splinting was an important factor in first aid.

First Aid: Equipment. (1) *Morphia.* The official equipment of the R.M.O. included a hypodermic syringe with two stout platino-iridium needles and several tubes of morphine tartrate in ¼-grain tablets, with a glass-stoppered phial for mixing. Apart from the syringe itself it was not a workmanlike outfit. Moreover, exact instructions as to the use of morphia in the field were at first entirely lacking, and among the many "rule of thumb" procedures recommended was the evil practice of "a tablet under the tongue."[100]

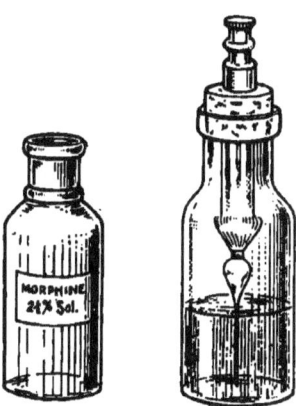

Hypodermic morphia outfit for field work, as used in Third Army. (From "The Early Treatment of War Wounds.")

(2) *The bandage.* That the "roller" bandage was in far more general use than the modifications of the "triangular" was probably due to the fact that, properly applied, it serves more effectively the purpose of *rest*. Training in its use and proper place in first aid as against

---

[97] See Vol. 1, p. 636.
[98] "Fractures of the shaft of the Femur," by Lieut.-Col. J. Colvin Storey, A.A.M.C., *M.J.A.*, 24th Nov., 1934.
[99] See "The primary treatment of compound fractures of the lower limb," by George Bell, *M.J.A.*, 22 Oct., 1932, p. 501.
[100] The question whether the soldier himself might carry an opiate was officially *taboo*. It was however widely debated in the Australian force before The Landing.

those of the triangular was "the first duty" of every R.M.O. An overtight bandage, which contracted when wet on a swelling limb under a splint, was, as the records show, the cause of many disasters.

For the severely wounded man his journey from the R.A.P. to the A.D.S. was critical of life and death. Treatment, confined to *adjustments, haemostasis,* and *sustainment,* was in battle carried out under stress of great urgency; the preoccupation of bearer officers in problems of movement and supplies at times interfered with their attention to treatment.

The Relay Posts and Collecting Posts

"With the progress of the war," says the *British Medical History*,[101] "the actual direct treatment applied to wounds in field ambulances became limited to the application of a simple protective dressing and adequate splintage; partial attempts at disinfection and repeated changes of dressing had been found to be productive of more harm than good. In fact, in the latter part of the war, the first field dressing applied by the regimental bearers was often deliberately left in place until the patient arrived at the casualty clearing station."

Dressing Station and Field Hospital

In general this statement is approved by the experience of the A.I.F. An experienced officer,[102] for example, writes:

"The chief business of a Field Ambulance is evacuation, its second business is again evacuation, and its third also. This cannot be sufficiently stressed. The ambulance may be tempted to do more professional work than it should, but it must not be forgotten that its chief aim is to form a link between the ever-changing front and the more or less fixed points where better conveniences exist for elaborate treatment. Though the ambulance officers may do a good deal of emergency surgery, still it must be remembered that this may not be done at the cost of rapid evacuation, and only to ease suffering or save life. The best ambulance is the one that gets its wounded out the quickest."

From 1917 onwards the guiding rule was that, apart from certain clearly defined essentials of first aid and surgical emergency and from some special types of wounds, until the casualty clearing station was reached treatment should be directed to *the man*, not to *the wound*: to procuring comfort, the alleviation of pain, promoting natural resistance, and conserving strength, without interference with movement to railhead by any attempts at a deliberate *restitutio ad integrum*. In this attitude (it is important to note) was no place for "mark

---

[101] Lieut.-Col. C. Max Page, *British Official Medical History, Surgery, Vol. I, p. 194.*
[102] Major James Sprent, 13th Field Ambulance.

time"; it was essentially active, a continuous campaign of constructive surgery based on a sound foundation of principles and practice built up with infinite pains and at cost of untellable sufferings by clinical observations and experiments on men and animals; and inspired by a vision which reached beyond the C.C.S. and Base Hospital to the orthopaedic and prosthetic problems of Roehampton, Sidcup, Southall, and the Base Hospitals in Australia. At no stage in that long course of surgical action was a combination of the triune forces of repair —reason, instinct, and the *vis medicatrix naturae*—more needful than in the posts of succour that intervened between the several stages of movement from the field of battle to the C.C.S. And in none was this sought with greater earnestness or achieved with greater success.

The following accounts, written for the Australian War Memorial adequately describe the work done in the field ambulance stations.

"A Main Dressing Station," writes Major Sprent, "is placed where routes of evacuation converge, conveniently close to the front. If too far back men die of exhaustion coming down, if too far forward . . . Red Cross protection cannot be expected from the most chivalrous enemy. . . .

"At the M.D.S. men are made safe for the long route back to C.C.S. Urgent amputations are performed, tourniquets removed if not already done at the A.D.S., vessels tied,[103] better and more elaborate splints are applied. Only the most exhausted cases are kept any time. Here operative surgical interference becomes feasible, anaesthetics are given, and a good unit can achieve asepsis. All cases are sent on shaved, clean, splinted, dressed and docketed. No field dressing, tourniquet, or improvised splint should pass the M.D.S. The clerks keep a careful record of all cases."[104]

The routine by means of which these functions could be conveniently carried out is described as follows:—[105]

"Make every effort to *avoid congestion*, which is bound to occur unless care is taken to prevent it. To avoid congestion the following essentials must be observed:—

[103] Warnings were issued by the consultants against prolonged endeavour to find bleeding points at the field hospital. The application of pressure, or tourniquet placed in position for adjustment by an orderly if required *en route*, were alternatives proposed; or the case might be retained for operation in a forward post.

[104] These records were kept in the Admission and Discharge books. The clerks also render the prescribed casualty wires and returns. (The penultimate sentence should be taken "by and large.")

[105] By Major J. H. B. Brown. This should be read in conjunction with the account given (*pp. 175-8*) of the work of the M.D.S. at Pont d'Achelles in the Battle of Messines.

"(a) The maintenance of an *In* and *Out* circular track for motor cars, so that all vehicles are moving the same way and do not have to turn round in their tracks.

"(b) Walking wounded, gassed cases, and stretcher cases to be kept separate and treated by separate staffs in separate departments, and to be evacuated to C.C.S. by a separate system of Transport.

"(c) Admission and Evacuating Rooms and staffs running same to be separate and distinct.

"(d) Painted notice boards to be placed in prominent positions with directing signs to assist in the carrying out of paras. (a), (b) and (c)."

Walking Casualties (Sick and Wounded). The walking wounded dressing station is "most conveniently situated at the M.D.S. though often at the A.D.S. or sometimes set apart by itself."

"Casualties passed first into the Admitting Room where every case is seen by a Medical Officer, the Field Medical Card is filled in, A.T.S. given, and they pass into the Dressing Room, where all wounded men are seen by an Officer who orders re-dressing if necessary. Thence they pass to the Evacuation Room to await transport, and are fed and made comfortable."

Stretcher cases "are carried to the Admitting Room by a special unloading party. Every case should be seen by a Medical Officer who writes on the Field Medical Card the diagnosis (in block letters), disposal (whether to C.C.S. or D.R.S.), and appends his signature, all other particulars having been filled in by the clerk. In this room every wounded man is given A.T.S. (1,500 units) by a specially trained orderly." [In a rush the serum is pooled in a sterile basin. A note of the injection with date is entered on the F.M. Card and a large T. marked with indelible pencil on the patient's forehead.] "Any morphia administered is recorded on his card with exact time and dose.

"From the Admitting Room cases pass to the Dressing Room where 1 to 4 tables may work. Every case is looked at by a Medical Officer who re-dresses if necessary. . . .

"After being dressed, cases pass to the Evacuation Room where every man should get a hot drink, food, and cigarettes. A buffet is usually run by the Y.M.C.A."

Gas Centre—Disposal of Gassed Casualties. [This, Major Brown states, should be sited as a special adjunct of the M.D.S. In view of the great importance of gas warfare the subject will be dealt with specially in *Volume III.*]

The Resuscitation Centre. "All urgent cases of shock or haemorrhage are at once sent to the Resuscitation Centre either from the Admitting Room or from the Dressing Room."

"**Triage**" **and the "untransportable case"**
The British system for effecting what the French and Americans called *triage*, the distribution of casualties to their appropriate treatment centres has been described in the previous chapter.

The question whether Field Ambulance or C.C.S. should be

responsible for the effective treatment of what the French and Germans termed the "untransportable case" was a matter of debate throughout the whole of the war. The fact that British policy strongly favoured concentration on the casualty clearing station makes it desirable to defer the consideration of it till the next chapter, which deals with the work of that unit.

SYNOPSIS OF CHAPTER XIII

EVACUATION: THE CASUALTY CLEARING STATION.

EVOLUTION, FUNCTION, AND WORKING OF THE C.C.S.
1. Function—strategy and tactics for the C.C.S.
   Problem of the "Untransportable case."
   March, 1915: before the C.C.S.
   Revolt from laissez faire.
   Early experiment: 1915.
   The Somme: "Abdominal centres."
   The tragedies of "Alberich."
   Field Ambulance or C.C.S?
   The advanced C.C.S. in 1917.
   C.C.S. strength in British offensives.
2. Structure: establishment and equipment of the C.C.S.
   Personnel.
   Surgical teams.
   Equipment, transport and housing.
3. The interior economy and working of a C.C.S
   Interior Economy—the departments.
   (a) Command and administration.
   (b) Clinical activities. Female nursing staff. X-ray department.
   Pathological department.
   (c) Quartermaster's department.
   (d) Pharmaceutical department.
   The working of a C.C.S.
   The receiving tent. The dressing tent.
   The C.C.S. group: rotation of duty.
   Technique for operation. Evacuation.
   Clinical Organisation.
   The surgical division.
   The task of classification and disposal.
   Treatment of the wounded man.
   Factors in "Resuscitation."
   The medical division.
   The C.C.S. and return to duty.
   The rôle of the C.C.S. in the prevention of disease.
   "Clearance."

THE AUSTRALIAN CASUALTY CLEARING STATIONS ON THE WESTERN FRONT, MARCH, 1916-MARCH, 1918.
Some "Imperial" adjustments.
The Units—Nos. 1, 2, and 3 A.C.C.S.
April, 1916-May, 1917.
In the Flanders Offensive.
The Winter of 1917-18,

CHAPTER XIII
EVACUATION: THE CASUALTY CLEARING STATION

THE medical units which in all the national armies in the Great War under various designations, and with slightly differing techniques, served the purpose briefly to be described in this chapter, were perhaps its most characteristic medical development. As an element indeed in an experience which may perhaps prove unique in the history of the human race, the C.C.S. of attrition warfare may be itself *sui generis*. Be this, however, as it may, in its general purpose the "Evacuating Hospital," represented in the British scheme by the Casualty Clearing Station, is assured of a place in the medical system of any nation which shall aspire to effect the systematic rescue of the casualties from its wars.

The general place of such a unit in any scheme of evacuation will be clear from foregoing chapters. It is not proposed to give a detailed account of the working of a casualty clearing station in the war of 1914-18 but rather to suggest the nature of the problems special to this unit, and to indicate the lines on which these problems were met. Some facts and figures are given from the general British experience on the Western Front; and in the last section of the chapter we follow the movements and special experiences of the three Australian casualty clearing stations from their arrival in France until the spring of 1918. In chapters of *Section III* their moves will be followed through the stirring events of the German break-through in March and April and in the Allied advance to Victory at the end of that year.

EVOLUTION, FUNCTION, AND WORKING OF THE C.C.S.

Historical note. Begotten in the South African War of 1899-1902, through conjunction of an avowed weakness in the medical scheme of evacuation with increasing military importance for a more effective system of rescue; born in 1905 at the hands of the Esher Commission as the "Clearing Hospital"; and reared in the peace time training of Lord Haldane's Territorial Militia, this very important military unit came of age as the "Casualty Clearing Station" in the war of 1914-18. As the focus of wound-treatment, the unit takes place of honour with the Motor Ambulance Convoy and the Command Depot, as the chief implements in one of the most striking and important medical contributions of the Great War to military medicine and to warfare, to wit, an effective and expeditious system of "return to duty" and "discharge" to civil life of the recovered and the unrecoverable soldier respectively.

As first conceived, the function of the "Clearing Hospitals" was set out[1] as

"Similar to those of the tent division of a field ambulance but on a larger scale. They form . . . the pivot upon which the whole system of evacuating sick and wounded turns."

As fully developed, in the last two years of the war, the casualty clearing station administered by "Army" had four distinct functions.

(1) Concentration and classification ("*triage*") of casualties and clearance to the ambulance train. (2) For the seriously wounded— resuscitation, effective operation, and adequate after-treatment. (3) Interim treatment of slightly wounded and "gassed" men, and of the sick. (4) The effective treatment and return to duty of minor forms of injury and disease, acting as "rest stations" and as special stations for the diagnosis and treatment of "N.Y.D.N.," "N.Y.D. Gas," S.I.W., ophthalmic cases, and various types of infectious disease, supplementing in this duty the "stationary" hospitals of the Lines of Communication.[2]

As the most important characteristic of life is a capacity for continuous structural development in adaptation to changing environment and to inherent functional urges, so in any war-time debate[3] on suggested changes in the constitution of the "units" composing the structural fabric of evacuation, we can discern the idea of the dominance of "function"—of the exact purpose to be served.

(1) The official view of the *function* of these new units is indicated in the strategic and tactical principles devised for their disposition along the battle-front, and for their administration

---

[1] In *Field Service Regulations, 1914, Part II p. 122.*
[2] The rôle of the "stationary hospital" in France when the Australian force arrived was ill-defined. This unit does not now appear in British establishments.
[3] *See e.g.* Report of the proceedings of the Interallied Surgical Conferences March and May 1917 (*Archives de Médicine et de Pharmacie Militaires, Vol. LXVIII* July-Sept. 1917. Paris: L. Fournier, 1917); *Report of the 11th Session of the Research Society of the American Red Cross in France Nov. 22-23rd. 1918*; *Report of the Re-organisation Committee, British Army Medical Services.*

and mode of employment; (2) their *structure* is represented by the "establishment," and equipment, provided on an increasingly extensive and ultimately enormous scale; and (3) a working *technique* was developed within the unit itself to enable it to exploit to the utmost the astonishing opportunities that soon presented themselves for augmenting the value of medical service within the Army zone.

The general nature of the functional urge that influenced the evolution of these units has been discussed in the two preceding chapters. Here, we deal with the strategical and tactical principles in which the official view of that function was expressed. What is to be said on the matter is taken largely from British records, since at this "level" of evacuation matters of policy lay outside the scope of Australian responsibility.

1. Function—strategy and tactics for the C.C.S.

Strategy. In the *British Official Medical History* the functions of the C.C.S. are epitomised as those, first, of a hospital; second, of an evacuating centre; and, third, of a sieve to protect the Army against loss of "cases of wounds and sickness likely to recover within a few days." These three spheres of action only gradually emerged from the primitive purpose first conceived. Sir William Macpherson states that the units "may be considered to have really embarked on their career" at the end of 1914, and thereafter their functions crystallised along the lines of movement and treatment described in the two preceding chapters. The opportunities and facilities for surgery steadily improved during 1915 and therewith the importance of these units and the manner of their employment. In June and July 1915 Nos. 10 and 17 C.C.S's were established at "Remy Siding" in tents and huts, and there formed the nucleus of a group which "made history" both military and scientific.[4] In preparation for the Loos operations (September 1915) two "Advanced Operating Centres" were established, but thereafter British practice swung away from the advanced operating centre, and made for the moving up of the main unit.

"From this time onwards it was the policy of the Army Medical Service to erect casualty clearing stations on open ground . . . with

[4] In Dec., 1917, No. 10 British C.C.S. was made a special "research" station for Second Army.

a railway siding for their own use, and with good road communication towards the front. Advanced operating centres were only erected when it was not possible to place casualty clearing stations sufficiently near the trench line, or when it seemed advisable to supplement the casualty clearing stations in anticipation of heavy fighting."

At the end of 1915

"the policy was finally adopted of not doing more operations than could be helped at field ambulances, and of consequently using the casualty clearing stations as front-line hospitals and transmitting wounded to them as quickly as possible."[5]

Tactics. The principles that should govern the strategic employment of these units having thus been established, tactical methods gradually crystallise in the crucible of Neuve Chapelle and Loos, the Somme, Arras, and Third Ypres. Chief among these was the system of *grouping,* and *alternation of duty.* This is well described by Sir Anthony Bowlby :—

"As soon as the first grouped casualty clearing stations were established at Remy Siding in 1915, it became possible to arrange that they should be on duty 'turn and turn about,' . . . during alternate periods of twenty-four hours. . . . From that time onwards the system of grouping two or more casualty clearing stations was adopted as a general principle. . . . During the Somme fighting in 1916 . . . it was arranged that each casualty clearing station of a group should take in wounded, not for a certain fixed period but up to a certain number, and when this number was reached the motor ambulances arriving with wounded were 'switched off' to the next casualty clearing station, until it also had received the allotted number. . . . The number that should be taken in before 'switching off' necessarily varied in proportion to the pressure and to the number of surgeons at work, but whereas at first as many as 400 were admitted before another casualty clearing station took on the work, the longer the war lasted the more the numbers tended to be reduced, so that 150 or 200 became a standard, and one severe case was often by arrangement counted as the equivalent of two patients able to walk. It was also found that when large numbers of wounded were arriving at the beginning of heavy fighting it was best to take in only 100 at first, or even less, for in this way the staffs of two or more casualty clearing stations got quickly to work instead of being kept waiting in idleness while the first casualty clearing station on duty took in a large number."[6]

The year 1916 and the Somme saw—as we have shown—the final move up of the surgical centre of gravity from the Expeditionary Base to the zone of the armies, and a surgical equilibrium—albeit somewhat unstable—established in the treatment of the prodigious mass of wounded men that flowed from a

---

[5] *Brit. Off. Med. Hist. Surgery, Vol. I, p.* 212.
[6] *Brit. Off. Med. Hist. Surgery, Vol. I, pp.* 217-8.

thousand R.A.P's set along the British front to a comparatively few highly organised Army groups of operating hospitals—the casualty clearing stations; thence to flow with a minimum of delay for sustainment, rest, operation and after-treatment by ambulance train to the several Expeditionary Bases. Meanwhile the potentialities of this unit in the sifting of convalescent sick for "return to duty" were exploited by developing both functionally and structurally its "medical" side.

The year 1917 saw the casualty clearing stations expanded to dimensions which staggered all precedent and expectation. Not only were the numbers of wounded immensely increased, but the new surgical technique made vastly greater demands on the stations as "operating hospitals." But by this time the system of technical direction by "consultants," medical as well as surgical, was an integral part of the medical organisation of the front as well as of the base. Acting in close *liaison* with the administrative staffs and executive units and with each other, these officers were admirably qualified to advise on the best means for meeting each new problem. Thus, in February, 1917, in preparation for the Arras campaign, the "lessons" of the Somme were epitomised by the Consulting Surgeons in a memorandum for the Director-General B.E.F. on "The treatment of wounds at the Casualty Clearing Stations."[7] In July those of Arras and Messines were similarly summarised in preparation for the Flanders offensive.[8]

The surgical "equilibrium" to which we made reference above was gradually stabilised on a more and more secure base of surgical technique, in particular by the excision of wounds and primary and delayed primary suture, implemented by improved *"triage"* and methods of transport and by appropriate staff and equipment. It was liable to interference from two directions. First by the development, in great operations of a serious disproportion between the number of casualties and the

---

[7] After proposing that "early operation on wounds requiring it should be done at the casualty clearing stations whenever possible," it was recommended that for heavy fighting the staffs of casualty clearing stations should be reinforced to a minimum of fourteen medical officers and fifteen nurses. It was suggested that these proposals should be implemented by the creation of "Surgical teams" to be drawn from other C.C.S's. At least 10 per cent. of the accommodation should be in beds and full provision made for anaesthesia by gas and oxygen.

[8] This recommended 8 operation tables in each C.C.S. instead of 4; a minimum of 24 medical officers and 25 nursing sisters to each C.C.S.; and increased teams and equipment. The provisions for the latter are dealt with in detail later.

staff and "equipment" available within the unit to deal with them; second, through impact of the problem of the "untransportable case." Excessive pressure of work—as in great offensives—was met by the organisation of "surgical teams," presently to be described.[9] In the "untransportable case" we renew contact[10] with a fundamental problem in evacuation, and one wherein British policy diverged in some respect from that of the other European Armies.

The history of the problem of the "untransportable case" reflects very exactly the whole history of medical work in this war. It is of more than academic interest, since the same road is quite likely to be travelled again in any future war. At first confined chiefly to chests, femurs, and particularly to abdomens the study of this problem came in time to embrace all those types of wound and wounding wherein the physiological or pathological time-constants or the gravity of the wound allowed too narrow a margin of safety to permit of their normal transfer from Field Hospital (Ambulance) to Evacuating Hospital (C.C.S.); broadly, a selection of abdomens, chests, multiple wounds and smashed limbs, tourniquets, ex-sanguined, "shocked" and "collapsed" men. During the phase of attrition warfare the steps taken in the B.E.F. may be indicated as follows:—

Problem of the "untransportable case"

(1) *March 1915: Before the C.C.S.* Memorandum No. 6 of the D.G.M.S., B.E.F., prescribed that "in wounds of the chest it is best to take the patient—if sufficiently well—to the casualty clearing station as quickly as possible, and it is desirable that he should in all cases be kept there for about a week at least." The memorandum went on to say that in wounds of the abdomen "as regards rest, the same applies." As regards operation "no fixed rule can be laid down, as much depends on the experience in surgery of the operator."

(2) *Revolt from laissez faire.* The next move adumbrates in respect of "regional" wounds the revolt from practice based on the South African War, and relates to the most imperative type of urgent wound—the "penetrating abdomen." When it is not immediately lethal the abdominal wound presents two specific and distinct time-constants—

---

[9] Priority in the idea of the "surgical team" can with some confidence be claimed for the Australian Service. The "first convoy" in Oct., 1914 included one of the leading surgeons of Australia (Mr. Fred Bird) and his team of 3 specially trained theatre sisters. With his son (Mr. Dougan Bird) as anæsthetist, Mr. Bird's team worked with the M.E.F. at Salonica in 1915-16. Another Australian surgeon, Mr. P. Fiaschi, enlisted in 1914 in the A.I.F. with his two specially trained assistants, and from 1915 worked with them as his "team" whenever opportunity permitted.

[10] *See pp. 247-250, 782-6.*

the first due to a physiological factor, the probability of death from haemorrhage—say 1-4 hours; the second due to a pathological one, the development of septic peritonitis—say 4-8 hours. In this war the chief cause of early death in abdominal wounds was *haemorrhage*.[11] This fact was first recognised officially by the D.M.S. First Army (Surgeon-General W. G. Macpherson), who in June, 1915, to promote early operation, arranged for the rapid transport of all abdominal cases to C.C.S.[12] Thereafter British procedure in this matter evolved along two lines, (a) rapid evacuation to C.C.S.; (b) the employment of forward operation centres.

(3) *Early Experiment: 1915.* The preparations for the Battle of Loos (September, 1915) included as we have seen the formation of "advanced operating centres."[13] The result of the experiment does not appear to have impressed the higher authorities in the B.E.F. and the idea was not further exploited at the time by G.H.Q.

"Better results were obtained by getting wounded into the casualty clearing stations before any operations were undertaken"—where they "could be in beds and well nursed."[14]

(4) *The Somme: "Abdominal Centres."* But the problem of the "urgent" case remained, and for the Battle of the Somme the D.D's.M.S. X and VIII Corps formed with their field ambulances "advanced operating centres" at Warloy and Authie respectively. These had, says the British Historian, "special surgical teams, for the purpose of immediate operations on abdominal wounds and other injuries." The centre at Warloy was known as an "abdominal centre." The staff of these stations did not move with the field ambulances to which they were attached for administration; the one at Authie subsequently (8th October, 1916) became an advanced post of No. 3 A.C.C.S. The centre at Warloy[15] occupied a "small but well built civil hospital with 75 beds, supplemented by accommodation for 375 other wounded." With 3 specialist surgeons, 9 nursing sisters, and a considerable staff besides, this was in effect a forward-placed C.C.S. rather than an advanced operating centre.

(5) *The Tragedies of "Alberich."* With "Alberich" we enter upon a tragic but extraordinarily interesting stage in the history of the "urgent" case. In the pursuit of the retiring Germans the advanced columns pushed far ahead of the C.C.S's and a double issue was raised: should the "urgent" case be treated at field ambulance or C.C.S.? And, if the latter, should the C.C.S. push forward an "advanced centre" or advance itself to a "forward" site? The problem was necessarily touched on in the narrative chapter[16] and here we may pick up the thread of

---

[11] *British Official Medical History, Surgery Vol. I pp. 478-9.* In a record of post-mortems done at No. 2 A.C.C.S. during 1916-17, kept by Lieut.-Colonel H. Skipton Stacy (*General Practitioner of Australia and New Zealand July-Oct., 1938*), haemorrhage as a primary cause of death was found to be "not common." Patients likely to die from that cause "would not reach the clearing station." There were however "many in which it was a contributing factor."

[12] "The number of abdominal wounds that reach an operating centre is not likely to exceed 2 per cent. of the total wounded received, provided that no segregation of such cases is practised." (*British Official Medical History, Surgery, Vol. I, p. 479.*)

[13] One station appears to have been staffed by Field Ambulance personnel.

[14] *loc. cit. Surgery, Vol. I, p. 212.*

[15] *See pp. 70-71.*

[16] *Chapter vi (pp. 111, 116-17).*

events with the reprimand administered by the D.M.S. of Fifth Army (General Skinner) to the C.O. 13th Australian Field Ambulance, for over-zealous action in the endeavour to mitigate the horrors of the Bapaume-Albert road for seriously wounded men.

Curiously enough within the casualty clearing station—No. 3 Australian—which itself at this very time was charged with the official care of such cases, we find an *advocatus diaboli*.

"At least one tent sub-division of the Ambulance doing the work of Main Dressing Station should be equipped and ready to perform any major surgical operation. The reason for this suggestion is:—during a big advance C.C.S's get left too far behind, and many factors arise causing delay in the treatment at C.C.S. of urgent cases. Owing to the present-day unwieldy nature of C.C.S's, usually at least 48 hours is required before a C.C.S. can take up its new forward position. It is during this time that many lives are lost owing to delayed operations. This could be obviated if the M.D.S. was prepared to attend to these cases until the C.C.S. had moved forward."[17]

(6) *Field Ambulance or C.C.S.?* So impressed was General Birdwood by the views of his Deputy- and Assistant-Directors of the need for operation on urgent cases including "abdominals" near the front, that he submitted to Fifth Army a proposal that the I Anzac Corps should organise "operating sections" which should be attached to field ambulances. General Skinner approved the general principle of the proposal but exempted "abdominals and severe chest injuries" since facilities for nursing and after-care could not be ensured without immobilising the field ambulance.

In the French Army the issue had by this time been decided in favour of a surgical accessory to the "Advanced Ambulance Group"; in the Belgian, by an "advanced post" of the C.C.S.—"Hôpital du Front."[18]

(7) *The Advanced C.C.S.* In the B.E.F. the Third Battle of Ypres saw a dramatic climax to the policy of advancing the C.C.S., in which an Australian unit, No. 3 A.C.C.S., was involved. In his preparations as D.M.S. Fifth Army, Surgeon-General Skinner, backed by the senior Consulting Surgeon (Sir Anthony Bowlby), pushed a group of stations to within five miles of the front line. The *dénouement* is vividly described by the sister-in-charge of No. 32 British C.C.S.[19]

---

[17] Memo by Captain F.W. Fay, No. 3 A.C.C.S. 26 September, 1916 to 26 March 1917.

[18] "The hospitals at the front are situated 10-20 kilometres behind the lines. They receive without distinction all the wounded and constitute in some degree a 'surgical barrier' behind the lines. Each of the larger formations has one or more annexes situated 3-4 kilometres from the front lines not far from the divisional aid-posts (*Postes de secours*) and designated advanced posts of the hospitals of the front. To these go the more seriously wounded unable to stand at once the long motor trip, abdominal wounds, wounds of the thorax or those with shock or serious haemorrhage not suitable for tourniquet. All other wounded are transported direct to the main hospital of which it is an annexe where begins the true surgical treatment of wounds." (M. Depage, Interallied Surgical Conference March, 1917: *Archives de Médecine et de Pharmacie, Militaires, Tome lxviii, p. 50.*) Though based on the methods of the Belgian Army (to which M. Depage belonged) the summary was accepted by the Conference as a general "appreciation" of the problem.

[19] Miss K. E. Luard, Q.A.I.M.N.S. *Unknown Warriors*: (Large gaps in the quotation are not indicated).

Third Army, near Arras, May 29th. We are to prepare to move
to another area and shall be near enough to the line
No. 32 to get them from the dressing stations direct, with-
British C.C.S. out long journey and waits which is what the C.C.S's
are out to prevent nowadays.
July 27th Brandhoek. Hospital has just been pitched and already
is splendid. This venture so close to the line is in the nature of an
experiment in lifesaving, to reduce the mortality rate in abdominal and
chest wounds. Hence this advanced centre to which all such wounds
come from a large attacking area instead of going on with the rest to
the C.C.S's six miles back. We have fifteen theatre sisters, thirty-three
in all. Sir Anthony Bowlby turned up to-day. It is his pet scheme,
getting operations done up here instead of further back or at the Base.
Our thirty medical officers include the largest number of F.R.C.S's ever
collected in any hospital in France before, with theatre teams to work
at eight tables continuously. *July 31st.* At 6.30 a.m. we began taking
in the first cases. *11 p.m.* We have been working in the roar of battle
every minute going at full pitch: twelve teams in the theatre. . . . Soon
after 10 a.m. "he" began putting over high explosives, they burst on two
sides of us not fifty yards away. It is going to be a tight fit; I thought
the work was going to get the upper hand of us. We get cases an hour
after injury, which is our *raison d'être* for being here. *August 2nd.* In
spite of the awful conditions (of wet and mud) a remarkable number are
doing well, especially those who came in first. *August 9th.* No. 44
C.C.S. is to open to-morrow and has thirty-five Sisters and lots of
teams. The Australians are at present working with us. They are a
handsome crowd and are very nice. We are now to take alternate
fifties of abdomens and femurs. *10th.* Sir Anthony Bowlby came round
to-day and seems pleased with it all. *August 11th.* He hasn't shelled us
to-day, and we have been able to get the wards straight. *13th.* The
Australians open their own unit to-morrow and we three C.C.S's take
in batches of fifty each, abdomens, chests and femurs. *August 16th.* Bombs
dropped on the Australian C.C.S., two killed. *August 18th.* The letters
to relatives of died of wounds reach 400 in less than three weeks. Miss
McCarthy (Matron-in-Chief, B.E.F.) came up to-day and was most
helpful and kind; she is much distressed at the conditions and thinks we
are too far up. *August 22nd.* A very bad day big shells coming over,
one burst between our wards and No. 44 and killed a night sister asleep,
and knocked out three others, another laid out the Q.M. in the Australians. The D.M.S. came up and had just said he would close No. 44
and the Australians and we would carry on with increased staff when
two more came crashing down. The Q.M.G. who was there said at
once—"All must clear out, patients and personnel."

The anticlimax appears in an abortive proposal that I Anzac Corps
should run an advanced operating centre at the M.D.S. at Dickebusch,
and the subsequent decision that the best solution of the problem lay in
developing the means of transport to the normal groups. Here
appropriately the matter may rest—as then it did—till the German
drive throws the issue again into the melting pot.[20]

---

[20] The problem of the untransportable case in the last stage of the war is dealt
with in *Chapter xxv (pp. 782-6)*.

The following table, slightly modified from that in the
British Official Medical History,[21] shows
C.C.S. Strength in British Offensives the number of casualty clearing stations in Armies at the commencement of offensive operations.

Army	Offensive operation	No. of C.C.S's	Austn. C.C.S's	No. of Divs. in Army	Austn. Divs.
First	Loos, 1915	12	—	16	—
Fourth	Somme, 1916	15	1	23	4
Third	Arras, 1917	13	—	16	—
Fifth	Arras, 1917	5	1	8	4
First	Vimy, 1917	11	—	14	—
Second	Messines, 1917	13	2	21	2
Fifth	Ypres, 1917	15	3	19	5
Third	Cambrai, 1917	14	—	25	—
Fourth	British adv. 1918	12	—	19	5
Third	"	12	—	18	—
First		12	—	17	—
Second		12	3	10	—

Personnel. The basic structure of the unit as first designed provided personnel and equipment sufficient for "the care of 200 sick,"[22] for which purpose a staff of 8 officers
2. Structure: establishment and equipment of the C.C.S. (including Q.M.) and 77 other ranks R.A.M.C. was provided. Early in 1915 nursing sisters were "attached" to the unit, at first five and then seven. The establishment laid down for Kitchener's Armies added 3 Chaplains, and slightly increased the number of "other ranks." But with the developments in the function of C.C.S's outlined above, this personnel and the equipment provided became hopelessly inadequate.

Surgical teams. The method consequently adopted for augmenting the personnel of the C.C.S. to meet general developments and special demands, such as those of major offensives, is described in the *British Medical History*[23] thus:—

"In preparing for an offensive, casualty clearing stations were reinforced by officers and men from field ambulances, from other casualty clearing stations . and from hospitals on the lines of communication.

---

[21] *General, Vol. II, pp. 50-1*   [22] *R.A.M.C. Training, 1911, p. 125.*
[23] *Brit. Off. Med. History, General, Vol. II, pp. 44-5.*

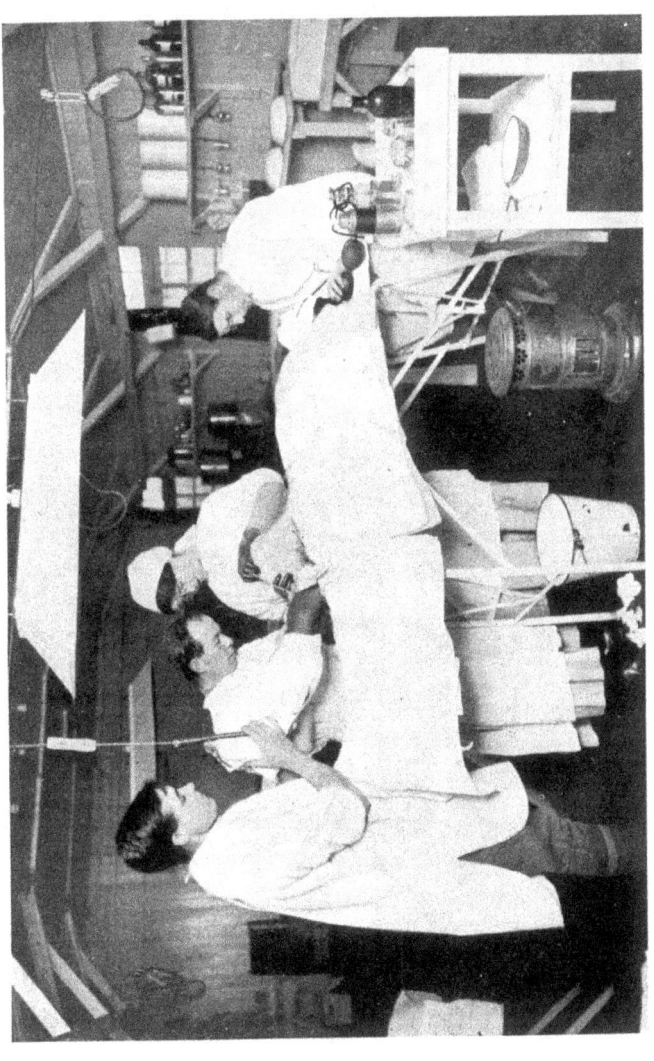

44. An operation at No. 1 A.C.C.S., Oultersteene, 23rd November, 1917
Major Fay Maclure is operating.

Aust. War Memorial Official Photo. No. E1304.

45. No. 3 A.C.C.S. at Gézaincourt, near Doullens, during the Somme battle, October, 1916

Lent by Captain R. P. Henley, No. 3 A.C.C.S. Aust. War Memorial Collection No. A2269.

To face p. 365.

This system of reinforcement, which at first was more or less of a haphazard nature, became in time regularized. From field ambulances one tent sub-division, or possibly two, would be allotted to each casualty clearing station receiving the wounded. One of the officers of a casualty clearing station was appointed a surgical specialist early in 1915, and a surgical team, or even two surgical teams with a second surgeon, could then be organized in each casualty clearing station; so that when personnel from one casualty clearing station was required to reinforce another, a surgical team was sent."

For the 1917 offensive in Flanders the system of "teams" was greatly extended, and arrangements made whereby the Base Hospitals should serve as a reservoir of teams for the front. The procedure to be adopted was set out as follows:—[24]

"To meet sudden emergencies at casualty clearing stations it is proposed to form 'surgical teams' from personnel of hospitals on the lines of communication. A 'Surgical Team' will consist of—1 Operating Surgeon, 1 Anaesthetist, 1 Sister, 1 Operating Room Attendant.

"The teams may be required to proceed at short notice to a casualty clearing station in the front area, and will be conveyed in motor ambulance transport provided from that at the Base concerned.

"The members will be trained to work together. They will be utilised only in times of great stress of work at casualty clearing stations in the Front Area, will be absent from their stations for a few days, and will return by road so that they will be back with their units again before the rush of patients arrives from the front.

"The teams may be drawn from Imperial, Colonial, or American units at the discretion of the administrative medical officer of the area.

"Will you please arrange to provide two such teams, which will be numbered 19 and 20. Kindly report when the teams have been selected and state the names of the members of each, and notifications should be sent to this office of any change in their personnel."

The development of the "team" system is one of the "high lights" of the surgery of the war and is in some sort reflected in post-war civil practice. It had repercussions in the Australian service, which will call for particular reference.[25] The operating surgeon of an A.I.F. team[26] records that his most inspiring experience in the war was when his team worked in No. 3 Canadian C.C.S. (Lieut.-Colonel R. J. Blanchard) at Remy Siding alongside teams from Great Britain, Canada, and the U.S.A., during the Third Battle of Ypres.

Equipment, Transport and Housing. It would serve no use-

---

[24] Memo. received by the C.O., No. 3 A.G.H. from D.D.M.S., L. of C.
[25] *See pp. 840-41.*
[26] Lieut.-Colonel D. A. Cameron, A.A.M.C. His team was drawn from No. 2 A.G.H., Boulogne. Between 23 July, 1917 and 28 Nov., 1917, this team operated on 610 patients. Later, "double teams" were found to promote rapid operating.

ful historical purpose to tabulate the equipment—tentage, technical instruments or apparatus, supply, ordnance and "Red Cross" stores—held "on charge" by a C.C.S. as a normal issue or acquired "additional to mobilisation store table." Not only were these units required to hold large reserves of blankets, stretchers, pyjamas, dressings and so forth, against emergency, but their "expansion" involved accretion practically without limit.

"There was no definite regulation limiting the amount of material and tentage which could be added to casualty clearing stations," says the British Historian.[27] "Individual commanding officers or D's.M.S. of armies requisitioned for whatever equipment they might consider necessary; and much additional equipment was obtained from the stores of the Joint Committee of the B.R.C.S. and Order of St. John."

It was found necessary to regulate this and in September, 1917, a schedule was drawn up to satisfy the requirements of the "three functions"[28] that a casualty clearing station was called on to perform. This was embodied in a routine order issued by the Q.M.G., G.H.Q. in November, 1917. It provided for each C.C.S.:—

"full hospital equipment and tentage for 200 seriously wounded, tentage and equipment for 800 less seriously wounded awaiting evacuation to the base, and shelter for the comparatively small number of trivial cases that the field ambulances failed to dispose of and who were awaiting transfer to divisional or corps rest stations."[29]

No transport was assigned to these units on mobilisation, but shortly after the commencement of the campaign in France and Flanders three 3-ton motor lorries were allotted to each. As first designed the Clearing Hospital had been equipped to move in eight or nine 3-ton lorry-loads. But the Somme soon changed all that—as the case of No. 3 Australian, presently to be described, will show—and by the end of 1916 (to quote again Sir William Macpherson)

"when the expanded units had to be moved . . . as many as 200 lorry-loads were used to move a casualty clearing station by road, or a complete train of goods-vans or trucks to move it by rail."

---

[27] *Brit. Off. Med. History, General, Vol. II, p. 43.*
[28] Those of a hospital, clearing centre, and sieve against wastage through slight casualties. See *p. 357*.
[29] *Brit. Off. Med. History, General, Vol. II, p. 44.* It was "decided" (*inter alia*) that "each Casualty Clearing Station shall be so organised that it is capable of moving forward at any time as a Casualty Clearing Station with accommodation for 200 wounded on the old scale, in order to form a nucleus pending the establishment of the bulk of the Casualty Clearing Station gradually on the new site."

The influence of all this on the course of events in the break-away from the attrition scrum, in 1918, belongs to a later chapter—*XX*—and will there be illustrated by the experience of the Australian units.

In the retreat from Mons 1914, owing to the absence of a motor ambulance convoy, the trains which carried the Clearing Hospitals became in effect themselves the "hospital."[30] Later the stations took over buildings—schools, institutions and so forth; but by the end of 1915 they were almost always housed in tents and huts. At the height of attrition warfare the housing of the C.C.S. was a stupendous business. The pitching of tents and "brigading" of the large marquees to form wards was a major feature of the unit's work, and increased—if it were possible—the importance of the Quartermaster's department. The diagrams on *pages 371 and 381* illustrate the usual lay-out of a C.C.S. in 1918.[31]

It is impossible within a few pages to conjure up an adequate picture of the social life and work of a casualty clearing station on the Western Front at the end of attrition warfare. The most that can be attempted is to create a framework which the reader must fill in, so far as he may, from reference to their work and experiences scattered through the narrative pages.

3. The interior economy and working of a C.C.S.

Hic labor, hoc opus est. Entering by way of the "receiving room," the waste products of attrition passed through these vast machines with speed and certainty until, assorted, and with their individual needs very exactly adjusted, they emerged from the evacuation room, for clearance to ambulance train as raw material for the further processes of "return to duty" or discharge to civil life. Wounded men were "resuscitated," wounds were effectively treated, the more severe by operation under anaesthetic, the procedure being controlled by X-ray, and allowing an adequate period of after-treatment. The sick for the most part were here diagnosed and classified for evacuation

---
[30] Speaking at a medical "meeting" held at the end of 1918 at the South African General Hospital, Abbeville, Colonel J. S. Gallie, R.A.M.C. recalled that a similar situation arose in the early operations of the A.E.F.

[31] For certain special features (*e.g.* the arrangements for internal communications) see the account of the work of the Australian units later in this chapter.

or convalescence. All passed on alleviated, rested, and—save in the heaviest rushes—clean. All the cases were accurately recorded; and systematic returns were made up for "Army" (on the one hand) and 3rd Echelon (on the other). The secret of the extraordinary success achieved we may discern not so much in individual skill and initiative—though these were important—but in order and system, achieved by exact "division of labour" among the personnel of the staff trained to combine an objective outlook in technique with the "human touch" in individual dealings. The primary division of the unit into spheres of labour was by "departments."

Interior Economy—the Departments of a C.C.S. The C.C.S. was commonly organised in four departments—(a) command and administration (including clerical department and "general" duties); (b) clinical (including the X-ray and pathology departments); (c) quartermaster's department; and (d) pharmaceutical department.

(a) *Command and Administration* do not call for particular comment save to note that, in the A.I.F., command of these units was held to call for clinical as well as administrative experience.

(b) *Clinical Activities* were organised and worked in two divisions, surgical and medical. The convalescent wards were common ground.

Female Nursing Staff. The addition of trained female nurses to the staff—the result it would seem of civil pressure—was unquestionably an important factor in the development of the unit as the chief operating centre in the scheme of evacuation. Duty with these units was the Mecca to which all good nurses aspired, and was a sphere in which in the Great War this Service played a part that, in spite of some obvious and considerable difficulties,[32] must ensure the permanence in some form of the association.

X-ray Department. The development of X-ray work in war follows very exactly the same curve as that of the general treatment of wounds. Cardinal points in this evolution are defined by the following statements from A.I.F. records:—

Wire to D.G.M.S., B.E.F., 12th July, 1916, from D.M.S., Fourth Army:—"Mobile X-ray unit absolutely essential for this Army. There is now no X-ray apparatus working either for Fourth or Reserve Army."

This was at the height of the Battle of the Somme.

"Without the help of X-rays the necessary clean operation is impossible." (From a "Preliminary report on research work," at No. 10 C.C.S., Dec. 26, 1917—Jan. 23, 1918.)

Readers of *Vol. I* will recall that No. 1 A.C.C.S. was in 1914 equipped with a portable X-ray apparatus, and that this worked in No. 1 A.S.H. at Lemnos and on Gallipoli in 1915.

---

[32] But *cf.* French and German systems (*Appendix No. 9*). *See also Vol. III.*

By 1917 an X-ray plant and expert radiologist were recognised to be an essential element in the interior economy of every C.C.S. In No. 2 A.C.C.S. in February, 1918, "almost all cases, except those with obvious e. and e. wounds without fractures," were X-rayed before operation.[33] But "the supply of X-ray equipment and of special officers was never equal to the demand, for while the apparatus itself could be readily obtained, difficulties in supplying suitable engines remained to the very end of the war."[34]

Pathological Department. Though not officially provided for, all the Australian units created a small pathological department chiefly with the purpose of performing post-mortems.

"The provision of a clean and well-lit post-mortem room is important in a C.C.S. as it encourages medical officers to study," says the War Diary of No. 3 A.C.C.S., February, 1918. At No. 2 post-mortems were done from the outset.[35]

(c) *Quartermaster's Department.* As in other Australian medical units, this was, when possible, in the charge of members enlisted from the Permanent A.A.M.C. or the Australian Instructional Staff, with "Honorary" commissioned rank. At the outset of the war, they were the only members of the A.M.C. with intimate knowledge of "supply," and of the accountancy required for dealing with the immense variety of stores. To the Quartermaster fell also the control of the kitchen, cooks, food and feeding, and also (in conjunction with Sergeant for general duties) of the erection of tents and the upkeep of the station. It is impossible in a general history to do justice to the importance of this work (admirable records of which were kept in the unit diaries) and, by common consent, it would not be easy to overstate the standard of attainment. The report of the Quartermaster of No. 2 A.C.C.S. (Hon. Captain J. H. Pollard) to his C.O. for February, 1918, included the following subject headings:—Foodstuff, Equipment, Buildings, Painting, Laundry, Red Cross, Sanitation, Agriculture, General.

(d) *Pharmaceutical Department.* In the Australian Service the position of pharmacist in the C.C.S. carried the rank of Honorary

---

[33] In the lecture at the I Anzac Corps School from which the above is taken Lieut.-Col. Balcombe Quick stated that he believed "this C.C.S. can claim the distinction of being the first in the British Army to use an X-ray apparatus in the field."

[34] *Brit. Off. Med. History, Surgery, Vol. I, p. 217.* The following note was furnished by Major G. C. Scantlebury, an Australian officer who served with the R.A.M.C.

" 'A *mobile* X-ray equipment' was a complete unit in which a lorry contained a dark room and special compartments for carrying all apparatus, a dynamo under the front seat worked by a whittle belt from the main shaft, and a dark tent attached to the back, which could be collapsed when moving and opened when stationary. A '*portable*' equipment was merely a small petrol engine which, along with a table and other apparatus, could be put on to a lorry and moved from place to place, but had to be removed and re-set on the ground whenever it was wanted. This meant that it took up to two days to get it going at each fresh place. In 1917 there were between 10 and 12 'Mobile' X-ray equipments and a great number of 'portables' at C.C.S's.

"Personally, from my experience, I cannot see how any X-ray unit could be worked in quite a self-contained way in any modern warfare. We found a hut or a big tent almost a necessity. True we did do up to 30 cases a day with a collapsible back-tent, but it was unsatisfactory. In March 1918 portables had to be abandoned while the mobiles packed up and moved off under their own 'steam'."

[35] A record of these has recently been published. See *footnote 11 on p. 361.*

Lieutenant. With the great extension of transfusion and infusion, and introduction of new specific sera and disinfectants, his duties became very responsible.

The Working of a C.C.S. The work of the C.C.S. will most readily be appreciated if it is visualised as a concurrent process of movement and treatment. We follow first the general course of a casualty:—

The process of clearing a motor ambulance convoy—or a hospital train at the base—and the reception, recording and distributing of casualties to wards, though always a strenuous procedure, became in the later stages of the war a familiar and exact routine—the handling of immense numbers of broken men had become a procedure almost as mechanical as that of breaking them. It was not that familiarity with suffering led to callousness, but rather that organisation had been perfected, and therefore eager anxiety was replaced by a confidence, born of experience, in a proved system of working.

"There was a definite route," says Sir A. Bowlby, "marked out for every man arriving in the casualty clearing station, and so well were arrangements carried out, that if a visitor entered when a convoy had ceased arriving he might find it hard to believe that the place was working at fever heat day and night."[36]

The following statement of the work of a casualty clearing station[37] belongs to the last eighteen months of the war.

The Receiving Tent. On admission all cases came into the receiving tent where they were recorded, relieved of their equipment etc., the *pack store* being sited as an annexe to receiving tent. Nourishment was available in an adjoining mess-tent.

Distribution: the Dressing Tent. From the receiving tent the men passed to the dressing tent where every man was seen by a medical "receiving" officer. Here the incoming stream of wounded was broken up into several.

(1) The slightly wounded who did not require operation were dressed and sent direct to an *evacuation tent* where they awaited the ambulance train.

(2) The cases that required operation were sent to the *pre-operative ward* if fit for operation. It was found to be a good plan to classify these, as they were seen, into A—urgent cases; B—Non-urgent cases which require operation as soon as possible; C—Cases which should be operated on if possible, but which should be sent on to the base if A and B class cases are waiting.

---

[36] *Brit. Off. Med. History, Surgery, Vol. I, p. 232.*
[37] Memorandum compiled for the Australian War Records Section by Major P. A. Stevens (Assistant Collator).

THE CASUALTY CLEARING STATION

(3) Cases needing Resuscitation were sent to *Resuscitation Ward*.
(4) Medical cases were sent to *Medical Wards*.
(5) Penetrating chests were sent to *Chest Ward*, whether requiring operation or not.
(6) Gas cases to *Gas Wards*.

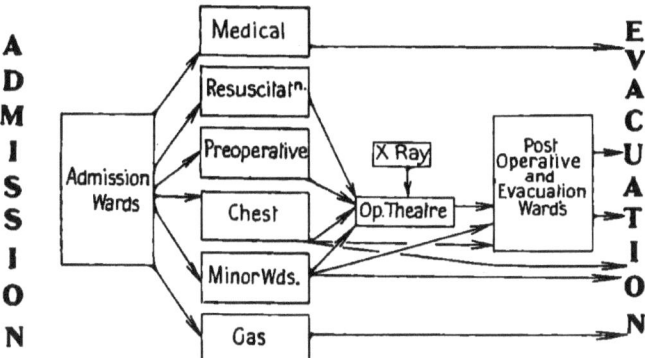

Working Scheme of Casualty Clearing Station. (*From notes by Major P. A. Stevens, A.A.M.C.*)

Careful judgment was required of the receiving officer in dealing with cases admitted—the main point being that the pressure of cases was the deciding factor in setting the standard for admission to the operating theatre. For example, while "through and through" and flesh wounds should not be sent to the pre-operative ward while compound fractures were waiting in large numbers, on quiet days with no rush of cases they should be sent through. Again abdominal cases with poor pulses should not be sent in while large numbers of penetrating joints and fractures were waiting.

The C.C.S. Group: Rotation of Duty. In quiet times each C.C.S. in the group received for 24 hours, but in rushes the reception was 150-250 cases. The unit was then closed and one of the others opened. When the C.C.S. closed, the receiving tent was cleared, all the cases proceeding either to ward, to evacuation tent, or to pre-operative tent.

Technique for Operation. The cases in the pre-operative tent were gradually passed through the X-ray room and the theatre, urgent cases going first. From the theatre, if fit to travel, they went into evacuation ward; if not fit, to post-operative (remaining) wards. While the pre-operative tent was being cleared at the rate, roughly, of 2 cases per hour for each surgeon, the resuscitation ward was looked through and cases brought into the theatre. The resuscitation ward would soon empty, for if a man was fit to operate on he was sent to the theatre, and then into the post-operative ward—on the other hand if he was unfit to operate on, the end was usually not far off. When the pre-operative ward was emptied, and the theatre emptied and the cases

Graph No. 1

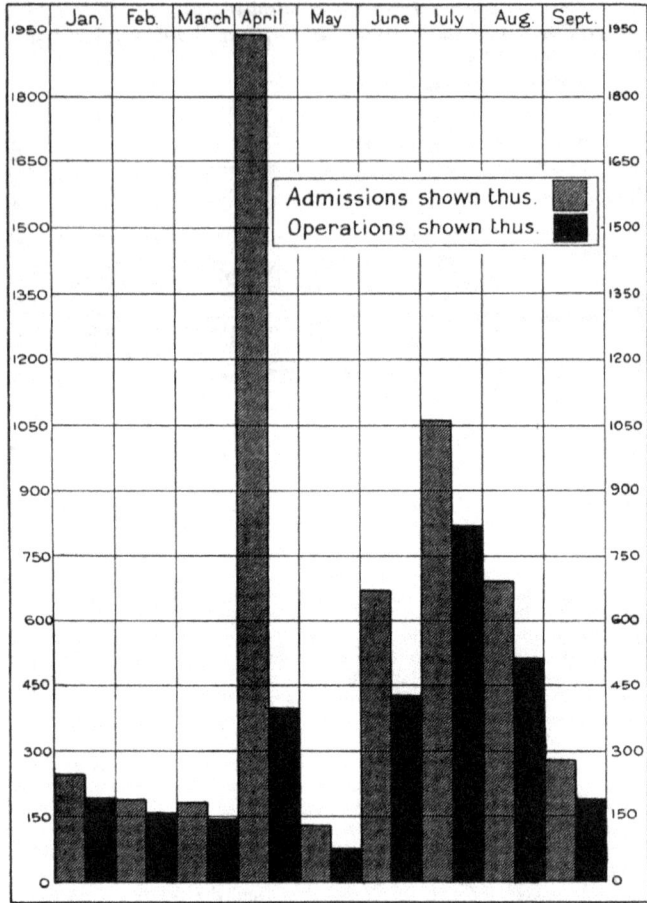

GRAPH SHOWING NUMBER OF WOUNDED (EXCLUDING GAS) ADMITTED EACH MONTH TO NO. 2 AUSTRALIAN CASUALTY CLEARING STATION, JANUARY TO SEPTEMBER, 1918, AND THE PROPORTION OF THESE WHO WERE OPERATED ON AT THE C.C.S.

Note.—Low proportion during April is due to overflow of cases during German Offensive.

From graph by 12408 Pte P. G. Samson in the unit war diary.

from resuscitation ward and chest ward done, there would be a lull. This, however, was rarely so, for usually in a stunt the C.C.S. opened again before the pre-operative ward was nearly empty.

Evacuation. The cases were sent off in ambulance trains, the idea being to keep accommodation in the C.C.S. for new cases.

The dominant idea in the work of the casualty clearing station was prophylaxis, an outlook which happily is being more studied in civil practice. On the medical side the early treatment of disease dove-tailed exactly with its prevention, so that the two may scarcely be separated. On the surgical side the prevention of sepsis made possible a vast increase in the proportion of wounds that should heal and permit return to duty without delay. At the same time (as has been well said by Sir Robert Jones himself) orthopaedic surgery begins at the C.C.S. in the prevention of functional deformities.[38]

Clinical organisation

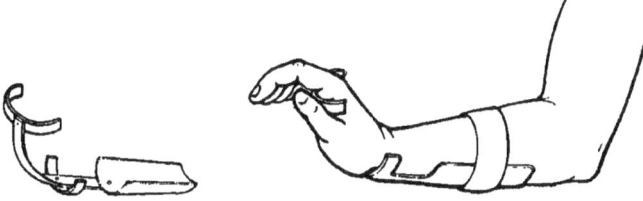

The Cock-Up Splint.

The surgical work at the casualty clearing station reflected very exactly the successive phases in the evolution of the general treatment of the wound, and of the wounded man. This is clearly shown by Australian records. Surgical work in the Third ·Battle of Ypres was definitely experimental;[39] at the Remy group B.I.P. and Carrel were in full vogue. The zenith of technical efficiency was not reached in the B.E.F. till the first quarter of

The surgical division

---

[38] Sir Henry Newland, whose experience in the immediate and late effects of war wounds was exceptionally varied and intimate, always strongly urged the importance of this principle in military orthopaedics. A favourite illustration was the value of the "cock-up" splint in wounds of the forearm in cases evacuated from C.C.S. to the Base in a rush.

[39] A particularly useful implement in the clinical experiment was the establishing of *liaison* between front and Base by the exchange of post-cards between the operating surgeon at the C.C.S. and the officer dealing with the case at the Base.

1918—the stage of the war to which our study in this volume has so far taken us.⁴⁰ Excision with primary or delayed primary suture had by then been accepted as the ideal procedure in the C.C.S., and the structure and operation of the evacuating machinery was being moulded to serve this technique. A generation of surgeons expert in the new methods was available, many of them young graduates who had grown up professionally with the war.⁴¹ The C.C.S. was the most advanced station at which ordinarily there presented itself the problem of regional surgery—penetrating wounds of the head and neck, thorax, abdomen, bladder, joints and limbs, injuries to large blood vessels, formal amputations, and so forth. The advances made in the general surgery of wounds was an *open sesame* to technical improvements in the special surgery of regional wounds.

The Task of Classification and Disposal. As the casualty clearing station was the heart of the system of clearing the wounded, so the receiving ward may be termed the sino-auricular node of the internal effecting mechanism. At the stage in the medical history of the war to which our study has reached, the most important factor in success was correct discrimination among wounds and wounded men, and ensuring that the action taken accorded exactly with the needs of the moment. The responsibility for this fell largely on the *Receiving Officer*, whose task has been well summed up⁴² as follows:—

"It is usual to select a surgeon of wide experience for this work, since, when the convoys are arriving in rapid succession, the duty of the 'spotting officer' becomes a task of great responsibility. He must be able, for instance, to gauge rapidly the general condition of a patient and the probable degree of seriousness of his wound. . . . He must keep a constant eye on the operation list. Should the latter be short, or the stream of patients be falling off, he can mark for the preparation room any cases which seem at all serious. In the contrary case, he must decide whether the individual and general interests would best be consulted by sending the case down to the base forthwith, should an ambulance train be waiting or expected, or by keeping him even though it is not likely to be possible to perform the operation for many hours."

Discrimination of Wounds. The following order of the C.O. No. 3 A.C.C.S. (Lieut.-Colonel R.D. Campbell), April 1918,

---

⁴⁰ Thus the diaries of Nos. 2 and 3 A.C.C.S's for Feb., 1918, report visits by their own surgeons along with "the surgeons of C.C.S's in this Army" to the research centre at No. 10 C.C.S. "to see the work that was being done there in connection with the early closure of wounds . . . in what class of case, with how much safety and success recent wounds may be closed after excision, or, when not judged safe to close at once, whether early secondary suture is not practicable."

⁴¹ *See p. 27.*

⁴² From an article by an anonymous author in *British Medicine in the War 1914-17* published by the British Medical Association Nov., 1917.

on advice of the Surgeon Specialist (Lieut.-Colonel W.G.D. Upjohn) closely reflects the general experience of the Australian casualty clearing stations:—

"The classification of wounded cases on admission by the Receiving Officer will until further notice be, in order of severity, as follows:—

Class "A"	Disposal	Label
1. Urgent cases	Preparatory Ward	URGENT
2. Penetrating Abdomen	Resuscitation or Preparatory Ward	ABDOMEN
3. Penetrating Chests	Acute Surgical Ward	CHEST
4. Compound Fracture Skull	Resuscitation or Preparatory Ward	"A"
5. Compound Fracture Femur	Resuscitation or Preparatory Ward	"A"
6. Spinal Injuries	Acute Surgical Ward	SPINE
7. Wounds of Large Joints	Resuscitation or Preparatory Ward	"A"

"All 'A' Class cases after admission to Preparatory Ward, Acute Surgical Ward or Resuscitation Ward will if possible be seen by the Senior Surgeon.
"The admission of 'URGENT or 'ABDOMINAL' cases will be notified by the Receiving Officer to the Senior Surgeon without delay.

"*Class 'B.'* This class of case is one that definitely requires operation before evacuation. It includes scalp and face wounds, non-penetrating thoracic and abdominal wounds, multiple wounds and wounds of extremities, (except tourniquet and haemorrhage cases, compound fracture femurs and penetrating wounds of large joints). These cases if much shocked *e.g.*, multiple wounds will go to Resuscitation, otherwise to Preparatory Ward. They will be labelled 'B' and will carry a number indicating precedence for operation based on order of admission.

"*Class 'C.'* A slighter class of case comprising minor flesh wounds, through and through bullet wounds of extremities without complications, finger injuries etc. These cases *will be dressed* before leaving the Receiving Tent, will be labelled 'C' and will be sent to a walking wounded ward. They will be operated on if pressure of work permits and if not, will be evacuated.

"*Class 'D.'* Minor surgical cases not requiring operation. They *will be dressed* before they leave the Receiving Tent, labelled 'D' and sent to a Walking Wounded Tent; during times of pressure all 'D' cases will be considered as for evacuation."

Treatment of the Wounded Man. The general surgery of wounds has formed the subject of the preceding chapter and, as already noted, it is not proposed in this work to enter upon any detailed account of regional surgery. Nor is it proposed to devote space to a description of the organisation of the operating theatre—rotation of duty, working of the surgical teams, and so forth. Such belongs more properly to a military manual. But the matter of the wounded man calls for more particular comment.

The *ultima thule* of high adventure, alike in the emotional and the scientific sphere in the treatment of severely wounded men, was the "resuscitation ward" of the C.C.S. Here were sent the men whose spark of life flickered—often to extinction. But if its tragedies were many and poignant, its triumphs were often dramatic, and success was surprisingly frequent, even among seemingly moribund men.

Factors in "Resuscitation." The evolution of resuscitation in the C.C.S. was due to (a) general recognition of the importance of wound shock and understanding of the factors in its production—in particular, the danger of immediate operation under anaesthetic without reviving treatment, such as rest. (b) Appreciation of the importance of artificial

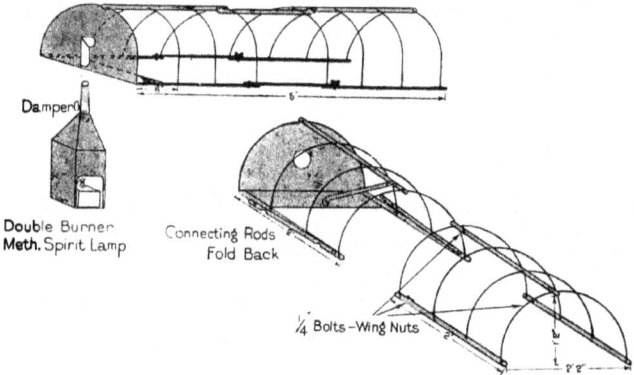

Portable hot-air cradle for use in resuscitation ward. (Designed by Pte. E. E. McMurdie, No. 2 A.C.C.S.; the drawing by Pte. A. E. Toyer, in the unit war diary for July, 1918.) For purposes of transport, one half of the cradle was placed within the other, the lamp, protected by a blanket, being fitted into the concavity.

warmth for the severely shocked man. (c) Appreciation of the significance of anoxaemia in wound shock and haemorrhage; and of the therapeutic utility, in shock, of increasing the fluid mass of the blood, as by colloidal saline infusions; and, in haemorrhage, also of replacing lost red blood corpuscles by transfusion; and in both, of supplying potential energy in the form e.g. of sugar. (d) The development of methods of technique of anaesthesia suited to the special requirements of wound surgery; in particular the general use of the nitrous-oxide oxygen mixture as a routine in operations not requiring complete relaxation—made possible by the introduction of apparatus designed in America—and by use of premedication. (e) The implementing of these discoveries by (i) the creation of administrative and executive machinery for ensuring the supply and distribution of apparatus suitable for field use and of materials for such—infusion-solutions, preserved blood, typing sera, and so forth; and (ii) by dissemination throughout the field-service of information on the nature, causes, and treatment of shock and collapse, and by instruction in the necessary technique. These latter were in full swing when the German break-through at the end of March, 1918, interrupted for some weeks the progress of scientific advance.

Some of these technical matters will be considered later.[43]

The graph given on *page 372* illustrates the work of an Australian casualty clearing station on the Western Front. The percentage of wounded operated on in C.C.S's during the Battle of Arras, April, 1917, is placed at 24, and at Messines, June, 1917, at 16. "During quiet periods" the proportion is stated to have risen to as high as 70 per cent.[44]

The difference in purpose which in front of railhead dominated the activities of the medical service toward wounding and disease respectively—namely, in wounds

The medical division

the motive of *treatment* with a view to saving life or limb, and in disease the motive of *prophylaxis* with particular reference to the prevention of Army wastage—is very clearly reflected in the work and even in the interior economy of the casualty clearing stations. The records of the Australian units make frequent comment on the unscientific and even casual arrangements for treating disease in the C.C.S., in contrast with the high professional standard achieved despite the conditions of the front in the immediate treatment of wounds. Briefly the history of the medical division was as follows:—

"Whilst the necessity for specialists for surgical work was early recognised to be essential in casualty clearing stations and base hospitals, the claims of medicine were longer in receiving special recognition."[45]

---

[43] *See Chapter xxv.*

[44] *Brit. Off. Med. History, Surgery, Vol. I, pp. 239-46.* The startling but highly misleading statistics of the proportion of wounded men that recovered as a result of all this work of rescue are given in *Chapter xxv* together with their explanation.

[45] The quotations are from the *Brit. Off. Med. History, Diseases, Vol. II, p. 499.* The post of "surgical specialist" was clearly defined, and the position held by an officer specially selected. His professional status was independent of his military rank. Thus Lieut.-Col. H. S. Newland, who in 1916 commanded No. 1 A.C.C.S. was, in 1917, appointed "surgeon specialist" to No. 3 under his whilom subordinate. Any relaxation of the professional issue in the selection was, in the A.I.F., strongly resented, as even General Howse had occasion to learn. The vexed question of the ranking and status of "specialists" is dealt with in *Chapter xxvi (pp. 834-9).*

Consulting physicians were appointed to G.H.Q., and to the Boulogne and Rouen Bases, in November, 1914, and in preparation for the Somme Sir Wilmot Herringham (Consulting Physician to G.H.Q.) was stationed in a C.C.S. at Heilly—"in connection with wounds of the chest"! For some time however the problems of surgery dominated the situation at the front and

"it was not until late in 1917 that a medical officer with special qualifications as a physician was officially appointed in each casualty clearing station. By this time the increase in the number of gas casualties had become so great that a definite and growing percentage of battle casualties, in addition to the ordinary sick was passing into the medical rather than the surgical side of the field medical units."

Their work was closely co-ordinated with that of the mobile laboratories, and with the administrative machinery for the prevention of disease. It may, indeed, be questioned whether, from the point of view of military wastage, it was not of equal significance with that of the surgeon specialist. With siege warfare, "gas," and the drive for exact discrimination in the interest of returning men to duty in the case of such "diseases" as "shell shock," trench fever, P.U.O., rheumatism, skin infections, trench foot, and nephritis, the amount of work done by the medical side came almost to rival the surgical, and greatly augmented the problems of housing, equipment, maintenance and transportation—in general the work of the Quartermaster's department.

The C.C.S. and Return to Duty. From the end of 1917 onwards in order to minimise the loss from the Army zone of both "non-battle" and minor "battle" casualties—in particular from the effects of gassing—the potentialities of the C.C.S. were increasingly exploited. C.C.S's were allotted for this special duty and some corresponding change made in their interior economy. Thus in the winter of 1917-18 both Nos. 1 and 3 A.C.C.S. were detailed by the D.G.M.S., B.E.F. to form "Corps Rest Stations" for I and II Anzac Corps respectively.[46]

War diaries of the Australian C.C.S's for the winter of 1917-18 disclose increasing attention not only to the discrimination

---

[46] On Jan. 1, practically all Australian troops having been transferred to the Australian Corps (formerly I Anzac) II Anzac became the XXII (British) Corps. The D.M.S., A.I.F. entered a protest against the allocation of two of the Australian C.C.S's to an "inferior" type of work as rest stations, and after three weeks No. 3 was relieved of this duty. No. 1 however continued to serve as a "Corps Rest Station" until the German offensive in 1918.

and treatment of gassed cases but to diagnostic refinements of all kinds, in particular to greater exactness in the analysis of P.U.O. As will be seen later this urge for exactness spread throughout the field units.

The Rôle of the C.C.S. in the Prevention of Disease. This aspect of the function of the C.C.S. was not prominent in the experiences of the Australian units, but was nevertheless one of great importance and will be clearly identified as such in the account of disease prevention to be given in *Chapters XVII, XVIII and XIX*.

Its rôle in *"triage"* and treatment completed, the C.C.S. had to fill the second half of its function—that of a "clearing" station. A proportion of light cases (more of the sick than of the wounded) were cleared back to duty by way of the "Corps Reinforcement Camp"; more serious cases, whose presence was embarrassing to the Army and hurtful to themselves, were sent on to the next stage of treatment, at the General Hospitals at the Base. Although passage through the station necessarily caused some delay in the onward flow of casualties, the urgency of "clearance" required that this check should be reduced to a minimum. Movement through the unit itself has been described. For unloading the motor ambulance convoy and on-loading the ambulance train men were obtained from such outside sources as diverse as the field ambulance bearer divisions, resting combatant units, labour companies, venereal convalescents, "T.B." and "P.B." men.

" Clearance "

The writer must unwillingly content himself with this bald account of a unit whose importance, as the focal point in the medical work of the Army zone in respect both to the treatment of wounds and the prevention of disease, and as well in the whole course of wounds and the welfare of the wounded man,[47] can hardly be over-estimated.

It remains briefly to outline the particular experiences of the three Australian casualty clearing stations in France and Belgium during the period of attrition warfare.

---

[47] Colonel Sir H. S. Newland whose experience covered a wide field of surgical work has recorded as his opinion (Australian War Records files) that, apart from actual rescue, the C.C.S. more than any other medical unit determined the fate of the wounded man.

THE AUSTRALIAN CASUALTY CLEARING STATIONS ON THE WESTERN FRONT

March, 1916—March, 1918.

From the point of view of service the Australian casualty clearing stations were "Imperial" units—using the term in its proper sense and not as synonymous with "British." They were an integral part of the second line of medical defence and their disposition and operations were directly controlled from G.H.Q. by the Director-General through the medical directors of the several Armies. Subject however to certain intra-imperial understandings[48] they were used in exactly the same way as the units raised in Britain and in other Dominions. But, except in the British advance of 1918, one at least was always found behind the Australian formations and a substantial proportion of Australian casualties passed through them.[49] Three stations only were raised by Australia instead of the normal one per Division. The deficit, however, was due not to any reluctance on the part of Australia to raise the stations, but to an impression, due to negotiations, such as those referred to later in this chapter,[50] that the War Office did not require them.

Some "Imperial" adjustments

In the matter of service it can be stated that the parts for which the Australian units were cast by the Director-General were nicely adjusted to meet at once the desires of General Howse and the aspirations of the units themselves and to give the most useful service within the B.E.F.; and that in this service each unit came to achieve the fullest confidence and regard of the D's.M.S. concerned. The D.G.M.S., B.E.F. and Army directors were keenly concerned to ensure that the Australian units developed homogeneously with the rest of the B.E.F. It has to be acknowledged that General Howse, imbued with the traditions of Gallipoli, was somewhat slow in appreciating the administrative difficulties brought about in the B.E.F. by the move up of the operative centre of gravity from the Base Hospitals to the C.C.S. He was moreover strongly (and not unjustifiably) sceptical of the plan to find teams from the Base for the front which should "double back," so to speak, in time to catch the rush when it reached the Base. Instead, he increased the surgical staff of the clearing stations themselves. At the end of 1917 a definite issue existed between the D.M.S., A.I.F. and the British Director General in France, in this matter. This will be followed later, but the outcome was that on 1st March, 1918, General Howse recommended for the approval of the G.O.C., A.I.F. (General Birdwood) "the appointment of six complete Surgical Teams to be drawn from

---

[48] See Chapter xxvi (pp. 821-7). [49] See Graph on p. 385.
[50] And in Vol. I, pp. 492 and 497-8.

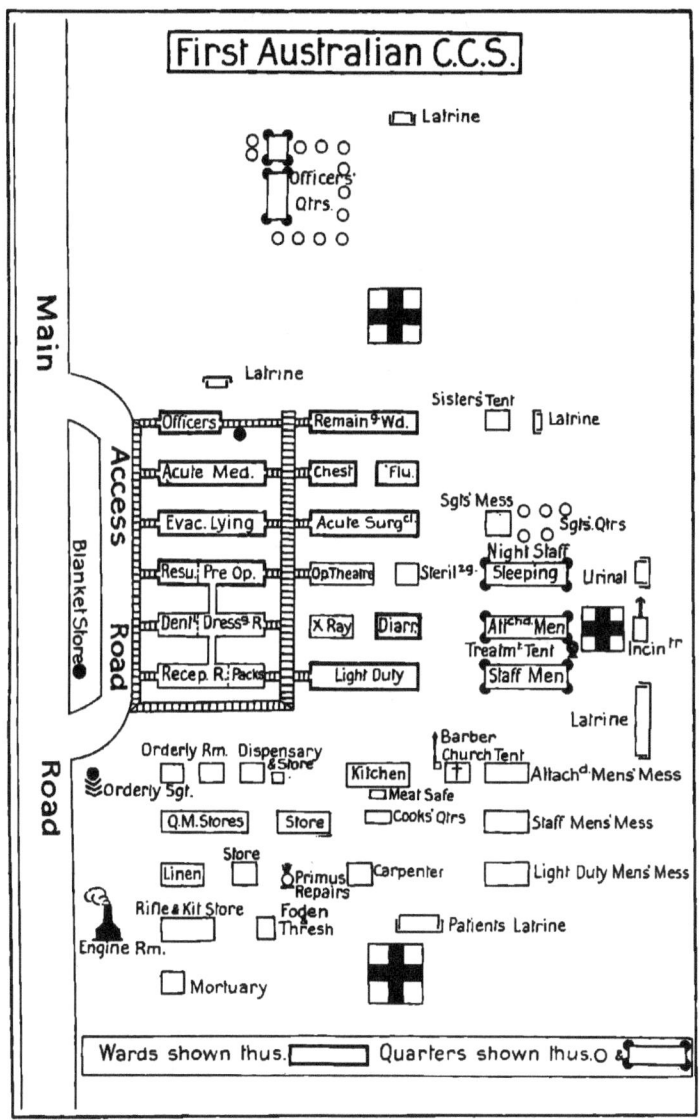

Plan of No. 1 Australian Casualty Clearing Station, at Frétin, at end of October, 1918.
This shows the station as reduced in the later stages of the war.
From drawing in war diary of No. 1 A.C.C.S.

A.A.M.C. personnel and to be available for use by the Imperial authorities when required; each team to consist of 1 Surgeon, 1 Anaesthetist, 1 Theatre Sister and 2 Orderlies." The teams were to be held at the three Australian General Hospitals and were ready for the great events of 1918. They comprised men who to-day are leaders in Australian surgery.

In the years of attrition warfare the *tempo* for the C.C.S's was set by three great British or Allied offensives: the Battles of the Somme, July 1916-November 1916; the battles around Arras April 1917-May 1917; and the battles in Flanders June-October 1917. One or another of the Australian C.C.S's was involved in each of these. The table at *page 364* and sketch map at *page 772* present at a glance their main history.

The Units April, 1916- May, 1917

Nos. 1 and 2, it will be recalled, arrived in France with the A.I.F. and were at once established behind the force in the British Second Army—almost literally "in the front line." In this solidly efficient Army, under Surgeon-General (later Sir) Robert Porter they worked till the end of the war—always in close conjunction, at times in double harness.

No. 1 A.C.C.S. (Lieut.-Colonel H. S. Newland) took over the Ecole du Sacré Coeur at Estaires in April, 1916. The nursing sisters joined and the unit opened immediately behind the I Anzac Corps for about 400 patients on May 17th. Here, during thirteen months, on a quiet front the unit built up, on the foundations of its Gallipoli experience, a technique and system on "western" lines that was afterwards to carry it with high credit through some of the most stirring experiences of any such unit in the war. During the winter 1916-17 it greatly expanded, running convalescent and isolation sections as well as dealing with the wounded from a divisional front.

"This C.C.S.," Colonel Dick notes in his diary, 11th April, 1917, "like many others, is virtually also a stationary hospital—owing to the long continued stage of stationary warfare such as has been necessary from trench warfare, which resembles for evacuation purposes all kinds of siege warfare. No unnecessary moves of similar C.C.S's are carried out—the damage to equipment of a highly technical kind is always considerable in any move, and C.C.S's now possess such."

No. 2 A.C.C.S. Lieut.-Colonel H. S. Stacy was allotted an undeveloped site at Trois Arbres near Steenwerck which it took over on June 17th.[51] Here the unit built up *de novo* a station which, within a month of its arrival, and ten hours after opening up, was able to deal with 900 wounded from the Battle of Fromelles.

"The laying out of the station; the erection of marquees on very

---

[51] The unit had been quarantined for some weeks at Marseilles owing to an outbreak of relapsing fever.

rough ground; the making of an in and out road consisting of a solid plank track; the building of bridges and the sinking of wells to ensure a good water-supply—involved very hard work. Two large tanks were installed on raised platforms giving a sufficient fall to enable water to flow freely where needed. A large Nissen was erected to serve for the operating theatre and X-ray department. Two long rows of double marquees were erected, and duckboards placed through the camp."[52]

A feature special to this unit was its use of a light trolley railway for its internal lines of communication, the rails being carried in sections as part of the unit equipment.

"Right through the period at this site, the work of construction was continually going on. Huts were erected for the special departments of the station—mortuary, quartermaster's stores, dental and staff quarters. At a later date, marquees were replaced by four large Latapee huts."

From August 1916 the unit received alternatively with No. 2 British C.C.S. at Bailleul. During the winter of 1916-17 this unit also served as a rest station with accommodation for 1,000 patients who might recover "within three weeks."

No. 3 A.C.C.S. (Lieut.-Colonel J. Corbin). This unit was raised in Australia with the 3rd Division[53] and arrived in England with that formation in July, 1916. On arrival the unit found itself for the time superfluous while the Division trained in England. But judicious importunity by Surgeon-General Howse gave it its chance,[54] and on September 26th the unit embarked for France, and arrived at Gézaincourt on October 5th, reporting to the D.M.S. "Reserve Army."[55] Thereafter the experiences of this C.C.S. were closely involved with the fortunes of this "stormy petrel" of British Armies and with the experiments of its adventurous medical director, Surgeon-General Skinner.

At Gézaincourt the unit replaced No. 11 British, and the C.O. took

---

[52] From a report drawn up for Colonel Stacy by Staff-Sergeant M. T. Baster. An excellent history of this station has since been compiled by Colonel Stacy and others.

It is claimed for this unit—it would seem justly—that it was the first in the B.E.F. to work with an X-ray outfit of its own. In 1916 the C.C.S's in Bailleul were served thus—"A lorry with X-ray apparatus came from Hazebrouck twice a week; if [urgent] the plate was developed in a small area on the lorry screened with black canvas. Otherwise the plate was brought to the C.C.S. on the next visit, or a telephone report might be made from Hazebrouck."

[53] *See Vol. I, p. 519.* Colonel Corbin had been second-in-command of No. 1 on Gallipoli, whence he was invalided to Australia.

[54] At this time the A.I.F. had four divisions in the line but only two casualty clearing stations. Early in August Surgeon-General Howse, through the D.A.G. at A.I.F. Headquarters, informed the D.G.M.S., B.E.F. (General Sloggett) that an Australian C.C.S was available, and desired that it should be accepted for service in France. Failing this (he stated) the unit—then doing nothing on Salisbury Plain —"would have to be disbanded and that would cause much discontent." On Aug. 16 General Haig advised the War Office that, on the basis of one C.C.S. per infantry division, the B.E.F. was two short of establishment; and that, if it were considered desirable to meet the views of the Australian and Canadian Governments in this matter, both No. 3 A.C.C.S. and No. 4 Canadian could be accepted. He stipulated, however, that it should be clearly understood that, for the time being, their duties would be confined to work at the Base, and to reinforce other units. Surgeon-General Howse, through the G.O.C., A.I.F. (General Birdwood), desired that the C.C.S. should be employed "as such" at an early date, somewhere in France; and on Sept. 19 he was advised that it could now be "placed" with one of the British Armies.

[55] Under General Gough. On Oct. 30 this army became Fifth Army.

over the command also of the Advanced Operating Centre at Authie.[56] After a few days to prepare, it opened on October 14th for "walking wounded." The first convoy of 250 arrived from the Battle of Beaumont Hamel, and the unit received congratulations from the adjacent 29th British C.C.S. "on the way in which its first convoy was handled."[57] In the first 48 hours 1,516 men were admitted and 1,400 evacuated; and from 14th to 30th October, 4,130 were admitted with 413 operations. After closing then for a week to install heating stoves the unit was "promoted" and took all types of case in strict alternation with the British 29th. For the rest of November, of some 3,000 admitted, 98 per cent. were wounded.

"Trains ran into the little siding loaded with wounded from the Somme battlefields. The weather was terrible and the mud near the line so bad that many came in for treatment literally covered from head to foot. . . . Sometimes 3 and 4 trains per day with loads of 200-400 cases. . . ." In December the sick began to come in numbers—trench foot, rheumatism, pneumonia. In spite of the terrible weather "the winter passed very pleasantly and with plenty of blankets and stores we managed to keep the cold out."

Move to Edgehill. On the 9th of February, 1917, the unit received orders to move to Edgehill. "Although we had arrived at Gézaincourt with three lorry-loads of equipment, when we came to move to Edgehill, instead of 3, there were 30 lorry-loads of gear to be moved." The new site "was on virgin ground and an entirely new C.C.S. had to be laid out" giving opportunity for exploiting original ideas.

The conditions of evacuation to this centre have already been described.[58] The unit worked here till April 7th when "orders were received to move forward to Grévillers near Bapaume, which had fallen some three weeks before. Shell holes were filled in to pitch the tents," and on the 9th the unit opened to receive "all classes of case. . . . The size of the camp was gradually extended to cope with the enormous number of wounded which were being received from Lagnicourt and Bullecourt." Subsequently the Australian C.C.S. was joined by Nos. 3 and 29 British, and with them formed the Grévillers "group."

As part of the general preparations for the Third Battle of Ypres on July 21st the unit was transferred to Flanders for special duty. At the same time Colonel Corbin handed over his command to Colonel R. D. Campbell.

No. 1. In preparation for the Flanders offensive, on May 19th No. 1 opened up in Bailleul, in the College of St. Joseph and on vacant land adjoining; 50 marquees were erected and some 300 yards of planking laid down. During the Battle of Messines this unit worked in conjunction with Nos. 2, 11, and 53 British, and between June 6th and 9th admitted 2,450 wounded. In July Bailleul was heavily bombed—hardly a matter for surprise—and the unit suffered a number of casualties in-

The Flanders Offensive, 1917

---

[56] 1 officer and 11 other ranks were detached for duty at this centre, which accommodated 60 cases, "mostly head, chest, and abdomen." The returns of this centre were rendered by it as a part of No. 3.
[57] This quotation and those that follow are (1) from the diary of the unit, (2) from a report by the commanding officer to the D.M.S., A.I.F., and (3) from a memorandum written for the Australian War Memorial by Capt. F. W. Fay.
[58] *See pp. 116-21.*

Graph No. 2

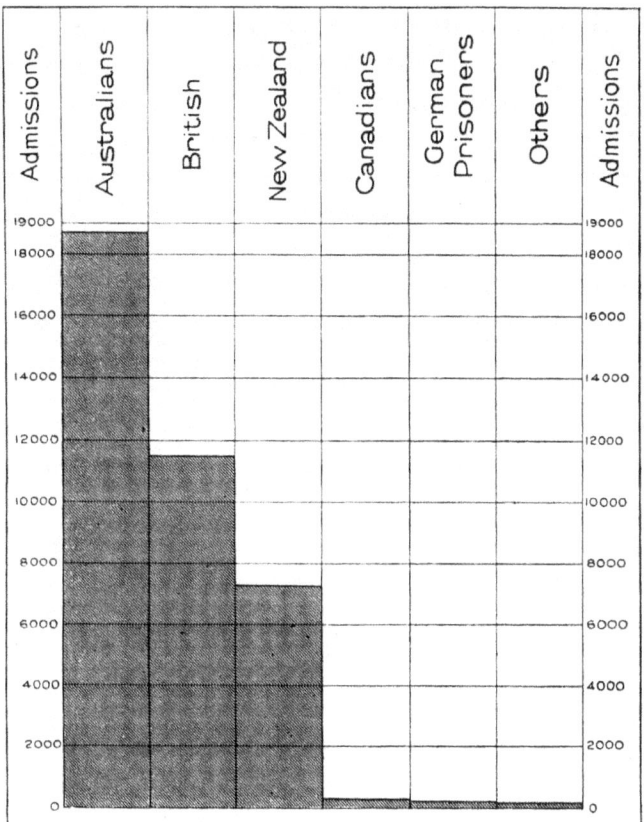

TOTAL ADMISSIONS TO NO. 2 AUSTRALIAN CASUALTY CLEARING
STATION FROM 1 JULY, 1916, TO 1 JUNE, 1918

Note.—The column "Others" includes B.W.I., Bermudians, French, Civilians, South Africans, Portuguese, and Americans.

The purpose of the graph is to emphasise the fact that, though the Australian C.C.S's were employed on a definitely "Imperial" basis and were wholly at the disposal of the D.G.M.S., B.E.F., the promise given by Britain to the Australian Government that when circumstances permitted they should serve the Australian force was faithfully kept. It may be noted that the proportion of total Australian casualties to British on the Western Front was roughly 1 to 15. The relative numbers of Australians treated by the other two, though not so high as in No. 2—which it will be recalled served the 3rd Division in the Battle of Messines—were quite comparable. The fact that the New Zealand Division saw most of its service in Second Army explains the large number treated in the Australian unit.

From graph by 12403 Pte. P. G. Samson in the unit war diary.

cluding one Sister wounded.[59] In consequence, all the stations were removed, No. 1 Australian to a site between Bailleul and Oultersteene; 108 lorry-loads of equipment were transferred to the new site, where a tented and hutted hospital was erected to accommodate 750 patients, and work was recommenced.

No. 2. Throughout the whole period of the Flanders offensive No. 2 had little respite—on the first day of the Battle of Messines 2,067 wounded were admitted and 2,000 evacuated in twenty-four hours. The work of the unit in this battle has been described;[60] and it played an important part in the subsequent fighting in this area. On the night of July 22nd two bombs were dropped on the station; two of the staff and 3 patients were killed, and 24 patients wounded. Thereafter, on the supposition that the bombing was deliberate, the use of distinguishing lights was officially stopped, and tents and huts were revetted.

The total admissions for sickness and wounds during June, July, and August, 1917, numbered 16,357 (including 1,077 gassed), of whom 452 died. Of 2,775 cases operated on during this period, approximately 1,600 were X-rayed "chiefly for the localisation of missiles."[61] During the year ending 30th August, 1917, 200 operations were done for penetrating wounds of the abdomen, of which cases 93 were evacuated to the Base, and 107 died in the station.

The subjoined table shows admissions of wounded and operations under anaesthetic for the months January to December, 1917.[62]

	Jan.	Feb.	Mar.	Apr.	May	June	July	Aug.	Sept.	Oct.	Nov.	Dec.
Admissions	232	218	305	387	937	6,267	2,168	2,067	547	358	347	550
Operations	131	142	144	211	397	1,052	790	933	254	200	169	331

In the Third Battle of Ypres in the later phases (September 20th-November 10th) both stations formed part of the evacuation scheme of Second Army which (it will be recalled) began in September to play the chief part. For the Battle of Menin Road Australian casualties went to the Remy group; No. 1 Australian and No. 2 British cleared for the British IX Corps, and No. 2 Australian and No. 53 British for the XVIII Corps. Both units worked at high pressure—so much so, indeed, that the C.O. of No. 1 (Lieut.-Colonel J. A. Dick) was constrained to note in his war diary of September 21st:—

"It is *always* difficult to get 'surgeons' to evacuate patients; also always difficult to get medical officers to perform fully the clerical part of their work. It is possible for medical men to be good surgeons or physicians or anything else, and still be bad 'medical officers.'"

No. 3. The selection of this unit by Surgeon-General Skinner for his experiment in forward emplacement, and its adventures therein at Brandhoek, have already received note.[63] After eviction, the staff was attached for a time to No. 10 British at Remy Siding; subsequently, in co-operation with a British C.C.S. as a "group," a very fine station was built up at "Nine Elms," behind Poperinghe.

---

[59] Sister Rachel Pratt, M.M.
[60] *See pp. 179-80.*
[61] The authority for this statement is a note in an (unpublished) history of this unit by the radiologist, Sergeant W. H. Jones. The claim is made by this unit that its X-ray Department was "the first of its kind with any C.C.S. in France."
[62] These figures are taken from an appendix to the unit diary of April 1918.
[63] *See pp. 187-8.*

The dominant military problem at this time was that of "strength." The reflection of this in the evolution of the C.C.S. has already been noted. Nos. 1 and 3 were at this stage wholly transformed to serve as Rest Stations, and No. 1 continued to act as such till the end of March, 1918. All three units were close behind the Australian Corps, and achieved close relations, personal and professional, with Australian field formations. Lectures were given and demonstrations arranged for medical officers of the field units.

Winter of 1917-18

The next phase in the experience of these units, in the German offensive, belongs to a later chapter.

SYNOPSIS OF CHAPTER XIV

EVACUATION: EXPEDITIONARY BASE, THE GENERAL HOSPITALS

BRITISH L. OF C.—MEDICAL ADMINISTRATION:
Ambulance trains—their control.
The trains.
The open truck.
"Improvised" and "Temporary Ambulance Trains."
The special "Ambulance" or "Hospital" Trains.

THE BASES.
Medical organisation.
The Consultants—Duties.

THE GENERAL HOSPITAL SYSTEM OF THE B.E.F.:
The Hospital centres.
Bed accommodation of General Hospitals.
Structure of a General Hospital.
    Establishment—Housing and lay-out—Kitchen—Sanitation—Equipment—Y.M.C.A. Hut and Red Cross Store.
Functions of a General Hospital.
The "Convoy"—Admission.
The duties of the staff.
    Commissioned officers—Nursing staff—Other ranks—Under-age boys—"P.B." men—Extra-unit personnel.
Evacuation:
Synopsis of disposal of cases and classification.
Disposal: return to duty.
Treatment at the Bases:
Notes on surgery in the Base Hospitals.
Venue for operation in rushes.
Provision for regional surgery.
    Femurs; injury of the eyes, face, and jaws; knee joints etc.
Operation to rectify deformities.
General surgery of wounds at the Base.
    The *bête noir*—"true sepsis."
Medicine at the Base.
    "Battle" or "Non-battle"?—Chemical trauma—Battle wounds—"Chest wounds."
The medical wards.
    Abbeville 1917-18—Trench fever—Gas—Respiratory—Nephritis—Other infections—Dysentery—Enterica—Meningitis.
Pathology in the Base Hospitals.

SYNOPSIS OF CHAPTER XIV

RESEARCH AT THE BASE:
Laboratory experiment and clinical observation
Research in problems of wounds.
Research into the aetiology of disease.

THE AUSTRALIAN GENERAL HOSPITALS IN FRANCE, 1916-17:
The D.M.S., A.I.F. and the Australian Hospitals.
Establishment of Australian General Hospitals.
Nos 1, 2, and 3 A.G.H.

RETURN TO DUTY—THE BASE DEPOTS:
"Australian General Base Depot."
Classification—System of training—Infectious disease—Statistics.

EMBARKATION.

CHAPTER XIV

EVACUATION: EXPEDITIONARY BASE. THE GENERAL HOSPITALS

THE disabled soldier whose wound, injury, or sickness was of such a nature or degree of severity as to make his retention in Army area undesirable—in view either of his own interests or the military situation—was transferred to the Lines of Communication, where he came under the control of the Inspector-General of Communications, and became the responsibility of the Director of Medical Services, L. of C. We visualise, then, a stream of casualties, sick and wounded, drawn from the vast system of treatment stations, major and minor, along the 100 odd miles of the British front passing by innumerable transport routes to converge, now chiefly by rail,[1] to some half-dozen centres of treatment and *triage* on the lines of communication and at the Expeditionary Force Bases. Here for a moment the casualty comes to rest in medical units—"General" and "Stationary"[2] Hospitals—not unlike those of civil life and under conditions not wholly alien from those.

BRITISH L. OF C.—MEDICAL ADMINISTRATION

The British Lines of Communication in France comprised a "two-way" traffic system by rail and sea, between the "Army" area and the Expeditionary Force Bases together with various subsidiary supply depots and medical centres behind the front. This was one of the most important spheres of medical activity, though at the beginning of the war the system was astonishingly vague.

The *British Official Medical History of the War* shows[3] that by October, 1914, confusion had become so confounded that the Director

---
[1] Though by far the greater number reached the Base Hospitals by rail, during 1917-18 31,563 were carried by barge and 52,841 by motor ambulance convoy.
[2] The rôle of the "Stationary" Hospital at the Base was even less defined than at the Front.
[3] *General, Vol. II p. 4.*

of Medical Services of the Expeditionary Force (Surgeon-General T. P. Woodhouse) "was represented in an administrative capacity both at G.H.Q. and on the headquarters of the L. of C., while he himself and his office were attached to neither"; the administration of the medical services at G.H.Q. was "practically in the hands of the Adjutant-General, assisted by a deputy director and deputy assistant director of medical services." "The situation" as Sir William Macpherson dryly comments "was not one which was conducive to smooth administration." At the beginning of January, 1915, a complete reorganisation of the administrative medical services was effected with a D.G.M.S. (Sir A. Sloggett) "as the responsible head at G.H.Q." and a Director of Medical Services (Surgeon-General Woodhouse) at the headquarters of the I.G.C. at Abbeville. The medical control of the several bases was placed under deputy directors.

With changes incidental to the development of the B.E.F. this arrangement persisted throughout the war.

The staff of the D.M.S., L. of C., included a D.A.D.M.S. for ambulance trains; after 1915 he was graded as an A.D.M.S. and had a small expert staff. Working in close conjunction with the

Ambulance trains— their control
Director of Transportation at G.H.Q., this officer controlled the movement of all the ambulance trains on the British front. The diagram on the next page indicates the channels whereby this stupendous task was carried out with unimpeachable efficiency and smoothness. An Ambulance Train Advisory Committee in France, with sub-committee at home, advised G.H.Q. and War Office respectively on the ambulance train requirements and problems associated therewith. A special inspectoral staff was also appointed in France.

The casualty clearing stations, at railhead, were linked to the system of General Hospitals by the ambulance trains.[4]

The Trains
The merging of Dominion with other British and Imperial casualties which began at the C.C.S.[5] was here complete since the service was supplied entirely by the War Office (or through it by private benevolence) and

---

[4] See pp. 28, 269. Railhead on the Western Front (it may be recalled) corresponded with the port of Mudros in the Gallipoli Campaign as a centre for classification and treatment; and the "black" ships and hospital ships corresponded to the ambulance train. For the student of military medical tactics and strategy no better exercise could be imagined than a comparative study of the transport and treatment problems of the L. of C. in the two campaigns.

[5] One feature of the arrangements on the ambulance trains went against Australian feelings; namely the unduly great difference in the matter of the comfort provided for the "commissioned" officer and for the rank and file. This "class" distinction between the wounded was strongly marked throughout the British Army medical system—*e.g.* in the provision for "Rest Hospitals" for officers at the Front, at the Base in France, and in Britain. The difference between British and Australian ideas is further seen in the activities of the British Red Cross Society and the Australian Branch respectively. It is fair to note that repugnance to these distinctions was not confined to the A.I.F. The following statement of opinion is that of an R.M.O. of the Guards. "The difference in our Army between the comforts and honours obtained and the hardships that have to be endured by the rank and file, and the easier lot of their officers, would be grotesque even if we were not all of the same race." (*Unwilling Passenger, p. 17*, by Lieut.-Col. Arthur Osburn).

the trains were staffed entirely by personnel of the R.A.M.C. and Q.A.I.M.N.S.[6] But to complete the picture of the evacuation of sick and wounded from front line to base a short account is given of the ambulance train system and service in France.[7]

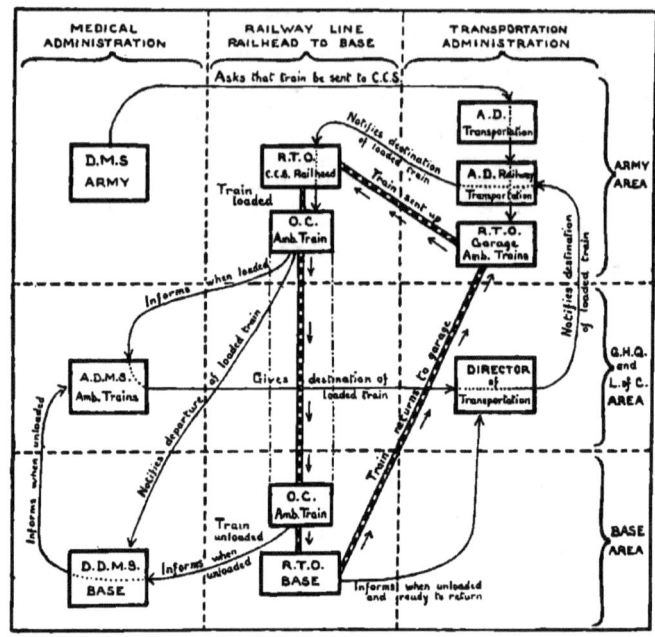

Scheme of method of running an Ambulance Train. (From British Official Medical History.)

The British Ambulance Train in the Great War evolved in three stages: (a) The haphazard use of open trucks. (b) Adaptation of coaches to take stretchers. (c) The construction and working of special ambulance (hospital) trains.

[6] Or by Dominion personnel lent to those services. In this way some members of the A.A.M.C. and A.A.N.S. did terms of duty on these trains. The experience of an Australian Medical Officer-in-charge of one is given in the narrative of March, 1918; see pp. 623-4.

[7] This is taken chiefly from the British Official Medical History and from the article by Surgeon-General Sir George Makins which deals with, inter alia, "Hospital Trains and Motor Ambulances" in British Medicine in the War 1914-17, published by the British Medical Association, 1917 (a reprint of articles in the B.M.J., April to Oct., 1917.)

(a) *The Open Truck*. The method of evacuation of wounded to the Base by open "supply" truck "returning empty" was perforce employed in the first week of the 1914 fighting. The plight of the seriously wounded evacuated thus seems to have created as painful an impression as that of the "black ships" from the Landing.[8]

(b) *"Improvised" and "Temporary Ambulance Trains."* In England at the outbreak of war there was one military ambulance train, constructed during the South African War.

"A small difference in gauge in the French and English lines prevented the prompt shifting of English hospital carriages across the Channel." Great difficulties were experienced in the initial stages of the campaign. "It seems as if both France and Germany had relied for the railway transport of the wounded on the same means which served the purpose in the war of 1870-71. In fact with the exception of the addition of frames for carrying stretchers placed on the floors of merchandise waggons, no special arrangements appear to have been made. [These trains] were provided with no permanent arrangements for cooking food, no sanitary conveniences, no provision for the carriage of water, and, in fact, consisted of a mere string of trucks, with no means of intercommunication."[9]

Even after the introduction of specially designed and constructed ambulance trains, the adaptation of passenger coaches to take stretchers was carried out, and after 1916 huge numbers of walking wounded were evacuated by the "temporary ambulance trains." At the end of the war the technique for adaptation had been standardised, and doubtless the methods adopted are embodied in "mobilisation standing orders" of all scientifically equipped nations. The Australian engineers had some experience in the "Somme winter" of 1916 in connection with evacuation from the Flers front by the broad-gauge train constructed by the I Anzac Corps.[10]

(c) *The Special "Ambulance" or "Hospital" Trains.* At the end of the war there had been specially constructed for the evacuation of British casualties between 40 and 50 ambulance trains, of which the larger number were working on the Western Front. At the end of 1917 the general organisation of a standard train was as follows:—[11] Each was composed of 16 bogie coaches varying from 58 to 61 feet in length. They were vestibuled throughout and heated by steam from the engine, and were fitted with electric light and fans. No. 1 coach was a brake van and lying infectious ward (18 patients); No. 2 a staff car with lavatories, dining and sleeping rooms for sisters and medical officers; and No. 3 a kitchen and "sitting sick officers' car." The following 8 coaches were "ward cars" with 36 beds in each (three tiers of twelve beds) with a lavatory and washing-up sink at the end. The remaining five coaches were, pharmacy and treatment car, sitting infectious car,

---

[8] *Vol. I, p. 179.* As late as May, 1915 (Battle of Neuve Chapelle) the D.M.S. First Army (Surgeon-General W. G. Macpherson) organised a special system for equipping and using empty supply trains for evacuation of wounded. *Brit. Off. Med. History, General, Vol. II, Appendix B.*

[9] Sir George Makins, *loc. cit., p. 58.*

[10] *See pp. 83n, 87-8.*

[11] *Brit. Off. Med. History Vol. IV, Chapter xxiii (pp. 560-665).* This chapter gives a detailed and informative statement of the various means of ambulance transport used in the British Army during the Great War. It is of interest that the aeroplane is not included.

kitchen and personnel mess car, personnel car (other ranks), brake van and store car.

In fact, as the *British Medical History* states,[12] "the ambulance trains were mobile hospitals complete not only in medical equipment but in medical personnel, stretchers, supplies and stores for use on the trains and to meet the emergency demands of D's.M.S. during active operations. They were used not only to evacuate the cases from the front area, but also to permit of treatment of the wounded during the journey."

Each train had a carrying capacity of 306 lying and from 56 to 64 sitting, and 36 to 39 personnel.

Most of the sitting cases were evacuated by the "temporary ambulance trains" ("T.A.T.") which had a capacity of 1,008 in third class carriages. The staff of the "T.A.T's" consisted of 1 Medical Officer, 1 N.C.O., and 8 privates of the R.A.M.C. from the regular ambulance train service. That for the ambulance train consisted of 3 medical officers, 4 nursing sisters and from 45 to 55 other ranks, R.A.M.C. After 1915 they were not marked with the Red Cross since this emblem provided an aiming point for bombing the railway track.

THE BASES

The British Expeditionary Bases in France comprised the ports of Calais, Boulogne, Rouen, Le Havre, Dieppe, and Marseilles; together with supply and reinforcement depots, chiefly at Etaples and Le Havre, and the "Third Echelon" of G.H.Q., B.E.F.—its records department—at Rouen.[13]

The medical organisation at the bases comprised:—
(*i*) Groups of General and Stationary Hospitals
(*ii*) Associated "Convalescent" Hospitals, Camps, or Depots[14]
(*iii*) Venereal, Dermatological, Infectious and other Special Hospitals
(*iv*) Ports of embarkation.

As with the medical stations at the previous levels of evacuation, the purpose of these at the Expeditionary Base was treatment, evacuation, and return to duty; but there was found here in addition exact and deliberate provision for research. The

---

[12] *Loc. cit., pp. 629-30.*
[13] Marseilles was the port for Indian Transports. Each port had its special function—meat, bread, oils and fats, etc. each passing through particular ports. After 1916 Australian reinforcements came chiefly through Le Havre. The homeward bound traffic passed—casualties via Calais, Boulogne, or Le Havre, men on leave mainly through Boulogne.
[14] The slovenliness of military-medical terminology noted in *Vol. I* was found also in France. No one knew what distinction was implied in Convalescent Hospital, Camp or Depot. The proper distinction, which should have been founded on the degree to which they were medical or military (and therefore protected or not by the Geneva Convention), was not observed.

deputy directors at the great ports—under the D.M.S., L. of C., and subject to the policy laid down by the Director-General— were responsible for the treatment and evacuation or return to duty of all casualties arriving by ambulance train or occurring within their area.[16] In most of this wide responsibility Australians had no part, but there was one important function in which the Australian Medical Service was directly concerned.

Reference has been made in various places to the work of the Consulting Surgeons and Physicians. Among these were three members of the Australian Service, Colonel Sir Alexander MacCormick and Lieut.-Colonel T. P. Dunhill, Consulting Surgeons, and Lieut.-Colonel E. W. Fairfax, Consulting Physician. The idea of these appointments originated at the Base and was brought about by the difficulty experienced in (i) securing continuity of action for the individual casualty throughout the stations on the line of evacuation and (ii) diffusing the results of observation and experiment throughout the medical service. This was a difficulty inherent in the organisation of services behind the front in strata or levels, each isolated from the one in advance or in rear of it. The appointment of Consultants was designed to overcome this isolation, and their work was entirely devoted to that end. The methods adopted are admirably set out in the following memorandum by the Consulting Surgeon to Rouen Base Lieut.-Colonel Dunhill, the Surgeon Specialist to No. 2 A.G.H.

"It was our duty to advise the D.D.M.S. on all questions relating to the surgical work of the area; to visit all hospitals and medical units regularly, and to spend much time there; to see that suitable men were placed in the positions of surgeons in charge of divisions and surgical specialists. A consultant must make himself familiar with the work of each of the officers working in his area. It is his duty to recommend changes or promotions. Men who are not deemed capable of filling the positions they occupy are shifted on his recommendation.

Duties—
supervise work

"On visiting a hospital, he calls on the O.C. first, as a matter of courtesy. Then he is met by the officer-in-charge of the surgical division. In times of rush, he does not allow this officer to be brought away from his work, but finds him at his work. He sees cases in consultation with the surgical officers. He watches carefully and notes

---

[16] Boulogne, Rouen and Abbeville, where Australian hospitals were sited, were bombed at various times. At Etaples a general hospital close to the railway junction sustained very heavy casualties.

the treatment and general management of cases. He helps and advises. If necessary he interferes to alter treatment or methods generally.

"When cases come down the line badly treated, he writes to the consulting surgeon of the area from which the case has come, unofficially. The work of the surgeon responsible for the incident is thus watched without any fuss, and a word in season prevents repetitions.

"In rush times it is quite impossible to see in consultation all the cases for whom it would be advisable; but in quieter times plans of work are discussed for the different types of battle injury, and as much individual work as possible is given.

"The consulting surgeon visits other areas and makes himself familiar with methods of treatment which are being carried out there, both at front and base. He meets, and discusses methods with, the consulting surgeons of these areas, and together they plan for continuity of treatment. He finds out the best and he distributes the knowledge acquired to the officers under his control. When there is time he encourages the officers under him to visit other hospitals in the district, or even to travel further afield to see special hospitals or men. In this way a high standard of efficiency is obtained, and a spirit of healthy rivalry induced. He sees that clinical research is kept going, *e.g.* delayed primary suture, methods of wound disinfection, bacteriological problems, etc.—anything that will result in a *saving of man-power for the army.*

To spread knowledge and promote research

"He advises the D.G. re the segregation of certain types of injury. Thus the segregation of fractured femur cases, of head injuries, chest injuries, etc., has immensely improved the methods of treatment in these types and the results obtained.

and advises as to system

"Thus the consulting surgeon, if he does his work conscientiously and sympathetically, ensures smooth and efficient surgical treatment from front line to home base."

THE GENERAL HOSPITAL SYSTEM OF THE B.E.F.

The Hospital Centres. The ultimate disposition of the general and stationary hospitals[16] and convalescent "depots" and "camps" of the B.E.F. was the result of numerous factors—of stirring events in the early months of the war; of the desire of the French authorities that casualties should so far as possible be evacuated to England; of the situation of military camps and "dumps"; of port and railroad facilities; and of the German submarine onslaught on hospital ships in 1917.

In August, 1918, of the 48 General Hospitals and 19 Stationary Hospitals of the B.E.F., 19 General and 8 Stationary Hospitals were

---

[16] The British Historian is emphatic that the function of "General" and "Stationary" Hospitals, as such, cannot be defined, being in both cases dependent on their distance from the front.

at Boulogne and Etaples; 15 General and 5 Stationary at Le Tréport and Rouen; and the remainder at fifteen other centres. In addition there were 7 Voluntary Hospitals and a number of Native Labour Contingent Hospitals.[17]

The great hospital centres at Trouville and Deauville were formed in the spring of 1917. Thereafter little change occurred.

Bed accommodation of General Hospitals

Hospital bed accommodation for the B.E.F. was provided by a system known as "crisis expansion" to meet emergencies. The total accommodation in its various classes of hospitals behind the Western Front varied from some 10,000 beds in 1914 to between 80,000 and 90,000 in 1917-18, and 95,000 at the time of the Armistice. The figures represent the capacity of the hospitals when expanded. The procedure of expansion was provided for by recognising four stages, as follows:—

"(1) The normal bed accommodation permanently established.

"(2) Expansion 'A,' or the number of fully equipped hospital beds, which could be added to each hospital by taking over more buildings or by increasing the number of tents or huts. This expansion was of a semi-permanent character.

"(3) Expansion 'B,' or the number of beds which could be added in an emergency by placing more beds in the wards and reducing the space normally allowed to each bed.

HOSPITAL CENTRES INCLUDING CONVALESCENT DEPOTS IN FRANCE MARCH, 1918, SHOWING ACCOMMODATION (*The numbers given are the maxima. Another centre was at Marseilles, for 5,000 beds; and there were nine others, each with less than 1,000 beds—at Bourg, Aire, Frévent, Doullens, Amiens, Cérisy, Cherbourg, Paris, and Cap Martin.*)

"(4) Expansion 'C.' The amount of additional accommodation available in an emergency by appropriating the huts for personnel, dining rooms and other accessory buildings and placing trestle cots and mattresses in them instead of hospital beds."

---

[17] The stationary hospitals in the forward area are not included in these figures.

At the end of 1916 the total thus provided was—"Normal beds 40,719; Expansion 'A' 7,947; Expansion 'B' 13,310; Expansion 'C' 9,048."[18]

In 1917 group "A" "were included in the normal permanent accommodation of the hospitals" and "B" and "C" became officially known as "crisis expansion."

When full to maximum capacity, including beds added by "expansion," a General Hospital at the seat of war might comprise a community of 3,000-4,000 or even more persons, and its intake and output of patients —its basic metabolism so to speak—might be as high as 800 a day. The most obvious general feature indeed of the series of medical units embraced in the scheme of evacuation will be seen in the increase in their size and complexity at each stage rearward from the front. From the Regimental Medical Establishment of 1 officer and 23 other ranks, through the Field Ambulance, 10 officers, 182 other ranks, and C.C.S., 8 officers, 7 nurses, 78 other ranks, we have now reached the General Hospital, an immense unit which, with the normal complement of 1,040 beds, comprised 34 officers, 73 nurses, 203 other ranks of the medical service. The professional staff is now exactly discriminated as "surgical" and "medical." A place is found for the "specialties" of civil life—eye, ear, nose and throat, skin. A pathological department is an integral part of each unit. In such respects, as well (as will presently be seen) in their method of working, these great units were as closely linked with the hospitals of civil life as with the military stations whose work has been reviewed in the preceding chapters.

Structure of a General Hospital

It follows that, though full of professional interest, the details of the internal structure and activities of these units are not so alien from civil experience as to call for detailed study here.[19] An account of some aspects of their work, however, based chiefly upon the experience of the Australian hospitals, will serve to indicate the nature of the particular problems of these units.

Their *structure*, like that of all military units, included three

---

[18] Quotations are from the *Brit. Off. Med. History, General, Vol. II, p. 67.*
[19] In its general features the work of a military general hospital in the Great War has been described, and illustrated by instance, in *Vol. I.*

elements: (*i*) personnel, (*ii*) housing accommodation, and (*iii*) equipment.[20]

Establishment. The establishment of medical officers and other ranks R.A.M.C. or A.A.M.C. of the "General" Hospital was subject to much change in the course of the war to meet special needs or the changing conditions of the war itself. Beginning with 520-bed hospitals staffed by 21 officers, 43 female nurses and 143 other ranks, in the last year of the war hospitals reached a normal bed-state up to 2,500 and a staff of 41 officers, 125 nurses, 138 other ranks and 124 women (domestics). In 1918 a sliding scale for staff and beds was introduced, the latter rising by accretions of 100 up to 2,500.

Housing and Lay-out. The General Hospitals in France were housed in tents or huts. In No. 1 A.G.H. in June, 1918, the hutting accommodation was as follows:—

Patients. 360 beds, Dining Hall, Cook-house.
Sisters. Quarters, Mess, Bath-house, Cook-house.
Officers. Quarters, Mess, Bath-house, Cook-house.
Other Ranks. Quarters, Recreation and Mess room, Cook-house.

Huts were also provided for one Bath-house for personnel (other ranks) and walking patients; Operation theatres; X-ray room; Pathological laboratory; Dispensary; Matron's office; Post office; and Quartermaster's office and Pack store.

The remainder were in tents.

For the planning and construction of General Hospitals the Engineers were responsible. Of three sites occupied by Australian units, the plan of No. 3 A.G.H. is selected for illustration, since it was designed without regard for exigencies of space and so forth. No. 1 at Rouen and No. 2 at Boulogne were not so exactly laid out.[21]

Kitchen. The importance of this feature in a General Hospital of 2,500 beds need not be stressed. An illustration of the kitchen at No. 3 Australian is given at *p. 428.*

Sanitation. "Sanitation" in these vast tent and hutted towns was a most formidable problem, especially in the winter. The system of

---

[20] That the question whether the first, or the second and third, of these constituted a "hospital," and which element was the more important, is by no means a purely academic one, was shown by Australian experience in the war. At no time was Australia able to provide, from her own resources, General Hospitals adequate to the requirements of her force in the field. Personnel was available, but much of the equipment—particularly tentage—must be obtained overseas. And it may be added that the most difficult problem for Australia to-day would still be the material rather than the human one. In this connection see *Vol. I, p. 89.*

[21] The following is taken from *The Work of the Royal Engineers in the European War 1914-18; Work Under the Director of Works (p. 158)* published for the Institution of Royal Engineers, Chatham. (This history may be commended for many useful specifications of medical constructive works.)

"*Sites and Lay-out.*—Generally speaking, sites for hospitals or groups of hospitals were selected as far as possible in proximity to railway stations, where special sidings could be laid to receive hospital trains, and whence there was good road access to the hospitals. . . . As a type, the plan of a general hospital of 1,500 beds, constructed at Abbeville, is given, as the site imposed no special conditions in the lay-out."

The plan reproduced in the abovenamed history is that of No. 3 Australian General. An exact model of this hospital made by German prisoners of war employed there, was on view for some time at Australia House and is now in the Australian War Memorial at Canberra.

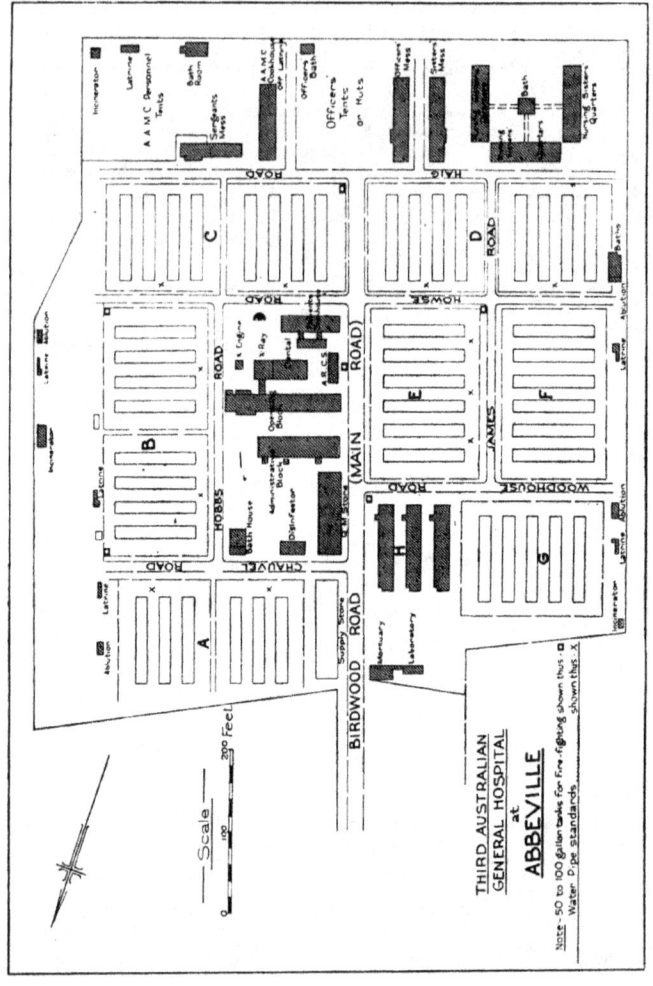

PLAN OF No. 3 AUSTRALIAN GENERAL HOSPITAL

From an Engineer plan which shows the layout and accommodation at the beginning of 1918. Tents are shown unshaded. At a later date, in Blocks E, F, and G, huts of the hospital Nissen type were substituted for the brigaded hospital marquee tents. The first hut in Block H was used for reception and discharge by convoy.

THE GENERAL HOSPITALS

conservancy was designed by the engineers, but was usually carried out by the unit personnel. Faecal disposal was commonly by incineration in destructors.

Equipment. The General Hospitals were equipped on a scale that permitted exact surgical and medical attention in the critical stage of the most serious types of case. The X-ray apparatus was adapted to all the refinements of localisation. In the Australian hospitals the official surgical equipment was greatly supplemented by the "Red Cross" and by special gifts.

Y.M.C.A. Hut and Red Cross Store. The "Y.M.C.A. Hall" was a structural feature whose importance in promoting functional efficiency may properly be stressed. In the Australian units a hut was provided for the representative of the Australian Red Cross Society.

Functions of a General Hospital

One feature of the working of these huge technical units which is not represented in that of the civil hospital calls for special note.

The "Convoy." The casualties arriving by ambulance train from the front reached the hospitals through the medium of a "convoy" of motor ambulances. These as will be recalled were provided at each base to link the ambulance train to the hospital and the latter with the hospital ship.

The arrival and departure of the convoy was the great event in the hospital day. The rotation of duty was much as in the C.C.S. groups and the frequency of convoys was in direct proportion to the pressure of casualties. From the office of the D.D.M.S., the hospital was notified by telephone of an impending "convoy," first when the incoming train was a few hours distant, again when it was about an hour away, and again when it was arriving at the station. The message noted the approximate number and nature of the casualties and their distribution; the hospital was informed if a loading party was required from it, in which case cars were sent to fetch the men, who, after loading, returned with the ambulances. The unloading of a hospital train in the later years of the war was a matter of minutes.

Admission. At the reception room of the hospital the routine of admission, classification, and distribution (*"triage"*) was organised with equal exactitude. As carried out at No. 2 A.G.H., the procedure was laid down as follows:—

"Every patient must be admitted through the Admission Tent, where the Admitting Officer will be in attendance with clerks. The Admitting Officer will fill up the Index Cards (and in time of stress, if the patient is one for classification, will complete the card by classifying him A. B. C. or D.) The classification letter should be written in the bottom right hand corner of the Tally Cards with red pencil. One clerk will fill up the Tally Cards, if classification is made by the Admitting Medical Officer. Another clerk will enter up the particulars in a Rough Admission Book. The patient will take with him to the ward to which he is allotted the Index Card, and, if classified, the duplicate Tally Cards. On admission to the ward, all cards with the patient will be fixed on to the chart board attached to his bed."

The duties of the staff may be illustrated by the instance of No. 3 A.G.H. in the last half of 1918.

Commissioned Officers. Of these this hospital had 28, as follows: The Colonel commanding; two Lieutenant-Colonels (Surgeon specialist and second-in-command); 12 Majors; 11 Captains, and 2 Lieutenants.

These officers were distributed for duty as follows:—Command (2), Registrar (1), Surgeon specialist (1), Operating surgeon (1), Anaesthetist (1), Surgical wards (8), Physician in charge of Medical section (1), Medical wards (2), Pathologist (1), Radiographer (1), Quartermasters (2), Dispenser (1), employed "on external duties" in the command under the D.M.S. Abbeville (6).

Attached. Dental officer (1), Chaplains (3). Two Surgical teams were also attached for administration and included 1 Operating surgeon and 1 Anaesthetist in each. The surgeons of the Surgical teams while at the hospital were employed in the general surgical work.

In addition a few officers were usually attached for "refresher" work in medicine and surgery.

Nursing Staff. The Principal Matron, the Head Sister, 20 Sisters, and 60 Staff Nurses; the total numbers varied at different times between 70 and 90.[22]

Other Ranks Department	Personnel N.C.O's	Ptes.	Attached (Under-age, "P.B.," etc.)	Total average
General Duties (a)	4	13	12	29
Ward Duties (b)	9	85	9	103
Q.M. Dept.[23] (c)	13	25	15	53
Clerical Dept. (d)	5	6	3	14
Messes (inc. Batmen) (e)	—	14	3	17
Sundry (f)	7	10	—	17
	38	153	42	233

(a) Includes R.S.M., Orderly Sgt., Orderly Corporal, General duties, Sanitary, Messenger, Picquet, Bugler,
(b) Includes Chief Ward-master, Assistant Ward-master, Blockmasters, Wards, Theatre, Dressing hut, Masseur, Operating team.
(c) Includes R.Q.M.S., "Chief Steward," "Q.M. Department," Cooks, Pack store, Carpenter, Bootmaker, Painter, Plumber, Fumigator, Tailor, Boilerman, Barber, Sailmaker, Gardener.
(d) Includes Clerical, Pay clerk, Postal.
(e) Includes Officers' Mess, Sisters' Mess, Sergeants' Mess, Patients' Mess.

[22] One V.A.D. was employed—Miss Nancy Birdwood, daughter of the G.O.C. A.I.F.
[23] The hospital diary suggests that some of the cooks might with advantage have been females specially trained.

(f) Includes Dispensing Dept., Pathological Dept., X-ray Dept., on command, at Schools, and Dental attached.

Under-age boys were employed in the following duties:—Batmen, Wards, Bugler, Sanitary, General duty, Q.M., Cooks, Sisters' mess, Officers' mess, Sergeants' mess, Clerk.[24]

"*P. B.*" *men* were employed in the following duties:—General, Cooks, Sailmakers, Carpenters, Officers' mess, Sisters' mess, Q.M., Batmen, Wards.[25]

Extra-unit Personnel. Convalescent patients were employed on many light duties in the wards and patients' mess tent and kitchen. In October, 1918, 63 were thus occupied at No. 3 A.G.H. During this month an average of 52 pioneers were at work under the Engineers in construction—chiefly of bomb-proof dugouts and revetments—and in the replacement of tents by huts. German prisoners of war were very freely employed in this unit, chiefly under the Quartermaster, in the repair of tents, maintenance of the grounds and so forth, and particularly in the construction of revetments.

Evacuation. The procedure, as laid down for this at No. 2 A.G.H. at Boulogne was:—

When orders from the Registrar are sent to a ward to evacuate so many "A" "B" "C" and "D" patients, the sisters will write up on the Tally Cards of the patients being evacuated the name of the ship and destination, and the Evacuating Medical Officer or the Medical Officer in charge of the case must sign these Tally Cards. The Index Cards, which take the place of History Sheets, must be signed by the Medical Officer in charge of case, and will be collected by the Sergeant supervising the loading of patients. (N.B. The classification "A" "B" "C" or "D" is only to be used for patients who are to be evacuated to England.)

Disposal.[26] The methods of disposal may be illustrated by a synopsis of those practised at No. 2 A.G.H.:—

SYNOPSIS OF DISPOSAL OF CASES AND CLASSIFICATION

1. *To be retained in hospital.*

Patients classified as ready for discharge under 7 days.	For disposal in France.
Ready for discharge under 14 days.	
" " " " 21 "	
Cases of fractured femur.	Till fit to evacuate to U.K.
Patients too ill to move.	

[24] A note in the hospital diary says that these boys "were an unmitigated nuisance" with "some brilliant exceptions."

[25] The hospital diary notes that it would have been better if these men had been "definitely A.A.M.C."

[26] The scheme of No. 2 A.G.H. set forth above was drawn up in 1916 and varied somewhat in details at different times. The arrangements also differed in some respect from those at Rouen, from which patients embarked at Le Havre; but it adumbrates accurately the work of a Base Hospital.

2. *Evacuate to U.K.*

All General Medical and General Surgical cases except as above:
Jaw and Face to Queen's Hospital, Sidcup.
Neurological (organic) to No. 4 London General Nephritis to St. Bartholomew's.
Organic diseases of or injury to Cerebro-Spinal system to King George's etc.
Rectal cases to St. Mark's.
Selected cases, Arterial Injury to No. 5 London General.
Gas shell cases (not mustard except with complications).
Men domiciled in Ireland (by Irish Convoy).
Orthopaedic cases (to be marked "Military Orthopaedic").
Internal derangements of Knee.

To be classified as
"A"—Stretcher cases needing special treatment on voyage.
"B"—Other stretcher cases.
"C"—Sitting cases.
"D"—Walking cases.

3. *Evacuate locally.*

To *Details Camp.*—Men fit for duty—for medical boarding.
To *No. 12 Con. Camp.*—Cases ready for duty in 4 or 5 days.
To *No. 1 Con. Camp.*—Cases requiring treatment and convalescence for over 4 or 5 days.
Clean operation cases awaiting transport to No. 25 General.
D.A.H. and V.D.H.
To *No. 7 Con. Camp.*—V.D.(G) and V.D.(S).
To *No. 25 General.*—Chronic skin cases. Scabies.
Cases (other than A.I.F. and N.Z.) requiring clean operation, Hernia, etc.
To *No. 8 Stationary.*—Mental cases. Fractured femurs.
To *No. 14 Stationary.*—Infectious cases.
To *Nos. 54 or 55 General.*—N.Y.D. Nervous. (On no account to be disposed of otherwise.)

From the wards in the "General" and "Stationary" Hospitals at the Base the casualty went, usually as a sitting case by ambulance convoy, to a British Convalescent "Camp" or "Depot" in France, and thence when discharged from convalescence through "Base Depot" back to the line; if not, he went by hospital ship to Britain, for further treatment.

Disposal:
Return to duty

In the "Convalescent" and "Base" Depot system in France we make touch again[27] with the system of convalescence under combined medical and military control, which, as organised for the Australian force, is described in a later section of this chapter.

---

[27] In its early crude beginnings it is seen in *Vol. I*, in operation in the Convalescent Depot systems at Zeitoun, at Lemnos, at Moascar, and in the Command Depot at Weymouth. *See also Chapter xvi.*

Regarded as a treatment station on the route of evacuation, the Base Hospital in France was not an end-point for wounded cases, save for the slighter ones and for a few special types—in particular femurs—to which further reference will be made. At this stage of evacuation treatment was not yet entirely an end in itself, but was intended also to promote removal for a further stage— this time the final one. But treatment at each stage was accompanied with the proviso—"return to duty" when possible; and the circumstances of the Base permitted the opportunity for effecting a useful short circuit in the case of men with slight wounds, whose treatment was often completed here, allowing their return to the front without going further. The conditions also allowed considerably greater scope than at the front in the selection of more serious cases for the benefit of continued treatment; the types of case for which treatment at the Base was favoured were those with fractures of the femur, penetrating wounds of the knee, "abdomens," "heads," and "chests," together with amputations, patients with retained foreign bodies, multiple or penetrating severe wounds, and the more urgent types of septic infection. For "disease" the Base was again a sorting house. Types of disease in which an end-point and complete cure might be reached without undue delay were held, treated, and returned to the front through the Convalescent Camps and Base Depots; the residue was cleared across the Channel to the hospitals in Britain.

Notes on Surgery in the Base Hospitals. The nature of the surgery done in the General Hospitals at the overseas base was determined in part by the conditions outlined above, but chiefly through the fact that, in ordinary circumstances, the wounded man would not reach these hospitals in less than 24 hours, commonly—even in 1918—48 hours or more after wounding;[28] and that, on the other hand, to reach the next stage he would have to face another 24 hours and the Channel crossing.

---

[28] In the early fighting of 1914 ambulance trains are said to have taken at times 56 to 72 hours on the trip. On the other hand No. 3 A.G.H., in the advanced general hospital centre at Abbeville, received in 1918 wounded men direct from the line, and even at Boulogne and Rouen the first operation was often at the General Hospital.

Venue for Operation in Rushes. Throughout the whole extent of the Lines of Communication from the R.A.P. to England, the work done in the treatment stations was in some measure at least determined by the mechanical factor of mass—of the size of the human wave passing at any one time over the transport routes into the widening reaches of the Lines of Communication. As has been seen, the number of casualties on whom operations could be done at the C.C.S. varied directly with the number of wounded men presenting. In lightly wounded men the question of the proper stage for operation had often to be determined by military rather than medical necessity; and it was a matter for debate whether or not they should be passed on for surgery at the Base. In this the French and British and American services tended to adopt different policies. A note, dated 1st January, 1918, from a senior operating surgeon of the A.I.F.[29] to the D.M.S., A.I.F. is here placed beside a statement in the *American Official Medical History.*

"So far as my observations go, the 'lying wounded' are promptly and efficiently treated [at the C.C.S.], so that contaminated wounds do not, in many instances, become grossly septic. The 'walking wounded' except in times of great slackness, do not receive the same prompt and efficient treatment. Very many 'walking wounded' with slight but contaminated wounds are dressed without any attempt to remove or treat the contaminated tissues, and these arrive at the Base in a more or less infected condition. Sepsis, thus established, greatly delays the return of the soldier to the firing line or to useful civil employment. In a military sense it is the slightly wounded man whom it pays to treat efficiently for he can then be returned in the shortest possible time to the firing line where the need for men is greatest.

"The French have done something to deal with this problem. Wounds of the soft parts are skilfully excised at what correspond to our Casualty Clearing Stations. In a very large percentage, 70 to 80 per cent. of cases, the wounds heal by pri-

"Our medical service did not accept the tenet of our Allies that the more lightly wounded should receive preferential attention in the zone of the armies because of the greater probability of their return to active service, and also because a greater number could thus be cared for in a given period. Increased knowledge of surgery proved that removal of devitalised tissue and foreign bodies from slight wounds could be accomplished successfully back of the zone of the armies. . . . No one questions the necessity for very prompt action in serious wounds, but it had also been believed that return to the colours would be expedited if the slightly wounded as well as the seriously wounded could be operated on within 12-hour limit of time. Later observations showed that practically the same results were obtained in the slightly wounded without foreign bodies, if operation were delayed 24 hours or even longer. Upon this knowledge was based the American policy of sending such cases farther to the rear for operation, if pressure was such that their numbers would overtax an evacuation hospital of approximately 1,000-bed capacity at the front.

---

[29] Colonel H. S. Newland in a personal memorandum dated 1 Jan., 1918. The quotation from the *American Medical History* is from *Vol. XI, Surgery Part I, pp. 112-3.*

mary union after 'delayed primary suture' and never become septic. Valuable men, valuable time and valuable dressings, etc., are thus saved."

The belief that early operation was essential in all cases (caused) the British and French to locate many large relatively immobile hospitals close to the front."[30]

Be this as it may, throughout the war, even in the British Service and as late as March-April, 1918, large numbers of less severely wounded came to operation first in the General Hospitals.[31]

Provision for Regional Surgery at the Base. While particular reference to regional surgery must again be excluded, it is desirable to note that at the Base many of the particular problems that derived from the anatomical or physiological features of the region or organ involved reached a climax so as to make some special provision necessary.

Femurs, Injury of the Eyes, Face and Jaws; Knee Joints, etc. The first move in this direction was induced by the terrible mortality in cases of fractured femurs in the hospitals in Britain. In 1917 provision was made to concentrate these in special hospitals in each centre in France. This was followed by arrangements for "specialist" treatment for some other regional wounds—such as injury of the eyes, face and jaws, and of penetrating wounds of the head, chest, knee joint, as well as for special methods of treatment, such as the "Carrel-Dakin."[32]

---

[30] The following statement by Médecin Inspecteur Général A. Mignon (*Le Service de Santé Pendant la Guerre, 1914-1918 Tome IV*, *p. 549*) has useful figures bearing on the above.

"Les délais d'opportunité de la suture ont augmenté avec l'expérience. Après avoir déclaré qu'une suture devait être pratiquée dans les six heures qui suivent la blessure, on l'a tentée et réussie le cinquième, sixième, huitième et jusqu'au onzième jour après la blessure. (*Bull. Soc. Chir., 1918, p. 657*). Sans aller jusqu'aux extrêmes, retenons que Delbet a obtenu de bons résultats dans son service de Paris, de la vingt-deuxième à la quarante-huitième heure; et Sencert, au Val-de-Grâce, de la vingt-quatrième à la soixante-sixième heure. (*Bull. Soc. Chir., 1918, p. 772*). La suture primitive a même été appliquée avec succès sur des plaies ayant été enflammées et dont tout symptôme inflammatoire avait disparu. (*Bull. Soc. Chir., 1918, p. 7*)."

[31] See pp. 621-22. The demand made on the surgeons in a great offensive is illustrated by the following note from the private diary of Lieut.-Col. D. A. Cameron, A.A.M.C., describing work at No. 2 A.G.H. at the time of the Arras operations.

April 8th, 1917. Large numbers of wounded arriving. Push at front evidently started. *10th.* Great numbers of Canadians . . . men arrive in helmets and with kit. *11th.* Very busy. *12th.* O.C. gave me a little theatre of my own at 6 p.m.—did 10 operations that night. . . . *13th.* Did 37 operations in the day—very busy—over 800 cases admitted during the night. . . . *14th, 15th, 16th.* Operations all day, *18th, 19th, 20th.* Very busy, though work lessening. *25th.* Very busy. *26th.* 28 operations in the day. *30th.* 28 operations. *May 1st.* During last month 8,091 admissions to No. 2 A.G.H.

[32] The history of "Carrel-Dakin" at the Base is worth a particular note. At a meeting of Consulting Surgeons at the office of the D.G., G.H.Q., 30 Nov., 1916, it was decided that every endeavour should be made to carry out the Carrel treatment of wounds. This advice was given effect to by an order of Dec., 1916, laying down procedures to be followed at "Clearing Stations," "on the Trains," and "at the Base." At each base "Carrel" cases from the front were to be concentrated

Operation to Rectify Deformities. A certain amount of regional surgery was also undertaken in the Base Hospitals in the "radical cure" of hernia, hydrocele, varicocele, varicose veins, haemorrhoids[33] and the like. These were found chiefly in men who, having been passed as "fit," developed the deformity—or, as was far more frequent, developed the "disability" from a pre-existing deformity—while on service. In this list we may include also the operation for appendicitis.[34]

General Surgery of Wounds at the Base. But, except for such developments in regional surgery, it was inevitable that the quest for asepsis, and the endeavour to break through the 12-36 hour time-limit that in most cases determined the onset of anaerobic infection, should result in the surgery of the Base becoming accessory to that of the front. It came to be concerned with the treatment of declared sepsis, and with measures for its limitation rather than its prevention; with antisepsis rather than asepsis except so far as, by "delayed primary suture" it completed the good work done at the front. Furthermore, in point of the actual *amount* of work, the Base remained the chief surgical centre, and the surgery done there was of profound importance to the welfare of millions of wounded men.

The bête noir of the Base—"true sepsis." It has been stated in short that surgery at the Base was concerned, above all, with the problem of the pyogenic cocci—in particular of the streptococcus, and that its great objective was to prevent re-infection,[35]

---

in special hospitals. The following is the experience of an Australian nurse who was for a time attached to one of these hospitals—No. 14 British General, at Wimereux, Boulogne.

"Early in 1917 we got on to the Carrel-Dakin method. I had a ward of 34 beds; every man had his bacterial chart as well as his temperature chart. The pathologist did the films and sent back a report on which we marked the chart up. When we got three negatives the wound was stitched up. The results were splendid. We had a great staff in the Carrel Ward, bigger than in most of the wards, as it was a show place, and the charting etc. took a lot of time." In the later months of 1917, though the hospital had increased in size, "the full Carrel treatment was ceased, as it kept patients too long and we couldn't manage the rushes." (From a memorandum written for the Australian War Memorial by Sister Leila Smith, A.A.N.S.)

[33] In the A.I.F. in France cases suitable for operation were operated on under supervision of the surgical specialist at each hospital. Unsuitable cases were sent to England, or returned to the front after boarding.

[34] 782 men were invalided to Australia during the war from this disease.

[35] Sir Anthony Bowlby (*Brit. Off. Med. History, Surgery, Vol. I, p. 246*) states that "while only about 10 per cent. of all open wounds were infected with streptococci on arrival from the front, within a week over 90 per cent. had become infected." A committee for the investigation of how this infection occurred was sitting at the time of the Armistice, and it had been already found that many of the nurses and orderlies were "carriers" of streptococci in their throats.

and to this end to achieve the early closure of all wounds. The discovery of a "royal road" to the goal of "prevention" through early closure may be recalled to give the proper setting to the picture of surgery at the Bases.

In this mental impression it should be recalled that for fully three years of the war the surgeon at the Base lived and moved and faced his task in a setting of sepsis. Three years of "trial and error" on the human guinea-pigs of the war passed before the wheel had turned in full cycle, and "immediate suture," the "big bad wolf" of 1914-15, had in 1918, as "primary suture" and "delayed primary suture" after excision, come to serve as the trusted watch-dog against secondary infection.[36]

Medicine at the Base. The numbers of battle and non-battle casualties admitted to medical units in the B.E.F. were: battle, 1,988,969, non-battle, 3,528,486—a total of 5,517,455; the number of these evacuated to Britain was 1,245,535 wounded, and 1,034,160 sick or injured. The corresponding totals in the A.I.F. were 142,206 battle and 207,978 non-battle casualties; of whom 130,960 and 147,294 respectively reached the Base. The nosological composition of this mass of "sickness," analysed for the A.I.F. so far as is possible in terms of pathogenesis, is given elsewhere.[37]

"Battle" or "Non-battle"? But, in addition to the officially "sick" by the time the Base was reached certain types of "battle-casualty" were becoming frankly "disease."

Chemical Trauma. In particular, gassed men were now in the stage of bronchitis or pneumonia, their condition differing little in its clinical features from that caused directly by infection. *Physio-psychic trauma.* In "shell shock" any possible "commotional" element had by now subsided, and the psychic or "emotional" element in the complex was dominant, and the disorder obviously now becoming fixed as a "functional" and frankly mental "dis-ease." *Physical trauma.* Types of non-battle casualty other than disease whose causation was less crudely physical than physical violence—for example trench foot and bronchial catarrh due to cold, and intestinal irritation due to food and dirt—came also into the medical wards.

---

[36] Humanity has been advised, above all things, to know itself. Of the moral "lessons of the war" none perhaps is more searching than this that in the matter of judgment man must be always aware of his emotions, reactions, prejudices.
The initial reaction of surgeons to the two great methods for treating contaminated or infected wounds, the Carrel-Dakin system of antiseptic lavage and secondary suture, and the method of aseptic excision with primary or delayed primary suture, reveal that not yet are the actions of man guided by reason alone but chiefly by prejudice. An Australian surgeon esteemed alike for his sound philosophy and his surgical judgment remarked to the writer anent this very thing that the trouble in the first few years of the war was that too few of the old men had young minds.

[37] *In Chapter xvii and Vol. III.*

Battle Wounds. Even wounds became at times the joint concern of physician and surgeon. The following note is from the records of No. 3. A.G.H.

"*Chest Wounds.* Penetrating chest wounds were treated in the *acute medical ward*, and from September, 1917, there were always a few of these cases in hospital. From the end of March, 1918, to October, 1918, this ward was continuously occupied by such patients, and for a short time they filled also two other wards. Most of these cases, if they reached the base, recovered; but there were a few deaths. In some, death was due to the severity of the wound, but in most it was due to *infection.*

"The following is a brief summary of the method of treatment employed. (1) Mild cases with small sterile haemothorax—rest in bed. (2) Cases with large sterile haemothorax—aspiration repeated as often as necessary. (3) Infected haemothorax—resection of rib and drainage: wash out.

"Except when the military situation required, all these cases were retained for three weeks after date of wounding."

In a not inconsiderable proportion of the sick reaching the Base, the morbific agent or influence—which in the great majority of cases was microbial—was well on the way to defeat by natural resistance, and the patients required only rest and food to reach "convalescence."

The morbid states which chiefly occupied the attention of physicians in the base hospitals in France are indicated by the following percentages of total B.E.F. admissions:—[38]

Influenza	7·04 per cent.	Trench fever	3·51 per cent.
Accidental injuries	6·57 per cent.	Scabies ..	3·11 per cent.
Coryza, acute bronchitis, tonsillitis, and laryngitis	6·40 per cent.	Trench feet	2·95 per cent.
		Fibrositis	2·67 per cent.
		Debility	2·57 per cent.
I.C.T. ..	5·69 per cent.	N.Y.D.N.	2·13 per cent.
P.U.O.	4·62 per cent.		

The Medical Wards. The following notes of work in the medical division at No. 3 A.G.H. at Abbeville during 1917 and 1918 compiled by Major F. Blois Lawton[39] will help to give form and life to these hospital returns. During 1918, 29,061 medical cases passed through this hospital.

Abbeville 1917-18. "From the time of the reception of our first patients in France the medical wards were usually busy, though at times for a few days they became slack. When there were few medical cases coming by 'convoy,' we were usually receiving local sick. When convoys of wounded were frequent, medical cases were few; sometimes the medical wards were full of surgical patients and *vice versa.*

---

[38] Venereal disease (18·79 per cent.) was treated in special hospitals.
[39] Major Lawton served with the unit from its inception to its disbandment.

"*Trench Fever.* The first patients admitted were 'light cases' transferred from the neighbouring hospitals. It was found that a number of these had 'trench fever,' and eventually they were evacuated to England. Trench fever varied much in its severity. Often enough the men did not appear very sick and had little or no rise of temperature, but complained of pain and undoubtedly had tenderness. Such patients were liable to be treated as mild and allowed out of bed, and some sent to convalescent camps, whence they returned to hospital with a recrudescence of their trench fever or presenting that syndrome known as D.A.H., and were lost to the Army for a long time. Trench fever disabled men for long periods, and must have been the most serious disease of the war in France. There were always cases of trench fever in the wards, but much less during the last year, though during this period many cases of trench fever were undoubtedly called 'influenza.'

"When the Hospital opened in France 'trench fever' was not a notifiable disease, but later it was notifiable. Many cases were sent on, however, with a diagnosis of P.U.O. or myalgia. This was due, partly to the fact that the signs and symptoms of the disease were not fully appreciated by many officers in General Hospitals, and partly to the necessity of filling up that cumbersome form A.F.W. 3110.[40]

"*Gas.* From the beginning we were receiving cases of gas poisoning, but in January, 1918, we were made a gas centre, and took all cases coming to this area as well as those sent down as 'N.Y.D. Gas poisoning.' Later in the year the gas centre was changed to one of the other hospitals, and we received no more. The worst cases of gas poisoning were received during the Cambrai offensive and just afterwards. At that time there were many deaths.

"*Respiratory.* At all times of the year there were usually a few cases of pneumonia, and sometimes there were large numbers. In the late winter of 1918 we saw a fair number of cases of broncho-pneumonia, presenting signs and symptoms which became only too common later in the year [in connection with the epidemic of "pneumonic" influenza].

"At all times there was 'influenza,' usually mild but often accompanied by laryngitis and tracheitis which persisted for some time. These patients required a long rest before they were restored to health.

"*Nephritis.* Always there were cases of nephritis in Hospital. These became more prevalent as the weather became colder. There were often severe cases, but there were few deaths. In February, 1918, there were several deaths. In the men who died it was found that there had been a chronic nephritis. Convulsions were uncommon, though other uraemic symptoms were encountered often enough.

"*Other Infections—Dysentery—Enterica—Meningitis.* In the summer of 1918 there was an outbreak of dysentery, and this hospital was made the dysentery centre for the area. Sixty beds were set apart and isolated for the patients and were sufficient for a time, but later another 30 were added. There were few acute cases, and all of them responded to treatment. All were examined pathologically, and all giving the necessary number of negative (3 in 3 days) results were sent to Con. Camp for further examination. The severe cases were

---

[40] A.F.W. 3110 was the form for notification of infectious disease. The danger of complexity in the notification form—*i.e.* neglect to notify—is not unknown in civil life. Major Lawton suggests, without doubt rightly, that a much simpler form would have served as well for an enquiry of this kind. See in this connection pp. 546-50.

evacuated. Nearly all those giving positive results had bacillary dysentery, but occasionally patients who had been in Egypt had amoebic dysentery. Apart from the epidemic, cases of dysentery were seen from time to time.

"Cases of meningitis came in occasionally, but there was never an epidemic. Occasionally cases of other infectious diseases were seen. Cases of Enterica were rare."

The pathology department was an important element in the routine work of the base hospitals as well as in the campaign of research. The Australian units were equipped for every type of work and were staffed by men of distinguished ability.

Pathology in the Base Hospitals

RESEARCH AT THE BASE

It would hardly be possible to exaggerate the importance in the Great War of scientific research, clinical and laboratory, into the war's medical problems. But, though the carnage of the war has often been referred to in these pages as a vast process of vivisection, the analogy with civil experiment cannot be pushed too far; for, from the millions of experiments made in the war on the reaction of the human body against infected wounds, in a minute fraction only were the results of the incision or of subsequent rational intervention by the surgeon and pathologist accurately observed and recorded. The same may be said, though perhaps less emphatically, of disease. The remarkable results in both were due rather to the vast resources, material and human, that were tapped, and to the urgent demand for "results."

Laboratory Experiment and Clinical Observation. After a war, from which came so little positive good, any constructive result has been seized on with pathetic avidity. And one result that was really worth much sacrifice was the re-discovery after fifty years of obscurity imposed by the over-powering success of Pasteur's analytical experiment, of the practical value even in exact "scientific" research, of the clinical outlook and synthetic method—the "general view" of medicine supported by Sir William Gull and the British tradition and drawn from Hippocrates through Sydenham, Linacre, Hunter; and which, sponsored by Sir Thomas Lewis since the war, has achieved a name and a professorial chair as "Clinical Science."

46. "NISSEN BOW" HOSPITAL HUTS AT No. 1 A.G.H., ROUEN
The huts are sandbagged for protection against fragments of aerial bombs.

Aust. War Memorial Official Photo. No. E3423.
Taken on 23 Sept. 1918.

47. PART OF THE TENT LINES OF No. 3 A.G.H., ABBEVILLE

Lent by Major F. D. H. B. Lawton, A.A.M.C.
Aust. War Memorial Collection No. C4539.   *To face p. 412.*

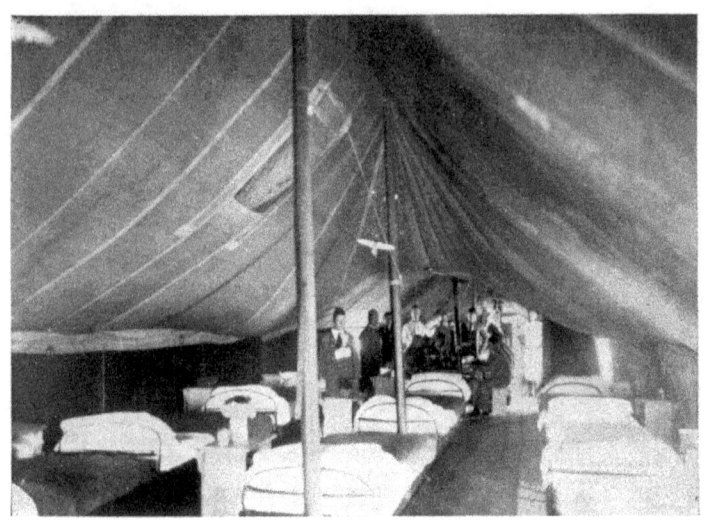

48. A TENT WARD AT No. 3 A.G.H., ABBEVILLE
The marquees are "brigaded" to form an extended ward.

Aust. War Memorial Official Photo. No. E2612.
Taken on 23 June 1918.

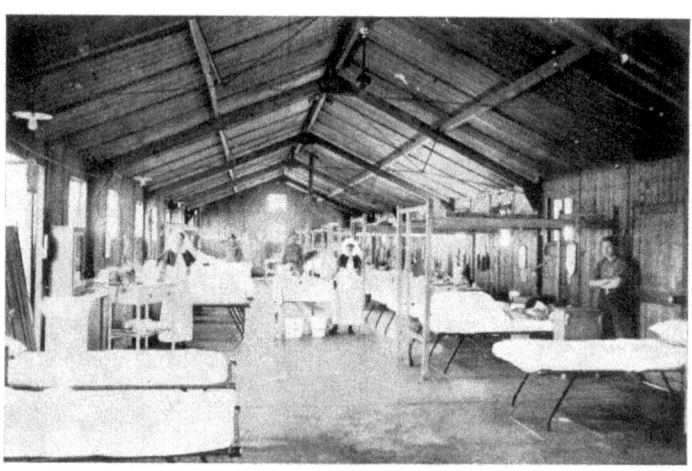

49. A HUT WARD AT No. 1 A.G.H., ROUEN
The wooden frames are for extension in cases of fractured femur.

Aust. War Memorial Official Photo. No. E3442.
Taken on 23 Sept. 1918.

In the previous volume an account was given of the work done at No. 3 A.G.H. at Lemnos under the direction of Lieut.-Colonel C. J. Martin, in which, as was there suggested, was seen the collaboration of clinical and experimental experts to a degree uncommon in civil experience. The same feature characterised some of the most fruitful episodes of investigation in France into both medical and surgical problems.[41]

Research in Problems of Wounds. In the early years of the war, research at the Base was directed almost entirely against the problems of wounding. It took two forms—first, the ultra-analytical, typified by the work of Wright; second, that of deliberate clinical research into methods of wound treatment. This, in the B.E.F., found its most exact exposition in the team work—pathologist plus surgeon—carried out in the clinical "research unit" established at No. 26 General Hospital at Etaples.[42] It was used to investigate the problems of wound healing, in particular the application of the Carrel-Dakin system, and subsequently of other antiseptic forms of treatment. Wright's work has already been described. His physiological experiments merged in the last year of the war with the search for an anti-serum against gas gangrene.

As with surgical technique the centre of gravity in organised research moved up, though much less decisively, to the zone of the field armies.

Research into the Aetiology of Disease. From the end of 1916 investigations were made into the causal factors in diseases prevalent in the Armies. In these, members of the Australian Army Medical Service played important parts. Of the historic studies of C. J. Martin and F. E. Williams into the aetiology of dysentery and the investigation of epidemic influenza at No. 3 A.G.H. a short account will be given in *Vol. III.*

THE AUSTRALIAN GENERAL HOSPITALS IN FRANCE, 1916-17[43]

Like the Casualty Clearing Stations, Australian General Hospitals were offered, accepted, and used by the Commander-in-Chief in France as "Imperial" units. The arrangement whereby, when possible, Australian soldiers should be sent to Australian units had been suggested by Australia in no parochial spirit. The advantages of "local" feeling had been recognised at the outset of the war by General Bridges and deliberately exploited in raising the field units of the A.I.F. It was believed

---

[41] As instance, Carrel's research at Compiègne, the investigation of wound shock on the British front, and the resolution of the clinical fog of P.U.O. in the rickettsial infection trench fever.

[42] In June, 1917, a small observation unit was provided here by the Joint War Committee (B.R.C.S. and Order of St. John). The moving spirit in this adventure in research was Major Sydney Rowland, whose death from C.S.F., while working here, was a tragic loss to British medicine.

[43] A full list of the Commanding Officers of these units will be given in *Vol. III.*

that apart from "sentiment" this instinct might be exploited to advantage of the common cause in the treatment of sick and wounded Australians overseas. There is proof that the British authorities were not unfavourable and that endeavour was indeed made by some administrative officers to implement it.[44] But in practice at the Base it was found impossible to carry out this policy to any considerable extent. Of the total admissions to Australian General Hospitals in the war 11·2 per cent. were Australians; and of all Australian wounded on the Western Front 6·5 per cent. were treated in the Australian General Hospitals. The matter was summed up in 1917 in a memorandum by Colonel C. T. C. de Crespigny, who commanded No. 1 A.G.H. in France:—

"No Australian General Hospital or Casualty Clearing Station in France is exclusively devoted to the treatment of Australians. Such selection and segregation would be difficult and inadvisable. We admit sick and wounded in precisely the same way that our British and American neighbours do, so that in the same ward one may see English, Scots, Irish, Canadians, Australians, New Zealanders, South Africans, Newfoundlanders, British West Indians and members of other overseas units. It is a most striking example of the Empire's 'far flung battle line.' The intimate contact that exists between hospital patients offers an admirable opportunity for men of various dominions and the mother country to know and understand each other."[45]

The D.M.S., A.I.F. and the Australian Hospitals. The control exercised by Surgeon-General Howse over these units was similar in every respect to that which, as already shown, he exercised over the casualty clearing stations. It was almost entirely concerned with establishment, promotions and posting,

---

[44] In some commands, however, more could perhaps have been done in this direction. Thus at Abbeville in 1918 many Australians were sent to the wards of the British Stationary Hospital half a mile from No. 3 A.G.H.—to the considerable inconvenience, for one thing, of the representative of the A.R.C.S.

[45] Colonel de Crespigny adds:
"The patience and stoicism of the wounded is remarkable. The quiet and restfulness of a hospital far from the battle line, with good nursing, cleanliness and considerable comfort appears to them so great a relief as often to counter-balance the pain and discomfort of their wounds.

"As an Australian addressing Australians there is no need for me to speak particularly of our own splendid men. We all know them. But I feel that I must add a word about the British soldier after more than two years' acquaintance with him. Remember that my impression of him is based upon observation of the man as a patient, when the heat of battle has passed and he has no regimental tradition to live up to and he is harassed with pain or sickness or both. And the longer one knows him the more one is struck by his pluck, endurance and ineradicable vein of quiet humour, which makes light of his own sufferings and helps his comrade in the next bed to bear his own. In hospital one sees him suffering bravely terrible and mutilating wounds and looking forward undaunted to a future which only too often must be a sad one in which both his capacity for earning his livelihood or enjoying his leisure will be permanently lessened or destroyed."

though with a "watching brief" for their general interests, in particular, that they should be given opportunity for effective employment. In the matter of their establishment some departure was made from British precedent, which opens up questions of some general interest.

Establishment of Australian General Hospitals. The establishment of the General Hospital was subject to some change in the course of the war, to meet special needs or the changing conditions of the war itself. That of the Australian hospitals, though based on British War Establishments, was never permitted by the D.M.S., A.I.F. to "cramp his style" or interfere with the distribution of his available personnel. He saw the problem of the Australian Imperial Force as a whole, and he would not hesitate to rob Peter at the Base to pay Paul at the Front. To this end the staff proper to an Australian General Hospital was never exactly defined, and was subject to a nice balancing by the Australian Director between four factors—the needs of the Base and the Front, the reinforcements coming forward to supply wastage in the medical service and, it should be added, the needs of the British Director General.[46] In one important respect also the staff of the Australian Hospitals differed from that of the British, namely in the more extensive substitution of members of the A.A.N.S. for male nursing orderlies, a difference which was reflected in the working of the wards. In the Australian Service it was found that the British establishment of medical officers might be reduced without detriment to efficiency.[47]

---

[46] An illustration of the attitude of General Howse on this matter of Imperial co-operation will be found in Chapter *xxvi*, (*pp. 821-3*) and *Appendix No. 2*.

[47] In 1916 the D.M.S., A.I.F. was sent by Sir Alfred Keogh a copy of a letter received by him from Sir Arthur Sloggett and was asked to comment on the following:—

"Twenty Australian doctors were asked for to complete the required establishment for the two Australian General Hospitals as now expanded.

"No. 1 with 750 beds has 20 M.Os. but requires 27—7
No. 2 „ 1,040 „ „ 19 „ „ „ 32—13
                                                                        20

"The Australian units are in a similar position to the Canadians who have been asked for 28 officers to complete.

"I hope the Colonies concerned will be able, not only to meet our present requirements but to maintain the establishment, otherwise our calls for R.A.M.C. will be correspondingly increased."

General Howse replied—"I found by experience in Egypt over a period of many months, that 25 officers were able to run a 1,040 bed General Hospital very easily. Australian M.Os. have been accustomed to very arduous work in the practice of their profession in civil life, and consequently find no difficulty in running a General Hospital with a smaller staff than that laid down in *Part VII—New Armies, 1915.*"

He added that "No. 1 A.G.H., equipped for 750, had sufficient officers to run 1,000 beds if necessary. . . . The O.C. No. 2 informs me that at no time has the staff been fully employed."

In fairness, the comment must be made that at times, especially in France, the whole staff might be at full stretch to cope with the work. Much depended on the type of casualties—in particular, on the proportion of wounded. But the considered opinion of the officer commanding No. 14 A.G.H. (Col. Walter Summons) on experience in General Hospitals throughout the war was that "the establishment laid down by the War Office for 1,040 bed hospital might with advantage be modified. The provision made for 30 medical officers in addition to O.C., Q.M., and Registrar is in excess of requirements. . . . At no time did the requirements of this unit demand more than 20." (*War Diary, March, 1918*).

With these provisos the Australian units complied with War Office establishment laid down in *Part VII New Armies* and modified at the end of 1916 by a sliding scale relating the staff to any convenient number of beds up to 2,500—the method adopted by the Australian Director-General in 1915 (*See Volume I, p. 406*). A table of establishments for the several medical units will be found as *Appendix No. 8*.

The prominent and even dramatic part played by No. 1 Australian General Hospital in the Gallipoli Campaign will be recalled. In April, 1916, under the command of Lieut.-Colonel de Crespigny, the staff arrived at Marseilles;

No. 1. A.G.H.

the unit's establishment was that for a 520-bed hospital with expanding limit to 1,000.[48]

On April 17th the unit took over the huts and tents occupied by No. 12 British Stationary on the Racecourse at Rouen, and on the 29th reported the hospital as ready to receive patients. Here, somewhat cramped as to space, it worked through three strenuous years, passing through its wards in that time more than 90,000 casualties.

Its most difficult time was in the winter of 1916-17. The site was an exposed one. "The winter of 1916-17," an officer relates, "will long be remembered as one of the most severe on record, and it was surprising how well most of the medical cases got on although they were nursed in tents. This was in a great measure due to the devotion of the nursing staff, many of whom suffered from minor degrees of frost-bite during the first three months of 1917. The cold interfered with the water supply, and the use of fuel was restricted owing to the shortage of coal. For weeks the temperature showed several degrees of frost and on occasion the thermometer registered 4° Fahrenheit."

A large proportion of the casualties from the Somme Battles passed through Rouen, and in the winter wounded were replaced by trench foot, pneumonias, nephritis, and trench fever cases, the latter chiefly sent in as "P.U.O."

The work done in the unit is shown in tabular form on *page 780*. Its experiences during 1918 belong to a later chapter

The personnel, officers, nurses, and other ranks, alike took part in the social life of this peculiarly interesting town and the hospital Rugby XV (it is recorded) "succeeded in winning a local competition."

In Egypt, as will be recalled, No. 2 Australian General Hospital was over-shadowed, on the military side of its work, by No. 1. But it had maintained throughout a very high professional and scientific standard—its clinical

No. 2. A.G.H.

records were unsurpassed in the Australian service.[40] This objective was maintained also throughout its

---

[48] In 1917 No. 1 and No. 2 were expanded to 1,040 and 1,500 bed hospitals respectively.

[49] The card record system of this unit was taken over by the Repatriation Department, and was found of great value in deciding difficult problems of attribution.

THE GENERAL HOSPITALS

service in France. Here the unit found itself so placed in relation to the stream of casualties as to be in a position to mould its own destiny.

Arriving at Marseilles on April 1st, established and equipped to form a 750-bed hospital, No. 2 was at once pressed into a service which gave it a place in the history of the B.E.F., in that, at a time of importance, it served as a sieve against the introduction of infectious disease from Egypt. An account of this important work is given elsewhere.[50]

Leaving behind a section thus engaged, the remainder of the unit took over a partly completed hospital site at Wimereux 2½ miles outside Boulogne. Here, at the most important base port of the B.E.F., and on the direct route of casualties from the Salient, the hospital maintained its tradition and built up a reputation for professional work which, even by the exacting standard of this base, was a high one. In particular a special study was made of fractures, especially of fractured femurs, and of perforating wounds of the joints.

The pathological department established a close *liaison* with that controlled by Lieut.-Colonel T. R. Elliott, the purpose of which was the study of surgical pathology of wounds and dissemination of results through museum specimens.[51] Figures illustrating the work of the unit will be found in the table on *page 780*.

No. 3. A.G.H.

Left behind in Egypt when the A.I.F. moved to the Western seat of war, No. 3 Australian General Hospital had the job of clearing up after the Gallipoli Campaign, and for a time also served as the General Hospital for Australian casualties from the fighting of the Light Horse. The circumstances under which it was brought to England and its initial work at the Kitchener Hospital Brighton are recorded elsewhere.

At the beginning of 1917 the submarine attacks on hospital ships and the urgent need to prevent wastage from the force in France brought about a general expansion of the B.E.F. Lines of Communication, and as a part of this the unit was sent to France.

Under the command of Colonel B. J. Newmarch with the establishment for a 1,500-bed hospital, the staff arrived at Abbeville on April 16th. Here under the immediate eye of the D.M.S., L. of C., Surgeon-General Woodhouse, it took over a hospital site which enabled it ultimately to accommodate more than 2,000 patients at one time; and, with the South African General Hospital and No. 2 British Stationary, it formed an advanced centre—almost an outpost—of general hospital work. Casualties were cleared through Rouen or Boulogne, and convalescents to the

[50] *Chapter xiv (pp. 542-6).*
[51] A considerable number of the preparations made in Australian units were included by Professor Arthur Keith in the museum of the Royal College of Surgeons in London. The Australian collection will be described in *Vol. III.*

great centre at Trouville. The unit served also, especially in the last phase of the war, a very large local population of moving and resting troops.

The work of this unit during 1917 was of a routine—not to say humdrum—type; but with the German push-through in 1918 it took a dramatic turn, so that, indeed, this centre held the limelight till almost the end of the war. The account of this is given later.[52] A matter which calls for record here is the formation of a pathological research laboratory, which was designed and organised under the immediate direction of the Adviser in Pathology of the Australian Imperial Force, Lieut.-Colonel C. J. Martin, whose work is recorded elsewhere. But researches carried out there belong to the later history of the service.[53]

RETURN TO DUTY—THE BASE DEPOTS

The setting up of four "Australian Divisional Base Depots" at Etaples has already been mentioned in recording the move of the A.I.F. to France, of which that incident formed part.[54] Throughout 1916 these formations remained there as an integral part of the British depot system. An Australian instructional staff, drawn from each of the Divisions, was pooled with the British, though each divisional depot had a small administrative staff of its own and a medical establishment on regimental lines. In June, 1916, the latter was augmented by an Australian dental unit—a quite dramatically successful move.[55] But the general working of the depots and in particular the system for dealing with convalescents, was only less crude and unsatisfactory than it had been in Egypt. The situation at the end of 1916 is disclosed in a report to the G.O.C., A.I.F.[56]

"According to returns furnished by the Base Depot, out of 1,275 in the 1st Divisional Base Depot 328 were sick, over 19 per cent. Enquiry into this appalling sick rate disclosed that it was due to the wrong classification of convalescents and casualties as sick. There are about 400 men not recovered from wounds or sickness, but who have been discharged from convalescent camps, hospitals, etc. to the depot. These men are useless for ordinary work in the depot, and should still be in convalescent camp. On the day of my visit there were 400 men awaiting dental treatment; many of these have never been to the front, many others had to be evacuated as dentally unfit shortly after their arrival. I am most strongly of opinion that more than half these should never have left England, or indeed Australia, in their present dental condition."

---

[52] See pp. 778-81, 800-1
[53] See p. 560 and Vol. III.
[54] See p. 34. A depot for the 3rd Australian Division was formed in Nov., 1916
[55] See also p. 655.
[56] By the A.A. & Q.M.G., 1st Australian Division, Colonel C. H. Foott.

Many of these men, it was found, "do not become fit as early as desired"—hardly a matter for surprise! The terrific experience of the Somme, initiating, as it did, for the B.E.F. the procedure of attrition, compelled in France as in England a drastic reorganisation of the whole system of numerical maintenance.

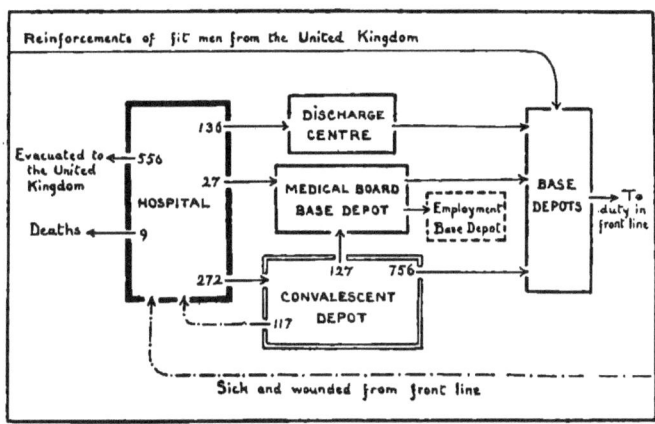

Disposal of sick and wounded received into hospitals and convalescent depots on the Lines of Communication in France. The numbers indicate the proportion per 1,000 admissions into hospitals and convalescent depots in 1917. (From British Official Medical History.)

The Base Depots in France had not only to ensure that reinforcements received from Great Britain were up to the standard of hardness and efficiency required by the Commander-in-Chief; they had also to receive men discharged from convalescent camps in France and to give them some hardening similar to that given in the depots in England. As part of a wide reconstruction in the B.E.F., in June, 1917, the Australian Base Depots were transferred from Etaples to Le Havre, reorganised as members of a single "*Australian General Base Depot,*" Lieut.-Colonel Burston, A.A.M.C., being appointed S.M.O. Shortly afterwards the function of putting reinforcements through a second training in drill was abandoned as unnecessary except in a few items and they were sent on to their divisional reinforcement camps close behind the front. But the hardening of convalescents in France was still necessary, and, though being designed for a simpler type of case it was less elaborate than that of the Command Depots in England, it nevertheless had some points of special interest.

When the Australian depots moved to Le Havre, reinforcements and convalescents still mingled with no exact procedure for insuring "fitness." It was not until 1918, long after the similar machinery of the Command Depots in England had been perfected, that the urgent call for effectives, brought about by the German offensive and by the diminished supply of recruits from overseas, compelled a more exact system.

The necessary reform was achieved by giving effect to the principle that few men discharged from *medical* convalescent camp or depot were fit to resume at once their place in the ranks, and that, in the promotion of their fitness and the selection of those who should be held fit for duty, the medical service must be given the controlling decision.

Australian Convalescent Depot

In April, 1918, an *Australian Convalescent Depot* was formed as part of the Australian depot system at Le Havre, and the duties of Colonel Burston were extended to include command of this convalescent depot in addition to his position as "S.M.O." of the whole depot system.

"Hardening" in France. The Convalescent Depot accommodated 2,000 men in two separate camps or "divisions," each under the full command of a medical officer. Each "division" was sub-divided into four companies, each one of which again was under a medical officer, who had the full disciplinary powers of a company commander, and was responsible for the interior economy of his company, and for the treatment, training, and classification of each man in his command.

Classification. Men marching in from "Con. Camp," if fit, were classed "A" and transferred at once to the Base Depots; otherwise they were classified "D," unfit for any duty; "C," fit for light fatigue and physical training; or "B," fit for physical training and route marching. Men were reclassified weekly, and if thought "unlikely to be fit within two months" went to the General Base Depot for medical boarding and appropriate action.

System of Training. This took the form chiefly of "physical training," and of games. The latter were organised on lines designed to "foster the spirit of healthy rivalry between companies in regard to both military duties and sport, and to ensure the active participation so far as desirable of every man." Inter-company competitions in boxing, wrestling, and most forms of sport were organised, and to a great extent replaced routine "physical jerks." The men were promised a fair deal and a reasonable spell in the depot, and that success in sports and competitions would not in itself involve early discharge as "fit."

Infectious Disease. For the depot a very effective sanitary organisation was provided and an exact system built up for detection and isolation of infectious disease and treatment of scabies. Fine baths and laundries were built, and controlled by the Corps and a particularly effective delousing system organised. The chief problem of the general depot work was to ensure that drafts to the front should be free from infectious disease deriving either from drafts from Britain or from local cases. From both sources in 1916 came outbreaks of mumps and measles sufficiently serious to interfere with military activities.[57]

During the last year of the war, by a rigidly enforced system of inspection and isolation, these cases of disease were effectively excluded from the front.

Statistics. The following table shows the work done in the Australian Convalescent Depot at Havre during its brief existence.

STATISTICS OF NO. 1 AUSTRALIAN CONVALESCENT DEPOT HAVRE

	ADMISSIONS FROM					DISCHARGES				
1918	Expedy. Front	Brit. Base Con. Hospls.	Base Depots in France	Depots in France	Total	"A" Class	Med. Board	To Hospl.	Died	Total
Apl.					1,157					22
May					2,023	2,870	275	361		1,399
June					2,063					2,085
July		850	660	54	1,564	1,479	277	102		1,858
Aug.		1,800	822	137	2,759	1,620	208	73		1,901
Sept.		762	196	48	1,006	1,597	142	67		1,806
Oct.	31	966	1,057	41	2,095	1,826	223	178		2,227
Nov.		1,051	77	20	1,148	1,258	67	60	1	1,386
Dec.		328	454	73	855	661	136	97	1	895
1919										
Jan.		56			56	614	83	34		731
Feb.		8			8	424				424
TOTALS					14,734[58]	12,349	1,411	972	2	14,734

Diminished by the moiety thus returned to duty, the overflow from the front passed through the Base for the most part

---

[57] The ultimate source of these outbreaks was the camps in Australia. These were followed by outbreaks on the transports, and these by others in the training battalions in England, from which cases reached the Base Depots in France. *See pp. 555-6.*

[58] Representing 38 per cent. of wounded and 62 per cent. of sick and injured.

rapidly; some without stay, others after partial treatment, some few again saved by prolonged care after the more desperate type of regional wound—femurs, abdomens, knee-joints, jaws, and so forth. These all went by special ambulance convoys or by ambulance train to embark on hospital ship for the British ports, Southampton and Dover.

Embarkation

SYNOPSIS OF CHAPTER XV

EVACUATION: LAST STAGE, DISTRIBUTION

THE CHANNEL CROSSING:
Embarkation.
Disembarkation: Distribution.

THE HOSPITAL SYSTEM IN BRITAIN:
Australian Patients and British Hospitals.
The Australian "Red Cross."
No. 3 A.G.H.

TREATMENT IN BRITISH PRIMARY HOSPITALS:
Secondary treatment of wounds and disease.
Prophylaxis in reparative surgery.
The treatment of diseases in British Hospitals.

THE NATIONAL ISSUES:
Reparative treatment.
Reparative surgery.
Types requiring reparative treatment.
Reparative Medicine.
The technical problem.

THE SPECIAL HOSPITALS:
The Australian Auxiliary Hospitals (Harefield, Southall, Dartford)
Work in the Auxiliaries.
For potential "effectives."
For "invalids."

THE PARTING OF WAYS—FINAL DISPOSAL OF AUSTRALIAN CASUALTIES:
The Medical Boards.
A poignant decision.
National wreckage and Army salvage.

CHAPTER XV

EVACUATION: LAST STAGE, DISTRIBUTION

THE CHANNEL CROSSING

THE next circuit of movement in evacuation, the determinant of "expeditionary" wastage, and the last stage in the long journey home was—the Channel Crossing.

In the history of the British race the English Channel has always been a symbol—as it is the origin—of that "insularity" which is held characteristic of at least the "English" moiety of the very diverse peoples whose national destiny it has bound together. Even casual mention calls to the imagination those attributes, good or bad, that depend on this geo-physical feature in racial environments and which were conspicuously present in the A.I.F. But as a material factor in European affairs the Channel has had its day. Its influence was hit hard when in 1913 Blériot made history in aviation—and in sea-power—by the first cross-channel flight; and harder still when on 21st March 1917 the Hospital Ship *Asturias* was torpedoed. From a stately tradition it passed to a standing joke when the cross-channel swim became a summer recreation for typistes. But it had a good ending. During the Great War the Channel stood as never before for the things that have most value with British peoples. As a record of achievement and endurance, the story of the Dover Patrol is hardly surpassed in dramatic and heroic interest even by Nelson's historic blockade; the maintaining of an unimpeded passage for troops and munitions to France, and for casualties and leave-men homewards, was a naval achievement second to none in its influence on the final result of the war. For the medical service of Great Britain the Channel provided problems of great importance and no little complexity, such as that brought about early in 1917 by the submarine sinkings of hospital ships and the consequent retention of British casualties in France. The mere physical transfer of casualties from France to England was a stupendous task—how great may in some degree be envisaged from the following figures:—[1]

The
English
Channel

---

[1] The figures are taken from the *Brit. Off. Med. History, General, Vol. I, pp. 372-3*. They differ from those given on *p. 409* (which are taken from the *Brit. Off. Med. History, Statistics, p. 15*). In the former, the total evacuated to the United Kingdom during 1914-18 is 2,232,997 and in the latter 2,279,695. Unfortunately no records were kept during the war of Australian embarkations from France to England except for the period March, 1918, onwards which are partly embodied *in diagram on p. 440.*

Total British and Dominion Troops Sick and Wounded Arriving Each Year in the United Kingdom from the Expeditionary Force, France.

YEAR	OFFICERS			OTHER RANKS			TOTALS	
	Sick	Wounded	Misc.	Sick	Wounded	Misc.	Officers	Other Ranks
1914	—	—	—	—	—	—	2,660	66,626
1915	5,577	5,630	—	120,675	131,567	—	11,207	252,244
1916	12,739	13,614	7	218,479	276,847	1,467	26,360	496,793
1917	15,283	17,335	4	320,876	346,941	123	32,622	667,940
1918	14,810	21,676	56	264,282	375,429	292	36,542	640,003
1919	3,886	419	—	107,854	6,528	5	4,305	114,387
1920	144	1	—	7,010	47	—	145	7,057
Total	52,439	58,675	67	1,039,176	1,137,361	1,887	113,841	2,245,050

The crossing of the channel by a casualty was an event of first importance in the problem of "return to duty," since it involved *ipso facto*—even for slightly wounded men such as were always sent across when a rush of casualties occurred—a much more prolonged absence from their unit than was usually required for similar casualties that were retained in France.[2]

The hospital ships were under the administration of the D.M.S. for Embarkation Duties, in England; embarkation was under the Deputy Director of Medical Services of the Base concerned.

Embarkation

During the period covered by this narrative the ports of embarkation were Calais, Boulogne, Rouen and Le Havre. Australian casualties went by the two latter, returning as reinforcements *via* Le Havre. From the General Hospitals, British and Australian, at these ports, men classified unfit for finalising in France, or else caught up in the rush from great battles, were taken to the dock by the cars of special motor ambulance convoys, driven for the most part by British women of the First Aid Nursing Yeomanry Convoy ("The F.A.N.Y's"), and embarked by admirably trained and efficient staffs, chiefly P.B. men of the R.A.M.C. As an administrative procedure embarkation was controlled by means of Army Forms—the *nominal roll* and *embarkation card*. By this means the records of 3rd Echelon in France were co-ordinated with those in Great Britain, and reciprocal action in the disposal of casualties at the ports of arrival was secured.

[2] The average time for the "round trip" by a minor casualty in France was put at about six weeks, but for the circuit that included Britain (Command Depots) it was estimated at some four months.

The efficiency of the cross-channel service of casualties may be gauged by the fact that, apart from enemy action of a kind that has been generally condemned, it has so little "history."

In the actual conduct of this stage of evacuation—and the motor ambulance convoys and ambulance trains of the preceding stages—the Australian Medical Service had no direct concern. Australian sick and wounded were conveyed to England as part of the great stream of British casualties; the cost of this service was included in the *per capita* payment whereby Great Britain and the Dominions arranged their respective financial commitments.³ From the moment he was taken over by the motor ambulance convoy at the front, the Australian casualty passed for the main part into the general stream of British casualties; not to be picked up again into any Australian unit or administration till the vicissitudes of primary hospital treatment had been safely surmounted. During 1916-1918, 155,000 Australian casualties went thus from France to England.⁴

Disembarkation: distribution

The hospital ships disembarked their patients at Southampton and Dover, Australians chiefly at the former.

Both of these great ports were admirably adapted for the purpose. Each had historical associations of great interest to men of British descent—well sustained by strong local sentiment whose roots reach to and draw life from every layer of English history. At the time of the war Southampton, on the Solent, most picturesque of British ports, was second only to the Port of London in its facilities for the rapid discharge of large vessels. Here it was that the *Aquitania* and the *Mauretania* disembarked in 1915 the "bye-wash" from Lemnos;⁵ and through Southampton in the course of the war passed more than 1,600,000 sick and wounded. The Port of Dover (serving Calais and Boulogne) was almost entirely given over to the hospital ship service, and during the war dealt with an almost equal number of casualties.

At both of these ports local services of succour, official and voluntary, were admirably organised and maintained under a Deputy Director of Medical Services. Patients were disembarked by special R.A.M.C. companies direct to the hospital train, which ran to the ship's side. To avoid congestion in times of rush, a "clearing hospital" was established at each

---
³ See Chapter xxvi and Vol. I p. 57.
⁴ These figures can only be given approximately. See note on p. 424.
⁵ See Vol. I, pp. 332, 500.

port. From these ports casualties were distributed throughout the British Isles by ambulance trains with a success that may be measured by the fact that in the course of the war nearly three million were so carried with only six deaths on the train.[6]

Distribution from the ports was controlled from the War Office by a special system of returns, whereby the destination of hospital trains was co-ordinated with the bed state in the various hospitals throughout the United Kingdom. All Australian casualties went direct to British Hospitals; nominal rolls showing their allocation went direct to Australian Administrative Headquarters, London.

THE HOSPITAL SYSTEM IN BRITAIN

The home hospital system of Great Britain was organised on a military basis, and the various hospital units were administered by the Deputy-Director of Medical Services of the "Command" in which they were situated.[7] The British soldier was given choice—conditioned by available accommodation—of the locality to which he should be sent, correct delivery being assured by affixing to his person a ticket with his address. Distribution was also influenced by the need for some special form of treatment, no less than twenty distinct classes being recognised and provided for. This system was extended to permit the despatch of a proportion of Canadian and New Zealand casualties to their own hospitals in England, but at no time during the war did Australia require this concession to "national" sentiment, or insist upon any differential treatment for her soldiers. The involvements of this policy were considerable, and it was the cause of much debate—in particular, of a divergence of view between the D.M.S., A.I.F. (Surgeon-General Howse), and the Director-General in Australia (Surgeon-General Fetherston). Though Australian sentiment both in the A.I.F. and at home called strongly, and naturally, for the treatment of Australians in their own hospitals whenever possible, it was realised by those responsible that to insist on direct admission would introduce a serious complication, and at no time was the pressure brought to bear such as to em-

---

[6] *Brit. Off. Med. History, General, Vol. I, p. 106.*
[7] *See Vol. I, p. 493n and Sketch Map at p. 17.*

barrass the D.M.S., A.I.F. or the War Office in their adherence to this policy—which was indeed compelled by the decision concurred in by the Australian Director-General, of sending the Australian General Hospitals to France,⁸ and of returning to Australia all men found unfit for duty for more than six months.⁹ The only concession desired by the Australian authorities was that, so far as was possible and expedient, Australian casualties should go to hospitals in the South of England. From early in 1917 it became the rule that they should be sent to hospitals in the Southern, Western and Eastern Commands, although this requirement could not always be fulfilled; nor—it may be added—was it "found possible to arrange" for Canadian and New Zealand patients in convoys from France to go direct to their own hospitals, though they were transferred thither at the earliest possible moment.

The decision was one that went to the root of Imperial relations, and the consideration which led to its adoption and the influences which conspired to maintain the policy are examined in the final chapter of this volume.

The combined effect of these various influences was to bring about the development in England of a system of Australian secondary or "Auxiliary hospitals." The chief purpose of these was to relieve the British General Hospitals of the Australian casualty—in particular of those suffering from a disability that incapacitated them for more than six months—so soon as he had reached a degree of recovery that would permit decision by a medical board as to his further destination. Their duty, as to which some particulars will be given later in this chapter, was to carry out only such *treatment* as would promote—or at least not interfere with—the prime purpose of *movement*.

In the Home system of hospitals in Great Britain¹⁰ there were treated during the war something over 3,000,000 sick and wounded. Of these, some 250,000 were Australians.¹¹ In the British hospitals, General and Convalescent, the Australian soldier was subject to British hospital discipline, was treated by British surgeons, physicians and specialists, and nursed by

---

⁸ *See p. 13n.*   ⁹ *See Vol. I, p. 507.*   ¹⁰ *Vol. I, p. 493n.*
¹¹ Exact figures are not available.

50. MODEL SHOWING THE EMBARKATION OF WOUNDED ON HOSPITAL FERRY AT BOULOGNE

From a series illustrating the evacuation of sick and wounded in the Australian War Memorial.

Aust. War Memorial Official Photo. No. J6436.

51. THE CENTRAL KITCHEN OF No. 3 A.G.H., ABBEVILLE

Aust. War Memorial Official Photo. No. E2563.
Taken on 23 June 1918.
                                                            To face p. 428.

52. A BRITISH HOSPITAL FOR AUSTRALIAN TROOPS

Bishop's Knoll, near Bristol, maintained by its owner, Mr. R. E. Bush, as an auxiliary to No. 2 Southern General Hospital.

53. THE ELECTRO-THERAPEUTIC WARD AT No. 1 A.A.H., HAREFIELD

Aust. War Memorial Official Photo. No. D40.   *To face p. 429.*

British nurses.[12] The work done in these undoubtedly varied somewhat in quality—the whole medical profession was mobilised in this service, and the British medical general practitioner is accustomed to a greater extent than in Australia, to rely on specialist help in major surgical problems.[13] In the eyes of medical officers of the staff of the D.M.S., A.I.F., the work done in some of the smaller hospitals had a "wait and see" quality that went beyond a legitimate *"non nocere."*

Australian Patients and British Hospitals. But it can be stated on adequate evidence that "speaking broadly," yet within limits that should fully satisfy Australian national sentiment, the Australian soldier received treatment that was not less careful than would have been the case had Australia made provision equivalent to a full establishment of general hospitals in England. Though he could not get the touch of Home in the British hospitals the Australian soldier got the best that England had to give and he got it (it may be noted incidentally) at an expense to Australia which was very far indeed below its cost to Britain.[14] Moreover through the system evolved by the British War Office, to permit to the Dominion Forces that *imperium in imperio* in respect of their own affairs that is the secret of British Empire, the Australian Director at Horseferry-road was enabled to maintain close touch with Australian casualties in British hospitals, through visiting officers.

During this stay of the Australian soldier in the British hospitals, General and Convalescent, adequate provision was made for ministration by his direct kith and kin. In addition to visitation by representatives of the Australian Medical Director, it was notified by Army Council Instructions that—

Australian "Red Cross" in England

---

[12] In modification of this general statement it may be recalled that some 200 Australian medical men and some 300 Australian nurses served with the R.A.M.C. during the war, and a proportion of them were in the British hospitals in England.

[13] "Large numbers of wounded men came under the care of medical officers whose previous experience had been limited to general practice in towns where all injuries and accidents of any degree of severity had been removed to the care of the surgeons in the county hospital. In the early days the activities of trained surgeons were confined to routine work in their own wards instead of being available for consultative and operative purposes throughout the hospital." (*Brit. Off. Med. History, Surgery, Vol. I. pp. 338-9*).

[14] For a statement of the cost of maintenance of A.I.F. patients in Great Britain, and of the financial arrangements in regard thereto made between the British and Dominion Governments, *see pp. 826-7.*

"The Australian Branch of the British Red Cross Society will undertake the work of attending to the comfort and requirements of the Australian soldiers while in hospitals. Its representatives will visit hospitals frequently and will work in conjunction with Australian administrative headquarters with the object of supplying any article that may be necessary or which will add to the comfort of the soldiers in hospital, but which is without the scope of the Ordnance Department."[15]

The general statement made above that no Australian General Hospital was available in Great Britain must be modified by reference here to one exception: during a brief period in 1916-17 an Australian General Hospital was established in England as a "primary" hospital. The circumstances of this call for brief notice.

No. 3 A.G.H.

In July, 1916, the rush of casualties from the Battles of the Somme brought about, in the Australian Medical Service as in the British, a crisis more urgent than any in the war, and this extended to the hospitals in Great Britain. At this time the Battles of Gaza[16] had resulted in a similar though less urgent crisis at the Australian Base in Egypt. No. 3 A.G.H. (which had just finished clearing up after Gallipoli) now became a bone of contention between the authorities of the A.I.F. in England and Egypt. Supported by the Director-General, A.M.S., the D.M.S., A.I.F. (Surgeon-General Howse) gained his point: the hospital was brought to England, and in October was established in the "Kitchener War Hospital" at Brighton as a General Hospital, receiving sick and wounded from France with some discrimination in favour of Australian casualties. Here it worked until April, 1917.[17] With the petering out of the Somme "offensive" the crisis that had brought the unit to England passed. Early in 1917 the submarine sinkings of cross channel hospital ships brought about an almost equally pressing situation in France. On May 9th the unit opened at Abbeville. Its important work there is recorded elsewhere.

---

[15] The work of the A.R.C.S. will be described in *Vol. III*.

[16] *Vol. I, pp. 615-26.*

[17] The buildings occupied ("Poor Law Institute and Infirmaries") had with successive re-buildings been used as a "workhouse" since 1690. They had been made available by the "Guardians of the Poor" for Brighton Parish in 1914 and were the first of the kind to be so used (*See Vol. I p. 493n*). The following note from the Clerk to the Board of Guardians shows the various uses to which the War Hospital was put—"December 1914-15 Indian troops; March 1916-October 1916 British troops; October 1916-April 1917 Australian Imperial Forces; 1917 onwards Canadian Imperial Forces."

For reasons explained in *Chapter xxvi* the idea of using this Australian hospital for Australian wounded, as was at first intended, was not carried out. Some 5,000 patients, British and Australian, were treated while No. 3 A.G.H. was in occupation. Surgical work was "chiefly the sequelae of chronic infection" and the results were "very gratifying." In four months—November to February—407 operations were done of which a large proportion were in fracture cases. Part of the medical work consisted in largely futile endeavour to obtain the required three "negatives" from cases of chronic dysentery, amoebic and bacillary.

THE LAST STAGE

TREATMENT IN BRITISH PRIMARY HOSPITALS

The *movement* of casualties through the British primary hospitals having been followed it remains to consider the treatment during this stage, which came but slightly within the general experiences of the A.A.M.C. Attention is directed to developments in the general surgery of wounds and not to the methods adopted and results obtained in regional wounds.

Secondary treatment of wounds and disease

The influence of treatment in Britain upon the ultimate condition of most wounded men, though of course considerable, was far less than that of treatment at the front, by which its character was in great measure determined. Its problems varied greatly in the different years of the war. In the first months hospitals in Britain received men with very heavily contaminated wounds—sometimes within 48 hours of a battle. Sepsis was practically universal, tetanus common (during the first 12 months of the war over 60 per cent. of all cases occurred in the hospitals in Great Britain). The subsequent progress at the front was accurately reflected at home. With the substitution of "more physiological methods" for strong antiseptics and drainage, the "almost universal anaerobic infections gave place to the coccal forms" and the wounded men showed much less constitutional disturbance. But the further course was much the same. From 1917 onwards the practice of excision or *débridement* had a profound influence on the condition of wounds reaching Britain and on results in final repair.

Effect of Transport and Time. Each of these was a vital factor in determining the methods and result of treatment in Britain. Every stage of movement was a period of retrogression in the septic wound. Even the Carrel-Dakin technique "showed serious draw-backs when the disturbances due to rail and sea transport had to be surmounted." These were much reduced when discreet provision for primary or delayed primary suture by *débridement* and light packing were adopted.

Delayed Infection: "Flares." Infected wounds which had healed by granulation were liable to this grave occurrence. In imperfectly cleaned wounds organisms became embedded in the granulation or scar-tissue and might cause recurrence of local sepsis when healed or partly healed. In old wounds it was found that closure was often promoted by B.I.P. and similar agents; but the most important step was the closing of granulating wounds by secondary suture. The older the wound, or the more fully established the physiological reaction, the more difficult it became to achieve asepis.

Prophylaxis in Reparative Surgery. Writers on the reparative surgery of war wounds are in general agreement that the importance of prevention in orthopaedic work was not at first appreciated. It was only at a comparatively late stage of the war, largely through the labours of Sir Robert Jones and his co-workers, that it began to be realised that every surgeon and every medical officer in charge of wounded soldiers must work not only on orthopaedic lines, but on orthopaedic lines of a preventive as well as a curative kind and that these "preventive" methods must be commenced in the earliest stages of wound treatment.[18]

The conclusion arrived at by the surgeons in Britain was that treatment directed to the excision of bruised and devitalised tissues, carried out within a short time after the infliction of the injury, which allowed the prompt closure of wounds and the exclusion of opportunity for renewed infection, "brought about the great revolution in wound treatment in the war."

The Secondary Treatment of Diseases in British Hospitals. The most striking feature of the treatment of sick men in the hospitals in Britain was a progressive differentiation of function to meet (*i*) the rapid advances in the knowledge of pathogenesis; (*ii*) the recognition of new clinical syndromes; (*iii*) the possibilities of advance in treatment by selection and concentration of special types of "disease" in special hospitals. Some account of these and of the clinical advances made in the war—as in the nature of "soldier's heart" and pathogeny of war-neuroses—will be found in *Volume III*.

Preceding chapters have been concerned chiefly with the medical problems involved in the prevention or repair of wastage, and to this end attention has been directed chiefly to the provisions made for those methods of treatment—excision of wounds, primary and secondary suture, treatment of trench foot, of I.C.T., of scabies, of acute and curable microbic diseases, and of "functional" disorders, physiological and psychical—which were of oustanding importance in promoting the return of the soldier to the front. At the stage now reached in the movement and treatment of the casualty—

The National issues: reparative treatment

---

[18] This point was emphasised by Lieut.-Col. H. S. Newland at the end of 1917 in a report to Surgeon-General Howse on the work of the Australian casualty clearing stations in France. The following note by Sir Robert Jones ("An Address on the Orthopaedic Outlook in Military Surgery," *B.M.J.*, 12 Jan., 1918, p. 42) puts the matter in a nutshell: "The orthopaedic problem can be divided, therefore, into two distinct parts—preventive orthopaedics and corrective orthopaedics. The latter is more especially the department of the trained orthopaedic surgeon. . . . The preventive requires the help of every surgeon who has to treat wounded men at any stage, especially the early stage."

namely discharge from a primary general hospital in Britain, with wound healed and disease if not "cured" at least restrained or defined—we have to do with problems of a different clinical order, and whose purpose is now more deliberately twofold, national as well as military. The national and the individual outlook come into prominence; the military objective, return to duty, fades out as the final quota of "fit" men is selected and "returned to duty" and the residue passed back, for what it is worth, to the nation.

Reparative Treatment of Australian Casualties in England. In the A.I.F. this end-point of treatment—as it may be termed —was a confused one. For the Australian soldier the last stage of his treatment—if that treatment was to extend over six months—and his final disposal were effected not, as then in the British Army, through a closely-knit system of administrative departments and medical units; on the contrary, they were carried out in two echelons of medical organisation and of professional activity, separated by 10,000 miles of sea and a considerable lapse of time. The treatment that should be carried out in England and in Australia respectively was ill defined, and continuity of medical action was maintained only by the system of interim-treatment built up in No. 2 Command Depot, and by that organised to cover the stage of sea-transport. The particular effect of all this on Australian surgery and the Australian soldier will be discussed in the next volume.

But reparative treatment was far from being confined to those who were unfit for further service, even for six months; and, even of Australians in these categories, a proportion was necessarily treated in Great Britain. A general reference to reparative treatment in Great Britain must therefore be made here.

Reparative surgery

With his discharge "convalescent" we reach a stage in the history of the wounded man when the wound has "healed" and wound-disease is at least in abeyance. But, though structural repair might in a rough fashion be complete, it still remained in almost all cases to recover functional perfection. And here we impinge upon the wide field of reparative or "orthopaedic" surgery, and of artificial replacements.

Types of Case Requiring Reparative Treatment. For practical purposes we may distinguish three groups of men recovered from wounds who required reparative treatment.

(1) Those whose wound though "healed" was left uncured—as with sinus leading to a sequestrum, faecal fistula, or foreign body *in situ*. Of these it need only be said here that many remain with us until this day. (2) A large body of men in whom structural repair, as of joints and bones, had passed the stage which H. O. Thomas called "unsound" and therefore plastic, or where fibrous reconstruction was complete; but in which the attainment of tissue normality was far from being synonymous with the restoration of functional efficiency or even a structural *restitutio ad integrum*. (3) Those men for whom functional restoration required no more than graduated re-training.

Of these groups, the first with comparatively few exceptions, were boarded for return to Australia as "invalids." The last went chiefly to Nos. 1, 3, or 4 Command Depots and thence again to France. The disposal of the second group, whether back to the front or home to Australia, provided the Australian Medical Service in England with its most engrossing and difficult task. For the most part this preoccupation had to do with methods of treatment whose purpose was individual and national rather than military and (as will presently be indicated) belongs more properly elsewhere.

At the same time this treatment became to an increasing degree definitive rather than general, in this respect allied rather to regional surgery than to the "general surgery of wounds" which, in the previous chapters of this section, we have set out to examine. For reasons connected with each of these the history of the evolution of reparative surgery in the Great War is followed in *Volume III*.

The chief distinction between wounding and disease, and, in less degree, between disease caused by infection and that due to some inborn or inherent factor, is that the former is self-limited, the latter often continuous or progressive. Hitherto for the most part we have followed the treatment and disposal of men suffering from disease of a kind or at a stage that admits sufficient check or recovery to permit *return to duty*. At the stage now reached we first make contact with a great problem of war

Reparative medicine

medicine, the cost of whose final solution bids fair to rival or even to exceed the total immediate costs of the war—the problem of continuing injuries which, in the terms of the Australian Pensions Act, are "due to or aggravated by war service."

Fuller discussion of this vast question is reserved for the next volume. But it is here that the problem is first sighted, and should therefore be defined.

The Problem. The problems of reparative "medicine," if less clearly defined and far more complex, were analogous to those of "surgery," and as important. Even plastic surgery had its analogue in medicine, as in the "cure" of the "carrier" state or in the restoration of the outward and visible signs of mental stability in men whose psychic structure could never attain to "normality." But, like reparative surgery, reparative medicine was concerned chiefly with the restoration of *"function."* And here medicine and surgery part in the meaning of the descriptive adjective "functional" as commonly used *i.e.* as a patho-genic description. For the present purpose we may adhere to the common sense usage which differentiates "function" from "structure."

The diseases involved in "reparative" medicine, as in reparative surgery, may with advantage be divided into three groups, and with the same significance. The *first* comprised those types of chronic and progressive disease or disorder in which recovery was incomplete or structurally impossible—nephritis, tuberculosis, mental disease, (psychosis), V.D.H., osteo-arthritis, and so forth. In a very large proportion of these the "disease" was "inborn" or of pre-war origin—"aggravated" by the war. With structural deformities such as hernia, varicocele, and flat-foot, accounted for the great proportion of men "invalided" for "non-battle" casualty during the war. This group is analysed, statistically and pathogenetically, and their disposal followed in *Volume III*. The *second* is a convenient group into which to place those men in whom recovery from an acute "disease" or "disorder," though accompanied by structural integrity adequate to ensure complete functional recovery in the military sense, was associated with continued delay in the attainment of such functional ability. Two clear-cut types present themselves, distinguished by their pathogenesis—*i.e.* whether physio- or psycho-genic. In the first were men convalescent from nephritis, gassing, respiratory disease, dysentery, trench foot, and many others. In the second are placed men in whom functional defects were wholly or chiefly psychogenic in their proximate, and perhaps their ultimate, causality. They included the great class of psychoneuroses, and—as predominantly psychogenic—"the effort syndrome" or "D.A.H."; and also many cases of "gassing." This second type which constitutes the dominant and characteristic problem of the war from the point of view of scientific medicine, is studied in a special chapter of *Volume III*, as also, in so far as their treatment is of interest, are those of the first type. The *third* group —"cured"—went to the Command Depot, distinguished now from "battle-casualties" only by the wound stripe worn by the latter.

THE SPECIAL HOSPITALS

For these various types of case and for primary as well as for reparative treatment, surgical and medical, the British War Office with the co-operation of the B.R.C.S. provided a great variety of *special hospitals*, to which—in particular to those for immediate treatment—many Australian casualties were sent on arrival in

Graph No. 3—AUSTRALIANS UNDER TREATMENT IN AUSTRALIAN AUXILIARY AND BRITISH HOSPITALS IN THE UNITED KINGDOM.

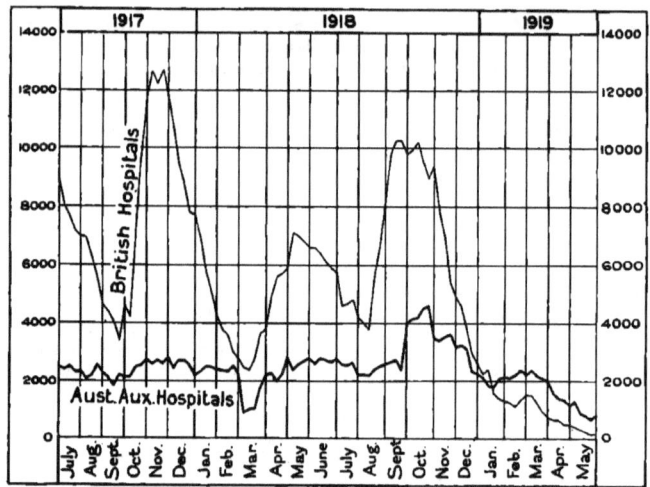

The figures are exclusive of patients treated in the camp hospitals of the Command Depots.

England from the front. For Australian convalescents, however, with few exceptions, both movement and treatment diverged from those of their British comrades, and became the responsibility of the Australian Government and the Australian Medical Service.

The British soldier, after treatment in a primary (general) hospital, was, if fit, given furlough and discharged to Command Depot; if still "unfit," he was sent to one of these special hospitals, or was finally discharged from the Army. Australian soldiers, on the other hand, returned to Australian control as follows.

Transfer to Australian Control. When they reached the stage of convalescence in the British primary hospitals (as also in No. 3 A.G.H. acting as such) they were roughly classified and—unless wholly crippled, as by spinal injury—were dealt with by discharge or transfer, in accordance with "Instructions" precisely laid down by the Army Council. These varied somewhat from time to time to meet Australian wishes; but ultimately the procedure was that all soldiers fit to travel as sitting cases, but not yet fit to be discharged to take furlough, were transferred, without being boarded and without delay, provided accommodation was available, to one of the three Australian Auxiliary Hospitals.

Cases considered unlikely to be fit for general service for a period of six months, and fit to travel but only as lying down cases, were specially reported to the D.M.S., A.I.F., who would then arrange for their transfer by hospital train.

Special provision was made for tubercular, mental and venereal cases and for amputations. Officers were dealt with by special procedure.[19]

Australian soldiers who were convalescent and in a fit state to proceed on furlough were discharged to Administrative Headquarters A.I.F., Horseferry-road, Westminster, where they were granted furlough, to report on completion to an Australian Command Depot.[20]

The Australian Auxiliary Hospitals[21]

During 1916 a large proportion of Australians, when discharged "cured" from the British hospitals, went direct to the Command Depots, and invalids boarded for Australia were in many instances embarked direct from the (British) General Hospital. But as the war progressed and submarine sinkings increased, and the food problem in Great Britain called with ever-increasing insistence for relief by the rapid clearance of unnecessary troops, the Australian D.M.S. became more and more convinced and determined in his policy of transferring Australians for the final stages of their recovery to the Australian Auxiliary Hospitals; and thus obtaining control of them at a stage when their movement onward might

---

[19] *See Vol. I. p. 502.* For an account of the various convalescent homes and hospitals for Australians in Great Britain, see *Vol. III.*

[20] Exception was made for hospitals in the neighbourhood of the Australian Command Depots from which Australian soldiers might be discharged direct to the depot.

[21] The development of the Auxiliary Hospitals to serve the requirements of patients boarded for Australia is dealt with in *Vol. III.*

be accelerated.[22] By the middle of 1917, indeed, the Australian Auxiliary Hospitals in England had come to act as an almost complete intermediary between the British hospital system and the Australian Command Depots for "B" class convalescents (Nos. 2, 3 and 4) and in particular, that for invalids (No. 2 at Weymouth).

The function of these hospitals in England has been stated in general terms.[23] It can be presented best in terms of *movement*, to which, to an inceasing degree, the claims of *treatment* were subordinated. In this chapter it is only necessary briefly to note the place of each of these units in the policy of the D.M.S., A.I.F., and with particular reference to the problem of "return to duty."

No. 1 Australian Auxiliary Hospital (Harefield). During 1916 the "Harefield Convalescent Hospital" was expanded,[24] to contain 1,000 beds, sub-divided into strictly convalescent, surgical, and medical divisions, and equipped and fitted out in a manner that enabled it to fulfil all the requirements of a first-class "auxiliary"—which permitted, indeed, a very considerable amount of intermediate and reparative surgery, and of special medical treatment.

No. 2 Australian Auxiliary Hospital (Southall). To relieve the pressure on Harefield, and in preparation to receive the wave of Australian casualties from the Somme after it had passed through the British hospital system in England, the D.M.S., A.I.F. acquired the St. Marylebone (Orphanage) Schools at Southall in the western suburbs of London for use as an Australian "Auxiliary." These were opened on August 4th as "No. 2 Australian Auxiliary Hospital, Southall," and staffed with surplus officers and men from the recently disbanded "Auxiliary Hospitals" in Egypt. At first purely auxiliary in function, to meet the situation created by the large number of limbless who were accruing from the Somme fighting, in November, 1916, the unit was staffed to specialise in the thorny problem of the fitting of artificial limbs, which hitherto had been carried out only at Harefield. During 1917 and 1918 the accommodation was almost exclusively devoted to this class of case.

No. 3 Australian Auxiliary Hospital (Dartford). In pursuance of his policy, at the end of September, 1916, the D.M.S., A.I.F.

---
[22] This policy was initiated by the D.M.S., A.I.F. in view of reports by his inspecting officers that there was unnecessary delay in the British hospitals. It is fair to say—*per contra*—that Medical Officers in British hospitals complained that the pressure brought to bear by A.I.F. Headquarters (D.M.S.) on the British hospital staffs to accelerate the passage of Australian sick and wounded militated at times against the interest of the patients. But a study of available records (which include admirable memoranda by members of the D.M.S's staff) points clearly to the need for close oversight. Some smaller British hospitals were staffed by men not highly skilled in surgery; and a definite part of the purpose of the D.M.S. was their transfer to the care of his own staffs in the Australian Auxiliary Hospitals.

[23] See also Chapter i and Vol. I, pp. 490-512.

[24] See Vol. I. pp. 497, 501.

successfully negotiated with the War Office for the provision of yet another Auxiliary Hospital on England and acquired from the Metropolitan Asylums Board a fine hutted hospital site, previously used for an infectious diseases hospital. On October 9th this was opened as No. 3 Australian Auxiliary by No. 1 Australian Stationary Hospital, which had arrived from Egypt in September; and before the end of the month it held 1,400 patients. Opportunity was given here for some special lines of clinical work, in particular in the surgery of nerves, and treatment of psycho-neuroses. Like Nos. 1 and 2, however, its purpose was essentially auxiliary—it was a clearing centre, to implement the "six months' policy."

Special Convalescent Hospitals for Officers and Nurses. In addition to the important units described above there were formed, chiefly through private benevolence, a number of small convalescent homes in private houses for officers and nurses of the A.I.F. awaiting final disposal after discharge from British hospitals.[25]

Work in the Auxiliaries
Though closely restricted by the D.M.S., A.I.F., to subserve the requirements of policy—both of reinforcement of the front and repatriation of invalids—the work of these Australian hospitals in Great Britain was both interesting and important, and of a most varied kind. A very brief summary must suffice here.

For Potential "Effectives." At Nos. 1 and 3 large convalescent blocks were organised, and, with the help of the Australian Red Cross Society (B.R.C.S.), excellent facilities were provided for amusement and recreation. Much of the surgery done in these units was connected with those types of case which might be made fit for duty: such as developmental defects or occupational deformities—hernia, hydrocele, varicose veins, haemorrhoids, and so forth. The special departments, eye, ear, nose, and throat, were well organised and active, and the X-Ray and Massage departments enterprising. On the medical side many of the patients were recovering from infectious disease in which the carrier state had supervened, in particular the dysenteries (amoebic and bacillary), typhoid, para-typhoid and malaria.

For "Invalids." Here professional interest, medical and surgical,

---

[25] Reference may, however, most conveniently be made here to the work of the British "Auxiliary Hospitals," through which passed during the war a large number of the Australian sick and wounded. An example of these which had a particular interest for Australians was the Bishop's Knoll War Hospital, Bristol—"an 'A' Class Auxiliary" to No. 2 British Southern General Hospital (*see Vol. I., p. 493*). This auxiliary was entirely maintained and conducted by a West Australian pastoralist, resident in England, and his wife (Mr. and Mrs. R. E. Bush). Organised in 1914 in a typical English country home, when in 1916 the A.I.F. was transferred to the Western Front, at the special request of Mr. Bush, arrangements were made that it should be reserved for Australian sick and wounded of all ranks and every degree of severity. It was admirably conducted as a hospital at the entire expense and under the direct supervision of Mr. and Mrs. Bush, who were able to create an atmosphere wholly congenial to the sick and wounded of the A.I.F. who were fortunate enough to be treated here. Mr. Bush informed all patients that they could obey a set of rules which he himself regarded as necessary or the official rules, whichever they chose. They invariably chose his rules, and, he says, 98 per cent. rigidly obeyed them.

centred largely on the devising of suitable interim treatment, and on procedures necessary to fit the war-damaged man for transportation to Australia. These are advantageously described together in the chapter in *Volume III* which deals with the special problems of the "invalid."

THE PARTING OF WAYS—FINAL DISPOSAL OF AUSTRALIAN CASUALTIES

With his discharge as "convalescent" from the British hospital system in U.K. to an Australian Auxiliary Hospital or direct (after furlough) to Command Depot, we arrive at a decisive stage in the movement of the Australian soldier

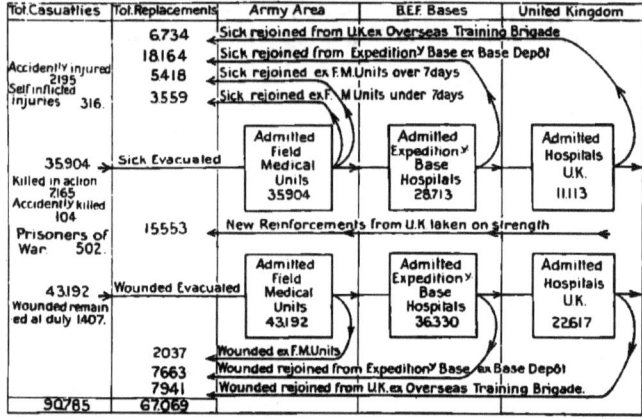

EVACUATION AND RETURN TO DUTY IN THE A.I.F. ON THE WESTERN FRONT—ILLUSTRATING EXPERIENCE DURING SIX MONTHS APRIL-SEPTEMBER, 1918.

Note.—The figures given are the actual numbers as disposed during the period under review being based on returns compiled by Australian Section of 3rd Echelon G.H.Q. The number (35,904) for sick evacuations includes 88 who died of disease; and of the wounded (43,192), 3,108 died. It will be noticed that the numbers do not balance. This is partly due to the fact (1) that the numbers remaining at the beginning and end of the period do not enter into the statement; (2) that local admissions to Base Hospitals are included in the admissions. In spite of such causes for inconsistency the diagram is of value as illustrating a vital procedure in modern warfare.

The A.I.F. strength on the Western Front at the beginning of the period was 122,426, and at the end 99,371.

evacuated through sickness or wounds. The stream of battle-casualties and sick has been followed from its source at the battle front through the various stages of collection in the field and clearance along the lines of communication; and it has been seen that at each stage—the Regimental Aid Post, the Field Ambulance, the Casualty Clearing Station, the General Hospitals in France—a moiety was separated[26] from their more seriously damaged comrades and, after suitable treatment, returned again to the front to renew the gaps created in the long line by the never ending process of "attrition." The point has now been reached where the stream finally divides into two, diverted hither or thither—back to the front or home to Australia—by the *ipse dixit* of the Medical Service: when recovery in the British primary hospital was complete the decision was made by the commanding officer of the hospital; when fitness for service was in doubt, by a medical board after the transfer of the convalescent to an Australian Auxiliary Hospital.

The final objective—so far as the Medical Service of the A.I.F. was concerned—of all recovered Australian casualties in their retreat from the front was the Australian "Command (Convalescent) Depots" on Salisbury Plain. Men found by the medical boards "likely to be fit for duty within three months" went to No. 1 (at Perham Downs), those likely to be fit within six months to Nos. 3 (Hurdcott) and 4 (Wareham).[27] Those adjudged unlikely to be fit for duty within six months, but not requiring hospital care, were sent to No. 2 (Weymouth). In these depots the soldier passed back from the protecting wing of the Geneva Convention and the Medical Service into combatant control—the "fit" class to undergo progressive training and hardening for the rough and tumble of soldiers' life; the "unfit," after various vicissitudes of reclassification and under appropriate medical supervision, to the transport for Australia, with the alternative, in a few cases, of "B Class" service overseas.

The Medical Boards. The final separation of the two streams of casualties differentiated by the "*six months*' policy" took place for the most part in the Australian Auxiliary Hospitals, and was the prime function of the A.I.F. medical boards. The work of these bodies was among the most vital

---

[26] The dimension of these "quotas" at each "level" in actual percentage of the whole stream, analysed by cause of disablement, will be found in the statistical chapters of *Vol. III*.

[27] The site occupied by the several Command Depots changed somewhat from time to time as did also, to some extent, their particular function.

and interesting features of medical responsibility in the war. Their function in the comity of the army may be compared to the part played in the social life of a civil community by its judiciary. By the judgment of the board was decided, justly or unjustly, the degree of guilt (in the "Erewhon" sense) of the soldier who should become injured or diseased in the service of war. The verdict and sentence of the board were given in terms of "fitness" for military service, and were expressed by means of a number of "categories" representing various degrees of such fitness (or unfitness). This system of medical categories formed the basis for the working of the great Command Convalescent Depot system—the military factory for repair and reconditioning.[28]

The circumstances of the sorting out of the heterogeneous collection of battle-casualties and diseases, that arrived at this final stage of retirement, is not only of great military importance, but is full of human interest to those in a position to see the wood for the trees; who can take an aeroplane view (so to speak) of the streams of convalescents and of invalids discharged from various British hospitals great and small, and converging, some by broad thoroughfares from great hospital centres, others in twos and threes, torn from happy hiding in almost unknown little country hospitals, to the toll gate of the medical board; thence again, on the judgment of the board, to diverge in two streams, the one back to the front for another throw of the dice with death,[29] the other, after various vicissitudes of "reclassification" and treatment, home to Australia. The tragedy of repeated woundings in battle, followed by the weary round of convalescence and retraining back to the tension of ever present death, was perhaps, in some part, the sacrificial substitute for the service of those who were unable or too precious to be enlisted; to that extent it was part of the price paid by Australia for escape from conscription. This freedom, perhaps, was worth the

A poignant decision

---

[28] Its operation is examined in the next chapter in connection with the practical medical problems met with in the process of repair. The working of the Australian system of medical boards in the A.I.F. is described in *Vol. III*.

[29] The highest number of successive journeys through the Command Depots and return to duty recorded of one individual was nine, though series of five or six were not uncommon—not necessarily in every instance for wounding. The number of multiple woundings recorded in the A.I.F. is stated to have been as follows: seven times, 1; six times, 10; five, 105; four, 807; three, 5,582.

THE LAST STAGE

price; but a plant of rosemary for remembrance should not be lacking from the pleasant garden that we have in testament from those who did the paying; and not the less because the toil of the treadmill has left its deforming mark on some of those who remain.

Of the two streams of convalescents referred to above, the "unfits" ceased to have interest to the military command as such; henceforth, though they remained an **Army wreckage and National salvage** official responsibility to the medical service, they were in the military sense "invalids," and were of practical concern to the nation only in a civic capacity; and their subsequent treatment and disposal were directed solely to the purpose of refitting them for return to civil life with as large a potentiality for self-help as could be conserved by reparative surgery, remedial treatment, or re-education. By the "six months' policy" this stream of invalids was deviated to flow as directly as might be to Australia. The account of the various stages and aspects of *"invaliding"* and *"repatriation"* of Australian sick and wounded soldiers belongs to the final volume of this work. The adventures of the other stream of men, *i.e.*, those found "fit for duty," call for present attention, since this body of soldiers furnished the reservoir of potential effectives which, as the war levied an ever heavier toll, and recruits from home fell off, became a factor of major importance in the striking power of the A.I.F. The machine which replaced the wastage from the Australian field force in France was the system of *Australian Depots in the United Kingdom*, or, familiarly, the "A.I.F. Depots in U.K."; through it passed, on their way to the front, both recovered casualties and also the new reinforcements, units, and formations, sent from Australia.[80]

---

[80] The work of the Command Depots is summarised in the relevant chapter (*xvi*). For detailed figures of the work of the Australian Auxiliaries in England see *Vol. III*.

SYNOPSIS OF CHAPTER XVI

THE HUMAN GRINDSTONE: REPAIRS AND REPLACEMENTS

THE A.I.F. DEPOTS IN U.K.:
The Knight's gambit.
Development of the Depots.
Effects of the Somme.
Developments during 1916.
Strength of the Depots.
Administration.
The D.M.S., A.I.F. and the Depots.
Health in the Depots.
Prevention of disease—Treatment of sickness—Venereal Disease.

THE COMMAND DEPOTS—FROM CONVALESCENT TO EFFECTIVE:
Early history of the Command Depots.
Disengaging the Invalid. Evolution of the categories.
The working of Command Depots.
Details of the categories.
Classification parades. Primary.
Weekly re-classification.
"Dental" fitness.
Comments on the system.
The professional problem in "Boarding."
  1. Unfitness through wounding.
  2. Unfitness caused by disease.
     The psychic element—Raw material for neuroses—War weariness—"D.A.H."—Trench fever—Trench foot—Other causes of disablement—Medical treatment.
Principles and practice of re-conditioning.
  Graduated training—Morale.
Final step of transfer: Hardening and training.
  The "Hardening and Drafting Depot." A cardinal development—The Overseas Training Brigade.
Constitution of the O.T.B.
Results.
"Home Service Personnel" (P.B. and T.B.)

THE TRAINING GROUPS—RECRUITS FROM AUSTRALIA:
Problem of unfit recruits—by-effects of Somme.
Medical reinforcements: the Training Depot.
  Recruits for A.A.M.C.—Reclaiming the "B" class.
  16th and 17th Field Ambulances.
  Training A.A.M.C.—Officers—Other ranks.

"DRAFT FOR FRANCE":
The journey completed.

LIST OF A.I.F. DEPOTS IN U.K.

Tidworth.—Headquarters.

Parkhouse.—A.A.S.C. and A.A.M.C. Training Depots, Convalescent Training Depot, Details Camp.

Sutton Veny Area.—1st Training Brigade, No. 1 Command Depot, Overseas Training Brigade (Longbridge Deverill), Reserve Brigade, Australian Artillery (Heytesbury), Pioneer Training Battalion, Group Clearing Hospital. (After Armistice No. 1 Australian General Hospital.)

Codford.—2nd Training Brigade, Group Clearing Hospital.

Hurdcott Area.—3rd Training Brigade, No. 3 Command Depot, No. 4 Command Depot, Group Clearing Hospital.

Weymouth Area.—No. 2 Command Depot consisting of (a) Monte Video sub-division, (b) Westham sub-division, (c) Verne sub-division, (d) Littlemoor sub-division.

Bulford.—Australian Dermatological Hospital.

Brightlingsea.—Engineering Training Depot.

Grantham.—Machine Gun Training Depot.

Other detachments e.g.—Railway details at Bordon, Heavy Artillery at Devonport, Engineer Training Depot (Signal Section) at Clifton, Bedfordshire.

Lewes.—Detention Barracks.

CHAPTER XVI

THE HUMAN GRINDSTONE: REPAIRS AND REPLACEMENTS[1]

THE A.I.F. DEPOTS IN U.K.

READERS of *Volume I* of this history will be familiar with the medical involvements of the problem of maintaining the strength of an army in the field, as seen during 1915 in the crude convalescent and training depots in Egypt.[2] Interesting and important as were these early local developments, they cannot compare in either respect with the remarkable system that was built up on Salisbury Plain to meet the demand for "effectives" on the Western Front in the attrition warfare of 1916-17, and the life and death struggle of 1918. Many medical officers of the field formations looked upon "the depots" as a despised domain of "categories" and cold-footers. Yet no more important medical work was done in the A.I.F. than here; no sphere of medical service presented more difficult problems; and in none were gifts for organisation and administration more brilliantly displayed.

The number of men dealt with in Australian Command Depots was very large, although figures for the whole period of their existence are not available. From July, 1917, to November, 1918, however, 134,104 were admitted into these depots; 46,871 of these were invalided to Australia; of the remainder the great majority after hardening in the depots were passed to France.[3] The figures give the measure of the medical problem, but no suggestion of its professional involvements; and perspective, not epigram, impels the statement that without an adequate

---
[1] The reader is recommended to read first *pp. 408-13 of Vol. I*. This chapter is in direct continuation of *pp. 16-20* of the present volume.
[2] The Corps Depot at Zeitoun for reinforcements and convalescents (*Vol. I., pp. 188-9, 265*), and the improvised "Divisional" Depots at Lemnos which dealt with the huge wastage from Gallipoli (*Vol. I., pp. 385-6*); later the problem was grappled in the more effectively organised Training Depot and Details Camp at Moascar (*Vol. I., pp. 656-7*) which served the Australian Light Horse.
[3] *See pp. 440-1 and Graphs at pp. 469, 480.*

description of the structure and working of the Command Depots an account of medical service in the war in relation to its duty toward the Army would be as *Hamlet* without the Prince of Denmark.

With his arrival in England by hospital ship the "casualty" was caught up in a complicated machinery of treatment and transfers, the purpose of which was to transform him with all possible speed into an "effective"—or to eject him as "unfit for further service." If he was transformed into an effective, he began, like the newly arrived recruits in the training battalions, that round journey to the front which he himself had already made at least once, and which has been aptly compared to the "knight's gambit" of the chess board—inasmuch as, for the great majority, it finished up at the original point of departure.

The Knight's gambit

The typical course of a recruit, who, after arriving at the training battalions by troop transport from Australia, reached the front and became wounded or seriously sick would be:—Draft for France, Base Depot in France, Corps Reinforcement Camp, Front Line. Becomes sick or wounded: Regimental Aid-post, Field Ambulance, C.C.S., Base Hospital in France, Hospital Ship to England, British General Hospital, Australian Auxiliary, Command Depot. There, as a "B class" man, he would traverse the maze of special treatments, graduated exercises and boardings, his course being determined inexorably by the "categories." On attaining "A" class he would reach the Overseas Training Brigade for "hardening"; and so again join a "draft for France." The total number of full round tours made by Australian soldiers on the Western Front was roughly 60,000.

For everything that happened to him in his retreat from the front, the medical service was wholly responsible; in the "right-about-turn" in the Command Depots it was the decisive instrument; with the soldier's transfer to the O.T.B. it took up again its normal brief to watch over his physical fitness for his military task.

This chapter is concerned with the medical involvements of the complicated military manœuvre of changing the retreat, as it may properly be termed, of these 60,000 troops into an advance. It deals, first, with the course of a recovered casualty through Nos. 1, 3 and 4 Command Depots to the "Overseas Training Brigade" to re-embark for France; second, with the medical responsibilities connected with reinforcements arriving by transports from Australia—in particular with the weeding out of unfits, the prevention or suppression of outbreaks and epidemics of infectious diseases, the training and distribution of reinforcements for A.A.M.C., and the medical supervision of reinforcement drafts for France. The work done at No. 2 Command Depot, Weymouth, devoted chiefly to "invalids" marked for return to Australia is dealt with in *Volume III*. It should however be clearly understood that, though this division corresponds to the actual separation of the two streams of casualties—the one destined for the front, the other for Australia —and of the executive staffs concerned with each, nevertheless the whole system was essentially a single organisation, under one Command and one Medical Director, the "A.D.M.S., A.I.F. Depots in U.K."

In previous chapters[4] we have traced the evolution of the A.I.F. Depots in England from the "Training Battalions" created in Egypt and the Australian and New Zealand Base Depot established under Sir Newton Moore at Weymouth to receive the sick and wounded from Gallipoli when they emerged from the hospitals in England.

Development of the Depots

During the nine months April-December, 1916, the losses in the A.I.F. on the Western Front through battle and non-battle casualty totalled 87,862 (from April to June 7,919; July to September 43,068; October to December 36,875). The terrific experiences through which the force passed had violent repercussions both in Britain and in Australia.

Effects of the Somme

The extent of the wastage had been expected neither by the Australian Command and Headquarters in Britain, nor by Australia. By the middle of August a crisis was reached: the training battalions had been drained and the mass of casualties was still passing through the evacuation stations in France and the British hospitals in England. On August 15th the Commandant A.I.F. Headquarters discussed with the War Office the calls that must be made on Australia if the crisis were to be met: the result was a cable from the Army Council advising the Commonwealth Government that the 3rd Division must be drawn upon to replenish the others; and recommending that, to make good the deficit and bring the 3rd again up

---

[4] See in particular *Chapter* i; also *Vol. I.*, as indexed under "Return to duty."

to strength, a special draft of 20,000 infantry additional to monthly reinforcements be sent and for three months the reinforcement rate for infantry be increased to 25 per cent. bringing the drafts from Australia up to 16,500 per month. The G.O.C., A.I.F., suggested that the Australian Light Horse be sent to France as infantry. The effects of the Somme, reaching Australia, were profound. It brought about, indeed, a change in the Australian attitude toward the war that influenced not only the immediate future of her force but her political and national history.

These effects were indeed more important than those concerning the immediate future of the formations. Though these immense demands could not be met—they proved in fact unnecessary—the national resources were still resilient. Partly by reinforcements, partly by recovered casualties, the losses were replaced, and by the end of the first quarter in 1917 they had been made good. But in these nine months the Australian Overseas Base had passed through a time of fiery trial, in particular, the medical service had been recognised as the key to the problem of "maintainence." From this time indeed the history of the Command Depots is that of a gradual imposition upon them of a share approximately equal to that of the training battalions in the task of supplying the calls of 3rd Echelon (G.H.Q.) to maintain the Reinforcement Depots in France.[5]

Developments during 1916[6]

The smooth and effective absorption in Britain of the huge mass of battle-casualties and sick from the A.I.F. during the summer and winter on the Somme was made possible by the agreement whereby all Australian casualties passed through the British primary hospitals.[7] Even so, and despite foresight and vigour on the part of the Director of Medical Services of the A.I.F., Surgeon-General Howse, the Australian Command Depots in U.K. were overwhelmed. By the end of September the battle-casualties from the Somme had reached the stage of convalescence and were ready for transfer to "Command Depot." By October the Australian Auxiliary Hospitals and the existing Command Depots were full, and thousands of men were await-

[5] "At the end of 1916 and beginning of 1917 there was a great preponderance of reinforcements. This lessened as fewer reinforcements arrived until the Depots consisted of approximately 50 per cent. reinforcements and 50 per cent. convalescents. Finally, the proportion of convalescents was considerably greater than the reinforcements." From a memorandum written by Colonel D. W. McWhae, A.D.M.S., A.I.F. Depots in U.K. 1917-19, for the purpose of medical history. This memorandum, and his reports to the D.M.S., A.I.F., are among the most complete and lucid in the Australian medical records of the war.

[6] *See Chapter i and Vol. I, Chapter xxiii.*
[7] *See Chapters xv and xxvi and Vol. I, Chapter xxiii.*

ing transfer from the British Convalescent "Auxiliaries" to Australian control.[8] On October 1st No. 1 A.A.H. (Harefield) held 1,000 patients, No. 2 (Southall) 400; on the 9th "No. 3 Australian Auxiliary" was opened at Dartford for 700 cases and within a week was treating 1,200. By October No. 3 Australian General had opened up at Brighton. About the same time No. 1 Command Depot at Perham Downs—receiving men "likely to be well within 3 months"—held 5,600, No. 2 at Weymouth, 1,800. On October 13th "No. 3 Command Depot" was opened at Wool as an overflow to No. 1, and at the end of the month this held 3,100. At the beginning of November this Depot was reorganised and was established at Wareham as "No. 4," to take the overflow from No. 2 (Weymouth) of men "likely to be unfit for periods from 3 weeks to 3 months."

In general, the new Command Depots were designed deliberately to serve the special needs of distinct classes of convalescents. But even at the end of this year, 1916, the term "crude" is hardly too strong to apply to the organisation and work of the depots. Colonel McWhae says:—

"It was during the early months of the existence of A.I.F. Depots in U.K.—when large numbers of troops were pouring into the Command from Egypt, from France, and from Australia, a period of rapid expansion of Command Depots, of closing down old and opening of new, of receiving large numbers of convalescents into camps already crowded, when infectious diseases [for the most part brought in transports from Australia] were widespread and many were dying of pneumonia in one of the most severe winters ever known—that the medical organisation of Command Depots and Training Battalions had to be built up, standardized, and made uniform. During this time of stress these and many other medical problems had to be solved, and no previous medical experience was available to help in their solution."

Even in January, 1917, patients were pouring into No. 1 Command Depot at the rate of 630 per week and large numbers reached the others; accommodation was strained to the utmost and over-crowding was kept down (and incidentally the demand from the front met) only by drafting to France any man fit to be sent, and recruits when half trained. But by February of 1917, both in the field and at the base, the A.I.F. was getting its "second wind"; and in the depots, as at the front, the spring of the year opened up a new phase in the history of the force.

The structure and working of the depots may conveniently be described as from this stage of their reorganisation.[9]

---

[8] The similar crisis created in 1916 by the wastage from Gallipoli is described in *Vol. I pp. 502-8*.

[9] On 20 Feb., 1917, Col. R. J. Millard was appointed D.D.M.S. on the staff of Surgeon-General Howse, D.M.S., A.I.F. at Australian Administrative Headquarters, Horseferry-road, and was succeeded as A.D.M.S. Depots in U.K. by Lieut.-Col. D. M. McWhae. On March 12 a new No. 3 Depot was opened at Hurdcott as an overflow for No. 1 "as a high category depot." It received men from hospital direct, or after furlough, or transferred from the "lower category" depots when "sufficiently progressed in their convalescence to have reached the needful classification to take them to a high category depot." (Diary of No. 3 Command Depot, Hurdcott.)

THE HUMAN GRINDSTONE

Strength of the Depots
"The total strength of A.I.F. Depots in U.K. rapidly grew from 2,000-3,000 in 1915, to 44,500 at end of 1916, and to approximately 60,000 early in 1917, remaining somewhere approaching this high figure until August, 1917, when the numbers steadily diminished, but the strength of the command never became less than 34,000. The number of medical officers employed in depots increased in proportion; from 4 during the first year to a maximum of 85, and never falling below 70."[10]

The general organisation of the Headquarters at Tidworth and hutted encampments on and about Salisbury Plain, comprising the twin system of the A.I.F. Depots in U.K. ("Training Units" for reinforcements and "Command Depots" for convalescents) has already been described.[11] These camps had been taken over from the War Office—the hutments were of a uniform type, with louvred windows; the men slept on wooden collapsible stretchers. The kitchens, of a standard type fitted with Wyles barrack cooking ranges, were well-appointed and convenient. The sanitary system was fully adequate.

Administration
The administration of the depot system was determined by the fact that the Australian Command Depots and Training Groups were separated from each other or from headquarters by distances of from 5 to 65 miles over the Counties of Wiltshire and Dorsetshire (No. 2 was 55 miles from Tidworth). Rail communications served conveniently both streams of arrivals: reinforcements from Australia, who arrived mainly at Plymouth and Devonport, came direct by the Great Western Railway; convalescents from Horseferry-road, London, came by a branch line from the neighbouring London and South Western Railway through Southampton.

To meet the situation on the medical side the administrative authority of the A.D.M.S. was deputed to "S.M.O's" of each Command.[12] These officers had large power of initiative subject to general principles laid down by the A.D.M.S., who represented on the one hand the General Officer Commanding the Depots—from 1916 onwards Major-General J. W. M'Cay—and

---
[10] From Col. McWhae's memorandum.
[11] *Chapter i and Vol. I, Chapter xxiii.*
[12] "A Senior Medical Officer was appointed to each of the 'Training Brigades' and to each of the four 'Command Depots,' and was responsible to the A.D.M.S. In Nov. 1917, separate 'S.M.O's' were appointed to the Sutton Veny and Hurdcott areas respectively, and from this date the number of S.M.O's responsible direct to the A.D.M.S. was reduced from seven to four, this making the medical organisation more stable." (From Col. McWhae's memorandum.)

Map No. 9

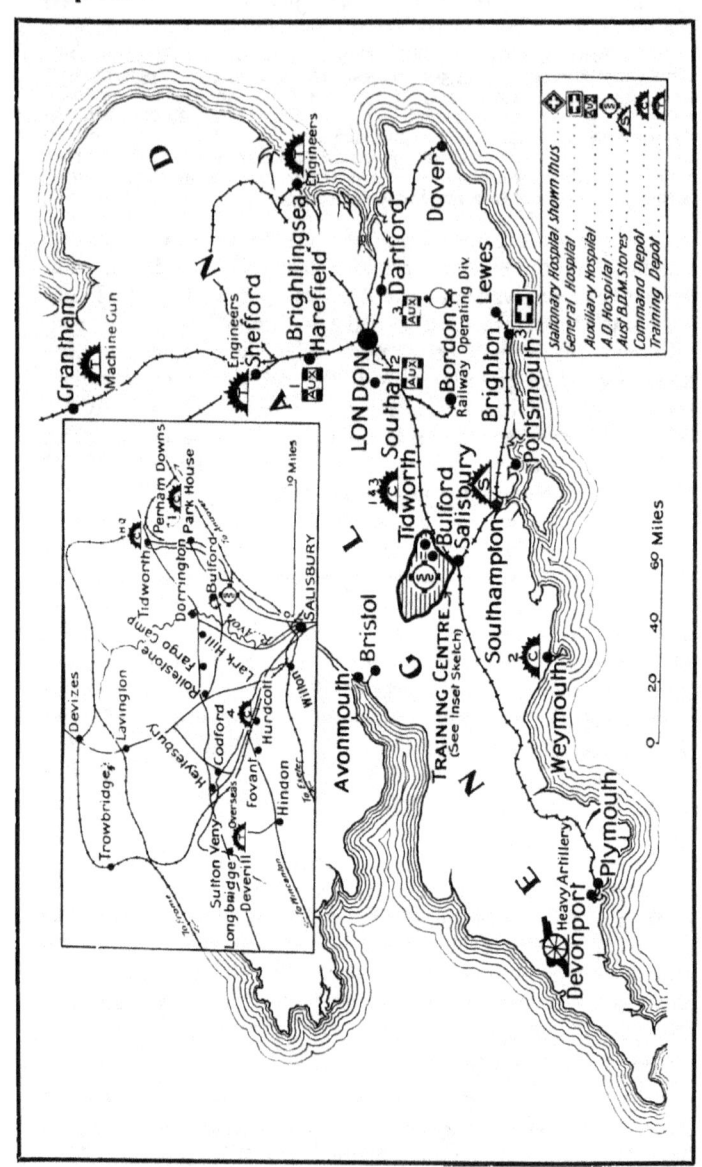

The Australian Auxiliary Hospitals and Command Depots in the United Kingdom.

No. 7 Camp, Codford, January, 1917.
*Lent by Pte. J. H. Case, and Pioneer Bn.
Aust. War Memorial Collection No. C1288.*

No. 2 Camp, Codford, May 1917. In the foreground are the tents of the isolation camp.
*Lent by Cpl. J. Lawrence, 59th Bn.
Aust. War Memorial Collection No. C1244.*

54-55. AUSTRALIAN CAMPS AT SALISBURY PLAIN

56. A "TEMPORARY DRESSING STATION" OF THE 17TH FIELD AMBULANCE (6TH DIVISION) DURING TRAINING IN THE NEW FOREST, AUGUST, 1917
Lent by Sgt. E. P. Grundy, A.A.M.C.
Aust. War Memorial Collection No. C4513.

57. MEDICAL EXAMINATION AT No. 4 COMMAND DEPOT, HURDCOTT
Aust. War Memorial Official Photo. No. D302. *To face p. 453.*

on the other the D.M.S., A.I.F.—Surgeon-General N. R. Howse.[13]

The D.M.S., A.I.F. and the Depots. The relations between the D.M.S., A.I.F. and the A.D.M.S. A.I.F. Depots (Colonel McWhae) come within the scope of *Chapter XXVI* which deals with medical administration within the A.I.F. abroad. It is only necessary to note here that, by methods of administration peculiarly his own, and by a flair for diplomacy unsurpassed in the Australian force, Surgeon-General Howse was able wholly to dominate the medical work of the depots and through this to impress personal views, gained on Gallipoli, regarding the place of the Australian Force in the war and in history, and the part to be played by the medical service in the attainment of this.

Prevention of Disease. The problem of maintaining the health of the troops differed remarkably in the Command Depots and the Training Groups. This matter being one of general interest will be examined in the next three chapters, those on preventive medicine on the Western Front.[14] The tremendous problem of venereal disease, and the experience of the depots in the pandemic of virus influenza, will be dealt with in the two chapters of the next volume concerned with those subjects.

Health in the Depots

Treatment of Sickness. As part of the British Southern Command the Australian depots were served by the British (R.A.M.C.) General Hospitals. These were situated at Fargo and Fovant, and it was soon found that between admission to

---

[13] It must be understood that the Australian depots were an integral part of the British "Southern Command." The "G.O.C. A.I.F. Depots" was responsible to the British "G.O.C. Southern Command" for maintaining discipline and securing efficiency; and similarly the "A.D.M.S. A.I.F. Depots" to the D.D.M.S. Southern Command (Surgeon-General W. G. Birrell, sometime D.M.S., M.E.F.). But matters of Australian policy remained with the G.O.C., A.I.F., Sir William Birdwood, and the D.M.S., A.I.F., Sir Neville Howse.

[14] In this connection, however, a special note is required. The selection of Salisbury Plain as the training ground for Australian reinforcements was the subject of much debate and strong criticism, and the outbreaks of disease of respiratory type, especially in the winter of 1916-17, were at the time, and have been since, a cause of bitter comment. But it seems obvious from a broad consideration of the problem that no other course was possible; and it may be pointed out that the authorities in Australia, who urged that Australian troops should convalesce in Egypt during the winter, were equally insistent that they should not do so in the summer. Moreover, although the heart-breaking problems, military and medical, that derived from the Somme and the Somme winter were not solved without bitter hardships and a heavy incidence of disease, the actual morbidity and mortality rates in these camps at their worst was little above that of Mena, or—it should be added—of the camps in sunny Australia at *their* worst. As has been urged in this work, the health of troops in camp is far less dependent upon environment than upon how the effects of environment are met.

them and treatment "in the lines" there was room for neglect of much potentially serious illness. This was indeed discerned as the chief cause for the grave morbidity and mortality from respiratory infections during the winter of 1916-17. A remedy was found in provision for the *early treatment of mild infections* in units corresponding to the C.C.S. or Field Hospital of the front, which were named "Group Clearing Hospitals."

Graph No. 4—SICKNESS IN THE A.I.F. DEPOTS IN THE UNITED KINGDOM, OCTOBER, 1916, TO DECEMBER, 1918.

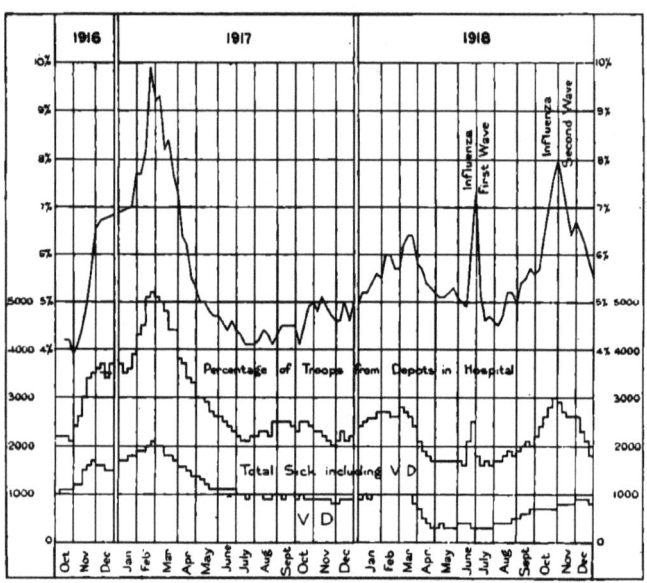

"These were organised in the early days of A.I.F. Depots. Their chief objective was to ensure that all sick soldiers, even if suffering from slight disabilities but not well enough to be treated as out-patients at sick parades, were admitted to hospital for observation and treatment. Except mumps patients, and during the influenza epidemic, all men needing more than 10 days' treatment were sent on to the British General Hospitals from these A.A.M.C. units. In September, 1918, at the outset of the influenza epidemic, those at Sutton Veny and Hurdcott were enlarged from 200 to 300 beds and nursing sisters (A.A.N.S.) attached for duty." (From Col. McWhae's memorandum).

The work of these units and results of treatment may be illustrated by the following example :—

In the first six months of 1918, the Group Clearing Hospital at Hurdcott admitted 3,368 patients, discharged 2,187 to their units, and sent on 1,010 to other Military Hospitals, the average number of patients in hospital being 172.[15]

Venereal Disease. On 16th October, 1916, the Australian Dermatological Hospital was established at Bulford Camp for the treatment of venereal disease.

The structure and general function of the "Depots in U.K." having been presented, it remains to give an account of the medical duties associated with the two elements in the command; (1) the *Command Depots* and (2) the *Training Groups*.

THE COMMAND DEPOTS—FROM CONVALESCENT TO EFFECTIVE

"A man who has been wounded or sick, and has been for a period of perhaps months in hospital with every want attended to and with no more arduous toil than assisting the nurse in ward duties, is in hardly a fit and suitable state for immediate return to the firing line or even to the fatigue of full training. It is at this point that the command depot steps in. After his discharge from hospital and subsequent furlough the man proceeds to a command depot where he receives training graduated in such a manner as to restore him once more to his former health and vigor."[16]

In its organisation the Command Depot was a military formation. The parades, discipline, messing, housing, the daily life and activities of the troops, were a military responsibility. But its purpose was essentially medical; and *a depot was successful in proportion with the degree to which the combatant command accepted the technical direction of, and co-operated with, the medical service, and the medical service on its side realised and accepted the priority of the military needs and the fact that the prime purpose of the depots was to provide drafts of fit effectives.*

Early History of the Command Depots. The chief function of the first "Australian Convalescent Depot" Weymouth in the early days—1915-16[17]—was to collect and despatch to Gallipoli drafts of recovered men, and to return "unfits" to Australia. In this period the little train-

---
[15] Complete figures are not available.
[16] From a memorandum by Lieut.-Col. H. H. Woollard, A.A.M.C.
[17] *See Vol. I, Chapter xxiii.*

ing given was carried out by combatant officers who were passing through the depot.

The original classification was: "A"—Fit for general service; "B"—Temporarily unfit for general service; "C"—Permanently unfit for general service. The procedure was crude. No accurate record was kept of the many men classed "B"; "reclassification" was carried out by a medical officer who walked along a line of men on parade and picked out those who looked fit. It was impossible to ensure that all "B" class soldiers were seen even in this primitive way. Early in 1916 the Commanding Officer of the unit was made responsible for parading all "B" class men once weekly and a system of four grades of training for these men was introduced—each grade walking a specified distance daily. Every soldier arriving in the depot was medically examined and reclassified, and, the crux of the problem, medical classification, was dealt with as soon as possible. During the period 1915-July 1916 dental work in the depot was carried out by N.C.O's or privates who in civil life had been dentists or dental mechanics.[18]

When the new Command Depots were formed in 1916 and Weymouth became "No. 2," the "temporarily unfit" soldiers were passed to others, leaving in No. 2 only soldiers of the "B1b" class and invalids awaiting return to Australia.

Disengaging the Invalid

The prime duty of the Command Depots was to disengage the "invalid" from potential reinforcements. The basis of this procedure was the "six months' policy"; the machinery was the Medical Boards, the Australian Auxiliary Hospitals, and No. 2 Command Depot; the implement was Army Form No. B. 179 (Medical Board paper) and the "categories." The working of the Australian system of "invaliding"—probably the most original, certainly much the most elaborate piece of medical work carried out by the A.A.M.S. in the Great War, will be examined in *Volume III*. But the system of "categories" whereby the "invalid" was disengaged from the recovered men, served as well to pass the convalescent soldier through the several stages of military fitness and so calls for note here.

Evolution of the Categories. The system of "categories" on which the working of the Command Depots in their dual purpose—"return to duty" and "invaliding"—was based must be regarded not as a prearranged formula into which the various elements in the stream of convalescents must somehow be fitted, but as the visible symbol of the inward and very vital needs and strivings of a system which, like the present day theory of the universe, could be understood best and put to practical use most simply and effectively by expression in a mathematical formula. And since the various categories stood for conditions that were essentially vital and dynamic, they were subject to change and atrophy in some directions, to development and growth in others. In

---

[18] An account of the work of the Dental Service will be given in *Vol. III*.

the evolution of the scheme from the simple "A" and "B" classes of the early war may be seen mirrored much of the history of this feature of army maintenance. Each new category was added to subserve a clear purpose: the fact that a special type of case was presenting in sufficient numbers, and that machinery became available for dealing methodically with it, might make worth while its differentiation by category; to be implemented by administrative, and even physical, segregation. Such, for example, were the "B1a4" and "A3" categories—dentally "unfit" and "fit" respectively—peculiar to the Australian force. As the war progressed the increasing importance of the Command Depots, and the need for gradual and closely controlled yet rapid ascent to fitness, brought about increasing complexity in the categories, each one of which (it must be realised) called for a special executive machinery to carry out the particular purpose for which it had been created.

The disengaging of the "invalid" from the military cosmos and his return to civil freedom was by no means a simple process, being often a gradual one. Thus "retrograding" to No. 2 Command Depot ("B1b" and "C") from the trial depots, Nos. 3 and 4 and even from No. 1, was by no means uncommon; and regrading in the opposite direction, i.e. towards "A" class as the result of unexpected improvement—or even of heavy calls from the front or a falling off in recruits—was a recognised though a much less common procedure.

The following description of medical work in the Command Depots is given verbatim from an account of that carried out at No. 1 Command Depot (Perham Downs).[19]

The working of Command Depots From it a general idea can be gained of the part played by the medical service in accomplishing the purpose of military convalescence. No fully satisfactory description is possible within the space that can be allowed: not only by reason of the complexity of the problems involved—administrative, professional, military, human—but, and chiefly, because the whole system, violently alive, was in constant flux; its functions and structure, and their output in work, changed rapidly in accordance with varying wastage of the A.I.F. and the resources available to replace it. Colonel Woollard writes:—

"Before considering the various medical parades which are essential for the working of a depot, it would be wise at this point to set out a list of those categories which are used upon such **Categories** parades, and which have been adopted for use by the A.A.M.C. Various alterations have been made from time to time, but the scheme given below is that which has evolved from simpler and less adequate systems, and has proved practicable and satisfactory in use over a period of several years.

"In general, the symbol 'A' indicates fitness for service, 'B' temporary unfitness, and 'C' permanent unfitness.

[19] "Medical work in a Command Depot" by Lieut.-Col. H. H. Woollard, A.A.M.C., S.M.O. Sutton Veny Area.

Category	Condition
A	Fit for general service[20]
A3	Physically fit, but in need of hardening.
B1a4	Medically fit, but dentally unfit.
B1a3 ⎫ B1a2 ⎬ B1a1 ⎭	Temporarily unfit for general service for less than six months, but fit for training. The degree of fitness for training varies and is least in "B1a1." As a rule men in these categories should be fit in at most two or three months.
B1b	Temporarily unfit for general service for less than six months; temporarily unfit for training.
B2a	Temporarily unfit for general service for more than six months; fit for home service.
B2b	Temporarily unfit for general service for more than six months; temporarily unfit for home service.
C1	Permanently unfit for general service; fit for home service.
C1 Aust.	Permanently unfit for general service; fit for home service in Australia. (This classification was adopted in October, 1917, but discarded early in 1918.)
C2	Permanently unfit for general service; temporarily unfit for home service.
C3	Permanently unfit for general service; permanently unfit for home service.

"With regard to the above categories it may be stated that 'A' class and 'B1a4' men receive full training; 'B1a3,' 'B1a2,' and 'B1a1' men light training, while 'B1b,' 'B2b,' 'C2,' and 'C3' men are exempt from all duty. Those belonging to the last three categories are returned to Australia.

" 'B2a' and 'C1' men are, in the ordinary course of events, employed in England upon home service duties, unless there is a superfluity of such category men, when those in excess of requirements are returned to Australia.

"Having thus considered the various classifications, it is now necessary to study the parades at which they are employed.

Classification Parades—Primary
"The first parade which a man attends after entering the depot, is the Primary Classification Parade, which is held every morning at 9 a.m. All those who marched into the depot the previous day are paraded at the Classification Room, which is usually situated in some central position in the camp. Here a separate card is made out for each man, who then passes through the hands of a dental officer. He enters a description of the man's dental condition upon the

---

[20] As the war progressed towards the exhaustion of available material and as the material available from convalescents, being picked over and over from R.A.P. to Base, became less and less amenable to medical reconditioning, categories were elaborated to fulfil increased refinements of medico-military treatment.
The categories given by Lieut.-Col. Woollard are those in use in the last six months of the war. Various sub-divisions of disabled men, with corresponding "categories," were used for a time and discontinued, or were used in certain depots only. Thus in No. 2 Command Depot, Weymouth, early in 1918 Category "A" (fit for general service) included "A1," actually fit for despatch overseas in all respects: "A2," fit for "A1" as soon as fully *trained*; "A3," fit for "A1" as soon as *hardened*; "A4," fit for "A1" as soon as of *military age*. At the end of the war it was found that the subdivision tended to defeat its own purpose through over-elaboration, and the trend was then towards simplification.

card, and marks him either 'dentally fit' or the reverse. This is because dental trouble is regarded as a cause for unfitness for service in the field.

"The man then passes through to the medical officers, being accompanied, as he is at all medical parades, by his medical card. Here he is stripped to the waist, and examined, both with regard to the particular disability from which he has just been suffering, and also with regard to his general condition. A brief description of his case is entered upon his card, and a category assigned to him. A corresponding entry is then made upon his A.F.B.178, or history sheet, and the man passes out, to receive the exercises indicated as suitable for him by the classification he has received.

"It is at this first or primary classification that the M.O. tries to weed out those who are likely to be unfit for some considerable time, from those whose disability is slight. The former are examined in conjunction with another M.O., thus constituting a medical board, and, if the case warrants it, a low category assigned.

"The majority of men examined at this parade usually receive one of the 'B1a' categories, very few being placed direct on to full training, in consideration of the fact of their recent discharge from hospital.

"Besides the mere classification, it is at this parade that a man is ordered massage or special exercises. It is a matter of no inconsiderable labour, and of the utmost importance, to see that each man is assessed as nearly as possible to his grade of physical fitness immediately upon his arrival in the depot. So that primary classification becomes the paramount medical parade of a depot, and, indeed, *it is upon the character of the work performed at this parade that the success or failure of the depot, as such, will depend.*[21]

"It will, however, be seen that primary classification is concerned only with the new arrivals in the depot, and that another parade is therefore necessary to determine the point at which the individuals composing the population of the depot have arrived at the stage of physical fitness. This function is fulfilled by the weekly reclassification.

Weekly reclassification

"All the 'B1a' personnel are called up in companies, or in some such definite grouping. Thus, if there are eight companies in the depot, over a company will be paraded daily. They are examined by two medical officers, other than the two who are employed upon the primary classification. If their health has improved, their categories are raised, until finally they become 'A' class, and are marched out of the depot. Those who are not improving, or who show signs of being unable to stand the training, are referred to the medical board of the depot. Thus every man in the depot is examined at least once a week.

"It is from this weekly examination that the depot obtains the majority of its output of 'A' class men for transfer to the Overseas Training Brigade, where they receive a final course of harder training before being drafted to France.

"But one must remember that a considerable proportion of men, although they have been classified as medically fit, have, for some reason or other, not yet been marked dentally fit by the dental officer concerned. These are in the main gum cases, and men awaiting dentures. They are therefore given the dental classification 'B1a4.'

"Dental" fitness

---

[21] The italics are the present author's.

"While men remain in this category, they do not parade for the usual weekly examination, as they have already been classified as medically fit. But when the dentist has completed his work, and they become dentally fit, they are the next morning paraded for a final medical examination. If their medical condition remains satisfactory, they are classed 'A3,' and are then ready for transfer to the O.T.B.[22]

Comments on the system

"It will thus be seen that there are at least three medical classification parades daily in a command depot, the primary classification, the weekly reclassification of a definite proportion of the 'B1' men in the depot; and the final medical examination and classification of those dentally fit the previous day.

"The ideal arrangement, if possible, is to have two different medical officers for each of these parades. The chief benefit of this is that each man then passes through the hands of several different doctors, and thus the chance of an unfit man being passed out of the depot as 'A' class is minimised. Besides this, these parades will be more or less simultaneous, thus rendering different groups of M.O's essential, although it is possible for the parade of dentally fit men to be taken along with either the primary or the weekly classification, if so desired.

"Mistakes have occurred, and of necessity must occur; but, when one considers the vast number of men handled by the depots in the U.K., it is a matter for surprise, not that there have been so many mistakes, but rather that there have been so few.

"As a general rule the duration of stay of a man with a slight disability (i.e. 'B1' class) in the depot is from three to four weeks. This is without reference to those who are dentally unfit, for the period of time taken up by a man who is a 'gum case' and the making and supplying of dentures, greatly prolong the stay of such cases.

"But, ignoring this, the average duration of stay for medical reasons is that given above. In this period each man is examined three or four times, and by different M.O's so that, unless he is wilfully concealing some disability,[23] it is extremely unlikely that he will be passed out as fit without such being the case."

The Professional problem in "boarding"

The medical man whose practice has lain in the treatment and certification of an industrial population will have no difficulty in translating in terms of his own experiences the physiological problems, clinical and psychic, of the Command Depot officer, engaged in the hutments of Salisbury Plain in the task of reconditioning for the front the soldiers of the A.I.F. No special purpose would be served by traversing in detail the problems involved, which in great part were identical with those of civil practice.

---

[22] Overseas Training Brigade.
[23] On the matter of "malingering" Lieut.-Col. Woollard comments as follows: "Considering the large numbers of men passing through a unit such as a depot, the amount of actual malingering is not great. The various devices that are used differ greatly." This matter is examined in *Vol. III*.

THE HUMAN GRINDSTONE

1. Unfitness Through Wounding. As to the difficulties in classifying wound cases, the following, according to Colonel McWhae's memorandum, represents the experience of Australian officers.

"So far as medical classification itself was concerned, it was necessary for it to be decisive, first to prevent unnecessary delays in grading men up to higher training and secondly to prevent delay in boarding invalids for Australia. However, in the cases of many injuries, the medical classification of the soldier was frequently doubtful. Within two months of injuries it was often impossible to say whether the resulting disability would, or would not, persist. Difficulties of medical classification were not slight and there was a tendency on the part of medical officers to keep men too long in temporarily unfit classes. The chief trouble was caused by the following:—

"1. Disabilities which, although functional, were persistent and far in excess of that which could be accounted for by the injury.

"2. Soldiers with apparently a slight disability only, who were probably exaggerating their disability.

"3. G.S.W. through fingers or palm of hand. In these cases even several months after the injury, the grip was remarkably weak or even absent altogether.

"4. When shot through arms or elbows with marked and persistent limitation of extension of the elbow due either to bone injury or contraction. There may also have been present loss of supination or pronation due to shattered bones or cicatrisation of muscles with, in the majority of cases, marked loss of power in the hands.

"5. Soldiers shot through the shoulder in whom stiffness and rigidity of shoulder movements were very persistent and possibly permanent.

"6. Soldiers with extensive scarring of the scapula where the scars may or may not have been adherent to the scapula and where there was often resultant loss of mobility at the shoulder joint.

"7. Soldiers with G.S.W. in back in whom there were deep scars causing, after long periods, limitation of forward flexion of body; or cases of concussion of the spine without physical signs, but where rigidity of the back persisted for long periods.

"8. Ankle injuries with marked and persistent lameness.

"9. Injuries to the knee joint with marked and persistent limp or stiffness of the joint or inability to fully extend the joint due to contracture, both with marked and persistent lameness.

"10. Men shot through the feet, in whom a limp persisted for long periods.

"11. Even cases of nerve injury, *i.e.* ulnar paresis with anaesthesia and paralysis of little and ring fingers, injury to posterior interosseous nerve. Neck injuries with injuries to brachial plexus and paresis and wasting of arm. Even slighter injuries to sciatic and external popliteal nerve with wasting of leg and foot drop.

"12. Soldiers with functional paralysis of the arms, *e.g.* useless hand; leg carried stiff and abducted in walking; and where there was apparently only a slight flesh wound, and who obstinately resisted suggestive treatment."

2. *Unfitness Caused by Disease.* The relative importance of various groups of "diseases" which brought about "wastage" at the several stages of evacuation will be shown by statistical tables in *Volume III*, where also a brief clinical study will be made of some of the most important of them. Here it is only necessary to identify the morbid states found by the medical officers in the Australian depots to be most important or most difficult to deal with.

The Psychic Element. Perhaps the most striking feature of medical work in the depots as revealed in the records was the very large proportion of "problem" cases in which the psychic factor was the chief cause of delayed recovery. This morbific agent was in evidence not so much in the form of frank cases of "nervous" disease or disorder, as of a component in many vague morbid states, such as "rheumatism," "neuritis," and in particular the great group of "chest cases"; it was also in evidence as a factor in the recovery of function after wounds or from the effects of "gassing." The wave of "shell shock" that swept through the field units in the Battles of the Somme, seems largely to have spent itself before it reached the depots, for Colonel WcWhae records:—

"The prevalence of functional cases was recognised early in 1918, when they were grouped together and a certain amount of suggestive treatment given with good results. It was not, however, until early in 1919 that a psychotherapeutic department was established at Weymouth, under an officer who had received a course of instruction at Seale Hayne Neurological Hospital."

The action there taken to deal with these patients belongs to the part of *Volume III* which follows the course of the convalescents earmarked for invaliding to Australia. It is desirable however to note here that, due chiefly to the personal views of Surgeon-General Howse, the "new psychology" had little place in the Australian medical service in Britain—nor, it may be remarked, is there any indication that, in the Command Depots at least, the objective and "commonsense" methods adopted would have been bettered by others more individual and subjective.

Raw Material for Neuroses. This is the most appropriate place for reference to a type of war disability which has received little attention but which, both during and after the war, was of great importance as forming the neural background to more striking features of psychic injury through the war. It was composed by a clinical group that bridges the gap between physiological and psychical sickness. These men were commonly marked up as suffering from "debility," but their functional unfitness was only in part physiological, though it derived from defect at a neural level lower in respect to volition than that from which came the "neuroses"—and still more, "malingering." The condition is described by a depot officer of exceptional insight as follows:—

"*War Weariness.* On the other hand, there was a proportion of men who had seen long service in the field, who, although showing no signs of organic disease, were yet unfit simply through strain and war-weariness. This class of case did not receive official recognition in the A.I.F., although it undeniably existed. It was useless to return them immediately to their units in France, and in this depot [No. 1 at Perham Downs] the practice was, in undoubted cases, to board them for periods of home service in England. And there is no doubt, in the mind of the writer at least, that this procedure was not only justifiable, but even beneficial to the record and efficiency of the A.I.F. as a whole."[24]

"*D.A.H.*" The more or less specific symptom-complex known before the Great War as "Soldier's heart," and in the British Army officially as "Disordered action of the heart" ("D.A.H.")[25] was early in evidence in the Command Depots as a cause of unfitness among "medical" cases from France. Eventually it proved one of the most clinically obscure among the "medical" conditions causing disablement and one of the most difficult to deal with. In the early months of 1918 (Colonel McWhae notes) "cases of D.A.H. accumulated in Command Depots, and S.M.O's were very doubtful as to the best method of dealing with them." The clinical work of Thomas Lewis during 1915-17[26] in the British special military hospital for heart disease at Hampstead, and later at Colchester, had been followed and, early in 1918, the system of treatment advocated by Lewis ("graduated drills") was studied at first hand and then tried in the depots. A number of "D.A.H. cases" were collected at No. 3 Command Depot and graduated training carried out "on the lines used at Colchester."

"The results, here at any rate," says Colonel McWhae, "were not satisfactory. It was found that under these circumstances the attention of the patients was unconsciously directed continuously to the cardiac condition by the very fact of their being grouped together, and by the observations of pulse rate which were made in order to determine their reaction to effort. It was decided, therefore, not to give separate training in special classes, or in special units to cases of this type, as it was considered that such methods had a powerful effect in suggesting unfitness." On 29th May, 1918, the use of the term D.A.H. was discontinued and in lieu thereof the term "Effort Syndrome" was used—in view of the fact that "there was no evidence that the condition was cardiac in origin." From this time a clear-cut policy was pursued.

"Soldiers with this disability were not given separate training in special classes, but received ordinary graduated Command Depot training. The majority were transferred to the O.T.B. and the number retrograded there as unfit for active service was, comparatively, very small. Except in the case of obviously ill soldiers, the only way to decide as to their fitness or otherwise for service was to give them graduated training in this way."[27]

[24] From Lieut.-Col. Woollard's memorandum. See also relevant chapters in *Vol. III*.

[25] In the "Annual Reports of the Health of the Army" as early as 1911. See *Vol. I p. 417* and *Vol. III*.

[26] Dr. (later Sir) Thomas Lewis worked as a member of the staff of the British Medical Research Committee. See *Annual Reports* of the Committee for 1916-17 and 1917-18, and preface to *The Soldier's Heart and the Effort Syndrome* by Thomas Lewis, M.D., F.R.C.P., F.R.S., September 1918. (Australian War Memorial copy; published in 1920 by Paul B. Hoeber, New York.)

[27] From Col. McWhae's memorandum. Further details of the experience of the Command Depots and observations made on cases invalided to Australia will be found in *Vol. III*.

Trench Fever. If not actually "new" in the sense that the living causal agent had not before the Great War been parasitic in men, this peculiarly interesting disease was at any rate the most dramatic "find" in the domain of diseases due to living agents. In spite of its comparative benignancy it was one of the most important causes of expeditionary wastage. The majority of men convalescent from the disease who reached the depots "carried on the usual Command Depot training." Some were re-admitted to the Group Clearing Hospitals, and closely observed.

Two classes of patients were identified:—

1. Those who presented a typical picture of the original condition and were diagnosed trench fever recurrences. These made a quick recovery after the pyrexia subsided; and the disease did not recur.

2. Those in whom the disease was followed by debility. These were apyrexial and complained of lassitude, shin pain, loss of appetite and inability to stand fatigue. Most were debilitated. In these the best treatment was found to be tonics, keeping the patients out of doors, encouraging exercise, treating the memories by suggestion, and discharging early from hospital.[28]

Trench Foot. During the winter of 1916-17 the A.D.M.S. reported "an accumulation of trench foot cases owing to their slow rate of recovery, which has impaired the output of fit men" (from the depots). The experience of the depots showed that the neuro-psychic effects of severe trench foot might be prolonged. This induced Surgeon-General Howse to advise against the retention of these cases in "Divisional rest stations" at the front, and influenced the estimate furnished by him to the G.O.C. A.I.F. of the wastage to be expected from sickness during 1918.

Other Causes of Disablement. From the records of the depots it is possible to identify in the "venereal" diseases one of the most important medical problems of reconditioning, as it was of every phase of medical work in the war, except at the front line. But the effects of this, and of *gassing,* in relation to return to duty from the Command Depots will be examined in due course in *Volume III.*

Medical treatment. "Reparative" treatment of all forms of disablement dove-tailed exactly with military re-training or "reconditioning" for return to duty, which was the particular function of Nos. 1, 3, and 4 Command Depots.

Principles and practice of reconditioning
"A man was never meant to contract his muscles for the sake of exercise. Muscular contraction should be the physical expression, the outer end of a plan. We should move to get something, or kill something, in work as in sport, and with the consciousness focussed always on the end, never on the means."[29]

In this present Year of Grace (1939) the civilised nations of the world are furiously expending their capital wealth in arms for

---
[28] Epitomised from Col. McWhae's memorandum.
[29] Richard C. Cabot, quoted in article "Physical Education" C. H. Hembrow, *M.J.A., 8 May, 1937.*

another World War and preparing their citizens for their part in it; the females by a sort of moral "training and hardening" for their important part in sustaining the chief brunt of its "horrors"[30]; the young males by "physical culture" to provide the perfection war requires. In Great Britain and Australia a badly belated and badly needed drive for physical improvement has been launched. The experience of the A.I.F. in the Command Depots has a bearing on the matter. A statement of this experience is given here; it is backed by authority, and a moral is thrown in.

Graduated Training. The rational measures taken to assist time and nature in effecting rapid restitution of "fitness" for military service present themselves in three forms; medical, military, moral. The following is abridged from McWhae (*loc. cit.*) :—

The first function of the Command Depots was to make convalescent soldiers fit for service. This was done chiefly by "graduated training" which was given to all men fit to receive it.

Men with special disabilities were given remedial gymnastic treatment, massage, or any necessary medical or surgical treatment.[81]

Military training was graded for "B1a1," "2," "3," and "4" men: 1-4 miles walk morning and afternoon; walks with a run of 100 yards, physical training and games. This scheme was tried for over a year. It was found however that the marches were carried out in an apathetic way, and were dull and uninteresting. In May, 1918, a new system was introduced in which organised games were made the basis of training, the games being divided into grades (by depots).[82] Quick changes were made—from games to physical training, then to quarter of an hour's rest, and so on. The new method was much more interesting. It claimed the attention of the men and was a great advance on the old. It was found so useful that soldiers awaiting return to Australia were, if fit, also given organised games under physical training instructors, and this had a big effect on their mental and physical condition.

The system tended ultimately to become somewhat top-heavy.

Morale. By no means of least importance were measures which may broadly be included under this heading. Of such were psychophysical tonics such as food and cooking, warmth and bedding, and other amenities noted under "Health"; and mental and "moral" tonics, designed to stimulate the social instincts—short leaves, concerts, lectures on current topics. In some depots garden plots were formed and

---

[30] *See The Lancet*, 8 Jan. 1938, sub-leader "The Red Cross; an End or a Beginning?"

[81] This comprised "massage," "remedial gymnastics," and other forms of physiotherapy, and was applied under the direct control of medical officers. The men in question were exempt from the weekly board and could be moved up to "A" grade by the M.O. in charge. Up to 500 men at one time were thus treated—the most for slight wounds—by a staff of depot-trained masseurs. (*See Vol. III.*)

[82] *E.g.*, for Category B1a1.—O'Grady, Do this-Do that, Chase Ball, Cock-fighting, Steps, Putty Nose, Three deep, Relay Races, Potato Race, Tunnel-Ball, and many others of the same kind.

potatoes and other vegetables grown, or fowls and pigs kept. The Y.M.C.A. built halls, organised plays and concerts, and helped with sports equipment. In each depot military bands were formed, most potent of all martial stimulants.

The lesson is that in the preparations for war as in warfare itself, "the moral is to the physical as 3 to 1." In physiological terms, "physical jerks" will make large muscles, but they will not *of themselves* promote endocrine balance, nervous tone, or moral "self-regard." Games, expressing both physical and moral attributes, will do all of these things.[33]

Subject absolutely to medical control of the categories, all this training was carried out by combatant officers. Nos. 1, 3 and 4 Command Depots were run on strictly military lines. At first the men were billeted and administered by categories, but in May, 1918, this futile method was changed: companies of 500 were then formed, in which a man remained until sent to the O.T.B. The company was paraded each morning and men of the various categories marched out to their respective training grounds.

When the convalescent soldier had reached the final Command Depot category, "A3," he was handed over to the military command for the final step—the hardening process, physical and moral, that should transform the recovered "A" class convalescent, still soft from the amenities of medical and semi-medical care and control, into the hard and highly efficient man-at-arms which the reputation of the A.I.F., and the place in British Arms assigned to that force by the Commander-in-Chief, now required.

Final step of transfer: hardening and training

Originally the convalescents, who passed out of the Command Depots as fit for further service, were sent, though themselves trained soldiers, to the Training Battalions consisting of newly-recruited reinforcements—there to be hardened before drafting to the front.

---

[33] In every Australian capital city the proportion of males who play "games" is limited, not by the number who wish to play but by the playing fields, baths, halls, gymnasia, and such like facilities available. These are inadequate to the demands, much more to the needs. The reason: that, in the peaceful times in which our fate is really determined, freehold and individual "rights," not the safety of the State or welfare of the community as a whole, is, with us, the "supreme law."

"This is the British system now,"[34] says a memorandum, in which the reason for its abandonment by the A.I.F. was set forth.[35] "It was found," this continues, "that:—

"(a) The training they needed did not fit in with the training of recruits.

"(b) A constant tendency existed to keep some of them with the Battalions, despite frequent instructions to the contrary, and even constant watchfulness did not stop this.

"(c) Men nearly always leave Hospital and Command Depots with relaxed mental energy and were not a good influence for recruits...

"(d) Medical and Dental examination to ensure fitness for overseas was split up, and mistakes kept occurring...

"I would point out that ... the training of recruits is fundamentally different from preparing men from hospital. In the former case, men are all taken as physically fit and the graduation of their training is based on degrees of knowledge; in the latter the men have to be taken as having the same degree of knowledge as a whole, and the graduation of their training is based on their physical fitness with special consideration too for reviving their relaxed mental energy. Hence the two sets of men cannot efficiently be trained together...."

Evolution of the "O.T.B." The "Hardening and Drafting Depot." For these reasons, late in 1916 a "Drafting Depot and Details Camp" was formed within No. 1 Command Depot. To this men who had reached the "A" class were drafted for training of a more military character than was given in other parts of the depots. It served its purpose sufficiently to meet the diminished, though still considerable, wastage of the autumn fighting in 1916. By February, 1917, the critical situation brought about in the A.I.F. by the battle-casualties of Pozières and Mouquet Farm had been resolved. But, though healed for the time, the problems created by the losses on the Somme were not cured—they were indeed never cured. With the Battles of the Hindenburg Line in 1917, the problem of wastage and replacements again became menacing, and the breaking up of the half-formed 6th Division did not fully resolve them. In May, 1917, General M'Cay, who had replaced Sir Newton Moore as G.O.C., A.I.F. Depots in U.K., wrote to General Birdwood as follows:—[36]

---

[34] The British "Regimental" system (*See Vol. I, p. 496n.*), provided for "Reserve" Battalions into which recruits and recovered men were drafted immediately. It was found in the A.I.F. that this system required a very large staff and that it tended to lower the standard.

[35] The memorandum was written at a later stage by Maj.-Gen. J. W. M'Cay.

[36] The sequence of paragraphs in this report has, for the sake of clarity, been slightly changed.

"I wish to bring under notice the present unsatisfactory organisation of the Drafting Depot and Details Camp at Perham Downs. . . .

"Experience has shown the following disadvantages in the old system:—

"(a) The detention of men fit for Hardening and Training at Command Depots, where they mix with unfit men, causes much difficulty in handling and training them.

"(b) It is difficult to maintain training and discipline, as officers and men look on a Command Depot as a sort of convalescent home.

"(c) All personnel show an inclination to avoid work when a large proportion have of necessity to perform only light duties, or none.

"(d) Owing to the insufficient training experience of officers and N.C.O's at Command Depots (they are mostly 'birds of passage') the training at these Depots has been of little real use. . .

A cardinal development— the O.T.B. "After considering the whole question with Brigadier-General MacLagan and the Assistant-Director Medical Services (Colonel McWhae), I have come to the following conclusions:—

"(i) It is sound policy from medical, disciplinary and training points of view, to pass the men out of Command Depots to a training depot as soon as they are medically, physically, and dentally fit.

"(ii) That this policy will best be carried into effect by forming, at Perham Downs, a Training Group to be organised and run on lines similar to the present Infantry Reinforcement Groups."

The advantages looked for were "more rapid return to the front"; improved discipline and *esprit de corps* "greatly lacking in Command Depots"; and the keeping of officers "up to the mark," a result "not least important or least needed." Most of all was desired a semi-permanent staff (or "cadre") of officers and N.C.O's, who should remain five or six months and be replaced by men brought over from the front, as was done in the Training Battalions.

"Read between the lines" the correspondence on the matter between the A.I.F. Depots in U.K. and A.I.F. Headquarters in France is illuminating. The proposal was

"considered sound but not practicable [to] put into effect at present. Divisions are unable to provide additional officers and other ranks" [for the training].

But at the end of June, 1917, General Birdwood himself went to England: the problem of maintaining Australian formations at strength was examined, and the importance of the two sources of replacement, recovered men and new drafts respectively, was assessed. As a result the Overseas Training Depot was approved and provision made for an adequate staff.

Constitution of the O.T.B. The Overseas Training Brigade comprised four camp battalions under the administration of a Brigade Headquarters. No. 1 Battalion consisted of "soft"-class men, *i.e.* those who had just marched in from Command Depot. After a week in this Battalion, during which time they were fully equipped, they were moved to No. 2 Battalion, "medium"-class men, where they spent another week. The next move was to No. 3 Battalion, "hard"-class men. On the completion of one week's training, and if passed by the M.O., they were considered fit for a draft, and were transferred to "A" Company of No. 4 Battalion.

Graph No. 5—SOURCE OF MEN FLOWING INTO COMMAND DEPOTS AND DESTINATION OF THOSE FLOWING OUT, JULY, 1917 TO DECEMBER, 1918.

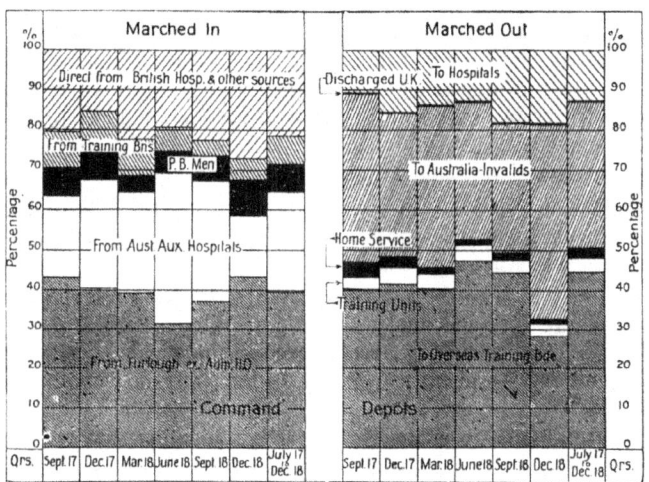

The medical staff consisted of an "S.M.O." and Regimental Medical Officers. Though only "A class" men were received, so rigid was the insistence by the D.M.S., A.I.F. that only men fit for the A.I.F. should leave the depots that in February, 1918 —the date is noteworthy—a standing medical board was formed to deal with doubtful cases brought up by the R.M.O.'s.

Results. The result of all this medical to-do in furtherance of the military demand for effectives is indicated by the following statement:—[37]

"From July, 1917, to December, 1918, the Overseas Training Brigade sent 32,893 infantrymen to France, and 20,259 fit men to their training units; the total output of men fit for general service being 53,152."

The figures show, as far as numbers go, the contribution of the A.A.M.C. in Great Britain in its "return to duty" activities in the critical stage of the war. On the other hand, in the tightening up of medical control over the quality of those let through, in the face of bitter demand for more men to avoid breaking up the A.I.F. formations, may be found a key to the character and influence of the Australian D.M.S. General Howse, whose policy was not without its effect upon the history of the A.I.F. during the supreme physical and moral test of 1918. The number of men caught in the final sieve during the severe training of the O.T.B. and "retrograded" as medically unfit was as follows: July-December 1917, 1,299; January-June 1918, 813; July-November 1918, 190. In view of the large number of convalescents dealt with and the high standard of efficiency required these figures indicate a notable success in the work of the Command Depots.

In the same period also over 50,000 convalescent men were returned to Australia as invalids.

In addition to these some thousands of men were classified "B2a" or "C1" and, under the title of "Home Service personnel," were employed in the depots constituting about 70 per cent. of the staffs, or were drafted for some special form of "B" class duty in England.[38] The discrimination, among men of lower category, of those fit for some form of military duty—in colloquial army terms "P.B." or "Permanent Base" men—and their employment and control was in the attrition warfare of 1914-18 a matter of major importance. In the A.I.F., for reasons that will appear later it was one of the most thorny of the medical problems.[39]

"Home Service Personnel" ("P.B." and "T.B.")

---
[37] From the memorandum by Col. McWhae.
[38] Permanent ("P.B.") personnel employed in France were taken from men boarded at the Base Depot Havre.
[39] The matter is introduced in its initial phase in *Vol. I, p. 412*. It is also discussed in *Chapter xxvi* of the present volume, and in *Vol. III*.

The procedure by which a proportion—in the A.I.F. a small one—of men were classified as "P.B." is admirably set out by Lieut.-Colonel Woollard:—

"The process of boarding does not finish with the finding of the depot medical board. If the man be given a 'B2b,' 'C2' or 'C3' category, he is, as has been stated, transferred to No. 2 Command Depot, Weymouth. Here he appears before a final board consisting of two of the consultants of the A.I.F. If this board concurs with the previous finding, he is returned to Australia on a hospital ship as soon as possible. On the other hand, he may be raised to a home service category and employed in England, or even brought up to 'B1a' or 'A' class.

"In the case of the home service men, that is, those of 'B2a' and 'C1' class, a three-monthly revision is held, at which those who have improved are brought up to a higher category, and those who have deteriorated are marked for Australia. . . . Other men, having been graded as fit for home service only, are transferred to London (Administrative Headquarters) or hospital or any unit in need of staff. . . ."[40]

THE TRAINING GROUPS—RECRUITS FROM AUSTRALIA

It remains to turn to the other side of the depot system— the Training Groups. Their general working does not come within the field of direct medical concern. Reinforcements "marching in" from the transports[41] were allotted to the "Training Battalion" or other training unit—corresponding with the front line unit for which they were destined.[42] Here they entered upon a course of training and mode of life intended to fit them for active service at the front.

Apart from the matter of health and the treatment of sickness, which have been dealt with earlier, the medical problems

---

[40] Re-grading from No. 2 Command Depot was not uncommon in 1918 in consequence of the improved boarding system and especially of the campaign of physical therapy carried out there during 1918 (*Vol. III*).

[41] The troops came by troop train direct from the transports. The arrangements for this movement and for their comfort *en route*, were controlled from Administrative Headquarters at Horseferry-road, which also directed the reverse movement— of invalids. During the first year of the depots, while *liaison* was imperfect, the "voyage health report" of the "Senior Medical Officer" of each transport arriving from Australia went to A.I.F. Headquarters and did not reach the A.D.M.S. at the depots, who was thus greatly hampered in the control of epidemic disease.

[42] Until the end of 1917 reinforcements for all "arms" other than the medical service arrived from Australia earmarked for particular units. After the heavy casualties of Third Ypres and the failure to send full quotas from Australia they were pooled and sent where most required. In pursuance of a deliberate policy, initiated by Surgeon-General Howse at Mena in 1915, of breaking down State rivalries and fostering Medical Corps *esprit*, from May, 1916, onwards A.A.M.C. reinforcements from all States, officers and other ranks alike, were sent as general medical reinforcements and were allotted to units at the discretion of the D.M.S., A.I.F. See *Vol. I p. 63n.*

special to this division of the depot system comprised, (1) the elimination of unfit recruits arriving by the transports from Australia; (2) training and distribution of A.A.M.C. reinforcements; and (3) medical oversight of the drafts for the front.

In the early pages of this chapter we saw in the mushroom-like growth of the Command Depots the direct results of the terrific wave of battle-casualties from the Somme that flowed to Britain from the Australian formations in France in the second half of 1916. We are to observe now a not less interesting and significant if less spectacular by-effect, namely a deterioration in the quality of the recruits sent from Australia, *pari passu* with a serious fall in their numbers; and, as obverse to this, a vigorous reaction on the part of the officers of the A.I.F. responsible for the physical efficiency of the force.

Problem of unfit recruits— by-effects of Somme

A proportion of men unfit for military service on account of disabilities existing prior to enlistment had always been found, sporadically, among the troops sent overseas from Australia.[43] So early as October, 1916, correspondence had passed between the D.M.S., A.I.F. (General Howse), and the Director-General in Australia (General Fetherston), giving presage of trouble.

"If," Surgeon-General Fetherston wrote in October, 1916, "we were to allow medical officers to reject every man in whom there was suspicion of tubercle or other disease we would have rejected an enormous percentage and you would be very short of reinforcements."[44]

The question did not however become acute till the beginning of 1917. In March the D.D.M.S. Southern Command (Surgeon-General Birrell) advised General Howse that a large number of the Australian reinforcements arriving in the depots were over-age, and of very poor physique. The Consulting Physician and the Consulting Surgeon, A.I.F., Colonels H. C. Maudsley and C. S. Ryan, also reported on the unfitness for front line service

---

[43] It may be recalled that as early as October, 1914, a number of men were weeded out from the "first contingent" during its voyage, at Albany in Western Australia. See *Vol. I, Chapter ii*. Other references will be found indexed under "Recruits."

[44] Correspondence, Fetherston-Howse 1915-18 (Australian War Memorial).

of men over 44 years. During the first six months of the year 785 men, who were found on arrival to be "unfit for general service," were immediately boarded for return to Australia. To 31st May, 1917, the total number of "unfits" arriving in Great Britain numbered 8,620, 3 per cent. of the total embarkations to that date.[45] In July, out of a "convoy" of 5,172 men, 143 were found "unfit for military service." Thenceforward the matter became a veritable "battle of standards." On 16th September, 1917, in response to repeated complaints from the training battalions, Colonel McWhae, the A.D.M.S., A.I.F. Depots, drew the attention of General Howse to "the large number of soldiers" who had arrived in August "quite unfit for any military service."

Of 269 men whose cases were referred to him from the training battalions, and who were personally examined by him, 14, found "permanently unfit for military work," were recommended for service in the A.A.M.C. Of the remaining 255, 251 were pronounced by boards to be "permanently unfit for general service," and 4 unfit for more than six months. These were men "concerning whom there can be no difference of medical opinion as to their unfitness for general service." 208 were transferred to No. 2 Command Depot forthwith for immediate return to Australia. 47 were classed "fit for home service"; but already there were in the Command "a large number of home service personnel in excess of requirements," who were being returned to Australia at the first opportunity.

The chief disabilities found were:—"Senility," 155 including 49 with bronchitis, rheumatism, etc.; "surgical disabilities" (fingers or thumb absent, stiff elbows, old fractures, hernia, etc.), 41; deformities of feet, 9; "medical disabilities" (heart and lung troubles, defective physique, etc.), 41; the remainder were cases of defective vision, or deafness, or were "mental." "With regard to senility," McWhae reported, "the majority are weak old men, not only permanently unfit for general service but quite unfit for employment on any military duties whatsoever, in England, and who should be returned to Australia before winter." The chief reason for these enlistments he found in the fact that the men had been encouraged by recruiting officials to under-state their correct age, or had done so "to encourage the young men to enlist." "It is very hard to understand," he added, "how medical officers have passed these old men as fit for general service."

It will not be found difficult when we come to study the conditions of recruiting in Australia.

In addition to these (who formed 6 per cent. of the total drafts for the month) 394 soldiers were reported as under-age,

---

[45] Consideration of this matter is continued in *Chapter xxvi*.

of whom 160 were under 18½ and thus debarred from serving in France.[46]

During 1917 1,673 recruits arrived from Australia who were found by the A.D.M.S., A.I.F. Depots in U.K., to be unfit for general service. The disabilities which caused their unfitness were as follows:—

> Over-age and senility, 488; diseases and injuries to legs and feet, and flat feet, 244; defective vision, 123; hernia, 114; debility, 104; diseases and injuries to arms and hands, 94; heart trouble, 83; rheumatism, 75; bronchitis, 59; deafness, 38; mental, 28; epilepsy, 28; asthma, 26; defective physique, 26; tubercular, 24; varicose veins, 20; haemorrhoids, 15; various, 84.

Of 4,400 reinforcements who arrived during September and October, 1917, no less than 1,700 were found "dentally unfit" for inclusion in drafts and requiring an immense amount of treatment.

To meet the problem of "over- or under-age" Colonel McWhae recommended that examining medical officers in Australia should pay attention to the *apparent* as against the *stated* age of the soldier—a proposal based on the soundest clinical principles but in the circumstances of recruiting at the time not without naïveté.

By the beginning of 1918 the debate on the question of "unfit" recruits had developed into a major dispute between the authorities in Australia and those of the A.I.F., in particular between the heads of the Medical Services at home and overseas, Generals Fetherston and Howse. This is followed further in *Chapter xxvi*. But in anticipation it may be stated here that *no dilution in the quality of the actual fighting units of the A.I.F. was at any time permitted.*

Medical Reinforcements: the Training Depot. The A.A.M.C. Training Depot at Parkhouse was formed in June, 1916.[47] On the 7th 4 officers and 656 other ranks, who had been released as a result of the disbanding of the Australian Auxiliary Hospitals in Egypt, marched in under Lieut.-Colonel J. S. Purdy. Thereafter all A.A.M.C. reserves were held here.

---

[46] The total reinforcements disembarked during this month were *Suffolk* 150, *Borda* 1,544, *Beltana* 580, *Hororata* 1,745, *Suevic* 1,569, a total of 5,588. These were men who were boarded immediately on arrival; a much larger number of disabilities became evident on training.

[47] See map at p. 452. In June, 1918, the depot was moved to Fovant.

Parkhouse served a dual purpose. (1) It was the depot for A.A.M.C. personnel, both reinforcements and recovered men, from which the Australian Director of Medical Services drew to meet his varied requirements in Britain and France. (2) It was the training centre for medical reinforcements arriving from Australia, and also for "unfit" men, "P.B." and "T.B.," from combatant units, who were used in large numbers in the last year of the war to dilute the medical units, and thus to permit the transfer of fit men for combatant service.

Recruits for A.A.M.C. The total number of men who passed through the depot cannot be ascertained.[48] The following note by the officer commanding the depot in 1918 sufficiently indicates, however, the number and source of A.A.M.C. reinforcements used on the Western Front in the last stage of the war.

"During 18 months ending December, 1918, 3,354 soldiers arrived at the A.A.M.C. Training Depot and 2,642 were sent overseas to France, the remainder being chiefly (Australian) 'home service personnel' who were discharged for employment on A.A.M.C. duty in England or on transport duty to Australia.

"During the first half of 1918, the A.A.M.C. other ranks reporting at the Training Depot consisted of approximately one third recovered casualties from the expeditionary forces, one third reinforcements from Australia, and one third transfers from combatant arms to the A.A.M.C. During the second period of 1918, casualties formed one fifth, the remainder being in practically equal proportions of reinforcements from Australia and transferred combatants."[49]

In October, 1917 the reserve in the depot was augmented from a source which merits particular note as being of more than passing interest.

Reclaiming the "B class." In February, 1917, with the idea of forming an "Australian Army," authority was given for the formation of two new brigades (16th and 17th) which were organised in the depots as the nucleus of a sixth division[50] and with them the 16th and 17th Field Ambulances, and a Sanitary Section. These were composed of "B" and "C" class men with an "A" class nucleus of carefully selected and experienced A.A.M.C. officers and other ranks.[51] The results of the experiment in the 17th Field Ambulance are recorded by the A.D.M.S. as follows.

16th and 17th Field Ambulances

---

[48] In particular no figures are available for the period 5 July, 1916 to 7 June, 1917.
[49] This note and the following are from memoranda by Col. McWhae (*loc. cit*).
[50] The project was killed by the losses in the fighting of Third Ypres.
[51] The units were commanded, the 16th by Lieut.-Col. A. H. Marks, the 17th by Lieut.-Col. R. W. Chambers.

"On 9th July there were 56 'A' class men and 218 'C' class in the unit. Every infantry battalion in the A.I.F. was represented except 10, every Field Ambulance except 1, and each General Hospital. It is interesting to compare these figures of 9th July with those of 25th October when the unit was disbanded. Then there were 197 'A' class men and only 50 'C' class men. [This was] due largely to improvement in the general health, as the result of several months steady training and instruction in A.A.M.C. duties under canvas in the New Forest in beautiful summer weather, combined with the impression of esprit de corps into the members. So successful was the experiment that all Medical Boards after that period were instructed to select suitable 'C' class men, permanently unfit for general service with a combatant unit, but fit for general service with the A.A.M.C. These men went to Parkhouse Training Depot and transferred to the A.A.M.C.—973 reinforcements were obtained in this way during 1918."

Training A.A.M.C. The training of the personnel for the Australian Medical Service was not one of the high-lights in its history: much time was wasted and the training itself was disjointed. This in some part was due to the facts that,

(1) the training was in two more or less insulated stages—in Australia in the several States, and overseas; (2) reinforcements allotted for the service were much below its wastage; and (3) unlike most other branches of the army, the medical service has no respite from its specific duties.

At first reliance was placed on training received in Australia and on the voyage. It was soon found that, as in the combatant arms, this must be supplemented by more informed and purposeful instruction in the depots. In January of 1917 there was in the depot no officer of any military experience and (as the A.D.M.S. reported) "training is therefore non-existent and the syllabus unsatisfactory." A permanent establishment was then authorised, and an endeavour made to instil at least some acquaintance with general military duties and "soldier-like smartness" in place of the slackness engendered by camp life in Australia and duty on the transports. By degrees Parkhouse found its place in the medical organisation of the A.I.F. Officers, commissioned and non-commissioned, of the splendid Australian Instructional Staff formed the backbone of the staff. Nevertheless throughout the war training was carried on "from hand to mouth."

During its whole existence the depot was seriously handicapped by a shortage of instructors. The permanent cadre consisted of 4 officers and 11 other ranks, and, except the C.O. and Quartermaster, these changed frequently. All other ranks were occupied in administration and routine duties except one Staff-Sergeant and one Sergeant-Instructor, other instructors being found from "casuals," chiefly convalescent N.C.O's passing through the depot. In April, 1918, 8 infantry N.C.O's of "B1a" class were employed with much advantage in physical training, games, squad and company drill, and anti-gas measures.

Medical reinforcements from Australia were found fairly well up in hospital work but "almost useless for the field."

Officers:—The training of medical officers was carried out by a series of Officers' Schools.[52] During the first six months of 1918 these had practically to lapse, inasmuch as when reinforcements arrived from Australia a similar number of officers temporarily employed in A.I.F. Depots were sent to France and the newly arrived officers had to take over their duties.

Other ranks. Training was carried out systematically except at the end of 1917 when, owing to the urgent demands from France, it was impossible to run any set scheme. Chief attention was paid to *physical fitness*, as it was necessary for men sent overseas as stretcher-bearers to be fit for their strenuous work at once. The men were instructed as to the dressing of wounds; application of the Thomas splint; bandaging; use and abuse of the tourniquet; carriage of patients with and without gas masks; protection of themselves and patients against gas; and sanitation. For the combatant personnel transferred to the Corps simple lectures were given on the circulation, respiration, and skeleton.[53]

"DRAFT FOR FRANCE"

Units and formations in the field reinforced themselves by making "demand" on the Australian Base Depot in France (Etaples, or Le Havre) through the Australian Section of 3rd Echelon, General Headquarters, B.E.F.[54] This office set in motion drafts from the base depot in France to feed the "Corps Reinforcement Camp," and itself made demand on the Depots in U.K. to refill the Base Depot.[55] The machinery of reinforcement was wholly a military matter; but the medical service was the determining authority in the matter of physical fitness.

It would seem a simple matter, says McWhae, to send troops a day or two's journey to their units in France. . . . But in the early days of the depots (1916-17) large numbers of men were struck off drafts at the last minute; mumps and measles broke out in drafts and an epidemic

[52] Initiated it would seem, by an adverse report from France by the A.D.M.S. 4th Aust. Division (Col. Barber). "All newly arrived officers from Australia were put through a 14 days' school of instruction—drill in the mornings, lectures in the afternoon." (From a note by Capt. A. C. Fraser, A.A.M.C.)
[53] Particular reference may be made to lectures by the Quartermaster No. 2 A.C.C.S. (Hon. Capt. J. H. Pollard, A.A.M.C.) on the "Duties of a Quartermaster attached to a Medical Unit."
[54] *See Vol. III.*
[55] After any heavy engagement, such as the Battles of the Somme, "drafts" went almost direct to the front from Britain.

of mumps [consequently] raged through the Australian Divisions in France; dentally unfits, and men whose "T.A.B." inoculation was unsatisfactory passed to France in large numbers.

This led, early in 1917 to a strong protest from G.H.Q. to the War Office against the irregular methods of the A.I.F. in respect to "T.A.B." inoculation. This was a bitter pill for among all the belligerents Australia had been the pioneer in compulsory inoculation against Typhoid ("T"); and also, in the face of strong opposition, in the education of the military command and the troops to the idea of protective inoculation as a wholesome measure of defence and a proper matter for military discipline. Moreover, through the admirable campaign of clinical and laboratory research at Lemnos the Australian Defence Department had been warned by its own medical service overseas 6 months beforehand that "T.A.B." must come, and had been furnished by Lieut.-Colonel C. J. Martin, A.A.M.C. with material for inoculating the 3rd Division, and with a thoroughly tested procedure. The unfortunate delay by Australia has been noted.[56] Its results are seen in a Report by the A.D.M.S. Depots (Colonel McWhae) to General Howse on "Soldiers arriving from Australia in August, 1917";—

"*Inoculation Against Typhoid and Paratyphoid:* I have again to report that it has been necessary to re-inoculate with Triple Vaccine all these troops immediately on arrival.

"I have made repeated representations that the methods of inoculation in Australia be made similar to those which it is necessary to adopt here. I am not permitted to allow a single soldier to proceed to France unless he has been fully inoculated with Triple Vaccine and unless the T.A.B. entries have been made in the correct way in Pay Books.

"In order to prevent the re-inoculation of troops from Australia in this Command, which should be entirely unnecessary, I again request that the following procedure be carried out in Australia:—

"(a) That Mixed Vaccine, Typhoid, Paratyphoid A, and Paratyphoid B be used; (b) that this inoculation be carried out by the two-dose system, i.e., ½ c.c. followed by 1 c.c. 8 to 10 days later; (c) that this inoculation be invariably entered up in Pay Books in the following form:—

| T.A.B. | 7.8.17 | J.H.G. (Initials of M.O.) |
| 2 | 17.8.17 | J.H.G." |

It was soon obvious that medical inspections just before the draft went overseas were too late. The precautions taken in consequence were "as simple as they were effective." A special *pro forma* was drawn up for the use of drafts as follows:—

No. Name	Rank	Unit	Inoculation	Vaccination	Are nec. Med. entries in Pay Book	Medical Fitness	M.O's initials	Dental Fitness	D.O's initials

This form was implemented by three special parades (1) The men were paraded for medical and dental inspection for the first time, *not*

---

[56] *Vol. I, p. 525-6.*

when they were warned for overseas, but within 24 hours of marching into a depot—so that all medical and dental treatment could be completed while they were carrying on their training. (2) *When they were warned for overseas* a second inspection parade was held, the same *pro forma* nominal roll being used. (3) A final inspection took place within 24 hours of proceeding overseas. The second practically resolved itself into striking off unfit soldiers, since inoculation, and dental treatment, etc., had then been completed. The final inspection, just before embarkation was chiefly for the detection of contagious disease, venereal, and scabies, and of contacts of infectious diseases (in particular mumps, measles, C.S.F). The medical officer carrying out this inspection signed a certificate that the men were medically fit, fully inoculated, and vaccinated, that the necessary entries had been made in pay books, and that they were not contacts of infectious disease.

"These medical duties in connection with drafts," says McWhae, ". . . were very successful in ensuring a high standard of fitness in drafts. Thus, from June, 1917, to November, 1918, during which period a record of unfit soldiers arriving in France was kept, 97,471 soldiers proceeded overseas and among these only 249 were found (in France) medically unfit. . . ." Of these 159 occurred from July to December, 1917, while from January to November 1918, with greater experience, only 90 unfit soldiers reached the Base at Havre. Of the total 93 were cases of gonorrhoea (probably infected after being warned for draft) and 83 of (treated) scabies (in which) the lesions (found) probably contained no live parasites.

The chapters of this section, as already stated, review the machinery for reconditioning the sick and wounded as it existed, when practically complete, in the early months of 1918. The situation at this stage was deeply affected by the failure, on 20th December, 1917, of the second attempt by the Australian Government to induce its people to accept the principle of manhood service: that project for replacing war wastage—first put to the people during the Battle of the Somme and now again after the Third Battle of Ypres—had been finally rejected. The effect of this upon the problem here dealt with is too obvious to need further emphasis; but the measures adopted for replacement of wastage in the remaining months of the war—when the A.I.F. like all other forces required its maximum strength for the final effort—will be dealt with in the last section of this volume.

From the depot at Le Havre—it may be recalled—the reinforcement, on demand being made by his unit through 3rd Echelon, would pass in a draft to the "Corps Reinforcement Camp" 5 to 15 miles behind the front line in the Army area. And with this process we complete our tour of the route

The journey completed

Graph No. 6

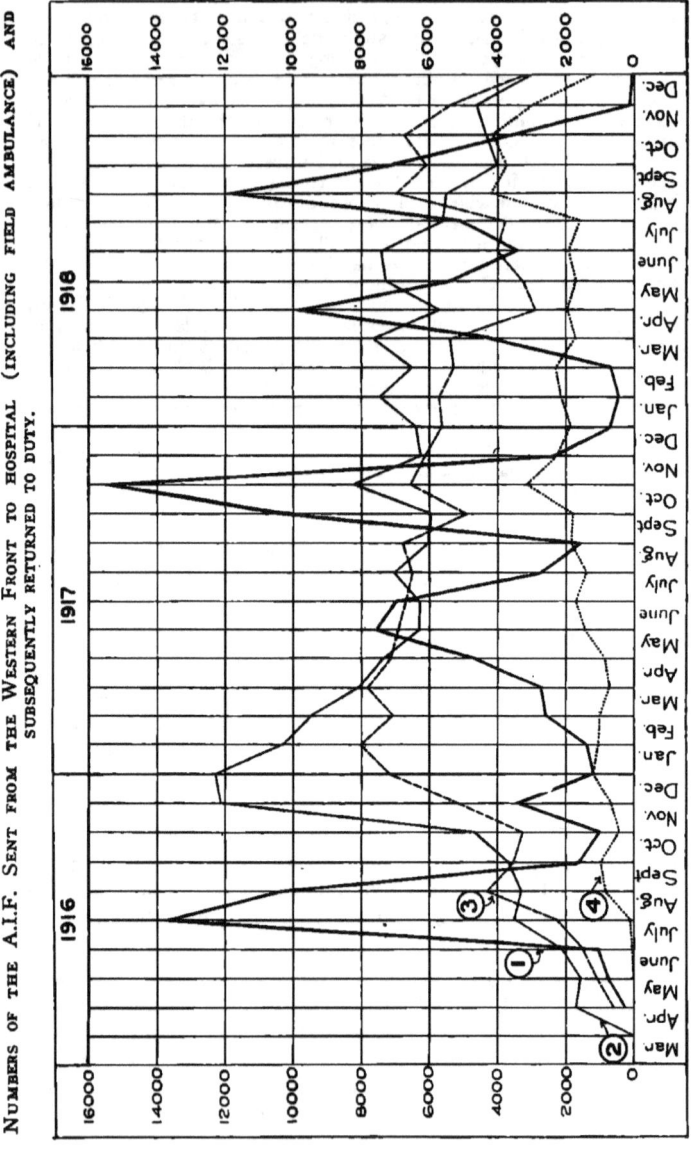

travelled by the Australian soldier in the Western Theatre of War who sustained some "casualty" of wounding or sickness. The diagram on *page 440* shows (from lack of data, only for the period April-September, 1918) the number of A.I.F. casualties who were returned to duty from the several treatment stations on the evacuation route.

In this technical retrospect of the route of evacuation we have been brought in contact with three prime factors in the production of wastage, namely, *wounding from missile or other weapon; gassing;* and *sickness or accidental injury.* It has been impressed that in the war of 1914-18 the medical service came to play a part of immense importance in the maintenance of man-power in face of the vast wastage of attrition warfare. Incomparably the most important part of this function was that of *prevention*—whether of wound infection and wound shock, of trauma through the inhalation of "poison gas," or of disablement through diseases and disorders incidental to the war-environment. In each instance, it is true, the *prevention* of casualty merged with its *treatment*. But it is necessary that the prophylactic *motif* be discerned as dominant in respect to the part played by the medical service in the maintenance of strength. The final chapters of this section, therefore, are devoted to a study of the evolution in the Great War of technical methods and procedures in respect to the major problems in military preventive medicine as indicated above.

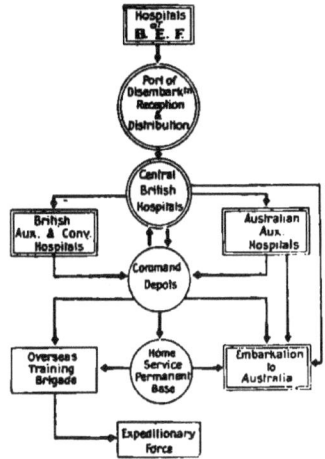

Distribution and Disposal of Australian Sick and Wounded Arriving in the United Kindom.

SYNOPSIS OF CHAPTER XVII

PREVENTIVE MEDICINE IN THE WAR—(I) THE FACTORS INVOLVED

THE GREAT WAR AND THE MEDICAL OUTLOOK:
Humani nihil alienum.
Aims in respect of man-power.
The pension aspect of prevention.
The triple responsibility.
Theories of pathogenesis.
Causes of disease; the extrinsic factor.
The inborn factor: neo-vitalism.
The era of preventive medicine.

THE ANTICIPATED CAUSES OF "WASTAGE."
From civil experience.
From military experience.
Actual wastage in the A.I.F. 1916-18.
The nosological principles here adopted.
Battle and non-battle casualties.
Wounded and sick evacuated to the base.
Admission to field ambulance, sick.
Primary analysis of wastage: "wounds" and "disease."
Definitions of "disease" and "wound."
The method of classification—"types" and "groups."
Table of battle casualties.

TABLE OF NON-BATTLE CASUALTIES:
Preventable casualties.
Scope of prevention in battle casualties.
In non-battle casualties.
The main problem on the Western Front.

ANALYSIS OF THE MAIN DISEASE TYPES:
1. Diseases due to living agents (Type III).
2. Diseases due to "psycho-physical" agencies (Type IV).

ORGANISATION AND METHODS OF THE SANITARY SERVICE:
Sanitary services of the B.E.F.
The keynote—co-operation.
Of medical department and Q.M.G's branch.
Sanitary Discipline.
Objectives—health promotion, disease prevention.
Prophylaxis by treatment.

CHAPTER XVII

PREVENTIVE MEDICINE IN THE WAR—(1) THE FACTORS INVOLVED

FLORENCE NIGHTINGALE writing in 1874 to the Secretary for India, Lord Salisbury, about the promotion of health in the British Army, quoted the Crown Prince Frederick of Germany as having said to her:—

"We could add to the strength and numbers of organised armies by sanitary works"; money spent on these works, he had said, "contributed to military forces as much as fortifications and direct military organisation."[1]

Since the "sanitary" reforms introduced into the British Army after the Crimean War the peace time sick-rate, abroad and at home, had been reduced by over four-fifths. No such advance was manifest in the field army. The Great War did for the army in the field what the reforms initiated by the report of the "Barracks and Hospitals Commission" of 1858 did for it in barracks.

THE GREAT WAR AND THE MEDICAL OUTLOOK

The effect of the war on the science of preventive medicine is chiefly discerned not in accretions to factual knowledge or in the discerning of new principles, but in its influence on the intellectual attitude and outlook of its generation. It encouraged *insistence upon reality*: in particular, insistence that pre-

---

[1] It is often forgotten that to this remarkable woman the British Army owed not only its re-introduction to the idea—accepted and implemented in the Continental nations—that a spirit of humanity might motivate the treatment of the wounded and sick in war without hurt to military efficiency; to her, with Sidney Herbert, it owed its return to medical sanity and remembrance of Sir John Pringle (1707-1782)—the father of military hygiene and originator of the Red Cross idea; and of Sir James McGrigor master of the technique of "return to duty," with whose help in the Peninsular War Wellington "brought the organisation and working of the medical service to a pitch of perfection till then unapproached in any European Army." (*Encycl. Britt.*)

ventive medicine shall be based upon exact knowledge of the origin of the various disorders that resulted in "wastage," military or national, or, ultimately, in national responsibility for the payment of a war-pension for disease "due to or aggravated by war service." As far as it is possible within their space, an endeavour will be made in this and the next two chapters to show the evolution of these processes[2] in connection with the problems of the Western Front.

It would be difficult to refute a proposal that the chief feature of preventive medicine in the Great War was this—that no aspect of the physical, mental, or moral make-up of man lay outside the sphere of its interest. The resources of every branch of medicine and surgery were enlisted in the task of maintaining the greatest efficiency in the greatest part of the available man-power. The results, though perhaps not so dramatic as has been thought, remain an impressive performance of international medicine and industrial organisation—of which, almost as much as of scientific progress, they were the reflection.

Humani nihil alienum

Aims in Respect of Man-power. The prevention of disease, like its nature, is most usefully studied in relation to a clearly defined standard of endeavour and of achievement, this being determined pragmatically, in terms of the purpose to be served.

In civil life the term "health" is largely an abstraction, and the objective of the private and public health activities concerned in preserving and promoting it—"preventive medicine"—is correspondingly vague. In the Army, at war, on the other hand, the problem of health presents, primarily, a quite clear-cut aim: namely to obtain and to maintain a body of men "fit" for the specific job of soldiering. This concept of health had determined the military medical organisation and methods, and was the motive in its activities throughout the war.

The study of disease prevention in war is thus largely confined to those procedures that will promote the maintenance "at strength" of a body of men under special and peculiar conditions—conditions that have but little relation to those which obtain in peace, and which in the war of 1914-18 contained elements, material, social, and individual that are seldom met with in a civil community. The conditions of the Great War favoured, it is true, confirmatory experiment and the exploitation of methods and hypotheses; but creative thought and original scientific research were possible only in a narrow field of interest. As Sir Henry Dale has reminded us, the Great War "diverted all scientific energies from their normal applications"[3] to the purpose of warfare. In effect,

[2] The *British Official Medical History* allocates two volumes to the subject of "The Hygiene of the War" alone.
[3] Sir Henry Dale: "Chemical Transmission of the Effect of Nerve Impulses," *The British Medical Journal,* 12 May, 1934, p. 835.

principles and practice of medical science evolved in peace were applied to the problems of warfare on a vast scale, and under widely differing conditions.

Wars for the most part are self-limited to a span of man's life too short to permit the emergence as a significant factor in wastage of those diseases that are the expression of degenerative **The pension** changes, the result of physiological wear and tear **aspect of** of life, or the expression of hereditary diatheses or **prevention** development of acquired morbid tissue habits, such as are so prominent a feature in the health picture of civil life. This fact further defines the scope of the problem of wastage from disease in war. But, as post-war medical history has proved, this is by no means to say that the influence of such "causes" of disease is in abeyance on active service. In the Great War indeed these "causes" of disablement in the manhood enlisted during its four years formed a definite element in the medical picture at the time, and in its aftermath have created stupendous problems in medicine and in statesmanship. And since in their national significance these problems of the aftermath of the war are second only to those involved in its prosecution, historical perspective requires that the factors concerned in the production through active service of *pension liabilities* and of *personal disablement and invalidity* shall form part of a study of its "preventive medicine."

The Triple Responsibility. We have to distinguish then, as concerns this matter of the genesis of disease and disablement in the war, and their prevention, two distinct forms of ill-health presenting widely different problems. First, those disablements due to injury, disease, and dysfunction, the clinical features of which made them a serious cause of wastage and a direct concern therefore to the Commander-in-Chief and War Cabinet. Second, those whose effects were not of a kind that should result in immediate functional disability, but rather of the type that would initiate morbid tendencies or minor structural changes which in after years should influence the onset of the degenerative changes proper to advancing age. With these went the crude sequelae of acute disease, and the late results of battle-casualty such as gassing, functional inabilities and deformities the influence of which might greatly be mitigated by early treatment, by relegation to "B" class service or otherwise "tempering the wind to the shorn lamb," or by discharge. *In the Australian Force military and national policy coincided to promote such action.* Indeed in this matter of disease prevention, without any deliberate definition of purpose, both the organisation and the efforts of the Australian Army Medical Service became differentiated along these two lines; and an account of the problem presented by sickness in the A.I.F. must, if it has regard for completeness, deal not merely with those matters that concerned the *immediate needs of the Commander-in-Chief* —that is with those diseases and disorders that influenced military wastage—but also with the influence of war experiences on *post-war national health* and the national pocket. Nor, we must add, can *the humanitarian aspect* of disease prevention be excluded from a study of preventive medicine in the war, though the emotional appeal of the sick man is of necessity less than that of the wounded.[4]

---

[4] The particular involvements of this sphere of preventive medicine in the war are examined in a chapter of *Vol. III.*

"We [may] remind ourselves of that most interesting, and, I think, fundamentally true conception of life in the physiological sense which was put forward by Claude Bernard in 1878 in his book *Les Phénomènes de la Vie* in which he wrote:— 'It is the constancy of the internal environment which is the condition of free and independent life... All the vital mechanisms, however varied they may be, have only one object, that of preserving constant conditions of life in the internal environment'... We have to study the varied influences which tend to disturb that optimum internal state on which depends the individual's sense of wellbeing, health, comfort, physical fitness, efficiency, and working capacity."[5]

Theories of pathogenesis

The Great War coincided with the vigorous adolescence of one of the most fruitful periods of advance in the science and art of medicine. Like every other great movement this had been initiated by a new philosophy, in the form of a new conception of "disease." The real significance of Pasteur's discovery, that a specific "disease" might be caused by a specific germ, lies in this—that the facts observed and the principles built thereon gave to the inductive science of medicine a logical base for deductive thought. "Give me a fulcrum," said Archimedes, "and I will move the world"; and the discovery in "infection" of an objective cause for disease had provided a rational fulcrum for a new era of thought and of progress in the science of medicine; a new source of intellectual energy which already had gone far to move the world on its intellectual and social as well as its medical foundations. With the discovery in bacterial and protozoal infection of an absolute cause of "disease" of a kind which, though essentially vital, conformed to the criteria of science and was susceptible to measurement and to forecast, pathology and epidemiology became candidates for promotion to the select group of exact sciences—the essential qualification for which was defined by Newton as conformity with the inductive method.

Causes of Disease: the Extrinsic Factor. The positive achievements of Pasteur and Lister, as well as being very practical boons to humanity, brought the vision of a science of disease based on a knowledge of

[5] "The Practice of Preventive Medicine in Industry" by Dr. G. P. Crowden, M.Sc., *B.M.J.*, 5 *Dec., 1936, p. 1156. Leçons sur les Phénomènes de la Vie communs aux Animaux et aux Vegetaux* was published in 1878 in two volumes. Claude Bernard died in the same year. (See *The Contemplative Works of Claude Bernard* in the *Bulletin of the Institute of the History of Medicine*—Johns Hopkins Press, May, 1935, *p. 335.*)

ponderable and measurable causes of specific morbid states.[6] The theory of infection had the same influence on pathogenesis as had Harvey's logical and experimental proofs of the circulation of the blood and Claude Bernard's concept of the *milieu intérieur* on physiology, the work of Vesalius, Schwann and Henle on anatomy, of Virchow on pathology, and of John Hunter on morphology. On the analogy of infection objective causes were sought and a rational mechanism was postulated for constitutional and metabolic types of disease, replacing vague concepts based by deduction on hypothetical diatheses, constitutions, or temperaments. And, on the other hand, the local "morbid histology" of Virchow was found inadequate to the idea of a pathology that was essentially functional and dynamic.[7]

The causal relationship of chemical substances and physical agents to morbid states were being studied inductively; the new sciences of bio-chemistry, of metabolism and nutrition, of endocrinology, even of psychology, illuminated the mechanistic theory of disease by promoting further triumphs of treatment and prevention. At the outbreak of the war all these wider involvements of the "germ theory" of disease were receiving recognition.[8]

The "Inborn Factor": Neo-vitalism. "Men are called healthy in virtue of an inborn capacity to easy resistance to those unhealthy influences that may ordinarily arise: unhealthy in virtue of the lack of that capacity."[9]

But if the most obvious effect of Pasteur's work was to exalt the mechanistic theory of disease and to emphasise the extrinsic factor in pathogenesis, it had a hardly less far-reaching influence in the other direction, namely to stress the importance of the "vital reaction," in other words of the "inborn capacity to easy resistance." The end of the 19th century and beginning of the 20th had seen in "neo-vitalism" the re-birth to a more scientific life of old theories of "humours" and "diatheses"—beloved of the French. Philosophic clinicians—British ones among them, Jonathan Hutchinson, the Garrods, Clifford Allbutt, J. S. Haldane, MacKenzie, Lewis—had sought by the inductive method to integrate the hypothesis of specific morbid tendencies, "inborn" and

---

[6] Thus—"When we speak of antigens, we mean substances of bacterial or viral origin which, as the result of their introduction into the living tissues of animals give rise to anti-bodies that are capable of re-acting either *in vitro* or *in vivo* with the corresponding antigens. . . . A dose of an appropriate anti-body will protect a susceptible animal from illness and death (against) many multiples of the lethal dose of a toxin." (*Recent Advances in Vaccines* by Fleming and Petrie. Churchill 1934.)

[7] "In the last quarter of the 19th century the conception grew clearer that morbid anatomy for the most part demonstrates disease in its static aspects only, and for the most part in the particular aspect of final demolition; and it became manifest, as pathology and clinical medicine became more and more thoroughly integrated, that the processes which initiate and are concerned in this dissolution were not revealed by the scalpel." Sir T. Clifford Allbutt, *Encyclopaedia Brittannica 1911* (Article on Medicine, *p. 55*).

[8] "On the subtle and insidious penetration of infections which corrupt the values of life perhaps a few more paragraphs might have been written. Every day is adding to our knowledge in this matter; how such agents undermine and disintegrate the fabric of the body, with ultimate effects not for many years perhaps making themselves known; and then often in disguise. Of such, as Sir Hermann says, are certain cardio-arterial degenerations; so that in the list of causes the part played by physical stresses becomes more and more restricted." Sir Clifford Allbutt—preface to the 5th Edition of Sir Hermann Weber's *Prolongation of Life p. xi.*

[9] Aristotle, *Categoriae, viii* (trans. Edgehill)—Quoted from *The Inborn Factors in Disease (p. 25)* by A. E. Garrod.

acquired, with the factual evidence of the morbific significance of mechanical factors and agents, physical, thermic, chemical, parasitic. In the domain of pathology Ehrlich had sought with approved success to bridge the gap between matter and life, mechanism and vitalism, by his "side-chain" theory of immunity to infection.

Thus, the new cardiology of James MacKenzie, wherein the living neuro-muscular apparatus replaced the mechanical leaking valve in the conception of "V.D.H." influenced the selection of recruits for the A.I.F.; while the side-chain theory, and its application by Bordet and Gengou in "complement fixation," had brought "606" and the "Wassermann reaction" to put the coping stone on Schaudinn's discovery of the "spirochaeta pallida" as the cause of syphilis.

On the other hand "disease" induced by specific deprivation of foodstuffs—avitaminosis—had not reached the stage of pathogenic analysis; even the science of endocrinology was still for the most part clinical.

The Era of Preventive Medicine. The practice of medicine has always reflected the current philosophy of the nature of life and of disease. The stress laid upon *prevention* rather than on palliation or cure by *treatment* was again a natural corollary to the discovery of extrinsic causes—microbial, chemical, physical, psychical—of specific diseases and disorders.

During the previous half century this new attitude to the problems of pathogenesis had opened up innumerable avenues of approach to the study of *aetiology*. The discovery of a specific extrinsic "cause" for a great number of definable diseases, had provided a rational basis and hence a greatly increased incentive to the practice of preventive medicine, both social and individual. It supplied a *point d'appui* for a vast system of public health services national and international. The achievements in preventive medicine in the Great War were wholly the result of this peaceful revolution. And if the medical fashion of the moment favoured unduly the mechanical factor in disease and exaggerated the significance of extrinsic causes, this, as it happened, accorded with the pathogenesis of the great majority of the disablements that actually brought about wastage in the war; whose morbific agents ranged from H.E., poison gas, and tight puttees, to wet and cold, the itch-mite, pathogenic germs, vitamin deficiency, and fear. On the other hand, it gave meagre assistance to the solution of the post-war problems of "attribution" or "aggravation" in degenerations and dysfunctions persisting in the "returned soldier."

Without some philosophic integration such as has occupied the preceding pages, an account of the vast paraphernalia of preventive medicine which permeated the whole structure of the warfare on the Western Front, must in great measure be little more than a compendium of facts and statistics. Marshal von Hindenburg has aptly entitled his war-memories *Out of My Life*; the Great War monopolised five good years of human progress. Apart from its help in similar future debauches, the only interest to humanity of such an account must lie in its contribution to the heritage of scientific medicine and to human progress in the art of living. And when all is told of the medicine of the Great War it is found to have little more constructive to its credit than but to point this moral—that "diseases" do exist, that they commonly have specific extrinsic "causes"; and that it is still supremely worth while to seek for these.

THE ANTICIPATED CAUSES OF "WASTAGE"

While few lines of action could be more subversive of victory in a great war than that preparations should be based exactly on the recorded experience of the last, on the other hand a "dead reckoning" made from current peace-time practice would be a not less risky foundation. Both must be used; both may be under- or over-stressed. From the point of view of communal health modern warfare like modern social life may be said to date within the last 100 years, and on its present plane within the last half century. The first conspicuous exception to the age-long experience, that in war more men die from disease than from wounding, was that of the German Army in the Franco-Prussian War of 1870-71.[10] The Japanese Army of 1904-5 may be said first to have demonstrated that the possibility of lessening disease might be an important factor in warfare. It is very pertinent that this change coincided with the introduction of the quick-firing small bore rifle.

The health experience of an army in the field will be the resultant of two components: the first, which may be termed its *milieu intérieur*, being the social pathogenic environment—the "public health"—of its era, together with its own inherent—racial—disease proclivities; the second, which may be termed its *milieu exotique* representing the physical conditions and particular disease environment of the campaign. Even a cursory survey of the wars of history shows that such an hypothesis should afford a safe guide to the experiences to be feared and preparations to be made; provided always that adequate account be taken of the special conditions of field service.[11] An appreciation of the disease to be expected and guarded against in a particular campaign should be based, not only on the analogy of civil experience, and on the experience

[10] 17,000 died from wounds and 15,000 from disease. Statistics of the French Army in that war are incomplete but the sick-rate was definitely higher than the German as the *morale* was lower.

[11] Thus while the absence of scurvy, typhus, and relapsing fever as major medical vicissitudes of more recent European wars reflects the modern era of nutrition and of personal hygiene, even so late as 1905 beriberi was a major disease wasting the Japanese Army in the war against Russia, reflecting the national deficiency in vitamin B1. (*Russo-Japanese War; Medical and Sanitary Reports* by Lieut.-Col. W. G. Macpherson, R.A.M.C. and other officers attached to the Japanese and Russian forces in the field issued by the General Staff at the War Office April, 1908.) And in 1915-18 typhus broke from its social moorings to run riot through Serbia and Russia, and malaria played havoc in Macedonia and Palestine.

of past wars, but on the special conditions likely to be met. Actually, in the case of most armies at the outset of the Great War it seems to have been based mainly on the experience of past wars.

From Civil Experience. Apart from statistics of *deaths* and of *notifiable (infectious) diseases* very meagre data are available to indicate the pathogenic factors in the normal morbidity of Australians. The position in 1914 in respect to quarantine and notification of transmissible diseases, which chiefly were concerned in army wastage, hardly calls for a particular note. Relevant facts will be found in various chapters of *Volume I* and in *Chapter XIX* of this. Six diseases—plague, cholera, smallpox, yellow fever, typhus fever, leprosy—were subject to quarantine and 33 in all were "notifiable" in the various States of Australia.[12] Morbidity not due to infection belongs chiefly to pension problems and such data as are available will be given in the relevant chapter of *Volume III*.

From Military Experience. The "sanitary" policy of the British War Office was based chiefly on the experience of the South African War and of the British Army in India and Indian Army. Some details of the first are examined in *Volume I*. It is not thought necessary to analyse the experiences of other wars.

British military manuals of 1914 reflected both past and present. The "chief diseases of soldiers" included plague and yellow fever, but not typhus or smallpox. The methods of "field sanitation" reflected exactly the civil experience of the 19th century and military experience of the Franco-Prussian, South African, and Russo-Japanese Wars, and made gastro-intestinal disease, in particular typhoid and dysentery, the basis of preventive medicine to the exclusion indeed of any other as a major problem of field sanitation.

The Nosological Principles Here Adopted. Statistical tables of disease[18] have been constructed to a nosology which relates each defined disease to its known cause, or (if this be not sufficiently specific or understood) to *that stage in its biological life-history or clinical cycle that is most amenable to preventive action or to curative treatment.* The defects and limitations of this method of presenting war-experience—not hitherto attempted in any work available to the author—have been appreciated in the first volume (*Chapter V*). These are not slight, and it is not suggested that outside the infective group of diseases more than a rough approximation has been achieved. In the sphere of secondary morbid states, degenerations, "vicious circles" and sequelae, not more than a working scheme has

Actual wastage in the A.I.F. 1916-18

---

[12] In N.S.W., 9, Tasmania, 17, Victoria, 20, Q'land, 23, S. Aust., 24, and W. Aust. 29.

[18] *See Vol. I Chapter v.* The plan of these was in the first place based on that of a weekly return rendered in 1916 to the D.D.M.S., I Anzac Corps, by the A.D's.M.S. of Divisions, of diseases evacuated from their field ambulances. It was designed to assist in the identification of profitable lines of prophylaxis, and served a useful purpose during the winter of 1916-17.

been attempted, from the point of view chiefly of *pensions problems*. Extenuating perhaps the defects of an experiment made under peculiar difficulties,[14] it may be contended that the statement of health experience of the force through disease in terms of causation has at least done this—it greatly simplifies the necessary account both of the methods adopted in the war for the prevention of various "diseases" and of the problems of the aftermath. In the present state of medical knowledge, and of its diffusion through the screen, the press, and in popular works, to know the effective cause of a morbid state and the circumstances of the population concerned is in no small measure also to know the lines of action involved in its prevention.

Indeed, after stating the diseases expected or experienced, what chiefly remains is to describe the developments in the machinery of preventive medicine in the A.I.F. on the Western Front and any outstanding features in its practice.

The total figures and detailed analysis of wastage from battle and non-battle casualties in the A.I.F. are given elsewhere.[15] Here the broad outlines of the problem of wastage are presented in graphic form:—

Battle and Non-battle Casualties. Graph No. 7 presents the relative proportions and total numbers of "battle" and "non-battle" casualties sustained by the A.I.F. during 1916-18 on the Western Front.[16] The battle casualties include killed, died of wounds, died of gas poisoning, prisoners of war, wounded, gassed, "shell shock 'W.'" Non-battle casualties—including deaths—consist of "sick" and "accidentally injured on service."

Wounded and Sick Evacuated to the Base. Graph No. 8 shows the wastage from wounds and sickness (on a percentage per week of the ration-strength of the A.I.F. in France) of men evacuated to the Base.[17]

---

[14] Owing chiefly to the destruction, in a British Government office, through misadventure, of the Australian statistical records (*See Preface* to this volume). The complete tables of morbidity are complementary to the present study of disease prevention, and with critical analysis will be found in *Vol. III.*

Since the publication in 1930 of the first volume of this work, the advantages and also the practical possibility of adopting teleological bases for the classification of diseases have been urged, *e.g.* by Mr. Wilfred Trotter, F.R.S. (*B.M.J.*, 28 *Jan. 1933*) and Dr. Parkes Weber ("Classification of diseases," in *Endocrine tumours and other Essays, 1936*). But each year sees a substantial reduction in the number of what may be called "diseases of uncertain origin." The last decade has been embarrassingly fruitful in such nosological vicissitudes.

[15] *See Appendix No. 1, and Vol. III.*

[16] These figures are based on the finalised adjustments (made in 1924) of the individual records of members of the A.I.F. kept by Australian Records Section of Third Echelon, B.E.F.; they may be treated as correct. In particular, all "missing" have been traced or allotted with a very high degree of certainty—a procedure made possible by the fact that it was carried out *during the war*.

[17] These figures are based on the weekly statement issued by the D's.M.S. of Armies on the consolidated returns from C.C.S's (A.F.W. 3185). *See p. 547.*

Admission to Field Ambulance, Sick. Graph No. 9 shows the rate per 1,000 of sick A.I.F. soldiers admitted to hospital (including field ambulance)[18] on the Western Front and in Gallipoli.

Graph No. 7—TOTAL CASUALTIES (BATTLE AND NON-BATTLE) IN THE A.I.F. ON THE WESTERN FRONT.

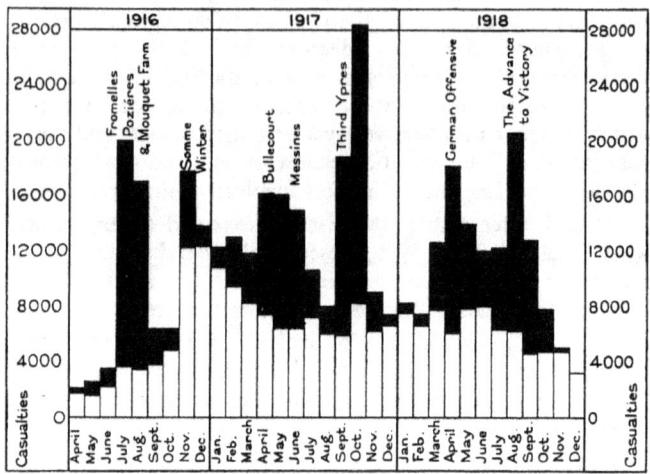

The casualties for each year were:

	Battle	Non-Battle
1916	42,267	45,657
1917	76,836	89,084
1918	60,352	73,237
Totals	179,455	207,978

(These include prisoners of war and killed as well as all medical casualties.) Black indicates battle casualties and white non-battle casualties.

Primary analysis of wastage: "wounds" and "disease"

For the classification of military diseases and disabilities by their causes the following definitions are here used. A disease is a clinical-pathological complex expressing the sum of the manifest results of the action, whether through injury or through deprivation, of a cause (*i.e.* agent) of disease, and of the vital reaction of the body thereto; when such results are sufficient to interfere with well-being and in particular with the performance of necessary social (in this case military) duties.[19]

[18] These figures, also from the Australian Records Section at Third Echelon, are based on the unit returns (B.213) and field ambulance returns (A.36).
[19] See also Dr. Parkes Weber, *loc. cit.*, footnote on *p.* 9.

Graph No. 8

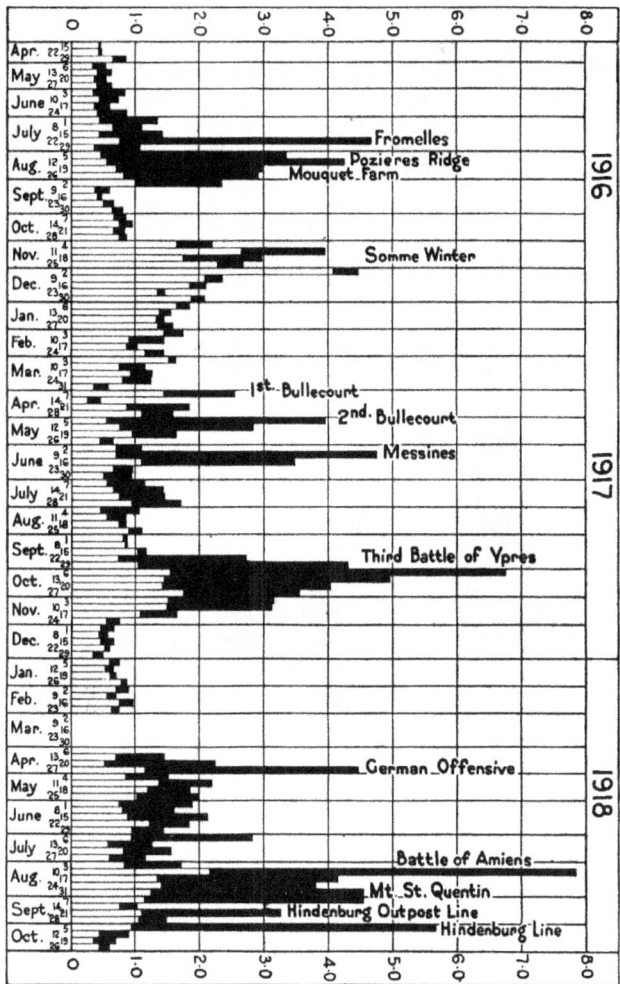

PERCENTAGE OF TOTAL EVACUATIONS (FROM ARMY AREA) ON THE
WEEKLY AVERAGE STRENGTH OF A.I.F. ON THE WESTERN FRONT

Note.—The figures used in the compilation of this graph have been obtained from reports of D's.M.S. of Armies, which, in their turn, were based on the details supplied on Army Forms W.3185 by casualty clearing stations. Particulars for the period of the German offensive of March-April, 1918, were not available from this source (see e.g. p. 625). It will be noted that there are some discrepancies between these figures and those shown elsewhere in the volume, which are compiled mainly from details supplied by the Australian Section of 3rd Echelon. The reports of the D's.M.S. were compiled *some days after* the occurrence of casualties.

The official definition of a wound has already been given.[20] *The Method of Classification—"Types" and "Groups."* In the tables given on *pages 495-7 and 501-4* are shown, analysed on an aetiological basis into "types," "classes" and "groups," the various traumata and morbid states that composed this wastage.[21]

Graph No. 9—COMPARISON OF THE A.I.F. SICK RATES IN GALLIPOLI WITH THOSE ON THE WESTERN FRONT.

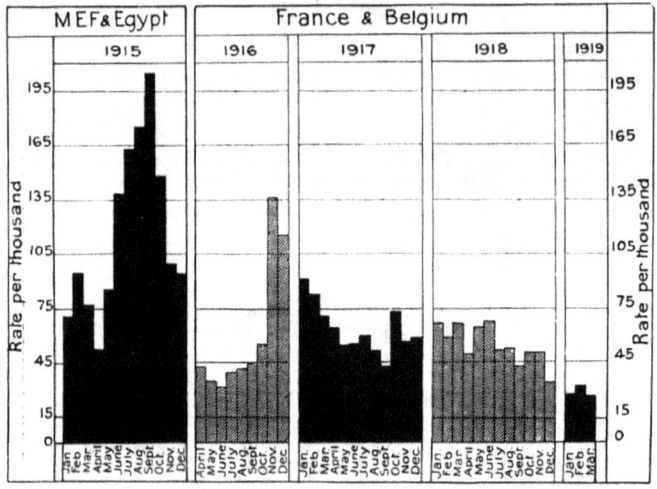

The graph shows the incidence of disease in terms of the monthly rate per 1,000 of men admitted to hospitals (including field ambulances).

Some 900 distinct disease entities[22] were entered in the "Admission and Discharge Books" used in compiling the statistical tables. These have been integrated into 181 groups of disease, and these again into 44 classes composing 8 teleological types.

The narrative contained in *Sections I and III* of this volume

---

[20] On *p. 270*.

[21] As an index of experience, the tables are in this respect misleading, in that they give little hint of troubles that "might have been"; nor do they *in themselves* show the results of the vast efforts devoted on the Western Front to the promotion of health and prevention of disease. Light is, however, thrown on these by a comparison of these tables, and the preceding graphs, with those given in *Vol. I* for Gallipoli and Palestine.

[22] The detailed "International Lists of Causes of Death," 5th Decennial Revision by the Health Organisation of the League of Nations (*Bulletin 1939, 7, Extract No. 34*) specifies 200 individual "titles." The "Tabular List" of terms under each title, based on the 2nd Decennial Revision (1909), includes some 8,000 morbid states or agencies. The *Nomenclature of Diseases drawn up by a Joint*

and also later in this chapter makes it possible for the reader to relate the incidence of the various diseases to seasonal and other conditions in the environment of the force. It may, indeed, at once be said that, in connection with the more chronic types of disease found in the A.I.F., either during or after the war—rheumatism, bronchitis, heart disease, "blood pressure," and such like—or even of such distinctive "war diseases" as "war nephritis," "pulmonary fibrosis," or the "effort syndrome," little more can be done to illuminate the problems of "attribution" and "aggravation" than to invite the attention of the reader to those narratives.

Admissions to field ambulances from A.I.F. in France (April, 1916-March, 1919)

(i) *Battle-casualties*

Class		Number	Percentage of total
1.	High velocity bullets (rifle and machine-gun)	48,309	33·93
2.	Shell fragments and shrapnel pellets	72,513	50·93
3.	Bombs and grenades	2,714	1·90
4.	Bayonets[23]	396	0·28
5.	Burial (by shellburst, mine etc.); and aeroplane crash[24]	—	—
6.	Fire (*flammenwerfer* etc.)[24]	—	—
7.	Chemical substances (gassing)	16,822	11·82
8.	"Shell concussion" ("shell shock 'W'")	1,624	1·14
9.	Infective agents (as bacteria)	—	—
	Total	142,378	100·00

Committee appointed by the Royal College of Physicians of London (London: His Majesty's Stationery Office, 1918) gives 3,120 "diseases," with an additional list of 500 "surgical operations," 119 "tumours and cysts," 354 "malformations," 230 "poisons" and 360 "parasites." The *Memorandum upon the Tabulations of Medical and Surgical Statistics of the War* by the Medical Research Committee (1918) allowed for 1,096 specific disease entities and 391 operations for wounding. Except such as are frankly alphabetical, all classifications—even that employed in the *British Annual Report of the Health of the Army*—are aetiological in form; though commonly so made as to confuse rather than to promote discrimination of "cause."

[23] Australian records do not discriminate the nature of the traumatic agent in wounds caused by missile or hand-weapon. The *British Official Medical History* gives two estimates—(1) *Statistics, p. 40*—Bullet 38·98 per cent., Shell 58·51 per cent., Bomb and grenade 2·19 per cent., Bayonet 0·32 per cent. (2) *Surgery, Vol. I p. 27*—27 per cent. bullets, 73 per cent. shells and bombs. Any estimate must be tentative and also will vary with the warfare. In arriving at the A.I.F. numbers and percentages, the first figures have been used here. The following figures, taken from the *German Official Medical History Vol. III pp. 70-73* have a general interest.

	Franco-Prussian	Great War German	Great War British
Bullet wounds	92 per cent.	54 per cent.	39 per cent.
Shells etc.	8 per cent.	46 per cent.	61 per cent.

[24] The considerable casualties sustained under this double heading cannot be discriminated. For infective agents (9) *see p. 498*.

(ii) *Non-battle Casualties*

Type I—*Defects and deformities of civilised life:*

Class 1. Age factors	53	0·03
2. Structural defects and deformities	4,524	2·14
3. Occupational diseases	—	—
4. Dental defects and diseases	2,772	1·31
	7,349	3·47

Type II—*Accidental injuries on service:*

5. All accidental injuries on service	15,648	7·39
	15,648	7·39

Type III—*Primary infections and infestations by living agents:*

6. Gastro-intestinal infections	1,558	0·74
7. Faucial and respiratory tract infections	41,300	19·49
8. The neurotropic ectodermoses	354	0·17
9. Rheumatic (nodular) fever	239	0·11
10. Tuberculosis	602	0·28
11. Specific muco-dermal infections	—	—
12. Infections of eye, ear, nose	2,671	1·26
13. "Septic" (pyogenic) infections	11,888	5·61
14. The venereal infections	13,105	6·19
15. Transmitted through an insect or other host	4,244	2·01
16. Helminthiasis (excluding Hydatid disease)	43	0·02
17. Skin infestations	20,533	9·69
18. Specific wound infections	21[25]	0·01
19. P.U.O. (Pyrexia of uncertain origin)	24,593	11·61
	121,151	57·19

Type IV—*Psycho-physical factors—"environment," nutrition and fatigue:*

20. Specific physical agents (heat & cold)	24,223	11·43
21. Physiological hardship	9,586	4·53
22. Specific food defects and deficiencies	34	0·02
23. Acute endocrine dysfunctions	2	—
24. Psycho-physical exhaustion	2,791	1·32
	36,636	7·30

Type V—*Disorders of the mind:*

25. Primary psychoneuroses (psychic environment)	6,290	2·97
26. Secondary psychoneuroses (end results)	21	0·01
27. Results of moral defects	751	0·35
28. Organised mental disease	143	0·07
	7,205	3·40

[25] Tetanus only.

1916-19] PREVENTIVE MEDICINE—THE FACTORS

Type VI—*Metabolic diseases, disorders and diatheses:*

Class 29. Degeneration of the endocrine glands ..	21	0·01
30. Disorders of hormonic secretion	13	0·01
31. Neoplasms	167	0·08
32. "Allergy" and other functional diatheses	1,016	0·48
	1,217	0·58

Type VII—*Secondary dysfunctions and degenerations, and terminal states:*

33. Diseases of the nervous system	746	0·35
34. The organs of special sense	5,856	2·76
35. Diseases of the skin	1,482	0·70
36. The digestive system	4,534	2·14
37. The respiratory tract	409	0·19
38. Diseases of the circulatory system ..	695	0·33
39. Diseases of the reticulo-endothelial system	41	0·02
40. Diseases of excretory system	720	0·34
41. Diseases and disorders of genital system	1,341	0·63
42. Chronic diseases of muscles, joints, bones	449	0·21
43. Impaired constitution	4,734	2·23
	21,007	9·91

Type VIII—*Sundries, undiagnosed, and unintelligible:*

44. Human idiosyncrasies, undiagnosed, unintelligible	1,609	0·76
	1,609	0·76
Total	211,822	100·00

It will be obvious that a large proportion of this disease mass would not be amenable to the methods of preventive medicine in the field or to the precautionary alertness of the recruiting officer however conscientiously applied. At the same time there is not one which the applicant for a pension could not claim to have been "due to or aggravated by war service."[26]

Preventable casualties

We may therefore, first, with advantage traverse the table of casualties with a view to identifying those concerned in preventable wastage.

(a) *Scope of Prevention in Battle-casualties. Classes 1, 2, 3, and 4 (bullet, shell, bomb, and steel)*: The prevention of wastage from battle-

---
[26] This matter will be examined in *Vol. III*.

casualties is a matter chiefly of military strategy and tactics, or else of effective treatment and of return to duty. But, remarkably enough, certain very important types of war "wounds," in particular *"gassing"* and *"shell shock 'W',"* came directly within the scope of "preventive medicine." *Class 6 (wounding by fire)* : In the late war *fire* as a weapon was for the most part confined to the use of "liquid fire" by flame-throwers. Very few Australians were wounded by these. The recognised method of avoiding injury was to lie low in the trench and let the flame pass overhead. Prevention was therefore, as often, a matter of morale. *Classes 7 and 8 (poison gas and "shell shock 'W' ")* : The "medical" measures taken to prevent battle-casualties from chemical protoplasmic poisons acting on mucous membranes, respiratory tract, and skin; and the supposed "commotional" effects produced by high explosive on the central nervous system, are examined in detail in the special chapters which deal with the clinical features of the lesions caused by them. "Shell shock 'W' ", for example, is dealt with in connection with the related conditions of psychic "sickness" under "war neuroses."[27] A note is, however, desirable here to show the place of these in the formal scheme of preventive medicine on the Western Front, since the promotion of morale (moral health) was found to be an important factor in the prevention of wastage from each of these two forms of "battle-casualty." And in each of them also, the Medical Service was involved in direct measures of prevention.

Gassing. The prevention of wastage from gassing ("anti-gas measures" or "defensive gas"), as well as its treatment, was for more than a year the responsibility of the Medical Service. The transfer in 1917-18 of the duty of preventing casualties from gas to the combatant side (Engineers) and the "Q" Branch cannot but have an important bearing on the future of war medicine.

"Shell Shock 'W'." The question of medical as distinct from strictly military measures taken to minimise wastage from this disorder opens up problems of the greatest theoretical interest. These measures comprised in particular the establishment of special diagnostic and treatment stations for "N.Y.D.N." and "N.Y.D. Gas" to receive apparently disabled soldiers whose symptoms were wholly or chiefly "nervous." The opportunity was thus given for discriminating between those in whom the condition was due to simple exhaustion or some definite physical trauma, or to acute and reversible psychic or psycho-physical dysfunction on the one hand and those in whom the condition was more or less organised on the other. The former received immediate treatment, the latter were evacuated.

Infective Agents as Weapons. The question of the use of disease germs as a weapon was present in the Great War of 1914-18 but was not a serious one.[28] Had it been used, it would have opened up a new field for "preventive medicine" in time of war.

---

[27] These will be dealt with in *Vol. III*.

[28] The only deliberate official action in this direction seems to have been in the distribution of cultures of the glanders bacillus in the British horse lines by German agents of which there is strong suspicion. The enemy's fouling of wells by horse manure during the retreat in "Alberich" was intended to deny them to the British rather than to spread disease. In 1916 a small portable test case was issued for the detection of metallic poisons and water was sometimes found to contain traces of arsenic. But as this substance was a constituent of several poison gases, its intended use was as a weapon by inhalation not by ingestion.

(b) *Scope of Prevention in Non-battle Casualties.* The very considerable proportion of the various morbid states which, as has been pointed out above, was not amenable to "preventive" measures during the actual course of the war, is therefore relegated for consideration elsewhere, as indicated hereunder:—

Type I. Defects and deformities of civilised life. Defined in terms of totalitarian warfare (attrition), a large proportion of all war wastage came from this type, but its prevention lies for the most part outside the scope of these chapters. Classes 1, 2, and 3 belong to *Volume III* (exclusion of "unfits") or to prophylaxis by treatment and operation. Class 4 (wastage from dental trouble) is dealt with in the chapter in *Volume III* devoted to that specialty. The Service of Dentistry became part of the preventive medicine of the war.

Type II. Accidental injuries on service. Though less important as a cause of wastage in the war than they are in peace to-day, "accidental injuries on service" accounted for no less than 7·39 per cent. of admissions to field ambulances in the A.I.F. The prevention of these casualties concerned the Medical Service no more than it did other soldiers. The important group of S.I.W. ("self-inflicted wounds") is included among "moral" defects (Type V).

Type III. Primary infections and infestations by living agents. Even more, probably, than in civil life[29] this cause of disease dominated the problem of health and efficiency in the army. It is the chief *raison d'être* and inspiration for the science of military hygiene and the art of military sanitation. With the next type it forms the main subject of this and the two following chapters.

Type IV. Psycho-physical factors—"environment" nutrition and fatigue. Though not so conspicuous or definite, the diseases included under this type were even more characteristic of the war on the Western Front than were those in the previous one. The two types were closely related.[30]

Type V. Disorders of the mind. This comprises a variety of morbid states, primary or secondary, in which the mental dysfunctioning is the most prominent clinical feature. Their identification as a type is in some respects a concession to convenience rather than a scientific integration. They are examined together in *Volume III*.

Type VI. Metabolic diseases, disorders and diatheses. The diseases associated within this type form groups which perhaps link

---

[29] It has been estimated by competent authorities (*Oxford Textbook of Medicine*, Vol. I pp. 180 et seq.) that more than 50 per cent. of all "disease" is "caused" by living agents—that is to say, would not occur without them. The proportion has been put very much higher, and the above figure is probably an understatement.

[30] Thus, "bronchitis" and "bronchial irritation"; "dysentery" and "diarrhoea"; "I.C.T." and "trench foot"; "trench fever" and "pediculosis"; infection and physical exhaustion or malnutrition.

Type V with Type VII.[31] It is used as a "dump" for aetiological conundrums.

Type VII. Secondary dysfunctions and degenerations, and terminal states. The large mass of disease and dysfunction included here represents for the most part morbid states that were secondary to and consequential on corresponding acute conditions, or else were "aggravations" of pre-existing diseases or diatheses (inherited or acquired). Thus "debility" was often the result of repeated acute states of exhaustion; "D.A.H." of continued physiological and psychic stresses; osteo-arthritis of "rheumatism." They did not come within the scope of measures for preventing wastage as interpreted in terms of "effectives"; their interest is in the sphere of the *national problems* and clinical research and belongs to the next volume.

The task in hand thus reduces itself to the problems of prevention in those groups of diseases that were caused directly by (1) *the various parasitic organisms,* uni-**The main problem on the Western Front** and multi-cellular, whose effects are seen in the diseases included under Type III, or by (2) *inanimate physical and physiological agents and agencies* which, in excess or in deficiency, and in conjunction with "psychic" influences, tended to reduce vitality and cause dysfunction, and thus to promote the development of "disease." These comprised physical substances such as wet, dirt, food-stuffs, poisons (extrinsic such as tobacco or alcohol, and endogenous such as the products of fatigue), and also physical forces and psychic influences, such as heat and cold, prolonged pressure, friction, or tension (*e.g.* by boots, puttees, or pack), excessive toil and strain, or want of food, sleep, and rest—in short "hardship." The dysfunctions, disorders and "diseases" which have been "attributed" to these as the primary factor[32] are comprised under Type IV.

By far the greater part of the specific diseases, disorders and dysfunctions, that were the cause of casualties that came within

---

[31] Thus, the treatment of neuro-circulatory asthenia (D.A.H., effort syndrome, "soldier's heart") by denervation of the adrenal gland (Crile, *Diseases peculiar to civilised man*) was, in part at least, inspired by the war, and must be regarded as a serious contribution to experimental pathology, and thus to nosology. The knowledge of the causal relations between fear and adrenal control, of the thyrotoxic influence of emotional states, and the work of Lewis and others on the mechanism of nervous control emphasise the intimate inter-relation of nerve and soma. During the war French military authorities accepted a causal relationship between the environment of the front line and acute hyper-thyroidism (*Reports of the Proceedings of the Interallied Sanitary Conference, 1917*). But it has to be confessed that with a few exceptions these aetiological advances have far outstripped current nosological systems.

[32] An endeavour is made by the arrangement of the "groups," to emphasise the close relation between infective, physical, and psychic agents in the production of the general disease picture.

the scope of "preventive medicine" in the armies in the field or in camps of training, were the direct, or "acute" effects of the action of one or the other or of both of the two types of cause whose results are assembled in more directly-related groups and sub-groups ("classes" and "groups") of our Types III and IV. Within these are various morbid states which in text books and nosological tables are identified by particular names and in medical art and practice are commonly associated with a particular therapy and prophylaxis. These are shown in the tables hereunder as individual or closely related disease entities.[33]

Analysis of non-battle casualties in the A.I.F. in France and Flanders, April, 1916, to March, 1919, for Types III and IV, showing causes of admissions and percentages of totals admitted to field ambulances.

	Field Ambulance Admissions	Percentage of Total Admissions
Type III—Primary infections and infestations by living agents		
Class 6—Gastro-intestinal infections:		
Group 21—Enteric group of bacteria	73	0·03
22. Dysenteric group of bacteria	819	0·39
23. Infective diarrhoea and acute enterocolitis	605	0·29
24. Cholera	—	—
25. Brucella group	—	—
26. Food poisoning	59	0·03
27. Amoebiasis	2	—
	1,558	0·74
Class 7—Faucial and respiratory tract infections:		
28. Diphtheria	409	0·19
29. Acute tonsillitis	3,060	1·45
30. Scarlet fever	28	0·01
31. Cerebro-spinal fever	152	0·07
32. Lobar pneumonia	688	0·33
33. Broncho pneumonia	276	0·13
34. Pleurisy, including empyaema	1,617	0·76
35. Coryza, acute bronchitis, laryngitis	8,866	4·19
36. Whooping cough	—	—
37. Influenza	21,947	10·36

[33] As explained elsewhere (*Vol. III*) the figures though approximately correct are not absolute. Their tabulation, as will be obvious, is tentative. How much, *e.g.*, of the "bronchitis" was caused by cold or poison gas, and how much by "infection?" What proportion of "diarrhoea" was really "dysentery"? In what proportion were "nutrition" and "parasitic invasion"—the "physical" or the "infective" environments respectively—responsible for the efflorescence of various "diseases," is in some measure a matter of informed conjecture only. *But informed conjecture is still in a great measure the basis of preventive medicine.*

	Field Ambulance Admissions	Percentage of Total Admissions
Class 7—Faucial and respiratory tract infections (contd):		
Group 38. U.R.T. Infection	429	0·20
39. Measles and rubella	495	0·23
40. Mumps (epidemic parotitis)	3,332	1·57
	41,300	19·49
Class 8—The neurotropic ectodermoses:		
41. Variola	2	—
42. Vaccinia	5	—
43. Encephalitis lethargica	2	—
44. Polio-encephalitis	2	—
45. Herpetic diseases	343	0·16
	354	0·17
Class 9—Rheumatic fever:		
46. Rheumatic fever—acute	44	0·02
47. Rheumatic fever—chronic	195	0·09
	239	0·11
Class 10—Tuberculosis:		
48. Tuberculosis pulmonary	602	0·28
49. Tuberculosis—other forms	—	—
	602	0·28
Class 11—Specific muco-dermal infections:		
50. Anthrax, glanders, actinomycosis	—	—
Class 12—Infections of eye, ear, nose:		
51. Local infective diseases of the eye	325	0·15
52. „ „ „ of the ear	1,484	0·70
53. „ „ „ of the mouth	862	0·41
54. Other local infective diseases	—	—
	2,671	1·26
Class 13—"Septic" (pyogenic) infections:		
55. General septic infections	59	0·03
56. Local septic infections—Abscess etc.	5,727	2·70
57. "Inflammation of connective tissue" (I.C.T.)	6,102	2·88
	11,888	5·61
Class 14—The venereal infections:		
58. Syphilis—invasion	54	0·03
59. Gonorrhoea	884	0·42
60. Chancroid	—	—
61. Unspecified	12,167	5·74
	13,105	6·19

	Field Ambulance Admissions	Percentage of Total Admissions
Class 15—Diseases transmitted through an insect or other host:		
Group 62. Malaria (Mosquito)	228	0·11
63. Filaria (Mosquito)	2	—
64. Trench fever (Louse)	3,811	1·80
65. Typhus fever (Louse)	—	—
66. Relapsing fever (Louse)	—	—
67. Sandfly fever	—	—
68. Bilharzia (Snail)	2	—
69. Hydatid (Dog)	11	0·01
70. Jaundice infective (Rat, etc.)	190	0·09
71. Plague (Rat flea)	—	—
	4,244	2·01
Class 16—Helminthiasis (excluding hydatid disease):		
72. Gastro intestinal	43	0·02
73. Anchylostomiasis	—	—
	43	0·02
Class 17—Skin infestations:		
74. Pediculosis (specified)	316	0·15
75. Scabies	19,920	9·40
76. Fungi (Tinea etc.)	297	0·14
	20,533	9·69
Class 18—Specific wound infections:		
77. Tetanus	21	0·01
78. Others (detailed figures not recorded)	—	—
	21	0·01
Class 19—P.U.O. ("pyrexia of uncertain origin"):		
79. P.U.O.	24,593	11·61
	24,593	11·61
Total—Type III	121,151	57·19
Type IV—Psycho-physical factors (environment) and fatigue		
Class 20—Specific physical agents:		
80. Traumatic abrasions	7,567	3·57
81. Heat effects	49	0·02
82. Frost bite (dry cold)	474	0·22
83. "Trench feet" (wet, cold, dirt)	7,202	3·40
84. Acute gastritis (food, hardship, strain)	1,810	0·86
85. Acute diarrhoea (food, hardship, strain)	7,121	3·36
	24,223	11·43

	Field Ambulance Admissions	Percentage of Total Admissions
Class 21—Physiological hardship:		
Group 86. "Rheumatism" and acute arthritis	3,835	1·81
87. Rheumatoid arthritis	—	—
88. Fibrositis ("muscular rheumatism")	2,846	1·34
89. War nephritis and albuminuria	868	0·41
90. Broncho-nasal irritations and non-specific infections	1,397	0·66
91. Minor cardio-vascular dysfunctions	628	0·30
92. Primary symptom states (dropsy etc.)	12	0·01
	9,586	4·53
Class 22—Specific food defects and deficiencies:		
93. Avitaminosis	34	0·02
	34	0·02
Class 23—Acute endocrine dysfunctions:		
94. Toxic goitre (acute)	2	—
	2	—
Class 24—Psycho-physical exhaustion:		
95. D.A.H. and Effort Syndrome	1,211	0·57
96. Acute exhaustion etc.	1,090	0·52
97. "N.Y.D. Gas" (gas-effect syndrome)	490	0·23
	2,791	1·32
Total—Type IV	36,636	17·30
Grand Total	157,787	74·49

As a necessary preliminary to an examination of the measures taken for their prevention a brief excursus is made into the nosological composition of the several "classes" of related diseases comprised in the two broad types (III and IV) which we have identified as calling for study in these two chapters.

1. *Diseases Due to Living Agents.* (*Type III*). The "absolute" and specific nature of acute disease due to "infection," which makes it in great measure *sui generis,* and, as well, the extraordinary predominance of this factor in disease and decay over all others, save only the ebbing of the tide of life itself, derive from the fact that the individual external agents or "causes" themselves possess "vital" attributes, in particular the power of "reaction" and of adaptation to their environment; and that this quality breeds approximately true in each species and variety of organism concerned. It is this fact that makes it possible to classify most if not all diseases due to infection by the *causal agent* itself, rather

than by the *organic reaction* of the body thereto or the structural changes induced by it, or simply by the particular organ affected. This quality of specific determinism is in a great measure lacking in "autogenous" disorders and diseases, as thyrotoxicosis, hyper-piesia, diabetes, eczema; and in disease of a secondary and chronic type—as chronic lung disease and upper respiratory tract infection ("U.R.T.I."); or in chronic joint, cardio-vascular and renal diseases. The exclusion, from this "Type,"[84] of morbid states which though definitely infective in their origins were not due to the primary parasitic invasion, permits the identification of a direct relation between "cause" and "effect" and a simpler line of approach to the study of the practical problem of their prevention on the Western Front.

But it may again be impressed that in the war no more than in peace was the prevention of infectious diseases found to be a straightforward matter of "hygiene and sanitation." The experience of Gallipoli had suggested that infectious disease might not be altogether a matter of "infection"; and with barely a score of cases treated for mild symptoms of avitaminosis, the troops in France, at the end of 1917 were being urged, failing more orthodox sources of vitamin "C," to eat salads made from dandelion leaves.

It is possible further to lighten these chapters by excluding certain groups of related infections, for consideration more profitably or conveniently elsewhere.

Of the several "classes" of infectious diseases, Class 14, the *"venereal" diseases*, calls for a special chapter by reason both of its complex "causal" relations, immediate and remote, and not less its great military importance. *Virus influenza* also, as distinct from "influenza" caused by Pfeiffer's bacillus and other bacteria, is kept apart as being a special "Act of God" and not an authentic element in military preventive medicine. For the most part the diseases and disabilities brought together in Class 8 (the "neurotropic ectodermoses"),[85] 9 (*rheumatic fever*), 10 (*tuberculosis*), 11 (*specific muco-dermal infections*), 12 (*infections of eye, ear, nose*), and 16 (*helminthiasis*) were, in the field or camps of training, amenable only to "treatment" not to prophylaxis. The *prevention of specific wound infections* (18) belongs with the treatment of wounds. For the rest (a) Class 6 (*gastro-intestinal infections*), (b) Class 7 (*faucial and respiratory tract infections*), and (c) Classes 13, 15, and 17 (*"septic"—pyogenic—infections, infections transmitted through an insect or other host*, and *skin infestations*) provided respectively the material for the three lines of action which, in effect, on the Western

---

[84] The classification is based on the *mode of attack*—pathogenesis—rather than on clinical and pathological syndromes produced thereby; which, as in Tuberculosis, Syphilis, or Streptococcal infection, cover almost the whole gamut of general and local "diseases." The widespread practice of referring to pulmonary tuberculosis as "T.B." (tubercle bacillus) has more than a *soupçon* of philosophic verity behind it. "Tuberculosis" is first and foremost an infection with the tubercle bacillus, though such infection can produce "diseases" clinically as far apart as "phthisis," *tabes mesenterica*, miliary tuberculosis, or Addison's disease.

[85] This class, as defined by Levaditi, was adopted in *Vol. I* (1930) when our knowledge of human virus diseases was but slight; and is retained here for convenience. For similar reasons a "class" of diseases caused by the "viruses" was not made. Encephalitis Lethargica was discovered during the course of the war and a few cases occurred in the A.I.F., but it did not come within the scope of preventive medicine. (*See Vol. III.*)

Front and in camps in England comprised the whole gamut of the measures for preventing infectious diseases.

2. *Diseases Due to "Psycho-physical" Agencies (Type IV)*. It is a commonplace of experience that, apart from gross trauma, or associated infection, the direct morbific action of physical agents is as a rule readily resisted. It is by reason of this astonishing adaptability to physical environment that the human species has been able to occupy the earth from the equator to the poles, and the soldiers on the Western Front were able to retain a satisfactory, even a high degree of health. Of all the diseases grouped under the aetiological title *physical environment* only one, "trench foot" was of first-rate importance. Apart from this condition the total is inconspicuous as a direct cause of wastage in the field army. But the influence of adverse physical agencies in the production of "disease"—whether acute and primary, or chronic—is almost inextricably interwoven with their effect in predisposing the body or the tissues to the onslaught of potentially pathogenic micro-organisms. Few indeed of the "diseases" here included were unequivocally the result of "environment" alone.[36] And in many—perhaps in most—parasitic diseases, some adverse physical influence (using this term in the wider sense indicated above) is a necessary or an important adjunct to successful parasitic invasion, whether exogenous, as in typhoid and dysentery, or autogenous, as in pneumonia, bronchitis, or "I.C.T." This held true of a large part of the infective disease to the risk of which the soldiers were exposed. In only a few of the transmissible diseases—trench fever, influenza, mumps, measles, scabies—was natural resistance to the infective agent so defective that the physical environment as such had no influence on their incidence. In practice, indeed, the distinction between measures to eliminate the causes of disease, and those designed to promote resistance overlapped. Baths and laundries, delousing, housing, warming, food and cooking, and so forth had their part in a common "drive" to promote health, physical and mental, and so became an essential element in Army structure.

It was chiefly against the morbific agents comprised under these two "types" (III and IV) that the vast system of Army "sanitation," and the efforts that were "the duty of every officer and man" were directed. They comprised 77 groups of disease, and some 300 morbid entities recognised as distinct "diseases."[37] Happily all of these may be reduced to a comparatively small number, presently to be identified, that were of prime importance, actual or potential, on the Western Front. Furthermore, the paraphernalia of military "sanitation" may itself be summed up and considered under two lines of "preventive" action corresponding with the twofold constitution of disease, namely the *protective reaction in the organism* and the *morbific action of the agent.*

---

[36] Even "trench foot," by the Americans absolutely identified with "frost-bite," was by the French, for a time, as confidently ascribed to infection by a fungus!
[37] These will be dealt with under "Statistics of the War" in *Vol. III.*

ORGANISATION AND METHODS OF THE SANITARY SERVICE

Whatever the mode of operation of a "sanitary" service[38]—and whether for peace or for war—three essential elements enter into it—*administration, executive action*, and *scientific knowledge*.[39] In this trinity "none is before or after the other, none is greater or less than the other." The sanitary machinery of the various nations in arms in the Great War differed widely in structure yet all contained these three prime elements.

Sanitary Service of the B.E.F. The medical personnel in the British Army charged with the prevention of disease was in a great measure self-contained and charged with this specific duty. The structure of the military "sanitary" system may be conceived as an arch. Based on the heritage of scientific medicine, embodied in military manuals, establishments, standing orders, and so forth, and in various advisory committees, specialists, and research units (within and without the Army organisation), and in the Great War supported also by conferences and advisory bodies, national and "Interallied," the two pillars of the arch—administration, and executive—met in the *Regimental Medical Officer*, the keystone of the whole structure, whose person and "establishment" combined administrative, executive, and advisory functions.

This structural analogy may be stressed. In the evolution of preventive medicine in the Great War the work of this officer stands out predominant; the keynote in its history, and as well, perhaps its most important "lesson" to the civil profession.

The components of this arch may be set out as follows:—

REGIMENTAL ESTABLISHMENT
(Commanding Officer, R.M.O., and Q.M.)

Five water-duty men (A.A.M.C.)
Q.M's "pioneers" and "fatigues"
Regimental sanitary detachment
Regimental medical orderlies
Company orderly corporal
Regimental aid-post
The sick parade

Administrative Personnel
Division: A.D.M.S. (*per* D.A.D.M.S.)

Executive Units
Sanitary Sections; Field Ambulance tent divisions, and transport.

---

[38] The general structure of the Sanitary Service of the British Army has been described in *Vol. I, Chapter i.*
[39] This is nowise invalidated by the fact that these may be contained in a single unit or even individual.

508   THE WESTERN FRONT   [1914-18

Corps: D.D.M.S. (per *D.A.D.M.S.*)

Sanitary Sections if allocated to Corps; and medical units if specially employed.

Army: D.M.S. (per *"A.D.M.S. Sanitary"*)

Mobile Laboratories (Bacteriological and Hygienic); special stations for inf. diseases (C.C.S. and Stationary Hospitals); clerical record staff.

L. of C.: D.M.S. (per *D.A.D.M.S.*)

L. of C. Sanitary Services (sanitary squads, etc.); Stationary Hospitals for isolation; clerical record staff.

Expeditionary Bases: D.D.M.S. (per *D.A.D.M.S.*)

Bacteriological and Pathological Laboratories and special wards in General Hospitals; Sanitary squads.

G.H.Q., B.E.F.: D.G.M.S.[40] (*A.D.M.S. for Sanitation; Adviser in Bacteriology and Pathology; Medical Advisory Committee B.E.F.; delegates to Interallied Sanitary Commission; etc.*)

Special clerical staff; Research Laboratories.

War Office: D.G., A.M.S. (*special department and staff; civil advisers.*)

Research organisations—of the Medical Research Committee, Lister Institute, the R.A.M. College, etc.; diagnostic laboratories; special wards in general hospitals for "carriers" of and men recovered from dysentery, typhoid, C.S.F., etc.

---

[40] The general administration of health matters in the British Armies in France centred in Abbeville, the headquarters of the I.G.C. The following is from notes kindly supplied by Lieut.-Col. C. J. Martin, A.A.M.C., Consulting Pathologist to the A.I.F.:

"The policy of disease prevention in the B.E.F. was by that time (summer of 1917) being carried out on very commonsense and elastic lines. The official authorities were Col. Leishman as Adviser in Pathology, afterwards succeeded by Col. Cummins as Adviser in Pathology and Col. Beveridge as A.D.M.S. Sanitary. There was division of labour, in connection with infectious disease, between these two. Col. Beveridge had charge of water, food, sanitation in general, and personal hygiene; Leishman or Cummins, of specific infections, etc.

"In addition to these, there was organised in 1918 an Advisory Committee to the D.G.M.S. in France. This consisted of Col. Leishman or Cummins ("Adviser in Pathology") and Lieut.-Col. Beveridge ("A.D.M.S. for sanitation") permanent Army officials; Generals Rose Bradford, Herringham and Elliott (Consulting Physicians); Generals Bowlby and Cuthbert Wallace (Consulting Surgeons). This committee met fortnightly, presided over by D.G.M.S., B.E.F. and, aided by preliminary unofficial meetings and discussions between the members, was largely concerned in the policy of disease prevention in the British Force in France."

It may with propriety be added that Lieut.-Col. Martin himself regularly attended these meetings, and his opinions carried great weight. The policy in connection with dysentery was, indeed, largely based on work carried out by him at Rouen.

1914-18] PREVENTIVE MEDICINE—THE FACTORS 509

Thus, at each level of army organisation from the War Office to the field unit, preventive medicine was represented by special "sanitary" officers, and by special executive units and personnel, for scavenging and conservancy, for diagnosis, and transport, for special accommodation and so forth. The whole constituted, with the other services of maintenance and the combatant units, a health system complete in itself; both for each executive level —division, corps, army, L. of C., Base, and Home—and also, in continuity, from the front line back to the United Kingdom.

Throughout the system the operation of preventive medicine—in Army terms "sanitation"—was based more and more exactly as the war progressed on co-operation between the medical services and the combatant branches. This co-operation involved, first, the services of maintenance other than the medical, in particular the Quartermaster-General's branch; second, the combatant command and the individual soldier. The elements in this co-operation can be summarised as follows:—

The keynote—co-operation

Of Medical Department and Q.M.G.'s Branch. The executive as distinct from the advisory responsibilities of the medical service were subject in the Great War to an evolution that is of great interest, both military and general. The trend of this evolution was to *delegate to the Quartermaster General's Branch and to Commanding Officers of combatant units* the executive responsibility for most of the measures available for preventing or minimising the immense mass of unfitness comprised in "personal hygiene." To the *medical service* were left the function of scientific initiative and advice, and executive procedures—such as the testing of water supplies, chlorination, and disinfection—whose due performance required a sanitary conscience developed by special knowledge and training to a professional standard of precision.

Sanitary Discipline. The *Manual of Elementary Military Hygiene, 1912*, laid down (*pp. 3-4*) that "Successful prevention of disease demands the co-operation of every individual, whether officer or man . . . this fact has not always been realised, an idea prevailing that it is a matter for the medical service and for it alone. Such a view . . . cannot be too strongly combated."

The development in the A.I.F. and the British Army of sanitary discipline and a sanitary "conscience," has been referred to from time to time in this history. It was an evolution continuous throughout the war. At first, of necessity, the Medical Service of the A.I.F., like the force as a whole, took its cues like its orders from the British, and, in its sick rate, for a time, floundered behind the formations of the British Army. But in this matter of health its eyes were opened by the Somme winter, as in fighting they had been by the Somme battles. In the matter of health, as in warfare, the force evolved a discipline and methods of its own, the chief characteristic of which was an intelligent appreciation of the end in view. By the end of the war, indeed, any report reflecting on the sanitary discipline of a unit was resented only less than if it had concerned its military efficiency.[41]

It may be doubted indeed whether any single factor was of greater practical importance in preventing wastage from disease than the implementing, in organisation as in discipline, in command as in obedience, of the relevant paragraphs of *Field Service Regulations*. The holocaust of battle-casualties in the Great War and the need to sustain the front resulted in this duty of "every officer and man" being made effective by a discipline that did indeed control every officer and every man, from the Commander-in-Chief downwards; and by dispositions and provisions that made "sanitary discipline" an element in military strategy.[42]

Such, in bare outline, were the scope of the problem and the two pillars of military-medical hierarchy, administrative and executive, that sustained the work. We must now consider the lines on which they did so.

An eminent British sanitarian, distinguished for his work alike in the war and in the subsequent peace[43] has defined the objective in preventive medicine as follows:—

Objectives—
health
promotion,
disease
prevention

"From its earliest beginnings, organised public health has run general and special measures in harness. However much action to secure the better general health and physical fitness of a population, and all that this implies may signify, there are always diseases the prevalence of which is little affected by the possession of a high standard of general, or even of individual healthiness."

The "general" and "special" lines of action suggested herein may more exactly be defined as comprising respectively (a) measures designed to accentuate the natural resistance to morbid agents by improving general health and vitality, physical and

---

[41] Thus in August, 1918, the O.C. of a sanitary section reported a battalion for breaches of sanitary discipline. The battalion commander is up in arms, and "in justice and fairness to officers and other ranks of this unit" desires "full details." From brigade the matter goes on to division, and thence to Australian Corps Headquarters. And while it appears that the report had been somewhat severe, the corps commander justifies the enquiry, and closes the episode with the minute—"It is exceptional to find infantry battalions reported, and the corps commander considers it discreditable when this occurs." As a contrast see *Vol. I, pp. 229-30*.

[42] A decision by the Commander-in-Chief to make a tactical or even strategic expenditure of health and morale (*e.g.* in the winter fighting on the Somme) is as clearly his prerogative and as much an element in the calculations of his general staff as the sacrifice of lives in battle; and the far greater immediate (though mainly temporary) wastage from disease than from battle-casualty made it a potential weapon in attrition.

[43] Sir George S. Buchanan; Presidential address to the Public Health Section at the Annual Meeting of the British Medical Association, 1931 (*B.M.J. 15 Aug., 1931*). Sir George played a leading part in the Interallied Sanitary Conferences during the war and later in creating and organising the Health Committee of the League of Nations, of which he was Vice-President.

mental, augmenting physical and moral efficiency and in particular combating the effects of deleterious physical and psychic factors in the environment, in other words—*promotion of health* —and (*b*) action taken against the causal agents of various diseases or groups of disease, or against their carriers—that is —*prevention of disease.*

These correspond closely with the constitution of the military machinery for maintaining health; and also with the broad lines of action that in their conjunction made up "preventive medicine" on the Western Front. To these two main lines of action, however, there was added a third—*prophylaxis by treatment*; and before discussing the chief measures, this may be dealt with summarily.

The dividing line between a bacterial "invasion" or a physical "disorder," and a full-fledged "disease," is hardly more susceptible to pathogenic discrimination than is the term "disease" to scientific definition. But it is proverbial—the "stitch in time"—that in much potential disease and disablement a space of time and a stage of morbid action presents in which nature, or the medical art, may intervene to remove or neutralise a potential cause of disabling disease. This line of approach to prophylaxis was much exploited in the war, and was found well worth while. The machinery involved in applying it at the front has been described in *Chapter XI*, but a note of its objective is appropriate here.

Prophylaxis by treatment

Prophylactic treatment presents itself in two aspects, the reflection respectively of the two major interests of military medicine, namely, from the point of view of *wastage in the field,* and from that of *post-war pension claims.* The prophylactic treatment, medical and surgical, that more directly influenced pension claims was that carried out in the hospitals, in No. 2 Command Depot, and on the transports, to prevent the onset in men already seriously damaged by wounds or disease, of irremediable deformity or disablement or irreversible disorder, physical or psychic. The consideration of this belongs to the next volume.

In the field the variety of conditions susceptible to prophylactic treatment was considerable. Among these may be instanced irritation and infection of the respiratory tract; superficial abrasions and minor pyogenic infections; pediculoses and other infestations of the skin; the minor degrees of "trench foot" and so forth; and acute physical and psychic exhaustion. In the case of two of the most important groups of diseases met with in the Great War—namely (1) those caused by psychic contagion (*i.e.* "suggestion"), such as the majority of "N.Y.D.N." and "N.Y.D. Gas," and (2) the venereal contagions ——prophylactic (*i.e.* "abortive") treatment in special clinics was in the A.I.F. the dominating feature in the medical campaign.

SYNOPSIS FOR CHAPTER XVIII

PREVENTIVE MEDICINE IN THE WAR—(II) THE PROMOTION OF HEALTH:
Environment—the Western Front.
Winter warfare in France.
Specific problems of health promotion.
Food and feeding.
    The Army ration—"Supply"—Schools for cooks—Distribution of food.
Housing and warmth.
Clothing and equipment.
    Items of clothing—material.
    Influence of clothing on health.
        The uniform—The puttee—The "Australian pattern" boot—The sock.
    Equipment—the problem of weight.
        Relation to physique—"Web equipment."
Other factors in health promotion.
    Care of feet and chiropody.
    Psycho-physical factors.
    Rest and sleep.
        Alcohol—The "Rum" ration—Use and abuse.
    The rational factor: education.
    Psychic amenities.

CHAPTER XVIII

PREVENTIVE MEDICINE IN THE WAR—(II) THE PROMOTION OF HEALTH

IT has been well said that

"Health at its best—for it is a variable state of being—is that condition of body in which all its organs and parts are sound and perform their functions duly, easily, and satisfactorily."[1]

With certain obvious reservations and corrections, measures for the promotion of health were applicable mainly to disease due directly or indirectly to pathogenic elements in the physical —as distinct from the parasitic—environment.

No question in relation to the health of the A.I.F. has been debated more persistently or more bitterly than this:—were there present in the Australian soldier's war experience, especially on the Western Front, physical factors that in themselves might legitimately be held to have initiated, immediately or remotely, a large body of permanent ill-health, or to have "aggravated" any existing tendency to disease? Such hypothetical disease states would doubtless include various forms of disability that reflected physiological or psychic dysfunction *per se*; "*morbi sine materia*," diseases without a lesion —causing disability but without structural change and capable of complete reversion or resolution. But it might well be supposed that they would also include many in which a permanent and irreversible degradation of function would ensue, with subsequent permanent degeneration of essential tissue cells and so of organs. To what extent, it is being asked with increasing urgency, can the effects of physical war environment be sup-

Environment— the Western Front

---

[1] Maj. Gen. Sir Robert McCarrison, "Nutrition in Health and Disease," in *B.M.J.*, 26 Sept., 1936, p. 611.

posed to have influenced the course of physical and mental senescence in the returned soldier?[2]

In the present state of our knowledge of the "causes" of disease other than by infection, and in the absence of exact data bearing on the matter in A.I.F. experience, it is impossible to give a clear answer to this important question. As will be seen later[3] the professional men responsible for deciding on questions of "attribution" or "aggravation" have found it necessary to rely almost wholly on a continuous personal history or on convincing *prima facie* evidence. Nevertheless, it would be unscientific to attempt to appreciate the problems in preventive medicine presented by the attrition warfare in Europe, or in the health history of the A.I.F. during and after the war without giving due weight to the effects of physical environment.

And while it is not possible to present an authentic picture of every element in this environment, one aspect may be selected as characteristic and a likely source of dysfunction and even of "disease." The following presents an accurate, if perhaps extreme, illustration of the front line in France in winter.

End of October, 1916. "'Wait till you get on the Somme,' said men who had been through Pozières. 'The rest is a joke.'... We left the motor lorries and entered the squalid village of Dernancourt.

Winter warfare in France
Here was the edge of the zone of death, newer and fiercer than Ypres. Out of Dernancourt we walked along a road deep in mud. 'Fricourt' was a notice on a signpost. Here for the first time I saw the appalling waste of modern war—stacks of bombs sinking into the mud—all man-

---
[2] The question is well presented in the following extract from a personal letter to the Medical Historian from the Medical Officer to an important municipal body—who was also the "Principal Medical Officer" of one of the Commonwealth Military Districts (Col. E. S. Stokes):—

"The question of the relationship of respiratory diseases, especially Bronchitis and Pneumonia, to exposure of the body to cold and wet, has recently arisen here in connection with some compensation cases. It has been contended that this morbid condition may be caused by such external influences, or, as an alternative, that these influences may aggravate the disease if the exposure occurs at any time, whether immediately before the receipt of infection, during the incubation period, or after the onset of symptoms. It has been further claimed that if such exposure was not the exciting cause, then it operated as a predisposing cause by establishing a lowered resistance of the body to invasion by the attacking organisms.

"War time experiences, where bodies of men have been exposed to extreme conditions of hunger, fatigue, wet and cold, either singly or in combination, have been quoted, and seem to shew that men under such circumstances do not suffer to a greater degree than others more fortunately placed."

[3] Under Pensions, in *Vol. III*.

ner of abandoned munitions. We debouched into a field of soft mud, and erected bivouacs, and there in rain and wind, we slept. . . . Next evening on our way again through an avenue of dead horses, mules, and wrecked wagons. No trees remained standing—only signs of death, more and more numerous as we went forward. Off the road on each side was a morass. Here was desolation beyond all compare. In the darkness our strung out line of heavily laden men trudged along the duckboards, great shell craters, water filled, below us . . . night and rain could not mask the stench that told its tale. The wood [Delville Wood] petered out on the forward slope—the duckboards ended at the edge of the valley. We plunged into mud from knee to waist deep churned to the consistency of pea-soup. . . . Here were our 18-pounders, emplaced against the further bank [which was] lined with dugouts. Fitful gleams of candle-light crept from the blanket-hung entrances. . . . [On again] with terrific effort we ploughed through the morass; our troubles were commencing. The front line was about three miles away, it took us seven hours of constant struggle to reach it. Shell craters on shell craters. Water filled them to varying depths. The pulverised soaked earth made every step a supreme effort. No two steps were ever on the same level. We fell, rose and fell again, soaked to our very hides. Every hundred yards or so, strength failed, as we tried to extricate a deep sunk leg. Then we would collapse and lie inert in the soft mud. Our sweaty faces would become cold in the chilly wind and wet clothes press icy against our skins. With a despairing effort we would rise and battle on. The slough of despond! I fought hard against an impulse to burst into childish tears. Hour after hour we struggled automatically. Later,[4] duckboards spanned this country in curving miles; but we unfortunates had no help. . . .

"At length we reeled and tottered into derelict shattered Flers. The shell-bitten road, a foot deep in slime, was grateful to our trembling legs. Again the muddied burdened line was moving ghostlike in the night. Sucking squelching noises of mud underfoot. The flares were much nearer now. . . . We blundered into the forsaken confines of Cheese Road. A narrow sap led to the front line. The churned mud was knee-deep. In places the arms and legs of dead men protruded, ghastly in the light of the flares. Where two men tried to pass they jammed. About 300 yards forward we came to an old German gunpit. A deep dugout ran down at the side. Fritz's Folly, just beyond, was occupied by the enemy. We stood on a plank track, waiting our turn to go down. A German flare hissed at us, and hung overhead. On its heels came a shell that burst redly on the bank. The shock toppled five of us into the mud alongside. I sank swiftly to my waist and was held firm. A roar of other approaching shells filled the air. . . . Squalls of metal ripped and thudded. I pressed the upper part of my body close along the mud. This then was the culmination of all my fears. I lay helpless and passive beneath the hot hail, picturing myself as those others we had seen. Red hot panic and cold clammy fear possessed me alternately. The shells ceased. . . . I groped for my rifle and reached the boards again. A board was laid out to the other four, and their heads were pulled clear of mud. Three were dead."[5]

---

[4] That is, in later months.

[5] The quotation is from *Backs to the Wall* pp. 12-18 (slightly abbreviated) by Captain G. D. Mitchell, M.C., D.C.M., 10th and 48th Battalions. (At this time he was serving in the ranks.) This experience may be contrasted with the experiences of the Light Horse related in *Vol. I* pp. 698-9—"Summer in the Jordan Valley."

In this account we can identify as conspicuous, physical exhaustion, exposure to cold, and wet, and dirt; strong and unrelieved emotion, and nutritional deficiency. This picture of a relief should be complemented by one of trench life and the struggle to keep dry and to get warm food; of the cheerless huts of the staging camp, and the long march of the relieved unit to the rest area, and back. It should be offset, by an account of the very successful efforts made to ameliorate the conditions of life and living: of food and feeding; of housing; of warmth and comfort; of clothing and cleanliness; of roads, transport, and reliefs; and (far from least) of psychic relaxation—leaves, amusement, sports, recreation, provided as part of the military machinery for preventing wastage or that of humane and patriotic bodies—Comforts Fund, Y.M.C.A., Red Cross, and the like.

All of these, in their sum, made up the vast machinery for promoting health in the interest of victory, and, perhaps, of humanity.[6] Stated in terms of scientific analysis their purpose was to promote and exploit the natural resistance to injury contained in the defensive mechanism of the body; whether *structural*, such as the skin, hair, cilia, mucous glands and so forth; or the self-adjusting *functional constitution* (*"milieu intérieur"*), such as the heat- and energy-regulating mechanisms; nutrition; immunity reactions; endocrine balance; basal (thalamic) nervous control; cortical inhibitions and sublimations, as of fear and sex; and the power of rational deduction from experience (educability)—and so forth.

No more is possible than to glance at this vast structure of social health activities built up behind the entrenched lines to implement the strategy of attrition. Nor is a serious study possible of the effect on this of the change to open warfare in 1918. The whole procedure of promoting health merges with the normal process of modern war. No more can be done than to select a few features for a suggestive note, as salient in the matter of health, or as pertinent to A.I.F. history.

---

[6] The environment of the Western Front, and the diseases associated with it as shown in the tables, may profitably be compared with those described in *Vol. I* of Gallipoli (*Part I Chapter xii*); Sinai (*Part II Chapter iv*), and Palestine (*Part II Chapter x*).

Two sets of factors were involved, those of material and those of action; thus:—*Food and feeding*—the ration, and its supply, preparation, cooking, and distribution.

Specific problems of health promotion

Protection and warmth—as by housing, heating, clothing, footwear. *Minor bodily repairs, and cleaning*—as by first aid for minor ailments, dental repair, care of feet, skin, and teeth, provision of underwear, washing, disinfection. *Rest and recuperation*—as by sleep, relief, relaxation. *Mental and moral tonics and anodynes*—such as entertainments, recreation, sports, leaves, alcohol. *Education*—as in schools of instruction, lectures, and so forth. *Spiritual ministrations*.[7]

The mere list of those with special medical interest suggests the vast expenditure of capital and labour, of time, constructive thought, administrative energy, and executive toil, involved in sustaining a major war.[8]

"He[9] sent out, in an unbelievably short time, the most perfectly equipped army that has ever taken the field. . . . Having sent forth this matchless little band of 100,000 men, he watched it grow day by day till it numbered some four millions. He watched it spread over . . . half the world, and for long harassed years he kept it fed, clothed and transported it, as no other army has ever been cared for in the history of the world."

Food and feeding

For the first time in the modern history of the world the problem of national food supplies was in the Great War a major factor in the international conflict. For the Allies, from 1916 food was an urgent problem, at the end of 1917 a menacing one. But though rationing in Britain, France, and Italy was much more drastic than Australians have ever troubled themselves to appreciate, it did not approach that which sapped the morale of the German people, and in Austria-Hungary brought about in children a degree of malnutrition for which a parallel must be sought in the wars of the Middle Ages—or in the industrial era of Great Britain.[10]

---

[7] Most of these have been the subject of some comment in *Vol. I* (*See index*). Only a cursory note can be permitted here.
[8] It may be recalled that the field armies of the nations involved in the Great War, for which some provision of the kinds mentioned was made are estimated at a total of over 50 million men.
[9] Sir John Cowans, throughout the war the British Quartermaster-General. From biography by Major Desmond Chapman-Huston and Major Owen Rutter, *Vol. I*, p. 288.
[10] *See Vol. I, pp. 465-6.*

A dietician of world-wide repute has said that "A primary purpose of the function of nutrition is to prevent, so far as its limitations permit, that disturbance or impairment of structure or function of organs or parts of the body which is disease."[11] It is relevant to the question of the influence of the war on health, and it is significant also for the future of warfare that, though civil communities might starve, by neither side was the ration of the soldier permitted to pass below the level of caloric adequacy. In the British Army indeed the ration was for a time based on an estimate of caloric requirements much in excess of that laid down as necessary in civil occupations.

The Army Ration.[12] In a discussion in the "Interallied Sanitary Conference," held in March of 1918, on the supply of foodstuffs available to the Allies, remarkable differences were disclosed in the Army rations of the various nations, in respect both to their "caloric values," and also in the relative proportions of proteins, carbohydrates, and fats.[13] National habits made any exact pooling of resources a very difficult matter. At this time (it may be recalled), though the place in nutrition of proteins, carbohydrates, and fats "was fairly well understood," speaking broadly "food value" meant "calories," as estimated chiefly on Atwater and Bryant's "tables,"[14] and nutritional requirements were provided for accordingly.

But by the second year of the war the impact of experience in Gallipoli and Mesopotamia, and the intellectual pressure of the new outlook on "nutrition," created by the pre-war discoveries and work of Eijkman, Gowland Hopkins, Casimir Funk, McCarrison, Chick, and a host of others, had begun to influence British Army outlook and practice. For the first time an exact investigation was made of the vitamin content of preserved and portable foodstuffs. It is not necessary to

---

[11] Maj.-Gen. Sir Robert McCarrison, "Nutrition in Health and Disease," *B.M.J., 26th Sept., 1936 p. 611.* For an authoritative opinion on the place of nutrition in the promotion of the public health in Australia *see Vol. III* in connection with recruiting in Australia.

[12] For Gallipoli ration, *see Vol. I, p. 242.*

[13] The Italian Army ration was stated to contain "3,303 calories with, and 3,087 without potatoes." The calorie value of the Japanese war ration was given as 3,206, 80 per cent. of which was obtained from rice. The average weight of the Japanese soldier was 57 kilograms (9 stone).

[14] An authoritative series of analyses had long been required, and the need became urgent during the war, when the army, in common with other sections of the community, was strictly rationed in 1917. Capt. R. H. Plimmer of the University of London, a recognised authority on analytical technique, was directed to make a series of analyses for the use of the army medical authorities. Until Capt. Plimmer's figures were available, the calculations of energy values appear to have been made by using those tables and figures given in a Report by the Royal Society on the Food Supply of the United Kingdom, and supplemented by analyses carried out in the Royal Army Medical College. The aim in the new investigation was to arrive at an average for each group of foodstuffs. The energy value for the analyses of protein, carbohydrates, and fat was calculated by multiplication with the usual physiological factors, namely, 4·1, 4·1, 9·3 respectively. An original feature of this important research (reflected in present-day teaching on food and feeding which is concerned with the *available* rather than the *total* units of food value) was the discrimination of the various elements in the crude foodstuffs. Thus, in the case of meat, the joints were separated into fat and skin and flesh and the proportion determined, and the proportion of the joints of the carcass also ascertained, so that the composition of any part and ultimately of the whole animal could be arrived at. The analyses numbered about 900. A full report of Capt. Plimmer's work was published in book form by the War Office in 1921. (The data here given are from the *Official History of the War: Medical Services, Hygiene, Vol. II, pp. 1-2,* and from Plimmer's work).

follow the effect of this impetus on the army rationing, nor of war experience on the scientific study of nutrition. In both it was profound.[15] In the B.E.F. the influence of the new outlook in dietetics was seen chiefly in an extension of the facilities given to the Director of Supplies for supplementing the "hard" army ration by "local purchase" of foodstuffs, in particular, of vegetables. Indeed, the "lesson of the war" in respect to nutrition would seem to be this, that reliance should be placed not only, or even chiefly, on providing artificially concentrated individual vitamins, but rather upon disseminating widely the knowledge of the sources and values in essential constituents of every type of foodstuff and upon elasticity in the arrangements for exploiting every available source.

In 1917 a great advance was made in the rationing by differentiating three classes of rationed persons, namely, the fighting troops, 4,200 calories, 130-150 grammes of protein; the troops in the Line of Communications, 3,570 calories, 120 grammes of protein; and the civil population at Home.

"*Supply.*" "Supply" was organised on highly scientific lines—the caloric value of foodstuffs being made the basis of rationing. This was implemented by a scheme whereby the Quartermaster of each unit made his "demand" on the divisional Supply Column for the "alternative" issues provided for in the army ration in terms of their "calorie values," and the Company cook made his complaint of deficiency in the same terms.

Schools for Cooks. One of the major advances in the feeding of the soldier was in the education and assistance given to the Company cook. In the winter of 1917-18, especially, schools for cooks were held in every division of the A.I.F. and ingenious recipes were devised for palatable dishes from the "hard" army ration. Field ovens for roasting the fresh meat ration (so as to displace the universal stew) were in general use.[16] The enormous extension of treatment in the field in "rest stations" (field ambulance or C.C.S.) made the position of the quartermaster in these units one of the most onerous and responsible in the medical service. Many of these positions were filled by members of the Australian Instructional Staff, and the high quality of the work of these officers—and it must be added of the cooks—is the subject of frequent comment by commanding officers.

Distribution of Food. The close relation between the problems of supply and of distribution does not require emphasis; in the attrition warfare of 1916-17 the distribution of food was a problem of major military importance. The introduction in the winter of 1916-17 of insulated hot-food containers had a military significance only less decisive than that of the "Mills bomb" or of poison gas.

[15] Reference may be made to the Presidential Address by Sir Robert McCarrison inaugurating the new Section of "Nutrition" in the annual meeting of the B.M.A. held at Oxford in 1936 (*B.M.J.*, 26 *Sept.*, 1936). ' See also *Vol. I, pp.* 462-5—work of the Lister Institute, observations at No. 3 A.G.H. at Lemnos, and experience in the Palestine campaign.

[16] Portable ovens for roasting were carried by most field ambulances in addition to the official "Soyer"—originally designed for Miss Florence Nightingale, by M. Soyer, the celebrated London *chef* who accompanied her to the Crimea. C.C.S's carried a complete cooking range. In the general hospitals the designing of kitchens and their relation to the wards were given close attention—in some more than 2,000 patients and personnel had to be served from a central kitchen.

In civil life housing serves many purposes, but for the soldier at the front, speaking broadly, only one—to give shelter from "the elements." For the "private" soldier "privacy" was non-existent; the "latrine" like the cook-house was a social resort. At "the front," to the primitive purpose of shelter from heat, cold, and wet was added protection from missiles of war and from gas; in the rear that from aeroplane bombs. The problem of "housing" thus merges insensibly with defence.

Housing and warmth

Housing as a Factor in "Wastage." From the point of view of the medical service the problem of housing presents two aspects which may very exactly be summed as serving respectively the prevention of casualties—battle and non-battle—and the treatment of casualties. Here we are concerned with the first, *i.e.* with "housing" as a factor in the prevention of wastage. The matter of accommodation for treatment of casualties on the line of evacuation from aid-post to base hospital is dealt with elsewhere.

Under this reference housing therefore starts at the front line with the *"trench,"* trench *"bay,"* and *"splinter-proof" shelter*. Immediately behind this—in the attrition warfare of 1916-17—was a vast system of *"deep dugouts"* where the front line troops lived; and a mile or so in rear the dugouts and concealed and *sandbagged* shelters, often of *"elephant iron,"* which held the battalion reserves. Thence through the sandbagged *"Nissen"* huts and ruins that sheltered the Divisional reserves we move back to the several "approach" and "staging" zones of the Corps and Army reliefs, and reinforcements, where the relieved and relieving formations sheltered in *hutments* and *tents*, sometimes camouflaged, and more or less broken buildings; and so to the *billeting villages* and *hutted camps* of the resting areas. Behind the Army areas, on the L. of C., and at the Base and at home, were the vast tent and hutted camps of the Reinforcement and Convalescent Depots, and the General Hospitals.[17]

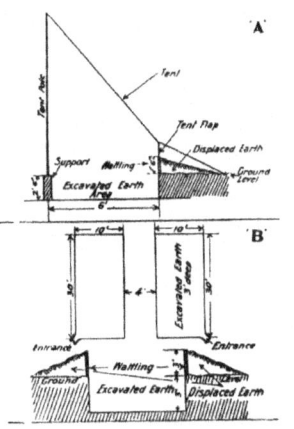

Methods of protection against shell and bomb splinters adopted by field ambulances (A) for bell and marquee tents; (B) for horse lines. (From war diary of 12th Aust. Field Ambulance.)

Save for its own personnel the medical service was not directly concerned in all this, however deeply it might be involved indirectly. How-

---
[17] An account of the problem of housing, from the point of view of the prevention of disease will be found in *Appendix No. 11*.

ever greatly protection might appeal as a means for the prevention of wastage from wounds, or from disease due to exposure, and as a rational line of endeavour, its concern was solely with the wasteful business of evacuation and repair.[18] The prevention of battle-casualties belonged to "G"; the housing of the soldier to "Q"; in each case the executive service was provided by the Engineers. Only in the matter of over-crowding and arrangement of bunks in the huts of the great depot camps at the seat of war and at the home base could its advice carry weight as against "the exigencies of the military situation." Yet it is not open to question but that in the circumstances of the war on the Western Front, as described in preceding pages of this and of *Chapter V* expenditure of money and energy on this—as on other matters of "maintenance"—"paid" in terms of efficient man-power and thus of "striking power." At any rate the construction of dugouts, huts, and shelters cannot but be regarded as a matter of first rate medical importance.

Warmth.—Closely allied with, and complementary to this matter of housing was that of providing artificial warmth, as by fuel stoves and hot food; and this again was allied with the promotion and protection of body heat as by food, clothes and blankets. This was a matter whose importance from a health standpoint comes second only to that of nutrition, and after nutrition, it was the chief preoccupation of the Q.M.G. The medical service lent a hand only when its advice was sought. Officially initiative lay first with the Command and the General Staff through the Adjutant-General's branch; but in practice close and immediate *liaison* with "Q" was found materially to promote their common purpose.

It is not possible to enter upon any detailed account of the vast business of providing warmth. By far the most important was the provision for hot food and drinks to which reference has already been made. The matter of clothing is dealt with later. The immense business of heating stoves calls only for two notes. First, to conserve heat, a "central" type of heating was essential.[19] Second, the business of *drying of clothes* was only less insistent than that of warming premises. The provision of drying huts for socks was an essential item in the prophylaxis of trench feet. Behind the front lines the heat from incinerators was sometimes made to serve a dual purpose.

Clothing and equipment

For men as they are to-day, clothing is necessary for protection against heat, cold, and physical trauma. To keep clean calls for washable underclothing.[20] And the soldier must carry a kit. In the field army each of these elemental factors had medical

---

[18] In the opinion of the writer it is gravely open to question whether, in the vast preparations for the "totalitarian warfare" foretold for the future, action would not with greater profit be directed more seriously than at present seems popular to the preventing of civilian casualties from H.E. as against preparations for their disposal and treatment.

[19] The fuel ration in the Australian Corps for both cooking and warmth was, in summer, at the rate of 1½ lb. of coal, 2½ lb. of wood; in winter 2½ lb. coal, 1½ lb. wood per man per day. In case of "shortage," preference was given to medical units. Solidified alcohol, for use in "Tommy's Cookers," was issued to troops in the trenches at the rate of 12,000 oz. weekly per division.

[20] The invention of the cotton gin ranks very high among the social factors that have helped to suppress scabies, lice, and fungoid skin disease.

involvements. Thus, the weight of the soldier's "kit" or "equipment" and the manner of its distribution to suit the erect posture might be expected to influence the development of circulatory and respiratory disorders; or of traumatic degeneration such as "osteo-arthritis," or "rheumatism," in the joint-structures of knee, spine and feet; or the incidence of non-septic traumatic inflammations such as fibrositis—"muscular rheumatism." All these conditions were so prominent during and after the war that it is difficult to exonerate equipment as a factor in the production of war-disability. The malign influence of unsuitable clothing—for example, of the puttee in producing trench foot—the advantage of washable underclothes in preventing the disease of dirt, the part played by the boot in the prevalence of or freedom from foot trouble, illustrate the direct concern to the medical service in this matter.

Items of Clothing. The clothes of the Australian infantry soldier comprised eight items as follows:—

(1) *Uniform*: tunic—known officially as "jacket, service dress"—of a soft woollen khaki-coloured cloth, with collar hooking at the neck; and cord breeches. As well as warmth and covering the military "uniform" gave the soldier the right to carry arms and to kill men.

(2) *Shirt*: soft grey flannel, without a collar, for warmth and "comfort."

(3) *Underclothes*: vest and drawers of cotton, or wool and cotton, and washable. Beside the minor purpose of preventing "body odour" these were a major rampart against skin disease.

(4) *Puttees*: These covered the leg below the knee with a winding spiral of woollen cloth. Their purpose was aesthetic—to complete the hiatus below the knee-breeches—and protective against cold and traumatic abrasion.

(5) *Boots*: bark-tanned leather (sole) and chrome-tanned (uppers). They were a factor of major importance in the efficiency of the foot-soldier. The artificial "aesthetic" kinks of civil "fashion" had very detrimentally influenced their structure.

(6) *Socks*: wool, cotton, or preferably mixed. These served the dual purpose of protection against traumatic abrasion and cold. As a washable article of underwear they were not only preventive of smell but prophylactic against *tinea albiginia* ("foot rot," athlete's foot, beach foot, soft corns, and so forth).

(7) *Greatcoat*: woollen, though officers usually provided themselves with a waterproof "trench-coat." The soldier's chief protection against cold and wet in the trenches; and, in moving warfare, often his only bedding. It was commonly carried in the "pack."

(8) *Hat*: behind the lines, Australian felt hat and a peaked woollen cap. In the line the "tin-hat" for protection chiefly against shrapnel.

The blankets and a rubber ground-sheet were sometimes carried on the "pack," but when possible by G.S. Waggon. In winter a special type of ground-sheet was issued which could be worn as a cape. For winter wear the Australian soldier was supplied from home with a lamb's wool jerkin to be worn in addition to the uniform. Balaclava caps, protecting the ears in the cold, were always, and in France mittens were often, part of the soldier's kit. The greatcoat, jacket, and shirt were made of the fine merino wool, in the production of which Australia leads the world.

The scope of this work does not permit of detailed study of the problems involved.[21] The following points, however, may be noted.

The Uniform. The Australian uniform is described in *Volume XI* of the *Australian Official History*.[22] The jacket was loose in body, neck, and sleeve, buttoned at the cuff. The breeches, on the other hand, were of riding pattern and gripped the leg below the knee—a feature which was not utilitarian, at least for infantry soldiers. The procedure of dis-infestation of underclothing, exchange and laundry—is also dealt with later. The average life of underwear was short so that provision had to be made for its frequent re-issue.

Influence of clothing on health

The Puttee. The weak point in this awkward piece of the soldier's clothing was revealed in the Somme winter when, as a prophylactic against trench foot the substitution, while in the line, of sandbags tied around the lower leg was officially recommended.

The "Australian Pattern" Boot. This boot as made in Australia was the subject during the war of a vigorous triangular debate between the Imperial authorities (War Office) who paid for the boots,[23] the Australian Government (Defence Department) which supplied most of them, and the Australian force in the field, which was shod with them.

Beginning in June, 1916, the controversy was still "going strong" in 1919. The chief points at issue concerned (*a*) durability, and ability to exclude wet; (*b*) Australian production; (*c*) comfort for general wear and marching, and appearance. All were of first rate importance but the question of most interest here is that of "fit." The problem of "fit" was largely due to the fact that, apart from congenital deformity, modern taste, dictated by the fashion makers, had caused the "normal" adult Australian foot to be commonly a deformed foot, and in adult males, unfortunately for military purposes, the degree of deformity varied greatly.

In this matter of foot-wear, as in "orthopaedics" generally, before

---

[21] Some are dealt with in *Vol. III.*

[22] It is of interest to note that Surgeon-Gen. W.D.C. Williams, A.A.M.S. "Director-General of Medical Services and Commonwealth Cadets," Australian Military Forces, 1906-11, took a leading part in the evolution of the Australian service jacket from the "shirt" with pockets designed for the "cadets" and worn also by the Citizen Force trainees.

[23] Under the agreement with the Australian Commonwealth whereby the British Government maintained the Australian Force in the field on payment of an agreed amount per head. *See pp. 826-7 and Vol. I pp. 44 and 57.*

58. A HUTTED CAMP AT DICKEBUSCH, NEAR YPRES
The huts are of the "Nissen Bow" type.

*Aust. War Memorial Official Photo. No. E1380a.
Taken on 15 November 1917.*

59. A COMPANY COOK-HOUSE OF THE 2ND BATTALION, YPRES, NOVEMBER, 1917

Aust. War Memorial Official Photo. No. E1064.   *To face p. 524.*

60. SUPPLYING FRESH VEGETABLES FOR THE 5TH DIVISION NEAR AMIENS

A lorry of the 5th Divisional Supply Column being loaded from the abandoned market gardens at Canon.

*Aust. War Memorial Official Photo. No. E2431.
Taken in May, 1918.*

To face p. 525.

the war America led the world; and the publication in 1912 of *The Soldier's Foot and the Military Shoe* by Major Edward Lyman Munson, of the U.S.A. Medical Corps, constitutes a landmark in the evolution of the Australian military boot as of the American.[24] It is true that the military bootmaker's "last" evolved but slowly along the physiological lines therein set out; but in 1914 the Australian Defence Department (Quartermaster-General) issued for the guidance of the officers of the citizen forces a pamphlet[25] which closely followed its teaching. The course of the development of the Australian military boot before and in the war is followed further in *Volume III*, but the following note made by an R.M.O. exactly and clearly sets out the two factors that matter.[26]

"*May, 1918.* While at Blangy Tronville a foot parade of the whole unit was held and 10 cases of ingrowing toenail and about 20 corns were treated. Most of the former were on the medial side of the great toe and in most cases were stated to have originated since joining the A.I.F. These could be avoided if the army boots were made with due consideration to the natural shape of the foot. Most of the boots have an inner line which deviates outwards slightly whereas the natural inner line of the foot is straight; and this causes friction and pressure. If the army boot were modelled on the American Army lines this trouble would to a great extent disappear. An aggravating factor also is the flatness of the toe of the boot. This is constantly complained of by the men themselves. The normal great toe is squeezed in a vertical direction by a boot which is otherwise well fitting. If these toes were blocked or made more roomy their efficiency would be improved."

The Australian boot: $A =$ defective; $B =$ corrected.

It is but fair to say at once that the Australian soldiers for the most part strongly favoured the Australian-made boot; and that the "lessons of the war" have been put to good purpose in the "new model" Australian military boot.

The Sock. The usage and wastage of this article were enormous. The supplementing of the official ordnance "issue" by voluntary aid and home efforts was a useful form of "war-work" as well as an emotional outlet. It should, however, be added that the socks knitted by "Sister Susie" were not always a comfort.[27] The importance of an ill-fitting or ill-shaped sock as a factor in sore feet was fully borne out by R.M.O's.

The overcoats first issued to the force were apt to become very heavy when soaked with rain. The "British warm," with a less felted surface, threw off the rain better.

---

[24] By American usage the term "shoe" includes boots.
[25] *Boots, Instructions regarding their fitting, preservation and care.*
[26] From report to the A.D.M.S. by Capt. G. P. Arnold, R.M.O., 51st Battalion.
[27] Instruction in this might well form part of the social scheme of education.

The Hat. In Mesopotamia Australian troops were equipped with solar topees. In Palestine, on the other hand, and throughout operations in the Sinai Desert they wore the felt hat which proved an adequate and convenient covering. For wear in Europe also the felt hat was found to be an exceptionally useful headgear.

Equipment—the Problem of Weight. In 1867 a Royal Commission enquired into the causes of the high incidence of heart and lung disease among soldiers during and after the Crimean War. Its views may be found summarised in one sentence:—

"The conditions of war demand that the marching powers and endurance of the soldier must not be lessened by unnecessary weight or a defective mode of carrying it. *Ceteris paribus*, the army that is least weighted and can move with the greatest rapidity must have the advantage."

The authority from whom this quotation is taken[28] opens his discussion on the significance of this military factor in the Great War with the statement that

"when further we come to examine the results of the huge load carried in the recent war on the physique of the troops engaged, we find a tragic tale of wastage."

It is true that it may not be possible to go all the way with this writer in his finding that excessive or improper loading was the most potent pathogenic factor in the "soldier's heart" and in most degenerative cardiac and pulmonary disease. It can, however, be said that the experience of the A.I.F. confirms the verdict that the soldier's loading is a factor of first rate importance in his efficiency and health.

The soldier's load tended sharply to rise throughout the war. To the rifle and bayonet, small-arm ammunition and entrenching tool were soon added the gas-mask, steel helmet, and Mills bombs. "Specialists" were laden with new offensive apparatus in the several types of quick-firing guns and so forth. In France, to permit of winter campaigns, the soldier's clothing and bedding were greatly augmented. The needs of exact organisation compelled each soldier to carry the full load assigned to him; and a study of the loads and of physique suggests

---

[28] Major N. V. Lothian, R.A.M.C. in "The Load carried by the Soldier" (*Journal of the R.A.M.C.*, Oct. 1921 *et seq.*) traces the evolution of the soldier's load from the beginnings of history, and makes a particular study of developments in the British Army in the 19th century and the Great War. In post-war studies of the subject, such as those by Cathcart and Orr, and Cathcart and Lothian, field experiments were checked by indirect calorimetry whereby the exact cost to the man of any special work could be arrived at.

great mal-adjustment between the weight the soldier was required to carry and his average physiological reserves of power. For while physique varied greatly, the load to be carried was absolute, and there was a definite tendency to arrange the load in terms of the highest rather than of average capacity. Australian experience endorses Major Lothian's statement that "it was a notable fact of the recent war that whenever great or continued exertions were required the kit had to be lightened."

The Load. The following table shows (approximately) the weight of the equipment actually carried by the soldier on the march.

Napoleonic Wars	Crimea War	South African War			
Circa 1800	1854	1900	1907	1914	1918
35 lb.	65 lb.	58 lb.	48 lb.	58 lb.	78 lb.

The infantry soldier's load at the outset of the Great War comprised:—(a) clothing worn (14 lb. 11 oz.), (b) arms (10 lb. 8½ oz.), (c) ammunition (9 lb.), (d) tools (2 lb. 9¼ oz.), (e) accoutrements (8 lb. 4¼ oz.), (f) articles in pack (10 lb. 1¾ oz.) (g) rations and water (5 lb. 13½ oz.).[29]

Field studies and experimental work both pre- and post-war would suggest one-third of the body weight, say, 45-50 lb. on an average, as the optimum load, with an effective maximum of 45 per cent. The British infantryman in the war commonly carried a load well above that figure and one which bore too high a relation to his weight to leave available energy for combat after the expenditure resulting from the march. There is, it would seem, an age-long tendency to issue to the soldier in peace an equipment weighing some 50-60 lb. on the assumption that he could support it in a battle, or that auxiliary transport might be available, or the excess discarded. In the Great War the men would not, on their own initiative discard their own property, though they sometimes discarded Government property (such as picks or shovels) very important for their fighting task; and only gradually did the discarding of part of the soldier's load become part of the official technique of battle or the march. When in 1914-15 the A.I.F. trained on the sands of the Sahara and "attacked" up the hills of Lemnos, it was assumed that the men would fight carrying full equipment.[30]

In the stationary warfare of Gallipoli and later in France provision was made for exchange from march to battle order and *vice versa*. The vast accumulation of equipment "additional to Mobilisation Store Table" was reflected also in the individual impedimenta of the infantryman. The solution indeed of the equipment problem in mechanised warfare

---

[29] *Field Service Pocket Book, 1914.*
[30] While the principle that men should be trained fully equipped for service has the support of history, ancient and modern, and as well of science and common sense, this assumption had untoward effects. At Mena it was a factor in the sick wave (*Vol. I, p. 76*). At the Landing the technique of adjustment for battle was so little understood that many battalions made no provision for a guard on the packs which were dumped near the Beach, and these were ransacked by "stragglers." The disasters of the famous trial march of the 14th Brigade from Tel-el-Kebir to Ismailia in 1916 were due to deep-seated errors in the military attitude toward the human machine.

would seem to be a twofold one; first, reduction in the weight of individual articles of equipment, second, provision for relieving the soldier of the part of his impedimenta not required at the moment: on the march his blanket, greatcoat, and the paraphernalia of battle; in battle the equipment required only for marching and camping. The equipment for static and mobile warfare respectively should be determined so that a quick change from one to the other can be made when necessary.[31]

Relation to Physique. The matter is obviously bound up with the question of physique in the selection of recruits. For weight carrying the soldier's weight and chest measurement rather than his height would seem important. But it is not difficult to conceive conditions in which men with certain qualities would be desirable recruits though they could not qualify for carrying weights.

The "Web Equipment." The British "web equipment" whereby men of the A.I.F. eventually carried their ammunition, tools, and surplus clothing had been introduced into the British Army with the Haldane reforms in 1907-8. It was an admirable implement and vastly better than the green-hide or leather apparatus. All these matters had important medical involvements, and the problem of loading the soldier should be a direct concern of the medical department.

Other factors in health promotion

We here impinge, both on the physiological and the psychic side, on the problem of disease prevention as distinct from health promotion. Such matters as treatment of minor injuries, cleanliness and hygiene of the skin, care of the feet, prevention of vermin, merge insensibly with the prevention of scabies, of trench fever, I.C.T. and of impetigo, sore feet, trench foot. At the same time the problems of securing sleep and rest, the exploitation of psychic amenities such as alcohol, or of such methods as education, blend with problems of *morale*, and of prevention of psycho-physical exhaustion, war-neuroses and debility. In the promotion of health by such means and by the treatment of minor injuries and disease the part of the R.M.O. was far more important than may be generally realised. For every soldier sent "sick" to field ambulance, on an average some 10 to 30 were treated by the R.M.O. at the aid-post. His influence in promoting health and morale can indeed scarcely be over-estimated. A table given below[82] may with advantage be compared with graph in *Volume I p. 348*.

---

[31] Statements by individual soldiers indicate that in the hurriedly organised counter-attack at Villers-Bretonneux (24 April, 1918) many soldiers found themselves too heavily equipped to execute the swift movements required by the battle plan without discarding some of their S.A.A. and bombs.

[32] From the experience of the R.M.O., 11th Battalion (Major L. May), 1918. Those ordered "medicine and duty" are not shown.

61. AUSTRALIAN SOLDIERS IN WINTER KIT
A drawing by Will Dyson of infantrymen in the Somme area during the winter of 1916.
Aust. War Memorial Official Photo No. J6649.

62. HOT FOOD CONTAINERS OUTSIDE THE COOK-HOUSE OF THE 57TH BATTALION, BETLHÉEM FARM, NOVEMBER, 1917
The scene is on the old Messines battlefield.
Aust. War. Memorial Official Photo. No. E1268.   *To face p. 528.*

63. AN OFFICER OF THE 30TH BATTALION INSPECTING FEET NEAR ZONNEBEKE, DURING THE THIRD BATTLE OF YPRES, OCTOBER, 1917

Aust. War Memorial Official Photo. No. E1120.

64. WATER CARTS AT THE WATER POINT, MONTAUBAN, DURING THE SOMME WINTER, 1916-17

Aust. War Memorial Official Photo. No. E57.   *To face p. 529.*

THE PROMOTION OF HEALTH

Analysis of statistics of the work of the R.M.O. 11th Battalion, February, 1918-January, 1919.

	STRENGTH	PARADED SICK		ORDERED LIGHT DUTY		ORDERED NO DUTY		TO HOSPITAL SICK		TO HOSPITAL WOUNDED	
	MONTHLY AVERAGE	No.	Daily per cent. of str.	No.	Daily per cent. of str.	No.	Daily per cent. of str.	No.	Daily per cent. of str.	No.	Daily per cent. of str.
1918											
FEBRUARY	750	767	3·65	171	0·81	97	0·46	61	0·29	—	—
MARCH	785	673	2·76	177	0·73	117	0·48	108	0·44	103	0·42
APRIL	759	488	2·14	87	0·38	80	0·31	64	0·28	48	0·21
MAY	721	530	2·37	110	0·49	94	0·42	61	0·27	22	0·09
JUNE	655	475	2·41	105	0·53	85	0·43	93	0·47	129	0·65
JULY	614	302	1·58	61	0·32	48	0·25	56	0·29	47	0·24
AUGUST	603	224	1·19	72	0·38	25	0·13	18	0·09	262	1·40
SEPTEMBER	426	197	1·54	49	0·38	48	0·37	24	0·19	61	0·47
OCTOBER	401	223	1·79	48	0·38	62	0·50	28	0·22	—	—
NOVEMBER	441	321	2·42	49	0·37	117	0·89	31	0·23	—	—
DECEMBER	416	342	2·82	81	0·63	110	0·85	26	0·20	—	—
1919											
JANUARY	390	371	3·05	39	0·32	219	1·81	15	0·12	—	—

Care of Feet and Chiropody. In spite of the extensive use of mechanised transport in the movement of troops, the care of the feet, closely involved as it was with the prevention of "trench foot," assumed an importance which can hardly have been surpassed in the wars of Marlborough or of Wellington. Yet, in contrast with the arrangements of the British Army, no official provision was made in the Australian force for the service of trained chiropodists. In some battalions a chiropody "kit" was purchased through the "Regimental funds," and a private detailed from the ranks for this duty. Some units arranged for their man to be trained, but in most he picked up a serviceable routine of foot care; the R.M.O. gave advice and treated the more severe cases. There seems to be no doubt that an appreciable amount of wastage could have been avoided by more exact and scientific professional attention to this matter. In particular, the wide diffusion of tinea—and its influences as a cause of foot-trouble and of "chafing" (tinea cruris)—were almost unnoticed.

Psycho-physical Factors: (a) *Rest and sleep.* The clinical features presented by the mass-disorders that derived from the attrition warfare of the Western Front confirm the general experience that, of all the physiological traumata inflicted by this type of warfare *per se*, long deprivation from sleep and absence while in the line of any surcease from physical and mental strain must be ranked very high as factors in the attainment of the desired "attrition," and therefore as a proper subject for defensive action, military and medical. The part played herein by the R.M.O., and the importance of provision for securing such rest, is a matter of frequent reference in the Australian records.

(b) *Alcohol.* The Great War was in this respect constructive, that it required the truth naked from any shroud of self-interest—except such as might promote victory. Thus both as a social and as a physiological problem the study of alcohol was materially advanced during the war. In particular, like the allied problem of venereal disease, the study was placed on a rational and scientific footing.

This was largely the direct result of the action of the British "Central Control Board (Liquor Traffic)" in appointing an advisory committee composed of some of the most eminent of living scientists and publicists to investigate the problem. Their report was published in popular form as a pamphlet, and their investigations were subsequently continued by the Medical Research Council of National Insurance.[33] The chief service performed by these councils was to bring out the fact that, in general, though its immediate effect on behaviour may be "stimulant," the *action of alcohol is essentially anodyne and depressant.* The social and the individual problems were generally illuminated by this scientific integration.

The "Rum" Ration. The consumption of alcohol was controlled in Great Britain by the Liquor Control Board (Civil) and the Committee of Imperial Defence (Military). In the field its general use and

---

[33] The original members of the Committee in 1918 were:—Lord D'Abernon (Chairman); Sir George Newman, M.D. (Vice-Chairman); Professor A. R. Cushny, M.D., F.R.S.; H. H. Dale, M.D., F.R.S.; Major Greenwood, M.R.C.S.; W. McDougall, M.B., F.R.S.; F. W. Mott, M.D., F.R.S.; Professor C. S. Sherrington, M.D., F.R.S.; W. C. Sullivan, M.D. Two further members were afterwards added, namely Professor E. Mellanby, M.D., and C. S. Myers, M.D., Sc.D., F.R.S.

The report was published under the title *Alcohol: Its Action on the Human Organism—1st Edition, 1918; 2nd, 1923; Revised and Enlarged, 1924.*

special "issue" were decided by the military command, with a quaint show of formal deference, but very little effective reference, to the medical service.[84]

The physiological evidence brought forward in the report of Lord D'Abernon's committee regarding the essentially anodyne action of alcohol was fully borne out in military experience. Its value lay wholly in euphoria, and the relief of anxiety. The continuous and compelling longing for some surcease, however temporary and partial, from war strain made the military use of the "rum ration" practically universal and, when not substituted for food, warmth and opportunity for rest, without doubt, often beneficial; and gave it a place in attrition warfare from which it would be difficult to expel it, even were it thought desirable to do so. At times the rum ration was used with the purpose of promoting action, not of inducing relaxation, its narcotic effect being called on to dull the edge of fear and anxiety before an attack.[35] It was, however, generally recognised by those who gave thought to the matter that the right place for the rum ration was after effort, not before, and in association with food, warmth, and rest; and this, emphatically, was the practice favoured in the A.I.F.[36]

In the A.I.F. it was the almost universal practice not to give it before but after attack. Commanders wanted clear heads on their men and feared the depressing effect on their men after a brief stimulation.

---

[84] Procedure in the A.I.F. was based on British Army orders. Commissioned officers were allowed to have spirits, "other ranks" were not. The following regulation obtained in Fifth Army in 1917:—

"*Liquor. Issue from Expeditionary Force Canteen.*

"1. Spirits shall only be sold for consumption by officers, and all orders for such shall be in the form of bulk orders on the nearest Expeditionary Force Canteen Branch, from Staffs of Armies, Corps, Divisions, or Base or Area Commandant on the L. of C. or at G.H.Q.

"2. . . . spirits will only be issued to messes on the production of a printed liquor voucher signed by a Staff Officer of the Formation. . . .

"3. No spirits will be allowed to be sold to sergeants' messes."

Beer was permitted in the sergeants' mess: privates got what they could pick up. Many units of the A.I.F. bought local beer in bulk and retailed it in their own canteens. The f₋ lowing is from the diary of the 3rd Field Ambulance (19 Oct. 1917): "Rest station inspected by 1st Anzac Commander, Lieut.-General Birdwood; he expressed approval. He commented especially on usefulness of canteen and importance of Q.M. department and the feeding. . . . A canteen is a very important part of a field ambulance. It is of great benefit to patients in rest stations. Beer is an important part of sales. It enables men to get good beer. It . . . minimises the desire for spirits."

[35] At times it was thought justifiable to exploit this action. *c.f.* C. E. Montague, *Disenchantment* (*p. 74*): "Isn't it (*i.e.*, the dulling of mental strain) just what more men'll get drunk for than anything else? And why the rum's double before you go over?"

[36] The official issue of "S.R.D." (Service Rum Diluted) was ⅓ a gill—2½ fluid ounces—and by General Routine Orders was "at the discretion of the G.O.C. on the recommendation of medical officers" (*Second Army, Routine Order*, No. 1363, 22 Nov., 1917). In the Australian force a daily issue was commonly authorised during the winter months to battalions in the line, artillery-men in gun pits and working parties. Lieut.-General Monash held strongly that the issue of alcohol must be with discretion; "as an effort to stimulate troops for a stunt 'No,' to revive them after heavy fatigue or stress when they could relax and rest 'Yes.'" A 3rd Division memorandum in 1917 placed the responsibility for the issue of rum directly on the "medical authorities." General Monash held strong views on the use of ardent spirits by officers in particular when work was to be done which required complete mental and physical fitness. But when the troops were resting he was "very human and companionable," and as he became assured of the discipline of his men, both as G.O.C. 3rd Division and of the Australian Corps, his rigour somewhat relaxed. (From notes furnished by Australian War Memorial. See also *Reveille*, "Liquid Rations," *July, Sept., Oct.*, 1938, and *Australian Official History, Vol. V, p. 598*.)

There were, however, important exceptions to the rule; where it was thought that troops were exceptionally tired or chilled before being called on for tense action a "tot" was sometimes issued to them.

Use and Abuse of Alcohol. Alcohol was not officially advised in first aid or in resuscitation, and when so used often did more harm than good. In the treatment of sickness medical practice did not differ from that in civil life, that is to say, the scope of usefulness of alcohol in treatment was very limited.

Useful and desirable as might be an appreciation of this side of the problem, the records do not provide material for an authoritative pronouncement. The following comment is based on what may be termed a consensus of impressions.

For commissioned officers, if we except senescence, dependence on alcohol was probably the most frequent immediate cause of failure to "make good" in the field. On Gallipoli it was the direct cause of one major military tragedy. The fall of the "pseudo-dipsomaniac," as he was then known, was early and complete; spirit soaking was laid bare by failure to stay the pace or rise to occasion. In the rank and file, forbidden the use of ardent spirits, the chronic alcoholics sometimes did good service—the cycle from private to sergeant and back was a quite authentic experience. In lads under 18 alcohol played havoc.

The Rational Factor: Education. "Education" was used in the Great War not only as a means for the dissemination of factual knowledge, but as in itself a source of mental and moral stimulation and sustainment. Beginning with "Divisional" and other schools established behind the lines as soon as the I Anzac Corps entered the line on the Western Front, the educational system of the Australian Corps, Divisions, and Brigades had (like those of British formations) become by 1918 a highly important organisation. In this campaign the medical service fully participated. The "sanitary" policy, indeed, of the Australian force was based on the idea of education in self-help chiefly through the medium of the sanitary sections. The Corps and Divisional school system included as a matter of major importance that of health.[37]

Psychic Amenities. As the war progressed these, like many other matters of health, became more and more the concern of the army as a whole and a matter of organisation even more than of discipline.[38] They included leave, local and to the British Isles or Paris, and the organised entertainment there, organised games and boxing, inter-unit competitions in military or sporting activities—particularly keen where they concerned horses—concerts, cinema shows, and on a lower level (sometimes in default of the organisation that should have been provided) "two up," "crown and anchor," and "housey-housey." Late in the war educational lectures were given and were appreciated.

---

[37] *See p. 614.* In the Corps school lectures on "water" by the O.C., No. 2 Sanitary Section (Major M. J. Holmes), furnish the most complete account of the subject in the Australian records. "Sanitary models" made in the 4th Divisional School were rescued from Meteren a few hours before its capture in April, 1918, and with a number of others are now in the Australian War Memorial, Canberra. *See plate on p. 581.*

[38] They are dealt with in the chapter of the next volume concerned with the psychic disorders of the war.

SYNOPSIS OF CHAPTER XIX

PREVENTIVE MEDICINE IN THE WAR—(III) THE PREVENTION OF DISEASE

The field for prevention.
The social milieu.
A triple campaign.

I. ARTIFICIAL IMMUNISATION.

Against smallpox and the enteric group.
Statistics of enterica—Appreciation of results—Attitude of Australians to compulsion.
Against Pneumonia.
Pneumonia and measles.

II. INDIRECT ACTION—THE HUMAN VECTOR.

Quarantine.
The "sieve" at Marseilles—Typhus detected and blocked.
Procedure in British Army.
Notification.
    Four methods.
    The notifiable diseases.
        Army Form W. 3110—Action upon notification—Experience in the A.I.F.
Implements of indirect action.
    The mobile laboratories—Isolation and segregation—Disinfection.
The "Carrier" problem.
Results illustrated in Respiratory Tract Infections.
Incidence of R.T.I. in Army life.
Aetiological varieties.
Experience of A.I.F. in France.
The main exemplar—THE DEPOTS IN U.K.
The influence of climate.
The problem defined.
Health machinery of the Depots.
Bronchitis and pneumonia—Cerebro-spinal fever—The epidemic virus diseases.

III. DIRECT ACTION—HYGIENE AND SANITATION.

Social hygiene.
Diseases of dirt and squalor.
    The morbid agents concerned.
    Incidence in the B.E.F.

SYNOPSIS OF CHAPTER XIX

Personal hygiene.
  Disinfection and dis-infestation in the field.
  The parasites.
    The body-louse—Scabies—Pyodermia.
  Apparatus of disinfection.
  Baths and laundries.
    Armentières, May, 1916.
    Australian Corps scheme of baths.
      Bathing routine—The "Shower."
    The type disease of squalor in the war—Trench fever.
Field sanitation.
  The gastro-intestinal infections.
    Comparison with Gallipoli.
    Prophylaxis of dysentery in B.E.F.
    "Diarrhoea" or "Dysentery"?
    Direct action against the fluxes.
  The water problem on the Western Front.
    Responsibility—The water supply—Purification—Chlorination—The "Horrocks test case"—Distribution—The petrol tin—The mobile water columns.

THE AUSTRALIAN SANITARY SECTIONS IN FRANCE.
  Beginnings—Allocation—Personnel.
  Control by Division? Corps? or Army?
    1916: Corps control—1917—Army control.
  Results of Australian policy.
  Functions of the Sanitary Section.
    Its place in water control.

PREVENTIVE MEDICINE—THE SIGNIFICANCE OF "P.U.O."

CHAPTER XIX

PREVENTIVE MEDICINE IN THE WAR—(III) THE
PREVENTION OF DISEASE[1]

The field for prevention

OF, the total non-battle casualties admitted to *field ambulance* from the A.I.F. in France, 57·19 per cent. were for diseases caused immediately by parasitic infection or infestation (shown in *Chapter XVII* under Type III[2]). Of this total, five classes of aetiologically-related diseases contributed some 50 per cent., and formed the chief objective in the campaign for the "prevention of disease" in the field.

Of this last total, *gastro-intestinal (faecal) infections* were responsible for 0·74 per cent., and constituted the chief *raison d'être* for the measures comprised in *"field sanitation."* Infection by mucus from the *respiratory tract or fauces* caused 19·49 per cent. Of these, specific air-borne respiratory infections, such as the exanthemata, were opposed chiefly by administrative measures, *notification and segregation*; the various non-specific infections, such as bronchitis, bacillary "influenza," coryza, tonsillitis, naso-pharyngeal catarrh, and laryngitis, were fought by measures calculated to prevent infection by promoting *"easy resistance"*—for example, by housing and ventilation, warmth and clothing, food and rest. *Contagious diseases of the skin, superficial coccal infections,* and *general diseases transmitted through a verminous host*[3] constituted approximately 17 per cent., and these three classes were mainly responsible for the vast army organisation built up to serve *"personal and social hygiene."* This leaves pyrexia of uncertain origin, "P.U.O." (11·61 per cent.), which on the Western

---

[1] The reader is commended particularly to *relevant chapters and pp. 413-15 of Vol. I.*
[2] *See pp. 501-3.*
[3] Malaria, hydatid, and infective jaundice are excluded.

Front comprised mainly undiagnosed trench fever and the sickness loosely classified at the time as "influenza."

The military scheme of preventive medicine in France and Belgium was closely modelled on the methods of civil life. It differed mainly in these two respects, that official control was extended to cover almost the whole gamut of social life in the "populations" concerned—the personnel comprising the military units —and that this military population was "regimented" to a degree impossible in democratic communities; the most significant result being that both the "rights" and also the responsibilities of the individual were far more restricted.

The social milieu

As in civil life, three distinct lines of action were exploited, and special personnel, procedure, and methods were developed to implement each of them. These lines of action were:

A triple campaign

(1) *Artificial immunisation*, the purpose of which was to increase individual resistance to certain specific infective agents.

(2) *Indirect (administrative) ·measures* to control the *human vectors* of infection. These measures comprised "notification" of cases of certain selected diseases, the immediate removal of such cases to field ambulance, and, if necessary after verification of the diagnosis by laboratory, their isolation in special medical units, and the segregation of contacts; also the search for "carriers." These measures were carried out through (a) international quarantine for troops moving by sea; (b) measures (of segregation and so forth) within the respective national armies.

(3) *Direct action*, attack or defence, was taken against the parasitic causes of disease, and this might be *immediate* (as by the destruction of the *acaris scabiei* in the skin) or *mediate*, through their vectors, whether these were animate (*e.g* lice or flies) or inanimate (food and water, blankets, clothing, dirt, air); as by "disinfection" or "spacing out."

Organised almost *de novo*, as was the machinery of health,[4] it worked at first stiffly even in the B.E.F., as is shown by the

---

[4] *See Vol. I, pp. 10, 229.*

Australian records of early 1916. At that time it required frequent adjustments and close oversight. But by the end of 1917 habitude had for the most part made its procedures a familiar, almost automatic, element in the social life of attrition warfare. In the open warfare of 1918, however, it was to receive a disconcerting jolt.

1. ARTIFICIAL IMMUNISATION

In the present state of our knowledge, rational measures for the *prevention of disease* have much less concern with the processes of natural resistance—the *vis medicatrix naturae*—than have those which subserve treatment.[5] But in two diseases of first-rate military potentialities rational procedure to promote resistance obtained results of decisive significance. That the "Jennerian vaccination" against smallpox carried out in all the great national armies prevented outbreaks of this terrible disease and was thus a decisive factor in the health history of the war, is proved by the history of smallpox in the Australian force at Mena.[6] The results of Almroth Wright's "anti-typhoid inoculation" are of no less interest. The experience in Gallipoli has already been fully dealt with, but that in France must be shortly referred to.

The Enteric Group (officially typhoid, paratyphoid "A" and "B," and "enteric group"). The following facts are pertinent to any inquiry into the part played by inoculation in the remarkable freedom of the A.I.F. in France from the diseases caused by this group.

Against the Enteric Group

In principle every member of the A.I.F. was "compulsorily" inoculated with "T.A.B." in the prescribed form.[7] The extent

---

[5] We may recall in this connection that "natural" (*physiological*) resistance, individual and racial, to parasitic invasion is only developed by close contact with the several organisms concerned. Both the *instinctive* and *rational reactions* against infection, on the other hand, tend for the most part to avoid contact with it—an infected person or animal is shunned, even outlawed. Thus—as has been stressed by Sir Almroth Wright—the creation of a national or racial resistance is delayed. Thence came the fact that in the French and the Australian armies *mumps*, in the British *roseola*, and in the American and Canadian *measles* in congested camps ran riot through the respective military communities. In the matter of cure, on the other hand, the line of demarcation between the *vis medicatrix naturae* on the one hand, and "instinctive" and "rational" lines of action on the other, is much less clearly defined.

[6] See *Vol. I, Chapter v.*
[7] See *p. 478, and Vol. I, p. 482.*

to which re-inoculation was carried out cannot be determined with exactness but was certainly high. Advantage was, for example, taken of the long rest, June-August, 1917, to give effect to Army Council Instructions, issued on 5th July, 1916, and 31st March, 1917, which enjoined a more efficient inoculation and re-inoculation of all troops. The procedure laid down in these instructions was embodied in I Anzac Corps Routine Order No. 1415, dated 14th April, 1917, as follows:—

"All ranks who have not yet been satisfactorily inoculated or re-inoculated against Typhoid and Paratyphoid fever within a year are to be inoculated as soon as possible, the following instructions being observed:

(a) Men who have been inoculated with two doses of mixed vaccine within a year need not be re-inoculated.

(b) Men whose last inoculation was performed with mixed vaccine more than a year ago should be re-inoculated.

(c) Men whose last inoculation was performed with a single dose of mixed vaccine more than six months ago should be re-inoculated.

"Men who are being inoculated for the first time will receive an initial dose of ½ c.c. and after an interval of 8-10 days a second dose of 1 c.c. of the mixed Typhoid and Paratyphoid Vaccine. In cases of re-inoculation a single dose of 1 c.c. will be given.

"In addition to entry on page 17 of Pay Books, nominal rolls will be prepared and kept up to date by all Units, showing the date of inoculation and re-inoculation of all members of the Unit.

"Regimental Medical Officers will indent at once on nearest Field Ambulance for amount of vaccine required."

The policy was based on

"the assumption that one dose protected fully for six months and partially for twelve months; and that two doses protected fully for one year and partially for two years." (Sir William Leishman, Interallied Sanitary Conference, 1917.)

In the British Army, in which inoculation was voluntary, from 1915 the proportion of men inoculated against enterica "fluctuated between 90 and 98 per cent."[8] The proportion of the A.I.F. on the Western Front inoculated with T.A.B. was computed by the War Office at "98·4 per cent. for 1917, and 95 per cent. for 1918," but almost certainly was never below 99 per cent.[9]

---

[8] *Brit. Off. Med. History, Pathology, p. 249.* Other references are taken from the Official History of the *Medical Department of the U.S. Army in the World War, Vol. IX* and the *German Off. Med. History, Vol. III.*

[9] *See Vol. I, p. 40.*

In the French Army anti-typhoid inoculation was tackled seriously only from the end of 1915. At the outbreak of war—through "military exigency"—it was optional, was not pressed, and at first one dose only was given. Two types of vaccine were employed, given in two doses.

In the German Army anti-typhoid inoculation was completed by January, 1915 (3 injections)[10]—"T.A.B." was not generally used till 1918.

In the American Army inoculation was compulsory and from July, 1917, a triple T.A.B. vaccine was used, three injections being given.

Statistics of Enterica. The experiences of the Australian force in France and Belgium in relation to the enteric group of fevers is shown in the following table:—

Table showing incidence of the Enteric Group of Fevers in the Australian Imperial Force, Western Front, 1916-1918.[11]

Nature of case	1916	1917	1918	Total	Deaths
Typhoid (inoc.) ..	26	18	6	50	4
Typhoid (not inoc.)	-	-	2	2	-
Paratyph. A (inoc. T.A.B.) ..	25	17	2	44	-
Paratyph. A (not inoc. T.A.B.)	7	1	-	8	-
Paratyph. B (inoc. T.A.B.) ..	21	21	2	44	2
Paratyph. B (not inoc. T.A.B.)	5	2	1	8	1
Enteric group (inoc.) ..	25	25	3	53	-
Enteric group (not inoc.)	2	-	-	2	1
TOTAL	111	84	16	211	8

Year	Average daily strength	Incidence of Enterica (from notifications)	Rate per 1,000	Total deaths	Case mortality
1916	86,163	111	1·29	2	1·80 per cent.
1917	118,454	84	0·71	5	5·95 per cent.
1918 ..	110,031	16	0·14	1	6·25 per cent.

Estimating the proportion of inoculated to uninoculated at 99 to 1 it is clear—for what it is worth in so small a group—that there is an advantage of nearly 10 to 1 in favour of the former.

The incidence of enterica in the British troops of the B.E.F.

---

[10] The period of protection was reckoned (after experiments) at about 6 months, and orders for re-inoculation were issued at the end of June, 1915—doses 0·5 and 1 c.c. The third and later inoculations were to be 1 c.c. (The number of organisms in each c.c. is not available.)

[11] The figures embodied in this table were most kindly made available to the Australian War Records Section in 1919 by the War Office. They were based on "notifications" by the D's.M.S. of Armies etc. to the D.G.M.S. B.E.F. The 3rd Echelon (A.I.F.) figures show 6 deaths only. It is impossible to ascertain the degree of accuracy of these figures, but there is no reason to believe that they are inexact to any material extent.

is shown in the following table (per thousand of ration strength):—

Year	Typhoid	"A."	"B."	"Enteric group"	Total death rate	Case mortality
1914 ..	—	—	—	—	—	12·1 per cent.
1915 ..	1·3	0·47	1·7	0·3	0·22	5·5 per cent.
1916 ..	0·57	0·45	0·7	0·27	0·02	1·12 per cent.
1917 ..	0·12	0·08	0·24	0·15	0·012	2·8 per cent.
1918 ..	0·03	0·015	0·06	0·015	0·007	5·9 per cent.

Total—20,149 cases with 1,191 deaths; all theatres; total case mortality 5·9 per cent.

In the French Army 45,200 cases occurred in 1914, 67,000 in 1915, 12,400 in 1916, 1,700 in 1917, 750 in 1918 (British Army *Manual of Hygiene and Sanitation, 1934*). The rate per 1,000 dropped from 39·37 in the first year to 7·18 in the second year and the case mortality from 12·08 to 2·5 per cent. (Interallied Sanitary Conference 1917.)

In the German Army 116,481 cases were treated in hospitals of whom 87·2 per cent. returned to duty, 10·1 per cent. died, 2 per cent. were discharged unfit. It would seem that paratyphoid was not included in the above. (*German Official History Vol. III, p. 99.* Figures are as given in the German text.)

The American Army (*Official History Vol. IX p. 17*) had a rate per 1,000 per annum of 0·37, with a case mortality of 14·85 per cent. This contrasted with—Civil War 29·86 per 1,000 and 36·92 per cent.: Spanish-American War 141·59 per 1,000 and 10·47 per cent.

Appreciation of Results. There is no valid reason for doubting the correctness of the unanimous conclusion based on the war experience of the medical profession in the nations engaged, namely that the observed rise in the titre of blood antigen (agglutinin) brought about by the injection of heat-killed organisms of this group will very often tip the balance against clinical infection in men exposed to risk; and that in the war this played an important and even decisive part in the very greatly diminished incidence of the disease.[12]

It seems desirable however to emphasise the need for clinical and scientific balance by recalling (1) the well known fact that *infection* depends on a number of factors, which may act independently of each other in producing "disease"[13]—mass infection, virulence, depression of individual, or immunity-state; (2) the fact that on the Western Front dysentery was also greatly reduced through general sanitation, and (3) the further fact that in the civil communities Typhoid had greatly decreased.

Attitude of Australians to Compulsion. There was little opposition to the procedure on the part of the Australian troops, many of whom had personal experience of similar prophylactic procedures in animals— against pleuro, black-leg, and tick fever. Oppsive propaganda in the civil community was most often due to the exploitation of half-baked

[12] The officer commanding No. 2 Australian Sanitary Section records that in his experience Typhoid was prevalent among the French civilian population both on the Somme and in Flanders, though it was often undiagnosed and the prevalence not officially recognised by the French authorities.

[13] As pointed out in this connection in *Vol. I, p. 525* "No greater danger besets the medical profession than that of premature wresting of evidence to suit current theory."

theories by individuals who were themselves in the happy position of having no responsibility for the welfare of the force or the winning of the war. In others it was undoubtedly based on sincere conviction and actuated by strong desire to put right what was looked on as an error. Opponents of the latter kind would welcome without mortification the resolution of doubts happily afforded by the results obtained during the war.

Experiments were made in the French Army in the use of anti-pneumococcus vaccine in the "native" troops (African and Indo-Chinese), using a "mono-vaccine" (single type) prepared by the Pasteur Institute from a strain which agglutinated 93 per cent. of cases of pneumonia occurring in Paris. The morbidity among the inoculated troops was found to be "sensibly diminished." After a year in France the native troops acquired a partial immunity.[14]

Against pneumonia

Pneumonia and Measles. Vaccines were used in the terrible outbreaks of pneumonia which marked the epidemics of measles in the American camps of training—due to both pneumococcal and streptococcal invasion. A brief account of this and some allied matters—as influenza—will be given in *Volume III*.[15]

11. INDIRECT ACTION—THE HUMAN VECTOR

The history of mankind has been greatly influenced, and at times dominated, by some half-a-dozen of the uni-cellular organisms which have evolved a parasitic existence upon his social habits.[16] These were the subjects of a greater organisation even than Army Procedure—namely the system of international quarantine, an institution too fundamental to be shaken even by the Great War.

The most important are typhus, relapsing fever, cholera, smallpox, yellow fever, plague, and influenza. With typhoid, malaria, and dysentery these diseases have dominated warfare in the past and it was against these chiefly that the system of International Quaran-

Quarantine

---

[14] Report of the Interallied Sanitary Conference, 1918.

[15] Inoculation against tetanus and gas gangrene is discussed as part of treatment of the wounded man. *See pp. 308-10.*

[16] The part played by epidemic diseases—in particular of the Rickettsia group—in wars of the past and in human history, and also the origin of disease in relation to parasitic life are discussed with great interest, if with some romantic licence, in Zinsser's *Rats, Lice and History.*

tine operated. It was dove-tailed in the war into an interallied scheme of quarantine[17] functioning chiefly at the ports of Marseilles and Taranto in connection with native troops from Africa and Indo-China and with the movement of troops from endemic centres in the East along the Allied sea Lines of Communication.

The negative history (as we may term it) of disease in the Great War is more significant than the positive, and the absence of certain diseases more impressive than the prevalence of others. It follows that the hitherto unrecorded medical events associated with a comparatively minor happening —the transfer of the A.I.F. at the beginning of 1916 from the Orient to the Occident—hold features of quite first-rate interest and significance. They do so on two counts: first, as an example in miniature of the vast problem of preventing epidemics of the major diseases of war on the Western Front which—as we have seen—has aroused the interest of military strategists; second and more particularly, as concerns Australian history, as in themselves of definite, possibly of great importance as an episode in the medical campaign—the holding of a breach against a potentially serious menace from exotic disease. This interpretation of the episode rests on the following considerations:—

The "sieve" at Marseilles

1. During the course of the war great epidemics occurred in the military and civil populations where and whenever preventive measures were inadequate or conditions specially unfavourable: smallpox in Russia and Turkey, typhus in Serbia and Russia,[18] malaria in the Palestine campaign, dysentery and enteric at Gallipoli and in Mesopotamia, epidemic jaundice at the Dardanelles, measles, mumps and roseola in concentration camps, and wound infections universally.

2. Until the influenza pandemic of 1918-19, among some 15 million men who served on both sides on the Franco-Belgian front under conditions inviting outbreaks of the pestilences characteristic of warfare, only one outbreak achieved general epidemic proportions, namely trench fever—epidemiologically identical with typhus.

3. Cases of all these diseases were brought from the East with the

---

[17] *See Vol. I p. 49.* The International Headquarters of this organisation was in the Commission Sanitaire d'Hygiène Publique which served as the Headquarters of the "Interallied Sanitary Commission" and as the venue of the annual "Interallied Sanitary Conferences" in the deliberations of which the problems of quarantine entered largely. In this connection *see also Vol. III.*

[18] *See p. 545.*

Australian and British troops, but failed to gain a hold. The reason why they did not do so reflects the campaign against the major diseases in the war.

Events at Marseilles.[19] During the months of April, May and June, 1916 the greater part of the Australian troops were brought to France from Egypt, where most had lived for some months. Many had served on Gallipoli. They had been subject to risk of infection from various diseases not met with in Western Europe, or else occurring here in a modified form, and cases of the following diseases had actually occurred, some as epidemics—smallpox, typhus fever, relapsing fever, typhoid, trachoma and infective ophthalmia, ankylostoma, malaria, dysentery (Shiga, Flexner and amoebic), infective jaundice, Egyptian chancroid. To prevent the introduction of these into France the following steps were taken.

(1) In Egypt,[20] close sanitary supervision during a period of 3-4 months. (2) Before embarkation (a) a vigorous campaign (chiefly carried out with Colonel Hunter's railway van steam disinfester) to free the force from lice; (b) a complete medical inspection; (c) inoculation with T.A.B.; (d) re-vaccination against smallpox. (3) By order of the D.D.M.S. Marseilles on April 4th, on the arrival at Marseilles of the first Australian brigades from Egypt, No. 2 A.G.H. was established at Moussot and well equipped for the isolation of infectious disease. (4) Inspection of troops before disembarkation by the medical officer in charge of transports.

Report by Major H.O. Lethbridge, A.A.M.C. "I had charge of the Isolation compound in No. 2 A.G.H. at Moussot, Marseilles, when the Australian and many British troops were passing through from Egypt to Northern France. Almost every transport would send us its quota of infectious diseases so that the importance of this hospital as a filter was great. Where the gravity of the infection warranted, the whole unit or formation was segregated and held up till deemed safe for it to travel north. The fact that most transports took a week (between Egypt and Marseilles) meant that most infections brought from Egypt would have shown up. At one time we had as many as 13 different diseases in the compound, including smallpox, typhus, measles and roseola, mumps, diphtheria, relapsing fever, scarlet fever, scabies, pemphigus contagiosus, cerebro-spinal meningitis, dhobie itch, and chicken pox.

"Three cases of typhus were detected," continues Major Lethbridge,
Typhus detected "all in troops from Sollum. A case of smallpox, admitted on the first day of his illness, was diagnosed by a typical prodromal rash."

Quite dramatic interest surrounds the inner history of the detection

---
[19] Epitomised from a report by the Medical Officer (Lieut.-Col. A.G. Butler, A.A.M.C.) representing Australia at the "Interallied Sanitary Conference" in Paris, May, 1917.
[20] See *Vol. I, p. 487.*

at No. 2 A.G.H. of these cases of typhus fever, which were all in British troops. The staff of this hospital had some previous acquaintance with the disease, since at Mena Camp, in 1915, several cases of typhus were identified by the officer commanding No. 2 A.G.H. (Colonel T. M. Martin) and demonstrated to his officers. At Marseilles, in 1916, the first of the cases was sent to the hospital with a diagnosis of cerebro-spinal fever. There, however, it was identified with the cases that had been seen at Mena, and though "the differential diagnosis was a little difficult, the suspicion was strong enough in our opinion to justify our immediate report that the case was one of typhus." The fat was in the fire! The D.D.M.S. for Marseilles base disputed the diagnosis. The hospital refused to budge: its diagnosis was typhus. The movement of a whole Brigade of troops was involved. G.H.Q., B.E.F. was urgently informed: the Adviser in Pathology (Colonel Sir W. B. Leishman) came post haste. The experts upheld the hospital. The Brigade from which they came was found very lousy, and two other cases occurred. The troops were segregated and deloused. "It is possible" (says Major Lethbridge) "that a grave epidemic of typhus was thus prevented." Whether this be so or not must remain conjecture. But it seems probable that against typhus fever the indirect line of defence is as important as the direct attack through "personal hygiene," which was to prove comparatively ineffective against the louse-borne disease "trench fever."

Comment. Why typhus did not become established among the troops in France has been the subject of much debate—*see e.g.* Zinsser, *Rats, Lice, and History*. Both lice and rats, the respective vectors in the human and murine strains of typhus, were plentiful enough to have supported an epidemic prevalence—as witness trench fever and the outbreaks of Weil's Disease. The following seems pertinent to the question "Can we say why epidemics appear and disappear? . . . It is of primary importance that this issue should be closely studied. If the decisive factor in an epidemic be the resistance of the population attacked, then measures must be devised to enhance that resistance. If, on the other hand, the inherent vigour of the virus be the only factor, then all agencies that affect the virus must be ascertained and enlisted for the campaign against the disease."[21]

It would seem that the answer is here to be found in the domain of mathematics rather than of biology. With a constant relative virulence in the infecting organism, until automatically checked by dilution of the population "exposed to risk" with "resistant" persons, the momentum of an epidemic augments in geometrical progression at a rate depending on the facilities for contagion.[22] The prime purpose in the mode of preventive medicine identified as "quarantine" is to achieve—so to speak—epidemic asepsis; to check the initial momentum of prospective outbreaks at their inception by reducing to zero the number of sus-ceptable individuals exposed to risk by contact with an infective host. It would seem that the prompt and vigorous action taken here and

---

[21] Dr. J. H. L. Cumpston, now Commonwealth Director-General of Health, in his Presidential Address on "The new Preventive Medicine" to the Section of Public Health and State Medicine, Australasian Medical Congress 1920. *M.J.A.* 4 *Sept., 1920*. The address admirably summed up the "lessons of the war" on "Public Health" methods.

[22] The fact that the rate of decline of an epidemic is also approximately in a geometrical progression, so that the curve is symmetrical, is due to causes of a "vital" nature. See Brownlee "Causes of epidemics and the laws which regulate their course"—*Proceedings of the International Congress of Medicine, London, 1913.* Section XVIII, *p.* 153.

THE PREVENTION OF DISEASE

elsewhere achieved this purpose. Typhus, the greatest epidemic disease known, lends itself more than any to methods of social control. Lice, highly organised multi-cellular creatures, are much less ubiquitous and pervading than the labile microbial or virus forms of life; and unlike the mosquito or the sandfly have but little mobility of their own. The experience of the Scottish Women's Hospital in Serbia in 1914-15 (*See Vol. I, p. 246*) proved that, now its life-history is known, even in war epidemic typhus is fairly readily checked if dealt with energetically by the methods of quarantine, and the disinfestation and "spacing out" of the louse-infected community.[23]

Only four cases in all are reported in the *British Official History* as having occurred in the B.E.F. in France. The experience of the German Army on the Western Front was the same as the British, but on the Eastern Front, where typhus was endemic, the Germans had many cases.

It would be difficult to propose a matter more worthy the attention of students of social evolution than this one of typhus. Its place in the history of past wars has been referred to. In the Great War and its aftermath the disease showed what it could do if social standards were relaxed. The epidemic in Serbia, 1914-15, was well up to reputation. Starting in November 1914, in February and March 1915—we quote from Zinsser—"the epidemic flowed with a speed and violence never equalled in any typhus outbreak of which we have reliable record." Over 150,000 people are stated to have died from the disease, a mortality of from 20 to 60 per cent. In Russia 154,000 cases were recorded during 1916; after 1917 the toll was enormous. In his well known articles[24] Dr. W. Horsley Gantt of the Johns Hopkins University paints an astounding picture of the effects of war and of famine. Under their combined influence, between 1917-21 there occurred epidemics "of a magnitude unrivalled in modern history. . . . It is impossible (he continues) to keep accurate figures, but conservative estimates by Russians put the morbidity from typhus alone at 20-30 millions with a mortality of 3 millions (Professor L. A. Tarassewitch). About a third as many suffered from recurrent fever"—also louse-borne. The conditions in Serbia and in Russia (it may be conceded) were "exceptional." But it is not irrelevant even to an Australian history to note that so late as 1914 a severe outbreak of typhus fever occurred in Ireland.

Leakage of Cases Despite Quarantine. Leakage of cases through the quarantine sieve were few, at least in the experience of the A.I.F. Two men who deserted from an Australian unit at Marseilles and pretended to be British were detected as Australians from Egypt two months later through the diagnosis of *relapsing fever* in a British General Hospital. Three other cases of relapsing fever occurred in the troops near Armentières. The battalions were deloused; no secondary cases were discovered. Two cases of mild *smallpox* in vaccinated Australian troops occurred after they had reached Second Army. The unit concerned was revaccinated; no secondary cases occurred. *Dysentery.* British and

---

[23] From a note by Dr. Elsie Dalyell, an Australian medical graduate who served with this unit and had experience also with the disease in Constantinople after the war.
[24] *British Medical Journal*, June 14, Aug. 23, Sept. 20, 1924; Feb. 5, Feb. 19, June 11, Oct. 22, 1927; July 22, 1936. See also Dr. Haden Guest, *Lancet*, 21 Nov., 1931, and Zinsser, *loc. cit.*

French authorities at the Interallied Conferences were in agreement that "carriers" among the troops from the East and coolie workmen from Indo-China were responsible for the wide-spread infection of the troops on the Western Front with both bacillary and amoebic dysentery.[25]

Notification in the Control of Preventable Diseases. Notification followed by appropriate action was exploited even more extensively in the British Army than in civil life; the object was both to direct local action (as in mumps, scabies, C.S.F., or trench foot) and also to determine general policy (as in tetanus, typhoid, and dysentery). But save for a few special diseases a precise or standard line of procedure was not laid down for the whole of the B.E.F.; in each sphere of administration—of G.H.Q., Army, L. of C., and Base— local policy was in a large measure determined by the needs of the moment, and the purpose was achieved by improvised methods. The exploitation of the method was thus far from exact; but from the point of view of medical tactics the flexibility and initiative bestowed by devolution may well have been an important factor in the considerable measure of success ultimately achieved.

Procedure in British Army

This method of report or "notification" of disease was used for a variety of purposes and in several ways. It was employed

Four methods

(*i*) as in civil Public Health practice, to initiate prompt action for preventing the spread of certain highly infectious or especially dangerous transmissible diseases, in particular those of the respiratory class. Notification was made on *Army Form W. 3110.*

(*ii*) To furnish a statistical barometer of the *general health situation* in units and formations. For this purpose various regular returns were rendered, daily or weekly. The most important of these was *Army Form W. 3185,* a daily return of sick evacuated from field ambulances and C.C.S's. Field ambulances sent it to the A.D's.M.S.; these officers condensed the field ambulance returns into a statement for "Corps"; and Corps similarly compiled the returns for "Army." Casualty clearing stations rendered the returns direct to the D.M.S.

(*iii*) To ascertain the prevalence of particular diseases—such as trench foot, scabies, diarrhoea, C.S.F., V.D.—in order to direct administrative action, or to indicate the need for an extension of special accommodation; and also as a basis for disciplinary action.

(*iv*) Certain returns based on those rendered under (*i*) were sent

---

[25] A sharp outbreak of bacillary dysentery occurred in New Zealand troops soon after their arrival on the Armentières sector in May, 1916.

on by Army to G.H.Q. where they were used for purposes of policy and statistics.

The three last may be dismissed briefly.

As to (*ii*): *A.F.W. 3185* showed by units—officers by name, others by numbers only—the sick and wounded admitted, evacuated, discharged, died, and remaining during the previous 24 hours. This return was the means whereby the *weekly sick rate* in all units was determined and published each week by Army Headquarters (D.M.S.). During the war the figure 0·3 per cent. per day—2·1 per cent. per week—was used empirically as a rough steel-yard for assessing the health and "sanitary discipline" of units and formations. Evacuations in excess of this figure were held to indicate an approach to the danger line, and to call for special enquiry.[26] The return was thus an important disciplinary implement and it was perhaps the most effective means for stimulating the sanitary conscience of units and formations.

As to (*iii*): "Special" returns were required from time to time by D.M.S. of Armies of such conditions as scabies, trench foot, V.D., diarrhoea, mumps, C.S.F. *Army Form W. 3185* was often used as a means for obtaining this information.[27]

In the wider field of the general medical policy and health administration of the B.E.F., the Director-General at G.H.Q. kept himself informed—somewhat precariously it would seem—through his special technical officers, of the prevalence of the most important endemic or sporadic infections—such as tetanus, C.S.F., dysentery, enteric—by "consolidation" of army returns and notifications.[28] Here however the subject merges with that of the permanent records of the war, personal and statistical.

(*iv*) The enormous number of casualties in the B.E.F.—in the case of non-battle casualties some 3,500,000—made complete statistical analysis impossible; consequently these administrative records kept in the field achieved considerable importance for statistical purposes. Certain diseases—in particular enteric, tetanus, C.S.F., and the major quarantinable diseases—were recorded and, so far as the exigencies of warfare permitted, tabulated by the technical staff of the Director-General B.E.F.

It remains to examine in some detail the first of these procedures namely that of specific notification of "cases" of disease followed by segregation of presumed infective individuals.

The first of these four methods, immediate notification of

---

[26] *See Graph No. 8 at p. 493.* Before the war this figure was employed differently. *Field Service Regulations, 1914 (p. 123)* laid down that "during periods of marching or halting without serious fighting, a steady inflow to the field ambulances of about 0·3 per cent. occurs daily, and . . . consequently a similar outflow from the field ambulances to the clearing hospitals, and thence to the stationary hospitals must be anticipated."

[27] Thus at the end of 1916 the D.M.S. of Fourth Army required that this return should include a statement of the number of cases of scabies, venereal disease, and trench foot; and of "the three most prevalent diseases."

[28] For the first two years of the war the records of tetanus and of typhoid were confused by reason of lack of co-ordination between the B.E.F. and the army medical system in Britain. The importance of ensuring co-ordination between the Expeditionary Force and its base is illustrated almost as forcibly by the experience of the B.E.F. as by that of the M.E.F.

specified diseases, was the only effective means available for checking the spread of those infectious diseases in which direct action against the agent was impossible. As such the procedure calls for particular note, and the more so because the methods adopted in the B.E.F. are open to constructive criticism. In the Australian force it was the means for a most effective internal campaign against epidemic camp diseases, a campaign in which infections brought in the troop transports from Australia—in particular, *mumps* and *measles* —were eradicated from the training battalions in Britain and drafts for France. We shall examine the working and machinery of this very important branch of military preventive medicine, first as it developed in the B.E.F., and subsequently in its quite dramatically successful exploitation in the A.I.F. reinforcement camps in England.

Army Form W. 3110. "Notification of infectious diseases," corresponded to the form of notification in civil practice. It was

(1) the implement whereby the machinery for the control of infectious disease by administrative measures was set in motion. (2) The instrument through which the "higher" medical administration kept its finger on the pulse of fluctuations in the transmissible diseases that held a menace for the armies in the field. (3) The source of special returns, and (4) was also used to ascertain the prevalence or existence of new types of disease within the force.

Action Upon Notification. In civil public health administration prevention of infectious disease by the indirect method of notification— followed by confirmatory diagnosis, the isolation of case and contacts, disinfection, and search for the previous case, carrier, or other source of disease—provides that the *practitioner* shall notify the occurrence in his practice of a case of such disease to the *health authority* by whom necessary action is initiated. Speaking broadly, in the army the procedure was reversed: specific notification, involving effective action, was made by the health authority (army or division headquarters) to the practitioner (R.M.O.) on information from the medical unit receiving the case. A positive diagnosis at the casualty clearing station, field ambulance, or by the mobile bacteriological laboratory was notified commonly through "Corps" to the A.D.M.S. and through him to the regimental medical officer for appropriate action. By this line of procedure such action was liable to be much delayed. Thus during the battles of the Somme in 1916, notification was "often not received until after an interval of from 10 to 12 days when precautionary measures are of little use."[29]

---
[29] From the personal diary of the O.C., No. 2 Sanitary Section, Major M. J. Holmes, dated 20 March, 1917.

By the end of 1916 the procedure was being speeded up by a short-circuit. A provisional notification of suspected cases by R.M.O. to A.D.M.S., was followed by direct action by the latter through his administrative sanitary officer, the Deputy Assistant-Director, to expedite diagnosis and if necessary to forestall it by segregation of contacts, search for carriers, and so forth. The effect of all this was, however, in a great measure offset by a peculiar hiatus in the chain of action which should follow notification. The defect lay in the fact that, apart from such steps as might be taken by the Deputy Assistant-Director to assist the regimental officer, an executive machinery was lacking for the difficult task of tracing the source of disease within or without the unit concerned, and of carrying through measures to prevent the further spread. This was brought about—as the A.I.F. in its experience under three armies discerned—by failure to exploit the possibilities of the *sanitary section*. Only, so far as can be ascertained, in Australian divisions was this public-health unit used for public-health purposes in the important field under consideration.

Shortly after the Australian divisions first entered the "nursery" front round Armentières, under Second Army, the staffs of I and II Anzac received the following order of D.M.S., Second Army, dated 14th June, 1916, which sufficiently indicates the regular practice in the B.E.F. In the matter of smallpox, typhus, relapsing fever, cholera and plague it necessarily followed the definite instructions of the D.G.M.S. at G.H.Q.

Experience in the A.I.F.

"In order to regularise the Notification of Infectious Disease the following procedure will be adopted dating from midnight 1st July, 1916.

"(1) Telegraphic notification is only required in the case of the following diseases—Suspected cases of Dysentery, Typhoid Fever, Paratyphoid 'A' and 'B,' Enteric Group, Cholera, Scarlet Fever, Cerebro-spinal Meningitis, Diphtheria, Dysentery, Typhus Fever, Relapsing Fever, Smallpox, Jaundice. It will be carried out as follows: Diagnosed cases of the above diseases will be notified by telegram to this office immediately a diagnosis has been arrived at. The notification will be sent by the Officer Commanding Casualty Clearing Station—or, in the event of a case being sent direct to No. 7 General Hospital, Malassise (for infectious cases), by the A.D.M.S. Division concerned—and will be in the form indicated. *Suspected cases of Dysentery* will also be notified.

"In addition to the notification mentioned above, on the diagnosis of a case of Diphtheria or Cerebro-spinal Meningitis, or on the admission of a case suspected to be suffering from one of these diseases, if the case has been diagnosed in the C.C.S., the O.C. of the C.C.S. will inform (by wire) the A.D.M.S. of the Division who will at once take steps in direct communication with the Officer-in-charge of the Mobile Laboratory concerned for the investigation of the carrier condition of the contacts in order that those found free from infection may be returned to duty without unnecessary delay and that the carrier contacts may be suitably dealt with.

"(2) A weekly nominal roll will be rendered direct to the D.M.S.

2nd Army by A.D's.M.S. and Officers commanding C.C.S's. It will include all officers and men diagnosed during the past week to be suffering from any of the following infectious diseases:—Anthrax, Cerebrospinal Meningitis, Cholera, Chicken pox, Diphtheria, Dysentery, Enteric Group, Erysipelas, Foot and mouth Disease, Glanders, Hydrophobia, Measles, Mumps, Plague, Paratyphoid fever (A & B), Pneumonia lobar, Relapsing Fever, Rose Measles (German M.), Scarlet fever, Smallpox, Tetanus, Typhoid fever, Typhus fever, Tuberculosis, Whooping cough.

"Should unusual evidence of any preventible disease manifest itself in any given formation, the matter will be the subject of a special report to this office by the D.D.M.S. of the Corps concerned, the fact of any unusual incidence of disease being reported by telegram."

In addition, a daily return of scabies was rendered to each Divisional A.D.M.S.[30]

The cases notified by army headquarters to I Anzac Corps during the period March, 1916, to February, 1917, are as follows:—[31]

Gastro-intestinal Infections		Respiratory Infections	
Typhoid Group		Scarlet Fever	19
Typhoid	41	Diphtheria	71
"Enteric Group"	5	Measles	211
Paratyphoid "A"	20	Mumps	1,658
Paratyphoid "B"	12	Cerebro-spinal Fever	51
Dysentery Group		Venereal Infections	1,194
"Shiga"	26		
"Flexner"	169	Miscellaneous Diseases	
"Mixed"	18	Acute Jaundice	18
Bacillary Unspecified	14	Trachoma	17
(Clinical) Unknown Origin	69	Tetanus	6
		Nephritis	50
Protozoal Group			
Amoebic dysentery	16		

Note.—During the period 3 cases of *smallpox*, 3 of *typhus fever*, 5 of *relapsing fever* were reported by Army or G.H.Q. as having been notified as occurring in Australian troops.[32]

As a means to early and exact diagnosis and disposal of

---

[30] Until 1918 no routine report of any kind was made by the regimental medical officers in France to the A.D.M.S. In the 1st Australian Division on Gallipoli a daily return was required by the A.D.M.S. (Colonel N. R. Howse), who was thus able to keep himself closely informed of the general health of battalions, and also of individual lapses from sanitary vigilance.

[31] The total evacuations from all diseases will be found in the statistical summary on *pp.* 496-7.

[32] The table was compiled by the D.A.D.M.S., I Anzac, from notifications by Army to Corps. It represents an approximation only, since such "notification" was not complete. The cases of typhus appear to have been credited to the A.I.F. in error. See *pp.* 543-4.

THE PREVENTION OF DISEASE

transmissible diseases an immense organisation was built up. Its scientific basis—research into the causes and pathology of "new" diseases, trench foot, trench fever, trench nephritis; into the conditions determining the spread of infective diseases, for example, the habits of the louse, the natural history of the house-fly, the existence or otherwise of the carrier state, the bacteriology of dysentery, the epidemiology of cerebro-spinal fever, and a host of other investigations; and the perfecting of technical measures such as disinfection and dis-infestation, sterilisation of water, treatment of carriers, and so forth—all this immense paraphernalia of research must for the purpose of this chapter be frankly postulated. It included the "mobile laboratories" at the front; those at the base in France, the latter for the most part departments of the general and stationary hospitals; the national research institutions, such as (to select among many) the laboratories of the Medical Research Committee in Great Britain, of the Institut Pasteur of France, and of the Academy Lucri of Rome; and the machinery of international co-operation—the permanent "Commission Sanitaire des Pays Alliées" and the annual deliberations of the "Interallied Sanitary Conferences."

The implements of indirect action

The Mobile (Bacteriological) Laboratories. These units, consisting of a senior and junior officer and one N.C.O. (laboratory attendant) together with a laboratory on a motor truck and a light car for the officers, were designed as strictly mobile units.[33] But during the years of static warfare they overflowed into huts or buildings and developed into a thoroughly organised rampart of diagnosis and of research along the whole front.[34] Australia supplied no such unit for her infantry in the *Western* theatre.[35] These mobile laboratories were "army" units, and, though allocated to serve the several corps, were administered directly by the D.M.S. of each army. Their work will be touched on in *Volume III*, but it may here be said that it made a lasting impression on the Medical Officers of the Australian Imperial Force. They were staffed for the most part by members from the teaching staffs of the medical schools. Combining routine work with "research" many of these men made important contributions not only to the medical

---

[33] The mobile hygienic laboratory had a precisely similar establishment.

[34] The place of the *pathological and bacteriological laboratory* in the prevention of disease in modern warfare has been sufficiently indicated by the study made in *Vol. I* of the problems of wastage at Gallipoli and in Palestine. On the Western Front also the history of the mobile laboratory is one of extraordinary interest, both military and professional.

[35] For the work of the Anzac Field Laboratory in Palestine see *Vol. I, pp. 603-4*. In France a Canadian unit (No. 5 Mobile Laboratory) achieved a high reputation.

history of the war but to medical science in general. A second line of scientific defence and attack was created in laboratories at the bases in France which have already been described.

Isolation and Segregation. This administrative procedure was carried out for the most part in "Stationary Hospitals"[36] or in casualty clearing stations set aside and specially staffed and organised for the purpose, and notified as such by "Army" to Corps and Divisions. Field ambulances were used as "scabies stations," and for the segregation of mumps—which disease provided at times a major problem in isolation.

Means of transport for infectious cases were arranged either by Division or—most commonly—by Corps, and were carried out by the horsed ambulance waggons of field ambulances or the motor ambulances of the motor ambulance convoy.

Disinfection. Next to the chlorination of water, the operation of disinfection, or "disinfestation," was perhaps the most important mechanical procedure in the preventive medicine of the war. The matter relates more closely to the technique of "personal hygiene" than to the present subject; but it may be said that the routine and haphazard "disinfection" of the fomites of "infectious" cases or of premises, was recognised for what most often it is—an administrative gesture, not to say a fetish. By the end of the war to "disinfect" meant in the Army to kill by well-attested means some specific agent of disease, in particular the strepto- and staphylo-cocci, the sarcoptes scabiei (itch-mite), and the pediculus vestimenti or corporis (body louse).[37] The pragmatic outlook of medical science to-day reflects, and doubtless also in some degree derives from this line of development in war-medicine.

In 1914 the cult of "the previous case" as the prime factor in the epidemic spread of diseases, including that of wound infections, had reached the standard text-books of medicine and pathology; and so had the theory of the "carrier" as the most important instrument in maintaining the endemic forms of transmissible disease. Successive editions of these books, and not less clearly the actual records of the war itself, show that these views on the nature of the biological mechanism which maintains the continuity of the various "infectious" diseases received an immense impetus during, and in some part through, the war. *Pari passu* with increased mastery of the "sanitary" situation, this indirect line of approach to the problem of disease prevention was more systematically exploited. The idea of the "carrier" came indeed largely to dominate the outlook in many important diseases, in particular in dysentery—bacillary and amoebic—in enteric fever, cerebrospinal fever, diphtheria, and (in France) in gonorrhoea. In

The "carrier" problem

---
[36] These were properly Line of Communication units, but when employed as above might be administered by "Army."
[37] *See p.* 575.

the researches connected with this evolution the Australian Army Medical Service was well represented.

What (it may be asked) was the exact value of this particular line of "preventive" activity? Did the immense expenditure of effort and resources involved in its execution play a material part in preventing infectious disease—for example, in the notable success on the Western Front of the campaign against gastro-intestinal infections, or in bringing about the comparative immunity from the carrier spread (droplet) infections of low infective virulence—C.S.F., diphtheria, scarlet fever, and perhaps lobar pneumonia, or in reducing the potential incidence of the more highly infective virus infections, measles, mumps, roseola, and virus influenza? A categorical answer in general terms to these questions would be of less service than an examination of its influence in preventing the two forms of infection chiefly concerned—gastro-intestinal and respiratory tract. Its part in preventing the first is examined later in this chapter.[38] But the question is particularly germane to the group of diseases in which infection is spread through the respiratory tract and fauces, in which, indeed, except for inoculation, "spacing out," and promotion of general health, this *"indirect" method of attack was the only one available.*

Results illustrated in R.T.I.

In the Great War, the Achilles heel in the armour of preventive medicine was, as it is to-day, the respiratory tract. To micro-organisms seeking parasitic relations with man the most effective mode of entry in all highly civilised communities is transportation by droplets of mucus exhaled as in coughing or transmitted by manual or other mechanical mode of vection.[39] Against organisms adopting these tactics, failing artificial immunisation and granted a sufficient margin of virulence in the attacker, even the most scientifically organised community, civil or military, is little less vulnerable than the barbarian.[40]

---

[38] *See pp. 580-87.*

[39] This last method of mucous interchange was recognised as being important in connection especially with diphtheria. Specific orders were issued in some armies for the disinfection of drinking cups in canteens.

[40] At the present time in public health circles opinions differ greatly as to the value and scope of notification and isolation as a means for controlling epidemic diseases of or their spread through the medium of the respiratory tract. For example in the various States of the Australian Commonwealth 37 distinct diseases are "notifiable"; but in the largest (New South Wales) only 13 of these are notifiable. ..*See also p. 490n.*

Incidence of R.T.I. in Army Life. The total deaths and disablings in the A.I.F. from infectious disease transmitted by respiratory tract mucus or—as in diphtheria—*materies morbi* from the fauces was very great. No more than in civil life was the army system able to cope with this form of infection and in all great camps it took the place, held elsewhere by gastro-intestinal infections, as "Public Enemy No. 1."[41] Thus the experiences of camp life in the A.I.F. Depots in U.K. have a definite military significance as well as medical interest, and it is to these, with a brief prefatory note on the problem of respiratory infection at the front that we now turn.[42]

Considered aetiologically the diseases of this class present a wide variety of biological powers for achieving their parasitic continuity such as virulence, tenacity, resistance, saprophytic potentiality, adaptation to environment and so forth—and these determine the form of rational reaction against them. Though these various mechanisms overlap, for the practical purpose of prevention the experiences of the A.I.F. suggest that the several disease groups can be roughly grouped as follows.

Aetiological Varieties of Respiratory Infections. (a) "Respiratory" diseases (in the aetiological sense) in which the infective virulence of the *materies morbi* or the susceptibility of the host to invasion is such as readily to bring about epidemic spread through indirect—*i.e.* air borne—"contact." Of such were mumps, measles, rubella, virus influenza, varicella; with, perhaps, a captive giant—variola.[43]

It is perhaps not mere coincidence that the causative agent in each of these is a "virus." (b) Minor variants—the coryzas and "febricula," pharyngitis, "septic sore throat," laryngitis and "influenza." (c) As a strictly pathogenic division a small group, but one of great importance presents itself in the secondary infections super-imposed on virus infections or physical traumata.[44] (d) Microbic infections of short range and typically spread by "carriers" and contact; cerebro-spinal fever,

---

[41] Though diseases of dirt (next to be considered) had the advantage in numbers from the point of view of "Divisional" wastage in the field, the heavy incidence of that type of disease was largely confined to the zone of the field armies.

[42] The problem presented by the prevalence of diseases of this nature does not lend itself as a whole to the compiling of exact statistics; but figures showing the incidence of diseases of this type on the Western Front and some account of the several disease classes will be found in *Vol. III*.

[43] Whether the disease is normally transmitted by air or by contact does not seem to be very clearly understood.

[44] For example, by the irritant and vesicant gases, or by measles, influenza, coryza. The most important of these complications (in general terms) were inflammations of the trachea, bronchi and lungs caused by streptococci, pneumococci, Pfeiffer's bacillus, and so forth, and infection of wounds by streptococcal "carriers" among surgeons or attendants.

diphtheria; rheumatic fever, "scarlet fever" and other haemolytic streptococcal infections (one of the great "discoveries" of the war), tonsillitis, occasionally lobar pneumonia; and we may include also Vincent's disease of the mouth and fauces. In these conditions direct "contagion" played a part possibly as important as infection through the air. (e) The morbid states comprised in the permanent pool of infection that has become notorious as chronic "upper respiratory tract infection" (U.R.T.I.), chronic tonsillar, nasal, and naso-pharyngeal infections, middle ear disease, sinus infections. With these we may place that strange pathogenic phenomenon, autogenous infection; wherein, under adverse physiological conditions, under infective pressure, or under impulse impressed by concurrent virus invasion, organisms of disease, tolerated as saprophytes, turn vicious and cause endemic infections such as "influenza," bronchitis, broncho-pneumonia, or lobar pneumonia. (f) Tuberculosis.

Each of these types was represented in the experience of the A.I.F. during and after the war as a source of specific problems. As a subject for study those included under (e) and (f) belong chiefly to the domain of clinical treatment and the prophylactic selection of recruits, and thus to the chapters of *Volume III*.

In the prophylaxis against this class of disease at the front, the most important question was whether it could be best fought by alleviating hardship or by combating infection. This question, together with the "carrier" problem will be examined in *Volume III*, where also figures are given showing the percentage of admissions of Australian troops to medical "units" for these diseases at the several levels of evacuation.

Experience of the A.I.F. in France

(a) *Mumps, Measles, Roseola, Virus Influenza.* Until checked by action in the A.I.F. Depots in the United Kingdom, mumps was a serious cause of trouble in the Australian force.[45] Isolation of cases and contacts did little to hinder its spread. The graph shows the inexorable course of such an epidemic through a susceptible military community, even in the field where contact was less close than in the camps or transports. The diffusion of mumps in the II Anzac Corps from the 3rd Australian to the New Zealand Division reflects, on a small scale, the spread of the influenza virus in 1918 throughout the civilised world. The impact of this latter disease on the A.I.F. troops in France has features of much interest, to which reference is made in later chapters. The pandemic itself is dealt with in *Volume III*.

(b) *"Minor Variants."* These "diseases" were responsible for a

---

[45] Very extensive outbreaks of mumps occurred among recruits in the French Army.

large part of the sick parade of the R.M.O. and "light duty" list of battalions; and also of the drug bill of the War Office.

(c) *Secondary Infections.* Under the conditions of the front this group was largely unpreventable and it therefore calls for no particular reference here.

Graph No. 10—THE COURSE OF A MUMPS EPIDEMIC IN THE II ANZAC CORPS DECEMBER, 1916, TO AUGUST, 1917.

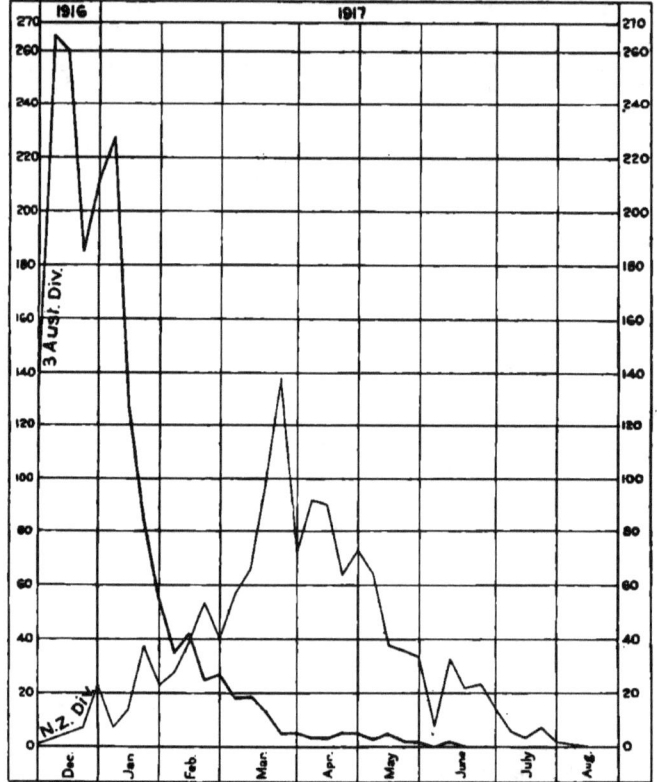

(d) *The "Carrier" Type.* Diphtheria, cerebro-spinal fever, scarlet fever, lobar pneumonia. Diseases of this type did not become unduly prevalent in the A.I.F. on the Western Front. In Circular Memorandum No. 19 dated 1st April, 1917, the Director-General, B.E.F. laid down periods of isolation and prescribed "throat sprays."

But the Great War showed that in this type of infection the treatment of contacts and search for carriers was of far less practical importance than the spacing out of potential cases, thus minimising the number of contacts made by each individual and also the "mass" of

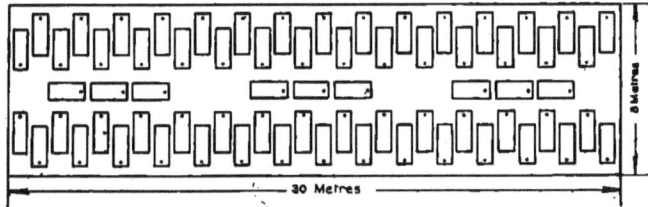

Beds arranged in "Adrian" hut to accommodate 69 men "head to foot" to avoid mucous interchange.

infective matter inhaled. A wide spacing was inherent in the conditions of life at the front; except for brief periods spent in the staging camps the troops lived in the open trench, or in scattered billets. To this fact may with confidence be attributed their comparative freedom from *cerebro-spinal fever, scarlet fever, lobar pneumonia,*[46] and perhaps *diphtheria*.

---

[46] In a discussion on respiratory diseases held in Paris in Sept., 1918, by the "Research Society of the American Red Cross Society in France," the A.D.M.S. Sanitation, B.E.F. (Col. W. W. O. Beveridge) emphasised this aspect of the problem and gave striking figures showing the result of tackling on these lines such diseases as diphtheria, C.S.F., and pneumonia. The American officers who spoke had not found it easy to apply this line of defence—by reason, probably, of the stupendous "mass production" of the A.E.F.

The following table shows "the incidence rate for pneumonia per 100,000 troops of the British Armies in France and that of the A.E.F.": taken from a report by Major Haven Emerson M.R.S. in *War Medicine, Vol. II, No. 3, p. 312.* This volume contained reports of the "Research Society" and other matter and was published by the American Red Cross Society in France.

	1917		1918	
	A.E.F.	B.E.F.	A.E.F.	B.E.F.
Jan.	—	8·67	392·3	17·16
Feb.	—	25·27	·155·3	5·65
Mar.	—	14·58	163·9	10·11
Apr.	—	10·40	59·0	11·80
May	—	8·93	16·5	7·65
June	—	6·23	82·2	10·24
July	66·6	7·35	44·6	—
Aug.	26·9	4·68	40·7	—
Sept.	20·4	3·49	—	—
Oct.	70·21	5·68	—	—
Nov.	66·0	6·65	—	—
Dec.	213·3	7·55	—	—

The report from which the figures are taken was published in October. Later figures do not seem to have been available at the time. They include the experience of the A.E.F. in camps in U.S.A., and on transports. The following are given as "known" contributory causes:—Crowding in camps, trains, and ports in U.S.A.; crowding, inadequate ventilation, insufficient inspection on the transports; crowding in barracks in France; drilling beyond the point of reasonable fatigue; sleeping in wet clothes, insufficient blankets, cold food; practice of waiting complaint of sickness by men instead of searching for early symptoms of infection; neglect of ventilation; promiscuous spitting, coughing, and sneezing.

Relevant experiences in the A.I.F. will be found in *Vol. III.*

(c) *Autogenous Infection.* We have here to do with diseases in which the specific means of "prevention" were much less significant than the *promotion of health.*

In (a), (b) and (c) as well as in (e) the most instructive experience of the A.I.F. abroad was in the A.I.F. Depots in U.K., and to this experience we may now turn.

The main exemplar—A.I.F. Depots in U.K.

"In peace and civilized conditions the spread of infection from man to man is restricted by the fact that the population is partitioned up into separate rooms and houses. . . . In war all this structural arrangement is swept away."[47]

During the winter of 1916-17, notorious in the AI.F. as "the Somme Winter," concurrently with the terrible experiences of the force in front of Flers, there occurred—in the curious medical parlance—"an outbreak of disease" in the A.I.F. Depots in U.K. such as brought these camps into disrepute which has persisted in spite of the fact that in the sequel they were the scene of one of the most ambitious and sustained and on the whole successful campaigns in preventive medicine in the A.I.F. The cause of the outbreak belongs to the general problems of military camps in war—one of the most important in military medicine.[48]

The Influence of Climate. That the various types of parasitic disease have seasonal predilections—*e.g.* the gastro-intestinal for summer and respiratory for winter—is a matter of common experience, and has, it would seem, some specific relation to the effect of temperature on the agents of disease (*e.g.* of warmth on the increase in water of B. Dysenteriae) or on the tissue of their host (*e.g.* of cold on the respiratory tract of man). Repeatedly during 1915-17[49] objections were raised to the wintering of Australian troops in Britain; and this in despite of the record of sickness at Mena camp in Egypt, and the fact that other troops—even Canadian—

[47] Sir Almroth Wright, in a special letter to *The Times*, 28 Sept., 1914. (*See* Vol. I, p. 74.)

[48] The experience of the Canadians in the camps of training in Britain in the winter of 1914-15 was a tragic one. And two years later, in 1917 and 1918, the experience of the American Expeditionary Force in the camps of training in U.S.A. records a morbidity and mortality from disease which (though figures for exact comparison are not available) cannot have fallen short of one-half of the total casualties, battle and non-battle, sustained by America in the world war. Up to May of 1918—that is before the pandemic of virus influenza—"of the total loss of days due to hospitalisation from sickness" 42.61 per cent. were due to "respiratory infections"—namely, mumps, measles, scarlet fever, diphtheria, meningitis, acute bronchitis, influenza, lobar pneumonia, tonsillitis, broncho-pneumonia, and acute pharyngitis. ("Sinusitis, otitis, and secondary involvements commonly following upper respiratory tract infections" were not included.) From report by Major Haven Emerson, *loc. cit. pp. 311, 313.*

[49] *See* Vol. I, pp. 429, 505.

seem to have suffered in English camps as much sickness as the Australians.

But the experiences of the A.I.F. in the war proved that the prevalence or otherwise of infective diseases in a force will depend on the *intelligence, foresight, and energy applied to the particular problems of health far more than on the influence of temperature and climate per se*.[50] Of camp outbreaks of respiratory diseases it can be said that the history of the A.I.F. tends to show that they were rather attributable to neglect—sometimes no doubt unavoidable—of well recognised principles of medicine—and of common sense. The fact that climate was not the crucial factor is illustrated by a comparison of sickness and deaths in the A.I.F. Depots in England with those in the recruiting camps in Australia 1914-18, the training camps at Mena and Zeitoun 1914-15 and the reorganising camp at Tel-el-Kebir, 1915-16.[51]

The records of the depots disclose two clearly defined groups of problems in preventive medicine.

The problem defined

(*a*) From the pool of fit men—recruits or recovered—in the training battalions and Command Depots came (1) outbreaks of bronchitis, broncho-pneumonia, and lobar pneumonia, and, supporting these, a very large sub-stratum of minor diseases from infection—"influenza" and a horde of coryzas; from irritation—tracheitis, bronchial catarrh, and so forth; (2) a considerable incidence of cerebro-spinal fever and some diphtheria; (3) a very large one of venereal diseases; (4) epidemic virus diseases brought with troops from Australia—mumps, measles, roseola; (5) the epidemic of virus influenza in 1918.[52]

(*b*) From the other group of soldiers in the depots, men of B2b, C, and border line categories awaiting return to Australia for discharge, there derived, in addition to the diseases listed above, two important problems: (1) that of preventing[53]

---

[50] The absence of dysentery on transports in the tropics may be instanced. England, it may be recalled, was at one time grossly malarious, and, in parts, mosquitoes are hardly less prevalent than in Australia.

[51] The medical history of these has been recorded in *Vol. I, Part I, Chapters v, xxi, xxii, xxiv*.

[52] In connection with the intestinal infections and the groups of disease whose prevention was mainly a matter of personal and social hygiene, it need only be said that the depots were "happy in having no history." At no time did trouble arise from gastro-intestinal infection. The camps had a reticulated water-supply and were served by the local civic sanitary services (pan). Heavy mineral oil was found very effective as a fly-deterrent. Scabies was prevalent in 1915 but, with the arrival of the main force from Egypt and of the A.I.F. Sanitary Section formed in Egypt under Lieut.-Col. J. S. Purdy—which became No. 6 Australian Sanitary Section—fully satisfactory control was maintained.

[53] Officers engaged in depot work definitely recognised these as presenting problems in *preventive medicine*.

the development of permanent functional disability from the effects of wounding—in joints, nerves, tendons—or from those of gas, or from those of disease—D.A.H., rheumatism, debility; and especially in preventing the neuroses; and (2) the problem, peculiar to Australia, of repatriating from the Western seat of war 60,000 invalids and some 150,000 troops, with a proportion of wives and families, 10,000 miles, through the tropics.

The problems under (b), and those of *venereal disease*, and of *virus influenza*, will be examined in *Volume III*. There remains to be dealt with here the general problem of respiratory disease as met with in the depots.

For three years these various problems extended to the utmost the abilities of as efficient a medical "team" as any that the war produced.

Machinery. The A.I.F. Depots were administered by the British D.D.M.S., Southern Command, but, in reality, full responsibility fell on the Australian "A.D.M.S., A.I.F. Depots" with the D.M.S., A.I.F. as the virtual director. The working of the depot scheme was indeed closely correlated with that of the boarding system and early treatment centres for V.D. at Horseferry-road. Early in 1917 fears of a widespread epidemic in Britain of cerebro-spinal fever and the arrival of many cases of the disease in troops from Australia (among other matters) led to the recall from Egypt of the A.I.F. Adviser in Pathology, Lieut.-Colonel C. J. Martin.[54] Under his direction a "Central Pathological Laboratory, A.I.F." was formed, under Captain Eustace Ferguson, to deal with Australian carriers and cases. It was accommodated in the Lister Institute and for some time acted as the Central Laboratory for the "London Command." The "S.M.O's" of the groups at Salisbury Plain, the Depot Medical Officers, and the R.M.O's, with their Sanitary personnel and Sanitary Squads completed the scheme which was built up during the last half of 1916 and first of 1917. To implement the campaigns against respiratory diseases in 1917, Australian "Group Clearing Hospitals" were formed clearing to the British hospital system of the Southern Command.

Bronchitis and Pneumonia. The conditions during summer in the hutted camps on Salisbury Plain were admirably adapted to the requirements of the incoming Australian force. In spite of crudities inseparable from the conditions brought about by the wholly unforeseen demands created through the immense casu-

The diseases involved

---

[54] The immediate reason for his recall was the accidental discovery of carriers in the staff at Horseferry-road. Col. Martin found that the incidence was the same in adjoining communities—as in the Army and Navy stores. No outbreak occurred.

alties of the Somme—demands for drafts to replace wiped-out battalions and for expansion in the convalescent depots to accommodate the incoming wave of recovered casualties—for the first six months little serious disease occurred, and what there was of it derived from the troop transports. But autumn found the depots quite unprepared for a winter on the Plain. Some camps were ill-sited—exposed and bleak—in particular Larkhill, Rollestone, and Perham Downs. But, most important, there had not been time to build up a staff capable of rising to the occasion; living, messing, training, sick parades, were mechanical—there was no vision.[55]

During the first quarter of 1917, 123 deaths from pneumonia and broncho-pneumonia occurred in the depot camps, out of a total of 158. In the second week in January the depot staff was reorganised. On February 13th the Right Honourable Andrew Fisher, the High Commissioner for Australia, desired a report on the circumstances of the outbreak and on health at the depots in general. In his consequent report to the D.M.S., A.I.F., the A.D.M.S. Depots (Colonel McWhae) pointed out that although the daily sick parade averaged over 4 per cent. of the troops in camp and the evacuation to hospital almost 2 per cent. per week, about half of the total sickness was mumps and venereal. The average number in hospital at any time was 7·5 per cent. of the troops in camp, of which number venereal cases comprised 3·5. Of the total sick sent to hospital for three weeks, January 12th to February 1st, 57 only were for pneumonia, broncho-pneumonia, bronchitis, and cerebro-spinal fever, but these furnished the whole of the deaths that occurred in the period. In concluding his report the A.D.M.S. gave his opinion that

"in view of the prevalence of influenza (*sic*) and the severe winter and the presence of over 10,000 invalids in the command, the health of the troops is good and the mortality not greater than would be expected in ordinary civilian life."

The general records, however, make it clear that this mortality from pneumonia was the expression of a great mass of minor infection, Pfeiffer's influenza, coryza, bronchitis, a

---

[55] *See pp. 446 et seq.*

result of conditions in which infection, physical trauma (as from cold) "chill," and lowered resistance cannot be distinguished; and that this minor sickness was an important factor in precipitating the more serious forms of disease. That this fact was observed and understood is seen from the measures

Graph No. 11—MORTALITY AMONG TROOPS IN A.I.F. DEPOTS IN THE UNITED KINGDOM, JANUARY, 1917, TO JUNE, 1919, SHOWING THE INFLUENCE OF EPIDEMICS OF RESPIRATORY DISEASE.

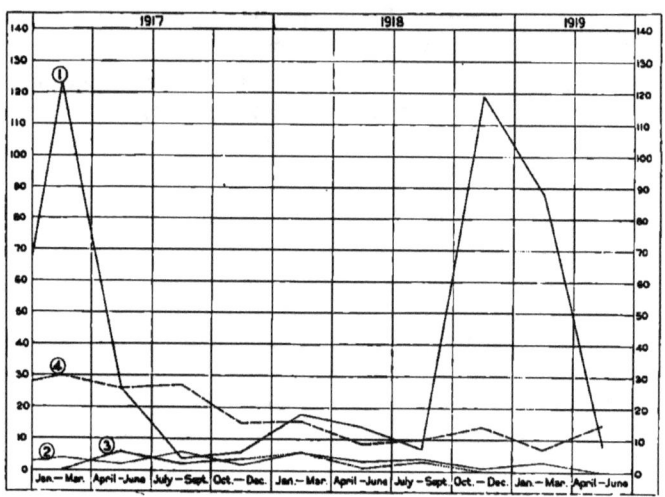

Numbered lines indicate: 1, Pneumonia and Broncho-Pneumonia; 2, Tuberculosis; 3, Cerebro-spinal Meningitis; 4, Other diseases.

taken to meet the crisis. These were stated by the A.D.M.S. in his report as follows:—

1. Breakfast was not to take place before 8 a.m.
2. Sick parades were held at 8.45 a.m. after breakfast.
3. No parade was allowed to be held before 9 a.m.
4. Special attention was paid to seeing that the men were provided with warm woollen underclothing and plenty of blankets, and a waterproof coat was issued to all.
5. Men were specially warned against standing or loitering about in the cold weather and parades in the open air were brisk.
6. All units received a light supper such as tea, soup, etc.

7. All medical officers were instructed that cases with a temperature over 100 degrees for 12 hours must be sent to hospital, and that all soldiers marked exempt from duty at the morning sick parade were to be again examined by them in the afternoon.
8. New arrivals from Australia were specially warned of the precautions to be taken against catching cold in the severe winter climate.
9. At a general meeting of medical officers early in February these precautions were impressed upon all and special attention was drawn to the necessity of sending cases early to hospital.

Attention was given to ventilation of huts by an order that at least diagonally opposite windows were to be kept open.

It was to implement these orders that there were formed the Group Clearing Hospitals, in which men suffering from minor sickness might be held instead of being treated in the lines.

Cerebro-spinal Fever. The A.I.F. depots escaped lightly in the world-wide diffusion of this curious disease during the war years. Of the cases which occurred, there were 114 deaths; the great majority had been infected on the troopships. Colonel McWhae says:—[56]

"During the week ending 22.3.17 it seemed that an epidemic of cerebro-spinal meningitis might break out; 10 positive cases occurred and 6 doubtful cases during that week, and there were 3 deaths. Steps were immediately taken as follows:—Special attention was called to existing instructions re ventilation and over-crowding. All windows and both doors of huts were to be open between 8 a.m. and 4 p.m. All medical officers in charge of troops visited commanding officers and discussed matters in connection with cerebro-spinal meningitis. A circular re ventilation, in which the position was explained to men, was posted up in huts."

Cases and contacts were dealt with by isolation and by a search for carriers in accordance with a routine designed by the A.I.F. Adviser in Bacteriology, Lieut.-Colonel Martin.[57]

The Epidemic Virus Diseases. If the first duty of the A.D.M.S. was to protect his depots, a not less important one was to secure from infection the drafts for France. As in 1915 in Egypt, the origin of this problem lay in Australia.

---

[56] In this and subsequent extracts, Col. McWhae's report is abridged and sometimes paraphrased. The extracts, however, are, for convenience, enclosed in inverted commas.

[57] The war-time studies of C.S.F., notably by Col. M. H. Gordon, materially extended the knowledge of the carrier state as well as of this disease itself; some details of the experience of the A.I.F. are given in *Vol. III*.

Each troopship brought its quota of contagion, and at first the conditions in the Command Depots made it impossible to urge an effective campaign in face of this constant reinfection from arriving reinforcements. "Mumps and measles were so widespread that it was impossible to exclude incubating cases from the drafts" [for France]. A solution to the problem was found in the creation of two "buffer zones": one of space and one of time. The spatial separation kept new arrivals away from the general depot system till they were clear of infection; the interval of time separated the medical inspection of the drafts from the date of their departure for the front. The latter process has already been described.[58] As to the former, to quote Colonel McWhae,

"The problems connected with infectious diseases did not arise from dangerous diseases such as cerebro-spinal meningitis but from 'ordinary diseases' such as mumps and measles. Except for a brief period practically all reinforcements from Australia were thoroughly infected with these diseases. Thus during January to March, 1917, 445 cases of mumps, 42 of measles, and 14 of C.S.F. arrived from the transports,[59] and cases in Command Hospitals increased from 300 on January 11th to 802 on March 5th. In this period the control of disease in the depots was in process of evolution. In the early winter months a great proportion of all men in camps were contacts. Effective isolation was impossible, the camps being crowded. . . ."

"By the end of March, 1917, the depots were reorganised. A thorough attempt was made to keep contacts from drafts. Contacts to the number of 8,600 were isolated, and in May it was possible to accommodate them in tented isolation camps in each training camp, which were placed out of bounds. Contacts of different dates were kept separate and did not mix with their units except in open air training. Nominal rolls showed the date of termination of isolation; cases among contacts were dealt with promptly and *their* contacts back-dated. The number in each tent was restricted and disinfection of blankets, etc. arranged."

The number of cases which occurred in the depots was greatly reduced; but the solution of the problem had to await "a yet more excellent way."

"Finally, (says the A.D.M.S.), to cut off at the fountain head the infection of troops in the depots, *all* drafts from Australia were isolated for 14 days in an isolation zone with their own training units instead of in separate camps, and thus could carry out their training. Cerebrospinal fever and diphtheria from the transports were dealt with as in Command Depots, isolation depending on the Bacteriologist's report."

[58] *See pp. 477-9.*
[59] The incidence of respiratory infections on the outward voyage from Australia was enormous (*see Vol. I, pp. 35, 39*). The problem was never tackled systematically at the Australian end.

This determined action was attended by most satisfactory results.

"These diseases ceased to cause any further worry despite the continued arrival of large numbers of mumps- and measles-infected troops from Australia. The (average) number of mumps patients in hospital decreased from 800 to 200, (and for) the first half of 1918 to 62. The total number of contacts lessened from 8,500 to 2,500 and during the first half of 1918 the average number was 1,765. The effectiveness of the isolation is shown by the fact that almost all the cases of mumps and measles occurred among troops already isolated, and very few indeed outside the isolated areas. Thus during August to November, 1917, when large numbers of infected convoys were arriving in England, 92 per cent. of mumps cases occurred in the isolation area and only 8 per cent. outside. The effect of these various measures on the overseas drafts was remarkable. Instead of large numbers of soldiers being struck off drafts prior to embarkation it became exceedingly rare for infectious disease to occur in troops who had finished their training. The great success however is shown by the fact that from June, 1917, to December, 1918, not a single case of mumps and only 5 cases of measles got to France among nearly 100,000 reinforcements."

The remaining health history of the depots belongs to venereal disease and the influenza epidemic. In August, 1917, a suggestion was made by the D.D.M.S.,

The experiences of 1917-1918

Southern Command that "no drafts from Australia be landed in this country between 1st January and 1st March." The D.M.S., A.I.F., agreed that there were "good medical grounds for intermitting the landing of Australian reinforcements in England in the winter"—December, January and February—basing his opinion on the analysis of the deaths from pneumonia and broncho-pneumonia in the first quarter of 1917. Of the 162, practically all occurred among troops recently arrived, the great majority in December, among whom the death rate was 8·7 per thousand per month of the troops arriving. "Owing to shipping difficulties" the War Office found it impossible to arrange for the suggested change; but "in view of the representations made by Surgeon-General Sir Neville Howse" the Army Council co-operated in providing improved accommodation for the next winter.

For the twelve months from July, 1917, to end of June, 1918, deaths numbered 141—3 per thousand per annum—as compared with nearly 300 for the first half of 1917.

III. DIRECT ACTION—HYGIENE AND SANITATION

We come now to the third and last of the procedures that make up the preventive medicine of the war. Of those types of disease that are amenable to direct action by sanitation or personal hygiene, only a few, and these commonplace ones, were prominent on the Western Front; but, as they were elemental in their social involvements, and were kept in check only by the social structure that has developed with civilisation, when this structure was violently deranged by warfare they could be dealt with only by laboriously improvising, or else by attempting actually to reconstruct it in the field. In mobile warfare these social ramparts had, of course, to be improvised; the successful experiments made in this direction in the Sinai and Palestine campaigns are described in *Volume I*. At Gallipoli, broadly speaking, all efforts at hygiene were ineffective. On the Western Front the static warfare compelled the construction, in the rear belt (say, between 5 and 15 miles behind the primitive zone of the trench line), of a system of feeding, water-supply, transport, housing, sanitation, cleansing, recreation, education and policing only less complex than that which sustains the social life of vast cities. Two types of "disease" have been identified above as having produced the impetus for this reconstruction—the diseases of dirt and squalor (calling for Social Hygiene); and the gastro-intestinal infections (the prime objective in Field "Sanitation").

The curious overlapping of the physical and the infective elements in the "cause" of the most important respiratory diseases, and the dominant part in their prevention played by the promotion of the natural resistance of the body, have no parallel whatever in connection with the type of disease next to be examined—the diseases of squalor: in these the "cause" was practically synonymous with the "agent."

Diseases of Dirt and Squalor. Colonel Soltau has written: "If some visionary could have foreseen the havoc the louse and the acarus would play, and had devised methods for their **Social hygiene** destruction, which could have been employed from the outset of war on an adequate scale, what a different story would have been unfolded in the medical history of the war."[60]

---
[60] "A note on Sick Wastage"—*Journal of the Royal Army Medical Corps, Aug. 1920, p. 155.*

The most obvious social difference and not the least important between highly and less highly civilised peoples, as also between wealth and squalor, Dives and Lazarus, is to be found in their respective washing-bills. And until the middle of the Great War the same might almost be said of the contrast between the cleanliness of the average bourgeois life of the day and the squalor of that in the field armies on the Western Front. This state of squalor is reflected in the callousness to minor crudities of life such as verminous infestation[61] and social promiscuity, and to the associated minor physical discomforts and disabilities—itches, rashes, ulcers, boils, sores, and so forth; and these again are reflected in the evolution of those parasitic diseases in which verminous infestation plays an essential part as vector of the morbid agent. These social conditions have been the "cause," in the aetiological sense, of the most terrible of the epidemic diseases that have scourged mankind, diseases which have destroyed vast armies and great nations and have changed the fabric of civilisation: in particular the Rickettsia (typhus) group, bubonic plague, and relapsing ("famine") fever. And on the Western Front in the Great War they were by far the most potent "cause" of temporary wastage—of a kind that did not, as a rule, take a man beyond the rest camp of his division. Their future is in the melting-pot with that of the human race; each will be determined by the triumph respectively of emotion and madness or of reason and sanity.

The Morbid Agents Concerned. The morbid states or "diseases" that compose this *group de convenance* are not difficult to identify though they come from various pathogenic groups. Most of the agents that have helped to create the universal instinct which manifests itself as "personal hygiene"—be this only a mud bath or a cat-lick—act on or through the *skin*. On the Western Front the most important of these diseases were scabies (caused by the acarus scabiei); inflammation of connective tissue, septic traumatic abrasion, and impetigo—the last often superimposed on scabies or on trench foot—and caused by strepto- and staphylo-cocci; sundry fungus (mycelial) diseases such as "dhobie itch," and "foot rot" (tinea albiginea). And in "trench fever" the Great War introduced a louse-borne disease quite new to medical science and, as a cause of temporary wastage, of first-rate military importance.

Incidence in the B.E.F. The most exact analysis of the cause of

---

[61] See *The Minor Horrors of War* by Prof. A. E. Shipley, a publication which was much used on Gallipoli. *See also Vol. I, p. 368.*

Army wastage made on a strictly pathogenic basis was that carried out during 12 months in a certain group of British casualty clearing stations which "tendered a monthly summary of diseases admitted." This summary was analysed by Colonel A. B. Soltau in "A note on Sick Wastage"[62] which sets forth more lucidly than any other writing known to the present author, the problem of preventive medicine in the Army zone in France. In relation to the immediate subject Colonel Soltau sums up thus:—

"[We arrive at] a total of 21,500 cases of trench fever. Adding to this total the 25,000 skin lesions originating in dirt, 'dirt disease' is seen to be the cause of 46,500 cases (out of 106,267 examined) or forty-four per cent. of the total incidence.[63] This mass of cases, so largely preventable, was a very serious factor in lessening the man-power of the Army. The methods of prevention were comparatively simple—careful inspection at frequent intervals, clean under-clothing, bathing facilities and disinfestation."

One further brief citation of Colonel Soltau's views will help to define an important type of disability which receives inadequate attention in military histories. Of the cases included in the group varicose veins, piles, hernia, appendix, eye, ear, and dental, Colonel Soltau remarks that "a very considerable number went to form the floating hospital population which was such a problem in the later years of the war. . . . Disabilities which in civil life do not prevent a man from being a wage earner, may on active service be a bar to fighting efficiency."

Re-grouped to permit some comparison with Australian figures Colonel Soltau's table is presented below.

DISEASE	Percentage	DISEASE	Percentage	DISEASE	Percentage	DISEASE	Percentage
Measles	0·74	Trench Fever	4·93	Local injury	5·22	Varicose veins	0·09
Mumps	0·42	Scabies	10·10	Synovitis	0·43	Piles	1·27
Influenza	3·41	I.C.T.	9·68	Trench foot	3·10	Hernia	1·23
Laryngitis	0·41	Boils	1·25	Myalgia	4·47	Appendix	0·66
Tonsillitis	1·34	Skin Diseases	4·27	Rheumatism	0·60	Total	3·25
Diphtheria	0·03	Total	30·23	Nephritis	1·53	Eye	1·01
Bronchitis	3·26	V.D.	6·34	Debility	2·39	Ear	1·32
Pneumonia	0·71	Dysentery	1·71	Total	17·74	Total	2·33
Pleurisy	0·60	Gastro-enteritis	0·56	Neurasthenia	0·36	Dental	2·45
T.B.	0·24			N.Y.D.N.	3·10	Sundry	0·17
Total	11·16	Diarrhoea	3·68	Cardiac	2·43	Grand	
P.U.O.	14·48	Total	5·95	Total	5·89	Total	100·00

The table shows percentage (for each class of disease) to the total admissions during twelve months to the C.C.S.'s in question.

---

[62] *Journal of the Royal Army Medical Corps, Aug. 1920, pp. 152-159* "A note on Sick Wastage" by Col. A. B. Soltau, Army Medical Service (T.F.). Col. Soltau was appointed Consulting Physician to First and Second Armies at the end of 1916, and was one of the clearest thinkers and most accurate observers on the consulting staff of the British Army. (He received his early education at the old High School in Launceston, Tasmania.)

[63] The comparable figure for the A.I.F. will be shown in the general statistical table in *Vol. III*. It should be noted that the tables given on *pp. 496-7, 501-4* represent admissions to field ambulance.

The system built up on the Western Front to promote escape from these scourges included organised provision for cleanliness of person and clothing together with prophylactic medical treatment. The first (and the most important) of these belongs properly to the history of the Quartermaster-General's Branch. Such a history is not known to the author.[64] Moreover, the relief of the medical service from this responsibility was a gradual and grudging concession by the military command to the facts, first, that a high standard of personal hygiene "paid" in terms of cannon fodder; and second, that military hygiene meant *organisation by the higher staff* at least as much as individual "discipline." From the "medical" standpoint, as distinct from the personal and aesthetic, "cleanliness" meant the destruction or removal of parasites as causes of specific diseases rather than as sources of discomfort and even of general ill-health. The medical service therefore remained deeply concerned in the technical adjuvants to baths and laundries—disinfection and delousing. But the comfort of cleanliness also had its medical involvements. The following account, therefore touches on A.I.F. experience in the general aspect of "cleanliness," as well as its more definitely "medical" side to wit, "disinfection" and "delousing" and the early detection and prophylactic treatment of scabies, pyodermia, I.C.T., trench fever, and so forth.

Personal hygiene

The war of 1914-18 did not differ from others less "great"

[64] Colonel Beadon's excellent work (*Vol. II* of *The Royal Army Service Corps*—Cambridge University Press) is as its sub-title indicates, "a history of transport and supply" and not a technical study. The history of the Services of Maintenance in the British Army is a sordid and disillusioning one; that of the A.S.C. is seen by so great an authority as Sir John Fortescue (*The Royal Army Service Corps*, *Vol. I, p. 265*) as "the long struggle of a great auxiliary service against the jealousy of Parliament and the prejudice of combatant officers." The most notable instance perhaps of this unfortunate British trait is the degradation of these services in the British Army after the Napoleonic wars. This is seen, *e.g.*, in the amazing contrast between the efficiency of the system of preventing wastage built up by Sir James McGrigor for Wellington in Spain, and the crudities of the Crimean War. Even to-day, with the "lessons" of the Great War still vivid, problems of maintenance are given little place in military training.

"Many historians would be hard put to it to give a clear account of the colossal work of 'Q' in the recent war. . . . The late Sir John Cowans [Quartermaster-General] speaking at Carlisle, complained with reason that in the thanks given by Parliament to the Army, no mention had been made of the work done by the Administrative Services, although as a whole the war was one of administration rather than strategy or tactics." ("The Load carried by the soldier" by Major N. V. Lothian, *Journal of the R.A.M.C. Jan. 1922, p. 17.*)

in being a physical and moral degradation to the primitive, though its circumstances permitted a more or less effective camouflage of this fact. Crude and primitive individualism commingled with the most highly sophisticated scientific co-operation in a curious emulsion of life that was neither civilised nor yet wholly primitive but an ill-assorted admixture of each—the murky twilight of the old gods, but a false dawn of the new. An excellent illustration of this strange assortment is seen in the subject under consideration.

Disinfection in the field

Apart from its place in surgery "disinfection" in the Great War signified essentially an attack on three specific parasitic pests. These were—

The parasites (i) The body louse, *pediculus humanus* var. *corporis* (*vestimentorum*).[65] This caused, directly, the morbid state known as "pediculosis"—with pyodermic complications; and, secondarily, certain major diseases—trench fever, typhus fever and relapsing fever.

(ii) The "itch mite" (*sarcoptes scabiei* var. *hominis*) causing "the itch," or scabies.

(iii) The pyogenic cocci (*strepto-* and *staphylo-cocci*), causing sores and suppurations—pyodermia—chiefly as impetigo, and I.C.T.

For the rest, it is, to say the least, doubtful whether the routine "terminal disinfection" of fomites (clothing and blankets) and premises after "infectious" diseases of the type of C.S.F., diphtheria, measles, mumps, or even typhoid and dysentery, was of any real significance as a factor in the stay of outbreaks.[66]

So far as concerns the present issue, namely, the prevention of wastage due to diseases attributable to these three parasites, we are concerned with—(1) the bionomics of the agents in three morbid states, *pediculosis, scabies, pyodermia*, with various permutations and combinations—the latter more important than the "pure" diseases; (2) the implements and apparatus for opposing these by "direct" action—to wit, various methods of "dis-infection" and "dis-infestation"; and (3) the arrangements in the B.E.F. for making these preventive measures available to the troops. These measures came to centre round the system of "Baths

---

[65] See MacCormac in the *Brit. Off. Med. History, Diseases of the War,* Vol. II, p. 89n.

[66] One of the strongest impressions that is gained as a result of study of "infectious disease" as a problem in the Great War, is the immense importance of direct contact with the "previous case"—whether as "case" or "carrier"—as a factor in contagion; that is to say, of personal contact between individuals, and the direct transfer of secretions containing so to speak "nascent" infection. Promiscuity, famine, and hygienic degradation, stand out pre-eminent as the major factors in epidemics of this type; in the Great War, on the Western Front, in the field armies, only the first of these factors, promiscuity, was effective. But the fate of Russia in and after the war suggests that in the next war it may be otherwise.

and Laundries," and the divisional establishment of Thresh steam disinfectors mounted on Foden lorries.

For what it is worth to humanity the Great War brought about this beneficent result—that the bionomics of the bodylouse and of the itch-mite were studied with an exactitude never previously approached in their history or man's, so that what we do not know of their intimate social and family life is scarcely worth knowing.[67] The consequent rise to fame of the streptococci does not require to be stressed.

The verminisation of a body of men thrust from civilised life into the promiscuity of mass warfare bears a close resemblance to the spread of "germs" in epidemic "disease,"[68] and this analogy carries through to the idea of "asepsis" and "antisepsis." The complete infestation of a battalion with lice or acari could be avoided only by the exclusion of "carriers"; a very few carriers—inevitable it would seem in our present social conditions—soon formed foci, and the general "rubbing of shoulders" and interchange of sleeping "pozzies," and other close contact involved in "active service" sufficed for the parasite, which spread by contagion with extraordinary rapidity in the population "exposed to risk."[69] The rate of their spread was influenced by various factors but chiefly by the population pressure, human and parasitic. The first Australian contingent was to some extent infested before it left camp, and at Mena much more widely so. Peacock found that, in 1916, 95 per cent. of British soldiers examined after six months' service at the front were lousy with an average of 20 lice per man; 5 per cent. were "dangerous carriers,

---

[67] Perhaps the most potent factor in the huge wastage caused by these parasites was failure to treat them seriously: the military command for long ignored them, the "scientific" medical profession disdained them. Though the rôle of the bodylouse in the spread of typhus fever was discovered (by Nicolle) in 1909, comparatively little was known of the bionomics of this insect. Professor Shipley's *Minor Horrors of War*, published in 1915, and then looked on as a mildly improper *jeu d'esprit*, was precursor to a larger literature on the louse, reflecting studies such as those of Bacot at the Lister Institute and of Prof. G. H. Nuttall at Cambridge and of Capt. Peacock in the field—as exact and scientific as those which elucidated the life history of malaria or of bilharziasis. Of scabies Capt. J. W. Munro, R.A.M.C., in a report (*R.A.M.C. Journal July 1919*) of a research carried out by him on the initiative of the D.G., A.M.S. in 1918-19, states that "in the [pre-war] literature relating to scabies and to the itch-mite no two accounts of the life-history of the mite agree, and there is a similar difference of opinion regarding its mode of spread or disposal." Hardly less pronounced was the clinical ignorance concerning this disease and its complications as these occurred among the troops in the field. For a very complete presentation of the progress made in the war in the aetiology, prophylaxis, and treatment of these conditions, the reader may be referred to the *British Official History* (*Hygiene Vol. II*), where an adequate bibliography is given. Instructions and memoranda were issued during the war—on pediculosis in 1916 and 1918, and on scabies in 1918.

[68] Compare also the extension of the plague of mice which in 1916-17 raged through the Australian wheat-stacks, and spread far and wide through the adjacent countryside.

[69] It was very widely held that some persons are repugnant to the louse and thus "immune" to pediculosis. There does not however seem to be any valid proof that such a condition exists as a physiological phenomenon; the freedom must be explained by extrinsic factors.

each bearing between 100 to 300 lice."[70] The efficiency of the survival technique of *sarcoptes scabiei* is shown by the fact that, of admissions for disease to C.C.S. those due to lice, scabies, or pyogenic cocci might on occasion be as high as 90 per cent., and that of men evacuated to the base for skin trouble almost 50 per cent. had scabies. Pyodermia was present as a primary or secondary infection in nearly 60 per cent. of all admissions to the Dermatological General Hospital at the base.[71] The pyogenic complications of pediculosis—*per se*—and of scabies were by far the most important elements in these two diseases, while lesions created through the scratch reaction against the parasites gave the pyogenic cocci of the skin their best opening to the dermis.

(*i*) *The Body Louse.* This insect is one of the most highly specialised of external parasites; its every organ and member is adapted for this purpose. Its strong preference for clothing rather than for body hairs[72] indicates the degree to which it is specialised to man. Apart from man the insect is wholly lost and forlorn; the longest period during which lice could survive separation from the human body was found by Peacock to be about 9 days.

"The louse," he says, "is a parasite which is utterly dependent upon man's blood for sustenance and man's body and clothing for prolonged prosperous longevity and reproduction."

Dissemination. The louse is very expert at "digging in" among the seams of the clothing to which it strongly adheres by hooked claws. Favoured sites are the seams at the fork of breeches and creases at the back of the shirt. Its spread from man to man is by a process of contagion with a range measured, in terms of space, by a few feet and, in terms of time, by a few days. Its powers of rapid diffusion—and incidentally of promoting that of smaller parasites such as rickettsia—lie, not in its own feeble and faltering movements, guided it would seem solely by a sense of warmth, but in its prodigious ability to make the most of its opportunities when established. Dugouts, blankets, bedding, and so forth were found to harbour very few lice, but one or two per man would suffice; with 8 or 12 eggs per day, and a cycle from egg to egg of 16 days, infestation was soon enormous. The solution therefore of the louse problem lay, as gradually became evident, in keeping the louse population per man at a minimum; and its crux lay in the egg, which will hatch out within 3 days, or as late as 30 days or more.

Vulnerability. It requires some force to crack a louse, so that to kill the insect by this means he must be found and caught. Through the

---

[70] *The Louse Problem at the Western Front,* by Lance-Sergeant A. D. Peacock, R.A.M.C., *p. 21.* Gross infestation reached as high as 1,300 to 10,000 counted lice as well as approximately 10,000 eggs on one shirt.

[71] No. 25 General at Hardelot. This hospital was in 1917-18 staffed by members of the A.A.N.S. These figures are from the *Brit. Off. Med. History, Diseases of the War, Vol. II, p. 68.* It should be said that the statistics of the Australian force do not reveal any incidence so high as this; *c.f. p. 496.*

[72] *Phthirus pubis* (crab louse) and *pediculus capitis* (head louse) were hardly more prevalent in the army than in civil life.

breathing pores (spiremata) it is vulnerable to oleagenous applications—exploited in the war in the form of vermijelli—and as with other insects naphtholene is highly toxic, and was used in "N.C.I." (naphtholene, creosote, iodoform) powder, or as a paste. It is killed by quite moderate heat, 55° C. dry heat in 5 minutes, 70° C. moist heat in 30 minutes. So far so good. But the catch in the louse problem lay first in the myriads of minute eggs; and, second, the fact that the rickettsia, if harboured in its excrement—their normal vehicle of contagion—were resistant to heat and antiseptics almost to the same extent as the pyogenic cocci.

Prophylaxis. The solution of the military problem of pediculosis was found to lie in the systematic mass disinfestation by the use of heat, as by ironing, hot air, or current steam. These amplified the individual efforts, which ascended through scratching, shaking, brushing, catching, applications, and scorching, to the home-made hot-air delouser (such as the "Russian Pit"), and so to the Foden lorry, steam hut, sulphur chamber, delousing train, and the system of "Baths and Laundries."

(*ii*) *Scabies.* The morbid condition known from time immemorial as the itch was found in the war to be a far more complex condition than had been supposed. The primary lesion —the "burrow" in the epidermis with underlying dermal reactive vesicle—is a minor and inconspicuous affair; the mischief came from infection of the scratch, and dermatitis from over-treatment. The crux of scabies as a medical problem lay in diagnosis by the R.M.O. and discrimination by the clinician; and in the education of these authorities. Few medical "lessons" of the war are more clear than this, that a practical knowledge of scabies in its every aspect is a matter of first-rate importance for every medical officer. This is far too large a matter to enter upon here but a few details as to the parasite are relevant.

Dissemination. Sarcoptes scabiei[73] lives in burrows in the human epidermis, but larvae, nymphs, and adult males wander when warm. As they are almost microscopic in size, transmission of the parasite is even more closely confined to contagion than in pediculosis. The vehicle most used by the itch-mite was the blanket, and next to this the underwear, both of which harboured the eggs as well as the acari, but direct personal contact was most important.[74] The life-cycle of the insect is 9 to 15 days —egg state 2½ to 3½, larval 1½ to 3, nymphal 1½ to 4, the adult female may live 4 to 5 weeks.

[73] All members of the sub-family sarcoptinae are parasitic in all stages, inhabiting the living tissues of their hosts. They are somewhat closely discriminating, but readers of *Vol. I* (*p.* 672*n.*) will recall an outbreak of camel mange in the Light Horse in Palestine.

[74] By no less an authority than Professor Darier (1917) the disease was classed, with *phthirus pubis* as "venereal." The data here given are taken chiefly from the article by Capt. Munro. It need hardly be recalled that there was an immense literature on scabies before the war.

Vulnerability. The clothing of persons suffering from scabies may remain infected for at least 11 days and blankets not less. "A fair amount of moisture is absolutely essential for the life of the mites and ova and this factor is as important as temperature." Acari, and in a less degree ova, are very susceptible to dry heat in the order of 50°-60° C. at 40 per cent. humidity. At 70 per cent. they are much more resistant. Of antiseptics, as is well known sulphur as ointment—1 in 15—was specific; but it was used with little discernment and too much stress on the sulphur.

Prophylaxis. Scabies alone of the three was attacked systematically by the indirect method of report and segregation, and this was implemented by regular scabies parades and scabies treatment stations—field ambulances or C.C.S's—as well as No. 25 General at the base. This was indeed the prime factor in prevention, far more important than disinfection; but it was full of pitfalls, in particular in the criteria of cure.

(*iii*) *Pyodermia*—the "pyogenic" cocci. In official war writings we find the term "pyococci" used to include both groups—streptococci and staphylococci. Since the war the immense accession of interest in the parasites that still are loosely associated under this title, has carried the subject of their related "diseases" almost to a new plane of scientific analysis, on a par with that of the rickettsial diseases and the salmonella group. In the war the pathogenic differentiation of the various "strains" of streptococci had scarcely commenced, and the wide field of parasitic action allotted to these, and the full appreciation of the powers of the staphylococci for sustained and malignant parasitism, are both largely post-war developments.

In the pyodermias we find the prime objective in prophylaxis—one which in the other two was secondary—namely, the protection of the man against himself. The mobility of the organisms being *nil* their chance in life lay almost wholly in the exploitation of local opportunity. Their mode of dissemination from man to man was and is still largely a matter of informed conjecture. The factors in their viability need not be traversed. The rôle of the two groups as a cause of septic skin lesions overlapped and from the point of view of prophylaxis by disinfection need not be discriminated. The most common skin disease at the front was impetigo which, MacCormac[75] states "as is well known . . . results from the streptococcal infection of the skin." "I.C.T." on the other hand was commonly staphylococcal. In both the prime factor in prevention was disinfection of the skin and of its immediate covering, the underwear; in other words baths and laundries.

The apparatus of disinfection ranged from that improvised

---

[75] *Brit. Off. Med. History, Diseases, Vol. II, p. 86.*

in the field units to the scientifically designed equipment of
the Sanitary Sections and the highly organised
Apparatus of disinfection mass-action of the baths and laundries. In
both spheres, improvised and designed, an
immense variety of apparatus was employed some of which
has received notice in the earlier volume. A technical description is not called for. Besides, SO_2 which was found of service
only at the Base, they exploited dry or moist heat.

Improvised Apparatus. The Serbian barrel was illustrated in *Volume I*. The "Russian Pit" hot air delouser reached the Western Front in 1918. Colonel Lelean's "boiler and sack" disinfector weighed only 50 lb., and worked on the principle of current steam passed through clothing by downward displacement in a collapsible water-proof sack in a hot-air chamber. (A diagram of the "Russian Pit" delouser is given at *p. 588.*)

Mass-action Apparatus. These may be classed as stationary and mobile. Of huts in which chiefly hot air was used various forms were designed, permanent or make-shift. The best known was that of Major Orr, C.A.M.C., which was heated by coke braziers placed in a central pit. Of mobile apparatus the Hunter railway van has already been illustrated at work in Palestine. For use on light railways at the front an admirable disinfesting truck was built at the I Anzac workshops under the direction of Captain C. D. Sheldon, R.E., for the A.Q.M.G. Anzac Corps (Lieut.-Colonel M. G. Taylor) early in 1917.[76]

The *"Foden" Lorry Thresh Disinfector.* The standard apparatus for disinfection and disinfestation on the Western Front was the well-known Thresh apparatus mounted on a Foden steam lorry. This employed the steam from the engine; and a temperature of somewhat over 100° C. at steam pressure of 5 lb. could quickly be attained. Its capacity was 100 blankets or 50 kits of clothing; the time required for each operation was about an hour. In the later years of the war they were used in conjunction with the Divisional baths.

Some five to fifteen miles behind the front, beyond the enemy's normal shelling, the social life of the military community merged more or less intimately—in billets,
Baths and Laundries estaminets, markets, social services and so
forth—with the normal communal existence of
the civil population of Northern France. A national social symbiosis developed; and in this a great system of semi-military "baths and laundries" had replaced the British house wife's "washing day"—by means of it several million males

---

[76] The chamber was of 125 cubic feet, the temperature attained 210° F. at a few pounds pressure of steam. Its capacity was 300 blankets in 2 hours. Lice were killed in half an hour. The blankets were dry on removal. A plan of this disinfector was shown at the Interallied Sanitary Conference in 1917, and was retained by the permanent Commission.

were kept reasonably clean and free from vermin. This had been, however, a very gradual development, and at the time with which we are dealing it had reached a very definite parting of ways.

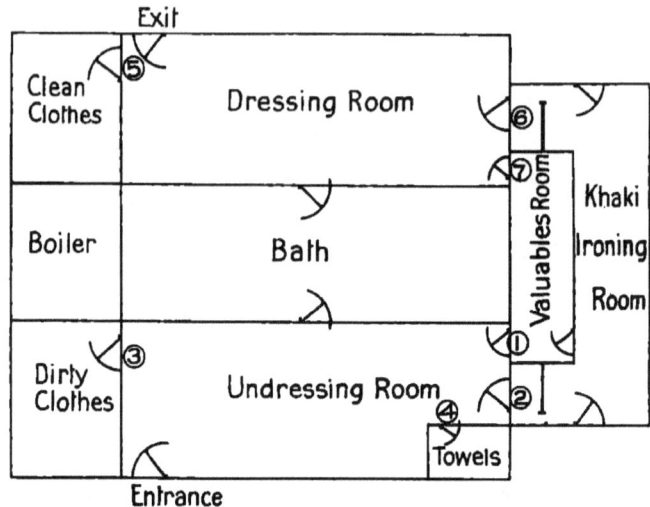

PLAN OF AUSTRALIAN CORPS BATHS AT LINDENHOEK, MARCH, 1918.

At (1) the bather hands in his cap, boots, puttees, and valuables, and receives a numbered disc with a string for hanging round the neck, the number corresponding with that on a pigeon-hole into which his property is put. At (2) he hands in his coat and trousers, which are numbered in accordance with the disc he has received at (1). At (3) he hands in his underclothes and receives a second disc bearing a number to correspond with the number of garments he hands in. The bather is now naked and enters the bath, which consists of showers only. Soap is provided in the bath and a disinfecting shower is used if necessary. On completion of the bath, the bather receives a towel and proceeds to dressing-room. At (5) he receives the number of pieces of underclothing corresponding with the number shown on the second disc; at (6) his coat and trousers, which have been ironed and brushed; at (7) his cap, boots, puttees, and valuables.

In the first rush of 1914 (the *British Official Medical History* notes) men washed when and how they could. "Ground sheets were used for improvising baths, and some battalions even carried large tarpaulins for the purpose," but such efforts were found "quite inadequate to deal with the problem as a whole." By November, 1914, "Divisional" baths were being organised by individual initiative on the principle that bathing and the provision of clean underclothes and the de-lousing of outer clothes should be combined in a single procedure. Such baths were established in all divisions of First and Second Armies in the winter of 1914-15. When the A.I.F. arrived in France in the spring of 1916, its medical service found itself responsible for the control of an extensive industrial organisation.

Of the arrangements with which the Australians first came in contact the D.A.D.M.S. I Anzac wrote:

Bathing arrangements Armentières Sector, May,1916
"Each Division has Divisional baths (in a blanchisserie if possible)—*e.g.* 1st Division at Sailly Laundry; 2nd Division, Erquinghem Laundry. A Medical Officer from Field Ambulance is in charge. He makes contracts for employment of women for ironing and sewing. The personnel to run the Laundry and Baths is supplied by Field Ambulances; 50-80 men are thus employed. [Application was made to Corps that P.B. men should be used for this work, with a few A.M.C. men to superintend, but the proposal was turned down.] Men give up their dirty underclothes and are given a clean set; they have a hot bath; their tunic and breeches are brushed and ironed to kill the lice; the dirty underclothes are washed and mended. Half a pound of coal is deducted for the baths from the [daily] allowance per man in the Division."

DIVISIONAL BATH RETURN FOR ONE WEEK

UNITS.	No. Bathed.	Garments washed.	Mended.	Ironed and disinfected.
1st Div.	7,150	35,034	4,995	5,391
2nd Div.	8,013	29,121	4,485	4,881

Australian Corps scheme of Baths
In this matter of bathing the B.E.F., "The Somme" created new conditions of life and a new outlook on its affairs. For the present reference these can be summed as follows:—

(*i*) The medical service was found too useful in other ways to be employed in running baths and laundries.

(*ii*) It was realised that the supply of clean clothes was an essential concomitant of bathing,[77] and that the job belonged properly to "Q" (Supply), not to the "A" Branch of the staff (personnel and discipline).

(*iii*) Proof that the louse was the vector of trench fever had called the attention of the General Staff.

---

[77] Of this change a high Australian authority says: "Until August, 1916, no attempt seems to have been made to go in for Baths and Laundries on a large scale. From time to time divisions had baths at which men might get clean garments in exchange for dirty as long as the stock of clean lasted, but stocks (supplied as they were from small Divisional laundries) were so limited that the clean clothing was seldom sufficient to go round. In those days every man was supposed to carry a spare set of underclothing plus an extra pair of socks, making 3 pairs in all—one pair worn and 2 pairs carried. . . . A small reserve of underclothing was allowed the division [from Ordnance] which was wholly inadequate [but at first] the men were able to wash their own clothing." (From note in War Diary of Corps Baths and Laundries Officer by Lieut.-Col. G. C. Somerville, later A.Q.M.G. Australian Corps.)

(iv) The "Corps" replaced the "Division" as the executive unit for tactics and administration.[78]

In the I Anzac Corps the "Q" branch embarked on a scheme of "baths and laundries" which in the Somme Winter assumed enormous proportions.

A Corps baths officer was made responsible for the running (chiefly by P.B. men) of all baths except such as might be improvised by the Divisions in the forward area, and for the laundry work and disinfection for the whole Corps, and for implementing the scheme of exchange of underwear. Large baths were established at Cagny and Heilly, and smaller ones at Fricourt, Montauban, Naours, Flesselles, and Coisy. The following notes were supplied by the A.Q.M.G., I Anzac for the Interallied Sanitary Conference, 1917.

"The ideal of a bath and change of underwear for men every 10 days involved the establishment of 5 baths with a capacity of 160 [men] each per hour. Nissen huts were equipped for steam sterilising with a capacity —each hut with twelve working hours—for 8,000 men; i.e. 32,000 pieces of clothing, plus 5,000 towels. The total *laundry* capacity per week (at the baths and by contract) totalled 265,000 pieces, i.e. the washing for 7,440 men per day. Contracts were let by weight or for pieces—the shirt, vest, drawers, socks and a towel were found to weigh—dirty 1·85 kilos, clean 1·70 kilos. Soap was not used. Washing was done with soda and ammonia. Women were employed for repairs."[79]

When the Corps went north its baths and laundries at Cagny were taken over by the Canadians, but they were resumed on its return south. Even while the front was fixed, the difficulties were stupendous; and with the rapid movement in "Alberich" the scheme was almost completely disorganised.[80] The Flanders offensive found the Corps again in control, but at the end of 1917 the Divisions resumed their normal executive autonomy, and the duty of establishing *baths* fell entirely on their respective D.A.Q.M.G's. The Corps however remained responsible for *laundry* work. The subsequent developments will be touched on in dealing with the open warfare of 1918.[81] Of the technical side of these enormous undertakings only a few facts can here be noted.

---

[78] *See pp. 66-69.*
[79] The officers responsible for this fine scheme were Lieut.-Col. M. G. Taylor, A.Q.M.G. and Lieut.-Col. S. G. Gibbs, D.A.Q.M.G.—two officers attached to the Corps from British units. The position of "Corps baths officer" created in August was filled by the appointment of Lieut. H. H. R. Macknight who held the position till the end of the war.
[80] *See p. 140.*
[81] *See p. 712.*

(i) *Bathing Routine.* The scheme was based on the principle that on entering the baths the soldier passed in his underclothes and uniform. The first were sterilised if possible and sent to laundry; the second was disinfested by ironing or steaming, while the soldier passed through the baths. A very exact method was required.

(ii) *The "Shower."*[82] The Australian soldier abroad found the apparatus of bathing different from those to which he had been accustomed. In Australia the "shower" is a normal installation in addition to a "plunge" bath; in Britain the usual provision was then a plunge bath or none. When the A.I.F. came to France the cult of the hot shower was in throes of evolution in the field, on the model—it would seem—of the mobile *bains douches* of the French Army.[83] By 1917 the hot shower had become general. It is not possible to enter upon a description of the various types of apparatus, stationary or mobile. The lesson of the warfare in France seems to be that improvisation and the exploitation of local resources can never be escaped, but standardised portable equipment for baths should be part of normal military impedimenta. The following note from the diary of the A.D.M.S., 4th Australian Division (Colonel Barber), sums up the situation at the end of attrition warfare:—

"Scabies is decreasing. This is apparently due to facilities for bathing. We have acquired four bathing sets. These weigh 7 cwt. and can be carried on one lorry with the Division. They can be erected in 24 hours and bathe about 60 men per hour. It is proposed to carry these sets with the Division, in which case there should be no more trouble on the bath question. Three rooms are necessary, one for bathing, one for undressing, and one for storing and serving out clean underclothes. If water [for bathing] is not available, as is the case with 12th Aust. Infantry Brigade at present, this is provided by water carts. It is hoped to provide an extra room for the ironing of the clothes."

The chief enemy against which all these medical defences were set up hardly appeared at all, or, if he did make his approach as in most of the great wars of history, he at least made no impression on the ramparts created by the medical service on the Western Front. Typhus was practically confined to the Eastern fronts.

The type disease of squalor in the war

Trench Fever. In his *Rats, Lice and History,* Hans Zinsser says: "Typhus had come to be the inevitable and expected companion of war and revolution; no encampment, no campaigning army, and no besieged city escaped it. It added to the terror of famines and floods; it stalked stealthily through the wretched quarters of the poor in cities and villages; it flourished in prisons and even went to sea in ships. And whenever circumstances were favourable it spread through countries and across national boundaries. As a matter of fact, until the last decade of the

---

[82] The provision for the very important matter of *"ablution"* (for example, of hands) was the responsibility of a man's unit, carried out in conjunction with the sanitary sections.

[83] The programme of the Interallied Sanitary Conference in 1917 included a demonstration of French portable *bains douches* at work near the front.

nineteenth century mankind changed very little as concerns those customs and personal habits which determine its relationship with typhus fever."[84]

In the Great War, the most bloody in human history, trench fever provides a burlesque anti-climax to the history of the exploits in destruction of one of the greatest among the "captains of the men of death" in the medical history of human wars. Typhus fever, chief actor in some of the greatest triumphs in the history of the parasitic exploitation of man by the underworld of life, was replaced epidemiologically, clinically, and aetiologically by trench fever, which, like typhus, was a "rickettsia" disease spread by lice. As a factor in the wastage of the Great War the story of trench fever is banal: though it incapacitated great numbers, it killed no one. In place of the terrific syndrome of typhus it presented, with vague pains and aches, an exasperating absence of objective evidence of "disease." But, as an episode in the age-long history of man's combat with his parasitic enemies, it stands out as the *raison d'être* and objective for one of the most clean-cut and successful campaigns in the history of rational scientific medicine.[85]

Trench fever may, indeed, well be termed the focal point of preventive medicine on the Western Front. It cannot be claimed that the A.I.F. had any special part in the researches that led up to this success. But the history of the campaign holds so important a "lesson" and is moreover so peculiarly fitted to impart a sense of life and purpose to the dry bones of the method and machinery which the Australians, like the rest of the B.E.F., employed, that a *résumé* of it will be given in a technical chapter in *Volume III*.

The Gastro-intestinal Infections. "In English there is a tendency to use the word 'sanitation' as if it were synonymous with scavenging, conservancy, and the removal of refuse and filth **Field sanitation** generally. . . . It is necessary to take a wider view of the subject."[86]

---

[84] Hans Zinsser, *Rats, Lice and History* (London: George Routledge and Sons Ltd., 1935), *p. 183.*
[85] The researches that elucidated the life history of trench fever have a close analogue in, and had their scientific and professional inspiration from, those by which the pathology of yellow fever was worked out by self-inoculation by a team of scientific experimenters from the Rockefeller Institute.
[86] *Manual of Elementary Military Hygiene, 1912, p. 1.*

65. Foden disinfectors at the Australian Corps Clothing Exchange, near Corbie

Aust. War Memorial Official Photo. No. E3450.
Taken on 10 September 1918.

66. BATH HOUSE OF THE 5TH AUSTRALIAN DIVISION AT
DAOURS, 21ST MAY, 1918

Men of the 51st Battalion bathing.

Aust. War Memorial Official Photo. No. E2314.

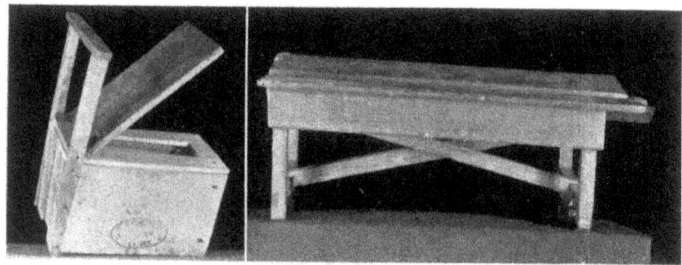

67. *Left*: FLY-PROOF LATRINE SEAT MADE FROM A BISCUIT BOX
Right: A STANDARD ABLUTION BENCH

These are photographs of models used in the Australian Corps School at Bailleul, February, 1918. (Now in the Australian War Memorial collection.)

Aust. War Memorial Official Photos. Nos. J6432 & J6431.

To face p. 581.

The "sanitary" policy and methods of the British Army in 1914 were in great part the result of a mental complex created by the sinister spectre of typhoid and dysentery in the history of British arms, in particular of the British Army in India and in the South African War; the story of cholera added an incentive to pay a perhaps undue attention to water.[87] That in general this apprehension was justified is shown by events at Gallipoli. It may come as a surprise to Australian medical officers that, though by the end of 1915 fear of typhoid had been dispelled, dysentery remained throughout the war the *bête noire* of the sanitary staff of the B.E.F.[88] Happily, as the figures show, it remained a "nightmare." Data are lacking from Australian experience to discriminate between "sanitation" and "T.A.B." as the reason for the low incidence of typhoid, and, after 1915, of paratyphoid in France. In the absence of cholera we are left with "dysentery" and "diarrhoea"—intestinal flux—as the *raison d'être* for the vast structure of "field sanitation" in France.

Before we enter upon an account of Australian experience —so far as it went—in France in these matters it is desirable to take a general survey of the problem of dysentery in the B.E.F.

Comparison with Gallipoli

The extraordinary contrast between the nosological composition as well as the extent of the sick wastage in the Gallipoli forces and that in the B.E.F.[89] must be taken to reflect some profound difference of environment or in the sanitary methods employed. Some differences are obvious. But to which is to be attributed the fact that while at Gallipoli dysentery, "dysenteric diarrhoea," and entero-colitis formed 20·8 per cent. of the total sick wastage and 30·2 per cent. of that from transmissible diseases, on the Western Front the figures are only 0·68 and 1·18 respectively?[90] It is obviously a matter of great importance that the precise reasons for the difference should be determined, but the distinction is by no means easy. It is as difficult to assign to any specific factor, or even to several, the pandemic of dysentery in the M.E.F. as

---

[87] It would seem, from observations by Australian medical officers in the advances to the Hindenburg Line in 1917 and 1918, that the Germans were far less concerned about this matter than were the British.

[88] This is clearly shown, for example, in the discussions of the Interallied Sanitary Conferences. A serious outbreak was indeed thought not impossible in 1918.

[89] *c.f. Chapter xxi of Vol. I* and this and the previous two chapters of the present volume.

[90] The percentages are based on figures given on *p. 451 of Vol. I and pp. 496, 501-4* of the present volume. If all cases diagnosed "diarrhoea" are included, the figures 0·68 and 1·18 will read 4·00 and 7·05 respectively. See also *p. 585n* this chapter.

it is to account for the comparative freedom of the B.E.F.[91] In *Volume I* responsibility for the Gallipoli pandemic was laid chiefly on two factors. First, that the *early cases of dysentery* were *not recognised* as such but were attributed to "irritation" from "clay in the water"—or by the D.M.S., M.E.F., to "excessive sea-bathing." Second, that when the trouble was recognised as dysentery, it was impossible to remove the *sources of infection*—men could not be evacuated until too ill to fight. In this way the whole community became infected but without the benefit of an acquired immunity. By a deductive process of exclusion—on a somewhat vague basis of factual evidence—the house-fly was incriminated as vector of infection from the open latrines; direct contagion by "dirt"—from lack of soap and water—was an accessory factor. Vitamin deficiency was referred to as a possible negative factor, and intestinal irritation and poor food as a positive pre-disposing one. Drinking water was there exonerated. In the following table the two experiences are compared.[92]

PATHOGENY	GALLIPOLI	FRANCE
Evacuation of infective persons	Only if too sick to be of use.	Every case of suspected dysentery was investigated and, if positive, evacuated.
Carriers	Conditions put control out of question.	The "case carrier" was controlled: all "diarrhoea" cases were suspect.
"Diarrhoea"	M.E.F. *Standing Orders* that "all cases of diarrhoea are to go sick" were not made effective.	Scientific and clinical discrimination were attempted, probably with considerable success.
Faecal disposal	Fully exposed in open pit latrines.	The use of "fly proof" latrines was a matter of discipline, but in front lines covering was often impossible or the order ignored.

---

[91] It is doubtful, indeed, whether even to-day we are exactly informed on the relative importance of the several biological and mechanical factors in the epidemic diffusion of dysentery and typhoid and even of cholera through a community. There is much in the recorded experiences of the war (it is convenient here to impress) to suggest that the part played by personal—so to speak hand to mouth—contact in the dissemination of all types of contagious disease has been much under-estimated and that the rôle of the house-fly has possibly been over-stressed. Unit outbreaks of typhoid (German, *Typhus abdominalis*) recorded in German unit histories—*e.g.* in that of the 202nd R.I.R., *pp*. *142-4* and the *German Official Medical History* seem to confirm more general impressions gained from Australian records that this mode of transfer may be dominant in quite extensive outbreaks of gastro-intestinal infection. In some forms of respiratory infection the rôle of the "spray" would seem over-stressed as against manual convection. We may instance diphtheria (*c.f.* Vincent's Angina), scarlet fever, tonsillitis, and other streptococcal infections of the naso-pharynx and respiratory tract.

[92] In the Gallipoli campaign the question of aetiology was burked by using the term "dysenteric diarrhoea." On Lemnos infection was as universal as on Gallipoli though, through circumstances, the disease was clinically somewhat less severe and was called "colitis."

1915-18]   THE PREVENTION OF DISEASE   583

PATHOGENY	GALLIPOLI	FRANCE
House-fly	Enormously prevalent.	Not considerable—kept in check by "sanitation."
Protection of of food	Practically non-existent.	A disciplinary matter, and reasonably effective.
Personal cleanliness (contagion)	"Soap and water" almost absent.	Except in the trenches facilities for cleanliness reasonably good.
Kitchens and messing	Cooks hopelessly handicapped.	For the most part clean, except in headquarters' messes.
Drinking water	Chiefly brought from overseas; presumed "safe"; not chlorinated.	Safety maintained by chlorination, with enormous effort, which, however, sometimes failed in the front line.
Food as a physical or physiological factor in the incidence of dysentery	Nominal ration identical with France, but as supplied was deficient in vitamins "B" and "C" and, as consumed, was "indigestible."	Greater variety; more fresh foods and much better cooking. A definite but certainly not a determining factor in the freedom from dysentery.
Promiscuity and crowding	Nothing approaching the crowding and promiscuity of Anzac was seen in France; but then Helles, Suvla, Lemnos, where these conditions were much less marked than at Anzac, were as badly infected.	
Climatic conditions	Summer continuously hot and dry.	Climate in summer moister and much more variable.
Seasonal incidence of fluxes	Practically confined to the summer months.	Seasonal incidence not so marked as at Gallipoli.
General factors	Continuous strain almost without any rest or relief.	Regular reliefs from the line to rest areas.

The initiation of prophylaxis and the research work in No. 3 A.G.H. on Lemnos have been described in *Volume I*. In France both lines of attack—on the human **Prophylaxis** sources of infection, and on the morbific agents **of dysentery** **in B.E.F.** themselves—were vigorously pursued. It is at this point that, although it comes outside the category of direct action, some reference must be made, as already foreshadowed in this chapter, to the method of *notification* as employed in the *prevention* of gastro-intestinal infections on the Western Front.

In the B.E.F. from the beginning of the war the policy was resolutely pursued of freeing the force from infection, and an elaborate organisation was built up to effect this. Cases of flux evacuated and found positive either to amoebic or bacillary dysenteric infections were not allowed to return to their units till after three consecutive negative findings. It must be said that in the experience of the medical service of the A.I.F., the policy was by no means easy to carry out. There were two reasons for this. First, the initial diagnosis as between diarrhoea and dysentery was often difficult or even impossible without exhaustive bacteriological investigation; and, second, it was not easy to ensure "disinfection" even if a man was clinically "cured."[93] In the first of these two reasons is bound up one of the major medical problems of warfare—which may indeed be identified as the type problem of military medicine.

As far back as authentic history can take us in the matter, the question of "cause" as between infection and irritation, "dysentery" and "diarrhoea," has been one of the major problems of military medicine. From the beginning of the Great War until the end, in almost every theatre, this was a cause of much anxiety, of acute differences of opinion[94] and of intense research. Medical literature of the war is greatly occupied with the problem in its various bearings. In the first year or two of the war euphemisms such as "clinical dysentery," "infective diarrhoea," "gastro-enteritis," "colitis," "diarrhoea," provided pigeon-holes for diagnosis whose multiplicity had a single origin—ignorance—and whose vagueness

" Diarrhoea "
or
" Dysentery "?

---

[93] Of such cases treated in No. 3 A.G.H. at Brighton, in particular of the amoebic infection, Major Lawton notes: "Many of the patients were there when we took over and remained when we left. Most of them had no symptoms except occasionally diarrhoea when having emetine bismuth iodide. . . . Practically, it might have been better to have let these men who had no symptoms join the other carriers in France, for there must have been any number of undetected carriers."

[94] The medical advisory committee of the M.E.F. held that much of the flux at Gallipoli was due to irritation—food *per se*—the same view was strongly pressed by the senior consultant physician of the A.I.F., Lieut.-Col. J. W. Springthorpe. The weight of evidence on the bacteriological side was strongly opposed to this. In the Sinai Campaign the same question was raised, sand being incriminated. Here again laboratory investigation proved such an hypothesis, to say the least, risky.

had one justification—military convenience. By the end of 1915 the situation had greatly changed as a result of the reaction against the terrible impact of intestinal disease in the Eastern theatres of war. Not only were facilities for the routine discrimination of the fluxes made available, but an immense body of new factual knowledge had been assembled and related. In these researches the Australian Medical Service was well represented. The clinical and bacteriological work at Lemnos, continued at Rouen by Lieut.-Colonel C. J. Martin, A.A.M.C., with Miss F. E. Williams, ranks among the most valuable contributions in the medical researches of the war[95] and is an important link in the chain which binds the discoveries of Flexner, Shiga, and their contemporaries to our present-day knowledge. Some account of these researches will be given in *Volume III*. For the present purpose it is only necessary to note that in this line of attack on the problem, procedure was greatly influenced by two discoveries; first that a negative result was often given in positive cases unless the stool was examined at once; second, that unless this was examined in an early stage of the disease it was often difficult, with the methods then in vogue, to identify the organism.[96] The tables given below and at *pages 501-4* and to be more fully set forth in *Volume III* analyse the records of intestinal fluxes in the A.I.F.

---

[95] *See Vol. I, pp. 457 et seq., and Vol. III* (work of Martin and Williams).

[96] It will have been observed that the diagnostic entry "diarrhoea" has been allotted a different place in the aetiological analysis of the figures of the B.E.F. from that given to the same "disease" in the records of Gallipoli. This apparent anomaly requires explanation. The different allocations are based on the assumption (1) that the great majority of men cleared to medical units at Gallipoli and therein recorded as suffering from "diarrhoea" were in fact disabled through some form of intestinal infection; and (2) that in the great majority of the cases cleared to field ambulance in France for "diarrhoea" the element of infection was absent or unimportant.

The first of these assumptions is based (*a*) on the fact that at Anzac until the last few weeks of the campaign men were treated in the battalion lines until too ill to be of use in the trenches; (*b*) on the hypothesis—upheld against some weight of opinion—that apart from its deficiency in vitamins "B" and "C" the Gallipoli ration was not *in itself* such as would cause continued and progressive intestinal disorder of epidemic proportions. The second assumption is based (*a*) on the fact that in France all cases of flux were closely observed and their diagnosis controlled bacteriologically; and (*b*) on the clinical records of rest stations and R.M.O's.

However this may be, it can be affirmed categorically—as will have been obvious to readers of *Vol. I*—that the experience of the war of 1914-18 fully justified the vigilant attitude adopted in the British Army toward "diarrhoea." Even of B.E.F. experience, the consultant quoted above (Col. Soltau) wrote: "It is probable that many of the so-called diarrhoeas were in reality true dysenteric infections in mild form."

Relative percentages (of total admissions of Australian soldiers to medical units) due to intestinal flux.

	M.E.F.	WESTERN FRONT			
	Primary admissions to all medical units	F. Ambs. Admissions	C.C.S. Chiefly transfers	Exped. Base Transfers	Hospitals in U.K. Transfers
Dysentery	9·96	0·39	1·06	0·64	2·58
Entero-colitis	4·02	0·78	0·67	0·45	0·69
Diarrhoea	6·52	2·90	2·17	0·97	0·63
Total evacuations for flux	20·50	4·07	3·90	2·06	4·10

Primary admissions of Australians with intestinal flux to field ambulances on the Western Front and transfers thence to C.C.S., General Hospital, or to the U.K.[97]

Dysenteric Group

	F. Amb.	C.C.S.	Exped. Base	U.K.
April, 1916-1917	250	275	411	555
April, 1917-1918	107	67	139	299
April, 1918-1919	435	951	361	620
Total Admissions	792	1,293	911	1,474
Percentage of total sick	0·38	0·85	0·58	2·30

Colitis and Enteritis

April, 1916-1917	606	394	274	105
April, 1917-1918	638	341	231	157
April, 1918-1919	327	233	193	135
Total Admissions	1,571	968	698	397
Percentage of total sick	0·75	0·63	0·44	0·62

Diarrhoea

April, 1916-1917	2,101	750	365	68
April, 1917-1918	2,239	662	506	89
April, 1918-1919	1,667	1,695	585	221
Total Admissions	6,007	3,107	1,456	378
Percentage of total sick	2·84	2·05	0·92	0·59
Grand Totals	8,370	5,368	3,065	2,249
Percentage of total sick	3·97	3·53	1·94	3·51

[97] These figures are based on a partial (over 33 1/3 per cent.) count of the Admission and Discharge books of medical units of the B.E.F.—Australian and British—dealing with Australian casualties. Fuller details will appear in *Vol. III*.

The prevention of the diseases of dirt by *social hygiene* involved, as we have seen, the stupendous task of keeping clean, in the unimaginable filth of attrition warfare, vast hordes of men closely concentrated along the entrenched lines. The problem of *field sanitation* in this form of warfare involved the reconstruction in some form of all the major conveniences of civilised urban existence. In terms of dysentery these may be defined as methods for preventing, directly or indirectly, the pathogenic organisms contained in faecal evacuations from being transferred from one soldier to another. Field sanitation centred on the following objectives. (a) The disposal of faeces. (b) Measures against the house-fly. (c) Providing for ablution. (d) Protection of food. (e) Protection and purification of drinking water. The immense labour involved in these tasks is reflected in the fact that a very great part of the medical records of the A.I.F. is concerned with their performance; and that in a great measure they monopolised the attention of the sanitary personnel.

Direct action against the fluxes

The small pit incinerator. This consisted of a conical or sloping pit in the ground, 4 feet to 8 feet in diameter at the top and some 5 feet in depth. This led by a tunnel—commonly a couple of oil drums— either to the side of a bank (as in the upper diagram), or to a raking-out pit approached by steps (as in the lower one). Two or even four passages were sometimes used to catch any winds. (The first diagram is taken from the war diary of No. 2 Sanitary Section; the second is drawn from a block model used in No. 4 Sanitary Section for instructional purposes. Each represents a mesial section.)

It is, however, neither necessary nor possible to enter upon a detailed examination of the activities connected with each of these functions except to record the experience of the sanitary officers of the A.I.F. as to the technical procedures found most useful—the most suitable type of latrine and method of disposal of excreta in stationary and moving warfare; their conclusions as to the incineration of refuse and disposal of manure; or as to the facilities for ablution *en masse*, fly-proof safes, or kitchen standards and methods. These are dealt with in *Appendix No. 12*.

The special interest of sanitation on the Western Front is however, contained in (*a*) the evolution of the method of direct chlorination for providing pure drinking water; and (*b*) the developments that took place in the machinery and methods for giving effect to the principles of field sanitation laid down for

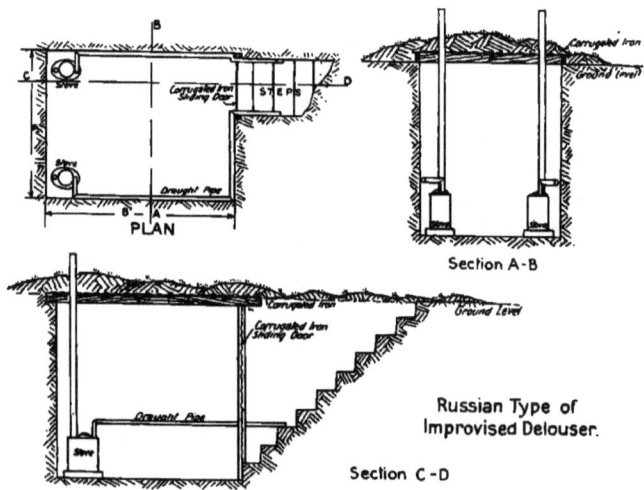

Russian Type of Improvised Delouser.

the force. These two features call for more particular notice since in each the Australian force made original contributions to the problem. It is true that each is intimately related to the change in the situation and in the problems of sanitation brought about by the moving warfare of 1918, which is described in later chapters. It will however be advantageous to include here the earlier aspects of each, together with certain other developments connected with the stationary warfare of 1916 and 1917.

The water problem on the Western Front
"Wholesome water in sufficient quantity was supplied under conditions often nothing short of appalling. There was no sewage so foul but what it was, when necessity arose, quickly converted into an important and safe drinking water supply in the face of unimaginable difficulty. . . . Let us think of huge armies of men and horses advancing through enemy territory with every source destroyed or fouled by the retreating enemy. A few hours without water and the advancing army would be brought to a standstill. Impure water would more slowly but just as surely stay its advance and lead to its impotence through disease."[98]

In the Army as in a civil community the problems of water supply are fundamental and can never be otherwise. Under favourable conditions the chief agents of gastro-intestinal diseases can live and within limits multiply[99] in this essential food-stuff; and in view of the facts that in warfare such contamination must be the rule, and that natural resistance is feeble, it is certain, notwithstanding any inferences that might be drawn from Gallipoli experience with water and inoculation, that measures to offset this factor in the environment must, as in the Great War, form the foundation-stone of the structure of field sanitation.

No writer could attempt to describe the work of the Services of Maintenance on the Western Front without a feeling of inadequacy; and this deepens when the subject is the steps taken to provide two million troops in the line with safe water —procured, stored, purified and distributed on the spot. No more can be done here than to identify those factors which

---

[98] From a lecture by Major M. J. Holmes, A.A.M.C., Officer Commanding No. 2 Sanitary Section, delivered to the Institute of Engineers (Canberra Division), Sept. 1932.

[99] Surprisingly little exact information is available regarding experimental investigation or epidemiological observation on this very important matter. The classical experiments of Dudgeon (quoted by Thresh, Beale and Suckling) in 1919 found Shiga bacilli able to survive in *sterile* water up to 3-4 weeks. Death (these writers state) would occur more speedily in "natural and impure water." H. W. Streeter (*Sewage Works Journal, 1930, Vol. II, p. 131*) discussing the natural purification of streams, notes an initial increase of bacterial density up to 10-15 hours, after which it decreased steadily, at least 8-10 days being required in the rivers studied for the bacterial content to become normal. Professor Harvey Sutton, to whom the author is indebted for the above, records an "epidemic of diarrhoea" in a unit of Light Horse in the Jordan Valley in 1916, which was proved to be due to infection of the water supply by a unit higher up the stream.

from the medical point of view most contributed to the astonishing success achieved.[100] If we accept the postulate that infected water is a major cause of gastro-intestinal disease,[101] then the part played by the medical service in this matter must take a high place as contributing to the successful prosecution of the war.

Factors in the Problem: Responsibility. Division of labour is the foundation of social life, and a modern army is perhaps the most exactly organised form of communal living that man has evolved. This is not to say that it is the highest form of development in the art of living; but that it is the most complete and compelling form of social co-operation on a great scale directed to the fulfilment of a specific social object. Its activities are motivated by an intensity of purpose unapproached in the pursuits of peace. The history of water on the Western Front is that of progress in co-operation between the several services concerned—engineers (supply), "Q" (distribution), medical (purity), A.P.M. (order); and in the creation throughout the force of that mutual understanding of aims and methods which constitutes the only useful basis of "discipline." Of the four factors involved the medical service had all to do with purity, and much with the creating and maintaining of "water discipline" under the various conditions of fighting and season.

The Water Supply. Water in France was derived from extraordinarily diverse sources—from shell-holes, moats, shallow wells[102] and streams foul beyond conception—in ascending scale up to huge specially constructed reservoirs, and deep wells, the supply from which was reticulated to "water points" within a few miles of the front line.

---

[100] A great part of *Vol. I* of the two devoted to the hygiene of the war in the *British Official History* is occupied by an admirable account of the water supplies in different theatres of war.

[101] The view held by Australian medical officers in France is indicated in the following extract from the lecture by Major M. J. Holmes: "In back areas, with troops in rest, there should be every chance of diarrhoea being eliminated, at least in the non-fly season, if water supplies are safe-guarded. With the advent of the fly and dust season, of course, food probably plays a greater part than water in the spread of the disease."

The following is from the report to the Fourth Plenary Session of the Inter-allied Sanitary Conference in 1919 by the A.D.M.S. Sanitary, B.E.F. (Col. Beveridge) whose opinion carried great weight:—

"The period of greatest prevalence [in France] has been 10 to 12 weeks of July, August, September which coincides with the fly season, the hottest weather, and often the greatest military activity." The incidence rate in the B.E.F. for 1918 was 618·6 per 100,000 per annum (12,211 cases with 46 deaths, the majority the Flexner type). In 1916 the maximum incidence was 124 per 100,000 in September; in 1917 54·76 per 100,000 in August; in 1918 180 in August.

The chief measures for control were stated to be "(i) attention to proper disposal of excreta so as to prevent the contamination of food and water; (ii) removal and treatment of all cases of diarrhoea as they occur."

[102] It was a not infrequent complaint by the owner of houses in which troops were billeted that the water in the household well was made undrinkable by disinfectants put in their family cesspit.

Purification. The Army scheme differs from that of civil life in that, however great the body of troops involved, the service is carried out, broadly speaking, on an individual basis,[103] the allowance for each man being rationed as strictly as his food.[104] The unit of demand in the infantry is the Battalion. At the outbreak of the war the unit of distribution and for purification was the 200-gallon water-cart fitted with clarifying and filtering apparatus (porcelain candles). The concentration of troops on the Western Front compelled new methods. A process of chlorination replaced the futile filter candles; the "step-by-step" battle made the two-gallon petrol tin the most important unit of distribution. The strategy of attrition required, since the matter bore on wastage, a new *standard of discipline* of which the Sanitary Section was the chief implement.

Of these elements in purification chlorination will be supplanted; the two-gallon petrol tin served a special purpose in the late war; but sanitary discipline was the answer to a human problem and will be required as long as armies. It was intimately bound up with the evolution of the Sanitary Sections, and will be examined in connection with the work of those units. The chlorination process and the two-gallon petrol tin call for a brief note.

Chlorination. Implemented as it was in the British Army by an admirable piece of military apparatus, the "Standard water sterilisation test case,"[105] the application of the chlorination process to the problem of water supply in the field must be held one of the great advances in military medicine and the agent in a new epoch of army sanitation. It replaced filtration through Berkfeld candles through which water was forced by hand pump—a rule almost invariably honoured in the breach, unless the candles were cracked! In the chlorination process water was sterilised by adding to the water-cart or other receptacle an amount of bleaching powder sufficient to combine with all the organic material contained—from 1 to 4 or 5 parts per million. The amount required was commonly determined by test on the spot after, if necessary, clarification from gross impurities by sedimentation—as with alum—and filtration through flannelette. Experimental work had been carried out before the war in the Royal Army Medical College and the amount of chlorine required in the form of bleaching powder had been roughly estimated.[106]

"Horrocks' test case."[107] This was based on the principles (1) that

---

[103] During the period of siege warfare in France some immense schemes of supply were created involving the construction of reservoirs, from which water was distributed under conditions which, in the "approach" areas, did not differ greatly from those of civil life. Such conditions can, however, hardly be held normal for warfare in the field.

[104] The official teaching in 1914 was that "each man would require daily"—in barracks, 20 gallons, in standing camps 3·5 gallons. On active service a gallon per head was the estimated requirement, with a minimum of 3½ to 5 pints daily for drinking.

[105] Commonly known as the "Horrocks' test case"—officially as "Case, water testing, sterilisation."

[106] Before the war the method of water purification by the use of chlorine had been chiefly exploited in America.

[107] This derived from suggestions made in 1914 by Professor G. Sims Woodhead of Cambridge University. The outfit designed by him was, however, found too elaborate for field work. A simpler "test case," based on the 4 oz. tins of chloride of lime ("bleach") already supplied to the troops, was designed by Colonel Sir W. H. Horrocks, Director of Hygiene at the War Office, and this became a general issue, for use both at home and in the field.

chlorine in water is "fixed" by organic material including bacteria which it kills; and (2) that with starch solution the presence of any free chlorine is shown by a blue colour. The purpose of the test was to determine the amount of bleaching powder required in any given sample of water. The apparatus could be used by "water duty" men or any intelligent soldier; but throughout the war its employment was almost wholly a responsibility of the Medical Service.[108] The chief reason was to ensure that it should be scrupulously done.

Distribution. Three distinct problems presented themselves in the reserve and approach areas and in the front line. The front line could be served only by hand-carry or pack animals -drawing by water-cart or otherwise from the reticulation points, or other source, where (under the direction of "water point men") the units obtained and purified their supply.

Front Line Supply—the Petrol Tin. The Australian force arrived in France at the moment that the British High Command and every service of maintenance was preparing for the Somme. Early in April, 1916, the I Anzac Corps was asked to suggest, on the basis of Gallipoli experience, a method for supply to the front line.

"Some means of carrying water to the trenches by hand is required, and it is proposed to adopt some form of receptacle for this purpose and issue to a scale of so many per brigade or division in front line trenches. Before proceeding further in this matter I should be glad of your opinion on the following points: (1) What form of receptacle should be provided? (2) What amount of water should it hold? (3) How should it be carried? (4) On what scale should provision be made?"

The two-gallon petrol tin was recommended by the Australians "or tins of similar shape and somewhat larger size." The two-gallon tin was adopted, and in May an issue of 1,600 per division in the front line was approved by the Quartermaster-General B.E.F. (Lieut.-General Sir R. C. Maxwell) "for the purpose of carrying water to the trenches . . . these to be considered as trench stores and to be demanded from the Deputy-Director of Supply and transport." In July an Anzac Corps dump of these tins was formed in Albert, with a repair shop, and units drew at the rate of 3,500 tins per Division, to be returned when empty to the Corps dump. The scheme

Two-gallon petrol tin. The dimensions were: base 9¼ in. by 5¾ in., height 11¼ in.

---

[108] Under certain circumstances the test was carried out by the Engineers. Chlorination at the source was sometimes adopted, as in the supply to the Somme battlefield from the Ancre. Mobile hygienic laboratories carried out special tests and advised on the technical questions that arose in connection with the large supply systems. In the last year of the war highly elaborate mobile apparatus and a special army service were organised to meet the needs of rapid movement of troops. In the French Army *eau javelle* replaced "bleach."

was soon greatly extended, and experiments made in transport. A special framework was fitted to water-carts; and special vehicles were also used. On the medical side a procedure was worked out for chlorination direct in the petrol tins, using a standard solution of bleach.

In this manner was instituted the system of supply by petrol tin to the front lines which served the British force, winter and summer, through every vicissitude of trench warfare and the advance to victory. The 200-gallon water-cart, chlorinated direct, remained the unit of supply for battalions on the move or in rest.

Collective Supply—the Mobile Water Columns. The individual system of supply described above and elsewhere was in France as in other theatres supplemented, or even at times superseded, by "supplies" provided wholly by the engineers and distributed, somewhat like other rations, by A.S.C. "water companies." Only a bare statement is possible of these stupendous activities.

From early in 1915 experiments were undertaken into the possibility of making water an A.S.C. supply. The purpose was achieved by the provision of "sterilising" and "water tank" lorries, and barges. Soon afterwards Water Tank (M.T.) Companies A.S.C. were formed to operate them.[109] Sterilisation was by chlorine—in the form of bleaching powder or gas—and the plant consisted of (*a*) pumping unit, (*b*) filtering unit, (*c*) chlorinating unit and contact tank, (*d*) dechlorinating unit (by sodium bi-sulphate and ferrous sulphate, or SO_3). Transport was by 150- or 500-gallon tanks on 30-cwt or 3-ton lorries. An establishment for the Water Tank (M.T.) Companies A.S.C. was approved at the end of 1915.

The capacity of these Water Companies may be judged by the fact that by the time of the Armistice No. 1 Company had sterilised 5,500,000 gallons of water and carried 35,500,000 gallons. Their organisation and equipment made them highly mobile and adaptable.

The fact that the Australian Imperial Force was organised, trained, and used almost wholly in front line work was very exactly reflected in the reaction of its personnel to the varied conditions of their warfare; and its influence is strikingly evident in the history of the important medical units whose

---

[109] In the companies first formed, complete arrangements were made for the detection and removal of arsenic and cyanides, copper and lead—from water "accidentally or purposely contaminated." The later formed companies were not so equipped.

The *British Official History* states that four Water Tank Companies were formed of which the first two and last two varied considerably in their capacity, equipment, methods and establishment. Nos. 1 and 2 consisted of 186 vehicles, of which 111 were lorries with 150-gallon water tanks, 19 3-ton lorries with clarifying and sterilising plant, 11 lorries with clarifying and anti-poison plant, and 20 3-ton lorries with 500-gallon tanks. The agent employed was "bleach." The staff consisted of Army Service Corps personnel, for carrying water, with R.A.M.C. attached who were responsible for the technical duties connected with sterilisation. Nos. 3 and 4 companies had 324 vehicles, and the personnel consisted of a headquarters, 6 sections A.S.C. "for carrying water," and 3 sections R.A.M.C. "for sterilising water." The agent employed was chloramine gas.

The Australian Sanitary Sections in France[110]

experiences on the Western Front we are now briefly to follow. Their development, indeed, has a permanent place in the wider field of the general evolution of military medicine. It is not proposed to undertake a systematic account of the technique of sanitation in the field[111] as this developed in the A.I.F. in France at the hands of the Divisional Sanitary Sections and the sanitary personnel of field units, but rather to use their experience to indicate the trend of development of preventive medicine in war as this was visualised and explored in the Australian force.

The place of the Sanitary Section and the Regimental sanitary details in the organised scheme of "sanitation"[112] in the field army has already been indicated.[113] No special account

---

[110] *Manual of Elementary Military Hygiene, 1912:*—"'Sanitation,' the synonym of hygiene, means health or health preservation, that is, the prevention of disease." In the *Army Manual of Hygiene and Sanitation, 1934*, "hygiene" is defined as "the science of the maintenance and promotion of health and the prevention of disease"; and "sanitation" as "the practical application of the science of hygiene to the varied conditions of life."

[111] The experiences of the Great War have been translated into present military practice in the official *Army Manual of Hygiene and Sanitation*. In this manual the methods and apparatus found most useful are described and figured. To those who live in the Australian country parts, details of apparatus have particular interest, and it may be noted that a paper on the "Application to civil life of the lessons of military hygiene derived from the Great War" was read by Major M. J. Holmes, sometime O.C. No. 2 Australian Sanitary Section, before the Section of Naval and Military Medicine and Surgery in the 11th Session of the Australasian Medical Congress held in Brisbane in 1920, and appears *in extenso* in the Transactions printed and published for the Congress by the Queensland Government Printer. This admirable study advocated the application in civil life of three principles found valuable in Army sanitation: (a) Uniformity and simplicity of administration—clear definition of responsibility, (b) Research, (c) Education. It may be regretted that a wider publicity was not secured for this study, in particular to its relevance in the sanitary problems of "bush" townships. These general principles had already been embodied by the Federal Director-General of Health (Dr. J. H. L. Cumpston) in his national policy, and they are to be seen to-day inspiring the advances that have been made in the wide field of Federal co-operation in promoting the national health of the Australian people.

[112] Every military unit of any size either had special "sanitary" personnel, or was required, in military parlance, to "detail" some of its personnel for sanitary duties. This was the case with the Field Ambulances, C.C.S's, and General Hospitals.

The status of the Regimental "sanitary detachment" has been a matter of debate in the British Army from its genesis in Cromwell's "New Model" Army in 1645. Its inception seems to have been in this wise. In the "Laws and ordinances of Warre" to govern the Parliamentary Army it was provided, as a punishment for "retreating before they come to handy-strokes" with the enemy, that if the fault lay with the officers "they shall be banished the Camp" for a period. If with the soldiers, "then every tenth man shall be punished at discretion, and the rest serve for Pioners (*sic*) and Scavengers till a worthy exploit take off the Blot." (Appendix to *Cromwell's Army* by C. H. Firth, 2nd Ed. 1912.)

It was laid down during the Great War (correspondence between Fifth Army and I Anzac Corps and 4th Australian Division, April, 1917) that "men belonging to Regimental Sanitary Squads should be trained [*i.e.* in Arms] as laid down in War Establishments, but it must be understood that their sanitary duties are to have preference."

[113] See *e.g.* pp. 507-10 and relevant references in Vol. I.

will be given of Regimental "sanitation," as carried out in France.[114]

The methods employed in the field units were those recommended by the Sanitary Sections, while *the development of an effective liaison* between the two is most conveniently followed as from the point of view of the Sections. It was, indeed, the major question in their evolution, far exceeding in its importance that of the methods and apparatus of field sanitation and only approached by their part in the problems of providing pure water for the troops in the field.

Beginnings. The Australian Sanitary Sections were created in 1915 as a new element in the medical system, not a part of the Divisional organisation. Their personnel belonged to the Medical Corps and were "non-combatants." They were raised on a basis of one per division, and were "attached" to divisions in much the same way as field ambulances to brigades. Though from the outset they were essentially "Divisional" troops, this "Divisional" association, which became so prominent a feature in their service, evolved rather as a functional urge than a structural heritage.

Allocation of Units. The early history of these units has in part been recorded. The 2nd Sanitary Section happened to be allotted to the 1st Division, and the 1st Section to the 2nd Division;[115] the others were

---

[114] Nevertheless, in sanitation as in all other matters, the battalions and other military units who carried out the real business of war were in a very high degree self-contained and responsible. Under each of the two theories regarding the place of the Sanitary Section in the preventive medicine of the front, it was accepted that, in the matter of conservancy, the duty of this new medical unit was to promote or to supplement, not to supplant, the internal "self-help" activities of the fighting units. This matter is dealt with in detail in *Vol. I.*

[115] *See p. 29.* On 28 Jan., 1916 the following was issued by the G.O.C. Anzac Corps.

"Approval is given for the inclusion of a Sanitary Section in each of the 1st and 2nd Australian Divisions. . . . The Sanitary Section, recently arrived from Australia, and now at Tel-el-Kebir, will be designated the 1st Australian Sanitary Section, and will constitute the Sanitary Section of the 2nd Australian Division. The Sanitary Section of the 1st Australian Division will be designated the 2nd Australian Sanitary Section, and its formation will be carried out by the Divisional Commander in consultation with the D.M.S., A.I.F., who will nominate a medical officer as O.C. Section. Any improvised Sanitary Sections previously authorised for these Divisions will cease to exist as such, and the personnel not absorbed in the Sections now authorised will be returned to the units from which they were drawn."

It may be recalled that on Gallipoli, in the absence of a specially enlisted Sanitary Section, a "sanitary" unit was improvised from Divisional personnel to fill a most pressing need. Stress is laid in *Vol. I (p. 357)* on the results of the failure— due in great part to lack of a trained Sanitary Section—to educate the personnel of battalions in sanitary self-help such as the construction of "fly-proof" latrines from biscuit-boxes. *See Vol. I, pp. 28n, and 251.*

allotted to the division with the corresponding number, and this allotment was adhered to throughout their subsequent administrative vicissitudes as "Army" and "Corps" troops.

Establishment and Personnel. The establishment of a Sanitary Section provided for 1 officer, 5 N.C.O's and 20 privates. On the Western Front throughout the war their command was given to legally qualified medical practitioners and the D.M.S., A.I.F. would permit no deviation from this principle.[116] It may be said at once that with notably little exception the selection of their personnel ensured a very high standard of achievement; these units were commanded and served with conspicuous ability. The outlook and ideals of a public health service of preventive medicine was ensured by an initial leavening of the command with medical officers of health, and of the N.C.O's with public health inspectors. Practical efficiency was assured by the inclusion of officers and men who had "made good" in general medical work in the divisions, of tradesmen and artisans, carpenters, tinsmiths, plumbers, draughtsmen and so forth, among the rank and file.

Up to the time of their arrival in France the Sections were administered directly by the A.D's.M.S. and had acquired a very definitely Divisional outlook.

This was quickly modified. It will be recalled that when at the beginning of 1916 the A.I.F. arrived in France the Western Front had settled down deliberately to siege warfare and this was enormously accentuated by the Somme battles and in particular the "Somme Winter" (1916-17). The shallow and labile Divisional fronts congealed into deep and relatively immobile "Corps" areas, within almost wholly static "Armies"; the Divisions themselves, the fighting formations, moved for the most part within the restricted gambit of the front, relief and rest areas of their own Army Corps. The whole front (as we have seen) was organised as a 100-mile-long town of varying depth, with some two million inhabitants. The conditions of life and the problems of "sanitation" in the Army Corps and Army areas became almost as stable as in a civil community. The effect of this is to be seen in a similar congelation in the outlook on the problem of disease prevention on the part of the army authorities; in particular—in the British service though not as a whole in the Australian —it brought about that the function of the Sanitary Sections became envisaged in terms of *material,* rather than of *men,* of apparatus rather than education. The indubitable need for some more or less permanent sanitary *cadre* to assist the "Town Majors" in maintaining the structural

Control by
Division ?
Corps ? or
Army ?

[116] In this the A.I.F. diverged from British practice and—it must be added—principle. See in this connection *Chapter xxvi,* and *Vol. I, pp. 609n. and 629.*

integrity of the permanent latrines, incinerators and grease-traps was met, not by the allocation of special personnel, but by immobilising the Sanitary Sections.

The consequent developments are noted here briefly; but the matter is considered to be of sufficient interest to justify inclusion of some relevant correspondence on the matter as an Appendix (*No. 12*).

(a) *1916: Corps Control.* The endeavour to exempt the sections from the rapid moves of the Divisions in and out of the line in the battles of August-September 1916 has been noted in *Chapter IV*; as three divisions only were concerned, and the Sections were allotted to areas controlled by the A.D.M.S. of the Division that happened to be passing through them,[117] the "personal touch" was not lost and the general control by the D.D.M.S. ensured continuity of policy. It was otherwise in Australian experience in the next development.

(b) *1917: Army Control.* As early as September, 1916, the authorities of Fourth and Fifth Armies had pressed for a revision of the order which (in 1915) made the Sanitary Sections Divisional units. In March, 1917, on the advice of the A.D.M.S. for Sanitation, instructions were issued by G.H.Q., B.E.F., as follows:—"In order to maintain continuity of sanitary work in Armies it has been decided to withdraw Divisional Sanitary Sections from their Divisions, and to constitute them as Army Troops Units. Instructions dealing with the employment of Sanitary Sections are issued herewith. Orders for the movement of these Sections between Armies will be issued by G.H.Q.; Orders for movements within Army areas being issued by Army Headquarters." The instructions implementing the order were put in force forthwith, and happened to coincide with the German retirement, "Alberich"; within three weeks the A.D's.M.S. of the four Australian Divisions issued a combined protest to the Deputy-Director—the gist of their complaint being chiefly the loss of personal touch with their Sections. The real clash came when the Divisions moved north, since the policy conflicted with that of Dominion autonomy. The matter was passed by Haig to the War Office, with the result that instructions were issued whereby, when such action was possible without dislocating the army arrangements, the Australian units were exempted from strict compliance with the order. Control therefore reverted to Corps, which commonly delegated it to the Divisions. Subsequent developments will be described when we come to the final stage of the war.[118]

Results of Australian Policy. The "national" involvements of the policy fortified a technical and service objection which grew in strength as the staff of the Australian service observed the effect of the authorised policy on the British units. The crux of the matter was that while the Australian units carried out a policy of educating the combatant units in self-help, pioneers and others from the battalions being attached to the Sections for training in sanitary methods and in construction and especially in improvisation of appliances, the British units became for the most part executive, constructing, far in the rear, sanitary and other appliances for delivery ready-made to the battalions.

---

[117] *See pp. 69, 73.*
[118] *See pp. 710-14.* New Zealand accepted the severance but made special Divisional arrangements. The Canadian Corps, like the Australian, secured the principle of "Corps" control of its Sections.

The nature of the duties of Sanitary Sections was clarified at the conference with the medical authorities of Second Army when I Anzac first reached France.[119] In the Australian service they gradually crystallised into three broad lines of action relating respectively to (a) co-operation in the indirect line of defence against infectious disease in general (by notification, and search for carriers or other sources of disease—in particular for sources in the civil environment and foci in the civil population), (b) disinfection and disinfestation, and (c) "direct" action against gastro-intestinal infections.

Functions of the Sanitary Sections

As to (a) Major M. J. Holmes says that, under the British system, as contrasted with that of the A.I.F.,

"the Sanitary Section was outside the notification scheme—it was concerned with scavenging, water control and so forth. In the Australian force, in particular in the 1st Division, the unit had a definite place in the control of disease by public health methods, the duty of the O.C. Sanitary Section being to trace contacts and carriers, to carry out terminal disinfection, and to investigate the origin of the case (under orders from the A.D.M.S. and in conjunction with the R.M.O.), especially in the civil population."

(b) Its duty of disinfection and disinfestation can also be dismissed briefly. In mobile warfare the "Foden lorry Thresh disinfector" was usually attached to the Section and moved with it, and Battalions had their blankets "disinfected" by individual arrangement; in static warfare the disinfector was generally attached to the Divisional baths, the Section usually allotting men to work it. The construction of improvised apparatus, such as the Russian Pit, was studied and taught to the battalions.

(c) The *raison d'être* of the Sanitary Section, however, was chiefly to promote "direct action" against gastro-intestinal infections. This has already been defined as the prevention of the contamination of food by flies or filth, and was ensured, in brief, by the disposal of excreta, prevention of fly-breeding, the protection of foodstuffs, the personal use of soap and water, and by achieving a safe water supply. The Sections developed a considerable degree of individuality in their methods of pursuing their purpose and in the relative prominence given to the

---
[119] See pp. 32-3.

several features of their work, but in all these matters the duty of the Section was interpreted in the Australian Force as comprising *inspection* and *supervision, education, construction* and *research,* with the purpose of promoting a high standard of sanitary morale and technical efficiency in the combatant units. The Sections experimented, with varying ingenuity and initiative, with old and new methods for achieving the simple "sanitary" purposes noted above. Some illustration of apparatus favoured or developed in the Australian force will be found in this chapter,[120] and an outline of the sanitary technique on the Western Front in *Appendix No. 12.*

It is only fair to record that some officers of the A.I.F. held views on the functions of a Sanitary Section which differed somewhat from that here presented. Thus the officer commanding No. 3 Sanitary Section[121] held that

Divergent views on the Sanitary Section

"the only usefulness of sanitary sections for front line or support line is to make latrine boxes, and get them taken up at night. . . . The limit forward of usefulness is at about reserve Coy. cookhouses, where grease traps, latrines, F.P. food boxes and water supply can be gone into. The most useful work is in camps and villages where troops are camped or billetted in large numbers."

He proposed that—

"The time has come for a radical alteration in sanitary sections to be considered: (1) cease to have a medical officer as O.C.; (2) enlarge the size of the unit and make it a working unit with power to demand material and the duty of making *all* sanitary appliances; or (3) do away with the section as a unit and simply have 12 inspectors attached to the A.D.M.S. staff to inspect divisional units and work under the D.A.D.M.S. of Division."

But on the other hand it is not less pertinent to quote the opinion of a British sanitary officer[122] who was closely associated with the Anzac Corps on Gallipoli:

"In trench warfare at any rate every division requires its Sanitary

---

[120] The hotly debated question of construction of apparatus for other units by the Sanitary Sections is touched on in *Chapter xxi, p. 654* and *Vol. I.*

[121] Major W. R. Kelly in a "Memorandum on Sanitation." The opinion of the D.D.M.S., Desert Mounted Corps (Colonel R. M. Downes, A.A.M.C.) has been placed on record by him in *Vol. I* of this work.

[122] From a copy of a letter to Sir Alfred Keogh contained in Surgeon-General Howse's private papers. At this time the Sanitary Section was a line of communication unit.

Section. . . . It must in future be an *integral part* of the divisional scheme, not to replace regimental sanitary duties and responsibilities but to give skilled assistance, to inspect, and to fill up gaps."

Even in France R.A.M.C. officers approved at times the Australian stand. Thus :—[123]

"15/7/18. This unit . . . is losing its special functions and is being forced into a constructional unit. . . . The latest XV Corps order provides that sanitary sections shall supply all sanitary appliances on demand by Area Commandants.[124]
"21/7/18. Had interview with D.D.M.S. re Corps order. . . . Pointed out that . . . the sanitary section is a medical unit primarily and not a branch of R.E. Put my views in writing for the D.D.M.S. who will bring the matter forward. 22/7/18. Again called to see D.D.M.S. at his request. This matter has been sent forward to the Corps for reconsideration. 29/7/18. Attended conference at XV Corps 'Q.' It was admitted by the Corps that sanitary sections should not be made to bear the responsibility of providing sanitary appliances on demand. Corps order will be amended accordingly."

In the very important matter of water control the Sanitary Sections were concerned chiefly with the problem of ensuring that the supply was made suitable for consumption and, in particular, **The Section's place in water control** that chlorination was carried out efficiently. The matter resolved itself into a problem of the organisation of supplies, and control of distribution—to ensure that the battalion water-cart and petrol tins were always treated, before consumption, with the amount of bleach found by the Horrocks' test to be required; and to minimise the use of untested and "illicit" supplies—as from shell-holes while in the front line. This last was partly solved by the two-gallon petrol tin. General organisation and control were effected in two ways :—

(1) There was established a system of *authorised water points* where representatives of four branches—Engineers, "Q," A.P.M., and Medical Service (Sanitary Sections)—co-operated to control and assist the distribution of the available supplies to the fighting units. There arose a question as to whether responsibility for chlorination rested with the regimental "water duty men" or the personnel of the Sanitary Section. It was found best to suit the rule to the circumstances, but with no weakening of regimental responsibility.[125]

(2) At the end of 1916 it was found necessary to test the efficiency of battalion chlorination by instituting a systematic campaign of in-

---

[123] From the personal diary of the O.C., No. 2 Aust. Sanitary Section (Major M. J. Holmes). His unit was attached to the British XV Corps, Second Army, July-Aug., 1918.

[124] These comprised ablution benches, latrines, urinals, incinerators, cook-houses, meat store-rooms, fly-proof meat safes, grease traps, cutting-up tables. They were required at times to make office furniture.

[125] British A.D's.M.S. insisted strongly on complete regimental responsibility, Australia inclined to facilitate co-operation by the sections. The first was less efficient but also less influenced by circumstances and must inevitably remain the first, and perhaps the most important line of defence. The question whether test cases should be issued to Engineer companies came up in the open warfare later in the war.

spection of Battalion water-carts as they went up full to their units. The result was at first disconcerting; improper chlorination or none at all was the rule. But by admirably organised and sustained efforts and Divisional co-operation, by the beginning of 1917 an efficiency approaching 100 per cent. was achieved. This standard could not in all conditions be maintained. But it can be stated that in chlorination, controlled water-points, inspection, and the two-gallon petrol tin, reinforced by the mobile water column and hygienic laboratory, the army had a rampart of defence against water-borne infection invulnerable save to the extreme vicissitudes of trench warfare on the one hand and moving warfare on the other.

A feature that marks out the Great War, from the medical point of view, from all others, is the degree to which exact diagnosis and pathogenic discrimination influenced the routine not only of medical work but of military life. In every campaign,[126] if with varying degrees of refinement, a soldier's sickness was diagnosed, and discriminated from that of his fellow "casualties." Each man and each "disease" received appropriate attention, whether of treatment or for prophylaxis.

Preventive medicine—the significance of "P.U.O."

Diagnosis and discrimination, on the surgical side in treatment, on the medical in "prevention," give the keynote to the medicine of the war and its most profitable "lesson." But (it may be asked) what of "P.U.O."—of which "disease" admissions to Australian Field Ambulances in France totalled 24,593 cases, 11·6 per cent. of all evacuations for sickness? What of "N.Y.D." and "N.Y.D.N."? Do these not invalidate the thesis?

Consideration of the facts makes clear that the reverse is more true. "Shots" at diagnosis were taboo. In N.Y.D., the service frankly said, "We do not yet know." "P.U.O." was a tribute to "reality." In great measure it replaced the civilian practitioner's bluff of "influenza." The diagnoses "N.Y.D.N." and "N.Y.D. Gas" illustrate the practical military purpose secured by frank acknowledgment of ignorance, and a determination to achieve the nearest approach possible to the facts of pathogeny. Medical intervention (it was observed) is successful in proportion as aetiological factors are exactly recognised and taken into account, and deliberate research for such

---

[126] Provision for exact diagnosis was by far the most important feature of the medical reorganisation that followed the first "wave" of disease at Gallipoli. See *e.g. Vol. I, p. 247.*

eminently "worth while" even in the throes of a World War. Evolution along these lines was indeed characteristic of this war, and was probably its most important, perhaps its only positive contribution to the science and art of living. In this contribution the profession of medicine was able to further its own broad and humane purpose in the world, even while serving the inhuman purposes of war.

SECTION III

THE WAR OF MOVEMENT: THE OFFENSIVES OF 1918

INTRODUCTION

IN this present series of chapters we resume the narrative of the experiences of the Australian Army Medical Service on the Western Front. It will be remembered that when it reached the end of 1917, this narrative was broken off to permit of a study of the developments in the Army Medical Service which had by then practically reached their culmination—in particular, the new place of the Service within the war machine. That study will help to elucidate the medical aspect of the new warfare of 1918, now to be described.[1]

In the Battle of Cambrai, with which the earlier narrative ended, we had discerned a "try-out" by both sides of military tactics almost amounting to a new art of warfare. The British High Command had lent an ear for the moment to the new "scientific" school of soldiers; the Germans in their counter-stroke applied methods to be used the next year in a vastly more powerful thrust. The leaders of the British Army Medical Service, not less than the High Command of the B.E.F., soon afterwards recognised that the war had entered upon a new phase. It was known that now, and for some time to come, at least, the Allied part would be that of defence; it was also discerned (though it would seem less clearly) that more or less rapid change and movement must now take the place of siege. The preparations made in the British Medical Service in France to meet these fundamental changes in the nature of its problems, and their actual *dénouement* in the events of March, April and May of 1918, form the subject of the first chapter; it also indicates the part played by the medical service of the Australian

[1] In the Canadian Official Medical Histories of the Great War the technical study of medical developments is based exclusively on the "Last 100 days."

force in the events of the two great German thrusts on the British front, on the Somme and on the Lys respectively. The second chapter describes, so far as they were seen in the Australian Corps, the readjustments imposed by the results of the German offensives and the preparations for a counter-offensive; from the viewpoint of the Australian Corps these developments appear as a natural and simple adjustment to the new conditions and technique of warfare. It was accomplished with a smoothness which in some measure masks its significance, but for which the reader of previous chapters will not be unprepared.

Pari passu with but unrelated to these general and technical developments we see in the A.I.F. the consummation of patriotic aspirations in the formation of a single "Australian Corps," and the replacement of the British by an Australian Headquarters Staff, including the appointment of an officer of the A.A.M.C. (Colonel G. W. Barber) to the position of Deputy Director of Medical Services. Associated with this appointment we find important changes in administrative methods, in part the impression of a forceful and self-reliant personality, but chiefly a reflection of remarkable developments in the Australian force as a self-contained and unique military formation. Through the integration of exceptional fighting qualities in the troops and of administrative and organising abilities of the highest order in its commander and his subordinate commanders and staff, we shall find the Australian Corps, swelled by external accretions at one stage to the size of an Army, taking a prominent part in the Allied counter-offensive and subsequent advance to victory.

The three subsequent chapters describe the successive blows in the British advance up the Somme to the Hindenburg Line. In this series of major battles we find the Australian Medical Service faced with the dual task; first, that of dealing within eight weeks with nearly one-seventh of the total battle-casualties sustained by the Australian force on the Western Front; second, that of sustaining the chief part in the problem of maintaining the fighting formations at a strength adequate for these stupendous tasks—and this in the face of not only casualties but of pandemic influenza. Not the least significant feature of its work in the war is revealed in the fact that, of the effectives that reached the front, no less than 60 per cent. were recovered men.[2] At the same time the new outlook on disease prevention, wherein "organisation" replaces "discipline" as the keynote of action, is reflected in the curve of disease in the force, and certain features of these activities special to this period of "open warfare" will call for a note. An account of the new gas warfare, which was so important a feature of this period, is relegated to the new volume.

Chapters XXIV and XXV take us to the end of the war so far as concerns the work of the medical service for the field army, and describes the interesting and important problem of combining the administration of two varying national forces, the Australian and American, and the preliminary steps in the repatriation of the Australian Imperial Force on the Western Front.

A final chapter deals with the "interior economy" of the medical service of the A.I.F. during the period under review in this volume; it leads up to the study in the final volume of what may be called the permanent social aspects of medical service in the A.I.F. in relation to the war of 1914-18.

---

[2] This estimate is based on *A.I.F. Statistics of Casualties, etc.* issued 30 June, 1919 by Records Section A.I.F. Headquarters, London, and compiled from figures kept and consolidated by the Australian Records Section of 3rd Echelon, B.E.F. The value of this compendium is unfortunately diminished by a number of arithmetical mistakes, but (though unofficial) it remains the only consolidation of the Australian statistical records of the war hitherto attempted.

CHAPTER XX

THE GERMAN THRUST FOR VICTORY

BY the time a play has reached the final act,[1] as this history of the Australian Medical Service in the Great War has now done, the *dramatis personae* should be familiar and the issues fairly well understood. In these the final chapters relating to military action the outlook will be rather that of "measures" than of "men": the experience of units, even of formations, are merged in an objective examination of the influence of the new warfare on the solution of the fundamental problems of the medical service in the field—the evacuation and treatment of casualties, and the prevention of wastage. It is perhaps inevitable, but is not the less embarrassing, that for this period the records of the service are such as to invite detailed and personal narrative. They are moreover adequate to a much more exact study of medical problems in the field than is possible in this work.[2]

1918; Stage directions
The salient features of the general and military situation in March of 1918 can be summarised in four items:—

1. The collapse of Russia and Roumania and the temporary defeat of Italy, together with highly effective tactics (both military and medical) in the conservation of force and prevention of wastage, had put the German High Command in a position to make available between 60 and 70 divisions for a thrust on any suitable part of the Western Front.[3]

2. As an offset to this, and to the adverse results of "attrition," the Allies had now a strategic reserve in the troops of the U.S.A. of whom,

---
[1] This chapter picks up the narrative of events from *Chapter x*.
[2] The war work of the Australian War Records Section of Administrative Headquarters, A.I.F.—which is now known as the Australian War Memorial—will be dealt with in *Vol. III*.
[3] On March 21 Germany had 192 Divisions on the Western Front, the Allies 175 (including 2 Portuguese).

when the German offensive opened, 4½ divisions were in France and about 40 in training camps in America. The American Army would not however be ready for any decisive part before the autumn of 1918 at earliest and in the meantime the Allied problem of man-power was urgent.

3. On the sea the method of convoy by warships, recently adopted, had in great measure solved the problem of the submarine blockade of Britain. At the same time the British sea blockade of the Central Powers was fully effective, and included as "contraband of war" practically every article necessary to human existence.

4. The Allied search for a strategic plan had reached a deadlock. In Britain the military strategy of 1917 had led to an acute conflict between the political and military "High Commands," with the result that reinforcements were held back by the Government in the United Kingdom.

German Preparations for an Offensive. From the moment when the Battles of Caporetto and Passchendaele and the Peace Treaty with Russia had made possible an offensive on the West, the German High Command had set itself to prepare, within the time-limit available, for a supreme thrust for victory on land. To implement the numerical superiority in fighting men, the General Staff had designed a tactical scheme the chief features of which were surprise, to be achieved by elimination of preliminary bombardments; by intelligent feints and "camouflaged" intentions; by the *immediate* exploitation of successful penetration; and by the more scientific employment of poison gas, in particular the utmost exploitation of "mustard."[4]

Allied Preparations for Defence. By the end of 1917 the French Army had recovered much of its resilience. General Pétain's slogan, "Wait for tanks and the Americans," was, however, accepted by the statesmen as the policy for the Western Front and this compelled both British and French High Commands to face up to the problem of defence. But beyond accepting the importance of co-operation in maintaining the continuity of the Allied front, strategic preparations for mutual support were chiefly concerned with the question of relative responsibility. In

[4] During 1918 some 50 per cent. of German shells contained poison gas.

January, 1918, the Fifth Army's front (which joined the French) was extended thirty miles to Barisis. Denied reinforcements by the Cabinet (to prevent his renewal in the spring of the Flanders offensive) Field-Marshal Haig found his front dangerously attenuated, in particular the sector held by Fifth Army, where early in March the British Intelligence Department confidently forecast a German thrust.

British Tactical Preparations. It was not till the middle of December that the British High Command turned from offence to defence, and not till the middle of January that this was seriously entered upon. Now, as throughout the war, whether for reasons of temperament, character, or training in the command of troops, the British military defence tended to rely to a less degree than the German on material protection, and therefore to a greater degree on the endurance of its troops.[5] Against one weapon defence was entirely adequate. In the new British "Small Box Respirator," with "N.C." container and a filter for the "Blue cross" arsenical smokes, and the new French Tissot mask, the Allies had found an effective counter to the lung irritants. Protection however against the external wounds produced by "mustard" was very imperfect.[6]

The possibility of a devastating break-through does not appear to have been entertained by G.H.Q., which prepared for a considerable bending, but not a breaking, of the line; and this optimism is reflected in the general medical preparations of the B.E.F. At the instance of the Director-General (General Sloggett), at a conference held on March 2nd, some individual action was taken by the D's.M.S.; but it was not till March 6th that specific instructions were issued from G.H.Q. of which the following were the principles.[7]

Medical preparations

(1) Casualty Clearing Stations. The king-pin in the British evacuation system being the C.C.S., the medical problems of retreat, as of advance, centred upon it. With only two 3-ton lorries of its own, each of these now vast tent and hutted hospitals depended for movement on lorries made available, on special requisition, by the Army "Director of

---

[5] *See p. 249.* The military tactics of defence were of vital concern to the medical service since they determined the strategic and tactical principles for the conduct of evacuation and disposition of medical units and use of transport in a retreat. Since however the Australian force was not involved in the retirements, it is unnecessary to describe the British defence in detail. Briefly three spheres of resistance were defined (1) A line of outposts. (2) A "battle zone" 2-3 miles behind this and 2,000-3,000 yards in depth. This consisted of bands of wire and mutually supporting strong posts or "keeps" permanently garrisoned, together with a partly occupied trench line. (3) A "rear zone" of strong posts and wire 2-5 miles behind this again was projected, but in the Fifth Army's sector, where labour was most scarce, this line remained largely a mere paper scheme. By far the greater part of the work was carried out by infantry, who at the time were being reorganised in "9-battalion" divisions and were also training in the tactical principles and methods of defence.

[6] *See Vol. III.*

[7] This account is based on orders issued to the A.C.C.S's and on the *British Official Medical History.*

Supply and Transport"; and its movement was a formidable undertaking. This was recognised, and action taken on two lines. (a) The number of C.C.S's. within a "danger zone" specified was to be reduced. (b) A G.H.Q. order of September, 1916, providing for the formation of a special mobile section of each C.C.S.[8] was brought again to the notice of Army Directors; and the D.M.S. "Fourth"[9] Army was instructed to hold six of his units ready to move at a moment's notice "for reinforcing" those in other Armies. No attempt was made to reduce the scope of these units; this would indeed have involved a reconstruction of the evacuation system on the British front. Most directors made a plan for a succession of sites on which to retire. Of the Fifth Army Director, General Skinner, however, the *British Medical History* records that, reluctant to abandon his "forward" policy he "displayed a tendency to prepare as much for an advance as for a retreat"[10] relying upon rapid removal of his units by train or road transport.

(2) *Motor Ambulance Convoys*. For the evacuation of casualties from the front attacked, armies "not actively engaged" were to be prepared to transfer one or more of these convoys to the areas of those that were attacked. The Director-General had at his own disposal special convoys for clearing by road to St. Omer, Amiens, Etaples, and Abbeville, in case of breakdown in the ambulance train service.

Field Units. The D's.M.S. of Armies prepared schemes whereby field ambulance stations should fall back on new positions—generally the advanced dressing station retiring to the former site of the main station. *More suo*, General Skinner of Fifth Army arranged instead to clear his "advanced" stations direct to C.C.S.[11]

Other matters mentioned in General Sloggett's order of March 6th concerned:—

"*Surgical teams*"—giving details of equipment for these, and appointing distributing centres; "*Special surgical sets*"—to augment C.C.S. equipment; "*Other personnel*"—renewing the obligation on field ambulances to augment the staff of C.C.S.; "*Stretchers*"—providing for reserve of 2,000 in each Corps and for replenishments; "*Blankets*"— reserves to be held with the stretchers, 2 blankets per stretcher; "*Primary suture of wounds*"—instructing all D's.M.S. to ensure that medical officers concerned "thoroughly understand what is required in this respect."

---

[8] After noting that these units, "so far as the transport required to move them is concerned," had "become extremely unwieldy" this order continued, "You will please arrange, therefore, for each C.C.S. to have ready now a list of the articles which are necessary for carrying on emergent surgical work and providing nursing facilities at main dressing stations or other suitable places in advance of its present position, whenever the necessity of moving a . . . station forward arises. This equipment should represent minimum requirements and should be limited to 9 lorry loads, to enable a casualty clearing station to open for work immediately without waiting till the bulk of its material arrives."

[9] Under Gen. Plumer this army had been called the "Second." Gen. Plumer and his staff were still in Italy. On their return on March 17 it again became the Second Army.

[10] See *General Vol. III, p.* 212.

[11] In Feb., in this Army at a meeting of Deputy-Directors "it was decided that for surgical reasons every effort was necessary to speed up the transit of wounded to C.C.S." In effect the advanced dressing stations would take the place of the main stations.

Ludendorff's Thrusts. The German offensive took the form of a series of independent thrusts on a vast scale at various strategic points of the British and French fronts in the northern half of the Allied line over a period from March 21st till July 15th. Working on the apprehensions of each of the Allied Commanders the German General Staff was able to mislead both. Save in the last two strokes, it thus achieved surprise, and within a few hours overran the main defensive zone. To this fact was due much of its tactical success—and much tribulation to the Allied Medical Services.

The German offensives

The several thrusts were made as follows:—

"Michael." The most extensive and important was that begun on March 21st against the British Third and Fifth Armies. The tactical objective was the railway junction at Amiens, and the original purpose, to separate the British and French Armies and crush the British, against which the whole strength was thrown. After penetrating to a depth of 35 miles, this attack broke in an ineffective assault against the Bastion of the Vimy Ridge and was held up 11 miles from Amiens. Some details are given later.

"George" (*"I" and "II"*). On April 9th a thrust was made on the depleted British front in Flanders, the brunt falling on the Portuguese in front of the Lys. The tactical objective was Hazebrouck railway junction, whose capture would have involved the main supply service of the British northern armies. The strategic purpose was penetration to the Channel Ports. The initial attack overran the defensive zone but failed against the Bastion of Givenchy Ridge. The advance was eventually held up before Hazebrouck. Renewed attacks to the north scored rapid tactical successes at Mont Kemmel, but the strategic gains were quite incommensurate.

In each of these operations decisive success appeared within grasp, but in each it was withheld with the British force fighting—as Haig said in the "order for the day" of April 11th —"with its back to the wall." In each of these operations also, partly by force of circumstances, but partly, too, through that fitness for the task which is the master of circumstance, the Australian Imperial Force played a rôle so spectacular as to give rise to legends that have obscured in some measure its real importance.

Three other thrusts were made: first on May 27th against the French front line between Soissons and Rheims. In three days this whirlwind advance swept nearly 25 miles, to the Marne, where its impetus died away.[12] Second, on June 9th Ludendorff thrust at the French salient in front of Compiègne but failed to "pinch it out." Third, on July 15th a double offensive was launched, east and west of Rheims, but was foiled by an elastic defence. On July 18th using some 400 light tanks and French and American Divisions Foch counter-attacked on a large scale against the German flank and, by an impressive victory, set the German commanders finally on the defensive.

At its close the German offensive had cost the British Army alone over 300,000 casualties and immense material losses, and the margin between success and failure had been a narrow one. But already on July 4th a blow had been struck at Hamel on the Australian front which, if minor in extent, proved a very effective rehearsal for the first thrust in the Allied offensive that ended the war. The events of these battles belong to the next and succeeding chapters; the present is concerned with the Australian part in "Michael" and "George."

Areas captured by Germans, 1918. 1, 2, and 3 mark the areas of "Michael," "George," and offensive against French respectively.

The Movement in "Michael": March 21st-26th. At the beginning of March, 1918, the British Army held a line from Houthulst Forest 125 miles south to the Oise where it joined the French.[13] The take-off

---

[12] The automatic slowing down of an advance through over-running communication and supplies was one of the most important strategic principles impressed in the Great War on the medical service which is peculiarly susceptible to its influence. (See, for example, *Chapters vi and ix.*)

[13] On March 21 from N. to S. the British "Armies" were commanded—the Second by General Sir Herbert Plumer, now back from Italy (D.M.S. Major-General M. O'Keeffe); First by General Sir Henry Horne (D.M.S. Major-General H. N. Thompson); Third by General Sir Julian Byng (D.M.S. Major-General Sir J. M. Irwin); Fifth by General Sir Hubert Gough (D.M.S. Major-General G. B. M. Skinner). The headquarters of the Fourth Army, Sir Henry Rawlinson, was now in reserve. The Third Army comprised the IV, V, and VI Corps, the Fifth Army the III, VII, XVIII and XIX Corps. The 1st, 2nd and 3rd Cavalry Divisions were in this Army.

for "Michael" was from the strongest sector of the Hindenburg Line, which had remained much as after the British offensive in 1917. The advance hinged on the British position on the Vimy Ridge, in front of Arras where a natural stronghold had been converted into a fortress. On the 44 miles front from Arras to the Oise 57 German Divisions were thrown against 20 British: the guns numbered 1 to every 11 yards. Infiltrating tactics were helped by a fog whereby the British posts and units were isolated and *liaison* impeded.

In spite of Cambrai the General Staffs of G.H.Q. and the Armies concerned were wholly unprepared for the rapidity of the advance. By the end of the first day the three lines of defence had been overrun. The Flesquières Salient, sole gain to British arms from Cambrai, was "pinched out"; and thereafter the way was clear, across the open grasslands traversed in "Alberich," to the line of the Somme, which was quickly forced, and thence to the waste of the old Somme battlefield of 1916. On March 23rd, however, dissatisfied with the outlook for rolling up the British, which had been planned for that stage, Ludendorff decided to continue with his left the effort to separate the British and French. Nevertheless on the Third Army's front as well as on that of the Fifth the immense pressure produced crises, and on March 26th, when the 3rd and 4th Australian Divisions reached the battle zone, the Allied strategy was in the melting pot.

March 26th: A Turning Point of the War. The events of so vast a battle cannot be summarised in a few sentences; nor is it easy to crystallise movement so rapid and diverse in a series of lucid intervals for description. Fortunately from the point of view of historical narrative it is possible to select a moment when events in three major spheres of interest, germane to this history, move to a focal point, thence to diverge and create a wholly novel field of outlook and action.

(1) On March 24th Ludendorff changed the direction of his thrust —towards the left flank of the French. General Pétain, the French Commander-in-Chief, who mistakenly feared an attack elsewhere, decided that he could no longer (as for 24 hours he had done) support the right of the British Fifth Army, but must uncover Amiens in order to protect Paris. This led Haig, who was vehemently opposed to such a policy, to issue on March 25th a provisional order for a corresponding movement of his own troops. Either movement, if carried out, would sever the two forces.

(2) On March 23rd Haig decided to use the Australian Corps as the main part of G.H.Q. reserve, and on the 26th the 3rd and 4th Divisions were being moved to the danger points in the Third Army's line.

(3) On the same date, at the famous conference held in Doullens, the decision was reached—with Haig's support and even at his suggestion—to appoint General Foch Generalissimo of the Allied Forces in France.

The position of the British front on this date is shown

in the sketch map. From this point the history of the British part in the offensive becomes intimately bound up with that of the Australian Divisions; and the account of the medical events of the Fifth Army's retreat is most conveniently picked up in this history when the medical units of the Australian divisions are caught into the stream.

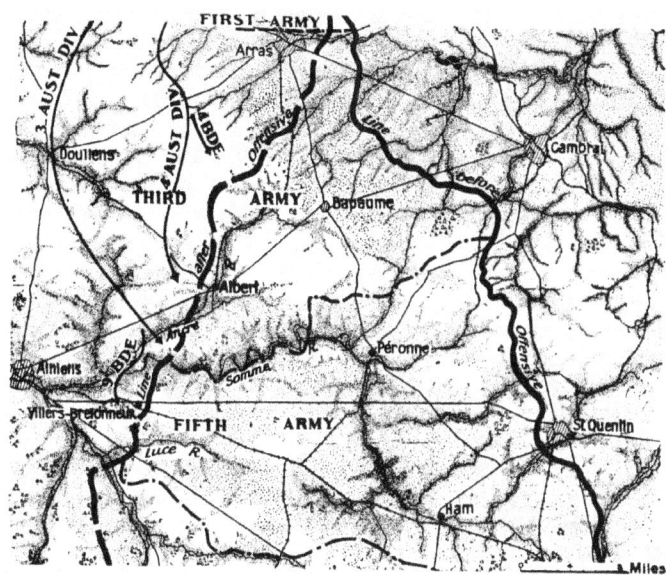

Winter of 1917-18. After the fighting of October, 1917, the five infantry divisions of the A.I.F. had taken over from the VIII Corps a front east of the Messines Ridge and in the valley of the Lys. During the winter, each unit in turn went for a fortnight's rest to village billets not far from Boulogne.

The Australian Corps medical units

At the front, beside the routine of trench-warfare and raidings reminiscent of the spring of 1916, the formations were kept busy with constructive work and training, and the A.I.F. staff in completing the reconstruction of the newly-formed "Australian" Corps. Though the work was heavy and the front low-lying and wet, and a suitable target for mustard gas, the conditions were infinitely more favourable than those of the previous winter. By the end of March the troops of all arms and services had fully recovered their resilience. Units and formations were at strength: all arms and every service had reached a standard that made the Australian force in France a weapon of tremendous striking power. *Esprit de corps* had been immensely augmented by the integration of the five Australian divisions and their ancillary services into the "Australian Corps"—the last stage of which was interrupted by the events reviewed in this chapter. On the physical side, the policy of the D.M.S., A.I.F., pursued with inflexible determination, and with a vision that had made him the trusted adviser of General Birdwood and his Chief of Staff,[14] had achieved striking results. Major-General Howse's contribution to the efficiency of the A.I.F. in the most critical moment of its service was this: that each quota in the diminishing tale of recruits from Australia as it arrived was inexorably cleared of all defectives; that the reserve of recovered men was sifted not less exactly; and that in the Command Depots a medical organisation had been built up that could transform a casualty into an effective with maximum efficiency in a minimum of time.

The health of the troops was incomparably better than in the previous winter. For the system of Divisional and "Corps Rest Stations" of the "Somme Winter" was substituted one of allocating a casualty clearing station to Corps for this purpose—for the Australian Corps No. 1 A.C.C.S. was chosen. Freed from this drudgery the medical service of the Divisions was able to concentrate on training. In January an admirable "Australian Corps Medical School" was formed in which a considerable proportion of the medical officers and N.C.O's of the Corps were given up-to-date training.[15] For all arms

---

[14] Major-Gen. C. B. B. White.
[15] The "Commandant" was Lieut.-Col. Clive Thompson. The course covered a week, and the syllabus included an introductory lecture by the C.O. followed by lectures on Military Law; Duties of a Medical Officer; Water; Map Reading; Hygiene of Troops; Care of Horses; Baths and Laundries; The Thomas Splint; P.U.O.; Mechanical Transport; System of Supply in the Field; Army Books and Returns; Military Operations; General Sanitation; and Wound Shock. Demonstrations were given of "Defensive" and "Offensive" gas, of C.C.S. work, and of aerial photography. At the close of the course an examination was held. The lecturers included, besides senior officers of the A.A.M.C., transport and legal officers of the Corps and Consulting Physicians of Second Army.

Schools of Instruction in cooking and in the best use of rations were held, a feature of which was the endeavour to eliminate, so far as possible, the depressing monotony of "stew."

Sanitation. By this time, with its baths and laundries, "sanitation" was *de facto*, as already it was *de jure*, a part of Army life. In this respect indeed, save when in the line, the troops tended to lose the art of self-help in field methods.

During the winter the actual fighting on Second Army front was confined to bombardments, raids, and patrols. At the end of the winter, the approaching hour of "Michael" was heralded by a harassing bombardment, of which a medical officer (Captain R. L. Forsyth) then with the 13th Field Ambulance at Bailleul has left a record:—

Rumours of war

"*March 4th.* I spent the next 10 days as orderly officer and played Badminton. Tilling was in the billet with me and the old lady was fat, red-faced and a brick. I got coffee in the morning and a comfortable bed. About March 14th the war started. I was in my digs writing when something went swish and the backyard tumbled down and the back wall went up in chunks. I cleaned the plaster out of my collar and went down-stairs. The old lady couldn't turn pale but talked harder than usual and waved her hands. I went into Bailleul square and patched up the remnants of 4 or 5 men. A lot more shells landed and bits of iron became common. I felt pleased when ordered off to the 4th Pioneer Battalion. Arrived there at 10.30 p.m. and found Whiting playing bridge. He gave me his blessing and his dugout and told me that everything was all right and nothing doing. I slept. Evidently the Kaiser's spies had been informed of my move as next morning, while the rest were telling me how quiet things were, a shell lobbed in front of the Mess, another splattered the R.A.P. The war was still on. Shells started to arrive with monotonous regularity—for 5 or 6 days 'woolly bears,' shrapnel, and 5·9's rained on the district. About March 21st we began to hear rumours, and an English artillery major told me that his boy was in Fifth Army and that they were hoping for an attack as they were ready to give the Hun hell. March 22nd was exceptionally warm and bright, I sat in the sun and read. That evening orders came through to embuss at Locre at 5 next morning."

On the following day the unit moved with the rest of the 4th Division south to the Somme.

Medical Units in Move to South. On March 21st the 1st, 2nd and 5th Divisions were in line at Messines, the 3rd and 4th in support and reserve. On March 24th, moving by brigades, the 4th Division embussed for village billets around Basseux (behind Arras) and on the 25th the 3rd entrained for Doullens, both being held in reserve behind the Third Army. With each brigade went the personnel of its corresponding field ambulance; horse and motor transport went by road.[16] From Basseux the 4th Brigade (4th Division), without its field ambulance,[17] was on March 26th detached and, with the New Zealand Division, was rushed into a gap in the IV Corps front near Hébuterne. On the night of the 26th-27th the 12th and 13th Brigades, with the 4th, 12th, and 13th Field Ambulances, route-marched immediately behind the barely established front down to Senlis near Albert, and in the afternoon of the 27th moved up by familiar roads past Vadencourt, Warloy, and Hénencourt to fill a breach which, through a misunderstanding of Haig's order of March 25th, was developing on the VII Corps front on the Ancre south of Albert. Hither also was hurried the 3rd Division. Each brigade as it moved up encountered the flotsam and jetsam, soldiers and civilians, fore-flung from the advancing wave of the German Army, and entered upon scenes and events admirably calculated to rouse in high-spirited and self-reliant men a strong determination and sense of responsibility—and in the staff officers exasperation at the inevitably conflicting and countermanding orders and instructions issued by every headquarters, a sentiment that is luridly reflected in the diaries of the A.D's.M.S.

The Allied Front, March 26th-27th. Looking—as now we can—behind the scene of these events, the cause of all this administrative confusion becomes clear. Next to the crisis on the Marne in 1914, the moment when the 3rd and 4th Australian Divisions reached the Somme was perhaps the most critical in the whole war. The effect of the orders of Pétain and Haig, tending to separate the British and French Armies, had to be repaired. The first action of General Foch was a peremptory order to both British and French leaders that there must be *"NO* withdrawal" of the general line, and it was in pursuance of this policy that on the night of March 26th the 12th and 13th Brigades of the 4th Division were sent to relieve the 9th Division which, in consequence of the misunderstanding above referred to, had retired across the Ancre; and the 3rd Division to form a front on the plateau between the Ancre and the Somme.[18]

---

[16] The ambulance horse transport that marched with the transport of the 4th Brigade took some 3½ days, as follows: *March 24*—Ravelsberg to Vieux Berquin, 20 kilometres, 8 hours; *25th*—to Hermaville, 80 km., 18 hours; *26th*—to La Cauchie, 15 km., 6 hours. Here it picked up the unit and marched with it to Baizieux, 45 km., in 12 hours, arriving at Baizieux at 2.30 p.m. on the 27th. On the *28th* it went with the unit to Toutencourt. "After a day's rest the horses were none the worse." (4th Fld. Amb. *War Diary*.)

[17] The absence of the field ambulance was due to an order of the Brigade or the Divisional Commander.

[18] On March 23 Gen. Pétain took command of the British Fifth Army and the front as far as the Somme. On the 28th Gen. Rawlinson superseded Gen. Gough, and a few days later "Fifth" Army became "Fourth." The D.M.S., Major-Gen. Skinner, continued to function till relieved on April 9 by Major-Gen. M. W. O'Keeffe. At the beginning of April Fourth Army came again under Haig's command.

Indeed, in Haig's acceptance of Foch; in Foch's "*NO* withdrawal" order; and in Haig's own orders which at this stage threw the Australian and New Zealand formations into the Third and Fifth Army fronts, we may perhaps see (as in the old nursery rhyme) that great moment when "the cat begins to kill the rat, the rat begins to gnaw the rope, the rope begins to hang the butcher . . ." leading, through the ups and downs of the failing German offensive and the Allied advance, to an auspicious *dénouement* on November 11th.

Local Situation on March 27th. The German advance on Third Army front on March 26th took it some 6 to 9 miles beyond that "Old front line of the English" from which on 1st July, 1916, the New Armies had kicked off for the Battle of the Somme: from the high land overlooking Albert the 4th Division saw the enemy issuing from that town. In the afternoon of March 27th the 12th Brigade with the 13th in support (and, a few days later, on its flank) took up a line along the railway touching Dernancourt, its rear resting on the bare hillside reaching up to the Albert-Amiens road in front of Laviéville. On that exposed slope lay the abandoned casualty clearing stations at "Edgehill." Crossing the Ancre at Heilly the 10th and 11th Brigades of 3rd Division straddled the peninsula from Méricourt l'Abbé to Sailly-le-Sec. Both found tired but far from defeated troops facing the enemy. Within 24 hours both formations had sustained heavy casualties which had been cleverly cleared by their medical units.

The Australians had been promised by one of their leaders "the fight of their lives"; the two divisional A.D's.M.S., in darkness and confusion, and faced (as they

The medical situation on the Somme believed) with the problem of clearing a flood of wounded from their two divisions, sought to ascertain the identity and location of the C.C.S's and M.A.C.'s on which to base their own schemes of clearance. To appreciate their task it is necessary first to outline briefly the course of the very instructive events in the Medical Services of Third and Fifth Armies during the German advance.

The Medical Service in the Retreat.[19] The effect of the 10 days, March 21st-30th, on the huge system of treatment-centres and transport units built up during three years of "attrition" was staggering. Caught in a rough-house, the units

---

[19] The happenings of the first five days are gathered from the *British Official Medical History*, supplemented by some Army and Corps orders, the *War Diary* of the D.M.S., Fifth Army, and some personal narratives.

of Third and Fifth Armies emerged denuded of much of their trappings, and much chastened of their "forward" spirit. But at the same time it is recorded that none of the wounded who reached a main dressing station or C.C.S. and who were fit to move, were abandoned; and none of the personnel of these units were captured.[20] This much, at least, was effected by motor transport in contrast to the limitations of horsed transport in the retreat from Mons.[21]

There were three phases in these medical events—

(1) *March 21-22.* The defensive line is "infiltrated" and many aid-posts and forward ambulance posts are cut off, and wounded lost through capture.

(2) *March 23-25.* The enemy drives the British Divisions across the open country, slowing down somewhat on the 24th-25th. In this stage the zone of the casualty clearing stations, and the first and even the second echelon of their new sites, are overrun.

(3) *March 26-May 4.* This phase, in the Somme area, includes the check on the line of the Ancre and south of the Somme to Hangard Wood, near the Luce; the renewed attempts to break through (March 26-April 9); and the subsequent desultory fighting to secure tactical advantage (April 10-May 4).

During the period March 21-April 30 the British losses totalled 302,869 of whom 28,128 were "killed," 181,338 "wounded" (1 killed to 6·4 wounded), and 93,403 are recorded as "missing and prisoners of war."[22]

Regimental Medical Establishments. Heavy casualties were incurred among R.M.O's and Regimental bearers. It is officially recorded that a serious cause of failure to clear wounded was—the old business—defective *liaison* between brigades and field ambulances.

Field Ambulances. The *British Official Medical History* records that in both Armies after the first day the medical services of Division and Corps worked methodically throughout the retreat, "falling back from post to post without confusion and according to plan." It is clear however that the term "methodical" connotes methods of a novel kind, in

---

[20] A number of Australian nurses were serving in the C.C.S's of Fifth Army and had highly "exciting" experiences—including withdrawal under field-gun fire—and did admirable service. Some of the details will be found in the chapter in *Vol. III* dealing with the Nursing Service.

[21] See in this connection *p. 288*.

[22] The figures are from *Statistics of the Military Effort of the British Empire, p. 362* (War Office, March, 1922). It has unfortunately not been found possible to resolve this last group; and, failing this, no attempt can be made to assess, from the proportion of killed to wounded and died of wounds, either the vigour of the British resistance, or the success of the arrangements and endeavours for rescue and clearance to the Base. For 1918 as a whole the British battle-casualties were (*Brit. Off. Med. History—Statistics, p. 168*) Killed 9·18 per cent., Died of wounds 5·26 per cent., Missing 7·26 per cent., Prisoners of war 12·28 per cent., Wounded less Died of wounds 66·01 per cent. The proportion of killed in action, died of wounds, missing, and prisoners of war to the total wounded (less died of wounds) was 1 to 1·9.

Mar., 1918] GERMAN THRUST FOR VICTORY 619

particular in the matter of transportation.[23] The vital duty seems to have lain in clearing stretcher cases from the motor loading posts to the ambulance treatment centre (whether "A.D.S." or "M.D.S.") and thence to the C.C.S.[24] After the war the opinion was authoritatively expressed[25] that "the uncertain link in the chain of evacuation was always bound to lie in the sector between the Regimental Aid-Post and the A.D.S.," and that "the common experience had been that the transport of the wounded man in this area was always greatly facilitated when motor ambulances could be pushed close up to the firing line."

The Motor Ambulance Convoys (for Stretcher Cases). Difficulty was experienced in keeping these very volatile units together, and in working them as units. In certain Corps the M.A.C. was split up and a section attached to Headquarters. In some Corps a "lorry convoy" was attached to the M.A.C. In both Armies whenever the C.C.S's were on the move and out of action, the M.A.C's chasing them with the stretcher cases were unable to cope with their task, and in consequence field ambulance transport had sometimes to clear to or even beyond the C.C.S. The *walking wounded* were cleared by 'buses and returning lorries.

The Casualty Clearing Stations. Only the barest outline is possible of the very instructive experiences of these units.[26]

In the Third Army the first echelon of moves was made on March 22nd-23rd from the forward zone comprising Ytres, Grévillers, Achiet-le-Grand, Boisleux-au-Mont, Agnez-lez-Duisans, about 7-8 miles from the front, to just beyond the old Somme Battlefield—Edgehill, Aveluy, le Bac du Sud. Later a second series of moves took them to a third echelon of positions—Corbie, Warloy, Puchevillers, Orville. On March 26th, when the Australian Divisions were arriving, these positions were

---

[23] An Australian surgeon serving with the R.A.M.C.—Major H. Boyd Graham, R.A.M.C.T.; *see Vol. I, pp. 89, 518,* found that the bearer divisions became, in effect, independent units, moving back in echelon on the A.D.S. as a separate link in the "chain" of evacuation. This officer records that in the 21st Division (VII Corps) a scheme was improvised whereby 3 bearer sub-divisions, together with 3 officers and 100 other ranks from Pioneer Battalions, formed a Divisional reserve of bearers. A bearer sub-division (1 officer and about 40 other ranks) formed a "Brigade bearer party" which was attached to Brigade Headquarters. It received operation orders from Division and submitted location reports to the officer-in-charge of the "Divisional" bearers. "By this means the close *liaison* so desirable between R.M.O's and Field Ambulances was comparatively easily maintained."

[24] A memorandum was issued on April 2 by the D.G.M.S. B.E.F. on "the experience of the last ten days of March." The most important lesson from the experience was stated as follows:
"Should our front line in the course of pressure by the enemy be forced back, the withdrawal of the main dressing stations will necessarily be in accordance with the general situation, but they should be established at suitable points in echelon during the withdrawal, so that there should always be a point to which the motor ambulance transport of the field ambulances can bring their wounded without having to go further back, and to which the M.A.C. can work without having to go further forward."

[25] In a discussion on transport of wounded in "open" warfare in the "War Section" of the Royal Society of Medicine presided over by the D.G.M.S., A.M.S., Sir John Goodwin (*Proceedings March 1922, p. 13*).

[26] The *British Official Medical History* gives a full and exactly charted account of these. Details of the moves of the three Australian casualty clearing stations in Second Army are given later in this chapter.

being abandoned in favour of a fourth echelon—Amiens, Vignacourt, Gézaincourt, Doullens, Frévent—20 to 30 miles or more by road behind the new front.

Here, for the most part, they remained till the advance to victory permitted a cautious move forward. In some instances the retreat was continued even as far back as St. Riquier and Pont Remy, near Abbeville.

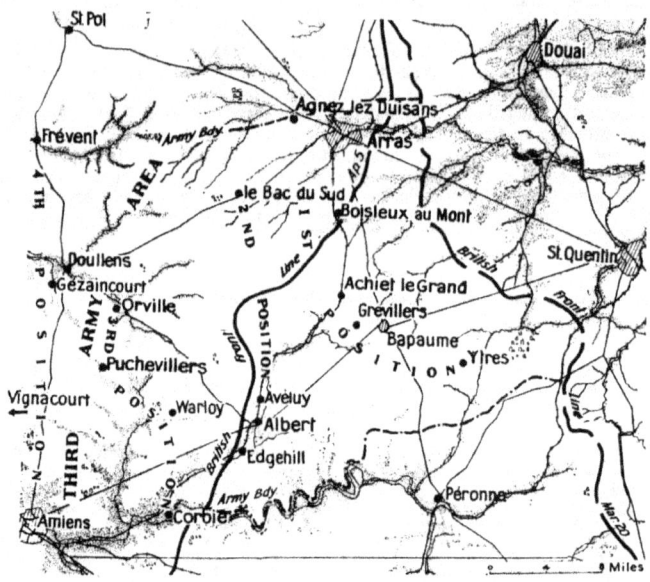

Movement of C.C.S's in Third Army during the German Offensive.

The retreat of the Fifth Army being much more rapid and more extensive than that of the Third, the medical difficulties were correspondingly greater. The clearing stations were no further forward than those of other armies and on March 21st occupied a zone Tincourt, Ham, Cugny, and Noyon—names that will be met again in the advance to victory—7 to 10 miles behind the front. A rear echelon was behind the Somme line at Marchelpot. The first withdrawal on 22nd-23rd took the first echelon back beyond the Somme line to Rozières, Roye, and Maricourt. On March 23rd the enemy rushed parts of the Somme line and the moves of the C.C.S's on March 24th-26th to Hargicourt, Villers-Bretonneux, Gailly, Corbie and Vecquemont were precipitate. Thereafter, in consequence of the military and administrative vicissitudes of this Army, of the French swerve to the south, and of the retreat of Third Army to the left, and the dreaded danger of a wide break between the British and French forces, these units were scattered. Some moved

Mar., 1918] GERMAN THRUST FOR VICTORY 621

north-westwards through Corbie to Third Army; some were pushed back through Amiens down the Somme, others south to Namps where a large entraining and treatment centre was formed from the remnants of seven units.[27]

Eddies from the Retreat: Casualties and Clearing Stations. The momentum from the impetus that carried both the casualties and the clearing stations through their concurrent echelons of moves, swept both far beyond the fighting zone. The danger of a gap opening in consequence of Pétain's order of March 24th and Haig's of March 25th had strong repercussions as far back as No. 3 A.G.H. at Abbeville, and the experience of that unit warrants a special note.

On March 27th the A.D.M.S. Abbeville area informed the Commanding Officer[28] that it was to "carry on as a C.C.S."

The officer-in-charge of the Surgical Division (Lieut.-Colonel H. C. Taylor-Young) stated in his report for March:—
"The number of cases admitted and the amount of work done have been greater than during any similar period since the arrival of the Hospital in France. The character of the cases has been more severe, and their condition more desperate, many arriving with only the field dressing applied. The majority were transported entirely by road, and in several cases the convoy was 36 hours and longer on the journey. During the earlier days of the rush the work was conducted on the lines of a Base Hospital, but owing to an order received (on March 27th) complete arrangements . . were made to conduct the place as a C.C.S."

During March 2,467 casualties were treated in this unit, of whom 536 were operated upon. Deaths numbered 21, and 2,381 cases were discharged or transferred. The report continues:—

"abdominal cases account for a large proportion of the deaths. They had all been transported by road, and had a long and very rough journey. All except one should have been hopeful cases for operation

[27] Four "units"—*i.e.* their staffs—were later sent to the Base to reorganise and re-equip. The D.M.S. of this Army, Major-Gen. Skinner, has been severely criticised for his methods, and it is true that the material losses were far greater than in Third Army and this under circumstances that made it a serious matter. Much however may be found to extenuate and explain this. The D.M.S. was involved in the strategic and tactical failures of Fifth Army. He himself attributed the loss of equipment—the value of which he placed at £200,000—to failure of the Transport Department to support him. (The war was costing some ten million pounds a day.) He suggested that in such a crisis the two 3-ton lorries of the C.C.S's be combined to form a column under the D.M.S. It may be added that as far back as 1916 officers of the Australian Medical Service, when they arrived on the Somme, had been unfavourably impressed by the attitude in this Army toward its Medical Department.

[28] This statement is from the hospital's war diary. Abbeville was the Headquarters of the I.G.C. and of the D.M.S., L. of C.

had they been tackled within a reasonable time. In almost every case instead of having merely dirty wounds to treat, they were very septic before reaching this Hospital."

The matron of the same hospital (Miss Miles-Walker) reported:—

"The routine of the Nursing Staff was as usual until the end of the month, when the influx of patients necessitated the extension of the Hospital to 2,000 beds." [Even the Y.M.C.A. Hut was filled with beds] . . . "11 English reserve Sisters were sent by the Matron-in-Chief, B.E.F. for four days' temporary duty during the heavy rush of work, which lasted for one week. . . . A great feature of this very strenuous week was the constant coming and going of refugee sisters, English as well as Australian, arriving without baggage from different C.C.S's to be accommodated."

On March 31st, under instructions from Headquarters L. of C., a board was appointed to report on the time required to move the hospital at (1) 48 hours', or (2) 7 days' notice. Lieut.-Colonel Taylor-Young's report for April says:—

"When my previous monthly report was submitted, no cases were coming to this area. The 65 remaining in Hospital were cases not fit to be evacuated; all others, many of them dangerously ill, having been, under urgent orders, evacuated. All Departments were prepared and ready for movement if so instructed. . . . On the 4th of the month, however, at 2.0 p.m. convoys began arriving and kept coming rapidly.[29] The following days were the most strenuous experienced by this Unit since coming to France.

"Four teams were available and started work at once continuing until midnight, after which hour, Major Matthews and I carried on throughout the night operating on urgent cases. Work continued at this very high pressure until the forenoon of the 8th, by which time, owing to representations made, the convoys were switched off to other Hospitals. . . . The number of anaesthetics administered [during the month] was 447

"The cases as a whole were severe and arrived in a bad condition, travelling by road. The great majority arrived untouched owing to 'forced evacuation' from the C.C.S's, and it was a marvel that some of them reached here alive. Considering these facts it is most gratifying that there were only 34 deaths ."[30]

The Ambulance Train. In the Great War (as we have seen) the whole "Army" scheme of evacuation hinged on railhead. In an advance the possible progress of railhead determined

---

[29] This was the day of the Second German Army's attack on the Fourth British Army, known in the A.I.F. as "First Villers-Bretonneux." The effort continued next day at Dernancourt—the last flicker of the "Michael" offensive.

[30] The report states: "A new class of case appears this month—delayed primary suture cases (D.P.S.); 18 of these came forward during the month and in every case the result was primary union."

the rate of movement of the Army; in a retreat, *vice versa*.[31] The movements of "No. 23" (Ambulance Train) during the week March 23rd-30th as told by the A.A.M.C. officer-in-charge[32] completes the picture of the movement of casualties to the base during the period of the retreat.

"No. 23 Ambulance Train left Abbeville at 2.45 p.m. on *Saturday, March 23rd.* At 8 a.m. *24th* it reached Edgehill (Dernancourt) where a T.A.T. [33] and another A.T. were loading. We started loading No. 23 at midday and at 2.30 left with a full load of 340 lying and 180 sitting cases, leaving No. 48 C.C.S. free to move back. No. 48 C.C.S. had the day before sent their nursing sisters back, and this unit had only arrived at Edgehill (from Ytres) 2 days before. . . . Many cases arrived in the trains that would under normal conditions remain at a C.C.S. for treatment. Six died, 2 head cases, 2 chest wounds, 1 abdominal and 1 thigh amputation. We took 25 hours to get to Amiens (*March 25th*), a distance of 15 miles, owing to a block in the traffic . . . arriving at Le Tréport at 4 a.m. on *Tuesday, 26th March.* We thus took 38 hours to do about 60 miles. Many redressings and resplintings were done and haemorrhages controlled by plugging, etc.

Journey of Hospital Train, March 1918.

"In a few hours after unloading we left and arrived Abbeville again at 10 a.m. leaving at 2.45 p.m. for Puchevillers, where, on arrival at 7 p.m., within 2 hours we loaded (240 lying and 17 sitting) and off again to arrive at Doullens at 2.15 a.m. (*27th*), where we picked up 170 walking cases. Here we put off 6 cases for urgent treatment—serious haemorrhage and chest that were doing badly on our tedious journey. We were kept here for five hours from traffic troubles, leaving at 7.30 a.m. and passing Montreuil before midday. Arriving at Etaples at 12.15 p.m. we unloaded in an hour and reloaded with 400 hospital cases by 3 p.m. when we left for Calais. The women motor drivers worked splendidly in connection with the transport of wounded. Arrived at

---
[31] The *British Official (Military) History* is emphatic in attributing the slowing down of the German advance largely to the problem of communications, in particular across the "devastated" area.

[32] Major W. W. W. Chaplin, A.A.M.C. This officer was detailed for the special duty from No. 3 A.G.H. The report is from the war diary, for March, of No. 3 A.G.H.

[33] Temporary Ambulance Train.

Calais 8 a.m. on *28th*, unloaded and left at 9 p.m. for Gézaincourt, arriving *29th* at 8 p.m. 6.30 a.m. (*30th*) we left with half a load 200 cases nearly all light. Arrived at Etaples at 11 a.m. and unloaded. . . . The Head Sister, 2 staff nurses, and 38 other ranks (R.A.M.C.) worked splendidly through our busy week."

Lessons as to Evacuation in a Retreat. From the welter of experiences of both armies there seems to emerge this fact, that in a rapid retreat the speed of the twofold movement— (1) that of the *casualty* along the chain of loading posts, treatment stations and transport circuits of the route of "evacuation"; and, concurrently, (2) that of the *whole evacuation system* itself, including *R.A.P and C.C.S.*—depends on the rapidity with which the casualty clearing station (if this be retained as the keystone of treatment) can make the sequence —break camp and move; pitch camp and clear stretcher cases by motor ambulance convoy. And the crux of the matter lies in the fact that success does not, as with the field ambulance, hang on the internal efficiency of the unit alone, but on this *plus* various extrinsic factors: in particular the relations between the D.M.S. and the Department of Supply and Transport, and Railway Operating Division.[34]

4th Division. Motoring on the night of March 26th-27th from Basseux to Baizieux the A.D.M.S., 4th Division, Colonel Barber, reported *en route* to the headquarters of the D.M.S. Third Army and subsequently to VII Corps headquarters at Montigny. He found the utmost difficulty in ascertaining the situation.

Medical arrangements on the Ancre

---

[34] The A.D.M.S. 4th Division (Colonel G. W. Barber) wrote in his war diary at the time:

"26th March. I have often urged the need for mobile C.C.S's—*vide War Establishments, Part VII*—and the necessity of the same under these conditions is becoming very apparent. The present fixed C.C.S's should in my opinion have been regarded as expanded stationary hospitals and mobile C.C.S's held in reserve. . . . If this had been done it would be strictly in accordance with F.S. Regs.—Medical Services. . . . All the trouble I have seen arise in the past has been due to non-compliance with these excellent regulations."

The British Official Historian states that in the experience of Third Army "severely wounded collected in advanced dressing stations could not be got away before the enemy captured the position; but all wounded admitted to a main dressing station were saved from capture. A.D's.M.S. of divisions and O's.C. of field ambulances strongly emphasize the importance of . . . field ambulances retaining their own ambulance transport solely for bringing wounded back from the front area and advanced dressing stations to . . . main dressing stations and no further." (*Brit. Off. Med. History, General, Vol. III, p. 246*).

Comments made by Australian units agree that in evacuation in a retreat it is vital that the proper transport circuits should be strictly adhered to.

"Medical arrangements in Third Army," he said in his *War Diary*, "seem to be totally disorganised—C.C.S's have been closed down, some apparently without justification, such as Puchevillers and Amiens; and in consequence all cases have to be evacuated a very long distance to Doullens and its vicinity. M.A.C. evacuations also unsatisfactory—16th M.A.C. appears to be working under orders of Army, 3rd M.A.C. under orders of Corps. There is no co-ordination of their work and consequently over-lapping occurs. . . . I am informed that there is a shortage of stretchers and dressings and no one seems to require any returns."

Though not unnatural in the circumstances, this ebullition, when read in the light of preceding pages, can be given its proper moral discount. It is clear that the confusion at the moment was largely due to the Corps Commander's misinterpretation of Haig's order of March 25th. But the picture of the confusion that reigned at this time behind the field ambulances is accurate enough.

The Field Ambulances (March 27th). The 12th and 13th Field Ambulances marched, and made their approach to the line, with their respective brigades. Moving up through Vadencourt and Warloy to Hénencourt, they found behind the British 35th and 17th Divisions a well organised scheme of Divisional clearance, and "heavy evacuation, going on satisfactorily."[35] After negotiations with the British units they took over the cellars of the great *Château,* and pitched tents in its grounds for an A.D.S. By mutual arrangement (pending instructions from the A.D.M.S.) the two Ambulance Commanders (Major F. N. Le Messurier[36] and Lieut.-Colonel H. K. Fry) worked out a scheme of clearance—the 13th to act as a "main" dressing station.

Bearer Captains moved off at 2 p.m. to Millencourt to get in touch with the R.M.O's. A motor loading post was formed at Millencourt at 5 p.m., and was clearing the R.A.P's by 7. A second loading post was taken over at Laviéville from the R.A.M.C., with stretchers and blankets salvaged previously from the C.C.S's at Dernancourt—now, by day, under rifle fire.

By March 28th a Divisional scheme was in full swing, with A.D.S. at Hénencourt (12th Field Ambulance) clearing the two brigade fronts to M.D.S. (13th Field Ambulance) at

---

[35] The quotations are from field ambulance war diaries.
[36] The O.C. 12th Fld. Amb. (Lieut.-Col. A. H. Gibson) was on leave; he returned on the following day and resumed command.

Warloy, which cleared to C.C.S. at Doullens. In the absence of a motor ambulance convoy the 4th Field Ambulance was used to form a "motor relay post" at Toutencourt at which casualties were transferred both to motor ambulances and to lorries.

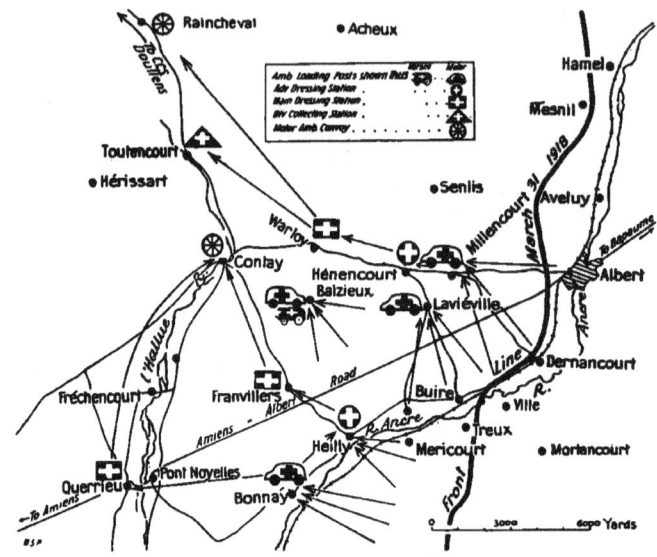

Evacuation Scheme of Australian Divisions with VII Corps in the last days of March.

3rd Division. Arriving at Franvillers with D.H.Q. on the night of the 26th, the A.D.M.S. 3rd Division, Colonel Maguire,[37] found less to work on than had Colonel Barber. On this front no scheme of Divisional clearance existed; the 9th and 10th Brigades were still *en route;* the D.D.M.S. VII Corps (Colonel Maguire records) "could give no further information" and "desired that A.D's.M.S. carry on independently." Colonel Maguire's operation order (March 27th) arranged for a temporary dressing station at Bonnay—it was

[37] The medical diaries of this division are models of clarity and system, reflecting the character of the divisional administration. General Monash had taken with him, in his advanced party to VII Corps H.Q., four staff officers including the D.A.D.M.S., Major W. Vickers.

formed by the 11th Field Ambulance and carried on till the 28th. Then, the 10th Brigade having completely moved up, its field ambulance took over the "forward" clearance, with A.D.S. at Heilly. Meanwhile on March 27th the 11th Field Ambulance formed an M.D.S. at Querrieu in time to meet the "steady stream of wounded" that began to arrive at 7 p.m. The ambulance diary states that officers were at first instructed that "cases are to be evacuated as rapidly as possible without re-dressing, unless urgently indicated"; later (on March 30th), on receipt of a report by the A.D.M.S. 4th Division that "the C.C.S's at Doullens were practically sending all cases through without re-dressing," orders were given "to clear up and dress all wounds as far as this is consistent with the rapid evacuation of casualties."

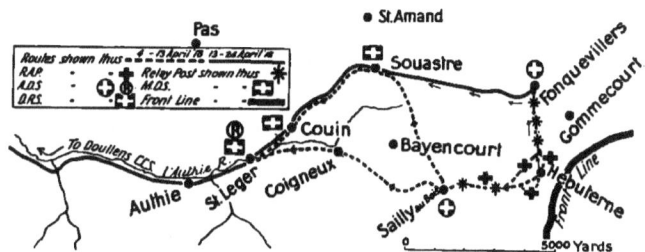

It is not possible to follow the kaleidoscope of events over this vast battle-front. The fighting by the 4th Brigade at Hébuterne may be passed over since no Australian medical unit went with the Brigade.[38] The scheme of clearance is shown in the sketch map. South of the Somme gaps in the line of the exhausted infantry of Fifth Army were being precariously caulked by the Cavalry Corps and "Carey's Force." But between March 28th and 30th events occurred in the military sphere which influenced the course of history.

**The check to "Michael":
March 28th-30th**

Operations: the Vimy Bastion. To effect his strategic aims—*i.e.* to roll up the British Force—on March 28th Ludendorff struck at the

---
[38] It was cleared by the field ambulances of the 62nd Division. On April 4 the bearer division of the 4th Field Ambulance rejoined the Brigade and cleared the R.A.P's working with a British field ambulance. The Brigade rejoined the Division on April 25.

bastion of the Vimy Ridge, minor thrusts being made at the same time farther south. The repulse at Vimy—fatal to the success of "Michael" —is not part of the history of the A.I.F. But on the Ancre and the Somme the pressure of the Australian troops was beginning to make itself felt.

Operations on the Ancre: 4th Division. On March 28th the 4th Division with the 35th British on the right defeated a strong attack at a cost to the 4th of 338 casualties. The wounded (259) were cleared without a hitch to C.C.S. at Doullens by the Divisional transport.

Between Somme and Ancre: 3rd Division. On the same day the 3rd Division sustained a loss of 65 killed and 266 wounded in a rash advance in daylight, somewhat reminiscent of "Krithia." On the 30th it repulsed with much greater "slaughter" a like assault by the enemy. On that part of the front the German advance was finally stopped. The work of the medical service calls for a note.

Evacuation: 3rd Division. Starting as they did on the 27th without any prior scheme in existence the medical units of this Division were hard put to deal with the heavy casualties. In particular the 11th Field Ambulance at the M.D.S. in Querrieu, had to bring out every trick in its bag. From four dressing tables and a "small theatre fitted up for urgent operations," cases passed out rapidly for evacuation. But at this stage they were held up owing to lack of transport.

During the night of March 28th-29th 400 cases, a large proportion serious, were accommodated in barns. The 3rd M.A.C. could only supply 6 cars. The stock of 600 blankets was soon depleted through the fact that M.D.S. and A.D.S. were close together, but M.D.S. and C.C.S. very far apart.

The first trouble (we are told) was resolved by "obtaining" the service of 8 motor lorries "which had come into the town in error" and which cleared 200 cases to Doullens; the second, by "salvaging" 2,000 blankets from the abandoned C.C.S. at Corbie. But by the morning of the 29th ample transport was available from the 3rd M.A.C., and by the 30th all evacuation was working smoothly and "owing to the efficient motor-transport service little surgical treatment was now required"; indeed the cars of the 11th Field Ambulance were being used to evacuate invalid civilians to the French Mission in Amiens.

The service of supply, both Army Service Corps and "Red Cross," functioned with extraordinary efficiency. From the Australian Red Cross depot at Frévent during April,

68. THE SOMME VALLEY NEAR CORBIE

From a painting by Sir Arthur Streeton. The view is from the high land between the Somme and the Ancre, looking south-westward over Corbie towards the Villers-Bretonneux plateau. A bombardment is falling near Marcelcave. Villers-Bretonneux is seen above Corbie Abbey on the right.

Aust. War Memorial Official Photo. No. J6165.

To face p. 628.

69. THE SOUTHERNMOST HUTS OF THE OLD "EDGEHILL" C.C.S. AFTER "MICHAEL"

They lay just within the Australian front line, which is seen on the hill. The line bent westwards along the railway seen in the foreground. This was the site of the Battle of Dernancourt.

*Aust. War Memorial Official Photo. No. E2499.
Taken on 14 June 1918.*

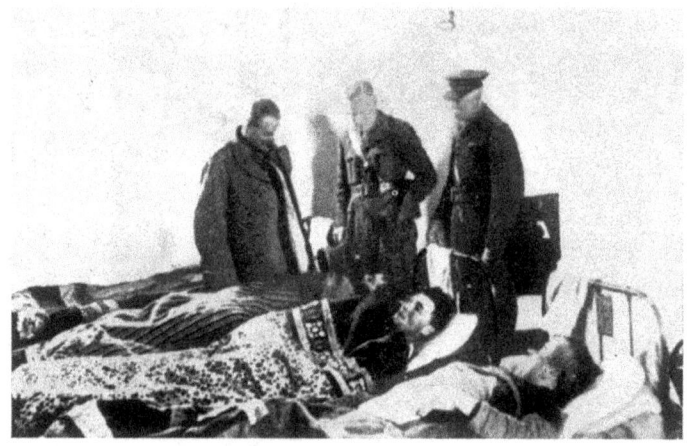

70. GENERAL BIRDWOOD VISITING A REST STATION

In attendance are the D.D.M.S. (Colonel Manifold) and Colonel R. B. Huxtable.

Aust. War Memorial Official Photo. No. E382.   *To face p. 629.*

the 10th and 11th Field Ambulances received for distribution:—

Pyjamas, 377 pairs; towels, 144; underpants, 50 pairs; carbolic soap, 120 lb.; cocoa and milk, 6 cases; coffee and milk, 6 cases; fancy biscuits, 9 cases; cigarettes, 25,000; socks, 723 pairs; hospital bags, 300; shirts, 50.

The ration issued by the A.S.C., comprising fresh meat, bacon, cheese, milk, vegetables, preserved meat, bread, jam, and sugar, was fully up to standard.

The 9th Brigade (3rd Division) had been guarding the VII Corps flank on the Somme at Corbie. On the 29th at 5.30 p.m. an urgent order took it post-haste across the Somme to Cachy to act as reserve to the XIX Corps of Fifth Army—to be, as things turned out, the advanced guard to an Australian invasion of the plateau south of the Somme that was to make history that will occupy most of the remaining chapters of this narrative. The Brigade was replaced in VII Corps by the 15th (5th Division) which had arrived on the same day from Flanders.

South of the Somme

On crossing the Somme the 9th Field Ambulance came under the A.D.M.S. 61st Division, XIX Corps (the only active corps left in Fifth Army). Except for a sharp counter-attack at Lancer Wood on the 30th, the Brigade was not seriously engaged in the fighting on this front till April 4th, when it played an important part in repulsing the southern thrust of the final effort in "Michael."

Last Kick in "Michael": the Thrust for Amiens. As was said above, the fate of "Michael" was sealed when on March 28th the attack of Prince Rupprecht broke against the bastion of the Vimy Ridge, and on March 30th the advance down the Somme was checked when almost in sight of Amiens. But against the advice of the field commanders Ludendorff decided on a further assault on the British-French junction, to be delivered as two converging but independent thrusts north and south of the Somme on alternate days. These produced two important actions— the "First" fight for Villers-Bretonneux (April 4th), and the Battle of Dernancourt (April 5th). In both these battles the Australian formations played a dominant part.[39] For convenience and continuity the operations on the Ancre are followed first.

The Battle of Dernancourt, April 5th. The attack made by the four divisions of the Second German Army mainly on the 12th and 13th Brigades of the 4th Division A.I.F. facing Dernancourt was unique in its action, fought to a finish in one day, and in a very exact sense within its sphere decisive in its result. Involving as it did an initial retirement

[39] At Villers-Bretonneux they shared that rôle with the British cavalry.

against enormous odds up the face of an open hillside, and a subsequent counter-attack down the crest of this slope, it resulted in heavy Australian casualties numbering 358 killed and 837 wounded, with 180 prisoners of war, many of whom also were wounded.[40] These losses must be held worth the while, for thereafter on this sector there was peace profound till the Australian troops began to "raid."

Clearance of Casualties. The collecting and clearing of the wounded from this strenuous battle were full of human interest and endeavour. Excellent accounts in the war diaries invite narrative—which cannot be indulged. Some ingenious technical adaptations however must be noted.

The first wounded from the front reached the *Waggon Loading Posts* within three or four hours, and throughout the day these posts cleared without incident. The *"A.D.S."* at Hénencourt Château had been badly shelled. To meet this (the 12th Field Ambulance diary records)

"the purpose of the station was changed. Casualties were treated in a cellar and the château converted into a motor-loading post and motor relay and reserve for bearers. The cars from Millencourt cleared direct to M.D.S. at Warloy provided the case did not need urgent attention, and were replaced from the reserve [held] at the château."

Some delay was caused when, to relieve congestion at the M.D.S., the cars from the A.D.S. were sent on direct to the "transport relay" beforementioned[41] at Toutencourt. At the M.D.S. (Warloy—13th Field Ambulance), before the first cases arrived at 10 a.m. from the front line, no less than 100 casualties had come in through the shelling of the back area, and the dressing station itself had been hit twice. Only three M.A.C. cars were available; lorries from the M.A.C. had been "withdrawn by Army (says Colonel Barber) without notice."

"By 11.30 a.m. the buildings and yard were full, with over 200 cases, and by permission of the Curé the Church near-by was used as a shelter. [Our] Ambulance cars were working forward, and an attempt to relieve congestion by sending the cars from A.D.S. straight through to Toutencourt caused congestion at the A.D.S.; 60 walking cases volunteered to walk to Toutencourt [4 miles] and were marched off."

Through the direct intervention of the Corps Commander

---

[40] An extremely interesting note in the *Australian Official History* (*Vol. V, pp. 395-6*) on the treatment of these men gives further instance of that curious phenomenon referred to elsewhere—the humane camaraderie of the medical service. It cannot too strongly be emphasised that Australian records give no support to any attitude of superiority on our part in this matter.

[41] *See p. 626.*

(Lieut.-General Congreve) Colonel Barber obtained cars and lorries. By 11 p.m. the M.D.S. was "clear and cases coming in slowly."

Between 8 a.m. and 11 p.m. of April 5th nearly 1,000 cases passed through the station. "Owing to the uncertainty of C.C.S. organisation," Colonel Barber notes, all cases were "thoroughly dressed" before being sent on. The tent subdivision personnel of this field ambulance, both officers and other ranks, had been trained to work in "teams," and the attempt was made to meet all requirements for the effective treatment of urgent cases.

The New Warfare. Indeed, reading between the lines of the war diaries of these two units, we can discern the germ of various medical developments at the front during this last phase of the war. These can be summarised as scientific adjustments of transport and treatment within Divisions and Corps to meet the problems arising from the prolongation of the time-distance factor—A.D.S. to C.C.S.[42]

The geophysical background for the chief events in the last scenes of the war in which the Australian force took a hand is found in the valley of the River Somme which also became the focal centre of Allied strategy.[43]

The Villers-Bretonneux front—and Somme Valley

From 30th March until the end of April the "Michael" offensive (save for the thrust at Dernancourt) resolved itself in a series of attacks on the British at Villers-Bretonneux and on the similar ground held by the French about Moreuil which together were the key to Amiens.

It is impossible to enter upon any general account of the attacks and counter-attacks and administrative adjustments that make up the confused history of the last stages of "Michael." Briefly, to pick up from March 27th when the French retreat and the retirement of the British VII Corps exposed both flanks of Fifth Army to attack, the Cavalry Corps was transferred from Third and crossed the Somme to Fifth Army. Partly by fighting, partly through exhaustion, the

[42] An illuminating comparison presents itself in the evacuation from Pozières and work of 1st Field Ambulance M.D.S. at Warloy in 1916—*Chapter iv, p. 69.*

[43] The terrain of this vast battlefield looking out from the heights north of the Somme towards Villers-Bretonneux is preserved in one of the finest pictures in the Australian War Memorial, "The Valley of the Somme," by Sir Arthur Streeton. *See plate at p. 628.*

German advance slowed down, and was brought to a decisive halt by the dramatic attacks and counter-attacks at Lancer Wood and Moreuil on March 30th. But it had left the Germans confronting, at a distance of less than two miles, the vital position of Villers-Bretonneux, overlooking Amiens.

First Fight for Villers-Bretonneux. On April 4th the Germans made a determined thrust on a wide front south of the Somme, which, though it failed in its main object, drove back the British Fourth Army on its whole front—at some points for nearly two miles—and the French for two miles beyond the River Avre. On the northern flank Hamel was occupied and Villers-Bretonneux was nearly reached, but it was saved by a brilliant counter-attack by the 9th Brigade and British cavalry. In the initial retirements and the subsequent advances the Brigade sustained 543 casualties, 99 killed, 444 wounded.

The 9th Field Ambulance. The medical unit with the Brigade was under direction of the A.D.M.S. 31st (British) Division, to whom it sent location reports for clearance to C.C.S. As generally, however, in this phase of the fighting, it worked as a part of the Brigade, and with a degree of tactical initiative that made up a wholly novel experience and imposed a great responsibility. In a battle in which retreat and advance followed in quick succession, the unit applied with distinguished success the principles of close medical and military co-operation. Its work and that of the R.M.O's[44] is given special notice in the *Australian Official History* and does not call for particular comment here.

During the first week in April the remaining divisions of the Australian Corps arrived from the north and came under command of the VII Corps of the Third Army and XIX (and subsequently III) Corps of the Fourth. It was significant of the military crisis that, south of the Somme, brigade after brigade was thrown in on arrival and strung out separately. With these detached brigades went their respective field ambulances.

The Australian Corps takes over the front

The 2nd and 5th Divisions Enter the Line. The 15th Brigade (5th Division), which had replaced the 9th in guarding the bridges across the Somme, south of Corbie, sustained casualties in front of Hamel in the German attack on April 4th and cleared them by its 15th Field Ambulance. On the evening of April 5th the 5th Brigade (2nd Division) entered the line alongside the 9th. The 2nd Division's other brigades (6th and 7th) went north of the Somme, and after the Battle of Der-

---

[44] Here, as elsewhere in this work, the term "R.M.O." includes the whole medical establishment of the battalion, unless the context makes clear that only the medical officer is intended.

nancourt relieved the 12th and 13th (4th Division), which had held that front since March 27th. On April 6th-7th the 8th and 14th Brigades of the 5th Division came south of the Somme, the 8th being for a few days sent south to Boves. Arriving on April 5th the A.D.M.S. of this Division established headquarters at Blangy.

Thus at the end of the first week in April the 2nd, 3rd, 4th and 5th Australian Divisions were strung out in a thin line before Amiens. From each division one brigade had been detached for some special emergency and was being used independently. On April 6th Australian formations held the line from Hangard Wood to Albert—the whole front of Fourth Army—as well as a small part of Third's. The 1st Division was then just leaving Flanders for the south. Arriving at Amiens on the 8th it was within two days turned right about to meet the crisis that had developed on the Lys.

Medical Arrangements: Fourth Army. In a situation so unstable as that which existed south of the Somme medical arrangements were still those of a mobile front. So late indeed as April 8th the D.M.S. Fourth Army named Abbeville as the next retiring point to which "the front line of C.C.S's would be moved and others later." The D.D.M.S. III Corps (Fourth Army), which on April 5th replaced the XIX at Villers-Bretonneux, noted on taking over that, "under the present conditions Advanced Dressing Stations change their positions so rapidly that it is impossible to give accurate locations from day to day." Casualties were being cleared under Brigade, Divisional and Corps arrangements, which often overlapped.

The Australian Corps: the New Deputy-Director. During these stirring events the Headquarters of the Australian Corps had remained at Flêtre in Second Army, denuded of its Divisions one by one. On April 3rd it came south and on the 6th relieved the VII Corps in Third Army, which had been holding its line with the 3rd and 4th Australian Divisions. Next day it became the left Corps of the Fourth Army and later took over from III Corps the sector of the 5th Australian Division south of the Somme.

The D.D.M.S., Colonel Manifold, came south with the Corps, but on April 8th handed over[46] to Colonel G. W. Barber,

---
[46] Col. Manifold returned to the Indian Medical Service and in June was made D.D.M.S. Southern Army, India. In 1922 he was knighted.

A.A.M.C.[46] The period of Colonel Manifold's direction in I Anzac, and for a short time, in the Australian Corps had seen immense changes and advance in military methods and technique. The medical units and administrative departments of the Corps and Divisions had reached a high grade of efficiency and war-wisdom; and in this growth Colonel Manifold had played a sympathetic and discerning part, and had filled his difficult position with great ability and unremitting energy. The new D.D.M.S. had been selected by the D.M.S. A.I.F. (Surgeon-General Howse) for his personal fitness not less than in virtue of his seniority in the service. As A.D.M.S. 4th Division Colonel Barber had shown a special aptitude for organisation, and in temperament and administrative methods was peculiarly fitted to take control of medical affairs in the Australian Corps at this juncture in its history.

"*Medical Instruction No. 10.*" As was his wont Colonel Barber lost no time in putting the medical situation on an exact basis. Two days after his appointment he issued "Medical Instructions" which outlined "the policy to be pursued during the present operations." In general these were intended to meet "the necessity of maintaining the mobility of medical units, and to meet medical problems consequent on the detachment of brigade groups," and to prevent wastage from Army area. "Divisional Rest Stations" were to be replaced by "Divisional Collecting Stations" (for patients likely to be fit for duty within 12 hours) and by a "Corps Rest Station" at the Corps Reinforcement Camp (to retain men who required a longer rest and treatment). The medical arrangements normal in the Australian divisions—one field ambulance clearing the front of each division and another running the M.D.S. behind it—were to be resumed. "First aid only" was to be given at the A.D.S., but "thorough dressing at the M.D.S., owing to the distance of C.C.S's." At the M.D.S. an officer was to be detailed "to sort out the patients" for C.C.S., D.C.S., or C.R.S. (if any), and to "hand over stragglers . . . to the military police." Use of the "misleading term 'Collecting Post' " for divisional collecting station, bearer relay post, or motor or horse waggon

---

[46] Col. Barber was replaced as A.D.M.S. 4th Division by Lieut.-Col. A. H. Moseley.

post, was prohibited.[47] A.D's.M.S. were made responsible for maintaining adequate reserves of equipment.

The front on the Somme: April 7th-May 3rd

Though no major operations took place on this front between April 7th and 24th the struggle for position was incessant, and at no time was the Fourth Army Commander (General Rawlinson) free from grave anxiety regarding the safety of the Amiens junction. The tremendous blows struck by Ludendorff in the north on April 9th and 10th had drawn thither a large part first of the British, then of the French, reserves. On March 25th, General Pershing agreed to permit the American divisions training in France to be used in emergency with the British or French[48]—a decision which afterwards furnished the Australian Medical Service with most interesting experience of the difficult problem of co-ordinating the differing administrative systems of separate national forces.

Struggle for Position: Hangard Wood. Between April 7th and 19th two detached Australian brigades were drawn into the fighting round Hangard Wood—where the Germans hoped to outflank Villers-Bretonneux. During this time the line on the Somme was gradually stabilised and organised as a defensive front. The Fourth Army now held its front with two corps, the III in front of Cachy and Villers-Bretonneux, and the Australian, astride of Somme and Ancre. A system of evacuation had been built up based on casualty clearing stations established on a line Vignacourt, Pont Remy, Picquigny, Longpré, and Namps, 20-30 miles behind the front. Main dressing stations were fixed, but advanced stations changed their site to accord with divisional arrangements. On April 17th No. 3 M.A.C. was placed under the immediate direction of the Australian Corps.

---

[47] In the maps and sketches which illustrate the further operations of the Australian Corps—*i.e.* from sketch map on *p. 626* onwards—the conventional sign for the "divisional collecting station" applies to the stations thus defined by Colonel Barber. (In spite of his order, the term "collecting post" or "divisional collecting post" retained an unofficial vogue and was applied to any rendezvous for walking wounded in advance of the "A.D.S.") In the *British Official Medical History* this sign is defined to signify a "walking wounded dressing station," a "divisional collecting post," or simply a "collecting post"—apparently indiscriminately. In this volume the conventional signs for the walking wounded stations have been brought in line with those for stretcher cases, and with the usage in the Australian Corps in 1918.

[48] Pershing: *My Experiences in the World War, pp. 319, 323.*

So uncertain was the military situation that, under instruction from the General Staff, the D.D.M.S., Australian Corps, made exact plans for clearing casualties northwards across the Somme in the event of the enemy's pushing to Amiens. His prepara-

"*Flying Fox*" *Transporter.*
(*Reproduced from a drawing in the war diary of the 9th Aust. Field Ambulance.*)

tions included a fleet of rowing-boats held in a backwater of the Somme, and a "flying fox" to carry stretcher cases across the river.[40] By the end of April the German artillery was again in great strength, and shell-fire from H.E., shrapnel, and gas shell on the exposed routes of clearance along the Somme valley led to a series of experiments by medical units in the use of underground or sunken posts and stations that will call for particular note in later pages.

The Battle of Villers-Bretonneux: April 25th. By the middle of April it was becoming clear to the German High Command that the thrust in the north must be helped by diversions elsewhere. Partly as such, but in the hope also of forcing some strategic result from so great a tactical gain, preparations were made for a revival on a lesser scale of the offensive against the British-French front, the objective being the heights and town of Villers-Bretonneux, commanding Amiens.

---

[40] The medical scheme envisaged two zones of retreat. In the first the advanced dressing stations would fall back to the sites of the "main," and these to the existing "divisional collecting stations," the siting of which was to be adjusted with this contingency in view. The second "zone" would place the M.D.S's almost in line with the present C.C.S. positions.

The Gas Offensive, April 17th-18th. Expected by the British Command since the middle of the month, offensive action began in a wholly unexpected form. On April 17th and 18th the town and adjoining wood were shelled with "mustard" gas on a scale not hitherto approached, and not exceeded at any time in the history of the Australian Corps. Little has been said in these pages of the gas weapon, in view of the fact that every aspect of this new form of warfare will be dealt with in a special chapter.[50] But it must be noted here that German technique and policy in this branch of warfare had by now reached a high degree of precision. It is true that a no less exact technique and training had been evolved in defence by both sides; nevertheless in the B.E.F. the number of casualties from this weapon had now reached such large proportions, and the complexity of the medical problems involved had been so greatly increased by the introduction of "dichlorethyl-sulphide" ("mustard" or "yperite") and the arsenes, that an elaborate system for dealing with gassed casualties had been organised. This included "gas centres" for the diagnosis of "N.Y.D. Gas," and special provision for immediate treatment and for the "decontamination" of casualties from "mustard."

But such a bombardment as was sustained at Villers-Bretonneux caught the Australian formations to some extent unawares, and, as the Official Historian puts it, "officers and men received a staggering object lesson in the need for precautions." Between April 17th and 24th some 1,700 gas casualties passed through the Australian field ambulances, involving immense labour and great dislocation of normal clearance. Gas shells were also largely used by the Germans in the subsequent operations.

The Attack, April 24th-25th. The actual assault came on the morning of April 24th—immediately preceding the stroke at Mont Kemmel in the north. Using tanks, for the first time with any effect, by 8 a.m. the Germans had captured Villers-Bretonneux—an advance of 2,000 yards, which put them in full view of Amiens. The task of recapture was allotted mainly to two reserve brigades (13th and 15th) of the two neighbouring Australian Divisions 4th and 5th),[51] acting under the III (British) Corps. It was achieved by the very unusual tactical expedient of envelopment under cover of darkness, the move-

[50] *In Vol. III.*
[51] After its relief by the 2nd Division at Dernancourt, the 4th Division had been in support. The 13th Brigade acted as Army Reserve.

ment being carried out by the two brigades independently. After a sweep which practically enclosed the town, and the wood of Aquenne—and most of their contents—the two brigades by dawn were strongly established beyond these places, and though heavy fighting continued until May 3rd in unsuccessful attempts by French and British to recapture Monument Wood and Hangard Wood, the action closed the German offensive on this front. This was indeed the last important attack on the British Army on the Western Front. The Australian casualties sustained were 2,473.

Medical Events of the Battle. The medical arrangements for the battle were under the D.D.M.S. III Corps and present no very special features. The 13th and 15th Field Ambulances came under the direction of the A.D.M.S., 8th Division, who saw to the work of clearance from the main dressing stations. The formation of advanced dressing stations and the collecting and clearance of casualties from each brigade fell on the two field ambulance commanders (Lieut.-Colonels H. K. Fry and K. Smith). The bearer divisions could do little at night; but with daylight (and victory) the clearing of advanced ambulance posts by the wheeled transport presented no special problem. The great difficulty lay in the rescue and first aid in the exposed forward area, of which task the onus fell on the R.M.O's; and in few actions was it more difficult. A graphic account of his experiences by the R.M.O. 52nd Battalion (Captain R. L. Forsyth) is quoted at length in the *Australian Official History*,[52] to which the reader is referred.

One medical officer (Captain P. B. Sewell), R.M.O. of the 50th Battalion, was killed, and another (Captain Forsyth) wounded. The death of Captain Sewell created one of those occasions—frequent enough to remain most often "unhonoured and unsung"—when the "rank and file" was called on to prove the mettle of its training and traditions. The following from the recommendation for an immediate reward (the D.C.M.) would apply *mutatis mutandis* to many such occasions.

"On April 24th, 1918, north-east of Cachy near Villers-Bretonneux, Lance-Corporal A. G. Forrester, M.M., was in charge of three squads of stretcher-bearers with the 50th Battalion when the battalion moved forward to attack the enemy's position. The advance was made under extremely heavy shell and machine-gun fire, and, before a regimental aid-post could be established, the R.M.O. (Capt. P. B. Sewell) was reported 'missing.' At this critical juncture Lance-Corporal Forrester, with the greatest coolness and resource, took complete charge of the

[52] *Vol. V, pp. 581-2, 585-6.*

situation in the absence of the R.M.O. He quickly organised the A.A.M.C. Details, established a Casualty Collecting Post, directed the work of the Battalion Regimental Stretcher-Bearers, and succeeded in getting in touch with the Battalion Headquarters and the Field Ambulance Posts in rear. He personally conducted these operations exposed to continuous heavy fire in an area which was devoid of shelter, showing complete disregard of danger. It was entirely due to his resource and masterly control of a most difficult situation that a serious breakdown in the evacuation of the wounded in the Battalion was successfully averted."

The Fourth Army Front in May, 1918. On April 25th the Australian Corps took control of all formations and of the whole Fourth Army front, from Monument Wood to Albert. But immediately afterwards the III Corps, withdrawn from Villers-Bretonneux, was put in again opposite Albert, the Australian Corps (with all its normal divisions except the 1st) side-slipping to become the southern corps of the army in order that it should have charge of this dangerous flank. The medical service entered upon the interesting task of adapting to the new conditions of warfare the technique of evacuation built up during the years of attrition and rudely jolted by the great retreat.

Meanwhile the 1st Division had been fighting heavily in Flanders, and this narrative must now turn to certain features of special medical interest in the operations that had caused its hurried return thither, the German offensive on the Lys.

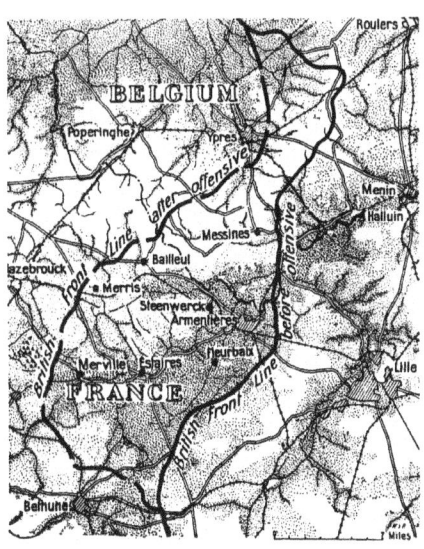

The Battle of the Lys, April 1918.

The Genesis of "George." An attack across the River Lys had been part of the original plan for the German offensive, and it was revived when the attack on Amiens failed. It was not expected at this stage either by the British general staff or by General Foch; and the front had been "milked" for the Somme and, in substitution, manned with battered remnants of the Third and Fifth Army formations, which had been previously engaged in filling their ranks from the reinforcements—chiefly lads of 19 or younger—now pouring into France. An offensive on this front had, however, been predicted by the Second Army staff as well as by that of the First (whose front was partly held by the Portuguese), and steps were taken to withstand or minimise the result of a possible break-through. The blow fell, on a wide front south of Armentières on April 9th, and north of it on the 10th, and rapidly developed. In this history we are concerned only with the "medical arrangements" to meet the expected German offensive and the steps taken when it occurred. Both, as it happens, are peculiarly pertinent.

Thrust for the Channel ports

In the second week of March, consequent on the order of the Director-General already referred to,[53] the D.M.S. "Fourth" Army[54] put in train a scheme of dispositions and adjustments of the casualty clearing stations. With the launching of "Michael" on March 21st and the subsequent thrust of "George" on April 9th these adjustments, still in process, merged with a series of urgent—not to say precipitate—moves to the rear. Nos. 1, 2 and 3 A.C.C.S.'s were intimately involved in all of these; and a report of their experiences therefore properly precedes such account as is necessary of the work of the field ambulances of the 1st Australian Division in helping to stop this offensive.

Medical preparations in Second Army

Before "Michael." We left the three Australian units[55] established in elaborately organised hutted and tented sites, No. 1 between Bailleul and Oultersteene (functioning as a "Corps Rest Station"); No. 2 at Trois Arbres near Steenwerck some 5 miles only from the front line; No. 3 at Nine Elms near Poperinghe. Nos. 1 and 3 were not involved in this first echelon of moves, and the events with which we are now concerned begin with the initial move of No. 2. No. 1, however, received instructions on March 14th to

The A.C.C.S's— first echelon of moves

---

[53] See pp. 608-9.
[54] This was almost immediately before this Army in Flanders resumed its old title of the "Second."
[55] See pp. 382-7.

"cease to function as a Corps Rest Station at midnight" preparatory to resuming as a C.C.S.

First Echelon of Moves: No. 2 C.C.S. At 10.40 p.m. on March 10th the O.C. (Lieut.-Colonel V. O. Stacy) received a message from D.M.S. "Fourth" Army.

"ordering," says the war diary, "the immediate closing down of this C.C.S. Sisters to be evacuated and all patients, fit to be moved, to be disposed of as soon as possible."

On March 12th instructions were received for a move to a site at Noote Boon near Oultersteene—within a "coo-ee" of No. 1—the transfer to be a "test of mobility."

On March 14th the Nursing Sisters were sent to a British Stationary Hospital at St. Omer.

"On the 15th instant 10 motor lorries began transporting material. By nightfall 50 loads had been dumped. By 11 a.m. on the 16th, 26 hours after receipt of orders, we were equipped and ready to receive 200 patients. On the 18th Colonel Manifold, D.D.M.S. Australian Corps, and on the 20th Major-General O'Keeffe, D.M.S. Second Army, visited the station."

The "station" formed by No. 2 at Oultersteene in this move was in the nature of an advanced operating centre. This was still in progress of transformation to a full-fledged casualty clearing station, and the old site was still being demolished, when "Michael" came—and, though the offensive was not on this front, there soon arrived orders for a second echelon of moves to "Ana Jana Siding" at Hondeghem near Hazebrouck.

Second Echelon of Moves (after March 21st). In this move No. 1 also was involved; it was serious business and was accomplished by both units with great celerity.[56]

"At 9.45 p.m. on the 25th instant," reported the O.C. of No. 2 to General Howse, "I received a wire to meet the D.M.S. at his office at 10 a.m. next day re another move still further back, and on the 26th I inspected with him the new site at Ana Jana Siding near Hazebrouck. O's.C. of No. 1 Aust. C.C.S. [Lieut.-Colonel A. H. Marks] and No. 17 British C.C.S. were also present and sites were allotted to them. This station is to move first. At 4.30 p.m. on the 26th 4 lorry loads of tents were shifted and the ground measured out for a tent-brigade area.

[56] The moves of all three units may be followed on sketch map at p. 772. It is very important that it should be understood that the moves described for the Australian units were only part of a hurried "general post" involving, within this Army, some 30-40 units—C.C.S's, Stationary and General Hospitals—British, Canadian, Australian and Portuguese.

"From work done yesterday 27th instant it would seem possible that a very workable C.C.S., accommodating from 200 to 250 patients could be formed on any new site in one day, if the necessary [material] arrived fast enough."

By the 28th 50 marquees had been erected, wards equipped, and electric light installed in the operating theatre and dressing room. Routine orders were published in the new camp on the 29th and "a start made on sanitation . . . which should turn out to be most perfect."

On April 5th the Sisters returned from St. Omer.

"By this time," continued Colonel Stacy's report, "the hospital hut for the theatre had been painted throughout but not equipped. Personnel huts commenced, water supplies brought from a stream filtered through sand and chlorinated and pumped into supply tanks in the camp. By April 8th the Oultersteene site was completely cleared and working parties brought back. Parties still working at the original site at Trois Arbres sending back timbers and huts to Ana Jana."

No. 1 A.C.C.S. was warned on March 26th "to be prepared to move in about 10 days"; but March 28th found this unit, also, moving under urgent orders to Hondeghem.

On April 9th came "George" and a stream of casualties: but it found the two units well prepared.

"On April 8th," says Colonel Stacy, "I sent for the party at Trois Arbres to rejoin unit. Some arrived the same night and the rest reported next morning after an exciting time. Tremendous bombardment in the Steenwerck-Bailleul area. No essential equipment left, only some out-buildings. On the evening of the 9th wounded began to arrive in large numbers—in lorries, ambulance cars, and walking—and continued practically all night. No. 1 A.C.C.S. and No. 17 British adjoining us also very busy. The whole staff worked incessantly from the evening of the 9th to noon on the 12th. Weather all the time cold and wet; 1,428 cases passed through—1,183 wounded, of whom 174 required a general anaesthetic—(a proportion, excluding the 212 gassed, of 1 to 5). Practically all had to be given A.T.S. since most were direct admissions and the rest [had] passed through Field Ambulances that had exhausted their supplies."

Third Echelon of Moves (during "George," April 12th). The next move was precipitate.

No. 2 A.C.C.S. "About noon on 12th April," the report continues, "while still very busy a telephone message was received that all patients were to be evacuated at once and the station packed up ready to move off by nightfall. By 5 p.m. all tents were down, patients evacuated, and sisters sent off in a bus to No. 10 Stationary St. Omer. A new site was given at Blendecques near Arques. Two lorry loads of tents and two trailers went straight off with a party. All officers except one

Apr., 1918]   GERMAN THRUST FOR VICTORY   643

at the new location by 8 p.m. The night was very clear, and a large scale air raid was in progress over Arques and St. Omer. Lorries plied all night, the journey taking 2½ to 3 hours. The roads congested with troops and refugees, the latter in hundreds. On April 13th the officer-in-charge at Ana Jana[57] got orders to leave the place at once. Marching out about noon the party reached Blendecques about 7 p.m. leaving a small guard behind. The men marched 15 miles with their packs up, and arrived in good order."

No. 1 moved at the same time. The site at Ana Jana did not come under shell-fire, and it was possible to salvage the equipment of both units and most of the huts, and also the trolley-tramway which formed a special feature of the equipment of No. 2.

We find from the same report that by April 17th No. 2 was again in working order with water and electric light laid on, tents pitched and equipped for 400 cases. By April 22nd a broad cinder road ran the length of the camp for evacuation cars. At the request of the D.M.S. Second Army a plan was drawn up showing the arrangement of traffic for Nos. 1 and 2 Australian stations which were opposite each other. The arrangement is said to have "worked remarkably well."

The records of No. 3 A.C.C.S., which was at Nine Elms, disclose a less strenuous time, but are not less informative of

No. 3 A.C.C.S.   the factors which make up that vital problem in evacuation—the *proper nature and place of the casualty clearing station.*

Writing on April 1st the C.O., Lieut.-Colonel R. D. Campbell says:—

"Under a new scheme, as a result of losses in the Somme, C.C.S's are being divided in Front Area and Back Area C.C.S.—the Back Area C.C.S. 10-15 miles behind the Front Area C.C.S. This C.C.S. remains a Front Area Unit, which is satisfactory on account of the better class of surgical work [i.e. dealing with a more serious type of case]. Preparations have been made—on paper—for an orderly evacuation of the Front Area C.C.S., if necessary, but its success, being wholly dependent on adequate transport, is problematical."

At midday on April 14th, "as a result of the enemy push-through at Estaires," orders were received[58] to shift to a new site at Esquelbecq, between Cassel and Bergues, and all patients (284 in number) were evacuated promptly by ambulance

---

[57] At this time the German advance had reached Oultersteene and the edge of Vieux Berquin and it was feared that Hazebrouck might be reached within 24 hours. That night the 1st Australian Division took up its position along the front defending Hazebrouck.

[58] With a view, it would seem, to the forthcoming evacuation of the Ypres Salient.

trains. The Nursing Sisters had been sent back to St. Omer a few days before.

"In view of such a move," says the unit diary, "some time previously 9 lorry loads of material, sufficient to house, feed, and surgically treat 200 patients, had been ear-marked[59] . . . The shifting of equipment was done by 8 lorries over a distance of 15 miles. . . . With this material, at the end of 48 hours it was possible, if necessary, to receive and treat patients on the new site. At the end of 72 hours we were ready for everything except X-ray work, this being held up owing to the lack of a suitable building."

When the order came to receive patients the hospital was well established, a tent operating theatre having been erected and X-ray work being done in a darkened "Armstrong" hut. The diary says:—

"It was found in most cases that it was possible to undertake only the 'A' class or more severe type of case. The Ambulance Train service [from C.C.S. to Base] being good this did not entail [undue] hardships on the patients. These arrived from the front in good time." Colonel Campbell concluded that when delay occurred it was before the patient reached the motor ambulance convoy.

Between April 26th and 30th over 1,200 patients were admitted of whom 800 were wounded; of these 138 were operated on, the rest dressed and evacuated.

During April the three Australian C.C.S's treated casualties as follows:—

	No. 1 A.C.C.S.	No. 2 A.C.C.S.	No. 3 A.C.C.S.
Wounded	1,812	1,959	1,407
"Gassed"	208	309	133
Sick	427	395	999

The 1st Division had begun to arrive on the night of April 12th after being heavily bombed while entraining at Amiens. While the division was coming up the defence rested largely on the 4th Guards Brigade,[60] which, for a time, held the enemy in a struggle which cost the brigade not less than 70 per cent. of the troops engaged. By the 13th, however, the Australian force was digging in on a line in front of Strazeele and Nieppe Forest, and behind this the remains of

---

[59] The detailed list attached in the report covered 4 foolscap pages of close typescript and comprised some 5,000 separate articles and packages, including 31 marquees and 39 bell tents.

[60] The rest of the 31st Division and the 29th were also in the struggle.

Map No. 10.

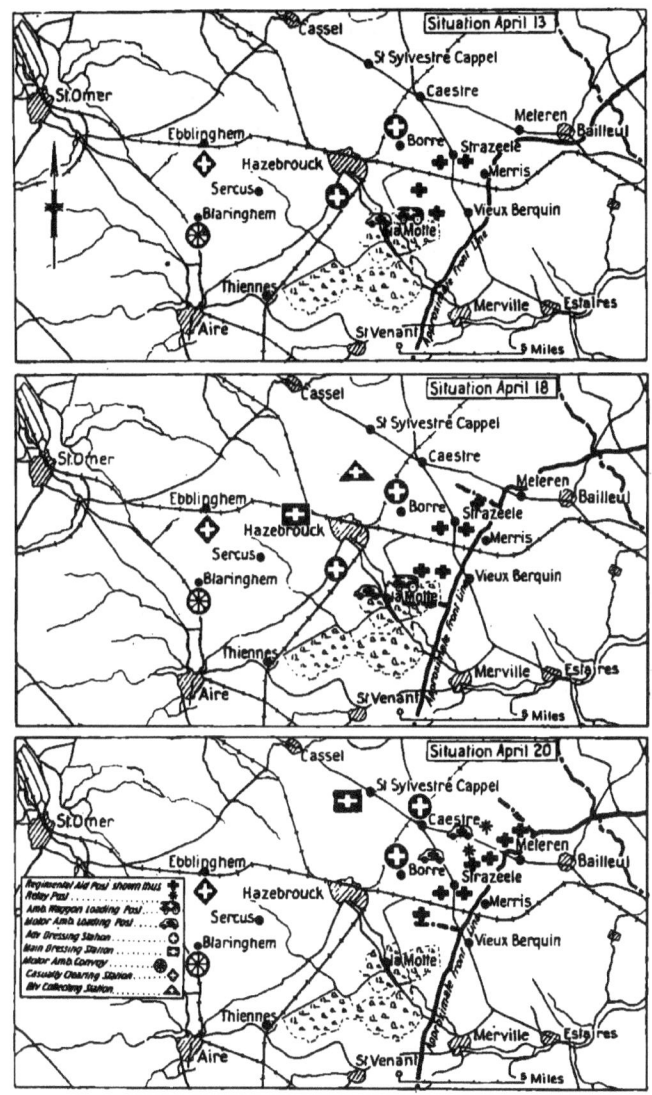

THE 1ST AUSTRALIAN DIVISION AT STRAZEELE—MEDICAL
ARRANGEMENTS, 13TH, 18TH, AND 20TH APRIL, 1918.

the defending troops that night retired to a security which in this sector never for one moment was again in jeopardy.

The 1st Division, with those beside it, repelled two first-class attacks on April 14th and 17th. Its four remaining months in front of Hazebrouck saw perhaps the most enterprising trench-warfare ever waged on the Western Front—a series of occasional minor attacks, all successful except the first, interspersed with spontaneous raids by the troops who almost daily brought in prisoners until on July 11th on their own initiative they "cut out" piecemeal half-a-mile of German front, taking over 150 prisoners.

The Medical Units. Though full of local incident and imposing at times a very heavy strain on the personnel of the 1st, 2nd, and 3rd Field Ambulances, the medical events of these operations do not call for special description since they illustrate no new developments, at least behind the lines. The division came under the direction of the D.D.M.S., XV Corps. On their arrival the field ambulances, working with their respective brigades, formed dressing stations which were cleared independently by No. 2 Motor Ambulance Convoy; but within a few days a normal divisional system was developed, based on casualty clearing stations at Ebblinghem. The "medical arrangements" in the 1st Australian Division for the dramatic warfare of "George I" are shown in the series of sketch maps. During the first two weeks the division sustained 1,610 casualties—441 killed and 1,169 wounded.

The comparative shortness of the German advance—at most 11 miles as against 40 on the Somme—involved a relatively longer evacuation route from M.D.S. to C.C.S., since the C.C.S's were far withdrawn but the M.D.S's were not driven very far. In contrast to conditions on the Somme, however, motor ambulance convoys remained intact and this in great measure determined the medical events of the crisis and the fact that at no time was there any difficulty in clearing the field ambulances. During May and June the 1st Division sustained considerable sick casualties from the first influenza epidemic.

On August 6th, in response to a demand as imperative as that which had sent it north, though of a very different kind, the division entrained for the south.

CHAPTER XXI

THE ALLIED COUNTER-OFFENSIVE: AUSTRALIAN CORPS PREPARES

THE events and action to be recorded in this chapter belong to that phase of the Great War in which the Allied Powers, backed by the first American Divisions and by the knowledge that this army of two millions was now constantly streaming across the Atlantic, wore down the German offensive and prepared for the counter-stroke that was to end at the Rhine. In point of time it covers three months from the Battle of Villers-Bretonneux, April 24th-25th, to the end of July, including the Battle of Hamel—a dress rehearsal for bigger things which came unexpectedly soon in the great Battle of Amiens, August 8th, "Germany's black day."

As they concern the history of the A.I.F. these events fall naturally in three groups :—

1. Certain changes of method introduced by the new Corps Commander, and in connection with these, various adjustments in the administration and direction of the Medical Services required by the new conditions and the new military outlook.

2. Inventions and innovations in the technique of the Medical Service.

3. The further development of these during the operations of this phase, which (as with the 1st Division at Hazebrouck) took the form of an extraordinarily enterprising patrol warfare punctuated by a series of raids and minor actions culminating in the Battle of Hamel. The medical arrangements for these operations present some features which call for note.

By the beginning of May the defence of Amiens had been secured by continuous systems of trenches, adequately manned and covered by large belts of wire and machine-gun emplacements. The French had extended from the south up to within half a mile of Villers-Bretonneux. The Australian Corps front reached from this point 10 miles northward across

The military situation: Fourth Army

both Somme and Ancre. The Corps Commander had at his disposal the 2nd, 3rd, 4th, and 5th Divisions which he disposed three in the line (one to the north and two mainly south of the Somme), the fourth division being in support.[1]

The New G.O.C. and Staff. Shortly after its replacement by that of Fourth Army the British Fifth Army headquarters, then in reserve, was reorganised; General Birdwood was promoted to its command, with the B.G.G.S. Australian Corps, Major-General White, as his Chief of Staff. He was succeeded in command of the Australian Corps on May 31st by Major-General Sir John Monash but retained the position of "G.O.C., A.I.F." The appointment of Australian leaders on the Staff had of late been proceeding rapidly under Birdwood and was continued by Monash, one of Birdwood's last changes being the replacement, already referred to, of Colonel C. C. Manifold, I.M.S., by Colonel G. W. Barber, A.A.M.C.

Staff changes in Australian Corps

"I joined the Corps," Colonel Barber says,[2] "under very favourable auspices. It had been brought to a great pitch of perfection by General Birdwood and the B.G.G.S., General C. B. B. White. I found that the staff worked in a most harmonious manner and that every assistance possible was given by one department to another.[3] . . . The D.D.M.S. had direct access to the Corps Commander and was his adviser and responsible for all A.A.M.C. activities within the Corps. The presence of the D.D.M.S. at the daily conferences of the Chief of General Staff was informative and helpful to all concerned."

Of the divisional administrations and executive units Colonel Barber says :—

"The A.A.M.C. had become highly efficient; A.D's.M.S., D.A.D's.M.S. and O's.C. Field Ambulances, and most of their officers and the R.M.O.'s, were experienced, the unfit and unsuitable having been eliminated. The other ranks were a fine body of men, bearer, tent, and transport divisions

---

[1] The lines of evacuation for these three divisional sectors are shown in sketch map on *p. 656.*

[2] In a memorandum to the D.M.S., A.I.F., already referred to. In this chapter and those that follow the author has borrowed freely from this memorandum, and from a special narrative written by Colonel Barber after the war for the purpose of this history.

[3] Colonel Barber specifies as "most valuable" the assistance given to the Medical Service during the succeeding months by the Engineer Service and "Signals." "Wherever possible adequate cover was provided for personnel and patients." The Assistant-Director of Signals "gave great assistance by providing telephonic communication between Dressing stations, which greatly facilitated evacuations and enabled one readily to furnish the Corps Commander with information as to casualties during an action."

It is to be noted that, while administratively under the "A" branch of the staff, the Medical Department was now in much closer touch with the "Q" branch.

well acquainted with their duties. The N.C.O's were particularly well qualified and efficient in spite of heavy casualties and loss by promotion to the commissioned rank in combatant units"
—which be it noted, apart from appointments as quartermasters, was the only outlet in the A.A.M.C. for promotion to officer.

In Major-General Monash the Australian forces had a commander whose aptitude for the type of warfare that had developed on the Western Front amounted to genius, and one who by nature and intelligence was prone to allot to the medical service its full share in every part of the task of warfare, and to call it in to every consideration. It was typical of him (and what a contrast to the proceedings of G.H.Q., M.E.F., in 1915!) that, when on March 26th he hurried south to the threatened gap between Somme and Ancre, a medical officer was one of the four who personally accompanied him.

Problem of Effectives. The problem of maintenance now became the outstanding factor in the military situation. Between March 21st and May 7th the losses by battle casualty in the Australian Force numbered 15,083.[4] During the same period wastage in the force from non-battle casualties totalled some 14,000.[5] By the end of May, with recruiting in Australia fallen to less than 2,000 a month, the Australian Depots in the United Kingdom were unable to keep pace with the demands of Third Echelon of G.H.Q. for reinforcements.

Reconstruction. It was now found necessary to begin a process of reduction in the numerical fighting strength of formations. The German, French, and British Armies had already in varying degrees taken this course, the reduction occurring mainly in infantry and cavalry. In the British Army, infantry divisions had been reduced from twelve battalions to nine, and in June the authorised strength of the battalions themselves was reduced, though Lewis guns, artillery, tanks, and other weapons had increased. After the Villers-Bretonneux fighting a begin-

---

[4] This figure is from the *Australian Official History, Vol. V, p. 657* and includes "missing," and prisoners of war.

[5] The cost to the B.E.F. of the two offensives (March 21 to April 30) was 302,869 battle casualties including—as is customary in British statistics—"missing" and prisoners. The non-battle casualties during the same period are not available from published British records. French battle casualties totalled 92,000. The German loss is estimated by the British Official Historian at 490,000. The British casualties from wounding were based on "admissions to hospital"—in effect to a field ambulance; the German, on evacuations from railhead. Thirty per cent. is allowed (as an estimate) by the British Official Historian as representing German casualties "not evacuated from the corps area."

ning of reduction was made in the Australian Corps also, three battalions being disbanded and used to reinforce others. This accretion, the comparatively small losses sustained during May and June, and the attention now being paid to the problem of "return to duty," combined to bring the remaining battalions, by the end of June, almost to full strength.[6] But the fear of disbandment of more battalions, to which the whole force was strongly averse, was constantly present.

Within the medical service inventions and innovations, to meet the new conditions and the expected offensive by the Allies, sprang from initiative in two distinct spheres of action—that of the administrative departments, D.D.M.S. and A.D's.M.S.; and that of the executive units, Field Ambulances, Sanitary Sections, and Regimental Medical Establishments. The innovations to be described were the almost automatic response of officers and men to a new situation. Through four years of varied warfare these officers and men had come to know their jobs and the place of the medical service in the scheme of things. Probably the outstanding feature of medical work in this period of the war was the prompt reaction of its administrative and executive sides to initiative in each other.

Preparations in the Medical Service

The new D.D.M.S. initiated his régime by tightening up medical administration within the Corps. In particular the status and function of the several administrative officers were defined more clearly than heretofore. For the medical service the Army Corps became more directly the military "unit."

Colonel Barber's administration

The duties of medical "directors" in the British military system were very diverse. To summarise, under the G.O.C. and the dual control of his "G" and "A.Q." staffs, they directed the activities of the medical personnel—including in the Australian force the dental; administered their interior economy; and exercised command of medical units.[7] The duty of a "Director"

---

[6] Thus, on June 30, the average weekly strength of the 4th Division, in which the 47th and 52nd Battalions had been broken up, was 15,631; the average strength of the ten remaining battalions was 860 (full strength being then about 930), and other arms were well up to strength. The only retrenchment made in the medical service in the B.E.F. was to withdraw the five "A.M.C. attached" for "water duties." Under a general order from G.H.Q., B.E.F. this was carried out in the Australian Corps. See p. 716.

[7] See Vol. I, pp. 5-6 (Statement by Major-Gen. Sir Edward Hutton) and Appendices Nos. 1 and 2.

and his deputies in connection with the "medical arrangements" for an offensive had been crystallised in instructions issued by G.H.Q., B.E.F., before the First Battle of the Somme ("Preparatory measures to be taken by Armies and Corps before undertaking offensive operations on a large scale") which are given in *Appendix No. 3* to this volume.[8]

Rôle of Corps and Divisions. On the main fronts in the Great War the Army Corps, despite its varying size, was the unit of action for the higher command.[9] The duties of the Deputy, the Assistant, and the Deputy-Assistant Directors of Medical Services—as understood in the Australian Corps, have been put on record by Colonel Barber.[10] The following summary is, so far as possible, given in his own words.

The Deputy-Director of Medical Services (D.D.M.S.), a specialist officer advising the Corps Commander, was also "deputy" to the Director of Medical Services of "Army"—in the case of Australian Corps, he was deputy to the D.M.S. of Fourth Army.

"The orders received by him from the D.M.S. Fourth Army, and which related chiefly to measures for the prevention and treatment of disease, were promulgated to his Divisions by Circular Memoranda. An important duty of the D.D.M.S. was administration of the Corps and Army troops and sanitation of 'Corps' areas. He was responsible for evacuation from M.D.S. to C.C.S. and he controlled the work of the Motor Ambulance Convoy attached to the Corps.[11] The D.D.M.S. Australian Corps had a special function, namely that of correspondence with the D.M.S. of the Australian Imperial Force concerning the welfare of the A.A.M.C. and the officers and other ranks in respect to promotion, reinforcements and leave. Orders to A.D's.M.S. relating to operations were issued as 'Medical Instructions' through the 'G' Branch.

"*A.D's.M.S. of Divisions* commanded the Medical Services and co-ordinated the regimental work of the officers and Field Ambulances, and were responsible for the evacuation from the line to the Main Dressing Stations.

---

[8] These arrangements for First Somme had, owing to the failure to break through, remained a dead letter. They were recently made available to the Australian War Memorial through the courtesy of the Historical Section of the Committee of Imperial Defence. They have been published in the *British Official History of the War: France and Belgium 1916 (I), Appendix 16.*

[9] A D.A.D.M.S. of the Australian Corps (Major W. H. Donald) has "appreciated," from the medical point of view, the position of the Corps in the military cosmos as follows:—

"The Corps was a most indefinite and jelly-like formation—its responsibilities were constantly revised and were never exactly defined. At times a highly complex formation, with duties far beyond the scope of the relatively small staff, at others it would subside into the merest go-between of the organic military formations, Division and Army. Relations were always more or less strained: the Corps was suspected of encroaching on Divisional duties with the object of justifying its existence—the Corps criticised the Divisional attitude as parochial."

[10] In the memorandum referred to on *p. 648.*

[11] Colonel Barber adds that throughout his own time as D.D.M.S. the Corps Motor Ambulance Convoy "was the 3rd British, whose admirable services should be recorded."

"An important officer of Corps and Division was the D.A.D.M.S. who was selected from officers with both R.M.O. and Field Ambulance experience. His duties were onerous and responsible, including general responsibility for sanitation within the area."[12]

"*Offices: Records and Returns.* The offices of D.D.M.S. and A.D's.M.S. were the clearing houses for the A.A.M.C. and were run on business lines. The office staff (Warrant Officer, 2 Other Ranks, and an Orderly) were mostly drawn from men of business education and clerks. The Warrant Officer was responsible to the D.A.D.M.S. for the important 'Field Return' and numerous other general returns."

No note on administrative medical duties in the field could be valid without special reference to this matter of returns and records. The misuse of "returns" is of course a hoary military joke, but it is not too much to say that the ordered life and activities of a modern army in a major war are absolutely dependent on the systematic rendition of returns and maintenance of records. The keeping of casualty records and rendition of corresponding returns were an important and onerous duty of the medical service. A special note on the subject will be included in *Volume III*.

Standing Orders for A.A.M.C., Australian Corps. On his becoming A.D.M.S. 4th Division Colonel Barber's first action had been to formulate "Sanitary Standing Orders"; after a few months' experience in France he had embodied his views on the medical administration of a Division in "Medical Standing Orders." Now, one of his first actions on becoming D.D.M.S. of the Corps was to integrate the various administrative instructions and precedents into *Standing Orders for A.A.M.C., Australian Corps*,[13] which with the approval of the Corps Commander, served as a ruling for the medical service throughout the Australian Corps;[14] all medical officers, in particular, those

---

[12] The following is from a D.A.D.M.S. of II Anzac:—
"It would appear to me that the duties of the D.A.D.M.S. Corps are what the D.D.M.S. makes them. I was D.A.D.M.S. II Anzac under both Roth and Begg. Under these two I found very different conditions. Roth made me do a great deal while Begg allowed me to do very little. In the latter case I was a clerk and nothing else. Roth on the other hand discussed everything with me and sometimes acted on my suggestions. A great part of our dealings with A.D's.M.S. Divisions was carried out by me by his direction. Also inspections of units occasionally. Sanitation and Health were dealt with by me under his supervision."

[13] *See Appendix No. 4.* These are not to be confused with "Medical Instruction No. 10" referred to in the last chapter (*p. 634*).

[14] Colonel Barber of course had no authority over Australian medical units outside the corps. In II Anzac Corps instructions corresponding to these were given in a pamphlet, "Lecture to Medical Officers," by the D.D.M.S., Colonel Mackie Begg.

Colonel Barber has recorded how, as A.D.M.S., 4th Division, he first became

recently joined, were required to make themselves familiar with it—and also, with *Field Service Regulations*.

Promulgation of Medical Instructions.[15] It was found necessary at this time to systematise the method for transmitting the instructions of A.D's.M.S. to the medical units.

"The chief mistakes (says Barber) made were the giving of too much information, imperfect paragraphing, inclusion of standing orders in routine, and the giving of orders calculated to cramp the initiative of Ambulance Commanders and Regimental Medical Officers."

Posting of R.M.O's. Closer rapprochement than heretofore was effected with the office of the D.M.S., A.I.F., and, as a consequence, the Deputy-Director secured a freer hand within the Corps. The important matter of the replacement of any Regimental Medical Officers who became casualties, was made automatic and immediate by leaving direct action to the Field Ambulance Commander. Reinforcing officers were to be posted to field ambulances before taking over regimental duties and at the same time experienced regimental officers were posted to field ambulance to qualify for promotion and future command.

"It seemed obvious," wrote Colonel Barber, after the war, "that we had done with stationary warfare and that we should be engaged in mobile warfare—advance or retreat. It was therefore urgently necessary to make arrangements in preparation." The "more important" of these, he said, were:—

Preparations for mobile war

"the mobility of medical units; the co-ordination of medical service within Corps and Divisions; the method of issuing medical orders; measures—in the form both of treatment and of transport—to combat the long distance from M.D.S. to C.C.S.; measures to ensure adequate medical supplies in a war of movement; and measures for preventing

aware of the need for such instructions which had been lacking under his predecessor.

"I drafted these as the result of attending a lecture on 'The R.M.O.' at one of the British Casualty Clearing Stations. The lecture was given in a humorous vein and was of little value, but in the discussion which followed many R.A.M.C. officers (T. and S.R.) expressed themselves very strongly concerning administration and complained that . . . they could obtain little or no information about their duties, regarding which many of them realised their ignorance. I returned to the Division determined that my officers should not have a similar complaint." He accordingly issued standing orders for the A.A.M.C. in his division. Other Australian divisions had issued—the 1st, a summary of rules; the 2nd, "Instructions for the guidance of all Medical Officers"; the 3rd, "Hints to Medical Officers"—extracts from G.R.O's, A.R.O's, D.R.O's, and A.D.M.S. Circulars; the 5th—a somewhat similar compilation.

[15] For the vague and anomalous position of the medical service with regard to the issue of "orders," see *p. 114n.*

sick wastage." In particular the work of Sanitary Sections required attention and the working of dental units had to be readjusted.

Some measures with the same object were taken by higher authorities—Army and G.H.Q. A few deserve special note. *Reserve of Equipment Formed.* To relieve the ambulance transport of equipment additional to the strict allowance and yet ensure special supplies for emergency, a special "Army" order permitted D.D's.M.S. to hold stores of stretchers and blankets. These, together with extra tentage, were dumped at the headquarters of the M.A.C., and lorries were specially attached to the M.A.C's for carrying them wherever the D.D.M.S. directed.

Effort for mobility

Changed Rôle of Sanitary Sections in Fourth Army. The views upheld in the Australian Divisions on the function and proper employment of the Divisional Sanitary Sections—that they should be rather instructing and directing units, like engineers, than skilled labour units[16]—were now accepted by Fourth Army. A standing order laid down:—

"To rectify a prevailing misapprehension, a Sanitary Section is not responsible for, and is not in a position to carry out, the provision and distribution of the various sanitary appliances that are necessary in an area. Every unit must be able to maintain satisfactory sanitation with improvised appliances until more permanent structures can be supplied."

The procedure that had previously been general in the British Army, of making these units stationary under "Army" control, was replaced in the Australian Corps by a judicious compromise, whereby, for administrative purposes they were made "Corps units" under the D.D.M.S. who might—and often did—hold them in an area other than that occupied by their own division. But normally the sections moved with and under the Divisional A.D.M.S., and were responsible for the sanitary efficiency of their own divisions.[17]

Mobility of Baths and Laundries. The prevention of what

---
[16] *See pp. 594-600.*
[17] The order for the transfer from Divisional to Corps control took effect as from April 21. For the purpose of giving instruction to battalion "pioneers" official provision was made for a workshop at the Headquarters of each Sanitary Section. A special Corps routine order (A.Q.) authorised supplies of material, arranged for indent and drawing, and provided for transport. (The 3-ton lorry originally provided had lately been replaced by an inadequate box-car.) "When these matters had been put upon a sound basis" (Col. Barber records) "one had little or no trouble with sanitation."

we have termed diseases of dirt and squalor was now fully taken in hand by the "Q" Branch of Corps and Divisions. A special "Baths and Laundries" sub-department of "A.Q.," with a commissioned officer (lieutenant) in control, was made fully responsible for these, under the D.A. and Q.M.G. Efforts were made to improve their mobility, a matter in which the British Army had lagged behind the French.

Of Dental units. During the siege warfare in common with all other units the dental units attached to Australian field ambulances had acquired far more equipment than could be carried, and they, too, believed this equipment to be essential. The result was that, in the rapid Divisional moves in the first part of 1918, not only the equipment but the dental units themselves (says Colonel Barber) "were scattered broadcast over the country." They were now assembled and steps were taken by the D.D.M.S. to ensure mobility, without loss of efficiency. These particulars, however, will more suitably be dealt with in the general account of the work and significance of these units in *Volume III.*[18]

The inventions and innovations referred to at the beginning of this chapter originated in the fighting of the field units during the warfare of May, June and July; and, to understand their development the reader will first require a short description of the medical arrangements of the Corps at that time.

Technical developments in evacuation scheme

During the period of intense minor activity on the part of the Australians during May, June, and July culminating in the Battle of Hamel, each of the three divisions in line developed its own scheme of evacuation, based on groups of casualty clearing stations at Crouy and Vignacourt. With slight changes in the position of the more advanced posts and stations the scheme remained unchanged until the general advance.

The Terrain: The River Somme. During the next five months the problems of clearance in the Australian Corps were dominated by the River Somme. Its wide wooded valley and partly canalised stream

---
[18] Equipment was cut down to 350 lb. Owing to the large number of British and American troops attached to the Corps the Australian dental units were overworked. It consequently became necessary to restrict the work done by Australian units for non-Australian troops to urgent cases.

divided the Australian front, each of the plateaux, north and south of the river, being held by one Australian division, with a third holding the valley between them and a fourth in reserve. Each sector was held by one division, usually on a two-brigade front.

A second important feature of the terrain presented itself in the old Roman roads Amiens-Albert and Amiens-St. Quentin which enticed all traffic towards the southern corner of the Corps area. The whole front was roughly eleven miles in length.

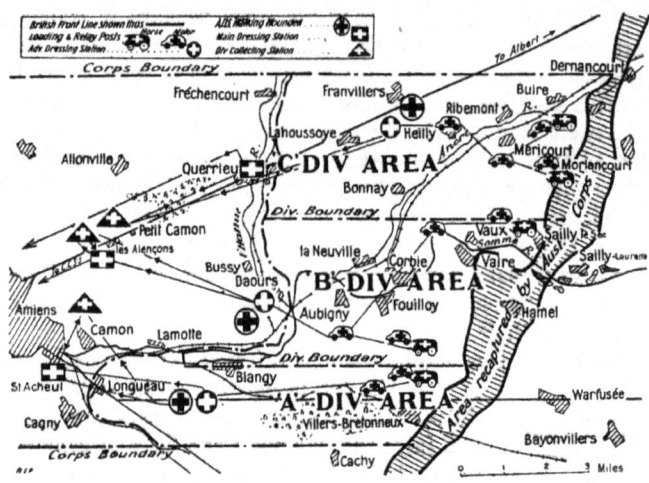

General Scheme of Evacuation from Divisional Areas, May-July. (The A.D.S. situated between Bonnay and Franvillers is that figured in plate and diagram at p. 660.)

The evacuation scheme was in great part determined by these geo-physical features—in particular in the central sector, where the position of the bridges decided medical sites and routes.

The accompanying sketch map shows the general scheme of clearance in the three divisions during May, June and July; only the main transport routes are indicated. "Main" dressing stations and "divisional collecting stations," sited on the two great roads, cleared from advanced dressing stations which lay within range of the enemy's 5·9-inch howitzers. A special feature of the forward clearance was that motor loading posts were pushed far forward: at times Ford cars even cleared some of the R.A.P's.[19] Much attention was paid to the problem of the *walking wounded*—in particular an endeavour was made to clear them to C.C.S. with a minimum of interim manipulation, leaving the stream of stretcher cases to pass down through the treatment centres and ambulance waggon routes. The 3rd British M.A.C. cleared for the Corps from main dressing to casualty clearing stations. Within the framework of this scheme were made the experiments in transport and treatment now to be described.

In this scheme the first innovation deserving mention was the "Corps Motor Relay Post." Four years of war had taught that, in heavy fighting, the ambulance transport of the field units and motor ambulance convoy sufficed only for stretcher cases; for the mixed group of "walkers" and "sitters"— most of whom had walked from R.A.P. to waggon loading post—other rolling stock must be found. The new war of movement, and the rearward emplacement of C.C.S. groups, compelled a more exact use than heretofore of "returning empty" ammunition lorries to supplement the buses supplied by "Army." The "motor relay post" at Toutencourt[20] gave the idea for an improved method of tapping the ammunition supply lorries, in particular those of the "Ammunition Parks"[21] on their return from rendezvous or refilling point to their own railhead.

Transport of Walking Wounded: Corps Motor Relay Post

"Full advantage was taken of returning ammunition transport," writes Colonel Barber, "but, as the ammunition railheads did not coincide with the location of the Casualty Clearing Stations, it was found necessary to establish ambulance posts where the routes diverged; one ambulance post each for the right and left sectors. These were christened Corps Relay Posts, and had establishment of one tent sub-division, with transport; they were administered by the D.D.M.S. as they were too far in

---

[19] The impressions of the warfare at this time, recorded by Capt. W. J. Newing who joined the Corps in May, offer instructive contrast to the records of the Third Battle of Ypres.

". . . One could not help thinking what a large unwieldy organisation a Field Ambulance is. Except when there is actual fighting the men do very little except clean up after themselves, and, from later experience with the 26th Battalion in actual fighting, one noted that the Ambulance bearers sometimes go all day without a carry. Ford Ambulances can get up so near to R.A.P's that it struck me that perhaps it would be better if bearers were battalion men, to be called upon in emergencies."

[20] See p. 626.

[21] In view of modifications in the method of ammunition supply since the war the detailed technique of *liaison* is not described. It must be emphasised however that medical officers should be closely familiar with the movements of the transport concerned in both forms of supply—ammunition and rations.

rear of their respective A.D's.M.S. Walking wounded were debussed here [*i.e.* removed from the lorries], and proceeded to Casualty Clearing Stations by lorries or buses obtained from the Army and kept at the Post for this purpose; this plan worked very well.

"Certain buses worked between Advanced and Main Dressing Stations, others from M.D.S. to C.C.S. When conditions allowed, patients were transferred direct from Advanced Dressing to Casualty Clearing Stations. Thus the 'Walking Wounded Dressing Station' might be an annexe of the A.D.S. or the M.D.S."

The Corps Relay Posts were moved or multiplied to meet changes in the routes. On occasion they served, in effect, as the "M.D.S." for walking wounded; kept "Admission and Discharge" Books, and furnished returns to Third Echelon.

The second innovation was the "standardised A.D.S." The history of ambulance work in France was, as the reader will already have gathered, largely the history of the "A.D.S." Yet that history can be understood only when dealt with in terms of facts and constants, and the meanings of the terms "advanced" and "main" dressing station were not constant. In evacuation the vital constant factors have been identified in *Chapter XI* as those of time and distance on the one hand and of the vital reaction to trauma on the other; and it was these that determined both the character of the "advanced" dressing station under various conditions of warfare, and also its location. During May, June, and July this problem of the A.D.S. was tackled scientifically in the A.I.F. The first experiment was undertaken by the 6th Field Ambulance when, at the end of April, it moved up from Warloy to clear the 2nd Division's front on the Somme and Ancre. The purpose in view was then to safeguard wounded who should be held up by enemy shell-fire at the A.D.S., and as well to minimise losses among the bearers. With the assistance of the A.D.M.S. (Colonel A. E. Shepherd) the commanding officer (Lieut.-Colonel H. L. St. Vincent Welch) secured the co-operation of the 2nd Pioneer Battalion in constructing a "model dugout" to house the A.D.S. on the exposed Franvillers-Bonnay road.[22]

The standardised underground A.D.S.

---

[22] The dugout was driven into the side of a slope some 30 feet underground, with independent entrance and exit, and accommodated some 50 stretchers on struts, in a gallery with two bays. A trolley track, with a reciprocating windlass at each end, admitted and discharged casualties. A model scheme with plans was designed to house underground all the posts, from the R.A.P's to the A.D.S.

The A.D.S. was completed by the end of May and served well the purpose for which it had been designed. It was found, however, that complete headcover was seldom required at the A.D.S., and it fell to the 14th Field Ambulance (Lieut.-Colonel C. W. Thompson), which took over the post on June 15th, to complete the scheme of "a standard type A.D.S." With the help of the Divisional Engineers, a new station was designed and was constructed to plan by the unit personnel helped by the Pioneers. The object of this new experiment was chiefly to obtain protection against fragments from the new German shells with instantaneous fuses ("daisy cutters," as they were called) and aerial bombs. This station was accordingly sunk only a few feet below ground level.

The principles which guided this unit were set out thus:—[28]

"Local conditions may indicate that a M.D.S. be the place where treatment is carried out. But in stationary warfare it is . . . desirable that the A.D.S. be designed for heavy shelling, situated, as it [the station] generally is, well within the shelled zone. It is a good plan to have an alternative dressing hut above ground since a wounded man may get handled much quicker on the surface." "It is highly necessary, we think," the writer adds, "that a patient should leave an A.D.S. fit to travel to C.C.S. That is an ideal to which one should approximate."

How from this station there was evolved the so-called "portable" station is told by Colonel Barber:—

"The idea was first conceived after inspection of the excellent tented A.D.S. constructed by Lieut.-Colonel Clive Thompson, C.O. 14th Field Ambulance. . . . Three wooden huts were constructed in sections and were kept in readiness at the Engineer dumps. As a rule one was erected in either sector if possible beside the A.D.S., which became the M.D.S. when we advanced. The other was kept in reserve to be 'leapfrogged' forward in event of an advance. It was found that the material could be transported in three lorries. When time allowed these huts were sunk and sandbagged. . . . In addition plans were drawn up (in consultation with the C.E.) for standard dugouts at R.A.P's, Bearer Relay posts, and Advanced and Main Dressing Stations. Relay posts were so constructed that by further digging they could be converted to an A.D.S. to carry 30 stretchers."

The third innovation was the Field Ambulance Resuscitation Team. Always difficult, the problem presented to the field medical units by the man whose wound called for prompt but effective surgery—"the problem of the tourniquet" as it might

---

[28] In an excellent study of the whole problem in the *War Diary* of the 14th Field Ambulance, 31 July, 1918.

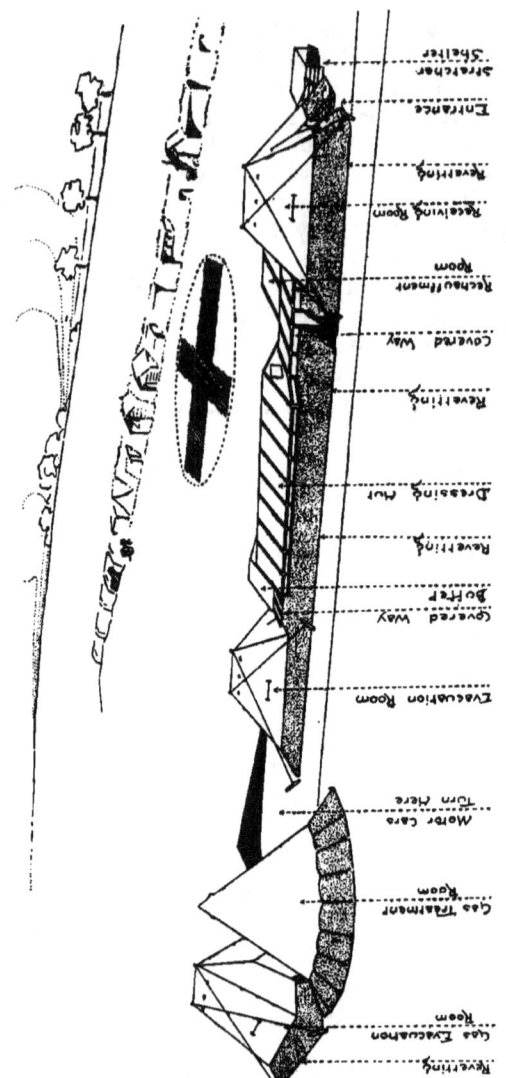

The Underground Dressing Station on the Franvillers-Bonnay Road

From drawing by Lance Mattinson in war diary of 14th Fld. Amb.

71. THE ADVANCED DRESSING STATION (14TH FIELD AMBULANCE) ON THE FRANVILLERS-BONNAY ROAD, JULY, 1918
This became the model for the standard A.D.S.

Aust. War Memorial Official Photo. No. E3877.

72. THE CONGESTION OF WOUNDED AT THE LOADING POST NEAR 4TH BRIGADE HEADQUARTERS DURING THE BATTLE OF HAMEL

Aust. War Memorial Official Photo. No. E2699.

74. GASSED MEN AT THE R.A.P. OF THE 42ND BATTALION IN VILLERS-BRETONNEUX, 27TH MAY, 1918

Aust. War Memorial Official Photo. No. E4850.

73. OPERATING ROOM IN THE MODEL DRESSING STATION, FRANVILLERS ROAD

Aust. War Memorial Official Photo. No. E2771.

To face p. 661.

be termed—with the equally prominent factor of wound shock, became in this phase of the war again a very pressing one. The partial solution effected by evacuation direct from A.D.S. to a C.C.S. placed far forward (as in the Third Battle of Ypres) was not now possible. It is true that the Thomas splint had provided a radical solution in the fractured femurs; and the "discovery" of warmth, transfusion, and rest had reduced the incidence of wound shock. But that there remained a very real problem[24] is shown by the urgency with which, so soon as the front had somewhat settled down, the field units set about to find a solution for what they held to be a professional *impasse*. From gropings at this time in all the medical units of the Corps there evolved the *Field Ambulance Resuscitation Team*—a purely Australian innovation, which not only played a most useful part in the work of evacuation during this phase of the war, but—what is even more important— had a high educative value for the personnel of the field ambulance.

The Field Ambulance Resuscitation Teams

A note on the constitution of these "teams," and an outline of their work and place in the medical scheme will be found in *Appendix No. 14*,[25] but the mode of their development must be described here. Two factors were equipotent in it, and these may be summed as "demand" and "supply."

Demand—and Clinical Experiment at the Front. From accounts of sundry strivings within the field units the following is selected to show "demand."

In the first weeks of May the 14th Field Ambulance (5th Division) "ran" the Main Dressing Station for the Central Sector of the front. This station was then at Daours.[26] Its Commanding Officer had formed the opinion that "on an average" in some 2 per cent. of battle-casualties "the long trip to the C.C.S." is excessively dangerous. In view of this he decided to provide effective surgical treatment in cases "of

---

[24] It might be argued that from the strictly military standpoint, or by the "totalitarian" standard of "humanity," the logical procedure in the severest types of wound would be euthanasia by an overdose of morphia; failing this, the remedy of No-Man's Land, a bullet. The ordinary standards of humanity, however, are deeply implanted in all civilised troops and great resentment follows their non-observance.

[25] *See pp. 953-7.*

[26] After being shelled on May 20 it was moved to Les Alençons. The note is from a report by the O.C. Lieut.-Col. Clive Thompson to the A.D.M.S. 5th Division (Col. M. H. Downey): "Operations performed at M.D.S. in Daours May 5-19, 1918." (Diary 23 May, 1918.)

haemorrhagic urgency" and in some others, including "selected abdominals." Through the Australian Red Cross Society the official equipment of the unit was augmented by a steriliser, a Shipway warmed ether apparatus, and a "Max Page" *réchauffement* apparatus. An operating theatre was fitted up and also rooms for post-operative treatment. During two weeks some 30 operations were performed and "on the experience gained" Lieut.-Colonel Thompson recommended to the A.D.M.S. that "an operating team" for each Division should be placed at the disposal of the A.D.M.S. for attachment to "suitably placed Main Dressing Stations."

The difficulty of providing early and effective surgical treatment for the seriously wounded in the Corps area was brought officially to the notice of the D.M.S., Fourth Army by the D.D.M.S., Australian Corps on May 21st but "without result."

Supply—and Scientific Research at the Base. Pari passu with these clinical experiments, advances in technical methods were moving other men toward the same ends.

Reference has elsewhere been made[27] to the research work on haemorrhage and wound shock carried out by the Medical Research Committee in association with various American and British workers; in particular its treatment by blood transfusion. The results of research were translated into practice in France first at the Bases, in particular at Boulogne where in January, 1918, surgeons at No. 2 A.G.H. were using the "whole blood" method. At the front, early in 1918, at No. 3 British C.C.S. at Gézaincourt (Third Army), under the Consulting Surgeon (Colonel Gray), Captain Kenneth Walker, R.A.M.C.(T.), had built up a "Shock Centre," which became a Mecca for front line medical officers, among them a number from the near-by Australian Corps. From these came the idea of field ambulance resuscitation teams—analogue of the C.C.S. "operating teams."[28]

Consummation: The Australian Resuscitation Teams. Towards the end of June officers of the 4th Field Ambulance took the initiative in applying this new line of treatment to field ambulance work. The matter was brought to a head by the occurrence of several unfortunate happenings. The following created a deep impression.

On June 24th, at Daours, the A.D.M.S., 4th Australian Division (Colonel A. H. Moseley) was wounded in the leg by a fragment of H.E. He was evacuated to the M.D.S. (4th Field Ambulance) at Les Alençons

[27] In *Chapter xii and Appendix No. 14.*
[28] The above is from a note by Lieut.-Col. Victor Hurley, A.A.M.C., who worked at this time with his "operating team" at Gézaincourt, and kept the D.M.S., A.I.F., posted in developments.

where under existing conditions no effort could be made to ligate the posterior tibial artery which had been severed in its upper third. Evacuation to C.C.S. at Crouy (18 kilometres) over bad roads involved several more hours before effective surgical aid was possible—and this when the division was holding a quiet front. The limb had eventually to be amputated.

With the approval of the A.D.M.S.[29] and concurrence of the Deputy-Director the Officer Commanding the 4th Field Ambulance (Lieut.-Colonel R. S. McGregor) now formed, unofficially, a "resuscitation team," directed by Major A. W. Holmes à Court.[30] Equipment for blood transfusion was obtained by various devices: serum for the typing of donors, gum and glucose solution, and so forth were supplied by No. 3 (British) C.C.S. The "team" was ready to undertake urgent surgical work in time for the Battle of Hamel; and during this action and subsequently it was kept fully employed at the M.D.S. at Les Alençons.

Early in July General Howse visited the Australian Corps, and unofficially approved the scheme.[31] Subsequent developments are recorded by Colonel Barber as follows:—

"With the consent of the G.O.C. Australian Corps (Lieut.-General Monash) a 'Corps Resuscitation Team' was formed for the purpose of performing urgent surgical operations, *réchauffement* and transfusion of blood. The necessary gas and oxygen apparatus for anaesthesia and equipment for transfusion of blood and gum solution were obtained and the team proved a complete success. As soon as it was thoroughly established and made mobile, it was detailed in turn to one Ambulance in each Division where it 'doubled up' with a similar team drawn from that Ambulance who received instruction, the necessary equipment being supplied by the D.M.S. Australian Imperial Force (from the Australian Branch of the Red Cross Society).

"Australian Corps 'Medical Instruction No. 14,' of August 23rd, authorised an establishment and equipment table. Thus in a short time we possessed a resuscitation team for each Division. That for the 1st Division, like the rest, was in full working order when that formation rejoined the Corps after the Battle of August 8th."

Within the Australian Corps these teams replaced the

---

[29] Lieut.-Col. R. S. McGregor acted as A.D.M.S. until July 6, when Col. Kenneth Smith was appointed to the position.

[30] To this officer is due the major credit for the creation of these teams, and for their successful development. The Australian war records are indebted to him for an admirable account of the origin and activities of these teams.

[31] The Consulting Surgeon B.E.F. (Surgeon-Gen. Sir Anthony Bowlby) and of Fourth Army (Col. G. E. Gask, and, later, Major G. Gordon-Taylor) co-operated *con amore* in the project and were of great help in overcoming some official inertia in the matter of Army supplies.

C.C.S. as centres for education in the prevention of wound shock—*réchauffement* and so forth; and they were an important element in field ambulance work throughout the advance to victory. In the great battle of the St. Quentin Canal the "Corps team" was attached to the 27th American Division.

On September 20th General Howse approached the Corps Commander with the recommendation that surgical resuscitation teams for the forward areas be made a permanent A.I.F. establishment. This recommendation was in due course forwarded to the D.G.M.S., B.E.F., who officially sanctioned the employment of the teams in the forward area of the Australian Corps.

The following is quoted from a statement by the Acting Consulting Surgeon, Fourth Army (Major G. Gordon-Taylor) in a report by the "Resuscitation Teams Committee" appointed by the D.D.M.S., Australian Corps:—

"Several months' experience in the Casualty Clearing zone behind the Australian Corps has enabled me to form an estimate of the excellent work of the resuscitation teams of that Corps. There can be no room for doubt that very many lives have been saved by the work of Major Holmes à Court and the members of the other resuscitation teams. Their experience in the Dressing Stations coincides with that of the Casualty Clearing Hospitals that in blood transfusion we have the most remarkable and valuable means of treating cases of severe shock and haemorrhage. Their results conclusively prove the value of these methods of resuscitation in the Field Ambulances."

On October 30th the following circular memorandum was sent from G.H.Q., B.E.F. to the Directors of Medical Services in all Armies:—

"The attached report on the organisation and work accomplished by Divisional Resuscitation Teams, Australian Corps, is forwarded for your information and consideration with your Consulting Surgeon. The employment or not of such Teams with Field Ambulances naturally depends on the factors imposed by the variations in the military situation—distance of Casualty Clearing Stations behind front line—time taken in transporting wounded from the latter to the former—number of Surgeons and other personnel available for the work etc. Where circumstances are such that the maximum good is likely to result by the employment of Teams as indicated in the report, you will no doubt be able to bring the principle into operation."

Thus three innovations instituted by the Australian Medical

Service at the front became an official practice throughout the Australian Corps, and, in this case, an authorised one in the British Army.

Health May-July
Apart from the first wave of the influenza epidemic, which struck the Australian troops in June, the health of the force was very satisfactory.[32]

"Good facilities for various sports were found to exist at the present location (says the diary of the 8th Field Ambulance in June), and these were fully availed of. Cricket, football, or baseball matches were arranged with the surrounding units. Daily bathing parades were held at a spot some mile and a half distance from the camp."

From the many and varied fights of this time, three may be selected for note as having particular points of interest, namely, the fighting north of the Somme on May 19th (Ville) and June 10th (Morlancourt), and the Battle of Hamel south of the river.

Military Operations

Fighting north of the Somme—Ville and Morlancourt. During May and June the 3rd, 2nd, and 5th Divisions in succession carried out a series of very successful "raids" and patrol actions, but the most important "set pieces," mentioned above, were both undertaken by the 2nd Division.

It is not possible to enter upon a particular account of the exceptionally varied and interesting medical events of these actions. It must suffice to say that they open up a new phase of field ambulance work in this war—it may even be said, in warfare. The main lines of evacuation were the same for both operations, modified to suit place and circumstances. An important factor in the success with which casualties were cleared through the "bearer" posts was the construction by the medical units, in conjunction with the engineer service and the pioneers, of safe and commodious shelters for R.A.P's and bearer posts. A feature of the *transport* work in these, as in later operations, was the forward emplacement of motor loading posts, whereby the bearer carries were reduced and clearance to the A.D.S. speeded up. What were called *"motor loading posts"* became, in effect, the pivot of clearance, all arrangements forward of the M.D.S. being adapted to the working of them.

---

[32] *See Graph No. 9 at p. 494, and Chapter xxiii.*

Both regimental and ambulance carries were short and evacuation correspondingly rapid.

In the operations at Ville on May 19th in which the 5th and 6th Brigades sustained 506 casualties, the 6th Field Ambulance (A.D.S. and motor loading post) with pooled bearers cleared 417 wounded to Querrieu (M.D.S. 5th Field Ambulance) in 12 hours, the wounded arriving, the war diary notes, "in excellent condition"; this was attributed by the O.C. to "the warmth of the day and the excellent *morale* of the service." For this "stunt" a special motor loading post had been constructed to accommodate 30 stretcher cases. Walking wounded arrived here two hours after the opening barrage and at the M.D.S. within three and three-quarter hours. From this stage of the war onwards German prisoners were always available for stretcher-bearing.[83]

In the operations near Morlancourt on June 10th-11th, the 7th Brigade had losses amounting to 487, the 397 wounded being evacuated by the 6th Field Ambulance through their new underground A.D.S. on the Franvillers-Bonnay road.[84]

By the end of June the Australian Corps, general staff and troops alike, were ready for a more ambitious effort, and the Army Commander (General Rawlinson), Lieut.-General Monash, and the tank commanders combined in devising a minor offensive which should serve incidentally to rehearse new tactical methods for the first stroke in the Allied offensive, for which the time would probably arrive before long.

The try-out;
Battle of
Hamel

Military Operations. The Battle of Hamel was the logical and inevitable outcome of Cambrai: a phoenix from the ashes of that brilliant but mismanaged effort. It was the first of the great series of battles undertaken during the next three months by the Australian Corps. The objective involved a German salient enclosing the village of Hamel; the advance was made on a 6,000 yard front to a depth, in the centre, of 2,000 yards. Secrecy was a special feature of the preparations for the battle. The G.O.C. 4th Division (Major-General Sinclair-MacLagan) was made responsible for its conduct. The tactical plan, worked out

---

[83] This was officially permitted but only for the journey *from* the line. It created the difficulty that the stretchers used were not returned. This was met by forming stretcher dumps at the motor loading posts and A.D.S. to "feed" the R.A.P's.

[84] This station has been described on *p. 658.* It was made the subject of a special report to his Minister (Senator Pearce) by the D.G.M.S. Australian Military Forces (Surgeon-Gen. R. H. J. Fetherston) who inspected it, during the course of these operations, on the occasion of his visit to the British and French fronts.

under General Monash with great care by the staffs concerned, involved parts of all three divisions in the line (2nd, 4th, and 5th), and the 11th Brigade of the 3rd Division was attached to the 4th Division for the operation. Part of the 33rd American Division was at this time attached to the Corps and four of its companies took part in the fighting. Tanks were used on a novel plan, operating on a general scheme but under the orders of each battalion.

As in other operations prior to the great advance, the normal divisional lines of clearance were used and improved to meet the special requirements of the action. Medical arrangements were put in the hands of the acting A.D.M.S. 4th Division (Lieut.-Colonel R. S. McGregor). Those for the 6th Brigade (2nd Division) were made by him in consultation with the A.D.M.S. (Colonel A. E. Shepherd) and the D.D.M.S., and were carried out by the 6th Field Ambulance (Lieut.-Colonel H. L. St. Vincent Welch). Evacuation was based on the main dressing station at Les Alençons (4th Field Ambulance, Major H. B. Lewers) clearing by 3rd M.A.C. to Nos. 5 and 47 casualty clearing stations at Crouy, and by light railway to Vignacourt. Arrangements were made for the surgical work at the M.D.S. to be controlled by Major Holmes à Court as a "try out" of the value of "resuscitation" methods by a specially trained and equipped "team." The "gas centre"—to which all gassed cases were sent—was worked from the M.D.S. A "divisional collecting station," now a regular feature of the evacuation scheme, was formed by one tent subdivision of the 12th Field Ambulance near Petit Camon.

Medical Arrangements for Hamel

Forward Clearance. The "Medical Arrangements" issued on June 30th by Lieut.-Colonel McGregor made the 13th Field Ambulance (Lieut.-Colonel F. C. Wooster) responsible for clearing the front of the 4th Division (4th and 11th Brigades). The A.D.S. on the Aubigny-Amiens road, four miles from the M.D.S., was of the new type. Two "Nissen" huts were specially dug in by the ambulance personnel to a depth of six feet. The station was also designated as the "M.D.S. for Walking Wounded,"[35] who were cleared thence by lorries direct to C.C.S. Much construction work was done forward.

[35] It would later normally have been called the "Walking Wounded Dressing Station" (or "W.W.D.S.").

Map No. 11

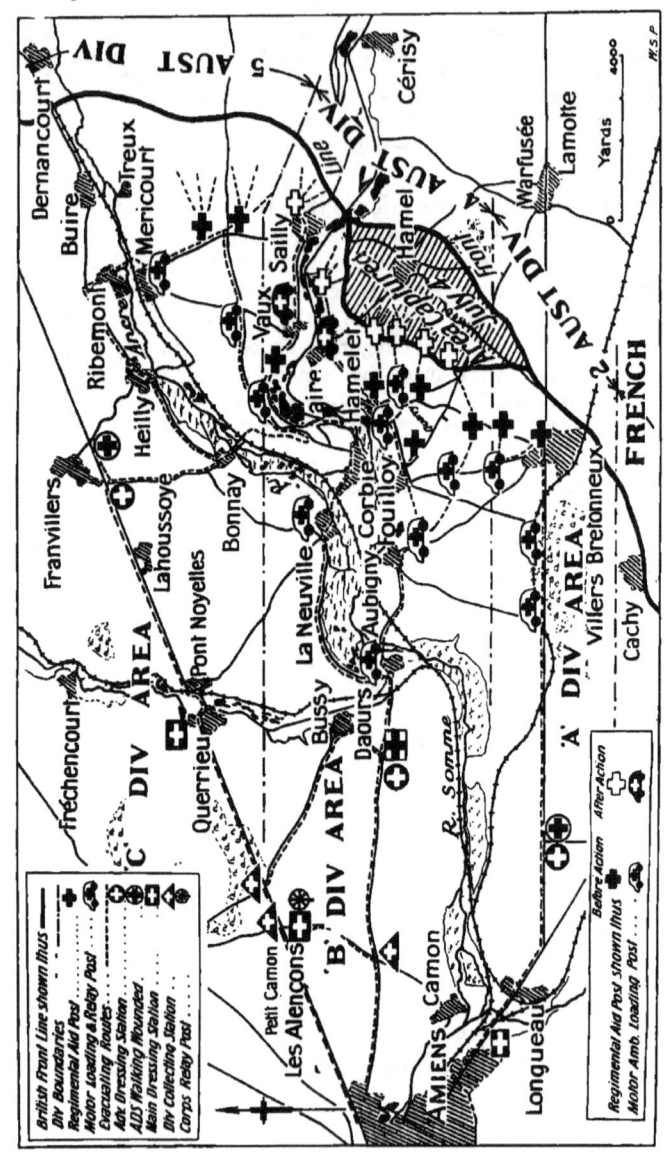

Medical Arrangements, Battle of Hamel, 4th July, 1918

"At each of the forward posts," says Lieut.-Colonel McGregor, "there was a safe accommodation for wounded varying from 15 to 100 lying cases, and a varying number of walking cases, and in addition cover for stretcher bearers, and also at Ambulance Posts for Ambulance cars [recesses cut into the bank at the side of the road]."

Sick and "Stragglers." Very exact arrangements were made by the A.D.M.S. 4th Division for dealing with sick. On and after "an hour to be named" walking sick were to be evacuated direct to C.C.S. unless likely to be fit for duty "within 2 to 3 days," in which case they would be sent to the D.C.S.

Five "stragglers' posts," to which medical officers were to send all stragglers were formed by the Provost Corps, for the most part between Corbie and Daours.[36] A "divisional stragglers' collecting station" was established at Daours. Here, "when required by the officer in command to do so" a medical officer from the A.D.S. would "medically examine all stragglers."

Records and Returns: "Died of Wounds." No casualties were to be recorded at the A.D.S. save and except that all men who died at medical posts in the forward area would be "advised to the A.D.S. and recorded in the A. and D. books of the W.W.M.D.S."

Transport. Three bearer divisions were in the forward posts or at the A.D.S.; the 11th Field Ambulance bearers were held at M.D.S. in reserve. In addition to the ambulance transport of the 4th Division, that of the 3rd was made available by the D.D.M.S.—a total capacity of some 140 stretchers. Cars were run in two circuits—between "forward Ambulance" (Motor Loading) Post and A.D.S., and between this and the M.D.S.

Clearance routes from the forward ambulance posts were arranged north and south of the Somme by two officers (Major L. B. Elwell and Major D. M. Steele) detailed by the O.C., 13th Field Ambulance. Transport was allotted as follows:—

South ("Quarry Post"). Complete Bearer Division of 13th Field Ambulance. Complete Bearer Division of 12th Field Ambulance. Seven large and four small motor ambulance cars—36 stretchers.

North. Two Bearer Sub-divisions of 4th Field Ambulance, three large and four small motor ambulance cars—36 stretchers.

[36] 4th Division headquarters were at Bussy. All Brigade headquarters were less than a mile from the front line.

The remainder of ambulance stretcher-bearers and ambulance cars were retained by the C.O. at the A.D.S. as a reserve and for evacuation of cases back to M.D.S.

Corps Motor Relay Post. For the evacuation of walking wounded "full use" (the D.D.M.S. instructed) was to be made of empty returning mechanical transport, which would carry cases to a corps motor relay post at Dreuil just behind Amiens. For clearing stretcher cases to A.D.S. the Ford cars and "Sunbeams" would to a great extent work in relay, the former replacing the horsed-waggons, for wounded.

To ensure effective co-ordination of the efforts of the three Divisions concerned, Colonel Barber conferred with the Assistant-Directors. On June 30th Lieut.-Colonel McGregor met the senior officers of the 4th, 12th, and 13th Field Ambulances and all the Regimental Medical Officers concerned. The latter were instructed to move forward with their battalions, and to select sites for new aid-posts in consultation with the respective battalion commanders, "notifying the site as soon as possible to O.C. Field Ambulance and to A.D.M.S." Direct *liaison* was arranged between Brigade Headquarters and Field Ambulance.

The Action (July 4th). The battle was one of the most dramatically successful of any fought by the Australian troops. "Zero" hour was at 3.10 a.m. By 5 a.m. all objectives had been captured with a loss in the 4th and 11th Brigades of 110 killed and 709 wounded, and in the 6th of 17 and 107. The total casualties at Hamel on July 4th were about 1,500. Prisoners numbered 1,472.

Medical Events of the Battle. Overwhelming military success involved the medical service—as did overwhelming failure—in special difficulties. The history of the medical events of this battle shows us an unpleasant and even dangerous situation met with the resource that derives from forethought and preparation.[37] The crux came in the central sector. Elsewhere everything went according to plan. On the right the 2nd Division cleared 132 stretchers and 111 walkers to St. Acheul by 10.30 a.m., and on the left the 5th evacuated a total of 173 to Querrieu even more quickly. The A.D.M.S. 5th Division records that, on this front, the enemy "scrupulously

[37] It is related of Napoleon that he once affirmed that his resourcefulness derived not from any peculiar faculty but from the fact that he thought out every contingency beforehand.

observed the laws of war," permitting bearers to clear across the open during heavy sniping.

The Quarry Ambulance Post. Casualties began to arrive at the Quarry post in less than an hour from zero. At 5 a.m. Major Elwell was asking for more bearers and, urgently, for stretchers. Then the trouble began. Wounded were brought in with quite abnormal rapidity from the R.A.P's, the stretcher squads being supplemented by German prisoners on their way to the rear as well as by infantry volunteers looking about for something to do; a number of urgent cases were brought in, through previous arrangement, by tanks.[38] Many cases drifted in also from the left flank. By 5.30 a.m. the incoming stream at the post was so great that the cars allotted to the circuit were quite unequal to the demand, and cases banked up until over 100 were waiting. Urgent communications from Major Elwell, and from the D.A.D.M.S. (Major Lind), who was sent up to report, as well as independent ones from 4th Brigade Headquarters near by, led to the transfer to this circuit of almost all the available ambulance vehicles. Through Brigade Headquarters there were even obtained from the Engineers six pontoon waggons, each of which did two trips with six stretcher cases. By 1.30 p.m. over 900 wounded had been cleared to the A.D.S., and this in turn banked up. By 3 p.m. "all the wounded were at the A.D.S. or behind it."

Advanced Dressing Station. The movement of events here cannot better be presented than from the report of the Commanding Officer (Lieut.-Colonel F.C. Wooster) to the A.D.M.S.

"*A.D.S.* (*N.4.c.9.2.*).[39] The first casualties arrived at 4.30 a.m. and thence continuously with increasing rapidity. The walking wounded were easily coped with, the standard dugout proving most suitable for the purpose. The lorries got away well and averaged about 3¾ hours for the trip to C.C.S. and back. Stretcher cases banked up until about 2 p.m. as the vehicles available could not keep up with the rapidity of their arrival. [At 1.30 p.m. the cars were switched to the rear circuit—A.D.S. to M.D.S.] At 3.5 p.m. O.C. was able to advise A.D.M.S. that Walking Wounded were clear, and stretcher cases rapidly clearing. At 5 p.m. A.D.S. was quite clear, having put through about 930 cases in 10 hours.

[38] For tanks as a means of evacuation at Hamel and Cambrai *see R.A.M.C. Journal* Oct. 1920, *p. 309*. See also *Brit. Off. Med. History, General, Vol. II, p. 110.* Like the aeroplane, though to a less degree, the tank created medical problems of its own of which a brief note is given in *Vol. III.*
[39] On the Aubigny-Amiens road, west of Vecquemont.

The proportion of stretcher to walking cases was about three to four, and there was a large proportion of abdominal and thigh wounds especially among the German wounded who numbered 180. A noteworthy feature was the very good condition of the wounded generally, due to the rapid evacuation and good weather. Casualty list of A.M.C. personnel (including attached) during the battle was only three O.R's."

Main Dressing Station. The first cases arrived at the M.D.S. at 6 a.m. Except for some slight delay about 2 p.m., "due (says Colonel McGregor) to the great distance cars had to travel to C.C.S.," evacuation was carried out "most expeditiously." Though the conditions were not such as fully to extend it, the work of the resuscitation team was considered by the A.D.M.S. "most excellent"—chiefly in the treatment of haemorrhage and shock and for urgent amputation.[40] The results achieved were such as to impel him to recommend a "special transfusion team" with each division; it should work at the M.D.S. "or even if possible," he adds somewhat naively, "at the A.D.S."

Casualty Clearing Stations. Colonel Barber has put on record that he was informed at the C.C.S. that the results were extraordinarily good, "in fact a record." Some cases were operated upon within 3 hours of being wounded; and the majority were evacuated to Rouen during the next 24 hours by ambulance train. On the experience gained in the battle the D.D.M.S. issued instructions as follows:—

"It has been noted that after prolonged occupation of a sector and consequent improvement at motor posts and A.D.S's there is an increased tendency among medical officers to redress wounds at these posts. Many cases do not require dressing between R.A.P's and C.C.S's. Commanders of medical units will be instructed that only such cases as require additional first aid shall be redressed at motor posts or A.D.S's and that all other cases should be forwarded to M.D.S's, pausing at A.D.S's for inspection by a medical officer who will order the unloading of any patient requiring further first aid. A double circuit (motor post to A.D.S., and A.D.S. to M.D.S.) is only permissible when it is desired to remove large numbers of patients quickly from a shelled area."

These instructions accord with "text book" procedure. Read in conjunction with the recorded views of field ambulance officers, they give further proof of the importance to

---

[40] Of 410 stretcher cases who passed through in 15 hours, between 6 a.m. and 9 p.m., "roughly 30 cases [7·3 per cent.] demanded immediate surgical interference . . . chiefly shattered limbs and other severe cases complicated by haemorrhage and shock."

the medical service at all times of keeping clearly in mind (1) the essential purpose of "evacuation"; (2) the factors and constants involved; and (3) the military and environmental conditions at the moment.

Apart from its considerable military importance, the Battle of Hamel has an interest which derives from a source which is novel to this narrative but which enters to an increasing degree into the history of the A.I.F., as it does also into that of the Great War. This was the entry on the British front, for training and fighting, of formations from the American Expeditionary Force— "A.E.F."[41] In this last phase of the war the experience of the Australian formations in France and that of part of the American Army was closely interwoven; so as to provide, indeed, material for a useful study in national co-operation. A description of the technical machinery of Anglo-American *liaison* on the Western Front is postponed till we reach its consummation in the last great battles of the war.[42] But the first association of the two forces, at Hamel, requires a short note.

The Americans

33rd American Division. At the end of June four companies of the 33rd American Division were attached for training to the 4th Australian —whose personnel they found "an independent, alert, energetic lot of men, and splendid fighters." This American Division was served by two improvised medical units, the 129th and the 130th American "Provisional Field Ambulances," which had been formed by combining two "Field Hospital Companies" with two "Ambulance Companies" from the 108th American "Sanitary Train."

The Americans in Action. Four companies of the 131st and 132nd Regiments, U.S. Infantry, were (as afterwards appeared, against the will of General Pershing)[43] attached for this battle to the 13th, 15th, 42nd, and 43rd Battalions, A.I.F. On the medical side some of the American regimental establishments took part in the action, and a company of American engineers also acted as volunteer stretcher-bearers. Their

---
[41] It may be recalled that the United States declared war on Germany on 6 April, 1917. The account which follows is largely based on *The History of the 33rd Division, A.E.F.*; see, in particular, *Vol. II, pp. 359, 379, 439, and Vol. III, p. 301.*
[42] See *Chapter xxiv.* A brief account of the organisation and methods of the American Medical Services will be found in *Appendix No. 9.*
[43] The story of this misunderstanding will be fully told in *Vol. VI* of the *Australian Official History.* Six other companies were withdrawn at the last moment.

experience in the battle was recorded by the R.M.O. of the 132nd American Infantry Regiment (Lieutenant F. E. Schram) :—[44]

"Reported to Major B. C. Kennedy, Medical Officer attached to the 15th Battalion, 4th Brigade, 4th Australian Division, at R.A.P., 6:00 p.m. as ordered. We moved from there to Battalion Headquarters at 10:30 p.m., accompanied by 5 hospital men and 2 stretcher bearing squads from Field Hospital. Those Field Hospital stretcher bearers were taken with us so as to let the Field Hospital know where our R.A.P. was.

"We moved from Battalion Headquarters about 12:45 a.m., accompanied by these men, to 'No Man's Land.' It had been previously arranged between Colonel MacSharry and Major Kennedy to do a 'hop-over' with the troops, as there was no suitable R.A.P. in their own present trenches without the carrying distance being too great, the idea being to establish themselves in an R.A.P. in the new trenches.

"We lay in 'No Man's Land' until the barrage started; then moved forward with the troops. We attended wounded men in 'No Man's Land' while the barrage was going on. We reached (the German) pear shaped trench with the troops, looked for a suitable dugout and could find none, so we started to do our dressing in the open trench. Cases were brought in rather fast, but we succeeded in dressing them and getting them out in rapid time.

"The carrying distance from our present R.A.P. to the A.D.S. was approximately a mile. To start with, there was no relay post established, but after a few trips a relay post was established midway between the R.A.P. and the A.D.S. We had some difficulty in getting rid of our dress cases. They were not evacuated fast enough. We had difficulty for a while in obtaining sufficient stretchers. Our supply of Thomas splints ran out and could not be replenished for a time. As a consequence we had to use rifles as splints. Of all the cases that I saw and dressed, no tourniquet was used. Pressure with the shell dressings was sufficient to check the haemorrhages.

"We had 12 stretcher bearers from each company, also one man in charge of each stretcher bearing detail from the company, which made 3 stretcher bearing squads. Four Americans were assigned to each bearing section, and these were mixed or distributed with experienced Australians, so that each stretcher squad had at least one American and experienced Australians. It is impossible to use diagnosis tags on each case, because they come in too fast, and to use diagnosis tags would delay them in getting out."

On his experience in this action Lieutenant Schram recommended that

"the present [American] Field packet be replaced by a larger dressing, similar to that used by the British."

The American Field Ambulances. The 65th Brigade group from the 33rd Division remained attached to the Australian

---

[44] For his work on this occasion Lieut. Schram was decorated with the British Military Cross.

Corps throughout July for training and experience, the "A," "B," and "C" sections of the 129th Provisional Field Ambulance being distributed among the Australian divisions in the line (2nd, 3rd, and 5th). Americans were also attached to the field ambulances of the 1st Division in Flanders. Cordial relations were established.

"One of the most important incidents [in July]," says the C.O., 3rd Field Ambulance (Lieut.-Colonel D. D. Cade), "was the arrival in the early part of the month, of a second party of American Medical Officers and personnel, who were sent to us to acquire information as to the method of work in our field medical units. These officers we found to be the best of good fellows, modest, unobtrusive, courteous in decision and very appreciative of any hospitality we endeavoured to show them. What particularly struck me in connection with them was the uniformly fine standard of physique both in officers and men and the keenness and intelligence of their faces. We parted from them with regret."

The D.D.M.S., Australian Corps (Colonel Barber), records that the Americans "did very good work. . . . Officers and men were of fine physique and were very keen to learn."[45] And of the "other ranks" a field ambulance officer (Captain W. J. Newing) writes:—

"After the Battle of Hamel the arrival of a batch of American bearers somewhat relieved the monotony—they were so keen, and were very amusing. I remember the first wounded man they brought in, at 3 a.m.—they woke everyone in the dugout to exhibit their prize. . . ."

As on the wider stage of the general war, events now move swiftly towards the final scenes. Two matters only need hold us here.

After Hamel

The Distance-time Factor in Evacuation. In the course of the fighting during May, June, and July an experimental investigation was initiated by the Officer Commanding the 7th Field Ambulance (Lieut.-Colonel A. M. Wilson) with the purpose of arriving at some exact data that should assist in determining the "medical arrangements" for an action.[46] Medical

---

[45] Col. Barber gained the impression that "the American Medical organisation was not so elastic as the British," and that "their Dental officers had far too much equipment."

[46] The use of "Macpherson's formula" (for deducing from the numbers of wounded expected and the distance to be travelled the amount of transport that would be required, or of calculating from the vehicles available the time that would be occupied) involves the possession of such data. The inventor of the formula (it may be recalled) was Lieut.-Col. W. G. Macpherson (universally known in the British service as "Tiger" Macpherson)—later Sir W. G. Macpher-

officers along the whole chain of posts and stations, from R.A.P. to C.C.S., co-operated in this enquiry into "the distance wounded travel" from front line to M.D.S. It was based on the "Field Medical Card" (*Army Form W. 3118*). He found that at that time a man wounded near the front line had to travel from 24 to 26 miles "before obtaining sufficient operative treatment"; that the time taken between the "advanced ambulance post and the C.C.S. is practically constant, and is about 4 hours" under the circumstances of this test.[47]

Chemical Warfare. Throughout the whole of this period German bombardments with gas-shell were a special symptom of the warfare and of the medical work. After Hamel this became "chronic."

On the night of July 16th-17th the enemy threw about 6,000 gas shells on the 2nd Division's front, producing some 200 casualties; again on July 22nd-23rd about 9,000 shells caused some 450 casualties. In each case a few "Blue Cross" shells were first thrown in order to cause sneezing and deaden the sense of smell, and they were followed by "Yellow Cross" containing dichlorethyl-sulphide ("mustard"). The nights selected were slightly wet, and misty.

"The advantages of night gas-shelling (an R.M.O.[48] comments) are obvious to anyone who has tried to move about with a respirator on in the dark.

"In each bombardment the first cases appeared at the Ambulance (Motor) Post three to four hours after the shelling commenced, and after that a steady stream followed and a few drifted in up to 24-36 hours later. Practically all were mild and showed varying degrees of conjunctivitis, laryngitis, bronchitis and gastric symptoms. Owing to congestion at the Advanced Ambulance Post most were made 'sitters,' but at the M.D.S. many were re-converted into stretcher-cases. At the Advanced Post the cases were given doses of the Soda Bicarb. and also their eyes were washed out with this solution—this treatment was also carried out at the R.A.P's. A few cases, in which the gas was obviously

son, Editor-in-Chief of the *British Official Medical History of the Great War*. His formulae were:
T = time allowed. W = number of sick and wounded.
t = time taken by transport for one journey and return.
M = units of transport required or available.
n = number of patients each unit of transport carries.
To find out the *time required*: To find out the *transport required*:

$$T = \frac{1}{M} \times \frac{W \times t}{n} \qquad M = \frac{1}{T} \times \frac{W \times t}{n}$$

[47] This valuable report is given in *Appendix No. 10*.
[48] Captain R. H. Crisp, R.M.O., 49th Bn.

present in the clothes, had their clothes removed at the Forward Ambulance Post, but the remainder were sent through as quickly as possible to the M.D.S. where they were completely bathed and changed. Theoretically, it would be better to bathe and change the patients at the Advanced Ambulance Post, but practically it is imperative to clear the forward area as soon as possible and only change a few of the worst cases. None of the cases showed any signs of collapse at the forward area, and restorative measures were not used to any great extent."

A much larger proportion of gassed cases were now being classed at M.D.S. as "N.Y.D. Gas" and sent to the special centre. During the period of minor operations from May to the end of July there were evacuated from Australian units in the Fourth Army 10,585 wounded (including 3,417 gassed) and approximately 20,000 sick (chiefly influenza). During the same period the 1st Division in front of Hazebrouck evacuated 2,192 wounded (325 gassed).

The Military Situation: Thrusts on the French Front. Although the months May to July had been comparatively uneventful on the British front, they were far otherwise on the French. Ludendorff had decided, before delivering a final blow at the British, to draw away all French and British reserves. Calculating on the psychological incubus of Paris on French strategy, he thrust on May 27th with terrific force and complete surprise straight for that city, and advanced to the Marne River with a rapidity greater than that of March against the British.[49] The fighting was unsurpassed in its intensity and the losses were tremendous: the exhausted British VIII Corps, which had been brought south to recuperate on part of this quiet front, was almost wiped out. Between the two salients created by this offensive and "Michael" the Germans struck the French again on June 10th, near Noyon, but with less success. Meanwhile American formations were being trained with feverish energy, and a number of them were thrown into the defence in the Marne area. The moment was arriving for the counter-offensive. News of Hamel reached the Supreme War Council at a moment tense with expectation, and was dramatic in its "psychic" uplift. On July 17th Haig informed Rawlinson of his intention that plans should be prepared for an offensive on the Somme. Meanwhile on the 15th the Germans made a last advance and crossed the Marne, but only to fall into the pincer grip of Foch's counter-attack on both flanks on July 18th. This battle was the try-out for the American Army. Its strategic plan envisaged the envelopment of the Germans in the Marne salient, but stubborn defence and some tactical failures defeated this. The Germans withdrew to the line of the Vesle (captured by them on May 27th).

---

[49] The British attached to the French Sixth Army had with them Nos. 37 and 48 Casualty Clearing Stations. In the break-through at Mont Notre Dame British and French casualty clearing stations and their wounded were captured together with their personnel. (*Brit. Off. Med. History, General, Vol. III, p. 276.*) No. 37 barely escaped. With these units were a number of officers of the A.A.M.C., "lent to the D.G., A.M.S., on March 24 by the D.M.S., A.I.F., as a gesture," the circumstances of which will be found on *p. 806*

The Australian Corps has the limelight. The terrible counter-stroke delivered by the French and American Armies on July 18th, on the Marne, made clear the fact that the moment was at hand for a general Allied advance. On July 21st General Rawlinson held a conference attended by the commanders of the Canadian and Australian Corps and a representative of the Tank Corps, and unfolded to these leaders a project, put forward by Haig and himself and provisionally accepted by Foch, for an offensive on the plan of Hamel but on "Army" scale. On July 24th Foch in his turn put forward the project as part of a much wider scheme of Allied offensives. Its scope was subsequently much enlarged, extending to two French armies as well as Rawlinson's.

In order to concentrate the necessary force—a much increased one—on the front of the intended operation, two British divisions of the III Corps relieved the 5th Australian between the Ancre and the Somme and at the same time a brigade of the 4th Australian Division temporarily replaced the 37th French Division south of Villers-Bretonneux. These moves were complete by August 1st. Starting from First Army on July 30th the Canadian Corps came south and by August 4th its brigades were moving into support behind these Australians who would screen them by holding the front line till a few hours before the attack. By August 6th the Canadian, Australian, and III British Corps stood ready for the Battle of Amiens.

CHAPTER XXII

THE BATTLE OF AMIENS

THE events that make the subject-matter of this chapter and the next form a phase in the history of the A.I.F. to which rapid movement gives a peculiar, dramatic interest. The variety of the problems, including those of the medical service, and the nature of the experience, as a kind of summing-up of the military "lessons" of the "Great" War, make this phase one of great military importance. The history of these three months stands out also as having given opportunity in the Australian force for a display of those special aptitudes, and attributes of temperament and character, that have evolved from the physical, social, and economic conditions of Australian national life.

The series of pitched battles and advances, whose medical events are now to be followed, formed part of a vast combined movement by the Allied armies on the Western Front. Beginning with the thrust on the Somme on August 8th (Battle of Amiens), which followed the decisive check to the Germans on the Marne and the French-American counter-offensive on July 18th, the campaign took the form of a rapid series of blows struck at the enemy on various parts of the British front, quickly followed by extensive thrusts by the French and Americans. The attacks by the British culminated in the breaching of the Hindenburg Line and the subsequent rapid (though orderly) retirement of the enemy over his whole front. Associated as they were with equally impressive defeats of the Central Powers and their allies in the other theatres of war—Salonica, Italy, and Palestine—these reverses brought about the military and national collapse of Germany.

The Military Situation: Allied Strategy

In this final phase of the Great War the Australian Corps had—mainly by reason of its own effectiveness—the good fortune to be located in a sector whose strategic importance gave fullest incentive to supreme effort. Also the nature of the terrain over which the fighting took place was peculiarly suited to operations by Australian soldiers.

From the first break-through on August 8th, until October 6th, the day on which—coincident with the first German armistice proposal—it was relieved by the II American Corps, the Australian Corps was engaged in almost continuous fighting. The course of this is followed in three chapters which may advantageously be summarised here.[1]

Chapter XXII describes the evacuation of wounded from the following operations:—
Battle of Amiens (August 8th) and the actions comprised in the immediate exploitation by Fourth Army up the Somme, hinging on Dernancourt, to attain by August 12th the line Lihons, Proyart, Dernancourt; the resumption, in conjunction with Third Army, of this advance on August 22nd, now as part of a wider offensive, followed by a German retire-

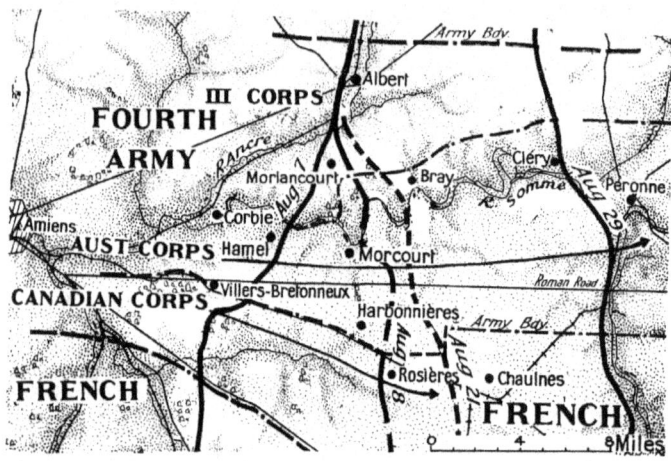

The Fourth Army's advance, Aug. 1918

ment which brought the front on August 29th to the "Line of the Somme"; the tactical manoeuvrings to dislodge the enemy from his positions including the Battle of Mont St. Quentin and Capture of Péronne (August 30th-September 2nd); and the subsequent retreat, begun

[1] In the *Report of the Battles Nomenclature Committee* the British battles are listed as follows: Those in which the Australian Corps took part are shown in italic type. ADVANCE IN PICARDY (8 Aug.-3 Sept.)—*Battle of Amiens* (8-11 Aug.) 1st, 2nd, 3rd, 4th and 5th Divs.; Battle of Albert (21-23 Aug.) 1st, 3rd 4th and 5th Divs.; *Capture of Chuignes* (23 Aug.); *Second Battle of Bapaume* (31 Aug.-3 Sept.) 2nd, 3rd, and 5th Divs.; *Capture of Mont St. Quentin* (31 Aug.-2 Sept.) 2nd Div.; *Occupation of Péronne* (1-2 Sept.) 5th Div. BREAKING OF THE HINDENBURG LINE (26 Aug.-12 Oct.)—Battle of the Scarpe (26-30 Aug.); Battle of Drocourt-Quéant Line (2-3 Sept.); Battle of Havrincourt (12 Sept.); *Battle of Epéhy* (18 Sept.) 1st and 4th Divs.; Battle of Canal du Nord (27 Sept.-1 Oct.); *Battle of St. Quentin Canal* (29 Sept.-2 Oct.) 2nd, 3rd and 5th Divs.; *Capture of Bellicourt Tunnel Defences* (29 Sept.-2 Oct.) 5th Div.; *Battle of Beaurevoir Line* (3-5 Oct.) 2nd Div.; Battle of Cambrai (8-9 Oct.). This nomenclature, however, has often been criticised.

by the enemy on September 4th, to the outer defences of the Hindenburg Line. *Chapter XXIII* deals with the part played by the Australian Corps in the capture of the outer defences and subsequent breaking of this line of defence, now as part of a general advance over the whole Allied front; and *Chapter XXIV* with the operations of the Australian Corps in conjunction with the 27th and 30th American Divisions (September 18th-October 6th), in the assaults on the main Hindenburg Line.

The evacuation of wounded and other activities of the medical service during these events very exactly reflected the tactical problems: first, that of the great "set-piece" Battle of Amiens; next of the scattered individual actions of the advance up the Somme; then, of the chase across the wilderness of the old French battlefield of the Somme and of "Alberich" to the Hindenburg Line; and finally of the bitter, highly skilled hand-to-hand fighting and "mopping up" that helped to loose the German grip from the lands of France.

For the Australian Corps the great battle of August 8th-11th was the logical and deliberate outcome of Hamel. But if, as for that battle its tactics largely came from Cambrai, its technique was built on that of the Battle of Messines. From Cambrai came secrecy, surprise bombardment, and the tanks, but the method of advance by "leap-frog" reflected Messines, to be achieved, however, with exactitude and success unapproached in that expensive action. And no one, who should have occasion to study the files and war diaries that record the preparations by the Australian force for the two battles, can fail to discern a strong family likeness in the precision and particularity of the orders, and the lucidity of the instructions that diffused the knowledge of task, place, and time-relations through each formation and unit down to each individual concerned. Such precise instructions could now safely be given since the units had sufficient experience to allow themselves freedom of interpretation, if necessary.

Battle of Amiens: genesis and kinships

The "medical arrangements" for the Battle of Amiens present the same qualities of foresight, attention to detail, and co-ordinated action as was noted in the arrangements by A.D.M.S., 3rd Division, for the Battle of Messines. The medical circumstances of the two battles, however, differed very greatly by reason of the manner in which the "Michael" attack had driven the casualty clearing stations to the distant rear.

When, on and after July 24th, Foch adopted and extended Haig's plan of an offensive on the Somme, neither of them foresaw the consequences that actually came through its overpowering success. The Battle of Amiens developed into a strategic offensive, drawing into its purpose, first, other British Armies, and then the whole Allied front.[2] The tactical plan for the battle provided for an advance by the Fourth British and First French Armies, the British starting a few hours earlier than their allies. The British advance would be in three stages leading to a final objective, comprising the old outer defence line of Amiens, and including the whole zone occupied by the German artillery. It involved the Fourth Army front[3] from the Luce to the Ancre, some eleven miles. The ensuring of secrecy was the more difficult since an important feature of the fight was the use of tanks in numbers unprecedented. It was achieved by devices that imposed formidable problems on the administrative departments, in particular, as always, on the medical service.[4] But in the Australian Corps at least there was no shadow of discrimination against the medical administrative officers. As responsible staff officers, Colonel Barber and his A.D's.M.S. were conversant from the beginning with every aspect of the plans which should involve the medical service.[5]

Tactics and Order of Battle: Fourth Army

Order of Battle: Fourth Army. The Fourth Army order of battle placed the Canadian Corps on the right opposite Hangard and Marcelcave, and the Australian in the centre, opposite Warfusée, with its left on the Somme. North of the river the 58th and 18th Divisions of III Corps would protect the left flank of the Australian Corps by advancing up the river on a frontage that should include the Chipilly peninsula, which protruded into the Australian front. On the right of the Canadian Corps the French First Army would launch its attack 45 minutes after the British. The several fronts and the three objectives, designated (from rear forward) the "Green," "Red," and "Blue Lines," are shown in the sketch map. "Zero" hour was fixed at 4.20 a.m. Further tactical details are given in connection with the preparations by the Australian Corps.

---

[2] It is generally agreed that a factor in the strategic failure of the German offensive was Ludendorff's inability to inhibit the emotive impulse to exploit a great tactical success. This failure was not unnatural in view of the fact that the extraordinary initial success of the German offensives was brought about by exploitation of the method of unrestricted advance along lines of least resistance. It fell to Haig to exercise the inhibiting influence, and to impose on Foch the halt of Aug. 12 to 20 for the development of a strategic plan before a further advance should begin.

[3] On Aug. 8 the composition of the Fourth Army was:—
Cavalry Corps: 1st, 2nd, and 3rd Cavalry Divisions.
III British Corps: 12th, 18th, 47th, and 58th Divisions, and 130th and 131st Infantry Regiments of 33rd American Division.
Canadian Corps: 1st, 2nd, 3rd, and 4th Canadian Divisions.
Australian Corps: 1st, 2nd, 3rd, 4th, and 5th Australian Divisions, and (from Aug. 9) 131st American Infantry.
Reserve: 17th, 32nd, and 63rd British Divisions.

[4] For a peculiarly interesting account of these, see *Secret Service*, by Major-Gen. Sir George Aston.

[5] For example, in the 4th Division the A.D.M.S. was informed of the situation at a conference at divisional headquarters on Aug. 1, when "the G.O.C. (Major-Gen. MacLagan) informed the Staff of the proposed offensive, and sketched his plan of operations." By way of contrast, see *Vol. I, Chapters vii and xiv.*

The technique as well as the tactics of this battle were in a great measure those devised by the Australian Corps for Hamel.

The Canadian Corps advanced on a three-, the Australian Corps on a two-divisional front. Each Australian division had two brigades in line.

The Australian Corps

On the Australian front the first objective ("Green" line)—roughly the enemy field-gun positions, about 3,000 yards from the start—was to be attained at 6.43 a.m.; the second, it was hoped, about 10.20. A short "hurricane" barrage (with a field-gun to every 16 yards) would be followed by the tanks and infantry at about 100 yards' distance. The 2nd and 3rd Divisions assisted by tanks would carry the advance to the "Green" line. Moving up immediately behind

Fourth Army's objectives, Aug. 8

this wave, and passing through it on the "Green" line at 8.20 a.m., the 5th and 4th Divisions would make for the "Red" line, using methods, rather, of open warfare. Successful occupation of the "Red" line would be "exploited" by advancing the two reserve brigades of these divisions to the "Blue" line[6]—the old Amiens defences. The greatest depth of the advance to the "Blue" line on the Australian Corps front would be six miles.

---

[6] For this purpose the 1st Brigade of the 1st Division, which was sent from Flanders to act as reserve, was specially attached to the 4th Division whose 13th Brigade was covering the assembly of the Canadians.

By G.H.Q. and Fourth Army. It is outside the scope of this narrative to examine the whole provision made by G.H.Q. and D.M.S., Fourth Army, and throughout this narrative of the advance the only casualty clearing stations whose moves will be described are those used by the Australian Corps.[7] For reasons doubtless of secrecy, the D.M.S., Fourth Army was informed of the impending operations only on August 6th. On the 7th over 4,000 sick were cleared from the C.C.S. groups to Abbeville and Rouen Base.[8] Evacuation from the Australian Corps was based on the 20th and 61st British Casualty Clearing Stations at Vignacourt, clearing thereto partly by light railway from Vecquemont, partly by M.A.C. After much importunity "in view of the distance from C.C.S." an additional convoy—the 11th—was attached to the Corps during the advance. On August 10th the 53rd and 55th C.C.S's opened at Vecquemont for the Australian Corps.

Medical Arrangements for the Battle of Amiens

By D.D.M.S., Australian Corps. Colonel Barber held several formal conferences[9] with his A.D's.M.S. and M.A.C. commanders at which major matters of policy were decided. The A.D's.M.S. conferred both formally and informally with their ambulance commanders. "Medical Instructions" for the battle were issued by the D.D.M.S. on August 4th, and corresponding "instructions" by the A.D's.M.S. Those of Colonel Barber were based, in accordance with his administrative methods, very closely on Corps operation orders and on his own general instructions and standing orders regarding procedure.

"D.D.M.S. Medical Instruction No. 35" issued "in accordance with Australian Corps battle instructions No. 1" indicated the disposition of the main and advanced dressing stations and

---

[7] The D.M.S., Fourth Army, had 12 casualty clearing stations for this advance, placed at Crouy, Longpré, Pernois, St. Riquier, and Vignacourt. No. 14 Stationary Hospital was at Pont Remy. In addition there were 6 motor ambulance convoys and 3 advanced depots of medical stores. During the first week no less than 48 surgical teams from L. of C. and other Armies, including a number from the Australian General Hospitals, and 64 additional Army Nursing Sisters, were attached to the C.C.S's of Fourth Army. Among the nurses were many members of the A.A.N.S., who at this time were being extensively used in the Q.A.I.M.N.S. In this connection, see *Vol. III.*

[8] This would be too late for the enemy to take advantage of information of this clearance. A feature of the "camouflage" was the earlier transfer, northwards to Second Army, of the 1st and 4th Canadian Casualty Clearing Stations.

[9] The D.D.M.S. and his A.D's.M.S. were included in all General Staff conferences in which medical matters were directly involved.

divisional collecting stations in each sector, (1) on "Y/Z" night;[10] (2) after capture of the "Green" line; and (3) after that of the "Red" line; and also the jumping-off position for the respective ambulances allotted for each duty at "zero" hour. In order that the Assistant Directors of Medical Services of the four divisions concerned might be free to use which ambulance they chose for the various duties, the ambulances of each division were denominated in Colonel Barber's order "X," "Y," and "Z."

As this was the most important and successful, and also—if it may so be termed—the most "sophisticated" battle in which the Australian force took part, the arrangements and instructions of the D.D.M.S., Australian Corps, and of the A.D.M.S. of a Division are given in *Appendix No. 3*, as typical of Australian Corps methods at the acme of its efficiency. With the

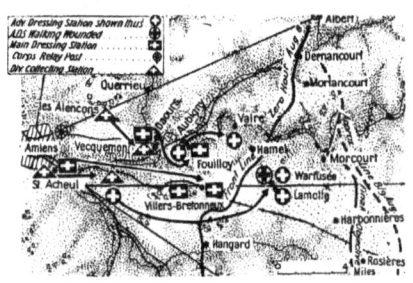

Leap-frogging of Field Ambulances, Battle of Amiens, Aug. 8-9

help of some general notes on the problem it will be possible, even for those untrained in military terminology, to follow the steps taken to translate the details of the plan for evacuation of casualties into exact orders defining the duties of all concerned, from highest to lowest.

The Medical Technique. The military technique of this battle was based on the "leap-frog"; and this depended on the exact *co-ordination of divisional action*. The two elements were reflected in the medical plans.

The "Leap-frog." The technique of a leap-frog in the medical services was an improvement on the instructions given in *Field Service Regulations, 1914*, which may be summarised thus:—

A tent sub-division may be sent forward to form an A.D.S. where

---

[10] That is, the night before zero day ("Z"). "Y" was the day before zero day.

seriously wounded are brought to the ambulance waggons. The rest of the tent divisions remain in rear as a link between the A.D.S. and the Clearing Hospital, or may be sent forward to expand the A.D.S. In the new procedure the field ambulance running the M.D.S. remained at work until its task was taken over by the reserve ambulance from the rear, which passed over it and occupied the position of the A.D.S. in front as a new M.D.S., the A.D.S. moving on; or, as more often, passed over both M.D.S. and A.D.S. to the M.L.P. to form a new A.D.S., the unit which had been "A.D.S." remaining as the new "M.D.S."[11]

First Method Before Leapfrog	No.3 F.Amb. (Res)	No.2 F.Amb.	No.1 F.Amb.	No.1 F.Amb.		
After Leapfrog		No.2 F.Amb. (Res)	No.3 F.Amb.	No.1 F.Amb.	No.1 F.Amb.	
Second Method Before Leapfrog	No.3 F.A. (Res)	No.2 F.Amb.	No.1 F.Amb.	No.1 F.Amb.		
After Leapfrog		No.2 F.Amb. (Res)	No.1 F.Amb.	No.3 F.Amb.	No.3 F.Amb.	

Two methods of "leap-frogging"

Co-ordination. The A.D's.M.S. arranged their plans to meet two alternatives—(1) complete success with few casualties but involving the necessity for rapid advance both of the A.D.S. and motor loading posts, to keep pace with the bearer carry, and of the M.D.S., to avoid undue strain on the divisional ambulance transport; (2) comparative failure, with heavy casualties, in which case all the medical resources of both the "Green" and the "Red Line" divisions in the sector concerned must co-operate to ensure effective evacuation. At a conference at Corps Headquarters between the D.D.M.S. and his A.D's.M.S. it was agreed that this dual purpose would be served by treating

---

[11] A somewhat similar procedure was adopted to secure "continuous action" in the casualty clearing stations during the advance. In the sketch maps, unless otherwise indicated, the moves shown are of stations, not of units.

each *sector* as a single administrative area for the purpose of evacuation, so that in each half of the front the combined resources of the two divisions "in tandem" would be used as one.[12] This would involve the pooling of 162 four-men bearer squads,[13] 18 horsed-ambulance waggons, and 12 Ford and 30 Sunbeam motor ambulances. It would further involve special arrangements for control and direction in various phases of the battle. Such a plan, original in conception, and ambitious in its demand alike on administration and executive, required for its success a very high degree of efficiency and co-ordination of effort in every element in the machinery of evacuation. The adoption of the scheme indeed reflected, not only the confidence of the administrative officers (at this stage of the war) in their ability to organise and give effect to it, but also their presumption of a corresponding ability in every unit, and every individual in the chain, from regimental stretcher-bearer to motor ambulance convoy. These were relied on not only to carry out their part in the working of the plan exactly and punctually, but also to adjust that part as required to the vicissitudes of battle. This confidence and battle skill, applied in the wider spheres of warfare, and operating with all the resources of science and human industrial organisation, made the working of a military *unit of action,* such as was the Australian Corps, the most stupendous example of concerted energy that the world had yet seen.

The Corps Resources for Medical Transport. The ambulance transport available to the D.D.M.S. comprised 77 cars of the 3rd and 11th M.A.C., distributed equally to the right and left sectors for evacuation from M.D.S. to C.C.S.; and 24 'buses and lorries (supplied by Army) to evacuate "walking wounded" as sitting cases either direct from A.D.S., or from the "Corps relay posts."

Divisional Arrangements and Dispositions. For the "Green Line" casualties, evacuation was based on the existing divisional schemes of clearance. The field ambulances of the leapfrogging divisions were kept closed, in readiness to move. The arrangements for the two sectors differed in the method adopted

---

[12] 2nd Division would combine with 5th, and 3rd with 4th.
[13] The field ambulances were at this time almost fully up to establishment.

by the respective A.D's.M.S. for the transfer of control in the successive phases of the advance. In the right sector the unit with the "leap-frogging" division was made responsible for evacuation only as far back as the "Green Line," whereas on the left it automatically took over evacuation to the main dressing station. Arrangements for the successive movements of advanced dressing station, and corresponding moves forward of main dressing station, are clearly set out in the operation orders. These operations provided a forceful illustration of the axiom noted in these pages—that in a great measure evacuation pivoted on the *A.D.S.;* the position of this station, and of the associated advanced dressing station for "walking wounded," in relation to the *Motor Loading Posts,* and the position of these latter with respect to the *R.A.P's*, were by far the most important factors in a successful divisional clearance.

A useful innovation, intended to promote *liaison* between the field ambulances and the battalions, was the attachment to each brigade in the line of an experienced senior officer from the ambulance that was responsible for the forward evacuation —R.A.P. to A.D.S.

Exact arrangements were made by Colonel Barber and the A.D's.M.S. for the supply of equipment, medical stores, water, food, and "comforts."[14] The "Advanced Depots" for the Australian and Canadian Corps were situated at Vignacourt and Crouy respectively.

A serious last-minute hitch threatened in the adjustment of boundaries between the Australian and Canadian Corps.

"Two days before the battle it was proposed that the boundary of the Canadian Corps on our right should include the Amiens-Villers-Bretonneux road. As the whole of the Australian Medical Posts had been carefully prepared on the southern side of the road, this meant the Australian Corps would, on extremely short notice, have to find fresh posts on the Northern side of the road, where there was no cover of any description. After much argument the Australian Corps was allowed to retain these posts, which was fortunate, as otherwise the whole of the arrangements would have been disorganised."[15]

The Battle—August 8. The first objective was everywhere reached

---

[14] The forward depot of the Australian Red Cross Society at Amiens was in advance of any other Red Cross depot, and served a definite and important purpose in promoting humane alleviation.
[15] Colonel Barber's memorandum.

8th Aug., 1918]   THE BATTLE OF AMIENS   689

by 6.20,[16] in a dense mist which helped more than hindered the advance. At 8 a.m. the mist quickly rose and the sun came out upon a beautiful summer's day. Until then the 2nd and 3rd Australian Divisions had carried forward the Australian advance. Now, at 8.20, the 4th and 5th, with supporting tanks, leap-frogged them to reach the second main objective. The III Corps had to face the additional task of recapturing ground lost on the preceding days; and its consequent failure to capture the Chipilly spur involved the left (4th) brigade of the 4th Australian Division, advancing along the Somme in the attack on the "Red Line," in considerable casualties from German batteries emplaced high on the ridge, and firing from its flank and rear. All save three of its tanks were put out of action, and it was compelled to throw out a defensive flank along the Somme. Before noon, however, the leading brigades of the 4th and 5th Divisions respectively were in the final "Blue Line," with patrols beyond.

From time to time there has been occasion to describe in these pages military events that held little of the pomp and circumstance of old-time war. The following, from the history of the 5th Australian Division,[17] describes a scene of a different kind on the 15th Brigade front shortly before the "Red Line" was reached.

"At half-past nine a great victory was clearly in sight. By this time, too, the splendid work of the road-making troops had borne full fruit, and, as the attack progressed, the most wonderful panorama of open warfare that the world had yet seen was disclosed to the observers. Up the long main road from Warfusée-Abancourt came a rapid stream of transport of all descriptions. Armoured cars racing after the infantry, cavalry streaming forward to play its part in the wonderful drama that was afoot, field guns galloping up, motor ambulances for casualties, motor lorries with supplies, and humbler transport with water, food, and engineering material—all pressed on and on, each with its appointed task and each straining every nerve to do it thoroughly and quickly. Tanks of all sizes and capacities were ploughing imperturbably along across country with the ludicrous look of anything that is in a hurry. Overhead the sky was thick with the aeroplanes of two nations, and the droning of their engines and the frequent patter of their machine-guns made the air as troubled as the earth. Ahead were the wonderful fighting tanks that had borne the brunt of the advance so far, and, just behind them, the long indomitable lines of infantry. But they were no longer to have pride of place. Soon the armoured cars went dashing through them; soon the fan-spread cavalry was circling out in front, rounding up bewildered prisoners, turning the enemy disorder into chaos. There in all its terrible splendour was yet another altar of the far-flung temple of Mars. . . .

"The immediate effect of the forward patrolling of the armoured cars and cavalry was to reduce still further the opposition to the in-

---

[16] The tactical schemes for the Canadian and III British Corps were more complicated than those of the Australian Corps, each having to provide protection for a flank.

[17] *The Story of the Fifth Australian Division*, by Captain A. D. Ellis, *p. 332*.

fantry. On the 15th Brigade front the red line was reached before half-past ten. Bayonvillers had provided no serious obstacle, the front line troops skirting to north and south of it and leaving to the 58th Battalion the task of mopping it up. This was accomplished without difficulty and by 2 p.m. a forward Y.M.C.A. centre was established in the village!"

Medical Part in the Operation. With minor exceptions, evacuation of casualties and movements of medical units went "according to plan." Inevitably some overlapping occurred at the boundaries of sectors. On the right, where the Canadian Corps joined the Australian, misdirection at a road junction brought about a very considerable influx of Canadian casualties to the 5th Australian Division. Prompt action was taken by the D.D.M.S. and mention is made of the occurrence only because it is almost the only significant departure from plan of which record can be found. The only "hold-ups" and "congestion" that occurred were brought about by the great distance to the casualty clearing stations. This necessitated in some instances the use of the divisional transport between M.D.S. and C.C.S., to the detriment of "forward" evacuation.

The main dressing station at St. Acheul, which, Colonel Barber notes, was "admirably planned and organised by Lieut.-Colonel H. L. St. Vincent Welch of the 6th Field Ambulance," passed through 600 casualties.[18] That of the 11th and 12th Field Ambulances at N.4.c.9.2. (near Bussy-Daours) passed through 300 wounded.

The plan whereby the bearers were pooled in each sector and allocated to battalions and brigades worked well. The vital arrangements for supplies, based on adequate and suitably distributed corps and divisional "dumps" and exact system of "demand," ensured not only that all demands were met during the course of the operation, but that the units, which passed automatically into reserve on the fulfilment of their special part, were promptly replenished and in a position to move forward at once on any task allotted to them in the exploitation of the success.

Liaison. In the problem of evacuation one factor, which in

---

[18] Comprising 400 stretcher cases (British and Australian), 100 walking wounded, and 100 prisoners of war (mostly stretchers). The casualties treated in the Australian units· included (Col. Barber states) "250 wounded Canadians who had drifted into our sector and 1,400 gassed Frenchmen."

this battle may appropriately be called the "essence of the contract," is revealed in the detailed reports of A.D's.M.S. and field ambulance commanders. The manner in which the adjustments were made from hour to hour to meet the fluctuations of the battle is such as causes surprise and compels admiration. Co-operation, which was as effective as in the combatant branches, was attained partly through the perfection reached by the "Signals" branch of the Engineers, with their field telephone; partly by the allotment of *liaison* personnel and a free use of "runners"; but chiefly through the fact that the medical service was accepted throughout as part of the essential machinery of war.

The following epitome of "remarks" by the A.D.M.S., 4th Division (Colonel K. Smith) are pertinent:—

1. All arrangements worked splendidly.

2. The placing of a senior Medical Officer at each Brigade H.Q. to act as *Liaison* Officer . . . will now be carried out in all future operations of this Division.

3. The only difficulty in the evacuation of casualties was caused by the great distance of the C.C. Stations.

4. These operations emphasised the necessity for the closest *liaison* between the "G" Branch and the A.D.M.S.

5. Ford Ambulance cars again proved their superiority for forward work.

6. Horse ambulances are too slow, and at least two should be replaced by Ford ambulance cars.

7. The installation of a telephone at the A.D.S. would have been an improvement—the officer in charge of evacuation being located there.

8. The greatest credit is due to the A.A.M.C. personnel of both Divisions in the sector for the manner in which each one carried out his allotted task.

A sector of the German front had been broken in this attack in a most complete and annihilating fashion—the moral effect of the battle has been recorded for all time by Ludendorff. Attacking south of the Canadians, the French extended the breach. But the High Commands, Allied and British, were not prepared fully to exploit so unexpected a success, and the British thrusts during the next four days were purely local.

The Thrust Continued: Aug. 9-20

On August 9th-10th the Canadian Corps continued the main advance, with the Australian swinging forward on its flank; and north of the

Somme the American 131st Regiment, acting under the British III Corps, attacked and captured the Chipilly ridge, and, advancing through Gressaire Wood, relieved the menace on the left. The 1st Australian Division had reached Corbie and Villers-Bretonneux on the 8th, its field ambulances accompanying their respective brigades. Though hurried orders reached its battalions as they marched towards Harbonnières on the morning of the 9th, it was found impossible to get them to the front in time to advance with the Canadians, but the 5th Division, which was still in excellent fighting condition, continued the advance towards Rosières, and met strong resistance. At midday the 1st Division took up the running, its 2nd Brigade pushing forward on the right of the corps sector, with part of the 2nd Division on its left. Advancing with tanks but without artillery support, the 2nd Brigade was held up on the wooded slopes before the hills screening the ruined village of Lihons. Here at a few thousand yards' range it came under fire of German batteries. Within a quarter of an hour the supporting tanks were disabled, but the position was captured by the method of open infantry advance in rushes. During the next two days the 1st and 3rd Brigades were thrown in; by August 11th Lihons and the adjoining heights had been taken, and the line lay upon the old cratered and much-trenched ground of the Somme battles of 1916. Next day Proyart was seized. The River Somme had proved—as always—a bad boundary, and from August 12th to 20th a special "Australian Corps Liaison Force"—roughly a division—of American and Australian troops commanded by Brigadier-General E. A. Wisdom took over the front north of it.[19] On August 12th the Canadians left to return to Third Army, their front being taken over by the French. The Australian Corps, including one British division, extended from north of the Somme near Bray to Lihons. For a week the line rested, awaiting the momentous order that should initiate a more general advance of the Allies. The divisions were in turn relieved and with them the divisional medical units, which were re-equipped and the bearer divisions rested.

Medical Events: Aug. 9–22

During this stage of the advance up the Somme, and increasingly as it progressed, the problems of evacuation centred in the collection of casualties to the regimental aid-posts, and their clearance from dressing to casualty clearing stations. The paralysis that had settled on the higher Medical Direction as a result of the German break-through in March, and the fear of further capture of casualty clearing stations, were too complete to be promptly resolved even by so signal a sign as that of August 8th, and the field ambulances "dragged at each remove a lengthening chain" of transport circuits which linked them with these units. On August 9th-10th the M.D.S's for the right and left sectors were moved up to the "White Château"

---

[19] The force was composed of the 13th Aust. Inf. Bde., and the 131st American Inf. Regt. (66th Brigade), with British artillery and the necessary auxiliary troops.

75. BEARERS OF A 5TH DIVISION FIELD AMBULANCE WAITING NEAR WARFUSÉE FOR THE SECOND STAGE OF THE INFANTRY'S ADVANCE, ABOUT 8.20 A.M. ON 8TH AUGUST, 1918

Note the tank tracks in the foreground. One of the fighting tanks is seen in the background.

Aust. War Memorial Official Photo. No. E2863.

76. Bearers of the 7th Field Ambulance attached to the 25th Battalion returning to Vauvillers close behind the front line, after the fighting on 10th-11th August, 1918

Aust. War Memorial Official Photo. No. E2916.

To face p. 693.

at Villers-Bretonneux and to Fouilloy respectively, after the 11th to function as gas centres. The A.D.S's had been advanced to Warfusée-Abancourt—"combined W.W.D.S. and stretcher cases"—and Lamotte (right) and near Hamel (left). The Corps relay posts were pushed up and No. 3 M.A.C. Headquarters advanced to Corbie. On August 12th by order of the D.D.M.S. the "pooling" of transport ceased—to be resumed if necessary "by mutual arrangement between the A.D's.M.S. concerned."

On August 10th Nos. 53 and 55 C.C.S's moved up to Vecquemont. The provision thus made appeared however to the Australian Deputy-Director quite inadequate and, to meet the chance of heavy casualties in an immediate advance, he formed a reserve of divisional cars to clear back from M.D.S. and secured accommodation between Les Alençons and Amiens for 1,500 patients.[20]

With the Liaison Force. During the nine days in which the Liaison Force existed, an Australian medical officer (Lieut.-Colonel R. W. Chambers) acted as its A.D.M.S., and Major T. C. C. Evans, A.A.M.C., as D.A.D.M.S. The 13th Australian Field Ambulance and 129th American "Provisional" Field Ambulance were attached to the force, and a new line of evacuation was established north of the Somme. Later this became the main route of clearance from the Australian Corps front.

Two features of his brief administration to which Colonel Chambers makes particular reference in his war diary have a bearing on matters of first-rate military importance.

Inspecting the lines of American battalions he found the military officers so oblivious to the need for sanitation that he was constrained to assert the authority of the regimental medical officers by personal appeal to the battalion commanders. The interest of this episode lies in its striking reminiscence of the early history of the Australian forces.[21]

The A.D.M.S. intervened, also, to check the flow through the A.D.S. of American soldiers evacuated as "gas," but without showing any symptoms of injury. The immediate cause of the needless wastage he discerned in a panicky attitude towards the dangers of "gassing" on the part of both medical officers and combatants, which was reflected in a divisional order to the effect that any man who reported

---
[20] This was not required, the casualties being far less than were expected.
[21] See, in particular, *Vol. I, pp. 230, 253*.

that he was gassed must be evacuated whether he showed any symptoms or not.[22] A revision of the order was arranged.

In preparation for open warfare Colonel Barber on August 12th issued a circular memorandum (No. M.2/8) replacing in some respects "Medical Instruction" No. 10 of April 10th. It outlined the practice to be followed in opening and closing main and advanced dressing stations.[23] These memoranda formed the basis of the Divisional arrangements made during the subsequent advance up to the Somme and thence to the Hindenburg Line.

The subjoined table shows the casualties sustained by the Corps between August 8th and 21st.

Date	1st Div. Gassed	1st Div. Wd.	2nd Div. Gassed	2nd Div. Wd.	3rd Div. Gassed	3rd Div. Wd.	4th Div. Gassed	4th Div. Wd.	5th Div. Gassed	5th Div. Wd.
8th Aug.	—	15	3	467	8	385	12	493	4	343
9th ,,	5	454	—	271	2	10	4	43	6	259
10th ,,	25	520	4	62	47	115	3	54	1	29
11th ,,	55	223	11	261	22	120	6	66	—	5
12th ,,	9	57	4	22	12	190	4	41	2	4
TOTAL	94	1,269	22	1,083	91	820	29	697	13	640
13th to 21st Aug.	29	126	16	136	11	90	39	264	7	166
TOTAL 8th-21st Aug.	123	1,395	38	1,219	102	910	68	961	20	806

GRAND TOTAL = 5,642.

Between 6 a.m. on the 8th and 6 a.m. on the 11th August nearly 16,000 British and 2,000 German wounded were received into the casualty clearing stations of Fourth Army.

After a short interval there began the series of hammer-strokes that were to end the war. The interval was due to the insistence of Haig. While Foch desired that an effort be made to repeat at once on the same part of the front the success of August 8th, Haig held that the local resistance was now too strong, and that he should strike elsewhere. His plan was

The Allied Strategy: Foch and Haig

---

[22] This extreme respect for "gas" by American units is the subject of comment in Australian medical war diaries. The reason, it would seem, is to be found partly in the excessive emphasis laid on the matter of "gas defence"; but more in the reaction of the unsophisticated soldier to the menace of the unknown. The matter is of first-rate importance in its bearing on the future of warfare. (*See Vol. III.*)

[23] Though issued by Corps it embodied and co-ordinated the experiences and views of the Divisional Directors. It is reproduced in *Appendix No. 3*.

accepted; the stroke was to be followed as soon as possible by other offensives by British, French, American, and Italian Armies.

The British Thrusts: August 21st-September 3rd. The first of this series of actions (Battle of Albert, August 21st-23rd) was undertaken by Third and Fourth Armies. The former attacked on a 9-mile front north of the Ancre, and penetrated deeply. On the 22nd the attack was widened, Albert being taken, and spread to Fourth Army, involving the 3rd Australian Division north of the Somme. On the 23rd it became an attack on a front of 33 miles extending southwards to the junction with the French at Lihons. This was followed by the "Second Battle of Bapaume" (Third and Fourth Armies, August 31st-September 3rd), which traversed the old battle-ground of the Somme, and the Battle of the Scarpe (Third Army, August 26th-30th), which threw the Third Army against the Hindenburg Line. The Germans had retired from the Lys salient, Fifth and Second Armies following; and an advance on September 2nd-3rd took First Army to within assaulting distance of the "Wotan Line" from Quéant to Drocourt, south-west of Lens. In the meantime the Fourth Army had crowned its extraordinarily effective operations by turning the flank of the strong German position on the Somme line and forcing its abandonment.

The activities of the Australian Corps in these operations comprised two major actions at the beginning and end of the phase, respectively; and in the interval a series of more or less disconnected attacks by smaller forces as the Army advanced along the river. Some of these operations were manoeuvres against villages situated within the re-entrant curves that marked the west-east course of the river. An important factor in the fighting, as in the work of the medical service, was the destruction of the bridges, in the repair of which the Australian engineers made some admirable achievements. The features of these operations which influenced most the problems of evacuation must be summarised briefly.

Advance up the Somme: The Australian Corps

Battle of Albert. On August 22nd in conjunction with the Third British Army the 3rd Australian Division attacked north of the Somme in the region of Bray. The outstanding success of the 3rd permitted the retention of heights on the northern bank safeguarding the flank for the attack in force south of the river on the 23rd. This attack—the Battle of Chuignes—was delivered on a frontage of 6,000 yards by the 1st Australian Division and a brigade of the 32nd British. An advance of two miles was made and 3,000 prisoners were captured. The Germans could not, however, be rushed into further retreat. They held on until August 29th, when they fell back to the line of the Somme west and south of Péronne, closely followed by the 5th and 2nd Divisions.

"*Line of the Somme.*" The next stand was made on the line of the Somme where it turns abruptly south, the same line being continued to the north by the Canal du Nord. Here the right and centre of the Australian Corps were for the moment brought to a complete stop, first, by the destruction of the bridges across the marshy southward stretch of the river; second, by the immense tactical strength of the right-angled bend in the vicinity of Péronne. These features of the terrain had important repercussion on the problem of evacuation. Successful action by the 3rd Division on August 30th north of the Somme in the neighbourhood of Cléry, however, led to enemy retirement on Mont

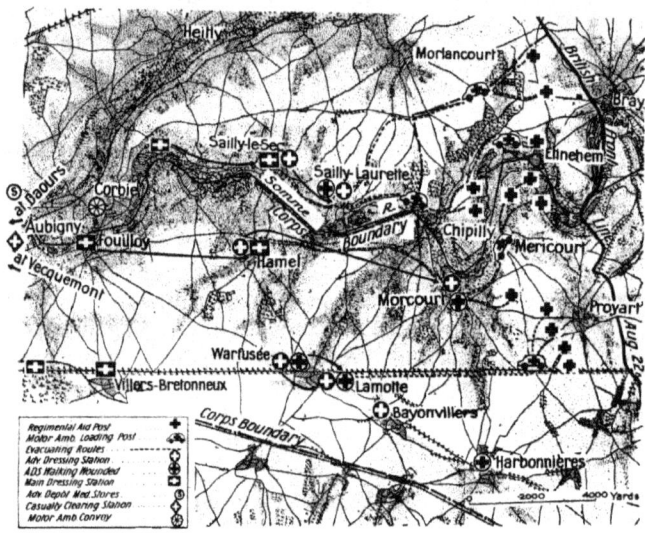

Scheme of Evacuation, Aug. 22, showing moves of Field Ambulances since Aug. 10

St. Quentin and Péronne. That night the river was crossed at Feuilleres by the 2nd Division, which, in three days of furious and brilliant fighting, completely carried the height of Mont St. Quentin, at the angle of the river, commanding Péronne, while that town was captured by the 5th Division on September 1st-4th by fierce hand-to-hand fighting—a real "soldiers' battle." This turned the flank of the Somme line.

Retreat to the Hindenburg Line. On September 5th the enemy in this sector retired—as in "Alberich"—fighting a strong rearguard action (though on a much more hurriedly prepared plan) against brigade advanced guards. By the middle of the second week in September his rearguards had reached without much hurt the forward defences of the Hindenburg Line—that is to say, the old British front lines against which had been launched on March 21st his great offensive against the Fifth Army.

The methods adopted for the evacuation of casualties, during the operations just outlined, conformed closely to the course of the fighting. It is unnecessary to describe in detail the special arrangements made for each phase in the advance. The series of maps shows the position of the several posts, stations, and routes of evacuation in the most important actions; and, for the reader who has studied the evolution of the problem of evacuation in the previous chapters, it will not be difficult to follow these. Generally speaking, the advance up the Somme basin was made on a two-divisional front, each division having in the later stages, with a view to resting the troops, only one brigade in the front line. Medical units progressed either by moving up direct to relieve the medical units immediately ahead of them, or by leap-frogging over them.[24]

Advance up the Somme: Medical Events

In clearance the crucial factor was transport. Not only was the distance from loading post to M.D.S. and even to A.D.S. often considerable, but the fact that the brigades were operating on unusually wide frontages made it necessary for transport to move laterally as well as from front to rear. In these circumstances the effective use of the M.A.C. was of even greater moment than hitherto; and the importance of the light Ford ambulance waggons is reiterated by ambulance commanders in their war diaries. During the advance to Péronne it was often possible to run these light divisional cars up to the regimental aid-posts and to evacuate the wounded direct to A.D.S.

The main routes of clearance are shown in the accompanying

---

[24] "Meanwhile a game of leap-frog was being played with the dressing stations. What was an A.D.S. to-day would be a M.D.S. to-morrow. The rearmost station, at a set hour, would shut down, and its staff, going in advance of where the A.D.S. was, would open up a new A.D.S. and, taking in all wounded, would evacuate them back to the original A.D.S., henceforth to function as a M.D.S. This system worked splendidly, and throughout the whole period of operations—lasting as they did some considerable time—not one hitch occurred." (From *The History of the Ninth Australian Field Ambulance, p. 52.*)

sketch maps. When the Line of the Somme was reached and the main fighting strength of the corps was transferred to the northern side of the river, the route for medical clearance was

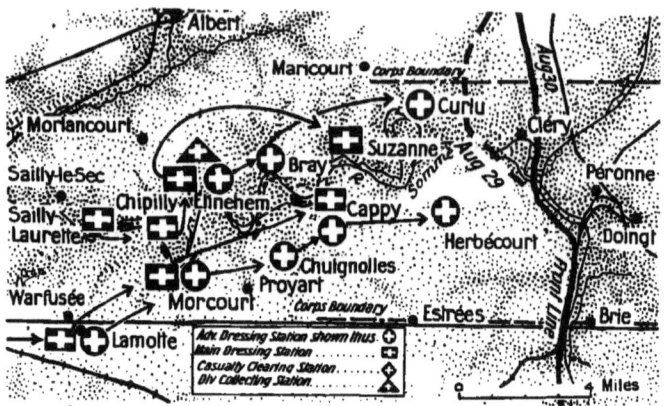

Advance of Medical Stations, Aug. 22-30 (Mont St. Quentin is situated a mile to the north of Péronne).

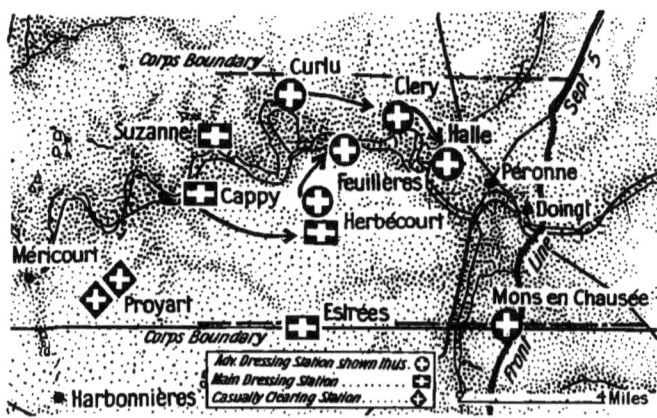

Advance of Medical Stations, Aug. 31-Sept. 5

also transferred thither—a process requiring very exact coordination—and the main St. Quentin-Amiens road, which so far had been the chief route, became almost unused.

In this advance Corps and Divisional Resuscitation Teams were an integral part of the machinery of treatment, and were employed chiefly at main dressing stations.[25] Throughout the advance much extra work was thrown on the medical service by its having to deal with large numbers of wounded Germans, who were evacuated by the ordinary channels with our own troops. Much of the medical work in these operations was in dealing with casualties from gas; this effective weapon was causing heavy wastage but very few deaths.

Certain events in the major actions of the advance may be noted. For the battle of August 23rd the 1st Division replaced the 5th, which had been temporarily holding the line immediately south of the Somme. Colonel Barber's instructions directed the A.D.M.S., 1st Division, after capture of the final objective to absorb the A.D.S. of the 5th for his M.D.S., and to ensure that motor posts be located with a view to their future absorption as A.D.S's. A failure to comply at the appointed time, though only by one hour, involved much congestion at the motor posts, since the divisional cars could not cope with the long trip over bad roads to the original M.D.S., then at Hamel.

In Battle of Chuignes

The operations at Mont St. Quentin involved the medical service of three divisions in an unusual dilemma. Assault across the Somme at Péronne being impossible, General Monash was attacking not only Mont St. Quentin but Péronne from the north of the river. He now therefore employed on that side of it not only the 3rd Division, which since August 22nd had advanced along that bank and won the foothold there, but the 2nd, which attacked Mont St. Quentin, and a brigade of the 5th (the 14th), which, from under the right wing of the 2nd Division, turned south-east and attacked Péronne. The capture of the town, which in its last stage was helped by the 15th Brigade attacking directly across the river, cost 178 killed and 1,084 wounded.

Happy Confusion at Mont St. Quentin

---

[25] One ambulance commander (Major H. B. Lewers) complained that the allocation of officers for team work was detrimental to the efficiency of his unit. It seems that experienced ambulance officers were being transferred elsewhere, and adequate provision had not been made for exchange between Regimental and Ambulance work.

On the southern side of the Somme, the troops of the 15th Brigade were under observed machine-gun fire from Péronne.[26] Since the river could be crossed by ambulance waggon only at Feuilleres, both the 2nd and 5th Divisions' assaulting brigades, as well as those of the 3rd Division on the left of the 2nd, were all cleared through motor loading posts north of the Somme at Cléry (captured by the 3rd Division on August 30th). The cars did not go north of the river all the way, but crossed to the southern side at Feuilleres, whence they followed the riverside road to the A.D.S. at Cappy, from which casualties passed north of the river again to the M.D.S. at Bray. Cars and casualties from all divisions commingled in a confusion which, being—happily—"insoluble," was resolved (like other emulsions) by natural laws—in this case the experience of their drivers and so forth—at the A.D.S. and M.D.S. farther on. Meanwhile the confusion served its purpose more effectively than could have been achieved without such admixture. Such things were possible only in the later stages of the war.

During this movement the corps advanced on a three-divisional front (from left to right—2nd and 5th Australian, and 32nd British), and the field ambulances became very mobile. On September 5th the D.D.M.S. issued instructions based on "Australian Corps Battle Instructions, Series 'D,' No. 1." The dispositions were much the same as those adopted in following the German withdrawal in March, 1917. The instructions were:—

Advance to the Hindenburg Line

"1. Bearer Divisions of Field Ambulances will move with their respective Brigade Groups.

"2. Dispositions of Field Ambulances, less Bearer Divisions, will be as follows:—

	32nd Div.	5th Aust. Div.	2nd Aust. Div.
M.D.S. & Gas Centre	X. Fld. Amb.	X. Fld. Amb.	X. Fld. Amb.
A.D.S. & Motor Posts	Y. Fld. Amb.	Y. Fld. Amb.	Y. Fld. Amb.
Reserve	Z. Fld. Amb.	Z. Fld. Amb.	Z. Fld. Amb.

[26] The Ford cars of the 15th Field Ambulance, clearing the brigade to A.D.S. at Herbécourt, were constantly sniped. In view, however, of their "forward" proclivities, this can hardly justify serious censure, though at the time it was resented.

"3. Tent Divisions of 'Z' (Reserve) Field Ambulances will be used to form new Advanced Dressing Stations in the event of advance, at which time 'Y' Field Ambulances will be converted to Main Dressing Stations, and 'X' Field Ambulances become the reserve.

"4. If considered necessary—
  (i) One tent sub-division from Reserve Field Ambulances will be used to form Divisional Collecting Stations.
  (ii) Tent sub-division personnel from Reserve Field Ambulances will move with Bearer Divisions attached to Brigades forming Advanced Guard.

"5. Attention is drawn to Australian Corps A.A.M.C. Standing Orders Section VI.

"6. O.C. 3rd M.A.C. will arrange evacuation from M.D.S's and W.W.D.S's.

"7. A.D's.M.S. will arrange that O.C., 3rd M.A.C., is at once notified of changes in positions of Main Dressing Stations and Walking Wounded Dressing Stations.

"8. Requirements of stretchers, blankets, and marquees will be drawn from 3rd M.A.C. Dump, A.D's.M.S. Divisions notifying this office of the amounts so drawn.

"9. Acknowledge."

Casualty Clearing Stations move up

On September 2nd the 5th British C.C.S. was opened at Proyart "for abdominal, chest, and fractured femur cases"; and on September 4th No. 61 also, for all classes of case. This advance for a time almost halved the transport problem.

The strength of the Corps was rapidly reduced by excess of casualties over reinforcements and rejoinings, and the problem of conserving strength by the retention of minor casualties—in particular those caused by gas and "N.Y.D.Gas"—and by the prevention of disease, became increasingly pressing. The Australian Corps was indeed approaching the limit of strength that would permit its continuance as a fully effective formation. The result of this, and measures taken in the medical service to minimise it, belong to the next Chapter.

Problems of wastage

The following summary illustrates the problem of evacuation, from August 22nd till September 4th, before the advance from Péronne to the Hindenburg Line began.

Summary of Casualties

Date	1st Div. Gassed	1st Div. Wd.	2nd Div. Gassed	2nd Div. Wd.	3rd Div. Gassed	3rd Div. Wd.	4th Div. Gassed	4th Div. Wd.	5th Div. Gassed	5th Div. Wd.
22nd Aug.	2	55	—	3	29	343	1	18	—	4
23rd ,,	114	882	—	1	4	83	1	15	1	26
24th ,,	119	60	—	2	47	130	26	9	2	18
25th ,,	488	120	—	1	73	127	219	1	—	2
26th ,,	51	37	3	7	30	81	53	—	—	1
27th ,,	15	11	1	35	8	61	1	—	7	73
28th ,,	6	5	5	33	2	63	—	1	2	43
29th ,,	12	1	2	132	5	45	2	—	2	69
30th ,,	16	4	3	53	16	118	—	—	1	32
31st ,,	8	—	7	331	42	197	—	—	9	59
1st Sept.	9	—	3	316	6	214	1	—	11	507
2nd ,,	30	—	15	431	2	5	—	—	35	377
3rd ,,	15	—	8	21	5	3	10	—	16	37
4th ,,	6	—	4	4	1	1	4	—	7	10
TOTAL	891	1,175	51	1,370	270	1,471	318	44	93	1,258

GRAND TOTAL, 6,941.

The last stand

During this time a general reconstruction of his line was being made by the enemy, involving retirement over its whole length. By mid-September the British force had come within striking distance of the Hindenburg Line, from near Cambrai to St. Quentin.

CHAPTER XXIII

"OPEN WARFARE" AND HARGICOURT—THE PROBLEM OF FIGHTING STRENGTH

IN this and the next chapter we are to follow the medical events of the last operations in which the Australian infantry took a part, and, incidentally, of the greatest battle in the final stage of the war. It is from a vast stage and one now crowded with the *dramatis personae* for the final scene, that the medical historian is required to abstract for particular description the part played in all this by the Medical Services with the Australian Imperial Force.

The battles now to be described ended with the "breaking" of the "Hindenburg Line." Coinciding as it did with the crumpling of the Austrian Army, the surrender of Bulgaria, and the Turkish debacle in Palestine, this event was quickly followed by the collapse of the German "home front." The Battle of Megiddo on September 19th was launched exactly twenty-four hours after the attack by the Australian infantry on the outposts of the Hindenburg Line.[1]

Within the previous fortnight both sides had called up their every resource of attack and defence, and collected their strength for the decisive clash; and before we pass to these operations and their medical events it is desirable to examine the resources, physical and moral, at this moment available within the Australian Corps.

THE PROBLEM OF MAINTAINING STRENGTH

To the student of warfare as a science and art, the means whereby military successes have been achieved is of greater importance than the national results of victories or defeats in

---
[1] *See Vol. I, Part II, chapter xi.*

themselves. Momentous as were the operations of the Australian Corps in this final campaign of the Great War, for the military student a still greater interest attaches to the question —what was the source of the tremendous striking power of the Australian formations at this time? Whence did this citizen army derive the vitality and resilience that made possible, during the whole of the terrific fighting of 1918, the remarkable achievements, individual and collective, which culminated in the battles that form the *raison d'être* of this chapter?

"Deprived of the advantage of a regular inflow of trained recruits, and relying practically entirely for any replenishments upon the return of its own sick and wounded," says Sir John Monash, "the Corps was able to maintain an uninterrupted fighting activity over a period of six months. For the last sixty days of this period the Corps maintained an unchecked advance of thirty-seven miles against the powerful and determined opposition of a still formidable enemy, who employed all the mechanical and scientific resources at his disposal."[2]

And if the present writer has correctly interpreted the part assigned to the Army Medical Service in a war of "attrition,"[3] and, in particular, if the claims made regarding the effect on the Australian force of the policy of Sir Neville Howse, as its Director of Medical Services, be accepted, then this question is one which must be held to have an intimate interest for the medical student of warfare.

In this matter of "fighting strength" we are really concerned on the human side with two distinct factors, namely, *man-power* and *morale*. We may recall, moreover, that Napoleon's well known estimate of the relative significance of these, as being in the order of 1 to 3, has never been challenged; and, since the medical service was concerned in both, the more important may be examined first. Morale has been stated[4] to be

Morale

"the product of able leadership, of success; of good organization, discipline and training, which produce self-reliance; of religious, or *other enthusiasm*, *superior numbers*, better armament, *physical fitness*,[5] national character, racial pride, early teaching; and, indeed, of any

---
[2] *Australian Victories in France in 1918, pp. 287-8.*
[3] The significance of this view to humanity and its significance in respect to the future of the military medical service will be discussed in *Vol. III.*
[4] By Maj.-Gen. Sir W. D. Bird, *The Direction of War*, 2nd edition, 1925, *p. 328.*
[5] The italics are the present writer's.

factor which tends to give the leaders and troops confidence in themselves and in their power to defeat the enemy. . . .

"Of these factors the most important is leadership, for it is generally not so much force as its effective employment that is decisive in war."

The records of the Australian Imperial Force and other national armies justify an addition to these—*confidence in its medical service.*

In this final phase of the war the Australian infantry was associated in the great battle of the St. Quentin Canal—presently to be described—as comrades-in-arms with two divisions of the American Expeditionary Force. The commander (and historian) of one of these, the 27th, has put on record his impression of the Australian soldier at this time.[6]

"This chapter on the Hindenburg Line Battle is an appropriate place to make some observations concerning the Australian soldiers, with whom we fought on that occasion.

"The Australian soldier was a distinctive type. . . The Australian army was solely a volunteer force. Not a man in it was present except by his voluntary action. This naturally affected his physical fitness and its morale. There were no troops in the war which equalled the physical standards of the Australians. The American army had thousands, perhaps some hundreds of thousands, of men who measured up to the very best physical specimens to be found among the Australians, but we also had many thousands of men drafted into the army who were not fighting men, and who knew they were not. The Australians had none of this class. It is true that the Australian soldier was lacking in 'smartness' of appearance and manner, and good humoredly took a seeming pride in the cold astonishment he created among others by his indifference to formality and his blunt attitude towards superior officers. But if by discipline we mean experienced and skilled team work in battle, then it must be said that the Australian troops were highly disciplined. Their platoons and companies possessed, as did ours, a highly developed gang spirit which prompted the members of 'the gang' to work together in mutual support, but in addition to this, and by virtue of their long experience in the war, they had come to realize the essential importance of military technique. They knew, from harsh lessons they had received in earlier battles from the harsh enemy instructor, that the shooting and bombing of the individual man at the front may be fruitless unless his group maintains contact with other groups on right and left, and at the same time sends a constant and reliable stream of information to the rear, so that the great auxiliary power of the division may be intelligently employed to aid them. The operations and the supply technique of the Australian divisions were of the very best, and so it was that the rough-and-ready fighting spirit of the Australians had become refined by an experienced battle technique supported by staff work of the highest order. Their record demonstrated, that for Aus-

[6] Maj.-Gen. John F. O'Ryan: *The Story of the 27th Division, Vol. I, p. 339.*

tralian troops at least, the refinements of peace-time precision in drill and military courtesy and formality were unnecessary in the attainment of battle efficiency. The Australians were probably the most effective troops employed in the war on either side."

In the creation and maintenance of that morale the medical service had a definite part.

(1) The policy of its D.M.S. ensured—so far as this could be done—that no man went to the front unless he was in a state of high physical fitness.

(2) The soldier himself knew that, if he was hit, nothing that flesh and blood could do toward saving life and health and alleviating pain would be left undone. He knew that by the medical service he would be treated as an individual and not *merely* as a pawn in the game of war; that few stretcher-bearers equalled the Australian ones in the devotion which they would show in his rescue whatever the danger of the battlefield; that the Australian Medical Service was thoroughly effective and peculiarly suited to his needs—the confidence of Australian soldiers in their own medical and nursing services, and their knowledge that their treatment would accord with the democratic principles that were part of their own fibre, were strong factors in ensuring their contentment.

(3) The efficiency of general methods for health and hygiene, laundries and baths, the encouragement of games, and similar methods in which the medical service shared with the "Q" Branch (as part of the "supply technique" so highly assessed by General O'Ryan), were an important factor.

The strategic methods of the European War of 1914-18 required that an uninterrupted front be maintained, however thinly held,[7] and the strategic history of 1918 deals largely with the juggling of formations and units to fill the whole front and yet permit of rapid concentration at certain points for attack or defence. "Fighting strength" in the common sense of the term was chiefly a matter of infantry. The main purpose of attrition warfare was to reduce their numbers as well as to break their spirits. In the A.I.F. the spirit of the troops had been little

Maintenance of Numbers

---

[7] For a graphic picture of the front at this time and of the Australian "digger" the reader may be referred to the *Australian Official History, Vol. VI, Chapter i.*

affected by the attrition of 1917, and was never so high as in 1918. But numbers had been so diminished that the strenuous open warfare of 1918 quickly completed the reduction of the battalions to a strength incompatible with efficiency as fighting units.

This problem was far from being peculiar to the A.I.F. When Ludendorff made his thrust in March, 1918, the relative strength of the German Army on the Western Front in divisions, as against the French, British and Belgian, was 192 against 175.[8] In May, after the thrust against the British, it was 206 against 173. But by the time the German offensive had ended both sides had been compelled to make a drastic break-up both of divisions and of battalions. In the final stage of lysis the progressive wasting of the divisions and battalions could not be stayed by the normal accession of recruits,[9] or by the improved methods for preventing wastage and promoting "return to duty."

In the B.E.F. In the British Army, so far as the effects of attrition could no longer be met by the inflow of recruits, even with standards of age and fitness lowered and with such combing out of civilians as was considered politically feasible, they were met by:—

(1) Combing out non-combatant services; (2) a limited conversion of mounted troops to infantry; (3) reducing the establishment of infantry battalions per brigade; (4) a temporary reduction of the number of divisions; (5) reducing the numerical strength of the battalion; (6) lowering the standards of "fitness," physical and functional, within the service; (7) extensive dilution of non-fighting and even of combatant units with permanent "B" and "C" class men.

Of these methods, (1), (6), and (7) intimately concerned the medical service.

Faced with the same problem as those responsible for the B.E.F., the General Officer Commanding and responsible administrative officers of the Australian force took a course which brought them at times into conflict with both the British War Office and the Australian Department of Defence. Briefly stated, the Australian Defence Department, as the flow of

---

[8] It cannot but be a cause for amazement, and incentive for study, that Germany was able to maintain so commanding a preponderance of man-power at the end of attrition warfare. From the medical standpoint there may have been two factors at least in this achievement (a) a greater concern to conserve man-power by strategic and tactical means, in particular by superior defences; and (b) possibly a more effective system of treatment in the field and return to duty.

[9] In relation to the numerical strength of the force in the field, national "lasting power" as distinct from military is determined by the number of males who in a given time shall reach military manhood and be found "fit" for service. Some relevant figures for the Great War will be given in *Vol. III*.

recruits became increasingly difficult to maintain, concurred in a lowering of the standard of fitness to a sufficient extent to cause the change to be marked by the Australian depot staffs in England. At the same time the British War Office was generally pressing on the A.I.F. leaders the policy that establishments and procedures for British and Dominion troops in the B.E.F. should be as far as possible the same—in particular, that the numerical strength and the organisation of Australian battalions and divisions should conform to those of the rest of the force. If battalions were allowed to fall to company strength, there occurred a heavy waste of staff, the same "overhead" being required by a battalion of 250 as by one of 750. The accepted British policy was to disband a proportion of battalions if reinforcements failed to maintain proportionate strength, and it was part of the duty of the Adjutant-General at the War Office, under instructions from the Army Council, to see that this should be done. The policy of General Birdwood, in which General Monash, after taking command of the Corps, fully concurred and co-operated, had, in effect, been—

(i) to defer indefinitely the disbandment of a Division, proposed in November, 1917; (ii) to side-track as long as possible the War Office policy for a reduction in the establishment of each infantry brigade; and the breaking up of 25 per cent. of battalions; (iii) to resist any lowering in the standard of physical fitness in front line troops.

For six months the Australian Corps had been continuously engaged in attack, which, contrary to the accepted military

In the A.I.F.   doctrine, many historians of this war have concluded to be more expensive than defence, even if sometimes more stimulating to morale. Wastage during this period is shown hereunder:—

BATTLE CASUALTIES April 1st-September 30th, 1918.

UNIT	Killed in action	Died of wounds	Died of gas	Prisoners of war	Wounded	Gassed	Shell shock	Wounded: remained at duty	TOTAL
1 Div.	1,662	724	18	28	6,683	1,539	8	250	10,912
2 Div.	1,495	622	23	86	6,204	1,872	20	262	10,584
3 Div.	1,160	512	42	124	5,898	2,541	20	239	10,536
4 Div.	1,451	587	14	236	5,690	828	12	299	9,117
5 Div.	1,256	579	61	12	5,649	1,814	34	309	9,714
Other Arms	141	84	8	16	730	375	1	48	1,403
	7,165	3,108	166	502	30,854	8,969	95	1,407	52,266

77. IN OPEN WARFARE

German prisoners carrying Australian wounded during the fighting at Bray, 22nd August, 1918. The fighting was just beyond the hill.

Aust. War Memorial Official Photo. No. E2951.

To face p. 708.

78. Wounded of the 34th Battalion being brought to the R.A.P. by German prisoners during the fighting of 22nd August, 1918, at Bray

The Germans are carrying a wounded man by their improvised method of using a waterproof sheet. (See illustration of "*Zeltbahntrage*," *German Official Medical History, Volume I, p. 295*).

Aust. War Memorial Official Photo. No. E3063.

NON-BATTLE CASUALTIES April 1st-September 30th, 1918.

UNIT	Accidentally killed	Died of disease	Accidentally injured	Self-inflicted injuries	Sick	TOTAL
1 Div.	20	12	433	43	7,439	7,947
2 Div.	20	18	373	90	6,478	6,979
3 Div.	15	8	429	55	7,098	7,605
4 Div.	20	22	308	60	4,621	5,031
5 Div.	14	14	307	61	4,706	5,192
Other Arms	15	14	255	7	5,474	5,765
	104	88	2,195	316	35,816	38,519

During this period 15,553 new drafts were taken on the strength of the formations in France. About 4,000 were made available by a reduction in battalion establishment from 976 other ranks to 900. This was ordered in June in the British Army, and in July was applied in the A.I.F.

In the same period 51,516 rejoined their units *ex* "sick and wounded." Of these latter, 14,675 came through the Overseas Training Brigade on Salisbury Plain; 25,827 rejoined from the hospitals at the Base in France through Le Havre; and the remainder, 11,014, returned to duty without having been evacuated from "Army" area.

By the middle of August most of the recovered casualties from the fighting of March, April, and May had come forward again to the depots at Le Havre, and were available to fill the demands of 3rd Echelon to reinforce the formations after the battles of August 8th to 23rd. Thereafter, however, the strength of the force was maintained chiefly through recruits and by local action. The administrative history of the A.I.F. in the last few months of the war was, therefore, a desperate struggle, in which the medical service was heavily involved, to maintain the infantry battalions at a strength compatible with their efficiency as fighting units, while avoiding any extensive resort to the device of disbandment. The following are certain of the measures by which this was attempted, including some of those above referred to.

The Measures Adopted. Some of these steps did not especially affect the medical service. Chief of them was the reduction, noted above, of the establishment of the battalion. But in the dreary business of stalling off impending dissolution the medical service was looked to as not before in any war. It was, moreover, doubly involved in this duty. In addition to its normal functions of *maintenance* and *humane alleviation* —carried out now under a pressure which increased with every dwindling of the fighting strength—it was actually required to act also as a "donor" of a large number of its own "A" class men to the fighting units, and at the same time to maintain its own efficiency unimpaired.

At this critical stage in the war the medical service was the chief agent in three distinct lines of action for supporting the strength of the forces in the field—(1) the prevention of sick wastage, (2) promotion of rapid return to duty, (3) the dilution of the fighting units with troops of inferior quality. Of these the Australian service energetically promoted the first two and as strongly opposed the third. Each must now be shortly discussed.

"*Sanitary*" *History*. The graph at *page 494* which shows the incidence of disease in the A.I.F. in France, presents this curious feature, that no rise marks the pandemic of influenza that occurred in 1918.[10]

(1) **Measures against sick wastage in the advance**
This is due to two facts. First, that the pandemic did not in fact produce any outstanding mortality or even morbidity in terms of "wastage" in the field units. Second that such additional wastage as occurred was masked by a fall in other diseases. In view of the enormous influence of the outbreak in civil life —so great as to be reflected in the general statistical tables of mortality—this must be considered remarkable. The development in the army of a "sanitary conscience," and a standard of "sanitary discipline" equivalent to that' which compelled the soldier to salute a commissioned officer, or to go "over the top" when required to do so, "paid" in terms of victory.

The bound volumes of the war diaries of the Australian Sanitary Sections during this period are tomes of formidable proportions, and their contents, narrative and appendices, present an admirably complete account of the varied activities of

Health problems in the advance

---

[10] The history of the epidemic as seen in the A.I.F. is followed in a special chapter of *Vol. III.*

the five units and of "sanitation" in general. But, save for certain features inevitable to the change from "stationary" to "mobile" warfare, the impression conveyed by their perusal is strikingly devoid of "highlights" of incident or experience. The same may be said of the records—war diaries, memoranda, instructions, correspondence files and so forth— which are concerned with more general problems in promoting health and preventing disease. So much is this the case that it demands a deliberate analysis to detect the reason for the apparent absence of "history" in an experience so full of incident and of work so obviously well done. With a necessary excursion into certain special problems, the result of such cogitation may be presented as the most useful contribution that can be made to the history of health in the advance to victory.

A Triumph of Realism. We have already seen that, in the A.I.F., organisation and administration were far more important in promoting sanitary morale and discipline than was the application of "disciplinary measures" so called. And this is the most striking feature in the medical records of this period, as it is of military ones. Administration merges insensibly with "discipline," organisation with executive. The problems of health (it is clear) have now become an organic element in the general problem of maintenance—taking place with transport, supply, water, engineering, and so forth. At this time, moreover, these latter were so highly developed and so efficient that the Australian Corps was accepted as a model. Its methods had the "noiseless tenour" of smoothly working machinery. But a few special problems came with the change to open warfare in the "Advance to the Hindenburg Line."

Rôle of Sanitary Sections Upheld. As will be recalled, after being placed temporarily under Corps control during the First Battle of the Somme, and then under Army during the German retreat in the spring of 1917, the Australian Sanitary Sections, differently from the British, were in effect restored to their divisions, though under general control of Corps. Throughout this advance they were administered by Colonel Barber. The Corps system worked well; the units were located in "sanitary areas" within the three echelons of Corps control—front, reserve, and rest—but in full *liaison* with the divisions. In the advance they were moved forward by a system of "leap-frog." Unit diaries are emphatic in urging the advantage of the Australian ideas of their function, and in recording how easily, if allowed to do so, the combatant units fell into the un-Australian practice of relying on the Sanitary Sections to do the work of sanitation rather than guide or instruct.[11]

Promotion of Health in the Units. The system of food supply in the Australian Corps and the manipulation of transport, two vital factors in health promotion, were at this time perfect.

---

[11] Thus the O.C., 4th Sanitary Section (Captain H. W. Franklands), in July notes that the units "began to look upon the Section as suppliers of sanitary conveniences. In any case the prevailing idea that Sanitary Sections operate 'latrine factories' is, and has been far too prevalent."

Disease Prevention in the Advance. Despite the fact that the conditions of the advance through a devastated area were highly unfavourable to personal hygiene, and that at times in the advance this got somewhat out of hand, the weekly reports of the R.M.O's show that on the whole a satisfactory standard could be maintained. Three matters merit a note.

(a) *"Baths and Laundries."* Arrangements for bathing were made within the divisions (by the "Q" Branch). The Corps "Baths and Laundries Officer" (Lieutenant MacKnight) maintained baths for Corps troops and for the divisional reinforcement camps, and in particular controlled the vast operations of the underclothing exchange between the divisional baths and the Army laundries. Clean underclothes were supplied in bulk to divisions in exchange for dirty, which were forwarded by rail, road, or barge to the Army laundries chiefly in Abbeville.[12] Baths of various types were obtained by Corps and lent to Divisions; a "standard" portable set was also designed and several sets were constructed.[13]

(b) *"Scabies Stations."* Even in the tremendous pressure of the advance the prevention of scabies by "early treatment" was very efficient. Scabies stations were associated with the divisional baths, and the "Foden" disinfector and clothing exchange were thus made available. A scabies report was required weekly from R.M.O's.

(c) *Dis-infestation. The "Russian Pit" Delouser.* In May the Director-General, B.E.F., issued plans and specifications for an improvised delouser which was said to be used by the Russian Army and to be serviceable. All divisions were required to experiment with the new method. Though by no means 100 per cent. efficient nor fool-proof,[14] the device was found useful.

Gastro-intestinal Infections: General Sanitation. From the "sanitary" point of view one of the most striking features of the change from static to mobile warfare, observed in the Australian units and even more (as would seem from reports) in the British, was the difficulty experienced by the battalions in readapting their habits to the sanitary technique of

---

[12] During the month of July, 1918 (Lieut. MacKnight records), the Australian Corps allotment from No. 1 Area Laundry at Abbeville, controlled by Army, which supplied the Australian Corps, had been increased to 140,000 pieces per week. On 20 Sept. 1918 a report shows that the stock of clean clothing at the exchange was approximately—shirts 13,000, pants 64,000, socks 70,000. The stocks held by the divisions were—shirts 7,000, pants 9,000, socks 26,000. At the same time the Abbeville laundry held on the Australian Corps account approximately 90,000 shirts, 145,000 pants, 85,000 pairs of socks. In the previous ten days 146,000 pieces had been received from it by the Corps—43,000 shirts, 39,000 pants, 54,000 socks, and 10,000 towels.

[13] With the rapid advance on August 8-9 the Corps had the opportunity of inspecting the former German baths. It was found (says Lieut. MacKnight) that the Germans made little use of portable sets, but installed instead "showers built in and supplied with hot water by some stationary arrangement. . . . In many instances there are delousing chambers, sometimes worked by steam and sometimes by dry heat, but no new ideas have been noticed."

[14] Thus the O.C., 5th Sanitary Section (Major V. M. Coppleson), records "results most satisfactory . . . an even temperature of 70 degrees Centigrade was maintained for ¾ of an hour. At the end of that time lice on underclothes were found in a dead condition and the eggs pulverised." *Per contra* in the 3rd Sanitary Section exact experiments carried out under the direction of the O.C. (Major W. R. Kelly) by Lance-Corporal L. E. Cooling showed that, while "under favourable conditions lice were killed, this was achieved by radiation and not by hot air or by convection"; that "the potency of the air [within the pit] as a pediculicide amounts to nil"; and that unless strict regard was had to its limitations it was likely to be "a snare."

moving warfare. They had, indeed, become almost as closely enmeshed in the technique of the "fly-proof box latrine" of stationary warfare as before the war in that of the cistern flush. In rapid moves the technique of the "shallow trench" latrine had in fact to be relearned.

Water. The most important feature of "sanitation" in the advance to the Hindenburg Line after August 8th—indeed the most striking part of "maintenance" in general—was the provision for maintaining supplies of safe water. It is generally accepted that no feature of the work of the Australian Corps was more striking than that of the field companies of the engineers in collaboration with the Sanitary Sections in (1) providing *supplies* of water, and (2) ensuring its *purity*.

(1) *Supply.* In the rapid advance forward from Villers-Bretonneux after August 8th reliance was placed on (*a*) the exploitation of any useful captured source such as shallow wells; (*b*) water tank lorries; (*c*) "sterilising lorries" to render fit for use water drawn from stagnant surface supplies.[15] Before the advance, a pipe-line was rushed up to water points behind the front at the rate of over one mile per day.

(2) *Purification.* This became more important than ever in the move across the devastated area between the Somme and the Hindenburg Line. Here almost the only supplies available were those obtained by opening up wells in the captured villages. A scheme of co-operation was developed, between the engineers, the sanitary sections, and the battalions, on the lines of that worked out in the I Anzac Corps in the advance in March, 1917. Arrangements were made for personnel of the sanitary section responsible for the forward area (in the final advance, No. 2) to follow up the advance in close *liaison* with the engineers, working commonly from the A.D.S. as a base. Samples sent back by "runners" from each captured source were tested; and, usually within a few hours of the capture of any well, the appropriate notice—whether fit for use and if so the amount of bleach required—was displayed on it. Chlorination was, if possible, carried out under the supervision of, or in some instances by, the water-point personnel of the Sanitary Section.

Two questions of permanent interest became prominent issues at this time:—

(*a*) Whether water should be issued to the troops chlorinated or unchlorinated. In the latter case chlorination would be the direct responsibility of the R.M.O. and his "water duty" men.[16] It was decided that, while it was often desirable that the chlorinating should be carried out by experts at the source, in general "the system which relies on the education and intelligence of each unit to chlorinate all water, and which holds each unit responsible for carrying it out, is the better system since under it the whole army is educated to carry out chlorination under all circumstances, and will not fail to do so under conditions where automatic chlorination by special plants is impracticable.

---

[15] *See p. 589.* Of the Fourth Army's advance in September the *British Official Medical History* (*Hygiene, Vol. I, p. 103*) states: "The sterilizers were practically the only important water points in the forward areas for several days until the engineers laid pipe line systems and got wells in working order. . . . A record for water delivered by the company [No. 1 Section of No. 1 Company] was reached during the week ending 6th September, 1918, on which date 500,000 gallons of water were sterilized, and 1,250,000 gallons of water were carried . . ."

It is to be noted that it was in this stage that the Australian Corps exploited so effectively the local village wells.

[16] For the "water duty" men, *see pp. 507, 600, and Vol. I, p. 10.*

... When all is said and done," writes Major Holmes, "the training of the individual to take intelligent action is the most reliable method in all matters concerning the protection of health."[17]

(b) The proposal was made and was supported by some of the A.D's.M.S. that the engineers themselves should be issued with apparatus for testing water for organic contamination. The proposal was rejected on the advice of the D.D.M.S., who held that, while the mechanical process of testing could quite well be performed by any instructed individual, this was very far from being the only question at issue in respect to the suitability or otherwise of the water for consumption, since it took no account of the nature of the contamination.

The freedom of the troops from dysentery in this advance was such as might well induce a false impression—that the problem was not a difficult one. No student of the prevention of water-borne infection in the Great War could for one moment be thus misled. If the price of freedom is eternal vigilance, the price paid in France for freedom from dysentery was not less exacting; nor will it ever be otherwise.[18]

The extent to which quick return to duty was being achieved is indicated in the figures on *page 709*.[19] In June, to free the mobile field ambulances for the more active rôle required in moving warfare, the D.M.S., Fourth Army, put a special casualty clearing station at the service of the D.D.M.S., Australian Corps, as a "rest station" for the reception of light, and gassed cases, who were likely to be able to return to duty within a short time. "This," Colonel Barber reports, "was a great boon . . . and it obviated the necessity for sending men who were likely to be well in a short period a long journey to the base." At the same time the "N.Y.D.N." and "N.Y.D. Gas" stations had so well served their incidental purpose of education, that these diagnoses were now shunned and men were dealt with, without hardship, at the forward stations.[20]

(2) **Measures for "return to duty" during the advance**

---

[17] From a paper by Major M. J. Holmes for the Australian Association for Advancement of Science, Melbourne, Jan. 1921, *p. 23*.

[18] The preservation of dental health during the advance, one of the most remarkable achievements of the Australian force in solving the problem of wastage, will be dealt with in the special chapter in *Vol. III* devoted to this speciality.

[19] Some corresponding figures for the German and other armies will be given in *Vol. III*. Those for the German Army are being compiled from the *German Official Medical History, Vol. III*.

[20] Thus Major C. L. Chapman, D.A.D.M.S. Australian Corps, lecture to Corps School:—"N.Y.D.N. . . . sparingly employed as every case must be sent to a special hospital (whose C.O.) is the only man who can mention the word 'shell shock' . Other cases to be diagnosed Fatigue, Exhaustion, etc."

The administrative involvements of this important policy, and its history in the A.I.F., belong to another chapter.[21] But its application as affecting the field units of the A.I.F. in France at this critical period must here be mentioned.

(3) **The question of dilution**

(a) *The "Under-age" Boys and "Over-age" Men.* A certain number of youngsters arriving from Australia were from time to time found to be under 18½ years, having overstated their age. These were held unfit for front-line service and were disposed of by attaching them to medical units, as also were chronic "V.D." convalescents. Dilution by "over-age" men was pressed on the A.I.F. by the authorities in Australia, but was as resolutely rejected.

(b) *Routing out the "A" Class Effectives.* Being in effect an overseas expedition, the Australian Imperial Force had little place for "P.B." men.[22] The only considerable departments in it in which such men could pull their weight were, first, the staffs of the depots in the United Kingdom and of Australian Administrative Headquarters, London, and second, the medical service.

The Service as a Donor. The "combing" of the depots (through the medical boards) has already been noted.[23] From its own ranks the medical service supplied "A" class men for the combatant arms under two arrangements; first directly, by transfer; second indirectly, by the use of "P.B." men instead of fit recruits in medical units. Direct transfer was chiefly of N.C.O's to schools for commissioned rank in the Infantry.[24] The indirect line of action had already been exploited in relation to the "A.A.M.C. attached for water duty" to combatant units.[25] In furtherance of this move, in June the D.M.S., A.I.F. (General Howse) permitted men below "A" standard to be sent from the depots to France, for service as "(a) A.A.M.C. details attached to battalions," and "(b) In . . . hospitals and medical units on the lines of communication."[26] The number of fit men thus released was probably not less than 1,000.

---

[21] In particular, *Chapter xxvi*.

[22] The physical standards for enlistment in the A.I.F. are examined in *Vol. III.*

[23] See *Chapter xvi*.

[24] The exact number transferred in this way is not recorded. Writing of June, 1918, Colonel Barber spoke of "50 in one division having been thus promoted in the previous year" from field ambulances. A considerable transfer took place also from General Hospitals and casualty clearing stations. Direct transfer of A.A.M.C. reinforcements to combatant arms was also carried out in the depots and in Australia. The records show that these men did exceptionally well, a remarkably high percentage of them being killed or wounded.

[25] See *footnote 40 on p. 256.*

[26] The criteria of "fitness" and types of disability which should permit employment as "B" or "C" class men in various forms of field work were exactly laid down by the D.M.S. in a memorandum which will be found in *Chapter xxvi* and *Appendix No. 7.* The position in the German Army is noted in *Appendix No. 9 (p. 924).*

In the British Army also the bearer divisions appear to have been fed with "Class 1" men from the General Hospitals and Base. But, although Class 1 was the highest category in the British Army, it cannot be assumed that these men were equivalent to the Australian "A" class; at this time the physical standards for the British Army had degraded to a degree that makes comparison with Australian standards misleading. On facts observed by himself in the course of his official visit early in 1918 the Australian Director-General (Surgeon-

Dilution in the Medical Service. In general, however, dilution of the A.A.M.S. with unfit men was stubbornly resisted by the medical authorities in the A.I.F. It appeared to the D.D.M.S. Australian Corps (Colonel Barber) and the, D.M.S., A.I.F. (Surgeon-General Howse) that the efficiency of the service was threatened by it, and resolute steps were taken by these officers to ensure that the policy of physical fitness enforced for the combatant arms of the A.I.F. should also obtain *in those departments of its medical service where— in their opinion—fully "fit" men were required*. General Howse successfully resisted all pressure to reduce the standard of A.A.M.C. reinforcements for the field units. In particular, the standard laid down for *stretcher-bearers* was to be *"the same as that required for 'A' class infantrymen."*[27]

In the matter of the *"A.A.M.C. attached"* to combatant units, at the instance of Colonel Barber the D.M.S. was able in September to secure for the Australian Corps a reversal of A.I.F. Order No. 1,000[28] and the return of the men to their original "attachments."

"Morale" v. "Strength." There thus emerges the important and interesting fact that, in this crisis in regard to "strength," the Australian Medical Service was insistent upon maintaining the moral element in strength at the cost of

---

Gen. Fetherston) reported to his Minister that "it was manifest that the interpretation of standard by the Imperial authorities was very low." In regard to new recruits, "Men were passed as fit for active service who would not have been taken for home service in Australia . . . the general physique of men coming up was very poor. . . . Thus very small light men or boys with no strength or stamina . . . were passed for class 1 (fighting line)."

Of "results as seen in the army" in England, France and elsewhere, he observed that "while men of some regiments are of good physique and well built, the majority contain very inferior specimens of men from a physical standpoint, many being small, light, under-sized, or narrow-chested. Whilst most are young, many being quite boys, there were always old, grey-haired men amongst them."

[27] But see, in this connection, the experience of the 16th and 17th Field Ambulances (*pp. 475-6*).

[28] The following note by Colonel Barber (*loc. cit.*) reflects the opinion of A.A.M.C. officers at the time: "The A.A.M.C. Corporal and other ranks attached to the battalions were drawn from our best men, and it is difficult to understand why they are not in the new organisation of the British post-war Army. They were the greatest help to the R.M.O. and Regimental Bearers and in addition to 'water duty' played a great part in the prevention of sick wastage and upkeep of medical equipment."

Correspondence files of the Australian Corps show that, when even this slight measure of dilution in the medical service was ordered, vigorous protests were made by ambulance commanders against reductions and postings that reduced the morale of their units.

numerical strength where access of numbers would have meant loss of morale.[29]

In spite of all such measures as were taken, the numerical strength of the Corps, after six months of continuous activity, could not be sufficiently maintained. Many battalions could summon for actual fighting no more than 200-300 men; and in the midst of these difficulties, just before the series of attacks on the Hindenburg Line were due to be launched, came two administrative bombshells.

Most surprising of these was the announcement from the War Office that some 6,000 of the earliest enlisted Australians were to be given furlough in Australia.

Though a matter chiefly of national and political interest, "Anzac Leave" demands notice on account of its serious repercussions in the medical service.

Early in September the Australian Prime Minister, Mr. W. M. Hughes, decided to enforce the Australian Government's wish that all Australians who had served continuously since 1914 should be given six months' furlough. This involved some 6,000 veterans. As launched by the Adjutant-General from the War Office the executive order giving effect to this decision was "a paralyser" to commanding officers. At 48 hours' notice every unit and formation was required to furnish forthwith the names of every man qualified by service who should desire to proceed at once on leave to Australia. Ultimately, those of the "veterans" who elected to take the leave in Australia left on or about October 12th. This invidious order, admirable in its intention, imposed on many men in "key" positions a most difficult conflict of allegiances. In the medical units its effect was most demoralising. At a time of intense pressure some units were almost denuded of their senior officers, non-commissioned officers and men. Many senior members of the nursing service also were involved. A tragic feature of the episode was the fact that these men were caught in the pneumonic phase of the influenza epidemic and many died.

The second bombshell was also an order from the Adjutant-General at the War Office—that seven Australian battalions, already marked for disbandment, must be broken up forthwith in order to furnish reinforcements for the rest. This measure, though applied in February to the British Army against the wish of the Commander-in-Chief, had thus far been avoided in the dominion forces, except for the disbandment of three battalions of the A.I.F. to make up for the losses at Villers-Bretonneux and Dernancourt. It was bitterly un-

---
[29] The *pros and cons* of this much debated policy are examined in Chapter *xxvi*, and also in *Vol. III*.

popular and was now resisted by open—though very orderly —mutiny, with the result that by leave of the Army Commander, disbandment was postponed[30] until after the coming series of engagements.

The Australian divisions thus entered their battles at the Hindenburg Line with their battalions at a strength of 200-300 effectives as against the normal 600.[31] In this, the decisive campaign, the Australian Corps was being kept in the line till physically incapable of further effort. By the sheer force of that fact, perhaps, as much as by the insistence of Mr. Hughes, who at this juncture came to France, the High Command had decided that, whatever the result of the coming engagements, all Australian divisions must be withdrawn after them for a complete rest. The operations fell into two phases, and the 1st and 4th Divisions would be withdrawn after the first phase. But the other three would not suffice to carry the whole effort through. In order to get out of them the last ounce of "fight," it was planned by Generals Rawlinson and Monash to attach to the Corps in the later phase the II American Corps, whose divisions would act under the Australian Corps—a very remarkable military adjustment whose medical involvements, far more complicated than might be imagined, will presently be described. The narrative must now turn to this famous series of battles.

OPERATIONS AT THE HINDENBURG LINE

The astonishing tactical success of the Battle of Amiens (August 8th) had determined Marshal Foch to thrust with all the forces at his command at a vital point in the enemy lines of communication. The German front depended largely upon the lateral railway through Mézières and Maubeuge. The French and Americans were to strike towards Mézières; the Fourth and Third British Armies towards Maubeuge; and the British Second, Fifth, and First Armies and the Belgians towards

---

[30] One battalion, the 60th, through the powerful influence of its brigadier, General H. E. Elliott, agreed to disband.
[31] During the course of a general offensive, the strength of battalions could seldom be maintained at a higher figure than this, and it was commonly lower.

Thielt farther north. All three blows were to be converging. This strategic plan was agreed to during the last week in August. Between September 12th and October 5th the Allies attacked in Flanders, on the Somme and Scheldt, and south on the Meuse.[82]

With accumulating successes this plan came to include the vision of victory in 1918. The consummation of this hope depended in great measure on the breaking of a vital element in the Hindenburg Line, between Vendhuille and Bellicourt on the Fourth Army front.

The "Hindenburg" (Siegfried) Line. The breaking of the "Hindenburg Line," the main fortification of the German foothold in north-western France, can be visualised as a strategic end in itself, or as a tactical element in a wider strategic purpose. But this may be affirmed with assurance, that the military effect of the battles, some of whose medical events are to be described in this chapter and the next, was final and decisive. The subsequent thrusts did little more than give the *coup-de-grâce*.

We are here interested only in that part of the line which extends from St. Quentin north towards Cambrai. Between these towns lies the watershed dividing the valley of the Somme from that of the Scheldt. Across that watershed, joining the two river basins, runs the Canal de St. Quentin—largely through a deep open cut—and behind this the Hindenburg fortifications on the Fourth Army's front mostly lay. Along the whole obstacle the Germans had constructed from ferro-concrete and barbed-wire a modern fortress line of immense strength and in great depth. But for 6,000 yards, between Bellicourt and Le Catelet, the canal passes through a tunnel; and, the obstacle being absent, the defences in this sector were particularly deep. Against these the Australian Corps was ultimately to be thrown. The defensive line in this sector comprised three zones; from west to east these were:—

1. The "Hindenburg Outpost-Line." This included—(a) the old British (Fifth Army) front of March 21st. Having been constructed under fire, this line was far less elaborate than was the German. (b) Some 1,000 yards behind (*i.e., east of*) this was the Hindenburg outpost-line proper, emplaced on high ground. Here, more or less parallel with and about 2,000 yards west of the line of the canal, the Germans had constructed an elaborate system of trenches with numerous dugouts, and concrete machine-gun and trench-mortar emplacements, together with "a perfect tangle of underground shelters and passages. Roomy dugouts were provided with tunnelled ways which led to cunningly hidden machine-gun posts, and the best of care was taken to provide numerous exits, so that the occupants should not be imprisoned by the blocking of one

---

[82] The official list of British battles is given on *p. 680n*.

or other of them by our bombardment."[33] Barbed-wire ran in great belts "cleverly disposed so as to herd the attackers into the very jaws of the machine-guns." Deep communication trenches led back to the main defensive line.

2. *The Main Hindenburg Line.* This lay mostly along and behind the canal, two-thirds of a mile behind the trenches of the outpost-line. In the tunnel sector a complete system of trenches and belts of wire followed roughly the line of the tunnel which lay deep in the ground below, with certain passages leading from it up to the trenches. In the tunnel the Germans had moored canal barges end to end, as living quarters and depots for stores and munitions. "The whole scheme," writes Sir John Monash, "produced a veritable fortress . . . defying destruction by any powers of gunnery, and presenting the most formidable difficulties to the bravest of infantry."

3. *The Le Catelet-Nauroy and Beaurevoir support lines,* respectively one and three miles behind the Hindenburg Line proper.

The whole Hindenburg system was, in this sector, from four to five miles across west to east. Far beyond it other lines of defence had been sited, but none was even nearly complete.

By September 11th the vanguard of the Australian Corps advancing on a frontage of 8,000 yards made contact with the outposts of this great fortress line, approaching the "open cut" between Bellicourt on the north and Bellenglise on the south, immediately south of the tunnel. The newly reconstituted British IX Corps was on its right[34] and the III Corps on its left. The task of fighting through these formidable defences took from September 18th to October 5th.

The operations fall naturally in three groups.

1. Reduction of the Hindenburg Outpost-Line (Battle of Epéhy, or Hargicourt—September 18th).

2. A general assault on the main Hindenburg Line in the sector of the St. Quentin Canal defences extending from Le Tronquoy tunnel on the south to Vendhuille on the north. This formed part of a wide offensive on the British front, from September 27th to October 2nd, involving Third and First Army fronts from Gouzeaucourt to Sauchy-Lestrée on the north (Battles of Canal du Nord, and St. Quentin Canal).

It was for this great offensive that the Fourth Army's strength was first augmented by the II American Corps. The central thrust against the tunnel sector of the St. Quentin Canal defences on a front of 6,000 yards, from Vendhuille to Bellicourt, was made by the II

---

[33] Sir John Monash, *Australian Victories in France in 1918, p. 217.* The account given of the Hindenburg Line is from this work and *The Story of the Fifth Australian Division.* The outline of the fighting is based on the section "Australian Forces in the War" by C. E. W. Bean in *Vol. III* of *The Empire at War,* edited for the Royal Colonial Institute by Sir Charles Lucas (Humphrey Milford, Oxford University Press). The volume of the *Australian Official History* dealing with this last stage of the war *(Vol. VI)* was not published at the time of writing.

[34] This corps had taken over the 32nd Division.

American and Australian Corps, under direction of the Australian Corps staff.

3. As operation (2) did not proceed as planned, it was found necessary to undertake on the Australian-American Corps front a further operation against the strong support defences on the high ground east of the canal—the "Beaurevoir Line," and the village defences of Montbrehain. This was carried out by the 2nd Australian Division on October 3rd-5th. The reduction of this last stronghold in the enemy's strategic base of offence and defence synchronised with the first German armistice proposal, the general Allied advance, and, incidentally, the withdrawal of the Australian Corps for rest and reorganisation, and its replacement in the Fourth Army line of battle by the II American Corps.

It is only with the first of these three stages that the present chapter deals. The battle of Epéhy (or Hargicourt, as it is best known to Australian writers) presents features of great interest, especially for Australians:—

Hindenburg "Outpost" Line

(1) The perfect example that it affords of the two-stage battle against entrenched troops—a "set-piece" assault on clearly defined objectives behind a devastating barrage; followed by exploitation towards a wider tentative objective by "open warfare" without barrage but supported by tanks.[35]

(2) the great depth of the "exploitation" objective against defences of such strength.

(3) The extraordinary success of the Australian assault.

(4) The tactical consequences of a local failure (III Corps) on subsequent operations.

(5) The automaticity with which at this stage of the war the medical service integrated with the military machinery of warfare.

The purpose of the attack was to advance the British front on the St. Quentin Canal to within immediate striking distance of the main Hindenburg Line. It was carried out on a 14-mile front, between Holnon and Epéhy, by the Fourth Army in conjunction with two corps of Third Army in the north and one of the First French Army on the south. Fourth Army order of battle placed the Australian Corps in the centre with IX Corps on the right and III on the left.

The Australian Corps. By September 17th the Australian formations had worked their way through most of the old British reserve defences, and faced the enemy who held the old British main and outpost lines of March 21st. Medical units had wormed their advanced positions—R.A.P's, loading posts, A.D.S's—forward to keep in touch. The Hindenburg Outpost Line proper lay beyond the old No-Man's Land of Fifth Army on the high ground that here overlooked the "open cut" south of the Bellicourt tunnel, some 4½ miles from the Australian front. North of this the British III Corps faced the 6,000 yards of tunnel sector and—though this was imperfectly realised at the time—

---

[35] In these battles, partly by reason of the immense losses suffered in the August fighting, the tanks were much less effective than on Aug. 8.

a far more elaborate system of outpost defences, in effect a protrusion from the fortress line itself. In the Australian Corps the 4th (right) and 1st (left) Divisions attacked, each on a two-brigade front; the two assaulting brigades to carry the attack through to the "red" line. A reserve battalion of each brigade was to carry out the final phase—"exploitation." The first objective ("green" line) was the old British front line; the second ("red") the old British line of outposts; the third ("blue"), 1,800 to 2,000 yards in advance, the original outpost defences of the Hindenburg Line. With "zero" at 5.20 a.m. the first objective was to be captured by 8.30 and the second by 9.50 a.m. The exploiting battalions would then begin their advance.

Sir John Monash has claimed[36] for the Australian contribution to this important battle that "there is no record in this war of any previous success on such a scale, won with so little loss." The following account of the military events[37] will serve to indicate the nature of the medical problem:—

The Battle

"The advance was to be so deep that it was necessary to arrange for the field guns to be moved forward during the fighting. The night was rainy, and, with the battalions reduced to a few hundred men each, the objectives so large, and the third stage of the plan—the attack on the Hindenburg Outpost Line itself—left almost optional in case the battalion commanders did not find themselves in a position to attempt it, even the Australian general felt little confidence that the attack could reach all the objectives intended. . .

"The 1st Australian Division attacked on the left and the 4th on the right, each with two brigades. The troops on the left flank of the 1st Division [III Corps] were held up short of their objective; and the left of the 1st itself after heavy fighting reached the old British Outpost Line and the old No Man's Land, ["red" line] but not the Hindenburg Outpost line ["blue" line]. The 4th Australian Division, however, although the troops on its right flank [IX Corps] were similarly impeded, rushed the Germans under the mist of smoke shell from both of the first two objectives, and then proceeded in full daylight and without the cover of artillery to work across a mile of No Man's Land towards the third objective—the Hindenburg Outpost Line. Only the left of the division was able to penetrate that line by day, the rest being unable to get through the heavy wire entanglement under fire. Shortly before midnight, however, the 46th Battalion of the 12th Australian Infantry Brigade attacked over the wire, took 600 prisoners (twice its own number), seized this very strong line of trenches from at least four times the number of German troops who had been freshly equipped and brought from St. Quentin, and established the British front on the heights looking straight down upon the St. Quentin Canal. Below it lay the mouth of Napoleon's Tunnel; and beyond—the main lines of the Hindenburg defences."

---

[36] *Australian Victories in France, 1918*, p. 233.

[37] From *The Empire at War*, Vol. III: Section II ("The Australian Forces in the War"), pp. 179-80.

The IX and III Corps were much less successful; in particular III Corps met with strong resistance, and failed to advance beyond the old British front line so that the left flank of Fourth Army's front facing the tunnel sector bent sharply back. In particular the strongly fortified positions known as Quennemont Farm, Gillemont Farm, and "The Knoll," which could be reinforced by underground routes from the main defensive line, remained uncaptured—a tactical failure which was to have many sad consequences.

The casualties of the two divisions for 18th and 19th September were :—

	Killed in action	Died of wounds	Died of Gas	Total	Wounded	Gassed	Prisoners of war	Total
4th Div.	89	32	—	121	557	6	—	563
1st Div.	107	37	—	144	489	5	2	496
	196	69	—	265	1,046	11	2	1,059

Medical Arrangements : Hindenburg Outpost Line

During the week before this battle, as the leading infantry of the pursuing Fourth Army brought up against the German outposts in the old British "reserve" line, the medical units also, from the front rearwards —R.A.P's, relay and loading posts, advanced and main dressing stations—had come to a halt, save for minor movements which conformed to the exploitation of the fluid front by enterprising battalions. At the same time the Corps stations—motor convoy and lorry relay posts, sanitary sections, scabies stations, baths and laundries, and so forth—and the various "Army" diagnostic and treatment centres, moving up more circumspectly behind the advancing divisions, felt in their turn the repulsive force of this hitherto "immovable obstacle," and closed in on a now again static front. The move up of the casualty clearing stations during the advance was carried out largely by leap-frogging, so as to avoid hiatus.

Pari passu the divisional transport routes, bearer, horsed, and motor relay circuits, and light railways—the last named thrown out like filaments before the broad-gauge railheads almost as fast as the divisional fronts could advance—telescoped up; and the same process went on more slowly with the Army motor and rail circuits in their rear.

MEDICAL ARRANGEMENTS 1st and 4th DIVI
LINE HELD:—From North to South A.25.d.o.o.—

BATTALION	REGIMENTAL AID POSTS	RELAY POSTS	MOTOR LOADING POSTS
Left Line Bn.	K.11.c.3.5	K.12.d.5.3	K.11.c.3.5
Left Support	K.15.a.7.3		K.16.a.7.3
Right Line Bn.	K.29.d.8.8	K.35.b.8.5	K.29.d.8.8
Right Support	K.35.c.5.2		

1st Division

DISPO

A.D.M.S. Office J.16.a.5.0
1st Aust. Field Amb., M.D.S., W.W.D.S. and Gas Centre (near Buire) J.28.a.5.4
2nd Aust. Field Amb. J.34.a.9.3. In reserve
3rd Aust. Field Amb. J.24.a.5.9. Evacuation from Divisional front
No. 18 Aust. Dental Unit J.28.a.5.4 (M.D.S.)
No. 2 Sanitary Section. (Bussu)

	LINE HELD:—L.26.d. central to R.15.b.5.8		Sheet 62C 1/40,000
Left Bn.	L.35.c.45.80 R.7.d.3.7		L.32.a.6.1
	L.30.c.cent		
	L.29.b.1.7		
	L.34.c.3.8		
Right Bn.	R.6.a.2.4.		R.8.c.8.8
	L.36.c.7.7		R.3.d.5.8
	R.5.c.2.3		(Horsed Amb.)
Support	Q.23.b.8.8		

4th Division

DISPO

A.D.M.S. Office Catelet (P.8.b.2.7)
4th Aust. Field Amb. M.D.S. Hancourt
12th Aust. Field Amb. A.D.S. Vendelles
13th Aust. Field Amb. Gas centre Q.13.d.7.7 (Beet factory) and in reserve.
No. 4 Sanitary Section. (Hénencourt)

D.D.M.S. Office N.16.a
3rd M.A.C. Villers-Carbonnel N.30.d.3.6
No. 18 Adv. Depot Med. Stores 62D/R.10.c
 (Also Depot for Oxygen and Sera) Chuignolles
Mobile Laboratory, No. 5 Can. (Bact.) Proyart
Infectious cases to nearest C.C.S.

Australian Corps and Fourth Army

[28] The map references mostly relate to posts and stations shown on one or other of the sketch maps in this chapter. The pro-forma employed is that used by most A.D's.M.S. in the Australian Corps to make their routine "disposition reports" to headquarters, and to issue their "medical arrangements" to the field units. The scheme was essentially dynamic and labile, changing almost from hour to hour as to R.A.P's and loading posts, and more

SIONS AS ON 17th-18th SEPTEMBER, 1918.[38]
G.l.b.7.0, G.l.d.6.5, G.8.c.5.5, G.14.a.6.0, G.20.b.7.0.   *Sheet 62C.*

ADVANCED DRESSING STATIONS	WALKING WOUNDED DRESSING STATIONS	MAIN DRESSING STATIONS	EVACUATION
J.24.a.5.9. (Tincourt) Reserve A.D.S. K.15.c.1.8 (Marquaix)	J.28.a.5.4 (near Buire)	J.28.a.5.4	From Relay Posts forward of R.A.P's to R.A.P's by hand carry or wheeled stretchers. From R.A.P's to A.D.S. by Divisional amb. cars. Stretcher cases to C.C.S., by M.A.C. cars; walking wounded to C.C.S. by lorries and 'buses.

SITION
No. 3 Aust. Dental Unit J.28.a.5.4 (M.D.S.)
No. 5 Aust. Dental Unit J.34.a.9.3 (2nd Fld. Amb.) (Halle Brusle)
Resuscitation Team J.28.a.5.4 (M.D.S.)
Australian Red Cross. Pernois
Gassed cases. All go to Gas centre J.28.a.5.4 (M.D.S.) near Buire
Records. All records kept at M.D.S. (J.28.a.5.4)
Medical Comforts and Stores. 2nd Fld. Amb. to draw for M.D.S. and A.D.S.

and 62D.

		Q.8.d.central (Hancourt)	Evacuation by hand carry to M.L. Post: thence to A.D.S. and M.D.S. by Motor Ambulance.
R.7.c.2.9 (Vendelles)		Q.8.d.5.4 (Hancourt)	

SITION
No. 19 Dental Unit with 4th Aust. Field Amb.
No. 27 Dental Unit with Div. Reinforcement Wing 0.8.b.9.0
No. 34 Dental Unit with 13th Aust. Field Amb.
No. 11 Dental Unit with 4th D.A.C. P.14.c.2.4.
Australian Red Cross Vecquemont, 62D/N.4.c.9.2.

No. 41 *Stationary Hospital* (Asylum) 62E/R.27.b.—N.Y.D.N., N.Y.D.Gas, S.I.W.,
  Venereal, Dysentery, Ophthalmic, Dental, Ear, Nose and Throat cases
C.C.S's. Nos. 5 and 41 Proyart
  Nos. 53 and 12 La Chapellette
  No. 37 Vecquemont (For overflow)

---

slowly in the case of stations in rear. A.D's.M.S. issued amendments as necessary, according with the rate of advance or of retreat. It was based on exact map references; place names could seldom be used in such orders in mobile or semi-mobile warfare, except for the larger stations in villages and towns. It should be noted that the method of map-reading differed from that now in use.

Even so, Army lines of communication were still unduly elongated—the shock of "Michael" was not yet spent! It was over forty miles from the front line to No. 41 Stationary Hospital—for "N.Y.D.N.," "N.Y.D. Gas," self-inflicted wounds, venereal, dysentery, ophthalmic, dental, ear, nose and throat cases—in the "Asylum" at Amiens.

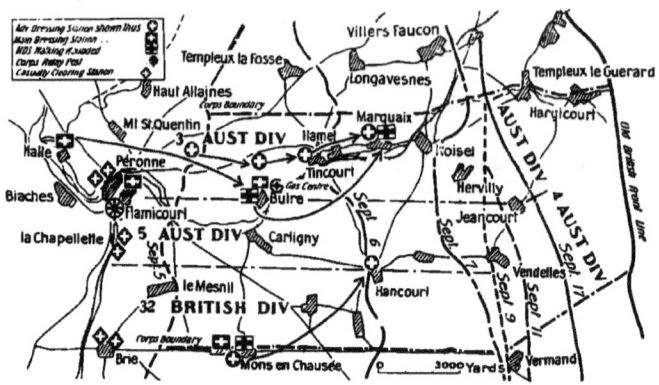

Stages of Advance and Moves of Medical Stations, Sept. 5-18

Fourth Army Medical Arrangements, September 18th. The general scheme of "medical arrangements" for the two divisions of the Australian Corps in the line is shown in the accompanying table. On it were based the special "arrangements" of the Corps for the attack on the Hindenburg Outpost Lines and also, *mutatis mutandis*, those for the great battle that followed it. The scheme may be taken as typical of the system of evacuation and treatment in "army" area in the B.E.F. at what would seem to be the most "normal" phase of the Great War in terms of future warfare.

The medical orders both of the Corps and the Divisions illustrate, by their simplicity, the understanding that by now had been achieved between the several administrative headquarters and the field units. The medical technique required for the "set-piece" battle in its two phases—first advance behind a barrage, and then exploitation by open warfare—was familiar to all concerned, whether carried out by leap-frog or by continuous advance. *Liaison* between direction and executive was automatic—a social "conditioned reflex"! The

Corps Medical Arrangements for Sept. 18

force of this observation will become apparent when we come to the events of the main battle.

Colonel Barber's "instructions" as D.D.M.S. dealt chiefly with the arrangements to be made for the evacuation of the "walking wounded"; as noted in his war diary, they illustrate the flexibility of medical tactics in this final campaign.

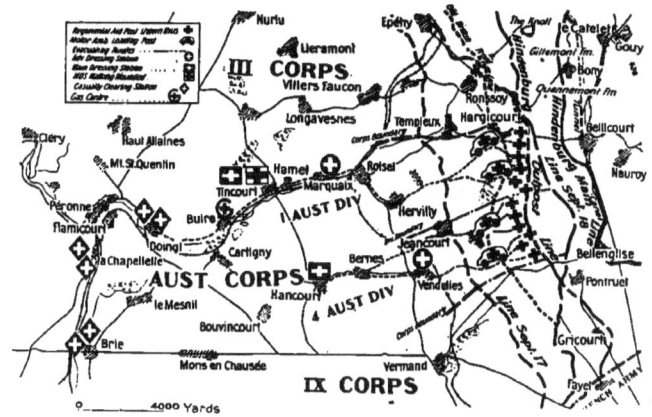

Scheme of Evacuation, Sept. 17-18. (Bearer Relay and Horsed Ambulance Loading Posts and Routes are not shown). The M.D.S. and W.W.D.S. of the 1st Division were situated on the Buire-Tincourt Road.

"September 15th. Received battle instructions for attack on German positions opposite Corps front. Decided to evacuate walking wounded from M.D.S. at Buire and Hancourt by light railway to Flamicourt, where a Corps Relay Station (one tent sub-division) could detrain the patients."

September 16th. This decision was implemented by "Medical Instruction No. 55" dealing with "The evacuation of Walking Wounded." The diary proceeds:

"September 17th. Attended conference presided over by Corps Commander, on offensive. Cancelled Medical Instructions issued yesterday, because Army decided to open C.C.S. at Doignt and Brie. These C.C.S's being reasonably close to M.D.S's at Buire and Hancourt, I have decided to rely only on M.A.C. cars and 'buses for evacuating wounded."

The Divisions. The A.D's.M.S. of the 1st and 4th Divisions disposed their field units in the way now normal in this type of battle. The 12th (4th Division) under Lieut.-Colonel A. H. Gibson, and 3rd (1st Division) under Lieut.-

Colonel D. D. Cade, with all the divisional resources at their disposal, were to clear their respective divisional fronts. Their clearance would be from A.D.S's, to be formed as soon as the situation should permit "on the main evacuation route" (4th Division) and at a "Reserve A.D.S." already selected at Marquaix (1st Division), to M.D.S's to be established for the operation at Hancourt and Buire.[39] The two reserve units remained closed, and furnished bearers and transport for the line. The divisional resuscitation teams were to work at the main dressing stations. The normal divisional institutions—gas centres, baths, disinfecting and scabies stations—were in full swing by September 17th. For example, for the 4th Division a "gas and scabies" station was established by a tent sub-division of the 13th Field Ambulance at Vraignes, in close association with the divisional baths. This gas centre was equipped with Haldane Oxygen Inhaler, and "laid out with chambers for the removal of clothing, treatment, feeding, and evacuation of casualties."

The Bearer Divisions. The outstanding feature of the medical problem in this battle was the comparative depth of the stage of exploitation—an additional mile—and the new problem was met by the mobilisation of all possible and available means of stretcher transport from the front line. Here we meet the final development[40] of an advance in the medical tactics of infantry warfare which seems to have come to stay, to wit, the method of using the "bearer divisions" of the field ambulances as brigade troops. This procedure was now general in the Australian Corps. The bearer divisions, working as "units," were attached to the headquarters of the corresponding brigades; each was under command of an officer attached to brigade headquarters, but himself and his command were controlled by the officer in charge of the "forward evacuation"—operating commonly from the A.D.S.[41]

From the medical standpoint this operation is happy in having no "history" to speak of. The D.D.M.S. notes laconically that "arrangements worked smoothly . . . 939 wounded, in addition to 314 wounded German

Evacuation

---

[39] See diagram on opposite page, which shows the lay-out of the M.D.S. at Buire.
[40] See also footnote 23 on p. 619.
[41] See in this connection *Appendix No. 3.*

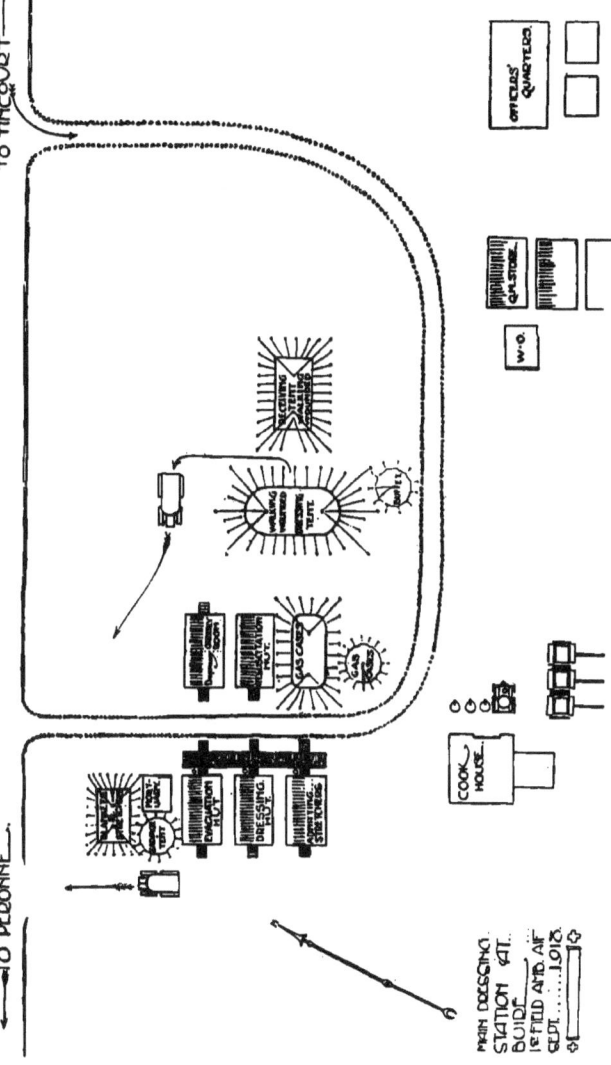

From War Diary of 1st Aust. Field Ambulance.

prisoners were evacuated from the 2 divisions in 24 hours." The war diaries of the A.D's.M.S. and of field ambulance commanders describe events as proceeding "according to plan," in close accord with the advances and checks of the battle as described above. On the 4th Division's front the O.C., 12th Field Ambulance, telephoned at 10.45 a.m. that he had established an A.D.S. at Vendelles on a site "suitable for expansion into an M.D.S. . . . Evacuation was proceeding smoothly." By 4 p.m. all new R.A.P's had been located. On the 17th the A.D.S. at Hancourt had been transformed to an M.D.S. with two good Nissen huts and three good dugouts. In the 1st Division the delayed "exploitation" held up the advancement of the dressing stations for some twelve hours, when the A.D.S. at Tincourt and the M.D.S. near Buire moved forward simultaneously to Hervilly and Marquaix respectively.

Some excellent descriptions of the medical operations in this division give a vivid glimpse of them.[42]

R.M.O., 11th Battalion.[43] *"16th September.* Very little to do here except sick parades. Bombed all night, shelled all day. Heavies in the village roaring and stolidly pounding away. C.O. and I go up the line at 4 a.m. and so get everything ready for the stunt—splints padded and the tally books written up as completely as possible. Fritz has gone back, so 'green' line cut out:[44] we (the 11th) with the 12th go for the 'red' line—about 3,000 yards; the 9th and 10th go on and exploit.

"17th September. During the night gas came over. 3.45 C.O. and I went reconnoitring with guide in the dark. Roads wet and muddy; looked round for an R.A.P. and found a crumpled cupola big enough for stretchers, but with only a single layer of sandbags. Fixed it up to use for the stunt. After sick parade go down to Tincourt; saw 3rd F.Amb. ['forward evacuation'] to give them my intentions and locations of my new R.A.P. and the proposed second one. All ready. Zero hour [will be] 5.20 a.m. on 18th: our [Bn.] front 800 yards, two companies attacking on high ground the others mopping up.

"18th September. 1.30 a.m. the O.C. and I rigged ourselves up for the line and set off across country with my 7 H.Q. bearers and 13 ambulance bearers [attached for the operation] with my own three orderlies bringing up the rear. Got the dressings and stretchers up to my cupola, settled down, and waited. At zero hour barrage started and was deafening. 6.10 a.m. came the first casualty—a Sergeant with left forearm lacerated. And then the cases began to come in and I did not look up again. No congestion—due to Fritz prisoners who poured in and carried

---
[42] Certain parts of the passages here quoted have, for brevity, been epitomised.
[43] Major L. May. At this time the battalion was in reserve near Marquaix.
[44] This was the case along only part of the front.

back. We put on Thomas, internal angular, and back splints, and dressed wounded, Germans and all. Sent my H.Q. bearers at 7 a.m. to find a new Aid Post. At 9.15 they returned, reported all clear and battalion headquarters to go on. Packed up, got 9th Battalion [in support] to do my cases, and we moved up 2,500 yards and got a pozzy in the sap which we roofed over, put our flag out and were ready. Few more cases, however, came, sewed up two Germans with perforated chest wounds, and put on a Thomas while two German M.O's came up and yarned. Later the 9th Battalion went on ahead and we moved up. Only 33 casualties, but many of the 10th, 9th, and 13th and Germans."

Lance-Corporal A.A.M.C. (attached 2nd Bn.).[45] *"17th September.* Going into action tonight. . . . Battalion strength now under 300.

"18th September. Moved up after midnight. Jeancourt on right, Hargicourt somewhere ahead. When passing a sunken road in single file a German bombing plane passed close overhead. To see the whole line of men in perfect time bend over and lie against the bank showed collective common sense. My section [*i.e.* the A.A.M.C. personnel] established itself behind a bank 70 yards from a tape, where battalion is lying waiting for zero. A number of casualties occurred immediately prior to this. [During the advance] was assisting M.O. to fix a Thomas splint when a salvo of whizbangs struck the bank—a flash of fire and all was blank. Later I discovered my steel helmet a battered wreck—the piece of shell incidentally taking a piece out of my scalp. Had slight concussion and a terrific headache. Had a nip of brandy and felt much better for same. Having tended casualties before zero, and those in the first few minutes of the advance, Doc. Rossell gave the word for our section to follow the advancing battalion. The movement forward of our particular section, was like rolling peas down-hill; the infantry in front had cleared the roads in no uncertain manner and in attending to casualties we lost touch with battalion which was well ahead, and still going strong. Moved forward 3,000 yards and found battalion advanced troops were still 1,000 yards ahead. It was rather unusual during the advance to witness the batteries of 18-pounders galloping into action, all smiles as if going to a picnic. Mick Carter of 2nd Bn., company cook, salvaged an old German cooker and went into action well loaded with hot soup and other rations for his company. He managed to get well up towards the front line and delivered a hot meal. The troops would have decorated Mick with a V.C. had they had their way. Plenty of dead Germans in evidence, and prisoners moving back—poor beggars seem pleased to have been taken.

"Was resting alongside bank when for the second time I knew no more, woke up in an ambulance (motor), by which I was conveyed to Main dressing station, received attention including anti-tetanus injection . . . had a good meal in the transport lines and a sleep and returned to duty next day. .

"22nd September. 2nd Battalion moving back into reserves into a wood behind Jeancourt and a sorry looking lot we are, haggard, drawn and war weary.

"23rd September. Relieved by American troops whose battalion being at full strength fairly dwarfs the shattered remnants of what was

---

[45] L/Cpl. R. Morgan (1st Fld. Amb.), attached for "water duties" to the 2nd Battalion. The 1st and 2nd Battalions occupied the extreme left of the Australian Corps front at the junction with III Corps.

once a full strength battalion 1,000 strong, now only just over 200. Moved to Tincourt."

R.M.O., 4th Battalion.[46] "17th September. After some days' relief the battalion went in again behind Templeux to join up for the attack on Hargicourt.

"18th September. I got some old French dugouts as R.A.P. close to the starting tape, and worked there in comparative comfort with R.M.O., 3rd Battalion (Capt. B. B. Blomfield), though the wood behind us was heavily shelled. No difficulty in evacuating stretcher cases as there were plenty of unwounded P. of W. soon collected round the R.A.P. I signed a chit to the C.O. that I had used 50 prisoners to carry wounded but I must have made use of a good many more. The wounded slacked off about 10 a.m., and I retained some prisoners of war to push my wheeled stretchers with stores, dressings and blankets towards the battalion objective at Hargicourt. This was quite against regulations of course—but perfectly safe. Discovered a good dugout right of Hargicourt and located the battalion headquarters and the various companies. The ambulance loading post was immediately in rear of my R.A.P."

3rd Field Ambulance War Diary (Lieut.-Colonel D.D. Cade; "Forward Evacuation" and A.D.S. at Tincourt and Hervilly). "18th September. Zero hour 5.20 a.m. 1st Division attacked on a two-brigade front. Wounded commenced to arrive at 8 a.m. Owing to heavy shelling of forward reserve dressing station at Marquaix, we could not open that station as an advanced dressing station as was originally intended. About 10 a.m. 2nd F. Amb. opened up in Tincourt adjoining, and took charge of all walking wounded. All our own wounded men cleared by 2 p.m. and all German prisoners by 5 p.m. After that hour casualties had fallen to normal.

"The rapid and successful advance of our troops had the effect of leaving our A.D.S. [at Tincourt] at the end of the first day too far in rear and, in accordance with A.D.M.S's orders, both M.D.S. and A.D.S. were moved forward at the earliest opportunity. On the evening of the 18th I chose an apparently ideal spot on the outskirts of a ruined village as the site for the A.D.S., but found that it really only served the right sector and it was decided to evacuate the left sector direct [from the loading posts] to M.D.S., which has been brought well forward to Marquaix—the site originally chosen by us for an A.D.S.!"

2nd Field Ambulance War Diary (Lieut.-Colonel Frank Lind;[47] W.W.D.S. at Tincourt, and M.D.S. at Marquaix). "On the afternoon of 17th September, in accordance with A.D.M.S's instructions, 'B' Section Tent Sub-division set up a Walking Wounded Dressing Station in proximity of 3rd F. Amb. at Tincourt. On arrival the section converted the three 'Swiss Cottage' tents, allotted to them for the purpose, into a very serviceable and neatly arranged W.W.D.S. The other tents were arranged in line parallel to road, with ammunition boxes, filled with earth, arranged around the sides to serve at the same time as seats and revetments. Patients entered into the first tent, where all the clerking was done; thence they passed to the second tent, where they

---

[46] Capt. J. I. Connor.
[47] It may be recalled that this officer commanded the Australian Contingent at the coronation of H.M. King George VI.

79. LOADING WOUNDED AT THE A.D.S., BRAY, ON 28TH AUGUST, 1918
Aust. War Memorial Official Photo. No. E3119.

80. AN M.D.S. BEYOND PÉRONNE IN MID-SEPTEMBER, 1918
This station, at Buire, near Tincourt, was then staffed by the 1st Field Ambulance.
From a water colour sketch in the diary of 1st Field Ambulance.

To face p. 732.

81. Engineers of the 5th Division repairing the plank road to Bellicourt on the battlefield of the Hindenburg Line, 1st October, 1918

Aust. War Memorial Official Photo. No. E3631.

were dressed; and finally to the third tent, where hot drinks in the form of cocoa and milk were given them with biscuits. Guides were posted at entrance and exit of station, the former to stop cars and lorries bringing down wounded and help them to clearing tent; the latter to check them into *char-à-bancs* to proceed to the C.C.S. . . . Later, on the afternoon of the 18th, the remainder of the unit still at Brusle moved to Marquaix to form a M.D.S. by 8 a.m. the next morning. Here the whole three tent sub-divisions worked hard in order to open the M.D.S. at the specified time. . . . [Here] cars bringing down stretcher cases entered by one gate into a courtyard in front of the M.D.S., and passed out by another. Stretcher squads were on duty—in front, to off-load cars on arrival; others inside, to load up M.A.C. cars, of which there were eight attached and which ran in and out on a complete circuit behind the station and quite distinct from the former. *There is little doubt that this [is the right] system, namely, the walking wounded and stretcher cases being kept entirely apart, [and] complete circuits for incoming and outgoing cars respectively.* . . .[48]

"118th Field Ambulance U.S.A. marched into Marquaix at 4.30 a.m. on the 23rd September and were followed later by their transport. They took over at 8 a.m. the next day. The following two days, during which we were waiting orders, the officers and N.C.O's gave the Yanks every assistance and much advice, for which they were very grateful."

During the next two days (September 21st-22nd) the two Australian divisions worked forward some 500-800 yards, putting that part of the Fourth Army's front on a line well placed for the final assault. Between the 23rd and 26th, however, the Australian Corps "side-slipped" to the north to place it *vis-à-vis* the Bellicourt tunnel sector, through which the Army Commander (General Rawlinson) proposed to thrust the combined Australian and II American Corps. They were to form a wedge which—with the co-operation of a fresh British corps (XIII) on the north—would expand right and left when clear of the canal and force the Germans out of their apparently more formidable positions behind the deep ravine where the canal ran through an open cut.

A change of front

The process of "side-slipping" formations in trench warfare involved a complicated series of infantry reliefs and interchange of medical and supply stations and transport routes behind the lines. On September 22nd-23rd the 4th Australian Division handed over its front to the 46th British (IX Corps). The order of the A.D.M.S. (Colonel Kenneth Smith), which

---

[48] Not italicised in the original.

is typical of such procedures, is reproduced in *Appendix No. 3.*[49]

On the night of September 23rd-24th the 1st Division handed over to the 30th American Division (II American Corps), and on the following night the 27th American Division, under Australian Corps, relieved the 18th and 74th British Divisions (III Corps). The 1st and 4th Australian Divisions moved back to rest near Abbeville; the 2nd, 3rd and 5th were behind the lines, still available for use, though at greatly reduced strength. For five days the American Corps held General Monash's new front; and for the first time since the A.I.F. had come to France no Australian infantry were in the front line.

---

[49] 4th Division, A.A.M.C., Order No. 1:2. *See p. 888.*

CHAPTER XXIV

THE HINDENBURG LINE—A STUDY IN CO-OPERATION

THE history of what might be termed the technique of American co-operation as a military ally with Britain and France in the war of 1914-18 is a subject worthy of close study, since the "total" warfare, which experts now prophesy, will involve for each side the intimate co-operation of various national armies, and these, apart from differences of language, will differ widely in their organisation and methods.

The II American Corps

The principle laid down by General Pershing—which reflected American national feelings—of an American Expeditionary Force of one or more armies with full lines of communication and all essential services, trained and organised on American lines and operating independently, was relaxed in January, 1918, to permit the training of American infantry units with British divisions under arrangements as to equipment, etc., somewhat similar to those made with Australia. The agreement was not implemented until March, 1918, when the II American Corps Headquarters Staff was created to train American divisions in the British zone. Some ten divisions passed through this corps, but all save two—27th and 30th—were afterwards diverted to American armies. These two at first served with British Second Army as the right and left divisions respectively of the British II and XIX Corps, and took part in the engagements associated with the retirement of the Germans from Mont Kemmel. In June Major-General Read was appointed to command the corps, which at the beginning of September was brought south, trained intensively round Beauval, and on the 22nd moved up for the assault on the Hindenburg Line.[1]

The Sanitary (i.e., Medical) Services of the A.E.F.

The American Sanitary Train. The Official Medical History of the United States Army gives the following summary of the medical organisation of the "Sanitary Train" of an American infantry division.[2]

---

[1] From the *History of the Medical Department of the United States Army in the World War, Vol. VIII, pp. 21 and 875;* and *The Story of the 27th American Division, p.* 176.

[2] The infantry of an American division consisted of two brigades, each comprising two regiments, each of three battalions, each containing 1,000 officers and men. The total strength of a division was 28,000. A short study of American army medical methods will be found in *Appendix No. 9*.

"The Sanitary Train is composed of a train headquarters, ambulance companies, field hospital companies, camp infirmaries, medical supply unit, and reserve medical supplies. The sanitary train is commanded by the senior medical officer on duty with the train. . . .

"*Ambulance Companies.* Ambulance companies push up close to the rear of the fighting troops and as near the line of regimental aid stations as possible, and establish dressing stations. In addition . . . they are charged with the transportation of the wounded back to field hospitals. . . . When field hospitals have not been set up and when sanitary columns or railway hospital trains of the line of communications are reasonably accessible, ambulance companies transport the wounded directly to them.

"*Field Hospital Companies.* Field hospital companies form part of the sanitary column. They are set up when conditions so warrant, ordinarily some 3 to 4 miles from the battle field, and are the places (*sic*) to which the wounded are transported by ambulance companies. . . . Field hospitals are not set up when the sick or wounded can be turned over conveniently to elements of the sanitary column or railway hospital trains of the line of communications."[3]

Sanitary Service of II American Corps. The corps was not joined by its sanitary service till the end of July and then by special arrangement this service was at half the normal strength,[4] being completed by the attachment of British Field Ambulances. When serving with British Second Army the medical transport seems to have been replaced by British.

"In some instances," the *American Medical History* states,[5] the motor ambulances were "found to be old, worn, and unserviceable, as most . . . had been in constant use for a long time." On their arrival on the Somme the two divisions (27th and 30th) turned in all medical property not carried by the personnel individually, and gradually received corresponding British equipment in its stead.

In the Battle of the St. Quentin Canal the American units were using both British and American equipment. An officer of the R.A.M.C. from Second Army was attached to each division to instruct the personnel in the methods of evacuation in France. Ambulance transport consisted of old British motor ambulances.

Thus the "sanitary" service of the formations which were now to co-operate with the Australians in this great battle was, by no fault of its own, composite in organisation, equipment,

---

[3] *Official History of Medical Department of the United States Army, Vol. VIII, pp. 1022-3.*

[4] This was necessitated by the fact that the transfer of the medical personnel of the A.E.F. to Europe fell far behind that of the combatant arms. At the end of the war, as pointed out in the Chief Surgeon's report, "the Armistice was the only thing that saved us from a disastrous situation resulting from personnel shortage." (*American Official Medical History, Vol. VIII, p. 25.*) It is to be noted, however, that from an early stage of the war America sent medical men to serve independently in British and French units or in "Red Cross" hospitals.

[5] *Vol. VIII, pp. 881-3.*

training, and methods, a curious hotch-potch of new-world and old, of peace and war.[6]

Medical Arrangements of II Corps on Relief. Both the American divisions on coming into the line took over and adapted the existing schemes of evacuation.

With his large staff the Divisional Surgeon of the 30th Division organised his front in two sectors, each with two Aid Stations and a Motor Loading Post. These cleared to A.D.S's at Jeancourt and Templeux-le-Guérard respectively. The Walking Wounded Dressing Station was at Jeancourt, and M.D.S. (118th "Field Ambulance") and Gas Centre (132nd British Field Ambulance) were at Marquaix.

The 27th Division cleared through a single A.D.S. at Ste. Emilie (106th Ambulance Company) to M.D.S., which moved from Longavesnes to Villers-Faucon on the 27th (105th and 106th Field Hospital Companies). This station served the division throughout the operations. Clearance to A.D.S. "was covered by Ambulance Companies No. 106 and No. 107 [less a detail to run the A.D.S.], reinforced by the litter-bearer section [Bearer division] of the 133rd British Field Ambulance and 100 men of the 108th Infantry [Regiment]." The motor transport consisted of 3 Fords and 11 Daimlers—none of them new cars.[7]

Australian-American Co-operation. The II American Corps was "affiliated" or "attached" to the Australian—both terms were officially used. The general staff

The Hindenburg Line : Battle of St. Quentin Canal, Sept. 29-Oct. 2

of the Australian Corps was made responsible for the plan and in a great measure for the conduct of this battle. The respective rôles assigned to the two corps were well adapted to get the utmost advantage from the combination. The Americans provided tremendous driving power, moral and physical, but lacked as yet war wisdom and skill in the technique of combat and service, and the automatic response to unexpected situations that comes with habitude. This the Australian Corps was able to supply, and the Americans to accept. The American soldier, like the Australian, was a realist: in this acceptance, and the high pride and self-regard

---

[6] The 27th Division was served by the 102nd Sanitary Train, which comprised Field Hospital Companies Nos. 105 and 106, and Ambulance Companies Nos. 106 and 107, together with the 133rd Field Ambulance, B.E.F. The 30th Division had two British field ambulances (132nd and 134th), as well as American units. The *American Medical History* (*Vol. VIII, pp. 891-2*) says: "The Sanitary train of the division did not join until August 1, 1918, when Field Hospitals No. 118 and No. 119 and Ambulance Companies No. 118 and No. 119, reported. In order to comply with the British Tables of Organisation, the field hospitals and ambulance companies were combined on August 14 and designated Field Ambulances No. 118 and No. 119."

[7] *American Official Medical History, Vol. VIII, p. 887.*

that alone made it possible, lay the possibility of success in this unique combination.[8]

The "Australian Mission." Liaison was effected through the creation of an "Australian mission," the rôle of which was "to act as a body of expert advisers on all questions of tactical technique and of supply and maintenance." The "mission" comprised a total of 217 officers and other ranks, with Major-General Sinclair-MacLagan (4th Division) at its head, and covered every technical arm and service except the medical. Co-operation between the medical services of the two corps was achieved by personal *liaison* between the departmental staffs, with a few formal meetings at which arrangements and orders were explained by Colonel Barber and his A.D's.M.S.

The Battle of St. Quentin Canal. Few battles of the A.I.F. can have more to teach of the science and art of modern war than that fought between September 29th and October 2nd.[9]

Plan. The 30th and 27th American Divisions were to attack at dawn and seize the main Hindenburg Line and the first support (Le Catelet) line, an advance of from two to three miles. The 5th and 3rd Australian Divisions would immediately move up and pass through them and seize by open warfare methods the Beaurevoir Line a similar distance ahead. The events, however, went very differently.

The Unreduced Outpost-line. In the first place the left division (27th) of the Corps had to start from a position less advanced than the right (30th). The failure of the British III Corps to reach its final objective on September 18th had not been made good—efforts by the III Corps to do this had failed; and though the 27th American Division, making another attempt on September 27th, had penetrated to its objective, its troops, like many of the British in the First Battle of the Somme, had failed to "mop up" and guard their flanks, and Germans had penetrated behind them. When the time came for the great attack on September 29th it was still believed that some Americans might be holding out in positions reached on the 27th. Consequently the American

---

[8] "It was certainly anomalous that a whole organised Corps should pass under the orders of a Corps Headquarters of another nationality but . . . General Rawlinson relied upon the good sense and mutual forbearance of the Corps Commanders concerned. I am bound to say that the arrangement caused me no anxiety or difficulty. General Read and his staff most readily adapted themselves to the situation." (Sir John Monash, *The Australian Victories in France in 1918, p. 243.*)
At a conference with his divisional commanders "Major-General Read . . . outlined the character of the offensive . . . and that the 27th and 30th Divisions were to be assigned to the Australian Corps for the purpose of leading the attack. General Read's spirit of co-operation in subordinating for the occasion his own rôle as commander of the II American Corps, and placing his two divisions at the disposal of the Australian Commander, created a most favourable impression at the time upon all who knew of the arrangement." (Maj.-Gen. John F. O'Ryan, *The Story of the 27th Division, pp. 253-4.*)

[9] The historian of the 5th Australian Division refers to the events of the 29th as "the most extraordinary day's fighting in the history of the Division."

commander preferred to have the barrage laid beyond those positions, although the attacking waves would start half-a-mile farther back. To help the waves to cross this half-mile a force of tanks, including No. 1 American Company in British tanks, was allotted.

The Main Attack. But when the attack was launched, at dawn on September 29th, the tanks ran into an old British minefield and nearly the whole line of them was destroyed. The American infantry pushed on in face of German machine-guns now firing with complete impunity. And when, several hours later, the time came for the 5th and 3rd Australian Divisions to move up in order to pass through the Americans (supposed by then to be on the first objective), the 3rd Division on the left was surprised to run into German machine-gun fire about the position of the old front line. It became obvious that the Germans were in strength close ahead. American dead and wounded lay thickly about the starting line and in front of it. Remnants of the 27th American Division were found a few hundred yards farther on, but none could give any information as to the position. A report, however, presently came back from an Australian observer that others had been seen two miles ahead, and this rumour had the same effect as at First Bullecourt—the Australian artillery was prevented unable to fire. Consequently the Australian battalions, with rifles, machine-guns, and bombs, had to use all their skill and audacity to make good gradually, by hard fighting, manoeuvring, and outflanking, the remainder of the 27th Division's objective. The 30th American Division and the right of the 27th had greater success than the left, the 30th passing the southern end of the tunnel and reaching Bellicourt. The 46th British Division did better still, crossing the canal south of the tunnel and reaching its objective. The 5th Australian Division, passing through the 30th American, had touch with these British on its right. The American casualties had been very heavy.

Next day, as there was no sign of Americans ahead, the artillery supported this difficult piecemeal fighting, and by October 1st the two Australian divisions had reached, roughly, the line originally laid down for the Americans. Their own original task, the breaking of the last support system (Beaurevoir Line) was still unaccomplished. The 3rd and 5th Divisions were worn out, and the job was handed to the last Australian division with the strength to carry it out, the 2nd.

For the Medical Service of the A.I.F. the contrast between this, their last battle, and the Landing at Anzac, their first, could scarcely have been sharper. At Anzac Cove in 1915 officers and men of the A.A.M.C. were receiving their first lesson in the difficult art of war; in this battle, three and a half years later, their advice was being sought and their direction accepted by the medical corps of a great nation justly proud of its own history. In the following pages it will be necessary among other things to describe aspects of the evacuation of wounded from the combined corps that fell short of the standard set for themselves by the Australian medical units in 1918. In doing so no vestige

Medical Arrangements

of blame can be attributed to those who, as inexperienced as were the Australians in 1915, were set to the undertaking of this complicated co-operative task; the sole object is to elucidate the facts and the lessons to be drawn from them.

That the clearance of wounded during the first 24 hours through the dressing stations was not wholly "successful" is undoubted. Australian diarists, official and individual, make no bones about this. Thus the personal diary of one of the most experienced and forthright A.A.M.C. officers, who had served in front-line units throughout the war,[10] has for September 29th the laconic entry:—

"Americans [*i.e.*, 27th Division] . . . jumped off 1,000 yards behind line [of the barrage] cut to blazes: our division [3rd] came in for a lot of machine-gun fire. Things generally mixed. Evacuation awful."

And the D.D.M.S., Australian Corps (Colonel Barber) permits himself the statement that "the Hindenburg Line evacuation was not so good."

Arrangements Made by Army and Corps. Casualty clearing stations for the two divisional fronts remained at Doingt and Brie for the right and left sectors respectively, with a forward echelon at Tincourt. Colonel Barber's medical arrangements for the two corps followed very exactly the military plan and envisaged a "leap-frog" battle for four divisions with two objectives. They were subject to the same inherent defects as led to the military misadventure—the unresolved menace of the left flank and the handicap imposed by imperfect integration of methods and machinery. For this latter Colonel Barber, it is true, made definite provision; but it is necessary to stress the fact that, as events proved, the problem of "affiliating" the medical services of two national armies is not met by issuing identical orders, if the two armies do not speak the same military language and think in the same terms, as applied, for example, to the constant factors in the business of evacuation. Colonel Barber's order ran:—

"*Australian Corps Medical Instructions No. 58* (dated 27th September, 1918).

"In accordance with Australian Corps Battle Instructions Series 'E' No. 2.

---

[10] Lieut.-Col. G. W. Macartney, commanding 10th Field Ambulance.

"1. Bearer Divisions of Field Ambulances will move with their respective Brigades.

"2. Dispositions of Field Ambulances, less Bearer Divisions, will be as follows:—

Right Sector	30th Amer. Div.	5th Aust. Div.
M.D.S. MARQUAIX	X. Fd. Ambce.	X. Fd. Ambce.
A.D.S. TEMPLEUX	Y. Fd. Ambce.	Y. Fd. Ambce.
Reserve	Z. Fd. Ambce.	Z. Fd. Ambce.
Left Sector	27th Amer. Div.	3rd Aust. Div.
M.D.S. LONGA-VESNES[11]	X. Fd. Ambce.	X. Fd. Ambce.
A.D.S. STE. EMILIE	Y. Fd. Ambce.	Y. Fd. Ambce.
Reserve	Z. Fd. Ambce.	Z. Fd. Ambce.

"3. The tent sub-divisions of 'Z' (Reserve) Field Ambces. will be used to form new Advanced Dressing Stations in the event of advance, at which time 'Y' Field Ambulances will be converted to Main Dressing Stations and 'X' Field Ambulances become reserve.

"4. On 'Z' day—(i) Divisional Surgeons of American Divisions will be responsible for evacuation from Green Line to M.D.S's. (ii) A.D's.M.S. Australian Divisions will be responsible for evacuation from Red to Green Line. (iii) After 5 p.m. 'Z' day, A.D's.M.S. Aust. Divisions will be responsible for evacuation from Red Line to Main Dressing Stations and will close all existing posts not required by them."

(Paragraphs 5, 6, 7, and 9 dealt with the *Corps Relay Posts*. The A.D's.M.S. of the two Australian divisions were instructed to open Corps relay posts by zero hour, the 5th near Roisel, the 3rd near Villers-Faucon; to be administered by the D.D.M.S. and to evacuate to C.C.S's by light railway.)

(Paragraph 8 concerned *No. 3 Motor Ambulance Convoy*. It was to evacuate all stretcher cases "from M.D.S. to C.C.S. by M.A.C. cars," and walking wounded from walking wounded dressing stations to the Corps relay posts by 'buses.)

"10. Os.C. 2nd and 5th Australian Sanitary Sections will attach water testing squads at Advanced Dressing Stations by zero hour."

Arrangements Made by the Divisions. It will be recalled that, in the somewhat similar battle of August 8th, divisional arrangements were made on the principle that for the purpose of evacuation the two divisions in each sector of the Corps front should be regarded as a single unit. In the battle of September 29th the Australian A.D's.M.S. envisaged the need for a similar alignment, but, by reason of the composite nature of the two attacking columns, they could give only partial expression to it in their instructions.

---

[11] Moved to Villers-Faucon on Sept. 27.

American Divisions.[12] The two American divisions were the two static elements in the "leap-frog" and consequently were concerned only with the collection of casualties from their respective fronts and their clearance to stationary treatment centres. Their dispositions for the battle were, broadly speaking, those already noted. The medical arrangements for the 27th Division's preliminary attack (Sept. 27th) on the outpost line were made and carried out entirely by the American staffs. The fierce fighting in that action, in which the 106th and 107th Regiments sustained 1,540 casualties, imposed a heavy and unexpected strain on the medical units as well as on the fighting troops of this hard-used formation, and subsequently compelled an intervention earlier than had been intended by its partner in the leap-frog—the 3rd Australian Division. From his observations of the situation that was arising in this division, Colonel Barber became seriously concerned as to the ability of the medical service to deal with the casualties from an operation such as that which he knew to be in prospect. Accordingly, after conference with the American Chief and Divisional Surgeons, he arranged that the 4th Division's resuscitation team (Major Holmes à Court) should be made available to assist the 27th American Division in the main offensive; his arrangements had ensured that on both divisional fronts all the Australian units should be in a position to co-operate from an early hour.

Australian Divisions. The two Australian A.D's.M.S. (Colonels Downey and Maguire) allotted to units of their divisions the task of carrying out Colonel Barber's instructions as follows:—

5th Division (right). The O.C. 14th Field Ambulance (Lieut.-Colonel C. W. Thompson) was put in charge of forward evacuation with base of operations "at the A.D.S." The tent division of this unit was to move on the 28th to a site near Templeux, and to be prepared to move forward on receipt of orders from the A.D.M.S. and to form an A.D.S. and W.W.D.S. in captured territory; "this will normally take place after consolidation of the ['red'] line."

The *8th Field Ambulance* was to move on the 27th to billets near the 30th American Division A.D.S. at Templeux and remain closed till the capture of the "red" line, when the American station would be taken over for conversion to an M.D.S. and gas centre. The *15th Field Ambulance* was to bivouac near Marquaix, one tent sub-division being held ready to open a Corps relay post near Roisel.

3rd Division (left). The orders of the A.D.M.S., 3rd Division, were based on the assumption that the take-off line on the 29th would conform to that of the right sector. Similar arrangements were made to those of the 5th Division—the 9th Field Ambulance (Lieut.-Colonel A. F. Jolley) to be in charge of forward evacuation and to form a new A.D.S. "at the junction of the blue and yellow roads west of Bony after 4 p.m. on zero day"; the 11th Field Ambulance (Lieut.-Colonel H. B. Lewers) was to transform the American A.D.S. at Ste. Emilie to an M.D.S. and W.W.D.S.; the 10th (Lieut.-Colonel G. W. Macartney) was to form a Corps relay post near Villers-Faucon.

In both divisions *bearer divisions* were attached to their respective brigades; *ambulance transport,* motor and horses, reported for duty to the unit clearing the front. Exact provision was made for the distribution of the Corps and Divisional reserves of stretchers and blankets. The

---

[12] Medical orders issued by the American formations are not with the Australian records.

location of the Red Cross Depot, Y.M.C.A., and Comforts Fund Depot were notified.

Australian commanding officers were instructed to collaborate with the Americans prior to taking over their own tasks.

This battle is a classical example of the "set-piece" battle which did not go "according to plan." What may be called the two-dimensional plan of the set-piece army corps battle, which presumed a series of more or less parallel objectives perpendicularly attacked by two parallel columns, supposed a series of medical stations aligned, in respect to their function of treatment, from side to side of the area controlled by the

Medical events of the battle

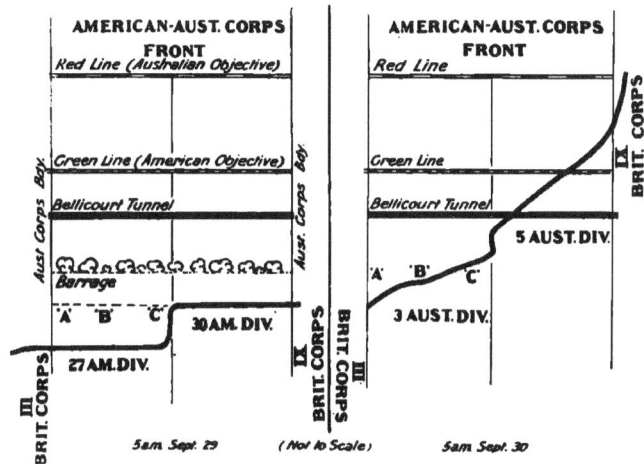

BATTLE OF HINDENBURG LINE, SHOWING SITUATION ON AUSTRALIAN CORPS FRONT ON 29TH AND 30TH SEPTEMBER, 1918.
"A" = The Knoll, "B" = Gillemont Farm, "C" = Quennemont Farm.

Corps, but, in respect of their function of clearance, aligned from front to rear. It will promote perspective if we first appreciate the general course of events as from front to rear before examining them in detail in the two columns, from right to left.

Through the failure to advance from "green" to "red"

line, save on the extreme right of the Corps front, section 4 of Army Corps instructions became meaningless. In effect 1st and 2nd echelons of medical stations telescoped, and on both divisional sectors—in particular the left—battle conditions did not, till more than 48 hours after zero, permit of the establishing of an effective A.D.S., sufficiently far forward of that already in use by the Americans, to make worth while or even possible any material change in the location of the treatment stations. The immediate effect of this was to throw the executive units of the American and Australian Corps together in mutual adjustment to the performance of a task in common instead of (as in a successful "leap-frog") in succession. The story of the evacuation of casualties from the wide and scattered fronts during these two days is largely concerned with the method and manner of this co-operation.

From the medical point of view, as from the military, the operations of the Australian Corps in this battle present themselves in three phases—

(1) The twenty-four hours from dawn on September 29th to dawn on the 30th, when no connected front line existed and the military situation was for the most part obscure. During this time no forward movement of the treatment centres was possible. (2) The next twenty-four hours, September 30th-October 1st, in which the situation was cleared up by a northward drive of the 3rd and 5th Australian Divisions assisted at first by detachments of Americans. R.A.P's and Relays moved forward, followed by the collecting and loading posts. At this stage the American divisions were withdrawn. (3) October 1st-2nd, in which the 2nd Division relieved the 3rd and 5th and advanced to confront the Beaurevoir Line and the Australian medical units carried out a modified leap-frog of their advanced and main dressing stations.

Casualties, September 29th-October 2nd. Though the Australian formations lost heavily in this battle—much more so than was expected—by far the greater number of battle-casualties were sustained by the Americans in the first twelve hours—a factor that greatly influenced the course of events. The evacuations were:—

Week ended	30th Amer. Division		5th Aust. Division		27th Amer. Division		3rd Aust. Division	
	Wounded	Sick	Wounded	Sick	Wounded	Sick	Wounded	Sick
28 Sept.	400	114	32	161	695	129	15	206
5 Oct.	2,018	189	1,179	177	2,652	359	865	229
Total	2,418	303	1,211	338	3,347	488	880	435

September 29th-30th. Conditions were very adverse to
the stretcher-bearers and transport. Passable roads were few and these were severely shelled and blocked by traffic.

Right Sector: 30th American- 5th Australian Divisions

"The congestion of troops and artillery on the roads leading to Bellicourt, when the Yanks were held up, was awful, and all under observation from Fritz. Naturally he shelled the roads heavily. . . . The bearers attached to the battalions, and the others, following closely on behind, experienced a nerve-racking time."[13]

During most of the time the weather was bad, days and nights wet and cold.

Forward Clearance. Failure to establish the "red" line left at most a small vaguely defined area—on the left none at all—in which during the first twelve hours the exploiting Australian divisions were (according to orders) to control evacuation. Within a few hours of "zero," therefore, the "digger" stretcher-bearers and "doughboy" litter-bearers had, to all intents, pooled their resources and were collecting and clearing casualties in common. The American bearers played their part with the same courage and *élan* as did the combatant troops. In spite of adverse conditions wounded reached the A.D.S. with unusual rapidity, this being due to the large numbers of bearers and prisoners available for carrying, some pooling of transport, and the restricted area of the American advance, in which the greater number of casualties were sustained.

Americans. In a special report on the operations in the right sector Major-General E. M. Lewis, commanding the 30th Division, describes the collecting of American wounded as follows:—

"Coincident with the advance of the troops, aid stations and ambulance posts were pushed forward. . . . By utilising the services of prisoners to bring back wounded on stretchers, and by the addition of 200 infantry stretcher bearers, the battlefield had been cleared of the wounded by nightfall. . . . The evacuation was accomplished under trying conditions; the men were not permitted to remain on the field over night and at no phase of the operation was the evacuation of the wounded not going well."

The casualties (wounded) are stated by General Lewis at 2,575—all "evacuated during the day." He comments—in premiss—"It is believed the evacuation of the wounded during this operation was as nearly perfect as possible under the existing circumstances."

Australians. Though within the limited area of the American occu-

---

[13] *The 8th Australian Field Ambulance on Active Service*, by L. W. Colley-Priest, *pp. 67-8.*

pation collection was rapid, it has to be confessed that Australian records do not paint so rosy a picture of the situation as a whole. Certainly, American wounded as well as Australians were arriving at Templeux in large numbers throughout the night of the 29th-30th.[14]

14th Field Ambulance. The officer commanding and tent division moved up to the American A.D.S. at Templeux at 10 a.m., but did not take over the forward evacuation till 5 p.m., nor, on account of the obscurity of the military situation, did he attempt to use his tent division to form a new A.D.S. Meantime, however, the officers-in-charge of the bearer divisions had found the situation as difficult as had the infantry, and the confusion was not fully resolved this night. By 7 p.m., however, the officers-in-charge of the three bearer divisions and the brigade headquarters detachment had linked up and were in touch with most of the battalions. The main line of clearance from the brigade fronts had by then centred in a "forward ambulance post" some 500 yards from Bellicourt, whence the bearer captains controlled their squads and kept touch with the R.M.O's. Through this collecting post for the next two days there passed "practically all the 5th Division's wounded, as well as American and German casualties; and the task of supplying stretchers, blankets and dressings was very difficult."[15]

September 30th-October 1st. The situation continued to be involved throughout the next 36 hours. On the 30th Bellicourt was still impassable to transport, but bearer posts were advanced to the Quarry. By October 1st "the military situation had become clearer, the road through Bellicourt passable"; cars were brought to the Quarry where, on this evening, an *"advanced dressing station"* was established. By this time, however, the attack was driving northwards and the task of clearance was moving to the left sector. On September 30th and October 1st the Americans, who (the 14th Field Ambulance diary records) "gave great assistance," were withdrawn. On the evening of October 2nd the 6th Australian Field Ambulance (2nd Division) took over from the 14th.

---

[14] In the account of the 30th Division's experiences in the *American Official Medical History* (*Vol. VIII, p. 892*), the historian states that "in the 24 hours from 6 a.m. September 29th to 6 a.m. September 30th a total of 2,075 cases were evacuated, and the following day 1,265"—with the definite implication that such evacuation was through American units. In the relevant map (facing *p. 884, Vol. VIII*) American "A.C. and F.H. 119" are shown as "A.D.S." at Templeux and at Jeancourt as from September 28th to October 1st, and "A.C. and F.H. 118" as "M.D.S." at Marquaix. Actually, no mention is made, in the American official account, of the nature of the medical operations—as a combined "leap-frog"—nor of the co-operation therein or even the existence of the Australian field ambulances. The American historian clearly regards the "assault on the Hindenburg Line" of September 29th-30th, so far as concerned the Australian and American Corps, as an American battle, with subsequent exploitation by Australian divisions, the American formations being withdrawn "presumably for rest and refitting." But however determined and gallant the American assault, and however important its contribution to the ultimate victory achieved, the interests of historical verity demand that the impression thus conveyed be modified to conform more closely with the facts as they appeared to the Australian units.

[15] Diary of the 14th Field Ambulance. This diary contains a wealth of detail, illustrating the confusion brought about by the military situation and its gradual resolution and the establishment of systematic bearer and motor relays and circuits. The following episode recorded by the 5th Division history, and noted in more than one diary, is illuminating. "About this time [midday, Sept. 29th] the bearers of the 15th Field Ambulance, operating under Major Craig and Capt. Le Souef, in searching for a suitable medical post in rear of the 57th Battalion, mopped up an enemy party of two officers and 40 other ranks." (*The Story of the Fifth Australian Division*, by *Captain A. D. Ellis, p. 373.*)

The Advanced Dressing Stations, Right Sector. Jeancourt and Templeux, September 29th and 30th. As indicated by the figures, the American medical units faced a huge task. The course of events at the A.D.S. on each of the divisional fronts in this battle throws into relief a defect in the British system as practised on the Western Front by the A.I.F. This was the failure to distinguish clearly in exact terms of treatment and transport, between an "advanced" and a "main" dressing station—a matter which affected the part to be played by the motor ambulance convoy. This important matter is dealt with in some detail in later pages,[16] but it will illuminate the narrative of events if we at once identify this lack of clarity as being in some measure at least the cause of a considerable degree of "confusion" and "congestion"[17] at the American stations, as noted in the Australian war diaries.

The Divisional Surgeon of the 30th American Division maintained his two advanced dressing stations at Jeancourt and Templeux-le-Guérard with the 119th American "Field Ambulance"[18] evacuating to M.D.S. at Marquaix.[19] The British 134th Field Ambulance ran the walking wounded dressing station at Templeux, clearing through the Australian Corps relay post.

Jeancourt. This station "saved the situation" for the 30th Division. It dealt almost entirely with American and German casualties. It was situated on the successful flank and evacuation went without a hitch save for some congestion on the 29th brought about by the fact that, being officially an "A.D.S.," it was not cleared by M.A.C. cars till September 30th when it was taken over by the 14th Field Ambulance. On October 1st

---

[16] *See pp. 764-6.*
[17] The term "congestion" had a very definite significance and usage in connection with the evacuation of wounded. The effect produced on the medical personnel by the development at any point of a "congestion of wounded," or any threat of such, may be compared as a spur to action with that evoked in the staff of a civil hospital by the arrival of an "acute abdomen."
[18] A combined "field hospital" and "ambulance company"—*see footnote 6 on p. 737.*
[19] The sketch map on *p. 749* shows the medical situation as about 7.30 p.m. on Sept. 29. Stations are designated "A.D.S.," "W.W.D.S.," "M.D.S.," etc., as officially recognised; the first cleared by field ambulance cars, the latter two by M.A.C. lorries and cars respectively. In the vital matter of records Australian units were instructed that "all cases will be recorded at the M.D.S. Templeux until A.D.S. and W.W.D.S. have been opened in captured territory; when opened Walking cases will be recorded there, provided M.A.C. lorries can be pushed up to that point." It is not clear where the Americans kept their A. and D. Books and sent off their casualty wires and returns.

as the front moved forward it was closed; and at the same time the M.D.S. and gas centre at Marquaix ceased to function and M.A.C. cars cleared only from the central M.D.S. at Templeux.

Templeux. Stretcher cases began to arrive here within one hour of "zero" and walking wounded half-an-hour later. From then onwards there flowed in a stream of casualties that at times was beyond the capacity of the large staff to clear without congestion.

Australians Take Over Templeux. The officer commanding the 8th Field Ambulance arrived at Templeux-le-Guérard about midday on the 29th with his tent division, his transport with that of the other two units having passed to the command of Captain Fay of the 14th at 10 a.m. A "standard A.D.S.," erected by the Australian Engineers in anticipation, had been put at the disposal of the American unit and used to accommodate stretcher cases while awaiting clearance. Heavy casualties and insufficient transport, and, perhaps, the inexperience of the Americans, had conspired—as it seemed to the incoming Australian unit—to put the situation almost out of control.

"When we arrived the place seemed to be in confusion. The car park was crowded with ambulances, full, empty, and loading or discharging wounded. Litters containing wounded men seemed to cover all available space."

By mutual arrangement the Australian unit began work at once, in an unused room; and, "owing to the accumulation of cases, the 5th Divisional Ambulance cars were loaned to the 119th American Ambulance," whose traffic was controlled by combatant officers. The congestion (so the 8th Field Ambulance diary states) "was soon relieved," and, in furtherance of Colonel Barber's scheme, between 5 and 6 p.m. the station was taken over by the Australian unit.

"By 7 o'clock our evacuations were keeping pace with our admissions." The A.D.S. was converted into an M.D.S. at 7.30 p.m., from which hour the names and particulars of all patients passing through were recorded and A.T.S. (1,500 units) given to all patients with wounds.

From the time of its conversion, though receiving casualties direct from the motor loading posts, the station was cleared by motor ambulance convoy to the C.C.S. at Doingt, those at

Tincourt having been filled up by 5 p.m. with American wounded. The W.W.D.S. remained in charge of the 134th British Field Ambulance, and the Americans retained the M.D.S. at Marquaix.

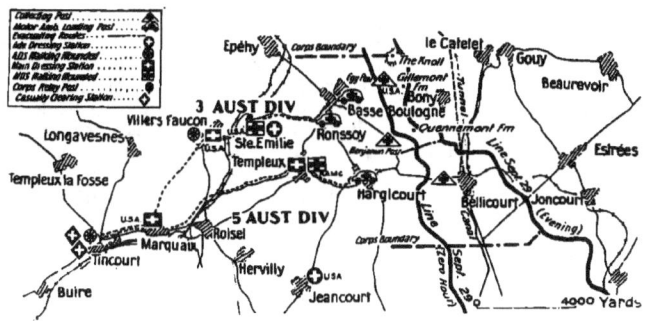

Medical Situation, 7.30 p.m., Sept. 29. (Where not otherwise indicated, the stations are Australian.)

The system of the dressing station now built up at Templeux, and the method of collection and clearance of which it was the pivot, seem to have been ideal for this type of warfare.[20] As it received direct from a minor first-aid treatment centre at Bellicourt, and evacuated by indifferent roads to C.C.S. some ten miles distant, it was necessary to provide effective "resuscitation" for the urgent "untransportable" types of case, and prophylactic *réchauffement*, refreshment, and necessary redressing and splinting for the less serious, while nevertheless ensuring a minimum check in the outward movement. Cases of gassing were diagnosed provisionally, treated and disposed of; walking wounded were passed to the "W.W.D.S." The creation of this combined classification[21] and treatment centre justifies a descriptive note, since it was the last important station formed by the A.A.M.C. in the war. The diary of the 8th Field Ambulance gives a full description, of which the following is a summary:—

An Ideal Station

---

[20] *See pp. 764-6.*
[21] *Triage*, as the French and Americans call it; see *Chapter xi*.

The dressing station consisted of a standard A.D.S. and of a number of "reinforced" (i.e., sandbagged) rooms contained within a semi-circle bounded on its diametrical side by the road and on the other by a crescent-shaped car-track, having an entrance at either end from the road. Cars passed in at one entrance and out at the other. All dressings were done in the reinforced rooms, the standard A.D.S. being set aside for the reception and treatment of gassed patients.

An exact one-way circuit was organised for cars and, within the station itself, for patients. From the admitting room the patient passed to one of three dressing rooms which contained trestles for the support of a total of six stretchers. If cold, the patient was detained in the dressing room and warmed by primus stove under the stretcher while hot air was conveyed to the lower limbs from another primus by means of bent piping beneath an improvised cradle. The manipulation of blankets with two folds above and two below was by now part of the technique-in-trade of field ambulances. Badly shocked patients and urgent types of case—abdomens, shattered limbs, chests, femurs—went to the resuscitation room for *réchauffement*, blood transfusion, or urgent operation by the "team." Such cases were evacuated with precedence.

From the same diary the following is gathered as to the experience on this occasion:—

Although a large proportion of the wounds were "punctured"—through and through bullet wounds[22]—and much less than usual contaminated with soil (a factor which it was thought "tended to the reduction of shock") there was an unusually large number of "perforated abdomens and chests and compound fractures of the thigh." . . . The "relatively larger number" of these on the second day was ascribed to the more rapid evacuation.[23]

Thomas splints were freely used for all serious injuries of the lower limbs and "could be put on with little pain. The boot was left on when possible and a clove hitch used for extension." "The American patients and the Germans especially seemed very appreciative of these splints."

Gassed Cases. Complete and exact arrangements were made for the treatment of every type of gassing, "all (it is stated) suffering from poisoning either by mustard gas or phosgene or a mixture of both. . . . Phosgene alone a rarity." Solution of sodi. bicarb. internally and externally was found effective, and "the patients all had great faith" in ammonia capsules!

September 30th-October 1st. The number of patients was not so great and the wounds were much more recent.

"Few [had been inflicted] more than 8 hours before," says the diary of the 8th Field Ambulance, "some as recently as two," whereas on the previous day many had been "about a day old. . . . One was struck by the mildness of the shock as compared with those of the previous

---

[22] In this connection *see p. 495.*
[23] It was probably for this reason that the mortality rate per cent. of "admissions to hospital" after wounding *increased* in the later years of the war.

night. . . . The patients talked more freely, were more optimistic and generally brighter, and complained about feeling cold, a rare complaint on the previous night. Morphia was injected less freely (*sic*)."

The station was inspected by the D.M.S., Fourth Army (Major-General M. W. O'Keeffe), and the Chief Surgeon (Colonel Clark C. Collins), and Consulting Surgeon and Physician (Colonel F. A. Besley and Colonel Mandel) of the American Corps, and by Colonel Barber. The W.W.D.S. was taken over from the 134th British Field Ambulance. The war diary records that, after October 1st, "nothing further happened at the M.D.S. or W.W.D.S. worthy of note during our control." At 8 a.m. on October 3rd the stations were handed over to the 5th and 7th Field Ambulances respectively, and at the same time the A.D.S. at the Quarry was taken over by the 6th. These belonged to the incoming 2nd Division. The 30th American Division had been relieved on October 1st.

The following table shows the casualties treated at the M.D.S. at Templeux while administered by the 8th Field Ambulance.

	Sick	Wounded	Gassed	Total
Australian ..	4	264	36	304
American	3	120	72	195
British	–	28	34	62
Prisoners of War	–	32	–	32
Total	7	444	142	593

September 28th-30th. It was on the left sector that the military situation was most difficult, and it was on this front especially that goodwill and mutual co-opera-

Left Sector : 27th American-3rd Australian Divisions

tion conspired to compel a fair measure of success from a threatened breakdown.

From the table on *page 744* it is seen that the losses sustained by the 27th American Division were heavier, and those of the 3rd Australian Division considerably less, than of the corresponding divisions in the right attacking column. The nature of the battle on this front created problems of a very unusual kind. The confused military situation on the day before the attack, the short advance achieved on the 29th—only 600-800 yards by nightfall—and the heavy casualties, brought a surge of wounded to the American medical posts and stations; at the same time the fact that individual parties penetrated somewhat farther imposed a tragic task on their litter-bearers. The medical units of the Australian division, pushing forward to effect the "leap-frog," either overshot the mark with their forward posts (as happened to the 9th Field Ambulance) or were held up, as the successive units telescoped, at points between the "advanced" and "main" dressing stations. The resulting confusion was not resolved till, on October 2nd, the American Corps was relieved. The wresting of a successful "clearance" from such conditions is a story of great technical interest.

Experience of the 27th American Division. The medical service of the 27th American Division was more handicapped than that of the 30th. To begin with, its establishment was smaller, and its organisation and equipment even less homogeneous.[24] Within three days of entering the line, with no opportunity of "learning the ropes" or getting the feel of this front, and without experience of a major engagement, it had been required to deal with the heavy casualties from the action of September 27th, and was now to bear the brunt of evacuation from one of the most difficult battles of the war.

Space does not permit of any account of the experiences of their bearers, or of the trials of their train transport ("ambulance section").[25] On the 29th after the first few hours—save possibly for bearers with detachments, if any, ahead of the general front—they were in effect part and parcel with the Australians. Their wounded arrived at the A.D.S. early and rapidly.

The Dressing Stations. On September 26th an M.D.S. was opened at Longavesnes (Field Hospital Company No. 106) and another was "prepared" at Villers-Faucon (No. 105). The latter was opened at noon on the 27th, the station at Longavesnes closing at the same hour. An A.D.S. was formed

---

[24] The division had one British field ambulance instead of two. Its "sanitary train" does not appear to have been reconstituted into "field ambulances." Its equipment was partly British, partly American. (*American Off. Med. History, Vol. VIII*; and memorandum by Major-Gen. Barber in Aust. War Memorial.)

[25] Some description of this is given in the history of this division (*loc. cit. pp. 322-3, 549, 552-3*). Australian and British wounded as well as American passed through the "aid stations." At 10 a.m. a "forward dressing station" was formed by the sanitary detachment of the 107th Infantry (Major R. A. Turnbull in command) on the Bellicourt road and a "forward station" in a dugout on the Gillemont road; the latter was used throughout the operation. A "collecting post" ("Egg Post") was formed at 4 p.m. "Ambulance head" (apparently the advanced post of motor ambulances) was at Ronssoy.

at Ste. Emilie on September 24th (Ambulance Company No. 106). From the 28th onwards the experience in these is so closely involved with that of the 3rd Australian Division that, *mutatis mutandis*, an account from either side should serve for both.[26] In what follows, the Australian records are relied on.

Experience of 3rd Aust. Division. Even more than commonly the account of events is beset by the difficulty of correlating in terms of their cause events coincident in time but separate in place and circumstance. This is due chiefly to the unstable balance brought about in respect both to treatment and transport by the uncertainty of the status and function of the A.D.S. at Ste. Emilie—the pivot of each set of activities. Events here, and in the two spheres of action respectively in front and behind it, are told so far as possible as recorded by the chief actors.

Forward Clearance in Left Sector, September 29th-October 1st—under 9th Field Ambulance (Lieut.-Colonel A. F. Jolley). The distribution of bearer divisions by brigades was carried out as in the 5th Division:—

"A Major, 2 Captains (bearer sub-division), 1 Q.M.S. or steward, cook with necessary cooking material, 2 runners (mounted orderlies), 3 ambulance waggons (horse), 1 limber, 1 water-cart, 5 horses to be utilised as pack train with pack saddles and water carriers, 50 petrol tins for water, 1 Transport N.C.O., all available (Ambulance) cars and 1 N.C.O. to control same, were detailed from each (Field) Ambulance" to its proper brigade.

These were distributed with a view to the early formation of an A.D.S.

The several brigade groups, after receiving instructions, joined their respective brigades on the 28th. Cars and pack-trains, with water cans and ambulance waggons, reported at "zero" to the "C.O. forward evacuation," and remained with his headquarters, which at 6 a.m. moved to Ste. Emilie. A special officer was charged with the duty of forming the new A.D.S. and had a complete section of a field ambulance placed at his disposal.

The problem of collecting and clearance took much the same form in this sector as on the right, but the features were

---

[26] See *The Story of the 27th Division, pp. 549-53*; and *American Off. Med. History, Vol. VIII, pp. 886-7.* With allowance for the natural *amour propre* of both sides, the accounts of the events accord very well.

more pronounced, since here the military situation was even more confused and cleared up more slowly.[27]

Summary of events—Forward Clearance, September 29-October 2

On the day of the battle traffic on all forward roads was closed till 9 a.m. At 9.30 Colonel Jolley reconnoitred forward. Information as to the situation was vague in the extreme, but near Ronssoy men of the 10th and 11th Brigades were found "dug in." A Red Cross flag was erected, more cars and personnel sent for from Ste. Emilie. The post thus sited (known as "Benjamin's Post") "became definitely established as a collecting post. It had the advantage of being seen from the surrounding country and was on the only decent road on the battle front. A position was found in cellars on the Bellicourt Road towards Ronssoy where cases could be held and where the front could be controlled."

A motor relay post was formed near Ronssoy and loading posts forward of Ronssoy and Basse Boulogne. At about 10.30 a.m. headquarters of 9th Field Ambulance moved up to the most forward of these. As the several Brigade Bearer Groups were located, pack-trains were sent up, but touch was not gained with all group commanders till about 5 p.m., nor till later still by these with all their battalions—some of which were out of reach. Colonel Jolley noted, for example: "44th Battalion S.E. of Quennemont Farm—too far forward to be of use and unable to be evacuated."[28]

A Move Back. In the late afternoon, as a result of sundry disasters, some posts and the car park were forced back, and the 9th Field Ambulance headquarters moved to Basse Boulogne. In spite of the fact that American cars were co-operating, the transport problem became serious, with consequent severe congestion at "the A.D.S. (*sic*) in Ronssoy."

This was brought about by trouble farther down the line, which caused an appeal from the 11th Field Ambulance, who "reported extreme congestion at the A.D.S." (at Ste. Emilie), and called, for relief, on the cars in the forward circuits.

A New "A.D.S." Urged. At 7.30 p.m. Lieut.-Colonel Jolley asked the A.D.M.S. (Colonel F. A. Maguire) that "the 11th Field Ambulance be opened as an 'M.D.S.' to bring M.A.C. cars forward. Present headquarters of 9th at Basse Boulogne to be called 'A.D.S.'"[29]

Night of September 29th-30th. The night was dark, wet, and cold, and full of excursions and alarms. Heavy gas shelling brought urgent calls, which were passed on to Ste. Emilie with a request for more cars. In response came a number of vehicles from the American Red Cross, some of which Colonel Jolley held at the car park "in case." But by 5 a.m. "all posts were cleared and evacuation proceeded normally." The medical situation eased with the military. M.A.C. cars now ran to Ste. Emilie, and, in spite of casualties at the front, a half-hourly circuit was

---

[27] A feature of the medical work was the heavy casualties in the draught horses from machine-gun sniping, and in the motor ambulance waggons through shell-fire. "I have not in my experience known braver men," Colonel Jolley notes, "than the drivers and orderlies. . . . The senior N.C.O. showed great resource in patching up cars . . . from parts of one partly destroyed."

[28] *See map at p. 760.*

[29] The quotation is from the diary of Colonel Maguire.

possible between the forward motor loading posts and the car relay post at Ronssoy.

On *October 1st* R.A.P's were all moving forward; the medical "leapfrog" was effected, and on *October 2nd* the post in Basse Boulogne was called an A.D.S.

Colonel Jolley comments: "The evacuations throughout were extremely difficult. The casualties were very heavy, 75 per cent. of them being Americans. Owing to the hold up of the Americans early in the fray, [our] advanced posts had been established too far forward, but when our infantry got busy and completed the work, they were in their proper position, and very many difficulties in the way of the evacuations were removed."[30]

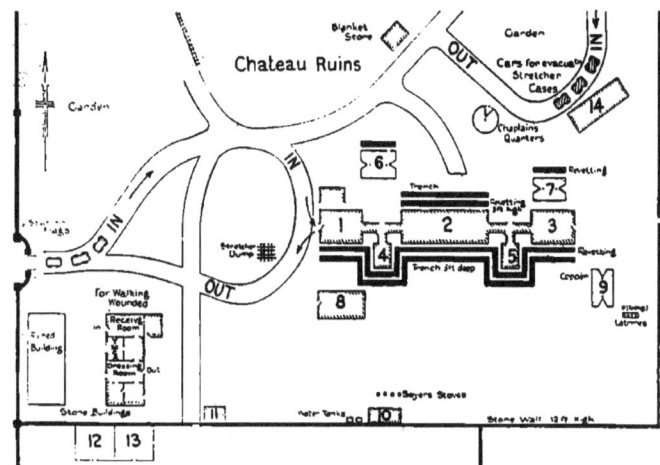

DRESSING STATION AT STE. EMILIE USED BY THE 3RD AUSTRALIAN AND 27TH AMERICAN DIVISIONS, 29TH SEPTEMBER-2ND OCTOBER, 1918.

The numbers indicate: 1. Receiving room; 2. Dressing room; 3. Evacuation room; 4. Dispensary; 5. Resuscitation room; 6. Gas treatment marquee; 7. Waiting marquee, gas cases for evacuation; 8. Nissen hut for overflow receiving; 9. Y.M.C.A. marquee; 10. Cook-house; 11. Post office; 12. Q.M's store; 13. Orderly Room; 14. Room for stretcher cases awaiting evacuation.

From War Diary of 11th Aust. Field Ambulance.

"Advanced" Dressing Station, Ste. Emilie. No records are available of events at the American A.D.S. at Ste. Emilie during the preliminary action on September 27th; the Australian diaries pick up the story on the 28th, with the arrival

---

[30] As in the 5th Division, the war diary of the clearing unit (9th Fld. Amb.) describes with admirable clarity the vicissitudes of its bearer and transport divisions in their endeavour to push forward the relay and loading posts, and to gain and keep touch with R.M.O's.

there of the 11th Field Ambulance to make, as required by Australian Corps orders, preparations for the "leap-frog"—that is, for the "transformation" of the A.D.S. (formed by the American unit representing "Y Field Ambulance" of Colonel Barber's orders) to an "M.D.S." run by Australians. In preparation for this event a "standard A.D.S." had already been installed by the Australian Engineers.

The diary of the 11th Field Ambulance (Lieut.-Colonel H. B. Lewers) says:[81] *"27th September.* Advanced party proceeded to Ste. Emilie to clean up, etc., the place which has been selected as an M.D.S.
"September 28th. 3 p.m. Remainder of personnel . . . arrived at Ste. Emilie. The site selected is in a destroyed Château. On arrival it was found that the 107th American Field Ambulance was working in a tiny brick room (an out-room to the Château) and using it as an A.D.S. The room appears far too small, and is draughty, badly lighted, and contains only one door for entrance and exit. With the large number of casualties congestion and confusion is bound to occur.
"September 29th. Attack on the enemy commenced 5.50 a.m. About an hour afterwards casualties began to come to the American station and as the day advanced the numbers increased, to a large extent."

At 9 a.m. (as his diary records) the A.D.M.S., 3rd Australian Division (Colonel Maguire), instructed Colonel Lewers "to open an A.D.S. at Ste. Emilie at once, and render every assistance to American A.D.S. in handling wounded." Colonel Maguire's diary continues:—

"10 a.m. visited A.D.S. Ste. Emilie. . . . The American organisation was quite inadequate to deal with any number of cases. They had ceased recording walking wounded, and were sending them to their own M.D.S. at Villers-Faucon to be recorded, instead of to No. 2 Corps Relay Post. Stretcher cases were all being handled by the 11th Australian Field Ambulance; 80 had been put through."

Going on to the American M.D.S. at Villers-Faucon he encountered a situation even more disturbing. The Australian resuscitation team, arriving there on the 28th, had found that the equipment and medical stores of the Field Hospital Company had gone astray and "only a thousand shell dressings" were available. Some instruments and apparatus were obtained from the American "Red Cross"[32] and some

---
[81] The narrative is slightly epitomised.
[32] As seen by the A.I.F. the American supply and transport department was the last to get into its stride—a reflex of the complexity and difficulty of supply and transport problems in war. The position of the "Red Cross" in the American medical organisation is examined elsewhere (*see Vol. III*). It was an important element in the work of their official medical service.

arrangements made for resuscitation work. Colonel Maguire says:—

> "Met Lt.-Col. Montgomery, Div. Surgeon 27th American Division, and Major Hutton his Assistant; with them proceeded to see their new M.D.S. at Villers-Faucon. It was totally inadequate to deal with any number of cases. One small Nissen Hut was being used as a Dressing Room with one entrance and only one table going. Arranged for them to make at the other end of hut an exit, and to install four tables and treble their staff. An Australian Resuscitation Team under Major Holmes à Court was working there—over seventy [stretcher] cases were awaiting evacuation."

It is convenient to conclude here what remains to be told of this American station at Villers-Faucon. The action taken in common by Colonels Maguire and Montgomery is thus outlined by the former:—

> "Arranged that no more walking wounded should go there—all to be recorded at A.D.S. and sent to No. 2 Corps Relay Post direct; Divisional surgeon will send 106 Field Hospital to Villers-Faucon and double the accommodation. Situation should clear up by 3 p.m."

This action had the desired result, but the situation in the meantime was disturbing. Lacking the preliminary *"triage"* provided by the combination "A.D.S." plus "W.W.D.S.," the American personnel had been attempting painfully to sort out slight from severe cases, and yet to treat and record them all. The 27th Division's history says:—

> "As the wounded kept coming in and it was impossible to provide shelter for all, the American Red Cross was called upon for 2,000 blankets in addition to the 1,000 furnished by the Ordnance Department, thus making it possible for the wounded to lie comfortably in the open while waiting transportation to the casualty clearing station. Hot drinks and hot water bottles were furnished those cases lying in the open, and ground sheets were also used as coverings." [33]

At 5 p.m. Colonel Maguire with Colonel Montgomery again visited all stations. The M.D.S., he found, "has been reorganised on lines suggested, and is now able to handle the situation."

The A.D.S. and W.W.D.S. We resume the narrative of the events of the forenoon. Returning to Ste. Emilie Colonel Maguire arranged with the American Divisional Surgeon for the 11th Australian Field Ambulance to assume full control of

---

[33] *The Story of the 27th Division, Vol. I, p. 551.*

the stations at once. The field ambulance says that soon after the wounded began to arrive the inadequacy of the arrangements made by the Americans had been realised,

"So, with the concurrence of the A.D.M.S., 3rd Australian Division and Chief Surgeon of the 27th American Division C.O. 11th Field Ambulance was placed in charge of the A.D.S. We then took over, having already placed the series of wooden huts, erected by Australian Corps, together with [our] staff at the disposal of the U.S.A. personnel to assist with their casualties.

"On our assuming control Captain Taylor, U.S.A.,[34] was placed in charge of motor transport and traffic. The American dressing station was turned into a walking wounded station only, and the stretcher cases were turned to the A.I.F. buildings. As a main station for walking wounded we kept their records. Cases came in large numbers and the strain of preventing congestion and keeping records was severe, owing to the inconvenience and limited accommodation under which the American personnel were working. American doctors and clerks were unaccustomed to our regulations, diagnosis, etc., and to the manner in which the Field Medical cards were made out."

Congestion did in fact occur from time to time. Walking wounded were cleared with ease, but for stretchers only the divisional cars of the two formations were available. An effort further to "pool" the resources of the two formations was made by putting all ambulance transport under the O.C. 11th Field Ambulance. This did not work well and on the 30th separate control was resumed.[35] By nightfall on the 29th, however, the evacuation of wounded was well in hand and "despite the numbers during the day the station was practically empty at 9 p.m."

"A pleasing feature at the W.W.D.S. was the efficiency whereby the wounded were refreshed by the American Red Cross. A liberal supply of hot cocoa, chocolate, biscuits, cigarettes, and tobacco was always on hand. Our own Y.M.C.A. catered for the requirements for the stretcher cases, and a sufficient supply of everything was always obtainable." •

September 30th. The number of cases "decreased some-

---

[34] Captain George E. Taylor, of the Ambulance Section, 102nd Sanitary Train.

[35] The episode throws light on the problem of co-operation. The 11th Field Ambulance records the circumstances as follows: "At 1 a.m. (30th) the C.O. 9th Field Ambulance came to Ste. Emilie, and on his request all cars, American and Australian, were sent up the line. It was subsequently found that the demand for cars was greater than the number of wounded justified. Naturally the Americans objected to being stacked all night at Australian posts with nothing to do, and lodged a protest. Next morning control of American cars passed to U.S.A. personnel, and that of Australian cars to 9th Field Ambulance. Matters then ran smoothly. Had more care been taken to differentiate the U.S.A. and Australian cars into watertight compartments, there would have been no misunderstanding. There was never any friction at all at Ste. Emilie."

what" on the 30th but a steady flow was maintained and the number of gassed cases increased. Particular comment is made as to

"the number of Americans who came down from the line complaining that they were suffering from the effects of gas. Not much material evidence could be gathered as to their real condition, and a lot of them were sent away as N.Y.D. Gas ... to the special C.C.S. 40 kilos distant." According to their own accounts, they "did not put on their gas masks for some time, others could not distinguish between gas and other shells."

Although the station remained an A.D.S., permission was given for clearance by the motor ambulance convoy. Among the stretcher cases were men who had been lying out for twenty-four hours.

October 1st. Very few casualties were passing through. "We could manage the place," says the diary of the 11th Field Ambulance, "with our own personnel." The American unit was withdrawn this night, and orders were issued by the D.D.M.S. recognising the transformation (i.e. to M.D.S.) that had actually taken place.

"All the time we were at Ste. Emilie we did M.D.S. work," says the diary of the 11th, "but technically did not become a main dressing station until 10 a.m. on 2nd October. Always we were too far behind the line to act as an A.D.S., and the 9th Field Ambulance were detailed to establish that. It would appear that their establishment was shifting and uncertain and led to [the] confusion."

Knowing, as now we do, the course of the military events, the true causes of the medical vicissitudes are readily identified, and do not call for comment.

The American medical units at the several stations were relieved on October 1st-2nd in stages. On the 1st the 10th Field Ambulance took over the M.D.S. at Villers-Faucon and the 11th full charge of the stations at Ste. Emilie. At 10 a.m. on the 2nd an A.D.S. was "formally opened" at Ronssoy (Basse Boulogne), and at the same hour (as stated above) the A.D.S. at Ste. Emilie became formally known as an M.D.S., "which simply meant that we kept a record of stretcher cases and gave A.T.S." The W.W.D.S. remained at Ste. Emilie; the M.D.S.

Relief of 27th Division

Map No. 12

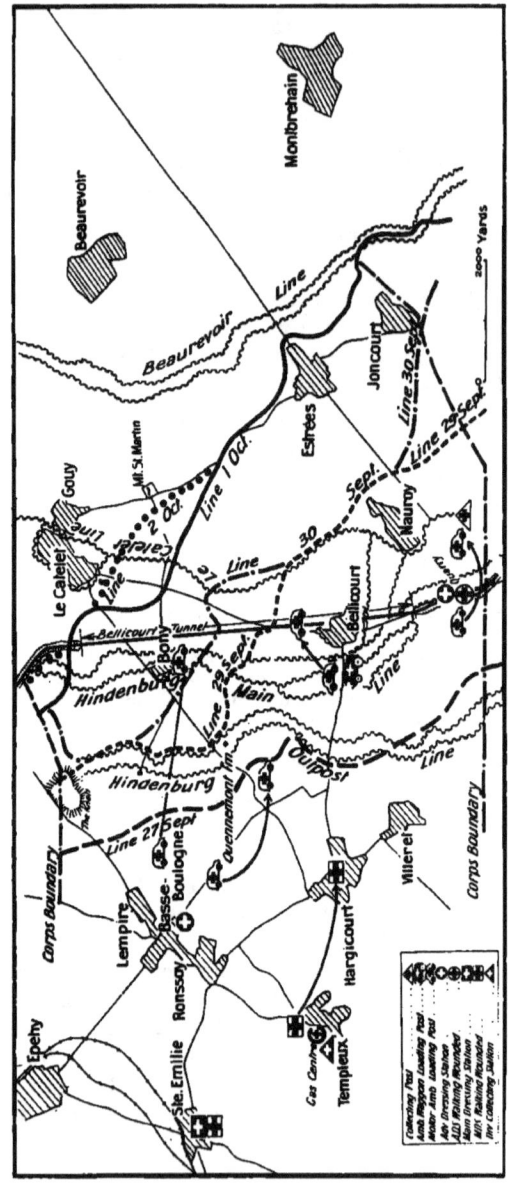

at Villers-Faucon closed at the same hour as the A.D.S. at Ste. Emilie became an M.D.S. The "leap-frog" was accomplished!

TABLE OF CASES TREATED, SEPT. 29TH-OCT. 2ND[36]

Main Dressing Station (Villers-Faucon)

	Wounded	Gassed	Sick	Total
Americans	1,332	320	160	1,812
Australians	233	32	31	296
British	248	45	44	337
Prisoners of War	66	–	–	66
Total	1,879	397	235	2,511
At W.W.D.S.	765	291	216	1,272
Grand Total	2,644	688	451	3,783

Walking Wounded Dressing Station (Ste. Emilie)

	Wounded	Gassed	Sick	Total
Americans	413	146	126	685
Australians	219	103	58	380
British	127	42	32	201
Prisoners of War	6	–	–	6
Total	765	291	216	1,272

Motor Ambulance Convoy. This large mass of casualties was cleared to C.C.S. by the cars and lorries of the 3rd Motor Ambulance Convoy and by light railway with a smoothness that under the circumstances seems remarkable. Indeed the mechanised transport of Army and Army Corps had at the end of 1918 reached a degree of efficiency that accorded with its now dominant rôle in warfare. The proportion of "stretchers" to "walking wounded" in this battle was approximately 1 to 4. The independent circuit for walking wounded by motor lorry and light railway through the "Corps Relay Posts" was now thoroughly organised to promote rapid "return to

Clearance to C.C.S.

---

[36] From *The Story of the 27th Division*, by Major-General John F. O'Ryan, Vol. I, p. 551.

duty"; and "over 4,000" were cleared without a hitch from the Australian posts, "No. 1" at Roisel (changed to Tincourt on the 30th) and "No. 2" at Villers-Faucon.[37]

Casualty Clearing Stations. The rush of casualties from the American Corps soon filled the first echelon of these at Tincourt (Nos. 12, 53, and 58), and casualties were then switched to the next echelon in rear (Doingt).[38]

When on October 1st the American Corps was withdrawn and the Australian divisions took up the advance on clearly defined fronts, medical events resumed much the same course as in the preceding operations. The services of maintenance surged forward with the general move—processes which at this stage do not call for particular description.

Australian Corps: Evacuation, Oct. 1st-2nd

On October 3rd the 5th Division was relieved by the 2nd, and the 3rd Division by the 50th British, and the Corps front was reduced to 6,000 yards. While the American Corps reorganised, the necessary task of ejecting the German from his last hold on the Hindenburg defences, the Beaurevoir Line and fortified village of Montbrehain, was allotted to the 2nd Australian Division.

The Beaurevoir Line was attacked at 6.5 a.m. on October 3rd by the 2nd Division (assisted by tanks) on a front of 6,000 yards, with the 50th British Division on its left. The 5th Brigade, after most of the tanks had been disabled, broke in fierce fighting through the German line at Estrées, but the 7th Brigade, though it took the uncompleted trench-line, could not seize Beaurevoir village. The penetration, however, was sufficient to be exploited. It was extended on the 4th by skilful manoeuvring, and on the 5th the last fit Australian infantry brigade, the 6th, attacked the dominating village of Montbrehain, well beyond the Hindenburg system. The fight was a very bitter one but the attack was entirely successful, though among the killed were many original "Anzacs."

The Battle of Beaurevoir and capture of Montbrehain

The cost of the Beaurevoir Line and Montbrehain was

---

[37] The diary of the Australian Corps Light Railways officer has the following entry for September: "Arrangements made for the conveyance of walking wounded from Corps Relay Posts . . . to casualty clearing stations at Tincourt. 46 trucks were covered with tarpaulins and covered with seats. On the 29th, 2,556 patients were carried, and on the 30th 707."

[38] "Abdominals and chests" from the 30th Division are said to have reached the C.C.S. in "an average of 4½ hours . . . from the time their wounds were received." (*Amer. Off. Med. History, Vol. VIII, p. 892.*)

14 per cent. of the 2nd Division's strength; 951 wounded were evacuated on October 3rd, 86 on the 4th, and 307 on the 5th.

For these operations evacuation was based on the system built up by the 5th Division; the new R.A.P's and loading posts cleared through an "A.D.S." at "The Quarry," four kilometres behind the line. The outstanding feature of the clearance, which was carried out by the 6th Field Ambulance, was the failure—chiefly owing to the state of the roads—of the divisional motor transport to cope with the casualties. As in the Somme Winter (1916-17), the convoy was called on to help it out.

Evacuation

On the night of October 6th-7th the 2nd Division was relieved by the 30th American Division. Major-General Read took over from Lieut.-General Monash, and the responsibility for the medical arrangements in the sector passed to his Corps Surgeon (Colonel Clark C. Collins). The place of the Australian Corps in the British line of battle passed to the II American Corps—which, it should be added, well sustained the part in the heavy fighting of October 17th-18th.[30] The Australian Corps was withdrawn to reorganise and recuperate in Fourth Army reserve area round Abbeville.

The Australian Corps hands over

The casualties, combatant and A.A.M.C., sustained by Australians in the battles of the Hindenburg Line were as follows:—

Australian casualties at Hindenburg Line

Casualties 3rd and 5th Divisions 29th September-2nd October

	Killed in Action		Died of Wounds		Died of Gas		Gassed		Wounded	
	3rd	5th	3rd	5th	3rd	5th	3rd	5th	3rd	5th
29th Sept.	106	95	15	20	1	–	81	70	528	702
30th Sept.	13	80	9	19	1	–	71	26	102	248
1st Oct.	13	25	2	13	3	2	27	16	56	150
2nd Oct.	1	3	5	8	–	2	12	7	3	3
	133	203	31	60	5	4	191	119	689	1,103

The last battle of the Australian Corps focussed with curi-

---

[30] For the week ending Oct. 12 the 30th Division had 1,784 wounded evacuated to the Base. For the week ending Oct. 19 this division evacuated 1,219 and the 27th Division 1,453.

ous perfection most of the major problems of evacuation met with on the Western Front.[40]

Comments and Conclusions Undoubtedly this battle showed up certain defects in both the British and the American systems. Seen as past history it may be said that all was well since it ended well. But projected to the future such soothing unction is not more permissible than it seemed to the Australian ambulance commanders who saw behind the scenes at Templeux and Ste. Emilie. In the circumstances any serious trouble was impossible, since any German counter-stroke on more than a brigade front, and over a few thousand yards in depth, was precluded by the success of the general offensive. But had the enemy, as at Lagnicourt or Cambrai, been in a position to deliver a smashing counter-attack, had even the success of the IX Corps on the right been less overwhelming, the congestion of wounded, actual and potential, at Ste. Emilie and Villers-Faucon, and even at Templeux, must have meant a medical disaster.

But the cause of such "failure" as there was, was not simple, nor was it one-sided. It went to the very root of the problem of evacuation.

The "Advanced" D.S. Cramped in style by its hybrid structure and training, the 27th Division in particular seems to have tried to apply American principles by British methods, and, in doing so, to have laid bare a weak point in the latter. The subject may be expounded by instance thus:—

In its diary for September, the 11th Australian Field Ambulance makes broad its phylacteries as follows:—

"The whole of these operations were characterised by the complete inadequacy of and the inexperience shown in the American medical arrangements. Had not the A.I.F. stepped in and converted the tinpot station at Ste. Emilie into a real A.D.S., the position of affairs would have been appalling. The Americans were very ready to learn and also to appreciate, and our relations were most cordial."

But, except the walking wounded, the patients who passed through this "real A.D.S." went thence direct to—and were promptly redressed at

---

[40] The diary of the D.D.M.S. for Oct. 6 has this entry:
"The following innovations in A.A.M.C., Aust. Corps, have been successfully introduced during the past six months:—
 (i) Abolition of Corps M.D.S's and Div. Rest Stations.
 (ii) Issue of Standing Orders for A.A.M.C., Aust. Corps.
 (iii) Introduction of standardised portable A.D.S., R.A.P. (Dugout), Bearer Relay Posts (Dugout), and A.D.S. (Dugout).
 (iv) The formation of surgical Resuscitation Teams for each Division.
 (v) Treatment of slightly sick and wounded at C.C.S."

—the M.D.S. at Villers-Faucon, not two miles distant! On American principles the most forward treatment centre should be formed not by the Field Hospital Companies (corresponding to the British tent division) but by Ambulance Companies (the bearer division), a very effective safeguard against the over-treatment and "re-dressing" of which we have heard somewhat throughout these chapters. The comment of the British medical historian upon developments in the British Service during this advance applies to the Australian Corps also. He says:

"During this period the D.M.S. [British First Army] carried out the policy of evacuation of wounded direct from advanced dressing stations to casualty clearing stations without an intermediate main dressing station; but what he had in fact abolished was the advanced dressing station, as the resources of the field ambulance tent divisions were concentrated at these dressing stations. The real advanced dressing stations were the collecting posts at which wounded were loaded on wheeled conveyances for transport to the dressing station. . . ."[41]

The "*Main*" D.S. But this, of course, is not the whole story. The Australian units did know their job, and the *American Official Medical History* points a moral for its own service. In connection with the very successful evacuation from the 27th Division on October 17th-18th the statement is made that:

"Use of a field hospital to operate the advance dressing station was due to the experience, on September 27th, at Ste. Emilie, where it had been learned that two ambulance companies were unable to spare sufficient personnel to operate such a formation during a period when a great many casualties were arriving. Employment of a field hospital as an advanced dressing station was also advantageous because this could be used later as a main dressing station if the main dressing station from the rear was 'leapfrogged' beyond it."[42]

And the A.D.M.S., 5th Division (Colonel Downey), after recording in his "summary" the fact that "owing to the military situation no A.D.S. was established" but that instead "car posts were pushed forward," concludes it with an apologia thus:

"*Deductions.* In an action in which the plans, as laid down, were so obviously upset, some confusion was bound to exist in the medical services. . . . The principle, of not establishing dressing stations in captured territory until definite objective has been gained, was amply justified in the operation under review."

"*A.D.S.*" v. "*M.D.S.*" The root of this very vital matter is to be found in the idea of the "leap-frog"—which itself implies movement, *advance*—expressed structurally in the "standard A.D.S." which served effective treatment. The Australian ideal was an "advanced" dressing station which should be prepared at the earliest possible moment to function as the real link between the collecting and loading posts on the one hand and the C.C.S. on the other—*i.e.* as a "main" dressing station. To ensure this the "A.D.S." must be so staffed and organised that the change to an "M.D.S." should come immediately the "military situation" made possible the *keeping of records* and the extension forward of the *motor ambulance convoy circuit*. On the furthest possible advance of the motor transport the success of evacuation in open warfare seemed

---

[41] *Brit. Off. Med. History, General, Vol. III, p.* 313.
[42] *Official History of the Medical Department of the United States Army in the World War, Vol. VIII—Field Operations—p.* 887.

to depend. In the case of the motor ambulance convoy, the standing rule was that it should not serve stations ahead of the M.D.S. On occasions, in order to get it there, it was, as we have seen, necessary either to obtain a special authorisation from army headquarters or for a station, which had been designated in orders as an "A.D.S.," to "be called" instead by Corps order a "M.D.S." The *treatment* given must be nicely adjusted to the *facilities for movement* to the goal, which is the casualty clearing station ("evacuating hospital") at railhead, or its therapeutic equivalent the "advanced operating centre." And the growing appreciation of this ended the uncertainties, the failures, and the "re-dressings" of 1916-17; and the problem of the "untransportable" case; and brought into being the Australian "resuscitation teams" of 1918. Some of these matters require a final word to link the experiences and the practice of the "open warfare" of 1918 with those of the static warfare described in *Section II*. What has to be said on this matter belongs however to the next chapter wherein we make final contact with the casualty clearing station and general hospital.

CHAPTER XXV

THE END OF THE WAR AND THE BEGINNING OF THE PEACE

WHEN on October 6th the Australian Corps handed over beyond Montbrehain to the II American, its troops had occupied some vital sector of the British front continuously for six months since March 27th when, in the later crises of "Michael" it was thrown in to maintain the French-British junction at Amiens. During this time it had performed services of great value to the Allied cause and had put the coping stone to a reputation for dependability gained on many fields, and in various seats of war and services[1]: to quote Sir Douglas Haig (when he informed the Duke of Connaught that they were among the best disciplined in the B.E.F.), "When the Australians are ordered to attack they always do so." And although it had not been called on to sustain that supreme trial of disciplined valour, an enforced retreat, the tasks set it were such as to make exceptional demands on both morale and man-power. When it was withdrawn in October it was apparently intended that, after a month's rest, with the reorganisation peremptorily required by the British Adjutant-General completed, it would again enter the line.[2]

By October 10th all five divisions were in Fourth Army rest area towards the coast, chiefly around Abbeville, and here

---

[1] An account of the work of the Australian Army Dental, Pharmaceutical, Nursing and Massage Services and of the service of Voluntary Aid; and that of the Australian Army Medical Service with the Australian Flying Corps and Royal Australian Navy will be given in *Vol. III*.

[2] That there were at this time no very general hopes of a decision in 1918 is shown by the fact that the D.M.S. A.I.F. (Maj.-Gen. Howse) was desired by the G.O.C. A.I.F. (Gen. Birdwood) to proceed to Australia to settle the question of substandard recruits. He left by the *Olympic* on Oct. 3 *via* America and was accompanied by the Commandant, Australian Administrative Headquarters (Brig.-Gen. T. Griffiths) and a number of officers on "Anzac leave." The party arrived in Australia on Nov. 11.

during some four weeks in happy surroundings, but under the menacing shadow of "pneumonic" influenza, battalions were broken up, the brigades reconstituted, the reorganisation of the field ambulances taken in hand, and 6,000 veterans launched on "Anzac leave."

During September and October, eight battalions were disbanded and their personnel distributed as reinforcements to other units.[3] Eleven of the 15 brigades were now of three battalions instead of four.

Reconstruction

Reconstruction in the Medical Service. This compulsory dissolution of combatant units and their reconstruction on an inferior plane of efficiency was made by Major-General Howse the opportunity for recommending a constructive experiment, namely, reversion to his own scheme designed to serve a like purpose in 1916[4]—that of the two-section field ambulance. The terms of the proposal, which was effected after the Armistice (forestalling post-war reorganisation) will be given in the next chapter.

In the meantime the retreat of the German armies on their home base, which had begun in the second week in October over the whole Western Front, gained increasing impetus. The successful attack on Valenciennes of November 1st and 2nd by the British Third and First Armies was followed by the advance of the whole British Fourth, Third, and First Armies across the Sambre on November 4th. In Flanders the British Second Army and General Birdwood's Fifth Army, with Belgian and French Armies, advanced towards Liége and Ghent. In the south the French and American Armies reopened their joint offensive in the Argonne. On November 9th Maubeuge was entered; appropriately enough the British First Army won the race for Mons which was captured by the 3rd Canadian Division on November 11th. On the same day Marshal Foch signed the Armistice which laid down the conditions on which the Allies would cease hostilities.

The last lap

On November 5th, after a month's rest[5] the 1st Division,

---

[3] Three battalions had already been disbanded, in April and May. The "original" formations—1st Division and 4th Brigade—were exempted from this reconstruction.

[4] *See pp. 33, 805.* The proposal was submitted to the Australian Corps by General Howse, through the D.A.G., A.I.F. in October. The same memorandum recommended a definite establishment for "resuscitation teams"—1 officer and 4 other ranks.

[5] The Australian artillery had remained in the line, and advanced with the II American Corps. The three Australian casualty clearing stations advanced with the British Fifth Army.

Map No. 13.

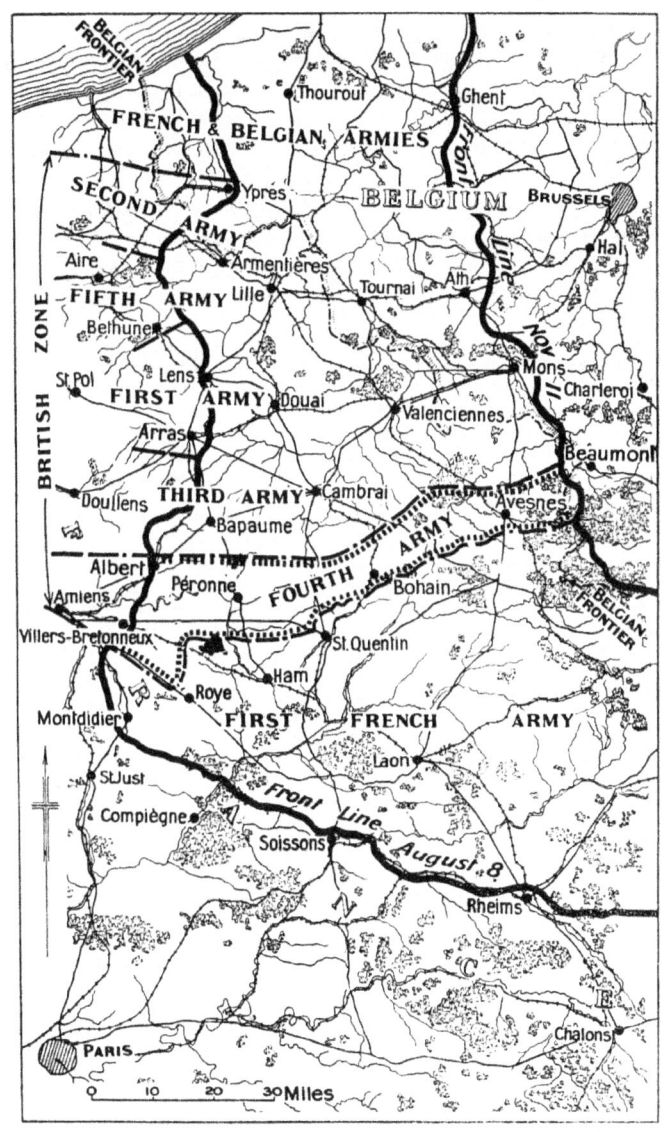

THE FOURTH ARMY'S ADVANCE, AUGUST-NOVEMBER, 1918

followed on November 9th by the 4th, moved up to rejoin Fourth Army. On the day of the Armistice the Australian infantry had reached to within a few miles of the front and Australian Corps Headquarters opened at Le Cateau. Concerning the Armistice itself, which left Australian soldiers, like all others at the front, outwardly quite unmoved, some unsophisticated ruminations are recorded in the diary of a medical orderly[6] who served in a front-line unit throughout the campaigns of the A.I.F. in France.

The Australian Corps in November

"*7.11.18.* Under orders to depart (under two hours' notice). Doc. Rossell has a confinement case in hand and has indicated that my services will be required . . . have been treating a number of cases for various complaints but confinement, 'Oh hell'! *8.11.18.* Marching orders apparently received, left Eaucourt for Longpré and entrained. Going into action once more. Detrained at Roisel. The army has advanced miles and miles beyond the old battle area and we are now within that area of France held by Germany since 1914. *10.11.18.* Travelled by bus from Roisel to Bazuel passing through liberated villages of Maretz, Reumont, Le Cateau, about 35 kilometres. . . . The population give a splendid welcome to the troops, the civilians are quite hysterical at having been liberated from the German yoke. *11.11.18.* Billeted in the ruins of the village of Baseul, the retreating German army have as far as possible devastated the country, mining houses, cross roads, railway embankments, etc. . . At about noon the sound of cheering aroused our curiosity, and upon enquiring was told an Armistice had been declared but had heard that yarn so often and so long that we were not to be caught. A little later Capt. Rossell beaming with smiles came along and certified that at last, long last, an armistice had really been declared at 11 a.m. and that hostilities had ceased. It was hardly credible as every few minutes a German mine would explode in the distance, bringing home the hated sound of war. Some of the section went souvenir hunting but I was not having any; too many mines and boobys for mine!

"And so to all intents and purposes the war is finished or seems so. And as one sits and ponders sadly of those many pals who are 'gone to that home from which no wanderer returns,' it seems so strange that it should be, that one's dearest pals should fall and that I should still be here. The very flower of our manhood have paid the greatest price, not willingly for not one of them but longed to live, return home and forget, just forget the past. Most of us enlisted for one of two reasons, Patriotism or Love of adventure, but not one had the slightest conception of the terrible price required of these Patriots or Lovers of adventure. Please God that this Armistice is really the end and that the sacrifices have not been in vain. Old pal of mine, would that you

---

[6] L/Cpl. R. Morgan, A.A.M.C., attached to 2nd Bn.

were here with me this day, but no, God willed it otherwise and so 'farewell.'
'We shall not forget,
While poppies bloom in Flanders fields.'"

For those who served with the A.A.M.C. in France and were left behind when the A.I.F. returned home, no better word could be found as epitaph than that subscribed by the Australian official artist, Will Dyson,[7] to his sketch entitled "Stretcher-bearers near Martinpuich"—

"They move with their stretchers like boats on a slowly tossing sea, rising and falling with the shell riven contours of what was yesterday no man's land, slipping, sliding, with heels worn raw by the downward suck of the Somme mud. Slow and terribly sure through and over everything, like things that have neither eyes to see terrible things nor ears to heed them. . . . The fountains that sprout roaring at their feet fall back to the earth in a lace-work of fragments—the smoke clears and they, momentarily obscured, are again moving on as they were moving before: a piece of mechanism guiltless of the weaknesses of weak flesh, one might say. But to say this is to rob their heroism of its due—of the credit that goes to inclinations conquered and panics subdued down in the privacy of the soul. It is to make their heroism look like a thing they find easy. No man of woman born could find it that. These men and all the men precipitated into the liquescent world of the line are not heroes from choice—they are heroes because someone has got to be heroic. It is to add insult to the injury of this world war to say that the men fighting it find it agreeable or go into it with light hearts."

Australian C.C.S.'s in the last phase
The movements and work of the three Australian casualty clearing stations in France have been traced through the years 1916 and 1917, and in 1918 up to the precipitate moves compelled by the German push through on the Lys in April. It is now necessary to furnish, from the very fine records kept, an epitome—tragically curt—of their peculiarly interesting experiences in the last seven months of the war.

In *Chapter XX* we left the three units in the northern sector of the British front, receiving and evacuating casualties from the Ypres, Armentières, Hazebrouck front in the Second Army; Nos. 1 and 2 at Blendecques, No. 3 at Esquelbecq. Their experiences fall into three periods.

---

[7] Will Dyson—brother of the poet and husband of an artist—combined in himself both these gifts together with deep insight in social and political philosophy and an understanding humour that made him a trenchant cartoonist and an unrivalled portrayer of the Australian soldier in the trials of the Somme winter and Passchendaele. Of the Australian official artists he was the one who lived with the troops through these trials, and his record of them (now in the Australian War Memorial at Canberra) is a monument to them and to himself.

(1) May-August. This period (it will be recalled) saw the final check to the German offensive in the north and the establishment of military dominance by a series of small- and large-scale raids, in which the 1st Australian Division played a very spectacular part. A large proportion of the Australian wounded were cleared through their own casualty clearing stations.

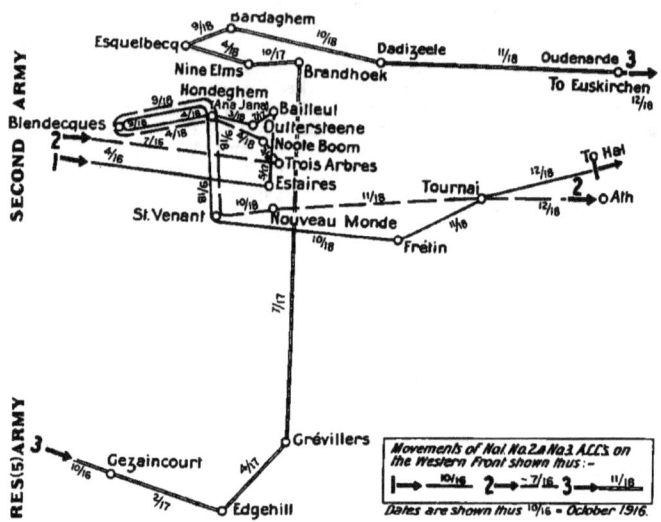

The events of "Michael" and "George" had been a serious shock to the medical administration of the B.E.F. and led to an endeavour to reconstruct, or at least to readjust, the casualty clearing station system to accord with the requirements of this new type of warfare. The effect of three years of attrition war in modifying the original intention for these units is illustrated in the following note by the officer commanding No. 1 in a report to Major-General Howse.

Personnel. "The establishment [*i.e.* staff] laid down is still for 200 sick, and consists of 86 all told . . . who by the establishment have to look after 200 sick, and, as actually happens and is recognised by the R.A.M.C., up to a total of 1,000. The modified scale of equipment for

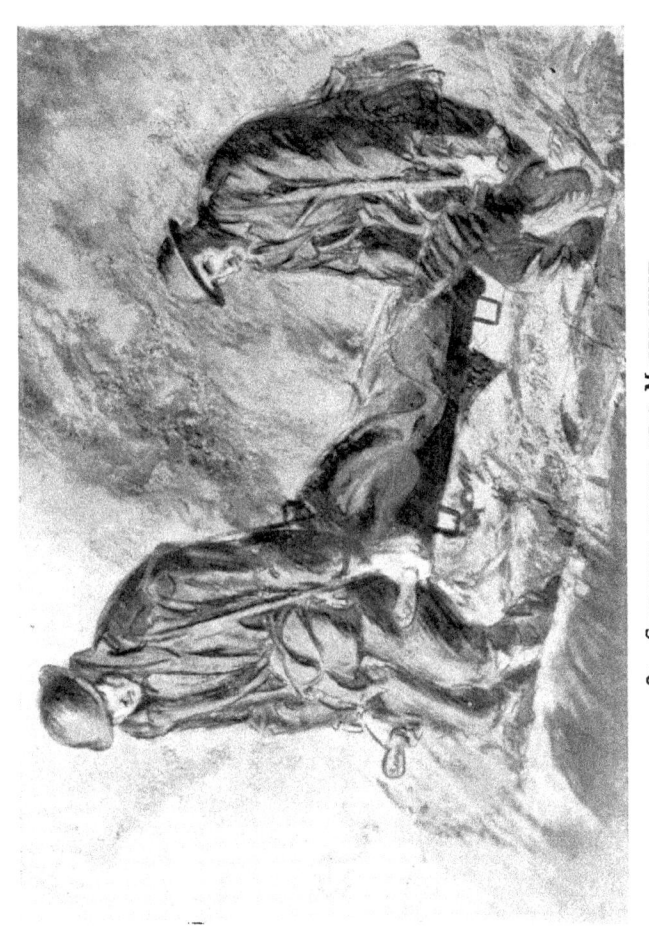

82. STRETCHER-BEARERS NEAR MARTINPUICH
From a drawing by Will Dyson

Aust. War Memorial Official Photo. No. J6450.

To face p. 772.

83. AN AUSTRALIAN AND AN AMERICAN STRETCHER-BEARER AT AN INFANTRY POST DURING THE BATTLE OF HAMEL, 4TH JULY, 1918
Aust. War Memorial Official Photo. No. E2691.

84. A RELAY POST DURING THE BATTLE OF THE HINDENBURG LINE
The embankment seen here lay above the canal tunnel. A wounded German has been carried by his comrades to one of the tunnel entrances.

Aust. War Memorial Official Photo. No. E3476. *To face p. 773.*

casualty clearing stations, on which we now draw our equipment, is for 800 patients in enlarged C.C.S., and 200 patients in hospital portion, a total of 1,000 patients. . . . The establishment for a casualty clearing station allows one theatre attendant, yet there are three surgeons on the staff, and surgical teams have to be kept in readiness to send away. . . ."

Housing. "A matter which has been brought to notice in the recent work is the tendency there has been for casualty clearing stations to become 'stationary' or almost 'general' hospitals. Huts are of course better than tents to work in, but, after a unit has been for, say, 6 months in one spot, the extra amount of stores and fixtures becomes very great, and the difficulty of transport is increased. . . ."

Equipment. "Now that casualty clearing stations are again mobile units it is of utmost importance to revise the modified mobilisation store table . . . which is more suited for a stationary hospital. Much of the equipment stated therein is useless for all practical purposes. Before the modified mobilisation store table was authorised, I had equipped this station for 1,000 beds by obtaining authority to draw additional and necessary equipment over and above the original table. I have carefully surveyed our equipment, and have returned to ordnance all stores which can be done without. As this is now a mobile unit, and it is necessary to do the maximum of work with the minimum of equipment, I would suggest that all casualty clearing stations be equipped to carry 500 patients. From recent experience, it is not possible to obtain sufficient transport to rapidly move the equipment of 1,000-beds C.C.S."

Reconstruction. On May 4th the D.M.S., Second Army, issued the following instruction:—

"Definite steps will be taken to reduce every article to the authorised scale of active service conditions laid down in the various *Field Service Manuals.*"

But the issue of such orders was clearly futile—the pivotal element in a vast system, such as had been built up in the B.E.F. to serve the current concept of "evacuation," could not be reconstructed with a stroke of the pen. As a matter of fact we find these stations within a few weeks swelled again to proportions not less than before. It is true that they had acquired insight into the adaptation necessary to meet the requirements of mobility on the one hand and of the improved military-medical processes and surgical technique on the other.

A more practical reform was a readjustment whereby the stations were grouped in two echelons, the more advanced— first echelon—receiving the severely wounded by M.A.C., while the second echelon some miles in rear was in effect a reserve but received sick and walking wounded. In the event of advance or retreat, the two echelons would, by a process of "leap-frog," reverse their respective functions.

The Australian Stations. No. 3 A.C.C.S. was included in the first echelon of a northern group (behind II Corps) with Nos. 2 Canadian and 10 British—a distinguished company—and during the next two months, with wounded and the first wave of influenza, had a very strenuous time. It was made a special centre for the severer type of influenza, which began to occur in June, just before the first wave subsided. Some useful observations then made will be included in the special study of this epidemic made in *Vol. III.* Of a total of 1,893 admissions in August, 1,177 were for sickness, and it was observed that, while the number of patients diagnosed "influenza" decreased, the duration of the disability and death rate from broncho-pneumonia was on the increase.

The increased attention given to the medical side of these units, and in particular the appointment of a Specialist Physician, had brought about a higher standard of endeavour and achievement. At the front as in civil life the problem of disease was first and foremost a matter of *diagnosis.* The signs of advance in this respect have already been referred to.[8] The acting C.O. of No. 3 A.C.C.S. (Major H. H. Woollard) in the monthly report to the D.M.S., A.I.F. for July, 1918, informs him that

"efforts are being made to stimulate M.O's to diagnose their cases and avoid subterfuges such as P.U.O., N.Y.D., etc. The importance of this is not so much in the direction of accuracy of diagnosis as increasing the observation of individual cases."

The report of the "Specialist Physician"[9] in No. 3 A.C.C.S. for August, 1918, puts the problem well:—

"In a large percentage of cases the differential diagnosis [in particular of P.U.O.] is very difficult and cannot be made with certainty at a C.C.S. under present conditions. If accurate diagnosis is essential, arrangements should be made for longer observation of the patients. This

---

[8] The significance attached to exact diagnosis has been the subject of comment elsewhere. *See, e.g., pp.* 601-2.

[9] Major Walter Fischel, M.R.C., U.S.A., who was attached for experience. The very important problem of how to short-circuit the medical "case" for return to duty within "army area" would seem indeed, in any form of entrenched warfare, best to be met by some such arrangement which should eliminate the ambulance train and the Base Depot—evacuation being by motor transport and return to duty through the regimental "reinforcement camp."

in turn would necessitate larger accommodation for medical cases. The logical thing would be separate Casualty Clearing Stations or Stationary Hospitals for medical cases."

During the summer of 1918 Nos. 1 and 2 A.C.C.S's, after a month's respite in second echelon behind XV Corps, from June 15th functioned as a first echelon, and received the casualties from the astonishing raids by the 1st Australian Division at Merris and Meteren. The two units worked in close co-operation, one each side of a central road, "receiving" on alternate days; and in June and July they dealt with some 8,000 casualties, sick and wounded. Each worked with three, and at times four, surgical teams attached, British and Australian, in addition to its normal surgical complement.[10]

(2) *August-November.* The northern force of the B.E.F. had been subdivided in June, the new Fifth Army Headquarters under General Birdwood, with Major-General Brudenell White as chief-of-staff, taking over a sector between First Army and the Second. From August 18th, when the Second Army attacked on the Oultersteene Ridge, military events on that front moved rapidly. On August 30th the enemy retired and Bailleul was occupied; by October the retirement had become a retreat. Most of the fighting devolved on Second Army, whose battle-casualties were heavy till the end.

The very dramatic events of these moves can only be outlined. Nos. 1 and 2 A.C.C.S's advanced with Fifth Army, No. 3 with Second Army. In general it may be said that, until the last stage of the advance, the standard of provision

---

[10] The following note by No. 1 A.C.C.S. has a general interest. "Three T.F.N.S. [Territorial Force Nursing Service] nurses joined from No. 54 General Hospital as partly trained anaesthetists . . . and have been very useful, not only as anaesthetists, but in relieving medical officers for other duties." The D.M.S., A.I.F., refused absolutely to participate in the scheme for training nurses for this duty, which was fairly extensively employed in the B.E.F., following American precedent.

No. 3 A.C.C.S. says: "The Surgical staff has been supplemented by Major R. G. Dixon, R.A.M.C. (T.F.) and surgical team, also by Lieut. J. H. Bloomfield, M.R.C., U.S.A., who is acting as surgeon in place of Lieut.-Col. W. G. D. Upjohn whilst the latter is on leave. Two attached surgical teams have been transferred to No. 62 Casualty Clearing Station, Arneke, and one to No. 20 Casualty Clearing Station, Vignacourt, on account of increase of work in those districts. Major W. Fischel, M.R.C., U.S.A., has been attached for instruction.

"The strength of the unit has been well maintained and now consists of 96 N.C.O's and men. The numbers of a Casualty Clearing Station on War Establishments are hopelessly inadequate and the staff is supplemented by 85 attached men as working patients. These men are gradually discharged to their lines and others retained in their places."

for casualties, and in particular for the surgical work, was little if at all relaxed. It was not till the second week in October that the retirement became sufficiently rapid to compel the drastic curtailment of gear and the final extrusion of the immense quantities of "lumber of all kinds." Casualty clearing stations entered upon a period of rapid moves, shedding equipment, till at the end of October we find No. 1 moved by five motor lorries with eight loads each, and with gear sufficient to equip a station of 100 beds and 500 stretchers. Only the operating theatre equipment, bedsteads, dispensary gear, and essential Q.M. stores were carried. The remainder was stacked under guard, though part of it was brought up subsequently.

Although in the advance in open country the number of battle-casualties greatly decreased, then, and throughout the rest of the year, the work thrown on these units was heavy through the second wave of influenza. No. 2 records:—

"November 11th happened to be one of the busiest days we have had for many weeks as the result of a final outburst of hostile shelling."

(3) Armistice and After. While Fifth Army advanced only as far as Ath, the Second continued its move into Germany, and on December 6th occupied Cologne. After the Armistice the constitution of casualty clearing stations was changed— they became mobile units for the clearance of sick. Tents were reduced from 154 to 98, the X-ray plant discarded, the operating theatre reduced from a hut capable of working eight tables to two tents containing one, the accommodation for patients was reduced to 50, material from 450 tons to 75, and the nursing staff from twelve to seven.

The 3rd A.C.C.S. was involved in the rapid advance of Second Army and on December 19th took over the deaf and dumb institute at Euskirchen (on the Rhine). Here it served the IX Corps till April 27th, when it was relieved and went to England for repatriation. Nos. 1 and 2 remained (at General Birdwood's special request) with Fifth Army at Hal and Ath until March, when they too were repatriated.[11]

---

[11] The procedure of repatriation and participation of medical units in the scheme of education and non-military employment are touched on at *pp. 797-801.*

Technical Advances in 1918. The following abridged report by the surgical specialist of No. 1 C.C.S.[12] for the month of August reflects the experience of the Australian units in the particular surgical problems of this period of the war. During the month the unit had been "working as a first line C.C.S." 1,240 surgical cases passed through of whom 579 came to operation. 481 X-Ray examinations were made. 151 were treated in the dressing room under anaesthetic, and 1,109 dressings were done.

"*Gas and Oxygen Anaesthesia.* This anaesthetic has been extensively used in cases of bad shock-haemorrhage. The Coxeter 'sight feed' apparatus and the apparatus constructed by Captain Wellman, A.A.M.C.,[13] have proved very efficient, and have enabled us to utilise this anaesthesia in all cases where its use has been indicated. The use made of these two plants has shown that *two* Gas and Oxygen sets are really an imperative need in every C.C.S."

"*Gas gangrene.* Twelve cases of gas gangrene have occurred during the month [of whom 9 had died]... The Welchii Anti-gas gangrene serum is still being used in a certain number of the cases received here," [with discouraging results.]

"*Transfusion of blood.* During the month a small annexe has been added to the hut for resuscitation, to be used as a Theatre for the transfusion of blood. The provision of this annexe would be of marked benefit during periods of battle crisis, as cases for transfusion could be dealt with separate from the main Operating Theatre, and thus free surgical personnel and equipment for operative purposes. The provision of Transfusion Teams during 'rush' periods would still further free the operative Surgical Teams. Bayliss' 6 per cent. Sterile Gum Acacia Solution in Normal Saline Solution has been used for the treatment of 'shock' cases.

"*Résumé of more serious cases during period 17/6/18 to 31/8/18.* Since this C.C.S. has acted as a first line C.C.S. the following more serious cases have been admitted. Many of these were suffering from Multiple Shell Wounds.

"*1. Cases of abdominal injury.* 70. A. Extraperitoneal wounds of abdominal viscera, and intraperitoneal wounds not included in Class B.

"B. Intraperitoneal wounds perforating hollow viscera.

"C. Cases dying on or slightly after admission.

"In class A. 24 cases have been admitted of which 17 were evacuated, 6 have died and 1 remains in the C.C.S.; a mortality rate of 29 per cent. In class B. (28 cases) 12 have been evacuated, 14 dying, a mortality rate of 57 per cent. The mortality rate of all cases of abdominal injuries including class C. (moribund) has been 58 per cent.

"*2. Fractured Femurs.* 68 cases have been admitted of which 6 were moribund. 17 of these have died (6 of which deaths were due to Gas Gangrene, and 6 moribund) or mortality rate of 25 per cent.

---

[12] Major George Bell.

[13] Capt. Wellman was induced to design and construct this apparatus in the field because the unit was unable to procure a "Coxeter or similar apparatus," the great advantages of which for some types of case over ether or chloroform had been demonstrated by a visiting surgical team. The apparatus, it was claimed, could "be used with complete success for administering the following anaesthetics:— O + E; N₂O; N₂O + O; N₂O + E; N₂O + O + E. Also for giving oxygen only...."

"Amputation of the thigh has been done in 32 cases, 19 of which were for severe G.S.W. of the thigh with severe comminution of the femur, and 13 for severe injuries of the leg and knee.

"3. *Fracture of Skull*, not including grazes etc. of outer table.

"Class A. where no penetration of the Dura had occurred, although a definite fracture of the skull was present. 14 cases, all evacuated.

"Class B. Penetration of Dura mater, 29 cases:—14 of these died and 15 were evacuated.

"Class C. 10 cases moribund.

"The total mortality rate of all head cases is 45 per cent.

"4. *Transfusion of blood*. This has been done 78 times, and 48 of the recipients have been evacuated.

"5. *Chest ward reports*. (1) Total number of Penetrating Chests (including Chest-Abdomens) 102. (2) Number evacuated 93. (3) Number of deaths 9. (4) Number requiring operation 17. (5) Mortality of operation cases 6. (6) Number of moribund cases 5."

The facilities in the Australian General Hospitals for helping to meet the effects of the German onslaught in 1918, were as follows:—

Australian General Hospitals in 1918 No. 1 (at Rouen, Colonel J. A. Dick) with a normal capacity of 1,040 beds, could expand to 1,300; about a third of the hospital was hutted—chiefly with the Nissen type; the remainder was in brigaded marquee tents. No. 2 (at Boulogne, Colonel H. A. Powell) could accommodate 1,900 patients in a crisis—1,300 in huts, 600 in tents. No. 3 (Abbeville, Colonel J. S. Purdy) had accommodation for 1,500 but had admitted up to 1,900, 50 per cent. in huts.

March to July. The German offensive in March, which so disorganised the structure of the medical scheme of evacuation at the front, involved to a lesser degree also the hospital centres at the Expeditionary Bases. Early in March, in view of the vulnerability of evacuation route from the Arras zone, hospital accommodation in the Boulogne base area was considerably expanded and on March 26th the Deputy D.G.M.S., Major-General Sir William Macpherson, advised the D.D.M.S., L. of C.:—

"Amiens is now the most dangerous point and can no longer be retained as a hospital centre." He must therefore "now be prepared to receive convoys of wounded into Abbeville, which will thus become very much a clearing station centre."

The main stream of casualties from "Michael" flowed for

the most part through Amiens direct to Rouen, where they were distributed locally or were passed on to other centres;[14] those from "George" flowed chiefly into the hospital centres at Boulogne and Etaples.

During March No. 1 A.G.H. admitted 5,029 patients which included 3,330 wounded; No. 3 at Abbeville took in 2,042 surgical cases and 1,043 "medical" (including 533 gassed.) During April No. 2, whose normal bed-state had been increased from 1,290 to 1,800, admitted 5,368 casualties.

During May, June, and July influenza became an important factor in evacuation, and in these months the flow of medical cases from the front exceeded the surgical.

August to Armistice. The opening of the British offensive on the Somme in August initiated a large flow of wounded through Amiens to Abbeville and Rouen, which later overflowed to Boulogne and Etaples.

Of this flood No. 1 A.G.H. at Rouen admitted 3,546 wounded, and No. 3 at Abbeville 2,691. In the Boulogne area a redistribution of hospital work arranged by the D.D.M.S. provided that No. 2 A.G.H. should admit stretcher cases only, and arrangements were put in hand to replace the tented part of the hospital with huts. During August the unit admitted 2,510 sick and wounded.

In September and October the three Australian General Hospitals admitted between them no fewer than 24,942 sick and wounded. On October 9th the war diary of No. 2 observes: "Influenza has broken out (*sic*) at other bases and is expected here." The course of the wave can be traced by the fact that in No. 3 2,222 admissions in September were for surgical treatment, and 1,161 for "medical," whereas in October the numbers were 1,126 and 3,186 respectively. This reversal is seen, though in a less marked degree, in the records of Nos. 1 and 2. On the whole, as has already been noted, the experience is striking for the inconspicuous effect of this disease on army wastage as compared with its influence on the work of the base hospitals and the life of the civil community.

The Armistice brought no relaxation for the General Hospitals; battle-casualties ceased, but the number of sick was more than maintained, chiefly from pneumonic influenza: in the post-Armistice period each of the three Australian General Hospitals admitted some 3,300 patients, of whom some two-thirds were sick. The tables given below show the extent, and some details, of their work during their period in France.

---

[14] *See sketch maps on pp. 397, 623.*

	1 A.G.H. 28.4.16-15.12.18 31 months	2 A.G.H. 9.7.16-9.3.19 32 months	3 A.G.H. 1918 12 months	TOTAL
Total admissions ..	90,298	90,399	28,292	208,989
Sick ..	46,187	—	18,653	—
Wounded	44,111	—	9,639	—
Average per month	2,913	2,825	2,358	2,787
Number of Australians admitted.[15]	9,030	9,040	5,660	23,730
Percentage of A.I.F.	10	10	20	11·35
Deaths	959	668	459	2,086
Average per month	30·94	20·87	38·25	27·81
Percentage of deaths to admissions	1·06	0·74	1·62	1·00
„ „ to sick	0·394	—	1·50	—
„ „ to wounds ..	1·754	—	1·87	—
Average daily cost of subsistence per patient	1/7			
Average duration of stay in Hosp.	6 days			
Number of cases examined by X-ray Dept.	11,488			

THIRD AUSTRALIAN GENERAL HOSPITAL

STATISTICS FOR THE YEAR 1918

At midnight on the 31-12-17 the number of patients
remaining were ..   769
The total admissions were   28,292
The total discharges were   27,639
The total deaths were .. ..   459[16]
The number of patients remaining midnight on the
31-12-1918 were   963

The above figures are divided into	Sick	Wounded
Remaining 31-12-17	467	302
Admissions	18,053	9,639
Discharges	17,878	9,761
Deaths	279	180
Remaining 31-12-18	963	—

---

[15] Of the total casualties in the A.I.F. in France, excluding K.I.A. and .P. of W., 6·5 per cent. were admitted to Australian General Hospitals in France.

While No. 2 A.G.H. was established at Wimereux the following number of cases passed through:—

British ..	65,756	A.E.F.	380	Civilian ..	36
A.I.F.	8,920	B.W. Indies ..	266	Portuguese	23
Canadian ..	6,645	Italian	137	Russian	13
New Zealand	2,699	Newfoundland ..	103	Bermudan	3
French ..	852	Belgian	61		
South African ..	391	Serbian	49		

[16] The total deaths which occurred at No. 3 A.G.H. are as follow:—

Period	From wounds	From disease	Total	Place
August 1915-January 1916 ..	41	102	143	Lemnos
February 1916-August 1916 ..	4	38	42	Abbassia
September 1916-March 1917 ..	5	8	13	Brighton
April 1917-May 1919	267	317	584	Abbeville
Totals	317	465	782	

1918] THE END OF THE WAR 781

Admissions are further classified as

	Sick	Wounded
From Front	7,469	9,237
From L. of C.	9,156	—
By transfer	2,028	402

Discharges are classified as

	Sick	Wounded
Died	279	180
To England	5,331	6,592
Convalescent Depots	5,276	1,790
Duty and Depots	4,691	367
Other Hospitals	2,580	1,012

The average admissions were
- Daily 77
- Weekly 544
- Monthly 2,357

The average discharges were
- Daily 76
- Weekly 540
- Monthly 2,341

The following British, Colonial and Allied troops and civilians were dealt with during the year ending 31-12-18:—

British Other Ranks	10,187
Australian Other Ranks	5,457
Australian Generals	2
Canadian Other Ranks	1,692
American Other Ranks	485
New Zealand Other Ranks	405
South African Other Ranks	209
Cape Boys	59
Indian Other Ranks	46
British West Indians	39
British Civilians	22
Chinese	15
Portuguese	11
Newfoundland Other Ranks	6
French Other Ranks	2
French Civilians	2
Italian Other Ranks	2
Russian (P. of W.)	1
Belgian Civilian	1

(*Note*: The Australian General Hospitals had no officers' wards.)

The admissions and discharges shown monthly:—

	Admissions	Discharges
January	909	949
February	950	743
March	3,084	3,944
April	2,467	1,852
May	831	1,193
June	1,639	904
July	1,021	1,659
August	4,123	3,313
September	3,383	3,337
October	4,312	3,969
November	3,310	3,768
December	2,263	2,467

The following number of operations were performed during the year:—

January	85
February	64
March	536
April	440
May	39
June	40
July	37
August	1,033
September	1,749
October	500
November	147
December	77

The Death Rate: 16·2 per thousand. Total number of operations, 4,747.

As a measuring-stick for gauging the significance of the part played by the Australian units in the British war-effort on the Western Front, the following figures are given in continuance of those presented in *Chapter XIV*.

During the last year of the war the number of general and stationary hospitals in the B.E.F. increased from 69 at the end of 1917 (44 general, 25 stationary) to 76 at the end of 1918 (48 general, 28 stationary). In the same period available beds—including "crisis expansion"—remained steady as between 80,000 and 90,000. The number occupied varied between 44,000 in January, 1918, and 74,000 in November, 1918. At the height of the German offensive in April, 1918, nearly 70,000 general hospital beds were in use. During 1918 the average ration strength of the B.E.F. on the Western Front was 1,900,000, including native troops. Of this number, 1,500,000 were fighting troops. At the beginning of the year the Australian fighting troops in France numbered 110,000. The figures at the Armistice are shown in the following table:—

British	1,561,803	South African	6,003
Australian	93,708	South African Natives ..	3,008
New Zealand	25,287	Indian	15,609
Canadian	153,828	Labour Units, etc.	107,481

Before we leave the problems of the war and enter upon a study of those that belong to the peace, there remains to be said a final word on the problem of the "un-transportable case"—a suitable subject for this last word in the study of the evacuation of wounded in the Great War, seeing that in it the "big three" in the problem of evacuation, *triage*, treatment, and transport, meet. It will be remembered that we left this problem at the beginning of 1918 "in the melting pot" into which it had been thrust by the German break-through. It is illuminated for us by several developments in the last eight months of the war, but particularly by the experience, already described, of the Australian "resuscitation teams" and by the association in the last battles of Australian medical units, with their British methods, and American units whose procedure was materially different. We are now therefore in a better position to dig down to the essentials of this interesting problem.

Evacuation of wounded: Some final conclusions

It was in an endeavour to do so that, speaking in May, 1917, at the Interallied congress of surgeons held in Paris, on the problem presented by the more serious types of wound, M. Duval, a leading French military surgeon, is reported as summing up the matter in the following epigrammatic pronouncement:

The "resuscitation team" and the "operating centre"

"Il est impossible que le blessé aille chercher son chirurgien; il faut donc que le chirurgien se porte au devant du blessé."[17]

---

[17] "It is impossible that the wounded man should go in search of a surgeon; it follows then that the surgeon must betake himself to the wounded man."

In the reaction of the British, French, and American services respectively to the idea contained in the above, it is possible to discern the origin of important points of difference between their outlook on evacuation in this war. It will promote clarity if we first "appreciate" the problem objectively, and then report, as a matter of history, the respective solutions arrived at.

The crux of the problem lay in this fact, that *two types of case* were concerned—

(a) First, a group wherein the need for special action arose by reason of physiological "collapse," as through excessive loss of blood; or by reason of uncontrollable haemorrhage; or of the onset or threat of wound shock; or the existence of injuries which, without special attention, in advance of the M.A.C., would involve an immediate threat to life, or irreparable hurt in transportation. In this group what was required was not *effective operation* but *effective first aid*—"resuscitation," with or without what may be termed "prophylactic" operation.

(b) The second group comprised those men in whom the prompt performance of a major operation under general anaesthetic afforded the only means for dealing with the emergencies described under (a) above, or for preventing pathological developments which would render recovery hopeless. Of these, the most important[18] were wounds of the abdomen, including the urinary system; some wounds of the chest; wounds of the thigh or leg (with or without retained foreign body) in which rapid swelling and tension in the limb has occurred; penetrating wounds of the knee joint; and any wound, with or without a fracture, with much laceration of muscle and particularly if a tourniquet had been applied. This group was determined by one essential fact—that a man is less fit for transportation after effective major operation under anaesthetic, than he is immediately before it; from this the proper deduction is that such operation should only be performed at a place where the patient can be held for after-care for some days—even for a week or more.

The problems involved in these two groups were in a great measure distinct, and the solutions arrived at can be dealt with separately.[19]

The "Resuscitation" Case. The scheme devised in the Australian Corps, and described in *Chapter XX*, for carrying out effective first aid in the field ambulance by the formation of "resuscitation teams," seems to have been the most systematic attempt made in the B.E.F. to deal with this problem of "resuscitation," as distinct from effective operation, in advance of the C.C.S. It has been reported in sufficient detail to enable the reader to relate this particular solution with the wider involve-

---

[18] This list is based on one given in a lecture to field ambulance officers by Lieut.-Col. Balcombe Quick, No. 2 C.C.S.; delivered at the Australian Corps "School of Medical Officers" at Bailleul, in Feb. 1918. Colonel Quick's list was of cases which were in his opinion "the most pressing in their need for intervention if a selection has to be made" of cases to be immediately evacuated to C.C.S.

[19] The relative proportion of these two groups to the total stretcher cases must depend on a variety of factors; in particular, the distance from C.C.S., and conditions on the transport circuits. In the Australian Corps the proportion of men thought suitable for treatment by the resuscitation teams was placed at about 2·3 per cent. For the "very urgent" operation cases 5-8 per cent. may be suggested.

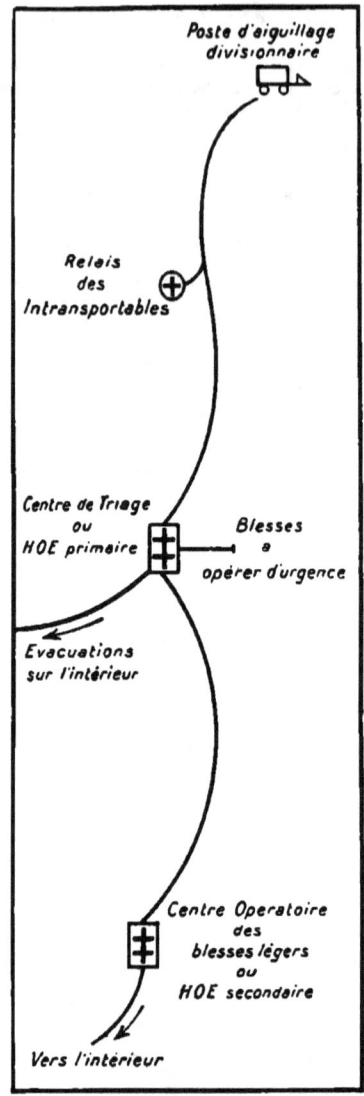

French method of Disposition in depth ("Echelonnement") of the Medical Stations behind the fighting force. (From "Le Service de Santé," Vol. IV, p. 809, by Médecin Inspecteur Général A. Mignon.) [20]

[20] A translation of the terms used in this diagram—reading from top to bottom—is as follows: Divisional distributing post; Relay post for those unfit for transport; Sorting centre (*triage*) or primary evacuating hospital; Wounded requiring urgent operation; Evacuations to interior (L. of C. or Base); Surgical centre for lightly wounded, or field general hospital; To interior (L. of C. or Base).

ments of the problem of the "urgent case" as these presented in the B.E.F. An examination of them will involve an appraisal of the distinctive features of the whole British system for dealing with battle-casualties.

The "Urgent Operation" case: (i) *Discrimination.* Australian records that deal with the evacuation of wounded from the Battles of the Hindenburg Line lay stress on what seemed to Australian officers to be an extreme preoccupation on the part of the American "ambulance companies" in the mechanical procedure of sorting and labelling the wounded at the "A.D.S."; to the Australians it appeared that this was the cause of some degree of "lag" in translating the results of *triage* into appropriate acts of treatment and transportation. Presuming the correctness of the observation, it may well have been that this defective co-ordination of the procedure of *triage* with that of disposal was due to the defective integration of American methods with British to which reference was made in the account given of this battle. Be this as it may, in the procedure of *triage* we meet a striking difference in French and American methods from British ones. The "classification" of casualties for disposal was quite as much a part of the British scheme, but was there carried out *curratim*—"while you wait"; it was not a special procedure and was as much a part of movement as of treatment.[21] Yet, far from being held of small account, it was recognised as being of the greatest importance, the whole experience of the A.I.F. on the Western Front confirming the lesson of Gallipoli, that the chief single factor in successful evacuation is the differentiation of the serious from the slighter battle-casualties, and the making of appropriate arrangements for the disposal of each.

(ii) *"Advanced Operating Centre," or C.C.S.?* Through this business of 'triage we are led to the second distinctive feature of the British system. This was the less exact "division of labour" in the medical service at the front. Though nowhere expressly laid down, it is to be discerned in the whole tenor of the records of the B.E.F., including the Australian, and is implicit in the following statement from the *British Official Medical History*:[22]

"The British system of handling all casualties was the establishment of a chain of medical units extending from the regimental aid post through field ambulances and casualty clearing stations to the base hospitals. Theoretically, every link in the chain was supposed to be capable of treating every type of wound or disease."

With some obvious provisos—*e.g.*, that surgeons should be concentrated at the C.C.S.—this statement seems adequately to present British policy, and in particular to reflect the attitude of the directing and

---

[21] This principle of permitting no check to movement is very well illustrated by the following note from the war diary of the A.D.M.S., 2nd Aust. Div., on 13 Oct. 1917:—

"The work at the A.D.S. [in the railway station Ypres] was of the ordinary routine type but great time was saved by having all cases examined in the road and classified 'A,' 'B,' 'C' [for appropriate disposal]. This allowed a large number being sent direct to C.C.S. or to the ambulance train at the Ypres station. Only those requiring fresh dressings, re-splinting, or those suffering from shock or threatened haemorrhage were brought in and attended to." (*See also Chapter x.*)

[22] *Diseases of the War*, Vol. II, p. 499. The article is concerned with the disposal of battle-casualties from gassing.

advisory staff of the B.E.F. towards this problem of the urgent case. The British leaders ultimately turned from the policy of improvising "advanced operating centres" towards that of improving the methods for bridging the gap between the A.D.S. and the C.C.S. This was done by special transport arrangements—even special transport vehicles; by an exact scheme for discriminating urgent cases; and by provision for prompt action at the C.C.S. Undoubtedly formidable difficulties were presented by the formation of advanced operating centres, with full provision for effective operation and after-treatment, and located sufficiently in advance of the C.C.S. to be worth-while. And the question of early operation should not be dissociated from the general problems of the C.C.S.[28]

The outstanding "lessons" that seem to emerge from Australian experience in the evacuation of wounded in the Great War may be summed up as follows: (*i*) In any great battle a proportion—which may be estimated at some 2-5 per cent.—of all battle-casualties other than from gassing will, if their lives are to be saved, require special arrangements for ensuring early operation or for effective first aid at a "field" hospital. (*ii*) For the rest, success in evacuation is in a great measure determined by the exact and early discrimination of stretcher cases, "sitters," and "walking wounded," and the making of special arrangements for the transport and treatment of each class. (*iii*) The basic principle—to ensure successful evacuation under all conditions and every combination of circumstance, the medical scheme must adapt its arrangements to the fundamental constants, physical, physiological, and pathological, which lie, and will always lie, behind the particular problems of all types of warfare and of every battle.

Some vital lessons

When all has been said as to the immense effort to save and repair the wounded, and as to the unquestionable improvements in method in which they resulted, the medical historian has to face frankly the tables summarising the mortality rates of men wounded and gassed in the B.E.F. and A.I.F. on the Western Front.

Results of wound surgery: A statistical paradox

---

[28] In their advance through the Argonne at the end of 1918, the Americans found it very difficult to give effect to their policy of advanced operating centres. This "appreciation" of the problem from the British standpoint may with great advantage be compared with the outlook and methods adopted in other nations; as given (*e.g.*) in *Appendix No. 9*.

MORTALITY RATE PER CENT. OF ALL ADMISSIONS TO HOSPITAL OF WOUNDED ON THE WESTERN FRONT[24]

British Troops			Australian Troops		
Date	Gassed	"Wounded"	Date	Gassed	"Wounded"
1914	Nil	6·16	Apr.-Dec., 1916	7·26	8·25
1915	2·40	6·40	1917	1·84	8·76
1916	16·77	7·30	1918	1·83	9·29
1917	3·42	8·70			
1918	2·35	7·15	1916-1918	1·92	8·80
			American Troops		
1915-1918	3·17	7·61	Feb.-Nov., 1918	1·73	8·25

These show this astonishing *prima facie* truth—that the "expectation of life" for wounded men who reached the field hospitals steadily deteriorated throughout the war. But though the truth, this is certainly not the whole truth. The explanation seems to be that, as the war went on, more and more of the seriously wounded men managed to reach the field ambulance. This interpretation has a striking confirmation in the comparison of the British and Australian figures for the last two years.

In successful warfare nearly all the victor's wounded lie within the ground seized by their own side; in unsuccessful fighting many seriously wounded are left in No-Man's Land or in the enemy's lines. In 1918 the Australians were advancing in nearly every battle and therefore presumably were able to rescue a high proportion of badly wounded men. The British, on the other hand, faced the brunt of two great German offensives, and therefore certainly had to abandon a proportion of seriously wounded. It would therefore be expected that among Australians the mortality of rescued men would be higher in

---

[24] The British percentages for "wounded" include admissions from gas poisoning. The Australian figures are for all wounds, less gassed. They are exact, being based on the finalised individual records. British figures are taken from the *British Official Medical History, Casualties and Medical Statistics*, pp. 111, 127, 141, 152, 161, 171. The figures for gassing are from Table 9 (p. 111) which shows the approximate total gas casualties admitted to Medical Units in France, with deaths, 1915-18, as follows: 1915, admissions 12,792, deaths 307; 1916, admissions 6,698, deaths 1,123; 1917, admissions, 52,452, deaths 1,796; 1918, admissions 113,764, deaths 2,673.

In the British history no explanation is offered of the exceptional figures for 1916, but it would seem to lie in the imperfect protection or education against phosgene. The gas problem is dealt with in the next volume of the Australian medical history, but it may be noted here that, although slightly over 93 per cent. of gassed cases admitted to C.C.S. required evacuation to the Base, the percentage ultimately returned to duty is stated by the British history to have reached 96·79 in 1915 and 92·90 for the later years of the war.

Statistics of wounding in the A.I.F. will be given in *Vol. III*. Partial figures will be found in *Appendix No. 1* of the present volume.

1918 than in 1917, and that in the British Army the position would be reversed. This is found to be the case.[25]

Before we leave the front in France and Belgium a final word is called for as to the treatment of the civil population, a note of which was made in *Chapter II*.

Medical Problems of the Civil Population   Indeed any student of history seeking data concerning the co-operation of democratic Allies—the most complex form of social co-operation—would find useful hints of the essential problems involved therein—social, psychic, even physiological—in the medical records of the "British Expeditionary Force" which invaded France in these years.

The Nature of the Relations. Continued successful co-operation will, it is suggested, depend on the possibility of establishing relations akin to those which exist within the "family"—the unit of the democratic society. Some such relation did, in the later years of the war, come to exist between the B.E.F. and the French and Belgian civilian populations. The analogue presents itself in two forms. First, in the family's right to "squabble" without any material disconcertion in the domestic menage. Second, the obligation to mutual assistance was on the plane of instinctive reaction rather than of rational or emotional appeal. This gave a natural even a common-place tone to medical interventions which as a fact held on occasion a high content of emotion. We shall do no more than summarise the points of contact.

The international aspect has been touched on in various places and need not be further examined.[26]

In the field formations the problem covered (*a*) mutual assistance in the prevention of disease and promotion of health in the respective populations involved; (*b*) assistance to sick or wounded civilians in the way of treatment and transport.

(*a*) The protection of the troops from infectious disease through contact was the subject of special orders and arrangements in each army. In general they provided for co-operation in ensuring the smooth working of the respective health machinery.[27] They were implemented

[25] The figures might conceivably be affected by variances in method of classifying the deaths of men who "died of wounds" in the advanced stations or in Great Britain: or by the progressive severity of wounds in the later years of the war. No evidence, however, is available of either of these circumstances.

[26] For example in *Chapter xviii* in connection with the interallied debate on the food problem. The problem of venereal disease is examined in *Vol. III*. The arrangements between the British and French Governments in connection with the establishing of treatment centres in France is touched on in *Chapter xiv*.

[27] Thus we find (*inter alia*) a Second Army order issued at the request of the Belgian Minister of the Interior instructing field ambulance commanders that infective cases among civilians should not be taken to civil infectious hospitals without first notifying the hospital as to the nature of the case, etc. And (for the other part) the French Mission at G.H.Q., B.E.F., arranges for the notification to the British military authorities, when expedient, of various infectious diseases of which we find record (besides V.D., a unique problem)—of typhoid, dysentery, diphtheria, scarlet fever, C.S.F., measles, and mumps among French civilians.

through the local machinery—the Maire of the Commune on the one hand and the administrative and executive agents in the B.E.F. (described in *Chapter XIX*) on the other.

(*b*) *Treatment and Transport of Civilians.* As already noted (*Chapter ii*), the matter of battle-casualties settled itself—rescue and treatment were automatic. But sickness provided curious problems, which, as it happened, came to a head about the time of the arrival of the A.I.F. At first (the British history states) "attendance and treatment were given by R.A.M.C. officers practically wherever and whenever they were asked for." With the establishment of siege warfare this became a cause of embarrassment on both sides, and a *modus vivendi* was worked out on lines whereby the normal professional and civic arrangements should so far as possible be preserved. Thereafter, each army made exact provision in accordance with the circumstances of the population—always with a wide range of discretion to the executive medical officers concerned. Civilians employed—as in laundries—were subject to exact arrangements between the British, French, and Belgian Governments.

In December, 1918, the D.G.M.S. through his Directors enquired by circular memorandum under several headings as to the assistance rendered to French and Belgian civilians in the way of organised and extempore medical attendance and provision. Replies by Australian units can be summarised in the following paragraph from that of the 15th Field Ambulance.

"During the period this Ambulance has been stationed in and around villages occupied by civilians, medical services have been rendered whenever required and drugs and dressings supplied. Patients requiring evacuation have been transferred to hospital by ambulance cars after authority for the patient's removal has been obtained from the Maire of the locality."

After the Armistice the influenza epidemic gave opportunity for more exactly organised assistance. Ambulance officers were detailed to work with the civilian practitioners in meeting this medical crisis.

Dental Treatment. The following summary of the situation from the dental side seems sufficiently apposite to quote.

"All A.I.F. Dental Officers in France. . . .

"For the information of all concerned it is pointed out that as the civilian dentists . . . in what is now the zone of the British Armies, have been called to the colours of our Ally, principally as combatants, the civilian population . . . is dependent upon the various Dental Services of the British Armies for the alleviation of pain of dental origin and it is incumbent upon A.I.F. dental officers to relieve such pain when civilians present themselves for treatment. The civilian population .

will invariably offer to pay in cash for dental attention. Under no circumstances will money be accepted. . . . To do so will bring the greatest discredit upon the Australian Dental Services. All ranks are warned that breaches of this instruction will be dealt with with the utmost severity."[28]

Summary. The records and correspondence files of the A.I.F. seem to show that in this matter generous sentiment should be exactly informed by commonsense business methods —in particular, that every medical officer with an Expeditionary force should be instructed in the matter of the civilian health services of the nation—whether Allied or enemy—in whose country he works.

REPATRIATION

The war ended, the concern of Australia for her citizen army centred on the reabsorption of its personnel at the earliest possible date into the peaceful social community and vocations from which they had been drawn. It is, however, one thing to let war loose and quite another to clear up after it. The aftermath of any great war is, in truth, in its social history apt to be more sordid and demoralising than the war itself, just as its political and international repercussions are more devastating. On the medical service of the A.I.F. and later, on the medical profession of Australia, was to fall a full share of the responsibility for conserving, in such degree as should be possible in this aftermath, the ideals for which the Australian soldier fought, and for fulfilling with generosity but with justice the pledges made to him by his country when he enlisted. These medical responsibilities began with the Armistice when the troops were concentrated within billeting areas in France, restive under restraints which, during the war, had not been resented; they were greatly enhanced when the service became involved in the wider problems of repatriation to Australia. For the medical service and medical profession it can be said—in way of foreword—that its steadfast adherence to professional probity has helped to maintain order and consistency in the conduct of restitution and

After the Armistice: First stage of repatriation

---
[28] Issued by the S.O., A.D.S. for the A.I.F. in France (Major L. B. Day) to all Australian dental units in France with copy "for information" to the D.M.S., A.I.F., 21 Aug. 1918.

reparation; and its responsibility will cease only when, some time in the third millennium A.D., the last "dependant" of the last pensioner shall have been paid his last penny by a grateful country.

The major problems of "demobilisation" and "repatriation," as they evolved in the Australian force and were faced in the hectic years that followed the Armistice, belong to the more or less "civil" repercussions of the war, which have been reserved for the final volume. But the immediate post-Armistice problems in France and the return of the troops to Britain must be examined here.

The Department of "Repatriation" and "Demobilisation."[29] The problems relating to repatriation and demobilisation of the A.I.F. had been a matter of concern to the G.O.C., A.I.F. (General Birdwood), and his advisers from as early as 1916, and a tentative plan had been designed by his chief-of-staff, Major-General White, whereby the return of the troops should dovetail in with the existing system of the Command Depots and of "invaliding." A small department of A.I.F. Administrative Headquarters had been formed to study the involvements of the problem—particularly that of adapting the machinery of Administrative Headquarters to the purpose of repatriation. An educational scheme had been devised and was already working. When the problem actually arose, however, on 21st November, 1918, the General Officer Commanding the Australian Corps (Lieut.-General Monash) was made by the Australian Government responsible for devising and carrying out the necessary plans, and on December 1st he was appointed "Director-General" of a new and largely independent "Department of Repatriation and Demobilisation." A great office was created with its premises in Victoria-street, London. Monash was in name under Birdwood and was in *liaison* with Australian Administrative Headquarters at Horseferry-road; in particular, it was agreed that the Department of the D.M.S., A.I.F.,[30] should be directly responsible for all action relating to the medical service in France.

---

[29] For the military significance of these terms and special Australian usage, see *Vol. III*.

[30] In the absence of Major-Gen. Howse in Australia Col. R. J. Millard was acting as D.M.S.

A Policy for Repatriation. As in all human enterprise the prime need was for a "policy." The line of thought that lay behind that designed by General Monash and his advisers, and set out by him[31] with characteristic clarity and insight, adumbrates very exactly the significance of the whole problem for the medical service, and has also much general interest.

"Long training and the excruciating stress of war had created a common morale of very high quality—a 'fighting morale,' which had turned the whole current of thought and individuality of every man into one single direction; the purpose of war to a victorious end was the paramount and dominating thought which filled the soul of every one. Instantly, upon the cessation of hostilities, this common outlook was violently extinguished, and, from the point of view of moral tendencies, these great compact war organisations became resolved into an agglomeration of individuals, each with his own different outlook upon the future, each animated by different aims, ambitions, desires, and tendencies. There was no longer any common purpose, any mutually binding force. To all who could appreciate these considerations, it was clear, from the outset, that the problems of demobilisation, full as they were of difficulties and technical details, of adapting ends to means, and of the creation of complex and untried machinery, were really dominated by moral considerations—that, in fact, the problem of demobilisation was, first and foremost, a psychological one."

Concentration after the Armistice. On the date of the Armistice the distribution of the members of the A.I.F. who had not already been repatriated to Australia either as invalids or on furlough was roughly as follows:—

In France and Belgium, 95,000; in the United Kingdom, in the form of sick, wounded, convalescents, partially trained reinforcements, and staffs, 60,000; in the Egyptian and other minor theatres of war, 30,000.[32]

The Australian force as a whole did not follow the Germans to the Rhine. The 1st and 4th Divisions, together with Corps Headquarters, remained in the neighbourhood of Le Cateau until December 7th, when they moved to Ham-sur-Heure in Belgium. The 2nd, 3rd, and 5th Divisions remained in billets round Abbeville, continuously depleted by drafts ("quotas") for Great Britain under the scheme of "repatriation" till April, 1919, when what remained of the 1st, 2nd, 4th, and 5th

---

[31] *The History of the Department of Repatriation and Demobilisation*; a report on the department's work. The introduction, from which quotations are here made, is by Sir John Monash.

[32] The figures are General Monash's. The repatriation of the troops from Palestine is dealt with in *Vol. I.*

Divisions was concentrated in the neighbourhood of Charleroi in Belgium, the 3rd remaining near Abbeville. Australian Corps Headquarters and the office of the D.D.M.S. were established in Charleroi.[83]

Demobilisation. Demobilisation, the reverse of "mobilisation," involves (*a*) the breaking up of the military formations and units comprising the force, and the discharge of its personnel from military control and responsibility; (*b*) the disposal of military equipment and stores not required for maintaining a peace-time force; and (*c*) the assembly and disposal of records—personal, administrative, and historical.

Only the preliminary stage of demobilisation could be carried out abroad, and for the most part this was done in France. That of the personnel is described presently under repatriation, of which it necessarily formed part. That of material involved the return to the British Ordnance Department, from which by far the greater part of it had come, of most of the military equipment and stores, whose provision had alone made possible the oversea service of the A.I.F.[84] Arrangements were made by the Australian Government.

The possibility of dealing fully with the immense and multifarious involvements of the war's aftermath in respect to reward and reinstatement, pension, medals, military status, preference for employment, and so forth was based wholly on retention of the "personal records" of the troops.

---

[83] At this stage an inquiry was made by the Collator of the Australian Medical Records into the opinion held by combatant officers concerning certain aspects of army medical organisation (the command of ambulance bearers, and discipline of field medical units). For the former, *see p. 284*. The latter subject will be touched on, in connection with the status of the medical service, in *Vol. III*.

[84] In this connection it has been said, with a germ of truth, that the experience of the A.I.F. was the worst possible preparation for self-defence. For this dependence, see *Vol. I, p. 55, and index entries under "Financial Relations."*

In its bulk and cost, and, in particular, in the industrial and technical organisation involved in its production, the *material* of war thus "demobilised" was of a dimension that should create the gravest apprehension to an imperfectly industrialised country such as Australia.

The following, from the *History of the 9th Field Ambulance, p. 61* (published in 1920), comes from the past as an authentic "lesson of the war."

"Boards of officers sat on the slightest provocation and seemed to take a delight in holding enquiries into deficiencies in mobilisation stores. The records of their deliberations built up a huge store of useful information, and with such things to guide the men at the head, the organisation of Ambulances in the next war should be on a much better basis than it was during this small mix-up. There will not be things included in the stores like Field Fracture Boxes, to be carried during the days of war . . and be dumped unused when the Armistice is signed."

Particularly important were the form "B.103," and the "medical history sheet" and other "administrative" records, in part maintained overseas, in part at home. Correspondence files, orders, memoranda, and so forth were held in the various record offices—at A.I.F. Headquarters in the field, 3rd Echelon, and A.I.F. Headquarters in London. The assembling and disposing of these was an important part of "demobilisation." With the end of the war came also an immense access of concern for *historical records* of all kinds, and to deal with these the Australian War Records Section was greatly augmented so that its activities came to form an important element in the tumult of demobilisation as they have in the shouting of the aftermath. An account of the medical involvements of all these will be found in *Volume III*.

Repatriation: "*Quotas*" *and* "*Cadres*." So much for demobilisation in respect to *material*. The first stage of demobilisation in respect to *personnel* was a reversal of reinforcement, and was part and parcel with the first stage of repatriation. To determine the order of precedence in which the members of the A.I.F. should be demobilised, the simple and essentially democratic principle was laid down that, so far as possible, "*The first to come out shall be the first to go home.*"

Procedure. The rule was perforce "applied in a rough and ready fashion." "Repatriation precedence rolls" were supplied to each division,[35] the period of service being reckoned by "full half-years." After the despatch of some 5,000 men in drafts the system of "quotas" was devised. The "quota" was fixed at a constant strength of 1,000 men—the average load of a railway train or transport, and of accommodation in a normal camp. Battalions and other units in each division, including the medical ones, were billeted and administered in "groups," from which in strict rotation the quotas were drawn. So soon as the strength of a unit fell below 40 per cent. of establishment, it was amalgamated with others, as were also the divisions themselves. Thus the field ambulances of each of the four divisions in the north were eventually reduced to one in each of two remaining divisional groups.

The last stage in this process saw units, groups, and ultimately divisions themselves, reduced to selected "*cadres*" of specialists charged with the final hand-over to the British and French authorities of such equipment, stores, camp sites and premises as should revert to each, and with the final disposal of unit records.

Medical Duties. With each quota went a medical detachment of one officer and at least five other ranks, A.A.M.C., equipped for first aid. Each soldier in a quota[36] was medically boarded and the findings were

---

[35] For the purpose of repatriation each division constituted a repatriating formation. The "Corps Troops," and "L. of C. Units" other than medical, were combined in a single administration. Some technical units, such as the Australian Flying Corps, were repatriated independently. The medical service was subject to special arrangements, as described below.

[36] Men other than those included in the quotas had their medical report filled in on the troopship home-bound.

recorded on A.I.F. Form 536, the purpose of which (it was laid down) was—

"(a) To ensure that each individual member of the A.I.F. is free from infection and fit to travel without danger to himself or others.

"(b) To permit of revision, and, where necessary, amendment of Medical Categories.

"(c) To assist the Pensions Department in assessing claims for pensions in respect to Disability due to Military Service."

The form was inspired from Australia and was designed to serve as a progressive record of the whole medical procedure of demobilisation, the final entry to be made on the soldier's discharge in Australia—where we shall meet with it again in connection with its application to the pensioning problem.

The personnel of each quota went first to the A.I.F. Depot at Le Havre[37] and, after being washed, deloused, and re-clothed, were assembled and organised as a "unit" on the lines of a battalion. The quotas retained this structure throughout their stay in the depots and (with the adjustments required by Non-Military Employment, discharge abroad, and so forth) until the final stage of demobilisation in Australia.

The elaborate and toilsome procedure described above was the price paid for the democratic policy "first come, first to return" instead of the simpler and far more "efficient" procedure of repatriation by existing units. It was a test at once of democratic ideals and of the Australian discipline; on the whole it worked well and was worth while.

Arrived in England, the quota, draft, or cadre "marched in" via the Overseas Training Brigade to the various camps of the A.I.F. Depots in U.K. on Salisbury Plain; and there, after their fortnight's furlough, its personnel awaited their turn to embark by troop-transport to Australia—although such as wished to take advantage of the scheme of Non-Military Employment could here be detached.

The machinery of the depots was both reversed, to serve "repatriation," and speeded up for invaliding. But this development, associated with return to Australia, will be discussed in *Volume III*. We have now to examine the medical problems in France during January to June, 1919, together with the "Non-Military Employment" of the personnel of the medical service and first stage in their demobilisation.

"God is forgotten and the doctor flouted" is as inevitable in the aftermath of a war as it is said to be after a sickness.

---

[37] *See pp. 420-21.*

"The period between December and April," records the D.D.M.S. Australian Corps, Colonel Barber, "was perhaps the most unpleasant of the war. The initial stages of demobilisation were carried out without much reference to welfare, health, or the needs of those services which were still working, the A.M.C., the A.S.C. (M.T. and Supply), and the Signal services; with the result that the officers responsible for the efficient working of those services found great difficulty in retaining sufficient combatant officers, men, and transport to carry on. The roads were in a very bad state, the troops scattered over an area of about 3,000 square miles; and when an ambulance broke down it was very difficult to get it repaired. The British C.C.S's were left inadequately staffed to deal with the grave problem of influenza. Some weeks earlier requests were made that Australian C.C.S's be sent to this Corps, but without avail."

Medical problems: After the Armistice

The British method of adjusting precedence in repatriation was by individual nomination to serve some social or industrial demand. It would seem that the Australian troops in France were hit both by British and A.I.F. methods.

"I had to lend 8 officers and about 170 men to various C.C.S's," Colonel Barber notes, "and as the majority were stretcher-bearers, and many of them recently drafted from the infantry, they were not much use as nursing orderlies. Owing to the demand by the A.I.F. in U.K. for officers and men of the A.M.C., it was extremely difficult to make arrangements for the satisfactory care of the troops. . . . This trouble was obviated by a Corps Routine Order which instructed that no A.M.C. personnel should leave the Corps without reference to the D.D.M.S. Without this I should have been unable to retain sufficient capable officers and men to carry on efficiently."

A set of "Medical Instructions," which had been issued by Colonel Barber on the 6th of October, 1918, to apply while the Corps was "in reserve," were found suitable for the rest of the time in France.

These provided for the treatment of patients "likely to be well within 5 days" in Battalion "rest posts," or "within 14 days" in field ambulances. The treatment of scabies and the prophylaxis and treatment of V.D. were made divisional responsibilities.

With the concentration of the troops round Charleroi and Abbeville the conditions became much easier; influenza subsided, the prevention of venereal disease became the chief problem and a very difficult one.[38]

"During all this period," Colonel Barber says, "the troops were very healthy, and had it not been for the epidemic of influenza the sick wastage would have been very low. . . . I think that the epidemic was

[38] This matter is dealt with in *Vol. III*.

to a great extent held in check by the wide dissemination of the troops over this large area."

Attendance on the civilian population, among whom the whole Corps were now billeted, became a great tax on the resources of the ambulance personnel. Happily, the sick rate in the troops was lower in these months than ever before in France.

A record of medical work during this trying period after the Armistice cannot but make special reference to the value of the services at this juncture of three voluntary organisations. At a time when the troops were "spoiling" for lack of occupation the Comforts Fund, Y.M.C.A., and Red Cross organisations made great efforts to provide games and entertainment, the Red Cross serving the medical units, the others the general body of troops.

Red Cross, Y.M.C.A., and Australian Comforts Fund

What may be termed the social problems of this period were immensely aided by the fine constructive project which became best known as Non-Military Employment or "N.M.E." The idea of re-creating in the soldier the constructive outlook proper to peace, and to prepare him for return to civil life, seems first to have been conceived in the Canadian force and to have acquired form and substance in the "University of Vimy Ridge" behind the lines of the Canadian Corps, whence the idea spread to the British and to other dominion armies. Its application in the A.I.F. was suggested by an officer of the 3rd Division (Lieutenant G. L. Mayman) to the Australian Official War Correspondent, who early in 1918 discussed the matter with Sir William Birdwood and Sir Brudenell White. A peculiarly interesting story must be reduced to a bald outline.

The Educational scheme and Non-military Employment

Early in May General Birdwood invited Chaplain the Right Reverend G. M. Long, Bishop of Bathurst, to draft proposals for an "Education" scheme for the Australian force. His proposals were examined by a "select committee" of senior officers of the A.I.F., and a scheme was devised to operate in two stages; first during the war, and second during the period of demobilisation.[39] A syllabus was drawn up, and units

[39] In cabling to Australia for authority, the cost was estimated at £100,000 for the first year. "This amount (it was added) may seem large, but the Australian Corps have on several occasions expended considerably more, in ammunition alone, in one day."

were invited and helped to institute classes and, as opportunity presented, to attend special schools. In the medical service, as the unit diaries show, the idea was embraced *con amore* as a relief from the strain and monotony of duties connected with battles and slaughter which by now had become inconceivably wearisome.[40]

Period of Demobilisation. Bishop Long's scheme, taken up vigorously by the Director of Demobilisation, and expanded by the Australian Prime Minister, Mr. W. M. Hughes, then in England, to include "Non-Military Employment," became a factor of major importance in the process of demobilisation overseas. "Non-Military Employment" was designed, as well as useful preoccupation and perhaps emolument, to augment the possibilities of "re-education" as a preparation for return to civil avocations by actual employment in various trades and professions.[41]

As material to be educated under this scheme the members of the medical service fell broadly into two groups—first, the medical and allied callings,[42] and, second, almost every other occupation. With a few exceptions noted below, the first comprised exclusively members of the service who held commissioned or warrant rank or, as nurses, a "relative" status as officer. For this group, on the advice of his A.D.M.S. (Lieut.-Colonel J. H. Anderson), who was largely responsible for the scheme, special provision was made by the D.M.S., A.I.F. The arrangements made for officers other than medical will be described in connection with the history of their special branch of the service. The scheme devised for members of the medical profession was the direct forerunner of the system of "post-graduate" courses developed in Australia after the war.

The Medical Services

For the rest it is only necessary to note that, so far as the engrossment of the service in its medical duties permitted, its members entered into the scheme with initiative and originality.

---

[40] As an example, in the 14th Field Ambulance classes were held in Bookkeeping, French, Arithmetic, Algebra, Salesmanship and Advertisement writing, Agriculture, Architectural draughtmanship, English grammar and literature, Latin, and Motor mechanics. "The classes are all well attended [the unit's war diary for Oct., 1918 states] and the interest shown both by students and instructors has been marked. . . . The establishment of our 'Ecole des Soldats' has been a matter of much wonderment and discussion amongst the villagers, the juvenile members of which gather round the windows and gaze at the students."

[41] Large numbers of men both in France and England availed themselves of the opportunity afforded them of taking up educational courses. Enrolments in A.I.F. Educational Classes on 22nd March, 1919, numbered 12,832, grouped as follows:— Trades, 3,003; Land pursuits, 1,276; Commercial, 1,915; Elementary, 3,565; University, 638; and General, 2,435. In June, 1919, 628 were undergoing a University course, including 210 medical; 2,788 were receiving instruction in technical training, 3,122 agricultural, and 3,936 industrial.

[42] Including dentistry, pharmacy, nursing, and "massage."

Not a few specialised in lines of work allied to those into which they had been pressed by the "exigency" of military service.[48]

At an early stage it became clear that the procedure for repatriation devised for the force as a whole could not be applied to the personnel of the medical service for the simple reason that for it, unlike the combatant arms, the Armistice brought little or no respite. The service became in fact at once a bone of contention between General Monash's Demobilisation headquarters in London, the D.D.M.S. (Colonel Barber) in France, and the acting D.M.S., A.I.F. (Colonel Millard), and as the only workable arrangement it was decided that the D.M.S. A.I.F. should direct all movements and postings, though the actual moves themselves should be arranged by General Monash's department. The general hospitals and casualty clearing stations were dealt with independently of the field units; and the personnel of the dental service along with the medical. Members of the Australian Army Nursing Service working in casualty clearing stations and British hospitals were assembled at Nos. 2 and 3 A.G.H. and were recalled to England by the Matron-in-Chief in drafts of ten. While awaiting their turn for this call they were given very free facilities for leave, and, under the aegis of their uniform, "hopping" lorries and helped by R.T.O's, they appear to have penetrated without misadventure to most accessible spots in Europe.

Repatriation of the Medical Service

For the *field units* the following arrangements were arrived at.

All officers other than those detailed for duty with embarkation quotas were to be withdrawn by name by the D.M.S. "as required for repatriation, duty in U.K. or elsewhere, educational leave, etc."

Other ranks were to be included in embarkation quotas as directed by the divisional commander under special regulation.

"On arrival at the depots in U.K., all A.A.M.C. personnel will be at

[48] Among these may be mentioned male nursing, electricity and massage, professional ambulance work, radiology, pharmacy, bacteriology, health inspection, the legal profession, teaching and invention. As a matter of considerable, if indirect, interest it may be noted that, quite apart from medical students who completed their course, at least 50 soldiers, from both medical and combatant branches, qualified in medicine after the war, many of whom began their preliminary studies at this time. Some have achieved high distinction in their new career.

the disposal of the A.D.M.S., A.I.F. Depots, for use on transport duty to Australia, but not necessarily with the embarkation quota of which they formed part."

All three *casualty clearing stations* carried on as going concerns until relieved by British units. Their break-up gave opportunity, lacking in most, for ceremonial occasions befitting the completion of a great task, in the course of which an "establishment" of officers, nurses, N.C.O's, and men had become welded into a unit and trained to work as a team by the discipline of an exacting professional technique applied in a service that made a high emotional appeal to "devotion to duty." Wider interests were touched on the occasion of the relief of No. 3 from duty with the "British Army of the Rhine" in the receipt by the Commanding Officer of the following letter from the D.M.S.,[44] dated 7th May, 1919.

"On the occasion of the departure of No. 3 Australian Casualty Clearing Station, the D.M.S., British Army of the Rhine, on behalf of the General Officer Commanding-in-Chief and Staff as well as all ranks of the Medical Services, wishes to express his high appreciation of the valuable and gallant services rendered by this unit to the British Expeditionary Force and to the Allied cause . . . on the battlefields of the Somme and Ypres . . . and in the recent general advance and military occupation. We of the Imperial Army now wish our brothers and sisters farewell and God-speed, and assure them that, though widely separated by the broad seas, they remain very near to our hearts."

The General Hospitals. No. 1 at Rouen closed down for patients on November 30th, and on January 9th was transferred as a going concern to Sutton Veny, where it replaced a British General Hospital and served the depots till its return to Australia. No. 2 remained at work at Boulogne till February 11th, its routine work interspersed with educational and "refresher" courses for officers and N.C.O's. It then closed for patients, wards were cleared, and boards were held to assess and adjust shortages in equipment. The personnel went off in drafts, the final "B" cadre leaving for London on the 26th with the unit records.

No. 3 at Abbeville served as evacuating centre for all Australian troops until the transfer of the divisions to Belgium, and as the final depot for the A.A.M.C. in France. The task of dismantling this vast institution, "boarding," and handing

---

[44] Major-General H. N. Thompson.

over its equipment—285 lorry loads[45]—was the more difficult inasmuch as, till May 7th, the unit was required to act as a 1,500-bed hospital. Wards were dismantled but the Sisters' mess quarters, its walls frescoed with paintings,[46] were taken over by Line of Communication Headquarters, B.E.F. To mark the occasion of the departure of the South African General Hospital a dance was held—the response to a toast of health being made by Captain Joubert, S.A.A.M.C., a nephew of the celebrated Boer General. The Matron, Miss Grace Wilson, and final cadre of sisters, left on May 23rd; records, and 38 cases of equipment, mainly instruments, given by the Red Cross but in excess of the amount laid down for 1,040-bed hospital, were returned to A.I.F. Headquarters. The final cadre moved off for Le Havre on June 9th.[47]

---

[45] Very full records were kept in this unit of the "lessons" revealed by the break-up and also of the interior economy and working of a General Hospital.
[46] By Privates W. C. Sharpen and H. Woollcott, who were later transferred to the Australian War Records Section. This mess had played an interesting part in the social life of the Australian Corps. During the 1918 fighting until the final stage of the advance it was a rendezvous on Sunday afternoon for Australians of all ranks from general to private.
[47] The following epitome of an entry in the records of this hospital on June 7 seems to justify inclusion as a "lesson of the war." *"Prisoners of War.* For the past 18 months 100 to 200 German prisoners of war have been employed at the Hospital. They come from No. 196 P. of W. Coy., the music of whose bands and singing are heard at night. Their duties tend more and more to embrace every department of hospital work. The present batch of men are mostly familiar figures and 'part of the show,' and the peculiar position has arisen that they are almost indispensable—or are thought to be so. (The Quartermaster reports that) 'all outside fatigues such as tent pitching, road and path making, and sanitary work went forward with a vim as soon as P. of W. labour became available . . . workshops a hive of industry.' Scrubbing, carpentry, stretcher-work, gardening, handling stores, most in fact of the routine general work and much about the wards has been done by the 'Fritzes' or 'Jerries.' Their discipline is excellent, they are intelligent and good workers, most of them good tradesmen; they keep themselves decent, march to their work like trained soldiers; their demeanour is good and they are easily managed. The effect of all this is demoralising. No one does any work if he can get a 'Jerry' to do it. The prisoners like it, and would sooner come up and work than stay in the cage. There appears to me in this an analogue of what would occur on a national scale if the need to labour in making good the destruction of the war is too greatly relieved by Peace terms. . . . The victors may eventually suffer more through the war than the vanquished, who will present a people brought through stress of necessity to a high pitch of individual and national efficiency while without this incentive we would deteriorate."

CHAPTER XXVI

AN ESTIMATE OF THE MEDICAL DIRECTION OF THE A.I.F.

IT remains to assess those aspects of Australian medical administration which had some direct bearing on the supreme military purpose, the pursuit of victory. The side of the department's work which served more particularly the needs of those men who, through wounds or sickness, could no longer usefully be employed on that quest, is one of the themes for the final volume.

The Director of Medical Services of the A.I.F. had to face two sets of problems: (1) those relating to the work and maintenance of the Australian Army Medical Services overseas; (2) those deriving from his medical responsibilities in connection with the physical efficiency of the Australian force. The account here given of the director's "reaction" to these must also touch on the final *modus vivendi* evolved—the heads of the Australian Service (in Australia and overseas) on the one hand and Sir Alfred Keogh, the head of the British Service, and his deputies on the other.

As related in the first chapter of this volume, Surgeon-General N. R. Howse, having been appointed by the Australian Government "Director of Medical Services" for the A.I.F., was attached to the Australian Administrative Headquarters, and his duties were defined by A.I.F. orders.[1] Here he proceeded to create an administrative department which gradually assumed complete responsibility for directing the work and

The Office of D.M.S., A.I.F.

---

[1] The appointment of Surgeon-Gen. Howse was published in the *Commonwealth Gazette* to date from 22 Nov., 1915. It is first noted in the British monthly *Army List* of July, 1916, appearing first as "D.M.S., Commonwealth Military Forces." The corresponding position in the Canadian Expeditionary Force at this time was filled by Surgeon-Gen. G. C. Jones as a "Director of Medical Services," and that in the New Zealand Expeditionary Force by Lieut.-Col. W. H. Parkes as "Deputy-Director."

maintaining the efficiency of the Australian Army Medical Service overseas except so far as these involved control of the actual medical-military operations of the forces in the field which belonged to the British medical direction. The control of the Australian force in Palestine (the Light Horse) was almost entirely delegated by General Howse to his representative at that seat of war. He himself, after his appointment as D.M.S., was subject only to "Army Council Instructions" and to the orders of the "G.O.C., A.I.F." (General Birdwood); whose own actions and decisions were governed by instructions from the Minister for Defence in Melbourne.

The Director of Medical Services, A.I.F. Official records and a wealth of personal testimony agree that the medical affairs of the Australian Imperial Force were administered with quite conspicuous efficiency; and that this was achieved moreover with extraordinary economy of means in the matter both of staff and organisation. It is not less clearly agreed that this was due to the fact that the department was the creation of a single mind of exceptional calibre, and was directed by one man whose force of character and powers of concentration were so exceptional as to amount, in their devotion at least to the particular purpose with which we are here concerned, to genius.

Surgeon-General Howse himself once said that his most important work in the war was the creation of his headquarters at Horseferry-road. But to such an extent was medical administration of the A.I.F. a reflection of the personality of its director that it is advisable to give here a study of General Howse himself and of his methods before describing the organisation and working of his department.

It may be doubted whether, since Baron Larrey directed medical affairs for Napoleon and Sir James McGrigor for Wellington, any head
Surgeon-General N. R. Howse of a medical service has gained so completely the confidence of the military command, or exercised so great a personal influence in military affairs, as did Surgeon-General Howse within the scope of the A.I.F. And it is a matter of more than passing interest to observe that, in each instance, the same causes operated to bring this about, namely, the combination of great professional and administrative ability with qualities of more directly military significance —personal courage and battle-sense, and flair as a soldier and "man of affairs" for understanding and dealing with the problems not only of

campaigns but also of the "home front."[2] The reasons for the very remarkable success of Neville Howse in the Great War are on the one hand to be sought in the war's actual events. *Si monumentum quaeris circumspice*: Howse's best biography of war service is the record and development of the Australian Army Medical Service itself, reflecting the personality, character, and abilities, and (we must add) the limitations, of its director, and his personal reaction to the problems of the Great War so far at least as they were presented to him in the experiences of the A.I.F. But it is equally due to the way in which his personality moulded events and environment.

Personal History. Neville Reginald Howse was an Englishman by birth and upbringing, an Australian by adoption and grace of a spiritual kinship, an imperialist through the interaction of these two allegiances, and not the less confirmed in this conviction that it was concealed in a pose of cynical nihilism adopted largely to aid him in the service of two masters, represented during the war by the Director-Generals of Medical Services at the British War Office and the Australian Defence Department respectively. He was born at Stogursey in Somerset in 1863 and received his medical education at the London Hospital.[3] He came to Australia in 1889, without capital or financial credit; and by energy and intensity of purpose—which were among the most striking elements in his make-up—dug himself into a general practice as a "bush doctor" in the small township of Taree on the Manning River (N.S.W.). In 1895 he went to England to take the Fellowship of the Royal College of Surgeons. Returning to Australia he settled in the country town of Orange where he built up a provincial surgical reputation on lines reminiscent of Berkeley Moynihan of Leeds, Robert Jones of Liverpool, and Rutherford Morison of Newcastle-on-Tyne. His service in the South African War has been noted in *Volume I*.[4] He valued the Victoria Cross there gained by him chiefly as it added weight to his counsel among combatant soldiers. On return he joined the Reserve of Officers but did no military training, and his knowledge of military organisation in its higher branches was in 1914 negligible.

Speaking of Howse's appointment in October, 1914, to the vague rôle of staff officer to accompany the D.M.S., A.I.F. (Surgeon-General Williams), an officer who more than any other was qualified to speak with authority,[5] wrote: "He was devoid of any higher military knowledge when he assumed that position. It is doubtful whether he knew of the existence of such a profound work as *Field Service Regulations, Part II*, but on the voyage in the transport *Orvieto* General Bridges had determined that everyone on his staff should be both exercised and trained, and no one answered the call more assiduously than Neville Howse. . . . He learned from whomsoever knowledge could be gained, and he gave in return all the keenness of an alert and active mind, and

---

[2] Larrey, it may be recalled, was himself a highly skilled surgeon—it is recorded that he once performed between two and three hundred amputations in one day. He reorganised the field medical service of his time. He had extraordinary success in maintaining the strength of Napoleon's army in Egypt and Syria. And he was Napoleon's trusted personal adviser and confidant in medical matters relating to the raising and maintaining of his armies.

[3] It has been stated that fellow students of the London Hospital diagnosed that Howse had gone to the war determined to get the V.C., and were assured that in that case he would certainly succeed in the quest.

[4] *See Vol. I, p. 33.*

[5] Major-General Sir Brudenell White, Chief of Staff of the A.I.F., in *The Argus*, Melbourne, 4 Oct., 1930.

all that wit and human kindness which made him the most lovable of men. . . . [When the force arrived in Egypt] it was soon evident that the A.I.F. was to be cast upon its own resources, and medical problems were for the moment paramount. Much talking there was, . . . but the arguments and journeyings had achieved little, and the brow of General Bridges grew clouded and his sarcasm more bitter. Then it was that the quiet surgeon with the humorous and kindly eyes and determined lips stepped into the breach. . . . Almost imperceptibly out of chaos came order. . . . General Bridges's eye grew bright whenever the staff officer, A.M.S., came to him, for he came not with problems but with their solution. . . . No praise can be too high for the man who without established military position . . . laid a firm foundation for the establishment of that great medical service than which there was nothing more loyal, efficient, and devoted in the forces of the Empire."

How quickly Howse seized the principles of military organisation and with what judgment he upheld them when seized, one among many incidents must suffice to show. On the voyage from Australia (it will be recalled) the D.M.S., A.I.F. (then Surgeon-General Williams), and his staff officer (Lieut.-Colonel Howse) together designed a field ambulance of two sections, completely motorised. The scheme was embodied in the establishment of the field ambulances for the force when it was reorganised after Gallipoli. The subsequent reversion on the initiative of Surgeon-General Sloggett to a "three section" unit has also been noted.[6]

"I was very angry," Howse writes to Fetherston on the 23rd of May, 1916, "with the War Office about 'C' Section, but possibly it is better to have same establishment for all Field Ambulances, and one could hardly hope that War Office would even consider our scheme. *We are correct, and I think* you will see that War Office accept it after this war."[7]

In September, 1918, General Howse, taking advantage of the drive for reduction of establishments, urged again—this time with success—that the three-section field ambulance "be reorganised on a two-section basis." The thing was done in the A.I.F. and it has become part of the British organisation after the war.

General Howse was supposed, and loved to be supposed, to be a supreme cynic. But he was capable of a singularly wise generosity. How, when the crisis in reinforcement forced a

---

[6] In *Chapter ii* (*p. 33*).
[7] The table of war establishments for a "Field Ambulance (two sections)" had been approved and issued with A.M.F. Military Orders of 14 March, 1916, and corresponding mobilisation store tables on April 4. These orders cancelled the existing establishment for a field ambulance (three sections).

slight measure of dilution in the A.I.F., he safeguarded the efficiency of the medical service, while making with medical personnel the gesture demanded in the interest of combatant strength, has already been told.[8] But less was known, even in the A.I.F., of a gesture made by him at a critical time for the British Army.

On 24th March, 1918, when the extent of the German break-through in the Somme region became known at A.I.F. Administrative Headquarters in London, General Howse called on the Director-General at the War Office, Sir Alfred Keogh. By him the gravity of the news was confirmed; even casualty clearing stations had been reported captured. The losses in the R.A.M.C. through casualty or temporary incapacitation and the military uncertainty had created a difficult situation. "What can we do to help?" General Howse asked. "Do you think you could spare 15 or 20 medical officers for a time?" "Thirty will be placed at your disposal; good morning, Sir." Returning at once to Horseferry-road, Howse sent for Lieutenant-Colonel Anderson,[9] his A.D.M.S. for personnel, and informed him of his promise. The men must be found, if it took himself and every officer and left the office boy in charge. It was a severe test, but Howse was not unprepared and extreme steps were not necessary. Several transports were shortly due to arrive with surplus medical officers on board—the result of a request made in February in case of possible emergency. The number required by General Keogh were found and served with the R.A.M.C., some of them till the end of the war.

It may be here added that this "gesture" was an unqualified success. Some of these officers did fine work and had exceptionally interesting service, including participation in the events of the Lys battle and the German break-through on the French front on the Aisne in July. In these operations Captain J. V. Duhig, A.A.M.C.—who served with the 51st (Highland) Division—has recorded that "four of us, my ambulance colonel, two Australian captains, and a Scottish captain, a dentist with a medical qualification who acted as anaesthetist, . . ran . . . an emergency C.C.S. serving two divisions for nearly a week."

The circumstances of Howse's appointment as A.D.M.S. to the 1st Australian Division and subsequently D.D.M.S., I Anzac, and—by the Australian Government—as D.M.S., A.I.F., have been recorded. His development and increasing grip of A.I.F. affairs in 1915 need not again be recalled.[10]

---

[8] *See pp. 715-6, 768.* His instructions on the standard of men of the A.A.M.C. for service at the front is included in *Appendix No. 6.*

[9] By whom the episode was related to the writer.

[10] *See Vol. I;* in particular *Chapter six of Part I.*

Major-General Gellibrand, an officer of outstanding judgment, has written:—

"Howse's value throughout Gallipoli was far beyond the medical sphere. His general life, his bearing, his endurance under disease and responsibility, his shrewd appreciation of character, his unofficial comments, his invariably cheery good humour, his natural gallantry had an effect I found it hard to estimate adequately. My own opinion is that his value would have been as great as a commander as it proved to be as a medical organiser."

Speaking also of Gallipoli, General White wrote:—

"Visiting medical officers quickly realised his complete grip of the problems."

One of them indeed recorded his impressions in the course of a personal letter to the Director-General, A.M.S. (Lieut.-General Keogh), at the War Office.[11]

". . . . Were we not for three unforgettable months a living quarter—living and dying—of ANZAC; and I an intimate of the D.D.M.S., now Surgeon-General Howse. Do you know him? In person I think not; but hope you will. He is one of the most forcible and effective A.M.S. officers I ever met or could conceive and, pretending to eschew the society of the combatants, carries, I find, great weight with them—owing to a clear head, a caustic wit, and an absolute dependence on fact and logic, regardless of ancient regulations. I imagine he must have the advantage there over Regular A.M.S. officers, who cannot be equally independent of King's Regs. But he appreciates their position and should be a valuable coadjutor both during and after the war, in making the Imperial Army a perfect machine as regards its medical service. I am sorry to be no longer under him. . . ."

We shall have occasion presently to observe some results that derived from this "casting of bread on the waters." A hoary tradition attributes to official army administration a greater concern that procedure should be correct than that the purpose be achieved. It would not be far astray to sum up Surgeon-General Howse's administrative method and outlook as the antithesis of this.[12] But there is good reason to believe that in the early days

The Evolution of Australian Medical Administrative Headquarters

---

[11] The letter was written shortly after the Evacuation of Gallipoli, and a copy was afterwards given by Keogh to Howse. It is among his personal records presented by Lady Howse to the Australian War Memorial.

[12] He held strongly that it was the place of the medical service in the army, and of the medical profession in peace, to initiate and secure reforms and improvements, not merely to advise and comment on technical matters. In the matter of means and methods his outlook was Machiavellian. Provocative overstatement or even misstatement was a favourite means for getting at the truth; bluff one of his favoured weapons of attack. It was characteristic that he was one of the finest bridge players in the medical profession.

of his A.I.F. administration—that is after Gallipoli—Howse was considerably handicapped by his lack of familiarity with the traditional technique of army procedure. In the reorganisation of the A.I.F. in Egypt, before its transfer to France, the medical department of General Birdwood's A.I.F. command "had," says General White, "to be helped along." Vision there was, but administratively it was still "very helpless." But, *per contra*, Howse had fought and won some important administrative battles, and had forced a wholesome acid tang of respect into the normal attitude of other departments with his own. From the British War Office he had gained administrative independence for the Australian Army Medical Corps. From the Adjutant-General's branch of the A.I.F., he had won the right of direct approach to the G.O.C. and General Staff; and in the Australian C.G.S. (Brig.-General White) he had gained as a friend and monitor one of the clearest and most constructive minds in the British Army. In the successive commandants of the Australian Administrative Headquarters in Egypt and in England he was brought into close association with men from each of whom in his own way there was much to learn.[13] From this combination, through the technicalities of reconstruction of the A.I.F. in Egypt after Gallipoli; the complex medical problems that arose in connection with the absorption of the force into the vast military cosmos of the Western theatre; the shock and disillusionment of the Somme; the sickness and wastage of the 1916-17 winter, there evolved, not (as General White says) without "inevitable mistakes," a medical department and a medical chief who together played a material part not only in the creation of "a service which grew to be famous," but in the evolution of the Australian Imperial Force itself.[14]

---

[13] Successive commandants under whom the medical department of the A.I.F. was administered were Brigadier-Generals V. C. M. Sellheim (19 Feb.-31 July, 1916), R. M. McC. Anderson (1 August, 1916-7 April, 1917), and T. Griffiths (8 April, 1917, till the end of the war). The first was a regular officer of long standing in the A.M.F. who had in effect "created the part" as officer-in-command of the "A.I.B.D." in Egypt. From him in the early days at Mena Colonel Howse had wrested the right to direct approach on medical matters to General Bridges. General Anderson was a successful Sydney business man who was appointed "D.Q.M.G., A.I.F.," to straighten out the business relations between Australia and Britain—a job which he carried out with great success but by methods which did not always make for smooth running. General Griffiths was a permanent officer of the A.M.F. whose character, ability, and "devotion to duty" made him one of the most trusted and regarded officers on the staff of the G.O.C., A.I.F.

[14] General Gellibrand has expressed the opinion that, in the general view, Howse was the only leader in the A.I.F. who could not have been replaced.

85. THE DISMANTLING OF No. 3 A.G.H., ABBEVILLE, MAY, 1919
Pulling down of "C" Block.
Lent by Pte. E. W. Gaut, No. 3 A.G.H.
Aust. War Memorial Collection No. C4787.

86. THE LAST DRAFT OF AUSTRALIAN SISTERS LEAVING FRANCE
FOR DEMOBILISATION
Third from the right is Principal Matron G. M. Wilson.
Aust. War Memorial Collection No. C4820. *To face p. 808.*

87. A.I.F. ADMINISTRATIVE HEADQUARTERS, LONDON

The front quadrangle. The building was a Methodist training college, in Horseferry-road.

Aust. War Memorial Official Photo. No. D941.

88. HORSEFERRY-ROAD, LONDON

The entrance to A.I.F. Headquarters was on the right, and those to the clothing store and War Chest Club on the left.

Aust. War Memorial Official Photo. No. D796.   *To face p. 809.*

The confused—not to say chaotic—administrative situation in the medical service of the A.I.F. at the end of 1915[15] was, speaking broadly, due to the coincidence of two strategic accidents:—

The Australian Medical Service achieves self-government (1) The diversion of the force to the Eastern theatre of war before its place in the army of the Empire could be effectively determined. The effect of this factor was augmented by failure on the part of the G.O.C., A.I.F., to recognise fully the importance of the base medical organisation, and to fill the medical section of the Australian Intermediate Base Depot. This omission—the effect of which was greatly enhanced by General Bridges's death—led to a temporary abrogation of the idea, with which the force had set out, of a medical service which should be self-contained and self-governing as to its "interior economy."

(2) The administrative separation of the Mediterranean Expeditionary Force and the Egyptian command. The situation thus created made nugatory all efforts on the part of General Birdwood and his local medical adviser—the D.D.M.S., Anzac Corps—to patch up a *modus vivendi* while the Gallipoli campaign was in progress.

The history of the striving—not to say "struggle"—for internal self-government, and its outcome in the appointment of Colonel Howse as "Director" of the combined medical services of the A.I.F. overseas, has been recorded in *Volume I*. The embryo Australian medical administrative headquarters constituted in 1914 in the person of Surgeon-General Williams, with a warrant officer and one clerk, in 1915 was wholly wiped out by the combined efforts of the Egyptian command, the War Office, and the Australian Defence Department. Thereafter, under Surgeon-General Howse, the history of this medical department is essentially pragmatic and utilitarian, reflecting a clear and constructive policy.

Structural Evolution. From the ashes of the old headquarters arose, early in 1916, two considerable independent medical departments. In Egypt, inspired by Colonel Howse and backed by the Director-General in Australia, there emerged a new department, which though then unrecognised by the War Office, became a *fait accompli,* an integral part of the new A.I.F. and wholly independent of any British administration. Aided by advice in administrative technique by the Australian chief-of-staff and by the commandant of the Australian Intermediate Base Depot,[16] the functions of the department and its Director, and the duties of the several sub-departments, gradually defined themselves

---

[15] See *Vol. I, Part I, Chapter xxii.*
[16] Brig.-Generals C. B. B. White and V. C. M. Sellheim.

under the stresses of the new conditions in the Australian force. The office (in fact) "just growed."

Meanwhile in Britain—also authorised by the Australian Director-General, but here with the imprimatur of the War Office and immediately under the British Director-General—Surgeon-General Williams, as D.D.M.S. for Australian troops in Britain, had created a similar department at Horseferry-road. This was deliberately and exactly modelled on the Army Medical Department of the War Office, the methods of which were very closely followed in the differentiation of duties, methods of procedure and correspondence, administrative relations, and so forth. The organisation of this office is shown in the following table:—

Establishment of Department of D.D.M.S., A.I.F., in
England, April 1916

	Officers	Other Ranks	Home Service Men	A.A.N.S.	Total
D.D.M.S.	1	5	7	—	13
A.D.M.S. (1)—incl. consultant staff	7	10	13	1[17]	31
A.D.M.S. (2) . .	2	—	2	—	4
Officer i/c Invaliding	1	3	1	—	5
Total	11	18	23	1	53

The duties of each officer were very exactly defined. Broadly those of the D.D.M.S. comprised "general administration under the D.G.M.S., War Office"; the A.D.M.S. (1) was for "personnel," but had also control of medical boards, dental treatment, artificial replacements, and so forth. The A.D.M.S. (2) was responsible *inter alia* for supplies and hospital premises. The officer-in-charge of invaliding dealt with all matters relating to invaliding to Australia.

The department was, indeed, designed to meet all the medical problems of an Australian force based on Britain.

Then came the transfer of the A.I.F's administration from Egypt to London and with it the wide expansion of the new A.I.F. Administrative Headquarters at Horseferry-road. The evolution of this great institution from the "Australian Intermediate Base Depot" has been followed so far as is necessary for the purpose of a medical history.[18] The developments of 1916-18 can only be shown here in figures.[19] The seven sub-sections in which the A.I.B.D. was designed by Colonel White in 1915 were in a great measure merged in "A" and "Q" branches, but with a wider control by the Commandant. The detailed establishment of Administrative Headquarters at the end of the war was as follows:—

---

[17] Principal Matron.

[18] See *Chapter i, and Vol. I (pp. 55-6)*. For a full description the reader is referred to the *Australian Official History, Vol. III, Chapter vi*.

[19] These are taken from a return rendered by each section to the Commandant in 1918. The return was called for at the instigation of the Chief Paymaster's Department in view of the fact that the headquarters had grown by irregular accretions and that no "establishment" had been laid down since April, 1916.

ESTABLISHMENT OF ADMINISTRATIVE HEADQUARTERS A.I.F.[20]

BRANCH or SECTION	Officers	Other Ranks	TOTAL	Auxiliary[21] and Civilian
Commandant	3	1	4	6
A.A.G.	13	103	116	42
Records (Personal) Section	15	200	215	760
Central Registry	2	76	78	220
Australian Provost Corps	2	138	140	15
War Records (Historical) Section	9	39	48	47
A.Q.M.G.	7	247	254	147
A.A.O.C. (U.K.)	8	247	255	33
Postal Section	5	176	181	488
A.M.T.S. (U.K.)	5	304	309	53
A.I.F. Canteens (U.K.)	6	30	36	5
Transport Section	4	22	26	9
Civilian Staff Control	1	3	4	31
A.I.F. and War Chest Club	1	139	140	—
Australian Club	1	15	16	—
Australian Red Cross	—	35	35	—
Australian Comforts Fund	—	4	4	—
Peel House	—	1	1	—
Aviation Section	5	4	9	9
Medical Section	20	60	82[22]	12
Finance Section	24	411	435	1,300
Audit Section	8	39	47	60
Demobilisation Section	4	7	11	6
Education Section	3	2	5	6
Total	160	2,349	2,509	3,249

It will be appreciated that in the war of 1914-18 the medical service was in a very considerable degree *sui generis*—ubiquitous and self-contained.[23] But as a matter of military organisation the department of the Director of Medical Services worked as an integral part of Australian Administrative Headquarters. It grew out of the conjunction of the two independent medical headquarters referred to above. Surgeon-General Howse, arriving with his small headquarters from Cairo, took over the headquarters and system already existing in England as a going concern, assimilated the staff with his own, and proceeded with

---

[20] The staff of Administrative Headquarters was greatly increased after the Armistice, quite apart from the independent Department of Repatriation and Demobilisation.

[21] Q.M.A.A.C. and Women's Legion.

[22] Two A.A.N.S. included in total.

[23] This is illustrated by the fact that the D.M.S. was as fully concerned with the activities of the A.I.F. Depots in the United Kingdom, an entirely independent administration, as with those of Administrative Headquarters.

circumspection to adjust orthodox administrative methods to meet the needs of the new situation and of new ideals.

Shortly after Easter, 1916 (says Lieut.-Colonel Anderson)[24] Surgeon-General N. R. Howse arrived in London. At that time the officers of the Medical Staff were at 72 Victoria Street. Colonel Giblin, who was "A.D.M.S. personnel," was at 130 Horseferry-road, and the D.M.S., A.I.F. established his own Headquarters there, closing the offices in Victoria Street. The whole Medical Section was then under one roof at 130 Horseferry-road, the transfer of offices being complete about 12th May, 1916. Lieut.-Colonel T. E. V. Hurley, who had been acting as Staff Officer attached to G.H.Q. B.E.F. in connection with the troops arriving in France, rejoined soon after, and the staff of the D.M.S. was then as follows:—

D.M.S	Surgeon-General Howse
D.D.M.S.	Colonel W. W. Giblin
A.D.M.S.	Lieut.-Colonel Hurley for personnel, dental services and nursing services.

Captain K. S. Cross—Officer for Medical Boards; Captain E. H. Rutledge—Officer for Invaliding; Chief Clerk, Warrant Officer J. R. Drummond. Principal Matron of A.I.F. in England—Mrs McHardie White.

In July, 1916, the following officers arrived from Egypt:—
Colonel C. S. Ryan, Colonel R. J. Millard, Colonel H. C. Maudsley, Matron-in-Chief Miss E. A. Conyers.

Colonel Millard was posted A.D.M.S., A.I.F. Depots in U.K., with his Headquarters at Tidworth. Colonel Maudsley Consulting Physician; Colonel Ryan Consulting Surgeon, A.I.F. The Matron-in-Chief was at 130 Horseferry-road.

The consultants formed the Medical Board for the invaliding of officers, and also at a later date visited A.I.F. Depots in U.K. each week for the purpose of reviewing all cases in which men had been marked for return to Australia as invalids.

This organisation continued throughout, though changes were made in personnel from time to time and additional officers appointed to deal with sub-sections which grew too large for control by one officer.

Thus in November, 1916, it was found that the growth of the Dental Services rendered it necessary for a Staff Officer to be appointed to control the whole of the dental services in the A.I.F. in England, France, and Egypt. This officer was stationed at Headquarters, A.I.F. Depots in U.K. from March, 1917, but finally took up his quarters at Horseferry-road in November, 1917.

It was soon found that a resident medical officer was required to deal with cases of sickness among members of the staff and men on leave and reporting from hospital for furlough. This department expanded greatly and two dental sections were added. In addition, an "early treatment" room for V.D. was opened and this office became

---

[24] Precis from a memorandum written in 1919. For an account of the parallel problem—the position of the "G.O.C., A.I.F."—the reader interested in the problem of "Imperial" co-operation may be referred to *Chapter vi of Vol. III of the Australian Official History of the War.*

the centre of an extensive campaign of prophylaxis among A.I.F. troops in Britain. Other specialist officers were added as required. The Base Depot of Medical Stores at Tidworth and that at Southampton were merged and moved to Horseferry-road.

The structure of the Medical Section at the end of the war in the distribution of duties of the staff are shown hereunder.

ESTABLISHMENT OF MEDICAL SECTION

1. *Administration*

	Officers	Other ranks	A.A.N.S.	Civilian	Total
D.M.S., A.I.F.	1				1
D.D.M.S.	1				1
A.D's.M.S.	3				3
Consulting Surgeons	2				2
Consulting Physicians ..	2				2
A.F.C. Boarding Officer	1				1
Staff Officer for Dental Services, and staff	1	2			3
Quartermasters	2				2
Matron-in-Chief and assistant ..			2		2
Clerical Staff		14		12	26
Total	13	16	2	12	43

2. *Executive Staff attached*

	Officers	Other ranks	A.A.N.S.	Civilian	Total
R.M.O's and staff	2	9[25]			11
Dental unit	1	3			4
"Early Treatment" (V.D) Centre	1	8			9
Base Depot of Medical and Dental Stores	3[26]	24			27
Total	7	44			51
GRAND TOTAL	20	60	2	12	94

I. DISTRIBUTION OF DUTIES AND RELATIONS

The Position of the D.M.S. The D.M.S. was the chief executive medical officer of the A.I.F.[27] and as such was on the staff of the G.O.C., A.I.F., though for purposes of administration it was found most convenient for him to have his headquarters in London, and to visit A.I.F. Headquarters in France at intervals according as work demanded.

He exercised a general control over all medical personnel in U.K.,

---

[25] Includes 1 staff-sergeant dispenser.
[26] A Quartermaster, in charge: an Hon. Lieut. and Pharmacist: and a Dental officer.
[27] *See* Vol. I, pp. 5-6.

France, and Egypt, and was responsible for advice on all matters referring to the health of the troops including their welfare in the field, their treatment in hospital, the length and nature of their convalescence and the arrangements for their return to Australia as invalids or their return to duty.

He directed (i) the activities of the Australian Auxiliary Hospitals in U.K. which were under the direct administration of the Commandant, Administrative Headquarters; (ii) the hospitals and medical units under the direct administration of the G.O.C., A.I.F. as far as staff promotions, movements of personnel, general matters of policy were concerned. In local matters the hospitals were under the control of the D.D.M.S. or A.D.M.S. of the area concerned, subject to appeal to D.M.S., A.I.F. where it was considered by the O.C. of the unit concerned that the procedure laid down by the local D.D.MS. or A.D.M.S. did not conform with A.I.F. practice.

He maintained *liaison* in the following way:—

1. *Australia.* By means of a monthly despatch to D.G.M.S. sent through the Commandant, Administrative H.Q.

2. *Egypt.* By means of intermittent despatches sent direct to D.D.M.S., A.I.F. in Egypt.

3. *France.* By means of frequent visits and frequent letters between the D.M.S. and chief medical officers of the A.I.F. in France.

4. *Units under Commandant, Administrative Headquarters* (Australian Auxiliary Hospitals). Direct.

5. *Units under G.O.C., A.I.F. Depots in U.K.* Through A.D.M.S., A.I.F. Depots in U.K. who visited the D.M.S. on a specified day in each week.

6. *War Office.* Personal visits of D.M.S. to D.G., A.M.S.

He advised the G.O.C., A.I.F. as to the standard of medical and dental fitness necessary for an "A" class man, and ensured that all ranks likely to be unfit for general service for more than six months be returned to Australia as quickly as possible. Such invalids were returned by hospital ship or hospital carrier. The staffs of these boats were made up mainly of Sea Transport Sections raised in Australia; when not available their places were taken by medical officers and other ranks of the A.A.M.C. who were being returned as invalids, or for other reasons of a private nature under directions from the G.O.C., A.I.F. With the growth in numbers of orthopaedic cases, "hospital carriers" were specially fitted and manned by a specially trained staff for their conveyance.

The examination of Australian Munition and War Workers was carried out at first by the R.M.O. at Horseferry-road, but later the amount of work involved rendered it necessary to attach a medical officer to the Officer-in-Charge Munition and War Workers specially for this duty.

The purchase of medical and surgical goods for shipment to Australia was carried out by the Base Depot of Medical and Dental Stores.

The A.A.N.S. was run entirely from Horseferry-road by the Matron-in-Chief under the D.M.S.

The duties of the medical headquarters staff at Horseferry-road were—[28]

D.D.M.S.	All matters of policy and hospital administration, and supervision of A.A.N.S.
A.D.M.S.1	All matters concerning personnel of A.A.M.C. Routine medical matters relating to the Administrative Headquarters and A.I.F. Depots in U.K.
A.D.M.S.2	Matters concerning movement of invalids in United Kingdom; arrangement for embarkation, administration of medical matters of A.F.C.
A.D.M.S.3	Transport arrangements for invaliding of sick and wounded to Australia; invalid boards on officers; transfers; pensions.
Q.M.1	Chief Clerk and confidential secretary to the D.M.S.
Q.M.2	Medical boards on officers and officers' convalescence; classification of other ranks.
Matron-in-Chief	All matters affecting A.A.N.S.
S.O.A.D.S.	All matters affecting Dental Service.

The Quartermasters were appointed as executive officers in connection with the several duties outlined above, including such matters as indents, artificial replacements, monthly and routine reports, board papers, and other documents required for invaliding and so forth.

The field of action of the several members of this staff comes largely within the theme of the next volume. Our subject here is almost exclusively those aspects of administrative responsibility in which the Director was himself most concerned, namely, *the supply and maintenance of medical units and personnel* and *posting and promotion of officers in the medical services;* and *questions relating to the physical standard of the force.*

---

[28] The authorities here are: (1) Lieut.-Col. Anderson (*loco citato*); (2) the return referred to in a previous note; and (3) a memorandum on the "Medical Section" of Administrative Headquarters, prepared under the instructions of the D.M.S. by the chief clerk. As has been noted, the duties of the several A.D's.M.S. were frequently changed and overlapped. Thus, the responsibilities connected with invaliding to Australia were shared by the A.D's.M.S. (2) and (3), the one dealing with personnel, the other with shipping. It must be noted that no complete list of the matters which came within the scope of the department is given. The A.D.M.S., A.I.F. Depots in U.K. is not shown as an officer on the staff of the D.M.S. though, in effect, he was. Another officer who does not appear, is the Consultant Bacteriologist A.I.F., Lieut.-Col. C. J. Martin, A.A.M.C., who for the greater part of the period under review was engaged on research work in France. An "A.I.F. Bacteriological laboratory" commanded by Major Eustace Ferguson, worked at the Lister Institute and came under the D.M.S. London Command. The officers who held the senior positions at the end of the war were:—D.D.M.S. (A/D.M.S. after October) Col. R. J. Millard; A.D.M.S. (1) Lieut.-Col. J. H. Anderson; A.D.M.S. (2) Major G. C. Willcocks; A.D.M.S. (3) Major L. W. Jeffries; Q.M's, Lieuts. A. Charlesworth and F. E. Bland; Physician, Col. H. C. Maudsley; Surgeon, Col. C. S. Ryan; S.O.A.D.S., Lieut.-Col. F. Marshall; Matron-in-Chief, Miss E. A. Conyers (Deputy, Miss G. M. Wilson). During the whole of 1917 Majors H. B. Lewers and A. E. Colvin held appointments as A.D's.M.S.

General Howse and most of his personal staff lived in a flat near Horseferry-road. The service was chiefly by batmen and the régime was severely simple. Here were invited for a meal men, on leave from the front, who could help to keep headquarters in London in touch with units in France.

In considering General Howse's administration it is not difficult, in the first place, for an informed observer to detect in all the activities of the department a keynote, to be discerned as clearly in the daily routine of each sub-department or office as in the minutes and correspondence of the Director himself. This motif we may identify as *purposefulness*. Expanded to a phrase this may be defined as the clear discernment of ends, and economy in the use of means to attain them.

The key-note in administration

General Howse's Administrative Technique.[29] It was noted at the time—"The outstanding features of General Howse's office are the entire absence of any formality or 'red tape' and his close personal control in matters of *policy*. His team is selected not so much for individual brilliance but because they have *savoir faire*, are good mixers, and know the front lines. To make sure that there shall be full co-operation, and no 'water-tight compartments' he arranges that their duties shall overlap, and occasionally readjusts or interchanges. From time to time also the General will require for a day to see *all* the correspondence etc., routine or otherwise, of a sub-department; so as to ensure that there has been no sub-conscious bias from the determined line of action, or his policy. But (on the other hand) in his methods he is an opportunist ingrain. He will ruthlessly scrap a carefully designed tactical plan to meet changes in the situation. But the broad lines of his purpose and policy have been clear and unchanged.[30] In any controversy he looks far ahead, in disputation prefers the approach oblique.

"A very important factor in his great success as D.M.S. has been his *flair* for discerning what is, and what is not, a medical responsibility. It is one of the first lessons his staff has to learn. This, indeed, is perhaps the keystone of his work in the war. He has made unprecedented claims for medical responsibility in military matters, and yet never lets himself or his staff be led to interfere in matters that are not 'their pigeon.' And if these claims have led at times to strenuous administrative battles (he has on more than one occasion made acceptance of his views a condition to his remaining in office), adherence to these principles has helped him to avoid entanglements.[31]

---

[29] This "appreciation" is from notes made at the end of 1918 by the "Medical Collator"; it was based on personal observation, or information supplied to him by members of Howse's staff, in particular, by Lieut.-Col. J. H. Anderson.

[30] An astute observer of men and personal friend of Sir Neville Howse, Sir John Gellibrand, has written of "his ability to absorb and use knowledge without apparent effort, and his talent for concentrating on what was essential and what was practical."

[31] He was adept at side-stepping that most detested of medical "duties"—promoting the supersession of a senior officer by finding him physically unfit for military service.

1914-18] MEDICAL DIRECTION OF A.I.F. 817

"His energy is terrific. He lives for work and maintains a remorseless drive on himself and his officers. He himself holds, and he impresses on his staff, that in return for the freedom from the risks and discomforts of the front, staff at the base should work twice as hard."

General Gellibrand has written:—

"No other man, that I have heard of, could have achieved an equal measure of success in maintaining effective control over medical details in France and co-ordinating and controlling the jumble of hospital matters in England—and all with an absence of serious friction."

We may well accept General Howse's own opinion, already cited, that his supreme achievement was the creation of his Medical Administrative Headquarters, *"as a means for getting things done"*; the relations built up around it with A.I.F. Headquarters in France, in London, and on Salisbury Plain, with the Defence Department in Australia, the Director-General, A.M.S., at the War Office, and the Director-General, B.E.F., in France.[82] Some note as to this method for maintaining each of these contacts is required.

Relations with G.O.C., A.I.F. The medical "service" was also a "department" of the Adjutant-General's Branch, and the official correspondence of the D.M.S., A.I.F., with the G.O.C., A.I.F., was submitted through the "D.A.G., A.I.F.,"[33] who was always at General Birdwood's headquarters on the Western Front. But at the outset of General Howse's administrative career as A.D.M.S., 1st Australian Division, he (then a colonel) was able to secure recognition *de jure* for the obvious fact that, whatever may be the position of the medical service in peace,

Administrative Relations

[32] Of his other achievements General Howse was wont to look back with special satisfaction on the co-operative relations established with the combatant command on the voyage from Australia to Egypt in 1914 (*see Vol. I, p. 42*); his successful insistence as A.D.M.S., 1st Division, on having direct access to the divisional commander, General Bridges; his successful contest with the brigadiers for the control of the field ambulances (Jan., 1915); his successful fight to establish the position of a "D.M.S., A.I.F."; the breaking down of interstate rivalry in the medical service, and creation instead of a "Medical Corps" *esprit* (1915-16); the creation of the Dental Service of the A.I.F., the first move in which was made by him in February, 1915; his insistence early in 1915 on a rigid standard of physical fitness for the A.I.F., and the subsequent maintenance of this against all assaults; the campaign against venereal disease; the implementing, during 1916-18, of the "six months' policy," through the Australian Auxiliary Hospitals; and the system of "invalid transport."

[33] The difficult and curious questions relating to the administration of the A.I.F., as distinct from command in the field of its constituent formations, and the general problem of its "interior economy" have received attention in some detail in *Vol. I*. Doubts as to the feasibility of combining field command of an army corps with administrative control of the whole Australian force were raised both

in war its responsibilities are so important and so technical that any attempt to press this administrative subordination unduly will result in trouble.[34] Thereafter he was meticulous in his care to ensure that neither he nor his officers should overstep either the spirit or the letter of the arrangement. A mutually serviceable *modus vivendi* was established. Besides his frequent visits Howse maintained a personal correspondence with both the G.O.C. (General Birdwood) and his Chief of Staff (General White). His correspondence with the D.G.M.S., B.E.F. also went through A.I.F. Headquarters in France.

In his general relations with the combatant side Howse was clear and quite determined. For him the medical service was an element *sui generis* in the structure of the Army, and he was adamant in resenting any attempt to weaken this position.[35]

---

by General Haig and the Commonwealth Government. Two important factors, however, combined to support this arrangement, which had been arrived at when the force was reorganised in Egypt: first, the strong conviction on the part of the Australian chief-of-staff, Brig.-Gen. C. B. B. White, that it "would work" and would avert the possibility of political interference, and, second, the personal support given to it by the Australian Prime Minister, Mr. W. M. Hughes, who was in England in 1916 when the matter was being finally determined. After much debate the decision was reached that the obvious difficulties involved in the dispersion of the force over two seats of war would be more than offset by the advantage to be derived from the unified administrative "command" of the whole Australian force overseas; and further, that the combination of the two commands in the person of General Birdwood—whose popularity was great and reputation for judgment and impartiality were high—could be effected by provision of an adequate Australian staff attached to his headquarters in the field in conjunction with an A.I.F. administrative headquarters in London. The personal appointment of General Birdwood as General Officer Commanding the Australian Imperial Force was made by the Commonwealth Government to date from 18 Sept., 1915. Lieut.-Col. T. Griffiths was made an "Assistant Adjutant-General, A.I.F.," and was retained at I Anzac Corps Headquarters in France and given adequate staff. He was subsequently made Commandant of A.I.F. Administrative Headquarters in London, being succeeded as A.A.G. in France in Dec., 1916, by Lieut.-Col. J. L. Whitham. The latter was succeeded in June, 1917, by Col. T. H. Dodds with the title of "Deputy Adjutant-General." On these officers rested the important responsibilities, first, of giving administrative effect to the policy and decisions of the G.O.C., A.I.F.; and, second, of serving as the official *liaison* between the Commonwealth of Australia and the commander of the Australian forces abroad. For consideration in detail of the important and interesting military and national problems involved in this arrangement the reader is referred to *Vol. III* of the *Australian Official History*.

[34] The results of such an attempt at the Landing have been narrated in *Vol. I*.

[35] One of several such occasions is recalled by the Australian Official Historian. When General Monash was creating the staff of the 3rd Division he required the medical officers (A.D.M.S. and D.A.D.M.S.) to wear the "colour patches" distinctive of the divisional staff, and issued an order to this effect. In a personal interview General Howse informed the divisional commander that he could not agree—they must wear the chocolate patch that was the insignia of the medical corps. The clash was sharp; General Monash, finding arguments failed, tried an appeal *ad misericordiam*. The result was characteristic; Howse won, but in such a way as to receive an augmented regard and respect. He fought a similar battle with Major-Gen. J. J. T. Hobbs of the 5th Division, with the same result.

Relations with the Commandant Australian Administrative Headquarters. The position of the D.M.S. on this Headquarters was laid down by the A.I.F. Chief of Staff in terms whose studied vagueness reflects the ubiquity of the service.

"The D.M.S., A.I.F. will be allotted to your headquarters and will advise on all medical questions and superintend all medical arrangements. He will also be attached, when possible, to General Birdwood's Headquarters as a *liaison* officer."

Howse's personal relations with the commandant—to whom he was senior in rank—were uniformly co-operative and cordial.

Dealings with G.O.C., A.I.F. Depots in U.K. No more instructive instance could be found to illustrate the nature of the relations established between the medical service of the A.I.F., and of its administrative head in particular, with the combatant command, than this. The structure of the depots themselves was anomalous—the system "worked" because it was intended to *work*. As part of the British Southern Command, this A.I.F. command was under the War Office, through which— or through the Australian A.D.M.S. at the depots—its D.D.M.S. communicated with "Adminaust."[36] On the part of the A.I.F., after much debate between the Depot Command, A.I.F. Headquarters, and the War Office, it was arranged that the A.I.F. depots should be an independent command under the G.O.C., A.I.F. (General Birdwood, in France). On the medical side, however, the salient fact was this, that however "medical" might be the functions of the Command Depots, their command was strictly combatant. Thus, neither, as an official of A.I.F. Headquarters, nor as Medical Director, did the D.M.S. have any direct line of contact with its A.D.M.S. And yet it is safe to say that in no field of his wide responsibilities did he make himself felt to greater effect. This was not achieved without some dust and heat and errors of judgment. During the first year—Colonel McWhae has himself stated—the depots hardly had a "fair spin" from Howse whose interest was otherwise fully engaged. The voyage reports of troopships from Australia went direct to A.I.F. Headquarters in London, while

---

[36] That this control was not a mere official figment is illustrated *e.g.* by the useful intervention of the D.D.M.S. recorded on *p. 472.*

the mumps, measles, and C.S.F. contacts went direct to the depots—to start new foci! But in 1917 the Director had achieved a tacit recognition as an authority determined to get things done. The losses on the Somme had concentrated the attention of all authorities on the depots and thereafter they had his close oversight.

General Howse maintained control of the depot system partly through systematic reports by the A.D.M.S.,[37] partly by personal inspections, but chiefly through the fortnightly visits of the A.D.M.S. to Horseferry-road, at which all questions of policy and procedure were thrashed out in "heart to heart" informal debates.

It may be said (in brief) that the policy of the depots reflected the mind of General Howse, while their extraordinary success was due chiefly to the organising and administrative ability of Colonel McWhae.[38]

With the Director-General, Australian Military Forces. (Defence Department.) The relations between the D.M.S., A.I.F. and the D.G., A.M.F. (Surgeon-General Fetherston) seem closely to have resembled those between the B.E.F. and the War Office. They were such as have been seen in the history of great wars throughout the centuries—the army in the field claims an independence which sooner or later brings it into conflict with the authorities at home.[39] In the A.I.F. the difficulties were greatly magnified by the distance-time factor. The authorities in Australia worked in a half-light of knowledge in an atmosphere highly charged with emotion; personal contact was chiefly through the flotsam and jetsam of invalids and fortuitous intercourse. In the later years of the war General Howse endeavoured, though with little success, to arrange a system of *liaison* with a constructive purpose—in particular to ensure agreement concerning unfit recruits and in the matter of orthopaedic treatment under the "six months'

---

[37] These reports are by far the best summary of medical work in any sphere in the records of the A.I.F.

[38] This statement can be made without any invidious comparison. Col. Millard's régime covered a period when permanent constructive work was impossible.

[39] The organisation of the British Army for war is essentially centrifugal, that of the Navy centripetal; and hence—it would seem—the administrative troubles of the M.E.F.

policy."[40] Besides the fortnightly report included with that of the Commandant and official correspondence—cables and letters—the two heads of the Australian Medical Service kept up a voluminous correspondence, personal and semi-personal. This dealt—with almost ultra-informality—with every matter of medical administration, from questions of policy of the highest moment to the details of individual efficiency or of political or other embarrassments.[41]

Relations with the Light Horse in Egypt. The chief issues here involved have been dealt with *in extenso* in *Volume I*. Important as is the matter, it is not possible to draw any particular "lesson" from the dispute between the D.M.S. and his staff officer. But a useful moral would seem to emerge, namely, that problems in administration such as were involved in the circumstances of the two parts of the A.I.F. can be solved only in an atmosphere of mutual co-operation, and with regard for the efficiency of the service rather than for uniformity of procedure. It was through the attainment, after unfortunate delay, of such an understanding that effective co-operation was ultimately achieved. Permission to Egypt to make temporary promotions and individual postings, and interchange of views by personal visit, were the practical methods by which the difficulty was solved.[42]

Relations with the British Medical Administration. We came "to holts" with this problem of "Imperial" co-operation early in *Volume I*.[43] In particular, we traced the development of the concept of an Australian Army Medical Service that should be self-contained in the matter of interior economy, and be directed by an officer of the A.I.F. who should be the head of a department within the command of the G.O.C., A.I.F., as defined in the "powers of the G.O.C., A.I.F." laid down by the Commonwealth Government in 1914 and imple-

---

[40] This matter is dealt with in *Vol. III*. Surgeon-Gen. Fetherston had desired such an arrangement as early as Feb., 1916. At the time the supply of medical officers would not permit of a suitable choice.

[41] Both Major-Gen. Howse and Major-Gen. Fetherston most generously and with admirable candour placed this correspondence at the disposal of the Medical Historian. That held by Gen. Howse has been given by Lady Howse to the Australian War Memorial. It forms a human and historical record of great interest.

[42] For details see *Vol. I, Part II, Chapter vii.*

[43] *Vol. I, pp. 86, 430*, and elsewhere as given under *Index* heading Great Britain.

mented early in 1915 by the creation of the "Australian Intermediate Base Depot."

When, in the face of strong opposition by the War Office, this policy was followed and Colonel Howse was made "D.M.S., A.I.F.," by Australia, "Imperial" relations were thrown into the melting pot. While not claiming any formal recognition of independence—indeed, while avoiding that issue—he actually maintained independence in any action that he considered essential to Australian interests.[44] But Howse was not disposed to accept offhand a position under the Director-General at the War Office[45] identical with that occupied by Surgeon-General Williams. Engrossed indeed in his immediate problems, the complexity of which will have been evident, the D.M.S. found little time at first to cultivate "Imperial relations." All he desired was to be allowed within his proper sphere to mould the A.I.F. to his own ideals; and to bring business methods to bear on the vast and varied problems which faced him in connection with the sick and wounded of the A.I.F. But—as in 1915—no attitude could better have helped to secure his position.

With the D.G.M.S., B.E.F. General Howse was however strongly desirous of establishing direct *liaison* with General Sloggett and, to further this end, before the A.I.F. had arrived in France he arranged that his senior A.D.M.S. (Lieut.-Colonel Victor Hurley) should visit the British headquarters and propose to the Director-General that a position should be made on his headquarters for an Australian medical *liaison* officer. General Keogh himself favoured the suggestion and commended its adoption to General Sloggett. The considerations which led the latter to decline this proposal were stated in a personal letter to General Keogh which, together with General Howse's comments, appears in *Appendix No. 2*. The relations ultimately established were, General Howse has stated, much on the lines of those already established by the

---

[44] Howse's refusal to work as staff officer under Surgeon-Gen. Babtie (*see Vol. I, pp. 478-9*) had in a great part been due to his conviction that the Australian Medical Service would not "get a fair deal" under that officer.

[45] At this time Sir Alfred Keogh. This officer was succeeded on 1 March, 1918, by Lieut.-Gen. Sir John Goodwin who, it may be recalled, was afterwards Governor of Queensland.

D.M.S. Canadian force[46] and which have been stated as follows:—[47]

"It was decided that the D.M.S. Canadians should have his headquarters in London, but that he should be at liberty to cross to the seat of war whenever necessary, under and with the authority of the D.G.M.S. overseas, to visit the Canadian Medical units in the various areas, and, conferring with the D.M.S's of these areas, through them and through the D.G.M.S. to initiate such changes in distribution of the units and personnel as should mutually be agreed upon."

With the achievement of stability in the administrative situation of the A.I.F. the relations between Howse and Surgeon-General Keogh became more deliberately constructive, and opened the way to deliberations on matters of high Imperial policy. On the 4th of September 1917, Lieut.-General Keogh addressed a "secret and confidential" letter to the administrative heads of the Medical Services of the Dominions, desiring their views on the possibility of establishing closer relations. He went so far as to suggest the ultimate possibility of a deliberate association in the control of an Imperial medical service.[48] The text of General Keogh's letter and of the replies by Australia and New Zealand[49] will be found in *Appendix No. 2*. That no action was taken during the war was due in some part to the fact that the Australian command was not prepared to support General Howse in this project, holding that a move of so fundamental a nature must form part of a general Imperial military adjustment.

The "Imperial" Hospital, Sidcup. An even more interesting, because successful, adventure in the technique of Imperial co-operation appears in the move which brought about the establishment of the Queen's Hospital, at Sidcup. Designed to deal on scientific lines with the terrible results brought about by wounds to the face and jaw, this hospital came to fill a unique place among the special hospitals in England. At the

An " Imperial " Medical Staff

---

[46] In the middle of 1918 a senior officer in the Canadian service was attached to British headquarters in France.
[47] By Col. J. G. Adami, C.A.M.C.: *The War Story of the Canadian Army Medical Corps, p. 82.*
[48] It was stated (personal records) by Gen. Howse that the action arose as the result of suggestions by himself to Gen. Keogh in the course of conversation regarding events of the Gallipoli Campaign.
[49] The reply by the Canadian Director is not available.

end of the war a surgical and dental staff from Great Britain
and each of the dominions and the U.S.A. worked, each in
their own pavilions, under the command of a senior officer of
the R.A.M.C. The letter which initiated the scheme appears
in *Appendix No. 2 (page 870).*

II. GENERAL HOWSE'S POLICY WITHIN THE MEDICAL SERVICE

The responsibilities of the Medical Director, A.I.F., have
been defined in two broad domains, namely, (1) to administer
the medical service and to direct its activities; (2) to advise
the G.O.C., A.I.F., on the physical fitness of his force, and to
implement such advice by appropriate action in the medical
sphere.

Hospital Policy for the Western Front.[50] General Howse
at once made up his mind that Australia should not follow
the lead of Canada and New Zealand by attempting to provide primary and secondary
hospital beds for all Australian casualties arriving in England. Instead, he determined, in
the interests of the "six months' policy," to concentrate on
the development of "auxiliaries" and on the rapid transfer
thereto of all Australian patients. The considerations which
led to this decision were stated by him as follows:—[51]

Medical units on the Western Front

"You know that they (Australian General Hospitals) belong to the
common pool and at present Imperial hospitals are treating 99 per cent.
of Australian cases. Had I offered to make arrangements for treatment of all our cases I should have been compelled to ask for ten general
hospitals costing £700,000 a year, and it would have been necessary to
keep many of these empty to meet any emergency that might occur.
I only quote these figures to show the expense of such a system. There
are many other reasons which make it hopeless to attempt to get control
of Australians until they are discharged from primary hospitals in
England. At present we have one general hospital of 1,040 beds, two
general hospitals of 520 beds, two stationary hospitals, and three
casualty clearing stations, for five divisions. Each division should have
two general hospitals of 520 beds, two stationary hospitals, and one

---

[50] The policy that governed the raising in Australia of medical units for the A.I.F. has been examined in *Vol. I, pp. 22-24,* and the present volume, *Chapters i and xv.* A compendium of all medical units raised by the Commonwealth will be found in *Vol. III.*

[51] In a letter to the A.I.F. chief-of-staff (General White), dated 19 June, 1916. Writing to General Birdwood on June 6 he had said: "In view of a prolonged war, I feel that my urgent duty is to reduce expenditure to a minimum whilst maintaining efficiency."

casualty clearing station. If I ask Defence for this number of units, it would mean a great increase of expense, and between ourselves I think Defence will have great difficulty in meeting necessary demands at end of 1916."

A Practical Problem of Empire. This decision was one that goes to the root of "Imperial" relations,[52] and its developments call for consideration.

It will be recalled[53] that in the first year of the war an arrangement was made that, instead of establishing Australian General Hospitals in England, Australian casualties from the M.E.F. should be sent to certain British hospitals in which "a section" should be staffed by Australian medical officers. But with the decision, approved by the D.G.M.S. in Australia,[54] that the Australian General Hospitals should go to France on their transfer from Egypt, the idea of a system whereby Australian casualties should be treated in Australian hospitals in England automatically lapsed. The Australian medical officers attached to British hospitals were then transferred by the D.M.S., A.I.F. to the Australian hospital units in France, or in the urgent calls from the Somme, were used to replace casualties in regiments or in the field units.

Thereafter, the calls from the front were continuous and exacting. In *England* the maintenance of the *status quo* created in 1915 was favoured by two factors, each of which (though for different reasons) tended to transfer the activities of the Australian Army Medical Corps in England from the *primary treatment* of Australian soldiers to the problems of *convalescence* :—

(1) The circumstances of the A.I.F. required a system whereby the recovered casualty should be transformed with the utmost speed into a soldier fit to take his place again in the field.

(2) The "six months' policy" laid down that those Australian casualties, whose disablement should be held to preclude for at least six months useful participation in the war, must be transferred with as little delay as possible to Australia. This necessitated the building up of a great system of sea transport, which had to be fed with a regular flow of "classified" invalids, for whom interim treatment in the depots and on the voyage must be provided.

These two considerations made necessary the formation of a vast special "intermediary" medical base in England. When, therefore, in 1916 as D.M.S., A.I.F., Surgeon-General Howse was called on to face the question anew, military and national considerations pointed strongly to the plan of making use of the almost unlimited facilities for treatment already available in the British "home base," instead of creating an immense independent treatment centre for Australian soldiers, intermediary between France and their antipodean home.

But as the war years went by a movement with a strong

---

[52] Early in the war King George V expressed the hope that all soldiers of the Empire should share in common the best treatment that Britain could provide, since they shared in common the duty of safeguarding British Imperial interests.
[53] *See Vol. I, pp. 498-500.*
[54] *See Chapter i.*

emotional appeal was launched to urge that Australians, at least on arrival in England, should be admitted primarily to hospitals staffed by Australian personnel. At the same time the specialists—physicians, surgeons and physiotherapists—both in the A.I.F. and in Australia were concerned for the results of the repeated breaks of gauge (as they may be conceived) at the treatment stations on the route of the Australian casualty.

This appeal for a complete Australian hospital system in England became so insistent[55] that the question of the possibility of giving effect to it was raised by the Minister for Defence, and was made a matter for specific inquiry by the Director-General (General Fetherston) and, among other matters, a reason for a special tour of inspection at the end of 1917. The result of this inquiry belongs to a later page. It is desirable, however, here to make a brief reference, but one which is very pertinent, to the financial arrangements between Great Britain and Australia.

The arrangement made by the British Government in the matter of payment for patients treated in British hospitals in the Gallipoli campaign was noted in the first volume.[56] In 1916, a similar general agreement was reached whereby the Australian force was maintained in the field, in all except pay, for a capitation payment to Britain per head of ration strength. The nature of the arrangement made concerning the treatment of Australian patients in British hospitals and *vice versa* is sufficiently displayed in the following correspondence.

Financial arrangements with Great Britain

---

[55] The same question arose in a more embittered form in the Canadian force. The difficulty of arranging for the primary segregation of all Canadian casualties was emphasised by successive commissions of inquiry. Thus, the "Babtie Commission" in November 1916, found the primary segregation of Canadian sick and wounded "not only impracticable but unwise." Ultimately, however, Canada sent overseas an establishment of hospital units approximately equivalent to full war establishment. Provision was made whereby a proportion of Canadian casualties from France went direct to Canadian units; the rest were to be transferred as soon as their condition permitted. Canada eventually had 16 General, 10 Stationary, 7 Special, and 8 Convalescent Hospitals overseas.

New Zealand attempted, with some success, though it would seem with much waste of space, to obtain control of her own sick and wounded in her own primary hospitals, of which she maintained a full complement.

It would seem doubtful whether within the A.I.F. itself there was at the time any very strong feeling on the matter, save on the part of some clinical specialists and the Australian Nursing Service. The question is examined from a different angle—that of "reparative" treatment—in *Vol. III.*

[56] *Vol. I, pp. 57, 492.*

Cablegram dated 10th July, 1917, from Defence Department, Melbourne, to Commandant, A.I.F. Headquarters, London. "Your letter April 19 No. 195, hospital charges British and Australian. Cannot agree in such proposal which entails considerable sums being paid by Imperial Government for treatment of Australian patients and which not charged to this Government. It is desired that arrangements be made fair to both Imperial authority and Australia."

The Commandant had reported that the cost of treating and maintaining soldiers in Australian hospitals, and presumably in British, would approximate 6s. per head per diem. The agreement fixed the charge at 2s. but, though the agreement was reciprocal, the number of British soldiers treated in Australian hospitals was negligible. General Griffiths's reply illuminates more than the question at issue.

"To sum up, the British suggested the low rate of 2s. per diem and preferred us to accept it. As it was not contrary to our interests to accept, I did so. All our adjustments with the Imperial authorities here are on the big-minded basis of mutual give and take. We always satisfy ourselves that the Commonwealth Government's interests are protected, and we leave it to the War Office to see that the Imperial interests are guarded, and as there is nothing antagonistic in the desires and sentiments of both parties, there is little or no friction."

The arrangement was then accepted.

It may be added that in the final "square up" after the war, Great Britain showed a like generous appreciation of the spirit in which Australia had entered the war: the fullest benefit of any doubt as to liability was conceded to the Australian representative.

It is doubtful whether, considered solely from the point of view of administration, the vast alternative scheme of Australian primary hospitals rejected by Howse would have involved as heavy demands on the energy of his headquarters as did the plan adopted. The vast business of the transfer of convalescent men from British hospitals to the Australian "auxiliaries," the problem of specialist treatment, of boarding, convalescence, furlough, and ultimate disposal, and last—but far from least—of visitation while in British hospitals, involved the creation of a system in which the work of each sub-department concerned must be correlated with a high degree of exactitude. Such a system was in fact created,

Treatment and disposal of Australian casualties

and so far as is necessary will be described in the next volume.

Among the services of a modern army the medical is unique in the variety of its responsibilities, and as a consequence in the complexity of its organisation and the variety of the necessary technical personnel.[57] We have to distinguish, as providing distinct problems of reinforcement for the Australian Army Medical Corps:—

Supply of personnel to the Medical Service

(a) Qualified medical men, including specialists in almost every branch of medicine, physicians, surgeons, pathologists, dermatologists, radiologists, and so forth.

(b) Warrant officers, Quartermasters and quartermaster-sergeants, rank and file, of medical units. These included as well as trained hospital orderlies men fit to meet the mental and physical demands of stretcher-bearing, skilled tradesmen of all kinds, horse and motor drivers.[58]

(c) Qualified dental practitioners and skilled dental mechanics. (d) Qualified pharmacists. In the A.I.F. these served with both commissioned and non-commissioned rank. (e) Trained nurses for service in the A.A.N.S. (f) Qualified masseurs and masseuses.

"Up to a short time prior to the Armistice," Howse's A.D.M.S. for Personnel[59] in 1917-18 has put on record, "there was never a surplus of medical officers over and above the actual requirements" (*i.e.*, for hospitals, depots, field units and administrative staffs). A statement, subjoined, shows the total number of medical officers, nurses and "other ranks" sent abroad with the A.I.F. up to 11th November, 1918.[60]

Supply of Medical Personnel for the Western Front

---

[57] The questions of "rank" and "status" in the medical services, and of the supply of personnel for the dental, pharmaceutical, nursing, and massage services are dealt with in relevant chapters of *Vol. III.*

[58] The fact that the transport service may be provided by the Army Service Corps does not affect the problem.

[59] Lieut.-Col. J. H. Anderson.

[60] Enlistment in the A.I.F. was not permitted outside of Australia. This regulation was strictly enforced. The medical men who in 1915 volunteered in Australia and were "lent" for "Imperial" service and commissioned in the R.A.M.C., were not permitted at the expiration of the period for which they had enlisted (one year) to re-enlist in the A.I.F. unless they returned first to Australia; and their seniority in the A.I.F. dated from re-enlistment. A very few exceptions to the rule were permitted. Col. Sir Alexander MacCormick for a time held a commission both in the R.A.M.C. and the A.A.M.C.; Lieut.-Col. (later Sir Charles) Martin, who at the time was Director of the Lister Institute, was permitted to join No. 3 A.G.H. in England. A considerable number of Australian graduates who were in England at the outbreak of the war enlisted in the R.A.M.C.; others formed the staff of the Australian Voluntary Hospital. Many of these officers had most distinguished service. It is hoped to give a list of them in *Vol. III.*

MEDICAL DIRECTION OF A.I.F.

Statement showing numbers of A.A.M.C. Units and Personnel embarked from Australia for service in the A.I.F.[61]

UNITS OR ESTABLISHMENTS / PERSONNEL

Nature of Unit.	Number	Medical Officers	Quartermasters	Dentists[a]	Pharmacists	Masseurs and Masseuses	Nurses	Other Ranks	Total
Regimental Medical Establishments	80	85	10	1	—	—	—	401	486
Field Ambulances	11	92	—	—	—	—	—	2,685	2,779
Rfcts., Dec., 1914-Dec., 1917	—	—	—	—	—	—	—	1,235	1,235
L.H. Field Ambulances	4	24	—	—	—	—	—	473	497
Rfcts., Dec., 1914-Dec., 1917	—	—	1	—	—	—	—	426	426
Camel Field Ambulance	1	2	—	—	—	—	—	93	95
Sanitary Sections	2	20	3	—	—	—	—	60	62
Casualty Clearing Stations	3	—	—	—	—	—	—	244	267
Rfcts., Feb., 1915-Mar., 1916	—	—	1	—	—	—	—	88	88
Stationary Hospitals[62]	2	15	—	2	—	—	—	186	202
Rfcts., Dec., 1914-Mar., 1916	—	—	1	1	2	—	—	131	131
General Hospitals[63]	5	100	4	—	—	16	326	620	1,054
Rfcts., Feb., 1915-April, 1916	—	120	1	—	—	—	340	1,305	1,783
Convalescent Depot (Harefield)	1	11	1	—	—	—	—	231	301
Dermatological Hospital	1	7	1	—	—	—	58	132	140
Rfcts., Feb.-April, 1916	—	—	—	—	—	—	—	38	38
Ambulance Workshop	1	—	164	—	—	—	—	18	19
Rfcts., June, 1916-Aug., 1917	—	—	—	—	—	—	—	14	14
Motor Drivers A.A.M.C.	—	—	—	—	—	—	—	124	124
Hospital Ships (& Transport Corps)	2	38	—	5	—	8[65]	102	486	640
Sea Transport Sections and Special Staff	—	—	—	—	—	14	57	229	319
General Reinforcements	10	19	—	—	1	5	1,403	3,147	5,356
		708							
Totals		1,242	23[84]	102	4	43[85]	2,286	12,366	16,066

[a] The following also embarked, for service with the A.N. & M.E.F.; medical officers, 35; dentists, 2; nurses, 9; other ranks, A.A.M.C. 101. In addition 35 other ranks A.A.M.C. went to Samoa in Nov., 1918 in the H.M.A.S. *Encounter*. 115 medical officers were enlisted in Australia for service in the R.A.M.C. and 136 nurses for the Q.A.I.M.N.S.
[62] With the exceptions shown in this column dental officers were allotted to medical or dental sections when they arrived overseas.
[63] Includes 11 M.O's, 1 dentist, 58 nurses and 5 staff-sgts., who embarked as members of No. 10 A.G.H., which, however, did not function as a General Hospital overseas. Its personnel were allotted to other A.I.F. units.
[64] Includes one M.T. Officer A.A.M.C.
[65] Includes one Stewardess.

In addition to these a considerable number of units were formed overseas, chiefly in the "duplication" of the A.I.F. after Gallipoli, from personnel sent in drafts from Australia and from transfers. The following table is an epitome of all new units whose establishments were filled by Australian personnel overseas.[66]

Units formed	No.	Units formed	No.
Regimental Medical Establishments ..	74	Australian Flying Corps Hospital	1
Field Ambulances	6	Auxiliary Hospitals	5
L.H. Field Ambulances	1	A.A.M.C. Convalescent and Training Depot, Parkhouse	1
Sanitary Sections	6		
Dental Units	118		
Anzac Mobile Field Laboratory	1	Base Depot Medical and Dental Stores	1
Group or Depot Clearing Hospitals	5	Australian Medical Administrative Headquarters	1

Further to these an Australian Section or staff was found for various British or Imperial units—the Queen's Hospital, Sidcup; No. 44 C.C.S.; Government Hospital, Suez; Springfield War Hospital; Nurses' Convalescent Hospital.

There must be added the large medical staffs required for the *Military* Convalescent ("Command") Depots in England, Egypt and France.[67]

During the war 66 medical officers died on service, and some 300 were returned to Australia. In the integration of the above figures, we have the problem of the D.M.S. and of his deputy in the East in connection with the maintenance of the medical service in commissioned officers, and apart from the principles adopted by Surgeon-General Howse for posting and promotion, and a few details of a general kind in connection with the situation at certain critical junctures, little can be done to re-create the problems of maintenance that faced the D.M.S., A.I.F., or to indicate the lines on which he dealt with them. From the point of view even of a technical history of the

---

[66] A comprehensive list of medical units formed with details will be given in *Vol. III*.

[67] In his report (1 Nov., 1916) to the D.G.M.S. in Australia General Howse states: "These Command Depots, although administered by the combatant branches of the services, are Convalescent Depots in all but name, and have the advantage over medical convalescent depots that the men in them can be disciplined in the ordinary way and not dealt with as hospital patients. The medical staff required for a Command Depot is practically the same as for a Convalescent Depot of the same accommodation." The staff of the several depots varied greatly and also in each from time to time.

Australian Medical Service, however, the loss is not one of major importance. It is shown that, with considerable wastage of medical officers resulting from casualties and from a rigid policy of return to Australia of medical men who, in the opinion of the D.M.S. were due for a rest and employment in Australia, or were not up to the exacting standard of the A.I.F., the reinforcements from Australia enabled him to maintain the units and establishments of the A.I.F. at strength.

What matters more, is the difference between this achievement, and the effort which the medical profession would have been called upon to make had Australia undertaken to provide the full medical establishment prescribed for a field force like the A.I.F.; and as well have attempted (as did Canada and New Zealand) to duplicate in Great Britain the home-base establishment of hospitals and convalescent homes required in Australia, on a basis of primary admissions from the front, as well as of finalising treatment, medical and surgical, and of repairs.

To assess this difference we may compare the tables on *pages 829 and 830* with the following rough estimate of the "complete outfit," units and personnel, required for such an effort.[68]

For the B.E.F. The staff for a mobile field bacteriological laboratory; motor ambulance convoy; 2 ambulance trains; 2 casualty clearing stations; 4-6 stationary hospitals; 2 1,040-bed general hospitals; convalescent hospital; hospital ship.

For the E.E.F. A C.C.S.; another (520-bed) general hospital.

In Great Britain. 8-10 general hospitals (500 to 2,000 beds) for primary admissions; 4-6 special hospitals, or blocks (each of 100 to 500 beds), for orthopaedic, cardiac, tubercular, and eye and ear cases and for mental disease and psycho-neurosis. 4 additional convalescent (auxiliary) hospitals, or annexes; an officers' general hospital of 520 beds together with certain miscellaneous units as camp and disembarkation hospitals. The orthopaedic and other special hospitals would require a staff of specialists.

3 Hospital ships (England and Egypt).

On a rough estimate the additional personnel would amount to a total of at least 500 officers and some 1,500 nurses and 3,500 medical orderlies. The medical officers would be almost entirely additional to those sent overseas during the war: nursing staff and other ranks partly

---

[68] The estimate represents *additional* medical units (which would involve corresponding reinforcement obligations). It is based on *War Establishments (Part VII —New Armies)*; the British official figures for hospital beds required in Britain; and on the medical units actually supplied by Canada.

so. In addition, a considerable number of pharmacists and members of the massage service would be required—not to speak of "voluntary aid."

As an offset must be put some transfer of specialist staff from Nos. 1 and 3 Auxiliaries; and the relief that would be given to No. 2 Command Depot. The effect of the last would, however, have been negligible: the sole purpose of the improvised staff maintained there was to promote the rapid transfer of invalids to Australia, and to minimise the effect of the break of treatment.

The difference between the two sets of figures gives the measure of the relief to the Australian medical profession; and thus the medical "man-power" freed for full or part-time work in the military hospitals in Australia: in other words, for implementing the six months' policy. The manner in which the medical profession, thus relieved, applied itself to this task will be told in the next volume.

A few points with regard to medical reinforcement must, however, be noted.

When the A.I.F. left Egypt, it left behind, as well as the Light Horse, the dregs from the immense and varied sick wastage of Gallipoli; and to clear this up No. 3 A.G.H. and three "auxiliaries" remained in Egypt. Presuming that, apart from its field units, the Light Horse would be served by British medical units, Howse arranged that, on the completion of their immediate task, the personnel of the Australian hospitals abovementioned would be available for the Western Front. With this curious, indeed unjustifiable, presumption began the administrative disputes between Egypt and Horseferry-road. But for the D.M.S. it must be said that, even with the reduction of the field ambulances to two sections, the duplication of the A.I.F. in February, 1916,[69] had left him with his hospital staffs below establishment, with a gross deficiency on normal establishment of L. of C. and Base units,[70] and with only the general decisions of the "Imperial Conferences"[71] to guide him as to the nature and extent of the provision he would be required to make in Britain.[72] And within a few weeks he was required by the

Supply of Medical Officers: Narrative of Events

---

[69] *See Vol. I, pp. 480-82.*
[70] *Ibid., pp. 203-4.*
[71] *See pp. 9-13.*
[72] It should be recalled that the total wounded in the Light Horse (after Gallipoli) numbered only some 3,500.

War Office to bring the Australian field ambulances up to three sections. This left him (as he cabled urgently in May) "with no surplus at all," and he pointed his demand for 60 young officers for field work with the statement that, if they were not quickly forthcoming, he would be obliged to call upon the British Service for assistance. On July 25th (during the Battle of Pozières) he asked for 50 more, "young active captains"—and for cabled advice when any batch embarked.

A despatch of October, 1916, gives in a nutshell both the difficulties of the Director and the principles on which he worked throughout the war.

"For some weeks, both Nos. 1 and 2 General Hospitals were working with nine to twelve Medical Officers and admitting patients often at the rate of 200 to 300 per day. Of the 110 (60 plus 50) Medical Officer reinforcements asked for in my two cables on this subject, about 65 have already arrived and have all been disposed of.

"The invaliding from France this winter is certain to be heavy. In addition also, there are many of the older and more senior officers who would probably not stand the winter, and I should think that the 110 already asked for, and promised by you to be sent, will barely see us until the end of the year, and even then will not permit me to staff the Nos. 1, 2, and 3 General Hospitals with as many Medical Officers as they should have. I should think as an absolute minimum, you should send 15 Medical Officer reinforcements per month and as far as possible distribute them equally over the transports leaving with reinforcements, not omitting to send some Medical Officer reinforcements to Egypt, where Col. Downes, the A.D.M.S., has been instructed to inform you from time to time of his requirements. In my previous despatches I have informed you that I propose to return to Australia, as soon as Medical Officer reinforcements are available, those Medical Officers who had received definite promises in Australia that they would be released at the end of 12 or more months of service, and those who desired to return because of urgent family or financial reasons,[73] as well as those who by reason of advancing years were not likely to stand further strain of active service. . . ."

In his despatch of October, 1917, Howse wrote:—

"The following are on list to sail (to Australia) during October:—2 Colonels, 3 Lieut.-Colonels, 10 Majors, 1 Captain. Amongst these are a few officers who have done very well, also a few who are really physically and mentally unfit for Active Service. We now have on the wounded list—14 Officers. The last ten days have been sad ones for us as we lost Lieut.-Col. J. J. Nicholas and Captain G. S. Elliott, probably two of our best officers. Nicholas was a brilliant man who will be sorrowed for by everyone. Am glad to hear that we may expect another

[73] Surgeon-General Howse returned to Australia every man who felt himself aggrieved by continued service, or who for legitimate family reasons appeared to be hampered in "pulling his weight." The very few first named pass into oblivion; of the second many returned later to the front or took up home service duties.

15 officers in October. Hope soon to get letter from you saying when you expect to send more. We are doing well—you have kept up a splendid supply and I have been able to send away (to Australia) most of the men who have applied, but if I had a surplus of medicos I should get permission for about ten more to return. I do not know yet, out of my lately wounded, how many will be able to resume work. A number of the officers mentioned in earlier part of this letter as returning in October, are on the sick list and have been boarded. Others would certainly break down if kept here during the Winter. I think most of the officers who are unlikely to be able to stand the winter in England or France have now been sent, with exception of 10 or 12 who will be sent on transport duty during November or December."

Officers: Promotion and Posting

In a democratic society with its ideals of intelligent co-operation the method of promotion is of great importance.[74] A sagacious and informed student[75] of the war and of the A.I.F. has observed that

"taking it by and large the conduct of war by Australians was in many respects governed by the principles of sound business. Fighting for a living in peace is no mean training for fighting for your life in war. . . . Promotion therefore turned on the future services to be rendered and not on rewarding the work of the past or consideration of length of service."

This judgment is applicable to the methods of the D.M.S. in the promotion of officers of the Medical Corps. The adjustments to be made are three:—

(1) If we except the few positions open to "quartermasters," commissioned rank was restricted within the medical and dental professions.[76] The problem of promotion, therefore, was definitely a twofold one, within commissioned and non-commissioned ranks respectively.

(2) In part as a consequence of the foregoing, seniority and previous service had considerably greater weight in the medical service than in the combatant arms, since the sphere of selection was more restricted.

(3) A matter of great significance was that promotion and posting within the A.I.F.[77] was the personal responsibility of the D.M.S.; and Surgeon-General Howse strongly impressed his personality and outlook on the service by his appointments to command or administrative positions.

---

[74] In the A.I.F. battalions promotion from the ranks was commonly like that of N.C.O's within the unit. This was a major factor in its efficiency.

[75] "Quail" in *Reveille*, May 1, 1939, *p*. 9.

[76] The question whether opportunity for attaining to commissioned rank should not be extended more widely to non-professional members of the medical service is examined on *p. 284* and in *Vol. III*.

[77] The position as regards the Light Horse is stated in *Vol. I, pp. 650-1*. Recommendation for promotion to non-commissioned rank was, of course, the right of the commanding officer of each unit, and was a privilege most jealously guarded as a main instrument in building up efficiency.

At the outset of his directorate, in 1916, General Howse took up the attitude that, apart from certain specialists, such as physicians and surgeons in L. of C. and Base units, promotion to the rank of major in the A.I.F. should be contingent on service overseas, and that none should be made without consulting him. To this principle the D.G.M.S. in Australia, in effect, agreed; and from 1916 onwards all promotion in the A.A.M.C., A.I.F.,[78] was by recommendation of the D.M.S. through the D.A.G., A.I.F., to the G.O.C., A.I.F.; and thence to Australia for approval and gazettal.

Though opportunity for promotion was "within establishment" of existing units, the field of promotion[79] was greatly extended by the creation of "auxiliary" hospitals, administrative and special appointments, and so forth, and by a liberal grading of such appointments.[80] Howse's aims were definite, namely, to create a corps of young men strongly imbued with the outlook of the front line.[81] To achieve this he facilitated and even on occasion accelerated the return to Australia of senior men who were past their prime or tired of war. Yet some senior officers with his approval "stuck it out" throughout the war.[82] Clinical positions were on the whole very evenly distributed. Thus officers aspiring to surgical and other desired posts had to take their turn at Bulford and in the Auxiliaries. In theory promotion within field rank was by selection, not by seniority. But in effect failure to achieve promotion in one or other of the many avenues open in the service meant return to Australia. The thorny question of rank and promotion for "specialists" is examined later.

The quality of the duty and service rendered to the A.I.F. by the commissioned officers of the Medical Corps was the

---

[78] Medical officers of the A.A.M.C. were commissioned by the King for service in the Australian Army Medical Corps at a rank not below that of "captain"; on recommendation by the Director-General, through the Adjutant-General and Military Board, transmitted through the Governor-General of Australia. In the R.A.M.C., it may be noted, medical officers were commissioned as first-lieutenants. The general problem of "rank" in the Australian Army Medical Services will be examined in *Volume III*. Promotion in the A.I.F. was "within establishment," which was authorised by the Military Board. Promotions were published in the *Commonwealth Gazette*, and this was the authority in any question of "seniority." Home service in the Australian Military Forces was entirely independent of service in the Australian Imperial Force, and had a special "seniority list."

[79] The rates of pay (excluding field allowance) for commissioned officers in the A.I.F. were as follows: major-general, £1,200 per annum; brigadier-general and colonel, £2 5s. per day; lieutenant-colonel, £1 17s. 6d.; major, £1 10s.; captain, £1 2s. 6d.; lieutenant, 17s. 6d. The rate for the rank and file was much higher than in the British Army.

[80] In the personal opinion of the writer, commissioned rank in the medical service of the A.I.F. was unduly high.

[81] His preference for his Gallipoli men was a cause of some resentment to officers who enlisted later or had not the opportunity of reaching Anzac. General Howse was not above the device of ensuring that some field "reward" should come to men who had served well in the drudgery of administrative positions.

[82] For example, Colonels J. A. Dick, R. B. Huxtable, B. J. Newmarch.

resultant of two factors—the quality and special features of the medical profession of Australia, and the method of promotion and posting. For the first we may select as outstanding characteristics, initiative, and adaptability, these reflecting the moderate extent of specialisation, and the nature of a "bush" practice. For the second, Surgeon-General Howse kept himself informed by confidential reports from commanding officers, by close touch with his deputy and assistant deputies, by careful selection of his A.D.M.S. for Personnel, and by personal interviews for which last he left himself time by delegating routine. A letter from the A.D.M.S. for Personnel to an officer commanding a casualty clearing station puts his mind and methods in a nutshell:—

"Dear—
"The G. has asked me to write to you about a move that will shortly be coming your way. He has nominated you for the position of A.D.M.S. —Division.............. [The present] D.A.D.M.S. is getting very senior and must get some other experience before further promotion becomes due to him. You will be asked to nominate someone as D.A.D.M.S. so please keep your eyes open for a man whom you would like to work with you. Three things are laid down to guide you in this connection.
"(1) The officer must be in your division.
"(2) He must not be from the same State as yourself.
"(3) He must be a junior Major so that he can remain in his place for some time.
"This has only been recommended so far, so something may come in the way and upset it."[83]

The A.A.M.C. and the "Scientific" Problems of War. The dislike evinced by most surgeons—Howse was essentially a surgeon—for the professional title "Doctor," reflects a fundamental difference in their mental outlook from that of physicians. This difference may perhaps best be summed up by proposing that the normal surgeon would reverse the ranks in the title of Charles Kingsley's book, *Madam How and Lady Why*, whereas the normal physician would retain them.[84]

The author is bound to record his own judgment that the

---

[83] The distribution, supply, and posting of dentists, pharmacists, and nurses is dealt with in Volume III.
[84] John Hunter cannot be accepted as invalidating the proposal—he was a biologist first, a surgeon for a living. Moynihan's "vital pathology" was essentially utilitarian. But Mr. Wilfred Trotter must be "barred."

Medical Service of the A.I.F. was not a highly "scientific" one; and that this defect—if defect it were—was in a measure at least due to the outlook, perhaps the limitations, of the Director. Surgeon-General Howse was not "scientific" in the popular connotation of the term, which supposes a considerable facility for abstract thought; he was essentially pragmatic and utilitarian, and this outlook was reflected in his administration. And, though the proposal will be distasteful to some, it is difficult to resist the conclusion that, in the circumstances of the Australian Medical Service on the Western Front, this was to the general advantage of the force, even though it was a source of regret, even of resentment, in the members of the service itself.

"For better or worse" the A.I.F. was essentially a frontline force; the first duty of its Medical Director was to ensure that the front line was efficiently served. Medical policy belonged to the British, and, without a far wider scope for cooperation than it was found possible to arrange in this war, it could not have been shared by the dominions. The fact that the dominions might voluntarily contribute scientific units and research centres or personnel could not diminish the responsibility of the R.A.M.C.[85] It may perhaps be suggested that the Australian School of Medicine—for such we may claim to possess—might in the early years of the war have supplied a useful "kick" to British preventive medicine, akin to that lent by the U.S.A. in 1917 in the matter of transfusion and trench fever.[86] Be that as it may, it has to be accepted that from the outset the A.I.F. presented few opportunities for "scientific" specialists or for specialisation; and that the advent of Surgeon-General Howse as D.M.S. did little to promote such opportunities.

So far as he concerned himself with the releasing of medical officers

---

[85] When such were offered they were accepted and used—for example, the mobile laboratory provided by Canada. Here the Australian Service was in the first place restricted by desire to meet exactly the wishes of the War Office (*see Vol. I, p. 498*). It is not generally known that in 1914 Howse desired to be sent with the first contingent of the A.I.F. in charge of a "sanitary section." The request was refused.

[86] An "appreciation" of the scientific work done by members of the A.A.M.C., and of the reasons which brought about some early failures and defects in the British Army, will be found in *Vol. III.*

for scientific work, it has been said[87] that two circumstances guided him:—
(1) Whether the man could be spared.
(2) The financial aspect.

With regard to the first, it was his policy to keep his field units at full strength in officers, other work, such as administration or at the Base units in England, being staffed as low as possible for this purpose. Till shortly before the Armistice, there was never a surplus of medical officers.

As to the second, he drew a careful line between expenditure for the benefit of the A.I.F. and expenditure on objects which might at some future date indirectly be of use to the nation.[88]

Training of A.A.M.C. It has to be acknowledged that the training of medical personnel for front-line service before they reached the front was not one of the highlights of the Australian effort. The chief cause of defect lay in imperfect co-ordination between Australia and the A.I.F. In "Notes on Medical Services in France" furnished, at his request, to General Howse in April, 1917, Colonel Barber, then A.D.M.S., 4th Australian Division, said:

Training and Distribution: The A.A.M.C. Depot at Parkhouse

---

[87] By Lieut.-Col. J. H. Anderson, in a special memorandum compiled for the Medical Collator in 1919.

[88] From the same source it is learnt that steps were taken for special training along the following lines:—

"*Operating Surgeons, Surgical Specialists, etc.* Junior officers with special surgical qualifications were trained at base hospitals under competent surgical supervision, and then sent for a time to Casualty Clearing Stations to enlarge their surgical experience. These officers were later available for positions as operating surgeons with surgical teams, surgeons in charge of resuscitation teams, and finally became qualified for positions as surgical specialists. This training depended very largely on the amount of work requiring to be done and was interfered with owing to the fewness of medical officers available. In periods of stress officers undergoing training were required to act in field ambulances or as R.M.O's when occasion demanded. Had a sufficient pool of surplus medical officers been available, this would not have occurred.

"*Pathologists and Radiographers.* Lists were carefully compiled and kept up to date of all officers possessing special knowledge as radiographers, pathologists, etc., and, as numbers permitted, these were afforded facilities for training along their special lines.

"*Specialists.* Specialists with expert knowledge of eye work, ear, nose, and throat work, neurology, etc., were kept as far as possible to their special lines, but in times of stress might be called on to do other work.

"*Other Ranks.* The above remarks mainly apply to officers, but similar lists of men with special knowledge in X-ray work, theatre work, pathology, insanity, etc., were kept in order that they could be readily drawn upon when required.

"On 18.12.17 special establishments of other ranks with regard to X-ray work and pathology were attached to various Australian units—see A.I.F. Order 1026. This was one of the earliest steps taken to establish complete pathological and X-ray departments in connection with these units.

"In connection with special work, the D.M.S. even prior to the Armistice placed every facility possible in the way of men wishing to study along certain lines. Officers wishing to proceed to the F.R.C.S. examination were granted special facilities in order to sit for the examination, and were helped in every way. Special facilities were also placed in the way of men wishing to publish original papers in any of the journals.

"Reinforcement officers arrive at a Division and, although they may have served with the A.I.F. for several months, they often know nothing whatever of their duties. . . . It is not always possible to place these officers in an Ambulance for training, nor is it always possible to train in the Field. An officer who has attended a course of Field Ambulance training such as laid down in the C.M.F. will quickly become efficient. I think every officer should be compelled to attend such a course."

The Australian end is dealt with in the next volume. In the A.I.F. on the Western Front Colonel Barber's strictures were met, partly by the more exact system at Parkhouse, already described in *Chapter XVI*, partly—in particular for medical officers—by the methods proposed by Colonel Barber —namely, the formation of divisional and corps schools of instruction—and by the issue of medical standing orders.[89]

Distribution: the Medical Pool. In war as in peace, the great problem of administration is how to prevent unemployment. The chief difference between these two social states regarded industrially is that in peace, save for the 10 per cent. who need not work, unemployment means destitution or the dole; in war it means full pay and inflated "overhead." And in war unemployment is the rule.[90] The question is not a small one—hence, for example, no small part of the national debts. These large matters have direct and very practical bearing on the administration of the medical service and one to which, as has been indicated, Howse was always alive. The question, how best to maintain medical reserves, was always present; and, though it related chiefly to medical officers, the problem of "other ranks"—in particular of N.C.O's—was far from simple and became more difficult as the war progressed and "duds" accumulated.

Reserve of Medical Officers. The normal channel for reinforcing A.A.M.C. units was the A.A.M.C. Depot at Parkhouse.[91] But the *locus*

"Subsequent to the Armistice matters were of course greatly changed. Every help was given to men wishing to proceed for examinations or to do research work. Several officers, asked for by name by the War Office for special lines of research, were detailed to proceed, and every help given to them and to the teachers who wished to obtain them."

[89] For *Standing Orders for A.A.M.C. Australian Corps, see Appendix No. 4.*

[90] Even in the A.I.F. the average time spent by a soldier with his unit at the front was perhaps four months; and of this time a small proportion only was occupied with fighting.

[91] The procedure has been described in *Chapter xvi*. An arrangement which greatly promoted the distribution of medical other ranks to the field, proposed by the D.A.G., A.I.F., and accepted *con amore* by the D.M.S., distributed A.A.M.C. reserves of other ranks—about 300—among the three Australian general hospitals in France instead of at Parkhouse and the general base depot at Le Havre.

where might best be held the reserves of medical officers was a difficult matter. R.M.O's were temporarily replaced by detailing officers from the field ambulances under divisional arrangement, and these in turn were replaced through 3rd Echelon chiefly from the base hospitals in France, which again drew on England. The selection of all officers for appointments was ultimately made or approved by General Howse.[92] Officer reserves were for the most part held supernumerary to establishment in base medical units. The case of the surgical teams, however, calls for particular note.

The Casualty Clearing Station Teams. Impressed with the importance of the surgical work at the Base, and imperfectly informed of the problems and purpose of the Director-General, B.E.F., Surgeon-General Howse proposed that, instead of holding surgical teams at the Base, he should strengthen the C.C.S. on the surgical side.

The Surgical Teams

"This step (he informed General Sloggett) is rendered necessary, as under the present system it is found difficult to keep the standard of operating in the Australian General Hospitals to the degree of efficiency deemed necessary."

He requested that in future no surgical teams be detailed from the Australian hospitals. Each Australian C.C.S. would carry, in addition to the personnel laid down in War Establishments, one surgeon specialist, two operating surgeons, and two anaesthetists—"all of whom are specially selected."

General Sloggett agreed to return all Australian teams to their units but under strong protest.

"I regret (he informed the G.O.C., A.I.F.) that I can give no undertaking to refrain in future from ordering up surgical teams from all classes of general hospitals on the L. of C. for duty with C.C.S's in times of pressure. This is in the interests of the Australian wounded equally with others, and if the surgical teams of the Australian hospitals do not take their share in the work of the C.C.S's in these times, the condition of the wounded on arrival at the hospitals at the Base will be very much worse."

After giving some details regarding the nature of his problem,[93] General Sloggett concluded:—

"I shall be glad if the D.M.S., A.I.F., would come and see me when he visits the B.E.F. in France. I would then be in a position to discuss with him questions such as this which he may desire to bring to my notice."

---

[92] Howse was generally advised by his A.D.M.S. for Personnel.
[93] *See Chapters xii and xxi.*

Something of an administrative impasse arose. It was resolved by a report to the D.M.S. by the officer commanding an Australian team at the Third Army Experimental C.C.S. at Gézaincourt,[94] and by a visit by the Deputy D.G.M.S. (Sir William Macpherson) to A.I.F. Headquarters in France. The *amende honorable* was made by Howse in a memorandum to General Birdwood on the 1st of March, 1918, recommending the formation of "six complete surgical teams . . . to be available for use by the Imperial authorities when required." Each team was to consist of a surgeon, an anaesthetist, a theatre sister, and two orderlies. During quiescent periods the teams would be carried supernumerary to establishment in the general hospitals—two teams at each—where they could work when not required elsewhere. The surgical staff of the casualty clearing stations was proportionately reduced.

"By the formation of such teams (he said) it is hoped to obviate dislocation of work incident on the sudden removal of medical officers from the duties on which they are employed at the moment."

The surgeons selected were young men who had shown surgical ability and self-reliance; the majority were officers who had been appointed to the original field ambulances—which at the beginning of the war were the centre for surgical field work. The Australian teams achieved a fine reputation in the British Service for readiness to rise to the occasion.

It should be noted that the real cause of the impasse lay chiefly in the curious relations that existed between the respective Directors-General at the War Office and in the B.E.F., the latter claiming—and securing—wide powers of initiative. The Australian Director sometimes found himself at a loss to discern where responsibility lay. As has been noted elsewhere, till the end of the war he had no pool of officers to play with in what at first he held to be a wasteful use of personnel. But it is clear from the history of these teams that the policy of organising the floating pool of technical experts, in teams which could be massed at strategic points, must be regarded as a permanent advance in the organisation of the technical branch of the medical service.[95]

As for the *Field Ambulance Resuscitation Teams*,[96] it is

---

[94] *See pp. 662-4.* The officer in question, Lieut.-Col. Victor Hurley—throughout the war one of Gen. Howse's most trusted lieutenants—had in 1916 been for a few days attached to Surgeon-Gen. Sloggett's headquarters and later was A.D.M.S. on the staff of the D.M.S., A.I.F.

[95] Such teams would have been valuable on the hospital ships and "black" ships at Gallipoli, as indicated in *Vol. I (p. 339)*.

[96] *See Chapter xxi and Appendix No. 14.*

worth noting that Howse's position as Chief Commissioner of the Australian Red Cross Society overseas enabled him to promote more effectively than would otherwise have been possible technical experiments of this kind.

Non-Commissioned Officers. In the matter of postings and appointments, serious difficulty arose, as the commanding officer of No. 3 A.G.H. at the end of the war noted, through

"the tendency for 'dud' officers and other ranks to accumulate in the General Hospital—the latter to a considerable extent due to the fact that the arrangement for reduction to the ranks of seriously inefficient N.C.O's by the Corps Commander was practically impossible in the Australian General Hospitals owing, I infer, to its having to go through the D.M.S's office, and to the great disinclination [for that office] to agree to strong action. I had N.C.O's who were a danger and a disgrace in the unit."

So far as concerned the N.C.O's the difficulty was largely due to the existence (partly through the disbandment of the mushroom "auxiliaries" in Egypt after the Gallipoli campaign) of a considerable surplus of N.C.O's. From the pool thus created the best men, as usually happens, quickly found their way into units and were retained there while the less efficient tended to be poured into it. By order of the D.A.G., A.I.F., before promoting their own men to fill vacancies, unit commanders were forced to draw on any available N.C.O's in this pool. The problem was not confined to the medical service and could only have been overcome by making more use of General Birdwood's powers to eliminate inefficients. He was given, in October, 1917, authority to reduce an N.C.O. for other reasons as well as crime, and to delegate this power. In addition, any member of the force could be returned to Australia for discharge on his decision that their "services were no longer required." But naturally these powers were cautiously used.

III. GENERAL HOWSE'S FIGHT FOR THE PHYSICAL STANDARD OF THE A.I.F.

In this, the second of the two major domains of responsibility into which for convenience we have divided the duties of the Medical Director, we pick up a parable whose story begins in the early chapters of *Volume I*.

At various junctures in this narrative[97] we have traced the development of the problem of the recruit found, on arrival overseas, unfit to serve at the front with the A.I.F. It first appeared as "a cloud on the horizon" in the preparations for Gallipoli; by 1917 it billowed out into a major issue between the A.I.F. and Australia. Some extracts from the correspondence in this long struggle are given in *Appendix No. 5*. The facts within dispute, as they presented themselves to the D.M.S., A.I.F., have been examined to the end of 1917.[98] We have now briefly to follow the further course of the dispute.

Recruits : The "Battle of the Standards"

Until the Somme the Director of Medical Services had had the support of the Director-General in Australia; as the official files clearly show, Surgeon-General Fetherston whole-heartedly tried to back up his D.M.S. overseas.[99] From the beginning of 1917, however, General Fetherston found himself more and more compelled to submit to a policy of dilution, which he was ultimately induced to support, but which General Howse resolutely refused to accept. On his side (it must also be said) General Howse made solid contributions to the solution of the problem in Australia. To check the practice of "impersonation," he urged examination immediately prior to embarkation. To promote correct discrimination he suggested that a board of experienced A.I.F. officers be appointed in Australia, and arranged that his Consultant Physician, Colonel Maudsley, should make available the results of his wide experience as a medical boarding officer. From this came one of the most useful Australian contributions to the clinical records of the war.

"Last night," wrote Fetherston to Howse on 12th July, 1916, "was delivered the extremely valuable paper by Colonel Maudsley which you sent, for which I shall ever be grateful. I would endorse his conclusions almost absolutely. Not only does he show men whom he considers have been wrongly enlisted in Australia, but admits that many of the defects could not have been discovered at the exam. here before they had had the stress of service. His paper will have great weight with the profession here for I propose to have it widely distributed to the M.O's throughout Australia."

---

[97] See, in particular, *Chapter xvi*; and *Vol. I* (under *Index* reference "Reinforcements").
[98] In *Chapter xvi*.
[99] See *Vol. I, p. 412.*

With a view to the education of examining officers the D.G.M.S. asked for a similar report on the surgical side of the problem, which later was compiled for the D.M.S. by Colonel Ryan.[100]

But the problem was not (as suggested by the Director-General) chiefly a clinical one. So early as October, 1916, he himself stated[101] as the crux, that "it is just a question as to whether it is best to send large numbers, or take no risks and send you smaller numbers." He added, "The Prime Minister, Mr Hughes, is very angry because we are rejecting so many."

It was, indeed, at the root a test of the moral fibre of the Australian people and of the vision and steadfastness of their leaders. There is no need to labour here the national involvements of the issue. They derived, in part, from the adherence of Australia to the principle of voluntary enlistment for service overseas, in part to the nature of this war of attrition.[102] But a third and even more potent factor appears in the stubborn refusal of General Howse to budge from the position taken up by him in 1914. By the date which we now have reached, the end of 1917, the matter had assumed the nature of a personal issue between the two heads of the Australian Medical Service, and statements and counter-statements of each side become, in some degree, the tactical thrusts in an administrative battle. In his confidential report to the Director-General on the 22nd of June, 1917, the D.M.S. "lets himself go" in entirely characteristic fashion.

"Am afraid you are still sending a large number of men away for a Cook's tour. They never get beyond Salisbury as they are absolutely unfitted even for service on L. of C.; in fact many are unfit for Home Service. You will admit that I have frequently called attention to the class sent, and now comes a knock-out. I am to make arrangements for an examination of the next lot of reinforcements immediately upon their arrival, and you will get a hell of a report if they are like the preceding ones, but I hope my frequent prayers to you will prevent a rotten lot coming forward. Why don't you put on a man like Giblin at £10,000 a year? It would save the Government that expense in a

---

[100] The chief features of their reports will be summarised in *Vol. III*.

[101] In a letter to General Howse.

[102] In most of the European armies considerable differences in the quality of the best and the worst fighting units became necessary, however much it was desired to avoid them—for example between the German offensive divisions and "trench divisions." In the British Army this differentiation was not carried so far, but still was considerable.

month. I only wish that you could personally examine many of the men sent forward. You would be paralysed with horror as many of the men are so palpably totally unfit for any service. In the days of rush you would certainly be excused, but in these days, when you have plenty of time, you should be able to produce some machinery to avoid such a public waste. I am writing to you strongly on this point because I feel certain you will be called upon later to explain, as it is now being generally talked about. I have referred to it frequently in my despatches only when compelled to do so. I know you have checked it, but it would make your hair turn white if you could see some of the men. Hope the official report after the examination of the July reinforcements will not cause your sudden death."

He added that some men were found unfit for service while still on the transports and were put ashore in South Africa. The Director-General ripostes with a formidable list of men returned "unfit" but in whom his officers could find no serious disability. It was being said, he wrote, that recruiting was "seriously prejudiced" by the return of these men without their having been given a chance to prove themselves.

The Evolution of the "B" Class Problem. The phase of the dispute which eventually led the Minister for Defence to bring it to an issue arose in connection with the employment of "B" class men in Britain and France. Early in 1917, with recruits diminishing and the need for them immensely increased by the vast casualties of the Somme, the proposal necessarily arose. On April 4th, on the instruction of the Minister, a conference of representatives of "State Recruiting Committees" was held at Defence Headquarters, Melbourne, with the Hon. Donald Mackinnon, Director-General of Recruiting, as chairman. Among the sixteen items discussed, which covered every aspect of recruiting, was a proposal to raise the age limit of recruits from 45 to 50.[103] The Director-General of Medical Services, in evidence, was "distinctly against raising the age limit," basing his opinion on the experience of recruiting officers and of information received from overseas. But his medical examining officers (he found) sometimes "winked at men of 48 years of age," and he himself would be "delighted to give special consideration" to the special enlistment of physically fit men between the ages of 45 and 50. He agreed to arrange that an order on this subject be issued.

---

[103] The Queensland representative reported that there were at least still 12,000 fit single men in that State.

The fat was in the fire. From this concession—unfortunate because unworkable—arose an embittered dispute which only ceased with the end of the war, and which has cost Australia a vast and useless expenditure of effort and money.

The next step was a minute from the Minister to the Secretary: "*Re* enlistment of men 45-50 years of age, please prepare a cable to War Office asking for their views." This was done, and, without consulting the A.I.F. Command (the second false step), the War Office replied on May 25th "entirely approving" the suggested enlistment up to 50 years, and commending "men found fit for general service after stringent medical examination" as a "useful addition to Australian forces." The cable continued: "Desire your earnest consideration that men found fit lower categories should be also accepted for duties of nature indicated[104] . . . so far as they can be used for auxiliary services with Australian divisions."

The Chief of the General Staff in Australia (Major-General Legge) took up this suggestion and urged that "recruiting should be thrown open as indicated," and all future recruits "fit for general service" excluded from these lower categories. This, of course, went far beyond Surgeon-General Fetherston's intention, and he submitted against it the views of Generals Birdwood and Howse.

"It has been a general practice," he wrote, "to ask and to follow the wishes of General Birdwood. If 'B' class men are sent from Australia they must be sent to work to Imperial units and not as Australians, and therefore must be handed over to the Imperial authorities entirely. . . . I very much doubt if the Imperial authorities would accept these men. They would be on a higher rate of pay than their own men and this would cause discontent. . . . If employed by the A.I.F. they would take the places now filled by temporary unfit men invalided from the fighting line."

Cabinet dropped the proposal to raise the age limit to 50, but as to recruiting men of lower categories a cable was sent to the War Office on July 10th desiring further information. The eventual reply was that "after consultation with General Birdwood and General Howse it is agreed that in present cir-

---

[104] These duties included: remount and veterinary work, motor transport work, supply duties A.S.C., canteens, clerical and account work, military police duties, building trades work, engineering work, railway work.

cumstances it is inadvisable for you to send men of lower categories."

But the mischief had been done. A considerable number of over-age men and under-age boys had been included among the recruits, and on arrival in England were found senile or immature—unfit for service in the A.I.F.

As for the men not over or under age but unfit for other reasons—from whom came the "Temporary Base" (T.B.) and "Permanent Base" (P.B) men—the problem of these, so far as the A.I.F. was concerned, dated from the time of the instructions given to General Sellheim, the Commandant of Administrative Headquarters, by General White (Chief of Staff of the A.I.F.) when those headquarters were transferred from Egypt to London:—

> "A definite policy as to the disposal of sick and wounded, and of men classed as 'temporary base,' 'permanent base,' and 'permanently unfit,' will be drawn up by the D.M.S. and promulgated."

But it was not till the end of 1916, after the huge losses of the First Somme, that the matter became urgent. By November large numbers of men had been boarded "B2a" and "C1"—in effect suitable for "T.B." and "P.B." The disposal of these men became an acute question and was made the subject of a letter by the D.M.S. to the G.O.C., A.I.F., which defined the position in the A.I.F. throughout the war.[105] For our present purpose it need only be said that the question was treated on a rigidly utilitarian basis. With the premise that four "P.B." or "T.B." men would be required to do the work of one "A" class man, save in a few selected duties, General Howse summed up the position as follows

> "I am very strongly of the opinion that the employment of P.B. men should be very carefully restricted, and limited solely to the officers and men with . . . special qualifications . . . I am strongly opposed to the indiscriminate employment of P.B. men on any large scale."

Practice in the A.I.F. was organised on this basis. In England a travelling medical board examined all soldiers employed as "P.B." once a month, and all classed "B1a" every week. In

---

[105] See Appendix No. 7.

France, by constant importunity, the D.M.S. was able to retain some hold on the exploitation of the "P.B." man.[106]

The action taken in Australia thus inevitably brought about a clash of policy between the A.I.F. and Australia which no projects for the employment of men of inferior category—for example, on munition work in England—could circumvent. While in Australia the gates were opened more and more widely for unfits by the lowering of standards[107] and recruiting laxity, at the other side of the world the D.M.S. was engaged in the vigorous campaign for their return to Australia. This was closely involved with the now stupendous problem of transport to Australia in the face of submarine sinkings which threatened summarily to end the war.

By the sending of a proportion of older, younger, and less fit men overseas the Australian Government was now faced with an awkward problem. These men if returned to Australia would seriously increase the discontent already due to this cause and contribute another factor in the already great difficulties of recruiting.

At the end of August, 1917, General Fetherston brought the matter to a head in the following minute to the Minister for Defence:—

"I have received a private letter from Surgeon-General Howse, in which he states that he is arranging to have all reinforcements medically examined on arrival in England with the object of finding men unfit for service.

"General Howse sets what standard he likes, and therefore the rejection or otherwise of large numbers is absolutely in his hands. If this is to be allowed, and no opportunity given to the men sent overseas to try and make good, then the Australian standard must be very greatly raised, as the standard as interpreted by General Howse for A.I.F. overseas is much higher than that which is being adopted in Australia.

"Some time ago I asked that a letter be sent to General Birdwood, asking if he desired the high standard maintained, which would mean a much smaller number of recruits, but I have not yet received any reply.

"For some time past the Department have been acting on the principle of giving men who had a reasonable chance of doing some service the opportunity to do so, and risking some breakdowns; but if

---

[106] The employment of unfit men in headquarters, and even in field units, quickly became abused, and constant "round-ups" were necessary.

[107] This matter will be dealt with in *Vol. III*. The reduction involved age and physical measurement and dental condition.

we are to be sure that no unfits land in England then every doubtful case must be rejected. This will certainly reduce the number of recruits by one half. Before issuing further orders to make the interpretation of the standard very high and only accept perfect men, I desire instructions in the matter."

On September 11th the G.O.C., A.I.F. Depots in U.K. reported that, of 5,600 reinforcements who arrived in England in the second half of August, 269 were beyond doubt unfit for general service—255 of them permanently unfit.[108]

The lists were set. A cable from the Minister for Defence to the War Office, dated September 25th, urged that "unfit" recruits be not returned to Australia "without being given an opportunity to prove their ability. They are volunteers." As the A.I.F. did not want them they were offered to the War Office for use at the expense of the Australian Government. The War Office asked that they should be put at its disposal and an instruction to this effect was passed by A.I.F. Headquarters to the G.O.C. Depots. Australia was informed that arrangements were being made for the War Office to have them examined, but neither the War Office nor the G.O.C. Depots appears to have taken the matter further. General Birdwood was not informed of these requests, but certain steps were taken in the A.I.F. on December 30th. Birdwood cabled that "all men physically fit to stand the strain of active service" were sent to France "notwithstanding that age is over 45 years." In addition, from April, 1917, a certain number of suitable men of the A.I.F. abroad, found unfit for active service, were transferred to industrial war work in the United Kingdom.[109]

At this stage occurred the Third Battle of Ypres with great successes on the part of the Australian divisions but tremendous casualties. In the same period came the "call-up" of men in Australia for home service; the subsequent failure of the second referendum, and a vigorous recruiting campaign with

---

[108] It was added that nearly 55 per cent. of all arrivals were also dentally unfit.

[109] Including a number of specialists who were taken over by the Ministry of Munitions from the A.I.F. irrespective of their being fit or unfit for active service, only 5 officers and 225 other ranks were absorbed as munition workers from the A.I.F. overseas. Under a system of civilian enlistment of men with certain military disabilities (*e.g.*, slight defects of one eye or of hearing) 6,000 munition workers were sent from Australia to England during the war. The experiment was successful although 600 had to be returned as unfit, whose selection had caused "endless trouble." (*See Aust. Official History, Vol. XI, p. 270.*)

progressive relaxation of the age standard. These events brought danger of the disbandment of one division to maintain the other four. But no more convincing proof could be sought of the rightness of the policy pursued by the D.M.S. than is seen in the resilience of the Australian divisions when they emerged from the filth and toils of that terrible battlefield[110]— the two chapters of this work devoted to it will not have been wasted if they serve to throw up into relief this moral victory. Its influence on the history of the A.I.F. has been recorded.[111]

In effect it settled also the question of reduction of standards. In that matter the climax came at the beginning of 1918. The Minister for Defence noted that of the soldiers returned to Australia up to the end of 1917, 10,333 had not been in any theatre of active operations. On January 12th he minuted:—

"I have for some time been much concerned with the large percentage of rejection of A.I.F. recruits recently in England. These recruits have been medically examined three times before leaving Australia so that it is extraordinary that any unsuitable men should get away.

"The matter is most serious in view of the shortage of recruits, and the effect on recruiting of the returned rejects is disastrous.

"In view of the above I wish General Fetherston to proceed to England about the middle of February to make full enquiry into this matter and any other medical questions that have been the subject of recent correspondence between H.Q., England, and this department.

"Colonel Cuscaden will act as D.G.M.S. during General Fetherston's absence."

As a result there arrived in England, early in May, a commission of enquiry from Australia in the persons of the Director-General of Medical Services (Surgeon-General Fetherston) and the Hon. J. C. Manifold. The D.G.M.S. was to inspect every part of the A.I.F. and to make preliminary enquiries in U.S.A. and Canada into problems of the home base, especially with regard to reparative surgery and artificial limbs.

General Fetherston chose to regard his mission simply as an

---

[110] This fact is brought out by the Australian Official Historian: see *Vol. IV, pp. 947-8.*
[111] In *Chapter x*.

inspection. He established an independent office and, from the outset, his relations with the medical department at Horseferry-road were critical rather than co-operative. He established independent relations with the War Office and G.O.C., A.I.F. His commission included, as well as the specific matters dealt with in the foregoing pages, every aspect of the work of the Australian Medical Services overseas, indeed every important feature of military medical work. Some of the recommendations made by him in his exhaustive and most able report to the Minister for Defence will feature in the account, to be given in *Volume III*, of the response made in Australia to the responsibilities incurred under the "six months' policy." Here it is only required that we follow through, to their final *dénouement*, the two major issues between Australia and the A.I.F.: the enlistment and military employment of men of inferior category, and the treatment of Australian sick and wounded in the Western theatre of war.

<small>Director-General's tour of inspection</small>

As to the first, General Fetherston found that the instruction to place unfit men at the disposal of the War Office had not been carried to its conclusion. He therefore wrote to General Birdwood on May 13th asking that the Minister's direction should

"be given effect to and no man returned to Australia who may be of service either to Australia or to the Imperial authorities. It is further desired that as many of these men as possible may be used in France. . . ."

In a second letter of the same date he took up the still more important question of the standards for the A.I.F. Which alternative would General Birdwood favour—"slightly lowering the standard of medical fitness," or "reduced numbers of reinforcements." He added that the Minister was most anxious that the five divisions should be kept up. These letters were passed to General Howse who on the same day informed General Birdwood that he was "very strongly of opinion that, if the present standard of medical classification in the line is lowered, the efficiency of the Australian Corps as a fighting force will be seriously impaired"; but that "the policy of keeping a large number of men other than 'A' class in France and

England is not a matter upon which, as D.M.S., I am entitled to express an opinion."

General Birdwood, after discussing the matter with General Fetherston in France,[112] insisted upon a standard of "physical fitness to withstand the rigours of the present campaign."

"We must remember that the practically unfailing success attained by the Australian troops must, to some extent at all events, be attributed to the fact that the ranks have been full of really fit men."

He even added that the experience proved it was unwise to enlist "for actual service" men of over 41. The fact that many men found fit in Australia were found unfit on reaching England might partly be due to psychological causes—in the case of a number of men the exultation of enlistment had worn off by the time they were trained and examined for service in France. As to the employment of unfit men, no doubt the British Government could find some service for them, but

"the effect on the A.I.F. of a policy of admitting of promiscuous enlistment in Australia and easy transfer to a labour unit in England cannot fail to be detrimental."

This interview and letter confirmed General Fetherston in the conclusion that

"no reduction in physique of Australians would be acceptable to the authorities overseas," and that, "though they did not say so, they preferred reduced numbers to getting men with poor physique."

On General Fetherston's return to London, a cablegram was sent to the Defence Department reporting the wishes of General Birdwood, and adding a suggestion that a final medical examination of all soldiers should be made at the moment of embarkation in Australia. On July 8th the Minister cabled to Fetherston:—

"Decided to adhere to age limit 45. No action to be taken reference passing unfits to Imperial authority, they should be returned to Australia for discharge. Birdwood's policy reserving class 'B' for men who have served concurred with. Desire that conference be arranged between War Office, A.I.F. authorities, Mr. Manifold and General Fetherston to determine definitely the standard required of recruits for general service."

---

[112] There was difficulty in obtaining permission in time for Mr. Manifold to go to France and he therefore remained in England.

But General Fetherston, who had already seen the War Office officials on this matter, considered that the germ of the matter was not the "printed standards" but their interpretation by examining medical officers; in Great Britain these admitted men "who would not have been taken for home service in Australia." He therefore suggested that General Howse should go to Melbourne to confer with the Minister for Defence.

The decision of the G.O.C., A.I.F., on the advice of his chief-of-staff (General White) and with the general approval of the corps commander (General Monash), that, in this question of physical standards, so far as military considerations would permit, he should be guided by the advice of his technical expert, must be held to accord with the principles which, in this technical age, must obtain in any great communal enterprise. The episode has the added interest that it seems to have been the first time on record that the commander of the military forces of a nation at war was materially influenced in a strictly military decision by his medical adviser.

While General Fetherston was returning to Australia matters developed quickly. The decision of the G.O.C., A.I.F. and reports by the commissioners had been backed by a vigorous continuation of the campaign by Administrative Headquarters against the recruitment of boys under 18 years of age and of men over 40, or of inferior category. On June 3rd the report of the A.D.M.S., A.I.F. Depots in the United Kingdom, after the inquiry undertaken by him, was presented. Colonel McWhae stated:—[113]

"Attached is a statistical report on the disabilities for which invalids have been returned to Australia from No. 2 Command Depot, Weymouth, for the period 6.10.15 to 21.4.18. During this period 39,000 soldiers were invalided, but this report deals with 31,718 only, the medical records for the remaining 7,282 being unavailable. Although the report is not a complete record, it gives a reasonably accurate idea of the chief causes of invaliding. The disabilities may be classified thus:—

I. Disabilities directly due to service   15,089   47·57 per cent.
II. Diseases acquired on service   8,542   26·93 per cent.
III. Disabilities existing prior to enlistment   6,170   19·45 per cent.
IV. Disabilities of which a considerable[114] proportion existed prior to enlistment ..   1,917   6·04 per cent.

[113] Only the relevant parts of the report are given.
[114] In view of the nosological composition of this group, as noted below, the term "considerable" is cautious. Eighty per cent. might be suggested.

"The details of the disabilities are as follows:—
I. Directly due to service: gun shot wounds, 12,469; gas poisoning, 358; trench feet and frost bite, 282; shell shock, 789; concussion of spine, 24; injuries not received by enemy action, 1,167.
II. Diseases acquired on service: general diseases and new growths, 3,313; respiratory diseases, 1,750; disease of the circulatory system, excluding V.D.H. and varicose veins, 1,352; diseases of the nervous system, including mental weakness, neurasthenia, and chorea, 736; diseases of the uro-genital system, 613; diseases of the digestive system, 545; miscellaneous diseases, 156; diseases of the skin, 67; diseases of the nose, 10.
III. Disabilities existing prior to enlistment: senility and premature senility, 3,130; deformities, 810; defective vision, 817; V.D.H., 607; epilepsy, 254; varicose veins, 157; trachoma, 151; pulmonary fibrosis, 87; emphysema, 22; hydatids, 15; spinal curvature, 18; locomotor ataxia, 8; obesity, 6; corns, 4; miscellaneous, 84."

The disabilities included under IV comprised: pulmonary tuberculosis, 580; hernia, 448; deafness, 315; otitis media, 312; miscellaneous ear diseases, 69; osteo-arthritis, 114; urethral stricture, 42; tuberculosis of glands and bones, 25; tuberculosis of testicles, 12.

The report fully supported the contentions of General Howse[115] and the relevant findings were cabled by Administrative Headquarters to the Defence Department in Australia.

"Howse states that 34 per thousand of all reinforcements arriving United Kingdom during 1917 were found unfit for service in France. During January and February this year 33 per thousand. Many of these cases are palpably unfit for any service at home or abroad. Have repeatedly called attention to thousands of unfits being sent during the last three years and nominal rolls have been sent monthly since January 1st 1917 showing full particulars of enlistment and disability of every man returned to Australia. Returned officers, Lieut.-Colonel Poate, New South Wales, and Major Turnbull, Victoria, can give valuable advice, both having examined many of those cases. He again strongly urges that action should be taken to prevent continuance this needless expense, and recommends that every reinforcement be examined seven days before embarkation by competent medical officers, who should personally certify such soldier is physically and mentally sound and appears to be within the age limit. The district commandant should be held responsible that no soldier leaves his district for embarkation as a reinforcement unless he is properly certified. Copy of signed certificate should accompany each reinforcement for information."

In August the Minister authorised a reversal of the policy

---

[115] Mr. Manifold also, in his report, after he had been to Weymouth "and seen the men rejected," said: "It seems impossible to think for one minute that these men could have ever been passed by a medical officer in camp although they may have got through in the rush of a recruiting depot. . . . A number stated they came from Broadmeadows Camp. Some, when asked who passed them in camp, said they had not had a medical examination. Some stated they had been in the 'cook house' as they 'broke down' when marching."

on both issues and a drastic tightening up of recruiting methods. Such account as seems necessary of the action undertaken to give effect to this decision belongs to the next volume.

A Critical Examination of the Issue.[116] It has been shown in this volume and the preceding one how the A.I.F. leaders—and strongest of them all in this, the head of its medical service overseas—resisted any lowering of standard whether by admitting physically inferior reinforcements or by diluting the force with unfit elements for its own wastage. It may be argued that, in pursuing this policy, the leaders were maintaining the prestige of the Australian force at the expense of its Allies—that the A.I.F. could better have helped the common cause by filling out its thin ranks, even if their quality had somewhat deteriorated. It can only be stated here that the D.M.S., who more than any other man was instrumental in having this policy adopted, was himself entirely of the opposite belief. He urged the policy because he believed that a smaller fit force would achieve more in the field than a larger one diluted with unfit men. He was never tired of insisting that the employment of unfit men could not "pay"; that their enlistment was false "economy."

Judgment on the point can only be conjectured; but the quite extraordinary success of the Australian infantry battalions in the last stages of the war must at least furnish a potent warning against any over-hasty assumption that he was wrong. The achievements of these skilled, high-spirited units of 200-300 men was certainly more far-reaching than most onlookers would have expected of units of normal size. The employment of small skilled units produced a salutary circle —the better the men and the leadership, the greater the achievement and the smaller the casualties. It would be, to say the least, a bold speculation to assert that battalions diluted with a proportion of less fit men to a strength of, say 400,[117] would have achieved more. On the other hand, it will probably be conceded that, had the A.I.F. been fighting in its own country, with its back to the wall, use would have been found—either in the infantry or out of it—for large numbers of men even less fit than many of those reinforcements whom its D.M.S. rejected.

Be this as it may, it seems permissible so far to support Surgeon-General Howse as to approve the claim made by him to the Australian Corps commander. "What a glorious record your Corps is making," he wrote to General Monash in September, 1918. "May I humbly say that I attribute a small portion of this success to your medical services. For four years I have set my face and every portion of machinery

---

[116] For this appreciation of the question, from a standpoint of general military history, the writer is indebted to the Australian Official Historian (Dr. C. E. W. Bean), who at the time was engaged on the history of the A.I.F. in the final advance.

[117] This figure would have meant the dilution of the infantry strength of the A.I.F. by a constant quota of about 10,000 men.

behind me to see that only men physically and morally fit should be sent to the front line."

During May, June, and July General Fetherston made a comprehensive and intimate inspection of all the Australian hospitals in Britain and France, and visited British units in which Australians were treated. As a result he urged in a memorandum to the G.O.C., A.I.F., that "an Australian General Hospital be established in England . . and that where possible all serious cases amongst Australians be concentrated either direct from France, or as soon as possible after their arrival in England." Failing the possibility of transferring one of the Australian General Hospitals from France to England and "bringing together some of our surgeons now working in non-Australian units"—which course he himself favoured—he was prepared to raise a new hospital for the purpose in Australia. The question was referred by the G.O.C., A.I.F., to the D.M.S. The latter advised against the step, and was supported in his attitude by General Birdwood. In a minute to the Minister for Defence Birdwood pointed out that in France it was "not feasible . . . to arrange for the A.I.F. to be wholly self-contained"; and for treatment in England urged that "it is advisable from the points of view of efficiency and expediency that the present system should continue . . .^{118}

"Australians to Australian Hospitals"

After completing his inspection and enquiries in Europe General Fetherston continued his tour of inspection of the A.I.F., visiting Salonica (where nurses of the A.A.N.S. were working in British hospitals), Egypt, and Palestine, returning to Australia via India, where also Australian nurses and pharmacists were employed. He arrived back in Australia on November 12th.

General Howse's Mission to Australia

In view, however, of General Fetherston's proposal that Major-General Howse should go to Australia, and in the belief that the interests, not only of the A.I.F. as a fighting force

---

^{118} The correspondence is epitomised in *Appendix No. 2*. A criticism by the Director-General on the food supplied in the Australian Auxiliaries was also referred by General Birdwood to the D.M.S. Some comparison with Canadian and New Zealand procedure will be given in *Vol. III*.

but of the men who had been crippled in its service, would be promoted by the personal influence and advice of General Howse, General Birdwood placed Howse's services at the disposal of the Minister for Defence and personally requested him to undertake the mission.[119] Accordingly, with the Commandant of Administrative Headquarters (Brigadier-General T. Griffiths) and a few other officers, he embarked for Australia via America.[120] He returned to England early in 1919 to assist in the repatriation of invalids and of the medical service; a subject which belongs to the next volume.

Howse's work for the A.I.F. in the war may, however, most properly be appreciated here. In *Volume X* of his monumental *History of the British Army*, the Hon. Sir John Fortescue sums up his account of the work and personality of Wellington's great "Chief of the Medical Department of the Army," Sir James McGrigor, as follows:—

Vale Howse

"McGrigor was indeed an able man in his profession, a thorough soldier and an excellent public servant. He was prompt in disencumbering the army of really disabled patients, and equally prompt in restoring the slightly ill or wounded to the ranks."

"The whole duty" of the head of a medical service could hardly be expressed more tersely and effectively, and his words may well serve as epitaph also to a great Australian.

The post-Armistice history of Australian medical administrative headquarters includes matters of great moment for the post-war problems of the Australian nation. Thorny questions at once arose concerning priority rights in repatriation as between the "invalids" and the rest of the force. The research was set on foot for authentic "lessons of the war" in the interests of the "post-bellum army."

The matter of medical records of the war, both "individual"

---

[119] General Howse was due for "Anzac leave." He himself believed that the war could not end before the summer of 1919.
[120] The party went as far as New York by the Atlantic liner *Olympic*. This vast steamship had arrived from U.S.A. the week before bringing 5,600 American troops, of whom 2,397 suffered from pneumonic influenza, and 141 died on the voyage, or within two days of their landing in England. The Hon. J. C. Manifold, who joined the Australian party at San Francisco, died of this disease on the first day out from San Francisco, but only two or three other cases developed. Arriving in Sydney Harbour on the morning of November 11, their vessel and its passengers were placed in quarantine for ten days.

records of casualty, required for the purpose of pensioning, and general records such as might help to gain some useful fruit of inspiration or of warning from the upas-tree of war, was given such attention as could be diverted from the scramble for the prizes of peace. The story of these, and other matters, which in the aftermath of the war have proved much more important to the nation than they seemed at the time, belongs to the next volume.

APPENDICES

APPENDIX No. 1

STATISTICS OF CASUALTIES IN THE GREAT WAR

(i) TOTAL BATTLE-CASUALTIES (INCLUDING DEATHS FROM DISEASE)[1]

Nation	Mobilised	Killed and died from wounds or disease	Wounded	Missing or Prisoners	Total
British Empire	8,654,467	929,812	2,097,994	32,391	3,063,664
France	8,407,000	1,109,000	3,025,613	252,900	4,387,513
Russia	12,000,000	1,700,000	4,950,000	2,500,000	9,150,000
United States	4,175,367	112,855	224,089	14,363	351,307
Italy	5,500,000	460,000	947,000	1,393,000	2,800,000
Belgium	267,000	104,779	77,422	10,000	192,201
Roumania	750,000	200,000	120,000	80,000	400,000
Serbia	707,343	322,000	28,000	100,000	450,000
Montenegro	50,000	3,000	10,000	7,000	20,000
Greece	230,000	15,000	40,000	45,000	100,000
Portugal	100,000	4,000	15,000	200	19,200
Japan	850,000	300	907	3	1,210
Germany	11,000,000	1,686,061	4,211,469	991,341	6,888,871
Austro-Hungary	6,500,000	800,000	3,200,000	1,211,000	5,211,000
Bulgaria	400,000	101,224	152,399	10,825	264,448
Turkey	1,600,000	300,000	570,000	130,000	1,000,000
Total:					
Allied Powers	41,640,177	4,060,746	11,535,718	4,434,857	20,934,995
Central Powers	19,500,000	2,887,285	8,133,868	2,343,166	13,364,319

[1] The table is taken from "Notes on the History of Military Medicine" by Lieut.-Col. Fielding H. Garrison, U.S.A. Medical Corps, published in *The Military Surgeon*, Aug., 1922. Col. Garrison was Librarian, from 1912 to 1930, to the Library of the Surgeon-General's office, United States Army.

CASUALTIES

(ii) APPROXIMATE BRITISH BATTLE AND NON-BATTLE CASUALTIES[2]

Campaign	Period	Force	Killed	Died of wounds	Died of disease or injury	Missing and prisoners of war	Wounded	Sick or injured	Total
France and Flanders	1914	Whole force	13,009	3,657	508	26,511	55,689	78,040	177,423
	1915		48,604	14,904	2,907	24,556	224,903	576,831	892,765
	1916		107,411	36,879	5,841	43,675	463,697	638,080	1,295,583
	1917		131,761	49,832	8,422	53,794	514,862	1,033,844	1,792,515
	1918		80,476	46,084	14,420	171,288	578,402	1,169,584	2,060,254
Italy	1917-18	British	1,230	58	759	344	4,689	50,552	57,632
Macedonia	1915-18	British and Dominion	2,797	1,299	3,744	2,778	16,888	477,518	505,024
Dardanelles	1915-16	British[3]	11,234	5,346	2,108	7,525	44,721	143,046	213,980
Egypt and Palestine	1915-18	British and Dominion	7,394	2,993	5,981	3,871	37,193	497,396	554,828
Mesopotamia	1914-18	Whole force	11,008	5,281	16,712	15,221	53,697	803,706	905,625
North Russia	1918-19	British and Dominion	187	24	121	177	505	9,461	10,475
East Africa	1914-18	All troops	2,689	754	6,558	1,301	7,777	330,232[4]	349,311
		Followers	376[5]	—	44,911	635	1,333	241,688[4]	288,943
South-west Africa	1914-15	Dominion	185	61	181	782	560	24,565	26,334
Total			418,361	167,172	113,173	352,458[6]	2,004,976	6,074,552	9,130,692

[2] This table has been compiled from details contained in the *Brit. Off. Med. Hist.* (*Casualties and Medical Statistics, p. 12*). In addition to the figures shown, no less than 1,965,646 cases of sickness and injury are recorded among troops in the United Kingdom. The number of deaths is not indicated. Some comparable figures for other national armies will be given in *Vol. III*.

[3] It would appear that the Australian casualties in the Dardanelles Campaign are not included. The A.I.F. figures for Egypt and Gallipoli during 1915 were as follows: Killed, 5,833; died of wounds, 1,985; died of disease or injury, 529; prisoners of war, 70; wounded, 19,441; sick or injured, 63,969; total, 91,827.

[4] 1916-1918 only.

[5] Includes died of wounds.

[6] This total includes 191,412 who were prisoners of war, of whom 16,332 died in captivity.

(iii) RELATIVE PROPORTIONS OF BATTLE-CASUALTIES

	1914	1915	1916	1917	1918	Whole period
Killed to wounded (including died of wounds):						
B.E.F. (including A.I.F.) ..	1:4.6	1:5.0	1:4.7	1:4.3	1:7.8	1:5.2
A.I.F. in France	—	—	1:3.1	1:3.9	1:6.2	1:4.3
Permanent battle losses to wounded less died of wounds:						
B.E.F. (including A.I.F.) ..	1:1.3	1:2.6	1:2.5	1:2.2	1:1.9	1:2.2
A.I.F. in France	—	—	1:2.1	1:2.4	1:3.7	1:2.7

The figures given in this table are derived, the British from the statistical volume of the *British Official Medical History*, the Australian from the records kept by the Australian Section of Third Echelon, B.E.F.

Permanent losses in battle-casualties (from the point of view of the commander in the field) include killed in action, missing, and prisoners of war, and men who subsequently died of wounds or were invalided. *Temporary losses* are the total battle-casualties less all permanent losses.

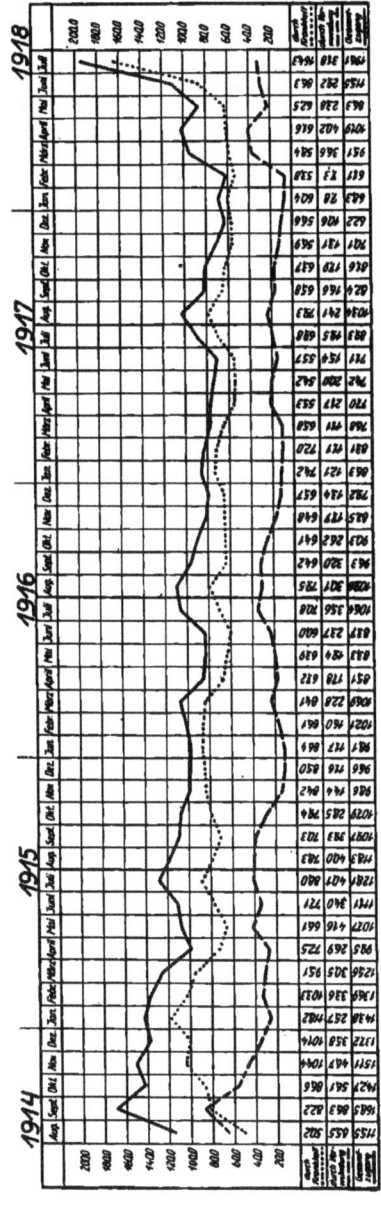

Graph No. 12

SICK AND WOUNDED OF THE GERMAN ARMIES IN THE FIELD

The sick are shown by the dotted line, the wounded by the broken line, and the total by the black line. The figures (which are given to one decimal point) indicate the ratio per 1,000 men.

From *German Official Medical History, Vol. III, p. 19.*

(iv) A.I.F. BATTLE AND NON-BATTLE CASUALTIES SUSTAINED ON THE WESTERN FRONT[7]

	Killed in Action	Died of Wounds	Died of Gas Poisoning	Wounded	Shell Shock (wounded)	Gassed	Prisoners of War	Total Battle Casualties	Died of Disease	Died of Other Causes	Sick	Accidentally Injured	Self-Inflicted Wounds	Total Non-Battle Casualties	Grand Total
1916—															
March	5	1	—	16	—	—	—	22	—	—	38	2	—	40	62
April	59	34	—	187	2	—	—	282	14	8	1,600	4	4	1,720	2,002
May	161	73	1	609	7	8	22	874	15	4	1,029	14	5	1,667	2,541
June	193	70	7	913	41	83	2	1,228	22	12	2,080	20	14	2,148	3,376
July	4,094	624	3	10,843	141	52	569	16,361	26	5	3,532	21	19	3,603	19,964
August	2,895	851	—	9,193	245	5	243	13,482	12	10	3,373	56	20	3,471	16,953
September	688	241	1	1,347	52	14	86	2,419	11	7	3,647	51	16	3,732	6,151
October	216	137	—	854	39	60	10	1,271	15	7	4,768	41	16	4,847	6,118
November	1,293	355	4	2,952	75	—	55	4,794	22	6	12,073	39	21	12,161	16,955
December	344	189	1	977	11	7	5	1,534	94	9	12,113	41	11	12,268	13,802
1917—															
January	335	163	—	1,164	24	4	16	1,706	51	10	10,261	71	14	10,407	12,113
February	619	295	6	2,285	19	44	60	3,328	64	13	9,546	80	13	9,716	13,044
March	652	350	—	2,370	44	28	101	3,545	37	13	8,058	76	13	8,197	11,742
April	1,890	459	3	4,218	34	69	1,829	8,502	32	7	7,420	107	17	7,583	16,085
May	1,908	531	3	6,744	136	159	61	9,542	12	—	6,280	113	17	6,427	15,969
June	1,449	424	2	5,951	77	526	22	8,451	9	5	6,310	70	18	6,433	14,884
July	535	198	1	2,183	20	292	50	3,279	8	26	7,092	80	20	7,206	10,485
August	335	181	3	1,325	12	97	10	1,963	13	8	6,031	38	6	6,096	8,059

[7] The table does not include casualties suffered by the two Australian Mechanical Transport companies before the arrival of the main force, in March-April, 1916. These units, with a total strength of some 10 officers and 550 other ranks, landed in France on 8 July, 1915. (See *Australian Official History, Vol. III, pp. 115-116*).

A.I.F. BATTLE AND NON-BATTLE CASUALTIES SUSTAINED ON THE WESTERN FRONT.—continued

	Killed in Action	Died of Wounds	Died of Gas Poisoning	Wounded	Shell Shock (wounded)	Gassed	Prisoners of War	Total Battle Casualties	Died of Disease	Died of Other Causes	Sick	Accidentally Injured	Self-Inflicted Wounds	Total Non-Battle Casualties	Grand Totals
September	2,570	666	3	9,067	255	332	25	12,918	5	7	5,906	32	15	5,965	18,883
October	4,411	1,233	28	12,378	245	1,675	91	20,061	11	7	8,299	36	23	8,376	28,437
November	323	205	34	1,032	26	1,086	12	2,718	9	10	6,142	17	15	6,193	8,911
December	135	85	1	431	3	150	18	823	17	19	6,401	33	15	6,485	7,308
1918—															
January	100	47	2	288	7	178	6	628	22	4	7,538	22	11	7,597	8,225
February	79	44	3	365	2	328	12	833	16	9	6,473	27	13	6,538	7,371
March	570	192	33	2,311	12	1,756	32	4,906	17	11	7,720	34	40	7,822	12,728
April	1,908	725	74	6,629	37	2,411	330	12,114	16	20	5,748	88	96	5,968	18,082
May	618	404	34	3,034	11	2,120	71	6,292	15	14	7,354	305	63	7,751	14,043
June	604	310	23	2,603	25	474	9	4,048	11	14	7,491	385	42	7,943	11,991
July	738	323	18	3,561	21	1,265	12	5,938	19	16	5,626	464	66	6,191	12,129
August	2,095	790	7	9,210	1	1,957	56	14,116	12	19	5,563	517	29	6,140	20,256
September	1,202	556	10	5,817	—	742	21	8,348	15	21	4,034	436	20	4,526	12,874
October	378	252	16	1,859	—	560	5	3,070	127	7	4,343	234	4	4,715	7,785
November	5	21	1	13	—	13	1	54	186	14	4,609	49	4	4,862	4,916
December	—	5	—	—	—	—	—	5	84	15	3,058	27	—	3,184	3,189
Totals by years—															
1916—	9,948	2,575	18	27,891	613	230	992	42,267	231	68	44,943	289	126	45,657	87,924
1917—	15,162	4,790	84	49,148	895	4,462	2,295	76,836	268	131	87,746	753	186	89,084	165,920
1918—	8,297	3,669	221	35,690	116	11,804	555	60,352	540	164	69,557	2,588	388	73,237	133,589
Grand Totals	33,407	11,034	323	112,729	1,624	16,496	3,842	179,455	1,039	363	202,246	3,630	700	207,978	387,433

APPENDIX No. 2

DOCUMENTS RELATING TO AUSTRALIAN ARMY MEDICAL SERVICES OVERSEAS

(i) CORRESPONDENCE RELATING TO IMPERIAL CO-OPERATION IN THE MEDICAL SERVICES[1]

Letter, dated 4th September, 1917, from Lieut.-General Sir Alfred Keogh, D.G., A.M.S., to the administrative heads of the Medical Services of the Dominions (marked "Secret and Confidential"):—

"For some time the Directors of the Medical Services of Australia, Canada and New Zealand have been in communication with me on a subject which is, I consider, of such importance that I should put it forward whether or not the statements I have to make commend themselves.

"I should premise, however, that many years ago I made an attempt to keep the Medical Services of the Dominions in touch with our own, because it was obvious that the newer services ought to mould themselves on ours—their destiny being to work with us. In the case of Australia this was effected by frequent communication of a personal nature between the Australian D.G. and myself. The former was then engaged in organising the Medical Service of Australia, and in all essential particulars it developed on lines similar to that of Great Britain. The connection with Canada was closer for we were able to secure that selected officers from that portion of the Dominions came to us for instruction in Administration, and were given opportunities of seeing the organisation and its constituent parts from Hospitals up to the W.O. branches. The result was a development in Canada along lines similar to our own. The service in New Zealand was a new formation, but the attitude of the Authorities has been sufficiently displayed by their demand that their Director of M.S. should be appointed from the Royal Army Medical Corps.

"When the present war broke out, the Canadian Divisions were the first to arrive and on my return to the War Office the old connection between the Canadian Medical Administration and myself was resumed. It soon became evident however that the Canadian Medical Service was expected to retain its complete individuality, and the connection was soon loosened. With the arrival of the services of the other Dominions, a similar condition was continued. My own instincts were against this separatist tendency but it was obvious that any attempt

---

[1] See pp. 821-4. The reply of the D.M.S., Canada, is not available.

on my part to weld all the Medical Services together for the common good would have been misunderstood and misinterpreted.

"These three and the other Services now work in Departments in complete isolation from the War Office although the administration of the Australian, Canadian, and New Zealand Medical Corps as well as myself much desire that it should be otherwise. The consequence as we see it is that the Empire does not receive the full benefit of what I may describe as Empire Medical Service. The very many distinguished men of the Dominions are not being effectively used with our own in the consideration of the scientific clinical and disease-prevention problems which have arisen and continue to arise—this is a failure in strength—the problems even in so far as they affect the troops of the Dominions are dealt with entirely by the British Medical profession— the professions of the Dominions are isolated.

"Having observed signs that the administration of the medical branches of the Armies of the Dominions were coming to recognise the disadvantages arising from a policy of isolation I asked them to discuss the question with me. This has been done, and I think I may say that so far as they are individually concerned they are of opinion that the medical resources of the Empire should be pooled for the common object. It is, however, not probable that the political heads of their respective Governments would concur. Nevertheless I think it well to put the facts forward and in a concrete form.

"(1) It is clear that in any scheme of combination with the Dominions, the Dominions would ask that their Medical Corps be not merged in the Royal Army Medical Corps and thus entirely absorbed and disappear, but that they should obtain a share in the control and management of what would be an 'Imperial Medical Administration.'

"(2) That there should remain the individual Medical Corps, British and Dominions, while the administration is combined.

"(3) That the individuals of the respective Medical branches should be available for scientific work, for clinical work and for administrative posts on their merits, irrespective of the services to which they belong.

"(4) That supplies should be furnished by one department instead of as at present—several.

"(5) That the waste of personnel which undoubtedly exists in the maintenance of several Medical Headquarters instead of one would be avoided by combination.

"(6) That while the personnel of the several Medical Corps would as a matter of good administration be kept at work with the Fighting Troops of their respective Armies, they could in fact be available for all and every service which might be thought necessary.

"Principles such as these necessarily mean that the administrators of the Medical Services of the Dominions would take a share in the medical administration at the War Office equal to that of the D.G., A.M.S. So far as I am personally concerned I have no objection, but as a firm believer in personal responsibility and a convinced opponent of Government by Committees, I consider this to be the weak point in the whole conception. I am not in the least anxious to evade my responsibilities, and would prefer to stand or fall by my own work, but the conclusion that the Dominions Medical Administrators must be equal to the D.G., A.M.S., is logical.

"It should be remembered also that my impression as to the possible success of the scheme outlined above is derived rather from the knowledge I possess of the characters and abilities of the present D's.M.S. of the Dominions—their successors and my successor might not work so amicably—moreover to secure the right men the appointments of the former could not be allowed to rest with the Dominions, but should be made by the Army Council. There are obviously great difficulties but I have thought it well to acquaint you as briefly as possible with all the facts."

Reply, dated 14th September, from Colonel W. H. Parkes, D.D.M.S., New Zealand Expeditionary Force:—

"I have perused your memo and consider the six reasons advanced in favour of the scheme for an Imperial Medical Service are so sound and convincing that they admit of no controversy. The real difficulty and one which is likely to meet with much opposition by the Higher Command, is the question of equal representation on a Council with yourself by the Overseas Dominions. It is quite possible that a deadlock might arise in matters where the opinion of the representatives are equally opposed, perhaps on a question not directly concerning the Dominions, and although this may be a remote chance it is a contingency which might occur.

"We have all realised with yourself how important is this objection to the scheme and I candidly do not consider that the D.G., A.M.S., who practically bears the responsibility of the Medical Services of the whole British Empire, should have a share no greater in the medical administration of the War Office than Overseas representatives. One would not expect such a proposal to receive the sanction of the Army Council, and for this reason I beg to suggest a modification of the scheme.

"Why not regard the representatives of the Dominion Medical Services as your Staff Officers with a status as such recognised and confirmed by the War Office? In this capacity they would be available as an advisory council and as representing the respective Services would be in a position to advise how best to promote the proper co-ordination of the Medical Forces in the various parts of the Empire. This cooperation would, I feel sure, prove of immense value in securing the full benefit of the medical talent available but which, under the present policy of isolation, is largely wasted.

"By excluding from the scheme as impracticable the point referring to equal representation, there remains nothing to which, in my opinion, the Army Council could object, and I feel sure that the respective Dominion Governments would welcome an Imperial Medical Service possessing greater possibilities for good as a result of combining the whole medical resources of the Empire."

Reply, dated 28th September, from Surgeon-General N. R. House, D.M.S., A.I.F.:—

"I purposely refrained from answering your communication of

OFFICIAL DOCUMENTS

8.9.17 until I had an opportunity of fully discussing the matter with the Directors of Medical Services of Canada and New Zealand.

"I have carefully considered the clear and concise principles enunciated by you and assuming that I am correct in thinking a Medical Council would be of assistance to the empire and admitting this presumption, I cannot see any logical solution of the question unless each member of the council had an equal share and responsibility in the administration of the Medical Service of the Empire. I am a strong believer in personal responsibility, but might I respectfully suggest that the War has become so vast and carried on under such varied conditions that it has become practically impossible for any one man to control effectively the Medical Services.

"I acknowledge the very great compliment paid me and recognise that it would be a very great honour to be associated with you in the administration of the Medical Services of the Empire, upon which the success of the War so greatly depends; from such an association I should gain much valuable information which would assist me in advising my Government on many of the important Medical questions which must necessarily arise at the termination of a long war."

(ii) CORRESPONDENCE RELATING TO CO-OPERATION BETWEEN THE D.M.S., A.I.F., AND THE D.G.M.S., B.E.F.

Letter, dated 16th June, 1916, from Lieut.-General Sir Arthur Sloggett, D.G.M.S., B.E.F., to Lieut.-General Sir Alfred Keogh:—

"In reply to your letter of 14th instant . . .

"2. With regard to an Australian officer on my staff—the principle has not been followed in the case of the Canadians, and the present arrangements have worked very well. If one Colony is allowed a Headquarters representative others will certainly want the same. The conditions are, I fancy, very different to what existed in parts of the Mediterranean, where nobody seemed to know who was at the head of anything!

"I shall be very glad to see Howse or any other Australian representative at any time in consultation, just as I see Carleton Jones.[2] The D.D.M.S. of the Australian Corps is in close touch with me in the same way that Foster of the Canadians is. I need hardly say that the wishes of the Colonial troops invariably receive my sympathetic consideration, and there has never been any friction.

"3. With regard to the return of Australian medical students there will be no difficulty if the Australian Authorities at home will issue instructions similiar to those for our own people."

Letter, dated 22nd June, 1916, from Surgeon-General N. R. Howse, D.M.S., A.I.F., to Sir Alfred Keogh, commenting on the above:—

"I have the honour to acknowledge receipt of your communication of 19th instant, with Sir Arthur Sloggett's letter attached. I respectfully submit for your consideration:—

"1. At my interview with the D.G., H.Q., British Army in the

---
[2] D.M.S., Canadian Army Medical Service.

Field, I was informed that every effort would be made to employ A.A.M.C. units

(a)
(b) ....

"2. Sir Arthur Sloggett states with regard to an Australian officer on his staff:—

"(a) That the Canadian system works well. As I informed you at my interview I understood the D.M.S., Canadians was approaching you with a similar request to mine as he did not find present arrangement at all satisfactory.

"(b) That if 'one Colony' is allowed a H.Q. representative, others will require the same. I presume this refers to the Dominion of Canada and the Commonwealth of Australia, these being the only Dominions represented by 20,000 troops in France.

"Nobody could have extended a more cordial welcome to me than Sir A. Sloggett and I appreciated it very much on behalf of our Corps. As you know the D.D.M.S. of either of the A. & N.Z. Army Corps cannot advise in any matter outside his Corps, as he would have no knowledge of Australian units attached to any Army or L. of C. I may add there never has been any question of friction—I only wish to be in a position to assist you in every possible way.

"3. . . . I have gone to some length in answering Sir A. Sloggett's communication, because he is probably not aware of my instructions from Defence, Melbourne, and I am anxious to get official information about our units which Defence expects me to communicate in my weekly despatch.

"I can assure you that I have no wish to force an Australian representative upon the D.G., but thought it would be of assistance to him in dealing with the Australian Medical Units. Possibly you can suggest some way out of the difficulty. I return Sir Arthur Sloggett's letter herewith."

(iii) CORRESPONDENCE RELATING TO THE TREATMENT OF AUSTRALIAN SOLDIERS IN GREAT BRITAIN

Letter, dated 18th July, 1917, from the heads of the Australian, Canadian, and New Zealand Medical Services overseas to the Committee of the British Red Cross Society:—

"We are of the opinion that it is advisable to provide a Special Hospital for the treatment of serious facial injuries, where troops from the Dominions of Canada and New Zealand and the Commonwealth of Australia, would be treated by surgeons skilled in plastic surgery. Such a special hospital would not only be of inestimable benefit to the wounded, but surgeons from Overseas would be given the opportunity of working with other members of the Staff, with the object of perfecting the treatment in this very difficult class of surgery.

"We are of the opinion that, if a portion of the money subscribed by the Dominions of Canada and New Zealand and the Commonwealth of Australia for the British Red Cross Society, were allocated for such a special hospital, this would meet the wishes of many of the subscribers."

OFFICIAL DOCUMENTS 871

Letter, dated 9th July, 1918, from Surgeon-General R. H. J. Fetherston, D.G.M.S., A.M.F., to the G.O.C., A.I.F.:—

"Commonwealth Offices,
Australia House,
LONDON, W.C.2.
9th July, 1918

"Memorandum to
General Officer Commanding,
Australian Imperial Force, France.

"*SUBJECT—Australian Hospitals in England and France.*

"Some time ago when the 3rd A.G.H. was first installed at Brighton, it was felt that a long-felt want had been met in that Australian soldiers could be concentrated and treated by Australian Army Medical Corps personnel. I understand that owing to the exigencies of the war, this hospital was moved to France and has since been working at Abbeville. None of the three Australian Auxiliary Hospitals in England can in any way be considered General Hospitals and do not receive patients direct from France.

"The three Australian General Hospitals in France do not have many Australian patients, probably not more than 2 to 5%, and no system of concentrating them in Australian Hospitals exists either in France or England, not even as is done with other Colonies or with special classes of cases such as shell-shock, epilepsy, thigh cases, etc. If it can be done for one colony or for one class of case, it can be done for Australian patients. Much changing and re-arrangement of Hospitals is now taking place owing to the extra danger from aerial attacks, and this is, in my opinion, a favourable opportunity to establish an Australian General Hospital in London or other selected place or places, possibly one each at Southampton and Dover, where serious Australian cases can be concentrated, some direct from France and others at a very early date after their arrival in England and before active treatment and often major operations have been undertaken. It would not be either advisable or practicable to have a hospital large enough to take all cases of Australians who are sick or slightly wounded, but a 2,000 bed hospital should easily be sufficient to attend and care for all serious cases of sickness and injury and work in conjunction with our Auxiliary Hospitals near London. Having patients so concentrated would present many advantages and it would be most gratifying to the invalids themselves to be nursed and attended by Australians. It would also make Australian authorities responsible for correct treatment. At present no real responsibility is placed upon anyone, and it is admitted by those in a position to judge, that the standard of the general hospitals in England varies considerably; and while a member of the staff may be highly skilled in one branch, he may not be competent to undertake difficult cases of another class. The same may be said of an Australian hospital but it should be within the power of those responsible to see that such specialists as are required, are available.

"I strongly recommend that an Australian General Hospital be established in England either by the transference and readjustment of the staff of one of our present General Hospitals, and that where possible all serious cases amongst Australians be concentrated either direct from France or as soon as possible after their arrival in England. Or if it is desired, I will recommend the Hon. Minister for Defence to raise an entirely new Hospital in Australia. This can be done without trouble and sufficient reinforcements be sent forward for the increased personnel. Should any further reduction in the personnel of the Australian Divisions take place, a considerable number of medical officers will be released for other work. Personally I much prefer using the present hospitals for this purpose and bringing together some of our Surgeons now working in non-Australian units."

Letter, dated 18th September, 1918, from Major-General Sir Neville Howse to Headquarters, A.I.F., France:—

"Reference your D.A.G. 87/60 of 24.7.18 forwarding copy of communication from Surgeon-General R. H. J. Fetherston, D.G.M.S. (Australia) dated 9.7.18.

"I have to report that when the Australian Divisions arrived in France in the Spring of 1916, the question of the treatment of Australian sick and wounded on the L. of C. in France, at the Base in France and in England, was most carefully and thoroughly considered from all aspects. It was immediately obvious that it was quite impossible to arrange that all our sick and wounded should be treated in Australian Casualty Clearing Stations and Base Hospitals in France. Unity of control of the evacuation and treatment of all sick and wounded from the British front, irrespective of what portion of the Empire they belonged to, was considered essential.

"With regard to England the former of the two alternatives outlined in General Fetherston's memorandum of 11th July last was decided on, *viz*—'To allow all invalids to be treated by the Imperial Authorities till they were fit to be transferred to Australian Auxiliary Hospitals.' Some of the more important reasons for this decision, were:—

1. The hardships which would be suffered by the invalids in immediately transporting them long distances from the port of arrival in England to an Australian hospital instead of effecting the transfer at a later date when they were in much better condition.
2. The large and unnecessary additional expense of such a policy.
3. The treatment received by our invalids in Imperial hospitals has always been of the best.
4. The great educational[3] value of treating men from the different parts of the Empire under the same arrangements in the same hospitals."

Letter, dated 17th September, 1918, from Major-General Sir Neville Howse to Headquarters, A.I.F., France:—

"Re Food in Australian Hospitals and
 Convalescent Depots in England.

"Reference D.A.G., A.I.F. memo. 87/60 of 24.7.18. Surgeon-General R. H. J. Fetherston, in his memorandum on the above subject dated 9.7.18, makes the following statements:—

---

[3] It is clear from Gen. Howse's correspondence and other records that the term "educational" employed here by him must be given a wide significance, and be understood to connote all the social and "national" adjustments that are involved in the continued possibility of a "Commonwealth of British Nations."

1. 'While this ration may be, and is, sufficient to keep men in health and to supply their vital needs, it is at least a short diet.'
2. 'I have been told by Australian invalids on several occasions that the food was not as much as they had had in some other British hospitals which they named.'
3. 'I know that the scale of food given in New Zealand Hospitals and Homes is much more liberal than in similar Australian Institutions.'
4. 'On my return to Australia I will recommend that such food as fruits, jam, butter, sugar and flour should be sent for use in Australian Hospitals.'

"In reply I have to state :—
1. I entirely agree.
2. Australian invalids may have stated that food was better in British hospitals, but I have repeatedly made enquiries from them in reference to the position and must admit that I have never heard an Australian say so.
3. This is correct, but my advisers are of the opinion, with which I concur, that the Army Council ration is physiologically sufficient and I do not think it justifiable to ask for preferential treatment for Australians over other troops.
4. If the recommendation is approved, and the articles arrive, they will be equally apportioned to all Australian Hospitals in England."

APPENDIX No. 3

ORDERS AND INSTRUCTIONS ILLUSTRATING THE TECHNIQUE OF MEDICAL ADMINISTRATION IN THE FIELD

(i) LETTER, DATED 31st JULY 1916, FROM SURGEON-GENERAL W. G. MACPHERSON, D.D.G.M.S., B.E.F., TO COLONEL C. C. MANIFOLD, D.D.M.S., I ANZAC, IN REPLY TO AN ENQUIRY BY THE LATTER REGARDING THE PROPER PROCEDURE FOR ISSUE OF MEDICAL "ORDERS"

"MY DEAR MANIFOLD,

"With regard to issue of orders, you should be guided by the following principles:—

"(1) All instructions affecting Medical Services only, and of a technical medical nature, you should issue yourself; but it would be well to consult other branches of the staff first, especially if it affects medical preparations for battle, etc. . . . Instructions you issue on this point should only be issued after consulting the general staff. Copies of instructions of this kind should be sent 'for information' subsequently to your D.A. & Q.M.G. and to G.S.

"(2) Any instructions of a general nature, which you wish to issue such as matters affecting billets, sanitation, food, clothing, etc. would be issued by the branch of the staff concerned; as both 'A' and 'Q' branch are controlled in Corps Headquarters by a D.A. & Q.M.G. you simply put up your recommendations or draft orders to D.A. & Q.M.G. for publication or issue 'if approved.'

Yours sincerely,
W. G. MACPHERSON."

(ii) MEMORANDUM PREPARED FOR THE D.G.M.S., B.E.F., BY LIEUT.-COLONEL S.L. CUMMINS IN JANUARY, 1916, AND EMBODIED OFFICIALLY IN INSTRUCTIONS ISSUED BY G.H.Q. BEFORE THE OPENING OF THE SOMME BATTLES

"*Preparatory Measures to be taken by Armies and Corps before undertaking offensive operations on a large scale.*

"25. *Medical Arrangements.*

"When active operations are contemplated, the Commander of a formation will take steps to convey to the Administrative Medical

Officers concerned as much of his plan as he feels justified in communicating, bearing in mind that successful medical arrangements depend largely on precise knowledge of the action proposed and close co-operation between Administrative Services and the Staff.

"Medical arrangements will proceed on the following lines:—

"*At General Headquarters.*

"The Director General, after consultation with the Adjutant General and the Quarter Master General, will arrange with the D.M.S., L. of C. for the accommodation of casualties on the scale anticipated in the Stationary and General Hospitals at Bases, these units being, if necessary, cleared by evacuation to Home Territory where this can be carried out without exciting comment or disclosing plans.

"He will arrange with the Director of Railway Transport for such railway facilities as will ensure the smooth working of Ambulance Trains and with the Director of Inland Water Transport for the use of Ambulance Flotillas when waterways are available.

"He will be prepared to supplement, as far as possible, the arrangements of Medical Services within Formations by holding in reserve spare personnel, vehicles, equipment and medical supplies, so located as to be available without delay, and will, when the information at his disposal indicates that an advance may be expected, make preparations for the sending forward of such additional medical units as may become necessary as the result of the forward progress of the troops.

"*At Army Headquarters.*

"The Director of Medical Services will, in consultation with the A and Q branches of the Staff, make such detailed plans as may be necessary for the collection and evacuation of wounded, the allotment of roads for use by Motor Ambulance Convoys, the Casualty Clearing Stations to which the wounded from the various Corps will be evacuated and the allotment of personnel for entraining duties at railheads. He will discuss with the A.D.R.T. of the railhead area concerned, the details of distribution of Ambulance Trains within that area and formulate, in consultation with D.D's.M.S. of Corps, plans by which co-operation may be obtained between Motor Ambulance Convoys, Clearing Stations and Ambulance trains with a view to avoiding delay of railway traffic.

"He will consider arrangements for equipping and staffing improvised ambulance trains or empty supply trains, these arrangements being made in consultation with the D.G.M.S. at G.H.Q. who will normally hold the medical personnel for this purpose in reserve outside the Army area.

"He will arrange with D.D's.M.S. of Corps, to what extent they are to control the Motor Ambulance Convoys and Clearing Stations in their areas during the operations contemplated and will convey through these officers to the A.D's.M.S. of Divisions as much of the general plan of Medical arrangements as will ensure co-ordination of Medical services at the front.

"When an advance is contemplated, he will arrange for certain of his Casualty Clearing Stations to be held in readiness for a move forward and will discuss with the Staff the best locations for these units in the area to be occupied. It will usually be possible to carry out these moves by road, the lorries of those Clearing Stations that are to remain in their positions being used to supplement the transport of those moving forward to new locations.

"As it usually happens that the strain of receiving and evacuating wounded falls more heavily on some Medical units than on others, the D.M.S. will as far as possible, augment the personnel of the units most actively engaged by transfers from other units in his area.

"*At Corps Headquarters.*

"The D.D's.M.S. of Corps will arrange with the branches of the staff concerned how best to give effect to the general instructions received from the D.M.S. of the Army and for such detailed arrangements as are necessary for the co-ordination of Medical Services within the Corps. They will arrange with the A.D's.M.S. of Divisions as to the points where wounded will be collected for transfer to Casualty Clearing Stations by the Motor Ambulance Convoys, these points being usually at selected Field Ambulances so placed as to be accessible to road traffic at all times and at which the casualties from Advanced Dressing Stations will be concentrated.

"They will see that the D.M.S. of the Army and the officers commanding Motor Ambulance Convoys are kept informed of any change in these arrangements necessitated by movements of the Corps.

"In anticipation of an advance, it may be necessary to hold one or two Field Ambulances or sections of Field Ambulances in reserve ready to move forward, and the question of pooling a certain number of Motor Ambulance vehicles from Field Ambulances for use as a Convoy within the Corps should also receive consideration.

"*At Divisional Headquarters.*

"The A.D.M.S. of a Division combines the duties of an Administrative Medical Officer at Divisional Headquarters with those of an Executive officer in command of a group of three units. When operations are contemplated he will make all administrative arrangements in consultation with the A and Q branches of the staff and will arrange directly with the G.S. branch as to the working of the Field Ambulances during the action.

"No detail that would apply to all situations can be drawn up in advance, but the following questions will always require to be considered.

"Provision of shelter in the form of shell-proof or splinter-proof dug-outs for the wounded at points as close as possible to the fighting line and the location and organisation of Regimental Aid Posts in consultation with the Brigadiers and Regimental Commanding Officers concerned. The provision of special communication trenches for the evacuation of wounded is most desirable where circumstances permit and the width of a stretcher should be borne in mind when these communication trenches are being made. The A.D.M.S. will ensure that co-operation is maintained between Field Ambulances and Regimental Medical Establishments and that the Advanced Dressing Stations are, when possible, so placed as to be accessible to road Transport. That precise instructions as to the use of roads by Ambulance vehicles within

MEDICAL FIELD ADMINISTRATION

the Divisional area are drawn up in consultation with the Q. staff and transmitted to all concerned and that a sufficient reserve in the shape of sub-divisions of Field Ambulances or complete units are held in readiness to cope with any situation that is likely to arise.

"Detailed plans for the co-operation of the bearer divisions or sub-divisions of Field Ambulances with the Regimental Stretcher Bearers will invariably be arranged in advance.

"The closest co-operation between the A.D.M.S. of a division with the D.D.M.S. of the Corps is necessary to ensure successful collection and evacuation of wounded."

(iii) MEDICAL ORDERS AND ARRANGEMENTS FOR AUSTRALIAN CORPS AND A DIVISION, FOR BATTLE OF AMIENS, 8th AUGUST, 1918

AUSTRALIAN CORPS
Medical Instructions No. 35

In accordance with Australian Corps Battle Instructions No. 1 d/1.8.18, the following dispositions will be made:—

1. Right Sector Ys Day	After capture of Green Line	After capture of Red Line
M.D.S. H.14.d.2.2	H.14.d.2.2	Villers-Bret. vicinity
A.D.S. N.26.d.1.3	Villers-Bret. vicinity	Warfusee A'court
D.C.S. M.18.a.5.6	N.26.d.1.3	N.26.d.1.3
Left Sector		
M.D.S. N.4.c.9.2	N.4.c.9.2	Fouilloy vicinity
A.D.S. 0.15.a.5.7	0.15.a.5.7	Hamel vicinity
D.C.S. Les Alencons	Les Alencons	N.4.c.9.2

Gas Centre—St. Acheul H.14.d.2.2

2. i. The disposition of Field Ambulances less Bearer Divisions at Zero hour will be as follows:—

	Right Sector		Left Sector	
	"C" Div.	"A" Div.	"D" Div.	"B" Div.
M.D.S.	X.Fd.Amb.	X.Fd.Amb.	X.Fd.Amb.	X.Fd.Amb.
A.D.S.	Y.Fd.Amb.	Y.Fd.Amb.	Y.Fd.Amb.	Y.Fd.Amb.
D.C.S.	Z.Fd.Amb. (1 t.s-d.)	—	Z.Fd.Amb. (1 t.s-d.)	—
Reserve	Z.Fd.Amb. (2 t.s-d's.)	Z.Fd.Amb.	Z.Fd.Amb. (2 t.s-d's.)	Z.Fd.Amb.

ii. The Reserve (Z) Field Ambulances will be used to form Advanced Dressing Stations in vicinity of Villers-Bretonneux and Fouilloy and will be converted to Main Dressing Stations as soon as situation permits, at which time (X) Field Ambulances will become the reserve.

iii. (Y) Field Ambulances will be used to form Advanced Dressing Stations in vicinity of Warfusee-Abancourt and Hamel.

3. *On "Z" Day.*
   i. A.D's.M.S. "C" & "D" Divisions will be responsible for evacuations from Green Line to Main Dressing Stations. A.D's.M.S. "A" & "B" Divisions will be responsible for evacuations from Red Line to Relay Posts established by them on the Green Line.
   ii. A.D's.M.S. "A" & "B" Divisions will arrange for Bearer Divisions to accompany their respective Brigades until arrival upon Green Line, and that tent subdivisions take over the Walking Wounded Stations at Main Dressing Stations and Advanced Dressing Stations.
   iii. A.D's.M.S. "A" & "B" Divisions will be responsible for evacuations from Red Line to Main Dressing Stations when command passes to their respective Divisions.
   iv. All Medical personnel at posts and stations will be under the A.D.M.S. responsible as laid down in preceding paragraphs.

4. A.D.M.S. "B" Division will detail a blood transfusion team (one Officer three other ranks) to the Main Dressing Station St. Acheul on "Y" day; this team will take charge of all blood obtained from C.C.S's and will be available on demand to the Main Dressing Station St. Acheul.

5. A.D.M.S. "C" Division will detail personnel in charge of Gas Centre St. Acheul. All Haldanes Oxygen Apparatus will be transferred to St. Acheul on "Y" Day.

6. *i.* M.A.C. will evacuate from Main Dressing Stations to C.C.S. Busses will evacuate Walking Wounded from Main Dressing Stations, and from Advanced Dressing Stations direct to Casualty Clearing Stations when situation permits, in which case records will be kept at Advance Dressing Stations.
   ii. M.A.C. at Main Dressing Stations will be reinforced and busses for Walking Wounded will report at A.D.S. N.26.d.1.3 and M.D.S. N.4.c.9.2 at Zero hour.
   iii. A M.A.C. Despatch Rider will be posted at each Main Dressing Station.

7. All sick unlikely to be fit for duty within 24 hours to be cleared on "X" day. No sick will be sent to transport lines, but will be disposed of through the usual medical channels.

8. A.D's.M.S. "C" & "A" Divisions and "D" & "B" Divisions respectively may pool horse and motor transport.

9. Acknowledge.

G. W. BARBER, Colonel,
D.D.M.S., Australian Corps.

Headquarters,
   4th August, 1918.

AUSTRALIAN CORPS
Medical Instructions—Routine No. 13

Reference Australian Corps Medical Instructions No. 35.

1. All patients will be sent to Nos. 20 and 61 Casualty Clearing Stations, VIGNACOURT after midnight 7/8th August, 1918.

MEDICAL FIELD ADMINISTRATION

2. Light Railway Ambulance trains will be available at VECQUE-MONT Light Railway Station on 8th August for walking wounded of Left Sector as follows:—

    5 a.m.—10 trucks, capacity 20 each
    10 a.m.—10 trucks,   20
    10 a.m.—10 trucks,   15
    Noon—10 trucks,   „   15 „

The above trains will run direct to C.C.S's Vignacourt, taking four hours on journey, and will return to be again available eight hours after departure.

3. The A.D.M.S. 3rd Australian Division will detail an Officer and sufficient personnel from Reserve (Z) Fd. Ambces, to receive, accommodate and entrain the walking wounded at Vecquemont Station. The Officer so detailed will make all arrangements direct with 2/Lieut. Anker, Light Railway Operating Officer, who will be posted at Vecquemont Station at 5 a.m. 8th August, 1918.

An orderly with minor dressings and comforts will accompany each train and return with it.

4. Wounded evacuated in returning empty ammunition M.T. from Right Sector will be debussed at Main Dressing Station, St. Acheul. From Left Sector will be debussed at Corps Relay Post.

5. Reference D.D.M.S. Aust. Corps. No. M1116, para. *iii* is cancelled and the following substituted:—

Corps Relay Post will be transferred to 62D/M.2.b.1.8 as from midnight 7th/8th August, 1918.

                                  G. W. BARBER, Colonel,
                                  D.D.M.S. Australian Corps.

Headquarters,
    7th August, 1918.

4TH AUSTRALIAN DIVISION.
Medical Arrangements No. 1
Map Reference Sheet 62D, 1/40,000 & Map "A"

In accordance with 4th Aust. Divisional Order No. 138 the 4th Aust. Division in co-operation with other Divisions of Aust. Corps and 3rd Corps will attack and capture enemy positions from Green to Red Line. Zero day and hour will be notified later.

For this operation, in accordance with Aust. Corps Medical Instructions No. 35, the following will be the Medical Arrangements:—

1. Tables 1, 2 & 3 appended show the disposition of Medical Units of 3rd and 4th Aust. Divisions at the different phases of the attack.

2. Command within the Sector passes to the G.O.C., 4th Aust. Division at Zero plus 4 hours, at which time the responsibility for the clearance of the Sector passes to the A.D.M.S. 4th Aust. Division, all Medical Units of the 3rd and 4th Aust. Divisions being at his disposal.

3. *When Command passes*: The O.C. 4th Aust. Field Ambulance will be responsible for the evacuation of casualties from the Red Line to the M.D.S., all bearer personnel of 3rd and 4th Aust. Divisions being at his disposal.

4. Distribution of 4th Aust. Divisional stretcher-bearer personnel will be notified later.

5. *Blood Transfusion.* Major Holmes à Court and 3 other ranks will be stationed at ST. ACHEUL as a Blood Transfusion Team, and will be available on demand from O's.C. Main Dressing Stations.

6. *Transport.* Horse and motor ambulance waggons of 3rd and 4th Aust. Divisions will be pooled under command of Capt. J. T. Jones, M.C., 12th Aust. Field Ambulance. This pool will be located at O.1.a.4.5 up to Zero hour, and will then be pushed forward as far as circumstances allow. All demands for additional waggons must be transmitted by O's.C. 9th and 4th Aust. Field Ambulances or through the A.D.M.S. in command.

7. *M.A.C.* (Located Sheet 62E/K.30.d.5.3.) Urgent demands for additional M.A.C. cars will be made direct to O.C. 3rd M.A.C. by O's.C. Main Dressing Stations (Aust. C.M.I. Routine 9 para. 1), a despatch rider for this purpose being attached by the O.C. 3rd M.A.C. Extra M.A.C. cars and 10 busses will report to O.C., M.D.S. at N.4.c.9.2, at Zero hour.

8. O.C. 4th Aust. Field Ambulance will arrange for direction boards for all tracks forward of Green Line.

9. *Records* will be kept at M.D.S's and W.W. Dressing Stations except—

(a) cases dressed and returned to duty;
(b) deaths in medical posts.

These will be kept by 13th Aust. Field Ambulance.

10. *A.T.S.* will be given at M.D.S's and W.W.D. Stations.

11. *Gassed Cases* will be sent to the Gas Centre ST. ACHEUL.

12. *Urgent cases* will be marked with a special label tied to the rear handle of the stretcher. Gassed stretcher cases will be similarly marked.

13. *D.C.S.* Only cases likely to be fit to return to full duty in 12 hours will be sent to the Divisional Collecting Station.

14. The A.D.M.S. 3rd Aust. Division has arranged for supplies of Dressings, Drugs, and Medical Comforts to be available at A.D.S. O.15.a.5.7. Dumps of Stretchers and Blankets are at P.13.d.1.5 and P.3.c.2.8.

15. All sick not likely to be fit for duty in 24 hours will be evacuated on "X" day. No sick will be sent to Transport Lines.

16. Field Ambulances acknowledge.

KENNETH SMITH, Colonel
A.D.M.S. 4th Aust. Division.

5 August, 1918.
11 p.m.

Secret

4TH AUSTRALIAN DIVISION

Table 1

	R.A.P's	Relay Posts	M.L. Posts	A.D.S.	M.D.S.	D.C.S.	Remarks
Right	P.21.a.9.2. P.16.c.1.9. P.16.a.1.3.	P.14.c.9.5. P.9.a.3.4.	P.13.d.1.5. P.8.b.2.3.	O.15.a.5.7. 9th Field Ambulance	N.4.c.9.2. 11th Field Ambulance	Les Alencons 10th Field Ambulance 2 Tent Sub-divisions in reserve	As soon as possible after zero hour W.W. Dressing station will be opened at Hospice FOUILLOY O.10.a.9.7 by the 13th Field Ambulance, being evacuated by busses direct to C.C.S.
Left	P.10.c.3.1. P.5.d.o.4.	P.4.a.4.5.	P.3.c.2.8.	13th Field Amb. 3 Tent sub-divisions	12th Field Ambulance 3 tent sub-divisions		This W.W. Dressing Station will also become the A.D.S. for stretcher cases as soon as circumstances allow. The 4th Aust. Field Ambulance Tent Sub-Divisions are at O.10.b.7.9 ready to push forward to establish an A.D.S. in HAMEL vicinity.

The O.C. 9th Aust. Field Ambulance is responsible for evacuation back to M.D.S.
The R.A.P's will advance as soon as possible and Motor Ambulances push forward along VAIRE-HAMEL-CERISY, HAMEL-WARFUSEE and FOUILLOY-WARFUSEE Roads.
3rd Divisional Stretcher Bearers will evacuate cases from GREEN LINE back to A.D.S.
4th Australian Divisional Stretcher Bearers will advance with the 4th Aust. Div. Bdes, but will not evacuate any casualties.
Evacuation from M.D.S. by 3rd M.A.C. cars; busses being used for Walking Wounded.
Gas and blood transfusion centre ST. ACHEUL.

5th August, 1918. 11.00 p.m.

KENNETH SMITH, Colonel,
A.D.M.S. 4th Australian Division.

4TH AUSTRALIAN DIVISION.

Table 2.

Evacuation scheme after capture of Green Line, *i.e.* after commencement of attack by 4th Australian Division.

A.D.S.	M.D.S.	D.C.S.	Remarks
Hospice FOUILLOY o.10.a.9.7 13th F. Amb. Also Walking Wounded Dressing Station.	N.4.c.9.2. 12th F. Amb. and 11th F. Amb.	Les Alencons (1 tent subDivision) 10th F. Amb. 2 tent subdivisions in reserve.	As soon as circumstances allow an A.D.S. will be established in the vicinity of HAMEL by the Tent Subdivisions of the 4th Aust. Field Ambulance, site being selected by O.C. 4th Aust. Field Ambulance. When this A.D.S. is established the FOUILLOY A.D.S. becomes the M.D.S. (2 Tent subdivisions 10th F. Amb. being brought forward to assist). N.4.c.9.2. then becomes the D.C.S. The 3 Tent Subdivisions of 11th F. Amb. and 2 Tent Subdivisions of 12th F. Amb. coming into Reserve.

The O.C. 4th Aust. Field Amb. is now responsible for evacuation back to M.D.S., 4th Australian Divisional stretcher bearer personnel being employed to evacuate cases back to the Green Line.

R.A.P's, Bearer Relays and M.L. Posts will be pushed as far forward as is possible.

Gas Centre and Blood Transfusion Centre ... ST. ACHEUL.

KENNETH SMITH, Colonel,
A.D.M.S. 4th Aust. Division.

5th Aug. 1918.
10 p.m.

MEDICAL FIELD ADMINISTRATION

4TH AUSTRALIAN DIVISION.

Evacuation scheme after capture of RED Line.

Table 3.

A.D.S.	M.D.S. and W.W.D.S.	D.C.S.	In Reserve
Hamel vicinity 4th Field Ambulance.	FOUILLOY 0.10.a.9.7. 13th F. Amb. and 10th F. Amb.	N.4.c.9.2. 12th F. Amb. (1 Tent Sub-division)	2 Tent Subdivisions of 12th Aust. Field Ambulance. 3 Tent subdivisions of 11th Aust. Field Ambulance. 3 Tent subdivisions of 9th Aust. Field Ambulance.

4th Australian Divisional stretcher-bearers evacuate casualties from Red Line to Green Line.
3rd Australian Divisional stretcher-bearers evacuate casualties from Green Line to A.D.S.
Gas Centre and Blood Transfusion Centre . . . ST. ACHEUL.

KENNETH SMITH, Colonel,
A.D.M.S. 4th Aust. Division.

5 August 1918.
11 p.m.

SECRET.
4TH AUSTRALIAN DIVISION.
Medical Arrangements No. 2—4th Aust. Div. Order No. 138.
The following arrangements will be instituted after Zero hour.
1. RECORDS. A. & D. Books for Walking Wounded will be kept by the O.C. 13th Aust. Field Ambulance.

A. & D. Books for stretcher cases will be kept by the O.C. 11th Aust. Field Ambulance.

When the location of the M.D.S. is advanced to FOUILLOY, the O.C. 11th Australian Field Ambulance will notify the O.C. 13th Australian Field Ambulance of the serial number of the last case admitted. 40 numbers will be allowed for cases on road and the A. & D. Books for stretcher cases opened with the resulting number by the O.C. 13th Australian Field Ambulance.

The complete set of A. & D. Books will be handed over to the Division holding the sector after the operation is concluded.

Should the circumstances not permit the establishment of a W.W.D.S. at FOUILLOY until some hours after zero, A. & D. Books for Walking Wounded will be kept by O.C. 12th Aust. Field Ambulance. Similar arrangements for continuance of serial number will be made when W.W.D.S. opens at FOUILLOY.

This continuous serial number for both Stretcher and Walking Wounded will ensure accurate knowledge of the total numbers of Stretcher Cases and Walking Wounded.

2. *BUFF SLIPS.* A.F.W. 3210 will be made out for each casualty by ambulances keeping records and filled by Divisions.

The 3rd Divisional Buff Slips will be collected by D.R. from 3rd D.H.Q. 2nd and 5th Divisional Slips will be delivered to the respective A.D's.M.S. by D.R.L.S.

The O.C. 13th Australian Field Ambulance will arrange to collect all 4th Divisional Buff Slips and distribute them to the units.

3. *CASUALTY WIRES & RETURNS.* To be sent to A.D's.M.S. 3rd and 4th Australian Divisions.

(a) at 6.00 a.m., 12.00 noon, 6.00 p.m. and 12.00 M'night Cas. Wires giving full particulars of Officers and numbers of Other Ranks by *Units* in case of 3rd Aust. Division, and full particulars of Officers and number of Other Ranks by *Divisions* in case of 4th Aust. Division.

(b) Routine D.D.M.S. Wires ⎫ The A.D.M.S. in command will
(c) Routine A.F.W. 3185 ⎬ be responsible for forwarding to
⎭ D.D.M.S. Australian Corps etc.

O.C's Field Ambulances keeping records will also furnish progressive totals of casualties of Officers and Other Ranks by Divisions to A.D's.M.S. 3rd and 4th Aust. Divs. by telephone every two hours.

KENNETH SMITH, Col. A.D.M.S.
4th Australian Division.

6th August, 1918.
3.30 p.m.

(iv) MEDICAL ARRANGEMENTS FOR OPEN WARFARE

Circular memorandum issued by the D.D.M.S., Australian Corps, 12th August 1918:

D.D.M.S. Australian Corps No. M2/8.

Some misconception appears to exist as to the formation, opening, and closing of Main Dressing Stations.

(i) A.D's.M.S. are at liberty to open Main and Advanced Dressing Stations when and where they consider most suitable but the D.D.M.S. and C.O. Motor Ambulance Convoy must be notified by telephone or wire of the intention to open Main Dressing Station, as early as possible, otherwise it will be difficult to clear Main Dressing Station satisfactorily.

(ii) Owing to the limited number of M.A.C. Cars, only one Main Dressing Station can be formed for each Divisional Sector, and, by mutual arrangement between A.D's.M.S. concerned the Main Dressing Station of adjoining Divisions should always, when possible, be in close proximity, to facilitate clearing by M.A.C.

(iii) When a Main Dressing Station opens in a Sector, the station previously acting as Main Dressing Station for that Sector must automatically close at the same hour, and become a Reserve Dressing Station. The M.A.C. will clear remaining patients, and afterwards should it be necessary to send patients to Reserve Dressing Station owing to congestion at Main Dressing Stations on application by C.O. or A.D.M.S. to O.C. Motor Ambulance Convoy.

(iv) In the event of a Division passing through another Division (leapfrogging as in recent operations) to attack a position beyond, tent division personnel of the attacking division must double up at the Main Dressing Station, Advanced Dressing Station, and all Posts of the Division through which the attacking Division passes.

(v) When walking wounded are recorded and evacuated direct from A.D.S. to C.C.S. this portion of the A.D.S. will, to avoid confusion, be known as "Walking Wounded Dressing Station."

(vi) Tent Divisions if desired, or holding parties (D.C.S. Personnel or Dental Units) must be placed in Reserve Dressing Stations, as these stations might again be required in the event of a reverse.

(vii) Notification of changes in location of M.D.S. and A.D.S. must be forwarded to D.D.M.S. at the earliest opportunity.

G. W. BARBER, Colonel,
D.D.M.S., Australian Corps.

Headquarters,
12th August, 1918.

(v) INSTRUCTIONS FOR THE DISPOSITION AND CONTROL OF BEARER DIVISIONS IN AN ADVANCE (ISSUED AS MEDICAL INSTRUCTIONS No. 14 BY THE A.D.M.S., 5th AUSTRALIAN DIVISION ON 20th SEPTEMBER, 1918)

Composition of a Bearer Division. During the continuance of the present mode of warfare, when a Bearer Division is ordered into action with its Brigade, it will consist of (a) 3 Officers. Each in command of a Bearer Subdivision and the senior to be O.C. the Bearer Division. If not more than two Bearer Officers be available, the place of the third may be taken by a competent Bearer N.C.O. at the discretion of the C.O. Field Ambulance.

(b) 3 Bearer Sergeants—1 Corporal—3 Nursing Duty men (1 N.C.O. and 2 men)—3 Drivers—1 Waggon Orderly—1 Q.M. Representative—1 Despatch Rider and 108 Bearers.

Bearer Transport. The Transport accompanying Bearer Division will consist of—1 Horse Ambulance waggon, 1 Limbered waggon, 1 Water cart (equipped with petrol tins).

Stores and Equipment. The Horse Ambulance Waggon in addition to forming the first link in the vehicle evacuation will carry the necessary Stretchers and Blankets. The Limbered waggon is invaluable for the transport of medical and surgical stores over rough or muddy country for the supply of R.M.O's. These stores should include such drugs as may be required to replenish R.A.P's.

Each Bearer Squad will carry forward a supply of first aid material for replenishment of R.A.P's. The total amount of stores and equipment to be carried by the Bearer Division, including Bearer Transport, will be determined by the O.C. Forward Evacuation.

O.C. Forward Evacuation. The Officer in charge of Forward Evacuation of wounded will be, unless otherwise stated, the O.C. the

Advanced Dressing Station. He will be responsible to the A.D.M.S. for the evacuation of casualties from the battlefield to the Main Dressing Station.

Disposition of Bearer Division.

(a) The Bearer Division will move forward under the direction of its O.C.

(b) A Bearer Division, when attached to a Brigade will detail forthwith 2 Bearer Squads and 2 Runners to each Battalion R.M.O.

(c) The remainder of personnel and Bearer Transport will be disposed of by the O.C.

(d) The Corporal will be attached to the O.C. Bearer Division.

Communications. The O.C. Bearer Division will keep close touch with Brigade and during absence from his headquarters leave his assisting Corporal to represent him. The R.A.P.—Ambulance should be made quite clear to R.M.O's by O.C. Bearer Division prior to the commencement of an operation.

Communications may be divided for description into six heads:—

1. Between O.C. Bearer Division and Brigade Staff.
2. Between Bearer Captains and R.M.O's.
    (a) The value of a Red Cross Pennant by day suitably placed cannot be exaggerated.
    (b) The improvisation of a Red Cross Light, by night, shining rearwards, by means of a small biscuit tin and red coloured paper is of value.
    (c) The use of a whistle with certain pre-arranged signals is of value in locating a Medical Post at night.
3. Between O.C. Bearer Division and R.M.O.
    (a) by telegram through Brigade Headquarters.
    (b) by runner.
4. Between O.C. Bearer Division and his Bearer Captains.
    (a) by telegram through R.M.O. of rear battalion.
    (b) by runner.
5. Between O.C. Forward Evacuation and O.C. Bearer Division.
6. Between Officer i/c Field Ambulance Cars and Waggons and O.C. Bearer Division and O.C. Forward Evacuation.

Rationing of Bearer Division. Each Bearer Division will join its Brigade carrying unexpired plus 24 hours rations. The bearers attached to Battalions will be rationed by their respective Battalions as soon as possible after their attachment to Battalions.

Bearer Captains will arrange this with each Battalion concerned and satisfy themselves that the new rationing has commenced and is maintained. The remainder of Bearer personnel will be rationed by Brigade and rations distributed as necessary by Bearer Q.M. Representative.

On a Bearer Division being ordered to rejoin its Field Ambulance the earliest notification should be given to the Ambulance in order that indent for rations may be promptly put in by Unit. This will be notified by O.C. Bearer Division.

MEDICAL FIELD ADMINISTRATION 887

Reports and Returns. 1. O.C. Bearer Division will furnish to the O.C. Forward Evacuation daily by midday a Disposition report showing state of Blankets and Stretchers, disposition of bearer personnel etc. on pro-forma "B" Aust. Corps A.A.M.C. Standing Orders.

2. On the completion of an operation, each O.C. Bearer Division will furnish forthwith a report to the O.C. Forward Evacuation who will report to A.D.M.S.

3. When C.O's Field Ambulances render the daily Ambulance waggon and car return (Appendix 5 A.A.M.C. Standing Orders) add columns for M.A.C. Cars M.A.C. Lorries; and Wheeled Stretchers.

M. H. DOWNEY, Colonel,
A.D.M.S., 5th Australian Division.

(vi) INSTRUCTIONS ISSUED BY THE D.D.M.S., AUSTRALIAN CORPS IN CONNECTION WITH THE ATTACHMENT, FOR TRAINING, OF AMERICAN MEDICAL PERSONNEL

AUSTRALIAN CORPS

Medical Instruction No. 29

In accordance with "G" Australian Corps 188/1872 and Australian Corps Order No. 132.

The 65th American Brigade Group will be attached to the Australian Corps for training and will be accommodated in the Army System from 20th to 23rd inst. On 24th inst. the Brigade Group will be attached to the Australian Divisions in line.

1. The O.C. 129th American Field Ambulance will distribute Sections to be attached to Australian Divisions for training, on 24th inst. as follows:—

"A" Section to "C" Division (5th)
"B" Section to "B" Division (3rd)
"C" Section to "A" Division (2nd)

Arrangements as to time and place of reporting to be made direct between respective A.D's.M.S. and O.C. 129th American Field Ambulance.

2. A.D.M.S., Support Division (4th) will arrange for evacuations from the 65th American Brigade Group while accommodated in the Army System, to the nearest Australian M.D.S. at which the records will be kept, and will detail a Medical Officer and one Sergeant Clerk to report to the 129th American Field Ambulance on 20th inst. for the purpose of giving instruction in A.M.C. Routine &c. during the period the 65th Brigade Group is in the Army System.

3. A.D's.M.S. will arrange that the American Field Ambulance Section attached to their Division reinforces or relieves similar elements at M.D.S., A.D.S., Motor and Bearer Posts; and that American R.M.O's attached to American Troops detailed to their Division, are afforded every facility for instruction in the duties of an R.M.O.

4. American Medical Personnel will invariably serve under the executive Command of their own Officers.

5. A.D's.M.S. will ensure that American Companies or Battalions serving with their Divisions are provided with a proper complement of Regimental Stretcher Bearers, Stretchers, and Medical Equipment.

6. Acknowledge.

G. W. BARBER, Colonel,
D.D.M.S. Australian Corps.

Headquarters,
July 18th, 1918.

(vii) MEDICAL ARRANGEMENTS FOR A RELIEF

A.A.M.C. Order No. 112 (Map Ref. 62C 1/40,000)

In accordance with 4th Aust. Divisional Order No. 149 the 4th Australian Division (less Artillery and 1 Bn. 4th Aust. Inf. Bde.) will be relieved by 46th Division between 21/23rd insts. Command within the Divisional Sector will pass at 10 a.m. 22nd inst. D.H.Q. will close at CATELET at 11 a.m. 22nd inst. and re-open at same time in CAVILLON Area.

1. (a) O.C. 12th Aust. Field Ambulance will hand over the A.D.S. (VENDELLES) and Forward Posts to the O.C. 1/3rd North Mid. Field Ambulance. 250 Stretchers and 500 blankets will be handed over to the incoming Unit—the O.C. 12th Aust. Field Ambulance if necessary, drawing on the M.D.S. to make up those numbers.

(b) O.C. 4th Aust. Field Ambulance will hand over the site at Q.&d. central HANCOURT to the O.C. 1/3rd North Midland Field Ambulance together with all drugs and dressings and oxygen cylinders. All supplies, stretchers and blankets and the Haldanes Four Way Oxygen Sets will be returned to the 3rd M.A.C. Dump. Reliefs in each case will be complete by midnight 21/22nd September, details being mutually arranged between Commanders concerned. Receipts for stores handed over will be forwarded to this office.

2. O.C. 13th Aust. Field Ambulance will be ready to move at 1 hour's notice after 10 a.m. 21st inst.

3. On relief Field Ambulances will be brigaded and will move under orders of the respective Brigade Headquarters and be billetted by them.

4. Casualties occurring while the Division is in the staging area will be evacuated through the 1st Australian Division Main Dressing Station K.15.c.1.8.

5. On arrival in new area O's.C. Field Ambulances will arrange accommodation in accordance with A.A.M.C. Standing Orders Section 11, para. 8.

6. Field Ambulances ACKNOWLEDGE.

KENNETH SMITH, Colonel,
A.D.M.S., 4th Aust. Division.

20/9/18.
5 p.m.

APPENDIX No. 4
STANDING ORDERS FOR A.A.M.C.[1]
AUSTRALIAN CORPS

I. D.D.M.S.

Will receive and transmit orders and instructions from Corps and higher formations. Issue instructions approved by Corps and Circular Memoranda on technical subjects.

II. A.D's.M.S.

1. Will receive and transmit orders from Divisions and higher formations, and issue instructions in the form of Routine and A.A.M.C. Orders, Medical Arrangements, Circular Memoranda on Technical Subjects, and draft Orders relating to the health of the troops, Prevention of Disease, and Medical Arrangements for insertion in Divisional Routine Orders with the approval of the G.O.C.

2. Will make himself acquainted with and apply the principles outlined under the heading Medical Arrangements in "The Training and Employment of Divisions, 1918," S.S.135, issued by the General Staff.

3. Will ensure that Medical Officers on first joining the Division are in possession of these Standing Orders, and such Circular Memoranda and Instructions as he deems necessary for the proper performance of their duties, *e.g.*, Instructions for Medical Boarding, Treatment of Gas Poisoning, Orders relating to the disposal of Mental Cases, Epileptics, N.Y.D.N. Cases, etc.

4. Will inspect the Field Ambulances under his command when the Division is in rest, and also, by courtesy of the Brigade Commander, the Regimental Stretcher Bearers, Sanitary Detachments, Water Details, Maltese Carts with Medical Equipment, and Water Carts of the Brigade.

5. Will ensure that Field Ambulances and the Regimental Service undergo courses of training on the lines suggested in Appendices 1 and 2. A minimum course of 14 days per annum will be carried out in the order indicated, but not necessarily consecutively.

6. Will hold a conference of Quartermasters of Field Ambulances on the second day of each month. C.O's. of units concerned may attend if they so desire.

7. Will ensure that Dental Inspections of all troops are carried out regularly as opportunity offers.

8. Will arrange when the Division is at rest for accommodation for 50 patients per Field Ambulance, and at least five patients per Rest Post of units with Medical Officer attached, and so obviate the necessity of forming a Rest Station.

9. Will post Medical Officers joining the Division for the first

---
[1] Issued on 1 June, 1918.

time, and without previous experience in the field, to a Field Ambulance in order that they may undergo training to fit them to take Medical Charge of a Battalion. As a rule Regimental Medical Officers who have served from six to twelve months with a Battalion will be transferred to a Field Ambulance and trained for Command. When possible Officers will be interchanged between Brigades and their respective Field Ambulances, and thus promote efficiency and harmonious working which is so essential to the successful evacuation of sick and wounded.

10. Will ensure that the D.A.D.M.S. is fully conversant with everything passing through the office.

III. Commanding Officers of Field Ambulances.

1. Will ensure that an Officer, in addition to himself, sees everything that passes through the office.

2. Will ensure that Officers, and particularly newly joined Officers, make themselves acquainted with all orders affecting them, and particularly those concerning Field Medical Cards and the disposal of patients. A file of such orders will be kept in the orderly-room, and will be initialled by each Officer.

3. Regulations regarding Surgical Operations will be strictly observed. No major operations will be performed at Main Dressing Station without the consent of the Officer Commanding, who will be responsible.

4. Will instruct Medical Officers in charge Bearer sub-divisions to accompany the same into action unless otherwise ordered. In the event of a Regimental Medical Officer becoming a casualty the nearest Bearer Medical Officer will take his place and notify O.C. and A.D.M.S. promptly. When casualties are heavy Bearer Medical Officers will assist R.M.O's.

IV. All Medical Officers.

1. Will make themselves conversant with:—
   (a) F.S. Regs. Part ii, Chap. xi (Medical Services).
   (b) K. Regs. paras, 1841-1845, 1857-1860.
   (c) R.A.M.C. Training 1911, particularly Parts ii., iii.
   (d) Regulations for the Army Medical Service, particularly Appendix 51.

Those not in possession of these books can view the first two at the orderly-room of the unit to which they are attached, and the two latter at the nearest Field Ambulance.

2. Returning from leave will report to the A.D.M.S. If unable to report personally owing to unit being too far from Divisional Headquarters, report will be rendered by wire. Officers will not proceed on leave until relieved.

3. Will make a practice of reading Divisional Routine Orders *daily*. Orders are frequently issued which affect them, their patients, or the health of their unit. They will also make themselves acquainted with G.R.O's, A.R.O's, and C.R.O's in so far as they affect the Medical Service.

4. Will render returns called for promptly, on correct date and signed.

5. In charge of R.A.P's and Relay Posts will be responsible for maintaining authorised supply of blankets and stretchers at their posts.

V. Regimental Medical Officers.

1. Will indent on nearest Field Ambulance for Medical Equipment,

STANDING ORDERS FOR A.A.M.C.

Drugs, Dressings, Comforts, etc.; if any difficulty is experienced in obtaining the same, they will at once report the fact to the A.D.M.S.

2. Unless specially ordered:—
   (a) Regimental Stretcher Bearers in action will not be allowed in rear of R.A.P's.
   (b) Field Ambulance Stretcher Bearers in action will not be allowed in front of R.A.P's.
   (c) Relay Stretcher Bearers in action will not be allowed in front of Relay Posts.

3. In event of an advance will instruct bearers with Companies to form Advanced R.A.P., and, when necessary move the R.A.P. to that point. R.A.P's, normally, will be in the vicinity of Battalion Headquarters. As a rule the 16 trained Stretcher Bearers will follow the Companies. The 16 surplus Bearers will be held in reserve.

4. Stretcher Bearers will be instructed to collect patients under cover during severe shelling, and to remove them when safe. Shell holes so used should be marked. A rifle with fixed bayonet, stuck in the ground near shell-hole makes a good marker.

5. When the front is narrow R.M.O's will arrange for their R.A.P's to be in close proximity in order that they may relieve one another. Two or more R.M.O's will not occupy the same R.A.P. unless perfect safety is assured.

6. During action applications for reinforcements, equipment, etc., will be forwarded to O.C. Advanced Dressing Station or to A.D.M.S. through Battalion or Brigade Headquarters.

7. Will at once inform A.D.M.S. and O.C. Ambulance i/c. Evacuation, of the location or change of location of R.A.P's.

8. Will at once notify regimental A.M.C. casualties to the A.D.M.S.

9. Will apply to the C.O. for the necessary material and labour for the construction of R.A.P's, which is a regimental matter.

10. Will forward broken stretchers and damaged equipment to the Field Ambulance, as these can be exchanged for new. All Medical Equipment must be accounted for and will not be disposed of without reference to the competent authority.

11. Will not retain patients in Rest Posts who are unlikely to be fit for duty within the period laid down in D.R.O's. Before a move or anticipated action all Rest Posts and R.A.P's will be cleared at least 24 hours previously.

12. Are responsible that Medical Equipment, Stretchers, Maltese and Water Carts are complete, and will at once report any deficiency or damage to same to the A.D.M.S. Water Details will always accompany Water Carts.

13. Will, after an action, at once indent to complete equipment and arrange with C.O. to complete establishment of stretcher bearers.

14. Will ensure that the infected blankets are sent with infectious patients to the Field Ambulance, others being drawn from the Field Ambulance to replace them.

15. Will train all the stretcher bearers in First Aid and Stretcher Drill, the Regimental Sanitary Detachment in Sanitation, and instruct the Water Details in the use of Poison and Water Test Cases on the lines laid down in Appendix 2.

16. Will make a daily sanitary inspection of the units to which they are respectively attached, and include any necessary remarks in the Daily Sick and Sanitary Reports, point out defects and suggest remedies

to the Orderly Officer. If no action results report in writing to the C.O., duplicate copy of report to A.D.M.S.

17. Will make arrangements for the Prophylactic Treatment of V.D. when the Division is at rest, and at all other times when possible.

18. When posted to a unit are under the orders of the C.O., and at the disposal of the A.D.M.S. Official correspondence will be forwarded through the C.O. Correspondence on technical subjects direct to the A.D.M.S.

19. Attached to Artillery Brigades will be disposed in action as follows: One at the waggon lines, and one forward with the guns, and arrange for mutual relief.

VI. Field Ambulances.

1. When moving in back areas will normally be ordered to move with and under the orders of Brigades with which they are grouped, who will billet them and their patients. When Brigades are employed tactically in forward areas, Field Ambulances will be disposed of to the best advantage by the A.D.M.S., after consultation with the "G" branch of the Division. When Field Ambulances are moving with the Division or a detached Brigade in enemy country, the following is the normal disposition:—

The Bearer Division with horsed ambulance waggons, one G.S. waggon, one water cart, and (if considered necessary) a proportion of a tent sub-division marches with and under the orders of their respective Brigades.

The Tent Divisions with transport less that detached to the Brigade, march with and in front of baggage sections of the Divisional Train and in rear of Divisional Ammunition Columns, and billets with the former.

The Motor Ambulances move up to the Brigade to clear patients at stated hours.

2. The composition of a Bearer Division if ordered on detached duty will be as follows, unless as otherwise stated:—

Bearer Division, less 7 waggon orderlies, 120 all ranks (less sick and men on leave)
Batmen 3
Transport Drivers 5

TRANSPORT

Horsed Ambulance Waggons 3
G.S. Waggon or Limber 1
Water Cart 1

VII. Sanitary Sections.

Sanitary Sections are normally administered by Corps and will be allotted fixed areas. In event of an Australian Division moving out of the Corps area, it will be accompanied by a Sanitary Section detailed by the D.D.M.S., and will be under the command of the A.D.M.S.

A Sanitary Section may be attached to an Australian Division within the Corps area, and will then move with and under the orders of the Division, and be responsible for the sanitation of the Divisional area.

When attached to Divisions, will be employed as follows:—

Personnel allotted to Brigades and Groups of units within the

STANDING ORDERS FOR A.A.M.C.   893

Divisional area as inspectors who will inspect, advise, and report daily to O.C. Sanitary Section.

Personnel allotted for the inspection, marking and testing of water supplies within the Divisional area, and the examination of storage tanks and water carts.

When possible a workshop will be instituted where instruction will be given in methods for the construction and improvisation of sanitary appliances from material readily available to the troops.

Cases of non-compliance with Sanitary Regulations will be reported to the A.D.M.S., who will obtain action by forwarding the report with his comments to the "A" Branch of the Division.

VIII. Dental Units.

Attached to Field Ambulances and Div. Artillery:—

1. Will be disposed to the best advantage by the A.D.M.S., and as far as possible be always allotted to the same Brigades or groups of Units.

2. Attached to Divisions will move with a maximum equipment weight of 350 lbs. Such surplus stores and equipment as are accumulated during stationary warfare will be disposed of under the directions of the S.O.A.D.S.

IX. Special Returns and Reports.

Will be rendered as follows:—

Pro-forma.	Detail.	By Whom rendered	To Whom rendered	When.	Appendix.
A.	Regimental and Field Ambulance Equipment	Q.M's.Fd. Amb.	A.D.M.S. Through C.O.	Last day of Month.	3
B.	Distribution Report	O.C. Fd. Amb. i.c. evac. from line.	A.D.M.S.	Within 3 days of taking over line.	4
C.	Ambulance Waggons.	O.C. Fd. Amb.	A.D.M.S.	Daily.	5
D.	Surplus Blankets and Stretchers.	A.D.M.S.	D.D.M.S.	Within 3 days of taking over line.	6
E.	Medical Arrangements	A.D.M.S.	D.D.M.S. and Copies to all concerned	Within 3 days of taking over line.	7
	Fd. Amb. R.O. (Copy)	O.C.Fd. Amb	A.D.M.S.	Daily.	
	Sick and Sanitary Report (Pro-forma at discretion of A.D.M.S.)	R.M.O.	A.D.M.S.	Daily.	

For the purpose of Return Pro-forma "A.," A.D.M.S. will affiliate units of the Division in proportion to Field Ambulances in addition to their respective Brigades.

X. Training.

Will be carried out on the lines suggested in Appendices 1 and 2.

APPENDIX 1.—Suggested Syllabus of Training for Field Ambulances of the Australian Corps.

Day	Morn. 7–7.30	FORENOON 9.30–11	FORENOON 11.15–12.15	AFTERNOON 2–4.30
1st	Phys. Exer.	Stretcher Drill R.A.M.C. Tg., Par. 380-384.	Squad & Com. Drill, Guard & Picquet Duties.	Practical Instruction First Aid R.A.M.C. Tg., Ch. 30-33 (Bandaging, etc.)
2nd	Ditto	Stretcher Drill R.A.M.C. Tg., Par. 384-397.	Squad and Company Drill Signalling.	Ditto
3rd	Ditto	Stretcher Drill R.A.M.C. Tg., Par. 397-399.	Squad and Company Drill Signalling.	Ditto R.A.M.C. Tg., Ch. 34 (Bleeding, etc.)
4th	Ditto	Stretcher Drill R.A.M.C. Tg., Par. 397-401.	Squad and Company Drill Signalling.	Ditto R.A.M.C. Tg., Ch. 35 (Fractures, etc.)
5th	Ditto	Stretcher Drill R.A.M.C. Tg., Par. 401-405.	Squad and Company Drill Signalling.	Ditto Ch. 35-36 and application of Thomas Splint.
6th	Ditto	Stretcher Drill R.A.M.C. Tg., Par. 401-406.	Squad and Company Drill Signalling.	Tent pitching and preparation of tents for Patients. R.A.M.C. Tg. Part IV. Ch. 25 Section 416-430
7th	Ditto	Stretcher Drill, R.A.M.C. Tg., par. 377-405.		Lecture, First Aid, R.A.M.C. Tg., Ch. 37-42.
8th	Ditto	Stretcher Drill R.A.M.C. Tg., Par. 377-405.	Lect. & Practical Demonstration. R.A.M.C. Tg. Transport of Wounded. Ch. 18, Par.295-300.	Checking equipment and examining contents. Water and Poison Testing cases and explanation of Sanitary Methods in the Field.
9th	Ditto	Stretcher Drill R.A.M.C. Tg., Par. 377-405.	Ditto Chapter 18, Par. 303-321.	Practical Instruction First Aid R.A.M.C. Tg. Ch. 30-33. (Bandaging, etc.)
10th	Ditto	Formation and Movement of Ambulances R.A.M.C. Training, Ch. 21.		Ditto R.A.M.C. Tg., Ch. 34-35, and application of Thomas Splint.
11th	Ditto	Stretcher Drill R.A.M.C. Tg., Par. 377-405.	Squad and Company Drill.	Tent Pitching, Guard and Picquet Duties, and preparation of operating tent and tents for sick.
12th	Ditto	Prep. of G.S. waggons, etc. for patients. R.A.M.C. Tg. Ch. 18, 337-348.	Pract. Dem. of Fld. C'k'g. R.A.M.C. Tg. Ch. 26.	Practical Sanitation R.A.M.C. Tg., Ch. 12.
13th	Ditto	Packing and loading Field Ambulance Equipment. Equipping Field Amb. Waggons.		Formation of Dressing Stn. and laying out of Fld. Amb. encampment for reception of wounded. Preparation of D.C.S., Bivouacs and Shelters. Chapter 15.
14th	Ditto	Route March—Formation and Movement of Ambulances. R.A.M.C. Training, Ch. 21.		

This Course should be carried out in the order indicated, but need not be carried out consecutively, but as opportunity offers. The training should be a minimum course of 14 days per annum. The C.O. will detail Officers, W.O's, & N.C.O's to carry out the training. In addition to this Course, Lectures should be arranged for on Duties of N.C.O's, Clerical Duties, Evacuation of Wounded, Field Medical Organisation, Sanitation, and Elementary Anatomy and Physiology, and by members of the D.H.Q. Staff to Officers on Military Law, Geneva Convention, Care of the Horse, Supplies, etc. Arrangements should be made for the attendance of R.M.O's.

STANDING ORDERS FOR A.A.M.C. 895

APPENDIX 2.

Suggested Training for
REGIMENTAL MEDICAL SERVICE

TEXT BOOK
R.A.M.C. TRAINING—1911

STRETCHER BEARERS

(a) *First Aid.*

PRACTICAL | REFERENCE
(1) Application of Splints. | Part V., Chap. 35
(2) Application of Dressings. | Part V., Chap. 32, 33.
(3) Checking of Haemorrhage. | Part V., Chap. 34.
(4) Bandages & Bandaging. | Part V., Chap. 30.
(5) Improvisation. | Part V., Chap. 44.

LECTURES
(1) First Aid. | Part V., Chap. 27, 28, 29.
(2) Transport of Wounded. | Part III., Chap. 18, especially Para. 306.

(b) *Stretcher Exercises.* | Part IV., Chap. 22, Paras. 380 to 402, Para. 405.

REGIMENTAL SANITARY DETACHMENT

PRACTICAL Improvisation of Sanitary Appliances.
Latrines. Grease Traps.
Refuse Pits. Incinerators.
Destructors. Ablution Places.
Urinals.

LECTURES
Sanitation of Camps, Bivouacs, Billets. Part II, Chap. 12.

WATER DETAILS

PRACTICAL
(1) Water and Poison Testing.

LECTURES
(1) Principles of Disease, Prevention. | Part II., Chap. 6.
(2) Control of Infection. | Part II., Chap. 7
(3) Water Supplies. | Part II., Chap. 8.
(4) Purification of Water. | Part II., Chap. 9
(5) Infectious Cases. | Part V., Chap. 46.
(6) Care of Feet. | Part II., Chap. 11, Para. 114.

C.O's Field Ambulances will furnish Drill Instructor on application by R.M.O.

APPENDIX 3.

AUSTRALIAN FIELD AMBULANCE.

Pro-forma A.

Monthly Report of Quartermaster on Medical Equipment of .... Field Ambulances and affiliated Units for Month Ending ....

UNIT	Water Bottles (medical)	Medical Companions	Surgical Haversacks	Field Medical Panniers	Reserved Field Med. Panniers	Field Surgical Panniers	Field Frac. Boxes	Res. Dressing Boxes	Haversacks with shell dressings	Cases, Water-testing poisons.	Cases, Water-testing Sterilisation.	"S.B." Armlets	Ammonia Capsules	Thomas Splints	Suspension Bars	Wheeled Stretchers	Oxygen Cylinders.	Oxygen Masks	Primus Stoves	Stretchers with Slings Complete	Remarks	Tents O.P.	Tents circ.
Scale for Reg. Unit	2	1	1	1 prs.	1 prs.	prs.			8	1	1	20%	10%	2	2				1	10	Such as under:—		
A.I. Bn.																							
Div. Train																							
D.A.C.																							
San. Sec.																							
Scale for Field Amb.	27	6	21	3	1	3	3	6	18	3	2			22	22	7		1	6	72	"All Shortages Indented for". "F.M. Panniers destroyed by shell-fire." 9-10-17. "1 Med. Companion unaccounted for."	3	12
Field Amb.																							

Q.M. .... Aust. Field Amb.   C.O. .... Lieut.-Colonel, Aust. Field Amb.

N.B.—Scales to be amended when necessary. Scale for Sanitary Sections need not be shown.

STANDING ORDERS FOR A.A.M.C.

APPENDIX 4.   Pro-forma B.

Distribution Report............Australian Field Ambulance.

Date............

Post	Map Location	Blankets	Stretchers	Ambulance Personnel at present at Posts	Ambulance Personnel wanted in case of heavy casualties	Evacuation Routes
R.A.P.						
R.A.P.						
R.A.P.						
Bearer R.P.						
Bearer R.P.						
Bearer R.P.						
A.D.S.						
R.A.P.						
R.A.P.						
R.A.P.						
Bearer R.P.						
Bearer R.P.						
Bearer R.P.						
A.D.S.						

(............Right Sector............) (............Left Sector............)

C.O.............Lieut.-Col.,
Australian Field Ambulance.

N.B.—When necessary add columns for M.D.S., Motor Posts, D.C.S., etc.

APPENDIX 5.

Pro-forma C.

Australian Field Ambulance.
Daily Return of Ambulance Waggons.

Date............

	Fords	Sunbeams	Horse Waggons	Motor Cycles	Remarks
Fit for duty	1	4	1	1	1 Ford } In Workshops
Unfit for duty	1	1	2	1	1 Sunbeam }
					2 Horse Amb. incomplete
TOTAL	2	5	3	2	1 Cycle proceeding to Workshops

C.O............ Lieut.-Colonel,
Australian Field Ambulance.

APPENDIX 6.

Pro-forma D.

AUSTRALIAN DIVISION.

Return of Stretchers and Blankets held by............Australian Division.
Surplus to Mob. Table Equipment.

	Stretchers			Blankets		
............Field Ambce.						
............Field Ambce.						
............Field Ambce.						
TOTALS						

Headquarters,
............, 1918.

A.D.M.S............ Colonel,
............Australian Division.

STANDING ORDERS FOR A.A.M.C. 899

APPENDIX 7. Secret. Medical Arrangements .... Aust. Div. .... Pro-forma E.
Line Held .... to .... Map References ....

LINE	R.A.P's	Relay Posts	Motor and Waggon Posts	Adv. Dressing Station	Main Dressing Station	Div. Collect'g Station	Evacuation
Left Bde.							Routes, Alternative Routes, and Method of Evacuation from R.A.P's to C.C.S. will be shown here.
Right Bde.							

DISTRIBUTION:
.... Motor Ambce. Convoy
.... Aust. Fd. Amb. .... Adv. Depot Med. Stores
.... Aust. Fd. Amb. .... Mobile Lab.
.... Aust. Fd. Amb. No............... C.C.S. Infectious Cases.
.... Dental Unit No............... No............... C.C.S. Ophthalmic, N.Y.D.N., N.Y.D.
.... Dental Unit No............... .... Gassed, S.I.W.
.... Dental Unit No............... with .... D.A.C. No............... C.C.S., Sick and wounded
.... Dental Unit No...............
A.D.M.S. Aust. Branch B.R.C.S. at...............

Headquarters, ..., 1918. A.D.M.S., ..., Colonel, Australian Division.

N.B.—Map Locations and distinctive names (if any) required, e.g. Under Column headed A.D.S. "I.9.c.6.6. Menin Road."

Under Column headed R.A.P. "J.2.d.I.I.," The Tunnels."

Columns will also be added for D.R.S. or C.R.S., etc., when necessary.
Under Distribution, Headquarters of Units will be shown e.g.—"Aust. Fld. Ambulance, A.D.S., Menin Road Evacuation, from Div'l. Front." No............... Adv. Depot Medical Stores—Picquigny.

APPENDIX No. 5

EXTRACTS FROM CORRESPONDENCE CONCERNING THE FITNESS OF RECRUITS SENT OVERSEA

THE report of Colonel Howse, as A.D.M.S., 1st Australian Division, upon the number of unfits found among the first and second reinforcements in Egypt before Gallipoli is referred to in *Volume I*. The reaction in Australia was the tightening up of examination of recruits. In October, 1915, the medical staffs of all Military Districts were instructed to exercise care

"that no man be allowed to pass the standard who is suffering from any disability, likely to be aggravated by service.

"The medical officers are personally held responsible for seeing that all questions on the attestation papers in reference to previous disease, fits, etc. are answered and the answers should be initialled by the examining medical officer. The whole liability is thrown on the medical examiners. This responsibility should be brought home to them."

(Other steps taken in relation to recruiting will be touched on in *Volume III*.)

Concerning a large number of men returned to Australia for medical reasons at the time of the transfer of the infantry divisions from Egypt to the Western Front, General Fetherston wrote to General Howse, now D.M.S., A.I.F.:—

(30th May, 1916) "We have received a list of men returned on the *Karoola* and *Runic* and who have since been medically re-examined. Apparently exertion and climate of Egypt must have had considerable effect on some of the men because men noted by you to be suffering from certain ailments are by the very highest medical opinion we are able to obtain in Australia found not to be suffering from those conditions on arrival. Still we have not had time to examine all the papers and will let you know. Many of them prior to going forward from Australia had been used to very hard work but climate must have had a bad effect. Every man before leaving Australia comes before three and generally four medical men or boards."

FITNESS OF RECRUITS

On August 16th General Fetherston informed General Howse that the question of fitness had been gone into. As to the unfits returned, excluding the wounded,

"reports of medical officers state that they consider between 60 or 70 per cent. should not have been returned, as they are quite fit for service. Every time a man is returned unfit he immediately swears that his condition did not exist prior to enlistment, was unknown to him, or was aggravated by service and claims a pension, which some manage to get—as you know the Defence Department has nothing to do with the granting of pensions."

(17th October, 1916) "Most of the men seem to have been enlisted towards the end of 1915 and early 1916. That was the time when large numbers of men were sent forward for the Remount Units, including officers also, whilst I was away. Large numbers of these were undoubtedly unfit. They were intended for employment as grooms in Egypt but were allowed to volunteer for other services. In this way they became mixed with general reinforcements. .

"If we allow medical officers to reject every man in whom there was a suspicion of tubercle or other disease we would have rejected an enormous percentage and you would have been very short of reinforcements. As it is, under the voluntary system, of all applicants in Victoria about 55 per cent. have been rejected; Queensland stands at about the same; but in N.S.W. they have not been so high, viz., about 40 per cent."

July 1916, General Fetherston to General Howse concerning Colonel Maudsley's report:—[1]

"I would endorse his conclusions almost absolutely. Not only does he show men whom he considers have been wrongly enlisted in Australia but admits that many of the defects could not have been discovered at the examination here before they had had the stress of service."

In November, 1916, Lieut.-Colonel Gordon Craig, O.C. of the Hospital Ship *Karoola* reported:—

"We carried back a lot of men to Australia who should never have left it. This fact should be known by all those Medical Officers who examine recruits. A thorough examination of the feet is not sufficiently appreciated by some. Numbers of our troops have never reached the firing line because route marches and training have proved too much for their tired feet. Unless a man can hop and walk on his toes for about a minute he should be rejected. The number of blind eyes, inguinal hernias, incisional hernias from previous operations, stiff joints, and other obvious defects that have caused the return of soldiers, reflect on the standard of examinations at this end. A keen recruit tries to hide his defects; the examining officer should be keen enough to detect them."

---

[1] *See Chapter xxvi, p. 843.*

30th March, 1917, General Howse to General Fetherston:—

"I am trying to arrange transport for two or three thousand "B" class men; they are absolutely unfit for service. Many of them do not disclose any organic disease upon a carefully conducted clinical examination, but are in and out of hospital, and are quite useless for front line, and practically useless for Home Service. . . . Far better no reinforcements be sent from Australia as they do no duty, and only cause congestion in our hospitals and Command Depots. The class of reinforcements you are sending are not up to the old standard.[2] Headquarters A.I.F. Depots report that 20 per cent. are unfit for the front line."

In May General Fetherston replied:—

"When in Egypt Birdwood put up a paper about the (in)advisability of employing 'B' class men who are Australians anywhere on account of high wages. Send back to Australia anyone you cannot employ fully. I wouldn't keep men in England who cannot do a full day's work for their pay. When they get back to Australia they will have to do some work, we will give them a pension but they will have to work. In my opinion it never pays with the high rate that Australians are paid to keep men who cannot give a full day's work for their pay. It is far better to let them be on pension. As you will see pensions are revised at the end of 6 months."

General Howse's letter of June 22nd has already been quoted.[3] On July 20th he wrote:—

"To-day I have nearly 100 officers and 5,000 men who will be returned before the end of September, and God knows how many more will crop up. This winter will clear out all crocks who have got any chest troubles. We pulled many of them through last year with nursing them, but if this winter is as severe as the last one, they will be cleared in many thousands."

16th October, 1917, General Fetherston to General Howse:—

"If you are only to get first class men, it is good-bye to reinforcements. You would not get 1000 a month of the type you apparently want. Any number of the men that go forward to you have only been from 10 days to 3 weeks in camp. It is just a matter as to whether it is better to send them on to you like that and allow you to do the medical work for them or to keep them in Australia; of course it is a matter of the orders issued by the C.G.S."

---

[2] Not unnaturally, seeing that the height standard had been reduced from 5 ft. 4 in. to 5 ft. 2 in., the standard of vision reduced, and men with minor defects accepted. For special units additional lowering had been approved. Thus men for railway sections and mining corps were accepted up to 50 years, and men with spectacles were allowed to enter the A.S.C., A.M.C., and ordnance corps. Men with minor and curable conditions suitable for operation could be taken into military hospital for treatment. The conditions under which treatment was given was that if the operation was successful the man forthwith enlisted for general service, if not successful agreed to be discharged and had no further claim for compensation or pension. (So many men pleaded disability, as a result of such operations, and were subsequently discharged, that this method was abandoned.)

[3] See pp. 844-5.

January, 1918, General Howse to Colonel Giblin:—

"Defence are annoyed at number of rejections but cannot for the life of me see why they still wish to send unfits unless it be a desire to quote big numbers independent of their fitness."

A later letter says:—

"It is not a question of a very high standard at all, as I went and saw a group of them (reinforcements rejected in England). Old men of 55 and 60, and they looked it, who were absolutely persuaded by the recruiting agents to put down their ages at 40. And similarly with boys of 16 and 17, who were told by the recruiting agencies that they were 21 and entered as such. It is simply a scandal. It is not the medical authorities I blame at all."

APPENDIX No. 6
PHYSICAL STANDARD OF A.A.M.C. PERSONNEL

Criteria laid down by the D.M.S., A.I.F., to regulate the dilution of Field Medical Units with men of inferior category:—

1. In future A.A.M.C. Reinforcements of the following standards will be included in Overseas Drafts.

"A" Class. Fit for General Service.

Grade 1. To be used as reinforcements to Field Ambulances and all Medical Units except those referred to in Grade 2. The standard of fitness to be the same as that required for "A" class infantrymen.

Grade 2. Unfit for employment as Stretcher Bearers but:—
(a) fit for duty with A.A.M.C. details attached to units for Water Duties.

Standard of Fitness.
(i) Able to keep up with Infantry battalions but not possessed of the physique or powers of endurance required of Stretcher Bearers.

(ii) All soldiers whose vision is less than that laid down for General Service with Infantry provided that:—
it is not less than 2/60 in either eye without glasses,
that it can be brought up to 6/18 in one eye with glasses, and that a good field of vision is present as tested by hand movements.

(iii) All soldiers with disabilities of the upper extremities of the following kinds:—
All soldiers whose trigger finger is absent, provided they have been actually tested and found unfit to handle a rifle.
All soldiers with a finger or fingers missing, or cases of injury to palm of hand or wrist, provided they have been tested and found unable to use a rifle or stretcher, but whose hand grip is fairly good and sufficient for the comparatively light duty required of A.A.M.C. Water Details.
All soldiers with injuries to forearm or slight limitation of mobility of the elbow joint but with strong and useful arms, except that after trial they have been found unfit for bayonet fighting.

PHYSICAL STANDARD OF A.A.M.C.

(iv) Soldiers with slight degree of flat feet, pes cavus, corns, hallux valgus, or bunions, who can walk well enough to keep up with infantry battalions but who are unfit for all the duties of an infantry soldier.

(v) Soldiers over the age of 45 provided they are sound and active enough to keep up with infantry battalions on the march.

(b) Fit for the staff of hospitals and medical units on the line of communications.

Standard of fitness.

(i) Soldiers fit for employment on sedentary duties. (Soldiers blind in one eye are fit for this class.)

(ii) All cases of Hernia with well fitting trusses.

2. (1) Area or Standing Medical Boards and S.M.O's of Areas will classify as "A" Class, A.A.M.C. Reinforcements specifying the grade according to the above mentioned standards, when they are examining the following:—

(a) Soldiers previously boarded B2a or C1 at their usual 3 monthly review by Area Medical Boards.

(b) Soldiers of Combatant Units who appear before Standing Medical Boards according to the normal procedure.

(c) All unallotted General Service Reinforcements on arrival from Australia.

(2) All soldiers so classified as "A" Class A.A.M.C. Reinforcements will be notified to this Office on A.M.C. Form 2 or 3, which will be accompanied by the Board Papers in the case of soldiers who have been previously boarded B2a or C1.

3. If the A.D.M.S. concurs in this classification the soldiers concerned will be transferred by these Headquarters to the A.A.M.C. Training Depot, Fovant, where they will be trained in their special duties while awaiting despatch Overseas.

4. All soldiers with Hernia with well fitting trusses will be notified to this Office forthwith without carrying out the procedure laid down in para. 1.

All cases of Hernia without well fitting trusses will be similarly notified to this Office the reason for the absence of a well fitting truss being stated in each case.

The nature of their present employment will be stated.

APPENDIX No. 7
EMPLOYMENT OF "B" CLASS MEN

IN May, 1916, General Birdwood advised the I.G.C., B.E.F. of the A.I.F. policy of returning to Australia all unemployed permanently unfit men owing to the high rate of pay, and in September 1916 requested that all A.I.F. P.B. men in France be sent to England for return to Australia. It was pointed out by G.H.Q., B.E.F. that the services of P.B. men were utilised for employment on the L. of C. and at the Bases in the British Army and that the numbers of Australians employed were proportionate to those used in similar British organisations. A scheme of allocating P.B. men to the Base Depots etc. was therefore drawn up to absorb 700 P.B. men, any in excess of this number to be sent to England for repatriation.

Early in January, 1917, General Howse found it necessary to act strongly in the matter. Both the problem and the policy accepted in the A.I.F. overseas are indicated in the following communication which he addressed to General Birdwood:—

"2nd January, 1917.

"I have to submit the following statement for your consideration in connection with the employment of officers and men of the A.I.F. as P.B. or T.B., that is cases which have been classified as either permanently or temporarily unfit for service in the field, but fit for duty at a base.

"From the point of view of the Medical Services and as a result of my observations since the commencement of the war, I have arrived at the following conclusions.

"*Permanent Base (P.B.) Officers and Men.*

"Officers and men of the A.I.F. who are permanently unfit for further service in the field should be returned to Australia at the earliest opportunity, with the exception of those Officers and men fit for home service and included in one of the following classes:—

    (a) Specially selected officers whose services can be profitably utilised with base units or at the A.I.F. Depots in the United Kingdom, as Instructors, Quartermasters or on Administrative duties.

"B" CLASS MEN

(b) N.C.O's and men specially selected for employment with base units or at the A.I.F. Depots in the United Kingdom, because of their special qualifications or trades, e.g. instructors, clerks, skilled tradesmen and cooks.

(c) Men over 44 years who by reason of their age are unfit for the strenuous work at the front, but who possess special qualifications for employment on Base duties.

(d) The Medical Services of the A.I.F. may recommend the transfer to the A.A.M.C. of specially selected P.B. men for employment at the Base hospitals and depots.

"Machinery for Classifying Officers and Men as P.B.

"The classification of Officers and men as P.B. should be made only after examination by specially selected Boards composed of Australian Medical Officers, and the following principles should be observed.

(1) No P.B. Officer or man should be retained on Base duty, if his disability is thereby likely to be further aggravated, e.g. cases of asthma, bronchitis, rheumatism, neurasthenia, shell shock. By continuing to employ cases such as these instead of returning them to Australia, irreparable injury to their health may be caused, and their pensions correspondingly increased. The Officers and men to be retained should be those whose disabilities will not be aggravated by further service, e.g. loss of a limb or an eye.

(2) All P.B. cases should undergo re-examination every month and possible re-classification. At this medical examination should be submitted a return by the O.C. under whom these cases have been employed, showing the number of days each P.B. man has been unfit for duty since the previous monthly examination.

(3) P.B. cases should be employed only in England or Egypt and not at all in France where the environment, employment and General Conditions are not so suitable and adequate control and supervision more difficult.

"Temporary Base (T.B.) Officers and Men.

"In this class are cases which in the opinion of a Medical Board are fit for Home Service, but unfit for service in the field for a period of *less* than six (6) months.

"Any case unfit for service in the field for a longer period than six (6) months is returned to Australia.

"T.B. Officers and men might be employed in England, France, or Egypt. Many of the temporary unfit cases, such as those after recovery from acute illnesses, those with slight contractions or stiffness of joints following illness or wounds, would be considerably benefited and more quickly made efficient for service in the field by being employed on suitable home service.

"T.B. Cases should be re-examined each month by the S.M.O. of the unit to which they are attached, to determine whether their health is being impaired by their employment or whether they should be re-classified in the light of their progress or otherwise.

"In France the classification of men as T.B. can best be carried out in the Divisional Base Depots. At present the Australian Medical Officer of each Depot sends cases for classification to a Standing Medical Board composed of Imperial Officers.

"As a result of two (2) years' experience I consider it is advisable for Australian Medical Boards to deal with Australians.

"The two Anzac Corps would forward their demands for T.B. men to the Divisional Base Depots, and each month T.B. men so allotted to corps and Divisions should be medically examined and possibly re-classified by the D.A.D's.M.S. of Corps and Divisions respectively.

"To sum up the position, I am very strongly of the opinion that the employment of P.B. men should be very carefully restricted and limited solely to the officers and men with the special qualifications referred to in the earlier part of this communication. I am strongly opposed to the indiscriminate employment of P.B. men on any large scale, for the following reasons:—

(1) It is frequently stated that by employing P.B. men on Base duties a corresponding number of men fitted for service in the field would thus be freed. My experience is that several P.B. men are required to do the same work as one 'A' class man, that P.B. men are more frequently off duty as a result of illness, while their cost of upkeep and rate of pay are the same as in the case of 'A' class men.

(2) By returning P.B. men to Australia many 'A' class men who cannot now be spared from their various civilian employments, would be freed to volunteer for Active Service.

(3) The services of P.B. men on general fatigue duties in Camps and training depots are not required as in every battalion there are from 20-50 men of the unit who are available, viz., those placed on light duties by the Medical Officer, those under detention, and those confined to their lines for disciplinary reasons. These men receive distinct benefit by being employed, for a certain number of hours each day, rather than idling about the camp.

(4) In view of the unsatisfactory results obtained in Egypt from the transfer of P.B. men to the A.A.M.C., I think it most unlikely, except in special cases, that I would recommend any further transfer of P.B. Combatants to A.A.M.C., unless a serious shortage of 'A' class men should occur.

"From a financial point of view the employment of P.B. men is wasteful in the extreme, and the Government does not receive in services rendered by the P.B. men a reasonable return for the money expended.

"With the exception of specially selected P.B. men one 'A' class man is worth at least four P.B. class men. For example, if 2,000 P.B. men are employed, their weekly cost of upkeep, at a moderate estimate, is £4 per week, that is a total annual cost to the Government of £416,000. The work done by these 2,000 'P.B.' Class men could be equally well performed by 500 'A' Class men at an annual cost of £104,000, showing a clear loss to the Government of over £300,000. This does not take into account the further damage to health and correspondingly increased pensions, resulting from the further employment of these 'P.B.' men.

I have purposely refrained from attempting any estimate of the economic value of 'P.B.' men employed in Australia.

"I shall be glad if the Lieut.-General will give this matter his earnest consideration. This matter has been under discussion for a period of more than twelve months and certain conflicting instructions on the subject now exist. . . .

"The practice of the Imperial Authorities as defined in various Army Council Instructions does not greatly assist us, owing to the fact that these Instructions have been drawn up to suit Imperial Conditions, and are not applicable to the Special Australian requirements."

The number of P.B. men was ever increasing and though the question was constantly receiving consideration, by June, 1917, the number employed in France had doubled the authorised allotment of 700 men. The approved allotment was decreased to 640, but by August there was a surplus of nearly 500. On 3rd December, 1917, the D.M.S. wrote to Colonel T. H. Dodds, the D.A.G., A.I.F.:—

The weekly Medical Report of Australian Base Depots, Havre, for week ending Nov. 22nd, 1917, shews that the Bases have an average daily strength of 4,704. Taking the daily average of 686 "P.B." men and 350 "T.B." medical; "T.B." dental; Light Duty Sick Parade; and Light Duty from hospital; and adding thereto a probable 100 "A" Class men on "Permanent Cadre"; we find that 1,136 men are available for full and light duty to look after 3,568—roughly, one (1) man for every three (3)! Apparently my estimate of the value of "B" class was grossly over-stated when I thought that four (4) "B" class men were equal to one (1) "A" class. Roughly speaking 6,500 invalids are now awaiting return to Australia; 3,500 are due to leave before Christmas and I am promised accommodation on Hospital Carriers for another 7,000 to 10,000 in January and February. Would it not be a good opportunity to send back every available "P.B." man? For instance:—

(1) The big excess which is usually carried at Australian Base Depots, Havre.

(2) Every "P.B." man with 2nd Anzac.

(3) Every "P.B." man with 4th Division, now in rest.

(4) Every "P.B." man carried with Anzac Corps (H.Q. and Divisions) when it is withdrawn from the line for rest.

Our present arrangement only admits of excess P. Base men for France being sent to Australia, and those are probably men who have not done long service in France, whilst a man who was made "P.B." in many cases over a year ago, when no excess existed, has no chance of getting back to Australia unless a medical examiner remarks the fact that he will be injured by climatic conditions. I think the present order has overlooked the fact that many of these men were made P.B's in the first case because they possessed unstable nervous systems, and if this be correct, they will probably be irreparably damaged by the unsuitable environment, even although they may not be actually under fire.

"P.B's" are being made so rapidly that if they were all cleaned out of France during December and January it would be quite easy to replace them in 1st Anzac H.Q. and in four (4) Divisions before they went into the line. I say four divisions for even if Referendum says "Yes," it is not probable that five (5) Divisions and Reinforcements will be available before September, 1918. What I wish you to respectfully bring under the notice of the General Commanding is that I have received a great number of complaints from "P.B's" of long service and their relatives that they have been kept in France for long periods whilst men of shorter service have been more fortunate in getting away.

I think this does occur in France; in England I believe it has been remedied to a great extent by selecting for return "P.B's" who have been long at a Camp and have not volunteered to remain. A large number of men are going to vote "No" at the forthcoming election, and I think if the Commonwealth Government gave a definite promise that all men detailed unfit for General Service, for a period of six (6) months would be given an opportunity to return, and selection was made according to date of Medical Board as each Hospital Carrier was available, it would do much to remove a real grievance which now exists, and very greatly decrease the negative vote.

On the 9th of January, 1918, the D.M.S., A.I.F., who had succeeded in getting France largely cleared of P.B's, again communicated with the D.A.G., A.I.F., as follows:

Am afraid you will soon transfer your portion of "P.B." hate to me, but this is really my last appeal for every "P.B." man you have. Report from Base Depots, France for week ending 4th January shews a daily state of 387 P.B. men. After end of this month I can see no transports available to Australia, and we shall probably be compelled to send them via Canada, consequently you will perceive my anxiety to make a complete clearance of any men in excess of those authorised. I hope to send off two transports next week and four at end of January. At present it looks as if these will be the last Hospital Carriers via the Cape.

In May, 1918, instructions were issued by General Birdwood that

"on the score of economy no B Class men are to be kept in France who are not physically fit to be employed on Class B duty; such men are to be evacuated without delay in order that they may be returned to Australia. Class B men physically incapable of giving a sufficient return for 6/- a day with rations, quarters and uniform are not to be kept one day longer than is necessary."

APPENDIX No. 8

MEDICAL ESTABLISHMENTS, A.I.F.

The following shows, in concise form, the chief B.E.F. and A.I.F. Medical establishments as in 1918.

	Officers		Other Ranks A.A.M.C.		Total Medical Corps Personnel	A.A.N.S. Female Nursing Staff
	Medical Officers	Quartermasters	Warrant and Non-commissioned Officers	Privates		
Regimental (Infantry Battalion) Medical Establishment[1]	1		1	4	6	
Field Ambulance[2]	9	1	23	159	192	
Dental Unit	1		2	1	4	
Sanitary Section[3]	1		5	20	26	
Mobile Laboratory[4]	2		1		3	
Advanced Depot of Medical Stores[5]	1		2	4	7	
Motor Ambulance Convoy[6]	4		4	14	22	
Casualty Clearing Station[7]	7		16	62	86	5-15[10]
Stationary Hospital	12	1	20	99	132	27
General Hospital—520 beds	21	1	23	122	167	32
1,040 beds	32	2	36	167	237	73[11]
2,500 beds	38	2	77	209	326	125
Convalescent Depot (Base)	7		4	11	22	
Base Depot of Medical Stores	2		1	7	10	
Dermatological Hospital	32	2	38	229	301	7
Sea Transport Section[8]	2		5	16	23	
Hospital Ship	11	1	19	64	95	21

Footnotes to Appendix No. 8 on p. 912.

[1] 16 combatants from the Battalion strength, including one N.C.O., were allotted as stretcher-bearers. While so employed they wore the Red Cross brassard and came under the Geneva Convention. The "Sanitary Squad" comprised a corporal and 7 other ranks (combatants). One Maltese cart was allotted for carriage of panniers and stretchers. A medical orderly (corporal) and a private (combatants but wearing brassards and protected) were allotted to assist the M.O. The private drove the Maltese cart.

A Field Artillery Brigade had one R.M.O. and 5 medical details attached. The Engineers of an infantry division had one R.M.O. and 6 medical details (2 to each Field Company).

[2] The Transport attached to a Field Ambulance comprised 3 horsed-ambulance waggons and 7 motor ambulances (2 Fords), 10 G.S. waggons, 3 water-carts, 2 motor cycles, 1 bicycle and 1 Maltese cart. The Ambulance was *not* allotted a field cooker—greatly to the detriment of its efficiency and its service to the wounded. With the A.S.C. personnel "attached" for transport, and 4 batmen, the total personnel in 1918 was 241. (For its complete organisation see *Vol. I, p. 8.*)

[3] One 30 cwt. lorry was allotted for tools—later a "box car" was substituted, to the detriment of efficiency.

[4] 1 motor laboratory, and 1 motor car were allotted to the Mobile Laboratory, and 3 A.A.S.C. were attached.

[5] The Advanced Depot of Medical Stores had 1 A.S.C. driver attached and requisitioned transport as required.

[6] The establishment comprised 50 heavy motor ambulances organised in two sections, a workshop lorry, one 30-cwt and 2 store lorries, 4 motor cars and 7 motor cycles. 4 officers and 146 other ranks A.A.S.C. were "attached."

[7] Three 3-ton lorries were allotted to each C.C.S. The personnel was augmented, as required, by surgical teams.

[8] This was the establishment early in 1918. When berths were not available for female nursing staff, the number of A.A.M.C. personnel was increased.

[9] Including Pharmaceutical and Dental officers.

[10] These were not carried on the establishment, but were "attached" when and in the numbers as required.

[11] In the A.I.F., the establishment of female nurses was considerably increased, as many as 92 being allotted to a General Hospital of 1,040 beds. The reason for this will be found in *Vol. I, p. 28*, and in the present volume, *p. 415.*

APPENDIX No. 9
SOME NATIONAL SYSTEMS FOR DEALING WITH CASUALTIES

(i) THE FIELD MEDICAL SERVICE AND METHODS OF THE FRENCH ARMY

THIS note deals with evacuation within the zone of the field armies; it is concerned with general principles and methods as these evolved in the war of 1914-1918. The information is taken chiefly from *Le Service de Santé* (Mignon); *Le Service de Santé, III Armée* (Bassères); and a report by the D.G.M.S., A.M.F. (Surgeon-General Fetherston) of a visit to the French front in July, 1918.[1]

As with the British, the organisation and methods of the French Army Medical Service underwent much development during the war of 1914-1918, this being due chiefly to the influence of the internal combustion engine, which made necessary the creation of the *Hôpital d'Evacuation*—in effect, the Casualty Clearing Station.

General Principles

(a) *Personnel.* The functions and status of the medical personnel of the French Army differed considerably from that of the British, the difference in part deriving from the universal obligation to military service in peace, in part also from the structure of the civil system of medicine in France. In the French Army the line of demarcation between combatant and non-combatant branches of the service is very definite; the cleavage is so great that the officers of equivalent rank are addressed differently. The Medical Service was included among the non-combatant services, together with the service of Supply, Veterinary Service, etc. The personnel of the Army Medical Service (*Service de Santé Militaire*) consisted of officers of the Army Medical Corps and of other ranks of the *Sections d'Infirmiers*.

1. Organisation

The former comprised (1) Physicians and Surgeons (Médecins) and (2) Pharmacists or Apothecaries (Pharmaciens). The ranks available to each were broadly equivalent. Officers belonged either to the "active" army, or to the "reserve." In addition "auxiliary" officers (médecins auxiliaires) were recruited from medical students.

[1] No official history of the Medical Services of the French Army has been produced. The two works used have a strongly personal outlook.

913

The principle of economising specialist personnel was implemented by the employment for non-technical work (administration, discipline, etc.) of officers of the "Intendance," of whom a proportion were allotted to each medical unit.

The "other ranks" of the service (Sections d'Infirmiers) consisted of privates and non-commissioned officers, allotted on lines not dissimilar from those in the British Army. They were organised as stretcher-bearers and hospital orderlies, but within the field units these appear to have been to a considerable extent interchangeable.

(b) *Units.* In the French Army, as with the British, the "Division" was the tactical unit. It had three infantry Regiments each, like our Brigades, of three Battalions. The Army Corps (Corps d'Armée—C.A.) appears to have been more systematically used as a unit than in the British Army, and during attrition warfare played an important part in medical arrangements.

The outstanding feature of the French system, as it evolved during the war of 1914-1918, was a *differentiation of function,* and a corresponding *diversity of structure,* in the medical units. Thus "medical," "supply," "light" and "heavy" mobile surgical field ambulances were distinguished, and specially established and equipped. This principle of specialisation was implemented by an elaborate provision for the *classification of casualties,* and by an appropriate system of "grouping" of medical units for the purpose of evacuation. An important feature of the French scheme was the care taken to ensure continuity of movement and treatment; the unification (as it may be termed) for medical purposes, of the several administrative echelons—Division, Corps, Army—is much in evidence in the endeavour to promote the rapid and exact distribution of wounded to the clinical echelons, the Hôpitaux d'Évacuation; "primary" (Army Corps and Army) and "secondary" (forward area of the Lines of Communication).

These principles emerged gradually in the course of the war and their evolution is instructive. In the pre-war reorganisation of the French medical service the Army adopted the principle of a uniform constitution for the field medical units; and that these should be disposed in echelon. Thus an ambulance when full of wounded would not move until it had cleared itself, but another ambulance, held in reserve, would pass in front of it and carry on its work; the first unit, meantime, carrying on as a stationary treatment centre.

The war "reversed this principle. It showed the need for the specialisation of ambulances (la nécessité de spécialiser les ambulances); to allot one section of them to surgery, another for sick, and a third for those gassed. It has also shown that an ambulance only requires the equipment necessary for its function. Thus, it is useless to equip every ambulance with a case of ophthalmological or otological instruments. . . ."

Some five types of treatment units were allotted to the Armies at the end of the war, in addition to the special treatment unit ("formation")—the Hôpital d'Évacuation.

The Hôpital d'Évacuation (H.O.E.). The history of this unit, as a cog in the medical machinery of war, is as dramatic in the French Army as in the British and German. It is impossible to enter upon this,

NATIONAL SYSTEMS FOR CASUALTIES 915

but the following note—a free translation from General Mignon—has a general interest:—

"The position occupied by the medical units behind the troops in the course of evacuation, was controlled according to the requirements of surgery; and the disposition in depth (échelonnement) of the units was so made that the wounded were placed in hospital earlier in accord with the gravity of their injuries.

"The first consideration in the evacuation of a casualty is to ensure that he is not subjected to a longer journey than he is able to undergo without aggravating his condition. Some must be stopped near the aid post: others can bear a journey lasting from 20 to 30 minutes without a risk of ill effects: the majority can be sent a distance of 100 or 200 kilometres.[2] In all serious wounds it can be said of the patient that —he is in a serious condition and requires prompt surgical treatment; or, that he is a medium, or a slight case and can wait from 12 to 15 hours for his first surgical treatment. Accordingly, the medical service must have three echelons of surgical units; first, near the front for the extremely serious casualties; another beyond the range of the artillery for the ordinarily serious case; the third 100 to 200 kilometres from the line for men whose treatment can be deferred for about 12 hours. These three echelons did in fact actually exist at the end of the war. They were called: advanced group of ambulances; hospitals of primary evacuation (H.O.E. primaire) and hospitals of secondary evacuation (H.O.E. secondaire)."

(c) *The Transport Units.* It is not possible in this note to describe the various special treatment units. The following refers to the element of transport ("Moyens de transport") in the scheme of evacuation; though they had much to do with all forms of first aid.

(i) *The Regimental Establishment.* This comprised both battalion and regimental personnel. The battalion staff comprised a Surgeon-Lieutenant and Auxiliary Surgeon with 4 medical orderlies and 16 stretcher-bearers; the regimental, a Surgeon-Major, Lieutenant-Pharmacist, and a dentist (auxiliary) with a bearer-sergeant and 38 bandsmen who acted as stretcher-bearers.

(ii) *The Division.* The field units comprised various "ambulances" and the divisional stretcher-bearer company (*Groupe de brancardiers divisionaire—G.B.D.*). At the end of the war this was composed as follows—3 military and 2 auxiliary medical officers, 7 apothecaries, 1 administrative officer, a dentist and 177 stretcher-bearers (brancardiers).

(iii) *The Army Corps.* The *Groupe de Brancardier du Corps* (*G.B.C.*), was completely changed in the course of the war. In 1914 it contained 205 stretcher-bearers (brancardiers); in 1918 150 medical orderlies (infirmiers); the officers then being 2 medical officers, 3 pharmacists, 2 administrative officers and a dentist. This *groupe* had no less than 7 horsed and 6 motor waggons for general purposes, including a travelling kitchen (cuisine roulante).

(d) *Motor Ambulance Transport.* Horse ambulance transport seems to have been little used in the field. Motor transport was organised on a dual basis. At first it was entirely controlled by the Army Transport Service. *Liaison* was, however, found so difficult that in November, 1917, the system was changed. Supply and upkeep of the

---

[2] *i.e.*, 62 or 124 miles.

medical motor sections (Sections Sanitaires Automobiles) remained with the Transport Service; their use (*usufruit*) was transferred in 1917 to the medical. Co-ordinating officers were appointed from each service—the *Officier du Service Automobile Regulateur*; and the *Médecin repartiteur des Automobiles*. This scheme appears to have worked well.

(*e*) *The Hôpital d'Évacuation* (*H.O.E.*). At the beginning of the war the establishment of this unit was as follows, and on it was based the vast structure of primary, secondary, and complementary hospitals that evolved with the war of attrition:—a senior officer of the active army (in command); 7 medical officers of the territorial army; 2 apothecaries; 2 officers of the administrative staff; and 40 orderlies.

The French system evolved along lines which can be educed from the above. It was based on the principles (1) that the zone of the Armies must be kept clear—"doctrine du déblaiement de la zone des armées." (2) That this clearance must be based on a comprehensive clinical organisation behind the troops. The special feature of the French field system of treatment centres, was the "grouping" (groupement) at each level (échelon) of evacuation, of ambulances (divisional and corps) and of evacuation hospitals, for various functions; these groups of treatment units being "fed" (so to speak) from a central classification centre or *triage*.

2. Scheme of evacuation

The Triage. "In 1917 *triage* became the pivot of the organisation of the field medical service. Special units were devoted to it; special instructions controlled its functioning; selected personnel was earmarked for it. It takes shape as an organisation apart in the *ensemble* of the medical organisation of the army." The system underwent various modifications at various points of the front and stages of the war; but the general principle became universal.

Ultimately *triage* became the particular function of the *Division* and the *H.O.E.*: in the former in relation with a station (the *poste de secours divisionaire*) which came to resemble our advanced dressing station, but with more exact provision for the treatment of special cases. In 1918 the immense treatment groups of the Corps dwindled, and all efforts centred on evacuation to the two groups of clearing hospitals ("primaire" and secondaire"). The needs of the "intransportables" at each level were met by the allocation of special surgical units or personnel. In common consent this service was admirably organised in the French Army.

Hôpitaux d'Évacuation. The subsequent course of evacuation cannot be carried further than to state that it was based on two groups of evacuating hospitals. The outstanding feature of the evolution of this unit in the French Army was their disposition, dating from the middle of 1918, in two echelons, Army, and L. of C. (D.E.); and the formation of special units which co-operated to implement their clinical functions. These functions are epitomised as follows:—(Mignon, *p. 444*). "The Primary H.O.E's which were placed in the most advanced positions, had two functions: the immediate *triage* of all those evacuated from the front, and the treatment of the wounded who required urgent operation. The Secondary H.O.E's, which were connected with the former by railway, and which were from 100 to 200 kilometres distant from them, were reserved for the reception and treatment of the lightly wounded sent to them by the Primary H.O.E's."

NATIONAL SYSTEMS FOR CASUALTIES 917

The Scheme at Work. The following is abbreviated from Surgeon-General Fetherston's Report—"The personnel of all ranks is smaller than the British and is used with great economy. They push their hospitals and ambulance far forward and deal very rapidly with the wounded. Altogether I formed a high opinion of the work of the French Army Medical Services near the firing line.

"The different units in the field were visited, starting at the regimental *poste de secours,* which corresponds to our regimental aid post. The zone of evacuation is divided into two areas—a forward one in the field—from the front line back to the advanced dressing station or *triage;* and a backward one—from the forward dressing station back to the hospitals of evacuation, or clearing stations.

"Their system of field hospitals, etc. is different from ours, and their so-called ambulances are really hospitals or groups of hospitals, while the bearer section of our field ambulances is [represented by] a separate unit operated by the Regiment (our Brigade), or by the Division.

"The Regimental aid posts are similar to ours, usually in houses, etc. Only emergency work was done—bleeding stopped, splints affixed, and antitetanic serum given. From here patients are sent back by stretcher or ambulance to the 1st Echelon or *Triage Avancé* (advanced dressing station), where emergency operations are undertaken; but cases which can wait are sent to the *triage* of 2nd Echelon—or Groupe d'Ambulances du C.E.—which was about 5,000 yards behind

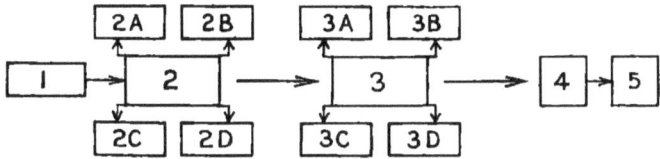

Diagram of Evacuation in Second French Army as at June, 1918.
Adapted from a sketch by Surgeon-General Fetherston.

The numbers indicate:—
1. Poste de Secours régimentaire (Regimental Aid Post); 2. Triage Avancé 1st Echelon (Advanced Dressing Station); 2A. Intransportables absolus (Too bad to shift); 2B. Récupérables, blessés et malades (For return to line within 21 days); 2C. Gazes (Gas Hospital); 2D. Point d'embarquement de C.A. éventuellement (Provisional evacuating point of Army Corps); 3. Groupe d'Ambulances du C.A. Triage 2nd Echelon (Main Dressing Station); 3A. Intransportables (Too bad to send back); 3B. Point d'embarquement de C.A. (Army Corps evacuating point); 3C. Fractures (in particular fractures of the femur); 3D. H.O.E.—Hôpital d'évacuation—primaire (Primary evacuating hospital or C.C.S.); 4. Zone de D.E.—direction des étapes (Head of the L. of C.) Hôpitaux d'évacuation secondaires et complémentaires (Secondary and supplementary C.C.S's); 5. Centres hospitaliers (Hospital centres in the interior).

the front line, where any necessary operations are performed, and X-ray photographs taken with a mobile X-ray plant. The patients, if very bad, are kept there until they are sufficiently recovered to be evacuated —chest, abdominal cases, etc., are kept from two to three weeks; others are evacuated by ambulance right away. Ambulances plying to regimental aid posts and *Triage Avancé* do not go further back than this advanced dressing station, where cases are labelled sitting, walking, or stretcher, and dealt with accordingly. Gas cases are evacuated to gas hospitals. From the *Triage Avancé*, patients who are likely to be fit for the line within two or three weeks are sent to a hospital near by, and not evacuated further. The absolutely untransportables are treated in the hospital until they are fit to be sent further back. All other cases go to the *2nd Echelon Triage*, either in buses (walking cases), or in ambulances. All cases in the advanced station who will not require to have their dressing removed until they arrive at the clearing station, are so labelled, and are not touched at the 2nd Echelon Triage.

"From the 2nd Echelon Triage, all thigh cases—fractures, etc.—are sent direct to special thigh hospitals, after being operated upon, if necessary, and put in suitable splints. The *Médecin Chef de Service* of the Army Corps (D.D.M.S.) said the feeling was that the 1st and 2nd Echelon Triage stations should in the future be amalgamated, so that there would only be one station between the regimental *poste de secours* and the *hôpital d'évacuation.*

"The whole system of evacuation as I saw it was very simple and very efficient, and all provision was made for feeding the patients, etc., at the different stations. There were specially heated "shock" rooms, where these patients are kept while recovering from or awaiting operation. The operating rooms at both advanced and rear dressing stations were specially heated and when the patient had been undressed and washed, he was sent right into the operating room without putting on fresh clothes. This is possible on account of the heating of the rooms, and saves a great quantity of laundry work. Fracture cases are thoroughly immobilised before being sent backwards."

(ii) THE MEDICAL DEPARTMENT OF THE UNITED STATES ARMY

The organisation of the American "Sanitary" (Medical) Service, for field work, has been described briefly but perhaps sufficiently in the text.[3] Their scheme of evacuation is illustrated in the diagram. A statement of the American conception of the place and purpose of the several treatment stations and of *Triage* will usefully supplement the study made in this volume of the British system of evacuation. (The italics used are not in the original text.)

The Field Hospital. "In trench warfare and in some quiet sectors the *field hospital* was of a semi-permanent character and was often elaborately installed with modern equipment and conveniences in well adapted commodious buildings or well arranged dugouts. . . . In open warfare . . . when equipment was sparse and of the simplest, often no patients could be held, and the work resolved into a problem of evacuation. On the other hand, in a few instances, . . . conditions obtained whereby the field hospitals were located in commodious buildings with clean, well-lighted operating rooms in which modern aseptic surgical work was done by attached special surgical teams, which included nurses."[4]

The Triage. "It is essential that all casualties from the front pass

---
[3] See in particular pp. 735-6.
[4] *American Official History, Vol. XI, Part I, p. 101.*

through the *triage*. . . . The function of a *triage* is, in general: First, the grouping of casualties as to degree, which determines whether they are (a) transportable; (b) non-transportable. Second, their classification as to type of casualty, i.e., (a) G.S.W.-S, (b) G.S.W.-O, (c) psychoneurosis, (d) gassed, (e) injured, (f) sick. *Other functions* of a *triage* are: 1. The rendering of *minor surgical aid* and medical treatment in emergencies, to make transportable, if possible, cases that would otherwise be non-transportable. 2. The *readjustment, or renewal of dressings* and of splints where necessary. 3. The administration of *antitetanic serum* for immunising purposes where it has not already been administered."[5]

The tactics of the *triage* (as we may say) were modified from time to time. The following from the Official History (*Vol. XI, Surgery, p. 109*) shows the trend of this.

"The chief change was one put into effect by the commanding officer of Field Hospital No. 127. This consisted in the placing of a *triage*, . . . a short distance in advance of the operating hospital for seriously wounded, thus separating it entirely from our advanced operative hospital to which it was attached in our former drive. All wounded were brought to this *triage* by the division ambulances. These ambulances were unloaded and immediately returned to the front stations for more wounded. In that way no serious blocking ever occurred at the advanced dressing stations.

"At the *triage* the patients were sorted out as to the degree of severity of their wounds. Accurate records were also kept of the wounded so that a report of the number, rank, organisation, and severity of the wounds could be made every six hours. It is imperative that the best and most decisive medical men available should direct this work. The severely wounded were sent to our *advanced operative station*, which was 12 kms. behind the front line at the beginning of operations. Inasmuch as the distance between the two stations was only about 200 yards, the mule-drawn ambulances were used for this purpose. The less seriously wounded were evacuated by truck and attached motor ambulance company to *Evacuation Hospital No. 5*, which was stationed 19 kms. farther in the rear. From here evacuation was carried out by *Train* to Paris."

The Evacuation Hospital (C.C.S.). The function of the Evacuation Hospital corresponding to the C.C.S. or H.O.E. is described thus (*pp. 112-13*).

"While in certain respects our field hospital continued to be an emergency hospital for the battlefield, it became more nearly a magnified and improved dressing station than a hospital. This made the evacuation hospital the actual theater of our surgical effort there, especially during very active periods. The *evacuation hospital*, plus the *mobile hospital*, and the *mobile surgical unit*, thus constituted the hospital for early surgery: upon it, to a very great extent, the patient's life and limb depended. It proved necessary to apply in this hospital with great rapidity, to the most urgent cases, the best treatment known to modern surgery, in order to secure satisfactory professional results, and at the same time, in order to secure the best administrative service, it was likewise necessary to evacuate its patients as quickly as possible to provide beds for incoming wounded. To a certain degree these needs

---

[5] *Loc. cit., p. 108.*

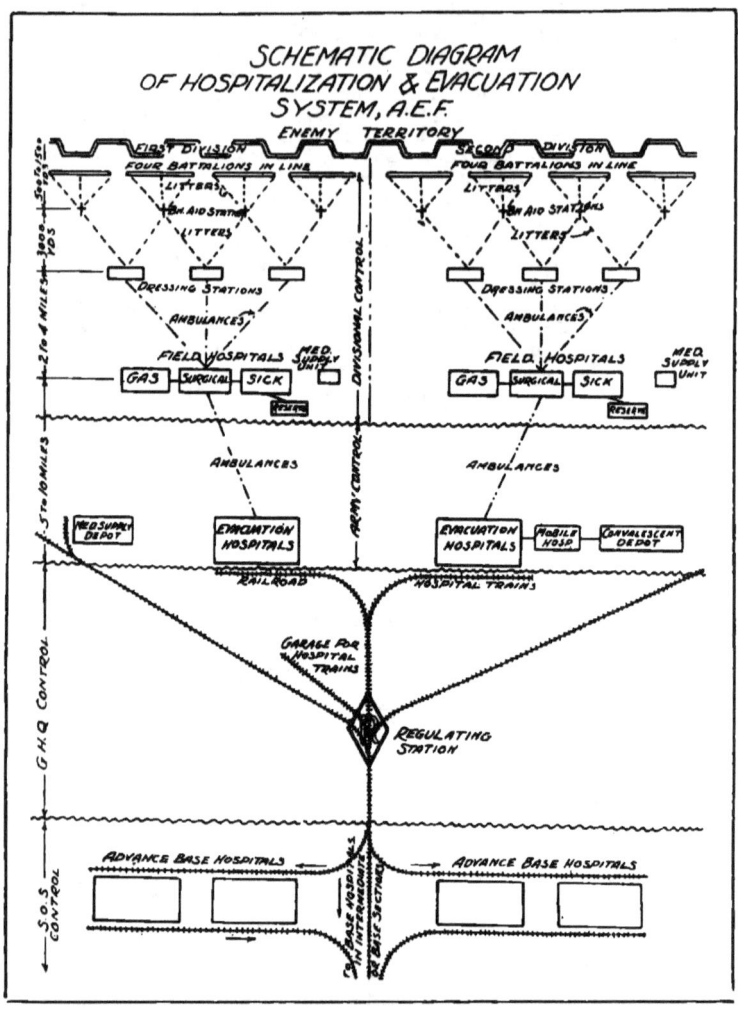

SCHEME OF AMERICAN EVACUATION

Reproduced from the *Medical Department of the United States Army in the World War*, Vol. VIII, p. 262.

NATIONAL SYSTEMS FOR CASUALTIES

conflicted, and it was only by the utmost diligence and perspicacity that they could be reconciled in periods of stress, or, that, if this proved impossible, their conflict could be reduced to a minimum."

(iii) THE FIELD MEDICAL SERVICE AND METHODS OF THE GERMAN ARMY[6]

Organisation of the German Army
Before the war the Army Corps was the tactical as well as the administrative unit of the German Army. Under the conditions of the war of 1914-18, when divisions were constantly being relieved and interchanged, that formation became the unit of tactical manoeuvre—*i.e.* the smallest self-contained unit of all arms. From 1916 the German Divisions were organised on a 3-regiment basis, the 3 infantry regiments (brigades) each of 3 battalions being grouped under one infantry brigade staff.

The Army Medical Service consisted of a Corps of medical officers (Sanitats-officier-korps) and the medical rank and file, *"Sanitätsmannschaft."* These comprised *"Krankenträger"* (stretcher-bearers) for field medical work and the *Militarkrankenwärter*—hospital orderlies.

Organisation of the Field Medical Service
The opening stages of the war of 1914-18 found the organisation of the field medical service inadequate to the requirements of this war, and at the end of 1916 it was reorganised. In the rapid advance into France and Belgium the ever increasing distance between the front and the L. of C. led to a great extension in the use of the "field hospitals" which in an advance took over the stations established by the "medical companies" and thus freed the latter to accompany their divisions. With trench warfare the medical companies took on a wider rôle of treatment—to hold "non-transportable" cases, and to do imperative major operations—estimated at 8 per 1,000 casualties. At the same time the field hospitals were pushed forward to co-operate more effectively with these. The field medical service comprised:—

The Regimental Medical Service. The medical establishment of a *Battalion* comprised 2 R.M.O's, 5 N.C.O's (medical) and 16 regimental stretcher-bearers—known as *"Sanitätern."* These latter were non-medical, and drawn from the unit and corresponded very closely with our regimental stretcher-bearers. The regimental (Brigade) medical staff comprised a Senior Medical Officer, *"Regimentsarzt,"* with small staff, with considerable powers of initiative.

The Divisional Medical Service. The "Medical Company" (Sanitätskompagnie). This unit was in effect the analogue of our Field Ambulance. During 1915-16 they were commanded by combatant officers, whilst the medical officers, with the exception of one R.M.O. were "attached." In January, 1917, a reorganisation placed medical officers in command and fixed the strength of a normal "company" at 8 medical officers and 221 other ranks—146 "privates," with 5 horsed and 6 motor ambulance waggons, and 2 field kitchens. The "unit" comprised elements equivalent to the British "tent" and "bearer" divisions and transport details, but had a very much wider field of action. The stretcher-

---
[6] This note is based on the official *Medical Report (Sanitätsbericht) on the German Army, Vol. I*, and from the *"Handbook of the German Army in War"* issued by British General Staff in Nov., 1918. The facts were kindly collected and collated by Maj.-Gen. Sir John Gellibrand. Assistance was also derived from particulars supplied by a German medical officer who served in the war of 1914-1918.

bearers were organised in two platoons each of 5 sections—1 N.C.O. and 12 privates with 3 stretchers. 6 stretcher-bearers were allotted for the ambulance waggons, 3 N.C.O's and 30 orderlies for work at the Dressing Station. The establishment included also 2 orderlies with 2 dogs, trained to find wounded; and a telephone detail for 3,000 yards of cable. Pigeons were also used. The Field Company stretcher-bearers commonly worked behind the A.D.S., but were often attached to regiments, and even worked in the front line.

Army Corps and Army Units. The *Field Hospital* (*Feldlazarett*) originally 12 per Army Corps, was—broadly—the analogue of our C.C.S. This unit had a chequered career. Originally they were subordinated to the A.S.C. for "discipline and administration," but were detached for duty by the divisional (or other) staff; or in emergency by the Regimental (Brigade) Senior Medical Officer. After various experiments, in March, 1917, they came directly under the staffs of the field formations—Division or Brigade—through the S.M.O. concerned. At the end of the war the composition of a Field Hospital was:—10 medical officers (1 dentist per division), 35 other ranks, 24 other ranks attached for transport with 12 vehicles and 34 horses. Its function was essentially that of *triage* and *treatment,* as the *Sanitätskompagnie* was of *movement.* The unit was, however, well equipped for the transport of its own technical *material,* and was much more mobile than our C.C.S., and its field of action much wider. It was thus able to co-operate effectively with the *Sanitätskompagnie,* on the one hand, and with the Lines of Communication on the other. In June, 1917, 2 Field Hospitals were definitely allotted to each Division, the remainder being Army Troops. A proposal to make *all* field hospitals "Army Troops" was unanimously opposed by all Armies, Corps and Divisions!

The diagram shows the general scheme of evacuation.[7] The following note applies chiefly to evacuation in stationary warfare. In the front lines each infantry company was allotted a shell-proof dugout as a company aid post—*Sanitätsunterstand.* This was manned by a medical N.C.O. and regimental stretcher-bearers equipped with a medical haversack, trench stretchers, blankets, restoratives and gas-mask spares. Five hundred yards behind the main defence line a larger dugout formed the "*Battalion-sanitätsunterstand*"—*the equivalent of our R.A.P.*—under the Battalion M.O's with a greatly increased quantity of medical stores. Here wounds were dressed, anti-tetanic serum was

System of Evacuation

---

[7] It indicates the stretcher-bearers' routes (*Weg der Krankenträger*) both for the infy. bearers ("*der Infant.*") and for the amb. bearers ("*der San. K.*"). The further route of evacn. can be followed from the diagram and text with the following elucidation of terms and conventional signs. *Verbindestellen* (*Sanitätsunterstand*) = coy. collecting stns. *Bataillons-Unterstand und Regiments-Unterstand für Verwundete, Zahlen deren Belegungs fähigkeit* = bn. and regtl. (bde.) dressing stns. ("aid-posts")—the numbers in brackets indicate accommodation. *Zwischenstelle* = bearer relay stns. or posts. *Unterstand Warterhalle: Leutnant mit Patrouille* = forward dugout (H.Q.) of bearer divn. (lieut. and party). *Wagenhalteplatz* = horse amb. rendezvous (loading post). *Krankenkraftwagen bei Bedarf* = motor amb. waggons with med. supplies. *Halteplatz der krankenkraftwagen* = motor amb. rendezvous. *Hauptverbandplatz* (*H.V.Pl.*) = main dressing stn. *Ortsunterkunft des San. Personals und zugeteilten Krankenträg* = billets of medical personnel and attached stretcher-bearers. *Ortsunterkunft der San. Komp. abseits vom H.V.Pl.* = billets of personnel of medical coy. not employed at M.D.S. *Krankenverteilungs-stellen* = classification centre or triage. *Feldlazarett* (*F.L.*) = field hospital (C.C.S.). *Krankensammelstelle* = collecting stn. for walking wounded and sick. *F.L. Gas* (*im Korpsbereich*) = fld. hosp. for gassed cases (in corps sector). *Fernsprecher* = telephone.

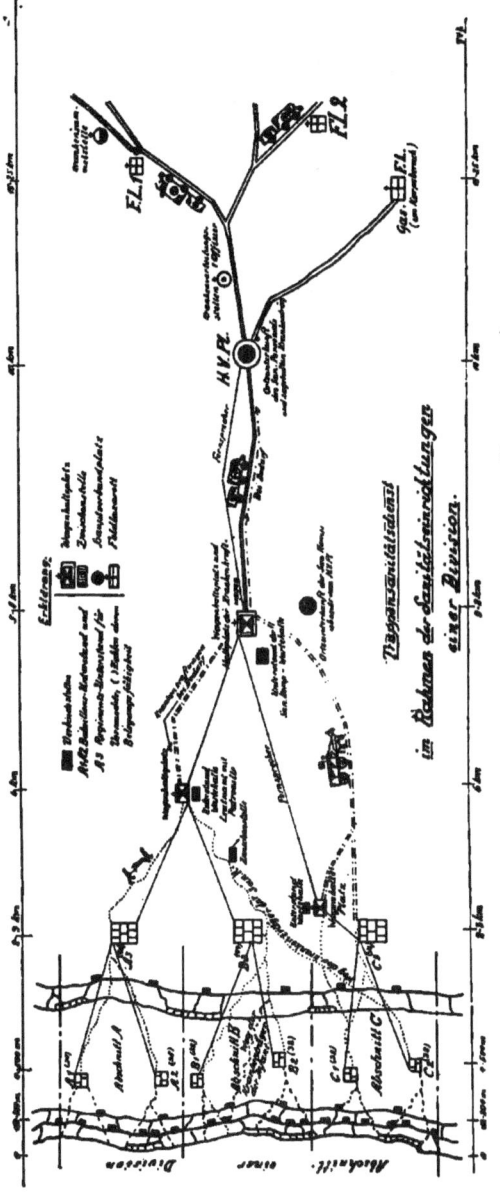

German Scheme of Evacuation in a Divisional Area

The diagram shows a divisional sector (*Abschnitt*) divided into three regtl. sectors (*Abschnitt* "A," "B," "C"), each subdivided into two bn. sectors ("A1," "A2," etc.). (See also footnote, opposite.)

German Official Medical History.

given, and, when possible, imperative operations were carried out. Serious cases were retained, if fire was heavy, up to the limits of accommodation (25 to 40 cases), but this was discouraged.

About 3,000 yards to the rear came the *"Regiments-sanitätsunterstand," equivalent to an A.D.S.*; generally in a deep cellar or bomb-proof shelter with accommodation for 100 cases under the Brigade S.M.O. staffed by personnel of the Medical Company or by reserve units allotted by the A.D.M.S. of the division. This sector was cleared by the stretcher-bearers of the Medical Company or of support or reserve units, or carrying parties returning from the front line. The evacuation route was marked by sign boards (Red Cross and arrow). These posts were linked through the *zwischenstelle (bearer relays)* and *wagenhalteplatz (horsed or motor ambulance rendezvous)* with the *Hauptverbandplatz—the approximate equivalent of our M.D.S.—* 7 or 8 miles in rear formed by medical officers and orderlies of the *Sanitätskompagnie* or *Feldlazarett*. The Waggon Rendezvous was commonly staffed and equipped to give food, treatment and shelter and resembled in some respects our A.D.S. The vehicles plied both forward and to the rear.

Walking Wounded. From the waggon rendezvous the slightly wounded walked, or got lifts, to the M.D.S. Here, or at a special *classification centre or triage (Krankenverteilungstelle)* they were classified and appropriately disposed.

The Sanitäts-Kraftwagen-Kolonnen. (Motor Ambulance Convoys). As in the British Army, these were a product of the war, and were apparently organised and used much as the M.A.C.

The *Feldlazarette* were disposed in two echelons—(*a*) in close proximity to the M.D.S. where they acted as Advanced Operating Centres for "untransportable cases," (*b*) in a rear echelon where they formed stations for dealing with every type of casualty. Female nurses were sometimes attached.

The foregoing were all within the "Zone of operations" of the "War Zone." Further evacuation, organised by an "Ambulance Convoy detachment"—800 motor ambulances—was per "ambulance train," "temporary ambulance train" or "passenger train with sick" to the *Lines of Communication area* of the War Zone; and thence through a "collecting station," situated on the boundary line of the War Zone, to the *Kriegslazarette* (War Hospital), Military and Red Cross.

General Comments

The German system was based on a *comparatively small technical medical (sanitäts) personnel which was expanded as required by temporary measures to meet periods of high pressure.* The zonal arrangement seems to have been less exact than in the British system and the medical machinery more self-contained. Though allotted to formations, units were available to render other units assistance by personnel and material. Very considerable latitude also was allowed to medical officers for supplementing regulation procedure (as by the use of buildings, requisitioned transport, etc.).

A special interest lies in the struggle between the medical authorities and the general staff for the retention by the service of men of standard physique. Eventually the general staff succeeded in substituting men of lower categories but at a cost of a 30 per cent. increase in medical establishments!

Perhaps the most important principle that can be gained from this flexible and apparently very efficient system is the importance of thinking in terms of *function* rather than of *structure*—

Lesson of the nature of the actual problem, in terms of existing constants, rather than of cut and dried schemes and "systems."

Lastly, it is interesting to note that special arrangements were made to prevent piracy of the practices at home, and that medical officers might be authorised by A.D.M.S. to receive fees for attendance from the inhabitants of occupied territories.

APPENDIX No. 10

SOME CONSTANT FACTORS WHICH DETERMINE THE ARRANGEMENTS REQUIRED FOR THE TRANSPORTATION OF BATTLE-CASUALTIES

(i) THE PROPORTION OF STRETCHER CASES TO OTHERS

As was observed in the text[1] it is difficult to set any exact figure for the relative proportion of stretcher cases, "sitters" and "walkers"—the two latter commonly constituting the "walking wounded." Thus, two Field Ambulances cited in the *British Official Medical History*[2] reported "walking cases" as comprising 16·2 per cent. and 44·2 per cent. respectively of "total evacuations" from 1st to 3rd July, 1916. In the second unit 34 per cent. were "sitting cases" and 21·8 per cent. "lying cases." Confusion is caused, for example, by failure to state the transport circuit to which the figures should apply. As with most questions relating to transport, the problem involves a number of variables, chiefly circumstantial, *e.g.* transport facilities (no man would walk if he could get a ride), proportion of sick to wounded, number of gassed cases, and so forth. The circumstances of each campaign, even of a battle, will influence the problem. No rule or any precedent can ever replace the need for adaptation to particular environment.

On the other hand, this is not to say that the human constants do not weigh. Quite apart from convenience, there must obviously be types of casualty for whom rescue, even to the R.A.P. and much more to A.D.S. or M.D.S., will require that they be carried on a stretcher. The figure has been set (*loc. cit.*) at 50-50, but this is not to say that a larger proportion of walking wounded need never be carried nor that a smaller proportion of stretcher cases could not otherwise be saved. Some data from various sources will help to a useful approximation.

In the Battles of the Menin Road and Polygon Wood (September, 1917), for the four divisions concerned not more than one-third of the total wounded passed through the A.D.S. for stretcher cases. Of 600 consecutive cases passing through this station on September 20th-21st, 350 were sent by the long "A" route to C.C.S.—some fifteen miles; 160 to the M.D.S. by the "B" route for immediate treatment for "shock, gas, haemorrhage, etc."; and 90 by the direct "C" route to C.C.S., chiefly for abdominals. Of 1,078 wounded passing through this station, 35 died at the station; 895 passed by the "A," "B," or "C" routes; and the remainder were sent on to C.C.S. without admission.

A ratio of 70 per cent. "sitting or lying down" to 30 per cent.

---

[1] *At pp. 273-4.*   [2] *General, Vol. III, p. 42.*

"walking" for the circuits forward of the "transfer station" (to M.A.C.) is proposed in the *British Official Medical History*³ as a provisional estimate "until experience is gained of local conditions." The comparable figures given by the *German Official Medical History* (*Vol. III, p. 61*) are "68 per cent. driving, 28 per cent. walking, and 4 per cent. 'untransportable' (*sic*)." Of American casualties carried by motor ambulance waggon, 5 were carried "recumbent" to 7 transported "sitting."⁴ The B.E.F. ambulance trains "over a long period" carried 58 per cent. sitting and 42 per cent. lying. For a period covering both active operations and quiet times, 75 per cent. of the sick, 90 per cent. of the wounded, and 81 per cent. of total sick and wounded required evacuation to the Base—the evacuation rising to 98 per cent. with active operations.

(ii) THE DISTANCE-TIME FACTOR IN THE EVACUATION OF WOUNDED

(*a*) *Report* (*slightly abbreviated*) *by the C.O., 7th Field Ambulance*:
"A.D.M.S.,
2nd Australian Division.

NOTES ON DISTANCES WOUNDED TRAVEL

"It has always been a subject of interest in this Unit as to how long it actually takes for a wounded man to arrive at the C.C.S. where he can obtain sufficient operative treatment. Accordingly, in July, 1918, an attempt was made to have the time recorded on the medical card (*A.F.W. 3118*) of every patient passing through the Unit. The R.M.O's were all seen personally and the matter explained to them and also the ambulance M.O's and, in addition, the C.O. of the M.D.S. and C.C.S's expressed their willingness to record the cases. In addition, the number of times a case was re-dressed was recorded on the card. This proved of value in showing how few times a case need be re-dressed before reaching the C.C.S. The diagram gives a representation of the evacuation scheme. The distances are, of course, the great points of interest, together with the mode of conveyance. During this tour in the line, the chief object was to get men as quickly as possible to the C.C.S., and also that a minimum of dressings should be done. Urgent cases were not removed from the cars at the A.D.S., but were sent straight through from the Advanced Ambulance Post to the Main Dressing Station. It will be seen that, on the right, a soldier near the front line had to travel a distance of 24 miles, and on the left 25 to 26 miles, before obtaining effective operative treatment.

"The figures of times taken for the patients to proceed from the forward area to the C.C.S. are as follows:—

"750 cases actually had their times recorded on the A.F.W. 3118. Gas patients were not included in the records, as they were frequently detained for bathing and treatment at the M.D.S. Moreover, of these 750 cases, 200 were obviously detained en route for some reason, either because of the lightness of their wounds; or because of their severity—to permit of restorative measures being taken. Of the remaining 500 cases, the statistics are strikingly in accord. The variations in time are

---
³ *Statistical Volume, p. 44.*
⁴ *American Official Medical History, Vol. VIII, p. 809.*

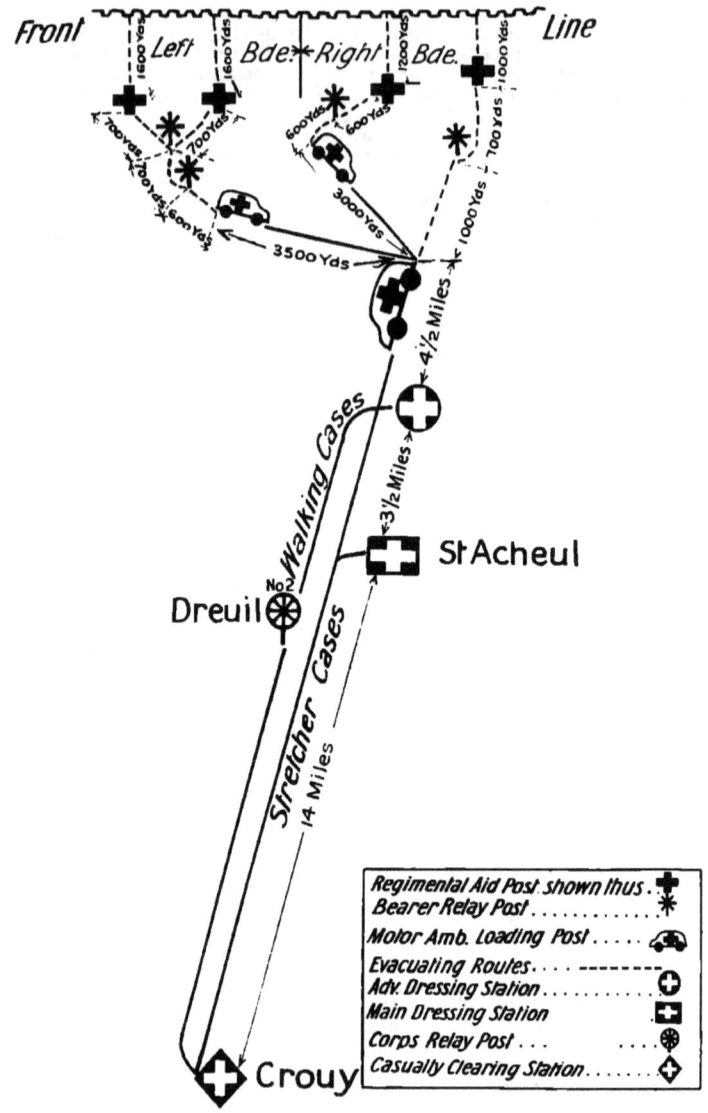

The Distance-time Factor in Evacuation: scheme of Movements

TRANSPORTATION OF BATTLE-CASUALTIES 929

due to the distance between the Advanced Ambulance Post (Motor Loading Post) and the place where the man was actually wounded. The time between the Advanced Ambulance Post and the C.C.S. is practically constant, and is about 4 hours, the first 1¾ being spent on treatment at the Advanced Ambulance Post, and the subsequent journey of 8 miles to the M.D.S.; the remaining 2¼ hours being expended in treatment at the M.D.S. and the subsequent journey of 14 miles to the C.C.S. Consequently, a man being wounded near a R.A.P. which was about 1 hour's journey from the Advanced Ambulance Post does not arrive at the C.C.S. until 5 hours have elapsed from the time of his being wounded. However, special cases, such as abdominal, often arrive at the C.C.S. in 1 hour less than this time, which, though satisfactory under present conditions, might be reduced by nearly 2 hours if an operating centre were nearer the line.

"The cases which arrived at the C.C.S. on July 4th, after the stunt of the capture of HAMEL, are of special interest. Zero hour was at 3.10 a.m., and the first cases arrived at the C.C.S. about 9 a.m. Owing to the early hour of the stunt, some considerable difficulty was experienced in collecting the wounded and the first Stretcher Cases arrived at the Advanced Ambulance Post about 5.30 a.m.—3½ hours later they were at the C.C.S. The average of 5¾ hours from the time a man was wounded till his arrival at the C.C.S. was maintained for the first batch of cases who were wounded near the jumping-off tape, but it gradually increased as the men got further toward their objective and finally reached about 9-10 hours for a few stretcher cases wounded just on reaching the final objective. Nevertheless, the time 3½ to 4 hours from the Advanced Ambulance Post to the C.C.S. was maintained during the whole of the day.

"The cases arriving at the C.C.S. from the stunt on the evening of 7th July are also extremely interesting as regards time. On this occasion the Zero hour was fixed at 8.30 p.m., just at nightfall. It was a very dark night with enough rain to make some of the roads impracticable for the Ford cars and, in addition, made things very difficult for the horsed ambulances. The first cases arrived at the C.C.S. about 2.30 a.m., having taken about 7 hours. Owing to the darkness and the rain, the times between the Advanced Ambulance Post and the C.C.S. was increased to 4½ to 5 hours, and the later cases of the stunt took 9-10 hours to arrive at the C.C.S. Had the weather conditions been favourable, the time would have been reduced considerably, as many of the cases were detained at the M.D.S. to allow of restorative measures being taken, as most of the patients were very wet and cold. In addition, another interesting fact was disclosed from the marking of the *A.F.W. 3118* in the particular way described. Practically all the men were dressed by the Regimental Stretcher Bearers, but a large majority of these cases—about 90 per cent.—were re-dressed by the R.M.O's, and acting on the Divisional Order, the majority of these cases were marked "O.K. for C.C.S." After leaving the R.A.P., only about 10 per cent. of the cases were re-dressed at the Advanced Ambulance Post and the A.D.S., and about 20 per cent. were re-dressed at the M.D.S. In this way the majority of the cases were only re-dressed once, and about 30 per cent. twice, and very few more than twice before reaching the C.C.S. The Consulting Surgeons at both C.C.S's were interviewed about the condition of the cases arriving at the C.C.S., and they expressed themselves as well satisfied with the system as adopted.

"However, the main point for which the statistics were collected is as follows:—

"The distance from the M.D.S. to the C.C.S. is about 14 miles and at least 1¾ hours in the car for a stretcher case. The road is extremely bad in parts and had not the C.O. of the 6th Australian Field Ambulance opened up the alternative route along the tow-path, many cases would have arrived at the C.C.S. in much worse condition. I should like to bring to your attention the advisability of establishing an *Operating Centre* as near as possible to the M.D.S.—for example at MONTIERS, thus saving the last trying 14 miles and two hours in the Motor Ambulances. In support of the suggestion, I should like to say that, during the operations at POZIÈRES in 1916, an operating centre was established at WARLOY, within a few hundred yards of the M.D.S. and undoubtedly was the means of saving many lives.

                    A. M. WILSON, Lt.-Colonel,
                    C.O., 7th Aust. Field Ambulance."

(b) The following figures are from British experience quoted from *British Medicine in the War, 1914-1917*, p. 31:—

Time of Evacuation to Casualty Clearing Station.

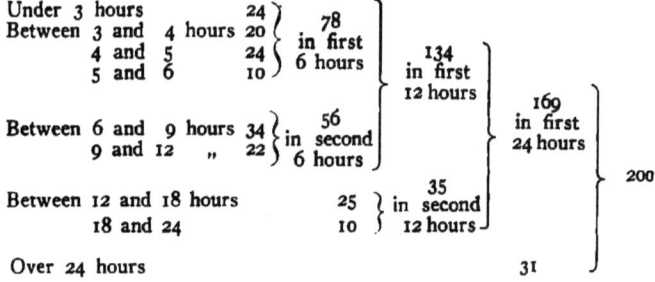

APPENDIX No. 11

VARIOUS TYPES OF HUTS AND TENTS IN COMMON USE[1]

(i) THE ACCOMMODATION OF TROOPS

The following study of housing as a problem in hygiene is from an article[2] by Colonel W. W. O. Beveridge—sometime Professor of Hygiene, Royal Army Medical College; and, during the war, A.D.M.S. Sanitary, G.H.Q., B.E.F.:—

"Overcrowding has always been recognized as a prominent factor in the spread of disease both in civil and military life. In England as long ago as 1861 the Royal Commission for Improving the Sanitary Condition of Barracks commented as follows:

" 'Before the soldier can be assured of having the amount of space required for health, there must be a distinct recognition that the amount given by regulation (i.e. 600 cubic feet) is on no account to be tampered with. No increase of regimental strength, no want of store rooms, libraries, or reading rooms, should for an instant be permitted to interfere with it. . . .'

"During the period prior to the war accommodation in barracks and hutments in Great Britain was provided on the scale of 60 square feet and 600 cubic feet per man. On the outbreak of the present war the great influx of recruits necessitated a somewhat less generous provision, and having regard to military exigencies 40 square feet or 400 cubic feet was fixed as the minimum accommodation which could safely be permitted in quarters. This has since come to be regarded as a war time standard which every effort should be made to attain.

"All epidemiological experience points to the very marked effect which overcrowding exerts upon the spread of infectious diseases, especially those affecting the respiratory tract. It is a matter of common knowledge that when diphtheria occurs among men who are crowded together, 'carriers' of Klebs-Loeffler bacilli are usually numerous, and

[1] Apart even from "enemy action" the problem of the housing or sheltering of two millions of British soldiers in the attrition warfare of the Western Front was a stupendous business. Thus, at the British Expeditionary Base in France alone— *ex pede Herculem*—more than 78 miles of hutment was constructed by the Royal Engineers.

[2] Entitled "Considerations in the Prevention of Respiratory Affections" published in the *Research Society Reports* by the American Red Cross Society in France (*Vol. II, No. 3, Oct., 1918*).

when these men are spread out in well ventilated quarters the 'carrier' condition rapidly disappears.

"The evil effects of crowding together in ill-ventilated wards, patients suffering from measles, are well known; the severity of the disease increases, and deaths from pneumonia as a complication may reach a high figure. Should such a state of affairs occur, experience has shown that it can be immediately remedied by the simple procedure of providing sufficient space and adequate ventilation. . . .

"By the simple expedient of allowing a space of 2 1/2 feet between each bed and by improving the ventilation of the quarters, the carrier rate, [in C.S.F.] in one instance, fell from 28 to 2 per cent. in 9 weeks, from 28 to 7 per cent. in 6 weeks in another, from 35·8 per cent. to 4·5 per cent. in 6 weeks in a third, and from 28 per cent. to 4·5 per cent. in 5 weeks in a fourth.

"A large number of similar experiments were carried out, all of which support the view that the distance between beds is of paramount importance and that quite a moderate degree of 'spacing out' of beds combined with simple methods for improving ventilation is highly effective in reducing carrier rates. . . . The important elements in 'overcrowding,' so far as the spread of infectious diseases affecting the respiratory passages is concerned, are, therefore, proximity of heads and defective ventilation. Ventilation may be improved within the limits short of creating a draught, but satisfactory results can only be expected when close proximity of heads is also prevented.

"Proximity of heads and degree of ventilation are, therefore, the criteria by which the adequacy of accommodation should be judged. . . .

"Hutting accommodation for the British Army on the Lines of Communication in France is provided on a basis of 4 feet of wall space per man, unless the huts are more than 20 feet wide, when 40 square feet of floor space per man is allowed. This includes accommodation for Labor Companies, both white and colored, and for prisoners of war and their escorts. Vigilance is exercised in preventing more men than the authorized number from being accommodated in any hut, particularly in the case of colored laborers who are specially susceptible to respiratory diseases.

"In ordinary hospitals 60 square feet of floor space with six feet of wall space per patient is provided, but during periods of pressure this may have to be reduced to five feet of wall space. In hospitals for infectious disease 100 square feet of floor space is allowed.

"Several types of huts for the accommodation of troops have been erected, the majority of which vary from 16 to 20 feet in width.

"The Adrian Hut is constructed in sections of 2 metres length which can be bolted together. Its extreme width at floor level is 27 feet 4 1/2 inches. A hut 30 metres long can accommodate 69 men giving each approximately 40 square feet of floor space, if the precautions referred to below are observed. Thirty beds could be placed down each side, and owing to the great width of the hut 9 can be arranged end to end down the centre. In order to make the best use of the available floor space it would be necessary for alternate men in the beds along the wall to sleep with their heads projecting towards the centre of the room. This arrangement could be still further improved by drawing alternate beds one foot away from the wall [*see page 557*]. To ensure this arrangement being adhered to, it would be necessary to fix the beds to

HUTS AND TENTS

the floor and to make the head end of each bed slightly higher than the foot so that men would be constrained to sleep with their heads at the proper ends. The difficulties of carrying out these refinements in actual practice are obvious. It has also been suggested that risk of spread of infection might be diminished by the erection of small partitions or screens between each bed.

"In army areas variations in the patterns of hut have lately been restricted for the sake of simplicity and convenience; the following are typical examples of huts utilized in army areas as shelter for troops.

Adrian Huts	30 metres ..	Men or Institutes
Standard Hut	60' x 16'	Men or Institutes
Nissen Bow	26' 10" x 15' 8"	.. Men
Nissen Steel Tent (Circular)	Diameter 14' 6 1/2"	Men

".... Ordinary circular bell tents, diameter 12' 6", usually accommodate not more than 12 men, but on occasion, 14 men may be placed in a tent. The wall space, floor space, and cubic space are thus below the standard prescribed for hutted accommodation. In warm weather when the tent flies are kept open, this is partly compensated for by free ventilation, but during wet and cold weather when the tent is closed the conditions both in regard to proximity of heads and ventilation are such as would favour the spread of disease affecting the respiratory passages. Owing to the men being grouped in separate tents, the danger of spread of disease is limited and the risk of an extensive outbreak is not so great as if the same degree of overcrowding occurred in a large hut or barrack room.

"It is obvious from what has already been said that overcrowding is a relative matter and no definite line of demarcation can be drawn between ample space and overcrowding; the two merge gradually into one another. For practical purposes, however, a compromise between military necessity and the ideal has to be made. The minimum standard of accommodation already referred to represents the practical compromise which has been effected; less accommodation than this increased enormously the chances of spread of infectious disease affecting the respiratory tract. ."

(ii) TENTS AND HUTS FOR HOSPITAL PURPOSES

At least 25 per cent. of the total force engaged (it was laid down in engineering manuals) will require hospital accommodation. Important as is this matter[3] it must yet be dismissed very briefly.

A great variety of tents and huts were in use, tents ranging from the "Tortoise tent" of the field ambulance (20 feet by 14 feet) through various types and sizes up to the immense "Bessoneau" hangar (45 metres by 21 metres[4]) used for the French H.O.E. The accommodation of rectangular tents could be increased almost indefinitely by the procedure of "brigading" whereby two or more tents were laced together, end to end or side to side.[5]

---

[3] The *Brit. Off. Medical History, Hygiene Vol. I* devotes 66 pages of letterpress, fully illustrated, to this subject.
[4] *i.e.* 147 ft. 7 in. by 68 ft. 11in.
[5] This is taken from an admirable account of "brigading" compiled for the Q.M. No. 2 A.C.C.S. (Capt. J. H. Pollard) by Sgt. T. Fitzpatrick and included in the war diary of the unit for Apr., 1918.

The most exacting unit in the matter of housing was the C.C.S. by reason of the varied nature of its work and environment. In November, 1917, a definite scale of tents was laid down in *General Routine Orders*

The "Brigading" of Marquees—a complete brigade of six tents joined end on.

for a C.C.S. This allotted 80 "Hospital" marquees which should accommodate 200 patients in beds and 800 on stretchers. The capacity of the tents and huts in common use was

Small marquee—8 beds or 12 stretchers;
Large marquee—14 beds or 20 stretchers;
Nissen ward hut—24 beds or 28 stretchers;
Adrian hut—40 beds or 60 stretchers.

In addition to these, various small huts were in use, the best known being the "Armstrong"—of two types, 24 feet by 15 feet and 12 feet by 9 feet 3 inches. Just before the Armistice the French "Bessoneau" tent and "hangar" were being introduced into the British Army in place of the "Hospital marquee large."

In addition to wards, operating rooms, reception and dressing rooms, accommodation had to be provided for officers and other ranks of the R.A.M.C., for the nursing sisters, and for convalescents, or "B" class men attached for duty. Many accessory constructions, usually of an improvised nature, were also necessary, such as lavatories, baths, latrines, blanket stores, stretcher dumps, sterilizing room, dentists' hut, X-ray huts, shed for disinfector, lamp and oil store, and so forth.

"*Dugouts.*" In one very important line of action British Army procedure differed greatly, even fundamentally, from the German. This was in the provision of underground shelter. Whatever arguments might be (and were) adduced to show that the sheltering of troops in dugouts tended to reduce their "offensive" spirit, the argument scarcely condones failure to provide shelter for the wounded while receiving treatment.

APPENDIX No. 12

SANITATION ON THE WESTERN FRONT[1]

I. CORRESPONDENCE RELATING TO THE FUNCTIONS OF SANITARY SECTIONS

Memorandum dated 12th March, 1917, from Adjutant-General, B.E.F., to Armies. "In order to maintain continuity of sanitary work in Armies, it has been decided to withdraw Divisional Sanitary Sections from their Divisions, and to constitute them as Army Troops units. . . . Orders for the movement of these Sections between Armies will be issued by G.H.Q.; orders for movements within Army areas being issued by Army Headquarters."

The Australian A.D's.M.S. were strongly opposed to the change; their arguments were presented to the D.D.M.S. I Anzac Corps in the following letters:—

"D.D.M.S.,
   1st Anzac.

"Considerable difficulty is being experienced in controlling sanitation in the Forward Area under the system and areas at present in operation.

"Two Sanitary Sections divide the 1st Australian Division area between them, in addition are responsible for a very elongated tract of country in rear extending over two Divisional areas as far back as Mametz and Fricourt—a distance from the front line of 14 miles.

"Even assuming that it is only occasionally necessary to visit this back area, its inaccessibility must cause considerable waste of time in travelling and time taken in travelling cannot be judged by distance as the congestion on roads very often hinders travelling tremendously. This time is urgently needed for placing the Sanitation of the newly occupied territory on a sound basis. Further the detachment of Sanitary personnel in this back area seriously weakens the section and hinders its work of construction and supervision.

"Again the partitioning of a Divisional Area into separate sanitary controls does not tend to uniformity of sanitation and complicates the provision of fatigues for conservancy work by the Division occupying that area.

"The close personal knowledge of Divisional Staff of the work being done by the Sanitary Section has been lost. Personal acquaintance with Sanitary Officers and officers of the Division and the personnel of

---

[1] *See pp. 587 et seq.*

the Sanitary Section with the personnel of Battalion Sanitary Details has been lost to a very large extent and thus the progressive training of Units in Sanitation interfered with.

"It is considered that more efficiency would be obtained in Australian Units under the old system of Sanitary Section working entirely with their Division. If this cannot be done it is suggested that Sanitary Areas should be shortened and made to conform more approximately to Divisional Areas.

R. B. Huxtable, Colonel,
A.D.M.S. 1st Aust. Div.
Divisional Headquarters, 23rd April, 1917."

"D.D.M.S.,
 1st Anzac.

"I am of opinion that the present arrangements for sanitation are unsuitable for this Division for the following reasons:—

"1. The A.D.M.S. is cut off from intimate association with the S.O. and therefore misses many opportunities of discussing sanitation and suggesting improvements.

"2. The S.O. is unacquainted with the C.O's of units or is not so intimately acquainted with them as under the Divisional arrangements, and therefore his personal influence is much reduced if not lost.

"3. In sanitation it is men not Areas that call for intimate knowledge of the S.O. and if he influences the C.O's the improvement of the Area is marked. No loss of continuity of policy need occur when a Division leaves an Area as it has always been our custom to hand over spot maps.

"4. Since the inception of the present plan of sanitation I have lost touch with the S.O., and am not so well acquainted with the state of the Area occupied by the Division as when I saw the daily reports sent in by the men of the Sanitary Section to the C.O.

"5. The Sanitary Area may embrace Areas occupied by two or more Divisions hence divided counsels and uncertainty of administration.

"6. The present plan is not popular with Units or Sanitary Officers. The S.O. is looked upon as an outsider and his counsel carries no weight. Indeed, if it be persisted in, I have reason to believe that great difficulty will be experienced in filling the office with capable men.

Alfred Sutton, Colonel,
A.D.M.S., 2nd Aust. Div.,
Headquarters, 21st April, 1917."

"D.D.M.S.,
 1st Anzac.

"Sanitary efficiency is likely to suffer owing to detachment of the Divisional Sanitary Section.

"Formerly I had a complete grasp of the Sanitary Condition of the Division, by means of daily reports from the C.O. Sanitary Section compiled from reports forwarded to him by his personnel attached for that purpose to the Brigades. By this means defects could be immediately

SANITATION

remedied, and defaulting Units brought to book without delay. I was also quite sure that every unit of the Division was under supervision.

"Under present conditions I have not got this staff at my command, and I cannot get the daily reports which are so necessary.

"Such reports as I receive often arrive after the Unit has moved out of the locality mentioned, perhaps into the area of another Sanitary Section.

"As the Sanitary Section has a huge area to inspect, the Divisional area cannot be inspected as it should, and what is most important, delay occurs, and delay means increasingly bad sanitation.

"The Divisional Area rarely seems to coincide with the Sanitary Area and I may have to deal with one or more Sanitary Sections, or the O.C. Sanitary Section with as many as three A.D's.M.S.

"The present arrangements might be fairly satisfactory under Peace conditions, or during Trench warfare, but when Divisions are mobile it is most unsatisfactory.

"I am of opinion that Sanitary Sections should remain with their Divisions. Sanitary work outside Divisional Areas could be carried out by L. of C. Sanitary Sections.

"The co-ordination of the work of Divisional Sanitary Sections would be simply an easy matter of organisation.

G. W. Barber, Colonel,
A.D.M.S., 4th Aust. Division.
April 22nd, 1917."

"D.M.S.,
1st Anzac.

"In reference to the disposition of Sanitary Sections, I have to report that the present plan of localising a Sanitary Section in a fixed area, independent of the Division is resulting in a very definite loss of that close relationship between the Sanitary Section and the Division, which counts for so much in the maintenance of a high standard of efficiency.

"Units get to know their own Sanitary Section and the Sanitary Section to know the difficulties as well as the shortcomings of the units, the triers and the non-triers, with the result that much can be achieved on the basis of mutual understanding which is hopelessly lost under the present system.

"Cases have occurred in my own Division when an Infectious case has been notified, instructions to disinfect the dugout, etc., have been sent to the Sanitary Section controlling the area in which the unit is located, the Sanitary Officer discovers that though the Headquarters of the Unit are in his area, the hut, etc., occupied by the man is in the next area under the control of another Sanitary Officer, obvious chances of friction or of delay thus occurring.

"Early in the present year, the G.O.C. this Division, in pursuance of a policy for raising the standard of Sanitation as high as possible, in addition to sanctioning the employment on water point duty Six (6) Regimental A.A.M.C. Water Details, authorised the attachment of 6 men from Battalions to the 5th Sanitary Section for instructional purposes, thus largely increasing the efficiency of the Sanitary Section and at the same time providing a means whereby, through the periodical changing of these men, the education of the units in Sanitation would be soon brought to a high level.

"Under the present method of fixing the Sanitary Section in a definite area, with consequent separation from the Division on moving out, it can scarcely be expected that the Divisional Commander will permit this very definite help to continue.

"It would appear to me that all the benefits of the present system could be obtained by Sanitary Section keeping records and maps and carrying out a system of 'handing over' similar to that adopted by Divisions and Battalions when taking over a new area or section of line.

"Knowledge of a new area can be quickly acquired; to get to know and gain the confidence of the personnel of a Division is a vastly more difficult matter.

W. W. Hearne, Colonel,
A.D.M.S., 5th Aust. Div.
21/4/17."

II. THE METHODS OF SANITARY[2] TECHNIQUE FAVOURED IN THE A.I.F. ON THE WESTERN FRONT

The following note on the technique of "sanitation" is complementary to the general study made in *Chapter XIX* and concerns the "direct" method of preventing gastro-intestinal diseases due to infection. Its purpose is to illustrate the principles adopted, not to serve as a synopsis of the various methods in use. The several procedures are described in accord with their place and sequence in the mechanical cycle of transmission of faecal matter from man to man.

Factors in the problem

The material agents concerned in the biological process of gastro-intestinal infection are—1. excremental matter (faeces and urine); 2. transmitting agents, (a) hands (b) flies, (c) dirt and dust, (d) surface and subsoil water; 3. immediate vehicles—food and drink.

The "sanitary" measures employed were designed to attack the cycle, infective individual (case or carrier)—susceptible individual, at these three points and are conveniently described in relation to each.

1. *The infective material: disposal of faeces and urine.* This was by far the most formidable problem of sanitary scavenging. The alternatives were—(a) disinfection; (b) incineration; (c) burial.

(a) *Disinfectants.* Used as fly deterrents, the cresols and heavy oil had a definite if a limited field of usefulness.

(b) *Incineration* was used in the larger medical stations, C.C.S's, General Hospitals, and Convalescent Camps; sometimes in occupied towns and villages; when the height of the subsoil water forbade the

---

[2] This term is used here, as commonly in the A.I.F., as, in effect, synonymous with "scavenging."

SANITATION

use of pits; and when burial might lead to the infection of the water supply.

(c) *Burial* was the general means of disposal of faeces and urine. Apart from aesthetic considerations the purpose of burial was to prevent the dispersal of faeces, as by the feet of man or of flies, or as dust and "dirt."

In effect the technique of faecal disposal by burial resolved itself into (*i*) the shallow trench 3ft. by 2ft. by 1ft., straddled; (*ii*) the single or double "fly-proof" seat, over a deep pit or a pan. (*i*) was universal in rapid movement. In stationary or semi-stationary warfare, the fly-proof seat, improvised or official, over a deep pit was the most favoured procedure.

The common practice at the several military levels can be stated thus:—

(*i*) The trenches: fly-proof box-seats over biscuit tins; or oil drums with individual self-fitting lid-seats. Faeces buried or deposited directly in shell-holes or shallow trenches in rear.

(*ii*) Support areas. Fly-proof box-seats over pit, pan, or biscuit tin. If the latter, burial in shell-holes or pits.

(*iii*) Back areas. Fly-proof box-seats over deep pits for camps; short shallow trench-system for troops on the move, or in camps until fly-proof boxes can be obtained; pan system and incineration for C.C.S's and for hospitals and other permanent institutions; fly-proof boxes over deep pits for villages, for troops billetted therein. The commendable French method of roofed pits with squatting holes was sometimes seen.

Some Constructional Notes. Latrine seats.[3] The most economical and easily made latrine seat is from a biscuit box. It can be fitted over deep trenches, is easily transported, and if desired can be made "fly-proof" and with self-closing lid.

"*Construction*: top and bottom are removed, projecting ends of stay battens sawn off. Two slats 2-in. wide are planed and rounded off at the inner edge and nailed, one along each side of top of box. Lids are made of spare boards or, preferably, only a framework is made for lid and a sheet of tin is nailed on the framework. A piece of tin is also nailed on inside of front of box to direct urine into pit. Hinges are of leather or webbing. Back rest is nailed on two slats nailed to sides of the box and inclining [preferably] backwards. The lid is therefore *not* self-closing.

"Reasons. (1) Slats are used instead of an oval hole in the seat because it is more easily made and does not require a key-hole saw; men cannot defaecate on the back of the seat even if standing up on seat; more easily kept clean and free from vermin. (2) Tin lid instead of wood and so not torn off for firewood. (3) Back rest sloping back and lid not self-closing—because soldiers will not put up with self-closing lids and always wrench off such lids. Compromise is necessary."

2. *Transmitting Agents.* (*a*) *The hands: Ablution.* Agents of disease contained in faecal matter and urine may be passed direct from man to man, as by the carrier-cook. There is much, if indirect, evidence that on the Western Front this was the most important mode of convection. Some sanitary officers believed that, in France, all other modes of infection were negligible. However this may be, it is certain that *soap*,

---
[3] See plate at *p. 581*.

hot water, disinfectant solutions for the hands and the *ablution bench* were in the first order of importance as implements in the sanitary campaign.

(*b*) *Flies.* Rightly or wrongly, an enormous amount of energy was devoted to preventing transmission of infection by flies; in particular, to controlling their *breeding in manure and kitchen refuse.*

Manure. Burning is mentioned only to be condemned. Never used in the A.I.F. *Spreading*—as on distant farm land. The purpose of this was to dry the manure—the larva of *musca domestica* requires moisture. Found "satisfactory." *Heaping* to promote fixation of ammonia and bacterial disintegration—the primitive biological cycle essential to continued soil fertility. This was favoured. (*a*) The manure was simply *"dumped"* at a distance from camp. (*b*) The fresh manure is *stacked* on the ground or a platform; the manure as stacked was packed down and covered with earth. By this procedure the larvae are killed or are forced to the edge by the heat of internal combustion and may be trapped or oiled.

Food and Other Refuse. The official procedure of "incineration" replaced dumping or burial of food, in order to check the breeding of *musca domestica.* It was tedious, laborious, unpopular, but universal behind the support areas.

Incinerators. A great variety of gadgets were used to promote combustion by creating a "draught"; from a simple cone as of coiled wire in a shallow pit to an elaborate destructor used for faecal disposal; "home-made" by the engineers, or portable as the "Horsfall."

Improvised Types. The *"pit"* incinerator figured on *page 587* appears to have been developed in the A.I.F. from the Welsh two-pit incinerator used by the 5th Australian Division at Tel-el-Kebir in 1916. "Very good. Burns well. Requires minimum of material, merely some iron bars for the bottom."

The open type built up of biscuit tins or oil drums filled with earth and wired together. Four sheets of corrugated iron wired together.

"An incinerator which requires the tins to be dug out each morning will always be late in starting the day's work."

In fixed camps incinerators were adapted (*a*) to heat water for ablution; (*b*) to provide the heat for drying rooms.

Disposal of Greasy and Soapy Water. Kitchen slops contained grease and bred flies; soapy water—as from ablution bench or "baths and laundries"—might pollute the water supply or make a bog. To promote disposal by soakage the "grease trap," improvised, as for kitchen use, or made by the engineers, was in universal use; in baths and laundries in conjunction with sedimentation, as by lime. Whatever the form the principle was the same—to pass the water alternately under and over a series of baffle-plates, so that solids sank to the bottom, grease congealed at the top—if the trap, box or pit, was large enough. For baths and laundries a double set of baffled pits was found desirable, each large enough to hold one day's ablution water.

(*c*) *Dirt and Dust.* Infective dust was not a major problem in France.

(*d*) The medical aspect of the water problem has been dealt with fully in the text.

SANITATION

3. *The Immediate Vehicle, Food and Drink.* (*a*) *The supply dump.* "Too much attention cannot be given to the sanitation of dumps and the method of holding food in dumps. The construction of dumps is important. They should be 3ft. 6in. above the ground so as to allow of the tailboard loading. Bread, etc., must be kept clear from water, mud and dirt. Meat must be cut up on proper blocks which must be scraped and cleaned daily. It is possible to erect dumps with fly-proof screens for perishable articles, and all food should be properly protected from flies. It is the duty of the O.C. Supply Unit, and dumps should be inspected by the D.D.M.S., Corps and the A.D.M.S., Division."[4]

(*b*) *The Kitchen.* Various standard types of improvised fly and dust-proof kitchen safes were in constant use. Facilities for cleanliness varied greatly. In the best battalions the cooks got a fair spin. In some they did not.

(*c*) *Distribution.* The efficiency of a battalion might be gauged by the way the men were fed. In the A.I.F. cooking by company and messing by platoons was almost universal. The food was thus received hot, clean, and expeditiously.

(*d*) *The Mess-tin.* In some units regimental funds were used to obtain extra boilers for providing hot water.

(*e*) *The Cooks.* When all is said for "sanitation" it may be proposed that the last word lay with the cooks.

---

[4] From a lecture on "Supply in the Field" delivered by Major C. J. Goddard, O.C. Australian Corps Troops Supply Column, at the Australian Corps School for Medical Officers, Jan. 1918.

APPENDIX No. 13

FRONT LINE APPLICATION OF THE THOMAS SPLINT

THE technique devised for applying the Thomas Splint in the field varied somewhat in different Armies, and a number of modifications and improvements were introduced. At the end of the war, however, a very exact procedure had been worked out and this was embodied in a system of drill, by numbers, for the instruction of stretcher-bearers. The subjoined diagram and directions were issued to No. 2 A.C.C.S. (then in Fifth Army) in October, 1918:—

INSTRUCTIONS FOR FRONT LINE APPLICATION OF THOMAS SPLINT. DRILL BY NUMBERS

The Thomas Outfit consists of:—
Stretcher on Trestles.
Blankets, 3. Primus Stove.
Thomas Splint (largest size).
Reversible Stirrup (Sinclair's).
Suspension Bar.

Flannel Bandages (6 yards), 3.
Triangular Bandages, 4.
Dressings.
Safety Pins.
Gooch Splinting ($10'' \times 6''$ and $8'' \times 6''$).

Personnel required:—
Operator 1. No. 1 Assistant. No. 2 Assistant (if available).

When not in use the splint is kept hung up. The five slings of flannel bandage are rolled round the inner bar of the splint, the leather is kept soft by saddle soap, and the iron bars are smeared with vaseline.

Indications of Front Line Application.

1. For all fractures of the thigh bone, except where there is an extensive wound in the upper part of thigh or buttock, which would interfere with the fitting of the ring.
2. In severe fractures about the knee-joint or upper part of the tibia.
3. In certain cases of extensive wounds of fleshy part of thigh.

I. Warming (Réchauffment).
II. Extension.
III. Modified Clove-Hitch over Boot.
IV. Splint.
V. Fixation of Leg.
VI. Dressing Wound of Thigh.
VII. Gooch Splints and Triangular Bandages.
VIII. Figure-of-8 and Stirrup.
IX. Spanish Windlass.
X. Pad in Ring.
XI. Suspension Bar.
XII. Hot Water Bottles and Blankets.

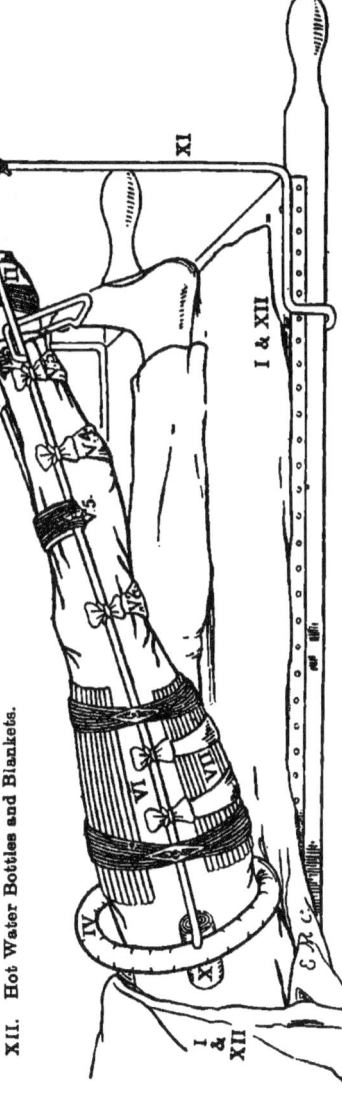

A FRONT LINE APPLICATION OF THE THOMAS SPLINT
(*See also Plates Nos. 39-40-41 at p. 348.*)

From diagram printed in France by the Army Printing & Stationery Services.

DETAIL OF THOMAS SPLINT DRILL

I.
Warming (Réchauffement).
On the word "One."—The stretcher, placed on trestles with a Primus Stove beneath, is prepared as follows:—The first blanket is folded lengthwise into three, two folds lie on the stretcher, one hangs over the side. The second blanket is arranged in the same way, one fold hanging over the other side of the stretcher.

The patient is now placed on the prepared stretcher and lies on four folds of blanket; the two folds hanging down form a hot air chamber. The third blanket is placed across the patient's chest, while the splint is being applied.

II.
Extension.
On the word "Two."—The No. 1 assistant stands at the foot of the stretcher facing the patient and opposite the injured limb. Grasping the heel of the boot with his right hand and the toe with his left, keeping the arms straight, he exerts a steady pull, thereby producing the necessary extension. The No. 2 assistant supports the injured part above and below the fracture.

III.
Modified Clove-Hitch.
On the word "Three."—To form the modified clove-hitch, the operator takes a length of 9 feet of flannel bandage. Holding it in the left hand by its mid-point, he grasps the centre of the left half with his right hand, palm to the right, and makes a loop which is carried up and passed behind the left hand, thus forming a clove-hitch with a diameter of 10 inches.

This is applied over the boot, with the short end on the outer side; the long end is carried under the instep, up and through the loop round the ankle. The two extension bands thus produced are ready to be attached to the splint later on. Care must be taken not to constrict the ankle.

IV.
Splint.
On the word "Four."—The operator threads on the splint; No. 1 assistant removing and re-applying upper and lower hands alternately to allow the ring to be passed over the foot. The splint should be pushed up under the buttock as far as possible, care being taken to keep the notched transverse bar horizontal. No. 2 assistant, as before, steadies the thigh.

V.
Fixation of Leg.
On the word "Five."—1. The extension bands of the clove-hitch are tied round the notched bar at the end of the splint as follows:—The outer band is passed over and under the bar, round the notch, drawn taut, and held over to the opposite side. The inner band is passed under and over the bar, then also round the notch where it crosses the first band and prevents it slipping. The two are finally tied off by a half bow.

2. The middle sling is tied off over the outer bar, No. 2 assistant keeping the knee partly bent.

3. and 4. The slings behind ankle and calf are tied, so that the leg rests in a shallow trough, half in and half out.

5. To prevent the leg rising off the splint a narrow fold bandage is placed across the leg, just below the knee; the ends are carried down between the leg and splint, brought up outside the bars, and tied off. The lower limb is now firmly fixed in a position of extension and it may be moved without causing pain to the patient or damage to the injured part.

VI.
Dressing Wound of Thigh.
On the word "Six."—The wound is exposed by cutting away the

overlying portion of trousers on the wounded part of the thigh, and the dressings are applied.

On the word "Seven."—The Gooch Splints are now applied. The short piece is placed behind, and secured by tying the remaining two slings. The long piece is placed on the front of the thigh, care being taken to avoid pressure on the knee-cap. The whole is now retained in position by two narrow fold bandages, carried round the thigh outside the bars of the splint. — VII. Gooch Splints and Bandages.

On the word "Eight."—The stirrup is "sprung" on to the splint above the ankle, its foot towards the stretcher. A bandage is then applied to form an additional sling, which by a figure-of-8-turn prevents lateral movement of the foot. — VIII. Stirrup and Figure-of-8.

On the word "Nine."—The extension bands are tightened and a small piece of wood or a nail is introduced to increase the tension by twisting up as required. — IX. Spanish Windlass.

On the word "Ten."—A pad is placed inside the ring on the outer side of the thigh to act as a wedge and prevent undue movement. — X. Pad in Ring.

On the word "Eleven."—The suspension bar is fitted to the stretcher with the "grip" away from the rackets. The splint is slung up not less than a hand's-breadth from the horizontal part of the suspension bar. To damp down the side movements, lateral tapes are tied to the uprights; they should not be tight. For the journey in the motor ambulance an additional band may be passed from the splint round one handle of the stretcher; this prevents excess of vertical movement. — XI. Suspension Bar.

On the word "Twelve."—Hot bottles are applied. The third blanket is folded into two lengthwise, and laid over the patient. The hanging folds of the first and second blankets are brought up over this so that the patient is evacuated with four folds of blanket on top as well as underneath. — XII. Hot Water Bottles and Blankets.

APPENDIX No. 14

WOUND SHOCK AND HAEMORRHAGE RESUSCITATION IN THE FIELD

THE subject matter of this appendix is complementary (*a*) to the general note in *Chapter XII* on *the concept "wound shock"* and (*b*) to the account given in *Chapter XXI* of experiments in field organisation carried out in the Australian Force during 1918, the purpose of which was to implement the conclusions arrived at as the result of experiment and research during 1917 and early 1918 regarding the most effective *treatment of haemorrhage and "wound shock."*

I. WOUND SHOCK AND HAEMORRHAGE

The contribution of the War of 1914-1918 to our knowledge of "wound shock." This at least cannot—on the medical side—be held against the War of 1914-1918, that the "scientific" interest of the many and varied experiments and observations of human behaviour under physical and psychic stress and strain was ever allowed to obscure their prime objective and purpose, namely, to serve as a guide to action. The sick or wounded soldier might suffer many and grievous hurts, and be the subject of much experiment and investigation; he would never be held to be "the uninteresting vehicle of a fascinating disease process." The campaign of research, experimental and clinical, into the essential nature of the disease-complex "wound shock"—for such, if we are to preserve a logical and consistent nosological outlook, the syndrome identified in this war as "pure" (secondary) wound shock must be regarded—had always in view this tremendous purpose, namely, to reduce the mortality in serious wounding consequential upon the evacuation of the wounded man to a field hospital for effective operation. This pragmatic and purposeful outlook is evident even in the highly "scientific" analytical researches undertaken in Britain (in the laboratories of the Medical Research Committee) and in America; as well as the clinical studies carried out in the various armies in the field. From the point of view of scientific progress it is perhaps open to philosophic doubt whether this exact definition of purpose were not a handicap. To the writer it seems, indeed, that we must candidly acknowledge that it was from the domain of clinical, rather than of analytical science that the most important and practical developments in the treatment of the physiological effects of wounding

1. The nature of Wound shock

and/or of haemorrhage chiefly derived. Certainly it is beyond cavil that much the most important contribution to the problem belongs wholly to the clinician. It was made at the end of 1914, by a British provincial orthopaedic surgeon; and was the use of the Thomas knee-splint in gunshot fracture-wounds of the femur; the very type and exemplar of shock-preventers. And (on the other part) the hypothesis of a toxic histamine-like "H" substance, set free in damaged muscle to act as a master-agent in the production of "pure" secondary shock, is a not unfair exemplar of the results of the search by analytical experiment for a pathogenic master-key in the production of the morbid state discriminated as "pure" wound shock. This hypothesis, indeed, held the field at the end of the war; it was—as we have suggested—inherent in the nature of the problem and inevitable that it should have failed to sustain the ambitious rôle assigned to it. And this was but one of the many hypotheses which, as the result of physiological analysis and research, were proposed as the basis for therapeutic experiment;— "acapnia," acidosis, fat-embolism, noci-association, adrenal exhaustion, adrenal excess, thermogenic failure (favoured by French physiologists), paralysis of the splanchnic circulation, cardiac failure, neural failure, and many more besides.

Under the acid test of clinical trial and experiment all failed to disclose the key to "exaemia"—the Hippocratic term proposed by Cannon to identify the problem of "the lost blood" in pure wound shock. The final report of the "Special Committee on Surgical shock" (on "Blood volume changes in wound shock and primary haemorrhage," published March 14th, 1919), opens thus:—"The fundamental cause of wound shock still remains obscure. No single aetiological factor has been suggested as the invariable cause"; and concludes as follows:—

"In shock without haemorrhage the reduction in blood volume indicates a marked disturbance of the normal mechanism by which the blood volume is maintained. . . . With a certain degree of shock, fluid supplied to the body will cause an increase in the blood volume. But in graver states of shock the smaller vessels of the vascular system are unable to retain an adequate amount of fluid. . . . Further knowledge is needed as to the cause of this alteration in the peripheral vessels, which appears to be a common feature in many shock-like conditions."

Between these two cardinal dates—December, 1914 and March, 1919 —in the Great War history of wound shock the historian finds himself confronted with a volume of clinical observation and of laboratory research which is in keeping with the medical and military significance of the problem. It is only possible here to attempt such brief outline of the evolution of the concept wound shock as will serve to link the advances made in the Great War with the stupendous problem that faces the world-in-arms to-day.

Evolution of the concept " wound shock "

Clinical observation and research. As a clinical phenomenon the "collapse" that accompanies severe wounding, and loss of blood, was studied by military surgeons as far back as Hippocrates, from whom the term "exaemia" was taken by Cannon. The condition was recognised in the 16th century; it was described by John Hunter in 1784, and the term "shock" was used much in the sense now employed by James Little in 1795. Larrey in 1800 knew the importance of removing shattered limbs before transportation (forestalling "a-noci-association"). The condition was exactly described and clinically analysed at the end of the 19th century: many of the theories, indeed, which even now rank as modern "were suspected and even enunciated at that time";—as those who were medical students in the nineties will recall. In 1899 Crile published his historic *Experimental Research into Surgical Shock*. At the outbreak of the war the existence of a clinical syndrome with features suggesting a definite pathological complex was clearly recognised, and its association with haemorrhage, cold, and extensive trauma (as by burns) was known.

Analytical experiment. We may date the first experimental study of the nature of wound shock to the beginnings of "scientific" medicine— the publication by Dr. William Harvey, in 1628, of his work *de Motu Cordis*. And, thereafter, until the beginning of this present century, the evolution of the concept "shock," as a pathogenic entity, is part and parcel with that of the ultimate physiological constants of life itself— of the "normal" temperature, "normal" blood-pressure, blood-volume, blood structure, p H balance, O/CO_2 interchange, basic metabolism, and so forth. We can identify the first specific observation bearing on the nature of shock as that of Goltz in 1870; that a tap on the exposed mesentery of the frog is followed by reflex dilatations of the splanchnic arteries; proving that the vaso-motor paralysis postulated as the result of "nervous shock" might be caused by an external trauma. In 1914 Crile enunciated the theory of "noci-association" to account for the peripheral stagnation of blood.

But, speaking generally, the position in 1914 as regards "shock" may not inaptly be compared with that which has been recorded of sepsis. Anaesthesia had in a great measure eliminated it from surgery; the motor car had not "arrived" to create it as a common disorder in social life. As a consequence, we find in the early years of the war a return to past history in wound shock only less striking than that observed in wound disease.

The problem set out. The consensus of opinions (it is proposed) from the late war and the late peace affirms the importance of visualising the development of wound shock as a continuous progress in physiological degradation. It is not less insistent that the primary trauma is essentially that of "nerve," as the secondary break-down is that of the circulation.

"Primary" shock is seen in its purest form in that caused by coronary embolus. "An outstanding feature of the onset is collapse. The patient is shocked, ashen grey, cold, and bedewed with sweat. The pulse may be rapid, small in volume, easily compressible, almost imperceptible, and there is usually a dramatic drop in the blood-pressure. The condition of shock may be so pronounced that life is in danger."

We need not follow the analogy further than to propose as legitimate the sequence, "nervous" shock, circulatory stagnation, tissue damage as the result of the impact of continued traumata of the kind which have been indicated in the previous letterpress dealing with this matter. The War and post-War research into the physiology of the peripheral circulation; or therapeutic discoveries as "continuous" infusion, or the chemio-therapy of Neo Synephrin, may concern this history only as they conspire to urge that a bounden duty and service to humanity rests on experimental physiology and pharmacology to combine with clinical science in the endeavour to fill the gaps still left by the late war and the late peace between theory and practice in the treatment of wound shock and haemorrhage. Especially (it is suggested) is it required that

WOUND SHOCK

the immense body of facts already revealed by experiment and observation be integrated in an endeavour to determine whether or no it is legitimate or profitable to conceive wound shock as a single clinical-pathogenic entity; and not rather as the resultant of inter-related failures in all or most of the several processes which combine to maintain corporeal life.

"Wound shock" and haemorrhage. One feature of wound shock as a practical problem calls, however, for comment, since it is inseparable from any attempt to meet the demands of treatment in the field. This is the relation between "wound shock" and haemorrhage. Throughout the history of wound shock the difficulty of distinguishing between the results of haemorrhage *per se* and the results of wound shock *per se* have been—as they are to-day—not less formidable in the sphere of action than of research. It can be stated categorically that whether or not haemorrhage in itself can be a *cause of shock*, it is certainly the most potent contributing factor in the development of vital collapse. It was demonstrated both by experiment and by clinical observation, that a minimal additional haemorrhage might reverse the course of a natural reaction to a rapid failure.

It is not proposed to enter upon a technical study of the methods adopted for the "resuscitation" of shocked and exsanguined men. The more strictly technical "lessons" of the war and results of post-war research have been embodied in official and semi-official schemes, as "blood-banks" and so forth, and implemented by exact organisation. But it is believed that it will be of interest and perhaps of use to follow the lines of development and to attempt a philosophic "appreciation" of the present significance of the observations then made.

2. Treatment of wound shock and haemorrhage

The field for experiment. The tenacity of life inherent in the human body was a constant source of amazement and of inspiration to those engaged in research work in the field. The tendency of the human being to recovery from the effects of injury is indeed astonishing.[1] It may be stated with confidence as an incentive for the future, that there remained at the end of this war a wide field of potential recovery for therapeutic exploration.

The factors in recovery. As discerning a "lesson" in the War of 1914-1918, we propose that from the point of view of treatment the most useful concept of wound shock (including here haemorrhage shock) is one which identifies clearly a dual structure in the morbid process, namely of *injury* and of *reaction.* This (at least) is certain; that in no morbid state met with in this war, whether through "wounding" or through "disease," was the natural process of recovery more clearly revealed as determining the issue of life and death. The *vis medicatrix naturae* is here, indeed, the biological mechanism of life itself. No observation of the War of 1914-1918 could be more pertinent and impressive for the War of 1939-.... than this—that, whatever its patho-

---

[1] The following experience is recorded by Major Noel Kirkwood: "After the 12th October stunt at Passchendaele I was doing the rounds of Ambulance relay points. ... I was [about to] take a stretcher from a dead man who had been there for three days. To my surprise I detected the faintest signs of breathing. He had a bullet through the chest. It 'had been three days of almost constant rain, and cold rain, and yet that man recovered."

genic constitution, wound shock is essentially a dynamic and vital *process* not a static structural *condition*, and is susceptible to "prevention" much more than it is to "cure." Each of the two factors concerned in anoxaemia and tissue-death—i.e. the *degree of "shock"* and its *duration* —may initiate a vicious circle. Unless, and until, the vessel walls should retain the infused or transfused fluid, or resorb the "lost" blood-plasma, and thus restore the normal "blood-volume" and circulation, neither colloidal saline nor even "whole-blood" can do more than maintain a precarious minimum of oxygenation. And the physiological time-constants of "shock" were found to be as inexorable as we have seen were those of sepsis. For, while "shock" or blood-loss, even of high grade, is very responsive to help, after severe or long continued anoxaemia the artificial restoration of blood-volume is but the beginning to a tedious recovery, which may extend over days, and is highly susceptible to added trauma; as through ether-anaesthesia, sepsis, operation, or secondary haemorrhage.

The rational implements in recovery. The rational processes of repair (as distinct from prophylaxis) which, as the result of clinical observation and experimental research established a claim to permanent value, were *the restoration of blood-volume* in wound shock and *the repair of blood-tissue* in haemorrhage and haemorrhage shock. Of the two the restoration of blood-volume was found the more important. 75 per cent. of blood-tissue—it was found—may be lost without necessarily fatal results, so the blood-volume and the circulation be maintained. This fact led to a curious divergence of practice which derived largely from pre-war developments, and which (it is suggested) must still be held to contain "an open question" for the "rough and tumble" of "total" warfare.

Pre-war developments. Credit for the scientific exploitation of blood transfusion as a therapeutic procedure belongs chiefly to America. Before the war, British surgeons and physiologists had strayed on the lines of saline infusion.[2] Between 1901 and 1910 experiments by Landsteiner, Moss and others into the phenomena of iso-haemolosis and iso-agglutination had discriminated four types of blood, and thus laid the foundation for a solution of the "donor" problem. By 1914 Alexis Carrel's method of "direct" transfusion, and Crile's cannulae had been replaced by the paraffined glass tube between donor-artery and recipient-vein, and the syringe method of Von Ziemssen. In November, 1914—a cardinal date—the first "transfusion" with whole "citrated" blood was carried out by Professor Agote, of Buenos Aires. Thus, for the greatest orgy of blood-letting in human history medical science had ready in "transfusion of blood" a means for its prompt replenishment which in the last two years of the war was widely exploited in the treatment of both haemorrhage and shock; which has, indeed, (God save the mark) been extolled as a triumph and "lesson" for peace from that vampire. If we may judge from recorded experience cases calling for such treatment were much more in evidence than in any previous war. This, we may suppose, was due to two factors; *first* to scientific attrition

---

[2] Thus Rose and Carless, *Surgery*, 9th Edition, 1911. "Success . . . *depends* on the introduction of a sufficient *quantity* of the fluid as a temporary substitute for the blood which has been lost, *rather than* on its *quality;* for it has been proved that the transfused blood of another person is rapidly destroyed and eliminated. Hence transfusion has now been replaced by what is known as infusion which consists of injecting some bland fluid isotonic with blood plasma." (The italics are as in the original.)

warfare, with its lacerating and multiple wounds and winter fighting; *second* (and the more important) to a medical service organised and accredited as never before for the succouring of wounded, whereby deeper levels (so to speak) of damage were "tapped" for treatment, and more precarious rescues attempted from that No-Man's Land of death and life that supplies the tragic and fluctuating figures for "died of wounds."

The lines of progress: transfusion v. infusion. The history of the treatment of wound shock and haemorrhage—which for practical purposes included shock with haemorrhage—by the artificial replacement of red blood cells and/or of blood-fluid, is one of which barely the salient features can be presented here. It may perhaps be summed up

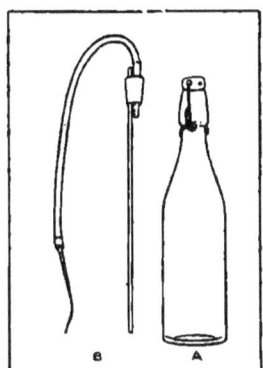 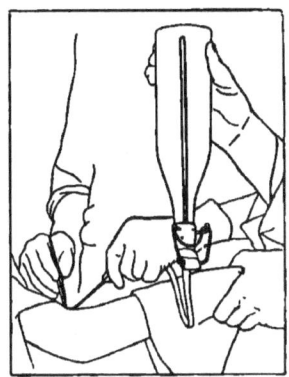

Glass milk-bottle adapted for the purpose of saline infusion. (From "A Practical Method for Supplying and Administering Intravenously Prepared Sterile Saline and Colloid-Saline Solutions in Cases of Haemorrhage and Shock in the Field," by Lieut.-Colonel P. Fiaschi, A.A.M.C., 1917.) This "gadget" was commended by Professor Bayliss in his report to the Medical Research Committee on "Intravenous Injections to Replace Blood," Nov. 1917.

as a co-operative competition between infusion—backed by the Old World—and transfusion, pressed by the New; with the latter dominant: but in the final stage converging toward a procedure which combined the two, in effect, blood cells suspended in colloidal fluid or colloidal fluid to which a proportion of blood cells was added.

The issue cannot better be stated than in the first paragraph of the first report of the "Special Investigation Committee on Surgical Shock and Allied Conditions"; by Professor Bayliss on "Intravenous Injections to Replace Blood," published by the Medical Research Committee on the 25th November, 1917:—

A necessary preliminary to a systematic study of the phenomena grouped together under the name "Shock" is to obtain some knowledge of the conditions requisite for the appropriate treatment of the simplest case, that of a fall of blood pressure due to haemorrhage uncomplicated by other states. As will be seen, however, in practice this simplification is scarcely possible, except in certain cases.

"Although, no doubt, the transfusion of blood itself is the ideal method of replacing that lost by haemorrhage, this procedure is not always practicable and requires caution or preliminary test of compatibility of the donor's blood with that of the recipient. Moreover, if it were possible to practice the intravenous injection of an appropriate artificial solution at Advanced Dressing Stations, many lives might be preserved. This aspect of the problem has been especially insisted on by Lieut.-Colonel Fiaschi, A.A.M.C., and by Captain Bullock, R.A.M.C."

The history of "Gum Saline." The fate of crystalloid infusions—as Ringer's—has been noted in the text (*Chapter XII*); physiologically and militarily they were rejected. The idea of adding a colloid to the solution was first exploited by Hogan, of Chicago; who, in 1915, carried out successful experiments with gelatine. The search by Professor Bayliss for a more convenient substance led him to conclude that "gelatine possesses no property of importance that gum arabic does not." Thereafter, "gum-saline" competed with whole blood—direct or citrated—as a treatment for wound shock, and the collapse due to haemorrhage.

The history of blood transfusion. As a practical procedure this came from the New World—both U.S.A. and Canada—in 1916, and having "caught on" at the Base moved up with the operative centre of gravity to the Front. Its development in the C.C.S. has been described (in *Chapter XXI*), its exploitation by the Australian Corps is the subject of the second part of this Appendix.

Comments

There is no reason to doubt but that in the organised schemes for injecting blood, gum, or glucose-saline into the veins of persons exsanguined or shocked the Medical Service of to-day has a weapon of high potential value. But the experience of the War of 1914-1918 suggests that the care and circumspection necessary in the material preparations for the procedure have a parallel in the mode of its employment; in particular that the purpose in view be clear—whether to supply blood-volume or haemoglobin. And it would seem desirable to point out that the experience of the late war proved that for the augmenting of blood-volume the par-enteral route is but a second string to natural absorption —*e.g.*, as promoted by the "forced absorption" introduced by Robertson and Bock (M.R.C. Report No. 25). There was much *post hoc ergo propter hoc* recording of experience in the joy of a new means of rescue. The Americans found that the results both from transfusion and infusion fell off greatly in their advance through the Argonnes from those observed in the previous war of position.

Be this as it may, it is to be accepted that both procedures in particular transfusion of blood by one of the various techniques now employed, have come to stay; and that the means for implementing their potentiality are to be exploited with energy and "brains." Both of these were employed in the organisation of the Australian Field Ambulance Resuscitation Teams.

The following is a list of the reports of the Special Investigation Committee on Surgical Shock and Allied Conditions appointed by the Medical Research Committee of National Health Insurance: presented between November, 1917, and March, 1919. The constitution of the Committee was as follows: Professor W. M. Bayliss, F.R.S.; Professor F. A. Bainbridge; Lieut.-Colonel W. B. Cannon, M.O.R.C., U.S.A.; Dr. H. H. Dale, F.R.S.; Colonel T. R. Elliott, F.R.S., R.A.M.C.; Captain John Fraser, R.A.M.C.; Colonel H. McI. W. Gray, R.A.M.C.; Dr. P. P. Laidlaw, F.R.S.; Major A. N. Richards; Professor C. S. Sherrington, F.R.S.; Professor E. H. Starling, F.R.S.; Major-General Cuthbert S. Wallace, A.M.S. (T).

3. Official Research on wound shock and haemorrhage

No. 1. Intravenous Injections to Replace Blood (W. M. Bayliss). 25th November, 1917.

No. 2. Investigation of the Nature and Treatment of Wound Shock and Allied Conditions: I. A Clinical Study of the Blood Pressure in Wound Conditions (Captain John Fraser, R.A.M.C., and Captain E. M. Cowell, R.A.M.C.). II. Some Alterations in the Distribution and Character of the Blood (W. B. Cannon, John Fraser, and Captain A. N. Hooper, R.A.M.C.). III. Acidosis in Cases of Shock, Haemorrhage and Gas Infection (W. B. Cannon). IV. The Initiation of Wound Shock (E. M. Cowell). V. A Consideration of the Nature of Wound Shock (W. B. Cannon). VI. The Preventive Treatment of Wound Shock (W. B. Cannon, John Fraser, and E. M. Cowell). 25th December, 1917.

No. 3. The Use of Intravenous Injections of Gum Acacia in Surgical Shock (Captain Hamilton Drummond, R.A.M.C., and Captain E. S. Taylor, R.A.M.C.), 7th January, 1918.

No. 4. Memorandum on Blood Transfusion (Captain Oswald H. Robertson, M.R.C., U.S.A.). 4th April, 1918.

No. 5. I. The Value of Haemoglobin and Blood Pressure Observations in Surgical Cases (Captain H. C. Bazett, R.A.M.C.). II. Observations on the Blood Pressure in Gas Gangrene Infection (Hamilton Drummond and E. S. Taylor). 25th April, 1918.

No. 6. Memorandum on Blood Volume after Haemorrhage (Oswald H. Robertson and Captain Arlie V. Bock, M.R.C., U.S.A.). 8th August, 1918.

No. 7. Acidosis and Shock (By the Sub-Committee). October, 1918.

No. 8. Traumatic Toxaemia as a Factor in Shock: I. Introductory (Cuthbert S. Wallace). II. The Action of Histamine: Its bearing on Traumatic Toxaemia as a Factor in Shock. (H. H. Dale, P. P. Laidlaw, and A. N. Richards). III. Supplementary Note on Histamine Shock (H. H. Dale). IV. Note on Muscle Injury in Relation to Shock (W. B. Cannon and W. M. Bayliss). V. Further Observations on the Results of Muscle Injury and their Treatment (W. M. Bayliss). VI. Some Characteristics of Shock Induced by Tissue Injury (W. B. Cannon). VII. Observations on Wound Shock, especially with Regard to Damage of Muscle (Major J. W. McNee, Captain A. F. S. Sladden, and Captain J. E. McCartney, R.A.M.C.). VIII. Blood Volume in Wound Shock (Captain N. M. Keith, R.A.M.C.). IX. Brief Summary of Changes in the Central Nervous System Occurring in Various Forms of Shock (Lieut.-Colonel F. W. Mott, F.R.S., R.A.M.C.). 14th March, 1919.

No. 9. Blood Volume Changes in Wound Shock and Primary Haemorrhage (N. M. Keith). 14th March, 1919.

II. THE AUSTRALIAN FIELD AMBULANCE RESUSCITATION TEAMS[3]

(a) *Report of meeting of the Australian Corps Resuscitation Teams Committee held on 14th October, 1918:—*

"In accordance with D.D.M.S., Australian Corps Medical Instruction Routine No. 15 dated 7.10.18, a meeting of the Resuscitation Teams

[3] Capt. N. M. Guiou, C.A.M.C., was instrumental in introducing similar, if less exactly organised, methods into the field ambulances of the Canadian Force.

Committee was held at Hallencourt on 14.10.18 to review the work of the Divisional Resuscitation Teams and to furnish a report thereon. There were present:—
President—Major A. W. Holmes à Court, a/D.A.D.M.S.
Members—Major ' Hayward (1st Aust. Divn.) Major Hutchinson, Capt. Wood (2nd Aust. Divn.), Major North, Capt. Stump (3rd Aust. Divn.) Capt. O'Regan (4th Aust. Divn.) Capt. Gray (5th Aust. Divn.) (Major Gordon-Taylor, a/Consulting Surgeon, Fourth Army, was also present.)

"Work of the teams since their inauguration was discussed and the appended report forwarded.

"Major Gordon-Taylor expressed appreciation of the work done and has furnished a special report (*q.v.*)

"*Report of the Committee:* A Surgical Resuscitation Team has recently been formed in each division of the Australian Corps for the purpose of performing urgent surgical work and resuscitation in the forward area.

"This has proved an effective means of treating many seriously wounded men otherwise difficult to deal with efficiently.

"Under the present conditions of warfare considerable time must inevitably elapse before a seriously wounded man can receive adequate attention at the C.C.S. This delay frequently involves loss of life or limb unless the case receives efficient early treatment at the Main Dressing Station.

"The class of cases particularly involved includes:—
i. Shattered limbs.
ii. Injuries to blood vessels involving the use of tourniquets.
iii. Cases of severe shock or haemorrhage.

"A team consists of two medical officers—one proficient in war surgery, blood transfusion, etc., another expert in administration of nitrous-oxide oxygen anaesthesia and in general resuscitation together with an N.C.O. and three orderlies who receive special training in this work at C.C.S.

"A team is attached to a Field Ambulance in each Division and is completely mobile moving with its equipment to A.D.S. or M.D.S. in a large Motor Ambulance Car.

"Operative work is restricted to necessary surgical procedures, ligatures of arteries, urgent amputations, etc.

"Resuscitation is effected by transfusion of blood from donors carefully selected from lightly wounded cases, injections of gum, sod. bicarb and glucose solution, etc. and *réchauffement.*

"Many limbs were saved by the early removal of tourniquets and it is found that severely shocked patients arrive at C.C.S. in much better condition after resuscitation, transfusion, etc. than would otherwise be the case.

"The use of nitrous-oxide oxygen anaesthesia does not involve any period of delay in recovery and patients can be evacuated almost immediately after operation.

"It has been found that teams working on these lines at M.D.S's or A.D.S's have expedited the work both of the Field Ambulances and the C.C.S's. The main work of the Ambulances in evacuation of the

WOUND SHOCK

wounded is not interfered with; moreover the transference of the serious cases to the team obviates congestion and delay in the main dressing room. The C.C.S. is enabled to concentrate its attention on abdominal, thoracic and other urgent surgical work as the cases dealt with by the teams are marked with distinctive labels and in many instances are found to be fit for immediate evacuation to Base Hospital.

"The lives of many men have undoubtedly been saved by this method of early treatment in the forward area and it is recommended that the principle of surgical resuscitation teams might with advantage be widely adopted throughout the Medical Services.

"Record of cases by teams in recent operations, Aug.-Sept., 1918 (exclusive of cases receiving general resuscitation, *réchauffement*, etc., closure of penetrating chest wounds, major dressings, etc.).

Operations 98: Blood transfusions 52: Gum and other intravenous injections 62.

"*Report of Consulting Surgeon, Fourth Army:* Several months' experience in the Casualty Clearing zone behind the Australian Corps has enabled me to form an estimate of the excellent work of the resuscitation teams of that Corps. There can be no room for doubt that very many lives have been saved by the work of Major Holmes à Court and the members of the other resuscitation teams. Their experience in the Dressing Stations coincides with that of the Casualty Clearing Hospitals that in blood transfusion we have the most remarkable and valuable means of treating cases of severe shock and haemorrhage. Their results conclusively prove the value of these methods of resuscitation in the Field Ambulances."

(*b*) *Establishment and Equipment of a Divisional Surgical Resuscitation Team.*

Establishment:

Medical Officers .. .. 2 } From T.S.D.
Other Ranks (including 1 N.C.O.) 4 }

Equipment:

Surgical Instruments (see Appendix A) 1 set No. 1 F.S.P. O/T.S.D.
Gas Oxygen apparatus .. .. 1 (Field Service Panier of the Tent Subdivision of the Field Ambulance concerned.)
Blood transfusion set (see Appendix B) 1
Gum infusion set .. 1
Bowls, Basins, etc. } Appendix C
Dressings }
Réchauffement Box 1

Transport:

1 Motor Ambulance to be available, for Divisional team for T.S.D. transport.

The whole to be a complete unit, mobile, attached for duty to M.D.S. or A.D.S. as required.

When Division is out of line, the team to remain attached to an Ambulance, *supernumerary to its establishment*, and to be available for ordinary ambulance duty if necessary.

When the Division is out of the line the team resumes duty with their T.S.D. or is detailed to a C.C.S. for instruction and practice.

APPENDIX A

Surgical Instruments [Minimum requirements]:
Operating set from No. 1 Field Service Pannier, of the Tent Subdivision.

From Red Cross.

Mosquito Forceps ..	4
Laves Toothed Forceps	2
Shimmelbush Mask	1
Mouth Gag	1
Tongue Forceps	1

Surgical Razors ..	2
Steriliser (20 inch)	1
Hypodermic Syringe ..	1
Gloves (Surgical) Pairs	6

APPENDIX B

Gum Infusion Set.
Gum Solution (18 doses)
Gum Infusion Set (Army)

From Advanced Depot Medical Stores

Blood Transfusion Set.
Blood Grouping apparatus.

Micro slides ..	6
Capillary Pipettes	2
Watch glasses	2
Serum groups II and III	

Distilled Water (bottles) 1
Sod. Citrate (Sol'n 1·5 per cent.)
                      1 bottle (4 oz.)
(*From Mobile Lab.*)

Transfusion apparatus.
Kimptons flasks   6

Robertson's Bottle

Soda Citrate solution 3·4 per cent.
(Sterile)

(These to be autoclared, and paraffined at C.C.S. and carried sterile.) for citrated blood.

(*Advanced Depot Medical Stores*)

(The use of preserved blood was recommended by the Committee.)

APPENDIX C

Bowls. Kidney	2
do. 10-inch	4
do. small	4
Acetylene Lamp Operating box	1
Surgical Gowns Jaconnet ..	6
Splints, Dressings, Towels, etc. } Ether, Chloroform }	

Dressing Containers 3
Basins, enamel, washing, 14-inch .. 3
Oil Cloth American .. .. 10 yards
                      (*A.D. Medical Stores*)
Stoves. Primus 2
                      (*Red Cross*)
To be requisitioned from ambulance running M.D.S.

Practically whole equipment can be packed in a Field Service Basket Pannier.

(c) *Representations submitted by the D.M.S., A.I.F. to Headquarters, A.I.F., for a permanent establishment:*—

Resuscitation Teams for employment in the Forward Areas: For some time past it has been felt that the lives of many wounded could be saved by instituting resuscitation and shock treatment at an earlier stage in the forward areas. For example, under the arrangements which existed in the 3rd and 4th Armies during the military operations in the Albert-Arras Sector, in July and August (1918), patients were received at several C.C.S's after a journey of 25 to 35 kilometres.

"Since the beginning of the war the C.C.S's have progressively lost their mobility, and have now reached the stage when they are practically Stationary or General Hospitals, with the result that they are not only unable to quickly follow up an advance of our own troops, but also in the event of a retreat are very likely to fall into the enemy's hands.

"At a rough estimate the wounded now arriving at C.C.S's fall into three groups—

1. 85 per cent. who suffer no appreciable hardship from the

WOUND SHOCK

journey to the C.C.S. after their wounds have been attended to at a Dressing Station.

2. 10 per cent. who arrive in varying degrees of recoverable shock but respond to treatment sufficiently to permit of their being successfully treated at C.C.S.

3. 5 per cent. are in such a "shocked" condition that they are practically hopeless.

"In many of the cases in Group 3, the long journey to C.C.S. has a great deal to do with the hopeless condition of the patients on arrival and these could be saved by resuscitation and shock treatment at the main dressing stations. Many of the cases in Group 2 would be greatly benefited by similar measures and their prospect of ultimate recovery increased.

"In addition to the resuscitation work lives could be saved by operating on the following cases at the Main Dressing Stations.

1. Cases of severe haemorrhage in which large vessels require ligation and so permit earlier removal of tourniquets.

2. Hopelessly shattered limbs requiring amputation after which they stand a journey to C.C.S. very much better.

"With these objects in view the Australian Corps has organised Resuscitation Teams on the basis of one (1) per Division, and in the recent fighting much valuable work was done by the Australian Corps Resuscitation Team under Major A. Holmes à Court, A.A.M.C. This work was rendered possible by the cordial support of Major-General Sir Anthony Bowlby and the Consulting Surgeon of the 4th Army.

"Much valuable work on this subject has also been carried out by the Shock Committee of the 3rd Army although the same opportunities for carrying their proposals into effect were not present.

"The Australian Resuscitation Teams consist of—1 Surgeon, 1 Anaesthetist and 4 Other Ranks (including 1 N.C.O.). The equipment necessary is not large and can be carried by one motor ambulance. Teams would be under the direction of the D.M.S. Army, and be attached to the Main Dressing Stations for duty.

"The coming winter affords a favourable opportunity for organising these teams before the more active operations and probable 'War of movement' next Spring, and I am so convinced of their value that I consider their continuance in the A.A.M.C. is essential, and would further respectfully suggest that these recommendations be forwarded to the D.G., B.E.F. for his consideration." (*Letter dated 20th September, 1918.*)

III. FRENCH ESTIMATE OF THE DEGREES OF URGENCY OF VARIOUS WOUNDS[4]

Classification of wounded. Triage being the classification of wounded according to the degree of severity of their condition and the operative urgency, the execution of it is facilitated, if one brings in advance under the eyes of the classifying officer, a table which shows the classification of wounded and which reduces the uncertainties of distribution. The prognosis of wounds may be reduced (*ramené*) to four degrees of

---

[4] From Mignon, *Vol. IV, p. 476*

severity: very serious, serious, moderate and slight. Correspondingly, the wounded may be classified as operative cases of extreme or of first, second, or third degrees of urgency.

The very seriously wounded, requiring very urgent operation are those suffering from large visceral wounds, from shattering of the limbs, perforation of the abdomen, active haemorrhage or haemorrhage masked by tourniquet, or from wound shock.

Seriously wounded of the first degree of operative urgency are sufferers from penetrating wounds of the head or thorax, from fracture of the spine, from fracture of the thigh, comminuted fracture of the leg or upper limb, or wounds of the pelvis.

Adapted to the scheme of evacuation, this classification determines the detention of the very seriously wounded, so-called intransportables, at an easy distance from the lines; the retention of the seriously wounded at the primary H.O.E. [forward C.C.S.] and the evacuation of the moderately and slightly wounded to the hospital centres of the D.E. [Lines of Communication]—the secondary H.O.E. [rearwards C.C.S.].

The proportion between the categories of wounded has been difficult to estimate. It seems that it may be placed at—10 per cent. very seriously wounded, 15 per cent. seriously wounded, 25 per cent. moderately wounded and 50 per cent. slightly wounded.

IV. AMERICAN EXPERIENCE WITH NON-TRANSPORTABLE CASES[5]

The American Official History records an exact observation carried out in 1917 on 340 cases of "non-transportable" wounded, in 79 of whom the time between the reception of the wound and the surgical treatment was known. The wounds were of similar severity. The figures showed a mortality of only 11 per cent. in cases treated within the first three hours; it rose to 37 per cent. when there was a delay of between three and six hours (though infection was not marked until after six hours); it was 75 per cent. in the eighth to the tenth hour. "Although during the first hour the cases were not in complete shock, they were in grave condition, anaemic and cold."

---

[5] From *The Medical Department of the United States Army in the World War*, Vol. XI, p. 207.

CONVENTIONAL SIGNS

Regimental Aid Post shown thus . .
Bearer Relay Post. . . . .
Collecting Post. . . . .
Amb. Waggon Loading Post . . . .
Motor Amb. Loading Post . . . .
Light Railway Loading Post. . . . . . .
Train Loading Post. . . . .
Evacuating Routes. . . . .
Adv. Dressing Station. . . . .
A.D.S. Walking Wounded . . . .
Main Dressing Station . . . . . .
M.D.S. Walking Wounded . . . . . .
Adv. Operating Centre . . . .
Corps Relay Post. . . . .
Motor Amb. Convoy. . . . .
Casualty Clearing Station . . . . .
Gas Centre. . . . .
Water Point. . . . .
Rest Station . . . .
Div. Collecting Station . . . .
Sanitary Section . . . .
Mobile Laboratory . . . .
Hygienic Laboratory. . . . .
Adv. Depôt Medical Stores . . . . . .
Baths & Laundries. . . . .
Stationary Hospital . . . .
General Hospital . . . .
Auxiliary Hospital . . . .
Dermatological Hospital. . . . .
Base Depôt Medical Stores . . . . . .
Convalescent Depôt. . . . .
Command Depôt. . . . .
Training Depôt . . . .

INDEX

PERSONAL

Ranks shown after surnames of officers and men are the highest attained by each.

Page numbers followed by *n* indicate that the reference is to a footnote on the page specified.

ADAMI, Col. J. G. (C.B.E., *Canad. A.M.C.*), 16*n*, 21*n*, 823*n*
AGOTE, Prof., carries out transfusion of whole blood, 1914, 950
ALLAN, Maj. R. Marshall (M.C., *R.A.M.C. & A.A.M.C.*), 289*n*
ALLBUTT, Rt. Hon. Sir Clifford (K.C.B., *F.R.S.*), 487
ANDERSON, Lt.-Col. J. H. (C.M.G., C.B.E., *A.A.M.C.*), *D.A.D.M.S., 3rd Aust. Div.*, 158*n*, 165, 166*n*, 170, 171, 176*n*; *A.D.M.S. for Personnel*, 798, 806, 815*n*, 816*n*, 828*n*, 838*n*; memo. by, 812
ANDERSON, Brig.-Gen. Sir R. M. McC. (K.C.M.G.), 808*n*
ANDREWES, Maj. Sir F. W. (O.B.E., *F.R.S., R.A.M.C., T.*), 309
APPLEYARD, Maj. S. V. (D.S.O., *A.A.M.C.*), 207
ARMIN, Gen. Sixt von, report on Ger. med. experience on Somme, 71*n*
ARNOLD, Capt. G. P. (M.C., *A.A.M.C.*), 525*n*
ASTON, Maj.-Gen. Sir George (K.C.B., p.s.c.), 682*n*

BABTIE, Lt.-Gen. Sir W. (V.C., K.C.B., K.C.M.G., *A.M.S.*), 822*n*
BAINBRIDGE, Prof. F. A., *F.R.S.*, 953
BARBER, Maj.-Gen. G. W. (C.B., C.M.G., D.S.O., V.D., *A.A.M.C.*), 132, 579, 630, 631, 635*n*, 672, 682, 715*n*, 738, 742, 748, 751, 752*n*, 756, 799, (Plate) 69; *A.D.M.S., 4th Aust. Div.*, 29, 120, 127, 174, 296*n*, 477*n*, 624, 634*n*, 711; advances R.A.P.'s, 62; keeps down sick wastage, 98; his orders, Hindbg. Line attack, 133; his memo. to D.M.S., 136; no special order by, Messines, 172; his opinion *re* med. arrngts. for Messines, 182*n*; Polygon Wd., 213; complains of physique of med. rfcts., 237*n*; comments on bearer sgts., 282; note on R.M.O., 294*n*; issues "Standing Orders," 137*n*, 652-3; his prepns. for mobile war, 653; his notes on: san. sectns., 654*n*, 936-7, dental units, 655, transpt.

BARBER, Maj.-Gen. G. W.—*continued*.
of wounded, 657, portable A.D.S., 659, "rest stn.," 714, *D.D.M.S. Aust. Corps*, 604, 633, 648; as an organiser, 634; narrtve. by, 648*n*; his adminstn., 650-51; his *Standing Orders for A.A.M.C.*, 652-3, 889, 889-99; account of resus. teams, 663; co-ordinates efforts of Divns., 670; his comments on Amer. med. service, 675; his *Med. Instn. No. 29, July 1918*, attchmnt. of Americans, 887-8; B. of Amiens: his orders, etc., 684, 685, med. arrangts., 688, 877-9, his comments, 690; his *Circ. Memo. 12 Aug.*, 694, 884-5; his instns. for B. of Chuignes, 699; measures for phys. fitness, 716; his instns. for 18 *Sept.*, 727; issues *Med. Instns. No. 58, 27 Sept.*, 740-1; difclts. after Armistice, 796; traing. of amb. offcrs., 838-9
BARRETT, Capt. A. H. (*A.A.M.C.*), 279*n*
BARTON, Maj. A. S. D. (D.S.O., *A.A.M.C.*), 332
BASTER, 7305 S/Sgt. M. T., 383*n*
BAYLISS, Prof. Sir William, *F.R.S.*, 339, 951, 952, 953
BAZETT, Capt. H. C. (O.B.E., M.C., *R.A.M.C.*), 953
BEADON, Col. R. H. (C.B.E., p.s.c., *R.A.S.C.*), 290*n*, 569*n*
BEALE, P. T. B., *F.R.C.S.*, 589*n*
BEAMISH, Maj. F. T. (O.B.E., *A.A.M.C.*), 124*n*, 125
BEAN, C. E. W., *Litt.D.*, 720*n*
BEAN, Maj. J. W. B. (*A.A.M.C.*), 71*n*
BEGG, Col. C. Mackie (C.B., C.M.G., *N.Z.M.C.*), *A.D.M.S., N.Z. Div.*, 29, 43; *D.D.M.S., II Anzac*, 48, 652*n*; his mthds. at Messines, 162, 164, 175*n*; at Broodseinde, 223; note on clearnce., 229; opinion *re* S.-B's., 249
BELL, Lt.-Col. G. (O.B.E., *A.A.M.C.*), 314*n*, 349*n*, 777*n*
BERNARD, Claude, 487; his concept of life, 486
BESLEY, Col. F. A., *Consult. Surg., II Amer. Corps*, 751

961

INDEX (PERSONAL)

BEVERIDGE, Maj.-Gen. Sir W. W. O. (K.B.E., C.B., D.S.O., *A.M.S.*), 508n, 557n, 590n; his article on housing, 931-3
BIGNELL, Lt.-Col. F. L. (D.S.O., *A.A.M.C.*), 112-13, 120
BIRD, Capt. D. (*R.A.M.C*), 360n
BIRD, Col. F. D. (C.B., *R.A.M.C.*), 360n
BIRD, Maj.-Gen. Sir W. G. (K.B.E., C.B., C.M.G., D.S.O.), 704-5
BIRDWOOD, F.-M. Lord, 11 *et seq.*, 89n, 142n, 362, 380, 383n, 453n, 468, 531n, 614, 767n, 768, 775, 776, 803, 809, 817, 819, 824n, 841, 842, 848, 849, 851, 856, 857, (Plate) 629; *G.O.C., I Anzac Corps*, 29, 39; *G.O.C., A.I.F.*, 808, 818n; attnds. W. Off. Confce., 12n; all Aust. Divns. serve under, 79; presses for their relief, 155; inspects 1st Div. Rest Stn., 246n; his understanding of Aust. desires, 259; commands Fifth Army, but remains G.O.C., A.I.F., 648; his policy as to reduced estabs., 708; his concern *re* repat. and demob., 791; discusses educatn. scheme, 797; Howse's correspce. with, 818; his views on recruitg., 846; insists on high phys. standard, 852; supports D.M.S., A.I.F., 853; returns "B Class" men to Aust., 906, 910
BIRDWOOD, Miss Nancy, 402n
BIRRELL, Maj.-Gen. (*A.M.S.*), 19n, 453n; on poor phys. of Austln. rfcts., *Mar*. 1917, 472
BLACK, Col. J. J. (D.S.O., V.D., *A.A.M.C.*), 144, 148, 149, 151, 152
BLANCHARD, Lt.-Col. R. J. (*Canad. A.M.C.*), 365
BLAND, Lt. F. E. (M.B.E., *A.A.M.C.*), 815n
BLOMFIELD, Capt. B. B. (*A.A.M.C.*), 732
BLOOMFIELD, Lt. J. H. (*Amer. Med. Res. Corps*), 775n
BOCK, Capt. A. V. (*Amer. Med. Res. Corps*), 952, 953
BOND, Col. C. J. (C.M.G., *A.M.S.*), 301n
BORDET, Jules, 488
BORST, 307n
BOWLBY, Maj.-Gen. Sir Anthony (Bt., K.C.B., K.C.M.G., K.C.V.O., *A.M.S.*), *Advisory Consult. Surg., B.E.F.* 155n, 302n, 321n, 332n, 358, 362, 363, 370, 408n, 508n, 663n, 957; commends work at M.D.S's, 70; supports Gen. Skinner, 187; agrees with Milligan on excision, 328
BOYD GRAHAM, *see* GRAHAM, H. B.
BRADFORD, Maj.-Gen. Sir J. R. (Bt., K.C.M.G., C.B., C.B.E., F.R.S., *A.M.S.*,), 508n
BRENNAN, Lt.-Col. E. T. (D.S.O., M.C., *A.A.M.C.*), 204, 220
BRERETON, Lt.-Col. F. S. (C.B.E., *R.A.M.C.*), 21n, 26, 287n
BRIDGES, Maj.-Gen. Sir W. T. (K.C.B., C.M.G.), 413, 804, 805, 809; reltns. with Howse, 817n

BROWN, Maj. J. H. B. (O.B.E., M.C., *A.A.M.C.*), 151, 274, 285n, 351n, 352
BROWNING, Prof. C. H., F.R.S., 324
BROWNLEE, Dr. J., 544n
BUCHANAN, Col. A. L. (*A.A.M.C.*), 209, 214
BUCHANAN, Lt.-Col. Sir G. S. (C.B. *A.M.S.*), 510n
BULLOCK, Capt. (*R.A.M.C.*), 32, 952
BURGHARD, Col. F. F. (C.B., *A.M.S.*), 313n
BURSTON, Col. S. R. (C.B.E., D.S.O., V.D., *A.A.M.C.*), 419, 420
BURTON, 8665 L/Cpl. O. R., 101n
BUSH, R. E., maintains hospl. for Austlns., 439n (Plate) 429
BUTLER, Col. A. G. (D.S.O., V.D., *A.A.M.C*), 195, 543n
BUTLER, Col. H. N. (D.S.O., V.D., *A.A.M.C.*), 56
BUZZARD, Col. Sir E. F. (Bt., K.C.V.O., *R.A.M.C.*), 293

CABOT, Richard C., 464n
CADE, Col. D. D. (D.S.O., V.D., *A.A.M.C.*), 325, 675, 727-8, 732
CAMERON, Lt.-Col. D. A. (*A.A.M.C.*), 365n, 407n
CAMPBELL, Lt.-Col. R. D. (D.S.O., *A.A.M.C.*), 334-5, 374, 384, 643, 644
CANNAN, Brig.-Gen. J. H. (C.B., C.M.G., D.S.O., V.D.), 284n
CANNON, Lt.-Col. W. B. (D.S.M., *Amer. Med. Res. Corps*), 947, 953
CARBERY, Col. A. R. L. D. (C.B.E., V.D., *N.Z.M.C.*), 16n, 223n
CARREL, Dr. Alexis, 950; his resches. 313n, 314, 319, 413n; "Carrel-Dakin" lavage, 320-22
CARRUTHERS, Brig.-Gen. A. (C.B., C.M.G.), 83n
CARTER, Pte. "Mick," 2nd Bn., 731
CATHCART, Lt.-Col. E. P. (C.B.E., F.R.S., *R.A.M.C.*), 526n
CHAMBERS, Lt.-Col. R. W. (C.B.E., *A.A.M.C.*), 475n, 693
CHAPLIN, Lt.-Col. W. W. W. (*A.A.M.C.*), 623n
CHAPMAN, Col. C. L. (D.S.O., V.D., *A.A.M.C.*), 200, 204n, 211, 714n
CHARLESWORTH, Capt. A. (M.B.E., *A.A.M.C.*), 815n
CHAVASSE, Capt. N. G. (V.C. with bar, M.C., *R.A.M.C.*), 277n
CHEATLE, Sur.-Rear-Adm. Sir Lenthal (K.C.B., C.V.O., *R.N.*), 313
CHEYNE, Sur.-Rear-Adm. Sir Watson (Bt. K.C.M.G., C.B., F.R.S., *R.N.*), devises "Borsal," *Feb.* 1915, 313
CHICK, Miss Harriette (C.B.E., D.Sc.), 324, 519
CHILDS, Maj.-Gen. Sir Wyndham (K.C.M.G., K.B.E., C.B.), 289n
COLLEY-PRIEST, 6618 Pte. L. W., M.M., 745n
COLLIER, Capt. F. W. D. (*A.A.M.C.*), 44n, 46
COLLINS, Maj. A. J. (D.S.O., M.C., *A.A.M.C.*), 238

INDEX (PERSONAL) 963

COLLINS, Col. Clark C., *II Amer. Corps*, 75a, 763
COLVIN, Maj. A. E. (C.B.E., M.C., *A.A.M.C.*), 815n
CONNAUGHT, Duke of, 767
CONNOR, Capt. J. I. (*A.A.M.C.*), 732
CONYERS, Matron-in-Chief E. A. (C.B.E., R.R.C., *A.A.N.S.*), 815n; arrives in Eng., 812
COOLING, 12967 L/Cpl. L. E., 712n
COPPLESON, Maj. V. M. (*A.A.M.C.*), 712n
CORDIN, Lt.-Col. J. (*A.A.M.C.*), 383, 384
COWANS, Gen. Sir J. S. (G.C.B., G.C.M.G., M.V.O.), 518n, 569n
COWELL, Col. E. M. (C.B.E., D.S.O., T.D., *R.A.M.C.*), 953
COX, Gen. Sir H. V. (G.C.B., K.C.M.G., C.S.I.), 29
CRAIG, Maj. R. F. (D.S.O., *A.A.M.C.*), 746n
CRAIG, Lt.-Col. R. Gordon (*A.A.M.C.*), 901
CRILE, 500n, 948, 950
CRISP, Capt. R. H. (*A.A.M.C.*), 676n
CROSS, Maj. K. S. (*A.A.M.C.*), 812
CROWDEN, Maj. G. P. (R.E., & *R.A.M.C.*), 486n
CROWTHER, Lt.-Col. W. E. L. H. (D.S.O., V.D., *A.A.M.C.*), 208, 214
CULLEN, William, on *vis medicatrix naturae*, 303n
CUMMINS, Col. S. L. (C.B., C.M.G., *A.M.S.*), 508n, 874-7
CUMPSTON, Dr. J. H. L. (C.M.G., *Aust. D.G. of Health*), 544n, 594n
CUNNINGHAM, Lt. K. S., 150
CUSCADEN, Maj.-Gen. Sir George (V.D., *A.A.M.C.*), *A/D.G.M.S., Aust.*, 850
CUSHNY, Prof. A. R., F.R.S., 530n

DAKIN, Prof. H. D., F.R.S., his researches, 314, 319; "Carrel-Dakin" lavage, 320-22; extolls Martin and Chick, 324
DALE, Sir Henry, C.B.E., F.R.S., 484, 530n, 953
DALYELL, Dr. Elsie, O.B.E., 545n
DARRIER, Prof., 573n
DAVENPORT, Capt. P. A. C. (*A.A.M.C.*), 65, 71n
DAVIDSON, 8811 Pte. G. L., quoted, 275, 276n
DAY, Maj. L. B., 140n, 790n
DEARDEN, Capt. H. (*R.A.M.C.*), 294
DE CRESPIGNY, Col. C. T. Champion (D.S.O., V.D., *A.A.M.C.*), 414, 416
DEHELLY, Georges, 319n
DE MONDEVILLE, Henri, 302n, 304n
DEPAGE, Prof. A., 362n; develops débridement, 326, 329n
DICK, Col. J. A. (C.M.G., V.D., *A.A.M.C.*), 382, 386, 778, 835n
DIXON, Maj. R. G. (O.B.E., *R.A.M.C., T.*), *Aug.*, 1918, 775n
DODDS, Maj.-Gen. T. H. (C.M.G., C.V.O., D.S.O.), 818n, 909-10
DONALD, Col. W. H. (V.D., *A.A.M.C.*), 651n

DOWNES, Maj.-Gen. R. M. (C.M.G., V.D., *A.A.M.C.*), 270n, 347n, 599n, 833
DOWNEY, Col. M. H. (D.S.O., V.D., *A.A.M.C.*), 661n, 742, 765, *11th Fld. Amb.*, 165, 171; *A.D.M.S. 5th Aust. Div.*, instrns. for 20 *Sept.*, 1918, 885-7
DRUMMOND, Maj. H., *R.A.M.C.*, 324, 953
DRUMMOND, Capt. J. R. (M.B.E., *A.A.M.C.*), 812
DUDGEON, Col. L. S. (C.M.G., C.B.E., *A.M.S.*), 589n
DUHIG, Maj. J. V. J., *A.A.M.C.*, attd. to R.A.M.C., 806
DUNHILL, Col. Sir T. P. (K.C.V.O., C.M.G., *A.A.M.C.*), 395; his note on B.I.P., 324
DUNSTAN, 14613 Pte. O. R., quoted, 111n, 154n, 282n
DUVAL, Pierre, 782
DYSON, Lt. Will, *Off. artist, A.I.F.*, 282n, 771, (Plates by) 528, 772

EAMES, Maj.-Gen. W. L'E. (C.B., C.B.E., V.D., *A.A.M.C.*), 314n
EDWARDS, 1001 Sgt. J. R., *A.A.M.C.*, quoted, 276n, 294n, 346n
EHRLICH, Prof. Paul, 301n, 324, 488
EIJKMAN, 519
ELLIOTT, Capt. G. S. (M.C., *A.A.M.C.*), 124n; killed 833
ELLIOTT, Maj.-Gen. H. E. (C.B., C.M.G., D.S.O., D.C.M., V.D.), 115, 508n, 718n
ELLIOTT, Col. T. R. (C.B.E., D.S.O., F.R.S., *A.M.S.*), 417, 953
ELLIS, Capt. A. D. (M.C.), quoted, 35n, 689n, 746n
ELWELL, Maj. L. B. (M.C., *A.A.M.C.*), 669, 671
EMERSON, Maj. Haven (*Amer. Med. Res. Corps*), 557n, 558n
ESHER, Viscount Rt. Hon., 50n, 288n
EVANS, Maj. T. C. C. (D.S.O., *A.A.M.C.*), 693

FAIRFAX, Lt.-Col. E. W. *A.A.M.C.*, 395
FAWCUS, Lt.-Gen. Sir H. B. (K.C.B., C.M.G., D.S.O. *R.A.M.C.*), 191
FAY, Maj. F. W. (M.C., *A.A.M.C.*), 362n, 384n, 748
FERGUSON, Maj. E. W. (*A.A.M.C.*), 560, 815n
FESSLER, 305, 348
FETHERSTON, Maj.-Gen. R. H. J. (V.D., *A.A.M.C.*), *D.G.M.S., Aust.*, 427, 472, 474, 666n, 715-16, 805, 821n, 853, 857, 900, 902; reltns. with Howse, 820; enquires re complete Aust. Hosp. system, 826; standards of phys. fitness: his attitude, 843, communicates with Howse, *Oct.* 1916, 901, reports on overseas attitude, 852, discusses with Birdwood, 852; writes to Howse *re* Maudsley's report, *July* 1916, 901, suggests Howse visit Aust., 853, attitude toward recruiting, *May* 1918, 846, writes to Howse

FETHERSTON, Maj.-Gen. R. H. J.—*continued.*
on shortage of fit recruits, *Oct.* 1917, 902, and to Min., 848; his mission overseas, 850-52, wants Gen. Hosp. in Eng., 856, writes to G.O.C., A.I.F., *July* 1918, 871-3, reports on French frnt., *July* 1918, 913, and on French med. methods, 917
FEWTRELL, Col. A. C. (C.B., D.S.O., V.D.), 112n
FIASCHI, Col. P. (O.B.E., V.D., A.A.M.C.), 314n, 360n, 952, i/c ward for shocked cases, 69; saline infusion method, 951
FISCHELL, Lt.-Col. Walter (*Amer. Med. Res. Corps*), 774n, 775n
FISHER, Rt. Hon. Andrew, 11n, 12, 561
FITZPATRICK, Maj. S. C. (M.C., A.A.M.C.), 275n
FITZPATRICK, 7316 Sgt. T., M.M., 933n
FLEMING, Capt. A. (R.A.M.C.), 486n, 487n
FLEXNER, Col. S. (*Amer. Med. Res. Corps*), 585
FOCH, Marshal F., 80, 611, 617, 640, 678, 682, 694; Generalissimo, *Mar.* 1918, 612; order to Allied Armies, 616; his stratgy., 718-9; signs Armistice, 768
FOLLITT, Lt.-Col. H. H. B. (A.A.M.C.), 174, 214
FOOTT, Brig.-Gen. C. H. (C.B., C.M.G., p.s.c.), 418n
FORRESTER, 4989 Cpl. A. G. (D.C.M., M.M.), 638-9
FORSYTH, Capt. R. L. (A.A.M.C.), 615; 638
FORTESCUE, Hon. Sir John (K.C.V.O.), 131n, 290n, 569n, 857
FOSTER, Maj.-Gen. G. L. (C.B., *Canad. A.M.C.*), 73, 869
FRANKLANDS, Capt. H. W. (A.A.M.C.), 711n
FRASER, Maj. A. C. (A.A.M.C.), 117, 477n
FRASER, Capt. Sir John (K.C.V.O., M.C., R.A.M.C.), 338, 953
FRENCH, F.-M. Viscount, 22, 131n; D.M.S., not on H.Q. of, 287n; Haig replaces, 8
FRY, Col. H. K. (D.S.O., A.A.M.C.), 195, 625, 638
FUNK, Casimir, 519

GALLIE, Maj.-Gen. J. S. (C.B., C.M.G., D.S.O., R.A.M.C.), 376n
GANTT, Dr. W. Horsley, 545
GARRISON, Lt.-Col. Fielding H. (*U.S.A. Med. Corps*), 860
GARROD, Sir Alfred, F.R.S., 487
GARROD, Col. Sir Archibald (K.C.M.G., F.R.S., A.M.S.), 487
GASK, Col. G. E. (C.M.G., D.S.O., A.M.S.), *Consult. Surg. Fourth Army*, 663n
GAUDIER, Dr., 326n

GELLIBRAND, Maj.-Gen. Sir John (K.C.B., D.S.O., p.s.c.), 115, 807, 808n, 816n, 817, 921n
GENGOU, 488
GIBBS, Lt.-Col. S. G. (R.A.S.C.), 578n; killed 209n
GIBLIN, Col. W. W. (C.B., V.D., A.A.M.C.), 844, 903; D.D.M.S., A.I.F., 812
GIBSON, Lt.-Col. A. H. (V.D., A.A.M.C.), 625n, 727
GLASFURD, Brig.-Gen. D. J., p.s.c., 87n
GODDARD, Maj. C. J. (D.S.O., A.A.S.C.), 941n
GODLEY, Gen. Sir A. J. (G.C.B., K.C.M.G., p.s.c.), 29, 39, 43
GOODWIN, Lt.-Gen. Sir John (K.C.B., K.C.M.G., D.S.O., A.M.S.), D.G., A.M.S., 619n, 822n
GORDON, Lt.-Col. M. H. (C.M.G., C.B.E., F.R.S., R.A.M.C.), 563n
GORDON-TAYLOR, Maj. G. (O.B.E., R.A.M.C.), 663n, 664, 954
GORDON-WATSON, Col. Sir Charles (K.B.E., C.M.G., A.M.S.), 315
GOUGH, Gen. Sir Hubert (G.C.B., G.C.M.G., K.C.V.O., p.s.c.), 52n, 115, 131, 133, 142, 184, 194, 383n, 611n, 616n
GRAHAM, Maj. H. Boyd (D.S.O., M.C., R.A.M.C., T.), 278n, 284n, 619n
GRAY, Col. Sir Henry (K.B.E., C.B., C.M.G., A.M.S.), on treatmt. of war wounds, 303n, 308n, 316n, 323, 326n, 327n, 328, 338n, 342n, 343, 344, 347, 348, 349, 662, 953
GRAY, Capt. J., A.A.M.C., 954
GREENWOOD, Capt. M. (F.R.S., R.A.M.C., T.F.), 530n
GRIEVE, Maj. K. H. (M.C., A.A.M.C.), 42n
GRIEVE, Capt. R. C. (V.C.), 167
GRIFFITHS, Brig.-Gen. T. (C.M.G., C.B.E., D.S.O.), 808n; A.A.G., A.I.F., 818n; Commdt. Admin. H.Q. 818n, 827; goes to Aust. 767n, 857
GRISTWOOD, A. D., quoted, 282n
GUEST, Maj. L. Haden (M.C., R.A.M.C.), 545n
GUIOU, Capt. N. M. (*Canad. A.M.C.*), 953n
GULL, Sir William, 412

HAIG, F.-M. Earl, 105, 145, 383n, 608, 612, 616, 694, 818n; replaces French as C.-in-C., B.E.F.; insist that Aust. divns. may serve separately, 31; passes Fromelles plans, 40; "wearing down" tactics, 51; autumn offnsve., 1916, 80 *et seq*; on repair of roads, 118n; spring offnsve., 1917, 129, 131; postpones Flanders offnsve., 138; his character and influence 138n, 140n; regards Bullecourt as great achievemt., 146; his intentions in Flanders, 158-9; appreciates human element 159n; his search for "effectives," *Aug.* 1917, 184n; B. of Broodseinde, 185; continues attck. to save French, 232, 235, 254; appreciates man-power prob. 254; his "backs to the

INDEX (PERSONAL) 965

HAIG, F.-M. Earl—*continued.*
wall" order, 11 *Apr.* 1918, 610;
accepts Foch as Generalissimo, 617;
his order of 25 *Mar.*, 621; informs
Rawlinson of his plans, 677; his project *July*, 678; imposes halt, 12-20
Aug., 682n; his appreciatn. of
Austlns., 767
HAKING, Gen. Sir Richard (G.B.E.,
K.C.B., K.C.M.G., p.s.c.), 42
HALDANE, Viscount, F.R.S., 278n, 356
HALDANE, J. S., F.R.S., 487
HARDY, Brig.-Gen. C. H. W. (D.S.O.,
V.D., *A.A.M.C.*), *A.D.M.S.*, 5th
Aust. Div., 29, 42, (Plate) 69
HARPER, Capt. J. C. M. (M.C.,
A.A.M.C.), 276n; quoted, 284n, 346n
HARRIS, Capt. H. R. J. (*A.A.M.C.*),
59n
HARRISON, Maj. E. S. (*A.A.M.C.*), 175
HARVEY, Dr. William, 487, 948
HAYWARD, Maj. L. A. (*A.A.M.C.*), 954
HEARNE, Col. W. W. (D.S.O.,
A.A.M.C.), O.C., 2nd Fld. Amb., 57;
on "shell shock," 72; works in Noman's Land, 86; *A.D.M.S.*, 5th *Aust.
Div.*, 86n, 153; his efforts for men,
91n; visits Glencorse Wd., 213; on
clearnce., 26th *Sept.* 1917, 215n; his
letter *re* San. Sects., 21 *Apr.*, 937-8;
killed, 236, 247
HEMBROW, Dr. C. H., 464n
HENDERSON, Capt. R. L. (M.C.,
A.A.M.C.), 58, 124n; mortly. wd.,
147n
HENLE, 487
HERBERT, Sidney, 483n
HERRINGHAM, Maj.-Gen. Sir Wilmot,
(K.C.M.G., C.B., *A.M.S.*), 378, 508n
HEYDON, Maj. G. A. M. (M.C.,
A.A.M.C.), 207, (Plate) 200
HINDENBURG, F.-M. P. von, 74n, 488
HIPPOCRATES, 301, 303n, 317, 412, 947
HOBBS, Lt.-Gen. Sir J. J. T. (K.C.B.,
K.C.M.G, V.D.), 198n, 818n
HOLMES, Maj. M. J. (D.S.O.,
A.A.M.C.), 141n, 548, 589n, 590n,
594n, 598, 600n, 714
HOLMES, Maj.-Gen. W. (C.M.G., D.S.O.,
V.D.), 137n
HOLMES à COURT, Lt.-Col. A. W.
(*A.A.M.C.*), 880, 955, 957; work with
resusc. teams, 663, 664, 667, 742, 757;
Pres. Resus. Teams C'tee., 954
HOOPER, Capt. A. N. (*R.A.M.C.*), 953
HOPKINS, Sir F. Gowland (O.M.,
F.R.S.), 519
HORNE, Col. G. (V.D., *R.A.M.C.*,
& *A.A.M.C.*), 314
HORROCKS, Brig.-Gen. Sir W. H.
(K.C.M.G., C.B., *R.A.M.C.*), 591n
HORSLEY, Col. Sir Victor (C.B., F.R.S.,
A.M.S.), 305
HOWSE, Maj.-Gen. Hon. Sir Neville
(V.C., K.C.B., K.C.M.G., *A.A.M.C.*),
19, 257, 377n, 380, 383, 414, 415n,
430, 432n, 449, 453, 462, 464, 470
et seq., 565, 599n, 634, 641, 768, 773,
791n; (Frontpce.); asks, in 1914,
to command a San. Sectn., 837n;
A.D.M.S., 1st *Aust. Div.*, 550n, 900;

HOWSE, Maj.-Gen. Hon. Sir Neville—
continued.
his advice, in 1915 on "abdominal"
cases, 312n; *D.M.S.*, *A.I.F.*, 11-13,
218, 900; apptmt. *Nov.* 1915, 802;
responsblties. defined, 15; attnds.
W.O. Conf. on disposal Austln. cas.,
12-13; estabs. reltns. wth. D.G.,
A.M.S., 15-16, 823; visits Allied
frnts., 15-16; suggsts. 2-sectn. fld.
amb., 33n; visits French frnt., 97,
140n; No. 3 A.C.C.S., 143; watches
evactn., 152; asks for report on
A.A.M.C. cas., 153; inspects rest
station, 246; his view on responsibty.
of Med. Serv., 249n; his reltns. with
G.O.C., A.I.F., 255, 817-18; insists on high standard in refcts.,
255; criticises holdg. cases at frnt.,
296; fosters Med. Corps *esprit*, 471n;
divergence of views wth. Fetherston,
427; insists on "fitness" of recovered
men, 470; contributes to efficiency of
A.I.F., 614; supports resusc. teams,
663, 664; effect of his policy, 704;
permits sendg. lower standard men to
France, 715; fight for phys. standard
of A.I.F., 716, 842-56; view on recruitg., 846; on employmt. of "P.B."
men, 847; claims for Med. Service
portion of A.I.F. success, 855-6; his
letters to Keogh, 868-70; to A.I.F.,
H.O., France *re* formtn. of A.G.H.
in England, 872; *re* food in Aust.
Hosps. in Eng., 872-3; to Gen. Fetherston *re* fitness of recruits, 901-2; to
Gol. Giblin on number of rejectns. in
Eng., 903; his statemt. to Birdwood
re "P.B." men, 906-9; and to D,A,G.,
A.I.F., 909-10; visits Aust., 767n,
857; character and achvmts., 803-7;
struggle for internal self-govt., 809;
forms new med. dept., 809, 811, 812;
his administrve. technique, 816-7; his
reltns. with: Admin. H.Q., 819,
A.I.F. Depots in U.K., 819-20, Aust.
D.G., A.M.S., 820-1, light horse,
Egypt, 821, Brit. med. administrn.,
821-2, D.G.M.S., B.E.F., 822-3; his
policy within Med. Service, 824-42; rejects scheme of Aust. primary hosps.,
827; arrnges. for hosps. to leave
Egypt, 832; his difficulties *re* personnel, 833; impresses personlty. on Med.
Service, 834; his attitude *re* promotions, 835, 836; essentially a surg.,
836; his outlook affects his administrn., 837; selects offcrs., 840;
strengthns. surg. side of C.C.S., 840;
recommends formation surgl. teams,
841; Chief Commr., Aust. Red Cross,
842
HOWSE, Lady, 807n, 821n
HUGHES, Rt. Hon. W. M., 798, 818n,
844; initiates second conscript.
refndum., 258; insists on Anzac leave,
717; on rest for A.I.F., 718
HUNTER, John, F.R.S., 301, 302, 303n,
412, 487, 836; on "wound shock," 947
HUNTER, Col. William (C.B., *A.M.S.*),
543

INDEX (PERSONAL)

HURLEY, Lt.-Col. T. E. V. (C.M.G., A.A.M.C.), 11-12, 662n, 812, 822, 841n
HUTCHINSON, Maj. E. L. (D.S.O., A.A.M.C.), 227, 234, 954
HUTTON, Lt.-Gen. Sir Edward (K.C.B., K.C.M.G., p.s.c.), 650n
HUTTON, Maj. Lefferts, 27th Amer. Div., 757
HUXTABLE, Col. R. B. (C.M.G., D.S.O., V.D., A.A.M.C.), 72; A.D.M.S., 1st Aust. Div., 126, 195, 205, 210, 835n, 935-6, (Plate) 629

IREDELL, 5593 Pte. K. J., 346n
IRVING, Maj. H. A. C. (A.A.M.C.), 85n
IRWIN, Maj-Gen. Sir Murray (K.C.M.G., C.B., A.M.S.), D.M.S., Third Army, 611n

JEFFRIES, Lt.-Col. L. W. (D.S.O., O.B.E., A.A.M.C,), 815n
JOFFRE, Marshal, wants prolonging of Somme Offensive, 80; Nivelle supersedes, 106
JOHNSON, Maj. M. B. (A.A.M.C.), 18
JOHNSTON, Col. W. W. S. (D.S.O., M.C., A.A.M.C.), 205, 276n, 278, 294n, 346
JOLLEY, Lt.-Col. A. F. (A.A.M.C.), 742, 753, 754, 755
JOLY DE LOTBINIÈRE, Maj.-Gen. Hon. A. C. de L. (C.B., C.S.I., C.I.E., R.E.), 83n
JONES, Maj.-Gen. G. C. (C.M.G., C.A.M.S., 802n, 869
JONES, Maj. J. T. (M.C., A.A.M.C.), 880; quoted, 83, 136, 173, 237, 277n
JONES, Maj.-Gen. Sir Robert (Bt., K.B.E., C.B., A.M.S.), 373, 431, 804; commends Thomas splint, 182; note on orthopaedic problm., 432n
JONES, 7460 Sgt. W. H., 386n
JOUBERT, Capt. G. J., S. Af. Med. Corps, 801

KAY, Col. W. E. (D.S.O., V.D., A.A.M.C.), 124n
KEITH, Prof. Sir Arthur, F.R.S., 342n, 417n
KEITH, Capt. N. M., R.A.M.C., 338n, 953
KELLY, Maj. W. R. (A.A.M.C.), 712n, his memo. on sanitn., 599n
KENNEDY, Lt.-Col. B. C. (A.A.M.C.), 674
KEOGH, Lt.-Gen. Sir Alfred (G.C.B., G.C.V.O., C.H., A.M.S.), 11, 301n, 415n, 599n, 802, 806, 807; D.G.A.M.S., 11n, 287n, 288n; Howse establs. reltns. with, 15; agrees to attach Aust. liaison officer to his H.Q., 822; letter on Impl. co-opn. 4 Sept. 1917, 866-8
KERR, Capt. F. R. (D.S.O., R.A.M.C.), 334n
KIRKWOOD, Lt.-Col. N. E. B. (M.C., A.A.M.C.), 86; reports on trench foot preventn. 100; his experience at Passchdle., 949n

KITCHENER, F.-M. Earl, 261n, 288n
KOLLOSCHE, Pte. O. R., see DUNSTAN, O. R.

LAIDLAW, Sir P. P., F.R.S., 953
LANDSTEINER, Dr. Karl, 950
LARREY, Baron, Napoleon's med. director, 330, 803; knew value of immed. suture, 304n, importce. of removing shattered limbs, 947
LAWSON, Col. C. B. (R.A.M.C.), 323
LAWTON, Maj. F. D. H. B. (O.B.E., A.A.M.C.), 410, 411n, 584n
LEANE, Brig.-Gen. R. L. (C.B., C.M.G., D.S.O., M.C., V.D.), 60
LEE, Maj. H. B. (D.S.O., M.C., A.A.M.C.), 125
LEGGE, Lt.-Gen. J. G. (C.B., C.M.G.), 29, 846
LEISHMAN, Lt.-Gen. Sir W. B. (K.C.B., K.C.M.G., F.R.S., A.M.S.), Adviser in Path., B.E.F., 313n, 508n, 544; his policy re inoculn. 538
LELEAN, Col. P. S. (C.B., C.M.G., R.A.M.C.), 575
LEMAÎTRE, René, first primary sutures performed by, 330n
LE MESSURIER, Maj. F. N. (D.S.O., A.A.M.C.), 625
LERICHE, René, credit of débridement claimed for, 326n
LE SOUEF, Capt. A. W. (A.A.M.C.), 746n
LETHBRIDGE, Maj. H. O. (M.B.E., A.A.M.C.), 543, 544
LEWERS, Lt.-Col. H. B. (D.S.O., O.B.E, A.A.M.C.), 667, 699n, 815n, 742, 756
LEWIS, Maj.-Gen. E. M. (D.S.M.), 30th Amer. Div., reports on colltg. wdd., 745
LEWIS, Sir Thomas (C.B.E., F.R.S.), 412, 463, 487, 500n
LINACRE, Dr. T., 412
LIND, Brig. E. F. (D.S.O., V.D., A.A.M.C.), 42n, 671; his account of 17-18 Sept. 1918, 732-3
LISTER, Lord, 301, 302, 303, 313n, 486
LITTLE, James, 947
LLOYD-GEORGE, Rt. Hon. D., 106
LLOYD, Col. Langford N. (C.M.G., D.S.O., R.A.M.C.), 71n
LONG, Brig.-Gen. Rt. Rev. G. M. (C.B.E.), drafts educn. scheme, 797, 798
LOTBINIÈRE, see JOLY DE LOTBINIÈRE
LOTHIAN, Maj. N. V. (M.C., R.A.M.C.), 526n, 527, 569n
LOWE, Maj. G. B. (A.A.M.C.), 209
LUARD, Sister K. E. (R.R.C., Q.A.I.M.N.S.), 362n
LUCAS, Sir Charles (K.C.B., K.C.M.G.), 720n
LUDENDORFF, Gen. E., 74n, 104n, 250n, 251, 610, 611, 612, 635, 677, 691, 707; aims to roll up Brit., 627; strikes 21 Mar., 333; attcks. Brit.-French junctn., 629

MACARTNEY, Col. G. W. (D.S.O., A.A.M.C.), 740n, 742

INDEX (PERSONAL) 967

McCarrison, Maj.-Gen. Sir Robert (C.I.E., I.M.S.), 514n, 519, 520n
McCarthy, Dame Maud (G.B.E., R.R.C., Q.A.I.M.N.S.), 363
McCartney, Maj. J. E. (R.A.M.C.), 953
M'Cay, Lt.-Gen. Hon. Sir J. W. (K.C.M.G., K.B.E., C.B., V.D.), G.O.C., 5th Aust. Div., 29; G.O.C., A.I.F. Depots U.K., 256n, 451, 467n
MacCormac, Lt.-Col. H. (C.B.E., R.A.M.C.), 570n, 574
MacCormick, Col. Sir Alexander (K.C.M.G., R.A.M.C. & A.A.M.C.), Consult. Surg. Boulogne Base, 314n, 315, 395; early use of Thomas splint, 349; officer in R.A.M.C. and A.A.M.C., 828n
McDougall, Prof. W., F.R.S., 282, 530n
McGavin, Maj.-Gen. Sir D. J. (C.M.G., D.S.O., N.Z.M.C.), 164n, 174
McGregor, Lt.-Col. R. S. (D.S.O., V.D., A.A.M.C.), O.C., 4th Fld. Amb., 663, 669, 672; A.D.M.S., 4th Aust. Div., 663n, 667, 670
McGrigor, Sir James, Wellington's med. dir., 483n, 569n, 803; compared with Howse, 857
Mack, Capt. B. H. (A.A.M.C.), 139
Mackay, Capt. E. R. (A.A.M.C.), 125
Mackay, Maj. J. S. (M.C., A.A.M.C.), 87
Mackenzie, Lt.-Col. D. S. (D.S.O., A.A.M.C.), 203n, 248n
Mackenzie, Sir James, F.R.S., 487, 488
McKillop, Maj. A. (D.S.O., A.A.M.C.), 37n
Mackinnon, Hon. Donald, 845
Macknight, Lt. H. H. R., 94n, 478n, 712
MacLagan, Maj.-Gen., see Sinclair-MacLagan
Maclure, Lt.-Col. A. Fay (O.B.E., A.A.M.C.), (Plate) 364
McMurdie, 7361 L/Cpl. E. E. 376
McNee, Maj. J. W. (D.S.O., R.A.M.C.), 324, 953
Macphail, Maj. Sir Andrew (O.B.E., Canad. A.M.C.), 16n, 256n
Macpherson, Maj.-Gen. Sir William (K.C.M.G., C.B., A.M.S.), 357, 361, 366, 391, 489n, 841; Russo-Jap. War, 261n; D.D.G.M.S., B.E.F., 90·1, 114n, 874; selects orders of D.D.M.S., II Ansac for reproductn., 181n; his comment, Third Ypres, 191; his distce.-time formula, 675n-6n; holds Amiens unsafe as hosp. centre, 26 Mar., 1918, 778; D.M.S., First Army, 393n; actg. head of R.A.M.C. and Brit. Off. Med. Histn., 288n
McSharry, Lt.-Col. T. P. (C.M.G., D.S.O., M.C.), 674
McWhae, Col. D. M. (C.M.G., C.B.E., V.D., A.A.M.C.), 451n, 453, 454, 461 et seq., 474 et seq., 563, 564, 820; S.M.O., Aust. Base Depot, Weymouth, 18; A.D.M.S., A.I.F. Depots in U.K., 450n, 561; extrcts. from his reports,

McWhae, Col. D. M.—continued.
449n, 450, on unfit men, 473, on Howse and Depots, 819, on low recruit standards, 853-4
Maguire, Col. F. A. (C.M.G., D.S.O., V.D., A.A.M.C.), 176, 754, 757; 9th Fld. Amb., 164, 175, 177, 178, 223, 231n, 239, 240; A.D.M.S., 3rd Aust. Div., 742, 756; his order Mar. 1918, 626.
Makins, Lt.-Gen. Sir George (G.C.M.G., C.B., A.M.S.), 302n, 314n, 315, 392n, 393n
Mandel, Col. II Amer. Corps, 751
Manifold, Maj.-Gen. Sir C. C. (K.C.B., C.M.G., I.M.S.), D.D.M.S., I Ansac Corps, 29, 132, 139, 154, 634, 874, (Plate) 629; his confnce. system, 69; suggsts. measures agst. trench foot, 83; consults D.A. & Q.M.G., 90; reports on large "sick" cas. list, 91; agnst, huge M.D.S's, 88n; for shortening divl. tours, 89n; tries to improve rest stations, 97; his "instructions" to A.D's.M.S., 114n; promotes baths, laundries, 140n; keeps touch with San. Sectns., 141; news re advance of stns., 142n; visits M.D.S. of 5th and 6th Fld. Ambs., 152; Third Ypres, 195; his orders re A.D.S. Menin Rd., 201; Polygon Wd., 218; Broodseinde, 225; the only Brit. "regular" in Aust. Med. Serv., 257; visits No. 2 A.C.C.S. 18 Mar. 1918, 641; Barber succds., 633, 648
Manifold, Hon. J. C., 850, 852, 854n; death, 857n
Mann, Dr. F. W., 305
Marks, Col. A. H. (C.B.E., D.S.O., V.D., A.A.M.C.), 2nd Fld. Amb., 86n, 16th Fld. Amb., 475n, No. 1 A.C.C.S., 641
Marshall, Lt.-Col. F. (C.M.G.), 815n
Martin, Lt.-Col. Sir Charles (C.M.G., A.A.M.C.), 99, 324, 413, 418, 478, 508n, 560, 563, 585, 815n, 828n.
Martin, Col. T. M. (C.M.G., V.D., A.A.M.C.), 314n, 544
Masefield, John, 49n, 51n
Matthews, Maj. W. F. (A.A.M.C.), 622
Mattinson, 17996 Pte. L., 660
Maudsley, Col. Sir H. C. (K.C.M.G., C.B.E., A.A.M.C.), consult. phys. A.I.F., 472, 812, 815n; his report on med. boardg. of recruits, 843; Gen. Fetherston's comment, 901
Maurice, Maj.-Gen. Sir F. (K.C.M.G., C.B., p.s.c.), on fundamentals of new warfare, 1n, 17
Maxwell, Lt.-Gen. Sir R. C. (K.C.B., K.C.M.G., R.E.), Q.M.G., B.E.F., 592
May, Maj. L. (D.S.O., M.C., A.A.M.C.), 205, 207; quoted, 124, 227, 528n; quoted, 283n, 730·1
Mayman, Lt.-Col. G. L., 797
Maynard-Smith, Col. S., see Smith, Col. Maynard.

968 INDEX (PERSONAL)

MEEHAN, Maj. A. V. (*A.A.M.C.*), 323*n*
MELLANBY, Prof. Sir Edward (K.C.B., *F.R.S.*), 530*n*
MIGNON, Med. Inspct.-Gén. A., 301*n*, 407*n*, 913; describes French med. dispositns., 784, 915, on degree of urgency of wds., 957*n*
MILES-WALKER, Matron, *see* WALKER, J. M.
MILLARD, Col. R. J. (C.M.G., C.B.E., *A.A.M.C.*), 799, 812, 820*n*; *A.D.M.S., A.I.F. Depots in U.K.*, 19, 453; *D.D.M.S., A.I.F.*, 450*n*; *Actg. D.M.S.*, 791*n*, 815*n*
MILLIGAN, Maj. E. T. C. (O.B.E., *R.A.M.C.*), 326-8
MILNE, F. M., Lord, 1*n*
MITCHELL, Capt. G. D. (M.C., D.C.M.), quoted, 97*n*, 516*n*
MOLIÈRE, 92
MOLTKE, F.-M. Count von, 262*n*
MONASH, Gen. Sir John (G.C.M.G., K.C.B., V.D.), 531*n*, 626*n*, 718, 720, 722, 734, 738*n*, 763, 799, 856; organises and trains 3rd Aust. Div. 158*n*; on Messines, as "set-piece" battle, 159*n*; personlty., 164; succeeds Birdwood, 648; co-ops. with med. serv., 649; consents to form resus. teams, 663; his preptns. for Hamel, 666; 667; Mont St. Quentin and Péronne, 699; maintains strikg. power, 1918, 704; carries on Birdwood's policy, 708; becomes D.G. of Repat. and Demob., 791; his insight, 792; conflict with Howse, 818*n*; agrees wth. Howse *re* standards of fitness, 853
MONTAGUE, C. E., 531*n*
MONTGOMERY, Lt.-Col. Walter C. *27th Amer. Div.*, 757
MOORE, Col. G. A. (C.M.G., D.S.O., *A.M.S.*), 315
MOORE, Maj. Gen. Hon. Sir Newton, J. (K.C.M.G., V.D.), 448; commands A.I.F. troops in U.K., 11, 14, 17, 18, 19; M'Cay succds., 467
MORGAN, 8353 Cpl. R., quoted, 58*n*, 124*n*, 145*n*, 147, 731-2, 770-1
MORISON, Prof. Rutherford, his "B.I.P." Paste, 323-4, 323*n*, 330, 804
MOSELEY, Col. A. H. (D.S.O., *A.A.M.C.*), *6th Fld. Amb.*, 85-6, 97, 157, 203, 221, 222, 226, 233; *A.D.M.S. 4th Aust. Div.*, 634*n*; wdd. 24 *June*, 1918, 662
MOTT, Lt.-Col. Sir F. W. (K.B.E., F.R.S., R.A.M.C.), 336*n*, 530*n*, 953
MOYNIHAN, Maj.-Gen. Lord (*A.M.S.*), 313*n*, 322*n*, 804, 836*n*
MUNRO, 13629 L/Cpl. E. C., M.M., 149
MUNRO, Capt. J. W. (*R.A.M.C.*), 571*n*, 573*n*
MUNSON, Maj. Edward L. (*Amer. Med. Corps*), 525
MURDOCH, Lt.-Col. A. W. (V.D.), 46*n*
MURRAY, Prof. Gilbert, 282*n*
MURRAY, Capt. J. F. S. (M.B.E., M.C., *A.A.M.C.*), 171

MYERS, Lt.-Col. C. S. (C.B.E., F.R.S., *R.A.M.C.*), 530*n*

NAPOLEON, 2*n*, 184*n*, 670*n*, 704, 803
NEWING, Lt.-Col. W. J. (*A.A.M.C.*), 657*n*, 675
NEWLAND, Lt.-Col. Sir Henry (C.B.E., D.S.O., *A.A.M.C.*), 312*n*, 373*n*, 377*n*, 379*n*, 382, 406*n*, 432*n*
NEWMAN, Sir George (G.B.E., K.C.B.), 530*n*
NEWMARCH, Col. B. J. (C.M.G., C.B.E., V.D., *A.A.M.C.*), 417, 835*n*
NEWTON, Maj. Sir Alan (*A.A.M.C.*), 302*n*, 486
NICHOLAS, Lt.-Col. J. J. (*A.A.M.C.*), 195; 209*n*, 833
NICHOLLS, T. B., 266*n*
NICOLLE, 571*n*
NIGHTINGALE, Florence, O.M., 520*n*; a pioneer of Army sanitn., 483
NIVELLE, Gén. R., 106, 129, 138
NORTH, Maj. H. M. (*A.A.M.C.*), 124*n*, 125
NORTH, Maj. R. B. (*A.A.M.C.*), 954
NUTTALL, Prof. G. H. F., F.R.S., 571*n*

O'KEEFFE, Maj.-Gen. Sir M. W. (K.C.M.G., C.B., *A.M.S.*), 611*n*, 616*n*; *D.M.S., Fourth Army*, permits M.A.C. cars in advance of M.D.S., 87*n*; visits No. 2 A.C.C.S., 641; inspects dress. stn., Templeux, 751
OLDFIELD, 9197 Cpl. W. A. S., wdd., 218*n*
O'NEILL, Col. E. J. (C.M.G., D.S.O., V.D., *N.Z.M.C.*), 164*n*
O'REGAN, Capt. S. V. (M.C., *A.A.M.C.*), 954
ORR, Dr., 323, 526*n*
ORR, Maj. (*Canad. A.M.C.*), 575
O'RYAN, Maj.-Gen. John F., D.S.M., *27th Amer. Div.*, 738*n*, describes Aust. soldier, 705-6
OSBURN, Lt.-Col. A. C. (D.S.O., *R.A.M.C.*), 272*n*, 289*n*, 391*n*
O'SHAUGHNESSY, Dr. L. F., 337*n*

PAGE, Lt.-Col. C. Max (D.S.O., *R.A.M.C.*), 350*n*, 662
PARÉ, Ambroise, 301, 302*n*, 303*n*
PARKER, Lt.-Col. K. S. (M.C., *A.A.M.C.*), 174
PARKES, Col. W. H. (C.M.G., C.B.E., V.D., *N.Z.M.C.*), *D.D.M.S., N.Z.E.F.*, 802*n*, 868
PASTEUR, Louis, 303, 322, 412, 486, 487
PEACOCK, Capt. A. D. (*R.A.M.C., T.F.*), 571*n*, 572
PEARCE, Rt. Hon. Sir George K.C.V.O., 666*n*
PENFOLD, Dr. W. J., 307*n*, 309*n*
PERCY, Baron, 274
PERSHING, Gen. J. J., 635, 673, 735
PÉTAIN, Marshal, French C.-in-C., 232*n*, 607, 612; his order 24 *Mar.* 1918, 621; tends to separate French and Brit., 616

INDEX (PERSONAL) 969

PETRIE, Dr., 487n
PHIPPS, Col. J. H. (D.S.O., V.D., A.A.M.C.), 59n, 151
PICKING, 16698 Pte. A. S. H., M.M., 173
PLIMMER, Capt. R. H. A., 519n
PLUMER, F.-M. Viscount, *Second Army*, 21, 159, 194, 611n; to Italy, 254n, 609n
POATE, Lt.-Col. H. R. G. (A.A.M.C.), 854
POLLARD, Capt. J. H. (A.A.M.C.), 369, 477n, 933n
PORTER, Maj.-Gen. Sir Robert (K.C.B., C.M.G., A.M.S.), D.M.S., *Second Army*, 168, 382; prlncples. adoptd. by his staff, 161; conservative policy of, 192, 195
POWELL, Col. H. A. (C.M.G., V.D., A.A.M.C.), 778
PRATT, Sister R. (M.M., A.A.N.S.), 386n
PRINGLE, Sir John, 483n
PURDY, Lt.-Col. J. S. (D.S.O., V.D., A.A.M.C.), 474, 559; O.C., *San. Sectn.* formed in Egypt, 18, *10th Fld. Amb.*, 165, *No. 3 A.G.H.*, 778
PYE, Lt.-Col. C. R. A. (D.S.O.), k. 247n

QUICK, Lt.-Col. Balcombe (D.S.O., A.A.M.C.), 324, 332-3, 369n, 783n

RAE, Capt. R. K. (A.A.M.C.), 207
RAWLINSON, Gen. Lord, 635, 677, 678, 718, 733, 738n; commds. *Fourth Army*, 52n, 611n; his advice on sickness, 90; replaces Gough 28 *Mar.* 1918, 616n; prepares for Hamel, 666
RAYSON, Maj. H. (M.C., A.A.M.C.), 46n
READ, Maj.-Gen. G. W. (D.S.M.), *II American Corps*, 735, 738n, 763
REID, Rt. Hon. Sir George, (G.C.B., G.C.M.G.), 11n
RICHARDS, Maj. A. N., 953
RICHE, P., 326
ROBERTS, W.-O., A. E., 85n
ROBERTSON, Capt. Oswald H. (*Amer. Med. Res. Corps*), 952-3
ROSS, Capt. D. M. (A.A.M.C.), 346n
ROSS, Lt.-Col. T. G. (D.S.O., A.A.M.C.), 70
ROSSELL, Capt. J. McF. (A.A.M.C.), 731, 770
ROTH, Brig.-Gen. R. E. (C.M.G., D.S.O., V.D., A.A.M.C.), 29, 48, 652n
ROWLAND, Maj. Sydney D. (R.A.M.C.), 413n
RUPPRECHT, Crown Prince of Bavaria, 159n, 629
RUSSELL, Capt. E. (A.A.M.C.), 45
RUTLEDGE, Lt.-Col. E. H. (A.A.M.C.), 812
RYAN, Maj.-Gen. Sir Charles (K.B.E., C.B., C.M.G., V.D., A.A.M.C.), 472, 812, 815n, 844

SALISBURY, Lord, 483
SAMSON, 12408 Pte. P. G., 372, 385n

SCANTLEBURY, Maj. G. C. (R.A.M.C.), 369n
SCHJERNING, Prof. Otto v., 302n
SCHRAM, Capt. Frank E. (*Amer. Med. Corps*), 674
SCHWANN, Theodor, 487
SCOTT, Prof. Sir Ernest, 262n
SEELY, Maj.-Gen. Rt. Hon. J. E. B. (C.B., C.M.G., D.S.O.), 50n
SELLHEIM, Maj.-Gen. V. C. M. (C.B., C.M.G.), 14, 17n, 808n, 809n, 847
SEWELL, Capt. P. B. (A.A.M.C.), k. 638
SHARP, Col. A. D. (C.B., C.M.G., A.M.S.), 95
SHARPEN, 6247 Pte. W. C., 801n
SHAW, Col. C. Gordon (D.S.O., V.D., A.A.M.C.), 57, 69
SHAW, Dr. Maurice E., 317n
SHELDON, Lt.-Col. C. D. (D.S.O., R.E.), 575
SHEPHERD, Col. A. E. (C.B.E., D.S.O., V.D., A.A.M.C.), *8th Fld. Amb.*, 85; *A.D.M.S.*, *2nd Aust. Div.*, 281n, 658; med. arrgts. for Hamel, 667
SHERRINGTON, Prof. Sir C. S. (O.M., G.B.E., F.R.S.), 530n, 953; on secondary shock, 334n
SHIERLAW, Capt. N. C. (M.C., A.A.M.C.), 278n
SHIPLEY, Prof. Sir Arthur (G.B.E., F.R.S.), 567n, 571n
SHOUBRIDGE, Maj.-Gen. T. H. (C.B., C.M.G., D.S.O., p.s.c.), 153n
SINCLAIR, Maj. Meurice (C.M.G., R.A.M.C.), 165n
SINCLAIR-MACLAGAN, Maj.-Gen. E. G. (C.B., C.M.G., D.S.O.), 468, 666, 682n, 738
SKINNER, Maj.-Gen. G. B. M. (C.B., C.M.G., M.V.O., A.M.S.), D.M.S., *Fifth Army*, 131, 186, 362, 383, 386, 609, 611n, 616n; his prepns. for *Third Ypres*, 187; his mthds. criticised, 621n
SLADDEN, Capt. A. F. S. (R.A.M.C.), 953
SLOGGETT, Lt.-Gen. Sir Arthur (K.C.B., K.C.M.G., K.C.V.O.), 383n, 415n, 608, 805, 841n, 879; D.G.M.S., *B.E.F.*, 11, 287n, 391; instructs that C.C.S's be beyond range of arty., 55; forms adv. op. centres in each army, 55; his memo. to D'sM.S., 25 *July* 1916, 66; enquires into sick wastage, 90-1; praises *II Anzac evacn.* for Messines, 181n; his prepns. for Third Ypres, 186-7; his order of 6th *Mar.* 1918, 609; questn. of *liaison* with Howse, 822; his problem *re* surg. teams, 840; writes to Keogh on Imp. co-op., 16 *June* 1916, 869
SMITH, Dr. J. Lorrain, F.R.S., 324
SMITH, Col. K. (C.M.G., A.A.M.C.), 638; *A.D.M.S.*, *4th Aust. Div.*, 663n, 691, 733; his med. arrangts. for 8 *Aug.* 1918, 879-84; for a relief, 20 *Sept.* 1918, 888
SMITH, Sister Leila G. (A.A.N.S.), on Carrel-Dakin treatmt., 408n

INDEX (PERSONAL)

SMITH, Col. S. Maynard (*C.B.*, *A.M.S.*), 155, 329-30
SOLTAU, Col. A. B. (C.M.G., C.B.E., T.D., *R.A.M.C.*), 193, 566, 567, 568
SOMERVILLE, Lt.-Col. G. C. (C.M.G., D.S.O., p.s.c.), 577n
SOUTHEY, Maj. M. V. (D.S.O., *A.A.M.C.*), 147, 284n, 348
SOYER, Alexis, designed Soyer stove, 520n
SPEARS, Brig.-Gen. E. L. (C.B., C.B.E., M.C.), 289n
SPRENT, Maj. J. (M.C., *A.A.M.C.*), quoted, 275n, 278n, 283n, 350n, 351
SPRINGTHORPE, Lt.-Col. J. W. (*A.A.M.C.*), 584n
STACK, Maj. (*R.A.M.C.*), 208n
STACK, Maj. W. J. (D.S.O., *A.A.M.C.*), 195
STACY, Lt.-Col. H. S. (*A.A.M.C.*), 361n, 382, 383n
STACY, Lt.-Col. B. O. (O.B.E., *A.A.M.C.*), 641, 642
STARLING, Lt.-Col. E. H. (C.M.G., F.R.S., *R.A.M.C.*), 953
STEELE, Maj. D. M. (M.C., *A.A.M.C.*), 237, 669
STEELE, Brig.-Gen. J. McC. (C.B., C.M.G., D.S.O.), 153n
STEVENS, Maj. P. A. (*A.A.M.C.*), 370n, 371
STOKES, Col. E. S. (*A.A.M.C.*), 515n
STOREY, Col. J. C. (O.B.E., V.D., *A.A.M.C.*), 182n, 349n
STREETER, H. W., 589n
STUMP, Capt. C. W. (*A.A.M.C.*), 954
STURDEE, Col. A. H. (C.M.G., V.D., *A.A.M.C.*), A.D.M.S., 1st Aust. Div., 29, 56, (Plate) 69
SUMMONS, Col. W. E. (O.B.E., V.D., *A.A.M.C.*), 415n
SUTTON, Col. A. (C.B., C.M.G., *A.A.M.C.*), A.D.M.S., 2nd Aust. Div., 29, 112n, 153, 195, (Plate) 69; Col. Barber opposes his advancing stns., 137; advances them, 142; directs evacn., 143; disposes units in echelon, 144; calls up resve. S.-B's, 149; extrcts. from diary 6-8 *Oct.*, 233, 249n; his letter *re* san. arrngts., 21 *Apr.*, 1917, 936
SUTTON, Capt. A. F. (M.B.E., *Dent. Service*), 88
SUTTON, Lt.-Col. Harvey (O.B.E., *A.A.M.C.*), 589n
SYDENHAM, Thomas, 412

TARASSEWITCH, Prof. L. A., 545
TAUNTON, Capt. H. C. D., *Dent. Service*, 171n
TAYLOR, Capt. E. S. (*R.A.M.C.*, T.F.), 953
TAYLOR, Maj. G., *see* GORDON TAYLOR
TAYLOR, Capt. George E., *Amer. Med. Corps*, 758
TAYLOR, Maj.-Gen. M. G. (C.B., C.M.G., D.S.O., p.s.c. *R.E.*), 94, 575, 578n
TAYLOR, Maj. R. J. (*A.A.M.C.*), 229, 239

TAYLOR-YOUNG, Lt.-Col. H. C. (O.B.E., *A.A.M.C.*), 621, 662
TEBBUTT, Col. A. H. (D.S.O., V.D., *A.A.M.C.*), 44
THOMAS, Albert J. (*R.N.* & *R.A.N.*), 182n
THOMAS, H. Owen, 434, *see* General Index under SPLINTS, Thomas
THOMPSON, Lt.-Col. C. W. (D.S.O., M.C., *A.A.M.C.*), 213, 614n, 659, 661n, 662, 742
THOMPSON, Maj.-Gen. Sir H. N. (K.C.M.G., C.B., D.S.O., *A.M.S.*), 611n, 800n
TILLING, Capt. H. W. (*A.A.M.C.*), 615
TIVEY, Maj.-Gen. E. (C.B., C.M.G., D.S.O., V.D.), 91n
TOLHURST, Dr. Jean C., 307n, 309n
TOYER, 17304 Pte. A. E., 376
TROTTER, Wilfred, *F.R.S.*, 491n, 836n
TUNBRIDGE, Brig.-Gen. W. H. (C.B., C.M.G., C.B.E., V.D.), 290n, 291n
TURNBULL, Maj. Raymond A. (*Amer. Med. Corps*), 752n, 854
TURNER, Lt.-Col. Sir George (K.B.E., C.B., *R.A.M.C.*, T.), 311n

UPJOHN, Lt.-Col. W. G. D. (O.B.E., *A.A.M.C.*), 375, 775n

VANCE, Major E. B. M. (*A.A.M.C.*), 349
VESALIUS, Andreas, 487
VICKERS, Col. W. (D.S.O., V.D., *A.A.M.C.*), 626n
VIRCHOW, Rudolf, 487

WALKER, Lt.-Gen. Sir H. B. (K.C.B., K.C.M.G., D.S.O.), 29
WALKER, Matron J. Miles (R.R.C., *A.A.N.S.*), quoted, 622
WALKER, Capt. K. M. (*R.A.M.C.*), 342n, 344, 662
WALLACE, Maj.-Gen. Sir Cuthbert (Bt., K.C.M.G., C.B., *A.M.S.*, T.), 310n, 508n, 953
WALSH, Col. R. W. W. (D.S.O., V.D., *A.A.M.C.*), 279n
WASSELL, Col. C. E. (D.S.O., *A.A.M.C.*), 236
WATSON, Col. Sir Charles G.; *see* GORDON-WATSON
WEBER, Dr. F. Parkes, 491n, 492n
WEBER, Sir Hermann, 487n
WELCH, Lt.-Col. H. C. St. Vincent (D.S.O., *A.A.M.C.*), 658, 667, 690
WELCH, Lt.-Col. J. B. St. Vincent (D.S.O., *A.A.M.C.*), 69, 88n, 236, 240, 330
WELLINGTON, Duke of, 803, 857
WELLMAN, Capt. A. R. S., *Dent. Service*, 777
WHITE, Maj.-Gen. A. T. (C.M.G., V.D., *A.A.M.C.*), 158n, 165, 171, (Plate) 69
WHITE, Gen. Sir C. B. B. (K.C.B., K.C.M.G., K.C.V.O., D.S.O., p.s.c.), 69n, 108n, 114n, 142n, 237n, 257, 258, 614n, 775, 804n, 809n, 810, 824n, 847, 853; A.I.F. chief of staff,

# INDEX (PERSONAL) 971

WHITE, Gen. Sir C. B. B.—*continued*.
15-16; defines responsiblts. of D.M.S., 15; sets out Corps scheme of works, *Nov.* 1916, 83; his view on responsiblty. of Med. Service, 249n; accomps. Birdwood to Fifth Army, *May*, 1918, 648; his plan for repat. and demob., 791; educn. scheme, 797; on Howse, 807-8, 818
WHITE, Principal Matron J. McHardie, (M.B.E., R.R.C., *A.A.N.S.*), 812
WHITHAM, Maj.-Gen. J. L. (C.M.G., D.S.O., p.s.c), 818n
WHITING, Maj. K. M. (*A.A.M.C.*), 615
WILLAN, Surg.-Capt. R. J. (O.B.E., M.V.O., V.D., *R.N.V.R.*), 323n
WILLCOCKS, Maj. G. C. (O.B.E., M.C., *A.A.M.C.*), 125, 815n
WILLIAMS, Sister F. E. (R.R.C., *A.A.N.S.*), her research, 413, 585
WILLIAMS, Surg.-Gen. Sir W. D. C., (K.C.M.G., C.B., *A.A.M.C.*), 11, 524n, 804, 809, 822; designs 2-sectn. Fld. Amb., 33n, 805; purchses. supplies of sera, 1915, 309n; forms med. dept., London, 810; Howse succds., 15
WILLIS, Maj. H. H. (*A.A.M.C.*), 207
WILSON, Lt.-Col. A. M. (D.S.O., *A.A.M.C.*), 675; on distce.-time factor, 927-30

WILSON, Principal Matron G. M. (C.B.E., R.R.C., *A.A.N.S.*), 801, 815n, (Plate) 808
WINN, Maj. R. Coupland (M.C., *A.A.M.C.*), 38n, 63, 174, 347
WISDOM, Brig.-Gen. E. A. (C.B., C.M.G., D.S.O., V.D.), 692
WOOD, Capt. D. (*A.A.M.C.*), 954
WOODHEAD, Col. Sir G. S. (K.B.E., *A.M.S.*), 591n
WOODHOUSE, Maj.-Gen. Sir Percy (K.C.M.G., C.B., *R.A.M.C.*), as D.M.S. refused attachmt. to French's H.Q., 287n; becomes D.M.S., L. of C., 391, 417
WOODS, Capt. E. W. B. (M.C., *A.A.M.C.*), quoted, 91n
WOOLLARD, Lt.-Col. H. H. (F.R.S., *A.A.M.C.*), 60, 455n, 457n, 458n, 463n, 471; on work of Command Depots, 457-60; No. 3 A.C.C.S., 774
WOOLLCOTT, W.-O. H., 801n
WOOSTER, Lt.-Col. F. C. (D.S.O., V.D., *A.A.M.C.*), 667, 671-2
WRIGHT, Col. Sir Almroth (K.B.E., C.B., F.R.S.), 313 *et seq.*, 413, 537, 558n, his mthds., 319-20; Wright *v.* Carrel, 321-2; quoted, 342n
WYLLIE, Maj. H. A. (M.C., *A.A.M.C.*), 124n

ZIEMSSEN, von, 950
ZINSSER, Lt.-Col. Hans (*Amer. Med. Corps*), 541n, 544, 545, 579-80

GENERAL INDEX

Plates, Maps, and Sketches referred to after places are those which best indicate their positions.

Page numbers followed by n indicate that the reference is to a footnote on the page specified.

ABBEVILLE (Sk. 10, 397), 430, 620, 633, 763, 767, 792, 796, 800; H.Q. of I.G.C. at, 22, 621n; 3 A.G.H. at 400, 410-11, 417, 621, (Plates) 412, 413, 428, 808; convoys clear to, 609, sick clear from, 7 Aug. 1918, 684; Amb. train via Mar., 623; laundries in, 712; wdd. evac. to, Aug., 779.
ABEELE (Sk. 75, 203), I Anzac H.Q. at, 74
ABRAHAM HEIGHTS (Map 224), 219
ACCIDENTAL INJURIES, 410, 481
ACHIET-LE-GRAND (Sk. 107, 620), 619; rly. reaches, 118n, 127
ACTINOMYCOSIS, 502
ACTS AND REGULATIONS Fld. Serv. Reglns., 66n, 191, 211, 356n, 510, 624n, 653, 804; health "the duty of every offcr. and man," 101; duty of Regtl. S.-B's, 275n; transpt. of wdd., 286; inflow to Fld. Ambs. etc., 547n; instns. for med. serv., 685-6
ADJUTANT-GENERAL'S BRANCH 12n, 34; Med. Serv. a "department" of, 817; of B.E.F., memo re San. Sectns., 12 Mar. 1917, 935
ADMINISTRATION 66-7, 75, 648, 817n-18n; I Anzac, 80, 116-17, B. of Menin Rd., 194-5, at Charleroi after Armistice, 793; records, in fld. and in London, 794; Admin. H.Q., A.I.F., 427, 437, 791. **Medical:** 114n, 802-58; scheme on W.F., 1918, 24; Col. Barber issues "Standing Orders," 137n; on Brit. L. of C., 390-4; organisn. and mthds. of San. ser., 507-12; Barber's, 650-53; for promotg. health, 711; med. sectn. at Admin. H.Q., 807-8, establt., 813; Howse's admin. technique, 816-17; the med. pool, resve. of M.O's, 839-40; employment of personnel in slack times, 839; orders and instns. re technique in the fld., 874-88; see also, ARMY MED. SERV.; AUST. IMP. FORCE; BARBER, G. W.; BRIT. ARMY; HOWSE; MANIFOLD
ADMINISTRATIVE SERVICES, see SERVICES OF MAINTENANCE
ADVANCED DRESSING STATIONS, see DRESSING STATNS.

ADVISORY COMMITTEE, MEDICAL, see COMMITTEES
AGNES-LEZ-DUISANS (Sk. 620), 619
AID POSTS, REGIMENTAL (Plate 709; Map 668; Sk. 57, 113, 123, 135, 144), 86, 120, 359, 447, 619, 657, 730, 732; at Fromelles, too far in rear, 58; described, 58, 147-8; longer carry to, 59; tactics of, 62; essential requiremts. at, 63; cleared by Ford cars, Mar. 1917, 119; illustratn. of siting, 133; number of squads at ea. group, 148; Engrs. help to build, 165; Thomas splints at each, 165; at Messines, 169, 170, 172, 173, 174; Menin Rd., 205, 207; Polygon Wd., 214; Broodseinde, 227, 228; and the R.M.O., 276-8; evacn. to M.L.P., 280-4; treatmt. at, by R.M.O., 346; many cut off, Mar. 1918, 618; standard dugouts, 659-665; see also BATTALIONS
AIR FORCE, supremacy of Brit., 53
AIRE (Map 769; Sk. 645), 397
"ALBERICH," 329, 361; code name for Ger. retirement, 108-9; initial stage of, 102
ALBERT (Map 68, 769; Sk. 10, 698), 81, 82, 140, 141n, 155, 592, 616, 617, 633, 639, 656; shelling of, 55; A.D.S. at school, 64; Gers. in, Mar. 1918, 617; B. of, 49n, 51, Aust. Divs. in, 680n, features of, 695-6, captured, 22 Aug., 695
ALBERT-BAPAUME ROAD (Sk. 57), 55, 117, 118n, 362; all routes converge on, 111
ALCOHOL, 528; for wounded, 345; "rum" ration, 530-32; use and abuse of, 532
"ALMA" (Map 224; Sk. 238), 228
AMBULANCE, see FIELD AMBULANCES
AMBULANCE CONVOY, MOTOR, 152, 161, 164, 265, 654; formtn. of, 25-6; nine for Somme Btle., 55n; park for, 69; use in advce. of M.D.S. permittd., 87n; patients for op. centres taken by, 121; numbers of liers and sitters carried by, 7 June, 1917, 175; five under D.M.S., Fifth Army, 186; B. of Pilckem, 190; Menin Rd., 208n; function and

GENERAL INDEX 973

AMBULANCE CONVOY, MOTOR—*continued.*
estab. of, 289-90, 911, 912n; numbers carried by, 390n; from Amb. train to Gen. Hosps. by, 401; in retreat, *Mar.-Apr.* 1918, 619; at B. of Dernancourt, 630; nr. Hazebrouck, 646; Battle of Amiens, 684n. **No. 3.** 667, 687, 693, 701, 724, 741, 759, 761-2, 880; under Aust. Corps, 635, 657; efficient service of, 628. **No. 6.** 71. **No. 11.** attd. to Aust. Corps, 684, 687. **No. 14.** at Fromelles, 41. **No. 20.** B. of Menin Rd., 197. **No. 21.** 252. **No. 27.** 87, 132, 143
AMBULANCE TRAINS, 287n, 359; number in France, 26; Somme Btle., 54, 55n; Messines 180; Third Ypres, 186-7; B. of Poelcappelle, 234; van for haemorrhage cases, 315; "Carrel-Dakin" treatment on, 321n, 322; their control, 391; scheme of running, 391-2; evolutn. of, 392-4; capacity and staff of, 394, 427, 927; not marked with Red Cross, 394; time taken, in 1914, 405n; journey of, 23-30 *Mar.* 1918, 622-4; good service of, *Apr.*, 644.
AMBULANCE WAGGONS, *see* MEDICAL TRANSPORT
AMERICA, UNITED STATES OF, declares war, 6 *Apr.* 1917, 138; exploits blood transfsn., 950
AMERICAN EXPEDITIONARY FORCE, 340, 606-7, 647; inoculn. in, 539; enterica in, 540; measles and pneumonia in, 541, incidnce. of pneumonia, 1917-18, 557n; health expercce. of, 558n; attck. wth. French, 18 *July* 1918, 611, 673-4, 677, 678; enter Brit. frnt. at Hamel, 673-5; obsessn. re gas, 693, 694n; Austrlns. assoced. with St. Quentin Canal, 705; with French on Argonne, 768; mortlty. rate, 787; total cas., 860; *see also* ARMY MED. SERV. CORPS, DIVISIONS, REGIMENTS
AMIENS (Plate 525; Map 668; Sk. 22, 607), 81, 96, 609, 617, 620, 621, 623, 625, 636, 644, 653, 656, 667, 670, 671n, 688n, 767, 779; hosp. centre, 397, too dangerous for 778; German thrust for, 629, 636, 637, 640, halted nr. 50n, 610; Pétain decides to uncover, 612. **Battle of,** 647, 679-702; Aust. divns. engaged, 680n; genesis and tactics, 681-2; leapfrogging of fld. ambs., 685; course of, 8 *Aug.*, 688-9; the thrust contd., 9-20 *Aug.*, 691-4; med. orders and arrangts. for Aust. Corps and a divn. for 8 *Aug.*, 877-84
AMMAN, raid at, 48n
AMMUNITION, 117; wastage, 515; S.A.A.: weight carried by soldier, 527, discarded, 528n
AMOEBIASIS, 501
ANA JANA SIDING (Sk. 772), A.C.C.S's at, 641-2, leave, 643

ANAESTHETICS, 162, 332n, 775n, 954; Capt. Wellman's apparatus, 777n; eliminate shock, 777, 948
ANCHYLOSTOMIASIS, 503, 543
ANCRE RIVER (Plate 628; Maps 88; Sk. 22, 613), 117, 139, 618, 628, 648, 658, 678; 9th Div. retire across, 616; 10th and 11th Aust. Bdes. cross, 617. **Battle of,** 49n, 79, 80, 81, 85-9, 90, Brit. offsve. to support French, 106
ANTISEPSIS, *see* TREATMENT
ANTHRAX, 502
"ANZAC" BLOCKHOUSE (Map 216; Sk. 189), R.A.P. at, 214, 217
ANZAC CORPS, *see* CORPS
APPENDICITIS, 408n, 568
APPOINTMENTS AND PROMOTIONS, *see* ARMY MED. SERV.; PROMOTIONS
AQUENNE WOOD, 638
ARGONNE, French-Amer. offsve., *Nov.*, 1918, 768, 786n
ARLEUX, BATTLE OF, 129n
ARMENTIÈRES (Map 164; Sk. 10, 639), 21, 546n, 771; trench lines near, (Plate) 33; attk. at *Apr.* 1918, 640
ARMIES, **British: First,** 130, 142, 344, 640, 678, 695, 718, 775; 5th Aust. Div. in, 40; proposed attk. by, 1917, 107, 108; B. of Vimy, 129; positn. of, 26 *Mar.* 1918 (Sk.) 613; advces., *Nov.* 1918, 768. **Second,** 21, 47, 79, 189, 193, 357n, 531n, 615, 633, 640, 641, 643, 695, 718, 771, 773, 775; Aust. sectors in, *Sept.*, 1916 (Sk.) 75; B. of Messines, 159 *et seq.*; Third Ypres, 184, 185, 186, 191-2, 194, 219, 232-3, 235-6; evacn. scheme, 386; advces., 768; at Cologne, 776. **Third,** 107, 108, 122, 130, 342n, 349, 610, 615, 621, 624, 632, 640, 662, 718; in B. of Scarpe, 129; crisis in *Mar.*, 612-13; med. serv., in retreat, 617; echelons of moves, *Mar.*, 619-20; med. arrangmts., 25-28 *Mar.*, 625; confusn., 625; line *Apr.*, 633; operns., 21 *Aug.*-3 *Sept.*, 695; advances, *Nov.*, 768. **Fourth,** 83n, 90, 91, 98, 114, 119n, 184, 185, 186, 191-2, 194, 219, 232-3, 718, 767, 955; resumes offnsve., 80, changes plans 84, ceases active operns. *Nov.* 1916, 85; Ger. attck., 622n; Germans drive back, 4 *Apr.* 1918, 632, 633; holds Villers-Bret. front, 635; situatn. *May*, 639, *Aug.*, 647-8; replaces Fifth, 648; B. of Amiens, 682-4; operns., 21 *Aug.*-3 *Sept.*, 695; Amer. Corps joins, 720; med. arrangts. 17-18 *Sept.*, 724-6; advces. *Nov.*, 768, 769. **Fifth (and Reserve),** 118, 120, 121, 140n, 143, 184, 187-9, 383, 531n, 608, 610 *et seq.*, 629, 640, 695, 718, 768, 776; in First Somme, 52, 53, 61, 72; in Somme Winter, 79; attacks, 80, 85; composn., 107; Ger. retiremt., 107, 108, 109, 110, 114; attacks outpost villages, 122; B. of Bullecourt, 130-2; prepns., 139; advces. med. stns., 141-2; Third Ypres, 194, 219, 232-3, 235-6; med. arrgts., 189-91;

44

GENERAL INDEX

ARMIES—continued.
D.M.S. advces. C.C.S's, 362; his "forward" policy, 609, 621; composon., 21 Mar. 1918, 611; crises in, 612; retreat of, 620-1; med. ser. in retreat, 617-18; exhaustn. of, 627; both flnks. exposed, 27 Mar., 631; replaced by Fourth, 648; Birdwood commands, 775. *See also* AMER. EXPED. FORCE; BRIT. ARMY; FRENCH ARMY; GERMAN ARMY
ARMISTICE, Ger. proposal for, 721; 11 *Nov.* 1918, Foch signs, 768; effect on Aust. soldiers, 770; no relaxatn. at Gen. Hosps., 779; problms. after, 790-5; concentrn. of A.I.F., after, 792-3
ARMY CORPS, *see* CORPS
ARMY COUNCIL, authorises formn. of 6th Aust. Div., 106; advice of, to Aust., 448-9
ARMY COUNCIL INSTRUCTIONS, No. 1023, dated 19 *May* 1916, 12n; issues *re* inoculn., 1916-17, 538; Howse subject to, 803
ARMY FORMS, nominal roll and embkn. card, 425; *A.M.C. Form 2 or 3* to accompany med. bd. papers, 905. *A. 36,* Fld. Amb. return, 177n, 492n. *B. 103,* 346n, 794. *B. 178,* med. hist. sheet, 459, 794. *B. 179,* med. board paper, 334, 456. *B. 213,* fld. return, 34, 492n. *No. 536,* 795. *W. 3110,* notifn. of infect. dis., 411n, 546, 548. *W. 3118,* fld. med. card, 162, 176n, 209, 334, 352, 676, 927, 929. *W. 3185,* rtn. of sick evac., 177n, 491n, 493, 546-7, 884. *W. 3210,* "Buff slip," 176n, 177, 884
ARMY MANUALS, 121n, *Fld. Serv. Manuals,* 773; *F.S. Pocket Book,* 527n; *Manual of Elementary Mlty. Hyg.,* 509, 580n, 594n; *R.A.M.C. Training,* 191, 266n; *Treatmt. of Wounded in Reg. Aid Posts and Fld. Ambs.,* 342n; *Memo. on treatment of Injuries in war,* 339; *Manual of Injuries and Diseases,* 337n, 338n, 340
ARMY MEDICAL SERVICE, 84n, 101, 110, 176, 191-2, 257, 290n, 357, 386, 382n, 499, 560, 603-5, 610, 625, 627, 640, 665, 686, 771, 793n; in modern war, 1-5, 603; orgn. from frnt. to base, 28; work in Somme btle., 50-74; in maintaining hlth., winter, 92; in preventg. wastage, 96-8; its functns., 117, 156; in maintaing. man-power, 140, 253, 263; mthds. of fightg. determine problms. of, 183; during attritn. war., 260-6; its allegiances, 263-4; technique and equipmt., 265-6; developmt. of surg. in war, 299-353; four stages in srch. for asepsis, 311-33; its part in water supply, 590; camaraderie in serv., 630n; final developmts., 631; new conditns., 6*Apr.* 1918, 639; reltns. with civilians, 33, 770, 788-9, 797; Imperial co-opn. in, 866-9. **American:** triage in, 291-2, 918-19; the evac. hosp. (C.C.S.), 299n, 919-21; tactics and mthds., Hamel, 673-4; the San.

ARMY MEDICAL SERVICE—continued.
(Medical) Services, 735-7, 918-21; the untransptble. case, 783, 958; of II Amer. Corps, 736-7; of 129th Fld. Amb., 887-8. **Australian:** 31, 55, 71, 93, 430, 617, 633, 646, (Plates) 32, 69; Howse takes control of, in Eng., 15-20; traing. in Eng., 18, 19; shortge. of M.O.'s., 19; units with I and II Anzac, 29; traing. in raids, 1916, 39; importce. of work of, 76n; co-ops. wth. "Q" Branch in winter prepns., 78-9; work under same conditns. as fightg. troops, 89; morale tested, 89; work in I Anzac, 1917, 104-28; med. situatn., 24 *Feb.,* 110; during Ger. retiremt., 111-14, 116-18, 124-5; at Bullecourt, 134, 135, 136, 146-57, work of S.-B's a high-light, 149-50, med. technique an interestg. example of A.D.S. work, 151; thanked by Brit. units, 153n; Austln. has limelight, 156; in B. of Messines; II Anzac med. arrgts., 162-6; gas barrage, 169; appreciatn. and criticism, 180-2; high standard, *Sept.,* 193n; B. of Menin Rd., 195, 200, 211-12; B. of Polygon Wd., 213-18; faulty *liaison* btwn. R.A.P's and Fld. Ambs., 217; some failure, *Oct.,* 219; B. of Broodseinde, 220-3, 230-1; work of amb. dvrs., 230; problms., 10-15 *Oct.,* 235; "lessons" from Third Ypres, 247-50; responsiblty. in deciding fitness, 249n; effect of Cambrai on, 250; M.O's sent to Italy, 254n; work of quoted by members, 274, 275-6, 279; tradition, *esprit de corps,* 203; views of combat. offcrs., 284n; motor amb. convoy not included in, 289; regtl. S.-B's not part of, 346; "Consultants" selected from, 395; employmt. of staff, 420; members contrib. in resch. work, 413, 553; its part in Aust. Conv. Depot, 420-1; its work in "repair and replcmnt.," 446-81; training and recruits for, 474-5, 477, 838-40; report of D.A.D.M.S., Depots, 478-9; its triple responsiblty., 485; its part in preventg. casualts., 497-500; evolves own mthds., 509-10; onerous duties of Q.M's, 520; its part in preventing dis., 535-602; acts as Brit. isolation hosp., Marseilles, 543; M.O's command san. secns., 596; effect of Ger. Offensve. on, 604; dual task of, 1918, 604; co-ops. with Amer., 605; interior economy of, 1918, 605; units in France, 1917-18, 613-15; Aust. Corps Med. sch., 614, 966; med. arrangts. on Ancre, 26-27 *Mar.,* responsiblty for maintaining resvs., 635; at Villers-Bret., 24 *Apr.,* 638; inventns., etc., 647, 664-5; co-opn. within Aust. Corps, 648; prepares for Allied defvc., 650; Col. Barber's adminstn., 650-63; his *S.O's for A.A.M.C.,* 652-3, 889-99; prepares for mobile war, 653; *Med. Instn. No. 14,* 23 *Aug.,* 663; B. of Hamel, 671-5,

GENERAL INDEX 975

ARMY MEDICAL SERVICE—continued.
co-ops. with Amer., 673-5; lends offrs. to R.A.M.C., 677n, 806; B. of Amiens, 682, 686-7, 690, 692-4; wth. Liaison Force, 693-4; Barber's memo. M2/8, 12 *Aug.*, 694, 884-5; in Somme advnce., *Aug.*, 697-9; advces. med. statns., *Aug.-Sept.*, 698; happy confusion at Mont St. Quentin, 699-700; its part in "open warfare," 703-34; maintains morale, 704-6, and strngth, 710-18, water duty men, 713, "A" class men, to combat. arms, 715, dilutn. resisted, 716; arrgmnts. for Hindbg. Outp. Line, 723-6, operns., 18 *Sept.*, descrbd., 730-3, co-ops. with Amer., 738, Landing and B. of St. Quentin compared, 739, med. events of btle., 743-4; 3rd Div. experce., 753-9; comments on mthds., 764-6; reconstrn. in, 768; repatrn., 790-5; later stages, 799-801; an estimate of med. directn. of A.I.F., 802-58; evolutn. of Aust. Med. Admin. H.Q., 807-15; units and personnel sent from Aust. for, 829; units formed overseas, 830; additnl. units needed to provide full med. estab., 831-2; supply of med. offrs. for, 832-4; promotn. and postg., 834-8; resve. 839-40; rank and status too high, 835n; promotn. of N.C.O's., 842; scient. problms., 836-8; employmt. of personnel in slack times, 839; Austln. D.G's tour o'seas., 851-3, 866-73; med. adminstn. in fld., 874-88; phys. standard of personnel, 904-5; med. estabs., A.I.F., 1918, 911-12; A.D's.M.S. desire divnl. san. sectns., 935-8; the resus. teams, 953-7. *See also* D.M.S., A.I.F. **British**: 261, 395, 398, 566, 568, 571n, 577, 603, 611n, 632, 643, 785, 876; organisn. of, in France, 22-34; scheme of med. adminstn., 24-5; Army Corps, the executive unit, 110; A.M.S. a *deus ex machina*, 254; its part in attrition, 159; developmts. in, 268-71; strtchr.-cases by motor, 286-90; unfair criticism, 288n; transpt. devlpmts. in, 290-1; struct. of, 326n; slovenliness in med. literature, 394n; crises in, 530; preventve. medicine, 483-512, promn. of health, 514-32; the San. Serv., B.E.F., 507-8; co-ops. with Q.M.G.'s Branch, R.A.M.C. agree with Aust. view, 600; water tank coys., 593n; purifying water, 591; prepns., *Mar.* 1918, 608-9; med. situatn. in Somme retreat, 617-24; confusn. in, 625; strngth. reduced, 650n; effort for mobility, 654; med. events, 9-22 *Aug.*, 692-4; the untransportable case, 783; Aust. graduates in R.A.M.C., 828n. **Canadian**: routes used by, 1915, 223; service directed by Canads., 256n; tries to treat all Canad. cas., 427-8; D.G., A.M.S. letter to head of, 4 *Sept.* 1917, 866-8. **French**, controls reschn. labs., Compèigne, 321; its credit for early steps in excisn., 326;

ARMY MEDICAL SERVICE—continued.
view on "untransptbles.," 783; disposn. of stns. behind line, 784; organisn. and mthds. of, 913-18. **German**, its experce. in Somme operns., 71n; its effort of humane co-opn., 134-5; organisn. and mthds. of, 921-5. **New Zealand**, 164n; tries to treat all N.Z. wdd., 427-8; D.G., A.M.S. letter to head of, 4 *Sept.* 1917, 866-8; reply, 14 *Sept.*, of D.D.M.S., 868. *See also* AMER. EXPED. FORCE; AUST. IMP. FORCE; BRIT. ARMY; CANAD. EXPED. FORCE; CASUALTIES; CONFERENCES; CORPS; DIRECTOR OF MED. SERV.; DRESSING STNS.; FETHERSTON; FRENCH ARMY; HOWSE; KEOGH; MED. OFFCRS.; REGTL.; SLOGGETT
ARMY SERVICE CORPS, 131n, 828n; degradation of, in 19th Centy., 569n; Water Tnk. Coys., 593. **Australian**, helps evacn. in Somme Winter, 85n; supplements horses of Fld. Ambs., 87; Amb. drvrs. members of, 193n; takes supplies to Fld. Ambs., *Apr.* 1918, 628-9; members attd. to med. units, 912n
ARQUES, 642, 643
ARRAS (Maps 10, 769; Sk. 22, 623), 106, 108, 114, 183n, 358, 363, 382, 612, 615, 778. **Battle of**, 104, 127, 128, 129-30, 138, 146, number passed through C.C.S's, 155n, percent. of operns., 179n, 332n, lessns., 359
ARTILLERY, **Allied**: bombardmts., 105n; superiority exploited, 159. **Brit. and Australian**, 692n; "box barrage," 37; in B. of Somme, 1 *July* 1916, 51, for assault on Hindbg. Line, 1917, 117, 127, 128, 129; First Bullecourt, 133, stops while wdd. collected, 135; Noreuil Vy., 139; prepns. for Flanders offnsve., 145; alleged shelling of Ger. Amb. Train, 154n; for Ypres offnsve., 180, 183, 184, 192; 15 in. guns nr. C.C.S's, 188; med. arrangts. for, 191-7; Menin Rd., 194n, 202; med. work with, 279-80; details attd. to, 912n, heavy arty., 279n; in B. of Amiens, 683; Hindbg. Line, 731, 739; Austln. with II Amer. Corps, 1918, 768n; 36th (1st Aust.) Siege Brigade, 279n. **Batteries**, 54th (1st Aust.) Siege, 279n; 55th (2nd Aust.) Siege, 252, 279n; 140th, 151st, Heavy, 155th and 353rd, Siege, 279n. **German**, 692; cas. from, 38; 1916, smashes local offnsves., 51; methods, 52-3, Aust. bearers avoid fire of, 59; bombardmts., 61, 125, 149-50, 207, 214, 226, 615, 636; loading posts sited in reln. to fld. guns, 285
ASEPSIS, *see* TREATMENT
ASSISTANT-DIRECTOR OF MED. SERV., *see* DIRECTOR MED. SERV.
ASTHMA, 99, 474
ATH (Map 769), 776
ATTRITION WARFARE, *see* STRATEGY AND TACTICS
AUBERS RIDGE (Sk. 36, 38), 35

AUBIGNY (Map 668; Sk. 656), 667, 671*n*
AUSTRALIA, recruitg. lessons in, 76; effort for conscriptn., 76*n*, 258, 479; number of Gen. Hosps. limited, 399*n*; mumps and measles in, 421*n*; effects of Somme in, 449; excessive individualism, 466*n*; quarantinable diseases in, 490, notifiable diseases in, 553*n*; attitude to compuls. inoculn., 540; failure in meeting diseases on transpt., 564*n*; national character helps mily. efficncy., 679; Howse's *liaison* with, 814; his mission to, 856-7
AUSTRALIAN GOVERNMENT, 844; its wishes *re* caslties, 9-13; confirms positn. of D.M.S., A.I.F., 15; discusses "death penalty," 259; financial arrangts. wth. Brit., 429; "Anzac Leave," 717; its arrangts. for demob., 793
AUSTRALIAN IMPERIAL FORCE, standard of health in, 32, 241-3; promotn. of health, 514-32; "compulsory" inoculn. wth. T.A.B., 537; disease experce. in, 549-50, 559; health, winter, 1917-18, 614; problem of "B" class, 1917, 213*n*; man-power and steps to maintain, 1917, 254-9, 1918, 703-18; preventn. of wastage, 293-6; standards of fitness, 469, Howse's fight, 842-56; questn. of dilution, 715-18; "Austlns. to Aust. Hosps.," 856; permntly. unfit to retn. to Aust., 906, 910; arrives in France, 7-8, 21, 27, 29-34; Aust. Govt's. concern for health in winter, 11; W.O. conf., 12*n*; a "national unit," G.O.C., A.I.F., 20; equipmt., etc., supplied by Brit. on capitatn. basis, 20; integral part of B.E.F., 31; new conditns., in Flanders, 31; raids, 39; Aust. effort on Somme, 52, 76; Somme Winter, 74-103; resourcefulness exhibited, 75; thwarted, 90; troops vote in referndm., 76*n*; in Arras offnsve, 129-57; qualities at Second Bullecourt, 142; med. ser. in Bullecourt btles., 156; at B. of Messines, 158; Brit. reglr. offcrs. replaced in, 256, 604; organism. and commnd., 256-8; no death penalty in, 259; L. of C. units in, 266; price paid for avoidg. conscriptn., 442; no provn. for chiropodists, 530; the rum issue, 531; its spectacular rôle, *Mar.-Apr.* 1918, 610; Amerns. at Hamel, 673; troops' special aptitudes, 679; Gen. O'Ryan's impressn. of Austlns.; *liaison* with II Amer. Corps., 738; demob. and repat. of, 791-800; distribn. at Armistice, 792; discpln. of troops, 795; estimate of med. directn. in, 802-58; med. ser. achves. self-govt., 809-15; hosp. units wth. the five divns., 824; hosp. charges, 827; enlistmt. in, not permitted outside Aust., 828*n*; rates of pay in, 835*n*; munitn. workers from, 849; standard of, the lesson of Third Ypres, 850; med. establts. in 1918, 911-12
—G.O.C., A.I.F., Birdwood becomes,
AUSTRALIAN IMPERIAL FORCE—*continued*. 18 *Sept.* 1915, 817*n*-18*n*; attends W.O. confce., 21 *Apr.* 1916, 12*n*; his policy, 708; concern *re* demob. and repat., 791; relns. with Howse, 817-18, as to phys. standards, 814, 853, informs I.G.C., B.E.F., 906. *See also* BIRDWOOD
—AUST. INTERMEDIATE BASE, 7-20, 809, 822; transfrs. to Eng. and becomes Admin. H.Q., A.I.F., 13-14
—AUST. ADMINISTRATIVE H.Q., A.I.F., 604, (Plate) 809; functns. laid down by Gen. White, 14; controls movts. of rfcts. and invalids, 471*n*; establt., 811. **Medical Section**, 14-15, 807-8, 830; its establt., 813; Howse's relns. wth. commdt., 819. *See also* DIRECTOR OF MED. SERV.; HOWSE
—AUST. CORPS, *see* CORPS
—A.I.F. DEPOTS IN U.K., *see* DEPOTS
—AUST. SECTION, 3RD ECHELON, 34, 157, 169*n*, 354, 440, 477, 479, 491*n*, 493; demand on for rfcts., 269, 709; its figs. for enteric, 539*n*
—WAR RECORD SECTION, 275*n*, 539*n*. *See also*, ARMY MED. SERVICE; BATTALIONS; BRIGADES; CASUALTIES; CAS. CLEARING STNS.; COLLECTING STNS.; CONVALESCENT DEPOTS; CORPS; DENTAL SERV.; DEPOTS; DIVISIONS; FIELD AMBS.; HOSPITALS; MASSAGE SERV.; MEDICAL TRANSPORT; NURSING SERV.; PHARMACEUTICAL SERV.; RECEIVING STNS.; REGIMENTS; SANITARY SECTNS.
AUSTRALIAN INSTRUCTIONAL STAFF, 369; at Parkhouse, 476; as Q.M's of med. units, 520
AUST. RED CROSS SOCIETY, *see* RED CROSS
AUST. WAR MEMORIAL, 175*n*, 532*n*, 807*n*
AUTHIE (Sk. 627), 361; advd. op. centre at, 384
AVELUY (Map 68; Sk. 620), 619; C.C.S's at, 138
AVESNES-LES-BAPAUME, div. rest stn. at 121; specl. centre for gas, 123
AVITAMINOSIS, 488, 504, 505

"B" CLASS, *see* CATEGORIES
BAC ST. MAUR (Sk. 41), 42, 43, 47
BACTERIOLOGY, A.I.F. Adviser in, 563; *see also* DISEASES; LABORATORIES
BAILLEUL (Map 164; Sk. 36, 772), 279*n*, 383, 384, 386, 615, 640, 783*n*; C.C.S's at, 161, 179; bombdd., 642; Germans withdraw 775
BAIZIEUX (Map 68; Sk. 626), 616*n*, 624
BAPAUME (Maps 68; Sk. 10, 613), 80, 116, 117, 118, 141*n*, 384; Germns. wthdraw., 114; rly. reaches 3 *Apr.* 1917, 118*n*; A.D.S. at, 119, 15th Fld. Amb. M.D.S. at, 121, 123; treatmt. centre for gas nr. 121-2; adv. rest stn. at, 140*n*; detraining point at, 151. Second Btle. of, 31 *Aug.*-3 *Sept.*, 1918, 680*n*, 695
BAPAUME-CAMBRAI ROAD, 126-7
BAPAUME POST, for slightly wdd. and strgglrs., 56

GENERAL INDEX

BARISIS (Sk. 607), 608
BASES, 358, 359; Egypt, 430; Calais and Boulogne, 22; med. organisn. and consults. at, 394-6; treatmt. at, 405-12; medcine. at, 409-12; resch. at, 412-13; *see also* BOULOGNE; DEPOTS; HAVRE; ROUEN
BASSE BOULOGNE (Map 760; Sk. 749), 754
BASSEUX, 615, 616, 624
BATHS AND LAUNDRIES (Map 93; Diag. 576), 73, 76, 140*n*, 421, 712; system of, 27; cdns. as exponents of, 74; infnce. on health, 78, 506; a med. responsiblty., 78*n*; provn., a "Q" matter, 78*n*, 94; evoln. on, 575-9, bathg. routine, 579; amt. of clothg. handled, Abbeville, 712*n*; Ger. inspctd. after adv. 8-9 *Aug.* 1918, 712*n*
BATTALIONS, AUSTRALIAN, water duty men of, 77; quick reliefs in winter, 89*n*; clear cas. to R.A.P's, 198; estab. reduced, 709; seven to be broken up, 717, disbandmt. postpnd., 718. **1st,** 731*n*; R.A.P. of, 86, (Sk. 123); trench foot in, 100. **2nd,** R.A.P's of Pozières, 58, 9 *Apr.* 1917, (Sk. p. 123); at Helles, 3 Oct., 227, descbd. by L/Cpl. Morgan, 58, 124, 147-8, 731-2; R.M.O. mort. wdd., 3 *May*, 147*n*; note by R.M.O., 284*n*; coy. cook-house at Ypres, *Nov.*, (Plate) 524; hot ratns. in action 18 *Sept.* 1918, 731; Amer. troops relve., 23 *Sept.*, 731-2. **3rd,** work of R.M.O., 124, 732, loses nrly. all S.-B's, Pozières, 275*n*. **4th,** R.M.O. of, 125, diary quoted, 17-18 *Sept.* 1918, 732. **7th,** R.M.O's reports, 20 *Sept.* 1918, 207. **8th,** R.M.O. wdd., 207. **9th,** 730, 731; cas., *Apr.* 1916, 37*n*; R.M.O. of, 207. **10th,** 516*n*, 730, 731; R.M.O. of 217. **11th,** R.A.P. "blown out," Menin Rd., 205; R.M.O's experce., 1918, 528*n*, diary quoted, 16-18 *Sept.*, 730-1; statistics of R.M.O's work, *Feb.* 1918-*Jan.* 1919, 529. **12th,** 730; R.M.O. nearly captured, 137; R.A.P. "blown out" and R.M.O. wdd., 205; statemts., by R.M.O., 276*n*, 278, 294*n*, 346. **13th,** S.-B's exchange wdd. with enemy, 64; R.M.O. mtlly. wdd., 278*n*; Amers. at Hamel, 673. **14th,** R.M.O. describes Bois Grenier raid, 38; regtl. S.-B's increased to forty, 63; fourteen S.-B's attd. to each coy., Pozières, 276*n*. **15th,** 674; Amer. at Hamel, 673. **17th & 18th,** S.-B's squad of 5th Fld. Amb. attd. to, *May* 1917, 149. **19th,** lends 100 men to help S.-B's, 207; C.O. k., 4 *Oct.* 1917, 247*n*. **21st,** lands 100 men to help S.-B's, 86. **24th,** extrcts. from hist. of, 62*n*, 276*n*; sick parade large, 90. **25th,** S.-B's, 10-11 *Aug.* 1918, (Plate) 693. **26th,** raid by, 6 *June* 1916, 27; R.M.O. de-

BATTALIONS, AUSTRALIAN—*continued.*
scribes R.A.P., 112-3, and clearnce. from Lagnicourt, 120. **27th,** 112; R.M.O's report, 3-6 *Nov.* 1916, 87; Sgt. Edwards' narratve., 276*n*, on sick parade, 294*n*. **28th,** 112; raid by, 6 *June* 1916, 27; notes by R.M.O. 276*n*, 284*n*, 346. **29th,** truce after Fromelles, 46*n*; C.O. complains abt. 14th Fld. Amb., 215*n*. **30th,** R.M.O's report, 91*n*; foot inspn. during Third Ypres, (Plate) 529. **31st,** R.M.O. wdd., 45. **34th,** wdd., brought to R.A.P. (Plate) 709. **37th,** Capt. Grieve on Messines, 167. **38th,** work of S.-B's, 238-9. **42nd,** gassed men, Villers-Bret., 27 *May* 1918, (Plate) 661; Amer. attd. to at Hamel, 673. **43rd,** Amer. attd. to at Hamel, 673. **44th,** 754. **45th,** its R.A.P., Messines, 173, 174. **47th,** help for S.-B's, 136; notes by R.M.O., 136, 173, 237-8, 277*n*; disbndd., 650*n*. **48th,** 516*n*; C.O.'s note on, 60; at First B'court, 133, Messines, 173, First P'daele, 237-8; C.O. wdd., 237-8. **50th,** wth. 51st captures Noreuil, 127; at Villers-Bret. 638. **51st,** 173; with 50th captures Noreuil, 127; men detailed from to assist S.-B's, 136; R.M.O's report on army boot, 525; men of, bathg. at Daours, (Plate) 581. **52nd,** R.M.O's diary, Villers-Bret., 638; disbanded, 650*n*. **55th,** wth. 56th captures Louverval and Doignies, 123; R.M.O. of, 124*n*; R.A.P. in "pill-box," 214. **56th,** wth. 55th captures Louverval and Doignies, 123; R.M.O. of, 124*n*; R.A.P. in "pill-box," 214. **57th,** 746*n*; R.A.P. at Cellar Fm. Av., 41; hot food containers, (Plate) 528. **58th,** R.A.P. at Pinney's Av., 41; "mops up" Bayonvillers, 690. **60th,** R.M.O's experce, at Fromelles, 44*n*; agrees to disband, 718*n*.
Pioneer Bns.: 83*n*; bld. shelter for R.A.P.; 120; **2nd,** 658; feat of sapping by, 145; **4th,** 615
BATTLES, ENGAGEMENTS, ETC., *see under names of places*
BAVARIA HOUSE (Map 224), 225, 229; Ford cars to, 6 *Oct.* 1917, 233
BAYONVILLERS (Sk. 683), 690
BAZENTIN (Map 68; Sk. 116), resve. area near, 116; evacs. to C.C.S's at Edgehill, 102; M.D.S. at converted to "entraining centre," 121
BAZENTIN-LE-PETIT (Map 88; Sk. 112), A.D.S. at, 101; S.-B's of 3rd Fld. Amb., at, 111*n*
BAZENTIN RIDGE, Btle. of, 49*n*
BAZUEL, 770
BEAULENCOURT (Map 68), 119
BEAUMETZ (Map 68; Sk. 123), cross rds. S.W. of, (Plate) 113; fightg. at, *Mar.* 1917, 118, cas., 119
BEAUMONT HAMEL (Map 88; Sk. 116), 384

BEAUREVOIR (Map 760; Sk. 749), 720; B. of Beaurevoir Line, 3-5 Oct., 1918, 680n, 721, capture of Montbrehain, 762-3
BÉCORDEL (Map 93; Sk. 82, 112), 81; clearce. to by rd., 87; treatmt. and displ. at, 88; A.D.S. at, 101; rest stn. at, 121
BÉCOURT CHÂTEAU (Map 88; Sk. 57, 82), work at main A.D.S., 65, (Plates) 65, 68, compared wth. A.D.S. at Charing Cross, 171n; Corps Mumps Stn. at, 110
BELGIAN ARMY, 104, 718; *Hôpital du Front*, 362; advces., 1918, 768; total cas., 860
BELGIAN BATTERY CORNER (Sk. 190), 198
BELLENGLISE, 720
BELLEVUE FARM (Map 93; Sk. 82), rest stns. at, 97, 110, 121
BELLEWAARDE FARM (Map 206), Austln. bties. near, 194n; horsed-waggons to, 208; 4th Div. clears to, 215.
LAKE (Map 216; Sk. 202), 194, 213.
POST (Map 216), 200, 215, 217.
RIDGE (Sk. 189, 202), 226, 233
BELLICOURT (Map 760; Sk. 749), 719, 733; 30th Amer. Div. reaches, 739; fst.-aid centre at, 749
BELLICOURT TUNNEL (Map 760), 600n
BENJAMIN POST (Sk. 749), 754
BERI-BERI, 489n
BERNAFAY WOOD (Map 88), 91n, 121; A.D.S. at, 84, trench feet patients at, (Plate) 77; med. dugouts, 101; evacn. by rly. from, 102
BEUGNÂTRE (Map 68; Sk. 135), M.D.S. at, 127, 136; 27th M.A.C. carries back to, 132; W.W. coll. stn. at, 142
BEUGNY (Sk. 116), A.D.S. at, 119, 123; M.D.S. moves to, 126, 138
BILHARZIA, 503
BIRR CROSS-ROAD (Map 206; Sk. 202), 196, 197, 199, 200, 201, 215, 217
BLANGY-TRONVILLE, 525
BLANKETS, 88, 203, 234, 628; dumps of, in 1916 Winter, 86; folding technique, 344, 345; carried on "pack," 524; distribn., 742; *see also* DISINFECTION
BLENDECQUES (Sk. 772), A.C.C.S's at, 642, 643, 771
BOARDS, MEDICAL, 264, 441-2, 456, 905; professl. problms. 460-64; formn., for doubtful cases, 469; process for P.B. men, 471; the Consultants, 812; *see also* CATEGORIES; CONVALESCENCE; INVALIDING; INVALIDS
BOILS, 568
BOIS GRENIER (Sk. 38), A.D.S. at, 37n
BOISLEUX-AU-MONT (Sk. 620), 619
BONNAY (Map 668; Sk. 626), tempy. D.-S. at, 27 *Mar.*, 1918, 626; A.D.S. nr., 658, 666
BOOTS, trench: inad. supply of, 91, drying and exchge. of, 94; material of, 523; controversy *re* "Austln. pattern," 524-5; *see also* CLOTHING
BORRE (Sk. 645), 646

BOSTAL HEATH, 18
BOULOGNE (Plate 428; Sk. 623), 425, 426, 613; conv. depots formed at, 27; hosp. base at, 161, 188, 394, 397, 662, 778, 779; lab. reschn. initiated at, 1914, 314
BOURSIES (Sk. 123), 122-3
BOVES (Map 68), 633
BOX RESPIRATOR, *see* GAS
BOYLE'S FARM, 174
BRANDHOEK (Sk. 76, 190), 75n, 186, 363, 386; M.D.S., 190; gas treatmt. centre, 223
BRAY (Sk. 680), 692; M.D.S., 700; (Plates) 708, 709
BREMEN HOUSE (Map 224; Sk. 238); 228, 229, 237
"BRICKFIELDS" (ALBERT), 67n
"BRICK-KILN," ZONNEBEKE (Sk. 238), 233, 237
BRIE (Sk. 726), 727, 740
BRIGADES, **American: 65th**, 674; **66th**, with Liaison Force, *Aug.*, 1918, 692n. **Aust., Artillery: 36th Heavy**, R.M.O's of, 279n; **2nd Field**, note by R.M.O. of, 59n; **4th Field**, R.M.O's death, 139. **Aust. Infantry:** served by "own" fld. amb., 75; responblty. to clear cas. to R.A.P's, 198; for fighting *see* BATTALIONS AND DIVISIONS. **Brit. Infantry: 4th Guards**, holds enemy, Hazebrouck, 644. **22nd**, Brig. thanks 2nd Aust. Div., 153n. **Canad. Infantry**, 1st and 6th Bdes. hold ground, 145. *See also* BATTALIONS
BRIGHTON (Map, 452), No. 3 A.G.H. at, 450
BRISTOL (Map, 452), 429
BRITISH AIR FORCE, supremacy of, 53
BRITISH ARMY, enlistmts. and caslts. to *Mar.* 1916, 7n; "New Army," 8; Commands in U.K. (Sk.), 17; G.S. disregards health factor, 1916, 80, 569n; enlistmt. age reduced, 254n; transpt. develpmts. in, 290-1; its debt to Flor. Nightingale, 483n; san. policy based on S.A. War and India, 490; caloric ratn. in, 519; inoculn. in, 538; procedure for prevn. of dis., 546-50; Serv. of Maintnce. neglectd., 569n; its san. policy, 1914, 581; follows scient. school, 603; faces dfce. problms., 607; war orgn. centrifugal, 820n; huts and tents in use in, 931-4. *See also* ARMY MED. SERV.; BATTALIONS; BRIGADES; CAS. CLR. STNS.; COLLECTG. STNS.; CONVALESCENT DEPOTS; CORPS; DENTAL SERV.; DEPOTS; DIVISIONS; FLD. AMBS.; HOSPITALS; MEDICAL TRANSPORT; NURSING SERV.; REGIMENTS; SANITARY SECTNS.
BRITISH EXPEDITIONARY FORCE, cas. evactd. to Eng. for treatmt., 9-10; develpmts. of, 21-7; "New Army" arrives W.F., 22; additnl. armies formed, 22; assimilates Aust. units, 31; cas. in 1916, compared with A.I.F., 103; extnds. frnt. by 20 miles, 106; its plan for spring offnsve., 107;

GENERAL INDEX

BRITISH EXPEDITIONARY FORCE—continued.
G.H.Q. approves II Anzac arrangts. for Messines, 181; C.-in-C's. hope for victory, 183; wasted in minor offsves 1917, 184; disbandmt. of bns., 254; develpmts. in med. ser., 268-71; the Gen. Hosps., 390-422; a Guard's offcr. comments on treatmt., offcrs. *v.* O.R's, 391*n*; bases in France, 394-6; an appreciatn. of Brit. soldier, 414*n*; G.H.Q. protests to W.O. *re* inoculn. in A.I.F., 478; proportn. of bullet to shell wds., 495*n*; orgn. of San. Service, 507-12; its policy in dis. prevn., 508*n*; new outlook in rationing, 520; typhus at Marseilles, 544; dis. notifble. in, 548-50; incidnce. of pneumonia, *cf.* Amer. 557*n*; effects of Somme, 577; sick exp., *cf.* Gallip., 581-3; tactical prepns. for defence, 1918, 608; "backs to the wall" order, 11 *Apr.*, 610; orders tend separate Brit. from French, 616; German offsve., 23-5; *Mar.*, 618; cas. 21 *Mar.*-30 *Apr.*, 618*n*; Cavalry's part in checking Gers., 629*n*; D.G.M.S. sanctns. resus. teams, Aust. Corps, fwd. area, 664; advces. 21 *Aug.*-3 *Sept.*, 695; maintnce: of strength, 704; numbers in France at Armistice, 782; proportns. of battle cas. in, 862. *See also* ARMIES; ARMY MED. SERV.; BATTALIONS; BRIGADES; BRIT. ARMY; CAS. CLR. STNS.; COLLECTG. STNS.; CONVALESCENT DEPOTS; CORPS; DENTAL SERV.; DEPOTS; DIVISIONS; FLD. AMBS.; HOSPITALS; MED. TRANSPORT; NURSING SERV.; REGIMENTS; SANITARY SECTNS.
BRITISH COMMONWEALTH OF NATIONS, *see* COMMONWEALTH OF BRIT. NATIONS
BRITISH EMPIRE, magnitude of its war effort, 1915-16, 7*n*; total btle. cas., 860
BRITISH GOVERNMENT, agrees to counteroffnsve., 1916, 8; defers to wish. of Def. Dept., 11; its financl. arrangts. with Aust., 429, 524*n*; co-ops. with French Govt., 788*n*; arrangts. *re* employmt. of civilns., 789. *See also* GREAT BRITAIN, WAR OFFICE
BRITISH NAVY, blockade by, 607; orgn. for war, centripetal, 820*n*
BRITISH RED CROSS SOCIETY, *see* RED CROSS
BROADMEADOWS CAMP, Vic., 854*n*
BRONCHITIS, *see* DISEASES
BROODSEINDE (Map 224; Sk. 185), 212, 213; Btle. of, 185, 219-31
BRUCELLA GROUP, 501
BRUGES, 159, 183
BUIRE (Map 668; Sk. 82), 81; rest stn., 84, 296; scabies stn., 110; M.D.S., 727, 728, (Plate) 732, (Diag.) 729
BULFORD (Map 452), 455; *see also* HOSPITALS (No. 1 A.D.H.)
BULGARIA, 104, 703, 860
BULLECOURT (Sk. 116, 135), origin of Btles. of, 122; objctve. of Fifth Army, 127; First Btle. of, 129*n*, 131-7; tnk.

BULLECOURT—continued.
carries wdd., 272*n*; Second Btle. of, 129*n*, 138, 145-57, (Plates) 150, salient captd. and held, 145, a "great achievement," 146; Btles., milestone in hist. of med. ser., 156; cas., by perlods and percentges., 156-7
BUSSY (Map 668; Sk. 54), 669*n*
BUTTE (WARLENCOURT), 117, 119

CACHY (Map 68; Sk. 656), 629, 635, 638
CAGNY (Map 68; Sk. 656), 94, 578
CALAIS (Sk. 10, 397), 161, 426; 188, 394, 425, 623, 624
CAMBRAI (Map 769; Sk. 107, 613), 612, 719; Btle. of, 5, 232, 680*n*, end of attritn., 250-3, new tactics, 603, tnks. for clearg. wdd., 671*n*, leads up to Hamel, 666
CAMPS, on Salisby. Plain, 17. *See also* CONV. DEPOTS; DEPOTS
CANADA, 866-8; Mily. Service Act, 255*n*
CANADIAN EXPEDITIONARY FORCE, 74, 256*n*; D.M.S. of, 802*n*, reltns. wth. D.G.M.S., B.E.F., 823; tragic exp, in Brit. training camps, 558*n*; Canad. Div. arrives W. Front, 22; div. baths as models in Brit. Army, 78; advces. railhd. to Anzac Rdge., 5 *Oct.* 1917, 227. *See also* ARMY MED. SERV.; DIRECTOR OF MED. SERV.; DIVISIONS
CANAL DU NORD (Sk. 107), 696; Battle of, 680*n*
CAP MARTIN, 397
CAPITAL PUNISHMENT, not inflctd. in A.I.F. for mily. crimes, 259*n*
CAPORETTO, 253, 254*n*, 607
CAPPY (Map 68; Sk. 698), A.D.S. at, 700
CARLISLE'S POST (Map 216), 222
CASSEL (Sk. 36, 645), 643, 78
CASUALTIES, mthds. of estimatg., 101; numbers passed through Corps Coll. Post, 7-8 *June* 1917, 178; Brit. and Ger. in Flanders Offnsve., 183; Brit. and Domin. arrivg. in U.K. each yr. from B.E.F., 425; preventn. of, 497-500; system for dealg. with gassed cas., 637; National systems for dealg. with, 913-25. Battle-cas.: definitn. of, 270-1, 491, scope of preventn. in, 497-8, 522; proportns. of, B.E.F. and A.I.F., 862; distce.-time factor in transptn. of, 926-30. Non-btle.: definitn. of, 491; scope of preventn. in, 499-500; analysis of 501-4. *See also* DEATHS; MED. ARRGTS.; STATISTICS; WOUNDED; WOUNDS
—ALLIED, during Somme operns., 102; total battle-cas., 860
—AMERICAN, 747, 761; total btle.-cas., 860; in B. of St. Quentin Canal, 739; propn. of "recumbent," to "sitting," 927; in 27th and 30th Divns.: 28 *Sept.*-5 *Oct.* 1918, 744; in 27th Div.: 27 *Sept.*, 742, wk. ended 19 *Oct.*, 763*n*; in 30th Div.: 29-30 *Sept.*, 745, 746*n*, wks. ended 12 and 19 *Oct.*, 763*n*
—AUSTRALIAN, from M.E.F., 7*n*;

CASUALTIES—continued.
genl. arrngts. on W. Front, 9-13; "Austlns. to Austln. Hosps.," 13; arrngts. fer, in Eng., 20; wkly. average, I Anzac, May 1916, 37; total May-June, 37; total Mar.-June, 39; plans for clearing, Fromelles, 42; heavy in Pozières and Mouquet Farm, 51-3; in capture of Pozières, July 1916, 59; number through 7th Fld. Amb., 22 July-16 Aug., 72; on Somme, July-Sept., 73; crisis in recruitg. due to, 76, 448-9, 467; sick and wdd. evacd. from Aust. Divs., Nov. 1916-Feb. 1917, 98; numbers, trench foot, Oct. 1916-May 1917, 99n; total Somme and Fromelles, July-Nov., 102; classifn., compared with B.E.F., 1916, 103; Malt Trench, 112-13; in Ger. retiremt., Feb.-Apr., 128; heavy among S.-B's, 149, 275n; Bullecourt, showg. ratios, 156-7; Messines, 167-8; number of wdd. through Corps stns., 175, admissns. to C.M.D.S's from II Anzac, 178; heavy at Passchdle., 186; numbers July-Aug. 1917, 191, 192; Menin Rd., 20-21 Sept., 205, number of wdd. through A.D.S's, 209-20, among Corps troops, etc., Sept., 213; Polygon Wood, 217-18; Broodseinde, 225-6, from gas, 14 Oct.-10 Nov., 235, total by mths., July-Dec., 243; wkly. incidnce. in Aust. Divs., Third Ypres, Sept.-Nov., 244-5; B. of Cambrai, 252; Flanders Offnsve., 255; number retd. to Aust., to 31 Dec. 1918, 264n; total btle. and non-btle. cas., A.I.F., 1916-18, 409, 864-5; per cent. of admissns. to A.G.H's, 414; displ. of in Eng., 427-8; treatmt. in Brit. hosps., 428; reparatve. treatmt. in Eng., 433; final displ., "parting of ways," 440-1; "knight's gambit," 447-8; total Apr.-Dec. 1916, 448; distributn. of A.I.F. in U.K., 481; analysis of causes, 491-2; comparison, Gallip. and W. Front, 494; admissns. to Fld. Ambs. 1916-18, 495-7, 501-4; analysis of figs. of an R.M.O., Feb. 1918-Jan. 1919, 529; percentage of dis. admitted to Fld. Ambs., 535-6; total, 24 Apr.-3 May, 638; Mar.-May, 649, wdd., gassed and sick, May-July, 677; in Aust. Corps, 22 Aug.-21 Aug., 694; summary, 22 Aug.-4 Sept. 701-2; 1st and 4th Divs., 18-19 Sept., 723; total btle. and non-btle., 1 Apr.-30 Sept., 708-9; number treated dress. stns., 29 Sept.-2 Oct., 761; total at Hindbg. Line, 3rd and 5th Divs., 763; per cent. to A.G.H's, 780n; mortality. rate on W. Front, 787, hosp. policy of D.M.S., A.I.F., for W. Front, 824-6; treatmt. and displ. of, 827-8; in Light Horse, after Gallip., 832n; figs. for Egypt and Gallip., 1915, 861n; reltve. propns., 862; total on W. Front, 1916-18, by months, 864-5; corres. re treatmt. in Brit., 870-3.

CASUALTIES—continued.
1st Div.: 9th Bn., Apr. 1916, 37n; numbers of walkg. wdd., 22-28 July, 72; at Pozières, 73; in Ancre Btle., Nov., 85; evacns. from, 5 Nov.-18 Feb., 98; Somme and Fromelles, July-Nov., 102; 27 Feb., 1917, 110; 2nd and 3rd Bns., Hermies, 9 Apr., 125; in Ger. raid, Lagnicourt, 137; number evacd., wdd. and gassed, 3-10 May, 146; Broodseinde, 4-5 Oct., 225; wkly. incidnce., Third Ypres, 244-5; Hazebrouck, 646; wdd. and gassed evacd., May-July 1918, 677, 8-21 Aug., 694, 22 Aug.-4 Sept., 702; 18-19 Sept., 723; total Apr.-Sept., 708-9; 11th Bn., 18 Sept., 731. 2nd Div.: deaths and gassed, 27 July-6 Aug., 1916, 61; at Pozières, 73; in Ancre Btle., Nov., 85; sick and wdd., by wks., Nov.-Feb., 98; Somme and Fromelles, 102; 6th Bde., Noreuil, 119; Laigni'ct., 120, 137; wdd. and gassed, 3-17 May, 146; Broodseinde, 4-5 Oct., 225, 226; Poelcappelle, 235; 5th and 6th Bdes., 19 May, 1918, 666; 7th Bde., 10-11 June, 666; 6th Bde., Hamel, 670; from gas, 6-9 June, 169n, addmissns. 8-21 Aug., 694; 22 Aug.-Sept., 702; total, 1 Apr.-30 Sept., 708-9; Beaurevoir and Montbrehain, 3-5 Oct., 762-3. 3rd Div., at B. of Messines: wdd. by days, 6-15 June 1917, 168, from gas, 6-9 June, 169n; admissns. to C.M.D.S's, 178, total 6-15 June, 180; Broodseinde, 4-5 Oct., 225, 12-13 Oct., propn. k. to wdd., 236, 238; Passchdle., 240; wkly. incidnce., Third Ypres, 244-5; total, 28 Mar. 1918, 628; in 9th Bdes., 4 Apr., 632; gassed and wdd., 8-21 Aug., 694, 23 Aug.-4 Sept., 702; total Apr.-Sept., 708-9; wdd. and sick, wks. ended, 28 Sept. and 5 Oct., 744, Hindbg. Line, 29 Sept.-2 Oct., 763. 4th Div.: at Pozières, 73; First Bullecourt, 134, Second, 146; wdd. by days, 6-15 June, 168; at B. of Messines: admissns. to C.M.D.S's, 178, total, 6-15 June, 180, total, 26 Sept., 217, 12-13 Oct., 236; wkly. incidnce., Third Ypres, 244-5; Ancre, 28 Mar., 1918, 628; 12th and 13th Bdes., 5 Apr., 630; 4th and 11th Bdes., Hamel, 670; gassed and wdd., 8-21 Aug., 694, 22 Aug.-4 Sept., 702; 18-19 Sept., 723; Apr.-Sept., 708-9. 5th Div., at Fromelles, 39-40, 47-8; sick and wdd. evac., by wks., Nov.-Feb., 98; Somme and Fromelles, 102; 15th Bde. at Laignic't, 120; 55th and 56th Bns., Louverval, Doignies, 125; wdd. and gassed, 3-17 May, 146; Polygon Wd., 215, 217; wkly. incidnce, Third Ypres, 244-5; gassed and wdd., 8-21 Aug. 1918, 694; 22 Aug.-4 Sept., 702; Apr.-Sept., 708-9; 29 Sept.-2 Oct., 763. A.A.M.C., 37n, 45, 139, 147n, 205, 207, 209n, 213n, 227, 236, 278, 622, 833; sustained by fld. ambs. and regtl. S.-B's, July-

GENERAL INDEX 981

CASUALTIES—*continued.*
Sept., 1916, 73; 11 *Apr.*-17 *May*, 136;
of Aust. divns., 11 *Apr.*-17 *May*, 153;
S.-B's k. and wdd., Messines, 173,
S.-B. capt. wdd., 174, 184n, S.-B's,
174; *July-Aug*, 1917, 192; brers., 18
Sept., 204n; enquiry into cas. amng.
Amb. S.-B's, Polygon Wd., 218; summary of wkly. incidnce., Third Ypres,
247; B. of Hamel, 672
—BRITISH, total sick and wdd.,
B.E.F. and M.E.F., 7n; evacd. to
Eng., 9-11; 61st Div., 19-21 *July*,
1916, 48n; concern in Britain at, 51;
XIV Corps in Somme minor operns.,
84n; total, and classfn., 1916, B.E.F.
and A.I.F. compared, 103; wdd. Arras
offnsve., 155n; 25th Div., Messines,
178; IX and X Corps, Messines, 180;
5 *Aug.*-9 *Sept.*, 184; II Corps, *Aug.*,
194; Menin Rd., 209-10; 66th Div.
cas. cleared by 3rd Aust. Div., 239;
III and VI Corps, Cambrai, 252; II
Corps, Mons, 22-23 *Aug.*, 1914, 286;
sick and wdd. admitted to med. units,
1914-18, 299; wdd. admd. to C.C.S's,
1917-18, 331; total, 1914-18, 409, 547,
860-1; in Ger. offnsve., 1918, 611,
618; wdd. admtd. Fourth Army
C.C.S's, 8-11 *Aug.*, 694; treated at
dress. stns., 29 *Sept.*-2 *Oct.*, 761;
mortality. rate of wdd. and gassed,
787
—CANADIAN, Mouquet Fm., 64;
evacd. by 5th Aust. Div., B. of
Amiens, 690
—FRENCH, at Verdun, 8; evacd. by
Aust. units, 690n; total, 860
—GERMAN, 61; during Somme
operns., 102; during retiremt., 109n;
in raid on Lagnic't, 15 *Apr.* 1917,
137; in Fourth Army C.C.S's, 8-11
Aug. 1918, 694; evacd. by ord. channels, 699; total, 860, ratio, 863,
propn. of drivg., walkg., and "untransptables," 927
—NEW ZEALAND, Messines: 180; admissns. to C.M.D.S's, 178; Passchdle.,
12 *Oct.*, 236
CASUALTIES, CLASSIFCN. AND DISTRIBN.
OF, 778-9; at Bécordel, 88; of total
B.E.F. and A.I.F., 1916, 103;
Pozières the pivot, *Mar-Apr.*, 1917,
121; of stret. cases, walkg. wdd. and
sick, Messines, 163, 178-9; at
M.D.S. 9th Fld. Amb., Broodseinde,
230; at A.D.S., Poelcappelle, 234;
A.I.F., by mths., *July-Dec.* 1917,
243; stret. cases and walkg. wdd.,
274; system of *triage*, 291-3, comparisn., French, Amer. and Brit.,
785, 913-25, C.C.S. as centre for,
300, 370, 374, 375; procedure at No.
2 A.G.H., 401, at B.E.F. Base, 403-4,
in Aust. Convlsnt. Depot, 420, at
dress. stn., Templeux, *Sept.-Oct.*,
1918, 749-50
CASUALTIES, COLLECTION AND CLEARANCE,
in 1914 to railhd., 286-7 at Fromelles,
44-7, effect of enemy barrage on, 53;

CASUALTIES, COLLECTION AND CLEARANCE
—*continued.*
mthds. on Somme, 56-7; heavy cas. to
S.-B's, Pozières, 58; S.-B's, Allied and
Ger., co-op., 60n; stret. and sittng.
cases by M.A.C., 71; med. arrangts.,
Somme, 83-7; in Ger. retiremt.,
111-12, 116-19; at Lagnic't, *Mar.*,
120, *Apr.*, 138-9; I Anzac 9 *Apr.*,
123-7; Bullecourt, 128n, 134-7, arrangts. *May*, 143-4, 147-8; at Messines: 3rd Div., 168-72, 4th Div.,
172-5; gen. arrangts. in attritn. warfare, 212; Menin Rd., 195-211; Polygon Wd., 215-18; Broodseinde, 225-30;
Passchdle., 236-40; Dernancourt, 5
Apr. 1918, 630-1; fwd. clearnce.,
Hamel, 667-9; Aust. and Amer., 28-30
Sept. 745-53; summary 29 *Sept.*-
19 *Oct.*, 754-9
CASUALTIES, EVACUATION OF, (Plates
293, 428, 661; Sk. 41, 62), in Army
Zone, 268-296; at C.C.S., 355-387;
at base, 390-422; in Britain, 424-
443; evolutn. of system, 25; C.C.S.
as surg. centre, 26; scheme, *May*
1916, 37, for Somme, based on Rouen,
54; problms. on Somme, 57-8;
transpt. for, 65-6; lack of co-ordn.,
70; effects of distce. on, 71; med.
arrangts. I Anzac, 82; distces. in
Somme Winter, 84; by bd.-gauge train,
101-2; light ttys. 111-12; by M.A.C.
and lorries, 121; by Amb. waggns.
and lorry, 132; a long evacn. route,
138; Bullecourt, arrangts. I Anzac,
143; med. problm., Bullec't, 146;
horsed waggon circuit, 151; Messines:
Second Army scheme, 161, II Anzac,
162-6; mthd., Pont d'Achelles, 176,
work at a M.D.S. descbd., 177, work
of C.C.S's, 179-80; "fwd." policy,
Third Ypres, 188; I Anzac scheme,
Menin Rd., 195-211; "A," "B," and
"C" circuits, 202n, 210, 273; Polygon Wd., (Map) 216; Broodseinde,
220-21, 230; technique of transpt.
and treatmt., Third Ypres, 247-8,
humanity *v.* efficiency, 248-9;
treatmt. and transpt. constants, 265-6;
movemt. within army zone, 268-96;
similarity in nat. systems, 270; function *v.* structure, 269-71; from
R.A.P. to M.L.P., 280-4; Gallip. and
Mons compared, 287n; in a retreat,
288n; co-ordn. of movt. and
treatmt., 291-3; developmts. in
treatmt. of wds., 299-353, stages,
340-53; the "untransportable case,"
352-3, 661-2, 785; the C.C.S. in,
355-87; the constant factors, 360; the
Gen. Hosps. in, 390-422; procedure
at No. 2 A.G.H., 403-404; the Channel crossing, 424-7, embktn., 425-6,
disembktn. and distribn., 426-7;
at med. prepns. in B.E.F., for *Mar.*
1918, 608-9; in retreat, *Mar.*, 1918,
618-24; Amb. train, 622-4; 3rd Div.
from Somme and Ancre, 628; Dernanc't 5 *Apr.*, 630; from Fourth

45

CASUALTIES, EVACUATION OF—*continued.*
Army, 633; *Apr.-May*, 635; route behind Hazebrouck, 646; technical develpmts. 655-6; risks of journey to C.C.S., 661; on Somme *May-June*, 665-6; in fwd. area, Hamel, 667-9, 671, 672; the distce.-time factor, 675-6, Macpherson's formula, 675*n*-6*n*; from Aust. units, *May-July*, 677; from Aust. Corps, on Brit. C.C.S's, Vignac't., 684; co-ord., B. of Amiens, 686-7, goes "according to plan," 690; Barber supplmts. med. arrangts., 693; terrain and problm. of, *Aug.*, 696; Aust. Divs., *Aug.*, 700; Amer. Divs., 737; med. arrangts. 1st and 4th Divs., 17-18 *Sept.*, 724-5, Col. Barber's instructns., 18 *Sept.*, 727, 3rd Fld. Amb. *re* "forward," 732; comment on for *Sept.* operns., 1st Div., 728-33; arrangts. of D.D.M.S. Aust. Corps, for St. Quentin, 740-1; signifnce. of term "congestion," 747*n*; comments and conclusns., 764-6; grouping of C.C.S's, 773, some final conclusns., 782; importce. of correct classfn., 785; fundmtl. princples. in Brit. system, 785-6; preparatory measures for a big offnsve., 874-7, Austln. for B. of Amiens, 877-84, instructns. for control of S.-B. divns., 20 *Sept.*, 885-7; some nat. systems, 913-25, French, 916-8, Amer., 918-21, Ger., 922-4; distce.-time factor, 926-30. **Walking Wounded:** at Vadenc't 70; by light rly. to Bazentin, 113; to the Butte, 117; to Pozières, 137; buses supplied by Army, 143; M.D.S. for, 5th Fld. Amb., 3-8 *May* 1917, 151; use of lorries, 161; at Messines, 166*n*, 172, 178, special provns., 163; by No. 32 Brit. C.C.S., 188; Menin Rd., 202, 208, 209, scheme of responsiblty., 197, lorries and buses, 198; cleared by rly., lorry and bus, 26 *Sept.* 1917, 217; arrangts. from R.A.P. to M.L.P., 280; developmt. of transpt. arrangts., 290-1; arrangts. for sick and wdd. at dress.-stn., 352; evacd. by tempy. amb. trains, 393; clearnce. to C.C.S., 657-8; by buses and lorries, B. of Amiens, 687; by light rly. and amb. trains, 879; arrangts. at 2nd Fld. Amb. dress. stn., Tinc't, 732-3; arrangts. 18 *Sept.*, 727; by motor lorry and rlys., 761-2; propn. to stret. cases, 926-7. **Stretcher cases:** to A.D.S., Contalmaison, *Mar.* 1917, 113; numbers through M.D.S., 137; 6th Fld. Amb. M.D.S., 3-4 *May*, 152; Messines: separated from walkg. wdd. and sick, 163, routes, 166*n*, from R.A.P. to A.D.S., 170; Menin Rd.: 208, 209; allocn. of responsblty., 197, A.D.S. to C.C.S., 202; Broodseinde: by horsed waggon, 4 *Oct.*, 227, by hand carry, 7 *Oct.*, 227; cleared by S.-B's, Passchendaele, 10-11 *Oct.*, 239; pro-

CASUALTIES, EVACUATION OF—*continued.*
portn. to others, 274, 926-7; S.-B. relays, 281; origin of motor conveynce., 286-90; arrangts. at M.D.S., 352. **Sitting cases:** to Pozières for distribn., 137; varies accordg. to transpt., 274; proportn. to lying cases, 927
CASUALTY CLEARING STATIONS, number provided for Somme Btle., 55*n*; evolutn. of tactics, 70-71; numbers evacd. from, to base, *Nov.* 1916-*Feb.* 1917, 98; journey to, *Mar.* 1917, longer than 1916, 117; evacn. to, 17 *Mar.*-2 *Apr.*, 120-2; at Grévillers, Edgehill, and Aveluy, *Apr.*, 138; improved mthds. at, 155; *point d'appui* of trtmt. 265; surg. work passes to, 316; functns. of, 355; structre., etc., 357; evolutn. of functn. and structre., 358; expnsion. of, 359; early operns. at, 359*n*; structre., estab., equipmt. of, 359*n*, 364-7; strength in Brit. offsves., 364; surg. teams, 364-5; equipmt., transpt., and housg., 365-6; interior economy and workg. of, 367-73; clinical orgn., 373; the surg. divn., 373-7; the med. divn., 377-8; specialists and consults., 377; discrimn. *re* return to duty, 378; equipmt. augmted. by surg. sets, 609; allocatn. to Corps for rest, 614; during retreat, *Mar.-Apr.* 1918, 619, keystone of evacn., 624; moves in Fourth Army, *Mar.* 1918, 641*n*; Hamel, 672; "abdominals and chests" from 30th Amer. Div. arrive in 4½ hrs., 762*n*. **Australian:** 355, 380-87, Imperl. adjustmts., 380; establt., 1918, 911, 912*n*; B. of Messines, 179-80; propn. of wds. operd. on at, 386; movts., 1916-18, (Sk.) 772; echelons of movts. *Mar.* 1918, 640-43; strategy and tactics of, 643; cas. treated at, *Apr.*, 644; surg. teams of, 840-41; in last phase of war, 771-8, advce. with Fifth Army, *Nov.*, 768; during demob., 796, 799; breakg. up of, 800; personnel embked. from Aust., 829.
No. 1: 41*n*, 368, 377*n*, 378, 382 *et seq.*, 614, 641; leaves Aust. wth. X-ray, 71*n*; arrives in France, 29; at Estaires, 30; Bailleul, 161, 180, admns., 6-9 *June*, 1917, 180, percentge. opertd. on, 248; Oultersteene, 179*n*, (Plates) 349, 364; "Corps rest stn." 6 *Dec.*, 246; moves back *Mar.* 1918, 640-1, Ana Jana, 641, 642, moves, 643; numbers treated at, *Apr.*, 640; Blendecques, 771; advces. wth. Fifty Army, 775; rapid moves, *Oct.*, 776; Frétin, *Oct.* 381; wth. army of occupn., 776; report of surg. work, *Aug.*, 777-8. **No. 2:** 361*n*, 374*n*, 382-3, 386, arrives in France, 29; Trois Arbres, Steenwerck, 30, 161, 164, (Plate) 349, recves. sittg. cases, Fromelles, 41, bombed, 22

GENERAL INDEX 983

CASUALTY CLEARING STATIONS—*continued.*
July, 1917, 179*n*, numbers passed through, 179-80, per cent. opertd. on, 248; report by surg. specialist, Feb. 1918, 332-3; post-mortems, 369; admns. and operns., *Jan.-Sept.* (Graph), 372; total admns., *July 1916-June 1918* (Graph), 385; admns. and operns., *Jan.-Dec.*, 386; moves back, *Mar.*, 640-3; total treated, *Apr.*, 644; Blendecques, 771; *June-July*, 775; advces. wth. Fifth Army, 775; on 11 *Nov.*, 776; with Army of Occupn., 776; list of serious wds. treated at, 783*n*. **No. 3:** 143, 361, 362, 366, 374, 377*n*, 378, 383-4, 386, 387; at Gézaincourt (Plate), 365; moves to Grévillers, 8 *Apr.* 1917, 132; numbers passed through, 3-9 *May*, 154; Brandhoek, 186, 188; Nine Elms, 230, 643; C.O's comment *re* morphia, 324-5; creates pathol. dept., 369; moves back, *Mar.* 1918, 640; Esquelbecq, 14 *Apr.*, 643-4, 771; total treated, *Apr.*, 644; C.O's report, *July*, 774; specialist phys., *Aug.*, 774-5; advces. with Second Army, 775-6; letter from D.M.S., Rhine Army, 800. **British:** 71, 132, 155*n*, 179-80, 328, 520*n*, 552, 625, 633, 640, 663, 684; treatmt. at, 26; nurses at, 26*n*; grps. at Grévillers, Achiet-le-Grand, 141; in B. of Messines, 161, 163*n*; dispositn. for Third Ypres, 186; surg. trtmt., 187; fwd. policy of, 187-8; grp. at Remy Siding, 203; at B. of Menin Rd., 210; risk capture, Cambrai, 252; the Brit. "evacg. hosps.," their functn., 299-300; numbers admttd. to, 1917-18, 331*n*; proportn. opertd. on, 332*n*, 377; analyse cause of army wastge., 568; transpt. and movt., 608; experces. in retreat, *Mar.-Apr.*, 617-21; at B. Dernanc't., 631; distce. behind Somme, *Apr.-May*, 635; captured, 677*n*; distce. to, causes congestn., B. of Amiens, 690; effect of Ger. break-through, 692, 772; move up *Sept.*, 701; open at Doignt and Brie, 727, 740, 748; at Tincourt, receive Amer. wdd., 29 *Sept.*, 748-9; clearnce. to, by M.A.C., 761-2; personnel, housing and equipmt. of, 772-3; estabts., 775*n*; effort for moblty., 776; problem of early opern. at, 786; Third Army experimtl., 841; time taken for wdd. to reach, 927-30; wdd. arrivg. at, falls into three grps., 956-7. **British C.C.S's:** *1/1st Midland*, 102; *No. 2*, 180, 383, 384, 386; *No. 3*, 384; at Gézaincourt, "shock-centre," 662; transfusn. serum supplied to resus. teams, 663; *No. 5*, at Crouy, 667; for abdominals, 701, 725; *No. 10*, 357*n*, 368, 386, 774; as resch. centre, Remy Siding, 203, 332; *No. 11*, 180, 383, 384; *No. 12*, 725, 762; *No. 17*, 203, 641, 642; *No. 20*, 684, 775*n*, 878; *No. 29*, 384; *No. 32*,

CASUALTY CLEARING STATIONS—*continued.*
188, 362, 363; *No. 36*, 83; *No. 37*, 725; barely escapes capture, 677*n*; *No. 38*, 83, 87*n*; *No. 41*, 725; *No. 44*, 188, 363, 830; *No. 45*, 102, 330; *No. 47*, 667; *No. 48*, 623, 677*n*; *No. 49*, 72; *No. 53*, 180, 384, 386, 725, 762, with *No. 55* at Vécquemont for Aust. Corps, 10 *Aug.* 1918, 684, 693; *No. 58*, 762; *No. 61*, 684, 701, 878; *No. 62*, 775*n*. **Canadian:** *No. 1*, 684*n*; *No. 2*, 774, at Remy Siding, 186, 203; *No. 3*, 365, at Remy Siding, 186, 203; *No. 4*, 383*n*, 684*n*. *See also* HOSPITALS
CASUALTY CORNER, 56, 63
CATEGORIES, MEDICAL, 12, 19, 442, 457-60, 795; evolutn. of, 456-8, med. control of, 466; problem of enlisting men of low standard, 846-50. **"A" Class:** 447, 466, 471, 475, 476, 814; dent. fitness, 459-60; combing out bases, 715; Brit. class 1 not equal to Austln., 715*n*; standards for A.A.M.C. rfcmts., 904-5. **"B" Class:** 447, 477, 559, 707, 905; problem of, 213*n*, 845-50; do water duty, 256*n*; graduated training in Commd. Depots, 465; objectns. to retaining o'seas, 902; "P.B." and "T.B." men, 470-1, 475, 715, 847-50, 906-10; employed in France, 470*n*; at No. 3 A.G.H., 403; "under-age" boys and "over-age" men, 715. **"C" Class:** 458, 470, 471, 475, 476, 559, 707, 905. *See also* BOARDS; INVALIDS
CAVALRY, 129, 131*n*, 141, 627. *See also* CORPS
CELLAR FARM AVENUE (Sk. 41), 41, 42, 45
CENTRAL ROAD, 130-1, 145
CEREBRO-SPINAL FEVER, *see* DISEASES
CÉRISY (Map 68), 397
CHALK PIT (Plate 64; Sk. 57), 58, 63
CHAMPAGNE (Map 10), 106
CHANTILLY, conf. at, 105
CHARING CROSS (Map 164), A.D.S., 165, 166, conditns. at, 169
CHARLEROI (Map 769), 793, 796
CHICKEN POX, 543
CHIPILLY (Map 68, Sk. 683), 689, 692
CHOLERA, 490, 501, 541, 549, 581
CHUIGNES (Map 68), B. of, 680*n*, 695, 699
CHUIGNOLLES (Map 68; Sk. 698), 724
CIVILIANS, reltns. wth., 33; med. trtmt. of, 770, 788-90, 797; evacd. by Germans, 140*n*; prevlnce. of Typhoid amng., 540*n*
CLAPHAM JUNCTION (Map 206), 196, 199, 200
CLASSIFICATION, *see* CASUALTIES, CLASSIFCN.; CATEGORIES; DISEASES
CLÉRY (Map 68; Sk. 680), 3rd Div. captres., 700
CLIMATE, *see* WEATHER
CLOTHING (Plates) 528, 680; cleang. and disinfectg. of, 78*n*, 94, 140*n*, 577, 578, 712*n*; items of, 523-4; inflnce. on

CLOTHING—*continued.*
hlth., 524-6; wght. of, 527; underclothg., 522, 523; the uniform, 523-4; shirt, 523; puttee, 523, 524; grtcoat., 523, 525; hat, 523, 526; socks, 523, importce. of, 78*n*, 91, 94; wastge. in, 525. *See also* BATHS AND LAUNDRIES; BOOTS
COLITIS, 99, 586
COLLECTING POSTS, trtmt. at, 350; at Cas. Cr., 56; at Bécordel, 84; nr. Mametz, 86, for slight and walkg. cases, 88; descripn. of, 150; at Messines, 164, 170, 172, 175, 178; Menin Rd., 207; Broodseinde, 222, 223; term prohbtd., 634; in Somme area, *May-July* 1918, 656; Petit Camon, 667; "Egg Post," 752*n*; Benjamin's Post. 754; disposns. for B. of Amiens, 877; for cases fit in 12 hrs., 880. *See also* CASUALTIES, COLLECTN. AND CLEARNCE.
COLOGNE. (Sk. 10), 776
COMFORTS FUND, AUSTRALIAN, 517, 743, 797
COMMAND DEPOTS (Map, 452), 356, 437, 446-7, 449, 451, 455-71; orgn. in Eng., 18-20; early hist., 455-6; evolutn. and orgn., 450-1; workg. system, 457-60, 465, 470, 614; prevention of disease in, 564; Howse's rept. on, 1 *Nov.* 1916, 830*n*. **No. 1**, 18, 434, 441, 457, 463, 464, 466, 467, 468. **No. 2**, 438, 441, 448, 450, 451, 471, 473, 832; Base Depot, Weymouth, becomes, 18; treatmt. carried out at, 341, 433, 511; "categories" in, 458*n*. **No. 3**, 434, 438, 441, 464, 466; opens 12 *Mar.* 1917, 450*n*; "D.A.H." cases collctd. at, 463. **No. 4**, 434, 438, 441, 460, 464, 466; med. exam. at, (Plate) 453. *See also* DEPOTS
COMMISSIONS, 356, 483, 526, 931; Interallied Sanitary, 452*n*, 551; "Babtie," on Canad. Service in Eng., *Nov.* 1916, 826*n*
COMMITTEES, on re-orgn. of Brit. Army Med. Serv., 356*n*; Med. Advisory of M.E.F., 584*n*; joint, of B.R.C.S. and Order of St. John, 366, 413*n*; Advisory to D.G.M.S., B.E.F., 508*n*; Health of League of Natns., 510*n*; Advisy. on Liquor Control, 530; Medical Research: 551, 946, on haemorrhage and wd. shock, 662, 947, 951-2, constitn. of c'tee, 953; resus. teams, 664, 953-5; on battle names, 680*n*; on shock, Third Army, 957
COMMONWEALTH OF BRITISH NATIONS, 7, Imperial co-op., 427-8
COMMUNICATIONS, 81; wth. frnt., complete, 94; light rly. extendd., 116; in "step by step" advce., 219-20; telephonic, importce. of, 283*n*, 691. *See also* LIAISON
COMMUNICATIONS, LINES OF, 30-1, 269, 417, 419, 520, 622; Aust. med. units of, 29, 266; transpt. for wdd. provdd. by Insp.-Gen. of, 286*n*; admins. on, 390-4; evacn. on, 390-422

COMPIÈGNE (Map, 769); French resch. labs. at, 319, 320-1; thrust agnst., 611
CONFERENCES, 832; at W.O. in 1914, 286; at W.O. *re* disposal of Aust. cas., 11-13; Allied, Chantilly, 105; Paris, 4 *May* 1917, 158; med. staff at Monash's confces., 684*n*; Col. Barber wth. Americans, 742; of recruitg. commtees., Melb., 845. **Interallied San.:** 551; *May* 1916, 32; problm. of food, 96; *Mar-May* 1917, 140*n*, 543*n*, 575*n*, 578; policy of inoculn., 538; in 1918, 541*n*, 542*n*; food stuffs, 519; on dysentery, by A.D.M.S. San., B.E.F., 590*n*; Sir G. Buchanan's part in, 510*n*. **Interallied Surg.:** *Mar.* 1917, 356*n*, 362*n*; French and *débridement*, 326; conclns. of, 330-1
CONJUNCTIVITIS, 676
CONNAUGHT SIDING, 166, 172
CONSCRIPTION, failure of fst. refndm. adds to work of med. ser., 76*n*; Aust. rjcts. secnd. refndm., 1917, 258; effect of failure on A.I.F., 442
CONSULTANTS, Cons. surgns. and physicians apptd. to B.E.F., 395, duties, 395-6; C. J. Martin's work, 508*n*, 815*n*. **Consulting Surgeons:** 187, 329, 359, 812, 844, 954, 955; commends work of M.D.S's, 70; demonstrts. Thomas splint, 155; pleased with patients arriving at C.C.S., 175*n*; Sir A. MacCormick at Boulogne, 314, 315; Sir G. Makins, B.E.F. Bases, 314*n*; Sir C. Gordon Watson, Second Army, 315; Col. Gray, Rouen and Third Army, 326*n*; Col. Maynard Smith, Fifth Army, on wd. trtmt., 329; Sir A. Bowlby suppts. D.M.S., Fifth Army, 362; Col. Dunhill, A.A.M.C., Rouen Base, 395. **Consulting Physicians:** 359, 378, 584*n*, 812, 843; of Second Army, lectres. on "mustard gas," 193; of B.E.F., Sir A. Wright, 315, Lt.-Col. Fairfax, A.A.M.C., Rouen Base, 395; Col. Soltau, First and Second Armies, 568*n*
CONTALMAISON (Map 68; Sk. 112), 52, 113
CONTAY (Map 68; Sk. 54), 53
CONVALESCENT DEPOTS, 18, 404*n*, 419, 441, 442, 829; orgn. of, in Eng., 16-20, control tightened, 258; their part in "rtn. to duty," 258; in France, 404, 830, formed at the Base, 27, 404. **No. 1 Australian:** formed *Apr.* 1918, 420-1; stats. of, 421; estabt. 1918, 911. *See also* COMMAND DEPOTS
CONVOY, *see* AMBULANCE CONVOY
COOKING, training for, discussed at San. Conf., 32; diffclts. in "staging camps," Somme, 89; Birdwood's comment on importce. of, 20 *Oct.* 1917, 246*n*; No. 3 A. G. H. suggests females for, 402*n*; schools for, 520,

GENERAL INDEX 985

COOKING—*continued*.
614-15; portble. ovens wth. Fld. Ambs., 520*n*; fld. cooker not allotted to Fld. Amb., 912*n*
CORBIE (Plates 580, 628; Sk. 54, 683), 619, 620, 628, 629; straggler's post, 669; No. 3 M.A.C. at, 693
CORDIAL FACTORY, ZONNEBEKE, 233
CORDUROY ROAD (Map 224; Sk. 190), 228
CORPS, ARMY, as a tactcl. unit, 66, 69; immense size of, 67*n*; controls baths and launds., 73; med. branch of, consolidates retns., 75; in Somme Winter, 82; mumps and scabies stns., 110; rôle of, 651. **II American:** 735, 737, 767; co-ops. with Aust. Corps, 718, 833; Aust. Corps relves., 1 Oct. 1918, 762; relves. Aust. Corps, 6 Oct., 679; wth. French attks. twds. Mézières, 718. **I Anzac** (Col. C. C. Manifold, D.D.M.S.): 69, 363, 378, 382, 575; arrives in France, 11, 29; wth. II Anzac at Armentières, 21; av. wkly. cas., May 1916, 37; joins Resve. Army, July, 39, 52; in attk. on Pozières, 51; replcrd. by Canads., 73; during Somme Winter, 74-103; relved. Canads., Ypres, 74; relieves XV Corps, 79; retns. to Somme, 80-2; scheme of works, 83, 92-4; in Ancre Btle., Nov., 85-9; tr. foot in, 91; baths and launds., 94, 577-9; training and re-orgrn., 101; 25 Feb.-17 Mar., 109-114; lght. rlys. of, Jan. 1917 (Sk.), 112; advced. guards of, 115-16; relfs. and moves, 26 Mar.-2 Apr., 120; advces, 2-9 Apr., 122-8; hvy. cas. in arty. of, Apr., 139; improvmt. in area of, 139-40; over 100 units in, 139; spearhd. of Second Army, 189; in rest and training, June-Aug., 193; in Third Ypres, 194-8; side-slips north, 212; B. of Polygon Wd., 213-18; again moves north, 218; B. of Broodseinde, course of, 225-6; B. of Poelcappelle, 233-5; Passchendaele, 235-6; system of schools in, 532; inocln. procedure in, 538; San. Sectns., 595*n*. **II Anzac:** 43, 378; arrves. in France, 29; med. units, 29; replces. I Anzac, 3 July 1916, 37; Col. Begg replces. Col. Roth as D.D.M.S., 48; 5th Div. goes south, 79; compositn., 158; B. of Messines, 160; med. arrangts., 161-6; its part in btle., 167-8; frnt. adjusted, 174; med. stns., 175-8; apprectn. and critcsm., 180-2; 3rd and 4th Divs. in, July-Aug., 191-2; B. of Broodseinde, 219; med. scheme, 223; clearnce. by 3rd Div., 228-30; Brit. Divs. replce., 3rd Aust. and N.Z., 232; B. of Passchendaele, 235-6; Canad. Corps relves., 21 Oct., 271; mumps in, Dec. 1916-Aug. 1917, 556. **Australian:** 636, 637, 641, 700-1, 770; formn. of, 5, 257-9, 604; mechan. transpt. coy. formed, 291*n*; plan and scheme of baths, 577-9; in G.H.Q. reserve, 612;

CORPS, ARMY—*continued*.
esprit de corps, 614; enters Somme battles, Mar., 617, 619; exerts pressure on Somme and Ancre, 628, 635; at Dernancourt, 5 Apr., 629-30; Col. G. W. Barber becomes D.D.M.S., 8 Apr., 633; astride Somme and Ancre, 635; takes over Fourth Army frnt., 639; Monash's methods, 647; prepares for enter.-offnsve., 647-78; changes in staff, 648; ready for B. of Hamel, 666; ready for B. of Amiens, 678; its part in final phase, 679-81; "Liaison Force," Aug., 692-4; advces. up Somme, 695-7, weakness of bns., 717; II Amer. Corps attd. to, 718; its part in Hindbg. Line attck., 721-2; side-slips north, 23-26 Sept., 733-4; co-ops. wth. II Amer. Corps, 737 et seq.; sitn., 29-30 Sept., 743-4; II Amer. Corps relves., 6-7 Oct., 763; innovatns. in A.A.M.C., 1918, 764*n*; Haig and Austln. discpln., 767; rest and reorgn., Oct., 767-8; disbandg. of bns., 768; strngth. at Armstce., 782; school for med. officrs., Bailleul, 783*n*, (Plate) 581; Howse's claim *re* success of, 855-6; med. orders and arrangts., 18 July, 887-8, B. of Amiens, 877-9, 12 Aug., 884-5. **British: Cavalry,** 611*n*, 631, 682*n*; provides advcd. gds., 119*n*; at Villers-Bret., 632. **II,** 53, 113*n*, 114, 132, 190, 194. **III,** 53, 56, 252, 611*n*, 633, 637, 638, 639, 720, 723, 731*n*; its D.D.M.S. adopts "forward" policy, 131; B. of Cambrai, med. arrngts., 251; at Cachy-Villers-Bret., 635; B. of Amiens, 678, 682, its thrust 9-20 Aug., 692; fails to reach objctve., 18 Sept., 738. **IV,** 22, 611*n*, 616. **V,** 22, 114, 122, 219, 290*n*, 611*n*; captres. Ecoust-Longatte, 127. **VI,** 252, 611*n*. **VII,** 611*n*, 619*n*, 624, 629, 632; in Ger. Offnsve. Mar.-Apr. 1918, 616, 629, 631, Aust. Corps relves., 633. **VIII,** 613, 677. **IX,** 160, 175*n*, 219, 386, 720, 723, 776. **X,** 160, 200, 219. **XI,** B. of Fromelles, scheme for, 40. **XIII,** 114, 733. **XIV,** 84*n*, 191, 219, 235. **XV,** 79, 83, 646, 775; tr. foot in, 91. **XVIII,** 190-1, 219, 235, 386, 611*n*. **XIX,** 190, 611*n*, 629, 632, 633. **Canadian:** 73, 74, 241, 256*n*, 678; B. of Passchdle., 185; adopts Corps control of San. Sectns., 597*n*; B. of Amiens, 682, 688, 691; strength at Armist., 782. **Indian,** arrves. in France, 29. See also ARMY MED. SERV.; CASUALTIES; MEDICAL ARRANGTS.
CORYZA, 90, 99, 410, 501, 559
CRATER, YPRES (Map 206), 208, 214
CRIMEA WAR, Royal Commsn., 1867, 526; wght. carried by soldr. in, 527
CROIX BLANCHE (Sk. 38), 42
CROUY, 688, 928; C.C.S's, 655, 663, 667, 684*n*
CULVERT, THE (Map 273), 196, 199, 200, 201, 214

GENERAL INDEX

DAOURS (Plate 581; Map 668; Sk. 54), 661-2, 669
DARDANELLES CAMPAIGN, 104, 109n, 494, 542, 581-3, 785; Brit. cas. in, 861
DARTFORD (Map 452), No. 3 A.A.H., 450
DEATHS, 87n; in A.I.F., France, to 30 *June* 1916, 39; in 5th Aust. Div., Fromelles, 48; of med. offcrs., 139, 147n, 209n, 227, 236, 247, 278n, 833; percent. among wdd., 248; from enteric gp., 1916-18, 539; among trps. in Depots, U.K., 1917-19, 563; from C.S.F., 563; from pneum. and broncho-pneum., *Jan.-Mar.*, 1917, 565; at No. 3 A.G.H., *Mar.* 1918, 621; percent. of all admissns. to hosps. of wdd. on W. Front, 787. *See also* CASUALTIES; STATISTICS
DEBILITY, 99, 410, 474, 500, 560, 568
DÉBRIDEMENT, *see* EXCISION; SURGICAL TREATMT.
DEFENCE DEPARTMENT, AUSTRALIA, 478, 852; its policy *re* Aust. cas., 10; issues pamphlet on boots, 525; cables London *re* hosp. charges, 827; Fetherston's comment on standard of recruits, *Aug.* 1917, 848-9; cables W.O. on retn. of "unfits," 849. *See also* WAR OFFICE
DELOUSING, *see* LICE
DELVILLE WOOD (Map 88), 516; B. of, 49n
DEMICOURT (Sk. 123), 122-3
DEMOBILISATION, *see* REPATRIATION AND DEMOB.
DENTAL SERVICE, 654, 767n, 829; creatn. of, 817n; its work in Depots, 19, 418, 456; a unit with ea. fld. amb., 29, 655, 893, and wth. ea. div. arty., 893; Staff Officer for, 812; D.D.M.S., I Anzac, confers wth. S.O., 140n; early and prophyl. trtmt. by, 295; dent. offcr. attd. No. 3 A.G.H., 402; its part in preventve. med., 499. **Dental Units**, 830, admine., 1918, 911; *Nos.* 3, 5, 11, 18, 19, 27, 34, 724-5; med. transpt. posts well run by dent. offcrs., 88, 166, 171n; treats civiln. popltn., 789-90; repat. of, 799
DEPOTS, Overseas Base and Conv. Depots, Egypt, 18, 446n; Aust. Base Depot, Weymouth, 18n, 448, becomes No. 2 Commd., 19; Aust. Gen. Base Depot, 447, 449, 470n, 477, 479; estab. at Etaples, 34, moves to Le Havre, *June* 1917, 258, 419, Col. Burston apptd. S.M.O., 419, retn. to duty through, 418-22, "B" Class men in, 909; 3rd Div. B.D., 418n; Corps Rfct. Camp, 477; training grps. for recruits from Aust., 471-7. **A.I.F. Depots in U.K.**: 443, 446-55, 477, (Plates) 18, 452; sites for, selected by Moore and Howse, 14; list of, 445; estabd. on Salisby. Pln., 17; organstn. of, 16-20, 560, in 1917, 450-1; med. organisatn., 19; sick wastge., Gen. M'Cay's estmte., 256n; strngth., 451; adminstn., 451, 453; health in, 453-5;

DEPOTS—*continued.*
commd. depots, from convlsct. to effctve., 455-71; hardening and training, 468; G.O.C's corresp. wth. A.I.F., France, 468-9; dis. preventn. in, 558-65; outpaced by rfct. demands, 649; repat. procedure 795; demand for A.M.C. men during demob., 796; D.M.S. keeps touch wth., 814, 819-20; G.O.C. and unfit rfcts., 849; A.D.M.S's rept. on causes of invalidg., 853-4. **Training Groups**: 76, 548; orgn. on Salisbury Pln., 16-20; prob. in maintaing. health, 453; re-conditning. in, 465; recd. recruits from Aust., 471-7; Training Bns. 448, 450, 466, 468, Brit. system, 467. **A.A.M.C. Tng. Depot, Parkhouse**, 476, 830, 838-40, (Plate) 18; formn., 474-5; its plce. in med. orgn., 476. **Overseas Training Brigade**: 447, 459, 463, 466, 467-70, 709, 795; constitutn. of, 469; evoln. of, 467; output fit for serv., 470. *See also* AUST. IMP. FORCE; CAMPS; COMMAND DEPOTS; CONVAL. DEPOTS; MED. STORES; TRAINING
DEPUTY-DIRECTOR OF MEDICAL SERVICES, *see* BARBER; BEGG; DIRECTOR OF MED. SERV.; MANIFOLD.
DERNANCOURT (Map 88; Sk. 54, 656), 515, 622n, 623, 625, 717; railhd. nr., 81; Austlns. hold rly., 617, (Plate) 629; B. of, 629
DHOBIE ITCH, 543, 567
DIARRHOEA, *see* DISEASES
DICKEBUSCH (Plate 524; Map 273; Sk. 76), 203, 363; A.D.S. at, 75n; B. of Menin Rd.: Corps Combined Convoy at, 197, C.M.D.S., 202
DIEPPE (Sk. 397), 394
DIPHTHERIA, *see* DISEASES
DIRECTOR-GENERAL OF MEDICAL SERVICES, **D.G., A.M.S.** (War Office), Sir A. Keogh recalled to positn., 11n; attnds. W.O. conf., 9 *Apr.* 1916, 12n; Howse offers med. officrs. to, 806; his letter to, *re* Howse, 807; suggsts. "Imperial" med. ser., 823, 866-8. **D.G.M.S., B.E.F.**, 90-1, 143n, 175n, 254, 270-1, 385, 539n, 547, 619n, 822-3; Sir A. Sloggett becomes, 11n, 287n; declnes. two A.S.H's offrd., 30; his memo to D's.M.S. Armies, 66; his prepns. for Third Ypres, 186-7; his circ. memo *Mar.* 1915, 316; presides at advisory c'tee meetgs., 508n; co-ops. wth. D.M.S., A.I.F., 869-70; memo prepd. for, on med. arrngts. for Somme btles., 1916, 874-7. **D.G., A.M.F.** (Surg.-Gen. *Fetherston*), his letter to Howse, *re* Aust. hosps. in France, 13n; his report on phys. of recruits, 715n, 716n; reltns. wth. Howse, Howse's report to, *re* Command Depots, I *Nov.* 1916, 830n; supports Howse, but compelled to submit to policy of dilutn., 843; his minute to Minister *re* rfcts., *Aug.* 1917, 848-9; tours A.I.F. o'seas,

GENERAL INDEX 987

DIRECTOR-GENERAL OF MEDICAL SERVICES—*continued.*
851-6; visits Salonica, Egypt, Palestine, India, 856; correspdce. re fitness of recruits, 900-2; his report on French med. evac. scheme, 917-18. **D.D.G.M.S., B.E.F.**, (*Maj.-Gen. Macpherson*), letter to Col. Manifold on issue of med. "orders," 874; suggsts. Amiens too dang. for hosp. centre, 778. See also *Personal Index* under FETHERSTON; KEOGH; MACPHERSON; SLOGGETT
DIRECTOR OF MEDICAL SERVICES, **D.M.S., A.I.F.**, *Surg.-Gen. Williams*: purchses. supplies of sera, 1915, 309*n*; wth. Howse suggests. 2-sectn. Fld. Amb., 805; his staff, 812; *Maj.-Gen. Howse*: A.I.F. Chief of Staff defines responsbties, 15-16; sends rep. to G.H.Q., B.E.F. to discuss A.I.F. med. arrangts., 11; attnds. W.O. conf., 12-13; his responsblts., 76*n*, 97; visits France, 140*n*, 143, 218, 246; criticises policy of keepg. sick at frnt., 296; protests agst. A.C.C.S's as rest stns., 378*n*; is critcl. of scheme for surg. teams, 380-2; his policy for Gen. Hosps., 414-15; for Austn. cas. in Eng., 437, 438*n*; his contrib. to A.I.F. effcncy., 614; permts. men below "A" class as bn. A.A.M.C. details, 715; resists dilutn. of A.A.M.C. wth. unfit, 716; the positn. of the, 813-16; his admin. technique, 816-17; his reltns. wth. D.G., A.M.S., 15-16, 821-2; wth. D.G.M.S., B.E.F., 16, 822-3, 869-70; wth. D.G.M.S. Aust., 427, 820-1, wth. G.O.C., A.I.F., 817-18, wth. Commdt. admin. H.Q., 819, wth. A.I.F. Depots, U.K., 453, 819-20, wth. Lt. Hrse., 821, 822; his policy wthin. med. serv., 824-42, for hosps. on W.F., 824-5, a practcl. problm. of Empire, 825-6; his mthd. of appointg. offcrs., 836; his fight for phys. stand. of A.I.F., 842-56; his corresp. with A.I.F. H.Q., France, on P.B. men, 906-9, 910; suggsts. permnt. estab. for resus. teams, 956-7; his missn. to Aust., 856-7; his responsblts. after Armstce., 791, 799; *vale* Howse, 857. **D.M.S., Canadian Exped. Force:** *Surg.-Gen. Jones*, 802*n*; his reltns. wth. D.G.M.S., B.E.F., 823. **D.M.S., M.E.F.**, attributes dysentery to "excessive sea bathing," 582. **D.M.S., B.E.F.**, not part of Gen. French's G.H.Q., 287*n*, 391. **D.M.S., L. of C.**, 417, 621*n*; staff includes an A.D.M.S. for Amb. Trains, 391. **D.M.S. for Embarkation Duties** (England), 425. **D.M.S., Lond. Command,** A.I.F. Bacteriolgcl. Lab., works under, 815*n*. **D's.M.S. of Armies:** Memo. of D.G.M.S., B.E.F. to, 66; med. arrangts. for Somme Btles., 1916, 875-6; prepare schemes for retreat, 1918, 609.

DIRECTOR OF MEDICAL SERVICES—*continued.*
D.M.S., First Army, 344, 393*n*, 611*n*, 765; originates "rest stns.," 295. **D.M.S., Second Army**, 41, 168, 195, 611*n*; his order, 14 *June* 1916, *re* notfictn. of infec. dis., 549-50; prinplcs. for evac. of wdd., Messines, 161; his policy, *Sept.-Oct.*, 192-3. **D.M.S., Third Army**, 547*n*, 611*n*. **D.M.S., Fourth Army**, 83*n*, 684*n*, 714, 751; records Austlns. "tired and exhausted," 90; B. of Amiens, infmd. of impendg. operns. only on 6 *Aug.*, 684. **D.M.S., Fifth Army**, 120, 143, 156, 330, 611*n*; the drivg. fce. in fwd. moves of med. units, 131; his views on disposn. of med. units, 131-2; his prepns. for Third Ypres, 186-9; pushes C.C.S. grp. to wthin. five mls. of frnt., 362; criticised after retreat, *Mar.*, 1918, 621*n*. See also `LESSONS OF THE WAR`
—DEPUTY-DIRECTOR, **D.D.M.S., A.I.F.** (*Surg-Gen. Williams*), reps. Aust. at W.O. conf., 12*n*; estab. of dept. in Eng., *Apr.*, 810; duties of, 815. **D.D.M.S. of a Corps,** duties defined, 651-2; changes and rlfs. of med. units initiated by, 69; med. arrangts. of, 876. **D.D.M.S., I Anzac** (*Col. Manifold*), 29, 83, 91, 143, 152, 156, 256*n*, 257, 874, 935-8; not in favour of huge M.D.S's, 88*n*; his effts. in the Somme Winter, 97; Order No. 51, 4 *Feb.*, 1917, 110; extct. from diary re evacn. from Martinpuich, 112*n*; his intentns. sent to A.D's.M.S. by "instns." not "orders," 114*n*; Med. Instn. No. 1, 114; not infmed. of impendg. attck. on Hindbg. line, 132*n*; responsblts. of, 139; his concern in promoting baths, laundries, 140*n*; confers with san. sectns., 141; frwd. move of med. stns., 142*n*; B. of Menin Rd., 195, dir. evac. aftr., 210; B. of Polygon Wd., 213, cause of cas. amng. S.-B's, 218; crse. of evnts., B. of Broodseinde, 225-6; arrnges. for extra S.-B's, 237*n*; high sick rate in 5th Aust. Div., 242*n*; wkly. dis. retns. rendered to, 490*n*. **D.D.M.S., II Anzac,** 29, 174*n*; Col. Begg replces. Col. Roth as, 48; B. of Broodseinde, 223, 229-30; his comment re S.-B's, 239*n*, 249; refers to C.M.D.S. as "Adv. Clearing Stn.," 248*n*. **D.D.M.S., Aust. Corps,** 662, 724, 727; mnthly. report by R.M.O's to A.D.M.S., 275; his note on R.M.O's, 294*n*; Col. Barber takes over from Col. Manifold 8 *Apr.*, 1918, 633; issues Med. Instn. No. 10, 634-5; has dir. access to Corps Cdr., 648; instn. on experncce. gained at Hamel, 672; his comment on Amer., Hamel, 675; B. of Amiens: med. arrangts., 684-8; Med. Instn. No. 35, 684-5; stops

GENERAL INDEX

DIRECTOR OF MEDICAL SERVICES—continued.
"pooling" of transpt., 693; Chuignies, 699; Hindbg. Line, 700-701, 740; rejcts. proposal tht. engrs. test water, 714; resists dilutn. of med. serv. wth. unfits, 716; innovatns. in A.A.M.C., 764n; Med. Instns.: of 6 *Oct.*, 1918, 796, No. 35, 4 *Aug.*, 877-8, Routine No. 13, 878-9, No. 29, 18 *July*, re attmnt. of Amer. personnel, 887-8, Routine No. 15, Resusc. Teams Cttee., 953, Circ. Memo M2/8, 12 *Aug.*, 884-5; duties of, 889. **D.D.M.S., N.Z.E.F.**, Lt.-Col. Parkes, 802n; corresp. re Imperial Med. Serv., 866-8. **D.D.M.S., L. of C.**, 288; enquires re 5th Aust. Div. sick evacns., 90. **D.D.M.S., Marseilles**, 543; disputes No. 2 A.G.H. diagnosis of typhus, 544. **D.D.M.S., I Corps**, attd. to Gen. French's G.H.Q., 287n. **D.D.M.S. III Corps**, 638. **D.D.M.S. Southern Command England** (*Surg.-Gen. Birrell*), A.D.M.S., A.I.F. Depots admin. by, 453n, 560; advses. Howse of poor phys. of Austln. rfcts., 472. —ASSISTANT DIRECTOR, **A.D.M.S., Sanitary, B.E.F.**, Col. Beveridge, 508n, 557n; his San. Conf. report quoted, 590n; extrt. from art. on housg., 931-3. **A.D.M.S., Abbeville**, 621. **A.D's.M.S., A.I.F.** (London), 806, 815. **A.D.M.S., A.I.F., U.K.** (*Col. McWhae*), in effct. an offcer. on staff of D.M.S., A.I.F., 815n, his reltns. wth. D.M.S., 453; his responsiblts., 560; reports to D.M.S., 561-5, 820, causes of invalidg., 853-4. **A.D.M.S. of a Division**, 164; duties vide, S.O's. for A.A.M.C., 889-90, in fwd. and back areas, 67; jealous of encrchmt. by Corps, 69; make own arrangts., 75, 876-7; subordntd. to Corps, Somme Winter, 82; concern in baths and launds., 140n; responsble. for evacn., 161; responsblts., Menin Rd., 197; admins. San. Sectns., 596. **A.D.M.S. 1st Aust. Div.**, 29, 724; Howse insists on access to div. commndr., 1915, 817n; B. of Menin Rd., 195, 198, 205, 210-11; 18 *Sept.*, 1918, 727-8; his letter re San. Sects., 935-6. **A.D.M.S. 2nd Aust. Div.**, 29, 143, 153, 927-30; B. of Menin Rd., 195; extct. from diary, 6-8 *Oct.* 1917, 233; Col. Sutton asks "when will generals learn that we are are but men," 249; re S.-B. coys., 281n, re classfcn., 785n; letter re San. Sectns., 936. **A.D.M.S. 3rd Aust. Div.**, 158n, 756, 860; attnds. staff confs., 164-5; experimnts. wth. Thomas splnt., 165n; medium of communicatn. Messines, 166; "plays for safety," Broodseinde, 230; B. of Amiens, 879; his arrngts., 29 *Sept.* 1918, 742.

DIRECTOR OF MEDICAL SERVICES—continued.
A.D.M.S. 4th Aust. Div., 29, 174, 296n, 682n, 724; issues orders, 7 *Apr.* 1917, 132-3; advses. agst. fwd. move, 137; B. of Polygon Wd., 213; circ. on "sick wastage" 8 *Oct.*, 242; corres. wth. D.M.S. re rest stns., 296; his comment on scabies, 579; diary, 26 *Mar.* 1918, 624n, report, 30 *Mar.* 627; Col. Moseley wdd., 662-3; B. of Amiens, 691; med. arrangts., 18 *Sept.*, 727; order No. 112, 20 *Sept.*, 734n, 888; notes on trng. of med. offcrs., 838-9; B. of Amiens, 879-84; letter re San. Sects., 936-7. **A.D.M.S. 5th Aust. Div.**, 29, 43, 156, 215n, 670-1; Col. Hearne, succeeds Col. Hardy, 86n; carries hot food to trenches, 91n; Polygon Wd., 213; inspcts. aid-posts, 213-14; Col. Hearne kld., 236; urges more freedm. for divl. admins., 242n; 20 *Sept.*, 1918, 885-7; 29 *Sept.*, 742; letter re San. Sects., 937-8. **A.D.M.S., N.Z. Div.**, sends help to 14th Fld. Amb., Fromelles, 43; B. of Messines, 164n, 172, 174. See also Personal Index under ANDERSON, J. H.; BARBER; DOWNEY; HEARNE; HUXTABLE; McWHAE; MAGUIRE; MILLARD; MOSELEY; SHEPHERD; SMITH, K.; STURDEE; SUTTON, A.; WHITE, A. T. —DEPUTY-ASSISTANT DIRECTORS, "sanitary" duties of, 507-8; of I Anzac, comments on bathing arrangts., May 1916, 577; of II Anzac, on med. arrangts., B. of Messines, 182n; of Aust. Corps on, "N.Y.D.N.," 714; of N.Z. Div., 164n

DISCIPLINE, 90; discussn. re "A.W.L." and death penlty., 258-9; R.M.O. importnt. in, 294; of Ger. P. of W. at No. 3 A.G.H., 801n; sanitary, essentially a matter of organisation, 90, 101, 711, its nature and factrs., 509-10, 590

DISEASE PREVENTION, 3, 32; preventve. med. in the war, 483-602; machnry. for, in B.E.F., 23, 490, 546-50; system for, 26-7, 77; prepns. in I Anzac, 1916, 78-9; measures for, in Corps scheme of works, 92-4; at end of 1917, 242-3; rôle of C.C.S. in, 379; notifcn., 411n; in A.I.F. Depots, 453; the factors invlvd., 483-512; aims in respct. of man-pwr., 484-5; the pensn. aspect, 485; scope of, 497-500; vitamin defcncy. dis., 505; not a simple matter of hygiene, 505; the san. serv. in, 507, 509, 508; policy in B.E.F., 1917, 508n; co-opn., 509-10; objctves. in prev. med., 510-11; discpln. and orgn. for, 510; prophlxs. by trtmt., 511-12; the promotn. of hlth., 514-32; trench foot, 522, (Plate) 529; a triple campaign, 536-7; artifcl. immunisatn., 537-41; indir. actn. in, 541-65; the "sieve" at Marseilles, 542-6; notfctn.

GENERAL INDEX 989

DISEASE PREVENTION—continued.
in, 546-50; segregatn., 552; disinfectn., 552; importce. of "spacing out," 557; in respir. infs., 557, 560-3; measures in A.I.F. Depots, 562-3; in the advce., *Aug.* 1918, 712; failre. in Aust. to tackle transpt. dis., 564n; dir. actn., hygiene and san., 566-93; disinfectn. in the fld., 569-70; importce. of "the previous case," 570n; vermin infestatn. in, 571-2; of dysentery, 583-4, 587-9; exact diagnosis, the keynote in, 601; "orgn." v. discpln., 605; of V.D., 796, 812-13; housg. in, 931-3; of gastro-intestinal dis., 938-41. *See also* BATHS AND LAUNDRIES; DISEASES; FLIES; INOCULATION; LESSONS OF THE WAR; LICE; SAN. SECTS.; SANITATION
DISEASES, definitn. of, 492; causes of, 486-7, 505n, 506, 567, the parasites, 570-4; classifctn. of, 99, 491n, 505n, by types, classes, and grps., 494-504, 506, 535-6; diagnosis of, 774-5; "carriers" of, 32-3, 408n, 546, the problm., 552-3, the type, 556-7, amng. surgs. or attndnts., 554n, in staff at Horseferry-rd., 560n, Gallip. and France compared, 582; secndry. infectns., 554n; causes of invalidg., 854; civiln. populn., 788n; agnst. fluxes, 587-9, primary admissns., 586; of dirt and squalor, 566-8, 579-80; reparatve. med. in, 435; system of detection in Aust. Conv. Hosp., 420-1; exclusn. of exotic from France by A.I.F., 32; diagnostic stns. for, 72, 295; specl. stns. for, 88n; due to phys. causes: 89, 496, 514-34, due to war serv., 90; In Somme Winter, 99-101, princpl. causes, 4th Div., 242; concealmt. a "crime," 293; types treatd. in fld. amb. rest stns., 295-6; to specl. hosps. in U.K., 404, in France, 725-6; types of btle. cas. become "disease," 409-10; aetiology of, 413; secndry. trtmt. of, 431-2; unfitness caused by, 462-4; psychic element in, 462; nature, and theories of pathogen. of, 486-8; the "inborn factor," neo-vitalism, 487-8; the era of prevntve. med., 488; morbific agents, 488; anticptd. causes of "wastage" by, 489-506, cvl. experce., 490, mly. expnce., 490; notifble. in Aust., 490n, B.E.F., 548-9; actual "wastage," A.I.F., 1916-18, 490-94, primary analysis of, 492-500, 501-504; infective agnts. as weapon, 498; the main problm., 500-501; did environment "aggravate"?, 514; effct. of clothg., equipmnt. on, 522-3; "natural" resistnce. to, 537n; importce. of "negative" hist. of, 542; infectious, at Marseilles, 543; varieties of resp. infs., 554-5; exp. of A.I.F., 555-8; infl. of climate on, 558-9; in A.I.F. Depots U.K., 560-5; Gallip. and France compared,

DISEASES—continued.
582-3; dysentery, colitis and diarrhoea compared, 586. **Accidental injuries**, 410, 481. **Actinomycosis**, 502. **Albuminuria**, 504. **Amoebiasis**, 501. **Anchylostomiasis**, 503, 543. **Anthrax**, 502. **Appendicitis**, 568, number invaldd. to Aust., 408n. **Asthma**, 99, 474. **Avitaminosis**, 488, 504, 505. **Beri-beri**, 489n. **Bilharzia**, 503. **Boils**, 568. **Bronchitis**, 78, 90, 99, 473-4, 499n, 515n, 555, 559, 568, in A.I.F. Depots, 560-3, due to gas, 676. **Bronchial catarrh**, 99, 504, 559. **Brucella group**, 501. **Cerebrospinal Fever**, 412, 413n, 479, 501, 543, 546, 547, 549, 550, 552, 556, 557, 562, 563, 564, epidemic feard., Brit., 560, steps to prevnt., A.I.F. Depots, 563, means to reduce carrier rate, 932. **Chicken pox**, 543. **Cholera**, 501, 541, 549, 581, subject to quarantn., Aust., 490. **Colitis**, 99, 586. **Conjunctivitis**, due to gas, 676. **Coryza**, 90, 99, 410, 501, 559. **Debility**, 99, 410, 474, 500, 560, 568. **Dhobie Itch**, 543, 567. **Diarrhoea**, 72n, 99, 499n, 501, 503, 546, 547, 586, Gallip. and France compared, 582, 586, or "Dysentery"? 584-5. **Diphtheria**, 501, 543, 549, 550, 552, 556, 557, 599, 564, 568, mucous interchge. import. in, 553n, "carriers," 931-2. **Dropsy**, 504. **Dysentery**, 72n, 411-12, 499n, 541, 542, 547, 549, 550, 568, 714, discussn. at San. Conf. 32, menace of, from water, 33, outbrk. in Fourth and Fifth Armies, 99, B.E.F. policy, 508n, Shiga, Flexner, Amoebic, 543, 550, 552; Bacillary, 546n, 552, on West Front, 545-6, the *bête noire* of san. staff, 581, B.E.F. and Gallip. compared, 581-3, 586, prophylaxis in B.E.F., 583-4, diffclts. of diagnosis, 584-5, numbers and percents. admittd. to Fld. Ambs., 1916-19, 501, 586. **Ear, Infs.**, 473-4, 502, 568. **Encephalitis Lethargica**, 502, 505n. **Endocrine dysfunctions**, 504. **Enteritis**, 99, 586. **Enteric**, 541, 542, 547, 549, 550, 552, rare, 412, immunisatn. agst., 534-41, stats., 501; 539-40, attde. of Austlns. to inoculatn., 540-1, inoculatn. in French, Ger. and Amer. armies, 539. *See also* **Typhoid** (below). **Epilepsy**, 474. **Eye, Infs.**, 473-4, 502, 568. **Exhaustion**, 99, 504. **"Febricula,"** 554. **Feet, sore**, 27, 57. *See also* **Trench foot** (below). **Fibrositis**, 410, 504. **Filaria**, 503. **Food**, 501, defcts. and defcncies. from, 504. **Frostbite**, 90n, 503, indistingble. from **Trench foot**, *q.v.*, 99. **Gas**, "gangrene," 310, 777. **Gastritis**, 99, 503, symptms. due to gas, 676. **Gastro-intestinal infs.**, 501, 550, 568, 580-4, 589, 590n, 598,

DISEASES—continued.
712-13; measures for prevntg., 938-41.
Glanders, 502. **Goitre**, toxic, 504.
Haemorrhoids, 99, 408, 474.
Heart, 526; *Cardiac*, 504, 568;
D.A.H., 435, 463, 500, 504, 560;
pathogenesis of, 500n; *Effort Syndrome*, 435, 463, 500n, 504; *V.D.H.*,
435, 488. **Heat**, effcts., 503.
Helminthiasis, 503. **Hernia**, 99,
408, 435, 473-4, 568, 905. **Herpetic
dis.**, 502. **Hydatid**, 503. **Hydrocele**, 408. **Impetigo**, 567, 570.
**Inflammation of the connective
tissue (I.C.T.)**, 27, 99, 410, 499n,
502, 567, 568, caused by pyogenic
cocci, 570, camflgd. much "trench
foot" (*q.v.*), 97. **Influenza**, 99, 410,
501, 505, 506, 541, 554, 555, 559, 568,
774, 779; virus, 542, 554, 559, 710,
768, exp. in A.I.F., 555, considble. in
1st Aust. Div., *May-June* 1918, 646,
many Anzac leave men die from, 717,
import. exp. in Aust. Corps, 796-7,
Amers. die from, 857n. **Jaundice**,
503, 542, 543, 549, 550. **Laryngitis**,
554, 568, due to gas, 676. **Leprosy**,
490. **Malaria**, 489n, 503, 541, 542,
543. **Measles**, 307n, 421, 479, 502,
506, 541, 542, 543, 550, 554, 559,
565, 568, epdmcs. in dfts. for France,
477, in Canad. Army, 537n, in rfcts.
from Aust., 564, eradicatd. from Trg.
Bns., U.K., 548, effcts. of overcrowdg., 932. **Mental disorders**,
88n, 435, 473-4. **Mouth, Infs.**,
502. **Muco-dermal Infs.**, 502.
Mumps, 88, 110, 421, 479, 502, 506,
542, 543, 547, 548, 550, 554, 559, 561,
565, 568, in rfcts. from Aust., 564, in
dfts. for France, 477, in A.I.F.
Depots, 19, epdmc. in II Anzac, 99,
(Graph), 556, in French and Austln.
armies, 537n, 555n. **Myalgia**, 568.
N.Y.D. Gas, 504, 512, 601, 677, 701,
diagnosis shunned, 714, Amers.
evactd. as, 759. **N.Y.D.N.**, 88n, 410,
568, 601, prophyltic. trtmt. for, 512,
diagnosis shunned, 714. **Nephritis**,
435, 504, 550, 568, gves. some concrn.,
154, Maj. Lawton's note on, 411.
Neurasthenia, 568. **Neuroses**,
462. **Neurotropic ectodermoses**,
502. **Ophthalmia**, infectve., 543.
Osteo-arthritis, 435, 500. **Pediculosis**, 27, 99, 499n, 503, caused
by body-louse, 570-3. **Pemphigus
contagiosus**, 543. **Pharyngitis**,
544. **Piles**, 568. **Plague**, 490, 503,
541. **Pleurisy**, 501, 568. **Pneumonia**, 99, 515n, 568, immunisatn.
agst. and experimts. in French Army,
541, incidnce rate, B.E.F., 2nd
A.E.F., 557n, in A.I.F. Depots, 560-3.
Broncho-pneumonia, 501, 555, 559,
774, dths. from in A.I.F. Depots,
561-2. *Lobar-pneumonia*, 501, 555,
556, 557, 559. **Polio-encephalitis**,
502. **Psycho-neuroses**, 435, 498.
Pulmonary fibrosis, 99. **Pyodermia**, 570, 572, 574. **Pyogenic**

DISEASES—continued.
Infs., 310, 502. **Pyrexia of Uncertain Origin (P.U.O.)**, 99, 296, 410,
503, 568, 774, trench fever oft. diagnosed as, 96, 154, 535-6, devlpmt. of
exact diagnosis, 379, its signifce., 601.
Relapsing Fever, 382n, 503, 541,
543, 545, 549, 570, escape "sieve" at
Marseilles, 32, 550. **Respiratory
tract infs.**, 99, 435, 453n, 454,
501-2, 550, Maj. Lawton's note on,
411, incdce. of, 553-5, 564n, mortlty.
A.I.F. Depots, 562, prevntn. of, 931-3.
Rheumatic fever, 502. **Rheumatism**, 99, 462, 473-4, 500, 504,
560, 568, common in 24th Bn., 90.
Rheumatoid arthritis, 504.
Roseola, 542, 543, 559, in Brit.
Army, 537n. **Rubella**, 502, 554.
Sandfly fever, 503. **Scabies**, 27,
99, 479, 503, 506, 522n, 543, 546,
547, 550, 567, 568, 796, caused by
"itch mite," 570, 571n, specl. stns. for
trtmt. of, 88n, 110, 712, 728, percent.
of admissns. A.I.F., 410, prevlnt. in
depots, 1915, 559n, dissemn., 573-4.
Scarlet fever, 501, 543, 549, 550,
556, 557. **Septic infs.**, 502. **Septic
Traumatic Abrasion**, 99, 567.
"**Shell Shock**," 39, 72, 73n, 154,
168, 178-9, 180, 270, 462, 495, views
of R.M.O's, 59n, 63, term "Shell
shock 'W'" introdcd., 73n, two types,
163n, measures to minimise, 498.
Skin infestations, 78, 503, 522n,
568. **Smallpox**, 490, 541, 542, 549,
cases in Austln. trps., 32, 545, 550,
immunisate. agst., 537, 543. **Synovitis**, 568. **Tetanus**, 431, 503, 547,
550, mthds. for prevntc., 309-10.
Throat infs., 554. **Tinea**, 503,
530, 567. **Tonsillitis**, 501, 568.
Tracheitis, 559. **Trachoma**, 543,
550. **Traumatic Abrasions**, 99,
503. **Trench fever**, 96, 296, 410,
499n, 503, 506, 567, 568, caused by
body louse, 570, type dis. of squalor,
579-80, offcly. recognsd., 154, in
Commnd. Depots, 464, Maj. Norton's
note on, 411, epidmc., 542. **Trench
Foot**, 27, 78, 91-2, 96, 97n, 99n, 113,
231, 242, 296, 435, 499n, 503, 506,
546, 547, 568, (Plate) 77, dominates
med. situatn., 1916, 87, a test of mily.
discpln., 90, camflgd., 97, prophylxs.,
Somme Winter, 100, 522, percent. to
Base hosps., 410, anti-tet. serum for,
100, in commnd depots, 464, Amers.
idntfy. wth. "frost-bite," 506n, care
of feet, 530. **Tuberculosis**, 435,
474, 502, 555, 568, (Graph) 562.
Typhoid [*see also (above)* **Enteric**],
33, 478, 538-9, 540n, 541, 543, 547n,
549, 550, 581, outbrk. in Ger. unit,
582n, *Paratyphoid*, 478, "A" and "B,"
549, 550. **Typhus**, 503, 541,
549, caused by body louse, 570, cases
interceptd. at Marseilles, 32, 543-5, in
Serbia and Russia, 489n, 542. **Vaccinia**, 502. **Varicella**, 554. **Varicocele**, 99, 408, 435. **Varicose**

GENERAL INDEX 991

DISEASES—*continued*.
Veins, 99, 408, 474, 568. **Variola**, 502, 554. **Venereal**, 99, 410*n*, 464, 479, 502, 512, 546, 547, 550, 559, 568; to be treatd. in France, 13, in A.I.F. Depots, 19, percent. in depots, 561, Aust. Dermat. Hosp. establshd. for, Oct. 1916, 455, early trtmt. centres for, 560, 812-13, convalscnts. attd. to med. units, 715, Brit. and French co-op., 788*n*, *Chancroid*, 502, 543, *Gonorrhoea*, 502, 552; *Syphilis*, 502, cause of, 488. **Virus**, 505, 563, *see also* **Influenza** (above). **War Weariness**, 462-3. **Weil's Disease**, 544. **Whooping Cough**, 501. **Yellow fever**, 490, 541, 580*n*. *See also* LESSONS OF THE WAR
DISINFECTION, 564, 569-70; as means of prevntng. disease, 552; of drinkg. cups, 553*n*; apparatus for, 574-5. *See also* SAN. APPLIANCS.; SANITATION; HYGIENE
DIS-INFESTATION, *see* LICE
DIVISIONS, mobile formntns., 30; relations wth. Corps, 66-7, 69, 75, 82, 164-5; responsblty defned., 163; normal functns., *Sept.* 1918, 728. **American:** composn. of, 735*n*; permttd. to be used in emergncy., 635; assist Allied cnter.-strke., 647. **27th**, 664, 740, 743; Gen. O'Ryan's impressn. of Aust. soldr., 705-6; relves. 18 and 74th Brit. Divs., 15 *Sept.* 1918, 734; B. of St. Quentin Canal: 738-9, med. arrngts., 737, 741, 742, expernce. of med. ser., 752-3; relf. of 1-2 *Oct.*, 759, 761. **30th**, relves. 1st Aust. Div., 23-24 *Sept.* 1918, 734; B. of St. Quentin Canal: 738-9, med. arrngts., 737, 741, line, 29 *Sept.*, 743, collectn. and clearnce., 745-6; its expernce., 746*n*. **33rd**, 674; part attd. to Aust. Corps, B. of Hamel, 667; trains wth. Austlns., 673. **Australian:** Base Depots establshd. at Etaples, 34; the call south, 79; all under one commnd., 79; responsblts. of A.D's.M.S., B. of Menin Rd., 197; disbandment temply. avoided, 259; system of schools establshd., 532; Resus. Teams, 664, 954. **1st**, 81, 113, 550*n*, 640, 663, 718, 727, 935-6; med. units of, 29; frnt. held, *June* 1916, (Sk.) 38; at Pozières: 52, 56, 59, entrains for north, 73; rtns. south, 79, 85, 86, 89; trench foot in, 99*n*; occupies The Maze, 24 *Feb.* 1917, 110; in rest, 114; operns., *Apr.*, 122-7; Lagnicourt, 137-8; 11th Brit. Div. relieves, 142; in rest, *May*, 155, 193; Menin Rd.: 199-200, 205-7, 210, 211; B. of Poelcappelle, 232-3, 235; 5th Aust. Div. relieves, 10-11 *Oct.*, 235-6; relieves 4th Aust. Div., 241; at Messines, 615; on Lys, 633; at Hazebrouck, 644-6, 647, 677; in raids, *May-Aug.* 1918, 772, 775; entrains for south, 6 *Aug.*, 646; rches. Villers-Bret., 8 *Aug.*, 692; B. of Chuignes, 695, 699; B. of

DIVISIONS—*continued*.
Hargic't, 722; 17-18 *Sept.*, 724-5; 30th Amer. Div. relieves, 734; in rest, 734; exemptd. from reconstrn., *Oct.*, 768*n*; its movts. after Armstce., 792-3. **2nd**, 75*n*, 112*n*, 114, 120, 137, 142, 143, 153, 241, 281*n*, 577, 633, 637*n*, 648, 658, 665, 670, 675, 676, 696, 701, 739, 744, 936; enters line, 27; med. units of, 29; relieves 1st Aust. Div., 59; Pozières Hghts. and Mouquet Fm., 52, cas., 61, 73: 4th Div. relieves, 61; entrains for north, 73; retns. south, 79; relieves 5th Aust. Div., 85-6; trps. exhaustd., 89; tr. foot in, 99*n*; relieves 15th Div., 101; cptures. Malt Trench, 110; in rest, 155, 193; B. of Menin Rd., 200, 204, 207-8, 210, 211; 4th relieves, 211; B. of Broodseinde, 222, 226-7; B. of Poelcappelle, 232-5; 4th relieves, 235-6; at Messines, 21 *Mar.* 1918, 615; on Somme, 4 *Apr.*, 632; B. of Hamel, 667; B. of Amiens, 683, 687, 689, 692; B. of Mt. St. Quentin, 699-700; 3-5 *Oct.*, 721, 762-3; 30th Amer. Div. relieves, 763; movts. aft. Armstce., 792-3. **3rd**, 29, 77, 232, 383, 448-9, 478, 531*n*, 615, 627, 633, 648, 665, 667, 669, 675, 699, 742, 743, 818*n*; arrives in Eng., 14, 16, 17, 20; trench foot in, 99*n*; B. of Messines, 158, 160, 164, 167, 171, 172; cas., 167-8; from gas, 169*n*; persnlty. of Commndr. dominates, 164-5; N.Z. Div. relieves, 180; *July-Aug.*, 184, 191-2; enters line, Third Ypres, B. of Broodseinde, 223; B. of Passchendaele, 236, 238-9; joins I Anzac Corps, *Nov.*, 241; mumps in, 555-6; moves to dang. point Third Army, 26 *Mar.* 1918, 612; Somme-Ancre, 26-28 *Mar.*, 616, 617, 627, 628; Corbie. 629; B. of Amiens, 683, 687, 689; med. arrgts., 879-83; attcks. nr. Bray, 22 *Aug.*, 695; Cléry, 696, at 700; B. of St. Quentin Canal, 738-9, 741; 50th Div. relieves, 3 *Oct.*, 762; movts. aft. Armstce., 792-3. **4th**, 61, 62, 75*n*, 101, 127, 152, 211, 238, 242, 477*n*, 615, 617, 627, 633, 634*n*, 648, 652, 674, 678, 718, 724, 936-7; med. units of, 29; attcks. Mouquet Fm., 52; entrains for north, 73; rtns. south, 79; prep. trenches for winter, 91; trench foot in, *Oct.* 1916-*May* 1917, 99*n*; cas., Stormy Trench, 109; in rest, 109; relieves 2nd Aust. Div., 120; First Bullecourt, 131-7; joins II Anzac, 137, 158; B. of Messines, 160, 164, 167-8; med. arrgts., 172-5; 25th Div. relieves, 180; *July-Aug.*, 191-2; rejoins I Anzac, *Aug.*, 193*n*; B. of Polygon Wd., 214-16; cas., 217; 10-11 *Oct.*, relieves 2nd Div., 235-6; First Passchendaele, 236; cas., 240; sick rate in, 242*n*; B. of Cambrai, 250; proposed as Depot Div., 259; decrease of scabies in, 579; moves to dang. point, Third Army, 26 *Mar.*, 612; relieves 9th Div., 616; Ancre, 26-27 *Mar.*, 624, 628; Dernancourt, 5 *Apr.*,

DIVISIONS—continued.
629-30; Villers-Bret., 637; 47th and 57th Bns. disbndd., 650n; A.D.M.S., wdd., 662; B. of Hamel, 666, 667, 669; Americans attchd. to, 673; B. of Amiens, 683, 689, 879-84; Hargicourt, 722; med. arrgts., 17-18 *Sept.*, 724-5, 20 *Sept.*, 888, 46th Div. relieves, 733; in rest, 734; rejoins Fourth Army, *Nov.*, 770; movts. aft. Armstce., 792-3. **5th,** 74n, 81, 110n, 114, 121, 145, 203, 235, 633, 648, 661, 665, 670, 675, 678, 699, 700-1, 885-7, 937-8, (Plates) 113, 525, 581, 733; med. units of, 29; wth. N.Z. Div. forms II Anzac Corps, 29; B. of Fromelles, 39-48; entrains for south, 79; at Flers, 79; 2nd Div. relieves, 85; relieves Guards Div., 90; discip. questned., 90; tr. foot in, 99n; operns. *Apr.* 1917, 122, 123; scheme of med. lectres. in, 140n; relieves 2nd Aust. Div., 153; in rest, 155, 193; to Hazebrouck, *Aug.*, 193; relieves 1st Aust. Div., 211; B. of Polygon Wd., 198n, 213-15, 217; First Passchendaele, 236; sick rate in, 242n; arrives Somme, 629; enters line, 632; Villers-Bret., 637; B. of Amiens, 683, 689-90, (Plate) 692; captres. Péronne, 696; B. of St. Quentin Canal, 738-9, 741; med. arrngts., 29 *Sept.*, 742; colletn. and clearnce., 29-30 *Sept.*, 745-51; 2nd Div. relieves, movts. aft. Armstce., 792-3. **6th,** proposed formn. of, 20n; ptly. formed, 106, 475; Bullecourt and Messines caused breakg. up of, 193n, 467. **British:** six new divs., to France, 106. **Guards,** 90, 191; Tr. foot in, 91-2. **7th,** 153n, 218. **8th,** 638. **9th,** 616. **11th,** 142, 152. **12th,** 682n, with 2nd Aust. Div. captures Pozières ridge, 52, 60. **15th,** 101. **17th,** 625, 682. **18th,** 682. **19th,** 56. **21st,** 218, 619n. **25th,** B. of Menin Rd., 194; B. of Messines, 158, 160, 164, 172, 180. **31st,** 632. **32nd,** 682n, 695, 700-1, 720n. **33rd,** 215. **35th,** 625. **46th,** 733, 739, 888. **47th,** 194, 196, 682n. **48th,** 52, 85. **49th,** 232, 236. **50th,** 762. **51st,** 806. **56th,** 682. **61st,** B. of Fromelles, 40, 43, 48n. **62nd,** First Bullecourt, 131, 142, 2nd, 145. **63rd,** 682n. **66th,** 232, 233, 236, 239, 240. **Canadian: 1st,** arrves. on W.F., 22; Mouquet Fm., 52, 63, 73; 3rd, cptures. Mons, 11 *Nov.* 1918, 768. **French: 37th,** 678. **German,** 104, 192; on W.F., 21 *Mar.* 1918, 606n; 57 thrown agnst. 21 Brit., *Mar.*, 612; number on W.F., *Mar.* and *May,* 707. **New Zealand,** 175, 180, 219, 232, 236; arrves. in France, 21, 29; in II Anzac, 29, 158; B. of Messines, 160, 164, 172, 173, 174, B. of Broodseinde, 223; mumps in 555-6; Hébuterne, 616; bet. Third and Fifth Armies, *Mar.*, 1918, 617. **Portuguese,** 606n

DOIGNIES (Sk. 123), 119, 122, 123, 124, 125, (Plate) 113
DOIGNT (Sk. 698), C.C.S's at, 727, 740, 762
DOULLENS (Map 68; Sk. 30, 613), 615, 620, 628; hosp. centre at, 397, 623, 625; confnce. at, 26 *Mar.*, 1918, 612; C.C.S. at, 626
DOVER (Map 452; Sk. 397), 10, 422, 424, 426
DOZINGHEM, 186
DRESSINGS, purpose of, 348; supply of, Somme, 56, 60, 86, B. of Menin Rd., 200; wdd. dressed too frqntly., 312n; fld., usually self-appld., 345; shell, appld. by regtl. S.-B's, 346; antisptc., out of favr., 348; oft. unsterlsd., 348; *see also* MEDICAL STORES
DRESSING STATIONS, fld. amb., *May* 1916, 37; distce. bet. advcd. and main, Fromelles, 42; Corps and Army, for particlr. condtns., 88n; med. trtmnt. stns. move up, 116-8; not to move too far frwd., 137; trtmnt. given at advcd. and main, 341, at divnl. posts and stns., 345-52; in Somme area, *May-July* 1918, 656; for Walkg. Wdd.: 658, 667n, adjoin M.D.S., 127, at Tincourt, 732-3, Jeancourt, 737, Templeux, 751; "died of wounds" records, 669; instns. re re-dressg., aft. Hamel, 672; leapfrogging of A.D.S's and M.D.S's, 697n; failre. to disting. bet. advcd. and main in Brit. system, 747; Templeux an ideal stn., 749-51; A.D.S. *v.* M.D.S., 765-6. **Advanced** (Plate 151; Sk. 57, 144): Fromelles, 46-7; Somme, 56; trtmnt. at, 64-5, overlaps M.D.S., 65; Thistle Dump, 84, 85; wide separation from "main," 117; clearnce. from., 10-11 *Apr.* 1917, 137; Gers. almost capture, 137; persnl. at, 150; example of work at, 151; B. of Messines, 165, 169, 170-1, (Plate) 172; obsvertns. of Gens., Macpherson and Fawcus on, 190; Menin Rd., 201-2, 208-9, 217, (Plates) 173, 201; Broodseinde, 221-3, 229; Poelcappelle, 233, 234; work at Ypres rly. stn., 292, classifctn. at, 785n; during retreat, *Mar.-Apr.*, 1918, 619. Henencourt, 625, 630; only "first aid" at, 634; Somme, *May-July*, 656, 658; the standardsd. undergrnd. A.D.S., 658-9, (Plates) 660, 661, (Diag.) 660; "portable," 659; new type, 667; at B. of Hamel, 671-2; B. of Amiens, 684, dispostns., and instns. *re* 884-5, 897; moves of, 693, 700; at Bray (Plate) 732; at Tincourt, Hervilly, 730, 832, Jeancourt, Templeux, Ste. Emilie, 737, 741, 747-50, Templeux describd., 750; Austlns. and Americans in, 752-7; comment on the "A.D.S." **Main** (Plate 112; Sk. 54, 135, 144), 143n, 148, 228, 362; siting and functns. of, 351-2; comment on, 765; surg. work at, 667; trtmt. at, 69;

GENERAL INDEX 993

DRESSING STATIONS—*continued*.
Fort Rompu, 37*n*, 42; Fromelles, 47, 48; Bécordel, 84, 88; Beugny, 126, 138; move fwd., 141-2; for walkg. wdd. and stretchrs., descrbd., 151-2; shelled, 154; Vaulx., 156; B. of Messines: 163, N.Z. at Westhof. Fm., 164, 175, "Corps" at Pont d'Achelles, 164, 175-8, 181-2, 185, Barber disapproves, 182*n*; descrptn. of lay-out, 176; arrngts. for, Fifth Army, *July-Aug.*, 1917, 190-91; B. of Menin Rd., 202; B. of Broodseinde, 223, 229-30, Warloy, 625-6, 630, Querrieu, 628; scheme for retreat, 636*n*; Daours, expermnts., 661-2; Les Alençons, 661*n*, 667; resusc. teams employd., 663; B. of Hamel, 672; B. of Amiens, 684, dispostns. and instns., 877, 884-5; Villers-Bret., 692-3, Bray, 700; Buire, 730, (Plate) 732, (Diag.) 729; Marquaix, 730, 732, 733, 737, 741; Amer. at Villers-Faucon, 737, 752, 757, Longavesnes, 737, 741, 752; Templeux, 751. *See also* COLLECTING POSTS

DREUIL (Map 68), 670, 928
DROCOURT-QUÉANT LINE (Sk. 122), 120, 131; Ger. "Wotan Line," 108*n*; B. of, 2-3 *Sept*. 1918, 806*n*
DROPSY, 504
DRUGS, *see* MEDICAL STORES
DUCKBOARDS (Plate 241), measuremts. and wght., 220*n*; tracks, 36, 82, 124, 220, 516, wire cvrd., 94, to dir. walkg. wdd., 201
DUGOUTS, *see* FORTIFICATIONS
DYSENTERY, *see* DISEASES

EAR INFECTIONS, 473-4, 502, 568
EATON HALL (Sk. 38), 42, 45
EAUCOURT-L'ABBAYÉ (Plates 77, 112), 770
ÉCOLE DU SACRÉ COEUR, 382
ECOUST-LONGATTE (Sk. 122), 122
EDGEHILL (Plate 629; Sk. 772), C.C.S. at, 120-21, 138, 384, 619
EDUCATION, 528; in promotn. of health, 532; sch. for med. offcrs., Bailleul, 783*n*; scheme of, 791; nonmily. employmt., 795, 799*n*, conceptn. and establshmt. of, 797-8; *see also* REPATRIATION
"EGG POST" (Sk. 749), 752*n*
EGYPT, proposed as A.I.F. med. base, 11; D.M.S., A.I.F. maintains control through A.D.M.S., 15, 814; training bns. in, 448; effct. of climate on trps., 900
ENCEPHALITIS LETHARGICA, 502, 505*n*
ENDOCRINE DYSFUNCTIONS, 504
ENGINEERS, 522, 659, 673, 912*n*; work on rds. and rlys., 113, 122, 196, (Plate) 733; thr. trials in "Alberich," 118; open sectns. of Hooge Tunnel, 200; prepare A.D.S., 221; construct cupolas, 222, R.A.P's, 655; plan and constrct. gen. hosps., 399; co-op. in water supply, 590, 713; constrct. 78 mls. hutmts. B.E.F. Base, 931*n*

ENLISTMENTS, in Brit. Army, 1916, 7*n*; age for, reduced, 254*n*; men understate age, 473; dispute *re* raising of age for, 845-50; in A.I.F., not prmitted outside Aust., 828*n*; as muntn. wkrs., 849*n*; *see also* AUSTRALIA; RECRUITS
ENTERITIS, 99, 586
ENTERIC, *see* DISEASES
EPEHY (Map 760; Sk. 749), B. of, 680*n*, 721-34
EPILEPSY, 474
EQUIPMENT, 86*n*, 265-6, 522-4, 655*n*, 662; for fst. aid, 349-50; of C.C.S's, 365-6, 773, 776, of Gen. Hosps., 401; the problm. of wght., 526-8; winter kit for Austlns. (Plate) 528; Amer. med. units use Brit. and Amer., 736; of a S.-B. divn., 885; compostn. of Thomas Splint outfit, 942; required by a div. resus. team, 955-6; *see also* MEDICAL STORES
ERQUINGHEM (Sk. 36), 27, 577
ESQUELBECQ (Sk. 772), 643, 771
ESTABLISHMENTS, 261, 831*n*; Dept. of D.D.M.S., A.I.F. Eng., *Apr.*, 1916, 810; of Admin. H.Q., A.I.F., 1918, 811, Med. Sectn., 813; of med. units, A.I.F., 1918, 911-12; of regtl. med. estabs., 398, 912; of San. Sectns., 596, of Motor Amb. Convoy, 289; of C.C.S., 359*n*, 364, 772-3, 911; of Resus. Teams, 768*n*, 955; of Amb. Trains, 394; of Water Tnk. Coys., A.S.C., 593; of Gen. Hosps., 11*n*, 399, 415-6, 911; *see also* STRENGTH
ESTAIRES (Sk. 36, 772), 382, 643; No. 1 A.C.C.S. at, 30, 41*n*; B. of, 332*n*
ETAPLES (Sk. 30, 397), 27, 395*n*, 397, 447, 609, 623, 624, 779; Aust. base depots establshd. at, 34; "research unit," 413
ETHICS OF WAR, Gt. War a retrogression of, 4
EUROPE, gen. mily. situatn. in, 1915, 7-8; btle. frnts., *June*, 1916, 9; the gen. situatn. in, 1917, 104, mily. plans, 105-7; *see also* WAR OF 1914-18; WESTERN FRONT
EUSKIRCHEN (Sk. 772), 776
EVACUATION, *see* CASUALTIES, EVACN. OF
EXAMINATIONS, MEDICAL, *see* BOARDS, MEDICAL; RECRUITS
EYE INFECTIONS, 473-4, 502, 568

FACTORY CORNER, 114
FARGO (Map 452), 453
"FEBRICULA," 554
FEET, 91, sore, 27, 97; care of, 100, 530, lectres. on, 140*n*; M.O's shd. make examn. of, 901; *see also* DISEASES **(Trench Foot)**
FEUILLERES (Sk. 698), 696
FIBROSITIS, 410, 504
FIELD AMBULANCES, 78, 348, 356, 358, 447, 609, 618, 685; organistn., 281, 284; as bde. units, 75*n*; transpt., 1914, 26; as A.D.S., 65; personnel attd. to C.C.S's, 71-2; S.-B. *liaison* with R.M.O., 278, policy dicsssd., 281; as trtmnt. stns., 295-6, 350-2,

FIELD AMBULANCES—continued.
552; surg. work passes to C.C.S., 316; in a retreat, 624; blood transfns. in, 664; two mthds. of leapfrogging by, 686. **American**: attd. to Austln. for training, 675; *65th Bde. Group*, 674. *Fld. Hosp. Coys.*, 736, 752, 757. *107th San. Train*, 756. *108th San. Train*, 673. *No. 118*, 733, 737. *No. 119*, 737*n*, 747. *129th Provisional*, 673, 675, 693, 887-8. *130th Provisional*, 673. **Australian**: 46, 56, 73, 144-145, 148, 162, 164, 165, 170, 177, 198-200, 201, 204, 231*n*, 285*n*, 577, 586, 675, 700-701, 728, 830, 877, 888, 890, 896, 897, 898; estab. of 1918, 911, 912*n*; two-sectn., 33, 805; sectns. work in tandem, 110; Bearer Divns.; attd. to respctve. bdes., 742, S.-B's pooled, 166, work as independnt. unit, 218, compon., disposn. and control, 885-7; motors replce. horses for transpt., 1917, 193*n*; *liqison* btwn. R.M.O. and S.-B's, 198; work of Q.M., 199*n*; M.O's k. and wdd., *Sept.-Nov.* 1917, 247; cost of rescue, 249; work of N.C.O's, 282, of offcrs., 283-4; work in, 351-2; admissns. to, from A.I.F. 1916-19, 495-7, 501-4, 535-6; resus. teams, 659-61, 953-7; desirablty. of 'phone at, 691; transfrs. to combatnt. arms, 715*n*; units and personnel embkd. from Aust., 829. **1st**, 29, 69, 125, 193*n*, 204, 230*n*, 231, 631*n*, 646, 724, 731-2; S.-B's k. and wdd., 204*n*; B. of Broodseinde, 220-2, 226; at Buire, *Sept.* 1918, (Plate), 732, (Diag.), 729. **2nd**, 29, 86, 123, 124*n*, 149, 204, 205, 241*n*, 247-8, 646, 724, 733; Somme, 1916, 57, 72; A.D.S., Beugny, 126; W.W. Stn., Tincourt, 732. **3rd**, 29, 56, 111*n*, 124-5, 126, 149, 151-2, 195, 198, 204, 205, 210*n*, 213, 227, 246, 283*n*, 296, 531*n*, 646, 675, 724, 727-8, 732; M.D.S. at Bapaume, 123; helps wth. harvestg., *Aug.*, 193*n*, A.D.S., stret. cases, Menin Rd., 201. **4th**, 29, 136, 137, 174, 178, 214-17, 240-1, 252, 516, 663, 669, 670, 880 *et seq.*, 888; W.W. Stn., Vaulx, 121, 127; A.D.S., Kandahar Fm., 177; accessory A.D.S., Ypres, 217; W.W. Stn, Vlamertinghe, 223; motor relay pst., Toutencourt, 626; M.D.S., les Alençons, 662, 667, at Hangcourt, 724. **5th**, 27, 29, 113, 119, 142, 144-5, 150, 193*n*, 195, 198, 204, 207-8, 210, 211, 214, 276*n*, 666; A.D.S., Martinpuich, 101; M.D.S., Pozières, 114, 120; M.D.S. for W.W., 151; A.D.S. for lghtly. wdd., Menin Rd., 201; M.D.S., Templeux, 751. **6th**, 29, 85, 117, 119, 120, 142, 203, 204, 221-3, 226-7, 233, 234, 658, 667, 690, 746; M.D.S. for strets., 145, descriptn. of work, 151, moves back to Beugnâtre, 154; work at A.D.S., Ypres, 292; A.D.S., Franvillers-Bonnay Rd., 666, Hamel, 751; clearnce., 3-5 *Oct.* 1918, 763. **7th**, 27, 29, 72, 85, 144, 149, 204, 675; M.D.S., Morbecque, moves to Fort

FIELD AMBULANCES—continued.
Rompu, 37*n*; M.D.S., Vaulx, 152; W.W.D.S., Templeux, 751; investigation of time-distance factor, 927-30. **8th**, 29, 43, 48, 154, 214, 665, 742, 745; M.D.S. at Fort Rompu, 42, at Bac St. Maur, 42; methods described, 85; A.D.S., Templeux, with Americans, 1918, 748-51. **9th**, 175-6, 228, 233*n*, 236, 240-1, 629, 632, 635, 697*n*, 742, 753-4, 793*n*, 881, 883; very exactly trained, 165. **10th**, 165, 627, 629, 740, 881, 882; gas trtmt. centre, Brandhoek, 223; Corps Relay post, Villers-Faucon, 742; M.D.S., Villers-Faucon, 7⁵⁰; unusual disposition at Messines, 166. **11th**, 165, 169*n*, 171, 628, 629, 669, 690, 742, 756, 758, 764, 881, 882, 883; M.D.S., "Red Farm," 223; temp. dress. stn. Bonnay, 626-7; M.D.S., Querrieu, 627; M.D.S., Ste. Emilie, 755, 759. **12th**, 29, 132, 136-7, 252, 616, 625-6, 630, 667, 669, 670, 690, 727-8, 881, 882, 883; A.D.S., Pozières Hts., 61, at Menin Rd., 236, at Vendelles, 724. **13th**, 29, 69, 132, 136-7, 252, 330, 350, 362, 615, 616, 625-6, 630-1, 638, 667, 669, 670, 724, 728, 880-4; A.D.S., Bapaume, 120; M.D.S., Vaulx, 121; A.D.S., Ypres, 236; Liaison Force, *Aug.* 1918, 693. **14th**, 29, 43, 44, 48, 213, 214, 215, 218, 660, 661-2. 742, 798*n*; A.D.S., Menin House, 208*n*; completes stand. type A.D.S., 659; takes over fwd. evacn., 29 *Sept.* 1918, 746; A.D.S., Jeancourt, 747. **15th**, 29, 48, 118, 214, 218, 632, 638, 700*n*, 742, 746*n*, 789; A.D.S., Bapaume, 117; M.D.S., transfrrd. from Bernafay to Bapaume, 121. **16th**, 106, 475. **17th**, 475, (Plate), 453. **Camel Fld. Amb.**, 829. **Light Horse Fld. Ambs.**, 829, 830. **British**: 152, 204, 233*n*, 619*n*, 627, 737, 747, 888. **New Zealand**, 164. *See also* ARMY MED. SERV.; AUST. IMP. FORCE; COLLECTING POSTS; DRESS. STNS.; LESSONS OF THE WAR
FIELD SERVICE REGLNS., *see* ACTS AND REGLNS.
FILARIA, 503
FINANCE, arrgts. btwn. Gr. Brit. and Aust., 426, 524*n*, 826-7; inoc. entered in pay books, 538; rates of, 835, 902
FIRST AID NURSING YEOMANRY CONVOY (F.A.N.Y's), 425
FITNESS, *see* RECRUITS, REINFORCEMTS.
FLANDERS, 31, 74, 382, 768, 861; Brit. offnsve. in, 138, 145, 158-231, 247-50, 384; Ger. thrust in, 9 *Apr.* 1918, 610; Allies attck. in, *Sept.-Oct.*, 719; *see also* WEST. FRONT
FLERS (Map 68; Sk. 51, 112), 74, 81, 111, 516; mud at, 228
FLESQUIÈRES, 612
FLÊTRE, 633
FLEURBAIX (Sk. 38), 37*n*
FLIES, prevntn. of breedg., 73, 565*n*, 582*n*, 940; Gallip. and France compared, 583
FOOD (Plates 524, 525), 32-3, 60, 96,

GENERAL INDEX 995

FOOD—continued.
210, 518-20, 614-15, 872-3, 940-1; hot food contnrs., 91n, 94, (Plate) 528; for wdd. man, 345, 522; its part in promotg. hlth., 506; protectn. of, Gallip. and France compared, 583; as a factor in incdnce. of dysentery, 583, 584n. *See also* COOKING; DISEASES; RATIONS

FORTIFICATIONS, Brit.: trenches, duckbds., tracks, etc., 35-6, Ger. dugouts used as R.A.P's, 58, 63, 84n, large med. dugouts, Needle Dump and Bernafay, 101, R.A.P. in old Ger. gunpit, Lagnic't, 120, Hooge Tunnel, 199, 200, 204, 205, 214, Ger. pill-boxes used as R.A.P's, 214-15; Ger.: three zones of Hindbg. (Siegfried) Line, 719, O.G.1 and O.G.2, 59, R.I, II, III, 108, 109, 118, concrete blockhouses, 108, 160, 183

FORT ROMPU (Sk. 38), 37n
FOUILLOY (Sk. 685), 693
FOVANT (Map 452), 453
FRACTURES, *see* WOUNDS, TYPES OF
FRANCE, *see* WEST. FRONT
FRANCO-PRUSSIAN WAR, propn. of bullet to shell wds., 495n
FRANVILLERS (Map 668; Sk. 54), 658, 666
FRÉMICOURT, 119, 123
FRENCH ARMY, 81, 184, 291-2, 299n, 362, 489n, 579, 607, 620, 627, 628, 713n, 718, 721; frnt. held, *May* 1916 (Sk.), 10; offsve. postpnd. until 17 *Apr.* 1917, 108, fails, 138; prob. of brk.-up of, 1917, 232n; recovers resilnce., 607; enlistmt. age reduced to 18 yrs., 254n; fem. nurses not used at frnt., 300n; *débridement* in, 322, 326n; immed. suturing, 330; dressgs. sterlsd., 348n; anti-typhoid inoc. in, 539; enterica in, 540; mumps in recruits of, 555n; Pétain's orders tend to sep. fr. Brit., 616; Foch cnter.-attcks., 18 *July* 1918, 611; Argonne Offsve., wth. Amers., 768; mthds. of med. serv., 913-18; estimate of degrees of urgncy. of wds. in, 957-8; total btle. cas., 860. *First Army*, 194, 682. *Second*, 106. *Sixth*, 114, 677n
FRENCH GOVERNMENT, reltns. wth. Brit., 9, 788n; arrngts. for employmt. of civilns. in Brit. Army, 789
FRESENBERG (Map 206), 240
FRÉTIN (Sk. 772), 381
FRÉVENT (Sk. 620), 397, 620, 628
FRICOURT (Map 68; Sk. 112), 81, 87, 116, 515, 578, 935
FRITZ'S FOLLY, 516
FROMELLES (Sk. 38), Btle. of, 35-48, 49n, 382
FROSTBITE, 90n, 99, 503; *see also* DISEASES, Trench Foot
FROST HOUSE (Map 224; Sk. 238), 229, 233, 237
FUEL, 89, 522n
FURLOUGH, Aust. trps. in U.K., 1916, 18n; "leave" as a factor in morale, 532; "Anzac Leave," 717, 768

GALLIPOLI, *see* DARDANELLES CAMPAIGN
GANGRENE, GAS, 310, 777
GARTER POINT (Map 224), 217, 222
GAS, med. serv. and, 23, 25; shell gas, 70n, 128n, 154, 167, 169, 50 per cent. of Ger. shells contain, 607n; "mustard" (yellow cross), 193n, 211, 235, 367, 637, 676, protectn. of skin agst. impfct., 608; thick in Glencorse Wd., 23 *Sept.* 1917, 214, *Oct.*, 241; inhalatn. of poisn. gas, a wd., 270; distressg. effcts., 333n; psychic element, 462; a prime factor in wastge., 481, prevention, 498; blue cross, 676; Americans and, 693, 694n, 759; symptoms of, 676; P.H. Helmet, 78; small box resnr., 78, 167n, 193n, 608, powerless agst. carbon monoxide in mines, 160n; early Austln. exp., 78, French Tissot mask, 608. Treatment, 59n, 70, 88n, 121-2, 123, 140n, 155, 162, 163, 203, 208, 295, 352, 411, 637n, 667, 676-7, 692-3, 728, 750, 878, (Plate) 661. Casltes., 59, 61, 168, 169n, 178, 179, 180, 495, 699, 787
GASTRO-INTESTINAL INFECTIONS, *see* DISEASES
GENERAL HEADQUARTERS, *see* BRIT. EXPED. FORCE, and Persnl. Index, HAIG
GENERAL HOSPITALS, *see* HOSPITALS
GENERAL STAFF BRANCH, 522, 691
GENEVA CONVENTION, 60n, 235, 305, 386, 441; episode at Fromelles, 46n; coll. of wdd. under white flag, 64n, (Plate) 68, med. serv. charged with minimising sufferg. under, 263; the internat. allegnce., 264; regtl. S.-B's come under, 275, 912n; provides for wdd. in a retreat, 289n; *see also* RED CROSS
GERMAN AIR FORCE, 1
GERMAN ARMY, 27, 35, 46n, 63, 159n, 183, 254n, 299n, 489, 718; its orgn., 921; its bid for victory, 1916, 8; respcts. Geneva Convention, 64n; retiremt., 1917, ("Alberich"), 102, 104-28, 612, its infl. on the war, 102, analogy wth. Gallip. evacn., 109n; withdrawal. 10-12 *June*, 168; Cambrai, *Nov.*, 251; fem. nurses not used at frnt., 300n; atats. *re* tetanus in, 310n; propn. of bullet to shell wds., 495n; anti-typhoid inoc. in, 539; enterica in, 540; offsve. of, *Mar.-Apr.* 1918, 603-46, object to sep. Brit. fr. French, 610, 612, "Michael": *Mar.* 26, critical day, 612, breach on the Ancre, 616-17, chckd., 28-30 *Mar.*, 627, 629, "George," 640, cost of offensve. to Brit., 611, factors in failure of, 682n, shock to med. admin., B.E.F., 772; double offnsve., 15 *July*, foiled, 611, 677; German troops obsve. laws of war, 670-1; gen. reconstruction of line, 702; strengh. *Mar.* and *May* 1917, 707; retreats *Oct.*, 768; total btle. cas., 860; total sick and wdd., 863. *First Army*, 108. *Secnd. Army*, 622n, 629. *Sixth*, 129, 145. *See also* ARMY MED. SERV.

GERMANY, 483; naval blockade of, 105, 607; U.S.A. declrs. war on, 6 *Apr.* 1917, 673*n*
GÉZAINCOURT (Sk. 54, 620), 383, 620, 624; No. 3 A.C.C.S. at, *Oct.* 1916, (Plate) 365; No. 3 Brit. C.C.S. at, 662
"GIBRALTAR" (POZIÈRES), 62*n*
GILLEMONT FARM (Diag. 743; Sk. 749), 723
GINCHY (Map 68; Sk. 112), Btle. of, 49*n*
GIRD TRENCH, 110
GLANDERS, 502
GLENCORSE WOOD (Map 206), 213, 214
GOITRE, 504
GOMMECOURT (Sk. 109), 49*n*
"GORDON DUMP" (Sk. 57), 56, (Plate) 65
GRAVENSTAFEL RIDGE (Sk. 189), 219
GREAT BRITAIN, 792; supreme effrt., 1916, 8; A.I.F. Depots in, 16-20; carries main burden on W.F., 1917, 104, 158; hosp. system in, 427-30; "Imperial" co-opn. in med. servs., 429, 866-9; Austlns. under trtmt. in, 436, 870-3; financl. reltns. wth., 426, 524*n*, 826-7; sickness and injury amng. trps. in, 861*n*; reltns. wth. France, 9, wth. Aust., 10-11, 12, 153*n*, 383*n*, 821-4, btwn. A.A.M.C. and R.A.M.C. 32-3. *See also* ARMY MED. SERV.; WAR OFFICE
GREAT WAR, *see* WAR OF 1914-18
GRÉVILLERS (Map 68; Sk. 51, 620), 110, 138, 139, 151, 384, 619
GROUND SHEETS, 234, 524
GUEUDECOURT (Map 68; Sk. 112), 74, 81, 101, 124
GUILLEMONT (Map 68; Sk. 51), Btle. of, 49*n*, 51
HAEMORRHAGE, 308*n*, 335, 783, 785*n*; effcts. augmtd., 303*n*-4*n*; trtmt., 162, 949-53, carried out at Coll. Post, Menin Rd., 207; arrest of, the duty of S.-B's, 346; fst. aid technique, 347; resus. in the fld., 946-58; *see also* SURGICAL TREATMT.
HAEMORRHOIDS, 99, 408, 474
HAGUE CONVENTION, reglns. of, broken, 264; *see also* GENEVA CONVNTN.
HAL (Map 769), 776
HAMEL (Map 668; Sk. 626), 699, 929; B. of, 611, 632, 647, 655, 663, 665, 666-7, 668, 673, 675-8; med. arrngts. for, 667-73, (Plate) 773; tnks. assist in carryg. wdd., 272*n*; cas. 670
HANCOURT (Sk. 726), 724, 727, 728
HANGARD WOOD (Sk. 683), 618, 633, 635, 638
HARBONNIÈRES (Sk. 680), 692
HAREFIELD (Map 452), No. 1 A.A.H. at, 20, 450, (Plates) 19, 429
HARGICOURT (Map 760; Sk. 726), 620, B. of, 721-34
HAVRE, LE (Sk. 397), 394, 425, 477; Aust. Conv. Depot at, 27; Aust. Base Depots at, 419, 420, 479, 909
HAZEBROUCK (Sk. 22, 623), 21, 610, 641, 644, 647, 771
HEALTH, defntn. of, 514; of A.I.F. on W.F., 32; during 1916, 72-3, 77; discip., 90; effcts. of adv. in "Albe-

HEALTH—*continued.*
rich," 1917, 116, of housg. and weather conditns. on, 140; *Mar.-May* 1917, 154; end of 1917, 241-3; in A.I.F. Depots, 453-5, 565; triple fld. of actn. in preservatn., 485; gen. admin. centres in Abbeville, 508*n*; infl. of clothg. on, 524-6; measuremnt. of, 547*n*; in A.I.F., 1917-18 winter, 614; *May-July* 1918, 665; probs. in adv., 710-14; low sick rate in Aust. trps., *Dec.* 1918-*Apr.* 1919, 797; responsblty. of D.M.S., A.I.F., *re*, 814; maintce. of, 77, 78, 92-4, 453; *see also* DISEASES
HEALTH PROMOTION, 91-6; in Somme Winter, 78, 79, 83; disrgd. of importce. by Brit. Gen. staff, 1916, 80; orgn. a fundmntl. factor in, 90; part of med. serv. in, 96-8; a cardinal phase, 101; "the duty of every officer and man," 101, 293; in 1917, 242-3; winter 1917-18, 258; exact aims of, 484; baths, launds., 506; prevntve. med. in, 510-11, 514-32; need for co-opn. in, 547*n*. *See also* BATHS AND LAUNDRIES; DISEASE PREVENTN.; LESSONS OF THE WAR
HEART, *see* DISEASES
HEAT, 503; *see also* WEATHER
HÉBUTERNE (Sk. 51), 427, 616
HEILLY (Map 68; Sk. 54, 626), 81, 83, 578, 617
"HELLES" (Map 216), 217, 222, 226, 227
HELLFIRE CORNER (Map 206; Sk. 189)
HELMINTHIASIS, 503
HÉNENCOURT (Map 68; Sk. 626), 616, 625, 630, 724
HERBÉCOURT (Sk. 698), 700*n*
HERMIES (Sk. 123), 119, 122, 123, 124, 125*n*
HERNIA, 99, 408, 435, 473-4, 568, 905
HERPETIC DISEASES, 502
HERVILLY (Sk. 726), 732
HIGH COMMISSIONER FOR AUSTRALIA, London, 12*n*, 561
HIGH WOOD (Map 88), 49*n*
HILL 40 (Map 224), 228
HILL 63 (Map 164), 163, 279*n*
HINDENBURG ("SIEGFRIED") LINE (Plates, 733, 773; Map 760; Sk. 116, 130), 104, 107-9, 127-8, 129*n*, 132, 467, 604, 612; descrptn. of, 719-20; Ger. retiremt. to, 109-128; Ger. retreat to, *Sept.* 1918, 696-7; Brit. adv. to, 604, 680*n*, 700-1, 702, 713; operns. agst., 718-34, med. arrngts., 723-6; breakg. of, 735-66; med. evnts., 743-4, commnts. and conclsns., 764-66
HONDEGHEM (Sk. 772), 641
HOOGE TUNNEL (Map 273), 199, 200, 214, 222
HORSEFERRY-ROAD, London, Admin. H.Q., A.I.F. at, 437, 451, 471*n*, 560, 791, 803, 812, 815, (Plate) 809; *see also* AUST. IMP. FORCE (ADMINISTRATIVE H.Q.)
HOSPITAL SHIPS, *see* MEDICAL TRANSPT.
HOSPITALS, 19, 57, 75, 156, 394, 397, 403-4, 405, 412, 447, 462, 545, 778; trtmt. at, in Eng. 341; system in

GENERAL INDEX 997

HOSPITALS—continued.
Brit., 427-30; Queen's, Sidcup, 823-4, 830; tents and huts used for, 933-4. **American:** 299n, 918, 919-21. **Australian:** 13n, 414-15, 827, 830, 856, 871-3; policy of D.M.S., A.I.F. for W.F., 824-5. **Auxiliary**, 437, 438, 441, 447, 452, 456, 830, 832, 871-2; trnsfr. of Austlns. from Brit. hosps. to, 13; system in Eng., 428; D.M.S., A.I.F. dir. actvties. of, 814, 824-5; at Bishop's Knoll, 439n. **No. 1** (*Harefield*), 20, 438, 439, 450, 832, (Plates) 19, 429. **No. 2** (*Southall*), 438, 450. **No. 3** (*Brighton, Dartford*), 438, 439, 450, 832. **Dermatological** (*Bulford*), 455, 829, 911. **General**, 11n, 395n, 407n, 413-18, 425, 614n, 778-81, 799; part of in evacn., 390-422; lay-out, 399n; establt., 415-16, 911, 912n; number of units and personnel sent from Aust. for, 829. **No. 1**, 203, 324, 414, 778, (Plates) 412, 413; arrves. in France, 29; at Rouen, *Apr.* 1916, 30; huttg. accommodn., *June* 1918, 399; short hist. of, 416; admissns., *Mar.* 1918 and *Aug.-Oct.*, 779; stats. of work in France, 780; to Sutton Veny, *Jan.* 1919, 800. **No. 2**, 365n, 395-6, 401-2, 403, 416-17, 799, 800; cases of typhus idntfd. in, 1915, 544; arrves. in France, 29; controls the "sieve" at Marseilles, 11, 32, 543; opens at Wimereux, *June* 1916, 30; capcty., *Mar.* 1918, 778; blood transfns. at, 662; admissns. *Apr* and *Aug.*, 779; stats. of work in France, 780. **No. 3**, 417-18, 437, 622, 779, 799, 828n, 871, (Plates) 412, 413, 428, 808; at Lemnos, 520n, 583; in Egypt, 832; at Brighton, Eng., *Oct.* 1916, 430, 584n; at Abbeville, 402-3, 405n, 621 (diag.), 400, work of med. div., 410-411; stats. of work in France, 780, 781; acts as final depot for A.A.M.C., 800-1. **No. 10**, 829n. **No. 14**, 415n. **Group Clearing Hosps.**, 454-5, 560, 563, 830. **Stationary:** 30, 158n; estabimt., 1918, 911; units and personnel embked. from Aust., 829. **Aust. Voluntary Hosp.**, 314-15, 828n, (Plate) 288. **British:** 315, 341, 427, 429n; trtmt. of Austlns. in, 20, (Graph) 436; number on W. Frnt., 1917-18, 782. **General**, 425, 437, 447, 453, 454, 641; estabmt. and structre. of, 398-401; functns., 401-4; system in B.E.F., 396-412; numbers, 396-7; accommodn., 397-8; importce. of kitchns. in, 520n. **No. 2 Southern**, 349n. **No. 7**, 549. **No. 11**, 314. **No. 13**, 314-15. **No. 14**, 315, 408n. **No. 25**, 404, 572, 574. **No. 26**, 332n, 413. **No. 54**, 404, 775n. **No. 55**, 404. **Special**, 341, 436-7, 439. **Stationary**, 552; rôle not specfd., 390n; numbers in B.E.F., 396-7. **No. 2**, 315, 417. **No. 7**, 315. **No. 8**, 404. **No. 10**, 642. **No. 12**, 416. **No. 13**, 315. **No. 14**, 404, 684n. **No. 41**, 725, 726. **Canadian**,

HOSPITALS—continued.
641n; number of, o'seas, 826n. **French**, *Hôpital d' Evacuation* (H.O.E.), 299n, 914-15, 916. **German**, *Feldlazarett*, 299n, 922. **Indian**, 315. **South African**, 367n, 417, 801. *See also* ARMY MED. SERV.; CASUALTY CLRNG. STNS.
HOUSING, in cmps. on Salisbury Pln., 17, 451; of advcd. op. centre, Warloy, 70-71; value of captured Ger. dugouts for med. Stns., 84n; Pnrs. con. stret. shlter. for R.A.P., 120; R.A.P. in shell crater, 174; in old French dugout, 732; "staging camps," Somme, 89; at B. of Menin Road: 203, 207, at Ypres Ramparts, 199, 204, A.D.S's for strtchrs. and W.W., 208-9; of C.C.S's, 365-6, 773, in huts and brigaded tents, 300; layout of a gen. hosp., 399, 400; problm. for trps. in fwd. area, 139-40; its part in promotg. hlth., 506, as a factor in "wastage," 521-2; model dugout for A.D.S., 658; types of huts and tents in common use, 931-4; need for ventiln., 932-3; "elephant iron" cupolas, 143, 200, 201, 222; huts: 186, standard, 933, Adrian, 932, 933, 934, arrngt. of beds in, 557, Armstrong, 934, Nissen, 114, 120n, 176, 667, 730, 757, 778, 933, 934, (Plates) 412, 524; tents: 84, 126, 564, 776, 933-4, bell, 933, Bessoneau, 933, 934; marquee, 97, 120n, 122, 178, 186, (brigading of), 778, 934, "Swiss Cottage," 732, "Tortoise," 933
HUMANITY IN WAR, 4, 153, 156; Ger. ordlies attnd. Austln. wdd., 134-5; v. effcncy., 248
HURDCOTT (Map 452), Grp. Clearg. Hosp. at, 454-5; No. 3 Cd. Depot at, 441 (Plate), 453
HYDATID, 503
"HYDE PARK CORNER," MESSINES (Map 164), 165, 172, 279n
HYDROCELE, 408
HYGIENE, 594n; in prevntn. of dis., 566-93; personal, 73, 78, 552. *See also* HEALTH; LESSONS OF THE WAR; SANITATION

IDEAL HOUSE (Plate 241), 222, 227-8
IMPETIGO, 567, 570
INCINERATORS, *see* SANITARY APPLNCES.
INDIAN EXPEDITIONARY FORCE, 11n, 782
INDO-CHINA, 541, 542, 546
INFLAMMATION OF CONNECTIVE TISSUE "I.C.T."), *see* DISEASES
INFLUENZA, *see* DISEASES
INJURY, *see* SICKNESS
INOCULATION, 478-9, 537, 538, 539
INSECT PESTS, *see* FLIES; LICE
INVALIDS, 19, 443, 470, 815n; the "six months'" policy re, 12, 441-3, 456, 814, 817n, 825; the med. bds., 441-2, 460-4; work in auxly. hosps., for, 439-40; effts. to prevnt. permnt. disablty. in, 559-60; machnry. in Depots speeded off. Armstce., 795. *See also* BOARDS; MED. CATEGORIES; STATISTICS
IODINE, PICRIC, 348

998 GENERAL INDEX

IRELAND, typhus in, 545
ITALIAN ARMY, 519n, 606, 860
ITALY, 104, 679; Brit. cas. in, 1917-18, 861

JAPANESE ARMY, 489, 519n; total btle. cas., 860
JAUNDICE, 503, 542, 543, 549, 550
JEANCOURT (Sk. 726, 749), 731, 737, 747-8
JORDAN VALLEY, 516n, 589n

KANDAHAR FARM (Plate 172; Map 164), 174, 176n
KEMMEL, MONT (Map 164; Sk. 185), 610, 637
"KNOLL, THE" (Map 760; Sk. 749), 723
KRUISSTRAAT (Map 224; Sk. 190), 190

LA CHAPELLETTE (Sk. 726), 725
LA CLYTTE (Sk. 76), 75n, 279n
LABORATORIES, MOBILE: bacteriolgl. and hygienic, 23, 55n, 186, 551n, 592n, estabmt., 1918, 911, 912n; *Anzac Fld.*, 551n, 830; *No. 13 Mob. Bact.*, 139n; *No. 14 Mob. Bact.*, 32; *No. 15 Mob. Hyg.*, 139n; *No. 5 Canad. Bact.*, 551n, 724; *A.I.F. Bact.*, 815n; *Central Path., A.I.F.*, 560. See also BACTERIOLOGY
LABOUR UNITS, number on W.F. at Armstce., 782
LAGNICOURT (Sk. 135, 144), 119, 122, 141n; captd., 120; Ger. raid on, 129n, 137-8
LAIES RIVER (Sk. 38), 40
LANCER WOOD, 629, 632
LARK HILL (Map 452), 17, 561
LARYNGITIS, 554, 568, 676
LATRINES, *see* SAN. APPLNCES.
LAUNDRIES, *see* BATHS AND LAUNDRS.
LAVIÉVILLE (Sk. 626), 617, 625
LE BAC DU SUD (Sk. 620), 619
LE BARQUE (Map 88; Sk. 109), 110
LE CATEAU (Sk. 607), 770, 792
LE CATELET (Map 760; Sk. 749), 719, 720, 724
LE SARS (Map 68; Sk. 116), 81, 101, 114, 119
LE TRANSLOY (Map 68; Sk. 116), 107, 110; B. of, 49n
LE TRÉPORT (Sk. 397), 397, 623
LEAGUE OF NATIONS, 325n
LEAVE OF ABSENCE, *see* FURLOUGH
LEBUCQUIÈRE (Sk. 123), 125, 126
LEMNOS, 426, 446n, 478, 527
LEPROSY, 490
LES ALENÇONS (Map 668; Sk. 685), M.D.S. at, 661n, 662, 663
LESSONS OF THE WAR, 258n, 281, 295, 377, 510, 790; of the Somme Winter, 79, 92; "hygiene" and "sanitation," 101; indignatn. wasted on "atrocities," 115n; "phys." and "moral," 140; wastge. in med. serv., 153; status of med. serv., 156; of Messines, 173, 180-2; importce. of Q.M., 199n; of Menin Rd., 210-11; of Broodseinde, 230-1; from Third Ypres, 247-50, 850; of Cambrai, 252-3; lessons of "attrtn.," 253n; "shoulder-high"

LESSONS OF THE WAR—*continued.*
carry, 272; bearer offcr., 284n; of 1914, 285; the "services of maintenance," 290n, 569n; "every officer and man," 293; of wd. infectn., 302; excsn. and tetanus, 309; trtmnt. of fractres., 314; no royal road to asepsis, 324; "infectn." and "contaminatn.," "asepsis" and "antisepsis," 329n; Thomas splnt. and shock, 348, 949-50; of the Somme, 359; the C.C.S., and orthopaedics, 373; the good med. offcr., 386; man and his emotns., 409n; and "clinical science," 412; enterprise in hlth., 453n; moral *v.* phys., 466; "diseases" do exist, 489; the R.M.O. and the "sanitary" system, 507; srces. of vitamins, 520; the mily. boot, 525; on alcohol, 530; of typhoid, 540; the social lessn. of typhus, 545; "spacing out" in respir. infectn., 557; scabies in eductn., 573; baths and launds., 578-9; of tr. fever, 580; on health for civil life, 592n; advance twds. exact diagnosis, 601; *festina lente*, 611n; of Mar. 1918, 619n; evacn. in retreat, 624; of 1918, 679; in med. tactics, 724-5; of Hindbg. Line, 764-6; from Austln. experce., 786, 783n; from German prisoner, on Winning of Peace, 801n; to politicians, 853; the G.O.C., A.I.F., and his medical adviser, 853; from the Ger. med. system, 925
LIAISON, btwn. R.M.O. and amb. S.-B's, 198, 211, 278, inefficnt., 217n; btwn. R.M.O. and rgtl. S.-B's, 281; duty of S.-B. N.C.O. to maintn., 283; R.A.P. focal point btwn. fld. amb. and regt., 280; btwn. R.M.O. and fld. amb., 283, 284, 346-7, 348, 619n; dfctve. betwn. bdes and fld. ambs., 618, btwn. frnt. and base, 373n; with depots imperfct., 471n; of fld. units, with san. sectns., 595; at B. of Amiens, 690-91, senr. amb. offcr. attd. to bde., 688; Aust. Corps *liaison* fcc., 692-4; with Second Amer. Corps, 738; of D.M.S., A.I.F. wth. Aust., Egypt, France, 814; communs. to be maintned. by bearer divs., 88; *see also* COMMUNICATIONS.
LICE, 522n; all armies infested, 32; provsn. for delousg., 78n, 94, 140n, 421, 506, 543, 552, 575; "spacing out" chcks. spread of typhus, 545; pub. hlth. mthds., 544n; the cause of pediculosis, trnch., typhus and relapsg. fevrs., 570-3; prophyl. agst., 572-3; crab-louse and hd.-louse, not more prevlnt. than in civ. life, 572n; system of baths and launds. to free trps. from, 575-9; expts. with Russian pit delouser, 712; *see also* DISEASES; SANITATION
LIGHT HORSE, Australian, suggstn. to send to France as infty., 449; reltns. of D.M.S., A.I.F. wth., 821, 832
LIGNY-THILLOY (Map 88; Sk. 109), 110
LINDENHOEK (Map 164), 576

GENERAL INDEX 999

LINES OF COMMUNICATION, see COMMUNICATIONS, LINES OF
LISTER INSTITUTE, 520*n*, 560, 815*n*, 828*n*
LOADING POSTS, horsed and motor, 137, 208, 285, 672, 754; horsed: 45, 56, 125, 128*n*, 135, 148, 200-1, 222, 228, forced back, Broodseinde, 225, immedy. in rear of R.A.P., 18 *Sept.*, 1918, 732; motor: 223, 280-4, 656, pivot of clearnce., 665
LOCRE (Map 164), 615
LONE PINE, 147; B. of, compared with Fromelles, 48*n*
LONGAVESNES (Sk. 749), 741
LONGPRÉ, 635, 684*n*, 770
LOOS, 357, 358, 361
LOUPART WOOD (Sk. 109), 110
LOUVERVAL (Sk. 123), 122, 123
LUCE, RIVER (Sk. 613), 618
LYS, RIVER (Map 164; Sk. 10, 639), 610, 613, 771; Brit. line in frnt. of, *May* 1916, 35; Gers. fall back on, 167; B. of, 604, 639, 640; Gers. retire from, 695

MACHINE-GUNS, GERMAN, 125, 133, 134*n*, 174, 700, 739
MAGGOTS, 63
MAIN DRESSING STATIONS, see DRESSING STNS.
MALARIA, 489*n*, 503, 541, 542, 543
MALINGERING, 460*n*
MALT TRENCH (Sk. 113), 110, 112-3
MAMETZ (Map 68; Sk. 112), 81, 935
MAN-POWER, see STRENGTH
MARICOURT (Sk. 698), 620
MARNE, RIVER (Sk. 10), crisis on, 1914, 616; Germans cross, 610, 677; French and Amers. cnter-strk., 18 *July* 1918, 678
MARQUAIX (Sk. 727), 728, 732, 737, 741, 747, 748
MARSEILLES (Plate 32), 394; quarntn. scheme at, 32, 542-6
MARTINPUICH (Plate 772; Map 88; Sk. 112), 101, 771
MASSAGE SERVICE, AUSTRALIAN, 439, 767*n*, 829
MAZE, THE, 110
MEASLES, see DISEASES
MÉAULTE (Map 88), 81
MEDICAL ARRANGEMENTS, for Austln. arty., 191-2; for dealg. wth. gas, 637; for a relif., 888; for a retreat, 636*n*; in an advce., 118-19; for Austln. cas. on W.F., 913; B. of Fromelles, 41-7; on Somme, 53-7, G.H.Q. instrns., 874-7; Somme Winter, 83-7, 101; I Anzac Corps *Feb.* 1917, 110 *et seq.*; Bullecourt btles., 131-7, 143-5; B. of Messines, 160-6, 180-2; Third Ypres: 186-9, B. of Menin Rd., 195-202, Polygon Wd., 213-15, Broodseinde, 220-3; B. of Poelcappelle, 233-6; B. of Cambrai, 251-3; on Ancre, *Mar.* 1918, 642-6; in Third Army, disorgansd., *Mar.*, 625; Villers-Bret., 638-40; Hamel, 647, 667-73; Aust. Corps, *May-July*, 1918, 655; B. of Amiens, 681, 684-91, 877-84; Hindbg. Outpost Line, 723-8; of II

MEDICAL ARRANGEMENTS.—*continued.*
Amer. Corps on rlf., 737; B. of St. Quentin Canal, 739-43; for open wfare., 884-5; see *also* ARMY MED. SERV.; CASUALTIES (EVACN. and CLEARANCE)
MEDICAL BOARDS, see BOARDS, MED.
MEDICAL COMFORTS, 31, 65*n*
MEDICAL OFFICERS, 42, 451; shortge. in A.I.F., 19; receive instrns. in gas defce., 78; as S.-B. capts., 284. **Regimental:** 44, 133, 137, 159*n*, 165, 173, 205, 207, 219*n*, 237-8, 529, 550*n*, 618, 619*n*, 632*n*, 638, 648, 653, 670, 676-7; *liaison* with S.-B. officrs., defectve., 42; 16 S.-B's allotted to, 56*n*; nature of ser., Pozières, 60; quals. needed by, 123; *liaison* wth. amb. S.-B's, 198; numbers k. and wdd., Third Ypres, 247; keep no official war diary, 275*n*; work of, at R.A.P's, 276-8, with arty. bdes., 279-80; their part in prevntg. wastge., 293-4; trtmt. gvn. by, and fnctns., 346-50, 890-2; the keystone of San. system, 507; their part in promn. of hlth., 528; chlorinatn. of water, 713
MEDICAL PROFESSION, 302-4, 799*n*; prone to wshful. thinkg., 540*n*; outlk. of physns. and surgs., 836
MEDICAL RESEARCH COMMITTEE, see COMMITTEES
MEDICAL SERVICE, see ARMY MED. SERV.
MEDICAL STORES, 56, 84, 126, 166, 170, 171, 725; supply govd. by transpt., 31; dffclty. of obtg., Somme, 59-60; essntls. at R.A.P., 63; strets. and blnkets., 86*n*, 123, 203, 222-3; "step by step" btle., 222; enormous wastge. of, 234*n*; disadvan. of large adv. dumps, 252; Advcd. Depots of, 186, 200, 684*n*, 688, 724, estabt. for, 911; Base Depots at, 813, 830, estabt. for, 911
MEDICAL TACTICS, see STRATEGY AND TACTICS
MEDICAL TRANSPORT, 23, 41, 53, 56, 113, 163, 280, 390*n*, 630, 665, 912*n*; effct. of intnl. combustn. engine on, 2; admirable orgn. of, 65-6; methods, 272; "flying fox" transprter., (Sk.), 636; G.H.Q. instructrs. *re*, for Somme, 875; by wheeled strets., 119; by lorries, 121, 132, 161, 209, 227, 229, 657; by Tnks., 272*n*; B. of Messines, 166; 171, 172*n*, 180; B. of Menin Rd., 197-8, 202; Polygon Wd., 214; Broodseinde, 221, 223; Poelcappelle, 234, 236; circuits of, 285-6, (Map) 273; for infect. cases, 552; in a retreat, 619, vital that circuits be kept, 624*n*; B. of Hamel, 669-70; B. of Amiens: pooling of, 687, ceases, 693; telescoped up, 723; prob. becomes serious, 754; condns. improve, 786. **Barges:** on Somme, 55; numbers carried by, 272*n*, 390*n*. **Horsed:** 56, 84, 117, 119, 126, 151, 217, 223, 227, 229, 234, 616, 618, 880, hvy. cas. amng. horses of, 754*n*.

GENERAL INDEX

MEDICAL TRANSPORT—continued.
Motor: 87, 132, 616, 618, 657-8, 737, 742, 748, 758n; origin of, 286, vol. aid, 287-8; dvlopmt. of, 290-1; use of char-a-bancs, 55, 65; pooling of, 65; strain on offcr. and men, Somme, 89; exhaust pipes of used to warm interior of vehcls., 155; replces. horsed transpt. 193n; "Corps com- combined convoy" formed, 223; M.A.C's formed, 25-6, estabt. 912n; women dvrs. of, 623; in French med. serv., 915-16; *Heavy*, 126, 223, 229, 233; *Light* (Ford), 26, 214, 215, 223, 229, 700n, aid-posts cleared by, 119, 126, replce. horsed wags., 670; importce. of, 697. **Hospital Trans-
ports:** 424, 426, 447; personnel embkd. from Aust. for, 829; estabt. for hosp. ship, 911. **Sledges:** for clearnce. over Somme mud, 85, 86, 87. *See also* AMBULANCE CONVOY; AMBULANCE TRAINS; RAILWAYS; STRETCHER-BEARERS
MEDICINE, PREVENTIVE, the factors invlvd., 483-512; the promn. of hlth., 514-32; the prevntn. of dis., 535-602; the signifce. of "P.U.O." in, 601-2; *see also* DISEASE PRE-
VENTN.; HEALTH PROMOTN.
MENA CAMP, 527n, 559
MENIN ROAD (Plates 173, 200, Map 206, Sk. 189), 74, 196, 201-2; con- gestn. on, 215; B. of, 184, 386, med. arrngts., 195-203, cas., 205, propn. of wdd. through A.D.S. for strets., 926, offcrs'. commnts. on evacn., 210-11
MENTAL DISORDERS, 88n, 435, 462, 473-4
MÉRICOURT (Sk. 54), 81
MÉRICOURT L'ABBÉ, 617
MERRIS (Sk. 645), 775
MESOPOTAMIA, 542, 861
MESSINES (Map 164, Sk. 167), 384, 386, 615; med. posns. reconnoitd., 39n; B. of: 158-182, (Plates) 172, 528; gen. prepns. for, 159-60, II Anzac's part in, 167-8, cas., 6-15 *June*, 180, percent. of deaths, 248; lessns. of, 359, tech. for B. of Amiens blt. on, 681
MESSINES RIDGE, 613, tactl. importce. of, 35
METEREN (Sk. 645), 532n, 775
MEUSE, RIVER (Sk. 10), 719
MÉZIÈRES, 718
"MILL COTT" (Map 224), 223
MILLENCOURT (Map 88; Sk. 626), 110n, 117, 121, 296, 625, 630
MINES, for B. of Messines, 159, 160n
MISSILES, 304-6; admissns. to fld. ambs. from various types of, 495
MOASCAR, 446n
MONS (Map 769; Sk. 10), B. of, 286, 288, 367, contrastd. wth. Somme, 618
MONTAUBAN (Plate 529; Map 88), 81, 87, 96, 124, 578
MONTBREHAIN (Map 760), captre of, 721, 762-3, 767
MONTIGNY (Sk. 82), 624
MONT ST. QUENTIN, *see* ST. QUENTIN

MONTREUIL (Sk. 22, 623), G.H.Q., B.E.F. at, 22
MOREUIL, 631, 632
MONUMENT WOOD, 638, 639
MORALE, 159n, 528, 716-17; defintn. of, 704; part of med. serv. in maintng., 705-6; "to the physical as 3 to 1," 138n, 704; highly favble., 80; Somme Winter, an extreme test of, 89, not comparble. with Flanders offnsve. 183n; of Austlns. *Sept.* 1917, 193n; of Gers., shaken by Flanders offnsve., 250; exceptnl quals. reqd. by S.-B's, 282; import. factor in prevntg. wastage, 498
MORBECQUE, 37n, 646
MORCHIES (Sk. 135), 138
MORLANCOURT (Sk. 656), 665, 666
MORPHIA, 63, 334-5; time and amt. to be noted, 162; gvn. by R.M.O. 346, equipt. for, 349, injctd. less freely, 1918, 751
MORVAL (Map 88), 49n, 81
MOTOR AMBULANCE CONVOYS, *see* AM-
BULANCE CONVOY
MOUQUET FARM (Sk. 57), 52, 63, 184, 467
MOUSSOT (MARSEILLES), 543
MOUTH INFECTIONS, 502
MOVEMENT, evacn. wthin. army zone, 268-96; of the wdd. man, 272-93; no attmpt. made to correlate with trtmt., 317n, 326n, 340; distce.-time factor in evacn., 928
MUCO-DERMAL INFECTIONS, 502
MUD, 108, 124, on the Somme: 81-2, 771, (Plate) 76, "troops literally stuck in," 83n, sledges for clearnce. over, 85, tenacious qual. of, 86, descrptn. of, 515-6, staging camps in, 89; S.-B's ordeal 1917, 111; individl. and elementl. in its malignity, 184n, 185; in B. of Broodseinde, 227-9, Passchendaele, 236, 238, 239, 240
MUMPS, *see* DISEASES
MUNITIONS, enormous distce. carried, 1916, 84n; Brit. rches. zenith in supply of, 105
MUNITION WORKERS, 814, 849n
MYALGIA, 568
MYIASIS, exp. of, at Pozières, 63

N.Y.D. GAS, 504, 512, 601, 677, 701, 714, 759
N.Y.D.N., 88n, 410, 512, 568, 601, 714
NAMPS, 621, 635
NAUROY (Map 760), 720
NEEDLE DUMP, 101
NEEDLE TRENCH, 91n
NEPHRITIS, *see* DISEASES
NEURASTHENIA, 568
NEUROSES, 462
NEUROTROPIC ECTODERMOSES, 502
NEUVE CHAPELLE (Sk. 36), 358
NEW FOREST (Plate 453), 476
NEW SOUTH WALES, number of dis. notifble. in, 553n; per cent. of volntrs. rejctd. in, 901
NEW ZEALAND, 12n; mily. serv. act in, 255n

GENERAL INDEX 1001

NEW ZEALAND EXPEDITIONARY FORCE, 866-68; outbrk. of dysentery in, 546n; arrngts. re san. sectns. 597n; D.D.M.S. of, 802n; see also ARMY MED. SERV.; DIVISIONS
NIEPPE FOREST (Map 164), 646
"NINE ELMS" (Sk. 203), 188, 230, 386, 640, 643
NISSEN HUTS, see HOUSING
NON-MILITARY EMPLOYMENT, see EDUCATN.; REPATRIATN.
NONNE BOSSCHEN (Map 206), 194, 196, 217
NOOTE BOOM (Sk. 772), 641
NOREUIL (Plate 150; Sk. 116), 119, 122, 127, 128
NOREUIL-LONGATTE ROAD, 150, 151, 152n
NOREUIL VALLEY (Plates 150, 151), arty. in, 139
"NORTH CHIMNEY" (Albert), 56, 65
NUN'S WOOD, 194, 196, 217
NURSING SERVICE, **Australian**: 363, 386, 408n, 454, 572n, 622, 641, 642, 644, 684n, 767n, 801, 810, 811n; numbers wth. Nos. 1 and 2 A.G.H. incrsd., 11n; some go to Italy 254n; serv. on Amb. trains, 392n; numbers on staff of C.C.S's and Gen. Hosps., 398; number wth. No. 3 A.G.H., 402; with Fifth Army in retreat, 618n; contrlld. by Matron-in-Chief, 814, 815; numbers who embkd. for o'seas, 829; numbers in Salonica, 856; numbers on estabt. of med. units, 911, 912n; repatn. of, 799, (Plate) 808. **British**: (Q.A.I.M.N.S.), attd. to C.C.S's, 26n, 188, 364, 368, 684n, to adv. optg. centres, 70, 120n, to Amb. trains, 392, 624; as anaesthtsts., 775n

OPERATING CENTRE, ADVANCED, 88n, 132, 357, 358, 359, 361, 782-6; at Warloy, 56, 70-1, 930; at Pozières dress. stn., 120, 121n; No. 32 Brit. C.C.S. for abdomens and chests, 188; trtmt. at, 341; at Authie, 384
OPHTHALMIA, 543
ORTHOPAEDICS, see SURGERY
OSTEO-ARTHRITIS, 435, 500
OUDERDOM (Map 273; Sk. 76), 75n, 213
OULTERSTEENE (Plates 349, 364; Sk. 772), 386, 640, 641, 642, 775

"P.B." MEN, see CATEGORIES
PACKS, 124, wght. of, 527
PAIN, see WOUNDS
PALESTINE CAMPAIGN, 104, 124n, 542, 584n, 679, 703, 861
PARA-TYPHOID, see DISEASES, **Typhoid**
PARIS, 31, 397, 612, 677
PARKHOUSE (Plate 18; Map 452), A.A.M.C. Trg. Depot at, 17, 18, 474, 476, 830
PASSCHENDAELE (Plates 232, 240; Sk. 185), tctl. importce. of, 35; adv. twds., 219; B. of, 235-40, 607, 771, 949n

PATHOLOGY, in the wdd. man, 304-10; in Base Hosps., 412; dept. of C.C.S., 369; B.E.F. Adviser in, 508n, 544; A.I.F. Adviser in, 418, 508n, 560
PAY, see FINANCE
PEDICULOSIS, 27, 99, 499n, 503, 570-3
PEMPHIGUS CONTAGIOSUS, 543
PENSIONS, 497, 526, 901, 902, 908; condns. liable to cause or aggravate dis., 89; factors in attrbtn., 485, 506, 523; prophylactic treatmt. inflces. claims for, 511; phys. environmt. of W.F. on, 514-15; prob. of prevntg. permanent. disablty, 559-60
PERHAM DOWNS (Map 452), 468, 561; Training Group "A" at, 17; No. 1 Command Depot at, 441, 450, 457
PÉRONNE (Plate 732; Map 769; Sk. 51, 698), occpn. of, 680n, 696
PERNOIS (Map 68), 684n, 725
PETROL TIN, 77, 343. See also WATER
PHARMACEUTICAL SERVICE, AUSTRALIAN, 402, 829; in C.C.S. carried rank of Hon. Lieut., 369; augmenting importnce. of, 370; to be dealt with in Vol. III, 767n; served in A.I.F. wth. commissnd. and non-commissnd. rank, 828
PHARYNGITIS, 554
PHYSIQUE, of A.I.F., 32; deteriortn. in, of recruits in depots, 472-5; reltn. of equipmt. to, 528; high standard of Austln., Amer. opinion, 705; Aust. concurs in lowerg. of stand., 708; questn. of dilutn., 715-16; Gen. Fetherston on Brit. recruits, 715n, 716n; Howse's fight to retain stand. of, 817n, 842-56; phys. stand. of A.A.M.C., 904-5; stands. of hght. and vision, reduced, 902n; stand. of rfcts. rejctd. in Eng., 903. See also HEALTH; RECRUITS; REINFORCEMENTS
PICARDY, 55n, 180; adv. in, 680n
PICQUIGNY (Map 68), 635
PILCKEM RIDGE (Sk. 185), B. of, 184, 189, 190, 191, 248
PILES, 568
PINNEY'S AVENUE (Sk. 41), 41, 42
PLAGUE, 490, 503, 541
PLEURISY, 501, 568
PLOEGSTEERT WOOD (Map 164; Sk. 36), 160, 165, 169, 279n
PNEUMONIA, see DISEASES
POELCAPPELLE (Sk. 185), B. of, 185, 232-5
POLIO-ENCEPHALITIS, 502
POLYGON WOOD (Map 216; Sk. 185), 194; B. of, 185, 213-18; enquiry into cause of hvy. S.-B. cas., 218; proportn. of wdd. passed through A.D.S. for stret. cases, 926
POMMIÈRES REDOUBT, 88
PONT D'ACHELLES (Map 164), 164, 166, 168, 172, 175-7, 181
PONT REMY, 620, 635, 684n
POPERINGHE (Map 273; Sk. 639), 386, 640
PORT À CLOUS (Sk. 41), 37n, 41
PORTUGUESE ARMY, 606n, 610, 640
POTIJZE (Sk. 224), 233
POZIÈRES (Plates 64, 65; Map 88; Sk. 57, 116), 92, 123, 132, 275n, 347,

POZIÈRES—continued.
467; captre. of, 58-9; "no longer in existence," 62n; entraining centre at, 113, 120, 121, 138; B. of Pozières Hghts., 49n, 51, 52, 59 et seq.
PREVENTION OF DISEASE, see DISEASE PREVENTN.; SANITATION
PREVENTION OF WASTAGE, see WASTAGE
PREVENTIVE MEDICINE, see DISEASE PREVENTN.; HEALTH PROMOTN.
"PRISON HOUSE," YPRES (Sk. 190), 190, 223
PRISONERS OF WAR, **Australian**, 39, 48, 59, 61, 134, 140n, 630, 708. **British**, 861n. **German**: 80, 167, 178, 209, 670, 672, 690n, 695, 728-30, 761, used for clearing wdd., 207, 215, 225, 226, 666, 730-1, 732, 745, (Plates) 708, 709, employed at No. 3 A.G.H., 403, 801
PROMOTIONS AND APPOINTMENTS, 791; in A.A.M.C., 648, 774; of med. offcrs., 834-8; of N.C.O's, 842. *See also* MEDICAL OFFICERS; NURSING SERV.
PROPAGANDA, 235n; Allied, 115n; Ger., 1
PROVEN (Sk. 203), 161, 179, 186
PROVOST CORPS, forms "Stragglers' Posts," 56, 634, 669; Asst. Provost Marshal, road control devlyes. on, 163n; prohibts. use of P. of W. as S.-B's, 226n; his part in water supply, 590
PROYART (Sk. 698), 692, 724, 725
PSYCHO-NEUROSES, 435, 498
PUCHEVILLERS (Map 68; Sk. 620), 619, 623, 625
PYODERMIA, 570, 572, 574
PYOGENIC INFECTIONS, 310, 502
PYREXIA OF UNCERTAIN ORIGIN (P.U.O.), *see* DISEASES

QUARANTINE, Internat. system of, 541-2; at Marseilles, 542; leakge. of cases despite, 545-6
QUARRY, THE (POZIÈRES), (Sk. 62), 64
QUARRY, POST (Map 760), 669, 671, 746, 763
QUARRY SIDING, MONTAUBAN (Sk. 112), 82, 87, 88
QUARTERMASTER-GENERAL'S BRANCH, 12n, 246n, 290, 306, 518n; importce. of, 367; its responsblty. in prevntn. of wastge., 27, in matters of hlth., 77; co-ops. with med. dept., 242n, 498, 509; baths and launds. under, 78n, 94n, 578, and road control, 163n; its part in housg., 522, in water supply, 590, 592. **Quartermasters**, 88, 369, 378, **815**
QUÉANT (Sk. 130), 108, 127
QUEEN ALEXANDER'S IMPERIAL NURSING SERVICE (Q.A.I.M.N.S.), *see* NURSING SERV.
QUEENSLAND, 822n, 845n; percent. of volntrs. rejctd. in, 901
QUENNEMONT FARM (Map 760), 723, 743
QUERRIEU (Map 668; Sk. 626), 627, 628, 666, 670

RADIOGRAPHY, 383, 386, 439; X-ray units, 71n, 186, 368-9, 644, 776, 777

RAIDS, 1916, 37-39; Aust., 27; Brit., 107; Ger. at Bois Grenier, 38; on Lagnicourt, 137-8
RAILWAY DUMP (Map 224; Sk. 238), 237, 241n
RAILWAYS, 88, 209, 219, 220, 451, 718; grwth. and med. use of, 23; trains delayed through derailmt., 117; gt. number of wdd. rch. Base hosp. by, 390n; importce. of reltns. betwn. Rail. Op. Divn. and C.C.S., 624; railbds.: adved. with vigour, 121, army area defined by, 269; evacn. schemes hinge on, 622; determine rate of movt. of army in advce. or retreat, 623. **Decauville**, 83n, 84, 132. **Broad gauge**, 83n, 87, 94, 113, 117, 118n, 120, 188, 221, 225-6, 233, 241. **Light**, 81n, 139, 165, 170, 172, 196-7, 202, 211, 226, 227, 285n, 575, 761, bring cas. almost from front line, 101, rlf. to S.-B's but distressing to patnts., 111-12, carry ammunitn., 112n, W.W. evac. by, 163, 171-2, 229, 762n, failre., B. of Menin Rd., 211. **French**, 81n, 113. *See also* AMBULANCE TRAINS
RANK, of med. offcrs., A.A.M.C., 834-5; opinns. re status of S.-B. offcr., 284
RATIONS, 82, 89, 222, 519-20, 886; schools for cooks, 520; calorie value of, 520; supplemented by local prchase., 31; problm. debated at San. Conf., 96; frnt. line trps. receive prefernce. in, 140n; fld. ovens for roastg. of, 199; wght. carried by soldr., 527; "rum," 530-1; high stand. of, 629; in Austln. hosps., Eng., 872-3. *See also* COOKING
RAVELSBERG (Map 164), 616n
RECEIVING STATIONS, *see* CASUALTIES; COLLCTG. AND CLEARNCE.
RECONNAISSANCE, *see* RAIDS
RECORDS AND RETURNS, 163, 626n, 725, 858, 880; orgn. and value of, 652; of wdgs. by sites, 47-8; gen. principles, 176; nom. rolls and daily wires, 177n; Corps Central Record Bureau, 203, 210-11, 248n; inoc. entry in pay book, 478, 538; tables of dis. based on wkly. retns., 490n; certain Austln. records destroyd., 491n; notifctn. of infect. dis., 539n, 546-50; daily retn. of scabies, 550; "died of wounds," 669; instns. re, 747n; in combined operns. with Amer. tps., 747n, 756, Amer. unaccustomd. to Austln. regs., 758; W.W. recordd. at A.D.S., importnce. of persnl. records, 793; demob. problms., 794; arrngts. for B. of Amiens, 883-4; to be rendd. by bearer divns., 887; spcl. rtns., 893 *et seq.*; A. and D. Bks.: 152, 177n, 883, nine hundred dis. entities entered in, 494, figs. for intestnl. fluxes based on partial count, 586n. *See also* ARMY FORMS
RECREATION, in training area nr. Albert, 96, 140; in *Sept.* 1917, 193n; in Aust. Corps, *May-July* 1918, 665; in Command Depots, 465-6; "Anzac Leave," 717, 768

GENERAL INDEX 1003

RECRUITS, 704, 709; corse. of, 447; the training grps., 471-7; qual. deteriorates, 254; signifce. of phys., 527; functnl. data, 528; lower stand. of, 715, 716n; fitness of: by effcts. of Somme, 472-5, Fetherston-Howse corresp., 472, 900-3, causes of unfitness, 473-4, Col. Soltau's remarks, 568, dent. unfitness, 418; the "Battle of the Standards," 843-56, a crit. examinatn. of the issue, 855; for A.A.M.C., 475. *See also* ENLISTMENTS; REINFORCEMENTS

RED CROSS SOCIETY, 326n, 577, 743; supplies med. comforts, 31; provides refreshmnts. for wdd., 210; diffce. bet. activties. of Brit. and Austln., 391n; value of work after Armstce., 797. **American:** 302n, 557n, 754, 757, instrumnts., etc., obtd. from, 758, wdd. refreshed by, 758, *Research Socty. Reports* by, 931n. **Australian:** 65n, 97, 140n, 401, 429-30, 439, 725, improve rest stns., 140n, works in fwd. zone, 65n, 628, provides surg. equipmnt., 401, 662, equipmnt. for resusc. teams, 663, 842, D.M.S., A.I.F. Ch. Commnr. of, 842, depot at Amiens in advce. of any other, 688n. **British:** 151, 208, 288n, 870. *See also* GENEVA CONVTN.

RED FARM (Sk. 190), 190, 229-30

RED LODGE ROAD, 279n

REGIMENTAL AID POSTS, *see* AID POSTS

REGIMENTAL MEDICAL SERVICE, 89, 169, 830; estabmt., 1918, 911, 912n; experce. of Somme cardinal in devlpmt. of, 70n; 3rd Aust. Div. scheme for Messines, 165; med. arrngts., Menin Rd., 198; responsble. for san. serv., 507; training for, 895; numbers embkd. from Aust., 829; German, 921. *See also* MEDICAL OFFCRS.; STRETCHER-BEARERS; TRAINING

REGIMENTS, **American:** *130th*, 682n. *131st*, 682n, at Hamel, 673, Chipilly, 692. *132nd*, at Hamel, 673, 674. **British:** *Devons* and *Gordon Highlanders*, 145, 153. *Suffolks*, 52. *Royal Welch*, 153. **German:** *Prussian Guards*, 145n. *202nd Res.*, 582n

REINFORCEMENTS, training of, 16, 471-7, 838-9; from Egypt, 20; Aust. Base Depots for, 34; effect of Somme on, 76, 448, 449; ancillary serv. combed for effctvs. for infy., 184n; 6th Aust. Div. personnel absorbd. as, 193n; A.A.M.C.: 237n, 474, 828, 904, med. offcrs., 832-4, numbers embked from Aust., 829, transfrs. to combatant arms, 715n; qual. as importnt. as strngth., 255; mainly recvrd. men, 1918, 258; system for ensuring fitness, 420-1; med. responsblty. re 447-8; supnly aft. Somme, 448; unfitness of, 473-4, 477, 844-5, 854; propn. of, to convalesnts. in depots, 449n; the professnl. problm. in "boarding," 460-4; recvrd. men and new drfts., 468-9, 477-8; qual. at critical stage, 470; deteriorn. in qual., 472; drfts. inoc.,

REINFORCEMENTS—*continued.*
478-9; from Aust., infectd. wth. mumps and measles, 564; depots unable to keep up drfts., 649, 708; bns. to be broken up to furnish, 717, 768; the "Battle of the Standards," 843-56; a critical exam. of the issue, 855; corresp. *re* fitness of, 900-3; not up to stand., 902, 903; I Anzac Corps Rfct. Camp, 379, 447, 479. *See also* ENLISTMENTS; RECRUITS

RELAPSING FEVER, *see* DISEASES

RELAY POSTS (Plates 150, 241, 773), 135, 727, 741, 747 756, 762; treatmt. at 350; motor, 670, 754; estab., admin., and orgn. at, 657-8

REMY SIDING (Map 203; Sk. 36, 203), 203, 357, 358, 365, 373, 386; C.C.S's at, 161, 179, 186, 195, 241, 332

REPARATIVE TREATMENT, *see* TREATMENT

REPATRIATION AND DEMOBILISATION, 443: early stage, 790; tentative plans, 791; Dept. of Repat. and Demob. formed, 791; policy, 792; involvemts., 793; drafts and quotas leave France, 792; disposg. of records, 794; provisn. for entitlement. problms., 795; diffclts., 796; of the A.A.M.C., 799-801; nonmily. employmnt., 776n, 795, 798

RESEARCH, 418, 484, 557n, 585, 661, 839n; initiatn. of experimt. 314; armies set aside experimntl. stns. for, 332n; on "wound shock," 335-7, 947-8; and haemorrhage, 953; into causes of dis., 486-8; into measures for dis. prevntn., 571; into life hist. of louse and itch-mite, 571n; into tr. fever, 580n; the A.A.M.C. and the scient. problms., 836-8; at the Base: 412, med., 394-6, into aetiology of dis., 413, scientific, 662, the srch. for antisepsis, 319-23; at C.C.S's: clinical, 26, renowned centre at Remy Siding, 203

RESEARCH COMMITTEE, *see* COMMITTEE

RESPIRATORY TRACT INFECTIONS, *see* DISEASES

REST STATIONS, 27, 72, 88, 90, 97, 110, 163, 414, (Plates) 293, 629; "special," at Fromelles (Port à Clous), 41; "Shell shock" at Vadencourt, 1916, 65; divisional, 75, 76, 110n, 121; replaced by "divisnl. collectg. stns.," 634; *Corps*, 90, 97, 163, 378, 640; at Buire, 1916, 84, 88-9; discomfort of, 97; at Reinfct. Camp, 634; prevent "army" wastage, 92; promote "return to duty," 246; C.C.S's, as, 258, 387, 714; fld. ambs. as, 295-6

RESUSCITATION, 352, 367; "Fld. Amb. Resus. Teams," 659-61, 663, 664, 699, 725; genesis of idea, 662-3, 953-7; A.I.F. estabmt., 268n; equipmnt., 955-6; work at Hamel, 672; lent 29th Amer. Div., 742; transfusn. of blood by, 777. *See also* SURGERY; SURGICAL TEAMS

RETURN TO DUTY, 76, 269, 356, 359, 367, 378, 404, 425, 438, 443, 449, 468, 774n; importce. in modern war, 3; the rest stns. in, 177, 246, 258;

GENERAL INDEX

RETURN TO DUTY—*continued*.
from C.C.S's, 296; from base depots, 258, 418-22; from A.I.F. Depots, U.K., 446-55; the "categories," 456-7; hardng. and trg. for, 466-70; during adv. to victory, 1918, 714, 761, 825. *See also* MAN-POWER; STRENGTH
Reveille, quoted, 200-1, 531n, 834n
RHEUMATIC FEVER, 502
RHEUMATISM, 90, 99, 462, 473-4, 500, 504, 560, 568
RHEUMATOID ARTHRITIS, 504
RIBEMONT (Map 668; Sk. 82), 81, 96, 124
RIENCOURT (Map 68; Sk. 122), 119, 122, 130, 139
RIFLE VILLA (Sk. 38), 42, 45
ROADS, 94, 121, 139, 196, 240, 241, 656, 658, 666, 671n, 745; in Somme Winter, 82, 85, 87; in "Alberich" adv., 111; Haig's order *re*, 118n; brk-down in thaw, 117; repair of, by fld. ambs., 125; traffic control on, 163n; plank circuit, Third Ypres, 220, 240n; some factors in repair, 220n
ROISEL (Sk. 749), 741, 742, 770
ROLLESTONE (Map 452), 17, 561
RONSSOY (Map 760), 754
ROSEOLA, 537n, 542, 543, 559
ROSIÈRES (Sk. 680), 620
ROUEN (Sk. 10), 161, 425, 672, 684, 779; Convlscnt. Depot at, 27; No. 1 A.G.H. at, 30, 426, 778, (Plates) 412, 413; Brit. scheme evacn. based on, 54; Third Echelon at, 394; Brit. Gen. and stat. hosps. at, 397
ROUGE DE BOUT (Sk. 38), 41
ROULERS (Sk. 10), 159, 184
ROUMANIA, 104, 606, 860
RUBELLA, 502, 554
RUSSIA, 104, 105, 138n, 542, 545, 606, 607, 860, 861
RUSSO-JAPANESE WAR, 261, 312

ST. ACHEUL (Sk. 685), 690, 928
STE. EMILIE (Map 760; Sk. 749), dress. stn. at, 741, 755-7, 761
ST. OMER (Sk. 22, 645), 22, 179n, 609, 642, 643
ST. QUENTIN (Sk. 620, 726), 719; capture of 31 *Aug.*-2 *Sept.*, 1918, 680n; B. of St. Quentin Canal, 29 *Sept.*-2 *Oct.*, 680, 699-700, 720-31, 737-62
SAILLY-LE-SEC (Sk. 656), 617
SAILLY-SUR-LA-LYS (Sk. 38), 577
SALISBURY PLAIN (Plate 452; Map 452; Sk. 17), 446, 451, 453, 460; camps on, 14, 17, 19, dis. in, 560-5; 3rd Div. orgnd. and trained on, 185n; A.I.F. Depots on, 795
SALONICA, 679, 856
SANDFLY FEVER, 503
SANITARY APPLIANCES, 600, 938-41; disinfctrs.: delousg. chamber, 94, Hunter's rly. van, 543, 575, Rus. Pit delouser, 573, 575, 712, (Diag.) 588, mass actn. apparatus, 575, the "Foden" lorry, 573, 575, 598, (Plate) 580; insulated shed for dryg. clothes, 95; incntrs., 587, 940; latrines, 939; *see also* SANITATION.

SANITARY SECTIONS, 73, 77, 186, 510n; O.C's of, attnd. San. confs. *May* 1916, 32; their plce. in water control, 77, 600-1, (Plate) 529; resp. for delousg., 94; work in Somme Winter, 96-7; new stand. of san. discip., 591; control and functns. of, 596-9, 935-8. **Australian:** 140-1, 475, 710-11, 830; establt. of, 596, 911, 912n; personnel embkd. from Aust. for, 829; control and fnctns. of, 141, 532, 892-3; thr. work in France, 593-601. **No. 1**, arrves. in France, 29, 96; allotted to 2nd Aust. Div., 595. **No. 2**, 587, 600, 713, 724, 741; arrves. in France, 29, 96; allotted to 1st Aust. Div., 595; mthods. adopted by, 141, 540n, 532n, 548n, 589, 594n. **No. 3**, 599, 712n. **No. 4**, 96, 587, 711n, 724; arrves. in France, 29. **No. 5**, 712n, 741; arrves. in France, 29, 96. **No. 6**, 559n. **Canadian**, 597n. **New Zealand**, 597n
SANITARY TRAIN, *see* ARMY MED. SERV., AMERICAN
SANITATION, 73, 140-1, 399, 401, 532n, 569-70, 595n, 615, 710-14; effct. of Crimea War on, 483; W.O. policy based on exp. of S.A. War, 490; evoltn. of, in Brit. Army, 490; ill reports, in Gallip., 32; Gallip. and France compared, 582; close supvsn. in Egypt, 543; San. Conf. on, *May* 1916, 32; in prev. of fly-breeding, 73, (Plate) 581; orgn. and mthds. of san. serv. B.E.F., 507-12, 580-93, 935-41; on the Somme, 73; A.I.F. San. depln., 90, 101, 509, 547, 590, 711; of a Gen. Hosp., 399, 401; system of dir. agst. dis., 506, 552, 566-93, 712-13, 938-41; co-opn. the keynote, 509-10; A.I.F. Depots camps svd. by civic san. serv., 559n; significe. of terms "san." and "hyg.," 594n; status of Regtl. san. detchmt., 594n, 895; Barber's "Sanitary Standing Orders," 652; establt. of a bn. "sanitary squad," 912n. *See also* BATHS AND LAUNDRIES; DISEASE PREVENTN.; FLIES; LESSONS OF THE WAR; LICE; SANITARY APPLNCS.
SAUSAGE VALLEY (Plate 65; Sk. 57), 52, 56
SCABIES, *see* DISEASES
SCARLET FEVER, 501, 543, 549, 550, 556, 557
SCARPE, RIVER, 106, 145; Btles. of, 129n, 138, 142, 680n, 695
SEA TRANSPORT SECTIONS, 814; personnel embkd. from Aust., for, 829; establt. 911, 912n
SEALE HAYNE, neurolgl. hosp., 462
SENLIS (Map 93), 616
SEPTIC INFECTIONS, 502
SEPTIC TRAUMATIC ABRASIONS, 99, 503, 567
SERA, use of by French and Gers., 309, 310n; anti-gas-gangrene, 309, 413, 777; anti-dysenteric, 309n; anti-tetanic 70, 126, 163, 177, 188, 352,

GENERAL INDEX 1005

SERA—continued.
642, 748, 880, D.M.S. A.I.F. purchses. supplies, 1915, 309n, gvn. for tr. foot, 100
SERBIA, 104, 542, 545, 860
SERVICES OF MAINTENANCE, 21-2, 762; importce. of med., 3, 260; admin. serv. of I Anzac, 53, 66-9; effct. on, of Gough's decsn. to attck. H'hurg Line, 115; neglect of, in Brit. Army, 569n; in water control, 589-93; see also ADMINISTRATION
"SHELL SHOCK," see DISEASES
SHOCK, WOUND, see WOUND SHOCK
SHRAPNEL CORNER (Map 206), 201, 209
SICKNESS, 33, 39, 73, 79-80, 90, 98, 113, 213n, 255-6, 367, 409, 418, 485, 547, 586, 646, 669, 709, 774, 779, 832; causes of, nosological tables, 495-504; defntn. of, 270-1; a major med. prob., 86-7; impfct. apprectn. of causes of brkdown, 91; camouflage of, 97n; rate in spring less than in winter, 154; prncple. causes, winter, 1916-17, 242; retntion. of sick men, 293-6; treated by R.M.O's, 294, 528, 529; percent. in base hosps., France, 410; in A.I.F. Depots U.K., 453-4, 561-5; prime factor in wastge., 481; comparison of rates B.E.F. and Gallip., 494, 581-3; dis. of dirt and squalor, 566-8; in adv. to victory, 710-14; see also DISEASE PREVENTION, DISEASES
SIDCUP, 341, 823-4, 830
SIEGFRIED LINE, see HINDENBURG LINE
"SIMON'S POST" (Map 216), 215
SKIN INFESTATIONS, 78, 503, 522n, 568
SLEDGES, 85, 86, 87
SMALL BOX RESPIRATOR, 78, 160n, 167, 193n, 608
SMALLPOX, see DISEASES
"SMITH'S ROAD," 220
SOISSONS (Map 769; Sk. 607), 610
SOLLUM, 543
SOMME, RIVER (Plate 628; Map 668; Sk. 115, 611), 361, 366, 382, 384, 616, 618, 620, 629, 633, 635, 658, 678, 696; river a bad boundary, 692. **Battles of, 1916**, 49-73, 358, 368, 430, 477n, 651; G.H.Q's preparatory measures for, 874-77; surg. moves up, 329; offnsve. opens 1 *July*, 51-3; Austln. partptn. in, 52 *et seq.*, ends, 89; cost, 73, 102-3; hlth. of trps. during, 72n; "lessons," 359; effcts., 447-9, 472; probs. created by, 467; moral and phys. domince. wth. Allies, aftr., 50. **Somme Winter:** 74-103, 614; mud in, 515-6, (Plate) 76. **"Second Battle" of Mar.-Apr. 1918:** 606-46; med. sit., 616n, 617-24; gaps in line, 28-30 *Mar.*, 627; focal point of Allied strategy, 631; crisis south of, *Apr.* 632; operns. *May-June*, 665; evacn. of wdd., 669; Haig plans offsve. on, 677; Allies adv., 695-8, 719, 779, med. evnts. in, 697-8; see also LESSONS OF THE WAR

SOUTH AFRICANS, in B.E.F., 782
SOUTH AFRICAN WAR, 261, 281, 312, 490, 527
SOUTHALL (Map) 452, 341
SOUTHAMPTON (Map 452), 10, 422, 426, 451
SPLINTS, often improvsd. by S.-B's, 63; cock-up, 373; Gooch, 349; Liston's long, 63; rt.-angle, 63; rifle, 348; **Thomas**, 155, 178, 182, 306n, 315, 317n, 329n, 349, 477, 661, 731, 750, (Plates) 348; applied in frnt. line, 162, 165, 170, 222-3; instructns. for, 942-5; regtl. S.-B's become expert at, 346; type and exemplar of shock prevntr., 947; small for arm, 348
"SPRING STREET," 173n, 174
STAGING CAMPS, 82n, 89, 111, 213
STANDARDS, see PHYSIQUE; RECRUITS; REINFORCEMENTS
Standing Orders for A.A.M.C., 652-3, 889-99
STATISTICS, **General:** A.I.F. troops in U.K. 1916, 18n; weight of soldiers' equipmt., 527; baths and launds., 577-8; Brit. war efft. on W.F., 782; analysis of R.M.O's sick parade, 529; evacns., B.E.F. to U.K., 1914-18, 409, 425. **Conv. Depots:** No. 1 Aust., in Havre, 421; *A.I.F. Depots in U.K.*, invalids to Aust. 1917-18, 446, strength, 451, sickness, 1916-18, 454-5, O.T.B., 1917-18, 470, of invalidg. from, 853-4, deaths, 1917-18, 565; "B" Class, 909. **Med. Units:** Fld. Ambs., 178; detailed analysis, 495-504; C.C.S's, 179, 384, 385, 568, 644, 774, 777-8; Gen. Hospa., 414, 778, 779-81. **Of Return to Duty:** 480; from Aust., 926n; **Recruits:** unfit, arrivg. in U.K., 473-5, 849; rfcts., *Aug.* 1917, 474; rtnd. without service, 850, 902; rejectns., 901. **Casualties (General):** of A.I.F. on W.F., 1916, 39, 448, 1917, 243-5, 1918, 649, 1916-18, 490-7, 864-5; Aust. and Amer. (Hindbg. Line), 744, 751, 761. **Casualties (Analysis of)** wounding, 304-5, 495; av. wastage (Graph) 493, *cf.* with Gallip., (Graph) 494; detld. nosological anal., 495-504; of dysentery, W.F. and Gallip., 581, 586, gastro-intestnl. dis., 590n; of wdd., death rate, 787; propn. k. to wdd., 47, 125, 157, 217-8, 225, 235, 236, 249, 305n, 618n; an import. feature, 138; a confusn. in terms, 275n; propn. stretchers to others, 137, 154, 179n, 210, 234, 274, 672, 761, 926-7; propn. of wdd. operated at C.C.S., 155n, 248, 372, 377, 386
—BATTLE CASUALTIES, Fromelles, 48; on Somme, 51, 59, 61, 72, 73; A.I.F. Ger. retiremt. *Mar.* 1917, 118, 125, 128; Lagnicourt, 137; Bullecourt btles., 134, 146, 151, 152, 156, 157; Messines, 167-8, 171, 175, 180, from gas, 169n; A.I.F. *July-Aug.* 191, 192; Menin Rd., 205; Polygon Wd., 217; B. of Cambrai, 252; wdd.

STATISTICS—continued.
admttd. to Brit. C.C.S's 1917-18, 331n; wdd. carried by barge and M.A.C., 390n; Brit. 21 Mar.-20 Apr. 1918, 618; gas, through Aust. Fld. Ambs., 637; 1st Aust. Div. Apr. 1918, 646; 2nd Aust. Div. May-June, 666; at Hamel, 670, 671-2; by gas July 1918, 676-7; number through 6th Fld. Amb., 690; Aust. Corps 8-21 Aug., 694; A.I.F. 22 Aug.-4 Sept., 702; A.I.F. Apr.-Sept., 708, 18-19 Sept., 723, 728-30, 2nd Aust. Div. 3-5 Oct., 762-3, A.I.F. 29 Sept.-2 Oct. 763, 27th and 30th Amer. Divs. Oct., 763n; in A.A.M.C., 136, 153
—NON-BATTLE, nosologcl. prncpls. adopted, 490-1; tr. foot. 91-2; A.I.F. evac. Nov. 1916-Feb. 1917, 98; sick rate I Anzac, 1917, 242; of tetanus, 309-10; case mortlty. from gas-gangrene, 310; percents. in base hosps., A.I.F., 410; A.I.F., 1916-19, 501-4, 535-6, 864-5; of enteric, 1916-18, 539; typhus, 545; in B.E.F., 547; infect. dis., I Anzac, Mar. 1916-Feb. 1917, 550; mumps, II Anzac, 556; incdnce. of pneumn. in B.E.F. and A.E.F., 557n; in A.I.F. Depots, 561-2, 564-5, from C.S.F., 563; of intestnl. flux, 586; A.I.F., 1918, 705
STEENWERCK (Map 164; Sk. 639), 161, 178, 179n, 382, 640, 642
STORES, see MEDICAL STORES
STORMY TRENCH, 109
STOVES, for heatg., 89, 94; primus, 343; Soyer's cookers, 345
STRAGGLERS, see PROVOST CORPS
STRATEGY AND TACTICS, in war of 1914-18, 1; entrnchd. lines in France and Flndrs. in 1915, 35; "Western" schl. of, 104n. **Allied:** strat. resve. of Allies, 606; raids, 39; Fromelles an "awful warning," 42-4; Haig's, in Somme Btle., 52, 102; Gough's tacts., 52, Mouquet Fm., 61; hlth. as a factor, 79-80; Haig's in 1917, 105; tanks, 131n; for Bullecourt, 145; Haig's for Flndrs. offsve., 158-9; the "leapfrog" battle, Messines, 160; Allied failure to brk. through, 240; effct. on med. ser., 268; new tacts., 1918, 603, 607, 608; Somme Vlly. Mar., 1918, 631; B. of Hamel, 666-7; Aug.-Oct., 1918, 679-83, 687; of Foch and Haig, 694-5; Hindenbg. Line operns., 718-21; for B. of St. Quentin Canal, 738-9. **German:** in retrmt., 1917, "Alberich," 50, 102, 105, 107-10; effect of Arras bttle. on, 129; conservatn. of fce., 606; Ger. plans for 1918, 607, 619; Ludendorff's aim, 28 Mar., 627; for Apr., 636. **Attrition Warfare:** 3-5, 49, 51, 61, 105, 232-59, 360, 367, 382, 406; technique of, 67n; results of "Somme," 80, 102; a maj. element in Allied, 138n; in Flanders Offsve., 158-9; "step-bystep" offsve., 183 et seq., 211-12; Third Ypres, logical consummatn. of mthds., 183n; price of attritn., 249-51;

STRATEGY AND TACTICS—continued.
end of B of Cambrai, 250-3; evolutn. in med. ser. during, 260-6; offset to reslts. of, 606; problm. of housg. in, 931n. **Medical:** 146, 190, 276, 301n; a useful illstrn. of, 127; impropr. interfce. by Army commndr. in, 142n; infice. by "stretcher cases" and "W.W.," 274; the R.A.P. and R.M.O., 276-8; prevntn. of Btle.-cas., 498; "san. dcpln." an element in, 510; med. system blt. up during, 617; in Aust. Corps, 634, reorgnd., 647; of Aust. C.C.S's, 643; "the leapfrog" technique, 685-6; med. arrgts., 18 Sept., 727; A.D.S. v. M.D.S., 765-6
STRAZEELE (Sk. 645), 646
STRENGTH, Brit. in France, Mar., 1916, 7n; A.I.F. in Eng. June 1916, 20; I Anzac, 1917, 193; avge. of A.I.F., July-Dec. 1917, 246n; A.I.F. Apr. and Sept., 1918, 440; avge. daily, A.I.F., 1916-18, 539; of Allies, on W.F., 21 Mar., 1918, 606n; of A.I.F., Mar. 1918, 614; reductn. of in Aust. Corps, 650n; . reln. to morale, 716-17; of Aust. Corps, cd. not be maintnd., 717; of Aust. units grtly. reduced, 718, 731, 734; of B.E.F. at Armstce., 782. **ManPower:** maintnce. of, 254-6, 607, 649-50, 701, 703-18, responsblty. of D.M.S., A.I.F., 97, part of med. ser., 140, 253, 263, 481, ancillary servs. combed, Aug. 1917, 184n, dis. prevn., 242-3, steps taken, 258-9, aims, 484-5, importce. of minor demobilities, 568. See also ESTABLISHMENT:; RETURN TO DUTY
STRETCHER-BEARERS, both sides oft. co-op., 60n; long carries of, 62, 126, in mud, 84-5, (Plate) 76, in the open, 85; thr. ordeal in Ancre morass, 111; "shoulder-high" carry, 58, (Plate) 288; regtl. and amb. co-op., 136; disposn. of, 5 May 1917, 152n; thr. morale, 153; work commended, 156; at B. of Menin Rd., 210, 211; Polygon Wd., 214; numbers reqrd., 249; hvy. cas., Mar.-Apr. 1918, 618; maintn. liaison btwn. R.M.O. and fld. amb., 619n; bravery at Villers-Bret., of, 666; Aust. effcy. as, 706, 716; work wth. Amers., 745; use of Thomas splnt. by, 942-5. **Ambulance:** work with rgtl. S.-B's, 58, 136, use wheeled strets., 58; work in mrng. mist, 60n; in Somme Winter, 85; relays of 6-8, 86, 111n; in relays, 120, 125; not allowed in frnt. of R.A.P's, 133; rsves., 144; hvy. tasks, 147; Bullecourt, the S.-B's day, 149; "shlder-high" carry, 149-50, (Plate) 288; shelling of, 154n; B. of Messines, 166, 170, 174, under gas barrage, 169; B. of Menin Rd., 199-200, 207; need for resves., 211; Polygon Wd., 214, 218, resves. and infty. used, 215, ineffcy. of

GENERAL INDEX 1007

STRETCHER-BEARERS—continued.
liaison wth. R.A.P's, 217n; engnrs. assist to prepare relay posts for, 222; Broodseinde, 223, 225, 227, 228-9, 231n, long carry, 226; Passchendaele, 237, 239-40, hdships of, assisting infty., 234, all availble. men assist, 13 Oct. 239; relays of, 281; quals. reqd., 282; status of S.-B. offcr., 283-4. **Regimental:** estab., 16 per bn., 77, 912n, increased, 60, 63; tactics, 37, 132, 198, in raids, 38; their work at Fromelles, 44n, 47; in Somme Btle., 58; at Pozières, 63; cas., 19 July-5 Sept., 73; mthds. of, 105n; special trg., 109n; long carries, 1917, 111; not allowed in rear of R.A.P's, 133; collect under white flag, 135; Amb. bearers co-op. with, 136; a dramatic illustration of work, 147; forward R.A.P's a help to, 164; rapid clearnce. Menin Rd., 207; Poelcappelle, 234, Red Cross disregarded, 235; Passchendaele, 238-9; specially selected men, 276; vital imprtnce. of their part in rescue, 341, 345-6; trg. of, 346, 895; their work described in *Austln. Off. Hist.*, 147, 638; not members of med. serv., 275. **German:** 60n, 71n. *See also* FIELD AMBS.; REGIMENTAL MED. SERV.; TRAINING; CASUALTIES, EVACN. OF
STRETCHERS, 37, 207; types of, 272; lge. dumps, Somme Winter, 86; snt. up to Armies, 187, 203; supply of, 742
SUBMARINES, German, effct. on evacn. of cas., 10; blockade of Brit., 105, 138, 607; attck. hosp. ships, 1917, 396
"SUGAR-LOAF" (Sk. 41), 40
SUPPLIES, MEDICAL, *see* MEDICAL STORES
SUPPLY, disorgn., Somme Winter, 82; lit. attn. devoted to, in peace trg., 290n; *see also* RATIONS
SUPREME WAR COUNCIL, 677
SURGICAL TEAMS, 132n, 329, 359n, 361, 364-5, 380-2, 402, 609, 775n, 841; evoln. of, 70-1, 953-7; orgn. of 360; incrse. in, 155; at C.C.S's, Messines, 161; Third Ypres, 187; C.C.S. grp. at Remy Siding, 203; provn. at A.D.S., 208; C.C.S's B. of Amiens, 684n; fld. ambs. resus. teams, 841-2
SURGICAL TREATMENT, 299-353; in R.A.P's and Fld. Ambs., 161-2; in C.C.S's, Thrd. Ypres, 187; constnts. in, 265; the srch. for asepsis, 310-340; resrches by Martin and Chick, 324; scient. antiseptics, 324-5; immed. and primary suture, 330-31; carried out at various stges. of evacn., 341; by R.M.O., 346-50; surg. divn. of C.C.S., 373-7; consltnts. supvse., 395-6; note on, 406-7; French view, 407n; prevn. of sepsis at the Base, 408-9; delayed inf., "flares," 431; at Command Depots, 465; at No. 3 A.G.H. *Apr.* 1918, 622; at M.D.S. 661-2, 672; at No. 1 A.C.C.S. *Aug.*, 777-8; blood trnsfson., 661-2, 664,

SURGICAL TREATMENT—continued.
777-8, 878, 880; by resus. team, 783n. **B.I.P.**, 162, 323-4, 325n, 341, 373. **Carrel-Dakin lavage,** 319n, 320-2, 341, 373, 407n, 408n, 413, 431. **Wright's method,** 319-22. **Salt-pack,** 323, 341. **Excision,** 325-31, 374, 431, 432. *See also* LESSONS OF THE WAR
SURGERY, gen., 299-353, 357, 358, 439, (Plates), 349, 364, 661; Aust. C.C.S's called on to undertke., 26; evoln. of, improvd. mthds., 155, 192; fall in incdnce. of gas gangrene, etc., 155n; in R.A.P's and Fld. Ambs., 161-2; amputns., 162, 778; percent. optd. on in C.C.S's, 155n, 179n, 248, 372, 386; at B. of Messines, 181-2; C.C.S. grp., Remy Siding, 203; trtmt. for haemorrhage, Menin Rd., 207; time factor dominates, 265; prophlctc., 301, 431-2, 783; effct. on professn., 302n; rifle bullet wds., 305-6; the surg. debacle, 312-13; reactn., 313-17; orgnd. expt., 1915-17, 317-31; moves twds. the frnt., 318; the efft. for continuity, 323-5; "antiseptic" and "aseptic," 329n; immed. suture, 330; exploitatn. 1917-18, 331-3; evoln. of technique, 359; delayed opns. and urgent cases, 362; surg. divn. of C.C.S., 373-7, 386; at Base hosps., 405-8; venue of confictg. views, 406-7; to rectify deformities, 408; pyogenic infs., 408; orthopaedic, 432-4; resus. team and optg. centre, 782-6; reslts., a stats. paradox, 786-8. *See also* WOUNDS, TREATMT. OF
SUTTON VENY (Map 452), 454
SYNOVITIS, 568

"TANK GUN POST" (Map 206), 214
TANKS (Plate 692), 131, 133, 611, 667, 678, 682, 689, 692, 721n, 739, 762; fst. used, 51; carry back wdd., 272n, 671
"T.B." MEN, *see* CATEGORIES
TEMPLEUX LE GUÉRARD (Map 760; Sk. 726), 737, 741, 748
TENTS, *see* HOUSING
TERRAIN, *see* TOPOGRAPHY
TETANUS, 309-10, 431, 503, 547, 550; *see also* SERA
THIEPVAL (Map 88; Sk. 51), Btle. of, 49n, 50, 51, 61
THILLOY (Map 88; Sk. 109), 110
THIRD ECHELON, *see* AUST. IMP. FORCE (AUST. SECTN., 3RD ECHLN.)
THISTLE DUMP, 84
THROAT INFECTIONS, 554
TIDWORTH (Plate 18, Map 452), 17, 451
TINCOURT (Plate 732, Sk. 726), 620, 732, 762
TINEA, 503, 530, 567
TOKIO RIDGE (Map 224), 213, 220
TONSILLITIS, 501, 568
TOPOGRAPHY, of Somme area, 50, 655-6, 696; of Ancre Valley, 81; effect of terrain on Bullecourt opns., 130

1008   GENERAL INDEX

TOUQUET BERTHE (Map 164), 165, 170
TOURNIQUETS, 177, 659, removed at M.D.S., 162, 351; excessive use of, Messines, 178; dangers of, 347; limbs saved by early removal, 954
TOUTENCOURT (Map 68; Sk. 626), 616n, 626, 630, 657
TRACHEITIS, 559
TRACHOMA, 543, 550
TRAINING, after Somme, 76; 4th Div. in new tactics, 109n; in Aust. Conv. Depot, 420; physical, 465; of A.A.M.C., 18, 477, 614-15, 838n; of regtl. S.-B's etc., 346, 347, 895; see also DEPOTS
TRANSFUSION, see SURGICAL TREATMT.
TRANSPORT, 247, 248, 271; developments in, 2, 288, 290-1, 697; goes hand in hand with treatmt., 25; horses bogged in mud, shot, 86n; struggle for, *Mar.* 1917, 113; Second Army scheme, Messines, 161; traffic control, 163n; traffic routes for, Menin Rd., 196-7; constants, 265; methods, 272; allotted to C.C.S's, 365-6; relns. btwn. C.C.S's and Dept. of S. and T., 624; American, 756n; efficiency of mechanised, 761; Aust. mechanical transpt. coys., 864n; with Bearer Div., 885, Fld. Amb., San. Sectn., M.A.C. and C.C.S., 912n; effect of internal combustion engine, 913; of French med. units, 915; of battle cas., 926-30; for surg. resus. team, 955. Ships mentioned: *Orvieto,* 804, *Runic,* 907, *Beltana, Borda, Hororata, Suevic, Suffolk,* 474n. See also MEDICAL TRANSPORT
TRAUMATIC ABRASIONS, 99, 503
TREATMENT, GENERAL, treatmt. of wds. and prevn. of dis. the maj. probs., 271; of sickness not specially characteristic, 3, 409; relegated to *Vol. III,* 432; hospital, in Eng., 20; reltn. to transpt., 25, 84, 247-8, 271; at C.C.S's, 26, 187; effect of Somme on, 50; at A.D.S., 64-5, 170-1, 209, 217; centres for, 69-70, 84; at Bécordel, 88; for trench feet, 100; improved mthds., 132, 155-6, 339-40; Schafer mthd. in mine warfare, 160n; use of picric acid, 161, 312n, 348; iodine, 161, 348; Second Army scheme for, Messines, 161-2; "Eusol" as stand. lotion, 161; at M.D.S., 177, 229-30, 692-3; comment on, Messines, 181-2; reparative, 264, 432-5; constants, 265; movt. co-ordinated with, 291-3, 766; in prevn. of wastage, 293-6; gen. surg. of wds., 299-353, of wounding, 310-40, of the wd., 310-33, of the wounded man, 333-40, 375-6, drg. evacn., 340-53; genesis of asepsis, 316; first aid, 341, 347-50; rest, wmth. and food in, 342-5, 750; by S.-B's, 345-6, the R.M.O., 346-50, at relay posts, 350, at dress. stns., 350-2, at the bases, 405-12, in Brit. prim. hosps., 431-2; reconditng. at Command Depots, 464-5; prophylaxis by, 511-12; of gassed cases, 676-7, 728, 750; confid-

TREATMENT, GENERAL—*continued.*
ence in, of Austln. soldier in own med. serv., 706; of scabies, 712, 796; at Templeux, 29 *Sept.* 1918, 749-51; of civil popln., 770, 788-90, 797; of Austln. soldrs. in Gr. Brit., 825n, 870-3, cost, 827; by blood transfusion, 661-2, 664, 777-8, 878, 880; of wd. shock and haemorrhage, 949-52; saline infusn., 951; by Fld. Amb. resus. teams, 953-7. See also DISEASES; SURGICAL TREATMT.; SURGERY; WOUNDS; TREATMT. OF
TRENCH FEVER, see DISEASES
TRENCH FOOT, see DISEASES
TRENCHES, see FORTIFICATIONS
Triage, see CASUALTIES, CLASSFN. OF
TROIS ARBRES (Plate 349; Map 164), 30, 163, 179, 382, 640, 642
TROUVILLE (Sk. 397), 397, 418
TUBERCULOSIS, 435, 474, 502, 555, 562, 568
TUNNELLING COMPANY, No. 1 Aust., 159n
TUNNELS, THE, see HOOGE
TURKEY, 104, 542, 860
TYPHOID, see DISEASES; INOCULATION; VACCINE
TYPHUS, see DISEASES

UNDERHILL FARM (Map 164), 169
"UNFITS," see CATEGORIES; RECRUITS; REINFORCEMENTS
UNITED STATES OF AMERICA, see AMERICA
"UNTRANSPORTABLE CASES," see WOUNDS, TYPES OF

VACCINATION, agst. Smallpox, 537
VACCINES, 478, 538, 539, 541
VACCINIA, 502
VADENCOURT (Map 68; Sk. 82), 57, 72, 616, 625
VALENCIENNES (Map 769), 768
VARICELLA, 554
VARICOCELE, 99, 408, 435
VARICOSE VEINS, 99, 408, 474, 568
VARIOLA, 502, 554
VAULX-VRAUCOURT (Plate 151; Sk. 116, 135), 119, 121, 128, 130, 132, 137, 142, 144, 149, 151
VÉCQUEMONT (Sk. 685), 620, 671, 684, 725, 879
VÉLU (Sk. 123), 125
VENDELLES (Sk. 726), 724
VENEREAL INFECTIONS, see DISEASES
VERDUN, Battle of, 8, 39, 50n, 74n, 183n
VICTORIA, 910
VICTORIA CROSS, not awarded for rescue work, 147n; bar awarded to Capt. Chavasse, 277n
VIEUX BERQUIN (Sk. 645), 616n
VIGNACOURT (Map 68), 81, 96, 620, 635, 655, 667, 684, 688, 775n, 878
VILLE-SUR-ANCRE (Sk. 626), 665, 666
VILLERS-BRETONNEUX (Plates 628, 661; Map 769; Sk. 653, 656), 620, 631, 635, 678, 693, 717; water-supply at, 713; B. of, 528n, 622n, 629, 632, 635, 636-7, 647, med. events, 638

GENERAL INDEX 1009

VILLERS-FAUCON (Sk. 749), 741, 742, 761
VIMY RIDGE (Sk. 107), tactl. importce. of, 35; B. of, 107, 108, 129; Germans adv. to, 610, 612, 627-8, checked, 629
VIRUS DISEASE, 505, 563
Vis Medicatrix Naturae, 92, 303*n*, 351, 537, 949
VITAMINS, 489*n*, 520, 585*n*; see also RATIONS
VLAMERTINGHE (Map 273; Sk. 76, 190), 75*n*, 190
VOLUNTARY AID, 23, 287-8, 402*n*, 767*n*. See also COMFORTS FUND; RED CROSS
VRAIGNES, 728

WAR OF 1914-18, effect of internal combustion engine in, 1; its infl. on present era of culture, 49; its course, 138; end of 1917, 253-4; evoln. in med. serv. in, 260-6; effect of, on human race, 262; prevntve. med. in, 483-602; "diverted all scientific energies from their normal applications," 484; numbers involved in, 518*n*; soldiers load tended to rise in, 526; a degradation to the primitive, 569-70; its gifts to humanity, 571; end of, and beginning of peace, 767-801; some national systems for dealing with cas., 913-25; its contribution to the knowledge of wd. shock, 946-7. See also LESSONS OF THE WAR; WESTERN FRONT
WAR CABINET, see BRITISH GOVT.
WAR OFFICE, its policy re disposal of A.I.F. cas., 10-13; advised agst. formation of 6th Aust. Div., 20*n*; policy re bns., 708; announces "Anzac leave," 717; means by which D.M.S., A.I.F., maintained *liaison* with, 814; raises age of enlistment, 846. See also BRIT. ARMY; BRIT. GOVT.; CONFERENCES
WAREHAM, No. 4 Command Depot at, 441, 450
WARFARE, new type of, created by intnl. combstn. engine, 3; nature of, 1914-18, 5; chrctr. of, in Somme Btles., 52-3; use of barrage in, 53; "wearing down" policy, 80; modern tech. rqmts. in, 139*n*; war of movt., 603-5, 703-34, (Plate), 708
WARLOY (Map 68; Sk. 620), 57, 70-1, 117, 361, 616, 619, 625, 658
WARLENCOURT (Map 88; Sk. 113), 111*n*, 116
WARMTH, 522; for the wdd. man, 342-5, 661
WASTAGE, defntn. of btle. cas. and sick, 270-1; in I Anzac, *Nov.* 1915-*Nov.* 1917, 98; causes of, 404, 481, 489-506, 567; primary analysis of, 492-500; housg. as a factor in, 521-2; problms. of, 701; prvntm. of: msres. for, 26-7, 94-6, 293-5, 530, in wnter. 1916-17, 92, rôle of med. serv., 96-8, Ger., 606. See also FORTIFICATIONS
WATER, dffclty. of obtng. at fnt., Pozières, 60; the two gall. petrol tin for, 61*n*, 166, 199, 592, 593; maintnce.

WATER—*continued*. of pure supplies, 77, 591, 713-14; from shell-holes, 89; shortge., at aid post, 148; bn. water duty men, 507; training of, 895; supplied by water carts, 579; Gallip. and France compared, 583; factors in the prob. of, 589-93; chlorination and the "Horrocks' test case," 591-2, 713-14; amt. reqd. by each man, 1914, 591*n*; san. secn's. plce. in control of, 600-1; supply in A.I.F. Depots, 559*n*
WATER TANK COMPANIES, 593
WEATHER, hot and dry, *July-Aug.* 1916, 50; dust rplced. by mud, 64; perfect summer in Picardy, *July* 1917, 180; the inflnce. of climate on dis., 558-9; condns., Gallip. and France compared, 583; fine at B. of Polygon Wd., 215; fine at B. of Broodseinde, until aftrnoon., 4 *Oct.*, 226; frosty and clear, 96, 110, 111; morning mists, 60*n*, 90, 689; rain, 80, 90, continuous during *Aug.* 1917, 184, begins aftrnoon., 4 *Oct.*, 219, 227-8, 232, "rain, rain, rain," 7 *Oct.*, 233, heavy, 11-13 *Oct.*, 238, and cold, 86, 126, 133, 231, 239, 241, 745, 754; snow, 90, 117, 121, 129, 136; thunder storms, 167, 239; effct. on time taken by wdd. to rch. C.C.S., 929
WEIL'S DISEASE, 544
WESTERN FRONT, the decisve. frnt., 1; gen. mily. sitn., 1915, 7-8; mily. dvlpmts., 1914-15, 22; Austlns. prepare for fst. winter on, 78-9; mily. sitn. *Sept.-Nov.* 1916 80-2; sitn., 1917, 104-5; Neville's Offsve. fails, 129; Brit. maintns. pressure, 158; mily. plan and mthds. for Flanders offsve., 158-9; Allied avtge. in manpower, 183; sitn., *Oct.*, 232; rslts. of attrition, the human material, 230; dvlpmt. of med. tech. on, 268-71; med. evac. within army zone, 268-96; comparison with Gallip., 391*n*, 494; the war of movt., offsves. of, 1918, 603-5; Ger. thrust, 21 *Mar.*-15 *July* 1918, 610 *et seq.*; *Mar.* 26, a turning point of the war, 612; sitn. 27 *Mar.*, 617; the Somme frnts., *Apr.-May*, 635; Allied cntr.-offsve.: Aust. Corps prepares, 647-78, Anglo-Amer. co-op., 673, the French frnt., *May-July*, 677, Allied strat., *Aug-Oct.*, 679-81, 694-5, 718-21, the thrust contd., 9-20 *Aug.*, 691-4, med. evnts., 692-4, Brit. thrusts, 21 *Aug*-3 *Sept.*, 695, uninterrupted frnt. to be maintnd., 706; Ger. armies retreat, *Oct.*, 768; Brit., Empire's war efft. on, 781-2; A.I.F. experce. on, confirms lessons of Gallip., 785; A.I.F. cas. sustnd. on, 864-5. See also LESSONS OF THE WAR
WESTHOEK RIDGE (Map 216; Sk. 189), 200, 215, 217, 221, 222, 226, 227-8
WESTHOF FARM (Map 164), 164
WEYMOUTH, formn. of spcl. "Med. coy." at, 18; No. 2 Command Depot at, 18, 438, 441, 448, 450, 456, 458*n*, 462, 471, 854*n*, early training at, 455-6

GENERAL INDEX

WHALE OIL, men's feet rubbed with, 91
"WHITE CHÂTEAU" (POTIJZE), 223
"WHITE CHÂTEAU" (VILLERS-BRETONNEUX), 692-3
WHOOPING COUGH, 501
WIMEREUX (Sk. 30), 30, 417
WIPPENHOEK (Plate 294; Sk. 76), 213, 246
"WOODCOTE HOUSE" (Sk. 202), 200
WOOL, No. 3 Command Depot at, 450
WOTAN LINE, 695; Brit. "Drocourt-Quéant Switch," 108n, 120, 127
WOUNDED, in A.I.F., France, to 30 June 1916, 39; B. of Fromelles: "saps" across No-Man's-Land, 43n; collg. of, 44, 46, during informal truce, 46n, numbers, 48; B. of Somme, 59, 61, infnty. fatigues, 58, addtl. S.-B's, 60, delayed rescues, 63, colln. under white flag, 64, in mud, 64, effcts. of distce. on serious cases, 71, specl. C.C.S. for lightly wdd., 72, evacn. hinges on transpt. routes, 84, unnecy. dressg. of, 88n; Bullecourt, terrible alterntves., 134-5, "put to death by merciful enemy," 135, 12 hrs. before rescue, 138; conditn. on arrival at C.C.S., 154, 956-7; numbers passed through Corps stns., 7-9 June, 175, avrge. stay, 176; B. of Menin Rd., 201, 209; in rain and mud, Passchendaele, 238, rescued 4-7 days aft. wounding, 239; percents. oprated. on at C.C.S's, 248; propn. of stret. cases to others, 274, 926-7; fine servce. of S.-B's, 274-6; dressed too frequently, 312n; distnctn. btwn. treatmt. of offcrs. and other rnks. excessive, 391n; emotionl. appeal of, grtr. than sick, 485; treated by enemy, 630; the "untransptable." case, 783n, 785; mortality of rescued, in advce. and retreat, 787-8; distce. time factor in evac., 927-30; French estimate of degrees of wd. urgency, 957-8. See also CASUALTIES; STATISTICS
WOUND SHOCK, 155, 334, 336n, 783, 785n; definitions of, 308n, 337n-8n; treatment of, 162, 247, 949-52; "secondary," 303n-4n, 334n; nature of, 335-40, 946-9; technique of the blanket, 344, 345; sepsis and haemorrhage impt. in, 347; first aid in, 348; "resuscitation" in, 376-7, 661-4, 777, 946-58; incidence of, reduced, 661
WOUNDS, definition of, 270-1; maggots in, 63, 325; factors in surg. of, 301-2; the pathology of, 304-10; specific inf. agents in, 307n; "infected" and "contaminated," 329n; concern of both phys. and surg., 410; research into probs. of, 413; unfitness from, 461-2; analysis of wastage from, 495, 497-8; causes of, 304-6, 481, 495; diseases of, 307-10, 325, 347n; pain in, 333-5; gen. surg. of, 299-353. **Infection of:** 311-12, 408n, 431, 542; "contamination" and "infection," 329n; fall in incidence of gas gangrene, etc., 155n; results of, prevn., 302; inf. agents on

WOUNDS—continued.
W.F., 307-8; effects of septic inf., 308-9; morbid states, 309-10; methods of treating, 313-31, "Carrel-Dakin" technique, 321. **Treatment of:** 3, 47, 356, 359, 360, 431-2; general surgery of wounds, 299-353; regional not dealt with, 300; treatment centres, 69-70, 120-1, 188, 350-2; lack of co-ordn. with movemt., in Somme, 70; policy of Fifth Army for, 131-2; improved mthds. of, 155-6; memos. on, 161-2, 316; at B. of Messines, 181-2; "lessons" from Third Ypres, 247-8; vis medicatrix naturae, 303n; reaction at the front, 316; developmt. of excision, 326-8; by R.M.O., 346-50; first aid, 348-9; prim. and delayed primary suture, 374, 622n; note on, by Col. Newland, 406-7; arrangemts. for regional wds., 407; at the Base, 408; at No. 1 A.C.C.S., 777-8; spec. hosp. for face and jaws, Sidcup, 823-4. **Types of:** 202, 306-7, 405, 434, 750, 782-6, 954, 957-8; percentages according to sites, 48; of P. of W., Menin Rd., 209; at No. 3 A.C.C.S., 375; cons. advised re, 396; C.C.S's for special, 186, 701; urgent cases, 202-3, 361, 375, 880. Abdominal: 71n, 162, 178, 188, 360, 375, 621, 672, 762n, 777, 783; centre for, 57, 361. Chest: 375, 410, 778, 783, 949n. Fractures: 65, 349; incidence of, 306n; of femur, 314-15, 360, 407, 777; Thomas splint, 155, 162, 182, 329, 348-9, 661. Jaw and face: 404. Missiles: 138, 229, 495, 498, 777. Skull: 316, 778. Spine: 375. Thorax: 162. Thigh: 672, 783. "Untransportable": 352-3, 360, 672n, 749, 782-3, Amer. exper., 958. See also SPLINTS; SURGICAL TREATMENT; SURGERY; TREATMENT, GENERAL
WULVERGHEM (Map 164), 279n
WYTSCHAETE (Map 164; Sk. 36), 159, 279n

X-RAY, see RADIOLOGY

YELLOW FEVER, 490, 541, 580n
Y.M.C.A., 178, 209, 210, 223, 352, 401, 466, 517, 622, 690, 743, 758, 797
YPRES (Map 216; Sk. 75 189), 78, 194, 292, 515, 771, 785n; salient at, 74-9, 159, 184, 189-90; Third Battle of, 183-231, 386, 661; cas. in, 243-5; "lessons" from, 247-50, 849-50
YPRES-MENIN ROAD, 234, 236
YPRES-ROULERS RAILWAY (Sk. 189), 189
YPRES-ZONNEBEKE ROAD (Sk. 189), 189, 222, 233, 236-7
YTRES (Sk. 620), 121, 252, 619

ZEEBRUGGE, 159
ZEITOUN, 446n, 559
ZILLEBEKE (Map 216; Sk. 189), 196, 201. LAKE, 191.
ZONNEBEKE (Plate 232; Map 216), 194, 220, 237

Halstead Press Pty Limited, 9-19 Nickson Street, Sydney

www.ingramcontent.com/pod-product-compliance
Lightning Source LLC
Chambersburg PA
CBHW070751300426
44111CB00014B/2374